Law, Sex, and Christian Society in Medieval Europe

Law, Sex, and Christian Society in Medieval Europe

James A. Brundage

The University of Chicago Press
Chicago and London

The University of Chicago Press, Chicago 60637
The University of Chicago Press, Ltd., London

© 1987 by The University of Chicago
All rights reserved. Published 1987
Paperback edition 1990
Printed in the United States of America

96 95   54

Library of Congress Cataloging-in-Publication Data

Brundage, James A.
  Law, sex, and Christian society in medieval Europe.

  Bibliography: p.
  Includes index.
  1. Sex and law—Europe—History.   2. Sex crimes—
Europe—History.   3. Sex—Religious aspects—Christianity
—History.   4. Law, Medieval—History.   I. Title.
KJ985.S48B78   1987   344.4'054   87-10759

ISBN 0-226-07784-5 (paper)

  This publication has been supported by the National Endowment for the Humanities,
a federal agency which supports the study of such fields as history, philosophy, literature, and languages.

For Tom

Contents

Contents

Illustrations

Abbreviations

AAS	*Acta Apostolicae Sedis*
ACA	Archivo de la Corona de Aragón, Barcelona
AKKR	*Archiv für katholisches Kirchenrecht*
Annales:	
é.s.c.	*Annales: économies, sociétés, civilisations*
Auth.	*Authenticum,* in *Corpus iuris civilis* (Lyon: Apud Iuntas, 1584).
Berkeley Proceedings	*Proceedings of the Sixth International Congress of Medieval Canon Law,* ed. Stephan Kuttner and Kenneth Pennington (Vatican City: Biblioteca Apostolica Vaticana, 1985)
Bieler	*The Irish Penitentials,* ed. Ludwig Bieler (Dublin: Dublin Institute for Advanced Studies, 1963)
BL	British Library, London
BMCL	*Bulletin of Medieval Canon Law*
BN	Bibliothèque Nationale, Paris
Boston Proceedings	*Proceedings of the Second International Congress of Medieval Canon Law,* ed. Stephan Kuttner and J. Joseph Ryan (Vatican City: S. Congregatio de Seminariis et Studiorum Universitatibus, 1965)
Boswell, CSTAH	John Boswell, *Christianity, Social Tolerance and Homosexuality: Gay People in Western Europe from the Beginning of the Christian Era to the Fourteenth Century* (Chicago: University of Chicago Press, 1980)
CCL	*Corpus Christianorum, series Latina* (Turnhout: Brépols, 1953–)
CCM	*Corpus Christianorum, continuatio medievalis* (Turnhout: Brépols, 1958–)
CIL	*Corpus inscriptionum Latinarum* (Berlin: G. Reimer [imprint varies], 1862–)
Clm	*Codex Latinus Monacensis*

COD	*Conciliorum oecumenicorum decreta*, ed. G. Alberigo et al. (Freiburg i/Br.: Herder, 1962)
Cod.	*Codex Justinianus*, in *Corpus iuris civilis*
Cod. Theod.	*Codex Theodosianus*, ed. P. Krüger and T. Mommsen, 3 vols. (Berlin: Weidmann, 1905)
Coll. 5L	*Collectio canonum in V libris*, ed. M. Fornasari (Turnhout: Brépols, 1970)
Coll. 74T	*Diuersorum patrum sententiae, siue Collectio in LXXIV titulos digesta*, ed. John Gilchrist (Vatican City: Biblioteca Apostolica Vaticana, 1973)
CSEL	*Corpus scriptorum ecclesiasticorum Latinorum* (Vienna: F. Tempsky, 1866–)
CSTAH	*See* Boswell, CSTAH above
DA	*Deutsches Archiv für Erforschung des Mittelalters*
DACL	*Dictionnaire d'archéologie chrétienne et de liturgie*, 15 vols. (Paris: Letouzey et Ané, 1907– 53)
DBI	*Dizionario biografico degli Italiani*, ed. Alberto M. Ghisalberti (Rome: Istituto della Enciclopedia Italiana, 1960–)
DDC	*Dictionnaire de droit canonique*, ed. R. Naz, 7 vols. (Paris: Letouzey et Ané, 1935–65)
DHGE	*Dictionnaire d'histoire et de géographie ecclésiastique*
Dig.	*Digestum seu Pandekta*, in *Corpus iuris civilis*
DMA	*Dictionary of the Middle Ages*
DTC	*Dictionnaire de théologie catholique*, ed. A. Vacant, et al., 15 vols. (Paris: Letouzey et Ané, 1908–50)
EDR	Ely Diocesan Records, in Cambridge University Library
Fournier and LeBras	Paul Fournier and Gabriel LeBras, *Histoire des collections canoniques en Occident depuis les fausses décrétales jusqu'au Décret de Gratien*, 2 vols. (Paris: Sirey, 1931–32)
FTeruel	*El fuero de Teruel*, ed. Max Gorsch (Stockholm: Almqvist & Wiksells, 1950)
Haddan and Stubbs	*Councils and Ecclesiastical Documents Relating to Great Britain and Ireland*, ed. Arthur West Haddan and William Stubbs, 3 vols. (Oxford: At the Clarendon Press, 1869–78; repr. 1964)
Hefele and Leclercq	Karl Joseph von Hefele, *Histoire des conciles d'après les documents originaux*, ed. Henri Leclercq, 9 vols. in 18 (Paris: Letouzey et Ané, 1907–31)
Hinschius, DPI	*Decretales Pseudo-Isidorianae et Capitula Angilramni*, ed. Paul Hinschius (Leipzig: B. Tauchnitz, 1863; repr. Aalen: Scientia, 1963)

Inst.	*Institutiones Justiniani*, in *Corpus iuris civilis*
IRMAe	*Ius romanum medii aevi* (Milan: A. Giuffrè, 1961–)
JE ⎫ JK ⎬ JL ⎭	Philip Jaffé, *Regesta pontificum romanorum*, 2d ed. by S. Löwenfeld (JL = A.D. 882–1198), F. Kaltenbrunner (JK = A.D. ?–590), and P. Ewald (JE = A.D. 590–882), 2 vols. (Leipzig: Veit, 1885–88; repr. Graz: Akademische Druck- u. Verlagsanstalt, 1956)
JEH	*Journal of Ecclesiastical History*
JMH	*Journal of Medieval History*
LAC	Gabriel LeBras, Charles Lefebvre, and Jacqueline Rambaud, *L'âge classique, 1140–1378; Sources et théorie du droit* (Paris: Sirey, 1965)
LC	Library of Congress
LQR	*Law Quarterly Review*
LThK	*Lexikon für Theologie und Kirche*, 2d ed., 14 vols. (Freiburg i/Br.: Herder, 1957–67)
Mansi	*Sacrorum conciliorum nova et amplissima collectio*, ed. Giovanni Domenico Mansi, 60 vols. (Paris: Hubert Welter, 1901–27)
Martène and Durand	*Veterum Scriptorum et monumentorum historicorum, dogmaticorum, moralium amplissima collectio*, ed. Edmond Martène and Ursin Durand, 9 vols. (Paris: Montalant, 1724–33; repr. New York: Burt Franklin, 1968)
McNeill and Gamer	*Medieval Handbooks of Penance*, ed. and trans. John T. McNeill and Helena M. Gamer (New York: Columbia University Press, 1936; repr. New York: Octagon Books, 1965)
MGH	*Monumenta Germaniae Historica* (Hannover: Hahn [imprint varies], 1828–)
Capitularia	Capitularia regum Francorum (= Legum sectio II)
Concilia	Concilia (= Legum sectio III)
Const.	Constitutiones et acta publica imperatorum (= Legum sectio IV)
Diplom.	Diplomata
Epist.	Epistolae
Epist. saec. XIII	Epistolae saeculi XIII e regestis pontificum Romanorum
Formulae	Formulae (= Legum sectio V)
LdL	Libelli de lite imperatorum et pontificum
LL	Leges nationum Germanicarum (= Legum sectio I)
Schriften	Schriften der Monumenta Germaniae Historica
SS	Scriptores
SS rer. mer.	Scriptores rerum Merovingicarum
SSRG	Scriptores rerum Germanicarum in usum scholarum

MIC	*Monumenta iuris canonici* (Vatican City: Biblioteca Apostolica Vaticana [imprint varies], 1965–)
Nov.	*Novellae leges,* in *Corpus iuris civilis*
Nov. Theod.	*Novellae Theodosiani,* in *Cod. Theod.*
Pauly and Wissowa	*Paulys Realencyclopädie der Altertumswissenschaft,* ed. August Friedrich von Pauly and G. Wissowa, 24 vols. in 49 (Stuttgart: A. Druckenmüller, 1894–1974)
PG	*Patrologiae cursus completus . . . series Graeca,* ed. J.-P. Migne, 167 vols. (Paris: J.-P. Migne, 1857–76)
PGO	*Patrologiae cursus completus . . . series Graeca et Orientalis,* ed. J.-P. Migne, 80 vols. (Paris: J.-P. Migne, 1856–66)
PL	*Patrologiae cursus completus . . . series Latina,* ed. J.-P. Migne, 221 vols. (Paris: J.-P. Migne, 1844–64)
Po	*Regesta Pontificum Romanorum,* ed. August Potthast, 2 vols. (Berlin: Rudolf de Decker, 1874–79)
Powicke and Cheney	*Councils and Synods with Other Documents Relating to the English Church, A.D. 1205–1313,* ed. Frederick M. Powicke and Christopher R. Cheney, 2 vols. (Oxford: At the Clarendon Press, 1964)
QFIAB	*Quellen und Forschungen aus italienischen Archiven und Bibliotheken*
QL	*See* Schulte, QL
RDC	*Revue de droit canonique*
RHC	*Recueil des historiens des croisades,* 16 vols. in 17 (Paris: Imprimerie Royale [imprint varies], 1841–1906)
Lois	Lois
Occ.	Historiens occidentaux
RHDF	*Revue historique de droit français et étranger*
RHE	*Revue d'histoire ecclésiastique*
RHGF	*Recueil des historiens des Gaules et de la France,* ed. Martin Bouquet et al., 2d ed. rev. by Léopold Delisle, 24 vols. in 25 (Paris: V. Palme [imprint varies], 1840–1904)
Salamanca Proceedings	*Proceedings of the Fifth International Congress of Medieval Canon Law,* ed. Stephan Kuttner and Kenneth Pennington (Vatican City: Biblioteca Apostolica Vaticana, 1980)
Schmitz	Hermann Josef Schmitz, *Die Bussbücher und der Bussdiciplin der Kirche nach handschriftlichen Quellen dargestellt* 2 vols. (Mainz: Franz Kirchheim, 1883–98; repr. Graz: Akademische Druck- u. Verlagstanstalt, 1958)
Schulte, QL	Georg Friedrich von Schulte, *Geschichte der Quellen und Literatur des canonischen Rechts von Gratian bis auf die*

	Gegenwart, 3 vols. (Stuttgart: F. Enke, 1875–77; repr. Graz: Akademische Druck- u. Verlagsanstalt, 1956)
SDHI	*Studia et documenta historiae et iuris*
SG	*Studia Gratiana*
SP	*Summa Parisiensis on the Decretum Gratiani*, ed. Terence P. McLaughlin (Toronto: Pontifical Institute of Mediaeval Studies, 1952)
ST	Thomas Aquinas, *Summa theologica* in his *Opera omnia*, ed. Roberto Busa, 7 vols. (Holzboog: Friedrich Fromann, 1980)
Stickler, Historia	Alfons M. Stickler, *Historia iuris canonici Latini institutiones academicae* (Torino: Pontificium Athenaeum Salesianum, 1950)
Strasbourg Proceedings	*Proceedings of the Third International Congress of Medieval Canon Law*, ed. Stephan Kuttner (Vatican City: Biblioteca Apostolica Vaticana, 1971)
SVF	*Stoicorum veterum fragmenta*, ed. Hans Friedrich August von Arnim, 4 vols. (Stuttgart: B.G. Teubner, 1905–24; repr. 1968)
Toronto Proceedings	*Proceedings of the Fourth International Congress of Medieval Canon Law*, ed. Stephan Kuttner (Vatican City: Biblioteca Apostolica Vaticana, 1976)
TRE	*Theologische Realenzyklopädie*, ed. Horst Robert Balz et al. (Berlin: W. De Gruyter, 1977–)
TRG	*Tijdschrift voor Rechtsgeschiedenis*
TUJ	*Tractatus universi juris*, 2d ed., 22 vols. in 28 (Venice: Franciscus Zilettus, 1584–86)
TUJ*	*Tractatus universi iuris*, 18 vols. (Lyon: Petrus Fradin, 1548–59)
ULC	University Library, Cambridge
VI°	*Liber sextus*, in *Corpus iuris canonici*
WA	Martin Luther, *Werke, kritische Gesamtausgabe* (Weimar: Hermann Böhlaus, 1883–)
Wasserschleben	Friedrich Wilhelm Hermann Wasserschleben, *Die Bussordnungen der abendländischen Kirche* (Halle: Ch. Graeger, 1851)
Whitelock, Brett, and Brooke	*Councils and Synods with Other Documents Relating to the English Church*, ed. Dorothy Whitelock, Martin Brett, and C.N.L. Brooke, 2 vols. (Oxford: At the Clarendon Press, 1981)

X	*Liber extra* (= *Decretales Gregorii IX*), in *Corpus iuris canonici*
ZRG	*Zeitschrift der Savigny-Stiftung für Rechtsgeschichte*
GA	Germanistische Abteilung
KA	Kanonistische Abteilung
RA	Romanistische Abteilung

Preface

This book began, as books frequently do, with casual queries and stray speculations. My earlier work on the history of the crusades piqued my curiosity about sexual behavior and the law. Why, I wondered, did the chroniclers who wrote about the recovery of the Holy Land spend quite so much time relating the crusaders' sexual adventures? Other moral offenses, even heinous ones, seemed not to fascinate them as sexual misbehavior did. Was it just because sex cases furnished titillating tidbits to spice up the narrative? Or did the chroniclers' treatment of these episodes represent some unspoken agenda?

As I read canonistic writers in an effort to understand how crusading armies worked, I wondered about the canonists, too. They seemed almost mesmerized by sexual behavior and insisted on examining it in stupefying detail. Furthermore, when Hostiensis, for example, discussed the case of the crusading harlot, was he simply using her as a bizarre specimen for his analysis of votive obligations? Was this just a device to catch the attention of law students and keep them awake in class? Or was there more to it? Did all the intricate detail in the Tree of Bigamy or the law about the affinal relationships of godparents, for example, serve some social purpose, or was it merely the spinning out of theories for theory's sake?

At the same time I also wondered about about my own society's sex laws. Why did we have those peculiar statutes banning fornication and contraceptives? Why did the courts fine prostitutes but let their clients off scot-free? Why on earth did some states prescribe the death penalty for sexual relations between consenting adults? Why did Nebraska castrate men who molested children? What was the point? Deterrence? Revenge? Or to pacify an angry god?

I suspected that such anomalies and curiosities must have a long history, that they had probably become embedded in law and folklore in the distant past. Certainly reason or equity seemed to have little to do with them. These peculiar statutes and the curious fascination with sex that I saw in the crusading chroniclers appeared to have common ground in medieval Christian morality. What I was seeing, I finally realized, was a system of legal theology rooted in medieval Catholicism but extending into modern statute law. My reading in the canonists also led me to wonder why Christians in general, and Catholics in particular, put sexual behavior so close to the center of their ethical systems. As I began to look for answers this book slowly took shape, over nearly twenty years.

The focus of the book is on the triangular relationship between sexual practices, theological values, and law.* One thesis of this book is that medieval canon law played a central role in shaping modern sex law in the West. The canonists rested their law concerning sex largely upon assumptions that they found in patristic writers and theologians. The canonists' contribution was to transform those moral teachings into law, to furnish a theoretical rationale for sexual norms, and to devise and implement systems for enforcing them. Many features of modern law about sex and marriage took shape during the twelfth and thirteenth centuries. By about 1250, the canonists had crafted much of the legal framework familiar in our own time. After 1300, civil governments began to play increasingly important roles in controlling sexual behavior. The Reformation speeded transition from Church control to civil control, but the process had begun about two centuries earlier and was already well advanced before Luther was born.

This book aims first and foremost to explore the historical development of medieval law dealing with sex, both within and outside of marriage. Because of the nature of the sources and the way in which the law itself developed, I have chosen to combine two rather different books into one. The first five chapters survey the development of Christian ideas about sex and society up to the mid-twelfth century. Although these chapters are based upon wide reading in the published primary sources, I have relied heavily on the work of specialists in the history of late antiquity and the early middle ages, as my notes make plain. Chapters six through nine, dealing with the classical period of the canon law, constitute the core of the book. Much of the material in those chapters (and especially in Chapters seven and eight) comes from unpublished manuscript summas, commentaries and glosses, as well as from printed texts. The scale of treatment in those four chapters is detailed and monographic. Chapters ten and eleven resemble the first five chapters in that they are based primarily on published sources and draw largely on studies by specialists in the period. The book thus comprises a monograph (Chapters 6–9) wrapped in a survey (Chapters 1–5, 10–11), with a final segment (Chapter 12) that summarizes the whole thing and draws conclusions from it.

I adopted a chronological structure for the book, since one of my primary aims was to show the development over time of legal constraints on various types of sexual activity. This approach inevitably involves some repetition, as each chapter in turn takes up themes treated in previous ones; although I have tried to keep this within bounds, some redundancies necessarily remain.

---

*My purpose is thus quite different from that of the late Michel Foucault, whose *History of Sexuality* centered on sexual experiences and perceptions, rather than on norms and behaviors; *Histoire de la sexualité* (Paris: Gallimard, 1976– ; 3 vols. to date) 2:9–10.

In writing this book I had several different audiences in mind. It is directed in part to specialists in the history of medieval law, society, and religion. But I have also tried to keep in view the needs and concerns of sexologists and practicing therapists who may be interested in the origins and development of law and public policy relating to sexual behavior.

James A. Brundage

Acknowledgments

I should like to thank the many individuals and institutions whose aid, support, and advice have made this study possible. Travel grants from the American Council of Learned Societies, the Graduate School and the Division of International Scholars and Studies at the University of Wisconsin—Milwaukee helped to underwrite much of my work in libraries and archives overseas. My department and the College of Letters and Science of the University of Wisconsin—Milwaukee from time to time gave me dispensation from teaching and other duties; without their help the task would have been far more taxing, more difficult, and more protracted. A visiting fellowship at Clare Hall in the University of Cambridge provided me not only with the base of operations from which I conducted much of my manuscript research, but also with congenial companionship and intellectual stimulus in one of this planet's loveliest settings. I am grateful to the president and Fellows for admitting me to their company. I wrote the first draft of this book in Chicago, while I was a Fellow of the Newberry Library. I should like to thank the president and staff of the Newberry, especially Richard Brown, Paul Gehl, Mary Beth Rose, Paul Saenger, and John Tedeschi, as well as the National Endowment for the Humanities, for their support, encouragement, and genial hospitality.

I have drawn upon material in the collections of numerous other libraries, in addition to the Newberry. I am particularly indebted to the patience and cooperation of librarians and staffs of the Institute of Medieval Canon Law in the Law School (Boalt Hall) of the University of California at Berkeley; the University Library in Cambridge; the Institute of Historical Research in London; the Memorial Library of the University of Wisconsin in Madison; the Golda Meier Library of the University of Wisconsin in Milwaukee; the Pontifical Institute of Mediaeval Studies in Toronto; and the foreign law division of the Library of Congress in Washington.

In addition I gratefully acknowledge permission from the following to publish excerpts from manuscripts in their collections:

The Stiftsbibliothek, Admont;

The Archivo de la Corona de Aragón, Barcelona;

The Bibliothèque Nationale, Paris;

The British Library, London;

The Syndics of Cambridge University Library;

The Syndics of the Fitzwilliam Museum;

The Master and Fellows of Gonville and Caius College, Cambridge;

The Henry Charles Lea Library, Department of Special Collections, Van Pelt Library, University of Pennsylvania;

The Provost and Fellows of King's College, Cambridge;

The Library of Congress, Washington;

The Master and Fellows of Pembroke College, Cambridge;

The Master and Fellows of Peterhouse, Cambridge;

The Master and Fellows of Trinity College, Cambridge;

The Prefect of the Vatican Library.

Both my readers and I have benefited from the willingness of friends and colleagues to read and comment on the manuscript of this book at various stages in its long gestation. In particular I wish to thank: Vern L. Bullough, Charles Donahue, Jr., DeLloyd Guth, Richard H. Helmholz, Michael Hoeflich, the late John F. McGovern, and Kenneth Pennington. I have also learned much—and shamelessly appropriated much—from discussions of this project with other scholars. The list of them is much too long to reproduce here in full; but I owe special thanks for ideas, insights, information, encouragement, and answers to various queries to: Martin Brett, Christopher Brooke, the late Christopher Cheney, Mary Cheney, Marjorie Chibnall, Giles Constable, Charles and Ann Duggan, Sir Geoffrey Elton, Richard Fraher, Gérard Fransen, Jean Gaudemet, John Gilchrist, Penny Schine Gold, Grethe Jacobsen, Sam Jaffe, Claudia Johnson, John Kenney, Julius Kirshner, Stephan Kuttner, Peter Landau, Jean Leclercq, Peter Linehan, Elizabeth Makowski, Knut Wolfgang Nörr, the Honorable John T. Noonan, Jr., Glenn Olsen, Dorothy Owen, Nancy Partner, Hans Pawlisch, Larry Rosen, Bernhard Schimmelpfennig, Barbara Seater, Carole Shammas, Michael Sheehan, Peter Stein, Kris Utterback, Sue Sheridan Walker, Alan Watson, and Rudolph Weigand, among many others.

My greatest debt of all is to my wife, Victoria Brundage; she alone knows just how great it is.

Introduction

Every human society attempts to control sexual behavior, since sex represents a rich source of conflicts that can disrupt orderly social processes. Human sexuality is too powerful and explosive a force for any society to allow its members complete sexual freedom. Some limits must be imposed, some rules agreed upon, and some enforcement mechanisms devised to implement the observance of the rules. Throughout the ages communities have used various combinations of law, religion, and morality to achieve control. Not surprisingly, the regulation of sexuality has been a central feature of virtually every known legal system.[1]

Historians and others in recent decades have begun to appreciate that sexual beliefs and practices exert power, not only over individual conduct, but also over the ways in which institutions themselves grow and develop. Marriage, adultery, fornication, prostitution, rape, sodomy, and celibacy—all have significant bearings upon property interests, household structure, and notions about morality, among many other things.

During the Middle Ages a peculiarly Western sexual ethos gradually took shape in Europe. The canon law played a crucial role in its formation, and much medieval sex law remains firmly embedded in modern law, thought, and practice. Early medieval intellectuals inherited and blended together notions about

---

[1]Thus for example Plato, *Laws* 6.783a. References to Greek and Latin classical texts, unless otherwise noted, are to the numbered sections in the Loeb Classical Library (London: W. Heinemann; Cambridge: Harvard University Press [imprint varies], 1921–). On sexual activity and law, see generally H.L.A. Hart, *The Concept of Law* (Oxford: Clarendon Press, 1961), pp. 151–207; Dennis Lloyd, *The Idea of Law* (London: MacGibbon & Kee, 1966), pp. 43–63; Arthur S. Diamond, *Primitive Law, Past and Present* (London: Methuen, 1971), pp. 47–54, 195–97; Sir Henry S. Maine, *Ancient Law: Its Connection with the Early History of Society and Its Relation to Modern Ideas*, 10th ed. (London: John Murray, 1884; repr. Boston: Beacon Press, 1963), pp. 22–29, 116–30, 342–47; Lon L. Fuller, *The Morality of Law*, rev. ed. (New Haven: Yale University Press, 1969), pp. 3–32, 95–151; Sir Carleton Kemp Allen, *Law in the Making*, 6th ed. (London: Oxford University Press, 1958; repr. 1961), pp. 389–96; Michel Foucault, *Histoire de la sexualité*. (Paris: Gallimard, 1976– ; 3 vols. to date.) 2:60.

sexual ethics and propriety that they found in the writings of ancient philosophers, lawyers, and moralists. On these foundations, later medieval authorities constructed a more comprehensive and systematic sexual doctrine. For better and for worse, major elements of this medieval doctrine concerning sex still dominate our lives.

Medieval beliefs about sexual morality rested upon basic ideas borrowed in large part from non-Christian sources in late antiquity. Many sexual beliefs and attitudes common in medieval Europe were Christian by adoption, not by origin. Jesus said remarkably little about sexual conduct, and sex was not a central issue in his moral teaching. But Jesus' followers during the first four or five generations after his death were far more concerned about sexual morality than Jesus himself had been. Christian writers appropriated numerous ideas and practices from pagan and Jewish sources. Among their borrowings was the perception that sex is closely related to the sacred, that sexual ecstacy is in some way linked to the sublime.[2] This belief figured in the cults of many ancient deities, and Christian thinkers felt a need to incorporate it into their religious system as well. Likewise they appropriated another ancient and primitive perception, namely that major dislocations in the ordinary course of life produced what the Greeks called *miasma*, or ritual defilement, from which the individual must be cleansed before participating in community activities. Sexual intercourse was a source of ritual impurity in many ancient religions, and Christian thinkers also carried over into their religious system the belief that sex was a source of impurity, even though purity laws had occupied only a marginal place in the religious teachings of Jesus.

Detailed treatments of ideas about sex and a well-developed rationale to support them did not appear in Christian literature until the fourth and fifth centuries, the patristic age. Sexual morality became a central Christian issue only during the generation of St. Jerome and St. Augustine. It is not coincidental that the period in which Christians began to formulate their ideas about sexual ethics clearly and explicitly was also the period in which Christianity secured the support of the Roman government. Christianity during this period became a Roman legal institution, both in the sense that Christians were protected by law from religious persecution and in the further sense that the Christian Church was beginning to create its own religious law, which relied heavily on the power of the state and was often enforced by public authority.

The attitudes and views of patristic writers about sexual morality were both original and derivative. They were derivative in that they echoed views about these subjects voiced by other educated people (some Christian, some not) in their own generation and the generations immediately preceding theirs. They were original in that they brought together elements that had never previously been combined.

[2] Mircea Eliade, "Chasteté, sexualité et vie mystique chez les primitifs," in *Mystique et continence: Travaux scientifiques du VIIe Congrès international d'Avon* (Bruges: Desclée de Brouwer, 1952), pp. 34–35, 49–50.

Christian notions about sexual morals consisted in large part of ancient notions about proper behavior cloaked in a soutane rather than a toga. Stoicism (or more accurately, certain varieties of Stoic thought) furnished the Church Fathers with many of their central ideas about sexual conduct. What was original in patristic sexual morality was its singular mixture of Stoic ethical ideas with ancient religious beliefs about ritual purity, supported by a theological rationale based in large part on the Hebrew scriptures. Christian sexual morality is a complex assemblage of pagan and Jewish purity regulations, linked with primitive beliefs about the relationship between sex and the holy, joined to Stoic teachings about sexual ethics, and bound together by a patchwork of doctrinal theories largely invented in the fourth and fifth centuries.[3]

Christian sexual morality began to take shape as doctrine during the fourth and fifth centuries; it gradually began to be transformed into law beginning in the mid-sixth century. When I say that sexual morality became doctrine, I mean that the views on sex expressed by the Fathers slowly took coherent form and began to be integrated into a larger body of theological ideas about anthropology, psychology, and cosmology. When I say that this body of beliefs commenced to be transformed into law, I mean that it began to be expressed as rules of conduct to which Christians were obliged to conform under penalty of disagreeable sanctions.

During the early Middle Ages, patristic doctrines on sexual morality were gradually accepted as part of the developing canon law of the Church. The nature and role of canon law, however, would undergo a dramatic transformation during the central period of the Middle Ages, as the Church gradually created a complex, sophisticated, and effective legal system. During the eleventh and twelfth centuries European material and intellectual life experienced remarkable alterations. From the time of Gratian, in the mid-twelfth century, Church law assumed a new place in European society. With Gratian, for the first time, canon law assumed the characteristics of a full-fledged legal system and, as this was happening, canonists began to explore systematically the juristic implications of patristic sexual doctrines. Their explorations resulted in a basic reshaping of Christian marriage practices and of the Western European concept of the family.[4] Canonists and the Church's legislators also attempted for the first time to impose criminal penalties on fornication as well as on adultery, to repress homosexual relationships, to regulate prostitution, and to penalize the sexual activities of the clergy.

Until the fourteenth century, canon law retained a virtual monopoly on legal control of lust and its physical manifestations. Laymen and secular courts prior to that time occasionally asserted jurisdiction over rape, more rarely over adultery and prostitution; otherwise they left sexual matters to the Church courts.

[3] Jacques Marie Pohier, *Le Chrétien, le plaisir et la sexualité* (Paris: Editions du Cerf, 1974), pp. 14–27.

[4] David Herlihy, *Medieval Households* (Cambridge, MA: Harvard University Press, 1985), p. 10.

After about 1300 and especially after 1350, however, municipalities and other lay authorities moved with greater urgency and increasing effectiveness into the business of imposing limits and controls upon sexual conduct, especially nonmarital or extramarital sexual relationships. The sixteenth-century Reformation gave still greater impetus to this laicization of jurisdiction over sex matters. Protestant princes welcomed the Reformers' attacks on canon law and took the opportunity to extend their jurisdiction over matrimonial litigation and sex crimes. Despite this, however, an astonishing amount of medieval sex law remained intact, even in the most staunchly Protestant regions.[5] In those parts of Europe that remained within the Roman obedience, jurisdiction over sexual transgressions also passed largely into the hands of lay authorities, although the Church retained control over marriage law in a few Catholic countries until late in the twentieth century. In the process of secularizing marriage law and sex law, modern states appropriated much medieval canonistic doctrine. A substantial part of legal doctrine about sexual activity and about matrimony in the Western world remains bound by its medieval Christian origins to this day.

The terms "Western" and "Christian" are sufficiently vague that I should say something about how I have used them in this study. "Western" includes, but is not limited to, the institutions, values, and especially the laws of Western Europe, together with the dominant cultures of regions successfully colonized by Europeans in modern times.[6] I have not attempted to deal with the sexual beliefs and laws of Eastern Christendom or of other non-Western religions, although I have included a brief sketch of Jewish sex law and its implications for Christian beliefs.

An even broader meaning is attached to "Christian" in these pages. When I refer to people and regions as Christian, I mean that they predominantly profess one or another brand of Christianity; but the label "Christian" also applies to many other individuals who, while not formally affiliated with any church, nonetheless subscribe tacitly (often unconsciously) to Christian values, including Christian sexual ethics.

As mentioned earlier, most medieval beliefs about sex bore little relationship

---

[5] See generally Wilhelm Maurer, "Reste des kanonischen Rechtes im Frühprotestantismus," *Zeitschrift der Savigny-Stiftung für Rechtsgeschichte*, kanonistische Abteilung [hereafter ZRG, KA] 51 (1965) 190–253.

[6] Certain non-Western peoples have also adopted (not always voluntarily) major elements of Western culture, including its legal systems. Japan is a particularly striking example. At the end of the nineteenth century, Japan restructured its traditional law. In that process, much old law was scrapped or refashioned into a series of codes closely modeled upon European, mainly German, civil law. Since 1945, Japanese law has also incorporated many features of the American brand of common law. See René David, *Les grands systèmes de droit contemporains*, 2d ed. (Paris: Dalloz, 1966), pp. 546–48; John Henry Merryman, *The Civil Law Tradition: An Introduction to the Legal Systems of Western Europe and Latin America* (Stanford, CA: Stanford University Press, 1969), pp. 5, 146.

to any statements of Christ. If "Christian" means what Jesus of Nazareth is reported to have taught, then there is not much Christian teaching about sexuality to discuss. Jesus was in favor of marriage (although apparently he did not practice it) and he opposed adultery (which is a special case of his general condemnation of deception and infidelity). He also seems to have disapproved of promiscuity and commercial sex, although he scandalized some of his contemporaries by befriending prostitutes. But it remained for medieval Church authorities, confident of the authenticity of their own beliefs, to wrap their views on sex and the family in the mantle of Christian orthodoxy. In effect, then, Christian sexual morality received its cachet of authority from the medieval Church.

Not every opinion aired by medieval canonists and theologians, to be sure, received official recognition. Medieval European society was notably pluralistic and encompassed diverse views about the morality of various kinds of sexual behavior and about the role that law (as opposed to less public and less formal sanctions) ought to play in controlling them. Despite claims to the contrary, Christian sexual ethics have been neither uniform nor static. Instead, Christian views of sex have changed over time as the Church has adapted itself to changes in society. It is not surprising that this should be true, but since the contrary is often asserted, it is important to be clear about the matter from the outset.[7]

Three major patterns of sexual doctrine underlie the diverse beliefs about sexual morality that have been current in Western Christendom since the patristic period. One pattern centered on the reproductive function of sex and established nature and the natural as the criterion of what was licit; the second focused on the notion that sex was impure, a source of shame and defilement; the third emphasized sexual relations as a source of intimacy, as a symbol and expression of conjugal love. Medieval writers placed greater emphasis upon the first two patterns, but at various times prior to the Reformation, and in many segments of Christian society since then, all three approaches and the consequences deduced from them have been held and taught in various combinations.

Another key element in shaping the medieval sexual ethos was the developed legal systems that arose in Western Europe after A.D. 1100. As noted above, the adjudication of sexual transgressions, whether in Church tribunals or in secular courts, turned upon norms that the canon lawyers enunciated. As legal regulation of sexual behavior in medieval Europe gradually changed over time, the views of ecclesiastical lawyers and law teachers largely shaped the changes that occurred.

The three approaches to sexuality outlined above shaped the main contours

---

[7] Assertions of this kind are a routine part of the rhetoric of papal declarations about sexual matters; see e.g., Pope Paul VI, *Humanae vitae* § 11, and Pope John Paul II, *Familiaris consortio* § 29. But cf. Willy Rordorff, "Marriage in the New Testament and in the Early Church," *Journal of Ecclesiastical History* [cited hereafter as JEH] 20 (1969) 193 and Jean-Louis Flandrin, "L'attitude à l'égard du petit enfant et les conduites sexuelles dans la civilisation occidentale: structures anciennes et évolution," *Annales de démographie historique* (1973) 195.

of medieval sexual teaching. The doctrines constructed by medieval thinkers have furnished the foundations for sexual theory and practice in the West today. Thus, the legal regulation of marriage and divorce, together with the outlawing of bigamy and polygamy and the imposition of criminal sanctions on fornication, adultery, sodomy, fellatio, cunnilingus, and bestiality—whether these activities are pursued for fun or profit—are all based in large measure upon ideas and beliefs about sexual morality that became law in Christian Europe during the Middle Ages. Other medieval legal doctrines have been abandoned altogether or modified radically during the past four centuries, as a result of changes in the economy, in social structure, in political systems, and in personal beliefs. Yet Western standards of acceptable sexual behavior have remained remarkably conservative, despite radical changes in the religious context from which they sprang. Basic innovations in this area of the law have been uncommon during the post-Reformation centuries.

As part of our medieval heritage, most of us still retain a deeply ingrained belief that sex is shameful and that respectable people should conduct their sexual activities in private, hidden in the dark. We normally do not mention sexual matters in polite society save in the most indirect ways. These attitudes and beliefs are largely consequences of patristic and early medieval religious teachings holding that sex was a source of moral defilement, spiritual pollution, and ritual impurity; hence, the argument ran, human sexuality was something to be ashamed of because it was both a result and a source of sin.[8]

The belief that sex, despite the superficial glamor sometimes attached to it, is at worst disgusting and at best absurd remains deeply ingrained in our cultural assumptions. Sir Thomas Browne (1605–82), for example, considered sexual intercourse a ludicrous contrivance and marveled at the Creator's lapse in taste when He made human reproduction depend on sexual coupling:

> I could be content [wrote Browne] that we might procreate like trees, without conjunction, or that there were any way to perpetuate the world without this trivial and worldly way of union: it is the foolishest act a wise man commits in all his life, nor is there anything that will more deject his cooled imagination when he shall consider what an odd and unworthy piece of folly he hath committed.[9]

The other side of this pervasive disdain for sex is the veneration (but not always the practice) of the ideal of chastity. The exaltation of sexual abstinence implies a rejection and disapproval of sex for pleasure, of recreational sex, and

[8] Apologists sometimes deny that Christians consider sex impure or unclean in itself; thus, e.g., Leonard Hodgson, *Sex and Christian Freedom* (New York: Seabury Press, 1967), p. 35. But although Christian authorities have been far from consistent in their handling of sexual questions, the notion of impurity itself has come to have an almost exclusively sexual meaning in Christian rhetoric; see generally Robert Briffault, *Sin and Sex* (London: Allen & Unwin, 1931; repr. New York: Haskell House, 1973), pp. 91–99.

[9] Sir Thomas Browne, *Religio medici*, pt. 2, in his *Works*, ed. William Swann Sonnenschein (London: George Routledge & Sons; New York: E.P. Dutton, n.d.), p. 80.

above all of promiscuity. Western Christians have historically accepted (and at some level most of us still maintain) an unarticulated allegiance to an ascetic ideal of sexual morals: the less sex, the better; the more, the worse. Implicit in this is a belief that virtue demands self-control, and self-control means a rejection of pleasure: whatever feels good is probably wrong.

Christian teaching since the patristic period has postulated a tension between salvation and pleasure: most influential Christian thinkers have nurtured a gloomy suspicion that the one cannot be attained without renouncing the other. Similarly the medieval Church long remained suspicious, even hostile, toward family ties. The Church's leaders suspected that conjugal affection and parental love often disguised sensual entanglements and worldly values. For that reason, theologians and canonists saw little value in family attachments. These views had momentous consequences for the ways in which medieval people defined and described their intimate relationships and emotions. The same notions continue to shape assumptions about sex and intimacy in the late twentieth century.[10]

Yet another common belief about sexual matters in the Western Christian tradition is the notion that "nature" constitutes a reliable test of the morality of various types of sexual behavior. What is "natural" often means whatever is thought (correctly or not) to be the usual practice of the majority. Thus heterosexual marital intercourse at night in the missionary position is identified as "natural" for human beings and hence morally acceptable. Other coital positions in other circumstances are morally dubious or wrong. But "natural," in this context, is ambiguous, and medieval writers used the term as inconsistently as unreflective moralists still do. Thus, for example, mammals other than humans do not usually copulate in the missionary position; many of them mate in such a way that the male penetrates the female from the rear. Moralists therefore reject dog-style coitus as unnatural for humans, because it is common among animals of other species. For other types of sexual behavior, however, the test of what is natural becomes, inconsistently enough, the sexual behavior of other animals. Thus homosexual relations and masturbation are labeled "unnatural" because it is widely (but incorrectly) believed that animals do not engage in these practices. In point of fact, every type of copulation that can be conceived, every posture that is anatomically possible, every "unnatural" deviation that can be imagined occurs somewhere in "nature." Despite this, the ambiguous distinction between "natural" and "unnatural" sex remains ingrained in the vocabulary and value systems of Western Christian societies.[11]

---

[10] Herlihy, *Medieval Households*, p. 114.

[11] On the other hand, sexual practices that many Westerners regard as "natural" sometimes strike members of other cultures as horrid, disgusting, and perverse. Thus in the 1950s, for example, a married woman complained to the Ndola Urban Court in Zambia that her husband was a sexual pervert; she also feared that his weird sexual practices might be a method of casting a spell on her. Upon examination of the facts it appeared that the husband's perversion consisted in his attempting to kiss and suck his wife's breasts as a preliminary to intercourse. The elders of the court agreed that this was un-

Western Christendom has been more restrictive in its interdiction of sensual pleasure than most other human societies. Western Christians have commonly associated sensuality with sin, guilt, and fear of damnation. This has, among other things, placed severe restraints in many Western societies on the display of affection between husband and wife, between parent and child, or between one friend and another, lest displays of feeling and affection arouse sexual responses or be suspected of cloaking lascivious advances. Virtue has come to be identified with sexual abstinence, purity with the rejection of sexuality, and emotional repression with maturity.[12] While other societies have sensed that sexuality involves great power—often represented by phallic symbols of various kinds—and hence must be exercised with restraint, few of them have carried the fear of sexuality to the point of loathing and disgust, as Western Christians have done.

Christian ideas about sex so permeate Western mentality that we generally accept them without examining them or identifying them as particularly Christian, although people in other societies find them distinctly odd as well as distinctively Western. One of these peculiar attitudes is the tendency to identify morals primarily, even exclusively, with sexual behavior. When, for instance, Lionel Smith Beale a century ago published a book under the title *Our Morality and the Moral Question*, neither he nor his readers seem to have thought it remarkable that the only moral questions raised in the book had to do with sex. Or, to cite a legal example, the legislators who drafted and adopted the Mann Act in 1910 knew perfectly well when they spoke in that Act of transporting women in interstate commerce "for any . . . immoral purpose" that it was exclusively sexual immorality that they meant.[13]

The medieval sexual tradition fabricated powerful taboos that have colored the lives of men and women for scores of generations. While these taboos have provided a framework within which people have been and continue to be able to make choices about their personal conduct, they have also exacted an enormous toll in misery and despair. Both individuals and Western society as a whole have been poorer as a result.

heard-of and intolerable behavior, and they arranged for the woman to have a police guard to protect her from her husband's unnatural pleasures; see A. L. Epstein, *Urbanization and Kinship: The Domestic Domain on the Copperbelt of Zambia, 1950–1956* (London: Academic Press, 1981), pp. 86–87. My thanks to my colleague, Bruce Fetter, for calling my attention to this case.

[12] Pohier, *Chrétien, plaisir, sexualité*, pp. 65–78; Briffault, *Sin and Sex*, pp. 47, 55.

[13] Lionel S. Beale, *Our Morality and the Moral Question* (London: J. & A. Churchill; Philadelphia: P. Blakiston, 1887; repr. New York: Arno Press, 1974). For the Mann Act see 18 U.S. Code §§ 2421, 2422 (1982). See generally Briffault, *Sin and Sex*, pp. 55–59; Ronald Dworkin, "Lord Devlin and the Enforcement of Morals," *Yale Law Journal* 75 (1966) 1004; Jean-Louis Flandrin, "Repression and Change in the Sexual Life of Young People in Medieval and Early Modern Times," *Journal of Family History* 2 (1977) 196–97, repr. in Robert Wheaton and Tamara K. Hareven, eds., *Family and Sexuality in French History* (Philadelphia: University of Pennsylvania Press, 1980), pp. 28–29.

Loading sexual relations with a freight of sin and guilt is not, of course, exclusively either a Western or a Christian phenomenon. Both traditional Jewish and Islamic cultures, for example, demand conformity to religious standards of sexual behavior and impose stringent moral sanctions upon those who deviate from the religious norms. But neither Judaism nor Islam has identified sex as something intrinsically evil or as the central element in morality, as Christian writers have often done.

The Christian horror of sex has for centuries placed enormous strain on individual consciences and self-esteem in the Western world. This tradition has had the effect of banishing sex from polite and rational discussion, making sexual relations something to be pursued secretly, furtively, and in the dark, even between married persons for whom these activities are usually legal. Christian morality has created sexual sin on a massive scale, with the bizarre result that well-intentioned married men and women have scarcely been able to beget a child without pangs of conscience and mortal dread, lest they enjoy the experience and die before they repent their pleasure.[14]

There is no necessary reason to label sex as either virtuous or vile. But although sex may be morally indifferent in itself, the devices adopted to control it are seldom morally neutral. Medieval society required, as all societies do, some kinds of control that would channel sexual drives into outlets that people were prepared to accept and tolerate. The appropriateness and value of retaining medieval sexual ethics in the modern world requires thoughtful evaluation, not unreflecting acceptance. The mechanisms employed in medieval Europe to restrain sexual behavior within acceptable limits were devised to meet needs and assumptions quite different from our own. The coercive power of Church and state at that time could scarcely ever be exercised efficiently or effectively over great distances or for long periods of time, as they can now. In addition, the rationale that underlay medieval mechanisms for restraining sexual activity depended upon assumptions about the nature of the universe, the workings of human psychology, anatomy, and physiology, and the relationship between God and man that are no longer widely shared in the industrialized societies of the developed world. This study will explore how the system of sexual control in a world we have half-forgotten has shaped the one in which we live.

---

[14] Friedrich Nietzsche, *Menschliches, Allzumenschliches* 1.141, in his *Werke*, kritische Gesamtausgabe, ed. Giorgio Colli and Mazzino Montinari (Berlin: Walter de Gruyter, 1967– ; in progress, 22 vols. to date) 4/2:134–35; Hans Zeimentz, *Ehe nach der Lehre der Frühscholastik: eine moralgeschichtliche Untersuchung zur Anthropologie und Theologie der Ehe in der Schule Anselms von Laon und Wilhelms von Champeaux, bei Hugo von St. Viktor, Walter von Mortagne und Petrus Lombardus* (Düsseldorf: Patmos-Verlag, 1973), p. 236.

1
Law and Sex
in the Ancient World

Scholars since the 1820s, following in the wake of such pioneers as Rawlinson, Champollion, and Schliemann, have gradually uncovered and deciphered the records of the Mediterranean civilizations that preceded the classical world of Greece and Rome. Their work tells us a great deal about long-vanished societies that flourished during remote antiquity in the areas that now comprise Iraq, Iran, Syria, Turkey, Israel, and Egypt. Collections of laws from those regions reflected the household structure and sexual mores of the elite groups that dominated their ancient societies. These ancient prescriptive norms for sexual behavior marginally influenced the development of the Greco-Roman ideas about sexual propriety that underlie so many medieval and modern beliefs about sex. We can begin, therefore, by sketching their broad outlines.

The Ancient Near East

Historians will probably never know when or under what circumstances it first occurred to some ancient king or priest that law would furnish a useful tool for the control of sexual conduct. The idea had already taken root by the time the so-called Code of Hammurabi was assembled in Babylonia around 1750 B.C.

Hammurabi's laws identified and prescribed punishments for a number of sexual offences. The Code provided, for example, that a married woman caught in adultery should be drowned: she and her lover were to be bound to each other and thrown into the water to perish together. Hammurabi also prescribed death by drowning for women who remarried while their husbands were prisoners of war or who refused to have sexual intercourse with their husbands.[1] Although Hammurabi's laws assumed that men normally had only one official wife at a time, the Babylonians did not define marriage as an exclusive sexual relationship. The laws envisioned stable sexual relationships between free men

---

[1] Hammurabi, *Code* § 129, 133a–135, 142–43, ed. and trans. G.R. Driver and Sir John C. Miles, 2 vols. (Oxford: At the Clarendon Press, 1952–55; repr. 1960) 2:51, 53, 57; Walter Kornfeld, "L'adultère dans l'Orient antique," *Revue biblique* 57 (1970) 96–97; Winfield E. Ohlson, "Adultery: A Review," *Boston University Law Review* 17 (1937) 330.

and concubines in addition to their wives. Concubinage in Babylonia was apparently permitted as an exception to the normal rule of monogamy when a wife failed to produce children or suffered from an incurable disease. The Babylonian concubine, who was normally a free woman, served as a supplemental, second-class wife.[2]

The slightly later laws of Ešnunna, like Hammurabi's *Code*, provided the death penalty for women who committed adultery; unlike Hammurabi's laws, however, Ešnunna's law prohibited husbands from pardoning their adulterous wives. Ešnunna did not treat extramarital sexual adventures by men as crimes, but the man who abandoned his wife forefeited his property and was condemned to exile. The property that the exile lost was assigned to the use of his separated spouse and the couple's children.[3]

Assyrian law, in contrast to Babylonian practice, treated adultery and other sex offenses as delicts, or private wrongs, for which the husband or father of the woman was entitled to receive compensation from the seducer. Although the Hittites treated most sexual offenses as delictual obligations, adultery was a striking exception to this rule. Hittite law required the death penalty for both the adulteress and her partner. This severity is unusual, for Hittite law generally avoided imposing the death penalty. The law also allowed the husband to slay the guilty parties if he discovered them in the sex act; this is also unusual, since the Hittites almost entirely prohibited self-help measures to avenge wrongs.[4]

Early Near Eastern religions also played important roles in shaping attitudes toward sex in antiquity. The peoples of the ancient Near East perceived a connection between sex and the sublime. They frequently described religious fulfillment in terms of the human experience of sexual ecstasy and accordingly worshipped great goddesses who were the apotheosis of their sexual ideals. Among the most influential of the ancient sex cults was that of the Phoenician deities Ishtar and Astarte. These androgynous goddesses personified the sexual experiences and yearnings of their devotees, who sometimes referred to Astarte as the Queen of Heaven. Her temples were served by sacred prostitutes, who provided worshippers with opportunities to experience the divine power of the goddess through the ministry of sexual pleasure. Incongruous as this may appear to modern Christian sensibilities, the cult of Ishtar-Astarte offered its devotees an opportunity to celebrate the joys of physical love and its power to transfigure sensual pleasure into something beyond the humdrum and the commonplace.[5]

Ancient Egyptian society was also concerned with sexual behavior and sought

[2] Louis M. Epstein, *Marriage Laws in the Bible and the Talmud*, Harvard Semitic Studies, vol. 1 (Cambridge, MA: Harvard University Press, 1942), pp. 34–35, 40, 45; Hammurabi, *Code* § 144–47, ed. Driver and Miles, 2:57.

[3] Kornfeld, "L'adultère." p. 100.

[4] Kornfeld, "L'adultère," pp. 101–2, 104.

[5] Herodotus, *Historiae libri IX* 1.105, 131. See also Walter Burkert, *Greek Religion, Archaic and Classical*, trans. John Raffan (Oxford: Basil Blackwell, 1985), pp. 152–53.

to bring it under control. Egyptian marriage was apparently monogamous, at least under the Old and Middle Kingdoms: the Egyptian language at that period had no terms for "concubine" or "harem," which suggests that these concepts were not a familiar part of life.[6] Adultery, however, was a familiar and troublesome problem. Some Egyptian texts referred to adultery as "the great crime" and prescribed death as the penalty for both parties—Uba-aner, for example, in Khafra's Tale had his unfaithful wife burned alive, while her lover was thrown to the crocodiles.[7] Other cases suggest that adultery, while considered serious, was not usually viewed as a capital crime, but rather was treated as a lesser offense involving the abuse of authority. In practice, adultery by Egyptian women most commonly resulted in repudiation and divorce, not in execution. Divorce was clearly quite common throughout ancient Egyptian history.[8] Prostitution was not a crime in ancient Egypt and, to judge from the racy tales that Herodotus related to Greek audiences, Egyptian prostitutes were highly regarded in the ancient Mediterranean world. Some of them apparently acquired wealth as well as fame from their trade.[9] One of Herodotus's spicy stories depicts the great pyramid-builder, Cheops, as forcing his own daughter into prostitution in order to raise money to pay for his architectural extravagances.[10]

Sexual Behavior in Ancient Greece

Legal regulation of sex amd marriage was part of ancient Greek life from the archaic period onward. The themes of sexual attraction, abduction, and sexual infidelity feature prominently in the Homeric poems, but reprisal for sexual peccadillos in Homeric society was a matter of private initiative. In the classical period, the great goddess Aphrodite became the patroness of love and sex among the Greeks. Like the Phoenician Ishtar-Astarte cult, the worship of Aphrodite celebrated the power of sexual experience to transcend the mundane. By the fourth century B.C. Greeks had begun to distinguish between two aspects of Aphrodite. Aphrodite *Ourania* personified the higher, celestial qualities of love and affection, while Aphrodite *Pandemos* celebrated the joys of sexual pleasure and served as the patroness of prostitutes.[11]

---

[6] William A. Ward, "Reflections on Some Egyptian Terms Presumed to Mean 'Harem,' 'Harem-Woman,' 'Concubine,'" *Berytus* 31 (1983) 67–74.

[7] W.M. Flinders Petrie, *Egyptian Tales*, ser. 1: *IVth to XIIth Dynasty* (New York: Frederick A. Stokes Co., n.d.), pp. 10–16; Ohlson, "Adultery," p. 332.

[8] C.J. Eyre, "Crime and Adultery in Ancient Egypt," *Journal of Egyptian Archaeology* 70 (1984) 92–105.

[9] Herodotus, *Historiae* 2.135.

[10] Herodotus, *Historiae* 2.126. Another story describes Pharoah Rhampsinitus prostituting his daughter; but Herodotus himself confessed doubts about the authenticity of this one; *Historiae* 2.121.

[11] Burkert, *Greek Religion*, p. 78; Sarah B. Pomeroy, *Goddesses, Whores, Wives, and Slaves: Women in Classical Antiquity* (New York: Schocken Books, 1975), pp. 6–7; Hans Herter, "Die Soziologie der antiken Prostitution im Lichte des heidnischen und christlichen Literatur," *Jahrbuch für Antike und Christentum* 3 (1960) 72–73.

Greek thinkers subjected sexual activity to considerable attention. They never considered sex an evil, nor did they place a high value on sexual continence, but they had a keen sense that some kinds of sexual activities under some circumstances were immoral.[12] One sex offense that Greek writers condemned in severest terms was adultery by a married woman. Public punishment of adultery was apparently unknown in the earliest periods of Greek history.[13] By the time of Philo Judaeus (ca. 13 B.C.–A.D. 45~50), however, adultery had become a serious crime, as had seduction of unmarried women and widows. These offenses could be punished by death or imprisonment; alternatively, the offended husband or father could require the malefactor to pay heavy compensation in order to avoid more unpleasant consequences. Although fidelity was demanded of wives, it was not required of husbands. Nevertheless certain obligations went with marriage: a law of Solon required married men to have sexual relations at least three times each month.[14] In addition, Greek opinion expected a married man to abstain from open or notorious relationships with women other than his wife, although flirtations and even sexual relationships with young men were not considered altogether incompatible with marriage.[15] But Athenian practice often failed to conform to Athenian ideals. Although Aristotle asserted that Athenian husbands had the same duty to observe sexual fidelity as their wives, neither law nor common practice penalized the straying husband as it did the unfaithful wife.[16] And despite the teachings of ethical writers, wealthy Athenian men often kept concubines; the law acknowledged their status and regulated their rights as well as those of their children. "We have mistresses for our enjoyment," Demosthenes (384–322 B.C.) declared, "concubines to serve our person, and wives for the bearing of legitimate offspring."[17]

Athenian law was particularly severe in dealing with the seduction of unmar-

[12] Foucault, *Histoire de sexualité* 2:57–58; Henri Jeanmaire, "Sexualité et mysticisme dans les anciennes sociétés helléniques," in *Mystique et continence*, p. 51.

[13] Hans Julius Wolff, *Written and Unwritten Marriages in Hellenistic and Postclassical Roman Law*, American Philological Association, Monographs, no. 9 (Haverford, PA: American Philological Association, 1939), p. 80; Ohlson, "Adultery," pp. 333–34. The laws of Gortyn, redacted on the island of Crete about 450 B.C., prescribed fines for fornication and seduction, as well as adultery. The adulterer might be punished by death if he was unable to pay his fine. *The Law Code of Gortyn* 2.10–44, ed. and trans. Ronald F. Willetts (Berlin: W. De Gruyter, 1967), p. 40.

[14] Plutarch, *Lives*, Solon 20.3.

[15] Foucault, *Histoire de sexualité* 2:163–65.

[16] Aristotle, *Oeconomica* 1.4.1; W.E.H. Lecky, *History of European Morals*, 2 vols. (London: Longmans, 1859; repr. New York: George Braziller, 1955) 2:313. Cf. also Euripides, *Andromache* ll. 177–80.

[17] Demosthenes, *Kata Neairas*, in his *Private Orations* 59.122. For a comparison of Greek concubinage with concubinage in the ancient Near East, see Louis M. Epstein, "The Institution of Concubinage among the Jews," *Proceedings of the American Academy for Jewish Research* 6 (1935) 176–77, as well as the same author's *Marriage Laws*, p. 67.

ried women. The Athenians in fact regarded seduction as a more serious offense than rape, both because the law presumed that rape was an act of unpremeditated impulse and also because the seducer not only ravished the body of his victim, but also turned her feelings and loyalty toward himself and away from her husband, father, or guardian. The male authority figures were treated as the aggrieved parties in Athenian actions for adultery and seduction; the woman's feelings were material and relevant only insofar as they affected the interests of her male authority figure.[18]

Treatment of sexual offenses was not uniform, however, among the Greek city-states in the classical period. Athenian writers, for example, told denigrating stories about wife-swapping among the Spartans, implying that both the moral and legal standards of Sparta were vastly inferior to those of Athens. In point of fact, Athenian reports of Spartan sexual practices probably exaggerated both the frequency and the indecency of extramarital sex among their Spartan rivals. Much of our information about the Hellenic world comes from Athenian sources, which emphasize the superiority of their sex rules to those of other *poleis*.[19]

Ancient Greeks generally disapproved of sexual relationships or intermarriage between close relatives, and Euripides (480–406 B.C.) characterized the lack of a law prohibiting incest as a feature of barbarian societies. Greek law also penalized rape, whether of a man or a woman, sometimes by fines, sometimes by more severe measures.[20]

Prostitution was a commonplace of sexual life in ancient Athens, as it was in other early societies. Temples dedicated to Aphrodite were apparently served by sacred prostitutes like those of Ishtar-Astarte in Phoenicia.[21] Quite apart from prostitution associated with temples and sacred places, commercial prostitution was also common in Greek antiquity. Ample evidence survives concerning well-organized and flourishing brothels, usually managed by women. These establishments were patronized by men of all types and social ranks, including philosophers and rulers. While most prostitutes were probably slave women, significant numbers of them were resident aliens who found commercial sex a rewarding enterprise.[22] Intelligent and ambitious women of higher social origin often made careers as *hetairai* and sometimes established long-term relationships with men of power and wealth.

Not all Greek prostitutes were women. Male prostitution was also common in ancient Greek society; this is scarcely surprising, given the near universality of homosexual relationships in ancient Hellas and the relative absence of social

---

[18] J.K. Dover, "Classical Greek Attitudes to Sexual Behavior," *Arethusa* 6 (1973) 62.

[19] Pomeroy, *Goddesses*, p. 37.

[20] William Burge, *The Comparative Law of Marriage and Divorce*, eds. Alexander Wood Renton and George Grenville Phillimore (London: Sweet and Maxwell, 1910), pp. 4–5; Pomeroy, *Goddesses*, p. 40; Euripides, *Andromache* ll. 173–76.

[21] Burkert, *Greek Religion*, pp. 152–53.

[22] Herter, "Soziologie," pp. 75–85.

stigma attaching to gay sex. It is at first glance a shade surprising that, while female prostitution was tolerated and free from penalty, a citizen who voluntarily had sex with another man in return for money lost his political rights; alien men who prostituted themselves were required to pay a special prostitution tax. This discrimination against male citizen prostitutes was apparently based on a belief that since most prostitutes were slaves or aliens, the citizen who chose to make his body available for hire was a traitor to his social class and hence deserved to lose his citizenship rights as a result of his disloyalty.[23]

Thus the Hellenic world regulated sexual behavior of many kinds by legal restrictions and imposed penalties upon those who transgressed the norms. It is popularly believed in modern times that legal restrictions upon sexual conduct are a creation of Christianity and that ancient sexuality was free from legal curbs on sexual expression, but the evidence does not support this myth. Limitations on sexual behavior in antiquity differed in many ways from contemporary restrictions, but pre-Christian societies had their own sense of right and wrong, shame and guilt with respect to sex, and their legal systems reflected those attitudes. Many ancient Greeks believed that pleasure, sexual or nonsexual, was not a worthy goal in itself. Indeed, classical Greeks esteemed chastity as a virtue and linked it to the capacity for other kinds of praiseworthy self-denial, such as foreswearing excessive eating and drinking. Greek thinkers also imposed limits even on legitimate sexual relations and laid great stress on restricting sexual pleasure to appropriate times and places.[24] The classical world scorned those who engaged in undisciplined sex as inferior creatures and ranked them with drunkards and gluttons, as persons who were incapable of self-restraint. Men who squandered their wealth on mistresses and dancing girls excited derision and indignation, rather than admiration, among respectable members of Greek society.[25]

Ancient Greek religious observances also imposed curbs on sexual behavior. Greeks of the classical period considered intercourse and other forms of sexual activity a source of *miasma*, or ritual defilement, and required that certain kinds of cultic observances be performed by virgins or by priests who were required to observe chastity during the times when they ministered in the temples. But sex also rendered ordinary people unclean, and custom required them to purify themselves after sexual intercourse before returning to ordinary business.[26]

PLATO

Prescriptions concerning sexual behavior in ancient Greece came mainly from philosophers, rather than from lawmakers. Plato (428/27–348/47 B.C.), by far

---

[23] Dover, "Classical Greek Attitudes," pp. 63, 67–68.

[24] Foucault, *Histoire de sexualité* 2:68–70.

[25] Dover, "Classical Greek Attitudes," pp. 60–61, 63–65.

[26] Burkert, *Greek Religion*, pp. 75–79; Jeanmaire, "Sexualité et mysticisme," pp. 54–55.

the most influential Greek writer on love and sexuality, has left a deep and permanent impression on Western beliefs about sexual morality. A profound ambiguity runs through Plato's treatment of sexual relations and love. At times he saw sex as a positive element in human nature, a benevolent force in mankind's psyche. But at other times Plato viewed sex as a distraction from the search for truth and beauty, a disturbing and negative feature of human experience, which men must learn to constrain within strict limits. In the *Symposium*, Plato treated sex as a positive force. He described sex as a manifestation of love, and thus considered it a component of mankind's eternal search for harmony between body and soul.[27] In his negative or "puritanical" mode, however, Plato viewed sex as a snare that distracted men from the love of wisdom. Sex, he maintained in the *Republic*, trapped men in a bog of sensuality, from which they found it difficult, or even impossible, to escape. Hence wise men should shun sex altogether or at least be wary of its allures. Men were better off when they were old, he added, since age cools the libidinal fires and this makes it easier for the elderly to seek true wisdom and love without sexual distractions.[28] In the *Republic* and in the *Laws* Plato argued that sexual relations ought to be restricted solely to procreative intercourse in marriage. Plato in these works voiced deep suspicion of sexual pleasure; pleasure, he thought, was excusable only when it was an unavoidable side effect of a virtuous act. Marital intercourse for the purpose of generating children produced enjoyment, he observed, and sexual pleasure under these circumstances was morally acceptable. But he strongly condemned promiscuity and any sort of sexual experience in which physical gratification was the primary goal.[29] Whereas in his *Symposium* Plato had sung the praises of homosexual love and indeed seemed to believe that love in a proper sense could exist only between two men, by the time he wrote the *Laws*, he had apparently reconsidered, for in the *Laws* he condemned gay sex as "unnatural" because it is not procreative. Moreover, he continued, gay sex is motivated solely by the desire for pleasure and thus lacks any redeeming virtue.[30] The restrictive side of Plato's treatment of sex later found an appreciative audience among the Fathers of the Christian Church.

ARISTOTLE

Aristotle (384–321 B.C.) dealt with sexual matters in the context of his discussion of the ethics of pleasure. Pleasure, Aristotle held, is not a good in itself and is certainly not the supreme good in human life. He was particularly critical of

[27] *Symposium* 189A–193E, 198A–D, 203C; cf. *Timaeus* 18D and 86D–E.
[28] *Republic* 329C.
[29] *Republic* 458C–E; *Symposium* 207D.
[30] *Symposium* 181B–182D, 191D–192B; *Laws* 636B–C, 836A–C, 839A–B, 841B–E. See also John Boswell, *Christianity, Social Tolerance, and Homosexuality: Gay People in Western Europe from the Beginning of the Christian Era to the Fourteenth Century* (Chicago: University of Chicago Press, 1980; cited hereafter as CSTAH), pp. 13–14; Singer, *Nature of Love*, 1:47–48, 74–79.

the pleasures produced by touch and taste. Humans shared these physical sensations with other animals, Aristotle maintained, and hence they should not be regarded as among the higher values of human life.

Aristotle also contended that seeking after enjoyable feelings leads to licentiousness and makes men brutish. He was sharply critical of sex, which he considered an especially corrupting pleasure, not only because it produces exquisite gratification and hence seems particularly alluring, but also because it affects the entire body, not just certain parts of it.[31] Physical pleasures, such as sex and eating, were irrational desires, Aristotle thought, precisely because reason played little or no part in the pursuit and enjoyment of them. Thus they were inferior to the higher intellectual enjoyments that constituted worthy goals for human striving.[32] Aristotle did not condemn love, however, although he regretted its frequent sexual manifestations. The desirable kind of love, the truly human kind, in his view, was love that transcended physical desire and sexual passion, love that was cool, rational, and nonsexual.[33]

THE PYTHAGOREANS

Other schools of Greek philosophy agreed with Aristotle's rejection of sexual pleasure as a proper human goal. The Pythagoreans considered intense sexual desire a special failing of the young, a phase that adults should outgrow as quickly as possible. They disapproved of sexual enjoyment even within marriage and held that married persons should voluntarily refrain from having sex for pleasure; when they copulated, they should do so solely in order to beget children. Even then couples should beware of the seductive allure of sex and should refrain from "excessive" intercourse, which meant any sexual act that did not aim at procreation.[34]

EPICURUS

Epicurus (342–270 B.C.), unlike Aristotle and the Pythagoreans, viewed pleasure positively. "Pleasure," he wrote, "is the standard by which we judge every good."[35] Thus Epicurus considered pleasure basic to ethical judgments.[36] But

[31] Aristotle, *Nicomachean Ethics* 3.10.18b.1–6 and 7.11.52b.6–24, ed. Hugh Tredennick, trans. J. A. K. Thomson (Harmondsworth: Penguin Books, 1977), pp. 137, 250.

[32] Aristotle, *Rhetorica* 1.11.1370a.16–26, ed. and trans. Médéric Dufour, 2d ed., 2 vols., Collection Guillaume Budé (Paris: Les Belles Lettres, 1960) 1:120.

[33] Aristotle, *Rhetorica* 1.11.1370b.14–15, 21–29.

[34] Sextus Pythagoraeus, *Sententiae* 10, in Friedrich Wilhelm August Mullach, ed., *Fragmenta philosophorum Graecorum*, 3 vols. (Paris: Firmin Didot, 1875–81; repr. Aalen: Scientia Verlag, 1968) 2:117; Dominikus Lindner, *Der Usus Matrimonii: Eine Untersuchung über seine sittliche Bewertung in der katholischen Moraltheologie alter und neuer Zeit* (Munich: Josef Kösel and Friedrich Pustet, 1929), pp. 29–30.

[35] Epicurus, *Pros Menoikeia* 129, in *The Extant Remains*, ed. Cyril Bailey (Oxford: Clarendon Press, 1926; repr. Hildesheim: Georg Olms, 1970), pp. 86–87.

[36] Epicurus, *Fragmenta* 6.59, ed. Bailey, pp. 134–35.

he sharply qualified this endorsement of pleasure as a human goal. Pleasure, he said, is not synonymous with sensual gratification; when he spoke of pleasure, Epicurus meant ease of mind and freedom from bodily pain, rather than "continuous drinkings and revellings and the satisfaction of lusts."[37] Gross physical satisfactions, he taught, do not produce the good life. Sensual reward, according to Epicurus, is simply not an adequate criterion for moral judgments. Transient fleshly joys, he thought, were treacherous and played no significant role in the ordering of a contented life.[38] Epicurus was particularly critical of the snares of sexual pleasure: "Sexual intercourse," he declared, "has never done a man good, and he is lucky if it has not harmed him."[39]

THE CYNICS

The Cynics were radical philosophers who rejected conventional Greek notions of morality and propriety. In contrast to the other Greek philosophical schools, the Cynics saw nothing wrong with enjoying sexual pleasure. Cynics believed that people ought to satisfy their sexual desires in the simplest and least complicated way. Sexual relations between any two people were morally acceptable, according to Diogenes (d. ca. 324 B.C.), so long as both parties consented. Marriage required mutual consent as well, but it need not be an exclusive union: extramarital relations were not immoral, the Cynics thought. Men and women should be allowed to have sex with as many or as few persons of either gender as they choose. Diogenes saw nothing wrong in masturbation or with sexual activity in public. The sole criteria of sexual morality, from the Cynics' point of view, were that sex ought to be simple, natural, voluntary and uncomplicated.[40]

THE STOICS

The sexual doctrines of the Cynics attracted fewer and less influential followers in the Greco-Roman world than did other philosophical teachings. For the subsequent history of Western beliefs and attitudes about sex, the most important Hellenistic philosophical school was Stoicism, and the Stoics took a stern and restrictive view of sexual pleasure, which they thought was of trifling value.[41] Although enjoyment was natural, leading Stoics considered it a mere side effect

[37] Epicurus, *Pros Menoikeia* 132, ed. Bailey, pp. 88–89.
[38] Epicurus, *Kyriai doxai* 10, ed. Bailey, pp. 96–97.
[39] Epicurus, *Fragmenta* 5.8, ed. Bailey, pp. 122–23.
[40] Diogenes Laertius, *Lives of Eminent Philosophers*, Diogenes 6.46, 69; Xenophon, *Symposium* 4.38; Pseudo-Lucian, *Cynicus* 10; Bion of Borysthenes, *Fragments*, ed. Jan Fredrik Kindstrand (Uppsala: Universitet; Stockholm: Almqvist & Wiksell, 1976), p. 274; John M. Rist, *Stoic Philosophy* (Cambridge: At the University Press, 1969), p. 60.
[41] Seneca, *De vita beata* 13.4–5, in his *Philosophische Schriften*, ed. Manfred Rosenbach, 3 vols. (Darmstadt: Wissenschaftlichen Buchgesellschaft, 1969–70) 2:30–32.

of more elevated human aims, comparing it to the hair of the armpits, a trivial accessory, not worthy of serious consideration.[42]

Chrysippus (ca. 277–204 B.C.) adopted a more nuanced analysis of pleasure. He distinguished between *hedone*, an unhealthy kind of physical enjoyment, and *hormai*, by which he meant rational enjoyment, which is under the control of the mind.[43] The goal of the wise man, according to Zeno (ca. 334–262/61 B.C.) should be to avoid both pleasure and pain, although even the wise might experience "suspicions and shadows" of these feelings. Freedom from pain (*apatheia*), however, was distinct, in Zeno's view, from insensibility. The *apatheia* that wise men valued meant an indifference to mere physical sensation, an indifference that resulted from an intellectual determination to free one's self from the vagaries of passion. Pleasure and pain, as Zeno thought of them, were outcomes of mental processes faultily controlled by the intellect. For the Stoics, sensations of all kinds resulted from an imperfect ordering of rational priorities. Those who strenuously pursued pleasure showed poor judgment. The senses, as Seneca remarked, are not proper judges of what is good, and it is a mistake to rely upon them.[44]

The Stoics considered sex a special type of pleasure. Sexual enjoyment was in itself morally indifferent, they believed, but they considered that men make poor use of their time when they occupy their minds with such matters. Sex, like wealth, was not a worthy goal for reasonable adults to seek, and the pursuit of sexual pleasure was not conducive to a healthy morality.[45]

Sexual relations belonged in the category of the "lower appetites," which the wise man refrained from indulging. The truly wise person, according to Stoic teachings, cultivated a sober and reserved demeanor; he abstained from sex and other lower concerns, such as eating and drinking, beyond the minimum essential for bodily health.[46] Accordingly, the wise man should strive to control his reactions to sensual stimuli, including erotic sensations. He should not, for example, be aroused by the sight of his neighbor's wife in the nude; rather he should censor these base feelings and discipline his reactions to bodily sensations. This mastery of the mind should be maintained even in marriage; it

---

[42] Sextus, *Adversus mathematicos* 9.73, in *Stoicorum veterum fragmenta*, ed. Hans Friedrich August von Arnim, 4 vols. (Stuttgart: B. G. Teubner, 1905–24; repr. 1968; cited hereafter as SVF) 3:155; Rist, *Stoic Philosophy*, p. 48.

[43] Rist, *Stoic Philosophy*, p. 38.

[44] Seneca, *Epistolae* 124.3, ed. François Préchac, trans. Henri Noblot, 5 vols., Collection Guillaume Budé (Paris: Les Belles Lettres, 1945–64) 5:98; Epictetus, *Discourses*, 2.11.19–21; Rist, *Stoic Philosophy*, pp. 32, 37, 52, 196.

[45] Seneca, *De beneficiis* 7.2.2, in his *Opera*, ed. Karl Hosius et al., 4 vols. (Leipzig: B.G. Teubner, 1900–1905) 1:189–90, and *Epist.* 104.34, ed. Préchac 4:168; Edward Vernon Arnold, *Roman Stoicism* (London: Routledge and Kegan Paul, 1911; repr. 1958), p. 348; Moses Hadas, *The Stoic Philosophy of Seneca* (New York: W. W. Norton, 1968), p. 54.

[46] Epictetus, *Discourses* 2.18.15–18; Arnold, *Roman Stoicism*, p. 314.

is wrong to lust after another man's wife, but it is equally wrong to lust after one's own.[47]

Because sexual satisfaction ranked low in their scale of values, Stoics considered chastity a virtue of correspondingly high importance. Even in marriage the sexual relationship between a man and a woman ought to be minimal, if not altogether nonexistent. Any departure from the ideal of chastity, marital or nonmarital, made a person feebler and less virtuous.[48]

Oddly enough, some early Stoics had accepted the practice of free love and asserted that sexual relations need not be restricted to marital intercourse. Zeno had argued that general acceptance of free love would eliminate the problem of adultery. Since the wise would be in control of their sexual impulses, he felt, freedom from restrictions on sexual partners would not lead to debauchery or sexual orgies. On similar grounds Zeno advocated nudity: he reasoned that since clothing concealed part of the body, individuals were unable to make informed decisions about the selection of their sexual partners. Zeno further argued that the use of clothing fostered unnecessary inhibitions, which a policy of public nudity would help to erase.[49]

Later Stoics sharply differed from Zeno on these matters. Musonius, for example, maintained that sexual relations are only moral and lawful within marriage and that free love would promote licentiousness. The impact of marriage and sexual relationships upon civic harmony and public order concerned many Stoic teachers. Marriage, they believed, required governmental regulation and attention. Designed as an institution for the procreation and rearing of children, marriage was too important to be left to the personal desires and whims of the partners. Likewise sexual relationships of all kinds had basic implications for public order; sex was a legitimate concern of the *polis*, and not simply the private business of the parties involved.[50] Indeed, sexual love (*eros*) was not only a legitimate interest of the *polis*, but because of its link to the birthrate was essential for the continued existence of the body politic. Sex, both in marriage and outside of it, was accordingly a proper matter for regulation.[51]

Seneca (ca. 4 B.C.–A.D.65), the foremost spokesman for Stoic views in the Latin-speaking world, warned that wise men should beware of the corrupting influence of pleasure, particularly sexual pleasure.[52] Wise men, he taught, certainly do not consider sexual pleasure the highest good; if they did so, there

[47] Rist, *Stoic Philosophy*, p. 45; Lindner, *Usus matrimonii*, p. 28.

[48] Epictetus, *Discourses* 3.22.76 and *Encheiridion* 33.8; Arnold, *Roman Stoicism*, p. 348.

[49] Marcia L. Colish, *The Stoic Tradition from Antiquity to the Early Middle Ages*, 2 vols., Studies in the History of Christian Thought, vols. 34–35 (Leiden: E.J. Brill, 1985) 1:38; Rist, *Stoic Philosophy*, p. 66; Arnold, *Roman Stoicism*, p. 276.

[50] Epictetus, *Encheiridion* 33.8; Arnold, *Roman Stoicism*, p. 349; Rist, *Stoic Philosophy*, p. 56.

[51] Arnold, *Roman Stoicism*, p. 317.

[52] Seneca, *De vita beata* 13.4–5, in *Philosophische Schriften*, ed. Rosenbach 2: 30–32.

would be no depravity they did not applaud, no perversion they scorned, and this would be delirium, not wisdom. "Unchastity," he wrote elsewhere, "is the plague of our time." Ironically, he penned these lines while in exile on Corsica, following his conviction for adultery.[53]

A fundamental Stoic precept, one that exposed them to amused derision from adherents of other schools of thought, was the teaching that "all sins (hamartemata) are equal." This paradox was the converse of another Stoic principle, that "all moral acts (katorthomata) are equal." The principle of the equality of immoral acts caused the Stoics embarrassment because it seemed to contradict common intuitive beliefs about the gradation of offences against the moral code. The paradox implies, for example, that murder is no more serious than jaywalking and, therefore, that both offenses merit the same punishment, a conclusion that most people would reject as absurd. Nonetheless the paradox of the equality of sins was basic to Stoic beliefs. Thus, given the principle of the equality of immoral actions, sexual offenses were neither more nor less serious than other delinquencies.[54]

The Stoics' generally disapproving view of sex rested on their belief that human reason vanished during the sex act. Yet they also insisted that love was a virtue. Zeno and other leading Stoics distinguished, however, between sexual love and the "higher" love that they esteemed. The wise man will love, they maintained, but they meant thereby that he would endeavor to be in harmony with a beautiful object.[55] This "higher" love was a moral imperative for attaining the peace of mind and spirit that was the overriding objective of human life, according to Stoic belief. Sexual love, then, was an inferior and potentially dangerous kind of love, a shallow surrogate for the intellectualized love that Stoics esteemed.[56]

Stoic teachings about sexual morality and its relationship to the goals of human life profoundly influenced the moral and ethical outlook of the Greco-Roman intellectual elite and were widely shared even by those who were in no sense Stoics themselves. As we shall see later, St. Paul's teachings about the role of sex in the moral order bear a marked resemblance to ideas that were common among Zeno's disciples. Paul and the Stoic teachers certainly agreed in their negative views about sexual pleasure and about sex as a potentially destructive temptation that virtuous persons should resist, save for procreative marital sex. But, as we shall also see, Paul was no Stoic; he rejected many basic Stoic doctrines and, moreover, his loathing for sex contrasted sharply with the Stoic premise that sex was in itself morally indifferent.[57]

[53] Seneca, *Epistolae* 124.2, ed. Préchac 5:97; Hadas, *Stoic Philosophy of Seneca*, pp. 107, 129.

[54] Rist, *Stoic Philosophy*, pp. 81–96; Colish, *Stoic Tradition* 1:44–45, 130.

[55] Epictetus, *Discourses* 4.1.143; Cicero, *Tusculanae disputationes* 4.72, in SVF 3:652.

[56] SVF 3:650–51; Arnold, *Roman Stoicism*, p. 318; Colish, *Stoic Tradition* 1:137, 151–53.

[57] Arnold, *Roman Stoicism*, pp. 425–26; Dover, "Classical Greek Attitudes," p. 70.

Sexual Behavior in Ancient Rome

ROMAN LITERARY TREATMENTS

Roman writers did not necessarily echo the moralistic attitudes of the Stoics and the other philosophical schools. Roman treatments of sexual themes have been described as "extraordinarily dispassionate," and indeed their discussions of bodily passions often displayed a decidedly matter-of-fact quality. Lucretius (ca. 97–54 B.C.) observed that human sexual urges are fundamentally insatiable. Lovers seek frantically for solace in the physical pleasures of sex, Lucretius noted, but ultimate satisfaction always eludes them. Nothing can cure the sexual itch; the best that men and women can do is to appease it momentarily, to satisfy the hunger for a time, but it will soon return to torment them. Marriage, Lucretius thought, provided the safest respite from this torment. Marital sex, he thought, quickly becomes routine and regular, devoid of grand passion, and this reduces the agony of insatiable longing that tortures the unmarried.[58]

Martial (ca. A.D. 40–104) wryly noted that lust frequently leads to mistakes. He and other Roman satirists shared a widely held view that sexual pleasure was not only a virtually universal preoccupation of humankind, but also that it was a goal that individuals could appropriately pursue, although they risked making themselves ridiculous in the process.[59] The public pursuit of sexual satisfaction outside of marriage furnished comic and satirical writers with a stock theme. The amused tone of Roman authors faded, however, when they talked about marriage. They considered marriage a serious matter in which sexual fulfillment and affection between the parties played subordinate roles. Roman marriage, at least among the upper classes, was concerned with property, politics, and power; it left little room for the pursuit of emotional satisfaction or sexual cravings. *Patresfamiliae* (male heads of households) had intercourse with their wives in order to produce heirs for their property who would continue the existence of their families. Married love and affection were, of course, important to many couples; but only scanty evidence survives of a concern with sexual and emotional fulfillment within marriage. Romans apparently regarded the emotional attachment between husband and wife as a private and confidential matter, not to be publicized or shared with outsiders.[60]

Married couples among the Roman elite lived in a social system in which the

[58] Lucretius, *De rerum natura* 4.1058–1287, ed. William Ellery Leonard and Stanley Barney Smith (Madison: University of Wisconsin Press, 1961), pp. 616–38; Singer, *Nature of Love*, 1:129–40.

[59] Martial, *Epigrammata* 11.9, ed. Ludwig Friedlaender, 2 vols. (Leipzig: S. Hirzel, 1886; repr. Amsterdam: Adolf M. Hakkert, 1967) 2:178: "Saepe solecismum mentula nostra facit." See also Boswell, CSTAH, p. 62.

[60] Philippe Ariès, "L'amour dans le mariage," in *Sexualités occidentales*, Ecole des Hautes Etudes en Sciences Sociales, Centre d'Etudes Transdisciplinaires, Communications, no. 35 (Paris: Seuil, 1982), p. 121.

family, as modern societies think of it, did not exist. The Roman *familia* meant a household, not a family in the modern sense, and households came in a great variety of sizes and shapes. Among the wealthy and powerful, the household often numbered hundreds of persons and things: children, servants, slaves, livestock, and other property were all part of the *familia*. But the head of household, the *paterfamilias*, was not part of the *familia*, although his wife and children were members of it and, like the servants and slaves, oxen and geese, and the rest of the *familia*, they belonged to the *paterfamilias*. Among the poor, however, households were apparently small, since they included no slaves or servants and little property. The *familia* of the humble often consisted simply of a woman and her children. Again, the male head of household was not part of his own *familia*.[61]

Roman upper-class men, upon whose activities the literary sources concentrate, typically sought sexual pleasure outside of marriage, not within it. While the upper-class Roman woman was expected to be a virgin at the time of her first marriage, boys usually received their sexual initiation in early puberty, often from prostitutes. In theory and in law, married men were forbidden to consort with women other than their wives during the republican period of Rome's history. The offense, however, carried no effective social or legal penalties and was generally ignored. Married women, by contrast, were considered tramps if they had intercourse with any men other than their husbands and their sexual dalliances could be punished by death, at least under certain circumstances. The sexual double standard was well established in Roman tradition, as in the rest of the ancient Mediterranean, from an early period.[62] Divorce, apparently uncommon during the early Republic, grew increasingly frequent and became socially acceptable from the first century B.C. onward. By the late imperial period, divorce was almost routine, at least among the propertied households about whom the poets and historians tell us most. Fragmentary evidence, mostly from inscriptions, however, indicates that divorce was considerably less frequent among the lower orders than it was among the wealthy and powerful.[63]

Romans, like most other ancient peoples, accepted concubinage as a basic institution alongside marriage. Concubinage during the imperial period was commonplace at all levels of traditional Roman society. From the early period of the Republic, Romans had viewed concubinage as an alternative to marriage. Most concubinage relationships involved a man of high social standing who cohabited with a woman of low status. The relationship could be terminated at

[61] David Herlihy, *Medieval Households* (Cambridge: Harvard University Press, 1985), pp. 2–4.

[62] Theodor Gottlob, "Der Ehebruch und seine Rechtsfolgen in den vorgratianischen Quellen und bei Gratian selbst," *Studia Gratiana* 1 (1954) 335.

[63] Iiro Kajanto, "On Divorce among the Common People of Rome," *Revue des études latines* 47 (1969) 99–113.

any time by the male partner.[64] As Roman society underwent basic changes during the late Republic, concubinage gradually became an alternative to marriage for single men who wished to remain unmarried but to have regular sexual partners. Marriage involved a union between persons of roughly the same social level, and brides or their fathers were expected to furnish dowries as a normal, even indispensable, part of the arrangements. As a result, couples who found it either difficult or impossible to fulfill these conditions might choose instead to live together as lover and concubine. Concubinage was particularly popular among soldiers, who could not marry during their term of service, and with *patresfamiliae* who lacked the financial resources needed to arrange advantageous marriages for their daughters. In the Republic and early Empire, concubinage was limited, at least in theory, to unions between a single man and a single woman; in the later Empire, however, it became possible, even common, for wealthy and powerful men to keep one or more concubines in addition to a legitimate wife.[65] Roman society strongly discouraged concubinage between high-ranking women and low-status men, for such unions offended Roman notions of propriety. A free woman who became the concubine of a male slave was liable to be reduced to slavery herself in consequence of her liaison. Concubinage that involved two free persons of the same or similar status was apparently uncommon.[66]

Concubinage carried no moral or social stigma, at least so far as the male partner was concerned. The relationship was accepted as commonplace and it was certainly no disgrace for a man to keep a concubine instead of a wife. The woman in the partnership, however, ranked far below a legitimately married woman. Despite this, talented and witty concubines of high-ranking men frequented the highest circles of Imperial society.[67] Many concubinage relationships were entered into simply for the sexual gratification of the man, who

[64] Paul Martin Meyer, *Der römische Konkubinat nach den Rechtsquellen und den Inschriften* (Leipzig: B.G. Teubner, 1895; repr. Aalen: Scientia Verlag, 1966); Adhémar Esmein, *Le mariage en droit canonique* 2d ed., 2 vols. (Paris: Sirey, 1929–35) 2:106; Epstein, *Marriage Laws*, p. 68.

[65] John P.V.D. Balsdon, *Roman Women, Their History and Habits* (London: Bodley Head, 1962; New York: John Day, 1963), p. 232; Epstein, "Institution of Concubinage," pp. 177–78, and *Marriage Laws*, pp. 68–69; Vern L. Bullough, *The Subordinate Sex: A History of Attitudes toward Women* (Urbana: University of Illinois Press, 1973), pp. 90–91.

[66] Tacitus, *Annales* 12.53, ed. C.D. Fisher (Oxford: Clarendon Press, 1906; repr. 1966; unpaginated); Balsdon, *Roman Women*, pp. 233–34; Beryl Rawson, "Roman Concubinage and Other de facto Marriages," *Transactions of the American Philological Association* 104 (1974) 279–305.

[67] Paul Gide, "De la condition de l'enfant naturel et de la concubine dans la legislation romaine," published as an appendix to his *Etude sur la condition privée de la femme dans le droit ancien et moderne et en particulier sur le sénatus-consulte Velléien*, 2d ed. by Adhémar Esmein (Paris: L. Larone et Forcel, 1885), pp. 564–65; Henri Leclercq, "Concubinat," in *Dictionnaire d'archéologie chrétienne et de liturgie*, ed. F. Cabrol et al., 15 vols. (Paris: Letouzey et Ané, 1907–53; cited hereafter as DACL) 3B:2498; Paul

could easily discard his concubine of the moment when a more attractive girl caught his eye. Yet evidence also reveals a few unions marked by deep, genuine, and long-lasting affection between lover and concubine.[68]

Prostitution, both male and female, was a flourishing industry throughout Roman history. In the early Republic, Romans made no distinction between a concubine and a female prostitute and used the same term, *paelex*, indifferently to designate a woman involved in any kind of nonmarital sexual relationship.[69] Gradually, however, the social and economic postion of the concubine improved. Differences were noted between long-term relationships outside of marriage and the transient liaisons that characterized prostitution.[70]

Two classes of prostitutes emerged in late republican and early imperial Rome. The established harlot normally lived and worked in a brothel, was required to register with the magistrates, paid a special tax known as the *vectigalia meretricum*, and received in return a prostitute's licence (*licentia stupri*). Unregistered prostitutes usually operated as streetwalkers, had no fixed address, and were reputed to be cheaper, but more dangerous and predatory, than their registered counterparts. Many prostitutes were slaves or women captured in war; brothel keepers purchased still others from suppliers among the barbarians.[71]

Higher-class prostitutes, described as *delictae* and *pretiosae*, were courtesans, patronized by men of wealth and high social position.[72] The fact that Latin had at least twenty-five terms for "prostitute" says something about the varieties and importance of prostitution in Roman society.[73]

Lacombe, *La famille dans la société romaine: étude de moralité comparée*, Bibliothèque anthropologique, vol. 7 (Paris: Lecrosnier et Babé, 1889), pp. 392–94.

[68] See, for example, the moving lament of Libanius (A.D. 314–91) on the death of his concubine in his *Autobiography (Oration I)* 278, ed. and trans. A. F. Norman, University of Hull Publications (London: Oxford University Press for the University of Hull, 1965), p. 141. A few memorial inscriptions also testify to special affection for a concubine; e.g., *Corpus inscriptionum Latinarum* (Berlin: G. Reimer [imprint varies], 1962– ; in progress; hereafter CIL) 1/2:601, 729, no. 1277, 2527.

[69] Harry E. Wedeck, "Synonyms for Meretrix," *Classical Weekly* 37 (3 January 1944) 116.

[70] Meyer, *Römische Konkubinat*, p. 10; Herter, "Soziologie," pp. 77–79.

[71] Herter, "Soziologie," pp. 77–79.

[72] Suetonius, *De vita Caesarum*, Caligula 40; Zosimus, *Historia nova* 2.38, ed. Immanuel Bekker, in *Corpus scriptorum historiae Byzantinae*, 50 vols. (Bonn: E. Weber, 1828–97) 30:104.

[73] Wedek, "Synonyms," pp. 116–17. Pierre Pierrugues, *Glossarium eroticum linguae latinae sive theogoniae, legum et morum nuptialium apud Romanos explanatio nova* (Paris: A.F. & P. Dondey-Dupré, 1826; repr. Amsterdam: Adolf M. Hakkert, 1965), whom Wedek surprisingly fails to cite, lists others, including *casalides, casorides, casonitae, charybdes, circulatrix, communis mulier, conciliatrix, diabolares, diabolae, Doris, famosa, gallina, junix, juvenca, libertina, limax, lupa, nonaria, paelex, peregrina, persuasatrix, procax, proseda, scorta, togata*, and *uxor*.

Not all Roman prostitutes were full-grown men or women; Martial twice refers to child prostitution as exceedingly common and derides the efforts of the Emperor Domitian (A.D. 81–96) to outlaw the practice of placing young persons in brothels.[74] Consignment of surplus children to the stews was a common resort of the poor at Rome and elsewhere in the Empire. For indigent parents it represented a means of earning money from unwanted progeny, at the same time reducing the drain on household resources.

How much Roman prostitutes earned from their trade is difficult to determine, for fees varied enormously between different classes of harlots. Martial mentions a payment of two gold pieces to a prostitute named Galla, but also indicates that some fatuous customers gave her five times as much.[75] Certainly some prostitutes accumulated sufficient savings to furnish attractive dowries when they married, but they were probably exceptional. Typical prostitutes seem to have made not much more than a living wage from their exertions.[76]

Differences in fee scales among different prostitutes reflected differences in social background; prostitutes from higher-class families usually fared better than their humbler coworkers. Diversity of fees was also related to the prostitute's skills and accomplishments. Numerous ancient sources refer to the *artes meretricae*, a phrase that has a variety of meanings. The ability to amuse clients and make them laugh was one component of the *artes*, and some prostitutes clearly were spirited and clever entertainers. The professional skills of the Roman prostitute frequently included the ability to play musical instruments (usually the flute or the harp), to sing, and to dance. Acting ability was also counted among the skills that an accomplished *meretrix* should have. In addition the *artes meretricae* presumably included more specifically technical skills, including artifices to avoid pregnancy, as well as a varied repertoire of sexual diversions.[77]

[74] Martial, *Epigram.* 9.6, 9.8, ed. Friedlaender 2:53, 54.

[75] Martial, *Epigram.* 9.4, and cf. 2.39, ed. Friedlaender 2:53 and 1:257. Martial's evidence is borne out by graffiti from Pompeii, where two gold pieces is the commonest price mentioned in advertisements for prostitutes: CIL 4:126 (no. 1969), 507 (no. 4023), 514 (no. 4150), 531 (no. 4441), and 577 (no. 5105). A Pompeian prostitute named Drauca could apparently be had for a penny (CIL 4:139, no. 2193), while others demanded as much as sixteen gold pieces (CIL 4:111, no. 1751). A male prostitute named Felix offered to perform fellatio for one gold piece (CIL 4:547, no. 5408), while Lahis (no. 1969) asked two gold pieces and Libanis demanded three for the same service (CIL 4:130, no. 2028).

[76] Herter, "Soziologie," pp. 80–85.

[77] Herter, "Soziologie," pp. 95–106; on the accomplishments expected from male harlots, see Cicero, *In Catalinam* 2.10.23. Some prostitutes clearly took pride in their professional standing and skills; see CIL 9:186 (no. 2029) and see also James N. Adams, *The Latin Sexual Vocabulary* (London: Duckworth, 1982), p. 194. It is not likely that many ancient contraceptive practices had much practical value in avoiding pregnancy; for descriptions of some of the methods prescribed in antiquity see John T. Noonan, Jr.,

The married man who patronized prostitutes or kept a concubine was not subject, by and large, either to moral or legal sanctions in Roman society. The husband who had an affair with another man's wife might be slain if he were surprised in the act by the woman's father, although the *Lex Julia de adulteriis* (18 B.C.) stringently restricted this right to certain specific circumstances. The husband who slew his wife's lover was guilty of murder, but the usual penalties for homicide might be reduced in these cases. Adultery, however, was primarily a female offense, and Roman law on this subject reflected the sentiments of upper-class Roman males.[78]

Romans generally tolerated a wide variety of other sexual practices. Masturbation by men or women was regarded as a blameless but unsatisfactory substitute for intercourse and carried no moral stigma, although the adult masturbator was sometimes ridiculed as immature or childish.[79] Homosexual relations were commonplace and likewise carried no social or moral opprobrium, with two important exceptions. Romans considered it disgraceful for a free man to adopt the passive role in anal intercourse. No disapproval attached to the man who played the active part in the relationship, and upper-class Roman males with a taste for sodomy were expected to recruit slaves or household boys to service their sexual desires.[80] The passive role in fellatio was even more strongly disapproved; again, the objection was not to the act itself, but to what was felt to be the incongruity of a free man acting the role customarily assigned to a slave or servant boy. No such disapproval appears to have attached to the man who performed cunnilingus on a woman.[81] Lesbian relationships excited greater opprobrium than did male homosexual liaisons, perhaps because upper-class Roman men found lesbianism threatening to their own sexual self-esteem.[82] Male sexual prowess was also linked to the size of the penis, and the man who boasted a large member was admired and envied by his more modestly endowed brethren.[83] Other sexual attitudes that figure in Roman literary sources have to do with men who preferred older women as their sex partners, a taste that Martial considered ludicrous.[84] Similarly scorned were Roman women who

---

Contraception: A History of Its Treatment by the Catholic Theologians and Canonists (Cambridge: Harvard University Press, Belknap Press, 1965), pp. 9–29.

[78] Ohlson, "Adultery," p. 336.

[79] Martial, *Epigram.* 9.41, 14.203, ed. Friedlaender 2:71–72, 341.

[80] Martial, *Epigram.* 3.71, 6.33, ed. Friedlaender 1:320, 444; Paul Veyne, "L'homosexualité à Rome," in *Sexualités occidentales*, p. 30.

[81] Martial, *Epigram.* 2.31, 33, 89; 3.87, 88; 4.84; 7.67; 9.63; 11.30, 47; 12.85, ed. Friedlaender 1:254, 255, 280, 328, 381, 507 and 2:86, 183, 190, 163; Veyne, "L'homosexualité," pp. 26–29.

[82] Martial, *Epigram.* 1.90; 7.70, ed. Friedlaender 1:219–20, 509.

[83] Martial, *Epigram.* 6.36; 9.33, ed. Friedlaender 1:445; 2:67; Adams, *Latin Sexual Vocabulary*, pp. 77–78.

[84] Martial, *Epigram.* 3.75; 9.66; 11.46, ed. Friedlaender 1:321 and 2:87, 189–90.

chose their lovers from the ranks of aliens and foreigners, whom conservative Romans regarded with contempt.[85] Again, it is not difficult to see in this latter attitude a defensive reaction to the sexual threat that foreign males might pose to Roman self-esteem and sexual prowess.[86]

Roman Law

Roman literary sources expressed skepticism that sexual activities should or even could be regulated successfully by law. Sex was too personal and intimate, sexual habits too varied, and ideas about sexual morality too diverse for the formal processes of the legal system to deal adequately and fairly with them at all. Martial, the sharpest and most perceptive critic of first century Roman sexual mores, ridiculed efforts to defend the sanctity of marriage by fencing it about with legal walls and barriers.[87] Besides, he pointed out, it was absurd to enact elaborate prohibitions of adultery and other extramarital sex when divorce was so simple and so common that a woman who was not yet thirty had already married ten husbands.[88]

Despite such reservations, Roman lawmakers and the learned jurists (many of them Stoics) who elaborated legal doctrine during the classical period of Roman law incorporated into the legal system numerous regulations to curb the sexual practices of Rome's subjects.

Roman law concerning sexual matters is permeated by symbols of patriarchal dominance. Legislators and jurists assumed that women were at the service of men, ministered to male pleasure, and accepted male gratification as their primary goal. Roman lawmakers, like Roman poets and orators, treated women as in some measure less fully human than adult males; they were particularly shocked whem women sought sexual pleasure for themselves. Classical Roman law reflected the beliefs and opinions current among the dominant male ruling groups.[89] We are best informed about the restrictions imposed on the sexual

[85] Martial, *Epigram.* 3.76, ed. Friedlaender 1:321–22.

[86] Martial, *Epigram.* 7.30, ed. Friedlaender 1:489.

[87] Martial, *Epigram.* 6.2, ed. Friedlaender 1:431.

[88] Martial, *Epigram.* 6.7, ed. Friedlaender 1:433: "Aut minus aut certe non plus tricesima lux est, / et nubis decimo iam Telesilla viro. / Quae nubit totiens non nubit: adultera lege est; / Offendor moecha simpliciore minus."

[89] The classical period of Roman law is usually deemed to run from the reign of Augustus (27 B.C.–A.D. 14) to the reign of Alexander Severus (A.D. 222–35). On its characteristics and major figures see Fritz Schulz, *History of Roman Legal Science* (Oxford: At the Clarendon Press, 1946), pp. 99–101; H.F. Jolowicz, *Historical Introduction to the Study of Roman Law* (Cambridge: At the University Press, 1932), p. 6; Roscoe Pound, *The Lawyer from Antiquity to Modern Times, with Particular Reference to the Development of Bar Associations in the United States* (St. Paul, MN: West Publishing Co., 1953), p. 46; Joseph C. Smith, "The Sword and Shield of Perseus: Some Mythological Dimensions of the Law," typescript of paper presented to the Faculty of Law of the University of British Columbia, 11 December 1983, p. 23. On class stratification and sexuality see

activities of the upper classes of Roman society, but there is evidence that lower-class women's sexual behavior was also curbed by legal restrictions. In Roman Egypt, for example, employers required their wet nurses to abstain from sex, either marital or nonmarital, during the term for which they were engaged. Wet-nursing contracts often featured stringent penalty clauses for nonobservance of the ban on sexual intercourse.[90]

Fornication

The basic category of sexual offence under Roman law was *stuprum*, that is, habitual sexual intercourse with an unmarried, free woman.[91] *Stuprum*, in other words, meant fornication, but only certain kinds of fornication. Fornication with slaves or servant girls did not count as *stuprum*, nor did intercourse with prostitutes or other women of degraded status.[92] Papinian (d. A.D. 212) insisted that *stuprum* must be distinguished from adultery. Adultery involved sex acts between a married woman and someone other than her husband, while *stuprum* was restricted to intercourse between any man, married or not, and an unmarried girl or widow.[93] Intercourse with a concubine was also excepted from the definition of *stuprum* according to the jurist Modestinus (fl. ca. A.D. 222–44), who somewhat inconsistently excluded homosexual intercourse from his definition of *stuprum* in one sentence and then appeared to include it in the next.[94] The basic statute on sexual offenses, the *Lex Julia de adulteriis* (18 B.C.) was vague and sweeping in its definition of illicit sexual unions; under its terms

---

also Veyne, "L'homosexualité," p. 30; Peter Brown, *Augustine of Hippo: A Biography* (Berkeley and Los Angeles: University of California Press, 1967), p. 390.

[90]Keith R. Bradley, "Sexual Regulations in Wet-Nursing Contracts from Roman Egypt," *Klio* 62 (1980) 321–25.

[91]Eduard Max Löwenstein, *Die Bekämpfung des Konkubinates in der Rechtsentwicklung*, Strafrechtliche Abhandlungen, vol. 20 (Bresslau [Wrocław]: Schletter, 1919), p. 6; Modestinus, in Dig. 48.5.35(34). Roman law texts will be cited throughout from the critical edition of the *Corpus iuris civilis* by Paul Krueger, Theodor Mommsen, Rudolf Schoell, and Wilhelm Kroll, 3 vols. (Berlin: Weidmann, 1872–95). In addition, citations of the Digest also refer to *The Digest of Justinian*, Latin text ed. Theodor Mommsen and Paul Krueger, English trans. ed. Alan Watson, 4 vols. (Philadelphia: University of Pennsylvania Press, 1985). The citation system is the standard one used in the *Bulletin of Medieval Canon Law* (hereafter BMCL).

[92]Guglielmo Castelli, "Il concubinato e la legislazione augustea," *Bulletino dell'Istituto di diritto romano* 27 (1914) 56–57. Many of the same terms and definitions remain current in modern civil law jurisdictions. See, e.g., the definition of *stuprum* in João Mestieri, *Estudo sobre o tipo básico do delito de estupro* (Rio de Janeiro: Apex, 1968), p. 11; Darcy Campos Medeiros and Arnoldo Moreira, *Do crime de sedução* (Rio de Janeiro: Freitas Bastos, 1968), p. 13.

[93]Dig. 48.5.6.1 (Papinian).

[94]Dig. 48.5.35(34) pr., 1: "Stuprum committit, qui liberam mulierem consuetudinis causa, non matrimonii continet, excepta videlicet concubina. Adulterium in nupta ad-

all sexual copulation, save for marital intercourse, might have been classed as *stuprum*.[95] The penalties prescribed for *stuprum* in the *Lex Julia* were severe; they included loss of half of one's property for persons who were classed as *honesti*; *humiles*, on the other hand, might be sentenced upon conviction to corporal punishment and exile.[96]

Both the *Lex Julia* and the interpretations of it by the jurists dealt differently with men and women in their treatment of fornication. Men could have sexual relations with prostitutes and concubines without penalty; they were debarred only from illicit intercourse with women of the higher classes. Upper-class women, however, were forbidden to have sexual intercourse with anyone at all, save for their husbands. The law was far from an abstract statement of ideals. Augustus himself penalized his daughter and one of his granddaughters for *stuprum*.[97] Some women of the upper classes so strongly resented the legal limitations on their sex lives that they registered with the magistrates as prostitutes in order to free themselves from harassment because of their nonmarital sexual activities. But such protests carried serious handicaps: registered prostitutes were barred from receiving legacies or inheritances and thus cut off from a share in familial property. The loophole in the law that enabled respectable women to escape punishment for *stuprum* was, in any event, closed by Tiberius (A.D. 14–37), who forbade upper-class women to enroll as prostitutes.[98]

Adultery

The *Lex Julia* itself did not define adultery or differentiate it clearly from *stuprum*.[99] The jurists assumed that adultery was a married woman's crime, while *stuprum* was a male offense. The married man who had sexual relations

---

mittitur; stuprum in vidua vel virgine vel puero committitur." But in Dig. 50.16.101 pr. Modestinus appears to limit *stuprum* to intercourse between men and women.

[95] Löwenstein, *Bekämpfung*, p. 4; Alexis Baumann, *Die zivilrechtliche Bedeutung des Konkubinates in rechtsvergleichender Darstellung unter besonderer Berücksichtigung des schweitzerischen, deutschen, österreichischen, und französischen Privatrechtes* (Coburg: Gedruckt im Tageblatt Haus, 1932), p. 9; Pál Csillag, *The Augustan Laws on Family Relations* (Budapest: Akadémiai Kiadó, 1976), pp. 77–81, 175–78, 180–84; Karl Galinsky, "Augustus' Legislation on Morals and Marriage," *Philologus* 125 (1981) 126–44.

[96] Inst. 4.18.4; Löwenstein, *Bekämpfung*, p. 6.

[97] Tacitus, *Annales* 3.24.2; Judith P. Hallett, *Fathers and Daughters in Roman Society: Women and the Elite Family* (Princeton: Princeton University Press, 1984), pp. 238–39.

[98] Tacitus, *Annales* 2.85; Pomeroy, *Goddesses*, p. 160; Lecky, *Hist. of European Morals* 2:303.

[99] J. A. C. Thomas, "Lex Julia de adulteriis coercendis," in *Etudes offertes à Jean Macqueron* (Aix-en-Provence: Faculté de droit et des sciences économiques, 1970), p. 637; Csillag, *Augustan Laws*, pp. 178–80; Castelli, "Concubinato," pp. 65–66; Amy Richlin, "Approaches to the Sources on Adultery at Rome," *Women's Studies* 8 (1981) 225–50.

with a woman other than his wife might be committing *stuprum*, but certainly
was not committing adultery. By contrast, the married woman who had sexual
relations with anyone other than her husband was guilty of adultery, whether
or not her illicit sexual partner was married.[100] Married women, moreover,
were specifically denied legal redress against their husbands because of their
husbands' extramarital sexual adventures.[101]

The *Lex Julia* sought to substitute punishment by public judicial process
for private vengeance in adultery cases. Prior to the adoption of the Augustan
statute the law had dealt rather leniently with adulterous women.[102] Roman
practice, however, was harsher than the law and had condoned the killing of a
wife if her husband caught her in an adulterous relationship. Roman cuckolds
sometimes killed their wives' lovers as well. The *Lex Julia* sought to limit the
wronged husband's *jus occidendi* by providing that if a married man caught his
wife in the act of intercourse with another man, the husband could kill his wife's
lover, provided that he did so at once; but the law forbade the husband to kill
the wife. Alternatively, the injured husband could detain his wife's paramour
for a period of up to twenty hours; at the end of this time, he must release his
prisoner, who presumably might by then be rather the worse for wear. The *Lex
Julia* accorded extensive rights to the father of an adulterous woman should he
discover the guilty pair in the act of adultery. The father in these circumstances
had the right to kill both his daughter and her lover, but he must slay both of
them, not just one or the other, and he must do it immediately. The father, like
the injured husband, had the alternative right to detain the adulterer for a
twenty-hour period.[103]

These complicated and rather odd-sounding provisions were designed to discourage informal self-help in adultery cases and to establish limits to the vengeance that the outraged male relatives of an adulteress could lawfully wreak
upon the unfaithful wife and her illicit consort. Husbands or fathers who ex-
ceeded the strict limits that the *Lex Julia* imposed upon their wrath were liable
to prosecution, although the penalties that might be imposed upon them under
these circumstances were lighter than the normal sanctions for acts of violence.
A husband who, contrary to the *Lex Julia*, killed his adulterous wife after finding her *in flagrante delicto*, for example, was spared the death penalty, but was
liable to perpetual exile and demotion in social rank.[104]

Not all married women were legally capable of committing adultery. The
wife of a slave, for example, could not commit adultery since marital unions

---

[100]Thomas, "Lex Julia," p. 637; Löwenstein, *Bekämpfung*, p. 6.

[101]Cod. 9.9.1 (Septimius Severus).

[102]Hallett, *Fathers and Daughters*, pp. 237–38.

[103]Thomas, "Lex Julia," pp. 640–41; Csillag, *Augustan Laws*, pp. 195–99.

[104]Thomas, "Lex Julia," p. 638; M. Andréev, "Divorce et adultère dans le droit
romain classique," *Revue historique de droit français et étranger* (cited hereafter as
RHDF), 4th ser., 35 (1957) 24–25; Csillag, *Augustan Laws*, pp. 185–95; Dig. 48.8.1.5
(Marcian).

among slaves lacked the dignity of legitimate marriage in a proper legal sense.[105] A concubine, for the same reason, was not guilty of adultery if she was unfaithful to her mate; some jurists held that infidelities committed by a woman who lived apart from her husband should not be classified as adultery.[106] Moreover, if a husband failed to repudiate his wife after discovering that she was having an affair with someone else, he was barred from bringing a criminal action against her for adultery and became liable for punishment himself for promoting immorality.[107] Yet, a married woman who wished to take a lover could not protect herself against an accusation of adultery by becoming the proprietress of a brothel or a theater.[108] The landlord who rented a property to persons who intended to use it for the purpose of committing adultery also became a party to their crime, subject to the same penalties as the principals.[109] Those who acted as go-betweens for an adulterous couple or who otherwise aided or abetted an adulterous union were also subject to punishment.[110] The Emperor Alexander Severus (A.D. 222–35) imposed a five-year statute of limitations upon prosecutions for adultery and this apparently applied to accessories as well as to principals in the crime.[111] An adulteress who, after a divorce from her husband, attempted to marry her partner in adultery faced legal problems in doing so, although such marriages were not explicitly forbidden until after Christianity had become the established religion of the Roman state.[112]

Marriage

Roman law punished *stuprum* and *adulterium* and ignored sexual relations between upper-class men and low-status women such as slaves or prostitutes, but it extended positive protection to sexual intercourse between married persons. Romans had traditionally considered marriage a private arrangement, and

[105] Henryk Insadowski, "Quid momenti habuerit Christianismus ad ius romanum matrimoniale evolvendum?" in *Acta Congressus iuridici internationalis VII saeculo a decretalibus Gregorii IX et XIV a Codice Iustiniano promulgatis*, 5 vols. (Rome: Pontificium Institutum Utriusque Iuris, 1935–37) 2:51–52.

[106] Wolff, *Written and Unwritten Marriages*, p. 80. Capture by enemy forces in war ruptured the marriage bond, so that sexual relations by the wife of a prisoner of war with someone other than her husband did not constitute adultery: Dig. 48.5.14(13).7 (Ulpian); Giuseppe D'Ercole, "Il consenso degli sposi e la perpetuità del matrimonio nel diritto romano e nei Padri della Chiesa," *Studia et documenta historiae et iuris* (hereafter SDHI) 5 (1939) 35.

[107] Cod. 9.9.1–2 (Septimius Severus); Dig. 48.5.30(29) pr. (Ulpian).

[108] Dig. 48.5.11(10).2 (Papinian).

[109] Dig. 48.5.9(8) (Marcian).

[110] Dig. 48.5.13(12) (Ulpian).

[111] Cod. 9.9.5 (Alexander Severus).

[112] Enrico G. Vitali, "Premesse romanistiche a uno studio sull'impedimentum criminis (adulterio e divieti matrimoniali)," in *Studi in onore di Gaetano Scherillo*, 3 vols. (Milan: Istituto editoriale cisalpino 'La Goliardica,' 1972) 1:274–98.

it became subject to legal definition and control only in the time of Augustus.[113] Romans were reluctant to allow public authorities to interfere in such a private and domestic matter as marriage, and this attitude presumably accounts for some peculiarities of Roman marriage law.[114]

The classical legal definition of Roman marriage was formulated by Modestinus: "Marriage is the joining of a man and a woman and their union for life by divine and human law."[115] While this definition has rightly been described as juristically unworkable, it does enunciate some important elements in the Roman notion of what marriage involved.[116] Modestinus's formulation implied that mutual consent of the parties was required and hence that marriage was a bilateral contract, notions that were developed more explicitly elsewhere in the law.[117] The statement that marriage was a permanent union was not intended to imply the later Christian notion of a lifelong indissoluble marriage that made any subsequent marriage void so long as the first spouse survived. Rather, the classical jurists meant simply that the parties at the time of marriage intended to live together on a lasting basis.[118] The couple's commonality of life that Modestinus described as a sharing referred both to an attitude of mind, a belief that the married partners formed a single social unit, and also to the notion that the couple might hold property jointly for their common use and enjoyment.[119]

Other jurists fleshed out Modestinus's definition more fully. The intention to have legitimate children was a central feature of classical Roman marriage law, and the jurists asserted that the procreation and education of children was the ultimate purpose of marriage.[120] Other texts make it clear that the feelings and attitudes of the parties were critical constitutive elements in Roman marriage, particularly *affectio maritalis* and *honor matrimonii*, concepts that we shall shortly discuss in greater detail.[121]

Roman marriage began with betrothal, an enforceable agreement between the heads of two households concerning the future union of two persons—a member from each group. The agreement normally involved arrangements for a

[113] Three major statutes of Augustus's reign asserted public control over marriage and related matters: the *Lex Julia de adulteriis* (18 B.C.), the *Lex Julia de maritandis ordinibus* (A.D. 4), and the *Lex Pappia Poppea* (A.D. 9); Bauman, *Zivilrechtliche Bedeutung*, p. 9.

[114] Andréev, "Divorce et adultère," pp. 29–30.

[115] Dig. 23.2.1 (Modestinus): "Nuptiae sunt coniunctio maris et feminae et consortium omnis vitae, divini et humani iuris communicatio." Cf. Dig. 1.1.1.3 (Ulpian); Inst. 1.2 pr.; and 1.9.1.

[116] Meyer, *Römische Konkubinat*, p. 5.

[117] Inst. 1.9.1; Dig. 1.1.1.3 (Ulpian), and 23.2.2 (Paulus).

[118] Károly Visky, "Le divorce dans la legislation de Justinien," *Revue internationale des droits de l'antiquité*, ser. 3, 23 (1976) 248–49.

[119] D'Ercole, "Consenso," p. 21.

[120] Dig. 1.1.1.3 (Ulpian); Inst. 1.2 pr.; Edoardo Volterra, *La conception du mariage d'après les juristes romains* (Padua: La Garangola, 1940), pp. 40–41.

[121] Notably Dig. 24.1.32.13 and 48.20.5.1, both from Ulpian (d. A.D. 228).

dowry (*dotum*) from the future bride's *paterfamilias* and a wedding gift (*donatio propter nuptias*) from the groom's *paterfamilias*, in order to provide an economic basis for the marriage. The betrothal, finalized by a ritual kiss, was binding on the parties and their parents. The future bride and groom were forbidden to marry anyone other than the person to whom they had been betrothed. The agreement terminated automatically at the end of two years if the parties had not married by that time, although it could be extended for good cause. The betrothal could be ended prior to the expiry of the two-year term by mutual consent of the parties and their fathers or guardians.[122] The consent of the father of an unemancipated child was essential to betrothal, although the consent of a woman's guardian was not required.[123] The woman's consent to her betrothal was expected but not absolutely demanded.[124]

Marriage normally followed soon after betrothal. It appears that girls often married in their early or mid-teens, for numerous inscriptions commemorate married women who died before the age of twenty. Roman men, on the other hand, often delayed marriage well into their twenties or thirties, and many of them never married at all.[125] The consent of both the bride and the groom, as well as their parents, was required for the legal validity of marriage.[126] Consent was, in fact, the sole essential requirement for Roman marriage; but this should not be taken to mean that the other usual and customary elements of the marriage rites were irrelevant or immaterial. Betrothal, dowry agreement, the ceremonial procession of the bride and her attendants to the groom's house, the wedding feast, and other rituals constituted external manifestations of consent. While these accessory actions were not essential, they nonetheless constituted vitally important evidence in order to prove consent to marriage.[127]

[122] Dig. 23.1.1 (Florentinus) and 2 (Ulpian), 10 (Ulpian), 17 (Caius); Cod. 5.1.1–4; Burge, *Comparative Law*, p. 9; Mary Brown Pharr, "The Kiss in Roman Law," *Classical Journal* 42 (1946/47) 395.

[123] Dig. 23.2.2 (Paulus), 18 (Julian), 35 (Papinian); cf. 23.2.20 (Paulus); Burge, *Comparative Law*, p. 7.

[124] Dig. 23.1.11 (Julian).

[125] Herlihy, *Medieval Households*, pp. 17–18; M.K. Hopkins, "The Age of Roman Girls at Marriage," *Population Studies* 18 (1965) 309–327.

[126] Dig. 23.2.2 (Paulus), 24.1.32.13 (Ulpian).

[127] Scholars have disagreed for nearly a century over the question of whether or not some portions of Ulpian's statement about marital consent in Dig. 24.1.32.13 may have been interpolated by Justinian's codifiers in the sixth century. See B. Kübler, "Emendationen des Pandektentextes," *Zeitschrift der Savigny-Stiftung für Rechtsgeschichte*, romanistische Abteilung (cited hereafter as ZRG, RA) 11 (1890) 49; Wolff, *Written and Unwritten Marriages*, pp. 93–94, 98; Franco Edoardo Adami, "Precizazione in tema di consenso matrimoniale nel pensiero patristico," *Il diritto ecclessiastico* 76 (1965) 211–12; Riccardo Orestano, *La struttura giuridica del matrimonio romano dal diritto classico al diritto giustinianeo* (Milan: A. Giuffrè, 1951), pp. 187–88; Gian Carlo Caselli, "Concubina pro uxore: Osservazioni in merito al C. 17 del primo concilio di Toledo," *Rivista di storia del diritto italiano* 37/38 (1964/65) 173; Volterra, *Conception*, p. 43; Emilio

Also vital to proof of matrimonial consent was what Roman jurists called *honor matrimonii*, the decorum with which a husband treated his wife and the social dignity that he accorded her.[128] Linked to *honor matrimonii* was the related concept of *affectio maritalis*, the bond that joined husband to wife, a tie that Roman jurists believed distinguished a true marital union from concubinage and other types of cohabitation.[129] *Honor matrimonii* was taken to be a visible and verifiable sign of the inward feeling that constituted *affectio maritalis*.[130] Roman jurists had difficulty with questions that involved intangible feelings, in large part because they raised such thorny problems of evidence; the law nonetheless accorded feelings and intentions legal importance in a number of different contexts. Ulpian, when dealing with a troublesome issue concerning the emancipation of slaves, observed that "We must suppose that the Aelian and Sentian law gave full scope to proper feelings (*iustis affectionibus*), but not indeed to infatuations (*deliciis*)."[131] Similarly marital affection and its expression in the form of matrimonial respect played decisive roles in Roman marriage law. Marriage in Roman law was virtually a formless transaction, for none of the customary ceremonies and usages connected with its celebration was required for the creation of a valid union.[132] Marital affection and matrimonial honor, however, were crucial elements in determining whether or not a marriage existed between two persons who were living together. That determination, in turn, had far-reaching practical consequences for the property rights of the parties, for inheritance claims, and for the status and property of the children of the union. So long as marital affection existed between the parties, they were married; if marital affection was absent, there was no marriage.[133] It was not even necessary for the parties to live together; so long as marital affection existed between them, they were married, regardless of whether they co-

---

Albertario, "Honor matrimonii e affectio maritalis," in his *Studi di diritto romano*, 6 vols. (Milan: A. Giuffrè, 1933–53) 1:198–99. See also Gordon Williams, "Some Aspects of Roman Marriage Ceremonies and Ideals," *Journal of Roman Studies* 48 (1958) 16–29.

[128] Albertario, "Honor matrimonii," pp. 197–98; D'Ercole, "Consenso," pp. 21–22; Volterra, *Conception*, p. 57; Gide, "De la condition," p. 551.

[129] Orestano, *Struttura giuridica*, p. 192; Volterra, *Conception*, p. 49; Visky, "Divorce," p. 241; D'Ercole, "Consenso," pp. 20–21; Caselli, "Concubina pro uxore," p. 174.

[130] Orestano, *Struttura giuridica*, p. 315.

[131] Dig. 40.2.16 pr. (Ulpian): "[N]eque enim deliciis, sed iustis affectionibus dedisse iustam libertatem legem Aeliam Sentiam credendum." See also the comments of Susan Treggiari, "Sentiment and Property: Some Roman Attitudes," in *Theories of Property, Aristotle to the Present*, ed. Anthony Parel and Thomas Flanagan (Waterloo, Ont.: Wilfred Laurier University Press, 1979), p. 76. I am grateful to my colleague, Professor John F. McGovern, for pointing this reference out to me.

[132] Percy Ellwood Corbett, *The Roman Law of Marriage* (Oxford: Clarendon Press, 1930), p. 68; Burge, *Comparative Law*, pp. 7–9.

[133] Dig. 48.20.5.1 (Ulpian).

habited or not.[134] Sexual union and consummation of the marriage were no more essential in Roman matrimonial law than a wedding cake is in ours.

Roman law conceived of marriage as a contract absolute: either it existed or it did not. Roman law did not recognize conditional marriage, where the contract became effective only upon fulfillment of some condition subsequent to the agreement itself.[135] Marriage was also a free contract; no one could legally be compelled to contract, or for that matter to dissolve, a marriage. Marital consent given under duress was insufficient to create a lawful union.[136]

Classical Roman law had complex rules that limited the choice of marital partners. Marriages between close relatives, whether by blood (consanguinity) or by marriage (affinity), were prohibited and the law spelled out the forbidden degrees of relationship in great detail.[137] In the classical law, intercourse between a man and woman prior to marriage did not create a legal affinity between them and hence was no bar to their marriage, even if the premarital intercourse was adulterous.[138] One large class of people was forbidden to marry at all: the sexual unions of slaves were defined as *contubernium*, rather than matrimony. *Contubernium* was not protected by law and created no juridical relationship between the parties; hence it provided no basis for inheritance or other property claims, nor could a slave owner be forbidden to break up such a union, for example by selling one of the partners to a distant owner.[139]

Marriages of free persons were subject to a number of further restrictions, in addition to the ones already discussed. A free man, for instance, was forbidden to marry a harlot, an actress, or other loose woman; senators and their children were forbidden to marry women of low birth, although a simple free man could marry such a woman. Likewise actors, men who practiced the *ludicri artes*, were ineligible to marry women of the senatorial class. Women over the age of fifty could not marry at all, although they could become concubines.[140] While remarriage following divorce or the death of a first spouse was allowed for most people, religious law as late as the Principate required the wives of the *flamines*

[134] Orestano, *Struttura giuridica*, pp. 76–77, 114.

[135] Rudolf Weigand, *Die bedingte Eheschliessung im kanonischen Recht*, Münchener theologische Studien, kanonistische Abteilung, vol. 16 (Munich: M. Huebner, 1963), pp. 28–64, 413–14.

[136] The forthright statement of Diocletian in Cod. 5.4.14 reiterates more clearly what had long been the teaching of the classical jurists; John T. Noonan, Jr., "Novel 22," in *The Bond of Marriage: An Ecumenical and Interdisciplinary Study*, ed. William W. Bassett (Notre Dame, IN: University of Notre Dame, 1968), p. 44.

[137] Burge, *Comparative Law*, p. 5, outlines these rules succinctly.

[138] Cod. 9.9.26 (Diocletian); cf. Dig. 48.5.12(11).13 (Papinian) and Gottlob, "Ehebruch," p. 336.

[139] Andres E. de Mañaricua y Nuere, *El matrimonio de los esclavos: Estudio histórico-jurídico hasta la fijación de la disciplina en el derecho canónico*, Analecta Gregoriana, ser. B.1, vol. 23 (Rome: Universitas Gregoriana, 1940), pp. 77–111.

[140] Caselli, "Concubina pro uxore," pp. 165–68.

of Jupiter to be married only once, and a *flamen* who married a widow was barred from exercising his priesthood.[141] Men who suffered from sexual impotence might contract legitimate marriages despite their handicap. Males who had been castrated, however, were legally barred from marrying.[142] Additional limitations on the right to marry resulted from the holding of certain offices. Imperial officials were forbidden to marry women from the province in which they held office, a disability that extended also to their sons.[143] Guardians were likewise forbidden to marry the women under their protection.[144]

Although Roman marriage centered upon a consensual agreement for which dowry was not required, dowry agreements were a customary feature of marriages among persons of property. By the first century of the Christian era the upper classes almost invariably prepared a written dotal instrument as part of the formalities of marriage.[145] Dowry strongly implied marriage; indeed, dowry without marriage was legally impossible. Any showing that a dowry had been given created a presumption that a marriage had been agreed upon.[146] After marriage, furthermore, gifts of property between husband and wife were legally no longer possible, so that any exchange of property between man and wife was either dowry or it was nothing.[147] Since property transactions were usually easier to prove than intentions, determination of marital status almost invariably hinged on a scrutiny of the property transfers between the partners.

Roman law assumed monogamy; so strong and basic was this assumption that classical Roman law simply ignored the possibility of bigamy.[148] Bigamy as a specific offense was introduced into the law only at a relatively late period, very likely under Christian influence.[149] When the law did begin to take cognizance of bigamy, the offense subjected the guilty parties to *infamia*. This legal taint made the bigamist incapable of holding public office or exercising any position

[141] Marjorie Lightman and William Zeisel, "Univira: An Example of Continuity and Change in Roman Society," *Church History* 46 (1977) 19–20.

[142] Ignatius Gordon, "Adnotationes quaedam de valore matrimonii virorum qui ex toto secti sunt a tempore Gratiani usque ad Breve 'Cum frequenter'," *Periodica de re morali, canonici, liturgici* 66 (1977) 191–95.

[143] Dig. 23.2.38 (Paulus), 23.2.57 (Marcianus), and 23.2.63 (Papinian).

[144] Dig. 23.2.62.1–2 (Papinian); Cod. 5.6.1 (Severus and Antoninus).

[145] Heinrich Brunner, "Die fränkisch-romanische dos," in his *Abhandlungen zur Rechtsgeschichte*, ed. Karl Rauch, 2 vols. (Weimar: Böhlaus, 1931; repr. Leipzig: Zentralantiquariat der DDR, 1965) 2:88–89; Carlo Castello, "Lo strumento dotale come prova del matrimonio," SDHI 4 (1938) 208–9.

[146] Dig. 23.3.3 (Ulpian).

[147] Dig. 24.1.1 (Ulpian).

[148] D'Ercole, "Consenso," pp. 46–47; Eduardo Volterra, "Per la storia del reato di bigamia in diritto romano," in *Studi in memoria di Umberto Ratti* (Milan: A. Giuffrè, 1934), p. 420.

[149] Volterra, "Per la storia," pp. 425–29, maintains that the references to bigamy in Cod. 5.3.5 and 9.9.18 are interpolations by Justinian's codifiers.

of trust or honor, from appearing in the courts, and from exercising a variety of legal rights. Continued existence of a prior legitimate union thus became an absolute bar to marriage in Roman law.[150]

Divorce and Remarriage

Classical Roman law generally allowed remarriage following the termination of a prior marriage by death or divorce. The law did, however, subject remarriage to certain limitations designed to safeguard the property interests of the children of an earlier marriage.[151] A difficult problem occurred when the first spouse disappeared under circumstances that made it probable that he or she was dead, but where death could not be proved. This situation arose most commonly when a husband serving in the army was reported missing in action. In this situation, classical law allowed remarriage of the presumed widow; if the first husband reappeared he could not bring action against his wife for adultery or bigamy, provided that she had remarried in good faith.[152] The second marriage in these circumstances was held to terminate the earlier one because *affectio maritalis* in the first marriage had ceased.[153]

Married Romans had a legal obligation to support their children, and the obligation extended to illegitimate offspring, where paternity could be proved.[154] Aside from support, however, classical law did not treat the bastard child as a descendant of its father; an illegitimate child's relationship to its mother was the same as that of a legitimate child. Concern for the welfare of bastards and methods of legitimizing them began to assume prominence in Roman law only after the reign of Constantine (A.D. 313–337).[155]

There is no evidence that Roman law ever forbade divorce, but divorces

[150] Dig. 3.2.1 (Julian), 3.2.13.1–4 (Ulpian); Cod. 9.9.18 pr. (Valerian); Alfred Louis Joseph Girard, *Des nullités de mariage d'après le Code civil, avec un exposé sommaire des principales théories du droit canonique et de l'ancienne jurisprudence* (Paris: Maresq, 1862), pp. 75–76.

[151] Henryk Kupiszewski, "Powtórne malzeństwo w konstytucjach cesarzy rzmskich w IV i V wieku" [Second Marriages in the Constitutions of the Roman Emperors in the Fourth and Fifth Centuries], *Analecta Cracoviensia* 7 (1975) 349–66.

[152] Dig. 48.5.12(11).12 (Papinian). Volterra, "Per la storia," p. 399, contends that several important clauses in this passage were inserted in the text by Justinian's codifiers and thus reflect a later stage in the law's development.

[153] Volterra, "Per la storia," p. 418.

[154] Dig. 25.3.5.8 (Ulpian). This passage has become the basis of modern child-support doctrine in Roman-Dutch law; J.E. Scholtens, "Maintenance of Illegitimate Children and the Exceptio plurium concubentium," *South African Law Journal* 72 (1955) 144, 148.

[155] Laurent Chevailler, "Observations sur le droit de bâtardise dans la France coutumière du XIIe au XVe siècle," RHDF, 4th ser., 35 (1957) 378; Horst Hermann, *Die Stellung unehelicher Kinder nach kanonischem Recht*, Kanonistische Studien und Texte, vol. 26 (Amsterdam: B.R. Grüner, 1971), pp. 45–49.

were apparently rare in early Roman history. The first known Roman divorce is said to have been that of Spurius Carvilius Ruga, who repudiated his wife in 230 B.C. As late as the time of Cicero (106–43 B.C.) the law required no special procedure for divorce actions, although certain customary formalities were usually observed and had a long history prior to Cicero's day.[156] A standardized divorce procedure first appeared in the period of Augustus. This procedure involved an oral repudiation of one spouse by the other in the presence of seven witnesses; written repudiation did not become obligatory until much later.[157] Informal separation and de facto divorce without legal formalities also continued to be common far into the imperial period.[158]

Classical Roman divorce law centered primarily on the property consequences of divorce and the division of goods between the spouses at the termination of their marriage. Although marriage was deemed to cease when marital affection ended, the property division required concrete action to disentangle the estates of the divorcing couple.[159]

Formal divorce was advantageous for the wife because it protected her from prosecution for adultery if she subsequently remarried during the lifetime of her first husband. Divorce terminated sexual rights between the couple, although until she remarried, a divorcée could be prosecuted by her former husband for sexual transgressions that had occurred prior to their divorce.[160] Classical law required no statement of specific grounds for divorce, although certain grounds were commonly understood to furnish an adequate basis for repudiating a spouse. Among these were adultery,[161] capture or enslavement of either spouse,[162] sexual impotence,[163] and insanity.[164]

---

[156] Visky, "Divorce," p. 240; Percy Ellwood Corbett, "Augustan Divorce," *Law Quarterly Review* (cited hereafter as LQR) 45 (1929) 178.

[157] Ulpian, *Ad edictum*, lib. 47, in Dig. 38.11.1 spoke of a *certum modum diuortii* prescribed by the *Lex Julia de adulteriis*, but just what that involved we do not know. Paulus referred to the seven witnesses; Dig. 24.2.9. See also Corbett, "Augustan Divorce," pp. 184–85; Csillag, *Augustan Laws*, pp. 127–38; Andréev, "Divorce et adultère," p. 17; D'Ercole, "Consenso," p. 45.

[158] Andréev, "Divorce et adultère," p. 11; Paul Frédéric Girard, *Manuel élémentaiire de droit romain*, 8th ed. by Félix Senn (Paris: Rousseau, 1929), p. 177.

[159] Csillag, *Augustan Laws*, pp. 138–43. In addition, divorce terminated the rights of the divorcée over her children; Hallett, *Fathers and Daughters*, p. 218.

[160] Visky, "Divorce," p. 242; Volterra, "Per la storia," p. 404; Wolff, *Written and Unwritten Marriages*, p. 68.

[161] Dig. 48.5.12 (Papinian); Volterra, "Per la storia," p. 402.

[162] Dig. 24.2.1 (Paulus).

[163] Dig. 28.2.6 (Ulpian); Gustave Leclercq, *Mariage des viellards et 'probati auctores'*, Biblioteca del 'Salesianum,' vol. 74 (Turin: Società editrice internazionale, 1967), pp. 18–19.

[164] Dig. 24.2.4 (Ulpian).

Concubinage

Along with marriage, and in some senses in competition with it, Roman law recognized concubinage. In the very ancient period the law had drawn no distinction between *paelicatus* with a concubine and with a prostitute. Only late in the Republic did legal texts begin to differentiate concubinage from prostitution.[165] Literary texts remarked upon the contrast much earlier—Plautus (d. 184 B.C.?) was apparently the first to use the term *concubina*, and in his comedies *paelices* normally refer to women involved in relatively transitory affairs, while long-term sex partners are called concubines.[166]

Legal systems have usually dealt with concubinage in one of three ways. In some systems concubinage is a tolerated institution, often an inferior type of marriage; other systems make concubinage an offense and subject participants in such unions to penalties. The third alternative is to ignore the matter altogether.[167] Early Roman law had opted for the last policy, but the adoption of the *Lex Julia de adulteriis* in 18 B.C. made it necessary to determine whether intercourse with a concubine constituted *stuprum* or not. Roman lawmakers chose to exempt concubinage relationships from the penalties for *stuprum*; concubinage thus became a legally tolerated institution.[168] When concubinage became subject to legal definition and regulation, it received a degree of legal protection as well.[169] Under the Augustan legislation, according to the interpretation that Paulus (fl. ca. A.D. 210) put on it, concubinage differed from marriage only in the intention of the parties.[170] Like marriage, concubinage was a

[165] Dig. 50.16.144 (Paulus); Baumann, *Zivilrechtliche Bedeutung*, pp. 7–8.

[166] Löwenstein, *Bekämpfung*, p. 4.

[167] Baumann, *Zivilrechtliche Bedeutung*, p. 5.

[168] Dig. 25.7.1 (Ulpian), 48.5.35(34) (Modestinus); Löwenstein, *Bekämpfung*, pp. 4–5; Baumann, *Zivilrechtliche Bedeutung*, p. 10. Castelli, "Concubinato," pp. 65–66, maintains that a concubine who was legally married to a man other than her lover might be prosecuted for adultery; but see contra Dig. 25.7.3.1 (Marcianus).

[169] Gide, "De la condition," pp. 548–49, followed by Caselli, "Concubina pro uxore," pp. 168–69, declares that concubinage, although tolerated, was not protected by Roman law and was in no sense a legal institution; at the other extreme, Balsdon, *Roman Women* p. 231, argues that Augustus's laws actively encouraged concubinage. Neither view seems entirely consistent with the texts. When Ulpian, for example, declares that, "[H]onestius sit patrono libertam concubinam quam matrem familias habere," and asserts that a man can have a concubine "sine metu criminis," (Dig. 25.7.1), it is difficult to see how Gide's and Caselli's interpretation can be tenable. Certainly if the patron of a concubine is exempted from punishment for illicit sexual relations, which otherwise he would be subject to, it is difficult to maintain that concubinage is not in some real sense protected by law. On the other hand, Balsdon seems to exaggerate both the intent and the result of the Augustan legislation. See also Csillag, *Augustan Laws*, pp. 143–46; Esmein, *Mariage* 2:105–7; Meyer, *Römische Konkubinat*, p. 89; and Pietro Bonfante, "Nota sulla riforma giustinianea del concubinato," in *Studi in onore di Silvio Perozzi nel XL anno del suo insegnamento* (Palermo: G. Castiglia, 1925), p. 283.

[170] Dig. 25.7.4 (Paulus).

long-term licit sexual relationship.[171] The lover might privately consider his concubine to be his wife, even though he was legally unable to marry her because of differences in social status or for other reasons of public policy.[172] The concubine, according to Paulus's commentary on the *Lex Julia et Papia Poppea*, was a woman whom a man kept in his house in place of a wife.[173]

Concubinage normally arose in one of three situations in Roman society. First, a continuing sexual liaison between two parties might constitute concubinage because marriage between the parties was legally impossible. This was true of unions between free men and actresses, adulteresses, convicted criminals, prostitutes, or women over the age of fifty. Second, there were cases of presumed concubinage, in which the law treated a relationship as concubinage, regardless of the intentions or beliefs of the parties—this happened with relationships between freeborn men and freedwomen or women of obscure origin. Third, there was voluntary concubinage; that is, a union between a free man and a woman who was also free in the eyes of the law, where the parties could legally have married one another but, for whatever reason, chose not to do so.[174]

The distinction between wife and concubine thus rested largely but not exclusively on the intentions of the parties.[175] Over time the gap between marriage and concubinage grew more tenuous, and concubinage tended to become in effect an inferior type of marriage, one in which the woman had fewer rights and less legal protection than a legitimate wife. Even in this regard the practical distinctions between wife and concubine gradually diminished.[176]

The touchstone for distinguishing marriage from concubinage was marital affection. Where there was marital affection a marriage existed in some sense, even though it might be one discouraged or disallowed by law (*matrimonium iniustum*); if marital affection was absent, the relationship was concubinage.[177] Moreover, in late Roman law, concubinage might develop into marriage if the

[171] Dig. 48.5.35(34) pr. (Modestinus); Girard, *Des nullités*, p. 83.

[172] Dig. 48.5.14(13).4 (Ulpian). The *Lex Julia et Papia Poppea* (A.D. 9) established legal impediments to marriage between upper-class men and socially inferior women; Caselli, "Concubina pro uxore," p. 164.

[173] Dig. 50.16.144 (Paulus).

[174] Caselli, "Concubina pro uxore," p. 168.

[175] Dig. 25.7.4 (Paulus); but cf. also Dig. 39.5.31 pr. (Papinian), 32.49.4 (Ulpian), and 24.1.3.1 (Ulpian), as well as Paulus, *Sententiae ad filium libri quinque* 2.20.1, in *Fontes iuris romani anteiustiniani*, 2d ed., by Salvatore Riccobono et al., 3 vols. (Florence: G. Barbèra, 1940) 3:346; Löwenstein, *Bekämpfung*, p. 6; Volterra, *Conception*, p. 52.

[176] Esmein, *Mariage* 2:107–9; Girard, *Des nullités*, pp. 9–10; Lacombe, *Famille*, pp. 197, 390–91; Wolff, *Written and Unwritten Marriages*, pp. 72, 96–97; Baumann, *Zivilrechtliche Bedeutung*, p. 13; Meyer, *Römische Konkubinat*, p. 60; Johannes Mullenders, *Le mariage présumé*, Analecta Gregoriana, vol. 181 (Rome: Università Gregoriana, 1971), p. 57.

[177] Percy Elwood Corbett, "Matrimonium iuris gentium," LQR 44 (1928) 309–10; Joseph Freisen, *Geschichte des kanonischen Eherechts bis zum Verfall der Glossen-*

couple came to regard one another with *maritalis affectio.* The phrase "marital affection," it must be emphasised, had a limited technical meaning: it denoted the special kind of regard that a husband has for his wife and was distinct from the other kinds of *affectio* that he might feel toward his children, his slaves, his friends, or even his concubine.[178]

Certain presumptions of fact also entered into the determination of the precise status of a sexual relationship in Roman law. The law assumed that a free woman who lived with a free man was married to him, unless there was evidence that she made her living by prostitution.[179] If a senator lived with a freedwoman, however, there was a contrary presumption that the relationship was concubinage, rather than a *matrimonium iniustum,* at least unless or until he lost his senatorial position.[180]

As concubinage came to be legally tolerated, it also became subject to regulations similar to those imposed upon marriage. A married man could not take a concubine, just as he could not take a second wife, until his first marriage ended.[181] This did not mean, of course, that Roman husbands had no sexual partners other than their wives; but those partners were classed as *paelices,* not *concubinae.*[182] And a man's decision to retain a concubine, in consequence, was held to disprove his intention to marry another woman.[183] As in marriage, the concubine must have reached the age of puberty[184] and must not be a close relative of her lover.[185] Just as tutors were forbidden to marry their wards, they were also forbidden to take them as concubines.[186] Likewise the law excluded

---

literatur, 2d ed., (Paderborn: F. Schöningh, 1893; repr. Aalen: Scientia, 1963), pp. 47–48.

   [178] Cod. 5.27.10–11 (Justinian); Corbett, *Roman Law of Marriage,* pp. 92, 95; Treggiari, "Sentiment and Property," p. 75, discusses several situations in which these distinctions operated.

   [179] Dig. 23.2.24 (Modestinus) as well as Dig. 25.7.3 (Marcianus) and 5 (Paulus). But cf. Giannetto Longo, "Presunzione di matrimonio," in *Studi in onore di Ugo Enrico Paoli* (Florence: Felice Le Monnier, 1956), p. 488.

   [180] Dig. 23.2.27 (Ulpian); Freisen, *Geschichte* p. 49.

   [181] Paulus, *Sententiae* 2.20.1, reinforced by later enactments of Constantine (Cod. 5.26.1) and Justinian (Cod. 7.15.3.2); Löwenstein, *Bekämpfung,* pp. 5–6; Volterra maintained that concubinage was not incompatible with marriage in the classical law: see "Per la storia del reato," p. 392. His argument is weak, however, for it disregards the evidence of Paulus as well as literary passages that tend to confute his views.

   [182] Dig. 50.16.144 (Paulus).

   [183] Dig. 24.2.11.1–2 (Ulpian).

   [184] Dig. 25.7.1.4 (Ulpian).

   [185] Dig. 25.7.1.3 (Marcianus), 23.2.14.3 (Paulus), and 23.2.56 (Ulpian).

   [186] Dig. 23.2.36, 59, 60, and 66 (all by Paulus); Baumann, *Zivilrechtliche Bedeutung,* pp. 10–11; Meyer, *Römische Konkubinat,* pp. 60–61; W. W. Buckland, *A Textbook of Roman Law from Augustus to Justinian,* 2d ed. (Cambridge: At the University Press, 1932), p. 115.

from concubinage status a woman who had previously been the concubine of a close relative.[187]

The concubine was obliged to be sexually faithful to her patron, although he was not obliged to be faithful to her. Sexual infidelity by a concubine might be punished as adultery under the *Lex Julia de adulteriis*.[188] Similarly, a concubine who left one lover for another was not *honesta*.[189] While the patron had a right to his concubine's services, she had virtually no claims on him. She had, in fact, most of the obligations, but none of the rights, of a legitimate wife. The woman did not form part of her consort's legal *familia*, she could be dismissed without formality, she enjoyed none of the honors that a wife was entitled to, nor did she have any claims to share in her patron's estate after his death.[190] One of the few economic protections that the law afforded her was a right to retain the gifts that she received—unlike a wife, a concubine could legally receive gifts from her lover during their relationship.[191] Neither her consort nor his heirs had a right to recover those from her.[192] If the concubine took property without permission, however, she could be prosecuted as a thief.[193]

The children of a concubine belonged to her and she had a right to their custody, although she lacked many of the supervisory rights that a legal wife enjoyed over her offspring.[194] Not only did a concubine have a right to have her children with her, but she also bore a positive obligation to support them and to provide them with food and other necessities. The father of progeny by a concubine, in contrast, had minimal obligations toward them since they were not part of his legal *familia* for inheritance and other purposes.[195]

Despite their legal disabilities, some Roman concubines enjoyed a considerable measure of honor and devotion from their consorts. One Cocceus Cassianus, for example, a man of senatorial rank, was so attached to his concubine, Rufina, that he left his estate to her in his will.[196] Even Roman bankruptcy law was so structured that insolvent men were permitted to retain slaves whom they held in affection; the purpose, almost certainly, was to allow the bankrupt to keep his concubine.[197] Concubines came to be such a normal part of Roman

---

[187] Dig. 25.7.1.3 (Ulpian); Cod. 5.4.4 (Alexander Severus).

[188] Dig. 48.5.14 (Ulpian); Corbett, "Matrimonium iuris gentium," p. 308; Baumann, *Zivilrechtliche Bedeutung*, p. 11.

[189] Dig. 23.2.41 (Marcellus); she could, however, depart if she received prior permission to do so, according to Dig. 25.7.1 pr. (Ulpian).

[190] Meyer, *Römische Konkubinat*, pp. 78–87; Gide, "De la condition," p. 563; Leclercq, "Concubinat," col. 2497.

[191] Dig. 24.1.3.1 (Ulpian).

[192] Dig. 39.5.31 pr. (Papinian).

[193] Dig. 25.2.17 pr. (Ulpian).

[194] Dig. 38.8.4 (Ulpian); Meyer, *Römische Konkubinat*, p. 52.

[195] Dig. 25.3.5.4 (Ulpian); Meyer, *Römische Konkubinat*, pp. 54–55.

[196] Dig. 34.9.16.1 (Papinian).

[197] Dig. 20.1.6 (Ulpian); Treggiari, "Sentiment and Property," p. 75.

society that Alexander Severus (A.D. 222–235) was said to have ordered that every unmarried provincial governor be furnished with a concubine at public expense as one of the necessities of life.[198]

Prostitution

Early Roman law, as previously noted, did not distinguish concubines from prostitutes, but the changes in the concubine's status that we have surveyed helped to clarify, if not to improve, the prostitute's status as well. Roman law was generally loath to admit that it was licit for respectable women to have extramarital sex, but prostitutes were by definition not respectable, and hence their sexual habits were not a matter of great concern. While the concubine slowly acquired some legal protection and concubinage gradually rose to the rank of an inferior type of marriage, the prostitute's legal status, conversely, remained depressed and degraded.[199]

The prostitute in Roman law was a man or woman who was available to anyone who wished to have sex without any ties of sentiment, affection, or commitment.[200] The law did not specify that payment was required in order to qualify these transactions as prostitution; hence the loose woman who gave sexual favors freely was just as much a prostitute as the pretty boy who demanded a fee in return for his services. This emphasis on indiscriminate availability as the determining characteristic of prostitution became fundamental for later civil-law definitions of the term. Prostitution itself was no crime, and no penalties attached to sex acts with a harlot.[201] Indeed, the pagan religious calendar contained festivals dedicated to prostitutes of both sexes: according to the *Fasti Praenesti*, the twenty-fifth of April was the feast day for male prostitutes, while the preceding day was sacred to female prostitutes.[202]

Sexual relations with a prostitute did not constitute *stuprum*,[203] but in classical law, sexual relations with a married prostitute might be prosecuted as adul-

---

[198] Gide, "De la condition," p. 546.

[199] Esmein, *Mariage* 1:105–6.

[200] Dig. 23.2.43 pr., 1–5 (Ulpian).

[201] Iwan Bloch, *Die Prostitution*, 2 vols., Handbuch der gesamten Sexualwissenschaft (Berlin: Louis Marcus, 1912–25) 1:15, 18; Löwenstein, *Bekämpfung*, p. 6.

[202] CIL 1:317; Veyne, "L'homosexualité," p. 28; Lactantius, *Divinae institutiones* 1.20, in his *Opera omnia*, ed. Samuel Brandt and Georg Laubmann, 2 vols, Corpus scriptorum ecclesiasticorum latinorum (cited hereafter as CSEL), vols. 19 and 27 (Vienna: F. Tempsky, 1890–93) 19:72–73; St. Augustine, *De civitate Dei* 2.27, ed. Emmanuel Hoffman, 2 vols., CSEL vol. 40, pt. 1 and 2 (Vienna: F. Tempsky, 1899–1900) 40/1:104–6; Ovid, *Fasti* 5.331–54; Valerius Maximus, *Factorum et dictorum memorabilium libri novem* 2.10.8, ed. Karl Kempf (Leipzig: B.G. Teubner, 1888), pp. 106–7; W. Warde Fowler, *Roman Festivals of the Period of the Republic* (London: Macmillan, 1899; repr. Port Washington, NY: Kennikat Press, 1969), p. 83; Jasper Griffin, "Augustan Poetry and the Life of Luxury," *Journal of Roman Studies* 66 (1976) 102.

[203] Dig. 48.5.14(13).2 (Ulpian); Castelli, "Concubinato," p. 59.

tery.[204] A rescript of Diocletian (A.D. 284–305) in 290 changed this policy, however, and provided that thenceforth no prosecution would be admitted for intercourse with a married woman who practiced as a prostitute.[205]

Prostitution in Rome necessarily implied moral and social degradation (*probrositas*) not only because of the harlot's sexual promiscuity, but also because of her way of life. The same type of social debasement was imputed to actresses and musicians, for example, as to prostitutes. To be classified as *probrosa*, a woman's turpitude must be manifest or notorious; a clandestine prostitute who accepted an occasional client on the sly might not be considered a *femina probrosa*. The licentious, irregular way of life that Romans considered typical of harlots was in itself sufficient to establish a presumption that persons who lived like that were prostitutes.[206] The law likewise inferred that anyone who lived in a brothel or served as a waitress in a tavern was a prostitute.[207]

While many, perhaps most, Roman prostitutes were freedwomen, foreigners, or slaves and thus marginal to the social hierarchy, some free women and even women of the senatorial class prostituted themselves. A free woman was entitled to a presumption that she was not a concubine or prostitute, unless she openly and publicly offered herself for hire.[208] The woman who did so lost status and was consigned to the marginal classes with whom she associated herself. There was clearly a feeling that a free woman who became a prostitute betrayed the social order and the class into which she had been born. This was especially true when the daughters of senators took up prostitution or such allied occupations as acting, singing, dancing, or public entertainment. Such women were socially degraded and stripped of the privileges that belonged to the senatorial order.[209]

Roman law was highly critical of married men who tolerated sexual promiscuity in their wives. The husband of an adulteress was considered an accomplice in her crime unless he took immediate action against her once he learned of her extramarital exploits.[210] If, instead of repudiating his erring spouse, he forgave her and sought a reconciliation, the cuckold was condemned as a pander (*leno*) and subjected to the social and criminal penalties attached to those who promoted prostitution.[211] Pandering (*lenocinium*) consisted in fostering and facilitating the practice of prostitution by providing housing for prostitutes, managing their business matters, or soliciting clients for them.[212] Panders,

[204] Dig. 48.5.11(10) (Papinian).

[205] Cod. 9.9.22.

[206] Dig. 23.2.41 pr. (Marcellus); Riccardo Astolfi, "Femina probrosa, concubina, mater solitaria," SDHI 31 (1965) 20.

[207] Dig. 23.2.43 pr. (Ulpian).

[208] Dig. 23.2.24 (Modestinus).

[209] Dig. 23.2.47 (Paulus).

[210] Dig. 48.5.14(13).5 (Ulpian).

[211] Dig. 48.5.2.2, 6 (Ulpian); Cod. 9.9.2 (Septimius Severus).

[212] Dig. 23.2.43.6–9 (Ulpian).

pimps, and brothelkeepers were classed as *infames*; this entailed loss of most social and civic privileges and also seriously limited their capacity to inherit property.[213]

Although a person need not accept money in exchange for his or her services in order to be regarded as a prostitute, most Roman prostitutes doubtless expected to be paid and lived on the income from their clients.[214] In some important ways the law restricted the property rights of harlots. The prostitute was deprived of inheritance rights and could not succeed to her parents' estate.[215] Nor could she inherit anything under the will of a soldier on active duty, even though Roman lawyers usually construed wills of this kind generously in order to give equitable effect to the testator's intentions.[216] Yet in other ways the law protected the prostitute's right to money or other goods that she received for her sexual services. While the jurists disapproved of the prostitute's activities and condemned her degrading life, they held that she did no harm in accepting money. The prostitute's title to her earnings was legally protected and the client who regretted his generosity had no right to reclaim the fees he had paid.[217] Nevertheless, the law provided no protection to the prostitute's person: if a client abused her or ravished her by force, she had no legal redress against him, according to Ulpian (ca. A.D. 160–228) because the client's motive was lust, not greed. So, too, if a client broke down the door of a brothel in his eagerness to bed a harlot, he incurred no liability for goods stolen by thieves who thereby gained access to the premises.[218]

Roman law reflected public policy, too, in imposing restraints upon those who procured girls or boys for a life of prostitution. Masters were forbidden to put their female slaves to work as prostitutes, unless the slave had been a prostitute by trade prior to enslavement. The slave who was forced into prostitution had redress against her owner and could secure freedom upon showing that she had been wrongfully prostituted.[219] Likewise a servant girl who was not a slave but who was held as security for the debts of her employer could not be forced into prostitution by the person who held her. If an attempt was made to prostitute her, she had a right to emancipation.[220] Contracts for the sale of slaves sometimes included clauses that barred the purchaser from prostituting the slave after purchase. If the buyer broke his word, the seller had a right to recover damages for injury, as well as for breach of contract.[221]

Roman jurists were anxious to sharpen the social distinctions between pros-

[213] Dig. 3.2.4.2 (Ulpian).

[214] Dig. 23.2.43.2–5 (Ulpian); Astolfi, "Femina probrosa," p. 22.

[215] Dig. 37.12.3 pr. (Paulus).

[216] Dig. 29.1.41.1 (Tryphonius).

[217] Dig. 12.5.4 pr., 3 (Ulpian).

[218] Dig. 47.2.39 (Ulpian).

[219] Cod. 4.56.1–3 (Alexander Severus). But a male slave who was prostituted by his owner apparently had no recourse.

[220] Dig. 13.7.24.3 (Ulpian).

[221] Dig. 18.7.6 pr. (Papinian); Treggiari, "Sentiment and Property," pp. 75–76.

titutes and respectable women. A passage attributed to Ulpian points up this concern: it prohibits matrons from dressing in the kinds of clothing favored by women of ill-fame—presumably this meant enticing, sexy garments that were felt to be unbecoming to women of high rank. Perhaps, too, Ulpian's prohibition sought to avoid embarrassing and distasteful encounters between respectable women and would-be clients who might mistake them for strumpets.[222] Similar desires to maintain dignity and social distinctions, as well as to avoid giving the appearance of respectability to the prostitute's trade, presumably underlay another passage in Ulpian. In the midst of a discussion of arbitration procedure, Ulpian declared that a party to a lawsuit could not be required to appear before an arbitrator in a brothel and should suffer no injury to his interests by failure to respond to a summons to appear in such an inappropriate venue.[223]

Raptus

Early Roman law appears to have tolerated rape—at least surviving legal documents do not suggest that forcible sex was severely punished. This may have reflected religious values as well as social conditions in the early Republic, for Greco-Roman paganism depicted the gods as practicing rape with lamentable frequency. Whether these legends simply embodied male aggressive fantasies or whether they reflected the realities of early Roman society is difficult to say.[224] In any event, society's tolerance of sex by force waned during the late Republic; during the early imperial period forcible ravishment became a serious offense. The praetorian edict had outlawed property transactions accomplished by force and fear[225] and Augustan legislation, especially the *Lex Iulia de vi publica*, extended the proscription to sexual relations. The law imposed capital punishment upon those who "ravished a boy or a woman or anyone through force."[226] Successful seduction of minors, when accomplished by persuasion and blandishments, rather than by crude force, was also punishable by death, while an unsuccessful attempt to seduce a minor merited the milder penalty of exile.[227]

---

[222] Dig. 47.10.15.15 (Ulpian). Antonio Guarino, "Ineptiae iuris romani," in *Daube Noster: Essays in Legal History for David Daube*, ed. Alan Watson (Edinburgh and London: Scottish Academic Press, 1974), pp. 126–28, argues that the text has been corrupted in transmission and that Ulpian originally meant to prohibit the wearing of lascivious garb by slave girls. At some point in the post-classical period, according to Guarino, the text was altered to forbid the wearing of such garments by matrons. Guarino suggests that the Empress Theodora (d. 548) may have been responsible for this alteration.

[223] Dig. 4.8.21.11 (Ulpian).

[224] Pomeroy, *Goddesses*, pp. 8, 12; A. Bride, "Rapt (Empêchement de)," in *Dictionnaire de théologie catholique*, ed. A. Vacant et al., 15 vols. in 30 (Paris: Letouzey et Ané, 1909–50; hereafter cited as DTC) 13/2 : 1666.

[225] Dig. 4.2.1 (Ulpian).

[226] Dig. 48.6.3.4 (Marcianus); Mestieri, *Estudo* p. 12.

[227] Dig. 47.11.1 (Paulus).

Raptus in Roman terminology included forcible abduction as well as forcible sexual relations. The emphasis in the law relating to *raptus* generally centered on the damage that the household suffered, rather than on the personal hurt and injury done to the victim.[228] It is characteristic of the Roman attitude toward *raptus* that forcible ravishment of a male or female servant gave the injured party's master a right to an action for damages; in general the father, employer, or owner of the victim of rape had a choice between seeking compensation for damages or criminal penalties for the offense.[229]

Paulus defined the force necessary to constitute *raptus* as "an assult that cannot be repelled,"[230] while Ulpian described the fear that a victim must experience in order to qualify the attack as rape as "mental alarm by reason of present or future danger."[231] Either abduction or sexual relations procured by force or fear, or any combination of these elements, counted as *raptus*. The crime, as Marcian (fl. ca. A.D. 250) noted, was more serious and more severely punished than adultery.[232] Although classical Roman law severely restricted the subject's right to self-help against an attacker, a specific exception permitted any person to resist and even to kill without penalty an assailant who sought to ravish the resister or a member of his household.[233]

Latin terminology, however, often renders the meaning of Roman law on *raptus* ambiguous. Ravishment sometimes consisted in the abduction of a girl from her parental home by a suitor of whom her father or guardian disapproved; in other words, what was sometimes at issue in actions for *raptus* was what we would call elopement. The importunate suitor who eloped with his sweetheart against her father's wishes was subject, in theory at least, to the same punishment as the genuine rapist with a knife in a back alley. The fact that the suitor's victim consented to his actions, or even desired them, might mitigate the penalty the abductor received, but his deeds exposed him to harsh reprisals from his intended wife's *paterfamilias*. If he escaped the most extreme penalties for his act, however, the admirer could still marry his beloved, provided that she freely consented to the union.[234]

Homosexuality

Roman society was not especially tolerant of gay sex, but the law did not impose special penalties upon same-sex relationships.[235] Instead, Roman legislation subjected homosexual activities to most of the same restrictions that it

---

[228] Dig. 47.9.3.5 (Ulpian).

[229] Dig. 47.10.9.4 (Ulpian); Cod. 9.20.1 (Antoninus Pius).

[230] Dig. 4.2.2: "Vis autem est maioris rei impetus, qui repelli non potest."

[231] Dig. 4.2.1: "Metus instantis vel futuri pericula causa mentis trepidatio [est]."

[232] Dig. 48.6.5.2 (Marcian).

[233] Dig. 48.8.1.4 (Marcian).

[234] Bride, "Rapt," in DTC 13/2:1666. This situation was changed by a rescript of Constantine in A.D. 320.

[235] Veyne, "L'homosexualité," p. 31.

imposed on heterosexual acts. The *Lex Scantinia* (149 B.C.) apparently imposed a fine on *stuprum* between males, but the penalty was not significantly different from that later prescribed for heterosexual *stuprum* by the *Lex Iulia de adulteriis*. The law probably sought to shield free adolescent boys from sexual harassment, much as it protected free adolescent girls.[236] The aim in both cases was to make it illegal to treat free youths in the same way that young slaves were habitually treated, and to preserve social distinctions between classes. The lawmakers do not seem to have envisioned imposing a ban on homosexual activities as such.

The attention of Roman law concerning adult male homosexuals centered on those who played the passive role in anal intercourse. Passive males might be cashiered from the army and were ineligible to practice law or even to appear in court on their own behalf.[237] The law here reflected a feeling that a man who submitted passively to sexual relations with another man betrayed the masculine virtues proper to free male citizens; he was penalized primarily for treachery to the social order.

Conclusions

Regulation of sexual behavior through law was common in all of the ancient societies surveyed here. Ancient sex laws tended to focus on a relatively narrow range of topics. They expressed particular interest in marriage and betrothal, as well as in adultery and concubinage, but took less notice of prostitution, rape, and gay sex. The central emphasis in ancient legal treatments of sex thus fell on marital and quasi-marital relationships, while nonmarital sex received only incidental treatment and was a matter of marginal legal concern.

All of these legal systems seemed more concerned about the impact of sexual relations upon the social order than with limiting or controlling sex acts in themselves. The stress that ancient law laid upon the property consequences of sexual relations is particularly striking. Lawmakers and jurists in antiquity also worried about the effects that extramarital sex might have upon social stability and used legal coercion as a weapon to combat the allures and temptations of nonmarital liaisons. Jurists were thus concerned that parents and elders should monitor the marriages and curb the sexual attachments of young people. Roman legislators and jurists displayed a firm resolve to use legal controls on sexual behavior in order to preserve the class structure. The law penalized those

---

[236] Cicero, *Epistulae ad familiares* 8.12.3; Suetonius, *De vita caesarum*, Domitian 8; Juvenal, *Satires* 2.43–47; *Paulys Realencyclopädie der Altertumswissenschaft*, ed. Georg Wissowa et al., 80 vols. (Stuttgart: J.B. Metzler [imprint varies], 1894–1980; cited hereafter as Pauly-Wissowa) 12:2413 and Supplement 7:411; Veyne, "L'homosexualité," pp. 28–29. Boswell, CSTAH, pp. 65–69, asserts that the *Lex Scantinia* had nothing to do with homosexual activity and attempts to explain away some of the evidence that supports the conventional interpretation of the statute, whose text, unfortunately, no longer survives.

[237] Dig. 3.1.1.6 (Ulpian).

whose sexual adventures across class boundaries threatened the social order. The law likewise discouraged sexual opportunists from alliances with social groups other than the one into which they were born. In accordance with Roman social norms, sex laws also helped to reinforce male ascendancy. As Ulpian noted, men customarily demanded from their wives a standard of sexual conduct that they did not observe themselves.[238]

Sex law as a means of enforcing ethical standards played only a minor role in the earliest surviving legal texts. Societies in remote antiquity apparently perceived morality as the sum of the kinds of behavior that preserved the social order, as defined by their own elite; concern about sexual ethics figures only occasionally in legal regulation of sex in the most ancient sources. The connection between religious norms and the legal regulation of sexuality was likewise weak in the ancient Mediterranean world. While religion might buttress society's claims to penalize those whose sexual activities transgressed the accepted standards of the elite groups, religious values had slight impact on the formation of those standards. Indeed, accounts relating the escapades of the deities often ran counter to the policies enunciated in society's laws about sexual behavior. The gods themselves would have run afoul of the law had they acted out their mythical adventures in the streets of Periclean Athens or Augustan Rome.

When Christianity emerged as the most favored religion of the Roman Empire during the early decades of the fourth century, many characteristic features of earlier legal regulation of sexual behavior in the Mediterranean world began to undergo profound and radical change.

---

[238] Dig. 48.5.14.(13).5 (Ulpian); Gottlob, "Ehebruch," p. 336.

2

Sex and the Law in Judaism and Early Christianity

Marriage and the Family in Ancient Judaism

"Wine and women make wise men fall away," observed Jesus ben Sirach,[1] and ancient Jewish law tried to restrict both, although the Mosaic law's interest in controlling sexual behavior was far stronger than its concern with drinking. The Hebrew Scriptures had a great deal to say about sex, and undertones of suspicion and distrust run through many of the scriptural passages dealing with it.

Scripture did not treat sex as sinful but as conducive to sin, a milestone on the road to the worship of false gods. The sacred texts described sex as a brutish business, an obsession fit for horses and mules and other creatures that lack understanding; for humans, however, it is unbecoming, even perverse, to dwell on the attractions of the bedchamber.[2] This aloofness should hold true even in marriage, where sex certainly plays a legitimate role, according to the sacred texts; yet that role should be limited to the serious business of reproduction. Marriage was not a game played for pleasure, but an institution that served both the social purpose of continuing the family line and the religious destiny of perpetuating God's chosen people. Marriage was not for fun, and neither was sex.[3]

Messages such as these recur under many forms in the scriptural revelation of Judaism and in rabbinical commentaries on the sacred writings. The rabbis were keenly aware of the dangers of sexual temptation. Accordingly they pre-

[1] Ecclus. 19:2. Scriptural citations throughout, unless otherwise specified, are to the Vulgate text in *Bibliorum sacrorum iuxta vulgatam Clementinam*, ed. Aloisio Gramatica (Vatican City: Typis Polyglottis Vaticanis, 1959). English translations generally follow those of the *Jerusalem Bible* (Garden City, NY: Doubleday, 1966), but are adapted where necessary to reflect the Vulgate version.

[2] Tob. 6:17; Eric Fuchs, *Sexual Desire and Love: Origins and History of the Christian Ethic of Sexuality and Marriage*, trans. Marsha Daigle (Cambridge: James Clarke & Co.; New York: Seabury Press, 1983), p. 52.

[3] Philo Judaeus, *De Josepho* 43; Anthony Kosnik et al., *Human Sexuality: New Directions in American Catholic Thought* (New York: Paulist Press, 1977), p. 14; Fuchs, *Sexual Desire and Love*, p. 62.

scribed that men and women should remain separate from one another, both in public and in private, in order to minimize opportunities for dalliance outside of marriage. "A man may not remain alone with two women," said one Mishnaic text, "but a woman may remain alone with two men," apparently on the theory that a man with two women might be tempted to make advances to both of them, but that a man in the company of another man would not dare to make sexual overtures to a woman out of fear that his jealous companion would report him to the community.[4]

Household structure among the ancient Hebrews, as among other ancient Near Eastern peoples, was polygynous. Men who could afford them kept numerous wives and concubines simultaneously, and monogamy was common because of poverty, not principle.[5] Josephus (37/38–after 100 C.E.), for example, when discussing the tangled marital affairs of King Herod (37–4 B.C.E.), who at one point had nine wives concurrently, observed, "It is an ancestral custom of ours to have several wives at one time," and he was right.[6]

Every adult Jewish male, according to rabbinical teaching, had a religious obligation to marry and to beget children, although the authorities differed about the number of children required to fulfill the obligation.[7] Marriage arrangements in ancient Israel normally began with betrothal, which involved an agreement between the fathers of the prospective married couple concerning property arrangements and other conditions of the marriage.[8] Traditional law concerning dowry was complex, for the future economic well-being of the household depended upon the care and forethought that went into these negotiations. Sexual attraction and charm played a minor role in these businesslike and serious contracts, but the Song of Songs vividly celebrates the joy and pleasures of marital sex and demonstrates that marital eroticism was no stranger in Israel.[9]

Jewish wedding ritual was a public acknowledgement of the bargain that had been struck and the family alliance that the union sealed. Once married, the husband had a moral and legal obligation to have sexual relations with his wife, and the wife had a right to demand sexual performance from him.[10] But accord-

[4] *The Mishnah*, Kiddushim 4.12–14, trans. Herbert Danby (London: Oxford University Press, 1933; repr. 1977), p. 329.

[5] Epstein, *Marriage Laws*, p. 49; Freisen, *Geschichte*, p. 45.

[6] Flavius Josephus, *Antiquitates Judaicae*, 17.9–15, 19–22.

[7] *Mishnah*, Yebamoth 6.6, trans. Danby, p. 227.

[8] Gen. 24:2–9 gives an early and striking description of conditions governing a betrothal agreement.

[9] The tractates Kiddushim and Kebutoth in the *Mishnah* deal primarily with betrothal and dowry law, while Yebamoth centers on the rules concerning consanguinity and other impediments to marriage. For celebration of the sensual joys of marital sex see esp. Cant. 1:15–2:6, 4:9–12, and 7:1–10.

[10] Harry C. Schnur, "Jüdische Ehe und Familie im Mittelalter," in *Love and Marriage in the Twelfth Century*, ed. Willy Van Hoecke and Andries Welkenhuysen, Medievalia Lovaniensia, ser. 1, no. 8 (Louvain: Leuven University Press, 1981), p. 97.

ing to some authorities, marital intercourse was only justified if its purpose was to beget a child. Intercourse solely for pleasure was wrong.[11]

Even marital relations for procreative purposes produced ritual impurity, however, and both husband and wife were obliged to undertake ceremonial ablutions after intercourse before they ventured to conduct either religious or temporal business. Unless purified, they might defile others and thus damage the community.[12] The ritual impurity attached to sex arose, according to Josephus, from a belief that intercourse causes a division within the soul; the ablutions were thought to heal this condition.[13] Other sexual incidents in marital life might also create impurity, particularly intercourse during menstruation, which the Mosaic law sternly forbade.[14] Priests, especially the high priest, were subject to special restrictions on their sexual activities within marriage.[15]

Ancient Hebrew law always permitted divorce, and while the formalities associated with the process were fairly complex, there was no question in Jewish tradition or custom that unsatisfactory marriages could be dissolved and the parties allowed to remarry. The major rabbinical schools disagreed sharply, however, concerning the grounds on which divorce might be authorized. The School of Shammai adopted a restrictive position and taught that a man might divorce his wife only if she were guilty of unchastity, while the School of Hillel took a more permissive view and allowed divorce on many grounds, so that a husband who was dissatisfied with his wife's cooking, for example, could lawfully divorce her for that reason alone. Rabbi Akiba (fl. ca. 135 C.E.) went so far as to declare that a man who sighted a woman more beautiful than his wife was justified in repudiating his spouse and marrying the more attractive rival. The property consequences of such impulsive actions no doubt restrained many men from taking advantage of this lenient interpretation of the divorce law. Women, on the other hand, had no legal right to take the initiative in dissolving an unsatisfactory marriage, so that divorce, as a matter of law at any rate, remained a male prerogative in traditional Judaism.[16]

The laws that applied to sex in Jewish marriage also applied to relations with

[11] Lindner, *Usus matrimonii*, pp. 25–26.

[12] Lev. 15:16–18; Deut. 23:10–11. On the vast and complex subject of ritual impurities in rabbinical thought see generally Jacob Neusner, *The Idea of Purity in Ancient Judaism*, Studies in Judaism in Late Antiquity, vol. 1 (Leiden: E. J. Brill, 1973), esp. pp. 14, 20–21, 24–25, 36–37; for relevant texts and detailed commentaries see also Neusner's *History of the Mishnaic Law of Purities*, Studies in Judaism in Late Antiquity, pt. 6, 22 vols. (Leiden: E. J. Brill, 1974–77).

[13] Josephus, *Against Apion* 2.203.

[14] Menstruation produced ritual defilement in the woman and anything she touched (Lev. 15:19–24), as did childbirth (Lev. 12:2–5); intercourse during menstruation compounded the defilement and affected both parties (Lev. 15:24, 18:19, 20:18).

[15] *Mishnah*, Yeb. 6.4, trans. Danby, p. 227.

[16] *Mishnah*, Gittin 9.10, trans. Danby, p. 321; *Babylonian Talmud*, Shabbath 64b, trans. I. Epstein et al., 7 vols. in 18 (London: Soncino Press, 1978) 2/1:307; Schnur, "Jüdische Ehe," pp. 98–99.

concubines, for Hebrew law generally treated wives and concubines similarly. There was a hierarchy of sexual and social relationships within households, running from the legitimate wife, or wives, to the concubine, the freedwoman, the female servant, and the female slave. All of these women might be sexually available to the male head of the household, and the law did not differentiate clearly or sharply among them. For many purposes the concubine was treated as if she were a married woman. The disparities, such as they were, between the concubine and the legitimate wife had to do mainly with their social origins and the formalities connected with betrothal, dowry, marriage ceremonies, veiling, and the like.[17] The concubine was typically an inferior consort from a lower social class than the legitimate wife and enjoyed lesser dignity and somewhat restricted rights in consequence of this.

In diaspora Judaism, there emerged a distinction between betrothed and unbetrothed concubines: the betrothed concubine was the lover of an unmarried man, while the unbetrothed concubine was the mistress of a man who already had a legitimate wife. A few concubines insisted on written contracts that governed their rights. These concubines generally brought dowries with them when they entered the household.[18] All concubines, dowried or not, had certain legal rights under Mosaic law. They were entitled to receive maintenance from their lovers and probably to share in his estate as well. The children of a concubine certainly had a right to inherit a portion of their father's estate, although their share was smaller than that of the children of a legitimate wife.[19]

Concubinage gradually faded from Jewish law during the post-Biblical period. Concubines are rarely mentioned in the legal sources after the second century of the Christian era, and the medieval rabbis simplified family structure by insisting that a long-term sexual liaison was either a full-fledged marriage or it was no marriage at all. Second-class marriage simply vanished from Jewish law in the Middle Ages.[20]

NONMARITAL SEX

While concubinage slowly disappeared from Jewish law, nonmarital sex did not. Neither the Scriptures nor the rabbinical authorities forbade simple noncommercial fornication between consenting partners. The writers apparently saw this as no great threat to marriage or to family interests, probably because they assumed that men would confine their extramarital adventures to servant and slave girls and would either not have access to free-born women of respectable status or be so irresponsible as to have affairs with them. When com-

[17] Epstein, "Institution of Concubinage," pp. 154–56, 159–60, 167–68, and *Marriage Laws*, pp. 35–37, 53; Freisen, *Geschichte*, pp. 46–47.

[18] Epstein, "Institution of Concubinage," pp. 157, 162–64, 186–87, and *Marriage Laws*, pp. 72–74; Mañaricua y Nuere, *Matrimonio de los esclavos*, p. 47.

[19] Epstein, "Institution of Concubinage," pp. 170–71, 173, and *Marriage Laws*, pp. 53–54.

[20] Epstein, "Institution of Concubinage," pp. 175, 180, and *Marriage Laws*, p. 62.

munities had to deal with couples who violated these expectations, they were far more severe than the treatment of extramarital sex by legal writers would have led us to expect and often censured cohabiting couples for immoral conduct. But the law's concern in dealing with nonmarital relations was mainly with rape or abduction of a virgin; lawgivers treated even these transgressions primarily as civil wrongs, not moral offenses. Actions in such cases lay against the man for stealing the woman's virginity, thus decreasing her value on the marriage market.[21]

Adultery was quite a different matter. Extramarital sexual relations by a married woman were considered a grievous offense against the whole community, not just against the woman's husband, and the community, not the husband, had the right to prosecute the wrongdoers. Adultery merited death by stoning for both the adulteress and her partner. An affair between a married man and an unmarried woman, however, was not subject to criminal penalties, although it might constitute a civil wrong against the woman and her family and could result in an assessment of damages against the man.[22]

The child of illicit intercourse was severely penalized in traditional Hebrew law. The term "bastard" (mamzer) had originally meant the child of a foreigner and also applied to the children of all mixed marriages, but by the beginning of the Christian era it was restricted to the progeny of illicit unions.[23] Bastards were deprived of inheritance rights and of most civil and juridical privileges in Jewish society, although exceptional illegitimate children, such as Jephthah the Gileadite, might rise to positions of power and authority.[24]

Prostitution, unlike concubinage, was forbidden to Jewish women by the Mosaic law, although foreign prostitutes were tolerated. Some authorities, notably Rabbi Elazar, regarded any woman who had intercourse outside of marriage as a harlot (zonah), but this view did not prevail among the commentators on the law.[25] Despite the Torah's ban on Jewish prostitution, the practice was tolerated in ancient Israel, although it may not have been conducted as openly as it was in pagan societies.[26] Contrary to legal prescription, Jewish as well as

[21] Deut. 22:13–21; Louis M. Epstein, *Sex Laws in Judaism* (New York: Ktav, 1967), pp. 167–68, and *Marriage Laws*, p. 305.

[22] Exod. 20:14; Lev. 18:20, 20:10; Deut. 5:18, 22:22–29; Kornfeld, "L'adultère," pp. 93–94; Anthony Phillips, "Another Look at Adultery," *Journal of Studies in the Old Testament* 20 (1981) 3–26. Philo, *De Josepho* 44, calls adultery "the greatest of crimes" (*tou megistou ton adikematon*).

[23] *Mishnah*, Yeb. 4.13, trans. Danby, p. 225; Epstein, *Marriage Laws*, pp. 279–80; Hermann, *Stellung unehelicher Kinder*, pp. 37–41.

[24] Judges 11:2–12:7.

[25] *Mishnah*, Yeb. 6.5, trans. Danby, p. 227; Lev. 19:29; Deut. 23:17–18. Prostitution by the daughter of a priest was punishable by death: Lev. 21:9; Epstein, "Institution of Concubinage," pp. 181–82, and *Marriage Laws*, pp. 280, 323. In *Sex Laws*, p. 143, Epstein argues that the Deuteronomic prohibition was aimed primarily at forbidding sacred prostitution, which was very common in the ancient Near East.

[26] S. Legasse, "Jésus et les prostituées," *Revue théologique de Louvain* 7 (1976)

Gentile women became bawds in Jewish communities. Popular songs cele-brated the charms of well-known whores, and the prophet Eli complained about his own sons' commerce with the prostitutes who plied their trade at the door of the meeting-tent.[27] The wisdom literature of the Scriptures describes vividly the wiles of prostitutes and warns of the dangers of doing business with them, but the warning itself is evidence that they did not lack clients. Prosti-tutes in Jewish communities during the biblical and talmudic periods appar-ently did not work in organized brothels, for the law has nothing to say about houses of prostitution. The prostitute in ancient Israel apparently encountered her clients in the streets and other public places.[28]

The Mosaic law forbade marriage between a Jew and a prostitute, a prohibi-tion applied to all, but with special force to high priests.[29] Reformed harlots who had given up their trade and sought to lead an honest life might marry observant Jewish men, but only after a three-month waiting period had elapsed between their reform and the marriage ceremony. Some later authorities ar-gued that even a priest might marry a Jewish harlot, provided that in the course of her career she had not had sexual relations with any gentiles, slaves, mem-bers of her own household, or married men of any kind. Partly because of the ritual impurity that they incurred through such contacts, prostitutes were forbidden to make gifts to the Temple or to participate in solemn religious observances.[30]

While ancient Jewish law viewed voluntary sexual relations, whether com-mercial or noncommercial, with considerable tolerance, it punished forcible rav-ishment of Jewish women severely. The rapist who assaulted a betrothed or married woman was liable to the death penalty; rape of an unmarried and un-betrothed virgin entailed a heavy fine and obligatory marriage to the victim. Seduction was also a serious offense, but was punished by milder sanctions, including a fine and, at the option of the girl's father, marriage to the victim. Practice seems to have followed theory, for the Scriptures relate the histories of two rape cases, in both of which the legal penalties were carried out.[31] Fines levied for rape or seduction were payable to the father of the victim, who was in effect deemed the owner of her now-vanished virginity and thus entitled to compensation for the loss. Women who were no longer under paternal au-thority might be entitled to keep the compensation for themselves. Neither rape nor seduction created a marriage impediment, although such circum-

141–42. Philo, *De Josepho* 42–43, and *De specialibus legibus* 3.51, claimed that ancient Israel punished prostitutes with death, but that is clearly an exaggeration; perhaps he was thinking of Lev. 21:9.

[27] Gen. 38:12–26; 1 Kings 2:22; 3 Kings 3:16–28; Josue 6:25; Isa. 23:15–16.

[28] Prov. 7:10–23; Ecclus. 9:2–9; Epstein, *Sex Laws*, pp. 157–58, 162.

[29] Lev. 21:7, 14; Josephus, *Antiquitates* 4:245.

[30] Deut. 23:18; Epstein, *Sex Laws*, p. 164, and *Marriage Laws*, pp. 305, 324.

[31] Gen. 34:1–31; Exod. 22:16–17; Deut. 22:25–29; 2 Kings 13:1–34; Epstein, *Sex Laws*, pp. 178–89.

stances diminished the price that the dishonored girl or her father might demand for her hand in marriage.[32] Two passages in Leviticus prohibit sexual relationships between men, and one of them prescribed the death penalty for same-sex intercourse.[33] Although Boswell has recently argued that this prohibition was based upon the purity law, not on moral grounds, and that its purpose was to emphasize the distinction between Jewish life-styles and those of Gentiles, the rabbinical commentators certainly considered homosexual activity a serious crime that merited death by stoning, a penalty not usually imposed for purity law violations.[34] The applicability of the prohibition to all Jewish males was never seriously questioned by authoritative commentators.

An Old Testament episode that Christian writers often cited as a further indication of the gravity of homosexual acts was God's destruction of Sodom and Gomorrah.[35] Modern commentators tend to consider the traditional interpretation of the Sodom episode problematical and ill-founded, since the tale seems to center on notion that it is wrong to mistreat strangers and travellers, rather than on sexual transgressions.[36] Putting aside the Sodom and Gomorrah story, however, scriptural and rabbinical disapproval of homosexuality is still clear and was echoed even by such a hellenized Jewish writer as Philo Judaeus (ca. 30 B.C.–A.D. 45).[37]

Although the Scriptures made no explicit mention of lesbian sex, rabbinical writers assumed that female homosexuality was forbidden and firmly registered their disapproval of it. Their disapprobation may be linked to the prohibition in Deuteronomy of the wearing of male attire by women or of female dress by men, a practice that the law labeled an "abomination before God."[38]

Law and Sex in Early Christianity

The Gospels have little to say about sex, and their silence implies that Jesus was relatively uninterested in the subject. He was apparently far more concerned with other matters and spoke at greater length on such topics as wealth and demonic possession.[39] While Jesus did not reject traditional Jewish beliefs about marriage and the family,[40] he differed from most traditional teachers in the emphasis that he placed upon love as a paramount element in marriage.[41]

[32] *Mishnah*, Yeb. 11.1, trans. Danby, p. 234; Epstein, *Sex Laws*, pp. 187–89.

[33] Lev. 18:22, 20:13.

[34] Boswell, CSTAH, pp. 100–02; but see the *Mishnah*, Yeb. 8.6 and Sanhedrin 7.4, trans. Danby, pp. 230, 392.

[35] Gen. 18–19.

[36] Boswell, CSTAH, pp. 93–96; even so, Philo Judaeus, for one, clearly saw the destruction of the cities as a result of homosexual intercourse by the Sodomites; see *De Abrahamo* 133–37.

[37] Philo Judaeus, *De legibus specialibus* 3.37–38; David Daube, "The Old Testament Prohibitions of Homosexuality," ZRG, RA 103 (1986) 447–48.

[38] Deut. 22:5; Epstein, *Marriage Laws*, p. 323.

[39] Boswell, CSTAH, p. 114; Kosnik et al., *Human Sexuality*, p. 17.

[40] Matt. 5:32 and 19:4–12; Mark 10:2–12; Luke 16:18.

[41] Matt. 19:3–6; Willy Rordorf, "Marriage in the New Testament and in the Early

Both Jesus and his early followers anticipated that Christian married couples would live within the context of traditional Jewish culture, but encouraged them to pattern their personal relationship upon the mutual self-giving that lay at the heart of the notion of *agape* among his early followers. Sexual relations in marriage formed part, but only part, of the sharing and loving relationship that seems to have been the marriage ideal of Jesus and the earliest Christians.[42]

A similar acceptance of the cultural context in which he lived characterized Jesus' treatment of divorce. While he did not ban divorce entirely, Jesus viewed it as a last resort rather than a routine solution to marriage problems.[43] He taught that grounds for divorce should be restricted, and here he was certainly at odds with the prevailing opinion among other rabbis. Adultery was the sole reason that Jesus would countenance for divorce; even when adultery occurred, he was loath to allow remarriage following divorce, although he apparently did not absolutely forbid it.[44]

Several passages in the Gospels condemn *porneia*. This word carried a number of different meanings. At times *porneia* means prostitution, at other times it refers to nonmarital sex in general.[45] It is difficult to be certain, for example, whether the term applied to premarital intercourse between persons betrothed to one another or, indeed, to any type of noncommercial, heterosexual relations of the kind conventionally labeled "fornication." Since neither the Torah nor most rabbinical teachers contemporary with Jesus prohibited intercourse between unmarried partners as a moral offense, perhaps *porneia* referred primarily to sex with prostitutes, adultery, and other promiscuous relationships.[46]

Church," *Journal of Ecclesiastical History* [cited hereafter as JEH] 20 (1969) 195–96; Fuchs, *Sexual Desire and Love*, p. 42.

[42] Rordorf, "Marriage," p. 198; P. A. Bonnet, "Amor coniugalis matrimoniumque in fieri prout Vetus et Novum Testamentum significat," *Periodica de re morali, canonica, liturgica* 65 (1976) 596–604; see generally Anders Nygren, *Agape and Eros*, trans. Philip S. Watson (New York: Harper & Row, 1969), esp. pp. 247–446.

[43] Matt. 19:7–9; Rordorf, "Marriage," p. 196.

[44] Matt. 19:9; D. R. Catchpole, "The Synoptic Divorce Material as a Traditio-Historical Problem," *Bulletin of the John Rylands Library* 57 (1975) 92–127; but cf. A.-L. Descamps, "Les textes évangéliques sur le mariage," *Revue théologique de Louvain* 9 (1978) 259–86 and 11 (1980) 5–50, and J.D.M. Derrett, *Law in the New Testament* (London: Darton, Longman, & Todd, 1970), pp. 187, 363–88; S. Schedl, "Zur Ehebruchklausel der Bergpredigt," *Theologisch-praktische Quartalschrift* 135 (1982) 361–65, who argues that the text of the Temple Roll, published by Yigael Yadin in 1977, indicates that in this context *porneia* must mean "unlawful marriage between close blood relatives."

[45] Esp. Matt. 15:19 and Mark 7:21. In Matt. 21:31–32, Luke 15:30, and probably in John 8:41, the reference is to intercourse with prostitutes. Bruce Malina, "Does 'Porneia' Mean Fornication?" *Novum Testamentum* 14 (1972) 10–17, lists and analyzes all occurrences of *porneia* in the New Testament.

[46] Malina, "Does 'Porneia' Mean Fornication?" p. 17; but cf. the very different conclusions of J. Jensen in an article also entitled "Does 'Porneia' Mean Fornication?" *Novum Testamentum* 20 (1978) 161–84.

Jesus clearly considered adultery a serious moral problem, but there too his teachings differed from traditional Jewish law, which prescribed the death penalty for the offense. Jesus spoke of adultery as a moral failure rather than a public crime and accordingly sought to treat offenders with spiritual remedies, rather than to punish them through public execution.[47]

Jesus' attitude toward prostitution was also atypical of conventional Jewish thought. Although he did not condone prostitution and showed no particular tolerance for it as an institution, Jesus did not condemn individual harlots. A well-known Gospel passage reports him as saying that publicans and prostitutes would enter heaven ahead of the religiously scrupulous pharisees.[48] This passage, of course, does not mean Jesus considered prostitutes somehow superior over others in their claim to salvation. Rather, he used the prostitute as a symbol for all sinners who, if genuinely repentant, were as worthy of divine mercy as scrupulous observers of the niceties of the law. Perhaps Jesus reasoned that the degraded nature of the harlot's calling assured that she had learned humility, which, in turn, predisposed her to receive the gift of salvation. In any event Jesus' tolerance for prostitutes and other social outcasts aggravated the hostility of conventional religious authorities toward his teaching.[49]

A few Gospel passages, particularly in Luke, give the impression that Jesus may have considered sex a barrier to salvation. In the parable of the invitation to the nuptial banquet, for example, Luke listed marriage among the unacceptable excuses offered by those who wished to avoid attending the festivities. A few lines later, Luke represented Jesus as insisting that a man who wished to follow him must reject the love of his wife. In yet another passage, Luke ascribed to Jesus a saying that appeared to mean that celibacy is necessary for salvation, a message that was bound to shock Jewish audiences. Luke's account thus presents the most radical treatment of Jesus' views on sex to be found among the evangelists, portraying him as sharply at odds with conventional rabbinical opinion on sexual matters.[50]

The growth of Christian beliefs and practices perceptibly distinct from and sometimes directly opposed to traditional Jewish teachings continued during the decades that followed the death of Jesus. The dominant figure in this development during the first generation of Christian teachers and writers was St. Paul. Although Paul is often said to have modified the message of Jesus, Paul's genuine letters were in fact written before any of the Gospels on which we depend for our knowledge of Jesus' teachings. Thus Paul's letters are the earliest surviving evidence of primitive Christian beliefs.

---

[47] Matt. 19:27–28; John 8:3–11.

[48] Matt. 21:31–33; Légasse, "Jésus et les prostituées," p. 137.

[49] Luke 7:36–50; Légasse, "Jésus et les prostituées," pp. 151–52.

[50] Luke 14:20, 25–27; 18:29; 20:34–35; cf. Matt. 19:10–12. See also Fuchs, *Sexual Desire and Love*, pp. 68–69; René Metz, "Recherches sur le statut de la femme en droit canonique: bilan historique et perspectives d'avenir; problèmes de méthode," *L'année canonique* 12 (1968) 92–94.

Paul's letters show far greater concern with sexual issues than the Gospel writers attributed to Jesus. Paul considered sex a major source of sin and a freqent impediment to the Christian life. Although he did not place sexual offenses at the top of his hierarchy of sins, they nonetheless occupied a prominent place in Paul's thought. He considered illicit sex almost as serious as murder.[51] In two different passages Paul sketched out a theory of sexual sins that distinguished among four types of offenders: prostitutes, adulterers, "the soft ones" (masturbators and others who use sex primarily for pleasure), and men (but apparently not women) who have sex with one another. All of these he considered sinful, and those who indulged in such practices were unworthy of God's kingdom.[52]

Paul's treatment both of illicit sex outside of marriage (*porneia*) and of marital sex itself was influenced by his conviction that the end of the world was imminent. Believing that the world would soon end, Paul took it as a corollary that all earthly concerns, including sex, should hold little interest for Christians. His strong disapproval of sexual misconduct did not necessarily represent a revulsion at its moral enormity; rather Paul seemed to feel that those who spent their time and energy in pursuit of sexual pleasure had their priorities wrong and should be attending instead to preparations for the final judgment.[53]

Although Paul considered sex a distraction from matters of greater importance, he gave considerable attention to the institution of marriage and to the sexual relations of married persons. One of Paul's best-known dicta declared that "It is better to marry than to burn." Paul implied in this statement that marriage was an alternative to eternal damnation, a thought more clearly enunciated in the less frequently quoted first clause of the sentence: "But if they cannot restrain themselves, let them marry."[54] By restraint, Paul here meant sexual continence. In Paul's hierarchy of virtues and vices, complete sexual abstinence was a preferred state, one that Christians ought to strive for; those who could not control their sexual passions, however, had the option of marriage, which would provide them with a legitimate sexual outlet, at the cost of forfeiting the higher virtue of virginity.

Paul then continued, in the sequel to this passage, to discuss some problems of marital ethics. Christians, he told the Corinthians, should not divorce; those

[51] Philippe Ariès, "Saint Paul et la chair," in *Sexualités occidentales*, pp. 35–36. This view was similar to ideas current among some Stoics. How much St. Paul knew about Stoicism is unclear, but since he was a native of Tarsus, the birthplace of two eminent Stoic teachers and a city famous for its schools, it is unlikely that he was completely ignorant of its main teachings. See Arthur Darby Nock, "Early Gentile Christianity and Its Hellenistic Background," in his *Essays on Religion and the Ancient World*, 2 vols. (Oxford: At the Clarendon Press, 1972) 1:125–26; Frank Bottomley, *Attitudes to the Body in Western Christendom* (London: Lepus Books, 1979), pp. 31–32.

[52] 1 Cor. 6:9–10; 1 Tim. 1:10; cf. 1 Thess. 4:3–7. See also Ariès, "St. Paul," p. 34.

[53] Rordorf, "Marriage in the New Testament," p. 195; Boswell, CSTAH, p. 115; Kosnik et al., *Human Sexuality*, pp. 17, 29; Fuchs, *Sexual Desire and Love*, p. 76.

[54] 1 Cor. 7:9; Fuchs, *Sexual Desire and Love*, p. 75.

who nonetheless did divorce should not remarry. Even Christians whose spouses did not share their faith should remain married and seek to convert their unbelieving partners.[55] Paul, or more likely one of his followers, also took up questions of marital ethics in the letter to the Ephesians. This epistle described the ideal marital relationship: wives should be subject to their husbands; husbands had an obligation to love and cherish their wives. Married couples ought to model their union upon the relationship of Christ with the Church: that is, each party had an obligation to love and respect the other.[56]

Still other passages in the Pauline letters dealt specifically with the role of sex in marriage. Sex united husband and wife both physically and spiritually and made them two persons in one flesh, just as the Christian's spiritual union with Jesus joined two persons in one spirit. Because of the sacred character of marital sex, Paul continued, sex outside of marriage was forbidden. The prohibition applied particularly to sex with prostitutes, for this was a species of defilement. Sex was good only within marriage, and indeed, wedded sex might even be an aid to salvation. Christians who were spiritual giants might be able to do without marital sex; more ordinary folk needed sexual solace and had a right to seek it in marriage.[57]

Marriage, in Paul's view, was good, though less good than virginity, but he frowned on remarriage. Upon the death of first wife or husband, Paul grudgingly allowed the surviving spouse to remarry, but he made it clear that he considered second marriages less than worthy of a committed Christian. Paul felt that remarriage of a widower disqualified him for high office in the Christian community.[58]

Paul's condemnation of extramarital sex was sweeping and unqualified. When he used the term *porneia*, Paul's meaning was unequivocal—it embraced any and all sexual relationships outside of marriage.[59] He singled out homosexual relations for special condemnation and declared that neither "the soft ones" (masturbators and other sensualists) nor men who have sexual relations with other men would enter the kingdom of God.[60]

[55] 1 Cor. 7:10–16; John T. Noonan, Jr., *Power to Dissolve: Lawyers and Marriages in the Courts of the Roman Curia* (Cambridge: Harvard University Press, Belknap Press, 1972), pp. 342–43.

[56] Eph. 5:21–33; cf. Coloss. 3:18–19; Ariès, "L'amour dans le mariage," p. 119.

[57] 1 Cor. 6:15–19; Derrick Sherwin Bailey, *Sexual Relation in Christian Thought* (New York: Harper Brothers, 1959), p. 119; Lindner, *Usus matrimonii*, p. 14; Fuchs, *Sexual Desire and Love*, p. 77.

[58] 1 Tim. 3:2; Tit. 1:6; Eph. 5:33; Rordorf, "Marriage in the New Testament," p. 198; Josef Trümer, "Bigamie als Irregularitätsgrund nach der Lehre der alten Kanonisten," in *Speculum iuris et ecclesiarum: Festschrift für Willibald M. Plöchl zum 60. Geburtstag*, ed. Hans Lentze and Inge Gampl (Vienna: Herder, 1967), p. 393.

[59] Jensen, "Does 'Porneia' Mean Fornication?" pp. 161–84; Fuchs, *Sexual Desire and Love*, pp. 73–74.

[60] 1 Cor. 6:9–10; Rom. 1:27; 1 Tim. 1:10. Boswell argues in CSTAH, pp. 106–12, that these passages do not refer to homosexual acts; his interpretation requires assigning

Early Patristic Writers

After the age of the apostles, evidence concerning the sexual ethos of the early Church becomes scanty for several generations. Then, during the second and third centuries, Christian writers gradually began to elevate sexual problems to a position of greater prominence than these had possessed in the thought of either Jesus or Paul. Several leading Christian writers in this later period viewed sexual relations as the prototype of all moral offenses. Those who adopted this position were often thinkers who had been influenced by Gnostic beliefs, which linked mankind's fall from grace to sexual intercourse.

The great Biblical exegete, Origen (ca. A.D. 185–253/55), and the anonymous author of the Gnostic *Gospel according to the Egyptians*, for example, believed that Adam and Eve had been innocent of sexual temptations or even sexual feelings in Paradise. When they committed the first sin by disobeying God's command not to eat of the fruit of the tree of knowledge, Adam and Eve introduced sex into the world and with it the evil of lust.[61] With sex came death. Since the Fall from grace, according to the Gnostics, sex was tied to reproduction and hence to the life-and-death cycle of human experience. Only a cessation of sexual activity in the world would bring about life without death. Thus so long as people marry and have sex, they will also die.[62]

---

to the words St. Paul used meanings that apparently escaped the early Christian writers who commented on them. For a telling, if somewhat overdrawn, criticism of Boswell's contentions see Warren Johansson, "*Ex parte Themis*: The Historical Guilt of the Christian Church," in *Homosexuality, Intolerance, and Christianity: A Critical Examination of John Boswell's Work*, Gai Saber Monographs, no. 1 (New York: Gay Academic Union Scholarship Committee, 1981), pp. 1–5. I am grateful to Dr. Peter Linehan for this reference.

[61] John Bugge, *Virginitas: An Essay in the History of a Medieval Ideal*, Archives internationales d'histoire des idées, series minor, vol. 17 (The Hague: Martinus Nijhoff, 1975), pp. 11, 16–18; Michael Müller, *Die Lehre des hl. Augustinus von der Paradiesesehe und ihre Auswirkung in der Sexualethik des 12. und 13. Jahrhunderts bis Thomas von Aquin*, Studien zur Geschichte der katholischen Moraltheologie, vol. 1 (Regensburg: Friedrich Pustet, 1954), pp. 10–11.

[62] St. John Chrysostom, *De virginitate* 14, in *Patrologiae cursus completus . . . series Graeca*, ed. J.-P. Migne, 167 vols. (Paris: J.-P. Migne, 1857–76; cited hereafter as PG) 48:544: "Where there is death, there also is marriage; when the latter disappears, the former will do likewise." This conclusion was evidently based on a reading of Gen. 2:17 and 3:19. See also Clement of Alexandria, *Excerpta Theodoti* 67.2, in his *Opera omnia*, ed. Otto Stählin, 4 vols., Die griechischen christlichen Schriftsteller der ersten drei Jahrhunderte, vols. 12, 15, 17, 39 (Leipzig: J. C. Hinrich, 1905–36) 17:129. Similar sentiments occur in Clement's *Stromata* 3.9.63–64, ed. Stählin 15:225, as well as in Lactantius, *Divinae institutiones* 6.23, in his *Opera omnia*, ed. Samuel Brandt and Georg Laubmann, 3 vols., in CSEL, vols. 19 and 27, pts. 1 and 2 (Vienna: F. Tempsky, 1890–93) 19:567. See also Fuchs, *Sexual Desire and Love*, pp. 90–91; Gerard Watson, "The Natural Law and Stoicism," in *Problems in Stoicism*, ed. A. A. Long (London: Athlone

In response to these teachings, mainstream Christian spokesmen replied that sex was a natural human function, sanctioned by natural law; hence they defended the propriety of marriage for Christian believers. Their reaction to Gnostic denials of the morality of marital sex introduced the concept of natural law into Christian discourse about moral problems. In taking this step, the early patristic writers adopted as Christian teaching a problematic element from pagan philosophy. This innovation would have far-reaching consequences for the development of Christian doctrine.

Members of the Encratite sect were extreme partisans of the view that sex was a major source of sin and moral corruption. Encratites considered marital sex invariably sinful and held that Christ had intended to abolish marriage altogether. Perfect chastity, Encratites held, was essential for salvation. At the other extreme were the followers of Basilides and Carpocrates, together with the leaders of the obscure Nicolaite sect, who argued that Christianity implied free love and lack of sexual restraint and preached a doctrine that involved total sharing of resources, including sexual favors, among the faithful. Orthodox teachers rejected the extreme views of all these groups, but clearly found doctrines involving sexual abstinence more palatable than those that favored sexual license.[63]

Few early patristic writers bothered to account for the dislike and revulsion that characterized their treatment of sex. They plainly felt that no explanation was required, that sex was inherently so filthy and degrading that the reason for condemnation of it was self-evident.[64] The negative attitude of patristic writers to sex has often been described as a reaction against the sexual license of pagan society and, indeed, against the legends of the pagan gods themselves.[65] There is some basis for this. Lactantius (ca. A.D. 250–after 317), for example, denounced the incestuous practices and other sexual delinquencies of the pagan priesthoods and characterized paganism as a licentious and sexually perverted religion that polluted both mind and body.[66]

Press, 1971), pp. 216–38; and Gerard Verbeke, *The Presence of Stoicism in Medieval Thought* (Washington: Catholic University of America Press, 1983), pp. 46–47.

[63] Jaroslav Pelikan, *The Christian Tradition: A History of the Development of Doctrine, I: The Emergence of the Catholic Tradition (100–600)* (Chicago: University of Chicago Press, 1971), pp. 84–90; Fuchs, *Sexual Desire and Love*, pp. 88–92; Georges Blond, "Les Encatrites et la vie mystique," in *Mystique et continence*, pp. 117–130.

[64] Bailey, *Sexual Relation*, p. 48; John H. Fowler, "The Development of Incest Regulations in the Early Middle Ages: Family, Nurturance, and Aggression in the Making of the Medieval West" (Ph.D. diss., Rice University, 1981), pp. 46–47, 184.

[65] Rom. 1:24–32; Rordorf, "Marriage in the New Testament," p. 208; Arnobius, *Disputationum adversus gentes libri septem* 4.21, in *Patrologiae cursus completus . . . series Latina*, ed. J.-P. Migne, 221 vols. (Paris: J.-P. Migne, 1844–64; cited hereafter as PL) 5:1041.

[66] Lactantius, *Div. inst.* 5.9.16–17, ed. Brandt, 19:427; Arnobius, *Adv. gentes* 3.9–10, in PL 5:947–50. These criticisms were, in fact, considerably exaggerated, for some

Nevertheless, the conventional interpretation that links Patristic disgust with sex to revulsion at pagan debauchery seems historically misleading. Many early Church Fathers considered sex disgusting and obscene by its very nature. Arnobius (d. ca. A.D. 317), whose obsessive fascination with carnal lust seems slightly bizarre, nonetheless reflected a not uncommon view when he declared that it would be blasphemous even to imagine that Jesus was "born of vile coitus and came into the light as a result of the spewing forth of senseless semen, as a product of obscene gropings."[67] Tertullian (ca. 150–ca. 240), another radical critic of sex, ultimately joined the Montanist sect, whose members rejected marriage as altogether incompatible with Christianity. Even before he left the orthodox fold, however, Tertullian's revulsion at sex led him publicly to renounce sexual relations with his wife. He expounded his reasons in a brief treatise addressed to her but clearly aimed at a wider audience. In his treatise Tertullian admonished his wife to put away lustful desires and to lead a celibate life. Sexual craving and delight, even in marriage, Tertullian declared, can have no place in Christian life.[68] In another treatise, this one in praise of chastity, Tertullian expounded more fully his belief that marital sex was incompatible with Christian virtue. He argued that coitus causes spiritual insensitivity: sexual intercourse drives out the Holy Spirit, and this deprives sexually active couples of the benefit of divine counsel.[69]

Both Origen and Tertullian blamed women for luring Christian men into sexual indulgence that they might otherwise have been strong enough to resist. Women, Tertullian, declared, are the devil's door: through them Satan creeps into men's hearts and minds and works his wiles for their spiritual destruction.[70] Origen's condemnation of women was equally severe. He believed that women are more lustful than men and that they are obsessed by sexual desire. Like Tertullian, Origen considered woman a primary source of carnal corruption in Christian society. "There are some women," he wrote, "though not all of them,

---

pagan cults advocated standards of sexual morality entirely comparable to those of the Christians; see Arthur Darby Nock, *Early Gentile Christianity and its Hellenistic Background* (New York: Harpers, 1964), pp. 20–21, for examples. See also J. H. W. G. Liebeschuetz, *Continuity and Change in Roman Religion* (Oxford: At the Clarendon Press, 1979), pp. 39–54, and more generally Ramsey MacMullen, *Paganism in the Roman Empire* (New Haven: Yale University Press, 1982).

[67] Arnobius, *Adv. gentes* 4.19, in PL 5:1039: "[Q]uod ex turpi concubitu creditis, atque ex seminis jactu ignorantem sibi ad lucem beneficiis obscoenitatis exisse." On Arnobius see also Liebeschuetz, *Continuity and Change*, pp. 252–60.

[68] Tertullian, *Ad uxorem* 1.1.4, in his *Opera omnia*, ed. E. Dekkers et al., in *Corpus Christianorum, series Latina* (cited hereafter as CCL), vols. 1–2 (Turnhout: Brépols, 1954) 1:373–74.

[69] Tertullian, *De exhortatione castitatis* 11.1, in CCL 2:1030–31. This view may well owe something to Stoic beliefs, too; see Epictetus, *Discourses* 4.1.143, ed. Oldfather 2:292, and Michel Spanneut, *Le stoicisme des pères, de Clément de Rome à Clément d'Alexandrie* (Paris: Editions du Seuil, 1957), pp. 212–13.

[70] Tertullian, *De cultu feminarum* 1, in CCL 1:343.

as we have noted, who are indiscriminate slaves to lust, like animals they rut without discretion. . . ."[71] These sex-obsessed women, he continued, procured the spiritual destruction of untold numbers of Christian men.

Denunciations of sexual feelings and activities in the writings of the early Fathers are often balanced against other passages that praise sexual abstinence as a peculiarly Christian virtue. St. Justin Martyr (ca. 100 ~ 110–ca. 165/66), for example, celebrated continence among Christians and found especially praiseworthy the example of one young man who asked to be castrated (presumably on the strength of Matt. 19:12) in order to ensure safety from sexual temptations.[72] Christian men did not commonly seek physical castration, but the early Fathers soon elevated virginity from the position of a rare, charismatic choice made by a few to a general virtue required of many.[73]

Praise of virginity was, of course, not altogether novel and certainly not unique to exponents of the Christian faith. Stoics and other non-Christians often spoke of sexual restraint and even total sexual abstinence as morally commendable. And despite the strictures of Christian apologists about pagan debauchery, non-Christian religious traditions in many parts of the Empire had identified sexual self-denial as evidence of spiritual strength and had venerated virgins as sources and symbols of spiritual power.[74] Christian writers nonetheless saw themselves as special advocates of chastity and virginity and endowed these virtues with preeminent importance.[75]

The Fathers were quick to dissociate themselves from the long-standing Jewish tradition of polygyny and sharply criticized contemporary Jews for continuing to practice multiple marriage.[76] Yet Christian apologists felt bound to explain away the fact that polygyny had not only been practiced by the Old Testament prophets, but had evidently been approved by Yahweh. Several second-century spokesmen dealt with this problem by arguing that polygyny among

[71] Origen, *In Genesim homeliae* 5.4, in PG 12:192.

[72] Justin Martyr, *Apologia* 1.29, in PG 6:373–74. The second-century Stoic, Sextus, advised castration for those whose lust was otherwise incurable; *The Sentences of Sextus: A Contribution to Early Christian Ethics*, 13, 273, ed. Henry Chadwick, Texts and Studies, n.s., vol. 5 (Cambridge: At the University Press, 1959), pp. 12–13, 42–43.

[73] Carolly Erickson, *The Medieval Vision: Essays in History and Perception* (New York: Oxford University Press, 1976), p. 190. The proof texts most commonly adduced to support this exaltation of chastity were, in addition to Matt. 19:12, Luke 20:34–35 and Matt. 24:19.

[74] Epictetus, *Encheiridion* 33.8; Joyce E. Salisbury, "Fruitful in Singleness," *Journal of Medieval History* (hereafter JMH) 8 (1982) 99, 105. It was a common belief in many ancient religions that certain sacred functions should be performed only by persons who practiced sexual abstinence or even total continence. Such beliefs are amply documented in numerous cults of the ancient Near East, Greece, and Italy, as well as in Africa and the Americas; see Arthur Darby Nock, "Eunuchs in Ancient Religion," in his *Essays on Religion in the Ancient World* 1:9–15.

[75] St. Athenagoras (late 2d cent.), *Legatio pro Christianis* 32, in PG 6:963–64; Lactantius, *Div. inst.* 6.23, in CSEL 19:570–71.

[76] Justin Martyr, *Dialogus cum Tryphone Judaeo* 134.1, in PG 6:785–86.

the prophets had been justified by the need during the early period of mankind's existence to fulfill the command to increase and multiply. Now, however, the argument continued, the duty to increase the human race is no longer pressing and, in any event, the new covenant of Jesus had outmoded the Old Testament injunctions.[77] In any case, they argued, the multiple marriages of the prophets had never been motivated by lust; indeed their acceptance of circumcision showed, according to Origen, that the prophets accepted the discipline of sexual restraint, since circumcision signified a commitment to cut off the lusts of the flesh.[78]

Despite the reservations of a few extremists, most Christians in the second and third centuries accepted marriage as a legitimate social institution.[79] St. Clement of Alexandria (ca. 150–ca. 200) enunciated the majority view when he taught that it was as wrong to condemn marriage as it was to seek indiscriminate sexual pleasure. Those who condemn sex within marriage, according to Clement, set themselves against the teaching of the Gospels.[80] Marriage, Clement maintained, was conducive to the spiritual well-being of faithful Christians.[81]

The early Church prescribed no specifically Christian wedding rites for believers, but rather accepted and adopted the ceremonies and forms of marriage and betrothal that already existed in the Roman world.[82] Yet as early as the time of St. Ignatius of Antioch (d. 107?) Christians had begun to supplement secular marriage rites with religious celebrations at which the bishop presided.[83] The early Church expected its members to marry publicly and some writers held that secret marriages were little better than fornication. This resistance to hidden unions rested in part on the belief that marriage in the Christian community was a concern of the whole membership, since it involved a change in the status of members of the group. It is also likely that disapproval of secret marriage reflected a belief that parents had the right and duty to select or at least approve the mates of their children.[84]

Although the orthodox Fathers of the second and third centuries accepted marriage as a legitimate option, they believed also that Christians ought to restrict the role of sex in their married lives. For St. Justin Martyr in the early

[77] Justin Martyr, *Dialogus* 141.4, in PG 6:797–800; Tertullian, *Ad uxorem* 1.2.2, in CCL 1:374–75; Clement of Alexandria, *Stromata* 2.99.1 and 3.82.3, ed. Stählin 2:167, 233; Jean-Paul Broudéhoux, *Mariage et famille chez Clément d'Alexandrie*, Théologie historique, vol. 11 (Paris: Beauchesne, 1970), pp. 88–91.

[78] Origen, *In Genesim homelia* 3.6, in PG 12:180–81.

[79] Origen, *In Numeros homelia* 23.3, in PG 12:749; Tertullian, *Ad uxorem* 1.3.3–4, in CCL 1:375; Bugge, *Virginitas*, p. 71; Fuchs, *Sexual Desire and Love*, pp. 88–89.

[80] Clement of Alexandria, *Stromata* 3.6.45; 3.12.80–81; 3.17.102–3.18.110, ed. Stählin 2:216–17, 232–33, 243–47; Broudéhoux, *Mariage et famille*, pp. 46–49.

[81] Clement of Alexandria, *Stromata* 2.23, ed. Stählin 2:188–94.

[82] George Elliott Howard, *A History of Matrimonial Institutions, Chiefly in England and the United States*, 2 vols. (Chicago: University of Chicago Press, 1904) 1:291.

[83] St. Ignatius of Antioch, *Epistola ad Polycarpum* 5, in PG 5:724.

[84] Tertullian, *De monogamia* 15–16, and *De pudicitia* 4.4, in CCL 2:1251–52, 1287.

second century, marital sex was designed to produce children: faithful Christians either married in order to have offspring or else lived in complete continence.[85] His contemporaries and successors reiterated this theme time and time again: marital sex was legitimate when employed for procreation but not when indulged in for pleasure.[86]

The most positive appraisal of marriage among the early patristic writers came from Clement of Alexandria, but even he took a narrow view of the place of marriage in Christian life. Moreover, Clement's views about marital sex were markedly restrictive. Although he had words of praise for conjugal love and for the beauty of the marital relationship, Clement also maintained that "voluptuous joy" had no proper place in Christian life. Sex for pleasure, according to Clement—who quoted the Stoic writer Musonius in support of his position—is contrary to justice, law, and reason. Christian couples will never have intercourse simply because they enjoy it and each other; they must make love only to beget a child.[87]

Not only did the Fathers of the first three centuries teach that the purposes of marital sex ought to be restricted, but they also warned that the times for marital relations should be curtailed. None of the early writers was specific about the precise periods when couples should forego intercourse; they simply stated that it was inappropriate, even sinful, to indulge in sex on holy days and Church festivals.[88]

Although most early patristic writers disparaged the physical pleasures of wedded life, several of them had high praise for marital love. The *Didascalia*, written in the latter part of the third century, probably in northern Syria, lauded affection between spouses. This early compilation of the rules of Christian conduct maintained that reciprocal love between husband and wife was the constitutive element of Christian marriage. The *Didascalia* added that couples should strive to enhance their emotional ties to one another because through their love they would find salvation.[89] Husbands should be faithful to their wives and treat them with consideration, not as servants or menials. The *Didascalia* admonished husbands and wives to remain sexually faithful to their

[85] Justin Martyr, *Apologia* 1.29, in PG 6:373–74.

[86] Origen, *In Genesim* 3, 5.4, in PG 12:175–80, 191–92; *In Psalmos* 49:18 and 139.6 in PG 12:1452, 1664; Tertullian, *De monogamia* 3.4–10, in CCL 2:1231–33, and *Ad uxorem* 1.3–5, in CCL 1:373–74; Athenagoras, *Legatio* 33, in PG 6:965–68; Lindner, *Usus matrimonii*, pp. 40–45.

[87] Clement of Alexandria, *Paedagogus* 2.83.1–2.115.5, ed. Stählin 1:208–26, and *Stromata* 3.57.1–3.60.4, 3.71.1–3.78.5, 3.96.1–3.99.4, 3.105.1–3.110.2, ed. Stählin 2:222–24, 228–31, 240–42, 244–47; Lindner, *Usus matrimonii*, pp. 35–40; Rordorf, "Marriage in the New Testament," pp. 206–7; Foucault, *Histoire de sexualité* 2:21.

[88] Origen, *In Genesim* 3.6 and *In Numeros* 23.3, in PG 12:180–81, 749.

[89] *Didascalia, id est doctrina catholica duodecim apostolorum* 1.8, ed. F.X. Funk, in *Didascalia et constitutiones apostolorum*, 2 vols. (Paderborn: F. Schöningh, 1905) 1:20–21; A. Montan, "Alle origini della disciplina matrimoniale canonica: Contributi per la ricerca," *Apollinaris* 54 (1981) 162.

mates; they should not seek to make themselves attractive to others, lest they fall into concupiscence and be tempted to sin.[90] The author particularly warned married women not to wear provocative clothing, like prostitutes, or to adorn themselves extravagantly in ways that might entice men other than their husbands to flirt with them.[91]

The Fathers of the first three centuries countenanced divorce, although reluctantly, when one partner had committed adultery. Remarriage following divorce, however, was forbidden. Indeed, the husband of an adulteress was expected to forgive his wife and take her back, provided that she performed appropriate penance; failure to take back a repentant wife was considered sinful.[92] Remarriage of widows and widowers was permitted though not encouraged.[93] Justin Martyr, in fact, compared second marriages to adultery and considered them positively sinful, but in this he differed from most orthodox writers.[94]

The Montanist heretics, especially Tertullian, their most eloquent champion, spoke out harshly against second marriages. Even in his treatise *Ad uxorem*, which dates from his orthodox period, Tertullian had criticized second marriages and labeled them an obstacle to faith.[95] After his conversion to Montanism, Tertullian's vituperation of those who married for a second time became increasingly hysterical. He compared remarriage by a widow to fornication, adultery, and murder and asserted that morally there was little difference.[96] The only possible reason for remarriage was sexual desire, Tertullian shrilled, and those who remarried were nothing but filthy sensualists.[97] All Christians, he asserted, were absolutely required to refrain from second marriages. Although St. Paul had forbidden only bishops to remarry,[98] Tertullian claimed that this prohibition was binding upon all Christians.[99] In reaction against the extreme disapproval of second marriages voiced by Tertullian and other Montanists, later patristic writers in the fourth and fifth centuries maintained that approval of second and subsequent marriages was an article of orthodox belief.

---

[90] *Didascalia* 1.3.1–9, ed. Funk 1:8–10; Montan, "Alle origini," p. 162.

[91] *Didascalia* 1.8.17–18, ed. Funk 1:24.

[92] Visky, "Divorce," p. 244; Charles Lefebvre, "Origines et évolution de l'action en déclaration de nullité de mariage," *Revue de droit canonique* [cited hereafter as RDC] 26 (1976) 24.

[93] Hermas, *Pastor*, mandatum 4.4, ed. and trans. Robert Jolly, Sources chrétiennes, no. 53 (Paris: Editions du Cerf, 1958), pp. 162–63; Rordorf, "Marriage in the New Testament," p. 205.

[94] Justin Martyr, *Apologia* 1.15, in PG 6:349–52.

[95] Tertullian, *Ad uxorem* 1.7.4, in CCL 1:381; André Rosambert, *La veuve en droit canonique jusqu'au XIVe siècle* (Paris: Dallloz, 1923), pp. 101–5.

[96] Tertullian, *De exhortatione castitatis* 9.1 and *De monogamia* 4.3, 10.7, 15.1, in CCL 2:1027, 1233, 1243, 1250.

[97] Tertullian, *De monogamia* 1.1. in CCL 2:1229.

[98] 1 Tim. 3:2.

[99] Tertullian, *De monogamia* 12.1–5, in CCL 2:1247–48.

Even so, most leading Christian authors of this later period held that second marriage, although allowed, ought to be discouraged.[100]

Marriages of the clergy posed special problems for Christian authorities. Although a few early writers expressed a preference that clerics not marry at all, nearly every third-century Christian clergymen whose marital status is known seems to have been married.[101] The first effort to prohibit clerical marriage appeared in the canons of Elvira in the early fourth century.[102] Nearly half of the Elvira canons dealt with sexual problems.[103] This legislation required a far stricter standard of sexual behavior from the clergy than from the laity. Transgressions that were lightly punished when committed by a layman were subject to severe penalties when a cleric was the culprit.[104] The Elvira canons deprived bishops, priests, and deacons who committed fornication of the right to receive communion, save on their deathbeds; the canons also required the higher clergy to divorce their wives and demanded that they cease marital relations if the wife had committed adultery. The canons forbade female servants to live in the same dwelling with a clergyman, unless the woman was a close blood relative.[105]

The most radical of the Elvira canons required that married clerics abstain permanently from sexual intercourse with their wives. Those who contravened this provision were to be deposed from office.[106] The Elvira celibacy canon be-

---

[100] Rosambert, *Veuve*, pp. 105–8; Lecky, *Hist. of European Morals* 2:326–27; Council of Elvira, c. 72, in *Concilios Visigóticos e Hispano-Romanos*, ed. José Vives, Tomás Marín Martínez, and Gonzalo Martínez Diez, España cristiana, vol. 1 (Barcelona and Madrid: Consejo Superior de Investigaciones Científicas, 1963), p. 14.

[101] Roger Gryson, *Les origines du célibat ecclésiastique du première au septième siècle*, Recherches et synthèses, section d'histoire, vol. 2 (Gembloux: J. Duclot, 1970), pp. 32–36.

[102] The date of the council is disputed. The editors of *Concilios Visigóticos* placed it between 300 and 306, while Samuel Laeuchli, *Power and Sexuality: The Emergence of Canon Law at the Synod of Elvira* (Philadelphia: Temple University Press, 1972), pp. 86–87, placed it in 309. Maurice Meigne, "Concile ou collection d'Elvire?" *Revue d'histoire ecclésiastique* 70 (1975) 361–87, argues that the received text of the Elvira canons is a composite of genuine conciliar enactments and two sets of earlier canons. Whether Meigne is correct or not, these canons circulated as a conciliar text in the early Middle Ages and were believed to represent an authoritative body of regulations concerning sexual problems. Without prejudice to Meigne's views, I shall continue to employ conventional usage and refer to the text as the canons of the Council of Elvira. See also Roger Gryson, "Dix ans de recherches sur les origines du célibat ecclésiastique: Reflexions sur les publications des années 1970–1979," *Revue théologique de Louvain* 11 (1980) 162–63.

[103] Laeuchli, *Power and Sexuality*, p. 61, table 4, presents a topical analysis of the legislation.

[104] Laeuchli, *Power and Sexuality*, p. 94.

[105] Council of Elvira, c. 18, 27, 65, in Vives, *Concilios Visigóticos*, pp. 5, 6, 13; Montan, "Alle origini," p. 165.

[106] Council of Elvira, c. 33, in Vives, *Concilios Visigóticos*, p. 7; Gryson, *Origines du*

gan a controversy that has troubled the Western Church down to the present. Although there is little evidence that the regulation had any immediate effect or that there was any serious or widespread effort to enforce it, the canon stated an ideal that a great many Christians ever since have seen as laudable, even sublime. Others, however, have denounced mandatory clerical celibacy as iniquitous and contrary to both human nature and the Scriptures.

The Elvira canons seem to represent an attempt to define a Christian self-identity. What made a Christian different from a pagan? Part of the answer, according to the Elvira canons, was that Christians observed a strict code of sexual ethics. Some writers have argued that the authors of the Elvira canons were also interested in asserting the power of the clergy as an elite group within the Christian community.[107] The celibacy canon identified complete sexual abstinence as a central characteristic of this new clerical elite. By requiring the clergy to abstain entirely from sex and by ousting those who failed to live up to that standard, the Elvira canons implicitly proclaimed the moral superiority of the clergy to the common run of the laity, who were by implication too weak-willed and too lacking in discipline to measure up to the moral standards required of their clerical leaders. The requirement of clerical celibacy strongly implied, in addition, that marriage was undesirable for churchmen because the sexual relations of clerics with their wives created a ritual impurity incompatible with the performance of Christian rites, especially the eucharistic liturgy.[108] The celibacy canon thus rejected sex as unworthy of the most dedicated and disciplined Christians, although it also implicitly acknowledged the importance of sex for the majority of humans.

Concubinage seems to have been common among Christians during the second and third centuries. St. Hippolytus (ca. 170 ~ 75–ca. 235) advised men who kept concubines to relinquish them and to marry, but he stopped short of condemning concubinage as sinful.[109] By the early third century the Church had not yet developed either a coherent marriage doctrine or a comprehensive matrimonial law and continued to treat concubinage as a normal social practice.[110] Concubinage was in any case part of Christianity's heritage from its Jewish past, and no strong moral imperative required Christians to reject this feature of the societies in which they lived.[111] Pope St. Calixtus I (217–22) ruled that the

---

célibat, p. 41, rightly rejects as unfounded the argument that this canon reflected current practice in the early fourth century.

[107] Laeuchli, *Power and Sexuality*, p. 90.

[108] Laeuchli, *Power and Sexuality*, p. 94; John E. Lynch, "Marriage and Celibacy of the Clergy: The Discipline of the Western Church," *Jurist* 32 (1972) 20–22; Gryson, "Dix ans de recherche," pp. 167–74.

[109] Montan, "Alle origini," p. 158.

[110] Jean Gaudemet, "La décision de Callixte en matière de mariage," in *Studi in onore di Ugo Enrico Paoli*, pp. 341–43, repr. in Gaudemet's *Sociétés et mariage* (Strasbourg: CERDIC, 1980), pp. 104–15 at 112–13.

[111] Freisen, *Geschichte*, pp. 45–46.

Church should accept as marriages all unions in which the parties were forbidden by civil law to marry one another—such as, for example, cohabitation between a free woman and a slave. Although civil law made it impossible for these persons to marry each other, the Church would nonetheless accept them as a married couple and would not penalize them for remaining together.[112] Thus the Church in the early third century had begun to assimilate concubinage to marriage, at least in some situations.[113]

Concubinage itself was undergoing change in this period. Civil rules requiring that concubines be chosen only from the ranks of lower-class women were becoming obsolete by the early third century; in that period a woman of the matron class might become the concubine of a lower-class man if she made her intention a matter of record.[114] Likewise *contubernium*, the nonmatrimonial coupling of slaves, came to be treated in the third century as concubinage though still not as marriage.[115] As the numbers of those involved in concubinage relationships increased because of changes in the legal definition of the institution, the Church found it appropriate to treat concubinage with tolerance and to accept it for ecclesiastical purposes as an alternative kind of marriage, rather than as a nonmatrimonial union.

The Church in the second and third centuries was not prepared to tolerate most other kinds of nonmarital sexual liaisons. Unchastity ranked with homicide and idolatry as the most serious offenses in the early Church's penal law.[116] Among the sins of the flesh, the Church's attention centered primarily on three: fornication, adultery, and the sexual corruption of young boys.[117]

Of these sexual sins, fornication was treated with the least severity, particularly fornication by young people, which counted as a fairly minor offense.[118] Fornication by older persons, particularly after baptism, ranked as a more reprehensible infraction and might constitute grounds for refusing to ordain a prospective clergyman.[119] Women who allowed themselves to be persuaded to have premarital intercourse with the men whom they later married were treated comparatively leniently, but those who had sex with other men incurred harsh punishment.[120] Christians who fornicated with non-Christians were likewise subject to severe penalties.[121] Clement of Alexandria, moreover, advised Christians to be cautious in their use of the public baths, since bathing in mixed com-

---

[112] Gaudemet, "Décision de Callixte," pp. 335, 343.

[113] Esmein, *Mariage* 2 : 109– 10.

[114] Gide, "De la condition de l'enfant naturel," pp. 558–59.

[115] Gaudemet, "Décision de Callixte," p. 340; Löwenstein, *Bekämpfung*, p. 16

[116] *Didache* 2.1–2 and 3.3, in *The Apostolic Fathers*, ed. Kirsopp Lake (Loeb); Henry Charles Lea, *History of Auricular Confession and Indulgences in the Latin Church*, 3 vols. (Philadelphia: Lea Brothers, 1896; repr. New York: Greenwood Press, 1968) 1 : 16.

[117] Michel Foucault, "Le combat de la chasteté," in *Sexualités occidentales*, p. 18.

[118] Council of Elvira, c. 31, in Vives, *Concilios Visigóticos*, p. 7.

[119] Council of Elvira, c. 30, in Vives, *Concilios Visigóticos*, p. 7.

[120] Council of Elvira, c. 14, in Vives, *Concilios Visigóticos*, p. 4.

[121] Council of Elvira, c. 78, in Vives, *Concilios Visigóticos*, p. 15.

pany might easily lead to more intimate contacts. Clement refrained, however, from prescribing abstinence from the bath altogether as a moral prophylactic.[122]

Adultery was a far more serious offense than fornication in the eyes of patristic writers and often counted on a par with murder in the scale of wickedness.[123] The *Didascalia apostolorum* forbade married men and women to dress or adorn themselves in ways that might attract lustful admiration and thus lead to adulterous temptations.[124] St. Athenagoras (late second century) characterized adulterers, together with pederasts, as enemies of Christianity and subjected both groups to the harshest penalties available to the pre-Constantinian Church, namely exclusion from its membership.[125] Women who persisted in adulterous relationships were excommunicated without hope of readmission; those who ended their adulterous unions were subject to a ten-year penance before readmission to communion.[126] The adulterous wife of a cleric, as noted earlier, was treated with particular severity. Her husband was required to expel her immediately and forever from their home and never to associate with her again; she was also permanently excommunicated from the Church.[127] The cleric who delayed action against his spouse and tried to shield her from the consequences of her folly was also excommunicated. Even a brief delay might result in a ten-year exclusion from the Church's fellowship.[128]

Male adulterers were also subject to stringent penalties. The Elvira canons distinguished between married men who were guilty of a single extramarital adventure and those who were habitually unfaithful. A single offense merited five years of penance, at the end of which the offender might be readmitted to communion. The man who repeatedly committed adultery, however, was condemned to lifelong penance and his restoration to communion had to wait until he was on his deathbed.[129]

[122]Clement of Alexandria, *Paedagogus* 3.31.1–3.33.1, 3.46.1–3.48.3, ed. Stählin 12:254–55, 263–64; likewise Cyprian, *De habitu virginum* 19, in his *Opera omnia*, ed. Wilhelm Hartel, 3 vols., CSEL, vol. 3 (Vienna: C. Gerold, 1868–71) 3/1:200–201; Broudéhoux, *Mariage et famille*, p. 192; Spanneut, *Stoicisme des pères*, p. 199.

[123]Rordorf, "Marriage," p. 204.

[124]The *Didascalia apostolorum* 2.1.3, 3.1.8, Syriac version, trans. Margaret Dunlop Gibson, in *Horae semiticae*, vol. 2 (London: C.J. Clay and Sons, 1903), pp. 3–4, 9–10.

[125]Athenagoras, *Legatio* 34, in PG 6:967–68; Spanneut, *Stoicisme des pères*, p. 111, demonstrates that Clement of Alexandria's treatment of adultery in *Paedagogus* 2.100.1 was borrowed directly from the Stoic writer Musonius.

[126]Council of Elvira, c. 64, in Vives, *Concilios Visigóticos*, pp. 12–13.

[127]Council of Elvira, c. 65, in Vives, *Concilios Visigóticos*, p. 13; but as early as the mid-second century the *Pastor* of Hermas, mand. 4.1.4–8, had recommended immediate repudiation of an adulterous wife, even by a layman; see *Apostolic Fathers*, ed. Lake 2:79.

[128]Council of Elvira, c. 70, in Vives, *Concilios Visigóticos*, pp. 13–14; this parallels prescriptions in an earlier rescript of the Emperors Valerian and Galienus (257) in Cod. 9.9.17.1.

[129]Council of Elvira, c. 47 and c. 69, in Vives, *Concilios Visigóticos*, pp. 10, 13.

Ecclesiastics during the Church's first three centuries had little to say about rape. From the fourth century onward, however, Church authorities joined the efforts of the imperial government to repress sexual assault.[130] The Council of Ancyra (314) required that a betrothed woman who had been forcibly abducted and assaulted be restored to her fiancé;[131] the Council of Chalcedon (451) prescribed that clerics guilty of rape be deposed from office; laymen who committed this offense were subject to anathema or excommunication.[132] These provisions were reiterated in the sixth century by Pope Symmachus (498–514).[133]

The early Church also banned prostitutes from the Christian community. Hippolytus, writing early in the third century, noted that those who practiced certain trades and professions were ineligible for reception into the Church unless they renounced their occupations; among those excluded were prostitutes, along with pagan priests, magicians, astrologers, gladiators, and soldiers.[134] The Elvira canons likewise stipulated that prostitutes might be admitted to the Church only if they had renounced their trade and married.[135] Pimps and panders were similarly ineligible for Church membership. If they took up these occupations after baptism, they were excommunicated.[136] Lactantius, more than any other Christian writer of his generation, showed some empathy for the prostitute's situation. Brothels, he declared, are diabolical establishments, and no one in them escapes the snare of sin. Both the client who yields to lustful abandon and the unfortunate women who suffer his odious attentions are mired in wickedness.[137]

Few Christian writers of the first three centuries had much to say about homosexual activities on the part of the Church's members, but St. Paul's condemnation of both active and passive gay sex apparently continued to represent the

---

[130] Cod. 9.9.20 and 9.12.3 (both by Diocletian).

[131] Council of Ancyra, c. 11, in Giovanni Domenico Mansi, ed., *Sacrorum conciliorum nova et amplissima collectio*, 60 vols. (Paris: Hubert Welter, 1901–27; hereafter Mansi) 2:531, and the *Decretales Pseudo-Isidorianae et Capitula Angilramni*, ed. Paul Hinschius (Leipzig: B. Tauchnitz, 1863; repr. Aalen: Scientia, 1963; hereafter Hinschius, DPI), p. 262.

[132] Council of Chalcedon, c. 27, in *Conciliorum oecumenicorum decreta*, 2d ed. by Giuseppe Alberigo et al. (Freiburg i/Br.: Herder, 1962; hereafter COD), p. 75.

[133] Phillip Jaffé, ed., *Regesta pontificum romanorum ab condita ecclesia ad annum post Christum natum MCXCVIII*, rev. ed. by Wilhelm Wattenbach et al., 2 vols. (Leipzig: Veit, 1885–88; repr. Graz: Akademische Druck- u. Verlagsanstalt, 1956), no. 764. Cited henceforth as JK (for letters to 590), JE (for letters from 590–882), JL (for letters from 882–1198). See also Bride, "Rapt," col. 1666–67.

[134] John Hegeland, "Christians and the Roman Army, A.D. 173–337," *Church History* 43 (1974) 155.

[135] Council of Elvira, c. 44, in Vives, *Concilios Visigóticos*, p. 9.

[136] Council of Elvira, c. 12, in Vives, *Concilios Visigóticos*, p. 4.

[137] Lactantius, *Div. inst.* 6.23.8–14, in CSEL 19:565–66.

Christian norm.[138] Sex with young boys was particularly disapproved, and the Elvira canons penalized such conduct severely.[139]

Conclusions

Although the scriptural tradition of ancient Judaism sought to constrain human sexual behavior within limits that would shield the community from the disastrous effects of unbridled lust, Hebrew tradition viewed marital sex as a divinely ordained component of human life. Since God wished humans to increase and multiply and since he had endowed their sexual organs with the capacity to produce exquisite pleasure, the rabbis saw no reason to limit the individual's enjoyment of sex, provided that it did not harm others. Hence Jewish law imposed relatively few limits on sexual relations, especially between married persons, and limited legal intervention in sexual activity primarily to behavior that seemed likely to injure or impair community interests or the rights of others.

Jesus, as we have seen, said remarkably little about sex and apparently found little to criticize in the conventional sexual ethics of first-century Judaism. Clearly he opposed adultery and sexual promiscuity, and he taught that divorce should be discouraged save for infidelity. But what little we know about his sexual views indicates that he made no sharp break with the commonly accepted practices of the Jewish communities in which he lived. St. Paul, on the other hand, was far more concerned with sexual issues than Jesus had been and considered sex a serious hindrance to spiritual perfection. Paul adamantly opposed sexual licentiousness and pleasure-seeking, particularly outside of marriage. Within marriage Paul felt that couples should keep their sexual passions under firm control. Still Paul considered marital sex sacred, a central feature of the bonding of husband and wife, a paradigm of the spiritual union of Christ with the Church.

In the post-apostolic period Christian writers began to express much more restrictive views of the role of sex in human life. The Church during he second and third centuries was beginning to formulate norms for Christian behavior and regulations for internal discipline. This legislation naturally remained sketchy during the early period, since the legal status of Christians was at best ambiguous and at worst precarious, with the Church's members subject to sporadic persecutions, especially during the reign of Diocletian (284–305). Even so, Church leaders needed to deal with the problems that sexual relations raised within the Christian community. There was broad agreement that marital sex was acceptable, although a number of important writers sought to discourage sex among the devout. A few aberrant Christian groups taught that Christians were not subject to sexual restrictions and might have relations with anyone whom they pleased. Other doctrinal deviants wished to ban all sexual

---

[138] *Epistle of Barnabas* 10.6–8, 19.4; Johansson, "Ex parte Themis," pp. 2–5.
[139] Council of Elvira, c. 71, in *Concilios Visigóticos*, p. 14.

relations, even in marriage. Extreme opinions at both ends of the spectrum were rejected by orthodox authorities, who denounced these beliefs as heretical.[140]

Although some patristic writers argued that virginity was a highly meritorious Christian virtue, no mainstream authority prior to the canons of Elvira demanded celibacy, even from the clergy.[141] Despite this moderate pose, the Church during the late third and early fourth century was clearly moving toward a more emphatic stress upon sexual abstinence as an ideal. Sentiment in favor of celibacy, particularly as a requirement for the clergy, drew upon arguments grounded in Pythagorean beliefs. Those who believed that virginity represented a spiritually superior state also seem to have adopted some of the reasoning of the Encratites and Gnostics, who perceived an incongruity between sexual activity and participation in the sacred mysteries of the Christian liturgy.[142]

Symptomatic of a growing body of opinion that depreciated marital sex as impure and debased was the practice of "spiritual marriage," which first appeared in the third century. Spiritual marriage referred to the cohabitation of ascetic men or clerics with consecrated virgins, a cohabitation in which the parties led a common life, but renounced sexual relations with each other or with anyone else. This life-style was criticized by many Church authorities, however, and the Elvira canons flatly forbade it. This prohibition, however, was no more effective in eliminating the practice of spiritual marriage than the canon on clerical celibacy was in persuading clerics not to sleep with their lawful wives.[143]

At the same time that Christian beliefs and practices relating to sex and marriage were changing, Roman civil law concerning marriage was also in flux. Even before the time of Constantine, public policy as enunciated in imperial rescripts and decrees had begun to place greater emphasis on marriage as a personal relationship. Roman law also began to assign greater value to long duration, even permanence, in marriage than it had previously done.[144]

The conversion of Constantine early in the fourth century profoundly al-

[140] Clement of Alexandria, *Stromata* 2.118.3–5, ed. Stählin 15:177; Fuchs, *Sexual Desire and Love*, pp. 88–91.

[141] Gryson, *Origines du célibat*, p. 42.

[142] Gryson, *Origines du célibat*, p. 43; Kosnik et al., *Human Sexuality*, pp. 18, 39; Fuchs, *Sexual Desire and Love*, p. 106.

[143] Eusebius, *Historia ecclesiastica* 7.30, in PG 20:715–16; Cyprian, *Epist.* 4.1–2, ed. Hartel, in CSEL 3/2:472–74. See generally JoAnn McNamara, "Chaste Marriage and Clerical Celibacy," in Vern L. Bullough and James A. Brundage, ed., *Sexual Practices and the Medieval Church* (Buffalo, NY: Prometheus, 1982), pp. 22–33.

[144] Philippe Ariès, "Le mariage indissoluble," in *Sexualités occidentales*, p. 123. Paul Veyne, "La famille et l'amour sous le haut empire romaine," *Annales: économies, sociétés, civilisations* 33 (1978) 35–63, argues that fundamental changes in Roman beliefs about sexual morality appeared in pagan society during the first two centuries of the Christian era, but that these changes were quite independent of any Christian influ-

tered relationships between the Christian Church and the Roman government. The Church soon became an integral part of the intellectual and cultural life of the Roman world and Christianity attained an intellectual sophistication and respectability that it had never known. As the Church became part of the mainstream of Roman life, it borrowed increasingly from the pagan world, from which it had formerly been almost totally estranged. In the process, both Christian institutions and thought were irrevocably altered. These developments also signaled the beginning of radical changes in the ways that authorities of both Church and government dealt with sexual matters.

---

ence. The Church, according to Veyne, simply adopted as its own the notions about sexual morals that were already current among educated pagans.

3

Sex and the Law in the Christian Empire, from Constantine to Justinian

Christianization of the Roman Empire and Romanization of the Christian Church

Constantine the Great (A.D. 311–37) set in motion a series of basic changes in both Roman government and the Christian Church. By the Edict of Milan in 313, Constantine proclaimed a policy of religious toleration. In short order, Christianity, which had been vigorously persecuted under his predecessor, became the most-favored religion of the Roman state. Constantine's personal and political objectives in favoring Christianity have been debated for centuries, but the result of his new religious policy was indisputable: Constantine integrated the Christian Church into the Roman governmental system. By the time of Constantine's baptism and death in 337, Christianity had grown from a relatively small, tightly knit band of persecuted believers into a flourishing, officially favored, publicly supported, branch of imperial government.

During Constantine's reign and those of his sons and successors, Christians secured numerous social and political advantages. By the end of the fourth century the Roman government, with the enthusiastic cooperation of Church authorities, was beginning to persecute pagans and other non-Christians, as well as Christians whose beliefs differed from the norms of an orthodoxy that was continuously engaged in defining itself. Early in the fifth century, Christianity became in law what it had for several generations been in fact: the official religion of the Roman state.[1]

[1] On Constantine's life and religious policies see generally András Alföldi, *The Conversion of Constantine and Pagan Rome* (Oxford: Clarendon Press, 1948); Jakob Burckhardt, *The Age of Constantine the Great*, trans. Moses Hadas (New York: Pantheon Books, 1949); Hermann Dörries, *Das Selbstzeugnis Kaiser Konstantins*, Abhandlungen der Akademie der Wissenschaften zu Göttingen, phil.-hist. Kl., ser. 3, vol. 34 (Göttingen: Vandenhoeck & Ruprecht, 1954), and Liebschuetz, *Continuity and Change*, esp. pp. 277–89. On the relationship of paganism to Christianity in the fourth and fifth centuries see also James J. O'Donnell, "The Demise of Paganism," *Traditio* 35 (1979) 45–88, as well as Charles Norris Cochrane, *Christianity and Classical Culture: A Study in Thought and Action from Augustus to Augustine* (London: Oxford University Press, 1944).

The transformation of Christianity from a persecuted minority sect to a legally established majority religion was accompanied by institutional restructuring of the Church itself. With enlarged membership and expanded civic responsibilities, the Church's leaders found it necessary to create an administrative system to match the new situation. Christian bishops became public functionaries, managers of sizeable assets, and controllers of increasing amounts of political power. The Church soon accommodated itself to the patterns of civil government. The organizational structure of Constantine's state, with its divisions into prefectures, dioceses, and provinces, furnished a framework that the Church adopted for its own administration. Bishops were invested with judicial authority and the government enforced their decisions as it did those of civil judges.

At the same time, Roman government itself changed as the Church gradually became for practical purposes a new branch of the administrative system. By the end of the fourth century, provincial governors, and even the emperors themselves, could ignore the wishes and policies of Christian bishops only at their peril. The Church had become a power within the state, one whose interests and aims government officials must accommodate, whether they agreed with them or not.

This dual process, whereby the Christian Church adapted itself to the apparatus of government, while civil administration modified its workings in order to assimilate the Church, involved momentous changes for both institutions. By A.D. 400, bishops were important, hard-working civil functionaries who attempted to act at the same time as spiritual leaders and spokesmen for the moral and religious values that the Church embodied. In their twin roles as government administrators and as religious authorities, bishops during the fourth and fifth centuries became burdened with power, laden with honors, and weighed down with responsibility. Lesser Church dignitaries, notably priests, deacons, and other clerics, also bore a share of the rights and duties that this transformation entailed.[2]

As Christianity grew in power, wealth, and respectability, and as the aims of the Church became increasingly entwined with the interests of the Roman state, it is scarcely surprising that some committed believers found the new situation disquieting. The growth of Church power bothered sensitive souls; many idealistic Christians felt themselves called to live a more demanding form of religious life than that led by the majority of the faithful. Dissatisfaction with ordinary routines of religious observance led them to create ascetic and monastic movements that came to play major roles in the spiritual life of the late ancient and early medieval world.

Christian asceticism involved renunciation of the pleasures and rewards of

[2]The most helpful general survey of institutional developments in the Church during the Christian Empire is Jean Gaudemet, *L'église dans l'empire romain (IVe-Ve siècles)*, Histoire du droit et des institutions de l'église en occident, vol. 3 (Paris: Sirey, 1958).

ordinary human society. The ascetic voluntarily chose to live a life of solitude, prayer, and discipline in the belief that only through subduing his body's yearning for comfort and denying its cravings for pleasure could a Christian hope to save his soul. Chief among the disciplines of asceticism was the renunciation of sex in favor of celibacy. Rejecting carnal pleasures and the usual social expectation that every free person would marry and reproduce, Christian ascetics dedicated themselves to total sexual abstinence. In place of children and family life, ascetics exalted the importance of virginity. Ascetics who considered virginity a cardinal virtue often deprecated the role of sex and marriage in the Christian life. Monks and hermits frequently looked down on married persons as spiritually inferior to those who sacrificed sexual pleasure in order to gain spiritual merit. As for sex outside of marriage, the unanimous verdict of Christian ascetics was that carnal transgressions inexorably doomed their perpetrators to the torments of Gehenna. The writings and teachings of monks and other ascetics did much to make Christians fearful and suspicious of sexuality.

At the same time, Christianity was experiencing a profound intellectual transformation. Christian writers in the first three centuries had begun the process of defining their religious doctrines; now Christian intellectuals were compelled to fashion more rigorous explications of their faith. Efforts to convince their Jewish and pagan rivals of the superiority of Christianity required them to present their religious views in terms to which rational persons could subscribe without blushing. Up to the beginning of the fourth century Christians had not yet created a systematic theology; now they felt the need to devise coherent and sophisticated justifications for their religious teachings in terms of current scientific and philosophical thought.

The Church Fathers of the fourth and fifth centuries took up this task with zest and vigor. They were determined not only to justify the teachings of their religion to others, but also to demonstrate to their own satisfaction that Christian beliefs accounted for the world and mankind's place in it more adequately than alternative explanatory systems. Out of the writings of such teachers as Sts. Gregory of Nyssa (ca. 335–ca. 395) and John Chrysostom (ca. 344–407) in the Greek-speaking East and Sts. Ambrose, Jerome, and Augustine in the Latin-speaking West, there would emerge by the sixth century a Christian world view that was far more systematic and rigorous than anything that had gone before. The theologizing of Christianity began in earnest during this period. This process required Christian intellectuals, among other things, to account for the place of sex in the scheme of creation and to define the role that sexual relations ought to play in the Christian life.

All of these developments—the acceptance of Christianity by the Roman emperors, its incorporation into the governmental system, its growth in numbers, wealth, and influence, the structural changes in its organization, the growth of asceticism and monasticism, and the intellectual refinement of Christian thought and belief—combined to produce basic changes in the ways that Christians dealt with sex and the place of sex in the Christian value system.

Christian Theories of Sexuality

The Church Fathers' views of sex were dominated by ascetic values, for most of the Fathers were, at one time or another in their careers, monks or hermits. The most important patristic authority on sexual matters, the one whose views have most fundamentally influenced subsequent ideas about sexuality in the West, was St. Augustine of Hippo (354–430). Augustine held strong, deep-seated convictions about sexual relationships and the role of sex in human history, convictions that flowed from his own experience and his reflections upon it, convictions that brooked neither denial nor dissent.[3]

Sexual desire, Augustine believed, was the most foul and unclean of human wickednesses, the most pervasive manifestation of man's disobedience to God's designs.[4] Other bodily desires and pleasures, Augustine felt, did not overwhelm reason and disarm the will: one can be sensible while enjoying a good meal, one can discuss matters reasonably over a bottle of wine. But sex, Augustine argued, was more powerful than other sensual attractions; it could overcome reason and free will altogether. Married people, who ought to have sex only in order to beget children, can be overwhelmed by lubricious desires that blot out reason and restraint; they tumble into bed together simply in order to enjoy the pleasure of each other's body. This, Augustine thought, was not only irrational but sinful.[5] Augustine's underlying belief in the intrinsic sinfulness of carnal desire and the sensual delight that accompanied sexual union became a standard premise of Western beliefs about sexuality during the Middle Ages and beyond.[6]

Not only was sexual desire a basic and pervasive evil, according to Augustine, but it was also a vice that no one could be sure of mastering. We are born with it and it lasts as long as we live. No one, whatever his age or position in life, can confidently claim to have conquered it.[7] "As I was writing this," Augustine noted in his polemic against Julian, "we were told that a man of eighty-four, who had lived a life of continence under religious observance with a pious wife for twenty-five years, has just bought himself a music-girl for his pleasure."[8]

---

[3] Peter Brown, *Augustine of Hippo: A Biography* (Berkeley and Los Angeles: University of California Press, 1967), pp. 390–91; Edward A. Synan, "Augustine of Hippo, Saint," in *Dictionary of the Middle Ages*, ed. Joseph R. Strayer et al., 13 vols. (New York: Charles Scribner's Sons, 1982– ; cited hereafter as DMA) 1:646–59. See also Bailey, *Sexual Relation*, pp. 58–59; Kosnik et al., *Human Sexuality*, p. 36.

[4] Augustine, *Contra Julianum* 4.5.35, in PL 44:756: "In quibus [cupiditatibus malis] libido prae caeteris est, cui nisi resistatur, horrenda immunda committit."

[5] Augustine, *Contra Julianum* 4.14.71, in PL 44:773–74.

[6] Müller, *Lehre*, pp. 22–23; Lecky, *Hist. of European Morals* 2:281–82.

[7] Augustine, *Sermo* 151.5, in PL 38:817: "Ergo semper pugnandum est, quia ipsa concupiscentia, cum qua nati sumus, finiri non potest quamdiu vivimus: quotidie minui potest, finiri non potest." See also St. John Cassian, *Conlationes* 4.11.2 and 4.15.1, in CSEL 13:105, 110, as well as his *Institutiones* 6.1, in CSEL 17:115.

[8] Augustine, *Contra Julianum* 3.11.22, in PL 44:713: "Nam cum hoc opus in manibus

Augustine and his contemporaries among the Fathers considered sex a grave moral danger in part because they believed that sexual feelings and urges, particularly the reactions of the genital organs, were not fully under the control of the human will. Since sexual desire was partly ruled by the will, Augustine felt that sexual urges could sometimes be mastered—the wish to have sex, the conscious desire for pleasure, these things required consent of the will before they became sinful. The sexual impulse itself, however, sprang unbidden from the depths of the human psyche and, since its appearance could not be anticipated, it constituted an ever present danger to morality.[9]

Sex, Augustine believed, was a shameful, sordid business. For this reason, he observed, people always try to carry out their sex functions in seclusion. Even brothels, he noted, provide privacy so that whores and their customers can do their dirty business in the dark. Likewise married couples seek seclusion when they make love: what they do may be perfectly legal, but it is also shameful. The shame of sex resulted from the ritual pollution that accompanied all sexual activity. Augustine and other Fathers argued that the Old Testament requirements for purification after marital intercourse or nocturnal emission meant that Christians, too, must cleanse themselves of sexual defilement before they could participate in religious services. The Fathers were careful to point out that this did not mean that sex was always sinful, but it did mean that sex left a stain of moral contamination that must be removed before entering holy places or participating in sacred rites. The genital organs themselves were both ritually and morally unclean, according to Augustine. Sexual passion was rooted in the genitals, and our very anatomy proclaimed that the physical sources of human life and reproduction were also the physical sources of sin and pollution.[10]

Christians therefore faced a moral imperative to avoid sex as much as possible, even though repression of sexual desires might encourage other moral shortcomings, such as greed.[11] The good Christian, according to Augustine and others, must lead a chaste life, even in marriage. Augustine was keenly aware of the difficulties that this entailed. He recalled in his *Confessions* his own ado-

haberem, nunciatus est nobis senex octaginta et quatuor agens annos, qui religiose cum conjuge religiosa jam viginti quinque annos vixerat continenter, ad libidinem sibi emisse Lyristriam." Brown, *Augustine of Hippo*, p. 405.

[9] Augustine, *De civitate Dei* 14.9, ed. Bernard Dombart and Alfons Kolb, CCL 47–48 (Turnhout Brépols, 1955) 48:441; *De nuptiis et concupiscentia* 1.23.25, in CSEL 42:237–38; *Contra Julianum* 4.2.10 and 4.7.38, in PL 44:741, 757; Müller, *Lehre*, pp. 24, 28; Brown, *Augustine of Hippo*, p. 389.

[10] Augustine, *De civ. Dei* 14.18–20, in CCL 48:440–43; *De bono coniugali* 20.23, ed. Joseph Zycha, in CSEL 41 (Vienna: F. Tempsky, 1900), pp. 217–18; *Serm.* 151.5, in PL 38:817; Daniel Callam, "Clerical Continence in the Fourth Century: Three Papal Decretals," *Theological Studies* 41 (1980) 49–50; Brown, *Augustine of Hippo*, p. 388.

[11] Augustine, *De bono viduitatis* 21.26, in CSEL 41:337–38; Brown, *Augustine of Hippo*, p. 351.

lescent yearnings, which had caused him to pray that God would "Give me chastity and continence—but not just yet!" And even as a mature man Augustine reported that he continued to be troubled by vivid erotic dreams and twitches of carnal desire. Nonetheless Augustine taught that, difficult as it might be, those who sought salvation must strive continuously to conquer their sexual passions and to overcome the spirit of lust.[12]

Augustine wrote eloquently on the theology of sex, but he was by no means the only patristic writer to deal with the subject. His contemporaries by and large shared Augustine's negative attitudes toward the role of sex in Christian life. A few were even more certain than he that sex was a root cause of sin and corruption. St. Jerome (ca. 347–419/20), for example, maintained that sex and salvation were contradictions. Even in marriage, coitus was evil and unclean, Jerome thought, and married Christians should avoid sexual contact whenever possible. St. Gregory of Nyssa was still more emphatic: he taught that only those who renounced sex completely and led lives of unblemished virginity could attain spiritual perfection.[13]

Such views as these owed as much to philosophy, particularly to Stoicism, as to religious teaching, and St. Jerome explicitly acknowledged in his treatise against Jovinian that he was drawing upon Stoic sources.[14] But although fourth- and fifth-century patristic writers borrowed heavily from pagan sexual ethics, they nevertheless sought to legitimize their borrowings by finding support for their conclusions in the Scriptures. This sometimes required ingenious feats of imaginative interpretation, but a Scriptural foundation for their ideas about sexuality seemed essential.

True, not every reference to sex in every passage of the Fathers was wholly disapproving. Some patristic writers commended married love as a virtue, and others praised procreation as a virtuous goal. It would require an artificial manipulation of the patristic texts, however, to fabricate from these scattered and fragmentary references a tradition of Christian tolerance toward sexual desires, much less a school of Christian eroticism, either in the patristic period or in the Middle Ages. Overwhelmingly the Fathers of the Church and their medieval successors saw sex as a danger to be combated, not a pleasure to be praised. Indeed it was the pleasurableness of sex that alarmed them most. But sex, un-

[12] Augustine, *Confessiones* 2.2.2, 3.1.1, 8.7.17, and 10.30.41, ed. Pius Knöll in CSEL 33 (Vienna: F. Tempsky, 1896), pp. 29–30, 44, 184–85, 257.

[13] Jerome, *Adversus Jovinianum* 1.13, 1.26, 1.28, in PL 23:229–30, 246, 249; Gregory of Nyssa, *De virginitate* 2, in PG 46:323–24; Bailey, *Sexual Relation*, pp. 45–46; JoAnn McNamara, "Cornelia's Daughters: Paula and Eustocium," *Women's Studies* 11 (1984) 12–13.

[14] Jerome, *Adv. Jov.* 1.49, in PL 23:280–81; Ariès, "L'amour dans le mariage," pp. 118–19; Philippe Delhaye, "Le dossier antimatrimonial de l'*Adversus Jovinianum* et son influence sur quelques écrits latins du XIIe siècle," *Mediaeval Studies* 13 (1951) 68. Jerome found some strands of Stoic ethics so congenial that he numbered Seneca among the saints; *De viris illustribus* 12, in PL 23:662. But his use of the Stoics was highly selective; Colish, *Stoic Tradition* 2:70–81.

like other pleasures, was not something that a Christian ascetic could take in moderation. Although those who vowed perpetual virginity might be said metaphorically to be socially dead, even the most austere ascetic could not completely forego eating and drinking without courting physical suicide as well; that, it was agreed, was immoral.[15] But, as St. John Cassian pointed out, it is quite possible to forego sex (at least overt genital sex) completely and still continue to exist.[16]

If fourth- and fifth-century patristic writing about sexuality was almost exclusively negative, the Church Fathers were emphatically positive in their praise of virginity. The notion that virginity possessed singularly powerful, almost magical, virtues was, like deprecation of sexual pleasure, a belief with pagan antecedents. Patristic writers diligently searched the Scriptures in quest of support for their exaltation of virginity. Not surprisingly they found what they were searching for, especially in certain remarks of St. Paul. Relying on Paul's authority, patristic authors created a theology of virginity that portrayed the asexual life as the summit of Christian perfection.[17]

But patristic sexual theories also owed more to heterodox teachings than orthodox writers cared to acknowledge. Gnostics and Manichaeans deeply influenced patristic theories of sexuality. The Manichaeans, whose beliefs Augustine had embraced as a youth, held that Adam and Eve knew no sexual desire, nor did they engage in intercourse, while they lived in Paradise. Human sexual organs are capable of coitus only when aroused by lust, they argued, and lust is a product of sin. Before the first sin, therefore, either there had been no sexual intercourse at all, or else arrangements for conceiving children must have been

[15] Peter Brown argues that the consequence of taking a vow of virginity was social death, that for purposes of property, inheritance, and the like, the celibate became a dead person; "Society and the Body: The Social Meaning of Asceticism in Late Antiquity," paper presented at the XXI International Congress on Medieval Studies, Western Michigan University, 9 May 1986. There is no question that ascetics were metaphorically described as dead, but while the ascetic who vowed perpetual continence ceased at law to be a person, he did not therefore cease to exist. Michael Blecker's argument that the law regarded the monk as a slave seems to account much more satisfactorily for the monk's legal status, or lack of it; P.M. Blecker, "The Civil Rights of the Monk in Roman and Canon Law: The Monk as 'Servus'," *American Benedictine Review* 17 (1966) 185–98; but see also B. Borgmann, "Mors civilis: Die Bildung des Begriffs im Mittelalter und sein Fortleben im französischen Recht der Neuzeit," *Ius commune* 4 (1972) 81–157.

[16] Boswell, CSTAH, p. 163; Foucault, "Combat de la chasteté," in *Sexualités occidentales*, p. 17.

[17] 1 Cor. 7:1: "Bonum est homini mulierem non tangere," as well as 1 Cor. 7:6–9, 25–27, and 29–36; also Gal. 5:16–21 and Eph. 5:3–4. See also Jerome, *Adv. Jov.* 1.41, in PL 23:282; Bugge, *Virginitas*, pp. 68–69; Joyce E. Salisbury, "Fruitful in Singleness," JMH 8 (1982) 97. The only early Christian writer who dealt with marriage in an entirely positive and approving way was the obscure third-century poet, Commodianus; Colish, *Stoic Tradition* 2:102.

different than after the Fall from Grace.[18] Jerome and many other patristic writers agreed with this analysis. Jerome understood the "innocence" of Adam and Eve primarily in sexual terms. Before the first sin there was no sex. The human race's first experience of sexual pleasure took place after expulsion from the Garden of Delights.

Sex thus came after sin and was its product.[19] Fulgentius of Ruspa (ca. 468–533) adopted a similar line of thought: the libido is a punishment for sin, a consequence of the Fall from Grace, and the root of all evil. John Chrysostom and Gregory of Nyssa enunciated similar views.[20] According to Augustine, however, Adam and Eve had known sex in Paradise, although it was a different kind of sex from the sort that we experience, for the very physiology of reproduction changed as a result of sin. Prior to the Fall the sexual organs had been under conscious control; but just as our first parents rebelled against God, so after the Fall our genitals rebelled against our will. Humans then became incapable of controlling either their sexual desires or the physical reactions of their gonads.[21]

The Church's struggle against heretical sects, especially the Pelagians and the Manichaeans, as well as the followers of Jovinian and the Stoics, did much to shape the marriage doctrines of St. Augustine and the other Fathers. Against the Pelagians Augustine defended the reality of the Fall from Grace and its dreadful consequences. Against the Manichaeans, the Abelonians, and the Priscillians, Augustine and other patristic writers upheld the holiness of marriage.[22] The Stoics presented special difficulties for patristic defenders of Christian orthodoxy, for while the Fathers certainly adopted some of their most dearly held beliefs from the Stoics, and were conscious that they did so, they also felt compelled to reject other Stoic teachings, such as the contention that all sins are equally serious.

[18] Augustine, *De Genesi ad litteram* 9.4.8, in PL 34:395–96; *De nupt. et concup.* 1.22.24, 2.13.26, 2.32.54, in CSEL 42:237, 279, 311–12; *De civ. Dei* 14.21, 23, in CCL 48:443–46; Bugge, *Virginitas*, p. 26; Müller, *Lehre*, p. 22; Brown, *Augustine of Hippo*, pp. 388–89; César Vaca, "La sexualidad en San Agustín," in *Augustinus magister*, 3 vols. (Paris: Etudes augustiniennes, 1955) 2:728; René Nelli, "La continence Cathare," in *Mystique et continence*, pp. 139–51.

[19] Jerome, *Epistolae* 22.19, in PL 22:406, and *Adv. Jov.* 1.16, in PL 23:235–36; Bugge, *Virginitas*, pp. 22–24.

[20] Fulgentius of Ruspa, *Ad Monimium* 1.17.2, 1.27.2, in his *Opera*, ed. J. Fraipont, CCL vols. 91–91A (Turnhout: Brépols, 1968), 91:17, 28, and *De fide ad Petrum* 16–17, in CCL 91A:721–22; John Chrysostom, *In Genesim homelia* 18.4, in PG 53:153, and *De virginitate* 14, in PG 48:543; Gregory of Nyssa, *De hominis opificio* 17, in PG 44:187–88; Müller, *Lehre*, pp. 14–15, 33; Bugge, *Virginitas*, pp. 16–17.

[21] Augustine, *De civ. Dei* 14.17, in CCL 48:439, and *De peccatorum meritis* 2.22.36, in PL 44:172–73; Müller, *Lehre*, p. 22.

[22] Augustine, *De haeresibus* 87, in PL 42:47; Jerome, *Adv. Jov.* 1:49, in PL 23:282; Clement of Alexandria, *Stromata*, 3.6.45, ed. Stählin 2:216–17; John Chrysostom, *De virginitate* 10, in PG 48:540; Müller, *Lehre*, p. 19; Callam, "Clerical Continence," p. 23; Brown, *Augustine of Hippo*, p. 192.

Conversely, the Jovinians agreed with the Stoics in considering all moral faults equally grievous, but also denied that the ascetic life had any special claim to be the preeminent Christian path to salvation. The Jovinians thus denied that monks and other ascetics were more virtuous and deserving than ordinary married Christians who had frequent sexual intercourse and even enjoyed it.[23] Jovinian's doctrine called forth one of the most blistering denunciations in all of patristic literature, the *Adversus Jovinianum*, in which St. Jerome savagely attacked Jovinian's beliefs. Indeed Jerome defended the celibate life so vigorously that he came close to condemning marriage. He also furnished generations of misogynist writers with a battery of elegant vituperation and ferocious mockery directed against the foibles and follies of women.[24]

Patristic discussions of the place of sex in the Christian life are shot through with a fundamental ambivalence about the place of women in the scheme of salvation.[25] Augustine agreed clearly and emphatically with other patristic writers in requiring that men observe the same norms of sexual conduct as women.[26] At the same time, however, Augustine, like other patristic authors, considered women frankly inferior to men, both physically and morally.

Women, he believed, were created by God in order to help men by bearing children. If this was not women's primary role in the scheme of creation, he asked, what reason could God have had for creating them? They were not as useful as men for agricultural work, and if God had intended Eve as Adam's helper in the fields, he would surely have created another man. As for the notion that women were destined to be man's companion, Augustine would have none of it. A man would have been better for that purpose, too.[27] "I fail to see what use woman can be to man," Augustine concluded, "if one excludes the function of bearing children."[28] Not only did women have no value aside from child-bearing, but they were, even worse, a source of sexual temptation, and

---

[23] Augustine, *Epist.* 167.4, in CSEL 44:591–92, and *De haeresibus* 82, in PL 42: 45–46; Delhaye, "Dossier antimatrimonial," p. 66.

[24] Delhaye, "Dossier antimatrimonial," pp. 71–86; Colish, *Stoic Tradition* 2:79–81.

[25] This ambivalence appears to be based upon the distinction between body and soul that was central to Augustine's concept of human nature. See esp. Kari Elisabeth Børresen, *Subordination and Equivalence: The Nature and Role of Women in Augustine and Thomas Aquinas* (Washington: University Press of America, 1981), p. 339; Rosambert, *Veuve*, pp. 94–95; and see generally Margaret R. Miles, *Augustine on the Body*, American Academy of Religion Dissertation Series, no. 31 (Missoula, MT: Scholars Press, 1979).

[26] Ambrose, *De Abraham* 1.4.25, in PL 14:431; Jerome, *Epist.* 77.3, in PL 22:691; Caesarius of Arles, *Sermones* 32.4, 142.3, ed. Germain Morin, 2 vols., CCL 103–4 (Turnhout: Brépols, 1953) 103:142, 186–87; John Chrysostom, *De verbis propter fornicationes* 4, in PG 51:214; Augustine, *Serm.* 9.4, 392.4–5, in PL 38:78 and 39:1711–12; Brown, *Augustine of Hippo*, p. 248.

[27] Augustine, *De Genesi ad litteram* 9.5.9, in PL 34:396.

[28] Augustine, *De Genesi ad litteram* 9.7.12, in PL 34:397; John Chrysostom, *De virginitate* 14, in PG 48:543.

had been ever since Eden. Eve's principal positive contribution there had been to sew together fig leaves to make the loincloths with which our first parents hid their shame at finding themselves naked.[29]

The notion that women were valuable only as mothers raised further questions about the role of females in a scheme of life that placed the highest value on sexual abstinence. If sexlessness was a requirement for perfection and virginity the surest credential for those who wished to be saved, as some patristic writers clearly thought, then what relevance did reproduction have for Christians who aimed at perfection? And if childbearing, the womanly virtue above all others, was ultimately inappropriate for Christian women, then what other function ought they to play in the plan of salvation? Patristic writers generally preferred to avoid these questions and gave no clear, unequivocal answers to them.[30]

They were clear, however, about the need to combat sexual desire and to avoid sexual sins, even if their designs for achieving these goals were far from consistent. The most common scheme involved strategies that limited marital sex to certain permitted times and situations, but otherwise advocated complete sexual abstinence, both in thought and deed. St. John Cassian (ca. 360–435) devised elaborate strategies for systematically avoiding situations that might bring sexual fantasies to mind, so as to achieve a totally asexual regime that monastic writers liked to refer to as the angelic way of life.[31] Cassian and others elaborated schemes of discipline to ward off dangerous sexual impulses. These plans regulated diet, clothing, social contacts, sleeping habits, posture, and other aspects of daily living with the aim of eliminating physical, mental, or emotional stimuli that might trigger sexual responses and sexual desires. The influence of such schemes upon the quality of spiritual sentiment, as well as the psychological and social well-being of Christians, is difficult to determine. Men and women who adhered to these plans would certainly be deprived of many kinds of human contact and would be subject to physical, social, and sensory deprivations that were likely to produce isolation, social maladjustment, and depression, to aggravate neurotic problems, and perhaps to precipitate even more serious disturbances. These possible outcomes, however, seemed lesser evils to those who devised such regimens than sexual lust would have been.

The one means of fighting off sexual temptations at which practically all authorities drew the line was castration. Although one or two extremists—Origen

---

[29] Augustine, *Epistulae* 243.10, ed. A. Goldbacher, 2 vols., CSEL, vols. 57–58 (Vienna: F. Tempsky; Leipzig: G. Freytag, 1911–23) 57:577; Jerome, *Commentarium in Evangelium secundum Mattheum* 19.10, in PL 26:140.

[30] Bugge, *Virginitas*, pp. 31–35.

[31] Caesarius of Arles, *Serm.* 45.4, in CCL 103:197; St. Basil, *Sermo asceticus* 2, in PG 31:873–74; Cyprian, *De disciplina et bono pudicitiae* 7, in PL 4:855–56; John Chrysostom, *De virginitate* 10–11, in PG 48:540–41; Foucault, "Combat de la chasteté," p. 20.

was the best known—had advocated and even practiced this radical method of combating sexual temptation, orthodox opinion held that this solution carried a good thing too far. Both the so-called Canons of the Apostles and the genuine canons of the Council of Nicaea (325) prohibited the practice.[32]

Marriage in the Christian Empire

During the fourth and fifth centuries, the Christian rulers of the Roman Empire initiated a series of changes in the civil law dealing with marriage. At least in part these changes reflected the impact of Christian beliefs upon public policy. Moreover, the administration of the law, as well as its formal provisions, were increasingly influenced by Christian religious values, especially since bishops, perhaps as early as the reign of Constantine, presided over courts in which they dealt with marriage and divorce litigation.[33]

One result of Christian influence on Roman marriage law was to make bigamy for the first time a crime in the Empire. The classical concept of consensual marriage, which depended upon marital affection and the continuing consent of both parties to remain married to each other, had made it nearly impossible for a Roman to contract a bigamous marriage. Under the Christian emperors, however, divorce became the sole procedure for terminating a marriage between living partners, and the grounds for divorce became more restricted. As a result of these changes, bigamy for the first time became a legal problem.[34] In addition, Constantine made it legally impossible for a Roman subject to have both a wife and a concubine simultaneously.[35] This alteration marked a break with earlier practice and illustrates, as does the development of the bigamy problem, the gradual enactment of Christian sexual teachings into public law.

At both ends of the social spectrum, the Christian emperors introduced laws that modified the ways in which people married. For the highest classes, the new legislation further restricted the groups within which marriage was permitted, thus narrowing the choice of marriage partner. For the lowest class of the population, however, the enactments of the Christian emperors made marriage for the first time legally available: successive laws transformed the informal couplings of slaves (*contubernium*) into legitimate matrimony, with all its rights and consequences.[36]

Further, marriage under the Christian emperors became a more formal con-

---

[32] 1 Nicaea (325) c. 1, in COD, p. 5.

[33] Volterra, *Conception*, p. 66; Gabriel Le Bras, "Observations sur le mariage dans le *Corpus* de Justinien et dans le droit classique de l'église," in *Etudes offerts à Jean Macqueron* (Aix-en-Provence: Faculté de droit et des sciences politiques, 1970), pp. 425–26; Noonan, "Novel 22," in *The Bond of Marriage*, ed. William Bassett (Notre Dame: University of Notre Dame Press, 1968) pp. 80–81.

[34] Cod. 5.17.8.4 (449) and 5.17.9 (497); Volterra, "Conception," p. 62.

[35] Cod. 5.26.1 (326).

[36] Cod. 5.5.7 (454); Mañaricua y Nuere, *Matrimonio de los esclavos*, pp. 154–74.

tract than it had been. Roman law prior to Constantine had not required any sort of ritual for contracting marriage, even though in practice ceremonies were in common use. During the fourth and fifth centuries, Church regulations began to require Christians to receive a nuptial blessing from a priest.[37] Christian wedding rituals first began to take shape during this period, and by the sixth century two varieties of ceremony had emerged. One type, commonest in Gaul, featured a nuptial blessing imparted by a priest while the newly wedded couple lay in the marriage bed. Nuptial ceremonies in Italy, by contrast, centered on a blessing bestowed upon the couple either in the church building or, more commonly, at the door of the church, at the time when they exchanged consent. Thus the symbolism of the Italian rites centered upon consent and the Church's role in marriage, while French wedding symbolism stressed consummation and treated the nuptial ceremony as primarily a domestic affair.[38]

Civil law also surrounded marriage with formal, contractual rituals. A dowry agreement became, at least for a time, a legal necessity. Both civil and religious authorities not only encouraged but even required a property agreement as a condition for recognizing a union as a marriage with full legal consequences. At the same time, the marriage market was changing, too. The value of dowries offered by the families of prospective brides was apparently rising, and in consequence men tended to marry earlier than they had in previous centuries, while the families of nubile women often postponed their daughters' marriages until later than had been customary.[39]

The Christian emperors also revised the rules relating to marriages between close relatives.[40] The new rules strongly discouraged marriage between kinsfolk. These rules may also have been intended to break down attachment to pagan customs, which had always been closely tied to the household and domestic rituals. Scholars have speculated that the new incest laws were designed to benefit the Church financially. The new rules, according to this argument, increased the likelihood that the Church would inherit property from wealthy persons who, under the new rules, would be less able to use intrafamilial marriage alliances to keep control of familial estates within their kinship group.[41] Whatever else they accomplished, the new laws on incest created a system of

[37] *Statuta ecclesiae antiquae* c. 101, ed. Charles Munier, Bibliothèque de l'Institut de droit canonique et de l'Université de Strasbourg, vol. 5 (Paris: Presses Universitaires de France, 1960), p. 100; St. Basil, *Homeliae IX in Hexameron* 7.5, in PG 29:160; and see generally Karl Ritzer, *Le mariage dans les églises chrétiennes du Ier au XIe siècle*, Lex orandi, vol. 45 (Paris: Editions du Cerf, 1970).

[38] Herlihy, *Medieval Households*, pp. 13–14.

[39] Herlihy, *Medieval Households*, pp. 18–23.

[40] André Lemaire, "Origines de la règle, 'Nullum sine dote fiat matrimonium'," in *Mélanges Paul Fournier* (Paris: Sirey, 1929), pp. 415–24; Wolff, *Written and Unwritten Marriages*, pp. 91–92; Carlo Castello, "Lo strumento dotale come prova del matrimonio," SDHI 4 (1938) 210.

[41] Jack Goody, *The Development of the Family and Marriage in Europe* (Cambridge:

reckoning degrees of relationship that persists in many jurisdictions to the present day.[42]

THE ROLE OF SEX IN MARRIAGE

Patristic writers generally viewed marriage with a degree of suspicion. Marriage, according to some, was an "indulgence," a concession to the moral frailty of those who were incapable of leading a life of perfect continence. Weaker members of the Christian community, those who were unable to renounce sex, married so that they could indulge their desires in a safely circumscribed situation. St. Caesarius (ca. 470–543) maintained that married people could be saved, despite their sexual activities, but only if they imposed stringent limits upon marital lovemaking and scrupulously observed God's other commands.[43]

St. Augustine was more positive in his appraisal of the married state than were some Fathers. Marriage, Augustine observed, was not morally wrong; indeed it even had certain positive values in the Christian scheme of things, for marriage produced children, it promoted mutual fidelity between the spouses, and it brought them together in a bond of love.[44] Two of these praiseworthy objectives of marriage, Augustine was careful to note, could be attained despite, not because of, the sexual element in marriage. Marriage, he wrote, might even be glorified because it made something good out of the evil of sex.[45] Sexual relations within marriage were a good use of an evil thing. Virginity, to be sure, was better, since that was a good use of a good thing. While marital relations were also good, they constituted a lesser order of good, because they employed the intrinsic wickedness of sex to achieve a morally valuable goal.[46]

Augustine judged the morality of marital sex in terms of the intentions of the parties. When married persons had sex for the sole purpose of procreation, they committed no sin. If they had sexual relations for mutual pleasure and enjoyment, they sinned—but only slightly. If they had sexual relations in some way calculated to avoid procreation, however, they sinned gravely.[47] Married

---

At the University Press, 1983), pp. 42–47 But see Appendix 2 below, as well as Herlihy, *Medieval Households*, pp. 11–13.

[42] Burge, *Comparative Law*, p. 21, outlines the complex rules concerning the degrees of relationship with unusual clarity.

[43] John Chrysostom, *De virginitate* 25, in PG 48:550; Caesarius of Arles, *Serm.* 6.7, in CCL 103:35; Bugge, *Virginitas*, p. 71.

[44] Augustine, *De nupt. et concup.* 1.17.19, in CSEL 42:231.

[45] Augustine, *De nupt. et concup.* 1.7.8, in CSEL 42: 219–20; *De bono coniugali* 3.3, in CSEL 41:190–91.

[46] Augustine, *De peccatorum meritis* 1.29.57, in PL 44:142; *De sancta virginitate* 20.19, in CSEL 41:253; Marie-François Berrouard, "Saint Augustin et l'indissolubilité du mariage: évolution de sa pensée," *Recherches augustiniennes* 5 (1968) 143.

[47] Augustine, *De nupt. et concup.* 1.15.17, in CSEL 42:229–30.

couples, he thought, should cease having sex as soon as they had produced a child or two. The sooner they stopped marital relations, the better for their moral health.[48] They would have been even more virtuous, of course, had they remained virgins; but once married, the less they yielded to sexual desire, the better.

Augustine's reservations about marital sex were almost certainly related to his own sexual experiences as a youth, experiences that he often reflected upon in his maturity. His tendency to isolate the sexual aspect of marriage, to treat it as an evil element lodged within the institution of matrimony, presumably mirrored his own feeling, when he was contemplating marriage himself, that he was a slave to lust. That feeling, in turn, seems to have been based upon disgust at his sexual cravings and desires.[49]

Augustine's treatment of marriage was measured and benign when compared with that of his great and influential contemporary, St. Jerome, whose treatment of marital sex was far more hostile and acerbic than Augustine's. While both Jerome and Augustine thought that sex for pleasure was immoral, even in marriage, Augustine saw values in marriage that would counteract and redeem the intrinsic wickedness of marital sex. Jerome and a few other patristic writers, however, found no redeeming value in marital sex: it was nothing more than a concession to human weakness, a remedy, and a poor one at that, for fornication.[50]

Since sex was a usual (and, in his view, a regrettable) feature of most marriages, Jerome and like-minded writers argued that couples had a moral obligation to limit marital relations to an absolute minimum. Jerome was bitterly critical of married men who loved their wives excessively. This was a "deformity," Jerome believed, and he cited with approval the Stoic writers Seneca and Sextus, who had declared that "A man who loves his wife too much is an adulterer." There can be little doubt in this context that Jerome identified love with sexual relations and that what he attacked so fiercely was immoderate indulgence in sex by married persons. Marital sex, Jerome thought, should be indulged in only very infrequently and then with sober calculation, not with hot desire. "Nothing," he asserted at one point, "is filthier than to have sex with

---

[48] Augustine, *De bono coniugali* 3.3, in CSEL 41:191.

[49] Brown, *Augustine of Hippo*, p. 390; Jean Leclercq, *Monks on Marriage: A Twelfth-Century View* (New York: Seabury Press, 1982), p. 13; Miles, *Augustine on the Body*, pp. 53–54, 70–75.

[50] Augustine, *De nupt. et concup.* 1.8.9, in CSEL 42:220–21; *De bono coniugali* 3.3, in CSEL 41:191; Caesarius of Arles, *Serm.* 32.4, in CCL 103:141–42; John Chrysostom, *Quales ducendae sunt uxores* 3.4–5, in PG 51:231–32, and *De verbis . . . propter fornicationes* 2, in PG 51:210; Lindner, *Usus matrimonii*, pp. 47–50; Müller, *Lehre*, p. 35; Berrouard, "Saint Augustin et l'indissolubilité," pp. 143–44. Jerome's aggressive denunciations of sexual activity of all kinds, in marriage and outside of it, strongly suggest a psychological immaturity that he never outgrew; Charles-Henri Nodet, "Position de Saint Jérôme en face des problèmes sexuels," in *Mystique et continence*, pp. 308–56.

your wife as you might do with another woman."[51] In this remarkable statement, which was to attract so much attention from so many medieval writers on marriage, Jerome had in mind qualitative as well as quantitative criteria for determining when marital sex was "excessive." He was denouncing not only too frequent marital intercourse, but also coital techniques and postures of which he disapproved.[52] Up to a point Augustine agreed with Jerome's strictures against "excessive" marital sex. Certainly he believed that married folk should curb their carnal desires; they ought to avoid arousing one another sexually; they ought to limit their lovemaking to proper times and places.[53] Intercourse during pregnancy, for example, he considered shameful in the extreme. But, he added, however immodest, shameful, and sordid the sex acts that married persons committed with each other, these were faults of the individuals, not blemishes attached to the institution of marriage.[54]

Among the Fathers of this era it was common ground that marital sex ought to be limited in frequency and duration. No one should have intercourse while undergoing penance for sins—and, considering that penitents might remain in that state for five or ten years, this was a significant limitation on sexual opportunities for many couples.[55] Indeed the Synod of Orleans considered that young people should be refused admission to penance because they might be unable to restrain themselves sexually during the prescribed period.[56] It was permissible, however, for those who had already completed penance to marry—or even to take a concubine in place of a wife—and to have marital sex.[57]

Earlier writers had stated vaguely that married couples should refrain from sexual relations during part of each year, but had failed to specify precisely what they meant. St. Caesarius of Arles elaborated this prohibition concretely. Sexual relations, he asserted, were forbidden throughout Lent and on the vigils of the major feasts of the liturgical year.[58] Coitus was also prohibited during

[51] Jerome, *Adv. Jov.* 1.49, in PL 23:281, relying on Sextus, *Sententiae* 231, ed. Chadwick, pp. 38–39; Fulgentius, *Epist.* 1.4, in CCL 91:190; Jean-Louis Flandrin, *Familles: parenté, maison, sexualité dans l'ancienne société* (Paris: Hachette, 1976), p. 157.

[52] James A. Brundage, "Let Me Count the Ways: Canonists and Theologians Contemplate Coital Positions," JMH 10 (1984) 82; Jean-Louis Flandrin, *Le sexe et l'occident* (Paris: Seuil, 1981), pp. 119–20.

[53] Augustine, *Contra Julianum* 3.14.28, in PL 44:716–17.

[54] Augustine, *De bono coniugali* 6.5, in CSEL 41:194; *De nupt. et concup.* 1.24.27, in CSEL 42:239–40.

[55] Council of Tours (461) c. 8, in *Concilia Galliae, A. 314–A. 506,* ed. Charles Munier, CCL vols. 148–148A (Turnhout: Brépols, 1963) 148:146.

[56] Synod of Orleans (538) c. 27(24) in *Concilia Galliae* 148A:124; Thomas N. Tentler, *Sin and Confession on the Eve of the Reformation* (Princeton: Princeton University Press, 1977), p. 5; Gottlob, "Ehebruch," p. 340.

[57] Leo I, *Epist.* 167, inquis. 13, in PL 54:1207.

[58] Caesarius of Arles, *Serm.* 1.12, 44.3, 187.4, 188.3, in CCL 103:10, 196, and 104:765, 768; Pierre J. Payer, "Early Medieval Regulations Concerning Marital Sexual Relations," JMH 6 (1980) 363.

menstrual periods and pregnancy, as well as on Sundays throughout the year.[59] The late fifth-century *Statuta ecclesiae antiqua* added that newly married couples should refrain from intercourse on their wedding night, out of reverence for the nuptial blessing that they received during the marriage ceremony.[60] This prescription, like the prohibition on sexual relations during penitential periods and festivals, implied that marital sex carried with it ritual pollution. For the same reason, St. Caesarius forbade newly married couples to enter the church during the first thirty days following their wedding.[61]

Neither the New Testament nor the patristic writers gave any indication that they counted marriage a sacrament, as they did baptism and the Eucharist. Although Augustine sometimes referred to marriage as a *sacramentum*, his meaning in these passages was clearly much different from his application of the term to the eucharistic and baptismal rites.[62] The belief that marriage was a sacrament appeared only much later.

Patristic writers assumed, as Roman law did, that consent made marriage. They rejected the notion that consummation was an essential part of marriage. It made no difference whether a couple ever went to bed together; so long as they consented to marry one another, that was what counted.[63] If consummation was not essential, it might follow that sexual impotence constituted no reason for holding a marriage invalid, and Augustine at any rate seems to have subscribed to this view.[64]

Christian authorities warned married couples that they should have sex only for proper reasons. Augustine pointed to the Old Testament prophets as examples for married persons of his own generation. The prophets, he claimed,

---

[59] Caesarius of Arles, *Serm.* 44.7, in CCL 103:199; Jerome, *Commentarium in Ezechielem* 6.18 and *Commentarium in Zachariam* 3.13.1, in PL 25:173, 1517.

[60] *Stat. eccl. ant.* c. 101, ed. Munier, p. 100.

[61] Caesarius of Arles, *Serm.* 44.5, in CCL 103:198.

[62] Augustine, *De nupt. et concup.* 1.17.19, 1.21.23, in CSEL 42:231, 236; Rordorf, "Marriage in the New Testament," pp. 208–209.

[63] Augustine, *De consensu evangelistarum* 2.1.2, in CSEL 43:82; *De nupt. et concup.* 1.11.12, in CSEL 42:224; Ambrose, *De institutione virginis* 6.41, in PL 16:316; D'Ercole, "Consenso," p. 28; Jean Gaudemet, "Indissolubilité et consommation du mariage: l'apport d'Hincmar de Reims," RDC 30 (1980) 29; William Joseph Dooley, *Marriage according to St. Ambrose*, Studies in Christian Antiquity, no. 11 (Washington: Catholic University of America, 1948), pp. 1–2.

[64] Augustine, *De bono coniugali* 7.7, 15.17, in CSEL 41:196–97, 209–10; Josef Löffler, *Die Störingen des geschlechtlichen Vermögens in der Literatur der auctoritativen Theologie des Mittelalters: Ein Beitrag zur Geschichte der Impotenz und des medizinischen Sachverständigenbeweises im kanonischen Impotenzprozess*, Abhandlungen der Akademie der Wissenschaften zu Mainz, Literatur, geistes- und sozialwissenschaftlichen Klasse (1958), no. 6 (Mainz: Akademie der Wissenschaften und der Literatur, 1958), p. 300.

[65] Augustine, *Contra Faustum* 29.4, in PL 42:490; *De nupt. et concup.* 1.8.9, in CSEL 42:221.

made love to their wives rationally and solely for procreative purposes.[65] Since marital sex is a favor, not a right,[66] couples should avoid making love merely for enjoyment or because they felt like it. Only propagation of the species, Augustine warned, entitled them to make use of their marital privileges blamelessly.[67]

But while Augustine and his contemporaries cautioned against intercourse for pleasure, they also reminded their married hearers that they were obliged to give their spouses sex upon demand. The marital debt was a right that either party could claim. The partner from whom it was demanded must accede to the spouse's request, and doing so was no sin. The other partner might sin in asking payment of the sexual debt for wrongful reasons or at inappropriate times, but the spouse who complied did not share the guilt.[68] If a couple agreed by mutual consent to cease having sexual relations and one of them later had a change of mind, however, the other party had no obligation to honor a demand for the resumption of marital intercourse. A mutual decision to forego sexual relations cancelled the marital debt, and neither party could thenceforth rescind that decision.

The marital debt created a parity of rights and obligations between the spouses. Each had an equal right to demand that it be paid; each had an equal obligation to comply with the other's demands. Equality of the sexes in marriage meant equality in the marriage bed, but not outside of it.[69] Just as each spouse was entitled to sexual service from the other on demand, so each was entitled to require sexual fidelity from the other. Neither had a right to seek sexual fulfillment outside of marriage, even if the other party was, for example, absent or ill and thus sexually unavailable.[70]

Cessation of marital relations did not break the bond of marriage, just as the beginning of sexual relations was irrelevant to the contracting of marriage.[71] The evident aim of patristic matrimonial theory was to separate marriage as far as possible from its sexual component, defining it as a contractual union, separate and distinct from the sexual union of the married persons.

[66] Augustine, *De nupt. et concup.* 1.14.16, in CSEL 42:228–29.

[67] Augustine, *De bono coniugali* 6.6, in CSEL 41:195; *De nupt. et concup.* 1.15.17, in CSEL 42:229–30; *De peccatorum meritis* 1.29.57, in Pl 44:141; Fulgentius of Ruspa, *Epist.* 1.6–8, in CCL 91:190–91; Caesarius of Arles, *Serm.* 42.4, 44.3, 5, in CCL 103:187, 196–98; John Chrysostom, *Homeliae XI in Epistolam primam ad Thessalonienses* 4.5.3, in PG 62:426. Herlihy, *Medieval Households*, p. 25, points out that the injunctions of Augustine and other Church Fathers against frequent marital intercourse produced the same demographic consequences as pagan avoidance of marriage, contraception, and infanticide. The rationale and the value systems were different, but both tended to lead to small numbers of children and a stable or declining population.

[68] Augustine, *De bono coniugali* 7.6, in CSEL 41:195–96; Fulgentius, *Epist.* 1.5, in CCL 91:190; Børresen, *Subordination and Equivalence*, p. 101.

[69] Augustine, *Epist.* 262, in CSEL 57:621–31; Børresen, *Subordination and Equivalence*, p. 104; Berrouard, "Saint Augustin et l'indissolubilité," p. 141.

[70] Caesarius of Arles, *Serm.* 43.7, in CCL 103:193–94.

[71] Augustine, *De nupt. et concup.* 1.11.12, in CSEL 42:224.

Divorce and Remarriage

Classical Roman law, as we have seen, based the existence of marriage on *affectio maritalis*. Where marital affection existed between a couple, they were married; when marital affection ceased, the marriage ended. In the postclassical period this concept of marriage underwent a slight but important change. Marriage in postclassical law continued to be contracted by consent, which implied marital affection; but once created, the marriage continued until the relationship ended by death or divorce. Classical Roman marriage, accordingly, required continuing consent of the parties, while postclassical marriage needed only initial consent.[72]

In consequence, divorce became far more central and significant in family law during the postclassical era, and it became more formal and more frequent as well. It was already common prior to the third century, but its frequency seems to have increased markedly after about A.D. 200. St. Jerome mentioned two extreme cases: one involved a man who had had twenty wives, the other the funeral of a woman who was being buried by her twenty-second husband.[73] While these were no doubt unusual, the incidence of divorce among the upper classes was clearly rather high.

Divorce began to come under closer public control from the time of Constantine, and there is little doubt that his reform of the divorce law reflected the policies of his Christian advisers.[74] Constantine's constitution of 331 regulated in detail the grounds on which divorce might be authorized. According to this statute a husband could divorce his wife because she had committed adultery, had administered poisons, or had procured prostitution. Wives, in turn, could divorce their husbands for murder, poisoning, or grave-robbing. Constantine also thought it necessary to specify three grounds that would *not* be accepted as a basis for divorce: a woman could not secure a divorce simply because her husband was a drunkard, a gambler, or an adulterer.[75] There was obviously a glaring disparity in the treatment of adultery by men and by women. Still, as Noonan has pointed out, the law probably did more to protect women than men, since under earlier rules it had been even easier for a husband to cast off his wife than it was under Constantinian legislation.[76]

Constantine's enactments imposed no restriction on remarriage following di-

---

[72] Volterra, *Conception*, p. 58.

[73] Jerome, *Epist.* 123.10, in PL 22:1052–53.

[74] D'Ercole, "Consenso," pp. 29–30. It does not follow, however, that the Church and the Roman government thenceforth were engaged in a continuing campaign to abolish divorce, as D'Ercole also claims. Neither the patristic writers nor the imperial legislation of the fourth and fifth centuries bear out this contention.

[75] *Codex Theodosianus* 3.16.1, ed. Paul Krüger and Theodor Mommsen, 3 vols. (Berlin: Weidmann, 1905; cited hereafter as Cod. Theod.); Visky, "Divorce," p. 246; Max Kaser, *Das römische Privatrecht*, 2 vols., Handbuch der Altertumswissenschaft, sect. 10, pt. 3, vol. 3 (Munich: C. H. Beck, 1955–59) 2:121; Noonan, "Novel 22," pp. 42–43.

[76] Noonan, "Novel 22," p. 43.

vorce, and there is no evidence to indicate that remarriage was much discouraged by extralegal pressures. Remarriage appears to have been the usual sequel to divorce, at least for men, and Constantine and his advisers unquestionably knew this.[77] A later generation of influential Christian writers, notably St. Augustine and St. Jerome, argued that marriage ought to be indissoluble and that the laws should support this view.[78]

The earliest clear formulation of a Christian doctrine of marital indissolubility appeared in Augustine, who held that the New Testament references to divorce (Matt. 5:32 and 1 Cor. 7:10–11) authorized separation, but not termination of marriage. Those who remarried following such a separation were adulterers.[79] Augustine's opposition to remarriage following divorce was predicated on his belief that people marry largely because of sex: his objections to remarriage, therefore, centered on the sexual opportunities that remarriage furnished.

Despite Augustine's arguments and similar ones voiced by Jerome, however, neither Church councils nor the Christian emperors made any move to prohibit divorce and remarriage during the fourth century. The Council of Arles (314), even before Constantine's divorce constitution, certainly discouraged remarriage following divorce on grounds of adultery, but stopped short of forbidding it.[80] Not until 407, nearly a century later, did the Council of Carthage rule that a divorced Christian might not remarry; the text of the canon, however, fails to make it clear whether this was a permanent prohibition, or whether it was limited to the lifetime of the first spouse.[81]

Public law was slower still to limit divorce and remarriage. The divorce law of the Emperor Honorius (395–423) in 421 technically liberalized the Constantinian constitution by allowing divorce without stated grounds. But since Honorius's law also penalized those who obtained such divorces by subjecting them to deportation, confiscation of property, and prohibition of remarriage, the clear intent of the law was to discourage baseless actions. The person who

[77] Noonan, "Novel 22," pp. 43–44.

[78] Noonan, "Novel 22," pp. 86–87.

[79] Augustine, *De nupt. et concup.* 1.10.11, in CSEL 42:222–23; *De bono coniugali* 7.6, 15.17, 29.32, in CSEL 41:196, 209–10, 227; and *De adulterinis coniugiis* 1.1, in CSEL 41:348. See also Ambrose, *Expositio evangelii Lucae* 8.5–6, in CSEL 32/4:394; Berrouard, "Saint Augustin et l'indissolubilité," pp. 139–55; Colish, *Stoic Tradition* 2:167–68. For earlier views on this matter see Charles Munier, "Le témoinage d'Origène en matière de remariage après séparation," RDC 28 (1978) 15–29.

[80] Council of Arles (314) c. 11(10) in *Concilia Galliae*, CCL 148:11; Carlo De Sanctis, "Il pensiero della chiesa sul problema del coniuge abbandonato senza sua colpa," *Apollinaris* 48 (1975) 205; Montan, "Alle origini della disciplina," p. 167; Hubert Mordek, "Ehescheidung und Wiederheirat in der Frühkirche: Zu Kanon 11(10) des Konzils von Arles (314)," RDC 28 (1978) 218–22; Rordorf, "Marriage in the New Testament," pp. 204–05.

[81] *Registri ecclesiae Carthaginensis excerpta* (407) c. 102, in *Concilia Africae, A. 345–A. 525*, ed. Charles Munier, CCL 149 (Turnhout: Brépols, 1974), p. 218; De Sanctis, "Coniuge abbandonato," p. 218; Montan, "Alle origini della disciplina," p. 173.

obtained a divorce because of demonstrated flaws and shortcomings in his spouse, however, could remarry after a statutory waiting period.[82]

In 439 the eastern Emperor Theodosius II (408–450) genuinely liberalized divorce and returned matters to the situation that had prevailed prior to Constantine: he allowed divorce by mutual consent without penalties and with the provision that divorced persons might, if they wished, remarry immediately.[83] The legal situation changed once more a decade later, when another divorce law of Theodosius II required that divorce actions demonstrate grounds. The law of 449 considerably broadened the basis on which divorce might be granted, notably by making adultery by either husband or wife a sufficient cause of action. If either party committed homicide, that was also sufficient reason for divorce, as were the traditional offenses of grave-robbing and poisoning.

The new legislation of Theodosius II added some novel justifications for divorce, including the charge that either party had plotted against the government or engaged in kidnapping. In addition, physical maltreatment of one spouse by the other was for the first time included among the accepted grounds for divorce.[84] The divorce law of 449 enunciated still another new principle: namely, that marriage could only be ended by divorce or death of one party, and this law for the first time required a formal public act for the termination of marriage.[85] Three years later, in 452, the western emperor Valentinian III (425–454) reinstated the old Constantinian constitution of 331 for his portion of the Empire. Since this radically restricted divorce rights once more, it seems plausible that, as others have suggested, Pope Leo I (440–461) may have inspired this action.[86]

These fluctuations in Roman divorce law raise the question of how successful even the most stringent of these enactments may have been in curtailing the frequency of divorce, or of remarriage following divorce. The law of Honorius, for example, contained punitive provisions that sought to discourage groundless divorces, but there was little in his constitution to prevent remarriage by anyone determined to do so, and there is no evidence that the Roman government actually attempted to carry out the deportation penalties or the prohibition of remarriage. Machinery for judicial enforcement was not built into the divorce act, and there is little reason to believe that vigorous efforts were made to carry out the sanctions. In short, even the most stringent of the anti-divorce measures seems to have been largely a dead letter.[87]

Roman divorce in practice continued to be mainly a private matter, despite this spate of legislative activity. Substantial numbers of Christians continued to

[82] Cod. Theod. 3.16.2; Noonan, "Novel 22," pp. 45–46.
[83] Nov. Theod. 12; Noonan, "Novel 22," pp. 48–49.
[84] Cod. 5.17.8 (449); Noonan, "Novel 22," pp. 49–51; Visky, "Divorce," pp. 246–47; Kaser, *Röm. Privatrecht* 2:121.
[85] Cod. 5.17.8 pr.; Volterra, "Conception," p. 60.
[86] Nov. Val. 35.11; Noonan, "Novel 22," pp. 52–53.
[87] Noonan, "Novel 22," pp. 53–54.

regard marriage as dissoluble and to act on that belief.[88] Sixth-century Church councils still distinguished between de facto separations, following which Church authorities were not supposed to allow remarriage, and *discidium*, or both separation and divorce of the parties by ecclesiastical authority. Following *discidium*, Christians often remarried.[89] Prohibitions of remarriage following divorce only gradually became effective in the West. Opposition to remarriage after divorce centered on the sexual opportunities that remarriage afforded and must be seen as part of a general effort by Church authorities to restrict sexual activity as far as possible.[90]

For the same reason, the right to remarry following the death of a husband or wife was also the subject of controversy. The Manichaeans had insisted that twice-married persons should be excluded from communion as adulterers. In reaction against Manichaeanism, the first Council of Nicaea (325) affirmed as a matter of doctrine that second marriages were permitted.[91] Yet many fourth-century Christians of unquestioned orthodoxy began to see widowhood as an opportunity for sexual continence; accordingly, they viewed remarriage as a renunciation of a chance to gain spiritual merit. St. Augustine, for example, maintained that second marriages ought to be discouraged. Again, as with his opposition to remarriage of divorced persons, Augustine's teachings about second marriages of widows and widowers focused upon the sexual opportunities that remarriage would afford. In his treatise on widowhood, Augustine counseled his readers that after they had lost the carnal delights of marriage they ought to replace those bodily pleasures with spiritual ones and renounce any thought of marrying again.[92]

St. John Chrysostom (ca. 344–407) also dedicated a short treatise to the problem of second marriages and, like Augustine, he strongly opposed them, not because they were wrong in themselves, but rather because they represented a concession to fleshly lust and a taste for sexual pleasure. For this rea-

[88] Noonan, "Novel 22," pp. 71–72, 85; D'Ercole's claim in "Consenso," pp. 23–24, that the Christian Church consistently prohibited divorce and remarriage from the beginning is simply not supported by the evidence.

[89] Council of Agde (506) c. 25, in *Concilia Galliae*, CCL 148:204; Gérard Fransen, "La rupture du mariage," in *Il matrimonio nella società altomedievale*, 2 vols. Settimane di studio del Centro italiano di studi sull'alto medioevo, no. 24 (Spoleto: Centro italiano di studi sull'alto medioevo, 1977), p. 610.

[90] *Reg. eccl. Carthaginensis* c. 102 in *Concilia Africae*, CCL 149:218 reports a conciliar canon of 407 that required divorced persons who remarried to do penance for their action. A century later the Council of Agde (506) c. 25, in CCL 148:204, prescribed excommunication for divorced persons who remarried—but only if they had secured their divorces without stating grounds and without seeking the judgment of their bishops.

[91] 1 Council of Nicaea (325) c. 8, in COD, p. 9; Montan, "Alle origini della disciplina," p. 168; McNamara, "Cornelia's Daughters," p. 18.

[92] Augustine, *De bono viduitatis* 21.26, in CSEL 41:337–38; Lightman and Zeisel, "Univira," pp. 27–29.

son Chrysostom strongly advised good Christians to abstain from remarriage; they should dedicate themselves after the deaths of their spouses to a life of penance and religious devotion. The implication was clear: those who had experienced the sensual delights of marital sex should now make amends for their past indulgence in the joys of the flesh by a life of mortification.[93] Conciliar enactments of the mid-fourth century reflected the views of Chrysostom and Augustine. The Council of Laodicea (ca. 360), for instance, cautioned that while second marriages were not forbidden, widows and widowers should not rush into them but should spend their time in prayer and fasting. If after a period of spiritual discipline they still felt inclined to remarry, the council grudgingly conceded that they might nevertheless be allowed to receive communion.[94]

But while ordinary Christians could remarry as a concession to the weakness of the flesh, those who aspired to receive holy orders were held to a higher standard. Opposition to the ordination of the twice-married found its scriptural basis in St. Paul's admonition (1 Tim. 3:2) that a bishop should be the husband of one wife, an ambiguous dictum that was widely interpreted to mean that remarried widowers should be excluded from holy orders. During the fourth century this Pauline prohibition was broadened to exclude from orders men who had married a widow or a divorced woman, on the theory that marriage to a previously married woman was tantamount to a second marriage for the man. This kind of constructive digamy was further extended by the Council of Gerona in the early sixth century to include cases in which a man had sexual relations with a woman other than his first wife, either in a second marriage or in some other relationship.[95]

Opposition to the ordination of twice-married men, although ostensibly based upon a scriptural injunction, seems in fact to have been predicated upon a belief that remarriage, or marriage to a sexually experienced woman, showed a lack of moral fiber, an unseemly proclivity to seek after sexual pleasure, and hence unfitness for the sacred functions of the Christian clergy.

CHRISTIAN CONCUBINAGE

Given the stern views of so many Christian authorities about sexual irregularities, one might have expected that the Church, once it gained power and authority, would abolish the long standing Roman practice of concubinage. In actuality, the reactions of the Fathers and the Christian Emperors to concubinage were more complex than that.

The Fathers of the fourth and fifth centuries disagreed about the moral status of concubinage. One view held that concubinage was an alternative form of marriage, created because civil law prohibited marriages between persons of

[93] John Chrysostom, *De non iterando coniugio*, in PG 48:609–20.

[94] Council of Laodicaea c. 1, in Mansi 2:564; Montan, "Alle origini della disciplina," p. 169.

[95] *Stat. eccl. ant.* c. 85, ed. Munier, p. 94; Council of Gerona (517) c. 8, in Vives, *Concilios Visigóticos,* p. 41.

certain social classes; hence Christians should accept these de facto unions and assimilate them to formal marriage by recognizing concubinage as a variant form of marriage. The other viewpoint held that concubinage was morally wrong, since it involved a continuing sexual relationship that was not sanctified by matrimony. Those who adopted this stance argued that a Christian man who lived with a concubine should marry her, if that was legally possible. If the law would not allow the man to marry his concubine, then the Church must demand that he dismiss her, do penance for his sexual transgressions, and marry someone else with whom he could contract a legal union. The problem that concubinage caused for Christian teachers and the ambiguity of their responses to it is revealed by the fact that some writers adopted both views in different contexts.[96]

In practice, the Church during the first two centuries of its existence had encouraged its members to marry according to the prescriptions of civil law, but had not frowned upon legally tolerated concubinage. The Church did, however, disapprove of concubinage between male slaves and free woman or free men with slave women; here, too, the attitudes of churchmen reflected the provisions of Roman law.[97] Pope Calixtus I (217–222) had attempted to revise the Roman Church's policy on concubinage by permitting the faithful to enter into relationships that civil law did not allow. Calixtus's decision was the subject of strident controversy and ultimately failed to prevail. A century later under Constantine, the Roman government strengthened its opposition to irregular concubinage, and the Church cooperated with this imperial attempt to preserve the class structure.[98]

From the time of Constantine the right of Christian Romans to keep concubines grew progressively restricted. Constantine himself in 326 forbade married men to take concubines, and at the end of the fourth century the first Council of Toledo adopted spiritual penalties to reinforce the civil prohibition.[99] Meanwhile opposition to concubinage among leading Christian writers became considerably sharper. St. Augustine once more became the spokesman for those who opposed concubinage as an unwholesome practice.

Augustine's personal experience again almost certainly shaped his views on concubinage. When he was about sixteen Augustine had taken a concubine with whom he lived for about fifteen years and by whom he had a son. Looking back upon this experience in maturity, Augustine described the relationship

---

[96] Esmein, *Mariage* 2 : 109–12.

[97] Miguel Falcão, "Atitude de igreja peranta as uniões conjugais da Roma clásica," *Theologica* 8 (1973) 1–20; Caselli, "Concubina pro uxore," p. 198; Brown, *Augustine of Hippo*, p. 62.

[98] Gaudemet, "Décision de Callixte," pp. 104–15; Falcão, "Atitude de igreja," pp. 20–26; Baumann, *Zivilrechtliche Bedeutung*, p. 13; Meyer, *Römische Konkubinat*, pp. 125–26; E. Jombart, "Concubinage," in *Dictionnaire de droit canonique*, ed. R. Naz, 7 vols. (Paris: Letouzey et Ané, 1935–65; cited hereafter as DDC) 3 : 1513.

[99] Cod. 5.26.1 (326); 1 Council of Toledo (397 ~ 400) c. 17, in Vives, *Concilios Visigóticos*, p. 24.

simply in terms of sexual passion; he says nothing to indicate that there was any deeper emotional bond between him and his mistress than a keen desire for sexual gratification.[100] Augustine eventually broke off this relationship in order to take a wife, and his former concubine returned to her home in Africa, leaving her child in Augustine's care. During the next two years the arrangements for his projected marriage became increasingly complicated, and the venture became more and more remote. Augustine then procured another concubine, with whom he lived until the time of his conversion to Christianity.[101] After his conversion, Augustine renounced sex altogether and abandoned his second concubine. Although he continued to experience strong sexual desires and vivid sexual fantasies, Augustine thereafter lived a life of strict continence.[102]

Augustine's sermons, letters, and other writings refer repeatedly to concubinage and do so in ways that clearly reflect his personal history. He condemned concubinage as nothing more than legalized fornication and made it clear that he considered such relationships grounded solely on sexual craving.[103] Augustine seems not to have felt much affection for either of his concubines. He discarded them when it suited his purposes, and he expressed neither compassion for his abandoned consorts nor concern for their welfare. The mature Augustine's disgust with the sexual life that he renounced at the time of his conversion surfaced in a passage of his commentary on the book of Genesis, where he questioned whether there was a real difference between a wife and a concubine—either one, after all, was simply a source of sexual temptation for a man.[104] The same attitude, equating female companionship with nothing more than sexual opportunity, appeared again in a letter that he wrote to a newly bereaved widower named Cornelius. Augustine warned his correspondent in contemptuous terms to beware of the wiles that Cornelius's slave girls were sure to employ in their efforts to distract him from grief at his wife's death.[105] Augustine's treatment of concubinage conveys the distinct impression that he regarded women fundamentally as little more than troublesome, though enticing, purveyors of sexual gratification for men.

Although Augustine discussed the institution of concubinage at greater length than most other Church Fathers, their treatments of the subject touched on many of the same themes. Jerome saw no difference between a concubine and a harlot: a concubine, he wrote to his friend and disciple Eustochium, was

[100] Augustine, *Conf.* 2.2.2, in CSEL 33:29–30; Brown, *Augustine of Hippo*, pp. 61–63.

[101] Augustine, *Conf.* 6.15.25, in CSEL 33:138.

[102] Augustine, *Conf.* 10.30.41, in CSEL 33:257.

[103] Augustine, *De civ. Dei* 16.34, in CSEL 40/2:186; *De bono coniugii* 5.5, in CSEL 41:193–94; *Serm.* 392.2, in PL 39:1710; *Serm. App.* 288.5, 289.4, in PL 39:2291–93; Børresen, *Subordination and Equivalence*, p. 108.

[104] Augustine, *Quaestiones in Heptateuchum* 1.90, in PL 34:571, commenting on Gen. 30:3, 9. Likewise in *Serm.* 224.3, in PL 38:1095, Augustine maintains that there is no real difference between a concubine and a prostitute.

[105] Augustine, *Epist.* 259.1, in CSEL 57:611.

nothing but a one-man whore; he added that he greatly feared that the women companions of the clergy fitted that description all too neatly.[106] Likewise, Jerome was disposed to treat the wives of pagan converts to Christianity as concubines, unless the new convert regularized his domestic situation by a proper Christian marriage.[107]

Indeed, Jerome saw little difference between a wife, a concubine, and a harlot under any circumstances. Living with a woman, regardless of the legal formalities, was for him a suspect business; having sex with her imperiled a man's chances of salvation.[108] Jerome thought it best to have as little traffic with women as possible and certainly no sexual relationship, even in marriage. If a man was so craven and weak-willed that he yielded to sexual desire, then as Jerome suggested to one correspondent, he might do better to keep his sweetheart as a concubine rather than marry her. After all, he declared ironically, your union with a wife may prevent you from receiving holy orders when you finally come to your senses, whereas a dalliance with a concubine will not.[109] Jerome agreed with St. Ambrose that relations with a concubine constituted adultery, whereas sex with a wife merely demonstrated a lack of moral fortitude.[110]

At the beginning of the fifth century, some moralists began to urge that concubinage should be eliminated from Christian society and sought to remove the legal protections that the institution enjoyed. Concubinage, as they saw it, amounted to a prolonged and continuous act of fornication. The first Council of Toledo, at the turn of the century, was a critical episode in the campaign to strip concubines of the cloak of legal toleration. Yet, at Toledo the anti-concubinage forces lost. The council finally adopted a canon that forbade married men to keep concubines—Constantine had outlawed it long before—under pain of excommunication. Unmarried men who kept a concubine (but only one at a time) in place of a wife, however, were not denied the right to receive communion. The council's language indicates that while the Fathers disapproved of concubinage and preferred that Christians marry, not cohabit, they did not regard the matter as a sufficiently grave moral offense to justify exclusion from the Eucharist.[111]

Caesarius of Arles and a few others asserted that, despite the civil law's tolerance of concubinage, canon law forbade the practice. But after the Council of Toledo, it was difficult to maintain that the Church's disapproval of concubinage was more than a counsel of perfection, and many Christians certainly under-

---

[106] Jerome, *Epist.* 22.14, in CSEL 54:161–62; cf. Augustine, *Serm.* 224.3, in PL 38:1095.

[107] Jerome, *Epist.* 69.3,6, in CSEL 54:684–85.

[108] Jerome, *Epist.* 69.4.2, in CSEL 54:685.

[109] Jerome, *Epist.* 69.5.6–7, in CSEL 54:688.

[110] Ambrose, *De Abraham* 1.4.25, in PL 14:431; Löwenstein, *Bekämpfung*, p. 10.

[111] 1 Council of Toledo (397 ∼ 400) c. 17, in Vives, *Concilios Visigóticos*, p. 24; Caselli, "Concubina pro uxore," pp. 163, 200, 212–18; Baumann, *Zivilrechtliche Bedeutung*, p. 16; Esmein, *Mariage* 2:40.

stood matters that way.[112] Even Caesarius acknowledged that concubinage was common among Christians—so common, indeed, that he conceded it would be impractical to excommunicate all those who practiced it.[113] Pope Leo I agreed with Caesarius. While he deplored the practice of concubinage, Leo felt that the custom was too strong to be overcome. Concubinage simply had to be tolerated, and the best that the Church could do was to prevent men from keeping more than one concubine at a time. Marriage was certainly preferable to concubinage, Leo continued, and Christian men would do well to abandon their concubines and to marry legitimate wives instead. That would be moral improvement. But those who elected to remain with their concubines need not be punished for making that choice.[114]

Meanwhile, imperial law under the Christian emperors made some modest improvements in the rights and legal status of concubines. This in turn helped to make concubinage more nearly similar to marriage, since it mitigated the legal disadvantages that concubines had suffered.

One critical area in which the concubine's situation improved markedly during the fourth and fifth centuries concerned the financial provisions made for her. As dowry was a critical element in differentiating a concubine from a wife, Roman courts were concerned to distinguish the conveyance of dowry property from the "loans" and "gifts" that men gave to their concubines. The distinction had serious implications for the rights of children, inheritance, and related matters. The great difficulty in making clear distinctions in this area underscored the seriousness of the problem.[115]

Neither a concubine nor her children, according to early Roman law, had any right to share in her lover's estate. But the Council of Gangra during Constantine's reign required Christian parents to provide support for all their children, legitimate or not, and civil law in the fourth century began to extend limited inheritance rights to illegitimates as well.[116] Valentinian in 371 ruled that a concubine and her children might receive up to one-quarter of the estate of the children's father.[117] This policy was temporarily reversed in 397 by the emperors Arcadius and Honorius, who cut concubines and their children out of the estate altogether, but in 405 the rule of 371 was reinstated.[118] Further changes in the early fifth century allowed the concubine and her children to receive a small portion of the estate; just how much they might inherit depended upon whether or not the father left any legitimate children.

[112] Caesarius of Arles, *Serm.* 43.4, in CCL 103:191–92.

[113] Caesarius of Arles, *Serm.* 43.5, in CCL 103:192–93.

[114] Leo I, *Epist.* 167, inquis. 4–5, in PL 54:1204–05; Jean Gaudemet, "Le lien matrimonial: les incertitudes du haut moyen-âge," RDC 21 (1971) 88–89, repr. in his *Sociétés et mariage*, pp. 192–93; Brown, *Augustine of Hippo*, pp. 88–89.

[115] Castello, "Lo strumento dotale," p. 213.

[116] Council of Gangra (before 341) c. 15, in Mansi 2:1103.

[117] Cod. Theod. 4.6.4.

[118] Cod. Theod. 4.6.5.

Legitimation of the natural children borne by a concubine remained barred by law until the end of the fifth century.[119] From the time of Constantine, however, the law began to take greater notice of natural children, although the notice that it took was not always very protective. The aim of much fourth-century legislation concerning illegitimacy was to separate the illegitimate child from the family and to exclude him or her from succession to either the mother's or the father's estate.[120] The children of concubines, or "natural" children, fared somewhat better in this legislation than did mere bastards (that is, the children of casual liaisons). The status of natural children improved notably when the Emperor Zeno in 477 granted them legitimate status if their parents married each other after the child's birth.[121] Theodosius II and Valentinian III further liberalized the legitimation rules so that formal acknowledgment of paternity either by the child's father or paternal grandfather bestowed legitimate status, together with inheritance rights.[122]

Sexual Offenses

Patristic writers saw fornication as the prototype of all sexual offenses; some of them considered fornication the root of all other evils. The spirit of fornication, they declared, was nearly impossible to eradicate and affected everyone, unlike other deadly sins that were alluring only to some. Fornication was also related to other deadly vices, particularly gluttony and pride. Pride was the source of man's inclination to fornicate, according to St. John Cassian, while gluttony resembled fornication because it involved the satisfaction of bodily desires. Since excessive eating ignites the fire of sexual desire, Cassian continued, fasting ought to be one of the primary defenses against fornication, for this would deprive the spirit of fornication of the fuel that it requires. Accordingly, Cassian made fasting the foundation of an ascetic system that was ultimately directed at eradicating sexual lust.[123]

Ordinary people who chose not to devote their lives to ascetic observances were often advised that their best defense against the ever present urge to copulate was to marry early. For this reason St. John Chrysostom warned parents to see to it that their children married soon after they reached the age of puberty.[124]

All sexual relations outside of marriage amounted to fornication. Patristic writers realized that fornication was exceedingly common, but they also viewed it as a grave moral failing. No kind of sexual experience, save for marital inter-

[119] Cod. Theod. 4.6.6; Caselli, "Concubina pro uxore," pp. 169–70; Meyer, *Römische Konkubinat*, p. 142; Gide, "De la condition de l'enfant naturel," p. 567.

[120] Cod. Theod. 4.6.2, 7; Cod. 5.27.2 (405); Baumann, *Zivilrechtliche Bedeutung*, p. 13; Chevailler, "Observations sur le droit de bâtardise," p. 379.

[121] Cod. 5.27.5 (477); Gide, "De la condition de l'enfant naturel," pp. 282–85.

[122] Cod. 5.27.3.1 (443); Baumann, *Zivilrechtliche Bedeutung*, p. 14.

[123] Foucault, "Combat de la chasteté," pp. 15–17.

[124] John Chrysostom, *Hom. in Epist. I ad Thessal.* 4.5.3, in PG 62:426.

course, was possible without sin, according to the Fathers, and this included premarital intercourse between persons engaged to be married.[125] Premarital intercourse, however, was not at this period considered an impediment to subsequent marriage.[126] Because of the ever present danger that social contacts might lead to sexual attraction and then to fornication, parents were cautioned to monitor the activities of their children. They were also encouraged to separate boys and girls in their households and to reduce contacts between them to a minimum. Boys and girls should not even be allowed to speak privately with each other. This separation of the sexes should apply to female slaves and servant girls, as well as to free women, for as St. Caesarius of Arles observed, the lower a woman's social status, the easier it was to corrupt her sexually.[127]

ADULTERY

The Fathers were not always precise in their terminology for sexual offenses and often used the term "adultery" indiscriminately to describe what was properly fornication (that is, sexual relations between unmarried persons) as well as extramarital sexual relations among married persons.[128] Adultery in the strict sense was increasingly defined as a serious offense both in Church law and in Roman civil law under Constantine and his successors. Reiterating the principle that men should be subject to the same penalties for adultery as women, St. Augustine urged married women to be assertive in dealing with their husbands' sexual infidelities. "You should not allow your men to fornicate," he admonished women. "Appeal against them to the Church—I don't mean to the public judges, the proconsul, the vicar, the count, or the emperor, but to Christ."[129] He went on to remind his audience of St. Paul's words (1 Cor. 7:4): "The wife does not have power over her body, but her husband does, and likewise the husband does not have power over his body, but his wife does."[130] St. Caesarius agreed with Augustine that married women should denounce their wandering husbands secretly to a priest, rather than making a complaint to public authorities.[131]

Adultery also became a more serious crime in civil law during the Christian Empire than previously. The *Lex Iulia de adulteriis*, as we have seen, had treated adultery largely as a private matter and exclusively as a female crime. Under Constantine both of these things changed. Adultery became a public

[125] Caesarius of Arles, *Serm.* 44.1, in CCL 103:196; Basil, *Epist.* 199.26, in PG 32:724; Fulgentius of Ruspa, *Epist.* 1.10, in CCL 91:192.

[126] Basil, *Epist.* 199.25, in PG 32:724.

[127] Caesarius of Arles, *Serm.* 41.3, in CCL 103:182.

[128] John Chrysostom, *De verbis illis apostoli*, "*Propter fornicationes autem unusquisque suam uxorem habeat*," 4, in PG 51:213–14; Basil, *Epist.* 199.21, in PG 32:721.

[129] Augustine, *Serm.* 392.4, in PL 39:1711: "Nolite viros vestros permittere fornicari. Interpellate contra illos Ecclesiam. Non dico, judices publicos, non proconsulem, non vicarium, non comitem, non imperatorem; sed Christum."

[130] Augustine, *Serm.* 392.4, in PL 39:1712.

[131] Caesarius of Arles, *Serm.* 142.2, in CCL 103:186.

crime, and heinous cases became punishable by death.[132] Lesser punishments were assigned for less serious offenses. In addition, as we have already noted, while adultery by the wife had long constituted grounds for divorce, a law of Theodosius and Valentinian in 449 made adultery by the husband also a legitimate basis for divorce.[133] The Christian emperors broadened the definition of adultery to include offenses other than marital infidelity. A law of Valentinian II in 388, for example, defined marriage between Christian and Jew as adultery and allowed anyone to lay an accusation on this charge before the magistrates.[134]

In his treatise *On Marriage and Concupiscence*, St. Augustine dealt with the question of whether a man guilty of adultery should be allowed to remarry. Augustine noted that civil law allowed a man whose wife had left him to marry another, but added that ecclesiastical law classified such a marriage as adultery. When the first spouse died, however, Augustine was prepared to allow the partners in adultery to marry each other.[135]

PROSTITUTION

The legislation of the Christian emperors dealing with prostitution made few changes in the earlier law on the subject. Constantine declared it illegal to place in a brothel Christian women who had dedicated themselves to virginity. He also deprived senators and other upper-class men who had children by prostitutes of their public honors and dignities.[136] But in general Constantine's attitude toward prostitutes was one of benign contempt. Loose women, he observed in a rescript of 326, should be spared judicial severity, because the vileness of their lives placed them beneath the law's concern.[137] It is characteristic of his pragmatic approach to prostitution that Constantine designated a section of his new capital city, Constantinople, as an official red-light district and required all of the city's harlots to remain within its confines.

Moral reprobation, social contempt, and practical toleration were the hallmarks of Constantine's policies on prostitution and these attitudes characterized imperial law throughout the history of the Christian empire.[138] Later rulers took some actions to ameliorate the situation of women who had been

[132] Cod. 9.9.29(30).4 (326); Winfield E. Ohlson, "Adultery: A Review," *Boston University Law Review* 17 (1937) 337.

[133] Cod. 5.17.8.2; Henryk Insadowski, "Quid momenti habuerit Christianismus ad ius romanum matrimoniale evolvendum," in *Acta Congressus iuridici internationalis* (Rome: Pontificium Institutum Utriusque Iuris, 1935–37) 2:75.

[134] Cod. 1.9.6; Noonan, "Novel 22," p. 74.

[135] Augustine, *De nupt. et concup.* 1.9.10, in CSEL 42:221–22; Gottlob, "Ehebruch," pp. 338–39.

[136] Cod. Theod. 15.8.1; Cod. 5.27.1 pr. (336); Paul Lacroix, *History of Prostitution among All the People of the World from the Most Remote Antiquity to the Present Day*, trans. Samuel Putnam, 2 vols. (New York: Covici, 1931) 2:187.

[137] Cod. 9.9.28(29): "[H]ae autem immunes ab iudiciaria severitate praestentur, quas vilitas vitae dignas legum observatione non credidit."

[138] Herter, "Soziologie," p. 110; Noonan, "Novel 22," pp. 82–83.

forced into prostitution. Theodosius II and Leo I restrained fathers and owners of slave girls from forcing them into prostitution and delegated to bishops the power to intervene in cases where a prostitute petitioned for release from involuntary servitude in a brothel.[139] At least until 439, however, prostitution remained a source of tax revenue for the imperial government.[140]

In the West, St. Augustine formulated the classical Christian rationale for a policy of practical toleration toward prostitution. Augustine noted in his *De ordine* that prostitution was an evil, but an evil that was necessary for the preservation of the social structure and the orderly conduct of civic life. "If you remove harlots from society," he predicted, "you will disrupt everything because of lust."[141] He reasoned that if prostitution vanished, sexual passion and desire would prompt men to turn their lustful attentions to respectable matrons and other virtuous women. He felt that governments should tolerate the evil of prostitution, rather than risk the even more serious evils that would follow its repression. Augustine's attitude toward prostitution contrasts strikingly with his uncompromising opposition to other forms of irregular sexual behavior. His treatment of prostitution probably reflects his class bias and indicates that his identification with the established order of Roman society was in this instance stronger and more compelling than his views on sexual morality.

Patristic writers cannot be accused, however, of lenience toward prostitution. Sex with a prostitute was a serious moral wrong, St. Ambrose maintained; he saw no excuse in pleas that intercourse with a harlot was merely answering a demand of nature. Sexual relations with anyone outside of marriage were wrong and grievously sinful. To consort with harlots was to indulge in wantonness, he believed. Ambrose's position typified that of other patristic writers.[142]

Prostitutes themselves, according to the Fathers, sinned each time they had intercourse with a client. The only way that a harlot could hope to merit salvation was to renounce her trade and to do penance for her past offenses. St. John Chrysostom, commenting on Matt. 21:32, pointed out that although Jesus had told the Pharisees that "Publicans and prostitutes will precede you into the kingdom of God," the Gospel promise applied only to those prostitutes who renounced their evil lives. But Chrysostom took care to reiterate the Gospel message that the reformed prostitute was eligible for heaven. He then regaled his audience with a cautionary tale about a wicked whore from Phoenicia who,

[139] Cod. 1.4.12, 14 (456); 11.41.6 (428).

[140] Nov. Theod. 18.1; Adolf Berger, *Encyclopedic Dictionary of Roman Law*, s.v. "meretrix," *Transactions of the American Philosophical Society*, n.s., vol. 43, pt. 2 (Philadelphia: American Philosophical Society, 1953), p. 581. On the origin of this tax see Suetonius, *Vitae caesarum*, Caligula 40, ed. Rolfe 1:466–68.

[141] Augustine, *De ordine* 2.4.12, in PL 32:1000: "Aufer meretrices de rebus humanis, turbaveris omnia libidinibus: constitue matronarum loco, labe ac dedecore dehonestaveris." Bloch, *Prostitution* 1:640.

[142] Ambrose, *De Abraham* 2.11.78, in PL 14:494; Dooley, *Marriage According to St. Ambrose*, p. 29.

"in our own days," had been overcome by remorse for her evil life, embraced a life of chastity, and saved many others by her example.[143]

INCEST AND RAPE

The fourth- and fifth-century Christian emperors made only minor alterations in the law concerning incest and rape; the changes seem to reflect broad considerations of social policy, rather than specifically Christian viewpoints.[144] Marriage prohibitions were extended in 355 to bring marriage of a woman to her brother-in-law under the incest ban, a change that affected observant Jews who still obeyed the Mosaic precepts on levirate marriage.[145] Indeed, Theodosius the Great in 393 forbade Jews to follow their traditional marriage law.[146] Other marriage limitations introduced by Constantine were designed to preserve class distinctions and to prevent conflicts of interest, rather than to promote specifically religious restrictions on marriage rights.[147]

As for rape, the principal innovation in the law under Constantine involved defining this crime as a public offense rather than as a private wrong. The victim of criminal rape might be punished along with the perpetrator. A woman who consented to abduction and carnal relations with her abductor—in other words a woman who was a willing party to an elopement—was to be burned to death along with her abductor. A woman who was abducted and ravished against her will was punished, but less severely, on the theory that she should have prevented the incident altogether by more vigorous resistance and hence was in some sense an accomplice, even if a reluctant one. Constantine's legislation also prohibited for the first time subsequent marriage between the abductor and his victim. Even if both the woman and her family subsequently agreed to marriage, it was held to be void.[148] To these public penalties, the Council of Chalcedon in 451 added further ecclesiastical ones; if the abductor was a cleric, he was to be deposed from office; if he was a layman, he was anathematized.[149]

---

[143] John Chrysostom, *In Matthaeum homilia* 67(68).3, in PG 58:636–37. St. Pelagia the Harlot and St. Mary the Harlot are two other reformed prostitutes whose careers were publicized respectively by James the Deacon and St. Ephraim of Syria; see Helen Waddell, *The Desert Fathers* (London: Constable, 1936; repr. Ann Arbor: University of Michigan Press, 1957), pp. 173–201.

[144] JoAnn McNamara and Suzanne F. Wemple, "Marriage and Divorce in the Frankish Kingdom," in Susan Mosher Stuard, ed., *Women in Medieval Society* (Philadelphia: University of Pennsylvania Press, 1976), p. 98.

[145] Cod. Theod. 3.12.1; cf. Cod. 5.5.5 (393).

[146] Cod. 1.9.7; Noonan, Novel 22," p. 79.

[147] Cod. 9.10.1; 9.11.1.

[148] Cod. Theod. 9.24.1.2.–3; Cod. 9.13.1; Pauly-Wissowa 12/1:250; Esmein, *Mariage* 1.391; Berger, *Encyclopedic Dictionary*, s.v. "Raptus," p. 667; Bride, "Rapt," col. 1666; Pomeroy, *Goddesses, Whores, Wives, and Slaves*, pp. 160–61.

[149] Council of Chalcedon (451) c. 27, in COD, pp. 69–70.

DEVIANT SEXUAL PRACTICES

The Christian emperors showed themselves bolder and more innovative in their legislation concerning sexual behavior, heterosexual or homosexual, which they considered deviant. In a tortuously worded decree of 342 the emperors Constantius and Constans prohibited sexual relations between man and wife in any fashion that did not involve penetration of the vagina by the penis. The intent, clearly enough, was to outlaw anal and oral sex between married persons, as well as other kinds of deviant sexuality.[150]

The early fifth-century *Mosaicarum et Romanorum legum collatio*, which sought to demonstrate that traditional Jewish law was compatible with Roman civil law, made a particular point of contending that homosexual activity was contrary to both legal traditions. Title five of the *Collatio* juxtaposed excerpts from the Torah with selections from Roman law sources in such a way as to construct a condemnation.[151]

This condemnation echoed the sentiments of the leading Church Fathers of the period. Augustine's verdict on all types of "unnatural" intercourse, heterosexual or homosexual, was that these morbid doings had no place either between a man and woman united in Christian marriage or, a fortiori, between persons of either sex outside of it. Augustine considered that deviant sexual practices could only be motivated by a quest for venereal pleasure. Since such conduct foreclosed even the possibility of procreation, it lacked any redeeming qualities and deserved the severest condemnation.[152]

Other writers were concerned about effeminacy among Christian men and taught that those who dressed like women or used feminine gestures or accoutrements should be forced to cease these offensive displays.[153] The Council of Gangra echoed the Deuteronomic prohibition of cross-dressing and forbade members of either sex to adopt the clothing styles peculiar to the other. The prohibition was directed not only against persons with deviant sexual preferences, but also against "holy transvestites," that is, pious women who disguised themselves as men in order to join male ascetic and monastic communities.[154]

---

[150] Cod. 9.9.30(31) (342).

[151] *Mosaicarum et romanarum legum collatio*, in *Fontes iuris romani antejustiniani*, Ed. Salvatore Riccobono, et al., 3 vols. (Florence: G. Barbera, 1940–43) 2:556–57. Title 5 begins with a paraphrase of Lev. 20:13 and joins with it a fragment from Paulus, *Sententiae* 2.12–13, forbidding the seduction of free boys, and a decree of Valentinian, Theodosius, and Arcadius (390) from Cod. Theod. 9.7.6, prohibiting homosexual brothels and prescribing the death penalty for passive homosexual intercourse. Given the deliberate conjunction of these passages under the rubric *De stupratoribus*, it seems reasonable to conclude that the compiler of the *Collatio* understood these laws to prohibit homosexual relations of all kinds.

[152] Augustine, *De nupt. et concup.* 1.8.9, in CSEL 42:220–21; *De bono coniugali* 11.12, in CSEL 41:203–04.

[153] Cyprian, *Epist.* 2.1–2, in CSEL 3/2:467–69.

[154] Council of Gangra (before 341) c. 13, in Mansi 2:1101; cf. Deut. 22:5; JoAnn

MASTURBATION AND SEXUAL FANTASIES

A new theme in Christian writing and thinking about sexual behavior during the fourth and fifth centuries dealt with masturbation and sexual fantasies. Neither pagan nor early Christian writers had paid much attention to these matters and apparently considered them trivial. With the rise in popularity and importance of monasticism and Christian asceticism during the generations following Constantine, however, writers on monastic discipline began treating masturbation and sexual fantasies, both conscious and unconscious, as serious moral problems.

St. John Cassian considered masturbation and nocturnal pollution central issues in sexual morality and devoted a great deal of attention to both matters. He considered nocturnal emission a critical problem because he believed that the frequency of erotic dreams and of nocturnal erections and emissions were indices of lust. A monk or hermit, he reasoned, might be able to overcome overt sexual temptations, but if he continued to experience sexual fantasies in dreams, and if he continued to have seminal emissions during sleep, then he had not yet overcome carnal lust. Hence, both his religious life and his salvation might well be in peril. But the monk who freed himself completely from these experiences had achieved a real victory over fleshly desires and consequently could be certain that he was on the right path to salvation.[155]

St. Caesarius of Arles agreed. Sexual fantasies and dreams, he warned, were insidious manifestations of lust that crept into the thoughts even of good and honest Christians and subverted morality from within. Sexual arousal, even if undesired, indicated that all was not well with the spiritual health of the individual. Caesarius considered any sexual longing, to say nothing of deliberate self-stimulation, a serious sin and placed it on an even footing with adultery or excessive indulgence in sex by married persons.[156] You can no more dwell on sexual thoughts during sleep without suffering moral damage, Caesarius warned, than you can hold on to burning coals without charring your flesh.[157]

If unwanted sexual fantasies were sinful, even worse were thoughts about

---

McNamara, "Muffled Voices: The Lives of Consecrated Women in the Fourth Century," in *Medieval Religious Women*, vol. 1, Distant Echoes, ed. John A. Nichols and Lillian Thomas Shank, Cistercian Studies Series, no. 71 (Kalamazoo, MI: Cistercian Publications, 1984), pp. 23–24.

[155] John Cassian, *De institutis coenobiorum et de octo principalium uitiorum remediis* 6.1–13, in CSEL 17:113–23, and *Conlationes* 22.1–7, in CSEL 13:614–27; Foucault, "Combat de la chasteté," pp. 20–21.

[156] Caesarius of Arles, *Serm.* 177.4, in CCL 104:720.

[157] Caesarius of Arles, *Serm.* 41.5, in CCL 103:184: "Quomodo enim si aliquis carbones ignis adprehendat, si eos cito proiecerit, nihil illum nocebunt, si vero diutius tenere voluerit, sine vulnere eos iactare non poterit, ita et ille qui ad concupiscendum oculorum defixerit aspectum, et libidinis malum in corde suscipiens moras in suis cogitationibus habere permiserit, excutere eas a se sine animae plaga non poterit."

sex that were deliberately provoked by suggestive words and sights. St. John Chrysostom vigorously denounced obscene spectacles in the theaters and warned that theater-going endangered the spiritual health of Christians. Almost as bad, in Chrysostom's opinion, were images and pictures, especially those that portrayed the naked body or, worst of all, sexual relations. Such images, he warned, infallibly lead to sin and to an unquenchable thirst for forbidden pleasures, even among married persons.[158]

SEX AND THE CLERGY

Shortly before Constantine came to power, as we have seen, the Council of Elvira (or the canons that circulated under its name) had first enunciated in an authoritative way the principle that Christian clerics should be required to renounce sexual relations with their wives.[159] Although Constantine subsequently repealed earlier Roman enactments that penalized adult men who failed to marry, there is no evidence that his action was prompted by a desire to impose mandatory celibacy upon the clergy throughout the empire, and in fact he never did so. Perhaps, however, one of Constantine's purposes in revoking the anticelibacy law was to regularize the position of Christians who voluntarily remained unmarried as part of their religious discipline.[160]

Apart from Constantine's repeal of the anticelibacy laws, imperial authorities made little or no effort to implement a policy concerning clerical marriage during the fourth and fifth centuries. Indeed it was not considered irregular or scandalous for clerics to found virtual sacerdotal dynasties; St. Gregory Nazianzen (d. 374), for example, succeeded his father as bishop of his native city, while one of the legendary lives of St. Patrick identified him as the son of a deacon, who in turn was the son of a priest. Ecclesiastical authorities at that time, however, began to move increasingly in the direction of encouraging the clergy either to remain unmarried or, if already married, to abstain from sex with their wives.

Local councils and synods, especially in North Africa and Gaul, took the lead in promoting clerical celibacy. A number of African councils in the late fourth and early fifth centuries required clerics in the ranks of deacon, priest, and bishop to refrain from marital sex. A rescript of Theodosius and Honorius, however, forbade them to abandon their wives.[161] In addition, some local churches

---

[158] John Chrysostom, *Homeliae in Epist. I ad Thessal.* 4.5.4, in PG 62:428.

[159] Callam, "Clerical Continence," p. 3.

[160] Cod. 8.57.1 (320); Cassiodorus, *Historia ecclesiastica tripartita*, ed. Walter Jacob and Rudolph Hanslik, in CSEL 71:28–29; Insadowski, "Quid momenti," p. 51.

[161] *Canones in causa Apiarii* c. 3 (version 2), c. 25, c. 30 (version 2), and *Registra ecclesiae Carthaginensis excerpta* c. 70, in *Concilia Africae*, CCL 149:108–09, 117–18, 126, 201; Gregorios Presbyter, *Vita sancti patris nostri Gregorii*, in PG 35:245–48. Several sixth-century councils in Gaul adopted similar provisions; see Council of Arles (524) c. 2, Council of Clermont (535) c. 13, 3 Council of Orleans (538) c. 7, 4 Council of

demanded that clerics in minor orders either vow celibacy or else marry when they reached the age of puberty. Those who elected to marry thereafter became ineligible for promotion to higher clerical ranks and only those who chose celibacy could proceed to ordination as deacons or priests.[162]

The Council of Chalcedon in 451 adopted part of this policy and made it binding on the whole Church. The Chalcedon canon stipulated that permission for clerics in minor orders to marry was a "concession," but indicated that in future this concession should be denied, especially to men who wished to marry Jewish or pagan women or women who belonged to heretical sects.[163] Although the Chalcedon canon is not entirely free from ambiguity, its primary intention seems to have been to ensure that minor clerics married within the orthodox fold, rather than to require that they not marry at all.[164]

The bishops of Rome did not begin to take a stand on clerical celibacy until the end of the fourth century, when Pope Siricius (384–398) addressed the issue in three different decretal letters. In a letter to Bishop Himerus of Tarragona, Siricius dealt with the general question of sexual abstinence. The pope praised celibacy as a virtue, but stopped short of requiring that clerics bind themselves to sexual continence.[165] In a subsequent letter denouncing the errors of the Jovinian heretics, Siricius approached sexual abstinence not as an ascetic discipline, but rather as a matter of ritual purity. But again in this letter he refrained from pronouncing a positive command on the subject.[166] In a third letter on the topic of celibacy, this one to the bishops of Gaul, Siricius combined the ascetic and purity themes that had figured separately in his previous letters, but once more failed to cast his praise of celibacy in the form of a positive command.[167]

Tours (541) c. 17, and Council of Tours (567) c. 11, in *Concilia Galliae*, CCL 148A:43–44, 108, 117, 136, 179–81. See also Johannes Quasten, *Patrology*, 3 vols. (Westminster, MD: Newman Press; Utrecht-Brussels: Spectrum, 1950–60) 3:236–37; Lynch, "Marriage and Celibacy," pp. 26–27, 205; Brian Brennan, "'Episcopae': Bishops' Wives Viewed in Sixth-Century Gaul," *Church History* 54 (1985) 314–15.

[162] *Breviarium Hipponense* c. 18 and *Can. in Causa Apiarii* c. 17 (version 2) in *Concilia Africae*, CCL 149:38, 122.

[163] Council of Chalcedon (451) c. 14, in COD, pp. 69–70.

[164] The Church in the Eastern Empire tended, as a rule, to make clerical celibacy a matter of choice, not a requirement; Cassiodorus, *Hist. eccl. tripartita* 9.38.26, in CSEL 71:563.

[165] Pope Siricius, *Epist.* 1.7.10–11, in PL 13:1139–40 (JK 255).

[166] Pope Siricius, *Epist.* 5.3, in PL 13:1160 (JK, p. 41, s.n.); Karl Joseph von Hefele and Henri Leclercq, *Histoire des conciles d'après les documents originaux*, 9 vols. in 18 (Paris: Letouzey et Ané, 1907–31; cited hereafter as Hefele-Leclercq) 2/1:71; Nicole Grévy-Pons, *Célibat et nature: une controverse médiévale*, Textes et études du Centre d'histoire des sciences et des doctrines, vol. 1 (Paris: Centre National de la Recherche Scientifique, 1975), pp. 11–12.

[167] Pope Siricius, *Epist.* 10.2.5, in PL 13:1184 (not in JK). Brennan, "'Episcopae',"

Fourth- and fifth-century councils reiterated earlier bans on the remarriage of clerics whose first wives had died; they likewise barred clerics who had married widows from promotion to higher office, a policy that Pope Siricius also favored.[168] These actions appear to have been predicated on the belief that remarriage was likely to be motivated largely by a desire to continue enjoying sex, a desire that was thought unseemly in a cleric; they also assumed that marriage to a previously married woman violated St. Paul's dictum in 1 Tim. 3:2 that a bishop should be the husband of one wife. The prohibition is reminiscent of a similar rule concerning the marriages of the Roman *flamines* of Jupiter.[169]

Another issue that prompted conciliar action during this period concerned living arrangements in which clerics shared a dwelling with women and the institution of "spiritual marriage." The first Council of Nicaea in 325 forbade bishops, priests, and other clerics to keep any woman in their households, "save perhaps for a mother or sister or aunt or such other person as may be immune from suspicion."[170] The Nicene canon was repeated in North Africa in the fifth century with special reference to widows, nuns, or other consecrated virgins who might dwell under the same roof with a cleric. All such suspect living arrangements were prohibited. Similar provisions were incorporated into the civil law in 420.[171] The Council of Carthage in the mid-fourth century further required that nuns and other women who had vowed chastity must live in strict segregation from laypersons of either sex, but especially from men. The Council applied similar rules to widows and widowers who had promised to remain unmarried after the deaths of their spouses.[172]

Local synods in Spain also adopted canons imposing penalties upon clerics who committed adultery and upon consecrated women who were guilty of for-

---

p. 312, asserts that these letters enunciated an "official policy of the Western Church," but the texts themselves are hortatory and stop short of establishing legal norms.

[168] 1 Council of Toledo (400) c. 3–4, in Vives, *Concilios Visigóticos*, pp. 20–21; Council of Thele (418) c. 4–5, in *Concilia Africae*, CCL 149:61; Pope Siricius, *Epist* 1.8.12 and 5.2.4–5, in PL 13:1141–42 (JK 255 and 258).

[169] See above, pp. 36–37.

[170] 1 Nicaea (325) c. 3, in COD, p. 6: "Interdixit per omnia magna synodus, nec episcopo nec presbytero nec alicui prorsus, qui est in clero, licere subintroductam habere mulierem, nisi forte matrem aut sororem aut amitam vel eas tantum personas quae suspicionem effugiunt." Cf. Cod. 1.3.19.

[171] *Breviarium Hipponense* c. 16, 24, in *Concilia Africae* CCL 149:38, 40; Cod. 1.3.19; Lynch, "Marriage and Celibacy," pp. 18–19; McNamara, "Muffled Voices," pp. 16–17, 20–21.

[172] Council of Carthage (345 ~ 348) c.3–4, in *Concilia Africae*, CCL 149:5–6; John Chrysostom, *Adversus virgines subintroductae* and *Quod regulares feminae viris cohabitare non debeant*, in PG 47:495–532; JoAnn McNamara, "Chaste Marriage and Clerical Celibacy," in Vern L. Bullough and James A. Brundage, *Sexual Practices and the Medieval Church* (Buffalo, NY: Prometheus, 1982), pp. 72–85.

nication.[173] These actions paralleled measures adopted by civil authorities during the same period.[174]

Sexuality and the Law under Justinian

On 13 February 528, the East Roman Empire's recently created ruler, Justinian (527–65), appointed a ten-man commission, headed by his learned legal adviser, Tribonian, to undertake an ambitious revision of Rome's entire accumulation of laws. By the early sixth century, Roman law had grown to such colossal proportions, had become so complex, and after nearly eleven centuries of growth was so riddled with perplexities, internal contradictions, and obscurities that few jurists could readily find their way through its maze of legislation and interpretation.

The commission proceeded first to the task of revising the statutes. In April 529, little more than a year after its creation, Tribonian presented the first fruits of its labor to the emperor: a systematic revision of the statutes under the title *Codex Justinianus*, or Code of Justinian. It comprised twelve books, each subdivided into titles that dealt with the statutes on a specific topic or problem. Four years later, on 16 December 533, an enlarged commission produced a further installment: the *Digesta* (known in Greek as the *Pandekta*), a massive anthology in fifty books of authoritative opinions and interpretations concerning the law, drawn from a whole library of juristic sources. A subcommission also produced in 533 the Institutes, a compact synthesis of the basic principles of Roman law in a mere four books. In 534 a revised version of the Code supplanted the first edition. A few years after Justinian's death an anonymous compiler added a fourth work, known as the *Novellae leges*, usually called the Novels in English. The Novels comprise 158 pieces of legislation supplementing the second edition of Justinian's Code.

These four works, the Code, Digest, Institutes, and Novels, collectively comprise what later generations came to call the *Corpus iuris civilis*, by far the most significant achievement of Justinian's reign. The *Corpus* remains to this day the basic source of all study of Roman law, for, aside from the texts in the *Corpus*, only scattered remnants of the pre-Justinian law have survived. Roman law since Justinian has meant essentially the law in the shape that he and his codifiers left it. Their work has been the basis of all subsequent jurisprudence in the Roman tradition and remains fundamental to the civil law systems based upon that tradition.

Justinian was vividly aware of the importance of sex in human behavior. He confessed in one of his enactments: "We know, although we are lovers of chas-

---

[173] 1 Council of Toledo (397 ~ 400) c. 16 and 1 Council of Tarragona (516) c. 9, in Vives, *Concilios Visigóticos*, pp. 23–24, 37. The ravishment of nuns was punishable by death from 354 onward; Cod. Theod. 9.25.1–3.

[174] Cod. 1.3.5 (364), 1.19.1 (420).

tity, that nothing is more vehement than the fury of love."[175] His codification of the law reflected both his awareness and his concern about the role of sex in human affairs.

MARRIAGE

Justinian inherited a doctrine of marriage that, as we have seen, made the intentions and attitudes of the parties critical elements of the marriage contract. Justinian reaffirmed that tradition explicitly several times. "Marriages," he declared in one passage of the Code, "are not contracted by dowry arrangements but by affection."[176] But Justinian was also aware that this doctrine created formidable problems: if the essence of the marriage contract resides in the intentions and feelings of the parties, then how can one prove with certainty that a marriage has in fact taken place? More to the point, how can a judge determine whether or not a child is legitimate if he cannot offer clear proof that his parents were married, rather than simply living together as lover and concubine?

These problems disturbed Justinian and his legal advisers, as they had troubled earlier generations of Roman jurists. In 538, Justinian attempted to solve this practical difficulty by making an abrupt break with long standing tradition. In a new law of that year Justinian changed the very basis of the marriage contract: henceforth dotal instruments, written agreements concerning the property arrangements for the marriage, were to be required in every case; persons who could not produce a dotal instrument would be deemed not to be married.[177] This proved to be a short-lived experiment. A radical break with the past, it cast doubt on the legal status of too many people to be a feasible reform. Accordingly, four years later Justinian partially altered the basic marriage law once again. In Novel 117 he ordered that citizens of the highest social ranks must contract marriages in future through written dotal agreements. Others were not forbidden to use dotal instruments as proof of their marriages, but were not required to do so. Persons of lower social rank might continue to marry "by affection alone," and their marriages would be held valid and their children legitimate.[178]

DIVORCE

Justinian's divorce policy, like his marriage policy, underwent gradual modification throughout his reign. His divorce legislation, in general, tended to in-

[175] Nov. 74.4 pr. (538); Noonan, "Novel 22," p. 55. The phrase is borrowed from Plato, *Laws* 839A.

[176] Cod. 5.17.11 (533): "Non enim dotibus, sed affectu matrimonia contrahuntur." See also Inst. 1.9.1; Nov. 22.3 (536); Emilio Albertario, "Honor matrimonii e affectio maritalis," in his *Studi di diritto romano*, 6 vols. (Milan: A. Giuffrè, 1933–53) 1:201; John T. Noonan, Jr., "Marital Affection in the Canonists," *Studia Gratiana* 12 (1967) 482–89.

[177] Nov. 74.3–4; Wolff, *Written and Unwritten Marriages*, p. 1.

[178] Nov. 117.4–6.

crease restrictions upon divorce, but there is no evidence that he considered marriage indissoluble or that he believed that marriage was a sacrament. His earliest divorce legislation in 533 amplified the grounds on which divorce could be obtained. This enactment specified that a man could divorce his wife if she procured an abortion, attempted marriage with another man, or made a habit of bathing in the company of men other than her husband.[179] Beyond this, Justinian also provided that a man might unilaterally abrogate his marriage by becoming a monk or hermit. This action did not technically terminate the marriage, even though it involved a legally sanctioned separation and also brought into force any prior agreement between the spouses concerning the division of property at the death of one of them. Justinian was also concerned to outlaw fraudulent divorces sought by married offspring who wished to gain control of property settled on them by their parents. For this reason he prohibited divorces without the consent of the parents of the parties, provided of course that at least one parent was still living.[180]

Justinian's next major divorce legislation was the complex and lengthy Novel 22 of 536. Novel 22 was particularly significant because it was based on the explicit premise that marriage was dissoluble. "In human affairs," Justinian declared, "whatever is bound can be dissolved," and marriage was a human affair.[181] Novel 22 outlined four possible avenues for terminating a marriage while both parties were still alive. A couple could dissolve their marriage either by mutual consent, or on grounds that Justinian refers to as "good grace," or for reasonable cause that was not "good grace," or without any grounds at all.[182] The law dealt no further with divorce by mutual consent, since in Justinian's eyes that was the business of the parties themselves. He disapproved of divorce without stated cause and required that in contested cases some justification be shown for the action. The bulk of Novel 22 then dealt with reasonable grounds for divorce and attempted to differentiate the acceptable ones from the unacceptable. Acceptable causes included inability to have sexual relations, capture or disappearance of one party during battle, adultery, homicide, grave-robbery, political conspiracy, sorcery, aiding and abetting bandits, attending the theater, dining, or bathing with other men, or spending the night away from home without permission of the husband, and activities that endangered the life of the spouse.[183]

[179] Cod. 5.17.11.2; Visky, "Divorce," pp. 249–50, 260; Noonan, "Novel 22," p. 90.

[180] Cod. 5.17.12 (534), reiterated in Nov. 22.19 (536); D'Ercole, "Consenso," pp. 40–41.

[181] Nov. 22.3: "Quoniam horum quae in hominibus subsequuntur, quidquid ligatur, solubile est." See also Noonan, "Novel 22," p. 57.

[182] Nov. 22.4: "Distrahuntur itaque in vita contrahentium matrimonia alia quidem consentiente utraque parte, pro quibus nihil hic dicendum est, pactis causam, sicut utrique placuerit, gubernantibus, alia vero per occasionem rationabilem, quae etiam bona gratia vocantur, alia vero citra omnem causam, alia quoque cum causa rationabili." See also Noonan, "Novel 22," pp. 58–59, and Visky, "Divorce," pp. 250–52.

[183] Nov. 22.6–16.

Justinian returned to divorce law once more seven years later when he published Novel 117. This enactment, which like Novel 22 is long and complex, concerned itself primarily with the economic consequences of divorce and paid particular attention to safeguarding the interests of the children. Novel 117 also revised the acceptable grounds for divorce enumerated in Novel 22 and substantially reduced the list of reasonable causes, eliminating most of the earlier grounds that had involved criminal acts against parties other than the spouse—thus sorcery, kidnapping, robbery, and other crimes against third parties disappeared from the list. Attempted homicide remained a valid reason for divorce only when the intended victim was the husband.[184]

The new divorce law retained the grounds enumerated in Novel 22 that involved acts whereby the wife created a suspicion that she might be engaged in an adulterous affair, such as attending entertainments in the company of other men, bathing or dining with them, and the like. But, interestingly enough, Novel 117 added to the list of reasonable causes similar actions by the husband that might create a justifiable suspicion that he was having an extramarital fling—frequent visits to other woman or, far worse, keeping another woman in the matrimonial home. If a man accused his wife of adultery but was unable to prove the charge, that also became a reasonable cause for her to seek divorce under the new statute. In general, Novel 117 restricted the possibilities for divorce and made it slightly more difficult to dissolve a marriage; in no sense, however, did it enunciate or even hint at a policy of indissolubility.[185]

Justinian's later legislation introduced further departures from traditional divorce law. Novel 127 in 548, which dealt with a variety of topics, included a provision stating the principle that men and women should be treated equally in divorce matters. In particular Justinian declared that there ought to be no difference in the penalties assessed against men and women who divorced without invoking one of the grounds recognized by law.[186] In 556, Justinian made a final and radical alteration in Roman divorce law. In Novel 134, the emperor abolished the longstanding practice of divorce by mutual consent and required that parties who thenceforth wished to divorce must plead a legally recognized cause for the action. And not only did Justinian abolish consensual divorce, but he also fortified his pronouncement with a series of penalties designed to ensure its demise.[187]

This repeal of consensual divorce lasted only a decade. After Justinian's death

[184] Nov. 117.8; Noonan, "Novel 22," pp. 65–67.

[185] Nov. 117.9; Noonan, "Novel 22," p. 68; Visky, "Divorce," pp. 253–56.

[186] Nov. 127.4: "Quia vero interdiximus dudum per nostram legem et viris et mulieribus repudia mittere et transigere matrimonia, nisi tamen quaedam sit causa nostrae legi cognita, et poenas hoc facientibus et viris et mulieribus imposuimus, mutationem quandam circa poenas viri et mulieris facientes et ad melius hoc transformantes sancimus, nullam esse differentiam quantum ad poenas inter virum et mulierem hoc praesumentes. . . . In delicto enim aequali proximas eis imminere poenas iustum putavimus esse." See also Noonan, "Novel 22," pp. 68, 90.

[187] Nov. 134.11; Noonan, "Novel 22," pp. 69–70; D'Ercole, "Consenso," p. 36.

his successor, Justin II (565–578) reinstated the consensual procedure. Justin noted that the abolition of divorce by mutual consent had created severe problems. Many persons had approached him, Justin declared, with complaints about the battles and struggles that raged in their homes because they were unable to prove that they had legal grounds for divorce. Marriages often deteriorated, he noted, because of irrational passions and hatreds, not because of any reasonable cause. In view of the complaints and petitions that had been submitted to him Justin decreed that the old practice of divorce by mutual consent should be reinstated. Justin also abolished the penalties that Justinian had attached to the practice, observing that if marriage was created by mutual affection, it seemed reasonable that it should be dissolved when affection died.[188]

The development of divorce law in Justinian's *Corpus*, then, was neither simple nor consistent. The early sixth century was a time of experimentation. Legislators were struggling to reconcile the contention of Christian doctrinal writers that couples should remain married for life with the practical realities of civil society and the Roman tradition of consensual marriage and consensual divorce. While the Church's spokesmen were successful in winning some slight modifications of the law to suit their doctrinal preferences, the reluctance—sometimes the inability—of Justinian and his successor to accommodate the views of the more rigorous moralists was also notable. Certainly the imperial government did not enact into law the comprehensive marriage and divorce policy that patristic writers advocated. This suggests that governmental policy may have reflected a reluctance on the part of many Christians, perhaps even a majority, to conform to the doctrinal views of a relatively small Christian intelligentsia on sensitive issues of family law.[189]

CONCUBINAGE

Other aspects of Justinian's law dealing with sexual behavior also suggest that the emperor was sometimes reluctant to adopt views urged upon him by his ecclesiastical advisers. While contemporary Christian moralists, as we have seen, deplored concubinage and equated it with fornication and prostitution,

[188] Nov. 140: "Plurimi autem nos adierunt inter se coniugium horrentes et abominantes et proelia discordiasque propter hoc domi contingere accusantes . . . dissolvere propter hoc precantes connubia . . . . quoniam vero difficile est inmutare semel detentos inrationabili passione et horrore . . . . Haec igitur aliena nostris iudicantes temporibus, in praesenti sacram constituimus legem, per quam sancimus licere ut antiquitus consensu coniugium solutiones nuptiarum fieri . . . . Si enim in alterutrum adfectus nuptias solidat, merito contraria voluntas istas cum consensu dissolvit . . . ." See also Noonan, "Novel 22," p. 70.

[189] D'Ercole, "Consenso," pp. 68–73, paints a far more glowing picture of the Church's success in remodeling imperial marriage doctrine to conform to ecclesiastical teachings than the evidence seems to warrant. Nor am I convinced by Lefebvre's assertions about doctrinal consistency among Christian writers during this period on the subject of divorce; see his "Origines et évolution," p. 24.

none of this appears in Justinian's legislation. While he did make major changes in the law dealing with concubinage, Justinian's legislation tended to improve the legal position of the concubine and her children, and the emperor refused to subject them to additional penalties, as the rigorists urged. Under Justinian concubinage was instead raised to virtual parity with marriage.[190]

In 528 and again in 529, Justinian liberalized the law relating to the inheritance rights of concubines and their children, especially by granting natural children the right to inherit up to one-half of their father's estate, as well as to succeed to property held by their mothers. The latter provision also enabled the father to increase the portion of his estate that his natural children would ultimately receive.[191] The concubine's situation improved further in 531 as a result of legislation that forbade the heirs of a deceased man to hold his concubine and her children in servitude, as earlier law had allowed.[192] Five years later, the right of concubines and their children to succeed to intestate estates was further enlarged.[193] In 539, Justinian granted them additional property rights, to the point that the status of a concubine and her children was only marginally different from that of a legitimate wife and her children.[194]

Justinian's legislation on concubinage reflected ecclesiastical advice only slightly. His repeated insistence that concubinage must be permanent and that men must not have more than one concubine at a time clearly accords with the views of Christian authorities.[195] For the rest, Justinian's legislation on concubinage was in no specific sense Christian. Tomulescu has shown analogs in pagan Greco-Roman and Syro-Roman sources, making it plain that Justinian in this area of legislative activity was influenced as much or more by non-Christian practices as by Christian ones.[196]

[190] C. S. Tomulescu, "Justinien et le concubinat," in *Studi in onore di Gaetano Scherillo* 1:301–02, succinctly outlines the scholarly disagreements on the importance and originality of Justinian's legislation on concubinage. See also Caselli, "Concubina pro uxore," pp. 170–72; Gabriel Le Bras, "Observations sur le mariage dans le corpus justinien et dans le droit classique de l'église," in *Etudes offertes à Jean Macqueron* (Aix-en-Provence: Faculté de droit et des sciences économiques, 1970), p. 427; Albertario, "Honor matrimonii," p. 204; Pietro Bonfante, "Nota sulla riforma giustinianea del concubinato," in *Studi in onore di Silvio Perozzi nel XL anno del suo insegnamento* (Palermo: G. Castiglia, 1925), p. 284; Castelli, "Concubinato," p. 68; Wolff, *Written and Unwritten Marriages*, pp. 98–99; Jombart, "Concubinage," cols. 1513–14; Laurent Chevailler, "Observations sur le droit de bâtardise dans la France coutumière du XIIIe au XVe siècle," RHDF, 4th ser., 35 (1957) 379; Olis Robleda, *El matrimonio en derecho romano: esencia, requisitos de validez, efectos, disolubilidad* (Rome: Università Gregoriana, 1970), p. 280.

[191] Cod. 5.27.8; 6.57.5.2; Baumann, *Zivilrechtliche Bedeutung*, p. 15.

[192] Cod. 7.15.3.

[193] Nov. 18.5 (536).

[194] Nov. 89.2–6.

[195] Cod. 7.15.3 pr.; Nov. 18.5; Tomulescu, "Justinien et le concubinat," pp. 324–26.

[196] Tomulescu, "Justinien et le concubinat," pp. 310–16.

SEX OFFENSES

Justinian's legislative record on sex crimes was rather mixed. He made it even more difficult for a cuckolded husband to kill his straying wife and her lover with legal impunity. Under the terms of Novel 117 (542), the husband must give three written warnings to the adulteress and her consort, each warning attested by three credible witnesses. If, after the third warning, the husband subsequently surprised his wife and her paramour in the husband's own house, in his wife's house, in the adulterer's house, or in a tavern, then the husband might slay the adulterer. The husband was still liable to the penalties for murder, however, if he killed his wife, although he could prosecute her for the crime of adultery.[197] Alternatively the husband had the right under a later constitution to beat his adulterous wife and to confine her in a convent. If he relented within two years, he could take her back; if he did not, she was obliged to become a nun.[198] A married man who committed adultery escaped with much milder penalties: he lost his rights to the dowry property and the nuptial gifts, both of which passed to his wife. She also had the right to bring a divorce action against him.[199]

Rape presented altogether different problems, and Justinian dealt with it more sternly than his predecessors had done. In a major statute of 533, he prescribed the death penalty for those convicted of abducting or ravishing any woman, whether slave, free, married, single, betrothed or not, dedicated to God, or living in the world. The penalty extended to accomplices in the act or in preparations for it; the family of the victim had the right to inflict the penalty if they apprehended the culprit in the act. The abduction or ravishment of a betrothed woman by her fiancé was likewise subject to the death penalty. If the victim was a lower-class woman the death penalty might be replaced by forfeiture of the property of the culprit and his accomplices to the family of the victim. If the perpetrator was a slave, he was to be burned alive.[200] Men who abducted or ravished nuns or other consecrated women were subject both to the death penalty and to confiscation of all their property, which was to be turned over to the victim's religious house.[201] Imperial officials were instructed to take special pains to pursue and capture rapists who fled and to ensure that they were remanded to the courts for punishment.[202]

In addition, Justinian in 533 made rape or abduction of a woman an impediment to marriage, even if the family of the victim subsequently agreed to the union. Here Justinian was evidently concerned with elopement rather than with forcible sexual assault:

[197] Nov. 117.15; Noonan, "Novel 22," pp. 67–68.
[198] Nov. 134.10 (556); Noonan, "Novel 22," pp. 68–69.
[199] Nov. 134.10 pr.
[200] Cod. 9.13.1 pr., 1, 3–5.
[201] Cod. 1.3.53(54) pr., 1, 3–5.
[202] Cod. 1.3.53(54).2.

Our Serenity will not in any way at any time agree to give a license to allow persons within our jurisdiction to contract marriage through hostile actions [the emperor declared]. It is proper that whoever wishes to take a wife, whether she be free or freed, should do so according to our law and ancient custom by asking permission from her parents or other appropriate persons and marrying with their consent.[203]

This law was apparently not successful in discouraging marriage by abduction, however, and thirty years later Justinian reiterated the policy in a further enactment, which he subsequently published yet again.[204] He also repeated, without elaboration, the criminal penalties of the old *Lex Iulia* against fornication with unmarried women and widows.[205]

PROSTITUTION

Prostitution was another facet of sexual conduct in which Justinian took an active interest. His concern was possibly related to his wife's earlier career as an actress, for his consort, Theodora, was also said to have been a prostitute prior to their marriage. Justinian sometimes speaks in his legislation in tones that express a surprising depth of feeling about the prostitute's situation. In an enactment of 535, he described in graphic terms the panderers who prowl through the provinces in quest of young girls who live in poverty and the wiles with which procurers deceive their victims by enticing them with shoes and clothes to come to the capital city. Once there, the emperor continued, they place the girls in bawdy houses, supply them with wretched food and ragged dresses, and turn them over to the lusts of any strangers who happen along. The whole passage has a ring of firsthand knowledge and personal emotion uncommon in legislative acts.[206]

---

[203] Cod. 9.13.1.2: "Nec sit facultas raptae virgini vel viduae vel cuilibet mulieri raptorem suum sibi maritum exposcere, sed cui parentes voluerint excepto raptore, eam legitimo copulant matrimonio, quoniam nullo modo nullo tempore datur a nostra serenitate licentia eis consentire, qui hostili more in nostra re publica matrimonium student sibi coniungere. Oportet enim ut, quicumque uxorem ducere voluerit sive ingenuam sive libertinam, secundum nostras leges et antiquam consuetudinem parentes vel alios quos decet petat et cum eorum voluntate fiat legitimum coniugium."

[204] Nov. 143, 150 (both 563).

[205] Inst. 4.18.4.

[206] Nov. 14 pr.: "Agnovimus enim quosdam vivere quidem illicite, ex causis autem crudelibus et odiosis occasionem sibimet nefandorum invenire lucrorum, et circuire provincias et loca plurima et iuvenculas miserandas decipere promittentes calciamenta et vestimenta quaedam, et his venari eas et deducere ad hanc felicissimam civitatem et habere constitutas in suis habitationibus et cibum eis miserandum dare et vestem et deinceps tradere ad luxuriam eas volentibus, et omnem quaestum miserabilem ex corpore earum accedentem ipsos accipere et celebrare conscriptiones, quia usque ad tempus, quod eis placuerit, observabunt impiam et scelerem hanc functionem implentes;

Far more than any of his predecessors, Justinian took active measures to protect women from involuntary impressment into a life of prostitution. If a master forced his servant girl to prostitute herself, according to a constitution of 531, the girl was to be freed and the master lost all rights over her.[207] In 534, Justinian required bishops to see that servant girls and others were not forced into careers as actresses or prostitutes. Should they find such women in their dioceses, the bishops were to see to it that they were freed and allowed to marry if they wished. Bishops were even empowered to overrule provincial governors in these cases.[208] In his constitution of 534 on prostitution, Justinian went further still. He prohibited the keeping of brothels and the practice of pandering within the city of Constantinople. The emperor imposed a heavy fine—ten pounds of gold—on those who operated houses of pleasure, forbade anyone to take money from prostitutes, and ordered pimps to be expelled from Constantinople.[209]

In addition to his legislation to repress prostitution and to penalize those who profited from the trade, Justinian also inaugurated a scheme to reform the prostitutes of his capitol. At the urging of Theodora, Justinian built a hospice, the Convent of Repentance, on the bluffs above the Sea of Marmora opposite the city, to serve as a refuge for women who wished to quit the life of sin. More than five hundred presumably repentant harlots, according to Procopius (ca. 490–ca. 562), soon found themselves confined within the convent, not all of them willingly. Some, he says, were so shattered by their enforced transformation into nuns that they leaped to their deaths from the convent walls.[210]

Homosexuality

Justinian also sought more vigorously than previous emperors to repress homosexual conduct. In the Institutes, he invoked the ban of the old *Lex Iulia* against "those who dare to practice abominable lust with men," and imposed the death penalty upon offenders.[211] In 538/539 and again in 559, Justinian returned to this topic in constitutions notable for their extravagant rhetoric. Homosexual relations, the emperor declared, are not only contrary to nature, dia-

---

quasdam vero earum etiam fideiussores expetere." Cf. the description by Procopius, *Buildings* 1.9.2–3.

[207] Cod. 6.6.1.4.

[208] Cod. 1.4.33; 5.4.29.

[209] Nov. 14.

[210] Procopius's public account in *Buildings* 1.9.5–10 contrasts sharply with the secret account in his *Anecdota* 17.5–6.

[211] Inst. 4.18.4. Boswell, CSTAH, p. 171, claims that this chapter of the Institutes was the first prohibition of homosexual practices in Roman imperial history; but Justinian's text pointedly stated that it was based on the old *Lex Iulia*: "Item lex Iulia de adulteriis coercendis, quae non solum temeratores aliarum nuptiarum gladio punit, sed etiam eos, qui cum masculis infandem libidinem exercere audet . . . ."

bolical in origin, and illegal in practice, but they also imperil the public safety, since, "Because of such offenses famine, earthquakes, and pestilence occur." Justinian therefore peremptorily commanded that such activities cease immediately. Men who had been guilty of sexual relations with other men, moreover, were to submit forthwith to ecclesiastical penance for their past deeds. Those who knew of others who had committed such actions should denounce the guilty parties to the authorities. In the second of these constitutions, Justinian expressly invoked divine authority for his legislation and pointedly referred to the Biblical account of the destruction of Sodom as a portent of the doom that faced the polity that failed to reform.[212]

Justinian's legislation also dealt with other sexual problems. In 558, he prohibited castration and the making of eunuchs, an oriental practice that had begun to fall into disfavor in the Empire.[213] While he made no attempt to impose celibacy on the clergy through direct action, he certainly tried to discourage clerics in major orders from marrying and having children; in a rescript of 530 he forbade the children of clerics to inherit from their fathers and he also inhibited them from receiving gifts from their parents as well.[214] It is arguable, however, that this rescript was as much concerned with preventing the diversion of Church property to private use as it was with the celibacy issue.

Conclusions

The sex legislation of Justinian was in many respects innovative and in some instances broke radically with past practice. His marriage laws underwent numerous changes, most of them seeking to make marriage easier to prove and hence more certain. At the same time, however, Justinian was constrained from departing too radically from the traditional concept that marriage was a private concern, a matter of intention, even of feeling, rather than of formalities. There is no evidence that he considered marriage a sacrament or that he accorded ecclesiastical authorities any special control over it. Certainly he considered marriage dissoluble, as his experiments with divorce law demonstrate. While his divorce legislation finally resulted in a tightening of the rules and restricted the grounds upon which divorce could be sought, Justinian was unable to abolish consensual divorce.

Justinian notably concerned himself with improving and enlarging legal protection for the children of divorced couples and with treating men and women more equally than earlier divorce law had permitted.[215] Justinian likewise contributed greatly to protecting and enlarging the property rights of concubines and their children. In the final analysis he made the status of the concubine closely comparable to that of the legitimate wife. Justinian likewise defended women who were forced into a life of prostitution and sought to shield them

[212] Nov. 77 pr., 1 (538/539); 141 pr., 1 (559).
[213] Nov. 142 (558).
[214] Cod. 1.3.44(45).3.
[215] Noonan, "Novel 22," p. 90.

from exploitation by pimps and madams. While he made it plain that he disapproved of prostitution, he did not vent his hostility upon the prostitute, but upon those who profited from her activities. Justinian's legislation against homosexual practices represented perhaps his most significant break with earlier sex law. Although his enactments against homosexual relations were not entirely unprecedented—as he himself pointed out—nevertheless the ancient world had not previously seen such a flat and comprehensive ban on sexual relations between men. Justinian's antihomosexual legislation is perhaps the area of his legislative activity where the influence of Christian authorities is most clearly evident.

Justinian's *Corpus* came into immediate force, however, only in that portion of the Empire (essentially its eastern half) that Justinian ruled, and few persons in Western Europe had any detailed knowledge of it for centuries after Justinian's death. Only in the eleventh and twelfth centuries did Justinian's codification become known in the West; but from that point onward the codification became the foundation for the study and teaching of law in European law faculties and enjoyed an enormous influence in shaping medieval legal systems throughout the Continent.[216]

By the time of Justinian's death, Germanic invaders had severed his realm from its former western territories. Despite energetic efforts, Justinian had been unable to reassert effective control over the Empire's former domains in the West. The Eastern Empire's government and legal system henceforth had little direct impact on institutions and events in the West. The remainder of this volume will focus, accordingly, on the law concerning sexual conduct in the West, to the virtual exclusion of eastern or Byzantine developments.

---

[216]Jolowicz, *Historical Introduction*, pp. 484–512; Kaser, *Röm. Privatrecht* 2:20–23; Barry Nicholas, *An Introduction to Roman Law* (Oxford: Clarendon Press, 1962), pp. 38–45; Buckland, *Textbook of Roman Law*, pp. 39–50; Gian Gualberto Archi, *Giustiniano legislatore* (Bologna: Il Mulino, 1970); Anthony M. Honoré and Alan Rodger, "How the Digest Commissioners Worked," ZRG, romanistische Abteilung [hereafter RA] 87 (1970) 246–314; and Anthony M. Honoré, *Tribonian* (London: Duckworth, 1978). On the disappearance of Roman law in the West during the early middle ages see Pierre Riché, *Enseignement de droit en Gaule du VIe au XIe siècle* (Milan: A. Giuffrè, 1965), vol. 1.5.B.bb of *Ius Romanum medii aevi* (Milan: A. Giuffrè, 1961– ; in progress; cited hereafter as IRMAe), pp. 4–5; Rafael Gibert, *Enseñanza del derecho in Hispania durante los siglos VI a XI*, in IRMAe 1.5.B.cc (Milan: A. Giuffrè, 1967), p. 17; and Giulio Vismara, "Le fonti del diritto romano nell'alto medioevo secondo la più recente storiografia (1955–1980)," in *Proceedings of the Sixth International Congress of Medieval Canon Law, Berkeley, California, 18 July–2 August 1980*, ed. Stephan Kuttner and Kenneth Pennington, MIC, Subsidia, vol. 7 (Città del Vaticano: Biblioteca Apostolica Vaticana, 1985; cited hereafter as *Berkeley Proceedings*), pp. 165–184.

4

Law and Sex in Early Medieval Europe, Sixth to Eleventh Centuries

The Germanic Invasions and Germanic Law

From the closing decades of the fourth century onward, the Roman Empire experienced a series of migrations in which non-Roman peoples forced their way into the imperial provinces of the West. The newcomers settled more or less permanently within the Western Empire's territories and gradually replaced Rome's administrative and legal systems with their own laws and institutions. These events are conventionally referred to as the "barbarian invasions" or the "Fall of the Roman Empire," but it should be emphasized that the incursions and the collapse were gradual processes, not abrupt, cataclysmic events. Migration and settlement took place over a period that spanned roughly three generations, and the displacement of Roman institutions happened even more gradually—so gradually, indeed, that many people who lived through these changes seem to have been unaware that the Empire had fallen at all.

It is conventional to refer to the groups who migrated into the Western Empire and settled there as "Germans" or "Barbarians." They were barbarians in the Greco-Roman sense of the term, because most of them did not speak Greek or Latin, and their customs were likewise alien to Roman sensibilities. As for their Germanic identity, the great majority of the immigrants apparently spoke tongues that fell into the family of Germanic languages, but they were by no means a homogeneous group, either in language or culture. Considerable numbers of non-Germanic people also participated in the invasions. Still, it is convenient to have some common label for the migrants as a group, and "Germanic" describes the majority of them reasonably well.

By the beginning of the sixth century, Germanic kingdoms had supplanted the highest levels of imperial government in the West. In place of a single Roman government, the West was now divided into competing successor states, ruled by Anglo-Saxons in Britain, by Franks in Gaul, by Visigoths in Spain, by Burgundians in the Rhône valley, by Ostrogoths in Italy, and by Vandals in the old Roman province of Africa.[1]

---

[1] See generally J. M. Wallace-Hadrill, *The Barbarian West, 400–1000* (London: Hutchinson's University Library, 1952); Ferdinand Lot, *The End of the Ancient World*

The Roman population of these regions, however, remained largely intact. Latin-speaking Roman Christians continued to live and work, to marry and raise families, and no doubt to worry a good deal during these decades. Nor did the displacement of Roman military power and government result in the immediate disappearance of Roman law courts, Roman traditions, or Roman social customs. Neither the immigrants nor the Romans among whom they settled had any wish to see Roman law or Roman society disappear. The Germanic settlers brought with them their own laws, customs, and traditional practices, but they did not seek to impose their law on their new neighbors; on the other hand, the Germans had no desire to adopt Roman ways, including Roman laws, as their own. As a result, the West became culturally and legally pluralistic.

Roman law and Roman law courts continued to function and to deal with problems that arose among people of Roman heritage; Germanic law and Germanic courts simultaneously handled problems that arose among people of Germanic heritage. But although both Romans and Germans preferred to retain their ethnic identities, including their laws, there was inevitably some spillover from one group to the other and from one law to the other. Roman law in the West became simplified and, especially after the disappearance of the Roman law schools, vulgarized or barbarized. At the same time, Germanic courts and rulers adopted some Roman ways of doing things. Each law influenced the other, each was modified by the other.

What little we know about Germanic folklaw prior to the migrations indicates that it was based upon two foundations: the collective responsibility of the kindred for the actions of its members and the principle of reciprocal revenge. The extended kinship group was prominent in archaic German society and remained fundamental to Germanic institutions for generations following the invasions. The kindred bore responsibility for fulfilling the obligations incurred by any of its members and for seeing to it that each member both paid what he owed and received what he had a right to. The group also tried to protect the peace and security of its members against outside interference.[2] Reciprocal revenge meant in effect that wrongs were avenged by inflicting injury upon the person responsible for the damage or, failing that, upon some other member of his or her household, or their kin.

---

and the Beginning of the Middle Ages, trans. Philip and Mariette Leon (New York: Alfred A. Knopf, 1931); J. B. Bury, *The Invasion of Europe by the Barbarians* (London: Macmillan, 1928); Robert Latouche, *Les grandes invasions et la crise d'occident au Ve siècle* (Aubier: Montaigne, 1946); Lucien Musset, *Les invasions: Les vagues germaniques* (Paris: Presses universitaires de France, 1965); Felix Dahn, *Die Völkerwanderung: germanisch-romanische Frühgeschichte* (Berlin: Safari, 1960); E. A. Thompson, *The Early Germans* (Oxford: Clarendon Press, 1965); Pierre Courcelle, *Histoire littéraire des grandes invasions germaniques* (Paris: Hachette, 1948); and Francis Owen, *The Germanic People: Their Origin, Expansion, and Culture* (New York: Bookman Associates, 1960).

[2] D. A. Bullough, "Early Medieval Social Groupings: The Terminology of Kinship," *Past and Present* 45 (1969) 3–18.

By the time that Germanic peoples began to settle in the West Roman Empire these institutional pillars of archaic Germanic law were already beginning to crumble, and the migrations hastened the pace of change. The kindred gradually lost many of its earlier functions, especially the protection of its members from wrongs done by outsiders. Increasingly Germanic kings began to assert their authority to safeguard their subjects and to intervene in quarrels and disagreements between members of the various households they ruled.

At the same time, a system of compensation for wrongs gradually replaced reciprocal revenge. Compensation was based on a calculation of the severity of the injury, usually expressed in money terms as a fraction of the *wergeld*. The amount of the *wergeld* varied according to sex and social status. In some Germanic law systems, notably that of the Salian Franks, age was also a factor in determining the *wergeld*. The king and his court determined which party had to pay and how much compensation was due in each case. Redress of grievances ceased to be the responsibility of the household and kindred; redress instead became the prerogative of king and court: successful complainants received property compensation for the damages they sustained, in lieu of taking physical revenge upon the offender.

Prior to the late fifth and early sixth centuries, Germanic law had been transmitted orally as custom from one generation to the next. Beginning in the late fifth century, Germanic kings in one region after another began to have their laws set down in writing in compilations that we usually refer to as the Germanic law codes. The codes that originated on the Continent were written in Latin; those from England, Iceland, and Scandinavia were usually written in the local vernaculars. These compilations furnish us for the first time with detailed evidence about the laws that Germanic courts were supposed to enforce. Germanic kings in the West, also authorized the publication of substantial extracts from Roman law texts for use among their subjects of Roman descent. These manuals of elementary Roman law document the process by which Roman jurisprudence in the West was gradually vulgarized during the generations that followed the invasions.[3]

[3]The most convenient and accessible editions of the Germanic codes are those in the *Monumenta Germaniae Historica*, Legum sectio, Leges nationum germanicarum, 5 vols. (Hannover: A. Hahn [imprint varies], 1835–1962; cited hereafter as MGH, LL nat. germ.). Recent editions of many of the codes, with German translations, can be found in the series *Germanenrechte: Texte und übersetzungen*, (Weimar, Göttingen: Akademie für deutsches Recht, 1934– ; 13 vols. to date). Four important codes are readily available in good English translations: *The Burgundian Code*, trans. Katherine Fischer Drew (Philadelphia: University of Pennsylvania Press, 1949; repr. 1972); *The Lombard Laws*, trans. Katherine Fischer Drew (Philadelphia: University of Pennsylvania Press, 1973); and *The Laws of the Alamans and Bavarians*, trans. Theodore John Rivers (Philadelphia: University of Pennsylvania Press, 1977). Earlier and less easily accessible translations of Germanic legal sources include *The Visigothic Code*, trans. S. P. Scott (Boston: Boston Book Co., 1910) and *The Laws of the Earliest English Kings*, trans. F. S. Attenborough (Cambridge: At the University Press, 1922). For texts of the Germanic manuals

Law and Sexual Behavior in the Germanic Kingdoms

Our knowledge of archaic German law dealing with sexual behavior comes mainly from a late first-century account by Tacitus, who gleaned his information secondhand from the tales of soldiers and travellers, supplemented perhaps by additional information gained from contacts with Germans who had settled within the Empire.[4] According to Tacitus, the Germans strongly disapproved of extramarital sexual adventures by their womenfolk. Women who transgressed the rules had their heads shaved, were driven from their homes, and received a public beating. There is no indication in Tacitus's account, however, that sexual adventures by men were similarly discouraged. Tacitus professed great admiration for the purity of sexual mores among Germanic women. His account implicitly contrasted their behavior with that of upper-class Roman matrons of his own time. Germans, according to him, did not allow their wives to gad about unescorted or to participate in late-night parties and drunken revels, nor did they consider adultery smart and up-to-date.[5] Tacitus portrayed the sexual habits of the Germans as upright and austere and marriage as a solemn undertaking in which monogamy was implicit, at least for women.[6]

Tacitus wrote nearly three centuries before the beginning of large-scale Germanic migrations into the West, and his account was colored by his tendency to idealize the rude and simple morality of the Germans. When our knowledge of Germanic law becomes fuller and more reliable, which is to say after the first phase of migration had ended, there had evidently been significant changes since Tacitus's time.

---

of Roman law see *Fontes iuris romani antejustiniani*, ed. Salvatore Riccobono et al., 3 vols. (Florence: G. Barbera, 1940–43) 2:655–750. See also Georges Chevrier and Georges Pieri, *La loi romain des Burgondes*, in IRMAe 1.2.b.aa.δ (Milan: A. Giuffrè, 1969); Jean Gaudemet, *Le Bréviaire d'Alaric et les Epitome*, IRMAe, vol. 1.2.b.aa.β (Milan: A. Giuffrè, 1965), and Giulio Vismara, *Edictum Theoderici*, IRMAe, vol. 1.2.b.aa.α (Milan: A. Giuffrè, 1967). On early Germanic law in general see also Hermann Conrad, *Deutsche Rechtsgeschichte: ein Lehrbuch* (Karlsruhe: C.F. Müller, 1954), vol. 1, *Frühzeit und Mittelalter*; Rudolf Hübner, *A History of Germanic Private Law*, trans. Francis L. Philbrick, Continental Legal History Series, vol. 4 (Boston: Little Brown and Co., 1918); Rudolf Buchner, *Die Rechtsquellen* (Weimar: H. Böhlaus Nachfolger, 1953), which is a supplemental volume of Wilhelm Wattenbach and Wilhelm Levison, *Deutschlands Geschichtsquellen im Mittelalter, Vorzeit und Karolinger* (Weimar: H. Böhlaus Nachfolger, 1952– ; in progress). For a brief and lucid sketch of domestic relations law in the Germanic codes see Katherine Fischer Drew, "The Law of the Family in the Germanic Kingdoms," *Studies in Medieval Culture* 11 (1977) 17–26.

[4] Ronald Syme, *Tacitus*, 2 vols. (Oxford: Clarendon Press, 1958) 1:126–28; Clarence W. Mendell, *Tacitus: The Man and His Work* (New Haven: Yale University Press, 1957), p. 216.

[5] Tacitus, *Germania* 19, ed. Rodney Potter Robinson, Philological Monographs, no. 5 (Middletown, CT: American Philological Association, 1935), pp. 295–96.

[6] Tacitus, *Germania* 18, ed. Robinson, pp. 294–95.

The Germanic law codes treat marriage as a union created by cohabitation, rather than by formal act. Marriage was a social fact, not a legal status, in fifth- and sixth-century German society.[7] Polygyny was also a common feature of Germanic domestic life, although most men probably contented themselves with a single wife because they could not afford to do otherwise. Among royal families and the upper ranks of the nobility, however, polygyny was common prior to the conversion of the Germans to Christianity. In many cases the practice persisted for several generations after conversion, and the law continued to ignore sexual promiscuity among men while penalizing it among women.[8]

Early Germanic law recognized three legitimate methods of contracting marriage: by capture (*Raubehe*), by purchase (*Kaufehe*), and by mutual consent (*Friedelehe*). Bride purchase involved an agreement between two families. An exchange of property was an essential part of *Kaufehe* and the Germanic law codes encouraged this type of marriage. Most of the codes envisioned a three-stage process of contracting *Kaufehe*. It began with an agreement (*Muntvertrag*) between the suitor or his father and the father or guardian of the prospective bride, concerning the compensation to be paid to the woman's family by the groom's family. This stage of the process corresponded more or less to *desponsatio* in Roman law. *Muntvertrag* was followed by a public transfer (*Anvertrauung*) of the bride to the head of the groom's family. This was followed by a wedding ritual (*Trauung*), during which the members of the bride's clan stood in a circle around her to witness the transfer and to signify their consent to the transaction. The process involved conveyance not only of the person of the bride to the family of the groom, but also of legal power (*Munt, mundium*) over her to the husband and his family group.[9] The bride's ties with her family of

[7]John F. Benton, "Clio and Venus: An Historical View of Medieval Love," in F.X. Newman, ed., *The Meaning of Courtly Love* (Albany, NY: State University of New York Press, 1968), p. 20; Suzanne F. Wemple, *Women in Frankish Society: Marriage and the Cloister, 500 to 900* (Philadelphia: University of Pennsylvania Press, 1981), pp. 13, 35–36; David E. Engdahl, "English Marriage Conflicts Law before the Time of Bracton," *American Journal of Comparative Law* 15 (1967) 109.

[8]Heinrich Brunner, "Die uneheliche Vaterschaft in den ältern germanischen Rechten," in his *Abhandlungen zur Rechtsgeschichte*, ed. Karl Rauch (Weimar: Bölaus, 1931; repr. Leipzig: Zentralantiquariat der DDR, 1965) 2:165; Wemple, *Women in Frankish Society*, pp. 38–40. The Visigothic laws alone among the Germanic codes forbade polygyny: *Leges Visigothorum* 3.4.9, in MGH, LL 1:150–51.

[9]Rudolf Köstler, "Raub-, Kauf- und Friedelehe bei den Germanen," ZRG, Germanistische Abteilung [hereafter GA] 63 (1943) 95–98; Brunner, "Die fränkisch-romanische Dos," in *Abhandlungen zur Rechtsgeschichte* 2:91; Christian Gellinek, "Marriage by Consent in Literary Sources of Medieval Germany," *Studia Gratiana* 12 (1967) 559; Wemple, *Women in Frankish Society*, pp. 12, 35; Baumann, *Zivilrechtliche Bedeutung*, p. 17; Burge, *Comparative Law*, pp. 10–11. Bride purchase was also common in Polish and other non-Germanic folklaw during the early middle ages; Marian Zurowski, "Einflüsse des kanonischen Rechts auf das ursprüungliche polnische Eherecht," *Oesterreichisches Archiv für Kirchenrecht* 25 (1974) 354; Sir Henry Maine, *Lectures on*

origin were, in effect, severed, and she was integrated into her husband's family. This type of union, involving active participation and control by the families of the parties, was the preferred type of marriage.

Marriage by capture or abduction (*Raubehe*) was accomplished by forcible abduction and ravishment without the consent of the woman or her family; it is therefore sometimes referred to as marriage by rape.[10] The law codes discouraged such marriages, and some of them imposed heavy fines on men who forcibly married free women.[11]

A man who did not wish to risk the legal and physical hazards of marriage by abduction and who was either too poor, too powerless, or too mean to purchase a bride had the alternative of marrying by consent. *Friedelehe* may in fact have been an outgrowth of *Raubehe*. The term *Friedelehe* designated marriage by elopement, to which the bride consented, but her family did not. It was distinguished from *Kaufehe* by the lack of a betrothal or dowry agreement and by the fact that the husband did not acquire *Munt* over his wife. In *Friedelehe* the woman's *Munt* remained with her family: she continued in effect to be a member of her family of birth, even though she lived with a man who belonged to another family.[12]

The distinction between marriage and concubinage in early Germanic society was unclear, both in practice and in law, a situation that has led some writers to claim that concubinage was unknown among the Germanic invaders. That claim, however, can only be sustained by artful definitions that distinguish marriage between free persons with full legal consequences from quasi-marriage

---

the Early History of Institutions, 7th ed. (Port Washington, NY: Kennikat Press, 1960), p. 59.

[10] Köstler, "Raub-, Kauf-, und Friedelehe," pp. 93–95; Simon Kalifa, "Singularités matrimoniales chez les anciens Germains: le rapt et le droit de la femme à disposer d'elle-même," *Revue historique de droit français et étranger* (hereafter RHDF), 4th ser., 48 (1970) 207–208, 214–15.

[11] *Pactus legis Salicae* 13.12–13, 15.2–3, ed. Karl August Eckhardt, in MGH, LL nat. germ. 4/1:63, 70; *Lex Ribuaria* 38(34).1–3, ed. Franz Beyerle and Rudolf Buchner, in MGH, LL nat. germ. 3/2:90–91; *Leges Langobardorum*, Rothair 186–87, ed. Alfred Boretius, in MGH, LL 4:44–45; *Leges Burgundionum* 12.1–2, ed. Ludwig Rudolf von Salis, in MGH, LL nat. germ. 2/1:51; *Lex Baiwariorum* 8.7, 16, ed. Ernst Heymann, in MGH, LL 5/2:356–57, 360; *Leges Alamannorum* 50.1–2, 51, 53.1–2, ed. Karl Lehmann, rev. by Karl August Eckhardt, in MGH, LL nat. germ. 5/1:111. *Raubehe* reappeared during the Viking invasions in the tenth century and persisted in Normandy for generations; Robert Bresnier, "Le mariage en Normandie dès origines au XIIIe siècle," *Normannia* 7 (1934) 89–91.

[12] Köstler, "Raub-, Kauf-, und Friedelehe," pp. 128–29; Volker Stückradt, *Rechtswirkungen eheähnlicher Verhältnisse* (Cologne: privately printed, 1964), p. 14; Löwenstein, *Bekämpfung des Konkubinates*, pp. 14–15; Wemple, *Women in Frankish Society*, pp. 12–13. By way of exception, however, *Friedelehe* in Burgundian law was accompanied by transfer of *Munt* to the husband; *Leg. Burg.* 100, in MGH, LL nat. germ. 1/2:113; and cf. *Leg. Visig.* 3.4.2, 7–8, in MGH, LL nat. germ. 1:147–48, 150.

between free and unfree persons without full legal consequences. The latter was for both practical and legal purposes equivalent to concubinage, and that is the term we shall use to describe it.[13]

Concubinage, in the sense of a long-term and more or less permanent relationship between a man and woman of unequal social status, was common in early Germanic societies. These unions were not necessarily sexually exclusive; married men commonly maintained one or more concubines in addition to their wives. The concubines were usually servant or slave girls, and the children of these unions could claim no share in their father's estate.[14]

Concubinage, like marriage, required no formal agreement or ceremony for its initiation, nor did Germanic law follow Roman law in resting the legal status of the relationship on the intentions of the parties. The notion of marital affection was unknown to Germanic law and played no role in defining marriage. What was essential to both marriage and concubinage in Germanic law was consummation, an element that Romans had largely ignored as irrelevant to the legality of a marital union. Sexual intercourse was essential to Germanic marriage, however, and no marital union was binding without it. Marriage in Germanic law consisted simply of sexual intercourse accompanied by an intention to live together permanently and to have children. The intention to form a permanent union was what distinguished marriage from concubinage.[15]

Germanic marriage operated with relatively few rules and restrictions. The most common prohibitions concerned marriages with close relatives by blood or marriage. Couples who married within the forbidden degrees of kinship were liable to have their marriages dissolved and their children declared illegitimate; in addition they might be fined heavily.[16] Although as late as the early

[13]Baumann, *Zivilrechtliche Bedeutung*, p. 17; Joseph Freisen, *Geschichte des kanonischen Eherechts bis zum Verfall der Glossenliteratur*, 2d ed. (Paderborn: F. Schöningh, 1893; repr. Aalen: Scientia, 1963), p. 53.

[14]*Leg. Langobard.*, Rothair 222 and Liutprand 104–106, in MGH, LL 4:54, 150–51; Löwenstein, *Bekämpfung des Konkubinates*, pp. 13–15; Jo Ann McNamara and Suzanne F. Wemple, "Marriage and Divorce in the Frankish Kingdom," in Stuard, *Women in Medieval Society*, p. 105; Hermann, *Stellung unehelicher Kinder*, p. 51; Freisen, *Geschichte*, pp. 55–56; Heinrich Finke, *Die Frau im Mittelalter* (Munich: Jos. Kösel, 1913), p. 52.

[15]Willibald Plöchl, *Das Eherecht des Magisters Gratianus*, Wiener Staats- und Rechtswissenschaftliche Studien, vol. 24 (Leipzig and Vienna: F. Deuticke, 1935), p. 50; Burge, *Comparative Law*, p. 12. The laws of the Alamans and the Bavarians, however, recognized love of another person as a legitimate reason for terminating a betrothal; *Leg. Alamann.* 52(53), in MGH, LL nat. germ. 5/1:110–11; *Lex Baiwar.* 8.15, in MGH, LL nat. germ. 5/2:359–60; Raymund Kottje, "Ehe und Eheverständnis in den vorgratianischen Bussbüchern," in *Love and Marriage in the Twelfth Century*, p. 37.

[16]*Pact. leg. Sal.* 13.11, in MGH, LL nat. germ. 4/1:62–63; *Leg. Visig.* 4.1.1–7, in MGH, LL nat. germ. 1:171–73; *Codex Euriciani* 2, in MGH, LL 1:28; Wemple, *Women in Frankish Society*, p. 36; P.D. King, *Law and Society in the Visigothic Kingdom*, Cambridge Studies in Medieval Life and Thought, 3d ser., vol. 5 (Cambridge: At the University Press, 1972), p. 233; and see generally John H. Fowler, "The Develop-

sixth century some Germanic kings managed to transgress the incest rules with impunity, by the end of that century even royalty could no longer do so. Polygyny likewise became subject to legal restrictions in the aftermath of mass conversions to Christianity among the Germans and by the late sixth century was becoming uncommon.[17]

Germanic law often regarded the first year of marriage as a trial period, at the end of which the union might be terminated unless a child was conceived during that time. If the bride became pregnant, the marriage was deemed permanent, and divorce became slightly more difficult.[18] In general, divorce was fairly easy for a man and quite difficult for a woman to initiate. The Burgundian woman who attempted to divorce her husband was to be smothered in mire, but the Burgundian man who wished to divorce his wife could do so on any of three grounds: adultery, sorcery, or tomb-violation. If he chose, however, he could also divorce his wife without citing reasons, but in this case he was required to pay her a sum equal to her marriage price and was also subject to a fine.[19] Visigothic women, by contrast, could repudiate their husbands for sodomy or for having forced the wife to have sexual relations with another man.[20] The provisions of the other codes varied, but all of them gave considerable latitude to the man seeking divorce, while severely limiting the right of women to initiate these actions.[21]

Early Germanic law treated bastard children by and large not much differently from legitimate offspring. Later, probably under the influence of Church authorities who were anxious to discourage irregular unions, the status of bastard children deteriorated markedly. The most notable exception to the general rule occurred in Lombard law, which remained extraordinarily mild in this respect. The Franks in the Merovingian period also tended to be relatively generous toward illegitimate and natural children and occasionally even permitted them to succeed to royal titles in preference to legitimate offspring.[22]

Fornication between unmarried persons was recognized as an offense in several Germanic codes and was normally punished by fines, sometimes fairly

---

ment of Incest Regulations in the Early Middle Ages: Family, Nurturance, and Aggression in the Making of the Medieval West" (Ph.D. diss., Rice University, 1981).

[17] *Pact. leg. Sal.* 13.12–13, in MGH, LL nat. germ. 1:63; *Leg. Visig.* 3.4.9, in MGH, LL nat. germ. 1:150–51; *Lex Rib.* 39(35).1, in MGH, LL nat. germ. 3/2:91.

[18] Heinrich Brunner, "Die Geburt eines lebenden Kindes und das eheliche Vermögensrecht," in his *Abhandlungen zur Rechtsgeschichte* 2:116–64; Wemple, *Women in Frankish Society,* p. 94.

[19] *Leg. Burg.* 34, in MGH, LL nat. germ. 2/1:68.

[20] *Leg. Visig.* 3.6.2, in MGH, LL nat. germ. 1:167–69.

[21] *Leg. Langobard.,* Grimwald 6, in MGH, LL 4:94; McNamara and Wemple, "Marriage and Divorce," pp. 98–100.

[22] *Leg. Langobard.,* Rothair 154–62, 225, and Liutprand 32.3, 105.2, in MGH, LL 4:35–37, 55–56, 123, 150–51; Brunner, "Uneheliche Vaterschaft," pp. 165–97; Hermann, *Stellung unehelicher Kinder,* p. 50; Chevailler, "Observations sur le droit de bâtardise," pp. 380–84; Baumann, *Zivilrechtliche Bedeutung,* p. 18.

heavy ones.[23] The Lombard laws even penalized sexual relations between a free man and a female slave, although the penalty was diminished if the slave was of Roman stock.[24] Male slaves who had sexual relations with free women, conversely, were severely punished. The Bavarian laws prescribed death for this offense.[25]

Adultery in early Germanic society was an exclusively female crime, although a few codes also penalized men for adultery under some circumstances.[26] Adultery was far more serious than fornication, since the adulteress cast doubt upon the legitimacy of her husband's descendants as well as offending his honor and pride. The husband who discovered his wife in the act of committing adultery had the right to kill both parties without legal penalty. The Visigoths, whose law on sexual matters generally echoed the *Lex Julia de adulteriis*, in this case went well beyond their Roman model and accorded the *ius mariti* to the woman's father and brothers as well.[27] Sexual relations with a betrothed woman might also be treated as adultery; in Lombard law this was true even if the espoused woman was a slave or bondswoman.[28] Sexual relations with a nun constituted adultery, presumably on the theory that a consecrated virgin was the bride of Christ; the brunt of punishment for this kind of adultery fell upon the man.[29]

Visigothic law provided that slaves who could furnish evidence about an adulterous liaison should be tortured in order to extract the information from them. An owner might not set his slave free in order to prevent him from testifying in an adultery case.[30] On the other hand it was a risky business to bring unfounded adultery charges against a woman; under Lombard law the accuser who was unable to prove his case lost all rights over the woman whom he falsely accused.[31] At the same time, the Lombards also penalized either men or women

---

[23] *Lex Rib.* 39(35).2–3, in MGH, LL nat. germ. 3/2:91–92; *Leg. Langobard.*, Rothair 189, in MGH, LL 4:45; *Leg. Burg.* 33, in MGH, LL nat. germ. 2/1:67; *Leg. Baiwar.* 8.8, in MGH, LL 5/2:357; *Lex Sal.* 36.1–4, in MGH, LL nat. germ. 4/2:74.

[24] *Leg. Langobard.*, Rothair 194, in MGH, LL 4:47; *Lex Salica 100 Titel-Text* 36.1, ed. Karl August Eckhard, (Weimar: Hermann Böhlaus Nachfolger, 1953), p. 148; cf. *Lex Rib.* 61.17, in MGH, LL 3/2:113.

[25] *Leg. Baiwar.* 8.9, in MGH. LL 5/2:357–58.

[26] *Leg. Visig.* 3.4.2, in MGH, LL nat. germ. 1:147–48; *Leg. Langobard.*, Rothair 179, 196, in MGH, LL 4:42, 47–48; *Lex Salica* (100 title text) 15.1, ed. Eckhard, p. 130.

[27] Tacitus, *Germania* 19, ed. Robinson, pp. 295–96; *Leg. Langobard.*, Liutprand 110.7, 140.2, in MGH, LL 4:152, 169–70; *Leg. Burg.* 36, in MGH, LL nat. germ. 2/1:69; Wemple, *Women in Frankish Society*, p. 11.

[28] *Leg. Langobard.*, Rothair 212–13, in MGH, LL 4:51–52; *Leg. Visig.* 3.4.1, 4, 5, in MGH, LL nat. germ. 1:147, 149.

[29] *Leg. Langobard.*, Liutprand 76.7, 95.12, in MGH, LL 4:138, 146; *Leg. Baiwar.* 1.11, in MGH, LL 5/2:283–84.

[30] *Leg. Visig.* 3.4.10–11, in MGH, LL nat. germ. 1:151.

[31] *Leg. Langobard.*, Rothair 196, in MGH, LL 4:47–48.

who condoned their spouses' adultery and failed to prosecute it.[32] The adulterer usually faced a heavy fine. In some jurisdictions and under certain circumstances he stood to lose all or a major part of his property.[33]

Rape, as distinguished from elopement (*Raubehe*), carried a variety of penalties, commonly a sizeable fine and sometimes whipping or other physical punishment in addition.[34] Rape of a free woman by an unfree man merited the death penalty under Salic law, which added, however, that if the woman went with her abductor voluntarily she lost her own freedom.[35] Visigothic law prescribed the death penalty for rape, but also provided that if the victim subsequently sought her ravisher's hand in marriage, and if her parents consented, he might escape alive.[36]

Germanic law codes had little to say about prostitution, except for the Visigothic code, which treated it in detail. The Visigoths prescribed that a free woman convicted of harlotry was to receive three hundred lashes; she could then be released, on condition that she never return to prostitution. If caught a second time, she received a further three hundred lashes and was to be given to some poor man, on condition that he never permit her to walk the streets again. Parents who prostituted a child received one hundred lashes. The master of a servant girl who failed to supervise her behavior and thus allowed her to become a prostitute might get fifty lashes; if he knowingly prostituted her and took any part of her earnings, however, he was subject to three hundred strokes. Prostitution seems to have flourished among the Germanic settlers in the West, although most of the available harlots were probably foreign girls taken as booty in military expeditions—many of them Slavs or Finns.[37] Since prostitutes were women whose origins and way of life cast them outside of the social networks of German society, it was considered a grievous injury to accuse a freeborn German woman of whoredom, and such an accusation was punishable by a large fine.[38]

[32] *Leg. Langobard.*, Liutprand 130, in MGH, LL 4:162–63.

[33] *Leg. Burgund.* 44.1, in MGH, LL nat. germ. 2/1:74; *Leg. Visig.* 3.4.12, in MGH, LL nat. germ. 1:151–52.

[34] *Pact. leg. Sal.* 13.14, 15.1–2, in MGH, LL nat. germ. 4/1:63, 70; *Lex Rib.* 38(34).1–3, in MGH, LL nat. germ. 3/2:90–91; *Leg. Langobard.*, Rothair 205–207, in MGH, LL 4:50–51.

[35] *Lex Salica* (100 title text) 14.6–7, ed. Eckhard, p. 128.

[36] *Leg. Visig.* 3.3.2, 7 and 3.4.14, in MGH, LL nat. germ. 1:140–42; Pierre Lemercier, "Une curiosité judiciaire au moyen âge: la grace par mariage subséquent," RHDF, 4th ser., 33 (1955) 464–74.

[37] *Leg. Visig.* 3.4.17, in MGH, LL nat. germ. 1:157; King, *Law and Society in the Visigothic Kingdom*, pp. 118, 202, 241; Gustav Jung, *Die Geschlechtsmoral des deutschen Weibes im Mittelalter: eine Kulturhistorische Studie* (Leipzig: Ethnologischer Verlag, n.d.), p. 217.

[38] *Lex Sal.* 49.4, in MGH, LL 4/2:88; *Pact. leg. Sal.* 30.3, in MGH, LL nat. germ. 1:118–19.

Sexual Behavior and the Christian Church in the Germanic Kingdoms

During the decades immediately following their initial settlement in the western territories of the old Roman Empire, Germanic kings and their subjects gradually accepted baptism and became, nominally at least, Latin Catholics.[39] From the late fifth century, then, increasing numbers of Germanic settlers came under the discipline of the Church in sexual matters. But the Germans were loath to discard their traditional customs, especially with respect to sex, marriage, and domestic relations. An uneasy tension resulted, punctuated by sharp clashes between the old traditions of Germanic society and the Church's demands for conformity to Christian concepts of sexual morality.

FAMILY STRUCTURE

The differences between German practice and Church discipline were particularly acute with respect to marriage and family issues. The clash grew sharper, moreover, between the sixth and the ninth centuries as a result of the emergence of a new kind of household structure and, consequently, a new definition of the family in western Europe. In the generation of Pope Gregory the Great (590–604) and St. Isidore of Seville (ca. 560–636) West European households still retained the characteristic features of Mediterranean antiquity. The households of the rich differed in structure from those of the poor, and the family, in the sense of a coresidential unit consisting of a couple and their direct descendants, had not yet emerged. By the generation of Charlemagne (771–814), this had changed. The family had come to mean a coresidential, primary descent group, and Carolingian administrators, when they set out to record the charac-

---

[39] Most of the Germanic invaders were still pagans at the time of their migration into the Western Empire, but a substantial minority—notably the Ostrogoths, Burgundians, and Visigoths—had adopted Arianism prior to the invasions. Tensions between Germanic Arian rulers and their Catholic subjects in Italy and Spain caused problems in those regions for generations following the invasions. Ultimately, however, the Arians capitulated and abandoned their heterodox tradition. The conversion of pagan Germanic settlers to Catholic Christianity was often quicker and less painful than the conversion of Arian groups. The Salian Franks embraced Christianity during the reign of Clovis (481–511) and his conquest of Burgundy in the early sixth century speeded the process of religious assimilation there as well. The conversion of Britain commenced even before the arrival of St. Augustine of Canterbury in Kent in 597; by the time of the Synod of Whitby (664) the process was far advanced. See H. St. L. B. Moss, *The Birth of the Middle Ages, 395–814* (London: Oxford University Press, 1935; repr. 1963), pp. 63–64, 73–78; Gustav Schnürer, *Church and Culture in the Middle Ages*, vol. 1: 350–814, trans. George G. Undereiner (Paterson, NJ: St. Anthony Guild Press, 1956), pp. 193–418; Gerhart B. Ladner, "The Impact of Christianity," in *The Transformation of the Roman World*, ed. Lynn White, Jr. (Berkeley and Los Angeles: University of California Press, 1966), pp. 55–91; Margaret Deansley, *A History of Early Medieval Europe, 476 to 911*, Methuen's History of Medieval and Early Modern Europe, vol. 1 (London: Methuen, 1956), pp. 59–60, 97–98, 103–108.

teristics of a population for tax assessments or other reasons, commonly did so in terms of family units. Moreover, rich families and poor families no longer differed enormously from one another in membership, although they often differed in size and of course in resources. But by the year 800 or thereabouts, the Western family had taken the shape that has characterized it ever since that time.

The family was greater than the sum of its members; its continuing existence, prosperity, and prerogatives transcended the interests of any generational segment within it. The sexual foibles of each member reflected upon the whole family, and marriage was a matter of family policy, not of individual choice.

By Charlemagne's time, moreover, European families were beginning to identify with the paternal lineage, rather than with both maternal and paternal lines. Also striking in the new family paradigm was the dawning consciousness of emotional bonding among family members as a central feature. In David Herlihy's phrase, the emerging family was marked by its symmetry (centered on the nuclear unit), its structure (identification with paternal lineage) and its sentiment (emotional bonding within the family).[40]

MARRIAGE

The altered structure of the family probably bred additional tensions between the Germanic approach to marriage and the Church's concept. Germanic folklaw treated marriage as a union that was contracted, sealed, and symbolized by sexual relations between the parties and dissoluble at will, at least for the man. Church leaders, in contrast, adopted the position that marriage created a lifelong bond between man and wife, contracted by their consent and that of their families.[41] Germanic custom and Christian teaching saw the role of marital sex quite differently. As noted earlier, the Germans considered sexual relations essential to the definition of marriage, whereas Christian teachers, under the in-

[40] Herlihy, *Medieval Households*, pp. 56–59, 61–62, 78, as well as "The Making of the Medieval Family: Symmetry, Structure, and Sentiment," *Journal of Family History* 8 (1983) 116–30; Georges Duby, *Medieval Marriage: Two Models from Twelfth-Century France*, trans. by Elborg Forster, Johns Hopkins Symposia in Comparative History, 11 (Baltimore: Johns Hopkins University Press, 1978), p. 3; James C. Holt, "Feudal Society and the Family in Early Medieval England: I. The Revolution of 1066," *Transactions of the Royal Historical Society*, 5th ser., 34 (1982) 199–200; Katherine Fischer Drew, "The Law of the Family in the Germanic Kingdoms," *Studies in Medieval Culture* 11 (1977) 17. Paul Veyne, "La famille et l'amour sous le haut empire romain," *Annales é.s.c.* 33 (1978) 35, contends that the nuclear family had become the basic unit of social structure in pagan Rome and would push the basic change back to some time prior to the end of the second century. He promises documentation to support his position in a forthcoming book.

[41] McNamara and Wemple, "Marriage and Divorce," p. 96; Paul Hinschius, "Das Ehescheidungsrecht nach den angelsächsischen und fränkischen Bussordnungen," *Zeitschrift für deutsches Recht* 20 (1861) 67; Wemple, *Women in Frankish Society*, p. 89.

fluence of patristic authorities, distrusted sex: they saw it as unclean, and incompatible with their ascetic values.[42]

Catholic writers in the eighth and ninth centuries were acutely aware of these conflicts about the role of sex in marriage, and some of them sought to harmonize Germanic tradition with Christian teaching. Archbishop Hincmar of Reims (845–882) made the most ambitious effort to do this. In a letter concerning a French marriage case about 860, Hincmar propounded a theory of marriage hitherto unknown in canon law, namely that an unconsummated marriage was incomplete and hence not fully binding:

> A true coupling in legitimate marriage between free persons of
> equal status occurs when a free woman, properly dowered, is joined
> to a free man with paternal consent in a public wedding [followed
> by] sexual intercourse.[43]

This formulation seems to have been original with Hincmar, although in framing it he borrowed phrases from earlier authorities, notably Pope St. Leo I and St. Augustine. But the writers whose words he appropriated and stitched together to suit his purposes would have been astonished at what he did with them, for Hincmar's coital theory of marriage was a novel attempt to give sexual consummation a central role in the formation of Christian marriage. He retained the Roman concept that marriage was made by consent. But although necessary, consent by itself was not sufficient, according to Hincmar. Marriage by consent alone, he held, was not permanently binding. Marriage in a full and complete sense began only when the parties united physically in an act of sexual intercourse. Perhaps reflecting this new reading of the nature of marriage, about the time Hincmar was writing it began to become common practice for nuptial ceremonies to take place at dusk, at the time of day his contemporaries considered especially propitious for intercourse and procreation.[44]

---

[42] Kosnik et al., *Human Sexuality*, p. 39; Bernhard Schimmelpfennig, "*Ex fornicatione nati*: Studies on the Position of Priests' Sons from the Twelfth to the Fourteenth Centuries," *Studies in Medieval and Renaissance History* 2 (1980) 5; Pierre Payer, "Early Medieval Regulations Concerning Marital Sexual Relations," JMH 6 (1980) 370–71.

[43] Hincmar of Reims, *Epistolae* 22, in PL 126:137–38: "Quibus sententiis evidenter ostendit, quia tunc est vera legitimi coniugii copula, quando inter ingenuos, et inter aequales fit, et paterno arbitrio viro mulier juncta, legitima dotata, et publicis nuptiis honestata, sexuum commistione coniungitur." Hincmar reiterated this formulation in his treatise *De divortio Lotharii et Tetbergae*, interr. 4, in PL 125:648–49. See also Gaudemet, "Indissolubilité et consommation," p. 34; Wemple, *Women in Frankish Society*, p. 83. On Hincmar's career see Jean Devisse, *Hincmar, archévêque de Reims, 845–882*, 3 vols., Travaux d'histoire ethico-politique, no. 29 (Geneva: Droz, 1975–76).

[44] Gaudemet, "Indissolubilité et consommation du mariage: L'apport d'Hincmar de Reims," RDC 30 (1980) 35–36; Sara Acuña, "La forma del matrimonio hasta el decreto 'Ne temere'," *Ius canonicum* 13 (1973) 149–50; Philippe Ariès, "Le mariage indissoluble," in *Sexualités occidentales*, p. 125.

Hincmar's coital theory of marriage possessed some juristic virtues: it enumerated a set of conditions for marriage that were, in large part, susceptible of verification by witnesses or by inference from circumstantial evidence. These features made it possible to resolve questionable cases by reference to actions, rather than impressions about intentions. The coital theory also harmonized Roman and Christian concepts of marriage with traditional Germanic practice. But Hincmar could not disguise the tension betweeen Christian and Germanic traditions inherent in his definition of marriage, tensions that flowed from conflicting views about the values and purposes central to marriage.

This conflict in value systems emerged openly in the rivalries between Germanic folklaw courts and prelates who sought to invoke theological principles in dealing with marital problems. Prior to the tenth century, the Church lacked jurisdiction over marriage in any technical sense. Ecclesiastical authorities could and did make judgments about marriages, of course, but the Church had not yet developed a juristic routine for dealing with matrimonial disputes. Few ecclesiastical writers in the eighth and ninth centuries entertained any illusion that the Church possessed an exclusive right to cognizance of marriage litigation. The Church's efforts to enforce compliance with its standards of Christian marriage were more hortatory than juridical.

Only during the tenth and eleventh centuries did Church officials seriously begin to assert exclusive jurisdiction over marriage.[45] Prior to that time, the Western Church limited its intervention in marriage cases essentially to reviewing the legitimacy of particular unions, especially those of prominent persons, whose irregular marriages could create public scandal. Churchmen employed various kinds of pressure to persuade couples to separate and imposed sanctions in order to insure conformity with the Church's marriage rules. Those who resisted could be excommunicated until they showed their readiness to obey and to do penance.[46] But all of this fell considerably short of full-fledged matrimonial jurisdiction.

In the years between 600 and 900 the church failed to secure clear-cut control of matrimonial matters, but ecclesiastical authorities continued to elaborate their opinions about sexual ethics. In retrospect it is clear that Christian spokesmen were in the process of formulating a theology of sex and marriage. Naturally enough the positions of individual writers varied according to each author's degree of sophistication, the circumstances in which he wrote, and the penetration of Christian viewpoints into his community.

[45] Pierre Daudet, *Les origines carolingiennes de la compétence exclusive de l'église en France et en Germanie en matière de juridiction matrimoniale* (Paris: Sirey, 1933); McNamara and Wemple, "Marriage and Divorce," pp. 106–107; Wemple, *Women in Frankish Society*, p. 75; Fransen, "Rupture," p. 609.

[46] Gérard Fransen, "Rupture," in *Il matrimonio nella società altomedievale* 2:608; Payer, "Early Medieval Regulations," pp. 354–55; J. M. Turlan, "Recherches sur le mariage dans la pratique coutumière XIIe–XVIe siècles," RHDF, 4th ser., 35 (1957) 480.

A few ecclesiastical writers in the sixth, seventh, and early eighth centuries were fairly positive in their valuation of marriage and marital love and even of the role of sex in marriage. St. John Damascene (ca. 675–749), a Byzantine theologian, was the most eloquent advocate during this period of the beneficent values of marriage and marital sexuality.

> Let every man enjoy his wife [he wrote at one point]. Nor should he blush, but let him go in and settle down in bed, day and night. Let them make love, keeping one another as man and wife, exclaiming: "Do not deny one another, save perhaps by mutual consent." [1 Cor. 7:5] Do you abstain from sexual relations? You don't wish to sleep with your husband? Then he to whom you deny your bounty will go out and do evil and his wickedness will be due to your abstinence.[47]

Fragmentary evidence from saints' lives, donations, wills, and burial inscriptions, suggests that many couples in the early Middle Ages valued marital love, including sexual love, as highly as Damascene. Loving sentiments embellished funerary monuments, husbands and wives were buried together, and some at least affirmed explicitly the tie between their sexual love and spiritual love.[48]

But sentiments such as those of Damascene were rare among the clerical intelligentsia, either in the East or West. St. Isidore of Seville expressed a more typical attitude when he repeated ideas that he found in Jerome and Augustine: sex for pleasure was wrong, even for married couples, Isidore warned; procreative sex, however, was a good use of an evil thing, and hence married couples should confine their sexual relations to the minimum required for procreation.[49] Isidore likewise voiced the Stoic view, earlier adopted and approved by Jerome, that excessive marital intercourse, beyond the needs of procreation, was sinful, although Isidore considered this only a minor sin, and compared it to eating more than required for sustenance.[50] Gregory the Great also sympathized with these ideas, but he was inclined to rate the moral danger more seriously than Isidore did. Although sexual intercourse, save for procreation, might be a minor sin in itself, Gregory worried that it could lead to graver, more serious kinds of sexual misconduct from which married couples could remain immune only if they renounced sexual relations altogether.[51] Better, he thought, for couples to agree not to consummate their marriages at all and thus

---

[47] John Damascene, *De sacris parallelis,* in PG 96:258; see also Damascene's disciple, Theodore Abucara, *Dogma de una uxore,* in PG 97:1555; Boswell, CSTAH, p. 159.

[48] Philippe Ariès, "L'amour dans le mariage," in *Sexualités occidentales,* p. 120; Leclercq, *Monks on Marriage,* pp. 49–50; Wemple, *Women in Frankish Society,* pp. 57, 103.

[49] Isidore of Seville, *Sententiae* 2.40.13, in PL 83:645; *De ecclesiasticis officiis* 2.20.9–10, in PL 83:812; Payer, "Early Medieval Regulations," p. 353.

[50] Isidore of Seville, *De ordine creaturarum* 14.11, in PL 83:949.

[51] Gregory I, *Moralia in Iob* 13.21 (12.18), ed. Marc Adriaen, in CCL 143A:597–98; Müller, *Lehre des hl. Augustinus,* p. 34; Flandrin, "Vie sexuelle," p. 103.

to avoid the temptations that sexual experience might generate. Several early medieval saints' lives picture couples who did in fact choose to live in unions that were both loving and nonsexual.[52] Those unable to make this sweeping sacrifice were at least advised to abstain from sexual relations for two or three days following their marriage and, in addition, to refrain from sexual activities at regular periods during each year of their married lives.[53]

Gregory of Tours (538–595) related an incident from his own experience that testifies eloquently to the way in which unsophisticated men and women might interpret ecclesiastical warnings about the spiritual dangers of marital sex. Gregory described a married woman who went to visit her widowed mother, who had become a nun. After talking with her mother, the younger woman decided to remain in the convent and sent her husband a message: "Go back and rear our children, for I shall not return to you. One who is joined in marriage will not see the Kingdom of Heaven." This message may have been doctrinally incorrect—Gregory certainly believed it was wrong—but the incident reflects conclusions that people could easily have drawn from ecclesiastical teachings about marital sex.[54]

Another Frankish bishop, Jonas of Orleans (ca. 780–843), the first Christian writer to devote a whole treatise expressly to the life of the Christian layman, firmly condemned those who sought pleasure in marital sex. Marriage is morally good, Jonas argued, but only when it is ordered toward procreation. Couples who have sex just because it feels good commit a wrong and must atone for it by penance.[55] Some people, Jonas continued, contend that because God created the genitalia therefore sex is natural, and God approves of it. Not so, according to Jonas. Sex for pleasure is an abuse of God's creation. The reproductive organs are precisely that and nothing else. Sex is allowed only to married couples, only at prescribed times and places, and only for reproduction.[56] Married men who believe that they can pleasure themselves and their wives whenever and however they wish are wrong. Such "immoderate" marital sex is a serious sin.[57] Jonas also appealed to the values of a warrior society to support limitation of sexual activity. Sex, he maintained, is not only fraught with moral danger, but it is also physically debilitating. Excessive indulgence in sex robs a man of his health, vigor, and equilibrium; it makes him nervous and soft. Thus Jonas ar-

---

[52] Leclercq, *Monks on Marriage*, p. 43, cites several examples.

[53] Hérard of Tours, *Capitula* 89, in PL 121:770; Payer, "Early Medieval Regulations," p. 355, and *Sex and the Penitentials: The Development of A Sexual Code, 550–1150* (Toronto: University of Toronto Press, 1984), pp. 23–28; P. Saintyves, "Les trois nuits de Tobie ou la continence durant la première ou les premières nuits du mariage," *Revue anthropologique* 44 (1944) 266–96.

[54] Gregory of Tours, *Historia Francorum* 9.33, ed. Wilhelm Arndt, in MGH, Scriptores rerum Merovingicarum 1:387.

[55] Jonas of Orleans, *De institutione laicali* 2.1, 6, in PL 106:167–70, 179–82.

[56] Jonas of Orleans, *De inst. laicali* 2.9, in PL 106:184–85.

[57] Jonas of Orleans, *De inst. laicali* 2.3, in PL 106:172–74.

gued that sexual restraint, even total abstinence, was a source of power and energy, a positive asset for the soldierly life as well as a moral virtue.[58]

Theological writers in the period between 600 and 900 were in the process of elaborating, slowly and haltingly, a sacramental theology. But none of the authorities of the age was prepared to see in marital activities any visible signs of operative sacramental grace. Tainted by lust and carnal desire, marriage did not seem to them a channel for the infusion of divine favor.[59]

Marriage was thus only a relative good: it served to prevent worse evils, such as fornication, but it had few positive virtues of its own, and those were offset by indulgence in sex. Consummated marriage fell far short of the ideal of virginity; married folk could only try to reduce their sexual activity to the minimum. That marriage was best in which the sexual element was least.[60] But to condemn marriage entirely was doctrinally unacceptable, and Church councils continued to insist that those who held marriage unchristian were guilty of heresy.[61]

One facet of marriage law that drew special attention from ecclesiastical authorities in this age involved the so-called impediments to marriage. Early medieval canon law had not articulated clearly its doctrine concerning obstacles to marriage. The Church now attempted to define its marriage rules more precisely. While it would be anachronistic during this period to call marriages that contravened the rules invalid, persons who infringed the regulations certainly came under considerable pressure to make amends for their action. Couples whose unions failed to meet the criteria that the Church established were strongly advised to separate.[62]

A growing number of these rules concerned marriages between persons related to one another through blood ties or linked together as in-laws or baptismal sponsors. The ostensible purpose of these regulations was to prevent incest, but the rules that came into currency during the seventh and eighth centuries forbade marriages where the relationship between the parties was so remote that incest seems unlikely to have been the central issue.

A group of texts attributed to Pope Gregory the Great were particularly important in defining the new criteria for consanguinity and affinity. These texts, often called the *Responsa Gregorii*, were known (at least in part) as early as the time of St. Boniface (680–755), and some of them probably predated his pe-

---

[58] Pierre Toubert, "La théorie du mariage chez les moralistes carolingiens," in *Il matrimonio nella società altomedievale* 1:254. The belief in the debilitating effects of sexual activity, especially for men, was a heritage from ancient medical lore.

[59] Toubert, "Théorie du mariage," pp. 269–70.

[60] Isidore of Seville, *Sententiae* 2.40.13–14, in PL 83:645; Müller, *Lehre des hl. Augustinus*, p. 35.

[61] 1 Council of Braga (561) c. 11, in Vives, *Concilios Visigóticos*, p. 68.

[62] Fransen, "Rupture," p. 607; David E. Engdahl, "Full Faith and Credit in Merrie Olde England: New Insight for Marriage Conflicts Law from the Thirteenth Century," *Valparaiso University Law Review* 5 (1970) 3.

riod.[63] One of the *responsa* enunciated the rule that marriages between blood kin within seven degrees of relationship were illegal and required married persons so related to separate. The seven-degree rule gradually became accepted during this period as the canonical norm on these matters, and as early as the tenth century it was beginning to dictate the marital strategies of the nobility in France.[64]

Both the dubious *Responsa Gregorii* and genuine Merovingian legislation, moreover, banned sexual intercourse, either in marriage or outside of it, between a married person and any of the blood kin of his or her spouse. Intercourse with the spouse's kin created a legal affinity punishable by lifelong penance, which effectively ended the sexual relationship between the married partners. Secular authorities also decreed that the property of those who offended in this way should be seized.[65]

To complicate matters further, an impediment to marriage was established between godparents and those for whom they stood as baptismal sponsors. In addition sponsorship established a tie of coparenthood between the godparent and all of the adult members of the godchild's family; the tie also carried with it matrimonial prohibitions. A similar relationship of cogodparenthood was created between the sponsors themselves and made marriage between them and any members of the other sponsor's family illegal. Even unwitting incest might be punishable. The Council of Verberie (753 ~ 756) provided that if a man slept with a woman whom his brother later married, the brother must repudiate his wife upon learning of her prior relationship, and in reparation he must do seven years of penance, at the end of which he might marry someone else.

[63]Lambertus Machielsen, "Les *spurii* de S. Grégoire le Grand en matière matrimoniale dans les collections canoniques jusqu'au Décret de Gratien," *Sacris erudiri* 14 (1963) 267–69; Paul Meyvert, "Les 'Responsiones' de S. Grégoire le Grand à S. Augustin de Cantorbéry," *Revue d'histoire ecclésiastique* 54 (1959) 879–94, and "Bede's Text of the *Libellus responsionum* of Gregory the Great to Augustine of Canterbury," in Peter Clemoes and Kathleen Hughes, ed., *England Before the Conquest: Studies in Primary Sources Presented to Dorothy Whitelock* (Cambridge: At the University Press, 1971), pp. 15–33.

[64]Hincmar of Reims, *De divortio*, interr. 12, in PL 125:706–707; Hinschius, DPI, p. 751; cf. JE 1978; Constance B. Bouchard, "Consanguinity and Noble Marriages in the Tenth and Eleventh Centuries," *Speculum* 56 (1981) 268–87; Herlihy, *Medieval Households*, pp. 61–62. On calculating degrees of relationship see Ernest Champeaux, "*Jus sanguinis*: trois façons de calculer le parenté au moyen âge," RHDF, 4th ser., 12 (1933) 241–90.

[65]Hincmar, *De divortio*, interr. 12, in PL 125:706–707; Hinschius, DPI, p. 571; Council of Worms (868) c. 32, in Mansi 15:875; Rabanus Maurus, *Epist.* 29, in MGH, Epistolae 5:446–47; *Leg. Visig.* 3.5.1, in MGH, LL 1:159; Charlemagne, *Capitularium missorum generale* (802) c. 33, in MGH, Capitularia 1:97; McNamara and Wemple, "Marriage and Divorce in the Frankish Kingdom," pp. 99, 101; Wemple, *Women in Frankish Society*, p. 76; Lea, *History of Auricular Confession* 2:110.

Other Gregorian (or pseudo-Gregorian) texts prohibited marriage to nuns or to infidels, which was also forbidden by genuine patristic texts.[66]

Church authorities insisted also in this period that marriage must be public. A letter doubtfully attributed to Pope Hormisdas (513–553) prohibited secret marriages and demanded that Christians celebrate their nuptials in public and receive the blessing of a priest, a practice already well established in the Byzantine Church by the seventh century.[67] Similar provisions appeared in the canons of some eighth-century councils in the West. These canons failed to solve the problem, however, and despite efforts to repress it, clandestine marriage remained common.[68]

Many Church leaders continued to oppose remarriage of widows and widowers. The Second Council of Braga (572) not only penalized men who indulged in second marriages by excluding them from holy orders, but also prescribed that all those who married more than once should do penance for their lascivious conduct.[69] Ecclesiastical authorities wrestled in addition with the problem of the vanishing husband who disappeared during battle or on a foreign journey. Pope Leo I allowed women whose husbands had been missing for a long time to remarry on the presumption that the vanished husband must have died. Should he reappear, however, the wife must abandon her second husband to rejoin her original mate.[70]

The Council of Verberie dealt with other complications of marital separation: if a man was summoned to distant parts by his lord, and his wife refused to accompany him, she could remain at home, but she must also remain single for

[66] Capitulary of Verberie (753 ~ 756) c. 18, in MGH, LL 1:23; Theodor Gottlob, "Der Ehebruch und seine Rechtsfolgen in den vorgratianischen Quellen und bei Gratian Selbst," *Studia Gratiana* 2 (1954) 340–41; JE 1941; Machielsen, "Spurii," p. 267; on godparenthood and co-parenthood see generally Joseph H. Lynch, "Spiritual Kinship and Sexual Prohibitions in Early Medieval Europe," in *Berkeley Proceedings*, pp. 271–88, as well as *Godparents and Kinship in Early Medieval Europe* (Princeton: Princeton University Press, 1986), pp. 219–57.

[67] A. Montan, "Alle origini della disciplina matrimoniale canonica: contributi per la ricerca," *Apollinaris* 54 (1981) 178; Acuña, "Forma del matrimonio," p. 148; Jean Gaudemet, "Originalité et destin du mariage romain," in *L'Europa e il diritto romano: Studi in onore di Paolo Koschaker*, 2 vols. (Milan: A. Giuffrè, 1954) 2:541, repr. in Gaudemet's *Sociétés et mariage*, p. 168; Antonio Marongiu, "La forma religiosa del matrimonio nel diritto bizantino, normanno, e svevo," *Archivio storico per la Calabria e la Lucania* 30 (1961) 3–10, reprinted with original pagination in his *Byzantine, Norman, Swabian, and Later Institutions in Southern Italy* (London: Variorum, 1972).

[68] Council of Metz (755) c. 15, in Mansi 12:583; Synod of Reisbach (799) c. 12, in Mansi 13:1027; Justina Ruiz de Conde, *El amor y el matrimonio secreto en los libros de caballerías* (Madrid: M. Aguilar, 1948), p. 6. For the problems that clandestine marriage gave rise to, see below, pp. 276–77.

[69] 2 Council of Braga c. 26, 80, as well as 2 Council of Seville (619) c. 4, in Vives, *Concilios Visigóticos*, pp. 94, 105, 165; cf. *Leg. Visig.* 3.6.1, in MGH, LL nat. germ. 1:166–67.

[70] JK 536; PL 54:1135–37; MGH, LL 1:23; Hinschius, DPI, p. 620.

the rest of her days. Her husband, however, after doing penance, might be permitted to remarry.[71] Clearly these provisions were not based upon a consistent doctrine of indissolubility. They demonstrate that the early medieval Church was prepared to adapt its policies to meet difficult situations. The Church's spokesmen sometimes acknowledged that it was exceedingly difficult, if not altogether impossible, to prevent people, especially young people, from engaging in sexual activity. Authorities, therefore, tried to adjust their policies to take into account the facts of experience.[72] For example, the Council of Worms in 868 decreed that married men who were doing canonical penance for their sins should not separate from their wives and that unmarried persons who found it impossible to practice continence should be allowed to marry, even while they were doing penance.[73]

DIVORCE

Mitigation of the principle of indissolubility was further apparent in the treatment of divorce during this period. In 726, Pope Gregory II dealt with the case of a man with a chronically ill wife who was unable to have sexual relations. The husband wished to divorce her and marry a sexually active woman. The pope cautioned the petitioner that it would be better for him to remain continent, but nonetheless authorized the divorce and remarriage, provided that the man continue to support his first wife.[74] Not all couples whose marriages were unsatisfactory sought ecclesiastical approval for terminating them. Divorce by mutual consent remained common in seventh and eighth century Gaul and probably elsewhere, too. Occasional efforts by churchmen and monarchs to restrict the practice seem to have had little effect. Adultery was generally recognized as adequate grounds for divorce, and authorities often allowed remarriage following divorce as a concession to human frailty.[75]

[71] Capitulary of Verberie (753) c. 9, in MGH, LL 1:23; Capitulary of Compiègne (753) c. 9, in MGH, LL 1:28; Council of Tribur (895) c. 39, in MGH, Capitularia 2:235–36; Fransen, "Rupture," p. 625; Hinschius, "Ehescheidungsrecht," pp. 80–82.

[72] Jean-Louis Flandrin, "Repression and Change in the Sexual Life of Young People in Medieval and Early Modern Times," *Journal of Family History* 2 (1977) 198; repr. in *Family and Sexuality in French History*, ed. Robert Wheaton and Tamara K. Hareven (Philadelphia: University of Pennsylvania Press, 1980), p. 28.

[73] Council of Worms (868) c. 30, in Mansi 15:874–75; Gottlob, "Ehebruch," p. 342.

[74] PL 89:524–25; JE 2174; cf. Stephen II, *Responsa* 2 (754) in PL 89:1024; McNamara and Wemple, "Marriage and Divorce," pp. 102–103; De Sanctis, "Pensiero sul coniuge abbandonato," p. 205; J. B. Sägmüller, "Das 'impedimentum impotentiae' bei der Frau vor Alexander III.," *Theologische Quartalschrift* 93 (1911) 94, continued in *Theol. Quartalschr.* 95 (1913), 568; Hinschius, "Ehescheidungsrecht," pp. 81–82.

[75] Council of Vannes (461 ~ 491) c. 2 in CCL 148:152; Council of Verberie (756) c. 2, 5–6, 9, in MGH, LL 1:22–23; McNamara and Wemple, "Marriage and Divorce," pp. 97–98; Francesco Delpini, "L'indissolubilità matrimoniale nei documenti ecclesiastici nell'età medioevale," *Sacra doctrina* 49 (1968) 75–79; Fransen, "Rupture," pp. 623–24;

Toward the close of the eighth century, however, both Church authorities and kings began to reassert older bans on remarriage following divorce for adultery. The Council of Friuli in 796, while acknowledging that adultery by the wife remained a legitimate reason for separation, disallowed remarriage by either party so long as the other lived.[76] Charlemagne adopted this policy in a capitulary of 802, thus extending the principle throughout his empire and placing imperial authority behind the rule.[77] Louis the Pious reiterated the policy, as did several of his successors later in the ninth century.[78]

The ability of married couples to have sexual relations gained renewed legal importance during the eighth and ninth centuries. When marriage was defined as a consensual contract, as it had been in Roman law, the sexual capacity of the parties was a secondary issue in determining whether they were married or not. Germanic concepts of marriage in which consummation was centrally important, however, made the issues of impotence and frigidity far more acute. A mid-ninth century text that circulated under the name of Pope Gregory the Great (it was actually an excerpt from a letter by Archbishop Rabanus Maurus of Mainz [ca. 776–856]) authorized the separation of couples who found it impossible to have sexual intercourse.[79] The policy stated in Rabanus's letter was supported by earlier rulings, beginning with a letter of Pope Gregory II in 726, and included in the canons of at least two eighth-century councils.[80] Companionate marriage was the preferred solution in such cases: in other words, the couple should remain together, despite their inability to have sex, and live a life of married chastity. Gregory II, however, was prepared to authorize the sexually capable partner in these situations to remarry.[81]

Hincmar of Reims introduced a further subtlety into the treatment of impotence and frigidity. When Hincmar dealt with two notorious divorce cases—the one between King Lothair II (855–869) and Queen Teutberga, and the other

---

Hinschius, "Ehescheidungsrecht," p. 85; Ariès, "Mariage indissoluble," p. 128; Wemple, *Women in Frankish Society*, p. 77; Willy Rordorf, "Marriage in the New Testament and in the Early Church," JEH 20 (1969) 204–205, points out that the Byzantine Church considered adultery the moral equivalent of the death of the guilty party and hence saw no obstacle to remarriage of the innocent party following divorce.

[76] Council of Friuli (796) c. 10, in MGH, Concilia 2:192–93; Delpini, "Indissolubilità," pp. 82–83; McNamara and Wemple, "Marriage and Divorce," pp. 103–104.

[77] *Capitularia missis dominicis data* (802) c. 22, in MGH, Capitularia 1:103; Wemple, *Women in Frankish Society*, pp. 81, 111.

[78] McNamara and Wemple, "Marriage and Divorce," pp. 104–105; Wemple, *Women in Frankish Society*, pp. 75–76, 81; Delpini, "Indissolubilità," p. 73.

[79] JE 1938; Rabanus Maurus, *Epistola ad Heribaldum episcopum Antissiodorensem* c. 29, in PL 110:491; Machielsen, "Spurii," pp. 254–55.

[80] JE 2174, text in MGH, Epist. 3:376; Capitulary of Compiègne (757) c. 20, in MGH, LL 1:29; Sägmüller, "'Impedimentum impotentiae'," pp. 93, 98–99; Löffler, *Störungen des geschlechtlichen Vermögens*, pp. 8–9.

[81] JE 2174 and MGH, Epist. 3:276; Sägmüller, "'Impedimentum impotentiae'," p. 100.

between Count Stephen of Aquitaine and the daughter of Count Raymond of Toulouse—he found it helpful to distinguish between natural impotence, that is an inborn incapacity for sexual relations, and acquired impotence, which Hincmar thought might be induced by sorcery. Natural impotence was permanent and provided adequate reason to allow separation and remarriage of the healthy partner, while the impotent party must remain unmarried. Acquired impotence, however, might turn out to be reversible. Hence the parties could separate but not remarry, so that in case the impotence was cured they might reconstitute their marriage.[82]

CONCUBINAGE

Concubinage remained common throughout this period, at least among the prominent and wealthy, and the Church's attitude toward these relationships continued to be ambivalent.[83] On the one hand, the Church treated concubinage as the functional equivalent of marriage for many purposes, including the determination of legitimacy for entrants into religious life or the priesthood.[84] On the other hand, ecclesiastical authorities were determined to restrict concubinage. They repeatedly warned married men that they must not keep a concubine as well as a wife. The Roman Synod of 863 also insisted that women must be free to choose whether to become concubines or not, since parents illicitly persisted in forcing their daughters into these relationships.[85]

---

[82] Hincmar, *De divortio*, interr. 15–16, in PL 125:716–25, and *Epistola . . . de nuptiis Stephani et filiae Regimundi comitis*, in PL 126:132–53; Löffler, *Störungen des geschlechtlichen Vermögens*, p. 9; Claude de Vic and J. Vaisette, *Histoire générale de Languedoc*, 10 vols. (Toulouse: J.-B. Paya, 1811–46) 2:277–78; Jane Bishop, "Bishops as Marital Advisors in the Ninth Century," in *Women of the Medieval World: Essays in Honor of John H. Mundy*, ed. Julius Kirshner and Suzanne F. Wemple (Oxford: Basil Blackwell, 1985), pp. 54–84. Sägmüller, "Nochmals das 'Impedimentum'," pp. 597–611, discusses another well-known case, that of the Emperor Henry II and Queen Kunigunde, a century later.

[83] Vern L. Bullough, *The Subordinate Sex: A History of Attitudes toward Women* (Urbana: University of Illinois Press, 1973; repr. Harmondsworth: Penguin, 1974), p. 164; Freisen, *Geschichte des kanonischen Eherechts*, pp. 68–69; McNamara and Wemple, "Marriage and Divorce," p. 108; Wemple, *Women in Frankish Society*, pp. 40, 78–80; Herlihy, *Medieval Households*, pp. 37–40, 52; Margaret C. Ross, "Concubinage in Anglo-Saxon England," *Past and Present* 108 (1985) 3–34.

[84] Council of Orleans (538) c. 10(9) in CCL 148A:118; Council of Rome (826) c. 37, in MGH, Concilia 2:582; Baumann, *Zivilrechtliche Bedeutung*, p. 16; Bishop, "Bishops as Marital Advisors," pp. 70–71.

[85] Jonas of Orleans, *De inst. laicali* 2.4, in PL 106:174–77; *Episcoporum ad Hludowicum imperatorem relatio* (829) § 54, in MGH, Capitularia 2:45; Council of Mainz (852) c. 15, in MGH, Capitularia 2:190; 1 Council of Toledo (397 ~ 400) c. 17, In Vives, *Concilios Visigóticos*, p. 24; Synod of Rome (863) c. 7, in Mansi 15:655; Löwenstein, *Bekämpfung*, pp. 17–18; Wemple, *Women in Frankish Society*, pp. 81–83.

Sex Offenses

That men ought to be held to the same standard of sexual conduct as women continued to appear as a theoretical norm in the moral manuals of this period. Society's practice, however, was entirely different.[86] The Third Council of Aachen (862) declared that it was rare, almost unheard-of, for a man to remain a virgin until marriage. But men remained largely immune to punishment for their sexual adventures, at least so long as those adventures did not infringe the rights of other men.[87] Women, however, were heavily penalized, even for minor sexual peccadillos, partly because of the danger of pregnancy, partly because female chastity had an appreciable market value. Sexual misbehavior by a woman not only constituted a moral offense, but also diminished her desirability, either as wife or concubine.[88]

Despite the Church's disapproval of nonmarital sex, fornication was commonplace in the early Middle Ages. We are best informed, of course, about sexual scandals among royalty and the higher ranks of the nobility; our information about the sexual practices of the lower classes comes mainly from clerical denunciations of their proclivity to lust. The Merovingian court had more than its share of lechers. A notable offender was King Dagobert I (623–638), who repudiated the wife his father had chosen for him and then married not only the beautiful Nanthild, but two other wives as well. For variety, he consorted with an Austrasian concubine whom he never married, but who bore him a son. The chronicler Fredegar was no doubt exaggerating, but perhaps not by much, in claiming that he could not include the names of all of Dagobert's mistresses in his book for fear of making the work too long. Dagobert's son, Clovis II (638–656), had an even more gaudy string of wives, concubines, and casual lovers.[89] Carolingian rulers, including Charlemagne himself, did not lag far behind the example set by the sexual adventures of the Merovingians.[90]

[86] Jonas of Orleans, *De inst. laicali* 2.2, in PL 106:170–72; Toubert, "Théorie," pp. 260–61; Wemple, *Women in Frankish Society*, pp. 75, 81.

[87] Council of Aachen (862), in Mansi 15:625, citing Augustine, *De bono coniugali*; Wemple, *Women in Frankish Society*, pp. 41, 93; Herlihy, *Medieval Households*, pp. 36–37.

[88] Wemple, *Women in Frankish Society*, pp. 70–71.

[89] Fredegar, *Chronica* 4.53, 58–60, ed. Bruno Krusch, in MGH, SS. rer. mer. 2:146–47; *Liber historiae Francorum* 44, ed. Bruno Krusch, in MGH, SS rer. mer. 2:315; *Gesta Dagoberti I regis Francorum* 22, ed. Bruno Krusch, in MGH, SS rer. mer. 2:408; Wemple, *Women in Frankish Society*, p. 39; Janet L. Nelson, "Queens as Jezebels: The Careers of Brunhild and Balthild in Merovingian History," in *Medieval Women, Dedicated and Presented to Professor Rosalind M. T. Hill on the Occasion of Her Seventieth Birthday*, ed. Derek Baker, Studies in Church History, Subsidia, vol. 1 (Oxford: Basil Blackwell, 1978; repr. 1981), pp. 46–48.

[90] Charlemagne had five wives, at least six concubines, and eighteen children; Wemple, *Women in Frankish Society*, pp. 78–79.

"It's hard to keep a pretty wife," declared Isidore of Seville, testifying to the frequency of adulterous liaisons in Visigothic Spain. Conscientious churchmen throughout the West continued to worry about the never-ending difficulties of repressing adultery.[91] While the early medieval Church continued to treat adultery as grounds for divorce or separation (with or without rights of subsequent remarriage), ecclesiastical writers in this period treated adultery primarily as a moral offense meriting penance, rather than as a canonical crime.[92] Secular law was harsher and might impose substantial fines upon the adulterer.[93] Germanic rulers preferred to keep family units intact, however, and discouraged couples from separating simply because one of them was involved in an extramarital affair. The discouragement was apt to be most effective when divorce on grounds of adultery entailed financial hardship.[94] Ecclesiastical councils were determined to prevent guilty parties in adultery cases from marrying their partners in crime, even after the death of the original spouses of both parties.[95]

Prostitutes seem to have carried on a brisk trade in the Germanic kingdoms, despite a flurry of Carolingian measures designed to discourage commercial sex. Louis the Pious attempted to repress harlotry in his Empire by making both prostitutes and their clients liable to public whipping, but his efforts were short-lived and ineffective.[96] The counts and judges of Visigothic Spain likewise had little success in banishing commercial sex from that kingdom, despite the law's insistence that they must prosecute every harlot who came to their attention, under pain of suffering disciplinary action themselves.[97] Where criminal penalties failed, the Church's efforts to exert moral pressure on wanton women were not much more successful. St. Columban attempted to express his indignation at prostitution by refusing to extend his blessing to the children whom

[91] Isidore of Seville, *De eccl. off.* 2.20.9, in PL 83:812: "Pulchra enim (ut ait quidam sapiens) cito adamatur et difficile custoditur, quod plures amant."

[92] 2 Council of Braga (572) c. 76, in Vives, *Concilios visigóticos*, p. 104; Council of Rome (826) c. 36, in MGH, Concilia 2:582; as well as a text of Pseudo-Gregory (JE 1956) conflated from a genuine text of the Council of Arles (314) c. 11(10), in CCL 148:11, and a letter of Pseudo-Zacharias; Delpini, "Indissolubilità," pp. 80–81; J.R. Reinhard, "Burning at the Stake in Mediaeval Law and Literature," *Speculum* 16 (1941) 186–209; Hans Bennecke, *Die strafrechtliche Lehre von Ehebruch in ihrer historisch-dogmatischen Entwicklung* (Marburg: N. G. Elwert, 1884), p. 34.

[93] *Lex Salica* (100 title text) 14.1, ed. Eckhardt, p. 130.

[94] Laws of Aethelbert 77(1), in *Die Gesetze der Angelsachsen*, ed. Felix Liebermann, 2 vols. in 3 (Halle a/S.: M. Niemeyer, 1903–06) 1:8.

[95] Council of Friuli (796) c. 10, in MGH, Concilia 2:192–93; Council of Tribur (895) c. 40, in MGH, Capitularia 2:236–37; Gottlob, "Ehebruch," pp. 341–43.

[96] *Capitularia de disciplina palatii Aquisgranis* (ca. 820) c. 3, in MGH, Capitularia 1:298; Richard Lewinsohn, *A History of Sexual Customs*, trans. Alexander Mayce (New York: Harper & Brothers, 1958), p. 145. An undated capitulary also banned prostitutes from bringing actions in the courts or testifying in actions brought by others; *Capitula Francia* 8, in MGH, Capitularia 1:334.

[97] King, *Law and Society*, pp. 81, 88–89.

King Theuderic II (612–613) had begotten by a woman alleged to be a harlot. But he succeeded only in enraging Theuderic's grandmother, Queen Brunhild, who expelled the saint from the court and the kingdom.[98] The best the Church could do, it seemed, was to try to restrain its own clergy from marrying divorcées or ladies of the street.[99]

The Church was active during this period in efforts to repress sexual violence, imposing its own penalties on rapists, in addition to punishments levied by secular authorities. Despite the efforts of both kings and bishops, however, the practice of seizing and making off with heiresses and other desirable women plagued early medieval society.[100] Evidently, too, not all of the cases reported as *raptus* by chroniclers and punished as *raptus* by the authorities involved ravishment of an unwilling victim. *Raptus* cases were often elopements of a girl with a suitor of whom her parents disapproved, a fact that helps to explain the apparent failure to prosecute many such occurrences and the frequent willingness, even eagerness, of victims to marry their abductors.[101] When cases were prosecuted, both victim and perpetrator sometimes ended by entering religion as a way of appeasing their families and preventing further discord.[102] Church authorities understandably strove to penalize the rape of nuns with the strongest weapons in their arsenal, but many of these rapes, too, involved the elopement of a nun (often a girl who had unwillingly entered the convent at the demand of her parents) with her lover.[103]

[98] Jonas, *Vitae sanctorum: Columbanus* 1.19, in MGH, scriptores rerum germanicarum in usum scholarum (hereafter SSRG) 34:187–91; Wemple, *Women in Frankish Society*, pp. 66–67.

[99] 4 Council of Toledo (633) c. 44, in Vives, *Concilios visigóticos*, p. 207; King, *Law and Society*, p. 153, n. 1.

[100] Council of Verneuil (844) c. 6 and Council of Meaux-Paris (845/46) c. 64, in MGH, Capitularia 2:384–85, 413–14; Kalifa, "Singularités matrimoniales," pp. 212–13; Wemple, *Women in Frankish Society*, pp. 34, 41.

[101] Fransen, "Rupture," p. 621.

[102] An eighth-century rape case, heard by Duke Hildeprand of Spoleto, illustrates several of these themes. Rabenno, son of Count Rabenno of Fermo, agreed to marry Halerana. A certain Hermifrid, however, took the girl by force of arms and made off with her. Rabenno sought judgment in the ducal court, where both the perpetrator and victim were seized and turned over to him. Rabenno agreed to spare their lives. He had Halerana put in a convent, but later changed his mind and married her. He pardoned Hermifrid, but subsequently regretted his generosity and killed him. As a result, all of Halerena's property and half of Rabenno's were forfeited to the king, who donated it to the monastery of Farfa. Rabenno then entered Farfa as a monk, while Halerana presumably returned to her convent. See Gregorio di Catino, *Il regesto di Farfa*, no. 144, 148, ed. I. Giorgi and U. Balzani, 5 vols. (Rome: La Società, 1879–1914) 2:121–22. I am grateful to Dr. Richard Ring for bringing this case to my attention. See also on these matters the Council of Meaux-Paris (845/46) c. 64, in MGH, Capitularia 2:413–14, and cf. *Capitularia incerta* c. 1, in MGH, Capitularia 1:315; Wemple, *Women in Frankish Society*, p. 82.

[103] Council of Lérida (546) c. 6, in Vives, *Concilios visigóticos*, p. 57; Council of Paris

The early medieval Church was also concerned over what one synod called "a new, unheard-of, and horrid wickedness," namely "unnatural" sexual relations, whether between men and women or between persons of the same gender.[104] Although this particular canon was unusually strident about the matter, Church authorities in the early Middle Ages certainly disapproved of and attempted to suppress all kinds of sexual practices that they regarded as deviant.

Occasionally Church authorities refrained from passing judgment on complaints about such behavior, as is illustrated by one case reported by Hincmar of Reims. During the reign of Louis the Pious, according to Hincmar, a noblewoman named Northild complained to the emperor about the peculiar sexual preferences of her husband, Agembert. The emperor, perplexed, referred the matter to a synod for advice. After discussing the problem, the bishops respectfully refused to determine whether Agembert's sexual practices were sufficiently bizarre to warrant a divorce. The bishops declared that they would prefer to leave such questions to the judgment of married layfolk, who were in a better position to decide about them. Besides, they added, lay authorities had adequate laws to punish Agembert, should they feel that punishment was required.[105]

Examples of such ecclesiastical restraint are uncommon; perhaps special circumstances made this case particularly delicate. But if Church authorities in the seventh, eighth, and ninth centuries were sometimes reluctant to deal with deviant sex practices, secular authorities were not so restrained.[106] In Spain the Visigothic laws prescribed castration for homosexual offenses, but homosexual culture seems to have flourished in Spanish cities during the eighth and ninth centuries.[107]

---

(614), Edictum Clotarii II, 18, in CCL 148A:285; Wemple, *Women in Frankish Society*, p. 158.

[104] 2 Synod of Aachen (860) c. 18, in MGH, Capitularia 2:468; but cf. Boswell, CSTAH, p. 202, who claims that early medieval censures of gay sex were not based on the belief that homosexual relations were unnatural.

[105] Hincmar of Reims, *De divortio Lotharii*, interrog. 5, in PL 125:655.

[106] An exception to the general rule was 16 Council of Toledo (ca. 693) c. 3, in Vives, *Concilios visigóticos*, pp. 500–501; Boswell, CSTAH, pp. 176–78, 202, argues that "sodomy" was loosely used in the vocabulary of this period to designate any type of sexual activity that an author particularly loathed. It is certainly true that the term was sometimes used vaguely, as in Hincmar, *De divortio Lotharii*, interrog. 12, PL 125:691, 693, and St. Boniface, *Epist.* 96, MGH, Epistolae 3:342–43. But Boswell seems to miss the point that this rhetorical device was effective precisely because the authors assumed that linking other sexual aberrations to homosexual practices would impress their readers forcefully with the wickedness of the particular sin they were denouncing. Had gay sex been viewed as an insignificant minor transgression, as Boswell argues, there would have been little point to this rhetorical trick.

[107] *Leg. visig.* 3.5.4, 7, in MGH, LL nat. germ. 1:163, 165; 2 Council of Braga (572) c. 81, in Vives, *Concilios visigóticos*, p. 105; Boswell, CSTAH, pp. 174, 176, 194, 202–3.

Sexual Activities of the Clergy

The early medieval Church achieved only indifferent success in its efforts to restrict clerical sex. Councils denounced the practice of allowing women to live with bishops and priests or to dwell in monasteries of men and decreed that clerics who permitted this practice should lose their clerical positions and suffer excommunication. Charlemagne incorporated similar provisions in two capitularies.[108] A few clerics attempted to circumvent these prohibitions by adopting the women with whom they cohabited, a subterfuge that the Second Council of Braga (572) condemned.[109]

No doubt some clerics who lived with female companions were involved in genuine spiritual marriages, in which carnal involvement was absent and in which the parties led a common life of prayer and asceticism. Nonetheless, there was a strong suspicion that cohabitation might lead to surreptitious sex. In many instances the women with whom clerics dwelt were their legitimate wives. Popes and councils strove to persuade married clerics to abstain from sex with their wives and imposed penances and punishments, including excommunication, upon those who refused to do so.[110] These enactments appear to have been founded upon a belief that it was inappropriate for clergymen to rush from the fleshly passions of the marriage bed to officiate at the sacred rites. The theme of ritual defilement resulting from marital intercourse by clerics runs through many of these punitive enactments.[111] The evidence suggests, however, that enforcement of this prohibition was neither uniform nor successful. Ecclesiastical dynasties in which the cure of a parish descended from father to son for generations seem to have been common, especially in rural areas.[112]

At least as common as the priest who kept a legitimate wife in his rectory was the priest who lived with a concubine to whom he was technically not married at all. Clerical concubinage presented a legal impediment to promotion and constituted grounds for dismissal, but these penalties were rarely enforced. A letter ascribed to Pope Pelagius II (578–590) declared that in regions suffering a shortage of clergymen, it was lawful to ordain men who kept concubines.[113] St.

---

[108] 2 Council of Nicaea (787) c. 18, in COD, p. 128; Council of Lérida (546) c. 15 and 1 Council of Braga (561) c. 15, in Vives, *Concilios visigóticos*, pp. 59, 69; 2 Council of Aachen (836) 2.11, in Mansi 14:682; Charlemagne, *Capitulare primam* (ca. 769) c. 5 and *Capitularium missorum generale* (802) c. 24, in MGH, Capitularia 1:45, 96.

[109] 2 Council of Braga (572) c. 32, in Vives, *Concilios visigóticos*, p. 95.

[110] 2 Council of Toledo (527) c. 3, and Council of Lérida (546) c. 5, in Vives, *Concilios visigóticos*, pp. 43–44, 56–57.

[111] Council of Orleans (538) c.2 in CCL 148A:114–15. Pope Siricius referred to the marital sexual relations of clerics as "contamination" as early as 386 in a letter to the bishops of Africa; PL 13:1160–61, JK 258. A similar reference to the spiritual pollution of clerical sex occurs in *Leg. Visig.* 3.4.18, in MGH, LL nat. germ. 1:158.

[112] Schimmelpfennig, "Ex fornicatione nati," pp. 8–9; Wemple, *Women in Frankish Society*, pp. 142–43.

[113] 2 Council of Braga (572) c. 27 and 4 Council of Toledo (633) c. 19, in Vives, *Concil-*

Boniface complained in a letter to Pope Zacharias (741–752) that some priests and deacons disported themselves with four or five concubines at once. Despite this outrageous behavior, Boniface complained, these men nonetheless advanced in clerical rank, and some of them even became bishops.[114] The pope in his reply deplored these scandals and instructed Boniface that he should by no means believe any priest who claimed to have papal permission to carry on in this way.[115] Neither the pope nor the saint had much success in the campaign against clerical concubinage, however, and two years later Boniface complained again to Zacharias that fornicating clerics now persecuted him for attempting to reform them.[116]

Local laymen sometimes took direct and forceful action against priests and their concubines. Public displays of displeasure might occur when the woman's family felt humiliated by having one of its daughters flaunted as a priest's concubine. Gregory of Tours relates the story of a concubine's family whose members laid hold of the priest, summarily imprisoned him, and redeemed family honor by burning his concubine alive.[117] But the issue in this tale, at least from the family's point of view, was not that the relationship was sinful or unlawful, but rather that it humiliated a proud family to have one of its daughters paraded in such a demeaning situation.

Male clerics were not the only offenders against the prohibitions of clerical sex. Church authorities and secular rulers alike campaigned against nuns and other consecrated women who indulged in fornication. But this battle, too, was only partly successful.[118] The Second Council of Aachen in 836 complained that certain convents were little better than brothels, a complaint repeated a century later in a letter from the Bishop of Würzburg to Rabanus Maurus.[119] A Frankish council hinted darkly that unchaste nuns might be subject to the same punishment that pagan Romans had imposed on Vestal Virgins who broke their vows, namely burial alive. But that savage reference was probably only a rhetorical flourish to show that the bishops took the matter seriously.[120] In any case there is little evidence that the situation greatly improved.

---

ios visigóticos, pp. 94, 198–200; Council of Orleans (541) c. 29, in CCL 148A:139; Ps.-Leo VII, *Epist.* 15, in PL 132:1086–87 (JE 3614); King, *Law and Society*, p. 153; Grévy-Pons, *Célibat et nature*, p. 13; see also the letter ascribed to Pelagius II (578–590) in his *Epistolae et decreta* 14, in PL 72:747–48 (JK 982)—the letter was in fact written by Pelagius I (555–560).

[114] St. Boniface, *Epist.* 50, in MGH, Epistolae 3:300.

[115] St. Boniface, *Epist.* 51, in MGH, Epistolae 3:305; JE 2264 (April, 743).

[116] Council of Rome (745) praef., in MGH, Concilia 2:39.

[117] Gregory of Tours, *Historia Francorum* 6.36, in MGH, SS rer. mer. 1:276.

[118] 2 Council of Braga (572) c. 31, in Vives, *Concilios visigóticos*, p. 95; *Leg. Visig.* 3.5.2, in MGH, LL nat. germ. 1:159–61.

[119] 2 Council of Aachen (836) 2.12, in Mansi 14:682; *Epistolae Fuldensium fragmenta* c. 6 (743), in MGH, Epistolae 5:525.

[120] Council of Tours (567) c. 21(20), in CCL 148A:186, citing Cod. Theod. 9.25.1–2; Wemple, *Women in Frankish Society*, p. 157.

Early medieval moralists believed that passion, especially sexual passion, posed a threat to the welfare of the individual and society. Since sexual passion impelled men and women to seek carnal satisfaction with almost anyone, at any time, in any way that they could contrive, Christian moralists and lawgivers, like their pagan counterparts, saw sex as a disruptive force in social life. Sexual urges, they believed, must be curbed and controlled; otherwise they were sure to result in irrational and frenzied couplings that would disrupt the orderly creation of families and the management of household resources.

Moralists of this era sought to adapt the views of the Church Fathers to the changed conditions of their own times. In the process they attempted to portray their sexual teachings as logical conclusions from Christian doctrine. These conclusions, however, often seemed to bear little relationship to the reasons marshalled to support them.[121] These characteristics were even more pronounced in the penitential literature that began to become a major focus for discussions of sexual behavior in Christian literature from the mid-sixth century onward.

Sexual Behavior and Moral Prescriptions in the Penitentials

Penitentials, a new genre of Christian moral literature, grew increasingly influential in shaping Catholic sexual doctrine between the end of the sixth century and the beginning of the eleventh century.[122] The handbooks of penance written in this period provided guidance for confessors in dealing with sinners who wished to be reconciled with God and to make their peace with the Church. The advice offered by the penitential authors was grounded on their practical experience as confessors, as well as on their reading in spiritual and doctrinal literature.[123] The penitentials, accordingly, focused primarily on pastoral con-

[121] Jean-Louis Flandrin, *Un temps pour embrasser: Aux origines de la morale sexuelle occidentale (VIe–XIe siècle)* (Paris: Éditions du Seuil, 1983), pp. 72–73, 116–17.

[122] Paul Fournier and Gabriel Le Bras, *Histoire des collections canoniques en Occident depuis les fausses décrétales jusqu'au Décret de Gratien*, 2 vols. (Paris: Sirey, 1931–32; repr. Aalen: Scientia, 1972) 1:347–58; A. Van Hove, *Prolegomena ad Codicem Iuris Canonici*, 2d ed., Commentarium Lovaniense in Codicem Iuris Canonici, pt. 1, vol. 1 (Malines, Rome: H. Dessain, 1945), pp. 283–90, 295–99; Alfons M. Stickler, *Historia iuris canonici Latini, institutiones academicae*, vol. 1: Historia fontium (Turin: Libraria Pontificii Athenaei Salesiani, 1950; no more published), pp. 86–92, 104–106, 112–13; António García y García, *Historia del derecho canónico*, vol. 1: El primer milenio (Salamanca: Instituto de historia de la teologia española, 1967), pp. 187–89, 254–59, 292–97. See generally Cyrille Vogel, *Les 'Libri poenitentiales'*, Typologie des sources du moyen âge occidental, fasc. 27 (Turnhout: Brépols, 1978). On the relationship of the penitentials to Germanic folklaw see also Harold J. Berman, *Law and Revolution: The Formation of the Western Legal Tradition* (Cambridge: Harvard University Press, 1983), pp. 68–75.

[123] Allen J. Frantzen, *The Literature of Penance in Anglo-Saxon England* (New Brunswick, NJ: Rutgers University Press, 1983), pp. 56–57.

cerns, on the means by which those who had offended God and the Christian community might make reparation for their sinful thoughts, words, and deeds.

Sexual offenses constituted the largest single category of behavior that the penitentials treated. Prominent among sexual problems were offenses against marital fidelity, failure to pay the conjugal debt, and sexual activities that were believed to offend God, whether they injured anyone else or not. The penitentials also sought to inculcate proper methods for channeling and controlling sexual impulses, so that the sinner might adopt a morally acceptable way of life.[124] The emphasis of the penitentials fell more heavily upon reparation for past offenses than upon reformation of future behavior, but penitential authors clearly hoped that the prescribed penances would change later conduct. In general the penitentials more commonly dealt with fornication, adultery, masturbation, and the like than with purely marital problems.[125]

The penitentials comprise a large and complex body of literature. The earliest ones are of Irish origin. The genre spread from Ireland in the late sixth century to England in the seventh century and thence to the Continent during the eighth century. Table 4.1 in the Appendix shows a classified list of the principal early medieval handbooks.[126] The growth in popularity of these handbooks paralleled the spread of a new type of penitential practice. The older discipline of the Church on the Continent had featured public acknowledgment of sins by the offender, followed by the imposition of public penance, in which the penitent was excluded from participation in the Eucharist and other sacramental functions. The guilty person regularly appeared clad in a rough penitential gown, at the entrance of the church, to beg forgiveness from the community for his or her offenses against the Christian moral code. In addition, public penitents often had to undertake prolonged and severe fasts, to abstain from sexual relations with their spouses, and sometimes to submit to public whippings and other acts of expiation prior to readmission to communion.

[124] Leclercq, *Monks on Marriage*, p. 69.

[125] Frantzen, *Literature of Penance*, pp. 3–4; Kottje, "Ehe und Eheverständnis," p. 25.

[126] The major published collections of penitential texts cited in Table 4.1 in the Appendix are (in addition to those in PL): Ludwig Bieler, ed., *The Irish Penitentials*, Scriptores Latini Hiberniae, vol. 5 (Dublin: Dublin Institute for Advanced Studies, 1963; cited hereafter as Bieler); Arthur West Haddan and William Stubbs, eds., *Councils and Ecclesiastical Documents Relating to Great Britain and Ireland*, 3 vols. (Oxford: Clarendon Press, 1869–78; repr. 1964; cited hereafter as Haddan and Stubbs); John T. McNeill and Helena M. Gamer, eds. and trans., *Medieval Handbooks of Penance*, Records of civilization, Sources and Studies, no. 29 (New York: Columbia University Press, 1938; repr. New York: Octagon Books, 1965; hereafter McNeill and Gamer); Hermann Joseph Schmitz, ed., *Die Bussbücher und die Bussdiciplin der Kirche*, 2 vols. (Mainz: Franz Kirchheim, 1883–98; hereafter Schmitz); Friedrich Wilhelm Hermann Wasserschleben, ed., *Die Bussordnungen der abendländischen Kirche nebst einer rechtsgeschichtlichen Einleitung* (Halle: Ch. Graeger, 1851; hereafter Wasserschleben) and *Die irische Kanonensammlung*, 2d ed. (Leipzig: Bernhard Tauchnitz, 1885; repr. Aalen: Scientia, 1966).

The new style of penance introduced by the Celtic Church featured private confession by the offender to a priest, followed by private acts of reparation.[127] The penitentials sought to guide confessors in assigning appropriate penances for different categories of sins; many of these handbooks consisted of elaborately detailed lists of offenses that the priest might expect to encounter in the confessional, together with tariffs of penances appropriate to each sin. In addition many sins, particularly those that were secret and known only to the sinner and the confessor, might be atoned for by "redemption" or "commutation," that is by the substitution of a money payment or other act that could be performed privately in place of the fasts or public acts of reparation stipulated in the penitential. A tenth-century English penitential, for example, allowed one day's fast to be replaced by the offering of one penny or the recitation of a few prayers, while a year's fast might be redeemed either by a payment of thirty shillings or by thirty masses. Similar schemes of commutation, some of them very fanciful, were common.[128]

MARITAL SEX

The penitentials by and large took a gloomy view of the sexual proclivities of both men and women. Many of their authors no doubt shared Pseudo-Gregory's belief that even in marriage sex is always pleasurable, always impure, and always sinful.[129] Marital sex was a concession, they believed: God allowed mar-

[127] John T. McNeill, *A History of the Cure of Souls* (New York: Harper Brothers, 1951; repr. Harper Torchbooks, 1965), pp. 112–35; Oscar D. Watkins, *A History of Penance*, 2 vols. (London: Longmans, Green & Co., 1920; repr. New York: Ben Franklin, 1961) 2:536–49, 603–31, 643–44, 688–92; Lea, *History of Auricular Confession* 1:20–49, 179–97, 2:73–114; but cf. Kate Dooley, "From Penance to Confession: The Celtic Contribution," *Bijdragen: Tijdschrift voor filosofie en theologie* (Louvain, 1982) 390–411. Confession of sins is a common and widespread feature of ancient and primitive religions. The practice is well represented in the religious institutions of every part of the world, but is especially prominent in the early religious systems of North America and Africa. In Mexico and Peru, confession goes back into the pre-Aztec and pre-Inca periods. In Egypt there is evidence for confession of sins as early as the XIX Dynasty (13th century B.C.). The sins confessed in ancient religions were almost exclusively sexual ones, with adultery playing a prominent role. See R. Pettazzoni, "La confession des péchés dans l'histoire générale des religions," in *Mélanges Franz Cumont*, 2 vols. (Brussels: Secrétariat de l'Institut, 1936) 2:893–96.

[128] Pseudo-Edgar, *Leges ecclesiasticae*, De poenitentia 18 and De magnatibus 2, in PL 138:512; Egbert, *Penitentiale* 13.11, in Schmitz 1:585–87; *Irish Canons* 2.1–12 and *Old Irish Table of Commutations*, in Bieler, pp. 162–67, 278–82; Boswell, CSTAH, p. 181.

[129] *Responsa Gregorii* in Gregory I, *Registrum* 11.56a, Paul Ewald and Ludwig Harmann, eds., in MGH, Epist. 2/1:340: "Non haec dicentes culpam deputamus esse coniugium. Sed quia ipsa licita admixtio carnis sine voluptate carnis fieri non potest, a sacro loco ingressu abstinendum est, quia voluptas ipsa esse sine culpa non potest."

ried persons to have sex only for procreation, never for pleasure. This opinion was consistent with the predominant teaching among the Fathers.[130]

Since marital sex was a concession, not a right, and since pleasure was an ever present incitement to lust, penitential writers maintained that sex in marriage must be strictly scheduled and closely monitored. Without periodic abstinence from sex, according to the Penitential of St. Finnian (written ca. 525–550), marriage itself lacked legitimacy and degenerated into sin.[131] Periodic sexual abstinence appears in the sixth- and seventh-century penitentials as a virtue. But while penitential writers of this period warned that married couples who failed to observe continence at certain seasons would feel God's wrath, they did not often prescribe specific penances for those who failed to heed these admonitions. By the end of the seventh century, however, married couples who failed to practice periodical sexual abstinence increasingly found themselves subject to penance; by the beginning of the eleventh century, periodic abstinence seems to have become common practice among conscientious couples.[132] Scheduled abstinence from sex, according to one authority, marked an essential difference between married sex and fornication. Moreover, children born of intercourse during forbidden periods were bastards in God's eyes, if not in human law.[133]

The penitentials usually specified the times when married people were expected to refrain from sexual relations according to two kinds of criteria: they defined some abstinence periods in terms of events in the wife's physiological cycle (see Appendix, Table 4.3); seasons in the Church's liturgical calendar determined most of the others (see Appendix, Table 4.4).[134] A few miscellaneous abstinence periods were defined by other criteria.

The major events in the female biological cycle that required married couples

---

[130] Kottje, "Ehe und Eheverständnis," pp. 32–33; John T. Noonan, Jr., *Contraception: A History of Its Treatment by the Catholic Theologians and Canonists* (Cambridge: Harvard University Press, Belknap Press, 1965), p. 163, concludes that the penitentials' treatment of sex offenses was more concerned with banning contraception and abortion than with punishing lust; but see below, pp. 168, 173, 174.

[131] Finnian, *Penitentialis* 46, in Bieler, pp. 90–93.

[132] Gregory the Great and Caesarius of Arles both commented on the nonobservance of the rather loosely-defined rules for sexual abstinence current in the sixth century; Caesarius, *Serm.* 44.7, in CCL 103:199; Gregory, *Dialogi* 1.10, ed. Umberto Moricca, *Fonti per la storia d'Italia*, vol. 57 (Rome: Tipografia del Senato, 1924), pp. 59–60. Jonas of Orleans, *De inst. laicali* 2.3, in PL 106:172–74, writing in the early ninth century testified that in his day most people observed the rules on sexual abstinence, which by then were much more complex and comprehensive than they had been earlier. See also Flandrin, *Un temps pour embrasser*, p. 142.

[133] Ivo of Chartres, *Decretum* 8.145, in PL 161:616; Jonas of Orleans, *De inst. laicali* 2.2, in PL 106:171; Flandrin, *Un temps pour embrasser*, pp. 117, 119.

[134] Flandrin, *Un temps pour embrasser*, p. 12; Payer, "Early Medieval Regulations," p. 364.

to practice continence included the menstrual period, pregnancy, childbirth, and lactation. Most penitential collections prohibited couples from having sexual relations while the wife was experiencing her menstrual flow. Those who broke this restriction were usually subject to a forty-day penance, though a few authors prescribed much shorter penances for this offense.[135] This prohibition was based on the purity rules of the Mosaic law, perhaps augmented by a belief in the terrifying physical effects of contact with menstrual fluid described in the *Natural History* of the elder Pliny.[136] Some early medieval writers believed that marital abstinence during menstruation was further justified because a child conceived during the menstrual period would be hideously deformed at birth. This notion may be original with Christian writers; it does not appear either in the Hebrew Scriptures or in the writings of ancient anatomists and biologists.[137]

Penitentials frequently prohibited sexual relations during pregnancy. The proscribed period usually ran from the first evidence of pregnancy to the birth of the child. This prohibition had no scriptural precedents either and probably represents another example of the influence of Greco-Roman views on sexual propriety during the early medieval period.[138] Some writers apparently believed that any sort of contact with a pregnant woman, whether unwitting or not, imparted ritual impurity. The *Bigotianum* insists, for example, that a cleric who came into contact with a pregnant woman must fast for forty days on bread and water; this clearly implies that ritual defilement was involved. Presumably the impurity resulted from the fact that pregnancy originated in a sex act and a belief that the resultant impurity remained contagious, so to speak, throughout pregnancy.[139]

Once a child was born, the penitentials required that the parents continue to abstain from sex for a substantial postpartum period.[140] The birth process it-

---

[135] *Merseburgense* (a) 96, in Wasserschleben, p. 401 (40 days); *Canones Gregorii* 107, in Wasserschleben, p. 172 (40 days); Bede 3.37, in Haddan and Stubbs 3:329 (40 days); Cummean 2.30, in Bieler, p. 116 (unspecified); *Old-Irish Penitential* 2.36, in Bieler, p. 265 (20 days); Ps.-Theodore 2.2.5, in Wasserschleben, p. 577 (30 days); *Escarpsus Cummeani* 13, in Schmitz 1:623 (40 days); Flandrin, *Un temps pour embrasser*, p. 12; Noonan, *Contraception*, p. 165; Lindner, *Usus matrimonii*, p. 86.

[136] Lev. 15:24, 18:19, 20:18; Pliny the Elder, *Historia naturalis* 7.15.

[137] Flandrin, *Un temps pour embrasser*, pp. 74–75.

[138] *Bigotianum* 2.93, in Bieler, p. 222; *Canones Gregorii* 80, in Wasserschleben, p. 170; Cummean 2.30, in Bieler, p. 116; Finnian 46, in Bieler, p. 92; *Old-Irish Penitential* 2.36, in Bieler, p. 265; Regino 1.328, in PL 132:256; Burchard, *Decretum* 19:155, in PL 140:1013; Ivo, *Decretum* 15.163, in PL 161:894; Flandrin, *Un temps pour embrasser*, pp. 13–16, 82–83; Lindner, *Usus matrimonii*, pp. 83–84; Noonan, *Contraception*, pp. 163–65.

[139] *Bigotianum* 1.6.2, in Bieler, p. 216; *Canones Hibernenses* 1.23, in Bieler, p. 162; Flandrin, *Un temps pour embrasser*, pp. 84–87.

[140] Cummean 2.31, in Bieler, p. 116; *Canones Gregorii* 126, in Wasserschleben, p. 174; *Old-Irish Penitential* 2.36, in Bieler, p. 265; *Collectio canonum Hiberniae* 46.11, in *Irische Kanonensammlung*, p. 215; *Bigotianum* 2.9.3, in Bieler, p. 222; Halitgar 24, in Schmitz 1:727; Regino 1.328, in PL 132:256; Burchard, *Decretum* 19.5, in PL 140:959.

self—as well, perhaps, as normal postpartum bleeding—apparently induced ritual pollution. The *Responsa Gregorii* seem to link the impurity attached to childbirth with the belief that the mother must have enjoyed pleasure from the sex act that resulted in the child's conception. This sexual pleasure may have been the ultimate source of the ritual contamination resulting from childbirth. Some writers prescribed a longer period of continence after the birth of a girl than after the birth of a boy. This disparity implies that the writers considered female sexuality itself to be a source of greater impurity than male sexuality.[141]

Once pregnancy was over, the child was born, and the postpartum continence period had passed, couples were still forbidden to have sexual intercourse, according to the *Responsa Gregorii*, until after the child had been weaned. Well-to-do women could avoid this prohibition, however, since they usually entrusted their infants to wet nurses shortly after birth—but the *Responsa* denounced that practice as immoral.[142]

In addition to ordaining abstinence periods linked to the female physiological cycle, the penitentials prescribed numerous and extensive periods of sexual continence required by the liturgical cycle. Early medieval Christians, to judge from the penitentials, seem almost to have been obsessed by a need to tie moral and behavioral prescriptions to liturgical events. This is scarcely surprising, since many societies, particularly rural ones, regulated their activities according to a calendar cycle linked to their cultic systems.[143]

Virtually all of the major penitentials required married couples to abstain from sex on Sundays; a substantial number of them prescribed sexual abstinence on Wednesdays and Fridays as well. A few added to this a requirement of continence on Saturdays.[144] Different rationales underlay these prescriptions. Wednesdays and Fridays were traditional days of penance, hence sexual abstinence on those days fitted into a regime of fasting and self-denial. Sundays, by contrast, were days of rejoicing—so much so that fasting and other penitential acts were often forbidden on Sundays. But as Christians were expected to participate in liturgical services on Sundays, and as sexual relations created ritual pollution which made the individual unfit to participate in divine worship, abstinence was not so much a penitential practice as a guarantee of ritual purity.

---

[141] Gregory I, *Registrum* 11.56a.8, in MGH, Epist. 2/1:338: "Voluptas etenim carnis, non dolor in culpa est. In carnis autem commixtione voluptas est; nam in prolis prolatione gemitus." Flandrin, *Un temps pour embrasser*, pp. 16–17, 80; Payer, "Early Medieval Regulations," p. 368.

[142] Gregory I, *Registrum* 9.56a, in MGH, Epist. 2/1:339; Flandrin, *Un temps pour embrasser*, pp. 17–19.

[143] Flandrin, *Un temps pour embrasser*, pp. 93, 160.

[144] Finnian 46, in Bieler, p. 92; Cummean 2.30, in Bieler, p. 116; *Collectio canonum Hiberniae* 46.11, in *Irische Kanonensammlung*, p. 215; *Valicellanum II* 40, in Schmitz 1:336; *Bigotianum* 2.10, in Bieler, p. 222; Egbert 7.3, in Haddan and Stubbs 3:423; Regino 1.328, in PL 132:256; Burchard, *Decretum* 19.155, in PL 140:1013; Kottje, "Ehe und Eheverständnis," p. 33; Payer, "Early Medieval Regulations," pp. 366–67; Flandrin, *Un temps pour embrasser*, pp. 21, 36.

This interpretation is borne out by the fact that some authors deemed the Sunday abstinence period to run only through the daylight hours, thus allowing married couples to have sex after sunset on Sunday evenings.[145]

In addition to these weekly periods of sexual abstinence, married couples were required to forego carnal relations during the so-called three Lents each year.[146] The first Lent consisted of the weeks prior to Easter, although the precise duration of this season varied considerably: in some communities Lent began as early as Septuagesima Sunday, while in others it commenced only on Ash Wednesday. Lenten fasting did not extend to Sundays, when fasting was in principle forbidden; but sexual abstinence during Lent was demanded on Sundays as well as on weekdays. Thus the period of sexual abstinence during Lent was substantially longer than the period of fasting. It might last as long as sixty-two days (where Lent began on Septuagesima) or it might be as short as forty-seven days (where Lent began on Ash Wednesday).

The second Lent referred to the season of Advent, that is the weeks immediately before Christmas. Here again various regions defined the period differently: some communities began Advent observances as early as St. Martin's Day (11 November), which meant forty-four days of sexual abstinence, while others postponed the beginning of Advent to the fourth Sunday before Christmas, which resulted in sexual abstinence for somewhere between twenty-two and thirty-five days.[147]

The third Lent was more variable still. This Lent centered on the feast of Pentecost: in some places the third Lent ran for up to forty days after Pentecost, while elswhere it comprised anything from seven to forty days before Pentecost.[148] Authorities who required sexual abstinence prior to Pentecost in effect prohibited marital relations for an extraordinarily long time indeed: if Lent began approximately four-and-a-half weeks before Easter, if couples were required (as they often were) to continue to abstain from sex during the week after Easter, and if they also had to abstain for forty days before Pentecost (which falls fifty days after Easter), this foreclosed marital relations for somewhere between eleven and thirteen weeks in the spring of each year.

Nor was this all. A good many penitentials also demanded sexual abstinence on all major feast days, the vigils of major feasts, and the quarterly ember days.[149] In addition, some penitentials required abstinence from sex for a period

---

[145] Flandrin, *Un temps pour embrasser*, pp. 98, 106–14.

[146] Finnian 46, in Bieler, p. 92; Cummean 2.30, in Bieler, p. 116; Egbert 7.4, in Haddan and Stubbs 3:423; *Collectio canonum Hiberniae* 46.11, in *Irische Kanonensammlung*, p. 215; *Capitula iudiciorum* 9.2, in Schmitz 1:660; Regino 1.300, 328, in PL 132:249, 256; Burchard, *Decretum* 19.155, in PL 140:1013; Lindner, *Usus matrimonii*, pp. 86–87; Payer, "Early Medieval Regulations," pp. 365–66; Flandrin, *Un temps pour embrasser*, pp. 22–25, 102–105.

[147] Flandrin, *Un temps pour embrasser*, p. 23.

[148] Flandrin, *Un temps pour embrasser*, pp. 24–27.

[149] *Casinense* 65, in Schmitz 1:413; *Capitula iudiciorum* 9.2, in Schmitz 1:660; Regino 1.328, in PL 132:256; Burchard, *Decretum* 19.5, in PL 140:960.

of time—usually three days—before receiving communion, although a few demanded as much as seven days of sexual abstinence prior to communion and a further seven days following it.[150] The abstinence in connection with communion may not have worked additional hardship on married couples during the early Middle Ages, however, because it was common practice at that time for laymen to communicate only at Christmas and Easter (the Lent and Advent penitential observances would in any case have prohibited sexual relations during the days immediately before receiving the Eucharist). As it became common to receive the sacrament more often—this began to happen after the Carolingian period—the sexual continence associated with communion imposed still further limitations on the sex life of married couples. Moreover, persons who performed penance for non-sexual sins were often required to abstain from marital intercourse throughout much or all of the period of penance—which for grievous sins might involve many years.[151]

There were still further limitations on marital sex. Newly married couples were strenuously enjoined to refrain from any sexual activity immediately following their marriage: the periods prescribed for postponement of consummation varied from one day to three or more. During this initial period of marriage the couple were advised to heed the admonitions given by the Angel Raphael to the Old Testament teacher, Tobias, and thus to spend their time in prayer and other penitential exercises.[152] Archbishop Theodore's *Penitential* required newlyweds to stay away from the church for thirty days following their marriage. Following that period, presumably dedicated to sexual exploration and delectation, they were to do penance for forty days, after which they could return to regular Church attendance.[153] These prescriptions, too, reflect the conviction that sexual relations, even in marriage, were irretrievably tinged with impurity and perhaps with sin as well. Accordingly after a short period of frolic immediately following marriage, sex should play a minimal role in the marital relationship.

The mandatory periods of sexual abstinence prescribed in varying combinations by virtually all penitentials had the result for those who obeyed them scrupulously of reducing the frequency of marital intercourse to remarkably low levels. Since many factors are involved—the woman's menstrual cycle

---

[150] *Old-Irish Penitential* 2.36, in Bieler, p. 265; Egbert 7.3, in Haddan and Stubbs 3:423; Halitgar 24, in Schmitz 1:727; Regino 1.300, in PL 132:251; Lindner, *Usus matrimonii*, p. 87; Payer, "Early Medieval Regulations," p. 367; Flandrin, *Un temps pour embrasser*, pp. 30–33.

[151] Columban B.14, 18, in Bieler, p. 102; Finnian 35–39, in Bieler, pp. 86–88; Cummean 22–24, in Bieler, p. 116; Regino 2.6, 2.29, in PL 132:287, 291; Burchard, *Decretum* 6.1, in PL 140:763–65; Payer, "Early Medieval Regulations," pp. 369–70, as well as *Sex and the Penitentials*, pp. 27–28; Flandrin, *Un temps pour embrasser*, p. 37.

[152] Tob. 6:16–22; Hérard of Tours, *Capitula* 89, in PL 121:770; Regino 2.153, in PL 132:312; Jonas of Orleans, *De inst.laicali* 2.2, in PL 106:171; Burchard, *Decretum* 9.5, 7, in PL 140:816; see also Saintyves, "Les trois nuits de Tobie".

[153] Theodore 1.14.1, in Haddan and Stubbs 3:187.

(which varies widely in frequency and duration), fertility, the age of infants at the time of weaning, and the liturgical seasons (which also varied considerably)—it is difficult to estimate precisely the number of days denied to sex, as well as the impact that these recommended limitations may have had on the married population as a whole, even assuming that people were generally aware of and made serious attempts to follow the prescriptions of the penitentials.

Flandrin has attempted to arrive at such an estimate, however, using statistical models that produce a reasonable approximation of a range of results for hypothetical couples. One model assumes a scrupulously observant couple who had intercourse at every available opportunity. The model further assumes that the woman had an absolutely regular cycle of menstruation and ovulation, and that she was maximally fertile, since pregnancy and childbirth would increase the length of the abstinence periods. Based on these assumptions and calculating results over a three-year period, the model shows that such a couple would have had sexual relations on an average slightly more than forty-four times a year, or in other words slightly less than four times per month. Using a more realistic model that assumes less than maximal fertility, a couple might have managed to have sexual relations a bit more frequently—slightly more than once a week, on average, over a three-year period.

A fertile couple who seriously attempted to follow the penitential prescriptions on marital abstinence would rarely have been able to make love more than five times per month during their years of maximum sexual activity. Modern populations whose sexual habits have been investigated shows much higher levels of marital sex among couples between the ages of twenty and thirty-five. In industrialized nations the mean frequency of marital intercourse in this age category runs close to three times the figures that Flandrin's models project. If the strictures on marital intercourse in the penitentials were generally known and observed, therefore, they would have had the effect of diminishing marital sexual activity to an extremely low level, without at the same time radically decreasing the possibilities of conception and thus the birth rate.[154] On the basis of Flandrin's calculations, the penitentials seem to have mandated an effective strategy for achieving the results that doctrinal writers favored: a reduction of sexual activity to a minimum in order to avoid its sinful consequences, while at the same time leaving unimpaired the reproductive function that would presumably populate heaven with saints.

The influence of the penitentials' prescriptions for sexual abstinence in marriage remains conjectural, for this depended on the degree of compliance. This variable is difficult to gauge. Flandrin argues, on the basis of admittedly tenuous evidence, that by the end of the tenth century many couples had begun to accept the periodic bans on marital sex advised in the penitentials.[155]

Beyond demographic considerations, the psychological impact of the prohibitions and sanctions attached to marital sex is even more difficult to measure.

---

[154] Flandrin, *Un temps pour embrasser*, pp. 41–54, 58.
[155] Flandrin, *Un temps pour embrasser*, pp. 128–58.

Certainly any couple who paid close attention to the rules outlined in the penitentials would have found the process of deciding whether or not they could in good conscience have intercourse at any given moment a complex, perhaps even frightening, process. Figure 4.1 displays in flow-chart form a schematic outline of the decision process, using criteria from a number of penitentials.

Any conscientious and moderately well-informed couple might well have approached their sexual encounters under such a scheme as serious, even solemn, occasions that required considerable deliberation and forethought. This regime seems well devised to rob marital sex of spontaneity and perhaps of joy. Those who stopped to examine all the contingencies involved in the decision to have sexual relations would presumably have been sobered by the process. Those who blithely ignored the complex web of prohibitions and sanctions might well have been prey to fear, apprehension, qualms of conscience, and guilt in the aftermath.

Aside from requiring periodic abstinence from sexual relations, the penitentials imposed numerous other limitations on marital intercourse. The handbooks encouraged couples to have sexual relations only at night and then to do so while at least partially clothed. One penitential stipulated that a husband should never see his wife naked.[156] The positions that couples assumed during their sexual relations were also regulated. Penitential texts repeatedly insisted that intercourse must not take place "from the rear."[157] Variations in the formulation of this prohibition suggest that it was intended to ban both vaginal intercourse from the rear and anal intercourse as well.[158]

The penitentials had little to say about heterosexual fellatio: only one of them mentioned it explicitly, although several dealt with oral sex between persons of the same gender.[159] The restrictions on marital sexual relations in nonstandard positions or employing unorthodox techniques may have been motivated by a desire to discourage sexual practices that were thought to hinder

---

[156] The references in many penitentials to intercourse at night imply an unarticulated assumption that sexual relations ought to occur only after sundown; e.g., Finnian 46, in Bieler, p. 92: "[E]t in nocte dominica uel sabbato abstineant se ab invicem"; Cummean 2.30, in Bieler, p. 116: [E]t sabbato et in dominico nocte dieque;" *Bigotianum* 2.9, in Bieler, p. 222: "iii. noctes abstineant se a coniunctione;" *Canones Gregorii* 181, in Wasserschleben, p. 179, "III. noctes abstineant a coniunctione;" Egbert 7.3, in Haddan and Stubbs 3:423: "[E]t in Dominica nocte;" Halitgar 24, in Schmitz 1:727: "[T]ribus noctibus ac diebus abstineant se." On nudity see Theodore 2.12.30, in Schmitz 1:547, and Ps.-Egbert, *Confessionale* 20, in Wasserschleben, p. 309; see also Payer, "Early Medieval Regulations," p. 361, and Kottje,"Ehe und Eheverständnis," p. 35.

[157] Cummean 16.15, in Bieler, p. 128; Theodore 14.21, in Haddan and Stubbs 3:189; Egbert 5.19, in Haddan and Stubbs 3:422; Bede 3.38, in Haddan and Stubbs 3:329; Burchard, *Decretum* 19.5, in PL 140:959, and *Corrector* 49, in Wasserschleben, p. 642.

[158] Payer, "Early Medieval Regulations," p. 358, and *Sex and the Penitentials*, pp. 29–30.

[159] *Old-Irish Penitential* 2.23, in Bieler, p. 264; Payer, *Sex and the Penitentials*, pp. 29–30, and "Early Medieval Regulations," p. 358.

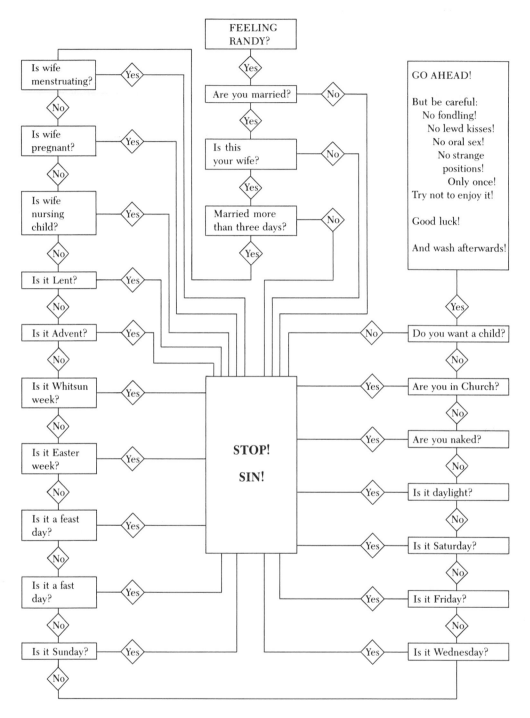

Figure 4.1. The sexual decision-making process according to the penitentials

procreation (or, in the case of oral and anal sex, made it impossible). More likely, however, these bans registered a suspicion that unorthodox variations and techniques involved the pursuit of more intense sexual pleasure.[160]

Whatever the position and whatever the technique, the penitentials clearly considered marital relations, and all sexual activities for that matter, a source of spiritual pollution. Symptomatic of this fear of spiritual taint was the requirement that persons who had engaged in sexual relations must wash themselves before entering a church or participating in religious services.[161] Both the notion that sex caused defilement and the belief that washing would restore purity have Old Testament sources.[162]

Aside from their treatment of sexual relations, the penitentials generally had little to say about marriage. The penitentials of Halitgar and Burchard forbade women to marry men to whom they had not been betrothed,[163] while the penitential of Rabanus Maurus repeated the First Council of Toledo's injunction that married men must not keep concubines.[164] Several penitential handbooks treated incest in considerable detail. Discussions of incest in the early penitentials tended to be less extensive than those in doctrinal treatises, however, and they usually banned sex only with close blood relatives: mother, father, brother, and sister are most often mentioned.[165] The later and more systematic handbooks, however, detailed a considerably wider range of relationships.[166] A few

---

[160] Payer, "Early Medieval Regulations," pp. 359, 371. Noonan, *Contraception*, p. 163, hazarded a guess (his word) that the ban on intercourse in anything but the so-called missionary position sprang from a belief that this position was the most favorable one for conception. While that rationale does appear in a few later treatments of the subject, the context of the prohibition in the penitentials suggests that the authors linked nonstandard coital positions, particularly the rear-penetration position, with bestiality rather than with contraception or abortion. See generally James A. Brundage, "Let Me Count the Ways: Canonists and Theologians Contemplate Coital Positions," JMH 10 (1984) 81–93.

[161] Theodore 2.12.29, in Schmitz 1:547; *Canones Gregorii* 182, in Wasserschleben, p. 179. References to sex as pollution occur in papal documents as early as 404, in a letter of Pope Innocent I, PL 20:476, JE 286. The notion was developed at length in the *Responsa Gregorii*; see Gregory I, *Reg.* 11.56a.8, in MGH, Epist. 2/1:340.

[162] Lev. 15:16–18. Early Christian doctrinal writers also allude to the theme occasionally; e.g., Lactantius, *Div. inst.* 6.23, ed. Brandt in CSEL 19:567.

[163] Halitgar 4.18, in PL 105:684; Burchard, *Decretum* 8.19, in PL 140:795. The objective of this prohibition was to assure that parents and families gave prior approval to marriage arrangements; Kottje, "Ehe und Eheverständnis," p. 37.

[164] Rabanus Maurus, *Poenitentiale Heribaldi* 28, in PL 110:490–91, citing 1 Toledo (397 ~ 400) c. 17, in Vives, *Concilios visigóticos*, p. 24.

[165] Cummean 2.7, in Bieler, p. 114; *Bigotianum* 2.3.1–2, in Bieler, p. 220; *Sangallensis tripartita* 1.6, in Schmitz 2:180; Theodore 2.12.24–28, in Haddan and Stubbs 3:201, extends the range of prohibitions to the fourth or even the fifth degree.

[166] Regino 2.184–85, 262, in PL 132:319–20, 334; Burchard, *Decretum* 7.1–6, 17–18; 17.1–26; 19.5, in PL 140:779–82, 919–24, 965–67; Burchard, *Corrector* 48, 95–96, 99–102, in Wasserschleben, pp. 641–42, 650–51.

penitentials, most of them from the Anglo-Saxon group, dealt with the problem of the impotent husband whose wife wished to remarry.[167] Only one penitential, the *Capitula iudiciorum* of Pseudo-Cummean, took up the problem of the sterile marriage; this handbook forbade infertile couples to separate, much less to remarry, on this account.[168]

Several manuals condemned divorce and remarriage as sins that required the imposition of lengthy penances: seven years was frequently recommended as an appropriate term.[169] But some penitential writers were willing to countenance divorce and to permit remarriage without penalty when the grounds seemed adequate. Archbishop Theodore's *Penitential*, for example, permitted a man whose wife had committed adultery to divorce her and marry another. The woman whose husband committed adultery, however, might divorce him only if she then entered a convent; she must not under any circumstances remarry.[170] Desertion constituted another acceptable reason for divorce according to some writers, and a few of them permitted remarriage in these cases, too.[171] The woman whose husband was missing in action, captured by enemies, or enslaved, could also remarry, according to Theodore.[172] He dealt more severely, however, with widows and widowers who wished to remarry. Although Theodore conceded their right to do so, he advised confessors to require remarried persons to abstain from meat on Wednesdays and Fridays for a year. A person who remarried for a third or subsequent time was subject to the same penance for seven years.[173]

NONMARITAL SEX

As one might expect in view of their strict limits on marital sex, penitential writers penalized nonmarital sex severely. They classified as sinful any sort

---

[167] Theodore 2.12.32, in Haddan and Stubbs 3:201; Ps.-Egbert, *Confessionale* 20, in Wasserschleben, p. 309; *Martenianum* 41, in Wasserschleben, p. 291; Rabanus Maurus, *Poenitentiale Heribaldi* 29, in PL 110:491; Hinschius, "Ehescheidungsrecht," p. 73; Löffler, *Störungen*, p. 8; Sägmüller, "Impedimentum impotentiae," pp. 92–93.

[168] *Capitula iudiciorum* 9.2, in Schmitz 1:660; cf. Finnian 41, in Bieler, p. 88; Kottje, "Ehe und Eheverständnis," p. 31.

[169] Finnian 42–45(s), in Bieler, p. 90; *Bigotianum* 2.6.1–2, in Bieler, p. 222; Theodore 1.14.8 and 2.12.8, in Haddan and Stubbs 3:188, 199; McNamara and Wemple, "Marriage and Divorce," p. 103. Note also the list in Table 4.2 in the Appendix. On the significance of the differences between penances for various sins, see Payer, *Sex and the Penitentials*, pp. 129–34.

[170] Theodore 2.12.5, in Haddan and Stubbs 3:199; Hinschius, "Ehescheidungsrecht," p. 68; Kottje, "Ehe und Eheverständnis," p. 27.

[171] Theodore 2.12.19, in Haddan and Stubbs 3:200; Halitgar 4.11, in PL 105:685; Hinschius, "Ehescheidungsrecht," p. 70; Kottje, "Ehe und Eheverständnis," pp. 28–29.

[172] Theodore 2.12.8, 23–24, in Haddan and Stubbs 3:199–201; Hinschius, "Ehescheidungsrecht," pp. 70–71; Kottje, "Ehe und Eheverständnis," p. 27.

[173] Theodore 1.14.2–3, and 2.12.9, in Haddan and Stubbs 3:187, 199. Theodore also noted, however, that St. Basil would reduce this penance to four years.

of activity that might lead to sexual intimacy between unmarried persons. Bathing in mixed company thus called for a year of fasting according to the author of the St. Hubert penitential.[174] Simple fornication, where neither person was married, required a moderately heavy penance—two years of fasting according to St. Columban, one year according to Theodore—but this might be increased or decreased depending on other factors.[175] The penance was halved, for example, in the case of a free man who bedded a servant girl; it increased to seven years, according to Cummean, if the man was in holy orders and climbed to twelve years if he was a bishop.[176]

Where one party to a nonmarital sexual relationship was married, the penance was significantly greater than that for simple fornication. The St. Gall penitential, for example, laid out a scale of penalties for adultery with a married woman, ranging from twelve years (three of them on bread and water) for adultery committed by a bishop, to ten years (three on bread and water, again) for a priest, and seven years for a monk. A layman or cleric in minor orders, however, must fast for five years (two of them on bread and water) for the same offense.[177] The husband whose wife took part in an adulterous affair was required by some authorities to divorce his unfaithful spouse; should he fail to do so, he also fell subject to penance, which involved fasting for two days each week for two years and complete abstinence from sexual relations until his wife completed the much longer penance required of her.[178] The penalties assigned for rape (either in the sense of forcible sexual assault or elopement without parental consent) were roughly equivalent to those meted out for fornication.[179]

MASTURBATION

The penitentials, unlike earlier Christian commentaries on sexual morals, devoted great attention to masturbation. This emphasis presumably reflected the experience that many penitential authors had as confessors to communities of clerics and religious. Penances assigned for solitary sex acts varied considerably—thirty days of fasting for boys and forty for young men, according to Theodore; the *Bigotianum*, however, increased the penance to a hundred days

[174] St. Hubert 47, in Wasserschleben, p. 383, and *Merseburgense* (b) 6, in Wasserschleben, p. 429; but Burchard, *Decretum* 19.138, in PL 140:1010, penalized mixed bathing with a mere three-day fast. See also Payer, *Sex and the Penitentials*, p. 61, and "Early Medieval Regulations," p. 362.

[175] Theodore 1.14.10, in Haddan and Stubbs 3:188; St. Columban B.16, in Bieler, p. 102.

[176] Theodore 1.14.12, in Haddan and Stubbs 3:188; Cummean 2.1–2, in Bieler, pp. 112–14.

[177] *Sangallense tripartita* 1.4, in Schmitz 2:179–80; but cf. Theodore 1.14.9, in Haddan and Stubbs 3:188; Bennecke, *Strafrechtliche Lehre von Ehebruch*, pp. 38–59, analyzes these provisions and their counterparts in other penitentials.

[178] Theodore 1.14.4 and 2.12.5, in Haddan and Stubbs 3:188, 199.

[179] Halitgar 4.16–17, in Schmitz 1:725; Burchard, *Corrector* 46, in Wasserschleben, p. 641, and *Decretum* 19.5, in PL 140:958–59.

for a first offender and a full year for repeated offenders.[180] Inconsistently, however, the *Bigotianum* in another passage imposed a mere three-week penance for masturbation by a priest.[181] St. Columban wished to see masturbation punished on the same scale as intercourse with animals and thought that nothing less than two years of fasting for laymen and three for clerics would constitute adequate reparation.[182] Mutual masturbation required increased penalties, as did femoral intercourse.[183] Even involuntary ejaculation during sleep called for penance, although the nature of the punishments assigned—often the recitation of psalms and a short fast—probably indicates that ritual defilement, rather than sin, was the underlying issue.[184]

HOMOSEXUALITY AND BESTIALITY

Many handbooks of penance dealt in detail with homosexual relations. This contrasts strikingly with the cursory attention these received from earlier moral writers. The increased attention to homosexuality presumably means that confessors felt a need for practical guidance in dealing with these particular penitents.

The homosexual practice that the penitentials condemned most often was anal intercourse, which they usually described as sodomy. This offense was sometimes linked to femoral intercourse as well. A good many handbooks prescribed a sliding scale of penances for anal sex, depending both on the age and the status of the penitent and on the frequency with which he indulged in the practice. Finnian, for example, prescribed two years of penance for boys who experimented with anal sex, three years for adult men, but seven years for those who made it a habit.[185] The *Old-Irish Penitential*, by contrast, assigned only two years of penance for the same act committed by grown men, but St. Columban in one passage called for ten years of penance and in another for seven for the same offense.[186] Columban also described the details of the penalties in greater detail than other authors—the first three years involved fasting on bread, water, salt, and dried vegetables, while the last four years of the punishment required merely abstaining from meat and wine.[187]

---

[180]Theodore 1.2.9, in Haddan and Stubbs 3:178; *Bigotianum* 2.2.3, in Bieler, p. 220; St. Columban A.7, in Bieler, p. 96, required a year's penance even for a first offense by a young man.

[181]*Bigotianum* 2.1.2, in Bieler, p. 218.

[182]St. Columban B.10, in Bieler, p. 100.

[183]Theodore 1.2.8, 11, in Haddan and Stubbs 3:178.

[184]Cummean 2.15–16, in Bieler, p. 114; but cf. *Bigotianum* 2.1.3–4, in Bieler, p. 218, where fasting is also required.

[185]Finnian 2*, in Bieler, p. 74; also Cummean 2.9 and 10.15, in Bieler, pp. 114, 128.

[186]*Old-Irish Penitential* 2.25, in Bieler, p. 264; Columban B.3, B.15, in Bieler, pp. 100, 102. The *Bigotianum* also adopted the ten-year term.

[187]Columban B.3, B.15, in Bieler pp. 100, 102; see also Theodore 1.2.4–7, in Haddan and Stubbs 3:178. The *Sangallense Tripartitum* 1.2, in Schmitz 2:179, details another

Theodore of Canterbury provided a range of alternatives for dealing with penitent homosexuals. He assigned fifteen years, ten years, and seven years for habitual adult offenders, four for those who offended but once; young habitual offenders merited four years of penance, while a first offense by a boy brought a penance of two years. Femoral intercourse, when treated as an offense separate from anal sex, generally received a considerably lighter penance—one or two years as a rule.[188] Incestuous relations between brothers ranked as an aggravated offense with correspondingly harsh penance.[189]

Oral sex, either homosexual or heterosexual, merited greater severity than anal intercourse. "Let him who puts semen in the mouth do penance for seven years," declared Theodore, for "this is the worst evil."[190] He added that other confessors would be far more severe and require lifelong penance (some say twenty-two years) for fellatio. Finnian and his compatriots were less harsh and judged fellatio or cunnilingus to deserve about the same penitential treatment as anal sex.[191] A few writers viewed sexual experimentation among boys as a relatively trivial offense, to be punished by brief periods of fasting or by corporal punishment.[192]

The penitentials occasionally mentioned female autoeroticism and lesbianism. They treated female masturbation in much the same way as the male act, although they were more censorious of female sexual play that involved dildos and other mechanical aids than they were of male use of mechanical devices in masturbation. Lesbian relationships, to judge from the few explicit treatments of the subject, seem to have been considered slightly less serious than male homosexual relationships.[193]

---

graduated list of penances for clerical sodomists. The penances ranged from 25 years for a bishop to 10 years for a simple cleric or layman.

[188] *Bigotianum* 2.2.2, in Bieler, p. 220; Theodore 1.2.8, in Haddan and Stubbs 3:178.

[189] Theodore 1.2.19, in Haddan and Stubbs 3:179, prescribed 15 years for this offense; in comparison, Theodore penalized mother-son incest with only 3 years: idem, 1.2.10.

[190] Theodore 1.2.15, in Haddan and Stubbs 3:178: "Qui semen in os miserit, VII. annos peniteat: hoc pessimum malum. Alias ab eo judicatum est ut ambos usque in finem vitae peniteant; vel XXII. annos, vel ut superius VII."

[191] Finnian 3*, in Bieler, p. 74; Cummean 2.8, 10.16, in Bieler, pp. 114, 128; *Bigotianum* 2.2.4, in Bieler, p. 220; *Old-Irish Penitential* 22, in Bieler, p. 264.

[192] Theodore 1.2.11, in Haddan and Stubbs 3:178; Bede 3.30–32, in Haddan and Stubbs 3:329.

[193] Theodore 1.2.12–13, in Haddan and Stubbs 3:178; Rabanus, *Poenitentiale Heribaldi* 25, in PL 110:490; Bede 3.23, in Haddan and Stubbs 3:328; Burchard, *Corrector* 142–45, in Wasserschleben, pp. 658–59; *Decretum* 19.5, in PL 140:971–72. Male masturbation with mechanical aids carried a penance of only 40 days according to Burchard, *Corrector* 111, in Wasserschleben, p. 653, and *Decretum* 19.5, in PL 140:968. By contrast, female masturbation with a dildo or other device carried a penance of one year if done alone, or three years if done with other women; Burchard, *Corrector* 142–43, in Wasserschleben, p. 658, and *Decretum* 19.5, in PL 140:971–72.

The comparative frequency with which penitential writers referred to sexual activity involving animals presumably reflected the rural character of early medieval society, where opportunities for sex play with domesticated animals were commonplace, while sexual opportunities with human partners were restricted. Some early penitentials, particularly the Irish ones, treated bestiality as a rather minor offense, and frequently linked it with masturbation.[194] The later collections, particularly those from the Continent, tended to associate bestiality with homosexuality and accordingly punished it with greater severity.[195]

The length of the fasts and other penitential acts for individual sexual sins prescribed by the penitential authors presumably reflected each author's assessment of the relative seriousness of offenses. A comparison of the punishments set down for each category of sin, therefore, outlines a rough hierarchy of sexual transgressions. Table 4.2 in the Appendix shows the penances attached to six types of sexual offense in ten penitentials. A comparison of these penances shows that virtually all of the authors represented in Table 4.2 ranked masturbation as the least grievous offense. In order of increasing seriousness, masturbation was followed by fornication between unmarried persons (considerably aggravated, however, if the man was in holy orders), then adultery, bestiality, anal intercourse, and oral sex. This analysis of sexual sins in the penitentials furnishes some insight into the ways that early medieval Churchmen applied the theories of patristic and doctrinal writers to the realities of human behavior.

The penitentials were intended primarily as pastoral guidance for confessors in evaluating the private revelations made by penitents. Confession not only represented personal spiritual counseling, but also counted as a quasi-judicial act: the penitent admitted his guilty deeds to the confessor, who judged their seriousness and, in light of his knowledge of the circumstances (enlarged where necessary by supplemental interrogation of the penitent), pronounced judgment in the form of a prescribed regime of penance. Much like a criminal sentence, penance involved both reparation for past wrongs and modification of future behavior.

Penance was believed to be simultaneously curative and reformative. The prescriptions compounded by confessors were calculated to make reparation for past offenses and thus to cure the penitent of the spiritual ills that resulted from his sinful behavior. The penitential regime also aimed to have a prophylactic action. In theory, at least, the penitent was supposed to emerge from the process chastened and prepared to avoid in future the activities that had infected him with spiritual illness in the past.

[194] Cummean 2.6, in Bieler, p. 114; St. Columban, B.10 and B.17, in Bieler, pp. 100, 102; Bede 3.25–26, in Haddan and Stubbs 3:328.

[195] Theodore 1.2.2–3, in Haddan and Stubbs, p. 178; *Bigotianum* 2.2.1, in Bieler, p. 220; *Sangallensis tripartita* 1.8, in Schmitz 2:180; Burchard, *Corrector* 113–14, 146, in Wasserschleben, pp. 654, 659, and *Decretum* 19.5, in PL 140:968, 972; also *Decretum* 17.33, in PL 140:925.

The authors of penitential manuals furnished explicit details about sexual practices in order to enable confessors to differentiate the degrees of seriousness involved in the wide range of transgressions that they encountered in confession. By the same token, however, these handbooks posed potential dangers, since they might suggest previously unexplored temptations to prurient readers. Hence, Pope Nicholas I (858–867) cautioned Bulgarian church authorities to see that penitential handbooks were kept out of the hands of laymen, who had no business perusing them.[196]

While written primarily for the instruction of confessors in administering private penance, the penitentials embodied rules and guidelines that had wider and more public import. Precisely because they formulated for the first time detailed advice concerning the relative seriousness of many offenses that Church authorities classed as canonical crimes as well as sins, the penitentials soon came to be used not only as pastoral guides but also as legal manuals. Prescriptions drawn from the penitentials quickly infiltrated collections of canon law and penitential writers came to rank as canonical authorities.

Sexual Behavior and the Early Medieval Canonical Collections

By the early tenth century the Western Church's accumulated body of behavioral and doctrinal regulations had grown unmanageably large. The thousands of canons adopted by synods and councils, together with the decrees and rulings of popes and bishops, the declarations of patristic writers and other spiritual authorities, and a considerable body of royal and imperial law dealing with religious and moral matters, all comprised what was vaguely thought of as canon law. The very bulk of these sources meant that a priest, bishop, or judge who sought an authoritative answer to nearly any problem arising in church administration or in ecclesiastical disputes faced a formidable task. A conscientious prelate who sought guidance in dealing with nearly any common problem—such as, for example, marital incest, adultery, rape, prostitution, property rights of concubines, or grounds for divorce—needed a large library. He had to resign himself (or more likely his clerks) to hours of tedious searching in order to unearth the relevant conciliar enactments, papal decrees, or patristic dicta. Information retrieval, to call it by its twentieth-century name, posed major and often insoluble problems for pastors, Church administrators, and ecclesiastical courts.

In response to the need for authoritative information about ecclesiastical policy and precedents, learned Churchmen had begun centuries earlier to compile guides and anthologies of canon law. The *Didache* or *Doctrine of the Twelve Apostles*, the earliest surviving example of such a handbook, dates from

---

[196] Nicholas I, Letter to the Bulgarians, c. 75, 13 Nov. 866 (JE 2812), in PL 119:1008. Ninth-century councils also worried about the effect of penitentials upon Christian morals and councils at Châlons and Paris condemned their use; see Payer, *Sex and the Penitentials*, pp. 57–59.

the end of the first or the beginning of the second century. The growth of Church law since that time had soon outdated brief and primitive summaries such as the *Didache*, however, and by the fifth century more ample digests and anthologies were in circulation.

The most influential canonical manuals of that age included the *Dionysiana*, prepared at Rome in the fifth century by a monk, Denis the Little, and the Spanish Collection, or *Hispana*, put together probably at Seville in the sixth or seventh century.[197] In France the *Collectio vetus Gallica*, written between 585 and 626/27, also enjoyed a degree of popularity.[198] These collections, though much fuller and more comprehensive than the earlier ones, remained sketchy and unsystematic; hence many authorities found them unsatisfactory. In 774 Pope Hadrian I (772–795) sent to Charlemagne a revised version of the *Dionysiana*, supplemented by more recent rulings and conflated with material from other canonical collections, as an authoritative guide to canon law for the Carolingian empire. The *Hadriana*, as this compilation was called, was itself outdated within a few years by fresh legislation.[199] Accordingly a

[197] Fournier and Le Bras, *Histoire des collections canoniques* 1:1–126; Gérard Fransen, *Les collections canoniques*, Typologie des sources du moyen âge occidental, fasc. 10 (Turnhout: Brépols, 1973), pp. 12–19; Stickler, *Historia iuris canonici*, pp. 22–105; Van Hove, *Prolegomena*, pp. 122–34, 150–62, 265–91; García y García, *Historia del derecho canónico* 1:43–48, 160–91, 283–94; Jean Gaudemet, *Les sources du droit de l'église en occident du IIe au VIIe siècle* (Paris: Editions du Cerf, 1985), pp. 134–37, 155–61; Michael Richter, "Dionysius Exiguus," in *Theologische Realenzyklopädie*, ed. Gerhard Krause, et al. (Berlin: De Gruyter, 1977– ; in progress; cited hereafter as TRE) 9:1–4. The *Dionysiana* circulated in three versions. The earliest has been edited by Adolf Strewe in *Die Kanonessammlung des Dionysius Exiguus in der ersten Redaktion* (Berlin: W. De Gruyter, 1931); the second can be found in PL 67:139–316; the third version apparently no longer exists, save for its preface, edited in Friedrich Maassen, *Geschichte der Quellen und Literatur des canonischen Rechts im Abendlande* (Graz: Leuschner & Lubensky, 1870; repr. Graz: Akademische Druck- u. Verlagsanstalt, 1956), pp. 963–64. The *Hispana* exists in two principal versions, with numerous variants. The *Hispana chronologica* is printed in PL 84:93–848, although the edition is not very reliable; no good edition of the *Hispana systematica* exists either, but there are excerpts from this version in PL 84:25–92. A critical edition is being prepared by Gonzalo Martinez Diez; see *La colección canónica Hispana*, Monumenta Hispaniae sacrae, vol. 1 (Madrid, Barcelona: Consejo superior de investigaciones científicas, Instituto Enrique Florez, 1966– ; in progress).

[198] Hubert Mordek, *Kirchenrecht und Reform im Frankenreich: Die Collectio vetus gallica, die älteste Kanonessammlung des fränkischen Gallien*, Beiträge zur Geschichte und Quellen des Mittelalters, vol. 1 (Berlin, New York: W. De Gruyter, 1975) includes a critical edition of this work, which was previously known as the *Collectio Andegavensis*.

[199] No modern edition of the *Hadriana* exists; the best available is an edition of the mixed version known as the *Dionysio-Hadriana* by François Pithou, *Codex canonum vetus ecclesiae Romanae* (Paris: E typographia Petri Chevailer, 1609). A conflated version of the *Hispana* and the *Hadriana* was prepared about 800 and is known as the *Dacheriana*, after its first modern editor, Luc d'Achéry; it has been mentioned previ-

stream of new canonical collections began to appear in the early ninth century.[200]

Among the new compendia was a group of influential but puzzling collections that consisted largely of forged papal letters and spurious conciliar canons. The largest and most influential of these collections is now known as the *Pseudo-Isidorian Decretals*. Although the collection circulated under the name of St. Isidore of Seville (ca. 560–636), who may in fact have been responsible for a now-lost early version of the *Hispana*, the Pseudo-Isidorian collection dates from the years between 847 and 852. Pseudo-Isidore confected his work somewhere in northern France, possibly in the ecclesiastical province of Tours, or perhaps somewhere around Reims—tantalizing clues point to ties with both regions, but it has not been possible to pinpoint its origin.[201] The collection circulated widely and was often copied; at least eighty-seven surviving manuscripts of the whole work, which is bulky and hence costly to produce, testify to its continuing use throughout the Middle Ages.[202]

In addition to the work of Pseudo-Isidore, two other compilations of forged laws appeared at roughly the same time: the *Capitula Angilramni* and the *Capitularies of Benedictus Levita*.[203] The interests of the forgers who produced these anthologies centered mainly on problems of ecclesiology, Church administration, and jurisdictional rights. They had little to say about sexual behavior, marriage, and related topics. Mixed in with the spurious material, however,

---

ously as a penitential, since it includes a substantial amount of penitential material. A revised edition of this work appears in the second edition of d'Achéry's *Spicilegium* 1:509–64. On its considerable influence see Raymond Kottje, "Einheit und Vielfalt des kirchlichen Lebens in der Karolingerzeit," *Zeitschrift für Kirchengeschichte* 76 (1965) 335–40.

[200] Fournier and Le Bras, *Histoire des collections canoniques* 1:234–347; Kottje, "Einheit und Vielfalt," pp. 338–40; Roger E. Reynolds, "Unity and Diversity in Carolingian Canon Law Collections: The Case of the *Collectio Hibernensis* and Its Derivatives," in *Carolingian Essays: Andrew W. Mellon Lectures in Early Christian Studies*, ed. Uta-Renate Blumenthal (Washington, D.C.: Catholic University of America Press, 1983), pp. 99–135.

[201] Horst Fuhrmann, *Einfluss und Verbreitung der pseudoisidorischen Fälschungen, von ihrem Auftrachtung bis in die neuere Zeit*, 3 vols., Schriften der Monumenta Germaniae Historica, vol. 24 (Stuttgart: Anton Hiersemann, 1972–74) 1:191–94; John Van Engen, "Decretals, False," in DMA 4:124–27.

[202] Schafer Williams, *Codices Pseudo-Isidoriani: A Palaeographico-Historical Study*, MIC, 3d ser., vol. 3 (New York: Fordham University Press, 1971), lists 80 MSS of the whole work, in addition to 49 MSS containing abridged versions. Five further MSS were noted by Mordek, "Codices Pseudo-Isidoriani: Addenda zu den gleichnamigen Buch von Schafer Williams," *Archiv für katholisches Kirchenrecht* 147 (1978) 471–78. Two others have since been added to this list: Vat. Reg. lat. 1038 (10th cent.) and Mantua, Biblioteca communale, MS 205 (16th cent.). For further information on one of the MSS listed by Williams see also John J. Contreni, "Codices Pseudo-Isidoriani: The Provenance and Date of Paris, B.N. ms. lat. 9619," *Viator* 13 (1982) 1–14.

[203] Fournier and Le Bras, *Histoire des collections canoniques* 1:127–45.

was a sizeable body of genuine papal letters, conciliar canons, and royal capitularies. Part of this authentic law dealt with marriage and sexual problems. The genuine canons dealing with sexual matters in Pseudo-Isidore's work seem to have been selected to emphasize the importance of clerical celibacy and the punishments to be inflicted upon clerics who failed to practice sexual continence.[204] Both genuine and forged portions of the collection mandated the practice of periodic marital abstinence from intercourse. In general the author(s) of Pseudo-Isidore made it plain that marriage should be both monogamous and indissoluble.[205] Still, the forged decretals added little to the development of sexual doctrine.

Most of the major genuine canonical collections of the ninth and tenth centuries shared with the forged decretals a relative disinterest in sexual problems. The leading Italian canonical collection, the *Collectio Anselmo dedicata* (ca. 882), paid only passing attention to marriage and sexuality; a similar cursory treatment of these topics characterized the principal French collection by Abbo of Fleury.[206]

In contrast, the major German canonist of the early tenth century, Abbot Regino of Prüm, who compiled his *Two Books Concerning Synodal Cases and Ecclesiastical Discipline* about 906, devoted the greater part of his second book to sexual matters.[207] Regino's work includes numerous excerpts drawn from the penitentials on the subject of marital chastity and periodic abstinence from sexual relations.[208] Regino's treatment of divorce was also substantial. His selection of material makes it clear that he considered marriage a lifelong commitment and wished to discourage remarriage following divorce.[209] Regino restricted the grounds for divorce to adultery and impotence and fiercely castigated informal

---

[204] Hinschius, DPI, pp. 32–33, 90, 340, 430–31.

[205] Hinschius, DPI, pp. 87–88, 265–66, 340–43, 351, 430, 738–42.

[206] Abbo of Fleury, *Canones ad Hugonem et Robertum ejus filium Francorum reges*, in PL 139:473–508; Stickler, *Historia iuris canonici*, pp. 148–50; Van Hove, *Prolegomena*, pp. 317, 420–21. The *Collectio Anselmo dedicata*, so called because it was dedicated to Archbishop Anselm of Milan (882–96) has never been published. Jean Claude Besse published a brief analysis of its contents under the ambitious title *Histoire du droit de l'Eglise au moyen âge de Denis à Gratien: Collectio Anselmo dedicata* (Paris: Sirey, 1957). See also Stickler, *Historia iuris canonici*, p. 150; Van Hove, *Prolegomena*, pp. 232, 314; García y García, *Historia del derecho canónico* 1:304–305.

[207] Regino, *Libri duo de synodalibus causis et disciplinis ecclesiasticis*, in PL 132:185–370; Stickler, *Historia iuris canonici*, pp. 146–47; Van Hove, *Prolegomena*, pp. 317–18; García y García, *Historia del derecho canónico* 1:303–304; Fuhrmann, *Einfluss und Verbreitung* 2:435–36. Another unpublished late Carolingian collection of texts dealing with marriage and related matters is the *De ratione matrimonii*, a selection of extracts from book 46 of the *Collectio Hibernensis*; see Reynolds, "Unity and Diversity," pp. 115–16.

[208] Regino 1.328; 2.153, 249, in PL 132:256, 312, 332.

[209] Regino 2.101–106, in PL 132:303–4.

separations without judicial process.[210] Regino was nearly unique among the canonists of his age in his attention to the reconciliation of separated couples and methods for bringing them back to marital harmony.[211]

Regino was a jurist of wider learning than most of his contemporaries. His discussion of marital and sexual problems relies not only on the conventional legal sources that other canonists of his period used—selected conciliar canons, papal letters, extracts from penitentials, and citations from patristic authorities, such as St. Augustine—but also refers with considerable frequency to Roman law, notably the *Sententiae* of Paulus and the Theodosian Code.[212] While Regino's discussion of adultery and fornication was fairly conventional,[213] he paid greater attention than was usual in his period to rape and the abduction of heiresses. His treatment of rape relies heavily on earlier conciliar rulings, but also draws upon the capitularies, as well as on papal letters.[214] Regino gave special prominence, as well, to homosexual offenses and masturbation, topics that earlier canonical writers took up briefly, if at all.[215] His concern for these issues doubtless reflects the influence of the penitentials, from which he drew heavily for this portion of his work.

Conclusions: The Church and the Regulation of Sexual Behavior in the Early Middle Ages

The work of Regino of Prüm typifies the common teaching of the Western Church concerning proper sexual behavior at the beginning of the tenth century. Churchmen had reached agreement by this period that only married persons should have sex and that they should do so primarily in order to conceive children. The Church stood the sexual teaching of the Manichaeans and Gnostic sects on its head. The Manichaeans had taught that sex for pleasure was acceptable, but they abominated procreation.[216] The rejection of pleasure as a legitimate purpose of sex depended in turn upon the dichotomy between body and soul, flesh and spirit, that is fundamental to late ancient and medieval Christian belief. This antagonism between the carnal and spiritual impulses of man, a notion that early Christians absorbed from Greek philosophy, likewise received

---

[210] Regino 2.111, 124, 128, 130–31, 133, 182–83, 242–45, in PL 132:306, 308–10, 319, 330–31.

[211] Regino 2.240–41, in PL 132:330.

[212] Regino 2.129, 148–50, in PL 132:309, 312 (Paulus); also 2.144–47, 175, in PL 132:311–12, 317 (Cod. Theod.); Van Hove, *Prolegomena*, p. 238.

[213] Regino 2.99, 116, 134, 138–40, 236–37, in PL 132:303, 307, 310–11, 329 (adultery); 2.132, 136–37, 141, 151, 172–74, 235, 246 (fornication), in PL 132:310–12, 316–17, 329, 331.

[214] Regino 2.155–62, in PL 132:313–14; on Regino's use of capitularies see García y García, *Historia del derecho canónico* 1:339; Van Hove, *Prolegomena*, p. 263.

[215] Regino, 2.248, 250–55, 257, in PL 132:332–34.

[216] Flandrin, *Un temps pour embrasser*, p. 125; Noonan, *Contraception*, pp. 107–15.

prominent emphasis in the penitentials, which were concerned, as we have seen, with ritual purity and the need to cleanse oneself from sexual defilement as a condition for participation in the sacred mysteries of the Church.[217]

The aversion to sex that had become a central feature of Christian thought by the tenth century reflected a further characteristic of the early medieval Church: the ascendency of the monastic ideal and the presumption that ascetic virtues represented the highest form of Christian life. By the tenth century, monks, who were bound to a rule of complete sexual abstinence, had imposed on Europe's married population rules of periodic continence that made marriage more sexually frustrating than celibacy. At the same time, influential figures in this period increasingly favored imposing celibacy upon the secular clergy as well as monks. Although marriage was not generally prohibited to clerics in the tenth century, authorities often exhorted clerics in the West to cast their wives, concubines, and children out of their homes and to embrace a celibate virtue that few secular clerics seem to have desired. The wives, consorts, and children of priests were as much the targets of this pressure as the priests.[218]

The penitentials, as we have seen, gave central prominence to sexual offenses; in so doing they implicitly told both confessor and penitent that sexual purity was the key element in Christian morality. The penitentials also reinforced the belief that there was a hierarchy of sexual offenses and subtly propounded a slightly different ordering of that hierarchy than appears in the writings of earlier Church authorities. Whereas earlier writers paid only scant attention to masturbation and homosexual practices, the penitentials often prescribed stern penances for homosexual activities and slight ones for masturbation. The implicit message was that homosexuality was among the most heinous offenses in the catalogue of sins.[219] Solitary masturbation, by contrast, ranked as the least serious sexual indulgence. The reordered emphases on masturbatory and homosexual activities that surfaced in the penitentials mirrored the experience and concerns of the monastic environment in which most penitential writers received their spiritual and intellectual formation. Their handbooks ensured that monastic beliefs about these types of sexual behavior would be imparted, both directly and indirectly, to the laity.

The penitentials also fostered the emergence of a distinctively ecclesiastical view of marriage. The clerical model of marriage promoted the concept that

[217] Mary Douglas, *Purity and Danger: An Analysis of Concepts of Pollution and Taboo* (New York: Frederick A. Praeger, 1966), pp. 130–33; Flandrin, *Un temps pour embrasser,* pp. 100–101.

[218] Flandrin, *Un temps pour embrasser,* p. 127; Wemple, *Women in Frankish Society,* pp. 127–28.

[219] Although Boswell, CSTAH, p. 180, maintains that the penitentials treated homosexuality as a commonplace and not terribly serious matter, the penances shown in Table 4.2 in the Appendix do not bear out his conclusion. See also the remarks of Payer, *Sex and the Penitentials,* pp. 129–34.

marriage was a lifelong committment; accordingly this paradigm restricted divorce, prohibited remarriage following divorce, and discouraged second marriages following the death of a first spouse.[220] The ecclesiastical view of marriage was by no means universally accepted in the tenth century, but it gradually secured endorsement even from lay authorities as the norm for Christian married conduct—this was reflected in Carolingian divorce legislation, for example, as well as in the penitentials and the dogmatic assertions of churchmen. Powerful and influential families among the laity viewed these matrimonial doctrines as a threat to their interests. Great families found it advantageous to keep marriage fluid, a union that could be dissolved when it was advantageous to one or both parties. An unforeseen and doubtless undesired effect of the increasing impact of the ecclesiastical concept of marriage on early medieval society was the increased competition among women for eligible husbands that resulted from the combined effects of monogamy and indissolubility. This drove up dowry costs and also increased the gap in status between a concubine and a wife.[221]

Although early medieval Churchmen sometimes linked ecclesiastical doctrines concerning marriage and sex to the reproductive needs of humankind, the clerical elite seemed largely indifferent to the social consequences of their matrimonial doctrines.[222]

But the restrictions that the Church placed on sexual activity, marital and nonmarital, entailed serious consequences. Ideas about sexual propriety that took shape during the early Middle Ages took solid institutional root in the following period. During the tenth century, civil authorities also began to adopt restrictive policies on sex and marriage propounded by earlier generations of churchmen. The process of systematically converting Church doctrines about sex into legal prescriptions was just commencing around the year 1000.

---

[220] Duby, *Medieval Marriage*, p. 3. Duby has expanded and modified the argument of this book more recently in *The Knight, The Lady, and The Priest: The Making of Modern Marriage in Medieval France*, trans. Barbara Bray (New York: Pantheon, 1983).

[221] Wemple, *Women in Frankish Society*, pp. 95, 193–94.

[222] Although Flandrin has contended that the Church's prescriptions about sexual abstinence in marriage may have imperiled the demographic equilibrium of Western society, it seems more likely that, as Herlihy has argued, medieval population size tended to be largely self-regulating and responded as much to market pressures as to theological ones. Flandrin, *Un temps pour embrasser*, pp. 69–70; Herlihy, *Medieval Households*, pp. 143–44.

5

The Era of Church Reform, Intellectual Revival, and Urbanization: 1000–1140

The Social and Intellectual Context of Church Reform

The generations who lived between the turn of the first Christian millennium and the appearance of the *Decretum* of Gratian about 1140 experienced a radical transformation in Western European culture. Thought and society by 1140 were far different from what they had been in the year 1000, although the full significance of the changes that had taken place was probably not apparent to most of those who lived through them. During that century-and-a-half, Europe's population increased enormously, and its patterns of settlement and economy began to change in fundamental ways. In the year of the millennium, no city of great size existed anywhere in the Latin West, and there had not been one for centuries. The largest, most prosperous European cities were in Muslim Spain—places such as Córdoba, with a population of perhaps 90,000, and Seville, with slightly more than 50,000 inhabitants. Northern European towns were much more modest in size: London's population in 1086, for example, probably did not exceed 8,000. Although Rome, the Eternal City, had only about 30,000 people at the first millennium, Venice and perhaps Milan seem to have been somewhat larger, with populations approaching that of Seville. But even towns of these modest sizes were few and far between. The overwhelming majority of Europe's people lived in small villages and hamlets that ranged in size from perhaps a dozen to one or two hundred families. The denizens of these rural settlements made their living, such as it was, from one or another form of agriculture: they were nearly all peasants, of whom a substantial fraction in many regions were serfs, legally bound to the land they tilled.

By the mid-twelfth century, however, Europe's total population had grown significantly. Even more important, the process of urbanization, or reurbanization, had commenced in earnest. Existing population centers—mainly the see cities of bishops—grew in size. In addition, new towns began to attract considerable populations. By 1140, there were still no large cities in Europe west of Constantinople, but Western towns elsewhere than in the Iberian Peninsula were larger and more numerous than they had been a century-and-a-half earlier. The populations of the greatest ones had grown to around 40,000. By 1140, the consequences of these changes were beginning to be felt in many depart-ments of life.[1]

Demographic alterations in settlement patterns had brought about impor-tant readjustments in European economy and society. Inhabitants of the new towns and the rapidly growing older cities depended primarily upon commerce and manufacturing, rather than agriculture, for their livelihood. As urban busi-ness activity grew along with the town populations, further changes in social structure were bound to follow—and so they did. Bourgeois townsmen were, by and large, legally free, not bound to the soil, as were many of their contem-poraries in rural areas. Townsmen in the prosperous urban centers sought, and most of them sooner or later obtained, rights of self-governance: they made laws and created courts to enforce them, they levied taxes and chose officials to collect and disburse them, they raised armed forces and allied with other towns for mutual defense.[2]

In the burgeoning towns of the eleventh and early twelfth centuries the be-ginnings of an intellectual revolution were slowly taking shape. Townsmen more than peasants had need of literacy. Growing numbers of secular clerics required schooling. The cathedral schools of bishops expanded in size and academic scope. Although there was a demand for greater numbers of people with exper-tise in the seven liberal arts, both lay and clerical students increasingly sought training in law and medicine, while interest in the "sciences" of theology and philosophy began to outstrip interest in the older arts of grammar, rhetoric, and dialectic.

The Roman Law Revival

This intellectual revolution, often labeled "the renaissance of the twelfth cen-tury," had far-reaching ramifications.[3] One component of it involved the study

[1] Josiah Cox Russell, *Late Ancient and Medieval Population*, in *Transactions of the American Philosophical Society*, n.s., vol. 48, pt. 3 (Philadelphia: American Philosophi-cal Society, 1958), pp. 69, 92–93, 99; Daniel Waley, *The Italian City-Republics* (New York: McGraw-Hill, 1969), pp. 35–37. The reasons for European population expansion in this period are not well understood, but at least one significant factor was probably a moderation in climate that began between about 750 and 800. The change brought milder winters, drier summers, and generally more favorable growing conditions for ce-real crops. The consequent improvement in food supply was, according to this theory, a necessary condition for long-term population growth between about 800 and about 1200 or 1250. See generally Robert S. Gottfried, "Climatology," in DMA 3:450–57.

[2] Waley, *Italian City-Republics*, pp. 55–86; M. M. Postan, *The Medieval Economy and Society: An Economic History of the Middle Ages* (London: Weidenfield and Nic-olson, 1972; repr. Harmondsworth: Penguin, 1975), pp. 235–45. For a more detailed treatment of town formation see M. W. Beresford, *The New Towns of the Middle Ages: Town Plantations in England, Wales, and Gascony* (London: Butterworth, 1967).

[3] The label comes from the title of an immensely influential book by Charles Homer Haskins, *The Renaissance of the Twelfth Century* (Cambridge: Harvard University Press, 1927; repr. New York: Meridian Books, 1958). See also the volume commemo-

and teaching of Roman law, as it was embodied in the texts of the *Corpus iuris civilis*, compiled centuries earlier at the command of Justinian.[4] Indeed, the legal revival arguably had a more profound, extensive, and lasting impact on European life and society than any other facet of the twelfth-century intellectual renewal.

The study and teaching of Roman law recommenced in Western Europe during the second half of the eleventh century. As late as the 1060s, Justinian's Digest remained virtually unknown in the West; then in 1076 it was cited in a judicial decision in Tuscany.[5] Within the next two decades, the Digest, along with the rest of Justinian's *Corpus*, was being studied avidly by a handful of legal scholars.

Shortly before 1100, systematic teaching of Roman law began in the northern Italian city of Bologna, where the earliest medieval law faculty took shape shortly after the turn of the century. The pioneer Roman law teacher was apparently a man named Pepo, about whom, however, little else is known with certainty.[6] The earliest Bolognese teacher and commentator on Roman law of

---

rating the publication of Haskins' work: *Renaissance and Renewal in the Twelfth Century*, ed. Robert L. Benson and Giles Constable (Cambridge: Harvard University Press, 1982), esp. the essays by Stephan Kuttner, "The Revival of Jurisprudence," pp. 299–323, and Knut Wolfgang Nörr, "The Institutional Foundations of the New Jurisprudence," pp. 324–38. For other facets of the twelfth-century revival see also David Knowles, *The Evolution of Medieval Thought* (Baltimore: Helicon Press, 1962), pp. 71–184, and Joseph de Ghellinck, *Le mouvement théologique du XIIe siècle*, 2d ed., Museum Lessianum, section historique, no. 10 (Bruges: "De Tempel," 1984).

[4]See above, pp. 113–14, and also Berman, *Law and Revolution*, pp. 120–23.

[5]The text of a 1076 judgment citing the Digest appears in Julius von Ficker, *Forschungen zur Reichs- und Rechtsgeschichte Italiens*, 4 vols. (Innsbruck: Wagner, 1868–74; repr. Aalen: Scientia, 1961) 4:99–100 (no. 73). See also Hermann Kantorowicz, *Über die Entstehung der Digestenvulgata: Ergänzungen zu Mommsen* (Weimar: H. Böhlaus Nachfolger, 1910), p. 20; J.A. Clarence Smith, *Medieval Law Teachers and Writers, Civilian and Canonist* (Ottawa: University of Ottawa Press, 1975), p. 5; Paul Fournier, "Un tournant d'histoire du droit, 1060–1140," RHDF, 3d ser., 41 (1917) 129–80.

[6]The scanty evidence for Pepo's career is analyzed by Hermann Kantorowicz and Beryl Smalley, "An English Theologian's View of Roman Law: Pepo, Irnerius, Ralph Niger," *Medieval and Renaissance Studies* 1 (1941; appeared 1943) 237–52, reprinted in Kantorowicz's *Rechtshistorische Schriften*, ed. Helmut Coing and Gerhard Immel, Freiburger Rechts- und Staatswissenschaftliche Abhandlungen, vol. 30 (Karlsruhe: C. F. Müller, 1970), pp. 231–44. Hastings Rashdall, *The Universities of Europe in the Middle Ages*, 2d ed. by F. M. Powicke and A. B. Emden, 3 vols. (Oxford: Clarendon Press, 1936) 1:111–12, credits Pepo with inaugurating the teaching of law at Bologna, but for this there is no sound evidence. See also Giorgio Cencetti, "*Studium fuit Bononie*: note sulla storia dell'Università di Bologna nel primo mezzo secolo della sua esistenza," *Studi medievali* 7 (1966) 795–96; Giovanni Santini, "La contessa Matilde, lo '*studium*' e Bologna, 'Città aperta' dell'XI secolo," in *Studi Matildici: Atti e memorie del II Convegno di Studi Matildici*, Modena-Reggio E., 1–4 maggio 1970, Deputazione di Storia Patria per le

whom we know much was a certain Warner, perhaps originally a German, whose name was Italianized as Guarnerius and then Latinized as Irnerius. By the early 1090s, Irnerius was preparing a copy of the Digest for his own use; before long he possessed texts of the Code and the Novels as well.

We know virtually nothing of the circumstances under which Irnerius began teaching law, but we do know the names of at least four of his students: Bulgarus Bulgarini, Martinus Gosia, Hugo da Porta Ravennata, and Jacobus. These "Four Doctors of Bologna" succeeded Irnerius as law teachers. They also served the rich and famous of their generation as legal advisers during the early- and mid-twelfth century—their best-known client was the German emperor, Frederick Barbarossa.[7] The teaching of Irnerius and his successors, as well as the appeal of the new civilian jurisprudence for powerful and ambitious rulers such as Barbarossa, stimulated a remarkable growth in the popularity of legal studies, first at Bologna and in relatively short order at other centers. During the opening decades of the twelfth century, the teaching and study of Roman law became a growth industry.

This revival did not occur in an intellectual or juristic vacuum. The demand for civilian jurisprudence was stimulated and enhanced by two closely allied currents of ecclesiastical life during the eleventh and twelfth centuries: the Church reform movement and the systematization of canon law.

The Church Reform Movement, Canon Law, and Sexual Behavior

Church reform represented in essence a reaction against the involvement of Church officials and ecclesiastical institutions in the affairs of feudal government and society. Reflective Christians, both clerics and laymen, felt that feudal institutions jeopardized the orderly functioning and administration of the Latin Church. As feudal potentates reached out to take control of lands and other assets that belonged to monasteries, dioceses, and parish churches, a growing body of reformers saw that the Church's ability to maintain its discipline and ideals, as well as the freedom to use its property for religious purposes, had been compromised. The reformers' fears were heightened by the mounting frequency with which tenth- and eleventh-century monarchs and noblemen were intervening in the selection of bishops, abbots, and other ecclesiastical officials.

---

antiche provincie modenesi, Biblioteca, n.s., no. 16 (Modena: Aedes Muratoriana, 1971), pp. 409–27; Giovanni de Vergottini, "Lo studio di Bologna, l'impero, il papato," *Studi e memorie per la storia dell'Università di Bologna*, n.s. 1 (1956) 23–41; Pietro Fiorelli, "*Clarum Bononensium lumen*," in *Per Francesco Calasso: Studi degli allievi* (Rome: Bulzoni, 1978), pp. 413–59.

[7] Hermann Kantorowicz and W. W. Buckland, *Studies in the Glossators of the Roman Law: Newly Discovered Writings of the Twelfth Century* (Cambridge: At the University Press, 1938), pp. 33, 68–111; Friedrich Carl von Savigny, *Die Geschichte des römischen Rechts im Mittelalter*, 2d ed., 7 vols. (Heidelberg: J. C. B. Mohr, 1834–51; repr. Bad Homburg: Hermann Gentner, 1961) 4:68–192.

By the mid-eleventh century those who feared and distrusted the power of feudal authorities had begun to take steps to combat control of Church property by laymen. In 1049, the reformers secured the appointment of one of their own number as bishop of Rome. Pope Leo IX (1048–54), the earliest of the reforming popes, gained the Chair of St. Peter through the intervention of the German emperor, Henry III (1039–56), a staunch supporter of reform. Once in power, Leo IX commenced to reorganize and strengthen the papal administration with a view to transforming the papacy into a center for the dissemination and implementation of reform policies. During the pontificates of Leo IX and his successors, especially Pope Gregory VII (1073–85), the reform papacy appealed to dedicated Christians to subscribe to the ideal of a Church organization free from secular interference. Independent of political ties to monarchs, the Church, according to the reformers, ought to be economically self-supporting, relying on the income from its own properties, Church taxes, and contributions from the faithful.[8]

The partisans of reform emphasized as a key element in their program the renewal of canon law, which they believed must play a key role in the governance of Christian society. From the very beginning, the reformers had sought to create a working system of Church courts and to expand the Church's jurisdiction, so as to bring into its courts a growing portion of the business of conflict resolution in the West. Reformers argued that the Church's courts ought to function as the primary forum for the settlement of disputes in any way affecting public or private morals, ecclesiastical institutions, or the administration of Church property. Church courts were to be a mechanism for the orderly regulation of Christian society.[9]

Such an organized system would require a comprehensible body of law to enforce. One characteristic product of the reform movement, therefore, was a stream of canonical compilations that stressed the new jurisdictional claims reformers made for canonical tribunals.

The earliest major canonical collection to respond clearly to the goals of the reform movement was the *Decretum*, compiled shortly after the turn of the millennium by Bishop Burchard of Worms (1000–1025). Burchard's vast work, which comprised 1785 chapters distributed among twenty books, drew upon earlier compilations, such as those of Regino of Prüm and the *Anselmo dedicata*, as well as penitentials, capitularies of the Carolingian monarchs, and some

---

[8] See generally Augustin Fliche, *La réforme grégorienne*, 3 vols., Spicilegium sacrum Lovaniense, Etudes et documents, fasc. 6, 9, and 16 (Louvain: Spicilegium sacrum Lovaniensis; Paris: E. Champion, 1924–37), as well as the more summary account in *La réforme grégorienne et la reconquête chrétienne (1057–1125)*, Histoire de l'église depuis les origines jusqu'à nos jours, vol. 8 (Paris: Bloud et Gay, 1950), and H. E. J. Cowdry, *The Cluniacs and the Gregorian Reform* (Oxford: Clarendon Press, 1970).

[9] Walter Ullmann, *Law and Politics in the Middle Ages: An Introduction to the Sources of Medieval Political Ideas* (London: The Sources of History, Ltd., 1975), pp. 133–34; António García y García, *História del derecho canónico: I. El primer milenio* (Salamanca: Instituto de história de la teología española, 1967) 1:280–83.

scraps of Roman law.[10] Burchard's *Decretum* was so huge, however, that few cathedrals, monasteries, and other centers of ecclesiastical learning and administration could afford to have copies made.

Everyday needs and humbler users required shorter, more succinct handbooks, and the reformers were not slow to supply them, cheerfully pillaging Burchard's work in the process. An early example of these manuals was the *Collection in Five Books*, written between 1014 and 1023, in central Italy, probably at the Benedictine monastery of Farfa.[11] An important smaller handbook was the *Collection in Seventy-Four Titles*, drawn up (at least in an early form) in Italy before 1076, probably by someone closely connected with the circle of Pope Gregory VII.[12] Among other notable canonistic handbooks of the era were the collection drawn up about 1083 by Anselm of Lucca, a nephew of Pope Alexander II (1061–73) and an ardent supporter of Gregory VII;[13] the *Collection of Cardinal Deusdedit*, compiled between 1083 and 1086 by another eminent supporter of Gregory VII;[14] and the *Liber de vita Christiana* written by Bishop

[10] Burchard of Worms, *Decretorum libri XX*, in PL 140:557–1058; Fournier and Le Bras, *Histoire des collections canoniques* 1:364–421; Stickler, *Historia*, pp. 154–59; Gérard Fransen, "Le Décret de Burchard de Worms: Valeur du texte de l'édition; essai de classement des manuscrits," ZRG, KA 63 (1977) 1–19; as well as his "Les sources de la préface du Décret de Burchard de Worms," BMCL, 2d ser., 3 (1973) 1–7, "Une suite de recherches sur le décret de Burchard de Worms," *Traditio* 26 (1970) 446–77, and "Les abrégés des collections canoniques: Essai de typologie," RDC 28 (1972) 157–66; Horst Fuhrmann, *Einfluss und Verbreitung der pseudoisidorischen Fälschungen*, MGH, Schriften, vol. 24 (Stuttgart: Hiersemann, 1972–74) 2:472–73; Mark Kerner et al., "Textidentifikation und Provenienzanalyse im *Decretum Burchardi*," *Studia Gratiana* 20 (1976) 17–63.

[11] *Collectio canonum in V libris* (cited hereafter as Coll. 5L), ed. M. Fornasari, in CCL, continuatio medievalis, vol. 6– (Turnhout: Brépols, 1970– ; in progress; 1 vol. to date).

[12] *Diuersorum patrum sententie siue collectio in LXXIV titulos digesta* (cited hereafter as Coll. 74T), ed. John Gilchrist, Monumenta iuris canonici (hereafter MIC), Corpus collectionum, vol. 1 (Vatican City: Biblioteca Apostolica Vaticana, 1973). Gilchrist has also published an English translation of his edition of Coll. 74T under the title *The Collection in Seventy-four Titles: A Canon Law Manual of the Gregorian Reform*, Mediaeval Studies in Translation, vol. 22 (Toronto: Pontifical Institute of Mediaeval Studies, 1980). See also Gilchrist's "The Collection in Four Books (4L)—The Source of the Collection in Seventy-four Titles (Coll. 74T)?" BMCL, n.s. 11 (1981) 77–80.

[13] Anselm of Lucca, *Collectio canonum una cum collectione minore*, ed. Friedrich Thaner, 2 vols. in 1 (Vienna: Wagner, 1906–15; repr. Aalen: Scientia, 1965); this edition is incomplete, for it includes only the first eleven books of Anselm's work. See also Fournier and Le Bras, *Histoire des collections canoniques* 2:25–37, Stickler, *Historia*, pp. 170–72, and John Gilchrist, "The Erdmann Thesis and the Canon Law," in *Crusade and Settlement*, ed. Peter W. Edbury (Cardiff: University College Cardiff Press, 1985), pp. 37–45.

[14] *Die Kanonessamlung des Kardinals Deusdedit*, ed. Victor Wolf von Glanvell (Paderborn: F. Schöningh, 1905); Fournier and Le Bras, *Histoire des collections canoniques* 2:37–54; Stickler, *Historia*, pp. 172–74.

Bonizo of Sutri and Piacenza around 1090.[15] In the middle of the last decade of the eleventh century, yet another major reformer, this time from France, turned his hand to canonistic scholarship and produced not one but three influential collections. The writer was Bishop Ivo of Chartres (1091–1116), whose canonistic works included the relatively brief *Collectio tripartita*, the enormous *Decretum*, and a popular, middle-sized book called the *Panormia*.[16]

The canon law collections from Burchard to Ivo were major tools for achieving the reformers' goals; they are for the historian one of the principal sources for understanding the thought of the reformers and the competing interpretations of the law current among the different reform groups.[17]

In general, the canonical compilations demonstrate that the reformers favored moral rigorism: as a group they considered sex and other pleasurable experiences tainted by evil and a potent source of sin. They were not merely suspicious of sex, but hostile to any sexual activity at all, save for marital relations undertaken expressly and consciously to conceive a child. The reformers, even more than the penitential authors and earlier patristic authorities, were intent

[15] Bonizo of Sutri, *Liber de vita Christiana*, ed. E. Perels, Texte zur Geschichte des römischen und kanonischen Rechts im Mittelalter, vol. 1 (Berlin: Weidmann, 1930); Stickler, *Historia*, pp. 174–75; G. Miccoli, "Un nuovo manoscritto de *Liber de vita Christiana* di Bonizone di Sutri," *Studi medievali* 7 (1966) 390–98; W. Berschin, *Bonizo von Sutri, Leben und Werk*, Beiträge zur Geschichte und Quellenkunde des Mittelalters, vol. 2 (Berlin, New York: W. De Gruyter, 1972); Hermann Schadt, "Eine neue Handschrift von Bonizo von Sutris Konsanguinitätstraktat und ihre Darstellungen," BMCL, n.s. 6 (1976) 72–75.

[16] Ivo of Chartres, *Decretum*, in PL 161:47–1036, and *Panormia*, in PL 161:1045–1344. The serious shortcomings of the Migne edition of Ivo's work are detailed by Peter Landau, "Die Rubriken und Inskriptionen von Ivos Panormie: Die Ausgabe Sebastian Brandts im Vergleich zur Löwener Edition des Melchior de Vosmedian und der Ausgabe von Migne," BMCL, n.s. 12 (1982) 31–49, and "Das Dekret des Ivo von Chartres: Die handschriftliche Überlieferung im Vergleich zum Text in den Editionen des 16. und 17. Jahrhunderts," ZRG, KA 70 (1984) 1–44. The *Tripartita* remains unpublished, save for its preface, which was edited by Augustin Theiner in his *Disquisitiones criticae in praecipuas canonum et decretalium collectiones* (Rome: In Collegio Urbano, 1836), p. 154. See also Fournier and Le Bras, *Histoire des collections canoniques* 2:55–114; Fuhrmann, *Einfluss und Verbreitung* 2:544–45, 554–57; Stickler, *Historia*, pp. 179–84; García y García, *História del derecho canónico* 1:318–20; Rolf Sprandel, *Ivo von Chartres und seine Stellung in der Kirchengeschichte*, Pariser historische Studien, vol. 1 (Stuttgart: Anton Hiersemann, 1962); Jacqueline Rambaud-Buhot, "Les sommaires de la Panormie et l'édition de Melchior de Vosmédian," *Traditio* 23 (1967) 534–36. Older but still useful are the studies by Alexandre Abry, *Yves de Chartres, sa vie et ses ouvrages* (Strasbourg: G. L. Schuler, 1841); Paul Fournier, *Les collections canoniques attribués à Yves de Chartres* (Paris: Alphonse Picard et fils, 1897), and *Yves de Chartres et le droit canonique* (Paris: Alphonse Picard et fils, 1898).

[17] J. Joseph Ryan, *Saint Peter Damiani and His Canonical Sources: A Preliminary Study in the Antecedents of the Gregorian Reform*, Studies and Texts, vol. 2 (Toronto: Pontifical Institute of Mediaeval Studies, 1956), pp. 158–75.

on limiting marital sex and on penalizing extramarital sex as severely as they could.[18] They reserved their harshest denunciations, however, for the sexual activities of the clergy. A central goal of reform was to abolish clerical marriage, to eliminate clerical concubinage, and to establish once for all the principle that clerical celibacy was not just a heroic ideal to be pursued by a few, but an absolute requirement to be imposed, by force if necessary, on every cleric in the Western Church.[19]

The sexual agenda of the reformers also included a strong commitment, not only to deny marriage to the clergy, but to reorganize marriage among the laity as well. The reformers were anxious, for one thing, to bring marriage under the exclusive control of Church courts and in so doing to replace customary marriage law with ecclesiastical law. The ecclesiastical model of marriage that the reformers so vigorously—and successfully—championed rested upon seven fundamental principles. First, marriage must be monogamous; second, marriage should be indissoluble; third, marital unions should be contracted freely by the parties themselves, not by their parents or families; fourth, marriage represents the only legally protected type of sexual relationship, and therefore concubinage must be eliminated, even among the laity; fifth, and as a corollary of the fourth principle, all sexual activity outside of marriage must be punished by legal sanctions; sixth, all sexual activity, marital and nonmarital, falls solely under ecclesiastical jurisdiction; and seventh, marriage must become exogamous, and intermarriage within related groups of families should therefore be eliminated.[20]

Laymen of all types resisted attempts to implement these propositions. Monogamy and indissolubility limited the capacity of families to repudiate existing marriages and to arrange new ones in response to changes in political and social circumstances. Noble families adamantly maintained that they must be free to shift alliances, including those sealed by marriage, in order to promote family interests. The reformers' drive to eliminate concubinage met opposition from many quarters. Laymen preferred to retain the option of contracting informal unions; laywomen feared (correctly, it turned out) that abolishing concubinage would intensify competition for marriageable men and thus decrease their own bargaining power in negotiating alliances; and clerics, seeing that the Church's leaders were intent on depriving them of their wives, stoutly withstood these endeavors, sometimes by violent means. Monarchs were reluctant to forego their jurisdiction over marriage, since this would deprive them of both the

---

[18] Leclercq, *Monks on Marriage*, pp. 13, 69.

[19] Baumann, *Zivilrechtliche Bedeutung*, p. 19; Michel Dortel-Claudet, "Le prêtre et le mariage: évolution de la législation canonique dès origines au XIIe siècle," *L'année canonique* 17 (1973) 338; Lynch, "Marriage and Celibacy", pp. 189–90; and see generally, Anne L. Barstow, *Married Priests and the Reforming Papacy*, Texts and Studies in Religion, vol. 12 (New York: Edwin Mellen, 1982).

[20] Duby, *Medieval Marriage*, p. 3; Jean Gaudemet, "La définition romano-canonique du mariage," in *Speculum iuris et ecclesiarum*, pp. 107–14.

revenues generated by marriage litigation and the right to enforce their own matrimonial policies among their subjects. And families, at every level of society, found it difficult, impossible, or impolitic in many situations to observe the reformers' rules on exogamy.[21]

In view of the objections raised against their marriage policies, it is remarkable that the reformers succeeded as quickly as they did in securing a fairly high degree of conformity to their unpopular principles. They achieved this success in the face of countless matrimonial scandals in high places—the sordid marital troubles of monarchs and eminent noblemen enliven the pages of eleventh- and twelfth-century chronicles, much as similar reports about the domestic tangles of wealthy notables abound in the popular press today. The two marriages of King Philip I of France (1059–1108), the amorous intrigues of his son, Louis the Fat (1108–37), or the well-publicized sexual adventures of Count William IX of Poitou (1071–1127), to mention only three notorious examples, provided ample material for gossip and spectacular scandals for reformers to denounce. It is clear, nonetheless, that by the early twelfth century the ecclesiastical model of marriage was achieving acceptance. Indeed the sexual cavortings of these magnates achieved notoriety, not because they were unprecedented or even particularly unusual, but rather because people had begun to accept the Church's marital norms.[22]

Gradual acquiescence in the Church's doctrine on marriage and sex was accompanied by a change in popular beliefs about conventional standards of sexual behavior for men and women. It is probably no accident that the ideal of romantic love was born in the same generations that gradually accepted the rigid rules of marriage advocated by Church reformers. Early twelfth-century poetry enunciated attitudes about sexual behavior and personal feelings that were foreign to beliefs current, say, a century-and-a-half earlier. The poetic typology of romance took shape in opposition to, and as escape from, a bleak marriage ideology that canonists and theologians championed.[23] Twelfth-century poets differed pointedly from the ecclesiastical establishment in regard to the nature of human sexuality and its role both within marriage and outside of it. Provençal poets, such as Count William IX of Poitiers (1071–1127), Macabru

[21] Duby, *Medieval Marriage*, pp. 7–21, and *Knight, Lady, and Priest*, pp. 43–44, 116–20, 133; Michael M. Sheehan, "Choice of Marriage Partner in the Middle Ages: Development and Mode of Application of a Theory of Marriage," *Studies in Medieval and Renaissance History*, n.s., 1 (1978) 7–8.

[22] Duby, *Medieval Marriage*, p. 45, and more cautiously in *Knight, Lady, and Priest*, pp. 5–19, argues that the turning point in the fortunes of the ecclesiastical model of marriage lay in the reign of Philip I. There is a case to be made, however, that the ecclesiastical model did not win a clear-cut victory until somewhat later—say, in the pontificate of Alexander III (1159–81).

[23] Duby, *Medieval Marriage*, p. 15; *Knight, Lady, and Priest*, pp. 211–26; C. N. L. Brooke, "The Gregorian Reform in Action: Clerical Marriage in England, 1050–1200," *Cambridge Historical Journal* 12 (1956) 1, 19–20.

(fl. 1129–50), and Bernart de Ventadorn (fl. 1150–80) idealized sensuality and carnal relationships, while canonists and theologians deplored them.

The views on sexuality that canonists and reform leaders adopted had their roots firmly planted in ideas expressed by St. Jerome and the author of the *Responsa Gregorii*. The sources of those ideas were ultimately to be found, as we have seen, in late ancient philosophical schools, particularly the Stoics.[24] Many eleventh century reformers propagated these gloomy views of sex. St. Peter Damian (ca. 1007–72), in particular, made the reform of sexual mores a major theme of his writing.[25]

Damian, although important, was scarcely alone in adopting a dismal outlook on human sexuality. His torrid denunciations of the dangers of sexual temptation and the sinfulness of intercourse, marital or nonmarital, found echoes in other writers of the period—Honorius of Autun (ca. 1080–ca. 1156), for example, and members of the school of Gilbert de la Porée (ca. 1075–1154).[26] Notable among these writers was Abbot Guibert of Nogent (ca. 1064–ca. 1125), who, like Peter Damian, seems obsessed with the filthiness of sex, returned time and again to the theme that the brush of lust has tarred us all. We are burdened and doomed, according to Guibert, by sexual fantasies that spring unbidden to our minds, even in sleep; sordid desires subvert our efforts to attain chastity and plunge us into ever deeper despair. Sex is a vice and a disease, Guibert believed; it taints and befouls every living person. Even when death finally delivers us from the grasp of lust, it is likely to pitch us into hell.[27]

Guibert was a bit peculiar, but even sober and well-balanced men of this age shared many of his notions. A chapter in the *Decretum* of Burchard of Worms, for example, listed the consequences of lust: it causes spiritual blindness, inconsiderateness, shiftiness of the eyes, hatred of God's commandments, attachment to worldly things, misery in this life, and despair for the future.[28] Even so

[24] Philippe Delhaye, "Le dossier antimatrimonial de *l'Adversus Jovinianum* et son influence sur quelques écrits latins du XIIe siècle," *Mediaeval Studies* 13 (1951) 86, also emphasizes Jerome's contribution, while Tentler, *Sin and Confession*, p. 166, stresses the contribution of the *Responsa Gregorii*.

[25] Lester K. Little, "The Personal Development of Peter Damian," in *Order and Innovation in the Middle Ages: Essays in Honor of Joseph R. Strayer*, ed. William C. Jordan et al. (Princeton: Princeton University Press, 1976), p. 332; K. Reindel, "Neue Literatur zu Petrus Damiani," *Deutsches Archiv für Erforschung des Mittelalters* (hereafter DA) 32 (1976) 403–43.

[26] Müller, *Lehre des hl. Augustinus*, pp. 58–59, 64–65. On Damian's obsessions with sex, money, and his own sinfulness see Little, "Personal Development," p. 339.

[27] *Self and Society in Medieval France: The Memoirs of Abbot Guibert of Nogent*, ed. and trans. John F. Benton (New York: Harper and Row, 1970), pp. 13–14, 65–67. Duby, *Knight, Lady, and Priest*, pp. 139–56. But see also the criticism of these views by M. D. Coupe, "The Personality of Guibert de Nogent Reconsidered," JMH 9 (1983) 317–29.

[28] Burchard, *Decretum* 19.6, in PL 140:977, citing (incorrectly) the *Penitential* of Archbishop Theodore.

ascetic a man as the philosopher-archbishop, Anselm of Canterbury (1033/34–1109) lamented in one of his prayers:

> There is one evil, an evil above all other evils, that I am aware is always with me, that grievously and piteously lacerates and afflicts my soul. It was with me from the cradle, it grew with me in childhood, in adolescence, in my youth it always stuck to me, and it does not desert me even now that my limbs are failing because of my old age. This evil is sexual desire, carnal delight, the storm of lust that has smashed and battered my unhappy soul, emptied it of all strength, and left it weak and empty.[29]

Fear and loathing of sex was common among the reformers and more generally among the Church's leaders during the eleventh and twelfth centuries, but condemnation of marriage because of its sexual implications was not. Indeed those who denounced marriage and advised laymen to abstain from it were considered heretics. A number of heretical sects during this period did, in fact, teach that no Christian could in good conscience contract marriage.[30] One sectarian group at Orléans in 1122 adopted the view that marriage was profane because it dealt with sex. The Church should therefore have nothing to do with it, they taught, and should leave marital matters entirely in the hands of the laity. This was not a view that Church authorities were prepared to tolerate—they made that point clear by burning fourteen heretics alive.[31]

[29] Anselm, *Oratio IV*, in PL 159:870: "Est et praeter haec, unum malum super omnia mala malum, quo tanto gravius et miserabilius laceratum et afflictum animum meum sentio, quanto et ab ipsis cunabulis semper mecum fuit, mecum crevit, in infantia, in adolescentia, in juventute mihi semper adhaesit, nec adhuc jam prae senectute membris deficientibus me deserit. Est autem hoc malum, desiderium voluptatis, delectatio carnis, tempestas libidinis, quae multis et variis modis infelicem animam meam maceravit, dissolvit et omni virtute destitutam inanem et debilem reddidit." Anselm's account of his own sexual yearnings in childhood seems to contradict his assertion in *De nuptiis consanguineorum* (PL 158:559) that small children experience no sexual feelings.

[30] Radulphus Ardens, *Homeliae in epistolas et evangelia dominicalia* 2.19, in PL 155:2011, refers to such a sect at Agen and describes them as Manichaeans. There were similar groups at Orleans and at Monteforte in Piedmont during the 1120s; Huguette Taviani, "Le mariage dans l'hérésie de l'an mil," *Annales é.s.c.* 32 (1977) 1074–78; Duby, *Knight, Lady, and Priest*, pp. 109–16.

[31] Andrew of Fleury, *Vita Gauzlini* 56a, ed. and trans. R.H. Bautier and Gillette Labory, *Sources d'histoire médiévale*, vol. 2 (Paris: Editions du Centre National de Recherche Scientifique, 1969), pp. 96–98 and 180–82; Radulfus Glaber, *Historiae* 3.8.26–31, ed. Marcel Prou, Collection de textes pour servir à l'étude et à l'enseignement d'histoire, no. 1 (Paris: A. Picard, 1886), pp. 74–81; Adhémar de Chabannes, *Chronicon* 3.59, ed. Jules Chavanon, Collection de textes . . . , no. 20 (Paris: A. Picard et fils, 1897), pp. 184–85. See also Raoul Manselli, "Il monaco Enrico e la sua eresia," *Bullettino dell'Istituto Storico Italiano per il medio evo* 65 (1953) 1–63, and Duby, *Medieval Marriage*, pp. 51–52.

A few atypical writers adopted more naturalistic views of human sexuality than were common among Catholic leaders. The late eleventh-century Benedictine monk and physician, Constantinus Africanus, for example, commended sexual intercourse not merely as natural, but even as necessary for good health, along with exercise, regular bathing, adequate diet, and sufficient sleep.[32] Folk medicine also prescribed sexual intercourse as a remedy for various ailments and afflictions, including snake bite, on the theory, apparently, that orgasm drained poisonous substances from the body.[33] Among the philosophers and theologians of the period, however, Peter Abelard was almost alone in denying the intrinsic sinfulness of sexual relations and in maintaining that sexual intercourse is both natural and beneficial.[34]

Sex and Marriage in the Canonists, 1000–1140

The canonists of the Church reform period subscribed to a definition of marriage borrowing from Roman law the concept that couples created their own marriages by free consent.[35] Marriage by consent was, of course, nothing new: the Fathers of the Church had long before adopted the notion. In addition, consensual marriage had been practiced in southern Germany and elsewhere long before the reformers made it a cornerstone of their program to reshape matrimonial institutions.[36]

During the second half of the eleventh century, both Anselm of Lucca and

[32] Constantinus Africanus, *De coitu*, in his *Opera* (Basel: Henricus Petrus, 1536), pp. 302–304; Joan Cadden "Medieval Scientific and Medical Views of Sexuality," paper presented at the XVIII International Congress on Medieval Studies, Western Michigan University, 1983, pp. 3–4.

[33] Albert of Aachen, *Historia Hierosolymitana* 5.40, in *Recueil des historiens des croisades, Historiens occidentaux*, 5 vols. in 6 (Paris: Imprimerie royale, 1844–95; cited hereafter as RHC, Occ.) 4:459.

[34] Hans Zeimentz, *Ehe nach der Lehre der Frühscholastik: Eine moralgeschichtliche Untersuchung zur Anthropologie und Theologie der Ehe in der Schule Anselms von Laon und Wilhelms von Champeaux, bei Hugo von St. Victor, Walter von Mortagne und Petrus Lombardus* (Düsseldorf: Patmos Verlag, 1973), pp. 81–82; Tentler, *Sin and Confession*, p. 167; Delhaye, "Dossier antimatrimonial," pp. 71–73.

[35] Ivo, *Decretum* 8.1 (= *Panormia* 6.1, citing Inst. 1.9.1) and 8.17 (= *Panormia* 6.107, citing Pope Nicholas' letter to the Bulgarians).

[36] Basic formulations of Roman consensual doctrine occur in two passages from Ulpian in Dig. 24.1.32.13 and Dig. 35.1.15 (= Dig. 50.17.30); on patristic adaptation of Roman consensual theory see Jean Gaudemet, "Originalité et destin du mariage romain," in his *Sociétés et mariage* (Strasbourg: CERDIC, 1980), pp. 153–63 and "La définition," pp. 107–14. On eleventh-century German practice see Christian Gellinek, "Marriage by Consent in Literary Sources of Medieval Germany," *Studia Gratiana* 12 (1967) 577; on the consent of the couple in Anglo-Saxon England see Christine Fell, *Women in Anglo-Saxon England and the Impact of 1066* (London: British Museum; Bloomington, IN: Indiana University Press, 1984), p. 58.

the author of the *Collection in Seventy-four Titles* included consent, not of the couple, but of parents, among the requirements for valid marriage and found authority for this position in one of the forged decretals of Pseudo-Isidore.[37] This view, however, aroused little enthusiasm among reform-minded canonists, who wished to minimize the role of parents in arranging marriages.

Another matrimonial issue that concerned the reform canonists was the role of sexual relations in the formation of marriage. Was an unconsummated union binding, or not? On this point opinions differed. Ivo of Chartres cited a letter of Pope Leo I, originally written in 458/59, in support of the theory that only consent of the parties was required. Ivo cited this letter repeatedly in both his *Panormia* and *Decretum*. According to Leo's letter, marriage exists between a couple whether they have consummated their union or not, for even an unconsummated marriage fully symbolized the tie between Christ and the Church.[38] This text, supported by a few others, became a key element in the reformers' teaching on marriage.[39] The leaders of the reform movement strongly opposed the coital theory of marriage that Hincmar of Reims had proposed about 860.[40] Although Hincmar's position found some support among theological writers on marriage in the late eleventh and early twelfth centuries, the canonists were less than enthusiastic about it. The coital theory found no place in the canonistic manuals until it was incorporated in the *Collection in Ten Parts*, a compilation of limited circulation written between 1123 and 1130.[41]

---

[37] Pseudo-Evaristus, *Epist.* 1.2, in Hinschius, DPI, pp. 87–88 (JK *20); Coll. 74T 62.271, ed. Gilchrist, pp. 164–65; Anselm of Lucca 10.2, ed. Thaner, pp. 483–84. The requirement of parental consent was a way of discouraging marriage by abduction, which was still a significant problem in many regions, particularly in frontier areas. See Duby, *Medieval Marriage*, pp. 4, 27; Heath Dillard, "Women in Reconquest Castile: The Fueros of Sepúlveda and Cuenca," in Stuard, ed., *Women in Medieval Society*, pp. 72, 80; McNamara and Wemple, "Marriage and Divorce," pp. 101–102.

[38] Leo I, *Epist.* 167.4, in PL 54:1204–1205 (JK 544); Ivo, *Decretum* 8.74 (= *Panormia* 6.23) in PL 161:599–600, and 8.139 (= *Panormia* 6.35) in PL 161:615. This text had appeared previously in Burchard, *Decretum* 9.1, in PL 140:815, and had been used by other canonists. On its history and the transformations it experienced, see Jean Gaudemet, "Recherches sur les origines historiques de la faculté de rompre le mariage non consommé, in *Proceedings of the Fifth International Congress of Medieval Canon Law, Salamanca, 21–25 September 1976*, ed. Stephan Kuttner and Kenneth Pennington, MIC, Subsidia, vol. 6 (Vatican City: Biblioteca Apostolica Vaticana, 1980; cited hereafter as *Salamanca Proceedings*), pp. 309–31, as well as his "Indissolubilité et consommation du mariage: L'apport d'Hincmar de Reims," RDC 30 (1980) 28–40.

[39] See also Ivo, *Decretum* 8.2–3 (= *Panormia* 6.14–15), in PL 161:583–84.

[40] Zeimentz, *Ehe nach der Lehre der Frühscholastik*, pp. 108–109; Gaudemet, "Indissolubilité," pp. 39–40, and "Recherche sur les origines," pp. 313–18, 329–30.

[41] Theological support for a version of the coital theory came mainly from the School of Laon; Zeimentz, *Ehe nach der Lehre der Frühscholastik*, p. 114; on the incorporation of Hincmar's doctrine in the *Collection in Ten Parts* see Gaudemet, "Indissolubilité," p. 38, and "Recherche sur les origines," pp. 326–27, citing Paris, Bibliothèque nationale (hereafter BN), ms. lat. 10743.

To Peter Damian the notion that marriage depended for its validity upon sexual relations seemed outrageous:

> If they [the defenders of the coital theory] maintain that marriage rests on intercourse [Peter fumed] then how is it that the holy canons forbid people to be joined in marriage without public weddings? Do they want the man to mount his wife in public? . . . If indeed marriage is made by coitus, then every time a man makes love to his wife no doubt they get married all over again.[42]

Damian and others insisted that consent must be at the center of marriage formation and that consummation merely affirmed consent.[43]

Reform canonists were also determined to establish the principle that marriage must be legitimate, that is, it must be contracted publicly and formally, with full solemnity, not entered into casually and secretly.[44] Legitimate marriage, according to the authorities that Ivo relied on, involved a public exchange of vows, marriage gifts, a wedding ring, and blessing by a priest.[45] Not all of these were necessary in every case, but a legitimate marriage must at least be contracted with public knowledge. Secret marriages were improper, and those who contracted them might be subject to penitential discipline, according to several of Ivo's authorities.[46] A number of councils in the late eleventh and early twelfth centuries reiterated the ban on secret weddings.[47] Save for one English canon, these prohibitions of clandestine marriage stopped short of ruling that

---

[42] Peter Damian, *De tempore celebrandi nuptias* 1, in PL 145:660–61: "Si enim jure in concubitu constare nuptias perhibentur, quid est quod sacri canones prohibent ut absque publicis nuptiis nunquam matrimonium copuletur? Nunquid hoc volunt, ut vir uxori publice misceatur? . . . Enim vero si concubitus nuptiae sunt, quoties vir mulieri admiscetur, toties procul dubio nuptias celebrare convincitur." See also Sara Acuña, "La forma del matrimonio hasta el Decreto 'Ne temere'," *Ius canonicum* 13 (1973) 154–55; Gaudmet, "Recherche sur les origines," pp. 320–21.

[43] Mullenders, *Mariage présumé*, pp. 11–12; Zeimentz, *Ehe nach der Lehre der Frühscholastik*, p. 114.

[44] Burchard, *Decretum* 9.2 (= Anselm of Lucca 10.3; Ivo, *Decretum* 8.140 and *Panormia* 6.36). The canonists cite Pope Leo as their authority, but the passage actually came from the forged capitularies of Benedictus Levita 3.179, in MGH, Capitularia 2:113.

[45] Ivo, *Decretum* 8.4–5 (= Anselm of Lucca 10.2 and *Panormia* 6.31) in PL 161:584–85, taken from Pseudo-Evaristus, decretal 2 in Hinschius, DPI, p. 87; see also Ivo, *Decretum* 8.6 (= *Panormia* 6.9) and 8.40–41 (= *Panormia* 6.33–34), in PL 161:585, 592–93.

[46] Burchard, *Decretum* 9.3 (= Ivo, *Decretum* 8.141 and *Panormia* 6.5), in PL 140:816; also Burchard, *Decretum* 19.5 (= *Corrector* 43), in PL 140:958.

[47] Council of Rouen (1072) c. 14, in Mansi 20:38; Council of Winchester (1076) c. 6, and Council of Westminster (1102) c. 23, in *Councils and Synods with Other Documents Relating to the English Church*, ed. Dorothy Whitelock, Martin Brett, and C. N. L. Brooke, 2 vols. (Oxford: Clarendon Press, 1981) 2:620, 677; Council of Troyes (1107) c. 7, in Uta Renata Blumenthal, *The Early Councils of Pope Paschal II, 1100–1110*, Studies and Texts, vol. 43 (Toronto: Pontifical Institute of Mediaeval Studies, 1978),

secret weddings were invalid.[48] Those who married secretly did so illegally, but common opinion held that they were nonetheless tied to each other by the marriage bond.

Formal betrothal was a usual preliminary to marriage in customary law and practice at this period, but the reformers refrained from making betrothal a requirement for ecclesiastically valid marriage.[49] They did, however, accord betrothals the status of valid contracts and prohibited those who had made such agreements from marrying anyone but the person to whom they were pledged.[50] The reformers encouraged the practice of giving dowries, which they linked to the requirement that marriage must be public. It was no coincidence that the earliest legal treatise on dowries in medieval Europe dates from just this period.[51] This recognition of the importance of dowries was consistent with practice; well-to-do families in the eleventh-century usually insisted that marriage must be preceded by a dowry agreement.[52] The acceptance of dowry by the canonists also helped to support the economic rights of the wife, which were eroding at that time. Changes in customary dowry practices during this period tended to extend the rights of the husband at the expense of his wife. In many families, the dowry that a woman received at the time of her marriage was the only share she would receive from her family's property.[53]

Nuptial rites also underwent considerable change during this period. Although marriage ceremonies originally were treated as private, family affairs (a character that they long retained in many regions) the clergy by 1100 played

---

p. 94; Michael M. Sheehan, "Marriage Theory and Practice in the Conciliar Legislation and Diocesan Statutes of Medieval England," *Mediaeval Studies* 40 (1978) 410–11.

[48] Westminster (1102) c. 23, in Whitelock, Brett, and Brooke 2:677: "Ut fides inter virum et mulierem occulte et sine testibus de coniugio data, si ab alterutro negata fuerit, irrita habeatur."

[49] Georges Duby, "Structures familiales dans le moyen âge occidental," in *Dokaldy Kongressa mezdoonarodnii istoricheskych nauk, Moskva, 16–23 augusta 1970 goda* [Proceedings of the Thirteenth International Congress of Historical Sciences, Moscow, 16–23 August 1970] (Moscow: Akademii Nauk SSSR, 1973), p. 156; Jenny M. Jochens, "The Church and Sexuality in Medieval Iceland," JMH 6 (1980) 380; Zurowsky, "Einflüsse," p. 355.

[50] Burchard, *Decretum* 9.31 (= Ivo, *Decretum* 8.169 and *Panormia* 6.18) in PL 140:819–20, citing Pope Siricius (JK 255). See also the early eleventh-century treatise on betrothal, "Be wifmannes beweddunge," in Whitelock, Brett, and Brooke 1:427–31.

[51] Burchard, *Decretum* 9.6 (= Ivo, *Decretum* 8.144 and *Panormia* 6.6) in PL 140:816. Both Burchard and Ivo ascribed this canon to the Council of Arles, but it came in fact from the forged capitularies of Benedictus Levita 2.133, in MGH, Capitularia 2:80. Martinus de Gosia, one of Irnerius' best-known pupils, wrote the treatise *De iure dotium* about 1140; the text is published in Kantorowicz and Buckland, *Studies in the Glossators*, pp. 255–66.

[52] Fell, *Women in Anglo-Saxon England*, p. 58.

[53] Duby, "Structures familiales," pp. 156–57.

more prominent roles in wedding rituals than they had in 1000.[54] Yet no major canonist of the period required a nuptial blessing for validity, although Ivo envisioned a wedding ritual in which the constitutive element was an exchange of oaths sworn by the parties.[55] An English council in 1076 did stipulate that a blessing by a priest was essential to marriage and that unblessed unions were invalid, but this appears to have been an isolated aberration.[56]

As festive occasions, weddings were prohibited during Lent, Advent, and other fasting periods. The canonists, however, did not link this prohibition explicitly to the older penitential practice that forbade sexual relations during Lent and other penitential seasons.[57] According to Burchard, priests and other clerics who were supposed to observe celibacy ought to avoid attending the feasts and entertainments that accompanied upper-class weddings. No matter what the season, Burchard maintained, they ought to shun exposure to love songs, obscene gestures, and the lewd jokes common at these affairs.[58] Even the laity, according to one canon, were forbidden to dance at weddings; rather they should dine solemnly, as befits Christians. This injunction, of course, represented no more than a pious hope, not a seriously enforced policy.[59]

Canonistic writers of the Church reform movement were greatly concerned with incest. Burchard devoted the entire seventh book of his *Decretum* to the subject and added an appendix to clarify the calculation of the seven forbidden degrees of relationship. Burchard's canons prescribed excommunication for those who contracted forbidden marriages, declared the contracting parties and their children legally infamous (*infames*), and held the marriages themselves invalid.[60] The anonymous compiler of the *Collection in Seventy-four Titles* found still further texts, and Ivo's *Decretum* contains massive numbers of additional authorities on this topic.[61]

[54] Karl Ritzer, *Le mariage dans les églises chrétiennes du Ier au XIe siècle*, Lex orandi, vol. 45 (Paris: Editions du Cerf, 1970), pp. 296–312, 447–50; Sheehan, "Choice of Marriage Partner," pp. 25–27; Jochens, "Church and Sexuality," p. 381; Duby, *Knight, Lady, and Priest*, 150–53.

[55] Ivo, *Decretum* 8.44 (= *Decretum* 16.142 and *Panormia* 6.7) in PL 161:594. This may, however, have been simply a display of Ivo's Romanist erudition, as the canon is taken from the *Epitome novellarum*.

[56] Winchester (1076) c. 6, in Whitelock, Brett, and Brooke 2:620; cf. Westminster (1101) c. 23, in ibid. 2:677, as well as "Be wifmannes beweddunge," c. 8, in ibid. 1:431; Sheehan, "Marriage Theory and Practice," pp. 410, 423–24.

[57] Burchard, *Decretum* 9.4 (= Ivo, *Decretum* 8.142 and *Panormia* 6.2), in PL 140:816.

[58] Burchard, *Decretum* 2.132, 134–35, in PL 140:648.

[59] Burchard, *Decretum* 9.10, in PL 140:817.

[60] Burchard, *Decretum*, book 7, in PL 140:779–88, comprising 30 canons and a chart to facilitate calculations of the degrees of relationship. For an analysis of Burchard's system of computing relationships see Ernest Champeaux, "*Jus sanguinis*; trois façons de calculer la parenté au moyen âge," RHDF, 4th ser., 12 (1933) 244–62.

[61] Coll. 74T 65.281–84, ed. Gilchrist, p. 170. These canons are taken from Pope Gre-

These prohibitions against incestuous marriage were by no means merely theoretical. Pope Gregory VII, for example, intervened in several cases to forbid consanguineous marriages that involved, among others, such powerful figures as Countess Matilda of Tuscany, Count Centullus of Bearn, and King Alfonso VI of Castile and León.[62] The letters of Ivo of Chartres likewise show him warning correspondents to avoid projected marriages that would expose them to the charge of incest.[63] Both Peter Damian and Anselm of Canterbury considered the issue of consanguineous marriages sufficiently pressing to devote special treatises to the problem. A number of local councils and synods also legislated on the subject, mainly repeating the prohibitions they found in the earlier canonical collections.[64] Two general councils during the early twelfth century enacted prohibitions against consanguineous marriage, and this legislation was reiterated by local synods.[65]

This vigorous activity by lawmakers, legal writers, and Church administrators demonstrates that the prevention of endogamous unions and the nullification of marriages between relatives, even distant ones, was a major concern of Church reformers. Their prohibitions and condemnations were couched in rhetoric designed to show that consanguineous unions contravened divine law, and the penalties they imposed on such unions involved mainly ecclesiastical sanctions—excommunication, *infamia*, and penances.

Worldly interests were also involved in the campaign against consanguinity. The eleventh-century reformers drew a firm legal line, for example, between bequests of land to the Church and the residual interests in those estates held by members of the donor's family.[66] Restricting the capacity of families to create

---

gory II's Roman Synod of 721 and the author of 74T found them ready to hand both in the *Dionysio-Hadriana* (PL 67:343–44) and in Pseudo-Isidore (Hinschius, DPI, p. 170). Part 9 of Ivo's *Decretum* deals almost entirely with consanguineous marriage and related topics; see PL 161:655–90.

[62] Gregory VII, *Register*, 1.5 and 2.35–36 (Matilda of Tuscany), ed. Eric Caspar, 2 vols., MGH, Ep. sel. vol. 2 (Berlin: Weidmann, 1920–23) 1:7–8, 170–71; 6.20 (Contulus of Béarn), ed. Caspar 2:431–32; and 8.3 (Alfonso VI), ed. Caspar 2:519–20.

[63] Ivo of Chartres, *Epist.* 129, 211, 261, in PL 162:139–40, 215–16, 265–66. On the last of these see also Anselm of Canterbury, *Epist.* 4.48, in PL 159:245.

[64] Peter Damian, *De parentelae gradibus*, in PL 145:191–208 = *Epist.* 19 in *Die Briefe des Petrus Damiani*, ed. Kurt Reindel, MGH, Briefe der deutschen Kaiserzeit, vol. 4, pt. 1– (Munich: Monumenta Germaniae Historica, 1983–) 1:179–99; Anselm, *De nuptiis consanguineorum*, in PL 158:557–60; Council of London (1074/75) c. 6, in Whitelock, Brett, and Brooke 2:614; Sheehan, "Marriage Theory and Practice," pp. 409–10.

[65] 1 Lateran (1123) c. 9 (repeating Pseudo-Calixtus c. 16, in Hinschius, DPI, p. 140) and 2 Lateran (1139) c. 17, in COD, pp. 167, 177. The Council of Westminster (1125) c. 16–17, in Whitelock, Brett, and Brooke 2:741, paraphrases the provisions of 1 Lateran c. 9.

[66] Jack Goody, *The Development of the Family and Marriage in Europe* (Cambridge: At the University Press, 1983), p. 107.

extensive webs of interrelations through marriage helped to safeguard Church property from the legal claims of numerous relatives. Ecclesiastical authorities demanded that families desist from intermarrying with members of their own clans in part, at least, to accomplish this aim and to break up the concentrations of landholdings that supported the economic and political power of the feudal nobility.

Although clear and explicit evidence for their rationale is difficult to come by, popes, bishops, church councils, and canonists seem to have reckoned that if blocs of feudal property were dispersed among large numbers of holders it would be possible for the Church to free itself from the power of the grand noble clans whose power rested squarely on the control of extensive landed estates. A policy of exogamy was well-calculated to achieve these goals, and Church reformers used the canon law on consanguinity to pursue them with vigor and tenacity.[67] The law of consanguinity proved to be a two-edged weapon, however: in the hands of the clergy it could prevent (or at least discourage) endogamous unions, but laymen quickly learned that they could use the consanguinity provisions of canon law to dissolve marriages that had proved unprofitable or unpalatable. Thus the weapon that the canonists forged to combat endogamy became a tool that laymen could use to combat clerically imposed indissolubility.

Closely linked to restrictions on consanguineous marriages was a battery of canonistic prohibitions against marriage with affinal, or fictive, relatives. Marriages with relatives by marriage or adoption had long been forbidden, and the major canonists included numerous earlier pronouncements on this topic in their collections.[68] The reform canonists placed much greater emphasis than had their predecessors on other and more tenuous affinity ties, notably the relationship between godparent and godchild or between co-godparents.[69] Since at least the Carolingian period, marriages between persons related by affinity contracted through godparenting had been forbidden; earlier generations of Christians disapproved of these marriages, but did not ban them.[70] Reform canonists, however, gave much greater prominence to the limitations on affinal marriages, and it seems likely that their reasons for this were not entirely theo-

---

[67] Cf. Duby, *Medieval Marriage*, pp. 53–54, 62–64, and *Knight, Lady, and Priest*, pp. 35–37, 48; Goody, *Development of Family and Marriage*, pp. 134–46.

[68] Burchard, *Decretum* 17.24 (= Ivo, *Decretum* 9.82, *Panormia* 7.66); 17.26 (= Ivo, *Decretum* 9.84); Coll. 74T 65.280, 282.

[69] Burchard, *Decretum* 17.23 (= Ivo, *Decretum* 9.81, *Panormia* 7.65); 17.24 (= Ivo, *Decretum* 9.82, *Panormia* 7.66); 17.25 (= Ivo, *Decretum* 9.83); 17.26 (= Ivo *Decretum* 9.84); 17.45 (= Ivo, *Decretum* 9.96, *Panormia* 7.67); 17.46 (= Ivo, *Decretum* 9.97); 17.49 (= Ivo, *Decretum* 9.100); all in PL 140:923–24, 928–29. In addition see Coll. 74T 65.279 (= Pseudo-Isidore, in Hinschius, DPI, p. 754; *Dionysio-Hadriana*, in PL 67:343), and Ivo, *Decretum* 9.28 (= *Responsa Gregorii* c. 6, in Hinschius, DPI, pp. 738–39), in PL 161:662–63.

[70] Burchard, *Decretum* 17.47 (= Ivo, *Decretum* 9.98) in PL 140:929. The earliest prohibition of marriage between godparent and godchild seems to be a rescript of Justinian, dated 530: Cod. 5.4.26.2.

logical. Godparent relationships involved, after all, a means of creating bonds between families. The bond was not as close and intimate as that created by marriage, but the relationship resulted nonetheless in a significant social linkage. The reform canonists may perhaps have seen the ban on marriages between persons related by affinity as a further means both to attack legal claims of donors' families to Church estates and to break up blocs of feudal property held by groups of families connected to one another by godparenthood.[71]

The cluster of developments in matrimonial law and practice championed by the Church reformers has led Georges Duby to postulate two theoretical models of marriage in eleventh-century society: an ecclesiastical model—marked by an insistence upon strict exogamy, indissolubility, and free choice of marriage partner—as contrasted with a lay model, whose characteristic elements included endogamy, the possibility of divorce and remarriage, and family control of the marital choices of young persons.[72] These are useful constructs for organizing and analyzing the evidence of law and practice in the eleventh century. Like any models, they achieve clarity by simplifying reality, which means that they disregard variables that do not fit the conceptual scheme. Eleventh-century popes and canonists worried a good deal about the matrimonial issues that feature in Duby's analytical scheme. But they were also concerned about other important issues that do not fit so neatly into the system.

One of those issues concerned the role of sex in marriage. Canonists of this period insisted that sexual intercourse, in marriage or outside of it, created a matrimonial affinity.[73] This concept seems to be rooted in the belief that sex creates a bond of intimacy between the partners, and that this bond ought to bar subsequent marriage between either partner and close relatives of the other. The social objective here was presumably to prevent rivalries between males of the same family over sexual access to females. None of the canonical sources spell out this rationale, but it seems implied in the law's provisions. The sources never speak of eliminating rivalries; rather they evoke notions of ritual purity.[74] Here again we may be seeing both an attack on immorality and an

---

[71] Joseph H. Lynch, "Baptismal Sponsorship and Monks and Nuns, 500–1000," *American Benedictine Review* 31 (1980) 108–14, surveys another facet of this whole topic; see also his *Godparents and Kinship*, pp. 219–57, as well as Fowler, "Development of Incest Regulations," pp. 152–77.

[72] Duby, *Medieval Marriage*, pp. 3–22.

[73] Burchard, *Decretum* 17.1–3 (= Ivo, *Decretum* 9.67–69); 17.8–9 (= Ivo, *Decretum* 9.70–71); 17.10–16 (= Ivo, *Decretum* 9.72–76); 17.19–21 (=Ivo, *Decretum* 9.77–79); and 17.22 (=Ivo, *Decretum* 9.80, *Panormia* 6.125), in PL 140:919–23.

[74] Thus, e.g., in Burchard, *Decretum* 17.8 (PL 140:920–21): "Si quis fornicatus fuerit cum duabus sororibus, vel cum noverca sua . . . abstineat se ab ingressu domus Dei annum . . . osculum nulli praebeat, sacrificium nisi pro viatico minime sumat." Again in 17.14 (PL 140:922): "Si frater cum muliere fornicatus fuerit, et frater nesciens cum eadem concubuerit, mulier diebus vitae suae poeniteat; post poenitentiam autem frater ignarus sceleris conjugium accipiat si vult." See also Ivo, *Decretum* 8.308, 313, in PL 161:651–52.

effort to prevent the perpetuation of closed systems of propertyholding through sexual conquest—perhaps even an attack on informal marriage by ravishment.

Impediment by reason of sexual intercourse was not just a speculative notion of lawmakers. Four actual cases discussed in the letter of Ivo of Chartres make this clear.[75] Two cases that Ivo dealt with concerned marriages between men and their concubines, while the other two cases arose out of more casual kinds of fornication. Ivo's treatment of these issues shows that he considered the question of affinity created by sexual intercourse difficult to deal with, for the law on this point was not well settled. Ivo's conclusion in each case turned on the point that intercourse creates what later authorities would call a prohibitive (or impedient), but not a diriment, impediment. In other words, previous intercourse was a sufficiently serious problem to block a proposed marriage, but if the parties were already married before the impediment came to light, the problem was not sufficiently grave to justify separating the parties and annulling their marriage.[76]

A substantial number of consanguinity and affinity canons appeared in Pseudo-Isidore. Burchard and Ivo were particularly important in the transmission of these from the Pseudo-Isidorian collection to later canonists, notably Gratian. Table 5.1 in the Appendix shows, for example, that twenty-four of fifty-three canons on consanguinity current in this period (about 45 percent) appear in Gratian, some of them more than once. Every one of the twenty-four canons that Gratian adopted had previously appeared in Ivo's *Decretum*, and all but three were also in Burchard's work.

Canonists of the reform era detailed other impediments to lawful marriage in addition to consanguinity and affinity. Nuns, as well as widows who had taken the veil and other women pledged to God, were forbidden to marry. If they attempted to do so, a Church court might hold their unions void.[77] Insane persons were likewise incompetent to marry.[78] Church authorities continued to disapprove of marriages between Christians and Saracens or other non-Christians. The evidence suggests, however, that that such unions sometimes did take place, particularly in the Crusader kingdoms of the Levant and in Spain.[79] Al-

---

[75] Ivo, *Epist.* 16, 148, 155, 188, in PL 162:28–29, 153–54, 158–60, 191–93; see also Duby, *Knight, Lady, and Priest*, pp. 166–72.

[76] Ivo, *Decretum* 8.10 (= *Panormia* 6.45), 8.36, 9.37, in PL 161:586, 591, 665; *Epist.* 16, 148, 232, in PL 162:28–29, 153–54, 235; Esmein, *Mariage* 1:209–10.

[77] Burchard, *Decretum* 8.30–31 (= Ivo, *Decretum* 7.49–50); 8.38 (= Ivo, *Decretum* 7.57); 8.46 (= Ivo, *Decretum* 7.64); 8.50 (= Ivo, *Decretum* 7.68), in PL 140:797, 799, 801, 803; Coll. 74T 65.276–78.

[78] Burchard, *Decretum* 9.30 (= Ivo, *Decretum* 8.168, *Panormia* 6.92). This canon comes from the *Sententiae* of Paulus, in Riccobono, *Fontes iuris romani anteiustinianae* 2:345.

[79] Burchard, *Decretum* 9.78 (= Ivo, *Decretum* 8.204), in PL 140:830. Examples in the Holy Land are mentioned by Fulcher of Chartres, *Historia Hierosolymitana* 3.37.4, ed. Heinrich Hagenmeyer (Heidelberg: Carl Winter, 1913), p. 748; Pierre Tudebode, *Historia de Hierosolymitano itinere*, ed. John Hugh Hill and Laurita L. Hill, Docu-

though no law at this point forbade Latin Catholics to marry Byzantine and other Eastern Christians, many contemporaries disapproved of these unions also.[80] Significantly, however, canon law protected the marriages of slaves and serfs, even when man and wife belonged to different masters, and forbade owners to break up these unions.[81]

Reform canonists maintained the Church's longstanding opposition to bigamy, but their position on digamy, or remarriage, was less clear-cut.[82] Several collections included canons that prescribed penances for those who remarried[83] and provided that widows who took second husbands might forfeit guardianship of their children.[84] They were, however, grudgingly prepared to allow second marriages "as a concession to human frailty," in the words of one Pseudo-Gelasian canon.[85] There was some doubt about third marriages, but apparently no attempt was made to ban them.[86] As a token of the Church's disapproval of second marriages, some authorities admonished priests not to participate in celebrating these unions.[87] Twice-married men continued, of course, to be ineligible for clerical office.[88]

---

ments relatifs à l'histoire des croisades, vol. 12 (Paris: Paul Geuthner, 1977), p. 109; Raymond d'Aguilers, *Historia Francorum qui ceperunt Iherusalem*, 7, ed. John Hugh Hill and Laurita L. Hill, Documents relatifs à l'histoire des croisades, vol. 9 (Paris: Paul Geuthner, 1969), p. 55; Albert of Aachen, *Hist.* 5.3, in RHC, Occ. 4:434. The Council of Nablus (1120) c. 15—the assembly was really a *parlement*, rather than a Church council in the ordinary sense—decreed that male Saracens who married Latin women should be castrated: Mansi 21:264. On the Nablus assembly see Joshua Prawer, *Crusader Institutions* (Oxford: Clarendon Press, 1980), pp. 15–17, and Hans Eberhard Mayer, "The Concordat of Nablus," JEH 33 (1982) 531–43. For the Spanish situation see Dillard, "Women in Reconquest Castile," p. 86.

[80]Odo of Deuil, *De profectione Ludovici VII in orientem*, 3, ed. and trans. Virginia Gingerick Berry, Records of Civilization, Sources and Studies, no. 42 (New York: Columbia University Press, 1948), p. 56.

[81]Burchard, *Decretum* 9.19 (= Ivo, *Decretum* 8.157) and 9.29 (= Ivo, *Decretum* 8.167, *Panormia* 6.40), in PL 140:818–19; also Ivo, *Decretum* 8.54, in PL 161:595.

[82]Ivo, *Decretum* 8.59, in PL 161:597–98.

[83]Burchard, *Decretum* 9.20 (= Ivo, *Decretum* 8.158) and 9.22 (= Ivo, *Decretum* 8.160), in PL 140:818); in addition, Ivo, *Decretum* 8.332, 15.72, and 16.125, in PL 161:655, 879, 929.

[84]Ivo, *Decretum* 8.271–74, in PL 161:644.

[85]Burchard, *Decretum* 9.21 (= Ivo, *Decretum* 8.159) in PL 140:818, cites Ps.-Gelasius c. 24 (Hinschius, DPI, p. 653): "Secundas nuptias, sicut [*fortasse*: licet?] saecularibus inire conceditur, ita post eas nullus ad clericale sinitur venire collegium. Alia est enim humanae fragilitati generaliter concessa licentia, alia debet esse vita divinarum rerum servitio dedicata." See also Burchard, *Decretum* 9.22 (= Ivo, *Decretum* 8.160) and 9.24 (= Ivo, *Decretum* 8.162), in PL 140:818–19; as well as Ivo, *Decretum* 1.42, 8.268–70 (= *Panormia* 6.59–62), in PL 161:77, 643–44.

[86]Burchard, *Decretum* 9.23 (= Ivo, *Decretum* 8.161), in PL 140:818.

[87]Burchard, *Decretum* 2.133 (= Ivo, *Decretum* 8.160, 315, and *Panormia* 6.67).

[88]Burchard, *Decretum* 9.24 (= Ivo, *Decretum* 8.162), in PL 140:819; Ivo, *Decretum*

Marital sex concerned many reform canonists, but there was no consensus concerning its proper role in marriage. At one end of the spectrum of opinion was the rigorist position, staunchly defended by Peter Damian. Damian held that sexual intercourse, under any circumstances, for any reason, was always sinful, even in marriage.[89] A more temperate opinion, based upon Augustine's teaching that procreation was one of the good purposes that marriage served,[90] held that marital sex was allowed only when the couple specifically intended to conceive a child.[91] St. Bernard of Clairvaux (1090–1153), who certainly could not be accused of encouraging moral laxity, added that a further reason for permitting marital sex, even aside from procreation, was to provide a legitimate outlet for sexual urges that would otherwise lead people into debauchery, incest, and homosexual relationships.[92]

At the other end of the spectrum of opinion about marital sex were a few writers who thought that it provided both a physical outlet for sexual energy and an emotional bond between the couple. Marriage, according to a certain William (writing between 1133 and 1135), is not merely a contract, but an agreement between two people to orient their lives toward one another. Love, including physical love, between man and wife, according to William, ought to be a central value in marriage.[93] Anselm of Laon (d. 1117) likewise praised the value of married love—love in marriage, he maintained, had a worth all its own, so that even a childless union had merit, so long as the parties loved one another.[94] Hugh of St. Victor (d. 1141), writing in the 1130s, added that marital

---

6.51, 55, 56, in PL 161:456; Coll. 74T 16.139, 143, 150–52, 155–56, ed. Gilchrist, pp. 94–96, 99–101; Coll. 5L 1.118–19, ed. Fornasari, p. 87.

[89] Schimmelpfennig, "Ex fornicatione nati," p. 10; Karl Mirbt, *Die Publizistik im Zeitalter Gregors VII.* (Leipzig: J. C. Hinrichs, 1894), pp. 328–29. Although Gregory VII expressed no opinion squarely on this point, his reference to the "fedam libidinose contagionis pollutionem" of sexual intercourse breathes disapproval; see *The Epistolae vagantes of Pope Gregory VII*, no. 9, ed. H. E. J. Cowdrey (Oxford: Clarendon Press, 1972), p. 20.

[90] Ivo repeated Augustine's analysis of the goods of marriage in *Decretum* 8.15 (= *Panormia* 6.30), in PL 161:587.

[91] Ivo cited two Augustinian passages to support the view that procreation was the only lawful purpose for marital relations: *Decretum* 8.77 (= *Panormia* 6.29) and 8.82, in PL 161:600–601. The same teaching appears in a gloss of Irnerius to Dig. 1.1.1.3 ad v. *procreatio*, published by Rudolf Weigand, *Die Naturrechtslehre der Legisten und Dekretisten von Irnerius bis Accursius und von Gratian bis Johannes Teutonicus*, Münchener theologische Studien, kanonistische Abteilung, vol. 26 (Munich: Max Hueber, 1967), p. 80.

[92] Philippe Ariès, "Le mariage indissoluble," in *Sexualités occidentales*, p. 126.

[93] Leclercq, *Monks on Marriage*, p. 7.

[94] Michael Müller, *Die Lehre des hl. Augustinus von der Paradiesesehe und ihre Auswirkung in der Sexualethik des 12. und 13. Jahrhunderts bis Thomas von Aquin*, Studien zur Geschichte der kath. Moraltheologie, vol. 1 (Regensburg: Friedrich Pustet, 1954), p. 47.

sex was a central part of married love, along with affection and fidelity, and that
sexual relations provided married couples with a focus for their loving union, a
view that echoed the sentiments of the eleventh-century author of the life of
St. Geoffrey of Savigny.[95]

But even those who defended the value of marital sex had reservations about
it. Hugh of St. Victor, for example, cautioned couples against immoderate
indulgence. He encouraged them to cultivate an attitude of conjugal chastity,
so that they could subordinate sensual enjoyment to the serious business of
procreation.[96]

The canonists of the reform period reiterated the principle, familiar from
patristic writings, that sexual rights and responsibilities were the same for men
and women.[97] This meant that both parties must abstain from extramarital affairs. In addition, both husband and wife had a positive obligation to respond to
the sexual needs of the other by paying the conjugal debt upon demand.[98] The
right to marital sex was taken seriously, and even powerful monarchs might be
compelled to make accommodations in order to enable their subjects to fulfill
the canonical requirements concerning marital debt. William the Conqueror
felt the power of this policy in 1068, when a group of Norman women successfully demanded that William release their husbands from the campaign to con-
solidate his English conquests so that they could return to Normandy in order
to satisfy their wives' sexual needs.[99]

Despite a generally warmer approach to marital sexuality, canonists during
the reform era reiterated one of the favorite themes of penitential writers on
marriage: the need for periodic abstinence from marital sex. The canonists
warned that those who failed to observe the rules on this matter would beget
bastards, not legitimate heirs.[100] The major canonists of this period borrowed
their sexual abstinence rules in large part from earlier penitentials, as Table 5.2
shows (see Appendix). The canons enjoined married couples to avoid sex during
the three Lenten seasons associated with Easter, Pentecost, and Christmas,[101]

[95] Leclercq, *Monks on Marriage*, pp. 25–28, 52.

[96] Hugh of St. Victor, *On the Sacraments of the Christian Faith* 2.11.9, trans. Roy J.
Deferrari, Mediaeval Academy of America, Publications, no. 58 (Cambridge, MA: Mediaeval Academy of America, 1951), p. 342. See also Ivo, *Decretum* 8.42, in PL 161:593.

[97] Burchard, *Decretum* 9.7 (= Ivo, *Decretum* 8.145), in PL 140:816; Ivo, *Decretum*
8.240 (= *Panormia* 7.3), and 8.263, in PL 161:594, 636, 642–43; Zeimentz, *Ehe nach
der Lehre der Frühscholastik*, p. 220.

[98] Ivo, *Decretum* 8.86, 130, 133–34, in PL 161:601, 612–13.

[99] Orderic Vitalis, *Ecclesiastical History*, book 4, ed. and trans. Marjorie Chibnall, 6
vols. (Oxford: Clarendon Press, 1969–80) 2:218–20.

[100] Ivo, *Decretum* 8.145, in PL 161:616; cf. Jonas of Orleans, *De institutione laicali
libri tres* 2.2, in PL 106:171.

[101] Burchard, *Decretum* 13.4, 19.5, 19.75 (= Ivo, *Decretum* 15.88), 19.155 (= Ivo,
Decretum 15.163), in PL 140:887, 960, 1000, 1013; Ivo, *Decretum* 8.46–47, 49, 89, in
PL 161:594, 602–603.

on all Sundays of the year,[102] on feast days,[103] prior to receiving communion,[104] while doing penance,[105] on their wedding night,[106] during the wife's menstrual period,[107] during pregnancy, and during lactation.[108]

The major reform canonists also condemned "unnatural" coital practices. They frowned on sexual experimentation and demanded rigorous standards of bedroom behavior. Burchard forbade the use of aphrodisiacs, including some rather exotic ones, by women who wished to stimulate their husbands' sexual ardor.[109] Ivo emphasized in his *Decretum* that marriage did not confer a license for unbridled sexual experimentation or lascivious comportment. Ivo adjured both husband and wife to observe modesty and to avoid indecent and immoderate use of their sexual rights.[110]

Divorce and Remarriage in the Canonical Collections of the Reform

Between the turn of the millennium and the appearance of Gratian's *Decretum* about 1140, canonistic policy with respect to divorce and remarriage underwent an important change. The canonists of the earlier reform period used consanguinity rules, as we have seen, to discourage endogamy. In fact, they were prepared on occasion to sacrifice the principle of indissolubility in order to solve problems posed by endogamous marriages. The later reform canonists, from Ivo of Chartres onward, reversed this tilt in policy: from Ivo's time canonists began to protect indissolubility, when necessary, by permitting couples to remain in endogamous marriages. The policy shift was slight, but the difference was significant.[111]

[102] Burchard, *Decretum* 19.5, in PL 140:960; Ivo, *Decretum* 8.83, in PL 161:601.

[103] Ivo, *Decretum* 8.84 (= *Panromia* 6.21), in PL 161:601.

[104] Burchard, *Decretum* 5.22 (= Ivo, *Decretum* 2.32 and *Panormia* 1.151), in PL 140:757; Ivo, *Decretum* 2.24, 8.87, in PL 161:166, 601.

[105] Burchard, *Decretum* 6.1, 6.35, in PL 140:763–64, 773.

[106] Burchard, *Decretum* 9.5, 9.7 (= Ivo, *Decretum* 8.145), in PL 140:816.

[107] Burchard, *Decretum* 19.5, in PL 140:959; Ivo, *Decretum* 9.119, in PL 161:688.

[108] Burchard, *Decretum* 19.5, in PL 140:959; Ivo, *Decretum* 8.88, in PL 161:601–602. .

[109] Burchard, *Decretum* 19.5, in PL 140:959; Ivo, *Decretum* 9.110 and 128, in PL 161:686–87, 690. In another passage of *Decretum* 19.5 (PL 140:974), Burchard also warned women not to mix menstrual fluid into food, or to allow a live fish to die on their pudenda and then serve the fish to their husbands, or to have another person knead bread dough on their buttocks prior to baking it and serving it to their husbands. The aphrodisiac effect, if any, of these practices presumably would depend upon the incorporation of pheromone traces into the food; see also Payer, "Early Medieval Regulations Concerning Marital Sexual Relations," JMH 6 (1980) 361; Peter V. Taberner, *Aphrodisiacs: The Science and the Myth* (London: Croom Helm; Philadelphia: University of Pennsylvania Press, 1985), pp. 244–46.

[110] Ivo, *Decretum* 8.234, 262, in PL 161:634, 642.

[111] Duby, *Medieval Marriage*, pp. 27–29, 64–65; *Knight, Lady, and Priest*, pp. 192–93 (but cf. pp. 163–65); Hinschius, "Ehescheidungsrecht," pp. 85–86.

All of the canonists of the period agreed that separations and divorces must be discouraged and that sanctions ought to be imposed upon those who divorced without cause or simply deserted their spouses.[112] It was common ground, too, that separation or divorce should be allowed only for serious cause—mere dislike or disgust with the appearance, habits, or character of the marital partner did not furnish adequate grounds for separation.[113] Anselm of Lucca maintained that the only proper grounds for separation were consanguinity, affinity, or impotence.[114] Ivo, however, still upheld the venerable tradition that considered adultery a sufficiently serious breach of marital vows to justify separation.[115] Even so, Ivo thought that separation ought to be discouraged and that every effort should be made to reconcile the parties.[116] Separation was clearly a last resort in Ivo's eyes, but one that must be allowed if all else failed in adultery cases. Although he cited one canon that permitted separation for consanguinity, Ivo, like Burchard, seems to have operated on the principle that the Church should prevent consanguineous marriages in the first place. But if they did occur, he believed they should be allowed to continue whenever possible.[117]

Separation, as Ivo described it, was just that and nothing more: the separated couple continued to be married to one another but were no longer expected to maintain a common life or to share the same household.[118] Here Ivo

---

[112] Burchard, *Decretum* 9.62 (= Ivo, *Decretum* 8.198), in PL 140:825; Ivo, *Decretum* 8.229, 8.328 (= *Panormia* 6.106).

[113] Ivo, *Decretum* 8.35, 8.231 (= *Panormia* 6.106), 8.232 (= *Panormia* 6.103), 8.235 (= *Panormia* 7.5–6), in PL 161:591, 633–35. In practice, of course, repudiation of spouses for personal reasons was scarcely unknown. A scandalous example was King Philip I's dismissal of his first wife because she was too fat; William of Malmesbury, *De gestis regum Anglorum* 3.257, ed. William Stubbs, 2 vols., Rolls Series no. 90 (London: Her Majesty's Sationery Office, 1887–89) 2:315. On this account, however, Philip was excommunicated three times and ultimately forced to do penance and make his peace with the church authorities; Duby, *Medieval Marriage*, pp. 29–45, and *Knight, Lady, and Priest*, pp. 3–18, examines the episode in detail. Earlier, Robert the Pious (996–1031) repudiated his Italian wife, Rozala (also known as Susanna), because she was too old; Richer of St.-Remy, *Historiae* 4.87, in MGH, SS 3:651; also Duby, *Knight, Lady, and Priest*, pp. 75–85.

[114] Anselm, *Collectio* 10.22–24, ed. Thaner, pp. 492–93; Fliche, *La réforme grégorienne et la reconquête chrétienne*, p. 466.

[115] Burchard, *Decretum* 9.63 (= Ivo, *Decretum* 8.199), in PL 140:825–26; Ivo, *Decretum* 8.9 (= *Panormia* 7.6), 8.43 (= *Panormia* 7.7), 8.109–10, 233, 239, 240 (= *Panormia* 7.1), 16.160, in PL 161:586, 593–94, 606, 633, 634, 654, 935. Cf. the Council of Nablus (1120) c. 19, in Mansi 21:264–65.

[116] Burchard, *Decretum* 9.81 (= Ivo, *Decretum* 8.217 and *Panormia* 7.41, in PL 140:830; Ivo, *Decretum* 8.237 (= *Panormia* 7.4), 8.242 (= *Panormia* 7.35–37), 8.243 (= *Panormia* 7.38), in PL 161:635–37.

[117] Burchard, *Decretum* 7.18 (= Ivo, *Decretum* 9.54 and *Panormia* 7.70), 7.27, and 9.80 (= Ivo, *Decretum* 8.216 and *Panormia* 7.89), in PL 140:782, 784, 830.

[118] Ivo, *Decretum* 8.200 (= Burchard, *Decretum* 9.64), 8.209 (= Burchard, *Decretum* 9.72), and 8.241 (= Burchard, *Decretum* 6.37). In addition see Ivo, *Decretum* 8.12–13

disregarded the authority of the Synod of Bourges (1031), whose canons allowed remarriage following separation because of adultery, but not on other grounds. Perhaps Ivo considered that the canons of a more recent council (Rouen, 1072), which forbade remarriage following repudiation for adultery, rescinded the Bourges canon.[119] But his treatment of separation and divorce rested, in the main, upon much older authorities than these two eleventh-century councils.

The canonists also drew upon earlier authorites for their treatment of presumption-of-death cases. But the earlier rules, they discovered, were inconsistent. A man whose wife disappeared could remarry.[120] Yet when a man disappeared or was absent for protracted periods, his deserted wife could remarry only if her husband's death was known with certainty.[121] Still other authorities taught that if a married man was taken captive by an enemy, and there was no reasonable expectation of his release, his wife might remarry; should the captive return, the wife must return to her first spouse, thus presumably terminating her second marriage. It is not clear in this situation whether the second husband was free to remarry or not.[122] Most authorities, however, took a middle position: they insisted that a wife who believed in good faith that her husband was dead could remarry. Should her belief prove wrong, she was required to leave her second husband and return to the first one. Again they left the status of the second husband uncertain.[123]

Most canonists of the later reform period were prepared to allow separation or divorce on grounds of adultery, consanguinity, affinity, or, under some circumstances, presumption of death. Insanity was sufficient reason for prohibiting a proposed marriage; if the couple married despite this, they were not to be separated.[124] If one party to an already contracted marriage subsequently went mad, the canonists refused to dissolve the union.[125] Several authorities explicitly excluded sterility as a basis for separation.[126] Impotence or frigidity, however, presented more difficult problems on which opinion was divided. One authority dismissed the case of a couple who were unable to consummate their marriage because of the wife's illness. The couple were urged to remain to-

---

(= *Panormia* 6.74), 8.131–32, 135, 221–23, 230, 236, 255, 257–58, in PL 161:625, 627, 636, 586, 612–13, 630–31, 633, 635, 640–41.

[119] Synod of Bourges (1031) c. 16, in Mansi 19:505; Council of Rouen (1072) c. 16, in Mansi 20:37–38; Delpini, "Indissolubilità," p. 74.

[120] Burchard, *Decretum* 9.54 (= Ivo, *Decretum* 8.189 and *Panormia* 6.91) in PL 140:824; Ivo, *Decretum* 8.246 (= *Panormia* 6.90) in PL 161:638.

[121] Coll. 74T 63.272 (= Ivo, *Decretum* 8.244 and *Panormia* 6.87), ed. Gilchrist, pp. 165–66; Ivo, *Decretum* 8.245 (= *Panormia* 6.89), in PL 161:638.

[122] Burchard, *Decretum* 9.55 (= Ivo, *Decretum* 8.190, *Panormia* 6.86), in PL 140:824.

[123] Burchard, *Decretum* 9.56 (= Ivo, *Decretum* 8.191), 9.57 (= Ivo, *Decretum* 8.192, *Panormia* 6.88), 9.58 (= Ivo, *Decretum* 8.193), in PL 140:824–25.

[124] Burchard, *Decretum* 9.30 (= Ivo, *Decretum* 8.168, *Panormia* 6.92), in PL 140:819.

[125] Burchard, *Decretum* 9.28 (= Ivo, *Decretum* 8.166, *Panormia* 6.93), in PL 140:819.

[126] Ivo, *Decretum* 8.254 (= *Panormia* 6.28) and 8.265, in PL 161:640, 643.

gether, despite their sexual problem. If they were unwilling to do so, however, they might separate, and the husband, who was sexually unimpaired, might remarry. He was required, however, to continue to support his first wife.[127]

Common opinion among the canonists held that when consummation was impossible due to a defect of either party, the healthy spouse might remarry, but the other might not.[128] If an impotent person attempted to remarry, the second marriage should be terminated. Ivo cited one authority who ruled that divorce on grounds of impotence required no formalities, but that view was distinctly eccentric.[129] Most commentators on impotence questions required positive proof of the alleged incapacity, although they differed sharply over the kinds of proof that were acceptable. A Merovingian council had held that where impotence was an issue the word of the husband should determine the outcome of the case.[130] Others preferred to rely on the wife's sworn statement and observations of the couple by neighbors in evaluating the merits of these cases.[131] Most authors who discussed impotence assumed that the condition was inborn and permanent. Hincmar of Reims, however, had raised the possibility that magic or sorcery might cause temporary incapacity. Couples thus afflicted were advised to fast, give alms, pray, and undergo exorcism. If these remedies failed, the couple might separate, but neither party might remarry.[132]

The only other justification that canonists in the reform era were prepared to recognize for the separation of married couples involved a decision by one or both parties to enter religious life. Discussions of this possibility emphasized that the decision must be mutual; no one could unilaterally terminate a marriage in order to enter a monastery or convent. Anyone who attempted to do so should be refused admission to the religious life and required to resume cohabitation with his or her spouse. After separation by mutual agreement to allow one party to enter religion, the other might not remarry. The authorities on this matter were reasonably consistent and the law seems to have been well settled by Burchard's time.[133]

---

[127] This is the decision of Pope Gregory II, referred to above, p. 143; it appears in Ivo, *Decretum* 8.78 (= *Panormia* 6.112), in PL 161:600.

[128] Burchard, *Decretum* 9.40 (= Ivo, *Decretum* 8.178, *Panormia* 6.115), 9.41 (= Ivo, *Decretum* 8.179, *Panormia* 6.118), 9.43 (= Ivo, *Decretum* 8.181, *Panormia* 6.120), 9.44 (= Ivo, *Decretum* 8.182, *Panormia* 6.116; see also Machielsen, "Les spurii," pp. 252–53); also Ivo, *Decretum* 8.79–80 (= *Panormia* 6.113–14), in PL 161:600.

[129] Ivo, *Decretum* 8.81, in PL 161:600.

[130] Burchard, *Decretum* 9.42 (= Ivo, *Decretum* 8.180, *Panormia* 6.119), in PL 140:821.

[131] Burchard, *Decretum* 9.40–41 (= Ivo, *Decretum* 8.178–79, *Panormia* 6.115, 118) and 19.5, in PL 140:821, 967.

[132] Ivo, *Decretum* 8.194 (= *Panormia* 6.117), in PL 161:624–25. See above, pp. 144–45, 188.

[133] Burchard, *Decretum* 9.45 (= Ivo, *Decretum* 8.183), 9.46 (= Ivo, *Decretum* 8.184, *Panormia* 6.82), 9.47 (= Ivo, *Decretum* 8.185 and 9.124), 9.47 (= Ivo, *Decretum* 8.185), 9.48 (= Ivo, *Decretum* 8.186, *Panormia* 6.84, and Coll. 74T 64.274), 9.49 (= Ivo, *De-*

By the end of the eleventh century, reform canonists had reached general agreement on divorce and remarriage law. They restricted the grounds for lawful separation or divorce to a handful of causes (adultery, consanguinity, affinity, and under some circumstances, impotence or entrance into religion). They circumscribed even more the right to remarry following divorce, for the canonists conceded this right only in some consanguinity or affinity cases and to the healthy party in congenital impotence cases; some would also allow remarriage in presumption-of-death situations.

This consensus among canonistic writers with respect to divorce and remarriage was not followed, however, by immediate or universal implementation. In regions on the fringes of Latin Christendom, such as Frisia and Iceland, Germanic practices that allowed divorce and remarriage for a wide variety of reasons continued to flourish well into the twelfth century. In most parts of the Continent, however, ecclesiastical authorities made vigorous efforts to enforce the newly consolidated divorce law, even on persons at the highest levels of society.[134]

Nonmarital Sex and the Reform Canonists

The vice of sexual sin as well as the virtue of sexual chastity is rooted in the spirit, not in the body, declared Ivo of Chartres in a paraphrase of an Augustinian dictum. But Ivo's contemporaries did not agree about how far sexual fantasies could be entertained before crossing the threshold of sin.[135] Among Ivo's contemporaries, only Peter Abelard and some writers of the School of Laon were prepared to maintain that carnal pleasure and the desire to experience it were natural and hence not intrinsically evil.[136] Sexual feelings that were not consciously desired and their physical manifestations such as, for example, a

---

cretum 8.128, *Panormia* 6.77, and 6.83), in PL 140:822–23; in addition see Coll. 74T 64.273, ed. Gilchrist, pp. 166–67; Ivo, *Decretum* 8.14 (= *Panormia* 6.16), 8.16 (= Ivo, *Panormia* 7.9–10), 8.127 (= *Panormia* 6.76), 8.129 (= *Panormia* 6.78), 8.220 (= *Panormia* 6.85) and 9.127, in PL 161:586–87, 612, 630, 690.

[134] Jochens, "The Church and Sexuality," p. 380; Grethe Jacobsen, "Sexual Irregularities in Medieval Scandinavia," in Vern L. Bullough and James A. Brundage, eds., *Sexual Practices and the Medieval Church* (Buffalo, NY: Prometheus, 1982), pp. 73–77; Hinschius, "Ehescheidungsrecht," p. 86; but see for example the case of Philip I of France, referred to above, p. 184, and the similar case of Raoul of Vermandois, discussed by Delpini, "L'indissolubilità," p. 65.

[135] Ivo, *Decretum* 8.11, in PL 161:586, citing St. Augustine, *De sancta virginitate* c. 8, in CSEL 41:242; cf. also Origen, *Commentaria in Epistolam Beati Pauli ad Romanos* 2.2, in PG 14:873–74.

[136] Abelard, *Ethica*, ed. and trans. D.A. Luscombe, Oxford Medieval Texts (Oxford: Clarendon Press, 1971), pp. 12–14, 18, 20–24; also D.A Luscombe, *The School of Pierre Abelard: The Influence of Abelard's Thought in the Early Scholastic Period*, Cambridge Studies in Medieval Life and Thought, n.s., vol. 14 (Cambridge: At the University Press, 1969), pp. 139, 176.

spontaneous erection, might produce no guilt, but any pleasure or enjoyment that resulted from sexual thoughts and feelings was clearly sinful according to the teaching current in the period.[137]

From these premises it followed that any voluntary action that might lead to sexual arousal or pleasure was sinful, whether or not the anticipated result occurred. The canonists of the reform period consistently supported this view and its juristic consequences. Thus, telling dirty jokes or laughing at them, singing suggestive songs or listening to them, and producing, performing, or attending entertainments calculated to arouse prurient feelings were all forbidden to laymen and even more stringently to clerics.[138] Canonists likewise repeated as legal injunctions the counsels of penitential authors against bathing in mixed company where men and women seeing one another in a state of undress might be sexually aroused.[139] Still more serious were touching, fondling, or kissing, especially if the breasts or genitals were involved.[140] The canonists were not alone in treating lascivious contact as a serious offense: the Icelandic law code, the *Grágás*, prescribed the same penalty for lewd kissing as for fornication.[141] Indeed, any kind of petting that led to orgasm was legally fornication.[142]

These prohibitions of carnal reveries and sexual contacts reflected the temptations as well as the values of a celibate clerical elite. The realities of social life among the laity in the eleventh and twelfth centuries were entirely different. The expectations of lay society militated against chastity. All classes of the medieval population included large numbers of unmarried men, for social and economic pressures forced many males to postpone marriage until relatively late in life. Among the nobility, about whose amusements we are fairly well informed, unmarried men rarely led lives of voluntary chastity. They had sexual access to servant girls, peasant women, bastard daughters of their relatives, and staggering numbers of harlots. The more presentable and ambitious of these young men might also offer consolation, sexual and social, to widows, possibly in the hope of marrying into wealth. Daring or foolhardy young men sometimes became involved with married women as well. The idealized dalliance that modern scholars depict as innocent or platonic courtly love masks

[137] Ivo, *Decretum* 9.123, in PL 161:689, citing Augustine, *De civitate Dei* 1.25, in CSEL 40/1:45.

[138] Ivo, *Decretum* 8.276, 11.79–81, in PL 161:645, 773.

[139] Burchard, *Decretum* 19.138 (= Ivo, *Decretum* 15.148), in PL 140:1010; cf. *Penitentiale Hubertense* 47 and *Merseburgense* (b) 6, in Wasserschleben, ed., *Die Bussordnungen der abendländischen Kirche nebst einer rechtsgeschichtlichen Einleitung* (Halle: Ch. Graeger, 1851), pp. 383, 429.

[140] Burchard, *Decretum* 19.137 (= Ivo, *Decretum* 15.147), in PL 140:1010.

[141] Jochens, "Church and Sexuality," p. 381.

[142] Burchard, *Decretum* 17.40–42, 19.5, in PL 140:927–28, 968, relying in part on Bede 3.33–36, in Arthur West Haddan and William Stubbs, eds., *Councils and Ecclesiastical Documents Relating to Great Britain and Ireland*, (Oxford: Clarendon Press, 1869–78; repr. 1964) 3:329.

the more fleshly reality of sexual mores among young men of good families.[143]

The canonists, however, wished to remake the sexual habits of lay society so far as possible in the image and likeness of the celibate elite. Sex, they taught, was permitted only between married persons and even for them should be hedged about by constraints. Sexual intercourse or other overt sexual activity by unmarried persons or by married persons outside of the marital relationship fell into the canonists' category of *moechia*, or illicit sex.[144] Some people can marry, said Ivo, quoting Augustine, and some cannot; but no one may fornicate or have illicit sex.[145]

FORNICATION

Fornication was, for the canonists of the reform period, the basic type of illicit sex, a sordid business that fouled the body while it sullied the soul; it slammed shut the gates of God's kingdom and turned men and women away from their maker.[146] Ivo was aware that he and other canonists were dealing here with new law, that in Christ's Church fornication was a far more serious offense than it had been under the Mosaic law of the old dispensation.[147] So serious was sexual sin that Burchard of Worms devoted the entire seventeenth book of his *Decretum* to fornication and related offenses; in addition sexual topics featured prominently in many of the other nineteen books of his work.

The fourth-century canons of Elvira furnished both Burchard and Ivo with penal guidelines on the subject of fornication: sexual relations between unmarried persons, according to the Elvira canons, merited a year's penance if the couple subsequently married one another. If they slept together but did not later marry, the penalty was increased to five years.[148] A later council modified this scheme and imposed a flat three-year penalty, and penitential writers added further modifications to cover other contingencies. But the underlying message remained clear: fornication is both a sin, requiring confession and penance and a crime, meriting public retribution and punishment.[149] Punishment

---

[143] Duby, *Medieval Marriage*, pp. 13–14, 94; *Knight, Lady, and Priest*, 219–26. The sources usually refer to bachelors as "young men" (*juvenes, juniores*), whatever their age, in contrast to "older men" (*seniores*), by which they meant married men, again irrespective of age.

[144] Ivo, *Decretum* 8.279, in PL 161:645.

[145] Ivo, *Decretum* 8.72 (= *Panormia* 6.4), in PL 161:599.

[146] Ivo, *Decretum* 8.275, 278, in PL 161:645; cf. St. Anselm, *De nuptiis consanguineorum*, in PL 158:559.

[147] Ivo, *Decretum* 8.310, in PL 161:651–52, citing Origen, *Homeliae in librum Jesu Nave* 5.5, in PG 12:849–50.

[148] Burchard, *Decretum* 9.14 (= Ivo, *Decretum* 8.152), in PL 140:817, citing Council of Elvira c. 14, in Vives, *Concilios visigóticos*, p. 4.

[149] Burchard, *Decretum* 9.68 (= Ivo, *Decretum* 8.205); 9.70; 17.5, 13; 19.5, in PL 140: 826–27, 920, 922, 957–58, 966; Coll 5L 2.64, 71, 78, ed. Fornasari, pp. 217–18,

for this offense might be meted out by ecclesiastical authorities or by other authorities vested with law-enforcement power, as happened, for example, on the First Crusade.[150] And if earthly rulers failed to take action, clerical writers seldom tired of reminding their readers that God was perfectly capable of reaching out and exacting terrible retribution from the sexual offender in this life as well as in the next.[151] The legal perils for criminal fornication were also greatly increased.[152]

Canonistic teaching about concubinage during the reform period was confused and inconsistent. The major collections included numerous citations from older authorities holding that concubinage was prohibited for all Christians, and the reforming synod of Gerona in 1078 went so far as to decree excommunication for any man who kept a concubine.[153] But eleventh-century canonists also reported numerous older authorities who treated concubinage as informal marriage and imposed no penalties on these unions.[154] While canon law, drawing upon earlier Roman law, forbade Christian men to have both a wife and a concubine simultaneously or to have more than one concubine at a time, it is not apparent that the church in the eleventh or early twelfth centuries, even at the height of reform fervor among its leaders, was prepared to outlaw concubinage among the laity.[155] What the canonical collections did make plain was that concubinage ought to be an exclusive relationship and reasonably

---

221–22, 225–27. Gregory VII, *Epist. vagantes*, no. 9, ed. Cowdrey, p. 20, declared that fornicating laymen should be banned from receiving the sacraments.

[150] Albert of Aachen, *Hist.* 3.57, in RHC, Occ. 4:378–79; Guibert of Nogent, *Gesta Dei per Francos* 4.15, in RHC, Occ. 4:182.

[151] Albert of Aachen, *Hist.* 3.46, and Guibert of Nogent, *Gesta Dei* 4.15, in RHC, Occ. 4:182, 370–71.

[152] Burchard, *Decretum* 17.3 (= Ivo, *Decretum* 9.69), 17.7, 17.8 (= Ivo, *Decretum* 9.70), 17.9 and 19 (= Ivo, *Decretum* 9.71 and 77), 17.10–11, 17.12–16 (= Ivo, *Decretum* 9.72–76), 17.17–18, 17.20–21 (= Ivo, *Decretum* 9.78–79), and 17.22 (= Ivo, *Decretum* 9.80, *Panormia* 6.125), in PL 140:919–23; Coll. 5L 2.79, ed. Fornasari, pp. 227–28.

[153] Burchard, *Decretum* 9.15 (= Ivo, *Decretum* 8.153, *Panormia* 6.43), 9.16–17 (= Ivo, *Decretum* 8.154–55), in PL 140:817–18; in addition, Ivo, *Decretum* 8.30, 34, and 62, in PL 161:590–91, 597. For the Synod of Gerona (1078) c. 9, see Mansi 20:519.

[154] Burchard, *Decretum* 9.1 (= Ivo, *Decretum* 8.139, *Panormia* 6.35), 9.18 (= Ivo, *Decretum* 8.156, *Panormia* 6.37), in PL 140:815, 818. Also Ivo, *Decretum* 8.64 (= *Panormia* 6.49), 8.65 (= *Panormia* 6.27), 8.66 (= *Panormia* 6.50), in PL 161:597–98. On Ivo, *Decretum* 8.64, drawn from 1 Council of Toledo (400) c. 17, see also the remarks of António Agustín (1517–86), *Dialogorum libri duo de emendatione Gratiani*, ed. Étienne Baluze (Paris: Franciscus Mugetus, 1672), p. 170. Perplexed by Ivo's willingness to tolerate concubinage, Agustín proposed a distinction between permanent concubinage, i.e. informal marriage, and casual concubinage, i.e. long-term fornication. The first he deemed acceptable, the second not.

[155] Ivo, *Decretum* 8.60 and 16.151, in PL 161:597, 933.

permanent. Under these conditions, concubinage remained an alternative to formal marriage.

Fornication, then, was a sexual offense in canon law, but concubinage was not necessarily an offense at all. The other principal sex offenses that the canonists censured were bigamy, adultery, rape, prostitution, pandering, sex with non-Christians, homosexual relationships, bestiality, and masturbation. The last three were by this time referred to commonly as "unnatural." Each of these offenses, if publicly practiced or generally known, carried with it the sanction of *infamia*, a deprivation of respectable status that involved unfitness for holding most kinds of public trust or office and the loss of rights to appear in court as a complainant or witness.[156]

The sources gave short shrift to both bigamy and miscegenation. Ancient authorities had flatly forbidden bigamy—in the sense of simultaneous marriage to two or more wives, as distinguished from constructive bigamy, or sequential marriage to two or more wives (digamy)—and the canonists simply repeated the ban.[157] Miscegenation, in the sense of sexual relations between a Latin Christian and a non-Christian partner who was also non-European, became a particular problem in the early twelfth century for Crusaders and settlers in the states created by the First Crusade in the Levant. Although Crusaders and Latin settlers in the Holy Land often entered into more or less casual liaisons with Saracen women from the region, both ecclesiastical and royal authorities opposed these arrangements. The Council of Nablus in 1120 prescribed harsh punishments calculated to prevent recidivism by offenders: a Latin man found guilty of miscegenation with a Saracen woman was to be castrated, while the woman was to have her nose removed.[158] Western canonists ignored miscegenation; presumably it was not a pressing issue.

ADULTERY

Adultery, however, was a matter of considerable concern. While adulterous fantasies were spiritual offenses, penalized in the privacy of sacramental confession, the canonists became concerned when sinful desires were acted out in carnal intercourse.[159] Drawing upon both ecclesiastical sources and Roman law,

---

[156] Burchard, *Decretum* 1.173 (= Coll. 74T 5.51, Ivo, *Decretum* 5.291, and *Panormia* 4.66), in PL 140:599–600.

[157] Burchard, *Decretum* 9.17 (= Ivo, *Decretum* 8.155), in PL 140:818, and Ivo, *Decretum* 8.63, in PL 161:597; cf. Council of Nablus (1120) c. 17–18, in Mansi 21:264.

[158] Council of Nablus (1120) c. 12, in Mansi 21:264. The narratives of the First Crusade furnish numerous examples of miscegenation, however; e.g., Fulcher of Chartres, *Hist.* 1.19.3, ed. Hagenmeyer, p. 243; Albert of Aachen, *Hist.* 2.37, in RHC, Occ. 4:327–28; Tudebode, *Hist.*, ed. Hill, p. 99.

[159] Ivo, *Decretum* 8.100, 101 (= *Panormia* 6.17), 102 (= *Panormia* 7.22), 103, 104 (= *Panormia* 7.19), 106 (= *Panormia* 7.27), 107 (= *Panormia* 7.23), and 108, in PL 161:605–606; Coll. 5L 2.67, ed. Fornasari, p. 220.

the canonists warned cuckolded husbands that they must not slay their adulterous wives, no matter how great the provocation; if they did so the Church was prepared to punish them as murderers.[160] Adultery constituted the second most serious offense after heresy, in the opinion of one authority, and could not be excused by procreative intent.[161] The offense entailed excommunication, removable only by submission to the required penance, by marital separation if the innocent spouse so desired, and by prohibition of future marriage between the adulterer and his paramour, even after the death of his or her earlier spouse.[162] Other authorities mentioned further types of punishment for adultery, including whipping and public humiliation of various kinds, as well as exile.[163] Adultery, like fornication and other sexual crimes, was also believed to invite direct intervention by God in human affairs and thus was blamed for numerous disasters.[164] As with fornication, too, the heinousness of the crime and the severity of the punishment might be increased if the relationship was also incestuous,[165] or if the offense was committed in a church.[166] The innocent husband of an adulteress was under considerable pressure to take action against

[160] Burchard, *Decretum* 9.73 (= Ivo, *Decretum* 8.210), in PL 140:827–28; Ivo, *Decretum* 8.111–12, 124–25 (= *Panormia* 7.14–15), in PL 161:606–607, 610.

[161] Ivo, *Decretum* 8.99 (= *Panormia* 7.21), in PL 161:604, citing Ps.-Clement c. 5, in Hinschius, DPI, p. 32; also Ivo, *Decretum* 8.105 (= *Panormia* 7.20), in PL 161:605. Cf. Ivo, *Decretum* 12.21, in PL 161:785, which compares adultery to other offenses, including perjury, sorcery, poisoning, defrauding laborers, and oppressing widows and orphans.

[162] Burchard, *Decretum* 9.65 (= Ivo, *Decretum* 8.201, *Panormia* 7.12), 9.66 (= Ivo, *Decretum* 8.202, *Panormia* 7.9), 9.67 (= Ivo, *Decretum* 8.203), 9.69–70 (= Ivo, *Decretum* 8.206–207), 9.74 (= Ivo, *Decretum* 8.211, *Panormia* 7.10–11), 17.51, and 19.5, in PL 140:826–28, 931, 957; also Ivo, *Decretum* 8.284 and 295 (= *Panormia* 3.143), in PL 161:642, 646; Gottlob, "Der Ehebruch und seine Rechtsfolgen in den vorgratianischen Quellen und bei Gratian selbst." *Studia Gratiana* 1 (1954), p. 344. Presumably the penalties and penances imposed upon adulterers account in part of the report of Albert of Aachen that those guilty of this offense flocked in great numbers into the ranks of the First Crusade; see Albert's *Hist.* 1.2, in RHC, Occ. 4:272.

[163] Thus Albert of Aachen, *Hist.* 3.57, in RHC, Occ. 4:379: "Deprehensi ibidem [*viz.*: Antiocheni] in adulterio vir et femina, coram omni exercitu denudati, et post terga manibus revinctis, a percussoribus graviter virgis verberati, totum circuire coguntur exercitum, ut saevissimis plagis illorum visis, a tali et tam nefario scelere ceteri absterreantur." Cf. Guibert, *Gesta Dei* 4.15, in RHC, Occ. 4:182. Albert's optimistic belief that savage punishment would deter other potential offenders was ill-founded. On exile as punishment for adultery, see Council of Nablus (1120) c. 5, in Mansi 21:263.

[164] Thus in the Levant blame for the military disaster of the Battle of the Bloody Field (1119) was laid on the marital infidelities of Roger of Antioch; Fulcher of Chartres, *Hist.* 3.3.4, ed. Hagenmeyer, pp. 622–24.

[165] Burchard, *Decretum* 17.4–6, 49 (= Ivo, *Decretum* 8.181 and 9.100, *Panormia* 6.120), 19.5, in PL 140:919–20, 930–31, 965–66; also Ivo, *Decretum* 8.256, in PL 161:641.

[166] Ivo, *Decretum* 3.14, in PL 161:202.

her, since if he failed to do so, he condoned her offense and might himself be punished.[167]

RAPE AND ABDUCTION

Despite generations of complaints about the frequency of *raptus*, the abduction and ravishment of women was still an urgent problem in the reform period.[168] Although *raptus* continued to mean any type of abduction, whether the victim was sexually molested or not, by the time of Ivo of Chartres, canon law had begun to equate abduction with sexual violation. Ivo cited a letter of his friend and patron, Pope Urban II (1088–99), in which the pope ruled that the abduction of a woman by a man created a presumption that the perpetrator sexually molested his victim; when apprehended, therefore, the malefactor was obliged to refute this presumption by proof, if he could do so.[169]

Evidently, therefore, by the last decade of the eleventh century the canonists had begun to redefine *raptus* as a sexual offense. Ivo's collections also indicate that the victim's consent to sexual intercourse was becoming an essential element in determining the nature of *raptus* and the severity of its punishment.[170] The principal penalties that the late eleventh-century canonists visited upon those guilty of *raptus* were excommunication, *infamia*, and (according to some) inability to marry the ravished woman, so that the ravisher might not benefit by his crime.[171] Churchmen guilty of *raptus* lost the benefit of their clerical status; accomplices and accessories to the crime were subject to the same punishments as principals.[172] The penalties increased if the victim was betrothed or married to someone other than her abductor, or if the woman had taken religious vows.[173] Civil authorities also treated rape as a grave offense, but frequently construed it as a crime primarily against the victim's father or male

[167] Burchard, *Decretum* 9.69 (= Ivo, *Decretum* 8.206) and 19.5, in PL 140:826–27, 959; Coll. 5L 1.122–23, ed. Fornasari, p. 88; Ivo, *Decretum* 8.114, 264, 266, in PL 161:607, 643.

[168] The complaints of Hincmar of Reims about the frequency of *raptus* in ninth-century France apparently still applied two centuries later; see *De coercendo raptu puellarum et sanctimonialium* in PL 125:1017–36.

[169] Ivo, *Decretum* 8.24 (= *Panormia* 6.109), in PL 161:589; Urban's letter is JL 5399.

[170] Ivo, *Decretum* 8.26 (= *Panormia* 5.63) is a conflated text that loosely paraphrases Isidore of Seville's *Etymologiae* 5.26 and the Council of Aachen (836) c. 65 (24), in MGH, Concilia 2/2:723. The text as it stands is apparently Ivo's work.

[171] Burchard, *Decretum* 9.33–34 (= Ivo, *Decretum* 8.171–72), 9.36 (= Ivo, *Decretum* 8.174, *Panormia* 6.55), 9.39, and 19.5, in PL 140:820–21, 958–59; Coll. 74T 65.285–86, 66.304 (= Ivo, *Decretum* 10.37), ed. Gilchrist, pp. 170–71, 175; Ivo, *Decretum* 8.25, in PL 161:589.

[172] Burchard, *Decretum* 9.35 (= Ivo, *Decretum* 8.173 and 322), 9.36 (= Ivo, *Decretum* 8.174, and *Panormia* 6.55), in PL 140:820.

[173] Burchard, *Decretum* 8.52 (= Ivo, *Decretum* 7.70), 9.32 (= Ivo, *Decretum* 8.170), 9.37 (= Ivo, *Decretum* 8.175), 9.38 (= Ivo, *Decretum* 8.176, *Panormia* 6.19), 9.39

guardian rather than as a personal offense against the victim, as canon law did.[174]

The canonists, however, were prepared to recognize the right of sanctuary for a man accused of *raptus*, should he manage to take refuge in a church, provided that he first released his victim and restored her to her family prior to claiming protection. Once on consecrated ground the abductor obtained a guaranteed immunity from retaliation by the victim's family, although he remained subject to ecclesiastical punishment for his deed.[175]

The most vexed problem in the ecclesiastical law concerning *raptus* during the reform period concerned marriage between the ravisher and his victim. Some authorities maintained that such marriages must be forbidden under all circumstances, even if the victim willingly consented to her abduction and to subsequent marriage with the abductor, while others argued that the possibility of marriage should not be foreclosed, particularly when there had been consent in the first place.[176] On this subject the law in the mid-twelfth century remained unsettled.

But Western authorities in the twelfth century evidently considered forcible rape a less pressing issue than their predecessors had. This lessened concern apparently reflected an alteration in the relations of the sexes. Suitors wishing to win the hand of a lady whose parents opposed their wooing were beginning to find more subtle ways of securing their goal. Where such a suitor a century earlier might have abducted the woman and pressed his suit by force and intimidation, early twelfth-century males seem to have been more inclined to resort to charm, blandishments, and acts of valor to win over the lady's heart. Ravishment was giving way to seduction as the preferred method of capturing an heiress against her family's wishes. This change in courting patterns is reflected not only in poetic praise of *fin'amors*, but also in canon law.[177]

PROSTITUTION

Prostitution was another topic of contemporary relevance for canonists of the reform era. The growth of population, the increasing flow of people into towns,

---

(= Ivo, *Decretum* 8.177, *Panormia* 6.56), in PL 140:803, 820–21; Ivo, *Decretum* 14.64, in PL 161:841.

[174] Council of Nablus (1120) c. 13–14, in Mansi 21:264; Dillard, "Women in Reconquest Castille," pp. 80–81; Anne L. Klinck, "Anglo-Saxon Women and the Law," JMH 8 (1982) 109; Fell, *Women in Anglo-Saxon England*, pp. 62–64.

[175] Ivo, *Decretum* 3.108 (= *Panormia* 2.72), in PL 161:222.

[176] Authorities forbidding marriage between ravisher and victim appear in Burchard, *Decretum* 9.33–37, in PL 140:820–21, and Ivo, *Decretum* 8.26, 8.171–75, in PL 161:589, 620–21, as well as Hincmar, *De coercendis raptu* c. 7, in PL 125:1021–22. On the other hand Ivo, *Decretum* 8.28–29, in PL 161:590, required that the abductors marry their victims (both of whom seem to have been willing participants in the incident) under penalty of harsher penalties if they refused.

[177] Ivo, *Decretum* 8.29 (= Coll. 74T 64.275), in PL 161:590; Duby, *Medieval Marriage*, pp. 105–106.

the severing of migrants to the towns and cities from their ties with friends and family in their villages of origin, and the greater anonymity that urban life entailed may have made both the practice and patronage of prostitution easier than it was in rural hamlets.[178] Even the armies of warriors under vows during the First Crusade were overrun by harlots, a situation that shocked and alarmed clerical chroniclers. The leaders of the Crusade tried time and again to expel the whores from their camps, but they succeeded only occasionally, and only at times when their forces were in peril. As soon as a crisis ended, loose women reappeared and took up their trade with the soldiery once more; brothels were clearly a normal component of the Crusaders' camps.[179] Even the appearance in a vision of Jesus, who excoriated the crusaders for their visits to the stews, was unable to put a stop to this traffic.[180] The lavish and numerous bordellos of Byzantium made a lasting impression, too, both on the participants in the Crusade and on those who heard their accounts of the sporting life in the Greek capital.[181] The stories and reminiscences of returning Crusaders probably had only marginal importance, however, for the apparent increase in prostitution in the West from the early twelfth century onward. That development was a product of population growth and changes in social structure in Western Europe, particularly its growing urban sector and rising numbers of women with meager resources and few marketable skills. The experience of the Crusaders with the elaborately organized prostitution industry in Byzantium and the Levant, however, may well have influenced the style of commercial sex in the burgeoning urban areas of the twelfth-century West.

In any case, the canonists of the reform period scoured their authorities to locate condemnations of prostitution and inserted into their collections as many suitable texts as they could find. Church tradition had condemned prostitution in no uncertain terms.[182] Roman law, however, had tolerated the practice, and what was more distressing to the high-minded, had protected the right of prostitutes to keep and enjoy the profits of their trade.[183]

But while Church reform canonists reiterated stock condemnations of prostitution from past authorities, writers of the period also advocated a more novel goal: the reform and rehabilitation of prostitutes. Associated with this zeal for rescuing harlots from a life of sin and leading them instead to salvation was a renewed interest in St. Mary Magdalen in the spiritual literature and liturgical

[178] Vern L. Bullough, *The History of Prostitution* (New Hyde Park, NY: University Books, 1964), pp. 111–14.

[179] Baldric of Dol, *Hist.* 1.24, 3.7, in RHC, Occ. 4:28, 66; Fulcher of Chartres, *Hist.* 1.15.14, ed. Hagenmeyer, p. 223; Albert of Aachen, *Hist.* 1.25, in RHC, Occ. 4:291; Guibert, *Gesta Dei* 2.8, in RHC, Occ. 4.142; Ordericus Vitalis, *Hist. eccl.* 9.7, ed. Chibnall 5:54; Ekkhard of Aura, *Hierosolymita* 11, in RHC, Occ. 5:19; *Gesta Francorum Iherusalem expugnantium* 12, 15–16, in RHC, Occ. 3:498–501.

[180] Ordericus Vitalis, *Hist. eccl.* 9.10, ed. Chibnall 5:98.

[181] Guibert, *Gesta Dei* 1.2, 4, in RHC, Occ. 4:127, 133.

[182] Ivo, *Decretum* 8.309, 311, 313, in PL 161:651–52.

[183] Ivo, *Decretum* 8.307 (= Dig. 12.5.4), in PL 161:651.

practice of this period. The Magdalen cult was actively patronized by Pope Leo IX and other reform leaders.[184] The impulse to rehabilitate harlots, rather than merely to condemn them, was particularly clear in the decision by Ivo of Chartres to include in his *Decretum* two canons that encouraged efforts to reform the daughters of joy. The canons not only sought to loosen the hold that pimps and panders had over prostitutes, but also declared it a meritorious act of Christian charity to marry a prostitute in order to redeem her from a life of sin.[185] Perhaps Ivo realized that in order to redeem prostitutes it would be necessary to weaken the power of those who profited most from the operation of brothels. At any rate he culled from his research a number of canons, drawn mainly from Roman sources, attacking the property rights and legal immunity of those who operated houses of ill-fame.[186] Other authorities in the reform period also legislated against pimps and panders.[187]

SINS AGAINST NATURE

A major moral concern of several influential reform leaders, notably St. Peter Damian, lay in the repression of "sins against nature." Unnatural sex acts, in Damian's view, included masturbation, femoral intercourse, anal intercourse, bestiality, and presumably (although he does not explicitly refer to them) fellatio and perhaps cunnilingus as well.[188] Although all of these practices are by definition contraceptive, the issue for Damian was not that these were substitutes for procreative sex, but rather that they were sodomitical and "against nature," a phrase that he used time and again in the *Book of Gomorrah*, the most explicit manifesto against deviant sexuality in reform literature. Damian's concern—indeed obsession might not be too strong a word for it—with masturbation, homosexual practices, and other "unnatural" sex acts was not shared or appreciated by other reform leaders. Pope Alexander II (1061–73), who on other issues was a staunch ally of Damian, even tried to suppress the *Book of Gomorrah*. The pope asked Damian to loan him the manuscript of the work, on the pretext that he wished to have a copy made for his own use; Alexander then locked the manuscript away and refused to return it to the author. Damian was understandably outraged and complained at length in an angry and impassioned

---

[184] Leclercq, *Monks on Marriage*, pp. 89, 95.

[185] Ivo, *Decretum* 8.37–38 (the latter = *Panormia* 6.57), in PL 161:591–92.

[186] Ivo, *Decretum* 8.304 (= Dig. 3.2.4.2), 305–306; 16.121 (= *Panormia* 5.56), in PL 161:650–51, 928.

[187] Council of Nablus (1120) c. 7, in Mansi 21:264.

[188] Peter Damian, *Liber Gomorrhianus* c. 1, in PL 145:161 = *Epist.* 31 in *Die Briefe des Petrus Damiani*, ed. Reindel 1:287–88; see also the recent English translation of this work by Pierre Payer, *Book of Gomorrah: An Eleventh-Century Treatise against Clerical Homosexual Practices* (Waterloo, Ont.: Wilfred Laurier University Press, 1982), p. 29. Damian directed his book particularly against deviant sex among the clergy, but his condemnations clearly applied to the laity as well.

letter to two of his curial allies, Cardinals Stephen and Hildebrand (the future Pope Gregory VII). After recounting the whole episode and after making a series of scarcely veiled threats about Pope Alexander's likely fate in this life and the next, Damian begged the two cardinals, successfully it seems, to retrieve the *Book of Gomorrah* and to restore it to its author.[189]

Damian's detailed and explicit diatribe against "unnatural" vice is unique, but the canonists of his period were also concerned with the issues raised in the *Book of Gomorrah*. The collections of Burchard and Ivo contained numerous canons condemning sodomy, bestiality, pederasty, and fellatio. They also prescribed penances, many of them severe, for those guilty of these practices.[190]

Sodomy (a term that included all kinds of deviant sex practices, but that was also used in a more specific sense to mean anal sex) drew special attention from legislators in the Crusader kingdom in the Levant. Authorities there decreed that men guilty of sodomy should be burnt to death.[191] Those who voluntarily confessed their guilt and performed the appropriate canonical penance, however, might be spared execution, but were condemned to exile instead. Men who suffered homosexual rape also escaped execution, but were nonetheless required to do canonical penance, presumably because of the ritual pollution that they had suffered.[192]

Canonists of this period also reiterated older penitential condemnations of lesbian relationships.[193] They paid only passing attention to sex with animals,[194] mutual masturbation,[195] and transvestitism.[196]

Although Peter Damian argued that solitary masturbation was a type of sodomy, because it was "against nature" and therefore deserved all of the severe

[189] Peter Damian, *Epist.* 2.6, in PL 144:270–72 (Reindel no. 156); Little, "Personal Development," pp. 333–34.

[190] Burchard, *Decretum* 17.30 (= Ivo, *Decretum* 9.88; cf. Damian, *Liber Gomorrhianus* c. 13, in PL 145:172–73 and Reindel 1:305–306); 17.31–37 (= Ivo, *Decretum* 9.89–95) 17.56, and 19.5, in PL 140:924–26, 930–31, 967–68; also Ivo, *Decretum* 9.105–106, 109, 115, in PL 161:685–86, 688. Boswell, CSTAH, pp. 205–206, asserts that Burchard counted homosexual offenses as less serious than corresponding heterosexual offenses and refers to *Decretum* 19.5 (PL 140:967) as his authority for this statement. His argument ignores the difference between the treatment of heterosexual and homosexual anal intercourse. *Decretum* 17.39 (PL 140:926–27), taken from Theodore's *Penitential*, assigns a much milder penance (3 years for adult offenders, 2 years for boys) for heterosexual sodomy than for homosexual sodomy (10 years for first offenders, 12 years for habitual offenders).

[191] Council of Nablus (1120) c. 8 and 10, in Mansi 21:164.

[192] Council of Nablus (1120) c. 9 and 11, in Mansi 21:164.

[193] Burchard, *Decretum* 17.27, 29 (= Ivo, *Decretum* 9.85, 87), and 19.5, in PL 140:924, 971–72.

[194] Burchard, *Decretum* 17.32–33 (= Ivo, *Decretum* 9.90–91), 17.38, 19.5, in PL 140:925–26, 968, 972; also Ivo, *Decretum* 9.107–108, in PL 161:868.

[195] Burchard, *Decretum* 19.5, in PL 140:968.

[196] Burchard, *Decretum* 8.60 (= Ivo, *Decretum* 7.78), in PL 140:803.

punishments visited on sodomy, his view found no following among the canonists.[197] Burchard's treatment of masturbation drew entirely on the penitentials and he dealt with it primarily as a matter for confession and penance, rather than as a criminal offense.[198] Ivo had even less to say than Burchard did about masturbation, although he included in his *Decretum* three brief statements concerning moral responsibility for seminal ejaculation during sleep.[199]

One English council during the period took the extraordinary step of classifying all unnatural sex acts as reserved sins, which could not be forgiven by an ordinary priest in confession, but must be referred to the bishop of the diocese for penance and absolution.[200] This canon, which accords fully with Peter Damian's views, seems to be the only instance in which Damian's rigorist position received explicit support from legislation.

Marriage, Sex, and the Clergy in the Church Reform Period

Abolition of clerical marriage and suppression of all sexual activity among the clergy were major aims of the leaders of the eleventh-century reform. Reformers called for the "liberation" of the clergy from their wives and concubines as an essential precondition for the liberation of Church property from lay control. Both aims, they believed, must be achieved in order to restore the Church to its rightful place in Christian society.[201]

The campaign against clerical marriage and against clerical sexuality generally was based upon both doctrinal and practical considerations. The doctrinal underpinnings of the campaign rested upon the familiar notion that sex was both impure and sinful. The married cleric who engaged in the sordid delights of the bedchamber sullied himself and the sacred mysteries. Those who officiated at the altar, reformers believed, must avoid carnal joys. The cleric who succumbed to fleshly temptation, even with the wife to whom he was legitimately married, became impure and his impurity contaminated every liturgical action he performed, sullied the sacred vessels that he touched, and defiled the sacred words that he spoke.[202] The font and source of this impurity, the reform-

---

[197] Peter Damian, *Liber Gomorrhianus* c. 22, in PL 145:183 and Reindel 1:319–20.

[198] Burchard, *Decretum* 17.41, 43, and 19.5, in PL 140:927–28, 968.

[199] Ivo, *Decretum* 9.111 (= *Panormia* 1.159), 112, and 113, in PL 161:687.

[200] Council of Westminster (1102) c. 29, in Whitelock, Brett,and Brooke 2:678–79; Henry Charles Lea, *History of Auricular Confession and Indulgences in the Latin Church*, 3 vols. (Philadelphia: Lea Brothers, 1896; repr. New York: Greenwood, 1968) 1:313.

[201] Walter Ullmann, *The Growth of Papal Government in the Middle Ages: A Study in the Ideological Relation of Clerical to Lay Power*, 2d ed. (London: Methuen, 1962), p. 297; Jean Gaudemet, "Le célibat ecclésiastique: le droit et la pratique du XIe au XIIe siècle," ZRG, KA 68 (1982) 10.

[202] Peter Damian, *Contra intemperantes clericos* c. 4 (Rindel no. 112), in PL 145: 393–94: "Manus, quae deputatae fuerant ad ordinandas in coelestis mensae ferculo vi-

ers asserted, was lust. Without lust there would be no sex, for the two were inseparable. Married priests betrayed their high calling and smirched their sacred dignity when they lived as married men, amid the reek and screams of snivelling brats, side by side with a smirking, randy wife, bedeviled by daily temptations to unclean thoughts, words, and deeds.[203] Peter Damian described this sordid scene; and the disgust at clerical marriage that pervades it became a central theme of reform propaganda.

Practical considerations, mainly economic, supported the drive for an unmarried clergy. Married clergy, the reformers declared, were expensive to maintain—married priests, after all, had to provide food, clothes, and housing for those bawling babies and slatternly wives, and the Church's resources were thereby frittered away, not in the service of God, but in catering to the whims of the wives and children of married clerics. Even worse, married priests, bishops, and others would be tempted to treat their ecclesiastical offices as family property and to convert their sacred dignity into the family heritage. This last charge was close to the mark. Sacerdotal dynasties were common, almost the norm, in some regions of eleventh-century Europe, and had been commonplace for centuries.[204]

Peter Damian was by far the most outspoken and most radical critic of clerical marriage. There can be little doubt that his vituperative remarks about clerical marriage were deeply rooted in his personal horror of sex. Damian

---

tales epulas angelorum, tractare non metuunt obscoenitates et spurca contagia mulierum. Ii, qui inter illa terribilia sacramenta choris admiscentur angelicis, mox tanquam de coelo ruentes, ad foeminae foeditati relabuntur amplexus, et velut sues immundae coenosis vermigenae luxuriae volutabris immerguntur . . . ." See also Damian's *Epist.* 5.13 (Reindel no. 141), in PL 144:359–72, as well as Pietro Palazzini, "S. Pier Damiani e la polemica anticelibataria," *Divinitas* 14 (1970) 129.

[203] Peter Damian, *Contra intemperantes clericos* c. 7 (Reindel no. 112), in PL 145:410: "Interea et vos alloquor, o lepores clericorum, pulpamenta diaboli, projectio paradisi, virus mentium, gladius animarum, anonita bibentium, toxica convivarum, materia peccandi, occasio pereundi. Vos, inquam, alloquor gynaecea hostis antiqui, upupae, ululae, noctuae, lupae, sanguisugae. Affer, affer sine cessatione dicentes [cf. Prov. 30:15]. Venite itaque, audite me, scorta, prostibula, saevia, volutabra porcorum pinguium, cubilia spirituum immundorum, nymphae, serenae, lamiae, dianae, et si quid adhuc portenti, si quid prodigii reperitur, nomine vestro competere judicetur. Vos enim estis daemonum victimae ad aeternae mortis succidium destinatae. Ex vobis enim diabolus, tanquam delicatis dapibus pascitur, vestrae libidinis exuberantia saginatur."

[204] Peter Damian, *Contra intemperantes clericos* c. 4 (Reindel no. 112), in PL 145:393; Schimmelpfennig, "Ex fornicatione nati," pp. 6–7; Barstow, *Married Priests*, pp. 59–64. On sacerdotal dynasties see Rather of Verona, *De nuptu illicito*, in PL 136:567–74; Brooke, "Gregorian Reform in Action," pp. 10–11. Orderic Vitalis, who was born in 1075 in the midst of the drive against clerical marriage and who was himself the son of a priest, furnishes evidence about the careers of the three sons of Archbishop Robert of Rouen; *Hist. eccl.*, ed. Chibnall 2:xiii, 30, 42, 118, 140.

stands as the principal eleventh-century advocate of the view that clerical marriage is heresy, a doctrine for which mainstream ecclesiastical thought furnished little support.[205] Damian identified the heresy of clerical marriage with Nicolaitism, an obscure first-century sectarian movement among Christians in Ephesus and Pergamon. Damian's writings popularized the use of this term to describe those who opposed the imposition of mandatory celibacy upon all Catholic clerics.[206] The usage took hold and became part of the standard vocabulary of propaganda and invective during the late eleventh century, as did Damian's use of such terms as "whore" and "harlot" to describe the wives of priests.

Extreme though Damian's position was, the fervor of his beliefs and the violence of his rhetoric made a strong impression upon his contemporaries. Moderate advocates of Church reform ultimately adopted many of Damian's ideas, but stripped them of the stinging rhetoric in which he dressed them.[207] Damian's attacks on clerical marriage and on all types of clerical sexuality found resonance in popular movements, notably the emergence in the mid-eleventh century at Milan of a politico-religious party known as the Patarines. This group rose up in arms against the married clergy of Milan and drove them out of their benefices and parishes.[208]

The attacks of Church reformers and the implementation of those attacks by popular movements, such as that of the Patarines, created something akin to a reign of terror among clerics and their families during the late eleventh and twelfth centuries. The frightened victims of the reformers' attacks on clerical marriage not only included clergymen, who were liable to be stripped of their positions and livelihoods, but also their wives and children, who were often the most bullied and fearful victims of the campaign against Nicolaitism. Women who had married clerics in good faith, women who were often themselves the

---

[205] Brooke, "Gregorian Reform in Action," p. 3.

[206] The Nicholas from whom the sect took its name was identified (no doubt erroneously) with Nicholas of Antioch; see Acts 6:5 and Apoc. 2:6, 15. See also Lynch, "Marriage and Celibacy," p. 190, n. 34; Martin Boelens, *Die Klerikerehe in der Gesetzgebung der Kirche unter besonderer Berücksichtigung der Strafe: Eine rechtsgeschichtliche Untersuchung von den Anfängen der Kirche bis zum Jahre 1139* (Paderborn: F. Schöningh, 1968), p. 143; Gaudemet, "Célibat ecclésiastique," pp. 7–8. Brooke, "Gregorian Reform in Action," p. 3, credits Cardinal Humbert (d. 1061?) with the first use of the term "Nicolaitism" to describe all unmarried clerics, but the usage appears occasionally in much earlier texts; see e.g., Council of Tours (567) c. 20(19) in CCL 148A:184.

[207] E.g., St. Anselm, *De presbyteris concubinariis*, in PL 158:555–56; see also Schimmelpfennig, "Ex fornicatione nati," p. 17.

[208] Christine Thouzellier, *Hérésie et hérétiques: Vaudois, Cathares, Patarines, Albigeois*, Storia e letteratura, no. 116 (Rome: Edizioni di Storia e letteratura, 1969), pp. 204–205. The term *patarini* was later applied during the twelfth century to heretical groups; Pope Alexander III was especially prone to label all Italian heretics "Patarines." The original Patarine movement, however, began in 1056–57 as an uprising against married and concubinous clerics and was supported by Bonizo of Sutri, among others.

daughters or grandaughters of priests or bishops, found themselves shorn of social position, driven from their homes, their marriages denounced as immoral from the pulpits, their honor ruined, their families broken, and their commitment to husband and children denounced as scurrilous and sinful. The children suffered a worse fate: their legitimacy was suspect, their capacity to inherit denied, their futures clouded, and their very existence deplored by public authorities and spiritual leaders. Reviled as the "cursed seed" of their fathers' lust, they were the innocent victims of high-minded idealists such as Peter Damian, Pope Gregory VII, and other reform leaders.[209]

As Ivo of Chartres was aware, clerical celibacy was a special ideal of the Western Church and had never been shared by Eastern Christians, who saw no problem in maintaining a married clergy.[210] The mingled traditions of the two churches in the canonical collections blunted for a time the thrust of the building attack upon clerical sexuality. Both Eastern and Western Churches had frequently forbidden clerics to live in the same household with women to whom they were not related, but this policy was directed primarily against those "spiritual marriages," that Church authorities had long viewed with suspicion.[211] Western authorities, moreover, even at the height of the reform movement tolerated marriage among the lower ranks of the clergy, although they preferred that men in minor orders should also remain celibate if they could.[212] Older authorities, too, even in the West, had ruled that clerics in major orders who were already married at the time of ordination might continue to have sexual relations with their wives after ordination.[213] Pope Gregory I had explicitly forbidden priests and other clerics who looked forward to ordination to dismiss their wives, and the Council of Gangra in the fourth century had warned the faithful not to refuse the ministrations of married priests, under pain of anathema.[214]

But the older law was inconsistent on all these points. Eleventh-century canonists included in their collections citations from earlier authorities that confuted each of these propositions, authorities who held, for example, that if married men were ordained, they must thereafter cease all carnal relations with their wives,[215] that married priests and deacons who failed to do this should be

---

[209] Laurent Chevailler, "Observations sur le droit de bâtardise dans la France coutumière du XIIe au XVe siècle," RHDF, 4th ser., 35 (1957) 381; Brooke, "Gregorian Reform in Action," p. 1; Gaudemet, "Célibat ecclésiastique, p. 10.

[210] Ivo, *Panormia* 3.84, in PL 161:1149.

[211] Burchard, *Decretum* 2.112–13, 115–16, in PL 140:645–46; Coll. 5L 2.16–39, ed. Fornasari, pp. 189–202; Ivo, *Decretum* 6.52 and 187–92, in PL 161:456, 487–88.

[212] Anselm of Lucca 7.133, ed. Thaner, p. 419; Coll. 5L 1.121, ed. Fornasari, p. 88; Ivo, *Decretum* 6.86 (= *Panormia* 3.108), as well as *Panormia* 3.102, 107, 109–11, in PL 161:465, 1153–54.

[213] Ivo, *Panormia* 3.85–88, in PL 161:1149–50.

[214] Burchard, *Decretum* 3.75 (= Ivo, *Decretum* 3.258) in PL 140:689; Ivo, *Panormia* 3.89, in PL 161:1150–51; Coll. 5L 1.124, ed. Fornasari, pp. 88–89.

[215] Burchard, *Decretum* 2.114, 2.148 (= Ivo, *Decretum* 5.59, 6.98, and 6.221, as well

deposed from office,[216] that all clerics above the rank of subdeacon were forbidden to marry,[217] and that clerical celibacy was mandatory for all men in major orders.[218]

Due to the confused state of earlier policy, the campaign against clerical marriage and clerical sexuality took shape slowly during the course of the century. Gradually older rulings in favor of clerical celibacy began to be reinforced by a stream of new legislation. In 1022, the Synod of Pavia forbade any cleric thenceforth to live with either wife or concubine under pain of deposition. This prohibition and others like it were taken seriously by bishops even in distant Hamburg, where Bishop Libentius ordered the wives of all his canons to leave town. His reform failed to accomplish much, however, for the ladies promptly resettled in nearby villages, where their husbands continued to visit them periodically.[219] Similar canons were adopted in 1031 by the Synod of Bourges and in 1068 by the Synod of Gerona.[220] In 1049 the newly-chosen reform pope, Leo IX, reportedly decreed that the concubines of Roman clerics should not only be separated from their lovers, but should be forced into servitude as chattels of the Lateran Palace.[221] A decade later at the Synod of Rome, Pope Nicholas II took the extreme step of overruling the Council of Gangra by forbidding the laity to attend Masses said by priests who remained with their wives or concubines. It is significant that the celibacy decree of Nicholas II equated priests' wives with concubines, for the pope thereby implicitly denied for the first time the validity of clerical marriage, although most canonists up to this point considered such marriages legally binding.[222] Pope Alexander II (1061–73) on three

---

as *Panormia* 3.100), in PL 140:645–46, 650; Ivo, *Decretum* 7.35 and *Panormia* 3.92, 95, 114–15, in PL 161:553, 1151–52, 1154–56.

[216] Burchard, *Decretum* 2.108 (= Ivo, *Decretum* 6.185, *Panormia* 3.91), in PL 140:645; Coll. 5L 2.68, ed. Fornasari, pp. 220–21; Coll. 74T 28.202, ed. Gilchrist, pp. 127–30; Ivo, *Decretum* 6.57 (= *Panormia* 3.137), in PL 161:456–57.

[217] Coll. 5L 2.69–70, ed. Fornasari, p. 221; Coll. 74T 21.170, 172, ed. Gilchrist, pp. 108–109; Ivo, *Decretum* 8.286 and *Panormia* 3.96, in PL 161:646, 1152.

[218] Burchard, *Decretum* 1.5 (cf. *Decretum* 2.148, as well as Ivo, *Decretum* 5.59, 6.98 and 221, *Panormia* 3.100), in PL 140:551, 645–46, 650; Coll. 74T 21.173, ed. Gilchrist, p. 109; Ivo, *Decretum* 6.119, 376 (= *Panormia* 3.97), in PL 161:474, 524; Ivo, *Panormia* 3.22, 93, 98–99, 105, in PL 161:1135, 1151–53.

[219] Synod of Pavia (1022) c. 1, in Mansi 19:353; Adam of Bremen, *Gesta Hammaburgensis ecclesiae pontificum* 2.61, scholion 43, ed. M. Lappenberg, in MGH, SS 7:328.

[220] Synod of Bourges (1031) c. 5–6, and Synod of Gerona (1068) c. 4, 6–7, in Mansi 19:503, 1071; Boelens, *Klerikerehe*, pp. 117, 133; Hermann Winterer, "Zur Priesterehe in Spanien bis zum Ausgang des Mittelalters," ZRG, KA 52 (1966) 375.

[221] Bernold of Constance, *Chronicon* s.a. 1049, ed. Georg Waitz, in MGH, SS 5:426; Peter Damian, *Contra intemperantes clericos* (Reindel no. 112) c. 7, in PL 145:411; Synod of Melfi (1089) c. 12, in Mansi 20:724; Grévy-Pons, *Célibat et nature*, p. 14.

[222] Ivo, *Panormia* 3.135 (cf. *Panormia* 8.142) in PL 161:1161; Roman Synod (1059)

separate occasions declared celibacy mandatory for all clerics above the rank of subdeacon, and the Synod of Gerona in 1068 required the deposition of any cleric in major orders who took or kept a wife or concubine.[223]

The campaign against the married clergy, their wives, and children intensified further during the pontificate of Pope Gregory VII (1073–85). At his Roman synod during Lent of 1074, Gregory proposed a lengthy, rhetoric-laden canon that forbade unchaste clerics to officiate at the altar and prohibited sexual intercourse for married clerics. Married clergymen who did not separate from their wives were to be deposed immediately.[224] The next year Gregory launched a vigorous effort to enforce these decrees. To this end he appealed for help not only from ecclesiastical officials, but also from German Dukes, the Countess of Flanders, and even, ironically enough, from the German Emperor, Henry IV, whom he was to excommunicate a year later.[225] In short order, local councils and synods followed up the Roman decree with supplemental legislation of their own, in an effort to publicize the new policy and to bring it forcibly home to the local clergy.[226] Gregory's successor, Urban II (1088–99), reinforced the celibacy policy when he met with groups of clergy in regional synods. Re-enactments of the celibacy decrees followed in the opening years of the twelfth century.[227] Pope Paschal II (1099–1118) slightly softened the harshness of earlier enactments, which had demanded the immediate, forcible separation of clerics from their wives and families. In a letter to the Bishop of Compostella, the pope declared that the sons of clerics who had married in the customary way before the promulgation of the recent celibacy decrees might be treated as legitimate and should not be denied the rights of lawfully born children, including the right to become candidates for ordination themselves, provided that they promise chastity, as was now required.[228]

---

c. 3, in MGH, Const. 1:547; Fliche, *La réforme grégorienne et le reconquête chrétienne*, pp. 28–29; Boelens, *Klerikerehe*, pp. 126, 134.

[223] Ivo, *Panormia* 3.103 (JL 4575), 3.138 (JL 4477), and 3.139 (JL 4612), in PL 161:1153, 1162; Synod of Gerona (1068) c. 6–7, in Mansi 19:1071.

[224] Roman Synod (1074) c. 11, in Mansi 20:413–15.

[225] Gregory VII, *Register* 2.45 (JL 4922), 2.67 (JL 4949), 3.3 (JL 4963), 4.10 (JL 5011), and 4.20 (JL 5030), ed. Caspar 1:182–85, 223–25, 246–47, 309, 328–29; *Epist. vagantes*, no. 6, 9, 11, 16, 32, and 41, ed. Cowdrey, pp. 14, 20–22, 26, 44, 84–86, 102.

[226] Primatial Council of Winchester (1076) c. 1, in Whitelock, Brett, and Brooke 2:619; Council of Poitiers (1078) c. 9, and Synod of Gerona (1078) c. 1, in Mansi 20:499, 517.

[227] Ivo, *Panormia* 3.101 and 104, in PL 161:1152–53, citing the Synod of Melfi (1089) c. 3, 12, in Mansi 20:723, 724; Council of Westminster (1102) c. 5, in Whitelock, Brett, and Brooke 2:675; Council of Troyes (1107) c. 3, in Blumenthal, *Early Councils of Paschal II*, p. 91.

[228] JL 5881, text in Mansi 20:1001. A few other authorities also opposed forced separation of married clerics from their wives; see Ivo, *Panormia* 3.113, in PL 161:1154, and Council of Winchester (1076) c. 1, in Whitelock, Brett, and Brooke 2:619.

The war against clerical marriage reached its climax in two stages early in the twelfth century. Up to this point the reformers had continued to treat the marital unions of priests as valid but illicit marriages. Priests were not allowed to marry, according to this view; but if they did so, the law nonetheless recognized their marriages as binding. In 1123, the First Lateran Council changed this policy. The council declared that ordination to the three higher grades of holy orders (priesthood, diaconate, and subdiaconate) created a diriment impediment to marriage. This meant that clerics in major orders could no longer marry at all and their unions were stripped of legal status and the protection of the law. The council prohibited clerical concubinage as well.[229] Local councils and synods during the ensuing few years reinforced these prohibitions.[230] The Second Lateran Council renewed the attack on clerical marriage and concubinage in 1139. This council decreed that the marriages of priests should be broken up, that both parties must do penance, and that those who resisted should be deprived of their clerical positions and benefices. In addition, the council adopted the policy of Pope Nicholas II and forbade the faithful to attend Masses or other services conducted by married priests or those who lived with concubines.[231]

The Lateran decrees of 1123 and 1139 thus transformed clerical marriage from a legally tolerated institution into a canonical crime. Sexual relations by a cleric in major orders, whether with his wife or not, henceforth were classed as fornication; women who had married priests and other clerics found themselves reduced to the status of concubines at best or, as some declared, of prostitutes.[232] The children of married clerics fared even worse. The Lateran decrees, reinforced by supplemental legislation from local synods, stripped these children of legitimacy; henceforth they were ineligible to enter the clergy themselves or even, according to some authorities, to marry.[233]

The early twelfth-century Lateran decrees decisively changed the law. Changing the social realities proved more difficult, for that required coopera-

---

[229] 1 Lateran Council (1123) c. 7, 21, in COD, pp. 167, 170; Grévy-Pons, *Célibat et nature*, p. 14; Gaudemet, "Célibat ecclésiastique," pp. 17–19; Dortel-Claudot, "Le prêtre et le mariage," p. 337.

[230] Council of Westminster (1125) c. 13, in Whitelock, Brett, and Brooke 2:740; Council of Clermont (1130) c. 4 and Council of Reims (1131) c. 4, in Mansi 21:438, 458.

[231] 2 Lateran Council (1139) c. 6–7, in COD, p. 174, anticipated by the Council of Rouen (1128) c. 1 and the Council of Reims (1131) c. 5, in Mansi 21:575, 459. But cf. Council of Gangra (ca. 324) c. 4, in Mansi 2:1101, cited by Burchard, *Decretum* 3.75, in PL 140:689; Coll. 5L 1.122–24, ed. Fornasari, pp. 88–89; Ivo, *Decretum* 3.258, in PL 161:258.

[232] Peter Damian, *Contra intemperantes clericos* (Reinndel no. 112) c. 7, in PL 145:411–12; Boelens, *Klerikerehe*, p. 161; Dortel-Claudot, "Les prêtres et le mariage," p. 339; Grévy-Pons, *Célibat et nature*, p. 14; Gaudemet, "Célibat ecclésiastique," pp. 19–20; Schimmelpfennig, "Ex fornicatione nati," p. 17.

[233] Synod of Bourges (1031) c. 8, 19, 20, in Mansi 19:504–505; Schimmelpfennig, "Ex fornicatione nati," pp. 18–19; Grévy-Pons, *Célibat et nature*, p. 13.

tion both from local authorities and from the great mass of the clergy themselves. Understandably enough, many of the Western clergy were shocked and resentful at these changes, which threatened their families, their comforts, and a centuries-old social system. Most of the lesser clergy had always married quite routinely and many had passed on their clerical positions and preferments to their children. The reaction of the lesser clergy to the imposition of reform was vigorous, sometimes violent. When the Bishop of Paris told his priests that they must give up their wives and children, they drove him from the church with jeers and blows, and he found it necessary to take refuge with the royal family in order to escape the wrath of his outraged clerics.[234] Archbishop John of Rouen was stoned by his indignant clergy when he ordered them to abandon their concubines, while in northern Italy some bishops simply did not dare to publish the celibacy decrees for fear of their lives. Their misgivings were not unrealistic: in a letter to Bishop Josfried of Paris, Gregory VII reported in 1077 that a proponent of clerical celibacy had been burnt alive by the outraged clergy of Cambrai.[235]

Nor were protests limited to assaults, demonstrations, and riots. Bishop Ulric of Imola (1053–63) directed an eloquent protest against mandatory clerical celibacy to Pope Nicholas II. Ulric denounced the policy as improvident, uncanonical, and unjust.[236] The so-called Anonymous of York likewise vigorously defended the right of priests to marry and asserted that both natural justice and canon law required that the sons of priests be accorded the full protection of the law and all the rights of legitimacy.[237] Lambert of Hersfeld attacked the reformers' celibacy program as madness and added that it ran counter to the Scriptures as well.[238] Other critics and opponents of mandatory celibacy included Gerald of Wales, Robert Courson, Thomas of Chobham, Giles of Corbeil, and Raoul Ardent.[239] But these learned champions were unable to prevail against the determination of the reformers. The *Rescript* of Bishop Ulric was formally condemned by the Synod of Rome in 1079, and the arguments of other adversaries of the celibacy rule were either ignored or dismissed as irrelevant

[234] Synod of Paris (1074) in Mansi 20:437–38; Grévy-Pons, *Célibat et nature*, p. 14.

[235] Gregory VII, *Register* 4.20 (JL 5030), ed. Caspar 1:328; Mansi 20:441–42; Ordericus Vitalis, *Hist. eccl.* 4, ed. Chibnall 2:200; Mirbt, *Publizistik*, pp. 271–72; Schimmelpfennig, "Ex fornicatione nati," p. 11.

[236] *Rescriptio Udalrici*, in MGH, Libelli de lite 1:254–60. The *Rescript* was later attributed to another Ulric, Bishop of Augsburg (d. 973); Fliche, *La réforme grégorienne et la reconquête chrétienne*, pp. 29–30.

[237] Anonymous of York, 1–2, in MGH, Libelli de lite 3:645–55; Grévy-Pons, *Célibat et nature*, p. 15; Brooke, "Gregorian Reform in Action," p. 14; Barstow, *Married Priests*, pp. 157–73.

[238] Lambert of Hersfeld, *Annales* s.a. 1074, in MGH, SS 5:217–18.

[239] John W. Baldwin, "A Campaign to Reduce Clerical Celibacy at the Turn of the Twelfth and Thirteenth Centuries," in *Etudes d'histoire du droit canonique dédiées à Gabriel Le Bras*, 2 vols. (Paris: Sirey, 1965) 2:1041–53; Barstow, *Married Priests*, pp. 105–55.

by the reforming party.[240] Critics of celibacy proved unable to organize an effective or coherent opposition group, while the policy's advocates had long since secured control of the Church's principal administrative positions.[241]

The eventual outcome was already clear to perceptive observers by the second decade of the twelfth century, even before the Lateran decrees were adopted. When Abelard and Heloise debated in 1118/19 whether they should marry or not, after their child had been born, Heloise found good canonical reasons for maintaining that if they married Abelard's clerical career would be irretrievably ruined.[242] A poem of Matthew of Vendôme vividly described the new state of affairs; Matthew depicted a cleric who pleads with the lady of his desire to fulfill his dreams by giving herself to him. The lady replies that she will do no such thing; she prefers to bestow her favors on a knight who will marry her, rather than on a cleric who cannot. "I don't want to sleep around," said she, "I want to get married."[243] Matthew's clear-eyed lady plainly realized that by this time a cleric could do the one, but not the other.

Although canon law had long penalized fornication by clerics and although the canonical collections of the reform period added little new to the existing regulations on clerical sex outside of marriage, the cumulative effect of the prohibition of clerical marriage and concubinage was to transform all sexual activity by clerics into fornication.[244] Since clergymen could no longer legally marry, they had no legitimate sexual outlet and every type of sexual union that they engaged in, no matter how stable or permanent, became both a sin and a canonical crime. Accordingly, the reform legislation on clerical marriage and concubinage greatly increased the scope of the criminal jurisdiction of the ecclesiastical courts and subjected every cleric who dallied with a woman to the threat of criminal sanctions.[245] In other respects, however, the canonical collec-

---

[240] Bernold of Constance, *Chronicon* s.a. 1079, in MGH, SS 5:436.

[241] Mirbt, *Publizistik*, pp. 274–305; Schimmelpfennig, "Ex fornicatione nati," pp. 42–43; Gaudemet, "Célibat ecclésiastique," pp. 13–14.

[242] T. P. McLaughlin, "The Prohibition of Marriage against Canons in the Early Twelfth Century," *Mediaeval Studies* 3 (1941) 94–100.

[243] Wilhelm Wattenbach, "Ein poetischer Briefsteller von Matthäus von Vendôme," *Sitzungsberichte der königliche Akademie der Wissenschaften zu München*, philosophische-, philologische-, und historische Klasse 2 (1872) 599; F. J. E. Raby, *A History of Secular Latin Poetry in the Middle Ages*, 2d ed., 2 vols. (Oxford: Clarendon Press, 1957) 2:33–34.

[244] Burchard, *Decretum* 2.117 (= Ivo, *Decretum* 6.57 and *Panormia* 3.137), 2.118 (= Ivo, *Decretum* 6.94 and 194, *Panormia* 3.94), 17.39, 19.43 (= Ivo, *Decretum* 6.397, *Panormia* 3.149), 19.150 (= Ivo, *Decretum* 6.400, *Panormia* 3.152), in PL 140:646, 926–27, 988–91, 1012. Also Ivo, *Decretum* 6.50, 80 (= *Panormia* 3.145), 6.193–94 and *Panormia* 3.134, 136, 139–42, 144, 146, 148, in PL 161:455, 462, 488–89, 1161–64.

[245] Continued meetings between a cleric and a woman might constitute grounds for sanctions, according to the Council of Westminster (1102) c. 6, in Whitelock, Brett, and Brooke 2:675. See also the remarks of Boelens, *Klerikerehe*, p. 88; Schimmelpfennig, "Ex fornicatione nati," pp. 45–46.

tions of the reform period added little that was new to existing law concerning clerical sexuality.[246]

The Enforcement of the Church's Sexual Regulations: Jurisdiction and Procedure

By the end of the eleventh century and the beginning of the twelfth the reformers had transformed the Western Church's law on sexual behavior. The ability of the church to translate that law into practical reality depended upon its success in asserting its jurisdiction over sex and in developing effective procedures to enforce its rules. By the mid-twelfth century the Church had achieved only partial success in these areas.

Canonical courts enjoyed their greatest success in securing exclusive jurisdiction during this period over marriage litigation. Although no detailed litigation records survive from this era, episodes reported by chroniclers make it plain that by about 1100 even kings and great nobles ordinarily brought questions concerning the validity of their marriages to ecclesiastical authorities and were often prepared, however reluctantly, to abide by their decisions. This monopoly on marriage questions represented a momentous victory for Church reform, as well as a source of considerable power for the Church's judicial system. Royal and local courts, to be sure, continued to exercise jurisdiction over some aspects of domestic relations—matters concerning marital property and (for some purposes) the legitimation of children continued to be handled by secular courts in most areas. But by 1100 the Church had secured virtual supremacy in the adjudication of issues relating to the formation of marriage and the separation, divorce, and remarriage of those whose marriages failed.[247]

Procedures and the law of evidence in the eleventh- and twelfth-century canonical courts remained fluid and lacked any great intellectual or juristic rigor. A notable exception to this general rule involved procedures for dealing with adultery, which were perhaps a shade more sophisticated than those employed for most other sex offenses. Two letters of Ivo of Chartres illustrate the more advanced nature of the procedures in adultery cases. In a letter to Archdeacon Gerbert of Paris, Ivo described the problems that courts faced when they dealt with adultery: it was difficult to secure reliable testimony from witnesses, Ivo declared, because people were afraid to give evidence out of fear of reprisal, while those who did testify were often motivated more by attachment

---

[246]They repeated longstanding bans on the ordination of twice-married men, denounced sexual activity by nuns, and censured homosexual practices by the clergy, but none of this was new.

[247]Pierre Daudet, *L'Etablissement de la competence de l'église en matière de divorce et consanguinité (France, Xème-XIIème siècles)*, Etudes sur l'histoire de la juridiction matrimoniale (Paris: Sirey, 1941), pp. 126–38; Philippe Delhaye, "The Development of the Medieval Church's Teaching on Marriage," *Concilium* 55 (1970) 83; Duby, *Medieval Marriage*, pp. 25–54.

to one of the parties than by love of the truth. Further, the *bona fides* of many witnesses were dubious, particularly those who managed brothels and were otherwise engaged in the prostitution industry. Still, Ivo continued, judges should make every effort to secure reliable testimony; should credible witnesses be lacking, however, defendants might refute the charges against them by undergoing the ordeal of the glowing iron, although Ivo had serious reservations about the value of this type of proof.[248] Despite respected authorities who taught that husbands were entitled to bring adultery charges against their wives on suspicion alone,[249] Ivo tried to discourage frivolous or poorly grounded actions of this sort. In another letter he advised a knight who suspected his wife of adultery that something more than mere suspicion and a bit of circumstantial evidence were needed. The woman in this case had carried a child a week longer than normal and delivered while her husband was absent from the kingdom. Moreover, the man suspected of corrupting her had suffered a burn when he attempted to purge himself of guilt in the hot-iron ordeal. Ivo advised his correspondent that this was insufficient evidence to warrant a divorce on the grounds of adultery. Ivo had consulted midwives, and they had advised him that there was nothing unusual in a child being born a few days later than expected. As for the ordeal, Ivo thought the procedure overrated, for the results might have a perfectly innocent explanation and did not necessarily indicate guilt. He advised the knight to drop the case and to accept his wife's sworn statement of her innocence.[250]

Questions concerning evidence in adultery cases were also under debate at about the same time among Irnerius's disciples at Bologna. Bulgarus cautioned judges to beware of discrepancies in the testimony of witnesses. He also maintained that in order to sustain an adultery charge the accuser must be able to show that the defendant knew that his extramarital sexual partner was married and that their relationship was in fact adulterous.[251] Both civilians and canonists in this period also maintained that complaints about adultery must be timely in order to be heard.[252]

Divorce actions brought before Church courts on the grounds of impotence presented peculiarly difficult evidential problems. One view current in this period held that the sworn statement of the husband in such a suit should prevail.[253] Other authorities were willing to credit the wife's statement, but only if it

---

[248] Ivo, *Epist.* 249, in PL 162:255. Ivo's *Decretum* 16.161, in PL 161:935, also suggests some procedural principles drawn from Roman law for use in adultery cases. The use of ordeals in these situations was, however, still common; Council of Nablus (1120) c. 4, in Mansi 21:263.

[249] Burchard, *Decretum* 16.37, in PL 140:918.

[250] Ivo, *Epist.* 205, in PL 162:210–11.

[251] *Quaestiones dominorum Bononiensium* 60, 81, in *Scripta anecdota glossatorum*, 2d ed. by Giovanni Battista Palmiero, 2 vols., Bibliotheca iuridica medii aevi (Bologna: Angelo Gandolpho, 1913; repr. Turin: Bottega d'Erasmo, 1962) 1:221, 255–56.

[252] Ivo, *Decretum* 8.113, in PL 161:607, citing Cod. 9.9.5.

[253] Burchard, *Decretum* 9.43 (= Ivo, *Decretum* 8.180, *Panormia* 6.119), in PL 140:821.

was supported by corroborative evidence, although they failed to specify what types of corroboration they required.[254]

Conclusions

By the mid-twelfth century, the advocates of Church reform had won at least partial victories on all of the major issues they raised. Canon law by 1140 was becoming a juristic system of greater effectiveness and sophistication than it had been a century or so earlier, when Burchard of Worms compiled his *Decretum*. The newer collections, especially those of Ivo of Chartres, gave prominent attention to the aims of the reform movement. In the field of marriage and family law, together with sex law, the emergence of new norms was particularly marked.

The law of marriage and divorce in the legislation and canonical collections of the late eleventh and early twelfth centuries gave primacy to the doctrine of indissolubility, save under exceptional circumstances. Divorce and remarriage were permitted only where a party to the first marriage proved impotent, where the original marriage seriously infringed the rules on consanguinity or affinity, and under some circumstances where one party was guilty of adultery. Exogamy and indissolubility clearly emerged as hallmarks of Catholic marriage during this period and the papacy and the Church's courts both worked diligently to implement these ideals. As a consequence the laity, even at the highest social levels, lost much of its former control over the marriages of family members. The old-style capacity of families to arrange the marriages, divorces, and remarriages of their members was rapidly disappearing by the 1120s and 1130s. Polygyny, too, was by now no longer common in Christian Europe, and, although concubinage among the laity was by no means rare, these unions were less common and subject to greater social disapproval than they previously had been.

The canonists of this period maintained, as did their predecessors, the Church's right to limit the sexual practices of married persons. Older regulations concerning licit times for marital intercourse continued to appear in the canonical collections of the late twelfth century, but the new law was relatively restrained, at least by comparison with the penitentials, in its treatment of other aspects of marital sex. Although the reform canonists included in their collections some earlier bans on deviant coital positions and "unnatural" marital sex, these regulations, too, were less emphatic than in the penitentials, and reform councils and popes rarely pronounced judgments on these matters.

Reform canonists regarded all nonmarital sex as criminal and subject to punishment. Church law in the early twelfth century became increasingly interested in penalizing nonmarital sex, although the effectiveness of its intervention was limited by its rudimentary enforcement system. Notorious sex crimes were occasionally prosecuted, but the Church had yet to develop an effective

---

[254] Burchard, *Decretum* 9.42 (= Ivo, *Decretum* 8.179), in PL 140:821.

system for detecting and arraigning routine offenders. Moreover, the Church's leaders in this period were prepared to tolerate, if not to approve, some kinds of extramarital sex, particularly prostitution and other casual sexual liaisons. A few reformers, notably Peter Damian, urged vigorous action against "unnatural" sex offenders, but this campaign failed to become an important focus of reform activity.

Reformers devoted their most strenuous efforts in the field of sex law to imposing mandatory celibacy upon the clergy. At the beginning of this period, earlier pronouncements about clerical celibacy remained ineffective; many, probably most, of the Catholic clergy were married or living in some type of relatively stable concubinage. By 1140 this picture had begun to change.[255] New laws against clerical marriage, particularly the canons of the first and second Lateran Councils, meant that clerics could no longer contract legally valid marriages. Certainly this did not stop many churchmen from attempting to do so, but their illicit marriages, if challenged, were almost certain to be pronounced void, and public opinion no longer accepted married clerics as willingly as it had done two or three generations earlier. Women who had been the wives of priests saw their status changed to that of concubines, and some reformers classed them with prostitutes. Priestly families were being broken up, and sacerdotal dynasties no longer controlled the succession to parishes and benefices as readily as they had in the past.

Changes in actual behavior occurred much more slowly, of course, than changes in the law. Repeated denunciations by local and regional synods of clerical concubinage and incontinence indicate that compliance with the new law was haphazard, particularly in rural areas where authorities visited infrequently, and among the lower clergy, where official vigilance was often lax.[256] Scofflaw clerics who ignored or flouted the law did exist, but the few who made it into the record almost certainly constituted only a fraction of those who failed to conform to the new discipline.[257] Gradually, however, celibacy became the norm, particularly among the higher clergy. Bishops who were married or who lived in open concubinage, for example, were becoming rare in many places by the mid-twelfth century.[258]

These changes in the church's marriage and sex laws during the reform era had far-reaching implications for social structure. Under legal pressure mar-

---

[255] As late as 1107, for example, Pope Paschal II, writing to Archbishop Anselm of Canterbury, complained that most English clerics were married and had children; JL 6152, Mansi 20:1063; Gaudemet, "Célibat ecclésiastique," pp. 3–6, notes further examples; see also Barstow, *Married Priests*, p. 77.

[256] Lynch, "Marriage and Celibacy," pp. 199–200; Grévy-Pons, *Célibat et nature*, p. 15.

[257] Among others see Ivo of Chartres, *Epist.* 65, in PL 162:81–82; Raymond d'Aguilers, *Liber* 18, ed. Hill and Hill, p. 154.

[258] Brooke, "Gregorian Reform in Action," pp. 7, 13, 18, and "Married Men among the English Higher Clergy, 1066–1200," *Cambridge Historical Journal* 12 (1956) 187–88.

riages became more stable and exogamy more common, while the church's law-givers pressed increasingly to promote freedom of contract as another essential feature of Christian marriage. Although nonmarital sex continued to be common, the canon law made it increasingly hazardous. And the sexual relationships of the clergy, as we have seen, were radically transformed as a result of the reformers' struggles on behalf of mandatory celibacy. The net result was to restrict the marriage options and to reshape the marriage strategies of a significant part of the population. As marriage became easier to contract (a long-term result of the canonists' emphasis on freedom to choose marriage partners), as the role of parents and family heads in arranging marriages decreased, as the ban on endogamy became increasingly rigorous, as divorce became more restricted, and as the clergy ceased to be acceptable marriage partners for women who had other options, the marriage market became more restricted. Prudent men were probably more cautious in choosing a wife by the mid-twelfth century than their great-grandfathers had been a hundred years before. Women found the number of potential husbands smaller than had their great-grandmothers.

These developments also prepared the ground for further changes, notably the emergence among elite groups during this period of increasing identification of the family with the paternal lineage, rather than the bilateral identification with both maternal and paternal kin common in earlier generations. From the late eleventh century the male line of descent becomes the primary factor in defining family relationships among the elite. In consequence wives and daughters become increasingly marginal members of the family, since they no longer transmited its identity to the next generation.[259]

Changes in marriage law and social practice, combined with changes in population densities and settlement patterns, altered the choices that people made when arranging their lives. Population expansion and increasing concentration of population in towns, combined with an extended ban on endogamy, encouraged the growth of prostitution, particularly as men became more cautious in choosing their wives because they could no longer easily divorce them if they made an unfortunate or impolitic choice. Men of wealth and social position may have found it possible, even desirable, to postpone marriage, particularly when they could do so without forfeiting the possibility of finding numerous partners for extramarital sex.

The Church's doctrinal development during the reform period, combined with the proliferation of new law reflecting the views of the reformers and the revitalization of the study of canon law, must be understood in the context of the social changes resulting from population growth and urbanization, as well as the intellectual changes that flowed from an increasing knowledge of and fascination with the revived Roman law among the Church's jurists. All of these were interconnected and each, in some degree, affected all of the others.

The period of Church reform, moreover, coincided with the emergence of new ideas about the nature of emotional and physical relationships between

---

[259] Herlihy, *Medieval Households*, pp. 82–88.

man and woman, the set of notions that is sometimes described as courtly love.[260] Again there seems to be a complex interconnection between the new ideas about love and the new order of marital and sexual relationships that resulted from the legal as well as the social changes of the reform period. Sexual doctrine and practice during the reform era represented the results of a complex interrelationship of conditions and causes.

Finally, theological understanding of traditional doctrines also underwent continual development during this period. Even the traditional Christian picture of Jesus, which concentrated on his divinity and ignored his masculinity, was altered as a result of St. Anselm's reinterpretation of the atonement. One result of this rethinking was a "sexualization" of the figure of Jesus in Christian devotional literature in the early twelfth century. The new style of devotional discourse found nothing incongruous in describing Christ metaphorically in terms of human sexual experience and in portraying Jesus as a lover who competed with other men for the affections of devout women (see, for example, Plate 15).[261] Thus Anselmian atonement doctrine in the long run had the paradoxical effect of integrating Jesus into the emotional, affective world of the twelfth-century love poets. The new *persona* of the sexual Jesus had significant implications both for later twelfth- and thirteenth-century views of marriage and virginity; concepts of celibacy and married love were both affected by the new notions concerning the humanity of Christ.

Up to 1140, however, the Church's legal writers had yet to come to grips with one basic juristic problem: how to explain and how to deal with the puzzling discrepancies in traditional law about sexual relations. The compilations of the reform canonists, from Burchard to Ivo, clearly demonstrated the lack of consistency between the views of councils, patristic writers, popes, and other authorities on virtually every major sexual issue that the canons dealt with. There was no coherent doctrine to account for the formation of marriage, for example, nor was there any unanimity of view on divorce and remarriage, on consanguinity, on impotence, on fornication, adultery, and other sexual crimes. Traditional canonists had collected divergent authorities, grouped together their teachings on various problems, and left the judge, pastor, or student to cope with the discrepancies as best he could. What was lacking was a synthesis that could give form, consistency, and coherence to canonistic tradition. That synthesis finally emerged about 1140 in the *Decretum* of Gratian.

[260] See generally Diane Bornstein, "Courtly Love," in DMA 3:668–74.

[261] Bugge, *Virginitas*, p. 83; see also Leo Steinberg, *The Sexuality of Christ in Renaissance Art and Modern Oblivion* (New York: Pantheon Books, 1983), pp. 1–9, 12–16, 27–35, 50–56.

6
Sex and Marriage in the *Decretum* of Gratian

Gratian and the Systematic Study of Canon Law

By 1140 or thereabouts—the precise date is unknown—a jurist named Gratian completed a textbook of canon law, which he entitled *A Harmony of Conflicting Canons (Concordia discordantium canonum)*. The title may seem odd, but its musical metaphor expressed accurately the work's leading contribution to canonical scholarship. For Gratian's book was more than just a compilation of conciliar canons, papal decretals, and citations from the Scriptures, the Church fathers, penitentials, Roman law, and other authorities. All of those things were there, to be sure, in the 3,823 chapters of the *Concordia*, but there was something else as well: in addition to assembling a vast array of authorities on canonical problems, Gratian added his own analyses and conclusions. His comments attempted to reconcile the differences among the legal rules enunciated by various authorities and to frame reasoned conclusions that resolved their inconsistencies. Gratian's work, then, furnished both a collection of canons and a synthesis of canon law.

Gratian's *Concordia* revolutionized the study of canon law and gave it an intellectual coherence that it had previously lacked. Earlier collections had produced a cacophony of dissonant opinions, from which lawyers, judges, and pastors could pick whatever suited their purposes, so long as they were content to ignore the rest. Gratian's book was something new and with its appearance we can, for the first time, begin to speak of canon law as a juristic science.[1]

About Gratian himself we know almost nothing. He probably lived and may have taught in Bologna. Very likely he was a monk, but the evidence for this is not conclusive. We can reasonably deduce from his book that he had some academic training in law, but where he studied and with whom is unknown. Probably he taught law—the *Concordia* has the earmarks of a work produced for the

---

[1] Stephan Kuttner, "The Father of the Science of Canon Law," *Jurist* 1 (1941) 2–19, and more generally *Harmony from Dissonance: An Interpretation of Medieval Canon Law* (Latrobe, PA: Archabbey Press, 1960). On legal science and Gratian's contribution to it, see also Berman, *Law and Revolution*, pp. 131–64.

classroom. Aside from the evidence of his book, Gratian remains a shadowy, insubstantial figure.[2] The date of the book's completion is reasonably well established from internal evidence; it includes extracts from the canons of the Second Lateran Council and hence must have been finished after 1139. Since the book seems to have been used in the mid-1140s it was probably finished early in that decade.[3]

The sources that Gratian tapped to create his *Decretum* (to use the short title by which his book is conventionally known) spanned a vast range of literature. Gratian must have had access to a considerable library when composing his work. He drew heavily from earlier canonistic collections in putting together the *Decretum*. He certainly relied on Ivo of Chartres and Anselm of Lucca, and apparently utilized collections of conciliar decrees and papal letters that have not thus far been identified and may no longer exist.[4] Whatever else he may have been, Gratian was certainly diligent and widely read.

The *Decretum* is oddly structured; its inconsistencies may well indicate that Gratian put the work together gradually over a long period of time. In its finished form, the *Decretum* seems to incorporate a number of shorter works stitched together to make the final product, which is in three parts.

Part I deals with the foundations and sources of canon law, its relationship to other types of law, the rights, powers, and obligations of the clergy, administration of Church property, and related matters. This portion of the *Decretum* is divided into units called Distinctions, of which there are 101; each Distinction is subdivided into chapters, and each chapter consists of a statement from some earlier authority dealing with the subject treated in that particular Distinction. A more or less logical scheme of development is apparent within most of the Distinctions.

Typically, Gratian presented a chapter or two explaining one interpretation of a particular theme and followed this with a second group of chapters advocating a different view or interpretation. Quite often these groups of chapters are separated by a *dictum* consisting of a paragraph or two in which Gratian ana-

[2]John T. Noonan, Jr., "Gratian Slept Here: The Changing Identity of the Father of the Systematic Study of Canon Law," *Traditio* 35 (1979) 145–72, presents a thorough and critical analysis of the scanty evidence and the ample legends that surround Gratian; but see also C. Mesini, "Postille sulla biografia del 'Magister Gratianus,' padre del diritto canonico," *Apollinaris* 54 (1981) 509–37. For conventional treatments see Stickler, *Hist. iuris canonici*, pp. 202–204, and Van Hove, *Prolegomena*, pp. 339–40.

[3]For critical evaluations of the evidence see Gérard Fransen, "La date du Décret de Gratien," *Revue d'histoire ecclésiastique* 51 (1956) 521–31; Gabriel Le Bras, Charles Lefebvre, and Jacqueline Rambaud, *L'âge classique, 1140–1378: Sources et théorie du droit*, vol. 7 of *Histoire du droit et des institutions de l'église en occident*, (Paris: Sirey, 1965; hereafter LAC), pp. 57–58; and Stanley Chodorow, *Christian Political Theory and Church Politics in the Mid-Twelfth Century: The Ecclesiology of Gratian's Decretum* (Berkeley and Los Angeles: University of California Press, 1972), pp. 255–59.

[4]LAC, pp. 51–74; Stickler, *Hist. iuris canonici*, pp. 207–10; Van Hove, *Prolegomena*, pp. 343–44; Fuhrmann, *Einfluss und Verbreitung* 2:566–72.

lyzed the argument of the preceding chapters and introduced the opposing views. He frequently inserted a concluding *dictum* toward the end of a Distinction, setting forth his own conclusions about the issue and the reasoning that supported them.

Part II, the longest section of the work, is arranged on a different plan. This section consists of thirty-six Cases (*Causae*). Each begins with a statement of a problem, often in the form of a brief story. Thus, for example, the last Case in Part II begins:

> A certain man lured someone's daughter with gifts and invited her to a banquet without her father's knowledge. After the meal the young man took advantage of the girl, who was a virgin. When her parents learned of this they presented the girl to the young man and, as is usual with persons getting married, the young man gave her a wedding gift and publicly took her as his wife.

Having set the scene by outlining this hypothetical situation, Gratian then formulated a series of questions about the legal consequences of the events described in the story. In Case thirty-six, for example, he framed two questions:

> Question I: Did the man ravish the young woman?
>
> Question II: Secondly, can a rapist marry his victim if her father gives his consent?[5]

Gratian then discussed each question in turn, citing authorities to support different views of the case. He also supplied *dicta* in which he analyzed the issues and presented his own conclusions about the way in which they should be resolved—he gave three authorities on the problem raised in Question I of Chapter thirty-six, for example, and explained his own views in three *dicta*. For Question II he adduced a dozen authorities and discussed the differences between them in four *dicta*.

Part II of Gratian's *Decretum* smells of the classroom. Its structure strongly supports the belief that Gratian taught law somewhere, very likely at Bologna. It covers a wide range of topics—judicial procedure, evidence, the powers of bishops, tithes, usury, the law of war, heresy, and more. Cases twenty-seven through thirty-six are sometimes referred to as the *Treatise on Marriage* (*Tractatus de matrimonio*), since those ten Cases deal primarily with problems in-

---

[5] C. 36 pr. Gratian's *Decretum* and the other texts of the *Corpus iuris canonici* are cited throughout from the standard edition by Emil Friedberg, 2 vols. (Leipzig: B. Tauchnitz, 1879; repr. Graz: Akademische Druck- u. Verlagsanstalt, 1959). For an explanation of the conventional citation system used here see *Traditio* 11 (1955) 438–39 and "Notes for Contributors" in BMCL 11 (1981) 137–39. My English rendition of Gratian, here and elsewhere, has benefited from the kindness of Judge John T. Noonan, Jr., who allowed me to consult his unpublished translation of the marriage cases (C. 27–36) of the *Decretum* and Book IV of the *Liber Extra*. Errors in translation are, of course, my own.

volving marriage and sexuality. It comes as a shock when reading through the *Treatise on Marriage* to discover that Gratian—or perhaps an early editor— inserted into the middle of Case thirty-three (which deals with marital impotence) a brief minitreatise on penance, the *Tractatus de poenitentia.* Stranger still, the *Treatise on Penance* is subdivided into four Distinctions, on the same pattern as the Distinctions in Part I. Students of Gratian's book have tried for eight hundred years to make sense of this peculiar arrangement.

Finally, Part III is subtitled *Treatise on Consecration (Tractatus de consecratione)* and deals with liturgical matters, the ecclesiastical calendar, and sacramental law. This section resembles Part I in that it is divided into Distinctions—only five of them this time—but, unlike both Parts I and II, includes no *dicta.* This absence of *dicta* suggests that Part III may have been an afterthought, tacked on to the body of the *Decretum* after the bulk of the work had been finished.[6]

Attempts to reconstruct the history of Gratian's work are greatly complicated by the fact that the *Decretum* continued to grow after Gratian had finished it. At various points in its formation, other hands revised the original. An early editor inserted about 100 chapters into the *Decretum* at some point in the early 1140s; these insertions are labeled *paleae* in the early manuscripts of the work. It is probable, but not certain, that other revisers made further alterations in the text.[7]

The *Decretum* soon became a standard canon-law textbook. It was studied as an authoritative exposition of the law in the schools of Bologna soon after Gratian finished it. The *Decretum* was an enormous success, and it became by medieval standards a best-seller all over Europe. Indeed it remained a best-seller for centuries, for it continued to be used as a basic textbook in canon law faculties until relatively recent times.[8] Despite its great success, however, Gratian's book

---

[6] For more detailed analyses of the structure of the *Decretum* see Stickler, *Hist. iuris canonici,* pp. 205–207; Van Hove, *Prolegomena,* pp. 340–42; and LAC, pp. 75–99. On Part III in particular see John H. Van Engen, "Observations on 'De consecratione'," in *Berkeley Proceedings,* pp. 309–20.

[7] Jacqueline Rambaud, "Les *paleae* dans le Décret de Gratien," in *Proceedings of the Second International Congress of Medieval Canon Law,* Boston College, 12–16 August 1963, ed. Stephan Kuttner and J. Joseph Ryan, MIC, Subsidia, vol. 1 (Vatican City: S. Congregatio de Seminariis et Studiorum Universitatibus, 1965; hereafter *Boston Proceedings*), pp. 23–44, and LAC, pp. 100–129; T. Lenherr, "Fehlende 'Paleae' als Zeichen eines überlieferungeschichtlich jüngeren Datums von Dekret-Handschriften," AKKR 151 (1982) 495–507.

[8] Rashdall, *Universities* 1 : 130–32. The popularity of the *Decretum* is attested by the hundreds of surviving manuscripts of the work, many of them with elaborate glosses and commentaries. The indispensable guide to the MS tradition is Stephan Kuttner, *Repertorium der Kanonistik (1140–1234): Prodromus corporis glossarum,* Studi e testi, vol. 71 (Vatican City: Biblioteca Apostolica Vaticana, 1937), supplemented by lists of additional MSS in most volumes of BMCL. On the early printed editions of the work see particularly Erich Will, "Decreti Gratiani incunabula: Beschreibendes Gesamtverzeichnis der Weigendrucke des Gratianischen Dekrets," *Studia Gratiana* 6 (1959) 1–280, and

was apparently never adopted formally and explicitly by Rome, although papal judges and the papal chancery certainly used it as a standard legal reference within a few years of its appearance.[9]

The book's popularity resulted primarily from Gratian's use of dialectical analysis to clarify canonistic regulations and to construct systematic legal doctrines from his raw materials. His conclusions did not always gain universal acceptance and his reasoning was sometimes muddled, as contemporaries were quick to point out, but the *Decretum* provided guidelines for interpreting the canons that were available nowhere else. Even at his most inept moments, Gratian provided twelfth-century canonists with points of departure for alternative and sometimes more successful interpretations of the canonical texts. At his best Gratian masterfully imposed a logical order on an unruly mass of material; he made legal sense out of his assorted texts in a way that none of his predecessors had managed to do.[10]

With the appearance of Gratian's *Decretum*, Church law may be said to have come of age as an independent intellectual discipline. Up to this time there had been no clear line of demarcation between theology and canon law. Hitherto those who had studied and taught theology had treated the canons as moral prescriptions and dealt with them as a kind of applied theology that furnished guidance to confessors, Church administrators, and other authorities in dealing with practical situations. Gratian's work for the first time established canon law as a discipline separate from theology, with its own subject matter and, to a degree, its own methodology as well.[11] In addition, Gratian's work successfully separated canon law from Roman law and established Church law as an independent juristic science. Canonists depended on Roman civil law for many of their basic ideas, conceptual categories, and intellectual tools, but Gratian's *De-*

Aldo Adversi, "Saggio di un catalogo delle edizioni del 'Decretum Gratiani' posteriori al secolo XV," also in *Studia Gratiana* 6 (1959) 281–451.

[9] John T. Noonan, Jr., "Was Gratian Approved at Ferentino?" BMCL, n.s. 6 (1976) 15–27, argued that the *Decretum* received papal approval in 1150 or 1151, but Peter Classen, "Das Decretum Gratiani wurde nicht in Ferentino approbiert," BMCL, n.s. 8 (1978) 38–40, pointed out some serious flaws in Noonan's argument. On papal use of the *Decretum* see Walther Holtzmann, "Die Benutzung Gratians in der päpstlichen Kanzlei im 12. Jahrhundert," *Studia Gratiana* 1 (1953) 325–49; repr. in Holtzmann's *Beiträge zur Reichs- und Papstgeschichte des hohen Mittelalters*, Bonner historische Forschungen, vol. 8 (Bonn: L. Röhrscheid, 1957), pp. 177–96; see also the remarks of Stickler, *Hist. iuris canonici*, pp. 210–12.

[10] See generally Kuttner, *Harmony from Dissonance*, as well as Gabriel Le Bras, "Le triomphe de Gratien," *Studia Gratiana* 1 (1953) 3–14; LAC, pp. 50, 266–68; Ullmann, *Law and Politics*, pp. 165–66; Rashdall, *Universities* 1:127–28; Martin Grabmann, *Die Geschichte der scholastischen Methode*, 2 vols. (Freiburg i/Br.: Herder, 1909–11) 2: 215–17.

[11] Rashdall, *Universities* 1:134–36; A. M. Landgraf, "Diritto canonico e teologia nel secolo XII," *Studia Gratiana* 1 (1953) 371–413; Ghellinck, *Mouvement théologique*, pp. 416–547; Berman, *Law and Revolution*, pp. 165–98.

cretum laid secure foundations for canon law's independence. Canonists continued to model their teaching and doctrines on patterns that originated in civil law and to draw upon civilians as a source; Gratian, however, gave canonists a colorable claim to separate identity as practitioners of an autonomous legal discipline that also had significant theological content, which even the Roman law of the Christian emperors never clearly claimed.[12]

Among the numerous problems Gratian explored was a welter of issues centering on marriage and sexuality. What was desperately needed and what Gratian labored to provide was a satisfactory theory to account for the formation of marriage—what made this couple married and that couple not married? Was it consent? If so, whose consent? The couple's or their family's? Was marriage a sacrament? If so, what did its sacramental character imply for questions of divorce and remarriage? Was sexual intercourse essential to marriage or not? What limits, if any, did the law place on the role of sex in marriage? Was concubinage still tolerable for the laity? Or for the clergy? How did concubinage differ from marriage? How did it differ from fornication, adultery, or prostitution? What rights did a concubine have? Did a concubine's children have a right to share in their father's estate? Was marriage by ravishment a real marriage? How about marriage following seduction? Was a secret marriage a real marriage?

The list of questions is long, and the problems that they address are serious, not only for individuals who were involved in these various situations, but also for the Church and for society at large. The answers that Gratian furnished were critical in the process of reshaping both law and practice during and beyond the twelfth century.

Gratian's treatment of these topics reflected the dynamic social developments of his period. In the late twelfth and early thirteenth centuries, marriage and the family were going through profound changes in Western Europe. Some theologians and spiritual writers were beginning to deal with marriage in terms of the couple's relationship, rather than the relationship between them and their families, and Gratian tried to take account of this changing emphasis.[13] There was debate, too, about the nature of the marital union and about the role that love ought to play in the couple's emotional and legal bonding.[14] The connection between marital love and marital sex was another issue that Gratian

[12] LAC, pp. 119–28, 168–69, 267–68; Rashdall, *Universities* 1:132–34; Smith, *Medieval Law Teachers*, pp. 21–22; Berman, *Law and Revolution*, pp. 199–224; Peter Weimar, "Die legistische Literatur der Glossatorenzeit," in *Handbuch der Quellen und Literatur der neueren europäischen Privatrechtsgeschichte*, vol. 1, *Mittelalter (1100–1500)*, ed. Helmut Coing (Munich: C. H. Beck, 1973), pp. 164–65; Savigny, *Gesch. röm. Rechts* 3:514–16.

[13] Benton, "Clio and Venus," pp. 20–21; Michael M. Sheehan, "Marriage and Family in English Conciliar and Synodal Legislation," in *Essays in Honour of Anton Charles Pegis*, ed. J. Reginald O'Donnell (Toronto: Pontifical Institute of Mediaeval Studies, 1974), pp. 211–12, and "Choice of Marriage Partner," pp. 7–8.

[14] Benton, "Clio and Venus," p. 21; Leclercq, *Monks on Marriage*, pp. 22–23; Müller, *Lehre des hl. Augustinus*, p. 78.

confronted, together with the distinction between marital and nonmarital love as expressed through sexual intercourse.[15]

Marital Sex in Gratian

Gratian's treatment of marital sex was conditioned by his attempt to construct a coherent theory of marriage. Basic to his theory was the proposition that the joining of man and woman in marriage is part of the natural law, ordained by God, and common to all peoples on the earth.[16] Gratian insisted that marriage ought to be monogamous. While he was familiar indirectly with Plato's argument in favor of men having wives in common, Gratian rejected this practice as inappropriate for Christian believers.[17] He also cited with approval early conciliar condemnations of heresies teaching that marriage was unsuitable or improper for Christians or that married persons could not be saved.[18]

Gratian, along with the theologians of his period, grounded his marriage doctrine on St. Augustine's teaching about the three appropriate goals of marriage. Marriage was good because it promoted and, indeed, made possible the virtue of conjugal fidelity; it provided a suitable moral and religious setting for the rearing of children; and it promoted mutual support and love between the married couple, who manifested their attachment to each other through their sexual union. These moral benefits of marriage differentiated it from adultery, fornication, and other nonmarital sexual relationships.[19]

Gratian outlined his theory about marriage formation in the second question of Case twenty-seven in the *Decretum*. An attentive reading of this section makes it clear that Gratian considered marriage came into being, not as the result of a single action, but rather as a two-stage process.[20] He distinguished between the initiation of marriage, when the parties exchanged words signifying consent to marry one another, and the completion or perfection of marriage through sexual consummation.[21] Both steps were necessary in order to create a binding marriage. According to Gratian, marriage is both a spiritual union, achieved through the exchange of consent, and a physical union, achieved

[15] Müller, *Lehre des hl. Augustinus*, pp. 66–67, 77, 82–83; Luscombe, *School of Peter Abelard*, p. 176; Gérard Fransen, "La formation du lien matrimonial au moyen âge," RDC 21 (1971) 114.

[16] D. 1 c. 7.

[17] D. 8 pr. and c. 1. For the history and transmission of this idea see Stephan Kuttner, "Gratian and Plato," in *Church and Government in the Middle Ages: Essays Presented to C. R. Cheney on His 70th Birthday*, ed. C. N. L. Brooke et al. (Cambridge: At the University Press, 1976), pp. 93–118.

[18] D. 30 c. 12; D. 31 c. 8–9.

[19] C. 32 q. 1 d.p.c. 10 and c. 11. For the influence of Augustine's marriage doctrine on twelfth-century theologians see Leclercq, *Monks on Marriage*, p. 12.

[20] John A. Alesandro, *Gratian's Notion of Marital Consummation* (Rome: Officium libri catholici, 1971), p. 1.

[21] C. 27 q. 2 d.p.c. 2, d.p.c. 29, d.p.c. 45; Alesandro, *Gratian's Notion*, p. 1.

through sexual intercourse. Coitus without consent to marry is no marriage; nor is an exchange of consent that is not followed by intercourse.[22] Gratian employed the dialectical method to reconcile two approaches to the definition of marriage that he found in his sources, namely the consensual theory and the coital theory. As Gratian explained matters, these two theories were not contradictory; rather, they complemented one another. Each described one facet and one stage in the process of creating a marital union, and neither was sufficient without the other.[23]

Although Gratian attempted to harmonize the conflict between consensual and coital theories, C. 27 q. 2 clearly makes consummation the key to marriage formation. Consummation transformed the union into a "sacrament" and hence made it indissoluble.[24] A marriage that was simply initiated but not consummated lacked the binding power of a consummated union. A consummated marriage, for example, could not be dissolved in order to enter religion, but an unconsummated union could be sundered for this purpose.[25] Likewise consummation created an obligation between the partners to pay one another the marital debt upon demand, whereas there was no such obligation between a couple joined in a merely consensual union.[26] Moreover, if one partner proved incapable of intercourse and hence could not consummate the marriage, the union could be dissolved and the partners (or at least the one who was not sexually incapacitated) could remarry. But if the marriage had been consummated by even a single act of sexual intercourse, then it remained binding even if one partner subsequently became impotent.[27] In addition bigamy was only possible if the bigamist was a party to a previously consummated first marriage. If the first union had been contracted by consent but never completed by sexual intercourse, then a second union by either party was not punishable as bigamy.[28]

Gratian thus opted for what came to be called the "Italian solution" to the problem of the relative importance of marital consummation and consent. In so doing he rejected the alternative "French solution," which held that prior consent to a first union, whether consummated or not, would invalidate any subsequent marriage so long as both parties to the first union remained alive.[29] Fi-

---

[22] C. 27 q. 2 d.p.c. 34; Bailey, *Sexual Relation*, p. 125.

[23] Alesandro, *Gratian's Notion*, pp. 79–81, compares Gratian's marriage theory with Roman law consent theory.

[24] C. 27 q. 2 c. 33–34, d.p.c. 34, and d.p.c. 39; Alesandro, *Gratian's Notion*, p. 89; Rudolf Weigand, "Das Scheidungsproblem in der mittelalterlichen Kanonistik," *Theologische Quartalschrift* 151 (1971) 53.

[25] C. 27 q. 2 c. 19–26 and d.p.c. 26.

[26] C. 27 q. 2 d.p.c. 18; Pietro Vaccari, "La tradizione canonica del 'debitum' coniugale e la posizione di Graziano," *Studia Gratiana* 1 (1953) 545–47.

[27] C. 27 q. 2 d.p.c. 28, c. 29, and d.p.c. 29.

[28] C. 27 q. 2 c. 30–32 and d.p.c. 32. Similarly, a woman who consented to marry one man, but then married another, was not guilty of adultery: C. 34 q. 2 c. 5; Alesandro, *Gratian's Notion*, p. 88.

[29] Alesandro, *Gratian's Notion*, p. 61; Weigand, "Scheidungsproblem," p. 53.

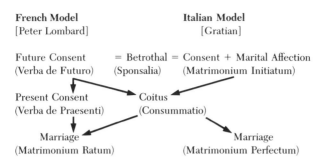

Figure 6.1.   Theories of marriage formation

nally, Gratian cited with approval a number of venerable authorities who had expounded the coital theory of marriage and indicated his agreement with their views.[30]

Gratian deliberately framed his theory of marriage in the particular form described here. His sources did not force him to adopt this construction, for he had readily available in Ivo's *Decretum* authorities who supported quite different views. Nor was it likely that oversight or indifference led him to omit from his discussion of marriage theory the distinction between present consent and future consent to marriage. That distinction originated apparently with Peter Abelard and was current in theological circles when Gratian wrote his book.[31] Parisian theologians were soon to adopt the present/future consent distinction as the cornerstone of their marriage theory, since it complemented their preference for emphasizing the spiritual, as opposed to the carnal, dimensions of marriage.[32]

Gratian deliberately ignored that model and, instead, assigned to physical consummation a primary role in marriage formation. His reasons for that choice are not altogether clear. Both oral agreements and sexual intercourse can present difficulties of proof. Agreements are often witnessed, while intercourse usually is not. On the other hand, it may well be easier to corroborate an alleged act of consummation by circumstantial evidence than it is to demonstrate that an agreement has been made, if there are no witnesses and the testimony of the parties conflicts. It was bound to be even more difficult to discover unequivocal proof in disputed cases as to whether consent, if given at all, had been cast in the present or the future tense. Although he made no mention of

[30] C. 27 q. 2 c. 16–18. On the origin and transmission of these canons see Jean Gaudemet, "Recherches sur les origines historiques de la faculté de rompre le mariage non consommé," in *Salamanca Proceedings*, pp. 326–31. Although sexual intercourse was necessary for consummation, sexual union under some circumstances might not consummate the marriage; see Alesandro, *Gratian's Notion*, pp. 87–88.

[31] Mullenders, *Mariage présumé*, p. 13.

[32] John T. Noonan, "Power to Choose," *Viator* 4 (1973) 424–25, 428; Georges Duby, "Le mariage dans la société du haut moyen âge." in *Il matrimonio nella società altomedievale* 1:25–26.

the problem of evidence in his discussion of marriage in C. 27 q. 2, Gratian's decision to place primary emphasis in his marriage theory on the tangible physical act of intercourse may have reflected concern with this basic juridical problem.

That Gratian gave primary emphasis to consummation in constructing his marriage formation theory did not mean that he ignored or depreciated the importance of consent. On the contrary, consent was an essential element of his definition of marriage, and he discussed consent issues at length. While he maintained that marital consent must be free and uncoerced,[33] Gratian recognized certain limits on the free choice of a marriage partner. First, both parties must be of an age where they could give meaningful consent; at a minimum this meant that both parties must have attained the age of seven before their consent could be considered binding.[34] Second, Christians could not marry infidels or Jews.[35] Third, those bound to observe celibacy could not marry anyone at all.[36] Fourth, no one could marry a person to whom s/he was related within seven degrees of kinship by blood or by a fictive relationship.[37]

Gratian left open the question of whether the consent of the parents was necessary for a binding marriage. Although he seems to have assumed that families would normally play an important role in the choice of marriage partners, he stopped short of making their consent essential to marriage.[38] He also failed to adopt a firm position on the question of whether previous sexual intercourse created a bar to marriage. Gratian seems to have inclined toward the belief that intercourse created some type of legal bond between the partners, but he stopped short of holding that such a relationship would prevent subsequent marriage between them.[39] He also implied that under some circumstances the creation of marriage might be made conditional upon some event subsequent to the exchange of consent. If the condition were not fulfilled, there was no marriage.[40]

Matrimony, in Gratian's eyes, created a social bond between the parties, and the constituent elements of that bond were consent and consummation.[41] He

---

[33] C. 31 q. 2 c. 1–4. Gratian explicitly affirmed his own conclusion at d.p.c. 4 : "His auctoritatibus evidenter ostenditur, quod nisi libera voluntate nulla est copulanda alicui."

[34] C. 30 q. 2 pr.; W. Onclin, "L'âge requis pour le mariage dans la doctrine canonique médiévale, in *Boston Proceedings*, pp. 237–40.

[35] C. 28 q. 1 d.a.c. 15 and c. 15–17.

[36] C. 27 q. 1 d.p.c. 43.

[37] C. 30 q. 1 d.a.c. 1; C. 35 q. 1 d.p.c. 1; C. 35 q. 2 & 3 d.a.c. 1, d.p.c. 21, and d.p.c. 22. On Gratian's method of calculating the degrees of relationship see Champeaux, "Jus sanguinis," pp. 262–88.

[38] C. 36 q. 2 c. 7–11; note also the *palaea* c. 11; Sheehan, "Choice of Marriage Partner," p. 12.

[39] C. 31 q. 1 d.p.c. 2 and d.p.c. 7; Esmein, *Mariage* 1 : 209–10.

[40] C. 28 q. 1 d.p.c. 17; cf. C. 32 q. 8 pr. On the development of conditional marriage see Weigand, *Bedingte Eheschliessung*, esp. pp. 414–23.

[41] The phrase "social bond" (*sociale vinculum*) is Augustine's: C. 32 q. 7 c. 27.

said nothing explicit about love as an essential element of marriage, although at one point he paraphrased a statement of St. Augustine to the effect that marriage was a school for love; this may well imply that Gratian expected that love could grow out of marriage, rather than that love ought to precede the marital relationship and form an intrinsic element of it.[42] Although Gratian was certainly no spokesman for courtly love ideas, his views in some respects paralleled notions about romantic love propounded by the poets writing during the period when Gratian composed his book. Gratian's insistence on freedom of choice in selecting marriage partners and his emphasis upon the notion of marital affection were notions compatible with those championed by the love poets of his age.[43] By marital affection—a term he borrowed from Roman law, but whose meaning underwent significant change in his text—Gratian seems to have understood, as Roman jurists had done, a habitual attitude of respect, deference, and consideration toward one's spouse that differentiated a marital relationship from casual cohabitation. But in addition, Gratian's use of the phrase is tinged with the sense of an emotional bond between the spouses, a mutual attachment and regard for the well-being of one another that seems closely related to the qualities poets invoked in their descriptions of love.[44]

Gratian's discussion of the marital relationship repeatedly emphasized its personal nature.[45] Couples contracted marriage by exchanging consent and consummating it through sexual intercourse, both decidedly personal matters. It was consistent with this personalist approach that Gratian was prepared, although reluctantly, to accept informal, clandestine marriages as valid. He was certainly not enthusiastic about clandestine unions and in one passage he labeled them void,[46] but elsewhere he insisted that once entered into they were just as valid and indissoluble as formal, public marriages.[47]

Gratian regarded intercourse as an essential element of marriage formation. Nevertheless, he believed that marital sex should be strictly circumscribed, al-

[42] C. 35 q. 1 c. un. In citing Augustine, Gratian represents him as referring to marriage as "quoddam seminarium karitatis," whereas Augustine had actually called it a "seminarium civitatis." The reading "civitatis" occurs also in Ivo, *Decretum* 8.39 (= *Panormia* 7.52), in PL 161:592. This discrepancy in readings was noted by the *correctores Romani*. See also Rudolf Weigand, "Liebe und Ehe bei den Dekretisten des 12. Jahrhunderts," in *Love and Marriage in the Twelfth Century*, pp. 41–42, 49, 51.

[43] D. 34 d.p.c. 3; C. 28 q. 1 d.p.c. 17; C. 32 q. 2 d.a.c. 6; C. 32 q. 5 d.p.c. 16; see also the important study by John T. Noonan, Jr., "Marital Affection in the Canonists," *Studia Gratiana* 12 (1967) 479–509.

[44] Duby, "Mariage," p. 37.

[45] But cf. Raymond G. Decker, "Institutional Authority versus Personal Responsibility in the Marriage Sections of Gratian's *A Concordance of Discordant Canons*," *Jurist* 32 (1972) 53.

[46] C. 30 q. 5 c. 6 and d.p.c. 6.

[47] C. 28 q. 1 d.p.c. 17 and C. 30 q. 5 d.a.c. 10; Alesandro, *Gratian's Notion*, p. 85; Noonan, "Power to Choose," p. 430; Decker, "Institutional Authority," pp. 56–57, 61;

though his treatment of the role of sex was less restrictive than that of many earlier authorities. In explaining the rationale behind earlier regulations that had forbidden women to enter the church immediately after childbirth, for example, Gratian cited a passage ascribed to Pope Gregory I that grounded the prohibition on the proposition that the pains of childbirth were retribution for the pleasure experienced in sexual intercourse. This passage argued that it was necessary for the new mother to be purified of the ritual pollution resulting from sexual pleasure prior to entering a sacred place. Gratian held, however, that these purity regulations were no longer in force and that they had never been part of the natural law.[48]

Gratian agreed with St. Augustine that sex must have been different in paradise than it is now. Sexual intercourse in Eden had taken place without heat; the marriage bed was then unstained by sin, and women gave birth without pain. With the first sin, however, all this changed. Sex could no longer be experienced without the itch of passion and the impurity that lust entails. Yet marriage must not on this account be condemned, Gratian cautioned, because sensual pleasure should play only a subordinate role in marital relationships.[49] The proper function of marital sex was for procreation, according to Gratian. Persons who married for sexual enjoyment he described as fornicators, a label that he justified with citations from St. Jerome and St. Augustine.[50] Although they may have been fornicators in spirit, they were married nonetheless, even if they married for unworthy and unacceptable reasons.[51] Gratian further qualified his theory about the motivations underlying marriage by granting that Christians could legitimately marry in order to avoid temptations to commit fornication or adultery.[52] In summary, Gratian felt that Christians ought to marry for a positive reason, namely in order to reproduce; they might marry for a negative reason, namely in order to avoid sexual temptations. But they should not marry primarily for sexual passion and physical pleasure.

Marital sex was a serious matter for Gratian. It must not be excessive in frequency, must not involve "extraordinary voluptuousness," or the "whorish pleasures" that St. Jerome condemned.[53] Above all, marital sex must not be

---

Plöchl, *Eherecht*, p. 46. Gratian's ambiguity about status of illegal clandestine marriages remained a problem for canonists up to the Council of Trent; Esmein, *Mariage* 1: 178–79. On the enormous practical problems that clandestine unions created see esp. Sir Frederick Pollock and Frederic William Maitland, *The History of English Law before the Time of Edward I*, 2 vols., 2d ed. (Cambridge: At the University Press, 1898, repr. 1968) 2:368–70, 385.

[48] D. 5 d.a.c. 1 and c. 2.
[49] C. 32 q. 2 d.p.c. 2.
[50] C. 32 q. 2 d.p.c. 1 and c. 2; C. 32 q. 4 c. 7.
[51] C. 32 q. 2 d.p.c. 5.
[52] C. 32 q. 2 d.p.c. 2 and c. 3.
[53] C. 32 q. 4 c. 5, 12, 14.

"unnatural," which Gratian apparently took to mean anal copulation and perhaps oral sex as well.[54] Unnatural sex in marriage was worse than adultery or fornication, according to the sources that Gratian cited.[55] His objection was not primarily that anal and oral sex were contraceptive; rather he reprobated these types of intercourse because they were an inappropriate use of the sex organs, and that, he believed, ran counter to natural law. Intercourse in a "natural" fashion but with contraceptive intent Gratian classed as a very slight sin, a moral blemish, much like such other *minuta peccata* as excessive talking, eating after one's hunger was sated, registering annoyance at an importunate beggar, or oversleeping and as a result being late for divine services.[56]

Much of Gratian's discussion of marital sex was based upon his concept of marital debt, that is the duty of husbands and wives to make themselves available for intercourse upon their spouse's request. Sexual intercourse in marriage was thus both a right and an obligation. The marital debt idea rested ultimately upon St. Paul's demand (1 Cor. 7:3–4) that husbands and wives pay each other what is due and Paul's further observation that the husband had power over his wife's body, just as the wife had power over her husband's. The right of one spouse to demand the conjugal debt and the obligation of the other to comply with the demand led Gratian to construct an elaborate theory of marital obligations. The conjugal debt arose, according to Gratian, at the moment when the marriage was consummated. Prior to that time there was no sexual obligation between the parties, and the exchange of marital consent by itself did not create a duty to consummate the union. Once an act of intercourse had taken place, however, a mutual obligation of sexual service sprang into being; thenceforth the spouses were bound to render sexual services upon demand.[57] The obligation was absolute: it made no difference, at least in principle, where or when the demand was made; the spouse from whom the debt was required had to comply.

[54] C. 32 1. q. 7 d.p.c. 10 and c. 11.

[55] C. 32 q. 7 c. 12–14.

[56] D. 25 d.p.c. 3 § 7. Although at C. 32 q. 2 c. 7 he quoted St. Augustine, *De nupt. et concup.* 1.15.17 (CSEL 42:230) to the effect that contraceptive intercourse is the moral equivalent of adultery, Gratian himself explicitly rejected this view at C. 32 q. 2 d.p.c. 5: "Sic econtrario datur intelligi de his qui coniugali affectu sibi copulantur, quod etsi non causa procreandorum filiorum, sed explendae libidinis conveniunt, non ideo fornicarii, sed coniunges appellantur." He reaffirmed this position once more at C. 32 q. 2 d.p.c. 16. Noonan, *Contraception,* p. 174, seems to imply that Gratian adopted Augustine's view, but this contention rests on the rubric that summarizes Augustine's text. Gratian's rubrics, however, do not necessarily reflect his own views, and in this case he clearly differed from Augustine's position.

[57] Thus C. 27 q. 2 d.p.c. 26 and d.p.c. 28; C. 32 q. 2 d.p.c. 2; C. 33 q. 5 d.p.c. 11; Elizabeth Makowski, "The Conjugal Debt and Medieval Canon Law," JMH 3 (1977) 99–114; Alesandro, *Gratian's Notion,* p. 88; Vaccari, "Tradizione canonica," pp. 533–47.

The marital debt was one area in which Gratian not only conceded but absolutely insisted that men and women enjoyed equal rights before the law. The wife had every bit as much right to demand sexual dues from her husband as he did from her. This parity in respect to the conjugal debt was Gratian's most emphatic venture in the direction of a doctrine of equality between the sexes.[58]

Gratian's treatment of abstinence from marital sex was conditioned by his ideas about the marital debt. Although he reproduced some earlier statements from the penitentials in favor of abstinence from marital sex during Lent and other penitential seasons, as well as prescriptions about sexual abstinence during menstruation, pregnancy, and lactation, his discussion of these texts made it clear that he considered them of secondary importance.[59] True, spouses should not demand payment of the marital debt during the periods of prescribed abstinence, but if one spouse made the demand, then the other was obliged to comply. Gratian thus subordinated periodic cycles of marital abstinence to the requirements of the conjugal debt and, whereas in the penitentials the abstinence regulations appeared as absolute commands, for Gratian they were a secondary issue in the sex life of married persons.

The theme of reciprocal sexual obligations extended into Gratian's discussion of voluntary separation in order to enter religion. His whole discussion of this matter centered on the proposition that such a separation required mutual consent. The husband who made a vow of continence without his wife's consent gave her in effect a license to commit adultery, and this he had no right to do.[60] The husband shared the guilt that resulted from his wife's misconduct and this would offset any virtue he might attain through ascetic observances.[61]

Divorce and Remarriage in the *Decretum* of Gratian

Gratian's treatment of divorce and remarriage reflected the novel concept of marriage that distinguished his work from that of his predecessors. Earlier writ-

[58] Both marital consent and marital affection involved a basic equality of the sexes in Gratian's thought, but the equality theme, although plainly evident, was not nearly so forcefully presented in those contexts as it was with reference to the conjugal debt. See also the remarks of Noonan, "Power to Choose," pp. 431–34. Gratian strictly limited the notion of equality between men and women in other contexts and, aside from the conjugal debt, marital consent, and marital affection, he considered the wife subordinate to her husband; C. 33 q. 5 d.p.c. 11 and d.p.c. 20.

[59] Gratian's principal discussion of periodic sexual abstinence occurs at C. 33 q. 4, where he cited authorities to support abstinence during Lent, Advent, Eastertide, Christmastide (c. 8–11), on feast days (c. 2–4), fast days (c. 1, 3, 7), and while performing penance. Prohibitions of intercourse during menstruation, pregnancy, and lactation are found in D. 5 c. 4 and *palea post* c. 4. But Gratian concluded his treatment of these matters by declaring at C. 33 q. 4 d.p.c. 11: "Hec autem servanda sunt, si uxor consensum adhibere voluerit; ceterum sine eius consensu nec causa orationis continentia servari debet." He then cited St. Augustine (c. 12) and the Council of Arles (c. 13) in support of this conclusion.

[60] C. 27 q. 2 c. 24; C. 33 q. 5 c. 1.

[61] C. 33 q. 5 c. 1–6, 11, and esp. d.p.c. 11 and d.p.c. 20.

ers had identified adultery, consanguinity, affinity, and sexual incapacity as the principal grounds on which marriage might be held invalid. Gratian's emphasis was quite different, and the differences flowed from his notions about the marriage bond. Nonconsummated marriages, in his view, were incomplete and hence dissoluble by mutual consent of the parties. The union that the couple had created solely by consent they could also dissolve by consent, provided that they had adequate reason for doing so, such as a desire to enter religion.[62] Further, even a consummated marriage, according to Gratian, might be terminated or held invalid if there were serious defects of consent. A marriage entered into under a misapprehension might be held null, Gratian declared, if the mistake was basic and serious. In order to justify a nullity ruling it was not sufficient to show, for example, that one had married a husband whom one thought rich and who turned out to be bankrupt. Even if a man married a woman whom he believed to be a chaste and pious virgin and then discovered that his bride had been a prostitute, this did not entitle him to be freed from the union, according to Gratian. On the other hand, if a man consummated his marriage with one woman (say, Jane) while believing her to be someone else (perhaps Joan), the marriage was invalid and the parties were free to remarry.[63] Marital consent given by a person who was under the minimum age for marriage or who was insane was likewise not binding.[64]

Gratian was also prepared to countenance divorce where one party proved to be sexually impotent, since in that situation the marriage could not be perfected by sexual union.[65] He was reluctant, however, to sanction divorce when the parties were related within the forbidden degrees of kinship, either by consanguinity or affinity, especially if the relationship was unknown or had been concealed by one party at the time of the marriage. In these situations Gratian believed that the illegal marriage should be remedied by the mechanism of dispensation; the marital defect ought to be healed by the exercise of the Church's power to permit exceptions to its own laws. Consanguinity and affinity regulations, Gratian maintained, were products of ecclesiastical legislation, not of divine or natural law. Hence the Church retained the power to waive these provisions when necessary in order to preserve marriages, and should exercise that power instead of dissolving marriages.[66] Divorces could be permitted on grounds of consanguinity or affinity, Gratian concluded, but the Church should authorize them only rarely.

Gratian's treatment of marriages between Christians and heretics was ambiguous. On the one hand he held that where a heretic had concealed his aberrant beliefs and the Catholic party had married him under the mistaken apprehension that he was a good Catholic, then divorce might be permitted, essentially

[62] C. 33 q. 5 d.p.c. 11 and d.p.c. 20.

[63] C. 29 q. 1 pr.

[64] C. 30 q. 2 pr.

[65] C. 33 q. 1 d.p.c. 3.

[66] C. 35 q. 8 pr. and q. 9 d.p.c. 2; more generally see C. 1 q. 7 d.p.c. 5 and c. 14–17, as well as d.p.c. 22.

because the deception amounted to fraud and hence vitiated good faith consent.[67] On the other hand when two pagans married and one of them subsequently converted to Christianity, while the other remained pagan, the situation was more complicated. Baptism, as St. Ambrose had observed, wipes out sins; it does not abolish marriages.[68] But Gregory the Great had ruled that if the pagan party to a mixed marriage railed against the Christian faith, then the marriage might be dissolved for that reason.[69] Gratian attempted to harmonize this conflict of authorities by distinguishing between situations in which the non-Christian party deserted the Christian spouse and situations in which the pair continued to cohabit. If the non-Christian walked out, then Gratian would allow the Christian to remarry. If they remained together, however, he would allow the Christian party to obtain a separation in order to secure unhindered freedom to practice his religion, but he would not countenance remarriage during the lifetime of the other partner.[70]

Many early authorities, as Gratian well knew, had allowed divorce on grounds of adultery,[71] but Gratian hedged this practice about with restrictive qualifications. When a woman had been ravished, for example, Gratian held that this forced coupling was in no sense adultery and that no divorce action could be grounded on such an incident.[72] Further, he invoked what we now call the clean hands doctrine in divorce actions based on adultery: a husband who was guilty of adultery himself could not prefer adultery charges against his unfaithful wife.[73] But even where he would allow separation on grounds of adultery, Gratian adamantly held that remarriage of either party should be disallowed. Those who divorced because of adultery by the other party must remain unmarried so long as the first spouse lived.[74] Indeed, Gratian's construction of the law of divorce on grounds of adultery placed the innocent party in a highly unenviable situation: once a husband, for example, became aware of his wife's adultery, he must either divorce her or at least refrain from further sexual intercourse with her until she repented and performed suitable penance. If he divorced her, he must remain unmarried so long as she lived; if he remained married to her, further sexual relations were contingent upon her reform. In any case the innocent party suffered the indefinite loss of sexual rights as a result of the extramarital adventures of his (or her) wandering spouse.[75]

---

[67] C. 29 q. 1 pr.

[68] D. 26 c. 4; paraphrased in C. 28 q. 2 c. 1.

[69] C. 28 q. 2 c. 2. This "Pauline privilege" (as it was later called) rested upon 1 Cor. 7:10–16.

[70] C. 28 q. 2 d.p.c. 2.

[71] C. 32 q. 5 c. 18–22; C. 32 q. 7 c. 10.

[72] C. 32 q. 5 d.p.c. 16.

[73] C. 32 q. 6 c. 1 and d.p.c. 5; Decker, "Institutional Authority," pp. 54–55.

[74] C. 27 q. 2 d.p.c. 32; C. 30 q. 5 c. 4; C. 32 q. 7 c. 1–10, d.p.c. 16, and d.p.c. 18.

[75] C. 32 q. 1 d.p.c. 10.

Gratian relied on the Council of Gangra as his authority for condemning informal divorce and separation.[76] These fourth-century rulings also furnished him with a basis for asserting that the Church forbade child abandonment and required that absent or separated parents furnish adequate support for their children.[77]

Finally, on the issue of remarriage following the death of a first spouse, Gratian advised that, although it would be better for widows and widowers to live a life of continence, second and subsequent marriages were not merely allowed by the Church's law, but were advisable if there were any danger that the surviving spouse might lapse into fornication.[78]

Gratian on Concubinage

In dealing with this subject Gratian found a great deal of ambivalence among his authorities. Concubinage among the laity continued to be common in Gratian's time and some perfectly respectable sources had held that Christian men were entitled to take a concubine in place of a wife, although all of them condemned men who had more than one concubine at a time or who kept a concubine as well as a wife.[79] But equally respectable authorities, and more of them, had condemned concubinage as fornication and urged Christians either to terminate such relationships or to regularize them by marrying their concubines.[80]

Gratian dealt with concubinage as a type of informal marriage, a de facto union that differed from fornication, say, with a harlot, because the concubine and her lover were bound together by marital affection.[81] Thus Gratian could reconcile the opposing teachings of his authorities even though secular law refused to grant union with a concubine the status of a formal marriage.[82] In this way, Gratian not only harmonized his sources, but he also treated concubinage relationships as permanent and binding unions so far as the Church's courts were concerned.

Nonmarital Sex in Gratian

Gratian considered the sex urge a defect, an illness or weakness of the human mind and body.[83] Voluntary yielding to sexual feelings he deemed culpable, but involuntary sexual experiences, such as wet dreams, involved no offense, al-

[76] D. 30 c. 3.

[77] D. 30 c. 14; Schimmelpfennig, "Ex fornicatione nati," p. 31.

[78] C. 31 q. 1 c. 10–13 and d.p.c. 10; C. 32 q. 4 c. 1; Rosambert, *Veuve*, pp. 118–19.

[79] D. 34 c. 4–5.

[80] D. 34 c. 6; C. 32 q. 2 c. 5, 11–12; C. 32 q. 4 c. 9.

[81] D. 34 d.p.c. 3; Plöchl, *Eherecht*, p. 50; but cf. Freisen, *Geschichte*, p. 65.

[82] C. 28 q. 1 d.p.c. 17; Plöchl, *Eherecht*, p. 51; Esmein, *Mariage* 2:113–14; Caselli, "Concubina pro uxore," pp. 218–20.

[83] C. 15 q. 1 pr. and d.p.c. 2.

though they might constitute a source of pollution.[84] Intercourse, whether in marriage or not, also produced ritual pollution, as Gratian knew from the *Responsa Gregorii*. Any experience that led to orgasm produced pollution and required cleansing before the person could receive the eucharist or enter a church.[85] Christians were obliged to keep their sexual impulses under control and to suppress any sexual promptings they might feel outside of the marriage bed. It behooved all Christians to maintain virgin minds in chaste bodies.[86] The rejection of sexual temptation was particularly important for women, who were even more susceptible to sexual corruption than were men, according to Gratian, and who could be led astray not only by overt sexual advances, but even by social gestures such as talking, kissing, and embracing.[87]

Sexual intercourse meant yielding to human frailty—it was always a sign of moral weakness. Gratian, like many of his contemporaries, had learned this lesson from patristic authorities and writers on penance. He had also learned that any kind of sexual play outside of marriage, no matter how trivial, was both sinful and criminal.[88]

Gratian's typology of sex offenses was conventional. The basic category was fornication, which included any type of intercourse save for that between husband and wife.[89] Adultery was an especially serious type of fornication in which a married person had sexual relations with someone other than his or her legitimate spouse.[90] Gratian was aware that his sources sometimes used both "fornication" and "adultery" metaphorically to refer to deviations from the Christian faith and that they often used these terms figuratively to describe sexual temptations and fantasies.[91] Gratian himself, however, generally used these terms carefully and literally. He categorized both adultery and fornication as major offenses against the Church's law and considered both of them punishable by the courts as crimes.[92] He outlined in the *Decretum* a hierarchical scale of sex crimes in which simple fornication (which some called "average incontinence") ranked as the basic offense, followed in order of increasing seriousness by adultery, incest, and unnatural sex.[93]

[84] D. 6 c. 1–3 and d.p.c. 3.
[85] C. 33 q. 4 c. 7.
[86] C. 32 q. 5 c. 11–12.
[87] C. 27 q. 1 c. 4.
[88] C. 32 q. 4 c. 4, 11; C. 32 q. 5 c. 15; D. 1 de pen. c. 12.
[89] C. 36 q. 1 d.p.c. 2; Esmein, *Mariage* 2 : 104.
[90] C. 36 q. 1 d.p.c. 2.
[91] C. 28 q. 1 c. 5; C. 32 q. 5 c. 13; C. 32 q. 7 c. 15.
[92] D. 25 d.p.c. 3; C. 32 q. 7 c. 16.
[93] C. 32 q. 7 d.p.c. 10 and c. 11. For "average incontinence" see Guibert, *Self and Society* 3.4, trans. Benton, p. 151. On the hierarchy of sex offenses see J. A. Brundage, "Carnal Delight: Canonistic Theories of Sexuality," in *Salamanca Proceedings*, pp. 361–85.

FORNICATION

Fornication, the commonest and most basic sex crime in Gratian's scheme, was a serious offense, comparable to perjury and even to some types of homicide.[94] Fornication, Gratian asserted, was prohibited by the Scriptures and, contrary to popular belief, could not take place under any circumstances without guilt, so long as the offender knew what he or she was doing.[95] More serious than fornication was adultery.[96] Like fornication, adultery was excused only by ignorance: it was a legitimate defense to an adultery charge to plead that the offender believed that the other woman was his wife.[97] It was not an acceptable defense, however, for the offender to plead that he had slept with a woman other than his wife only in order to beget children.[98] A procreative intention did not excuse the crime.

ADULTERY

Just as men and women were equally bound by their conjugal duties, Gratian considered that each bore equal guilt if he or she strayed into adultery. Since adultery by a man was just as much a crime as adultery by a woman, the punishments for both should be the same.[99] When the innocent partner became aware of the spouse's infidelity, he or she was obliged to refuse further marital relations, unless or until the unfaithful one broke off the outside relationship and did penance for it.[100]

Gratian noted that earlier writers had differed on the question of whether adultery constituted a bar to subsequent marriage between the participants. Some authorities had claimed that an adulterous couple could never marry each other,[101] others ruled that an adulterer could marry his mistress provided that he had done penance and that the former spouse was dead.[102] As usual, Gratian attempted to resolve the conflict of authorities by distinguishing different types of situations. If the adulterer and adulteress had plotted the death of the first spouse, or if they had agreed during the lifetime of the first spouse that they would marry once the spouse was dead, then they should not be allowed to wed. If, however, there had been no prior agreement and no involvement in

---

[94] C. 3 q. 11 d.p.c. 3.

[95] C. 34 q. 2 d.p.c. 7; C. 32 q. 4 d.p.c. 10; C. 14 q. 6 c. 4; C. 27 q. 1 c. 20.

[96] C. 32 q. 5 d.p.c. 14 and c. 15–16; Alesandro, *Gratian's Notion*, p. 88.

[97] C. 34 q. 2 c. 6.

[98] C. 32 q. 7 c. 27.

[99] C. 32 q. 5 d.p.c. 22 and q. 6 pr., as well as C. 32 q. 4 c. 4; C. 32 q. 5 c. 23; and C. 32 q. 6 c. 4–5.

[100] C. 22 q. 4 c. 21; C. 32 q. 1 c. 4–8 and d.p.c. 10.

[101] C. 31 q. 1 c. 1 and 3.

[102] C. 31 q. 1 c. 2.

the first spouse's death, then the adulterous pair might marry, provided they first did penance for their offense.[103]

Gratian strongly disapproved of private vengeance for adultery and cited several authorities who had forbidden Christian men to slay their unfaithful wives. Punishment of adultery was the business of public authority, not a private right to be exercised by aggrieved husbands—it would be better for a man to commit bigamy, according to St. Augustine, than to slay his unfaithful spouse.[104] Gratian stood firmly by his authorities in rejecting self-help doctrines rooted in both Roman and Germanic law.

The status of the children of an adulterous union posed difficulties. Again Gratian found conflicts among his sources: some had held that the sins of the parents should not be visited upon the children; others contended that the offspring of adultery should be excluded from positions of honor and especially from the priesthood. After setting forth numerous authorities on both sides of the issue, Gratian came down on the side of those who taught that adultery created an irregularity in the offspring that precluded their ordination.[105] Here again, as with consanguineous marriage, Gratian relied upon the power of dispensation to temper the punishment that strict law required.[106]

PROSTITUTION

Gratian adhered to patristic precedent in his treatment of prostitution. He defined prostitution through a citation from St. Jerome, who had emphasized the notion that the essence of prostitution lay in promiscuity, rather than in the mercenary nature of the transaction between the harlot and her client.[107] Thus a woman who took many lovers was a prostitute, whether she took money for her favors or not. Financial gain was a secondary consideration in Gratian's treatment of the topic.

Although he quoted St. Augustine's statement that it was an offense either to be a prostitute or to patronize one of them, Gratian was more keenly concerned with other aspects of the subject, especially questions about marriage to prostitutes.[108] While he cited authorities who either strongly discouraged marriage to a prostitute or flatly forbade it, Gratian was prepared to distinguish between different situations. It is one thing, he reasoned, to marry a harlot with the intention of profiting from her continued practice of her trade. Certainly this should be discouraged. Likewise a married man ought to repudiate his wife if

[103] C. 31 q. 1 d.p.c. 2 and d.p.c. 3, as well as c. 4–5; Esmein, *Mariage* 1:209–10; Gottlob, "Ehebruch," p. 347.

[104] C. 23 q. 5 c. 40; C. 33 q. 2 c. 9; Bennecke, *Strafrechtliche Lehre von Ehebruch*, p. 63.

[105] D. 56 c. 3–8, 10, and d.p.c. 13; Schimmelpfennig, "Ex fornicatione nati," pp. 22–23.

[106] D. 50 d.p.c. 36; D. 56 d.p.c. 1 and d.p.c. 13.

[107] D. 34 c. 16; Bloch, *Prostitution* 1:19.

[108] C. 32 q. 1 d.a.c. 1 and d.p.c. 10.

she made herself available to other men, since he could not trust her fidelity, which was one of the essential goods of marriage.[109] It was quite another matter, however, for a Christian man to marry a prostitute who promised to reform and to give up her life of sin. Such a marriage ought not be forbidden, Gratian believed; indeed it might be considered praiseworthy to rescue a harlot from moral turpitude.[110] But the task of rescuing strumpets, he warned, should be undertaken warily, for such women find it difficult to tear themselves away from evil habits and associates. For this reason, Gratian argued, men who married former prostitutes, praiseworthy as their actions might be, should not subsequently be ordained, lest the former activities of their wives dishonor the sacred dignity of the clergy.[111]

Practicing prostitutes, according to Gratian's authorities, were tainted with *infamia* and thus suffered all the legal disabilities attached to that condition.[112] The children of prostitutes, however, should not be punished for the sins of their mothers,[113] although they were ineligible for ordination.[114]

RAPE AND ABDUCTION

Raptus meant for Gratian either abduction of a girl without her parents' consent (even if she was a willing party to the abduction) or intercourse with her against her will.[115] He thus distinguished between rape and other kinds of sex crimes on the basis of the violence employed against the persons who had rightful control over a woman's sexual relations, namely either the woman herself or her family.[116] By his willful act, the rapist violated both the rights of his victim and of her family, stealing something over whose disposal they had rightful control.[117] Gratian also distinguished between rape, where violence was used to secure the attacker's will, and seduction, where a girl was induced by guile and promises to agree to illicit sexual relations.[118]

Violence was thus a necessary element in the offense of rape, regardless of whether the force was directed against the victim's family or against the victim herself. Marriage procured by force or threats of force against the girl's family

[109] C. 32 q. 1 c. 1–4.

[110] C. 32 q. 1 d.p.c. 13 and c. 14; Freisen, *Geschichte*, pp. 621–22.

[111] D. 34 d.p.c. 8.

[112] C. 4 q. 1 c. 1; C. 4 q. 2 & 3 c. 3. On canonical infamy in this period see generally Peter Landau, *Die Entstehung des kanonischen Infamiebegriffs von Gratian bis zur Glossa ordinaria*, Forschungen zur kirchlichen Rechtsgeschichte und zum Kirchenrecht, vol. 5 (Cologne: H. Böhlaus, 1966).

[113] D. 56 c. 4.

[114] D. 56 d.p.c. 13.

[115] C. 27 q. 2 d.p.c. 47 and c. 48–49; C. 36 q. 1 c. 1–2 and d.p.c. 2; Esmein, *Mariage* 1:392.

[116] C. 27 q. 2 d.p.c. 49; C. 36 q. 1 d.p.c. 2.

[117] D. 5 de cons. c. 26.

[118] C. 36 q. 1 d.p.c. 3.

likewise constituted rape, according to Gratian's reading of the law.[119] But marriage resulting from duress was, as Gratian saw things, no marriage at all and should not be considered binding, since free consent, which was essential to marriage, was absent.

According to some earlier writers marriage between a rapist and his victim remained forever impossible, even if, after the rape episode, both the girl and her family consented to it.[120] Gratian had serious doubts about this teaching. Certainly, he maintained, if the victim had previously been betrothed or married to someone other than her abductor, then she ought to be restored to her husband or fiancé when she was liberated from her abductor's control.[121] If the victim of an abduction or of forcible sexual intercourse later consented to marry her assailant, however, and if her parents also consented to this marriage, then Gratian was prepared to allow the marriage, provided that the rapist repented of his unlawful actions and performed appropriate penance.[122]

Gratian knew, of course, that royal law and folklaw often prescribed the death penalty for rape or abduction, but he emphasized that in ecclesiastical law the appropriate remedy for rape was excommunication.[123] He considered the rape or abduction of nuns especially heinous and apparently felt that the extreme penalties for rape should apply in these cases, whether the nun was a willing accomplice to the episode or not.[124] Although he expressed no opinion as to whether the death penalty was justified in ordinary rape cases, Gratian maintained that if the abductor and his victim took refuge in a church, the perpetrator must be granted immunity from capital punishment.[125]

A woman victimized by forcible sexual molestation, Gratian added, should not be held guilty either of fornication or adultery, since she had not been a willing participant.[126] But even an unwilling victim of sexual duress, he concluded, could not subsequently be considered a virgin; even if she incurred no blame in the incident, she was ineligible to become a consecrated virgin, since, without any fault on her part, she had forfeited that status.[127]

OTHER SEX OFFENSES

Gratian paid scant attention to other sexual offenses among the laity. While he noted the civil law penalties for sexual corruption of either boys or girls and cited some authorities who reprobated homosexual intercourse and other "unnatural" sex acts, Gratian gave little space to these matters. He made it plain

[119] C. 36 q. 1 d.p.c. 3.
[120] C. 27 q. 2 c. 34; C. 36 q. 2 c. 1, 4, 11, and d.p.c. 10.
[121] C. 27 q. 2 d.p.c. 45, c. 46–47, and d.p.c. 47.
[122] C. 36 q. 2 d.p.c. 6 and d.p.c. 11.
[123] C. 27 q. 2 c. 33; C. 36 q. 2 c. 2, 5–6.
[124] D. 1 de pen. c. 6 and d.p.c. 18; C. 36 q. 2 c. 3.
[125] C. 36 q. 1 c. 3 and d.p.c. 2 § 5.
[126] C. 32 q. 5 c. 1–10 and d.p.c. 14.
[127] C. 32 q. 5 d.p.c. 13 and c. 14.

that he considered deviant sex more heinous than either adultery or fornication, but he failed to specify penalties for these offenses.[128] He also included without comment an early conciliar condemnation of cross-dressing.[129]

Sex and the Clergy in Gratian's *Decretum*

Since the Church required clerics in major orders to observe celibacy, twelfth-century writers warned repeatedly that they must be wary of dealing with women and ought to shun their company so far as possible. Gratian's contemporary, St. Bernard of Clairvaux (ca. 1091–1153) cautioned his monks that "To be always with a woman and not to have sexual relations with her is more difficult than to raise the dead. You cannot do the less difficult; do you think that I will believe that you can do what is more difficult?"[130]

With this sentiment Gratian was in complete agreement and his *Decretum* reiterated numerous warnings that clerics must refrain from forming relationships of any kind with women, lest they expose themselves to sexual temptation and, even worse, succumb to it.[131] Not only should they avoid female company, including that of their own relatives, but they must decline even to talk about them, much less discuss their physical attributes and attractions.[132]

Gratian applauded the Church reform movement's views on celibacy: he collected in the *Decretum* a battery of authoritative prohibitions of clerical marriage and concubinage, including the celibacy decree of the Second Lateran Council (1139), and warned that clerics in holy orders who kept wives or concubines were subject to dismissal from their posts and degradation from clerical rank.[133] He likewise repeated the warning of the Roman Synod of 1063 that had forbidden the laity to attend Mass or other services conducted by married or concubinary priests, together with Gregory VII's condemnation of bishops who failed to enforce the celibacy rule.[134] Gratian included in his work a virtual handbook of decrees and decisions supporting the reformers' views on the celibacy issue, including the penalty of enslavement for the wives, mistresses, and children of clerics in sacred orders.[135]

---

[128] D. 1 de pen. c. 15; C. 32 q. 7 c. 12–14.

[129] D. 30 c. 6.

[130] St. Bernard of Clairvaux, *Sermones in Cantica canticorum* 65.2.4, ed. Jean Leclercq et al., vols. 1–2 in Bernard's *Opera* (Rome: Editiones Cistercienses, 1957– ; in progress) 2:175; translation from Caroline Walker Bynum, *Jesus as Mother: Studies in the Spirituality of the High Middle Ages* (Berkeley and Los Angeles: University of California Press, 1982), p. 145. The passage is reminiscent of St. Jerome, *Epist.* 22.14, in CSEL 54:162.

[131] D. 32 c. 16, 18; D. 34 c. 1; D. 81 c. 20–21.

[132] D. 32 c. 17 (*palea*); Joris Backeljauw, "De uxoris statu sociali in iure canonico medii aevi," *Divus Thomas* 89 (1968) 272.

[133] D. 27 c. 8; D. 28 c. 2 and c. 9; D. 32 c. 10, 11, 16; D. 33 pr. and c. 1; D. 82 c. 2.

[134] D. 32 c. 6, c. 10; D. 83 c. 1.

[135] D. 81 c. 30; C. 15 q. 8 c. 3. At D. 56 d.p.c. 13 Gratian remarked that the law treated the children of priests more harshly than it did adulterers.

Gratian also stressed the point that the clergy were forbidden to have casual sexual affairs.[136] Although fornication may have been a common consequence of enforced celibacy, Gratian clearly believed that even a single instance of sexual transgression by clerics demanded severe punishment.[137] Violation of the obligation to celibacy was more serious for a cleric than adultery was for a layman, he thought, and required correspondingly more severe punishment.[138] True, the penalties prescribed by Gratian's authorities for clerics guilty of fornication or adultery were less severe than those visited on married or concubinary priests, but the differences were slight. The cleric convicted of a transient sexual offense lost his ecclesiastical office and could expect confinement in a monastery for the remainder of his life.[139] The offender did not, however, suffer degradation from holy orders, which was prescribed for those involved in long-term relationships. Gratian's authorities also established severe punishments for those who attempted to seduce or marry religious women and consecrated virgins, while nuns who succumbed were subject to the penalties for incestuous adultery.[140]

Gratian saw no bar, however, to the ordination of men who had been married or who had kept a concubine prior to assuming holy orders, provided that before they were ordained their wives or concubines had died or agreed to a separation.[141] Gratian's work included an important exception to the rule that previously married men could be ordained: a man who had married twice, or who had married a widow or a divorcée, or whose wife had committed adultery was deemed guilty of constructive bigamy and hence was barred from ordination.[142] Digamy, or ecclesiastical bigamy, as Gratian called it, consisted in having had sex with more than one woman or in having relations with a woman who had slept with another man. It made no difference whether the relationship occurred in a solemnized and valid marriage or not, nor did it matter which party had participated in the affair. The physical act of intercourse with a woman who had known another man or with more than one woman was a bar to clerical orders, as Gratian read the law.

Constructive bigamy was not a crime or an offense; but it gave rise to an irregularity, much like the irregularity incurred, for example, in having been born to an unwed mother. The affected person might not even know the cause of his irregularity. Gratian did not explicitly link the ban on the ordination of men tainted by constructive bigamy to notions of ritual purity, but this idea probably underlay the sources that he cited. Gratian's commentators would soon

---

[136] D. 50 c. 29, c. 33; D. 51 c. 5; D. 81 c. 1.

[137] Flandrin, *Familles*, p. 184.

[138] C. 27 q. 1 c. 21; cf. C. 30 q. 1 c. 9.

[139] D. 81 c. 10, 11; C. 3 q. 2 c. 4; Esmein, *Mariage* 2:114–15.

[140] D. 27 c. 9; C. 27 q. 1 c. 23–25, 27–30, 34–35, 37, 40 and d.p.c. 40.

[141] D. 33 d.p.c. 6, as well as D. 33 c. 6–7 and D. 26 c. 1.

[142] D. 26 c. 2, 3, 5; D. 32 c. 12; D. 33 c. 1, 2, 17; D. 51 c. 5. For Gratian's own comments on the matter see D. 26 d.p.c. 4; D. 34 d.p.c. 12 and d.p.c. 14.

point out the difficulty in accounting otherwise for this policy.[143] In any event, Gratian left open the possibility that candidates for ordination who had incurred the irregularity of constructive bigamy might receive papal dispensation from the strict application of the law, particularly if a shortage of clergymen seemed to require such a concession.[144]

Procedure and Evidence in Sex Cases

Gratian had little to say about specific procedures in sex cases. He opposed the use of ordeals in ecclesiastical courts and sought to explain away conciliar canons that prescribed them.[145] Gratian was grudgingly prepared to accept the evidence of compurgation, if more positive evidence was unavailable, but he preferred that Church courts rely upon proof through the testimony of witnesses and he included in his work several canons relating to the evaluation of their evidence.[146] Certain classes of persons were barred from giving testimony, notably those who had been found guilty of rape, adultery, and other heinous crimes and, in general, all persons tainted with *infamia*.[147] Although he believed that women were inherently incapable of exercising jurisdiction, Gratian was willing to allow them to testify, particularly in adultery cases.[148] The testimony of all witnesses, he believed, should be critically examined, and judges ought to be skeptical of the evidence supplied by witnesses who might be swayed by emotional attachment, affection, family ties, or by less genial sentiments, such as self-interest, fear, or greed.[149]

Both with respect to the law of evidence and with respect to judgments, Gratian appears to have believed that ecclesiastical courts ought to strive to achieve equity, "the mother of justice," as he called it, rather than be bound by

---

[143] Stephan Kuttner, *Kanonistische Schuldlehre von Gratian bis auf die Dekretalen Gregors IX.*, Studi e testi, vol. 64 (Vatican City: Biblioteca Apostolica Vaticana, 1935), p. 105.

[144] D. 34 c. 7, 18.

[145] C. 2 q. 5 c. 24–25, which must be read in the context of C. 2 q. 5 d.a.c. 22 and d.p.c. 26. See also Paul R. Hyams, "Trial by Ordeal: The Key to Proof in Early Common Law," in *On the Laws and Customs of England: Essays in Honor of Samuel E. Thorne*, ed. Morris S. Arnold et al. (Chapel Hill: University of North Carolina Press, 1981), pp. 90–126, and Robert C. Van Caenegem, "Methods of Proof in Western Medieval Law," in *Academiae Analecta: Medelingen van de Koninklijke Academie voor Wetenschappen, Letteren en Schone Kunsten van België*, Klasse der Letteren 45 (1983) 85–127.

[146] C. 2 q. 4 c. 1 and *dictum post*.

[147] C. 3 q. 4 c. 4; C. 3 q. 5 c. 9; C. 6 q. 1 c. 15–19 and d.p.c. 19.

[148] C. 3 q. 7 d.p.c. 1; C. 15 q. 3 c. 2; C. 33 q. 5 c. 17; Filippo Liotta, "Il testimone nel Decreto di Graziano," in *Proceedings of the Fourth International Congress of Medieval Canon Law, Toronto, 21–25 August 1972*, ed. Stephan Kuttner, MIC, Subsidia, vol. 5 (Vatican City: Biblioteca Apostolica Vaticana, 1976; cited hereafter as *Toronto Proceedings*), p. 87; Backeljauw, "De uxoris statu socialii," p. 273.

[149] C. 3 q. 5 c. 12; C. 35 q. 6 d.a.c. 1; Liotta, "Testimone," p. 88.

a narrow legalism.[150] In marriage law, particularly, achieving equitable solutions to human problems might require generous use of the power of dispensation, through which the pope and other ecclesiastical authorities had the power to derogate the law in special cases in order to achieve a fair and just resolution of the problem.[151]

Conclusions

Gratian composed his *Decretum* at a time when the Church's law of marriage and sexual offenses was undergoing considerable change. Two quite different theories about the formation of marriage were current when he wrote, and, characteristically, he attempted to reconcile them and to produce his own marriage theory, which combined elements of both schools. Similarly the mid-twelfth century was a period of uncertainty about the sacramental character of marriage. Theologians contemporary with Gratian were not agreed on the question of whether it was a sacrament at all and, if it was, what implications that might have for marital indissolubility.[152]

Gratian's treatment of divorce and remarriage reflects these uncertainties in contemporary thought.[153] His discussion of clandestine marriage likewise reflects the uncertainties of his generation about the nature of marriage as a public institution. Should some sort of public ceremony be required as an essential condition of marriage? Or was marriage primarily a private agreement between the parties, in which case it would be inconsistent to require public rituals? Gratian was apparently undecided on these issues, although his sympathies leaned in the direction of considering marriage an essentially private affair.[154] While Gratian accepted the rules that barred marriages between persons related within seven degrees of consanguinity, he was surely not unaware of the potential problems that those rules posed, since few marriages can have been entirely immune from attack under the seven-degree rule.[155] All of these issues

---

[150] C. 25 q. 1 d.p.c. 16 § 4; Charles Duggan, "Equity and Compassion in Papal Marriage Decretals to England," in *Love and Marriage in the Twelfth Century*, p. 60.

[151] Gratian grounded his theory of dispensation in large part on ideas that he found in the work of Ivo of Chartres; see Ivo, *Decretum*, prol., in PL 161:51, 57; also Fournier, *Yves de Chartres*, pp. 8–10; Sprandel, *Ivo von Chartres*, pp. 77–85. On dispensation more generally see J. Brys, *De dispensatione in iure canonico praesertim apud decretistas et decretalistas usque ad medium saeculum decimum quartum* (Bruges: C. Beyaert; Wetteren: J. De Meester, 1925).

[152] Delhaye, "Developpement," p. 85; Mullenders, *Mariage présumé*, p. 14.

[153] Ariès, "Mariage indissoluble," p. 131.

[154] Ariès, Mariage indissoluble," pp. 134–35.

[155] Flandrin, *Familles*, p. 29, provides calculations to show the consequences of these rules; even under a set of restrictive assumptions, designed to minimize the effects of the rules, a prospective bride or groom might easily have nearly three thousand relatives within the forbidden degrees of blood relationship alone.

impinged on family structure, which itself was undergoing important changes in Catholic Europe during Gratian's generation.[156]

The *Decretum* outlined a scheme of sexual morality that was disciplined and austere, grounded on the premise that sex was licit only within marriage, and then primarily for procreation, never for sheer pleasure. All extramarital sex was not only sinful, but also criminal and subject to punishment by ecclesiastical authorities. The social realities were, of course, quite different. Twelfth-century men, particularly those of the higher social classes, typically enjoyed extensive sexual freedom. Few upper-class males were likely to be penalized for their non-marital sexual activities. We are poorly informed about the sexual practices of bourgeois and peasant society in the mid-twelfth century, but there is no evidence to suggest that men in those groups were seriously deterred from seeking sexual pleasure outside of marriage by the laws of God or man.[157] The law concerning extramarital sex, as Gratian described it, was a set of prescriptive norms supported by little effective machinery for their enforcement. Developing that machinery was one of the challenges that his successors faced.

Women in twelfth-century society were far more circumscribed in their sex lives than were men and this was probably true at all levels of the social hierarchy. "The woman has no power," Gratian declared at one point, "but in everything she is subject to the control of her husband."[158] Here Gratian described quite accurately the realities of his time for the great majority of women, save perhaps for a small handful of those among the highest nobility and royalty.[159] To this broad generalization, however, Gratian admitted two important exceptions: so far as sexual rights within marriage were concerned, women, he taught, had absolute equality with men. The sex life of the married couple was, or ought to be, an island of comparative privacy where equal rights prevailed, within a larger society where women's rights were severely curtailed. And men and women were equal so far as the law was concerned when it came to sex crimes, particularly adultery. Again, however, it remained for Gratian's successors to contrive mechanisms to secure effective implementation of the limited equality that he believed women were entitled to.

---

[156] On contrasting developments in family structure in France and England, for example, see Charles Donahue, Jr., "What Causes Fundamental Legal Ideas? Marital Property in England and France in the Thirteenth Century," *Michigan Law Review* 78 (1979) 83–84; Holt, "Feudal Society and the Family," pp. 193–212. Maitland's scathing comments about Gratian's marriage theory in "Magistri Vacarii Summa de Matrimonio," LQR 13 (1897) 135, give Gratian less credit than he probably deserves for fashioning a bridge between tradition and the current realities of his day.

[157] Duby, *Medieval Marriage*, p. 92.

[158] Rubric to C. 33 q. 5 c. 17: "Nulla est mulieris potestas, sed in omnibus uiri dominio subsit."

[159] Backeljauw, "De uxoris statu sociali," p. 272.

7

Sexual Behavior and the Early Decretists, from Paucapalea to Huguccio (1140–1190)

The Decretists and the Teaching of Law

With the appearance of Gratian's *Decretum*, canon law began to assert its independence from theology and civil law. During the second half of the twelfth century it assumed a prominent place in the curricula of the new universities that were just taking shape. Students of canon law at Bologna were using Gratian's *Decretum* as their basic textbook soon after its completion. By the 1160s, it was similarly employed in the schools of Paris; before the end of the twelfth century teachers at Oxford and in the Rhineland were expounding the *Decretum* to rapidly increasing numbers of students.

The early history of the law faculty at Bologna remains dim; some type of university organization, in which the study of canon law played a major role, had begun to emerge there by the 1160s.[1] Paucapalea seems to have been one of the earliest canon-law teachers in the Bolognese law faculty, and before 1148 he had written a short commentary on Gratian's work.[2] Paucapalea's *Summa* was

[1] Rashdall, *Universities* 1:146–49; Ullmann, *Law and Politics*, pp. 163–64; Vito Piergiovanni, "Il primo secolo della scuola canonistica di Bologna: Un ventennio di studi," in *Berkeley Proceedings*, pp. 241–56. On other Italian centers of legal study during this period see Peter Classen, "Italienische Rechtsschulen ausserhalb Bolognas," also in *Berkeley Proceedings*, pp. 205–21.

[2] *Die Summa des Paucapalea über das Decretum Gratiani*, ed. Johann Friedrich von Schulte (Giessen: E. Roth, 1890); also J. F. von Schulte, *Die Geschichte der Quellen und Literatur des kanonischen Rechts bis auf die Gegenwart*, 3 vols. (Stuttgart: F. Enke, 1875; repr. Graz: Akademische Druck- u. Verlagsanstalt, 1956; cited hereafter as Schulte, QL) 1:109–14; Kuttner, *Repertorium*, pp. 125–27; R. Naz, "Paucapalea," in DDC 6:1268–69. John T. Noonan, Jr., "The True Paucapalea?" in *Salamanca Proceedings*, pp. 157–86, argued that the text of Paucapalea published by Schulte was in fact a slightly later work, excerpted from the original *Summa* by an unknown redactor. The original text of Paucapalea, according to Noonan, is the so-called *Summa Sicut vetus testamentum*, discovered by Kuttner in the National Library at Florence. But Noonan's argument has been strongly criticized by Rudolf Weigand, "Paucapalea und die frühe Kanonistik," *Archiv für katholisches Kirchenrecht* 150 (1981) 137–57.

no doubt a byproduct of his teaching. Other canon-law teachers at Bologna soon followed his example and produced further expositions of Gratian's text. Among them were the shadowy Rolandus (fl. ca. 1150),[3] the better-documented Rufinus, (active in the late 1150s),[4] Joannes Faventinus (fl. ca. 1171),[5] Simon of Bisignano (fl. ca. 1177 ~ 1179),[6] and Huguccio (fl. ca. 1188).[7]

At about the same time that Rufinus was finishing his *Summa*, the teaching of canon law was commencing at Paris.[8] There, too, Gratian's *Decretum* was the

[3] *Die Summa Magistri Rolandi nachmals Papstes Alexander III.*, ed. Friedrich Thaner (Innsbruck: Wagner, 1874). Rolandus was also the author of a theological treatise, *Die Sentenzen Rolands nachmals Papstes Alexander III.*, ed. F. A. M. Gietl (Freiburg i/Br.: Herder, 1891). See also Kuttner, *Repertorium*, pp. 127–29; Schulte, QL 1:114–18; Marcel Pacaut, "Roland Bandinelli (Alexandre III)," in DDC 7:702–26. The conventional identification of the Bolognese Master Rolandus with Rolandus Bandinelli, who became Pope Alexander III, has been seriously challenged by John T. Noonan, Jr., "Who Was Rolandus?" in *Law, Church, and Society: Essays in Honor of Stephan Kuttner*, ed. Kenneth J. Pennington and Robert Somerville (Philadelphia: University of Pennsylvania Press, 1977), pp. 21–48. Rudolph Weigand, "Magister Rolandus und Papst Alexander III.," *Archiv für katholisches Kirchenrecht* 149 (1980) 3–44, supports Noonan's argument with further evidence.

[4] Rufinus, *Summa decretorum*, ed. Heinrich Singer (Paderborn: Ferdinand Schöningh, 1902; repr. Aalen: Scientia, 1963); Schulte, QL 1:121–30; Kuttner, *Repertorium*, pp. 131–32; Robert L. Benson, "Rufin," in DDC 7:779–84.

[5] The *Summa* of Joannes Faventinus remains unpublished; see Schulte, QL 1:137–40; Kuttner, *Repertorium*, pp. 143–46; Alfons M. Stickler, "Jean de Faenza," in DDC 6:99–102; M. B. Hackett, "An Unnoticed Johannes Faventinus Fragment," *Traditio* 14 (1958) 505–508.

[6] Simon's *Summa* has also never been published; see Schulte, QL 1:140–42; Kuttner, *Repertorium*, pp. 148–49; and "An Interim Checklist of Manuscripts," *Traditio* 11 (1955) 441; A. Lambert, "Bisignano, Simon de," in DDC 2:900–901; Walther Holtzmann, "Zu den Dekretalen bei Simon von Bisignano," *Traditio* 18 (1962) 450–59; Josef Juncker, "Die Summa des Simon von Bisignano und seine Glossen," ZRG, KA 15 (1926) 326–500.

[7] Huguccio's *Summa*, although highly original and immensely influential, has never been published in full, although excerpts from it have appeared in numerous books and articles; see esp. J. Roman, "Summa d'Huguccio sur le Décret de Gratien d'après le manuscrit 3891 de la Bibliothèque Nationale, Causa XXVII, Questio II," RHDF, 2d ser., 27 (1903) 745–805; Schulte, QL 1:156–70; Kuttner, *Repertorium*, pp. 155–60, supplemented by "An Interim Checklist of Manuscripts," *Traditio* 11 (1955) 441–44, 12 (1956) 563, 13 (1957) 469, and "Notes on Manuscripts," *Traditio* 17 (1961) 534. See also C. Leonardi, "La vita e l'opera di Uguccione da Pisa," *Studia Gratiana* 4 (1956/57) 37–210; Alfons M. Stickler, "Uguccio de Pise," in DDC 7:1355–62; and Giuseppe Cremascoli, "Uguccione da Pisa: Saggio bibliografico," *Aevum* 42 (1968) 123–68.

[8] Stephan Kuttner, "Les débuts de l'école canoniste française," *Studia et documenta historiae et iuris* (hereafter SDHI) 4 (1938) 193–204; André Gouron, "Une école ou des écoles? Sur les canonistes français (vers 1150–vers 1210)," in *Berkeley Proceedings*, pp. 223–40. Gerald of Wales, *De rebus a se gestis* 2.1–2, in his *Opera*, ed. J. S. Brewer, 8 vols., Rolls Series, no 21 (London: H. M. Stationery Office, 1861–91) 1:45–48, testifies

basic text, and Parisian teachers soon fashioned their own expositions of Gratian's work. Some of these *Summae* and gloss *Apparatus* circulated as independent books; others were copied into the margins and flyleaves of students' copies of Gratian's work. The *Summa* of Stephen of Tournai and the anonymous *Summa Parisiensis*, both composed about 1160, seem to be the earliest surviving products of the Paris canonists.[9] In the late 1170s, another anonymous *Summa* of the Paris school appeared, this one known from its opening words as *Inperatorie maiestati*.[10] Sicard of Cremona, another Paris teacher, produced a *Summa* around 1180, and at roughly the same time, Peter of Blois was writing his *Distinctiones decretorum*.[11] During the 1180s, further anonymous canonistic treatises emerged from the Paris school, including *Tractaturus magister, Et est sciendum*, and *Omnis qui iuste iudicat*.[12]

While French canonists were creating a law faculty at Paris, systematic study and teaching of canon law also began in England and Normandy. The early products of the Anglo-Norman school, like those of the French school, were often unsigned. One of the earliest Anglo-Norman canonistic works, the *Summa De multiplici iuris diuisione*, written during the 1160s,[13] was followed in the

---

that he studied and taught canon law at Paris about 1177 and gives a colorful account of the popularity of the subject—and of his own lectures. Daniel Morley, who visited Paris at about this time, indicates that canon law was a well-established field of study and that it attracted throngs of students; Rashdall, *Universities* 1:321.

[9] Stephen of Tournai, *Summa über das Decretum Gratiani*, ed. Johann Friedrich von Schulte (Giessen: Emil Roth, 1891; repr. Aalen: Scientia, 1965), presents a partial edition of Stephen's text. The other major work of the early Paris school is *The Summa Parisiensis on the Decretum Gratiani*, ed. Terence P. McLaughlin (Toronto: Pontifical Institute of Mediaeval Studies, 1952; cited hereafter as SP). See generally Kuttner, *Repertorium*, pp. 133–36, 177–78, supplemented by "An Interim Checklist of Manuscripts," *Traditio* 11 (1955) 440–41, 12 (1956) 563, 13 (1957) 469, and 17 (1961) 533. See also Kuttner's "The Third Part of Stephen of Tournai's Summa," *Traditio* 14 (1958) 502–505; G. Lepointe, "Etienne de Tournai," in DDC 5:487–92; LAC, pp. 278, 282–83; and more recently, H. Kalb, *Studien zur Summa Stephans von Tournai: Ein Beitrag zur kanonistischen Wissenschaftsgeschichte des späten 12. Jahrhunderts*, Forschungen zur Rechts- und Kulturgeschichte, vol. 12 (Innsbruck: Wagner, 1983).

[10] Kuttner, *Repertorium*, pp. 179–80; LAC, p. 283; W. Stelzer, "Die Summa Monacensis (Summa 'Inperatorie maiestati') und der Neustifter Propst Konrad von Albeck: Ein Beitrag zur Verbreitung der franzözischen Kanonistik im Frühstaufischen Deutschland," *Mitteilungen des Instituts für österreichische Geschichtsforschung* 88 (1980) 94–112.

[11] Kuttner, *Repertorium*, pp. 220–22, and "Zur Biographie des Sicardus von Cremona," ZRG, KA 25 (1936) 476–78; also Stephan Kuttner and Eleanor Rathbone, "Anglo-Norman Canonists of the Twelfth Century: An Introductory Study," *Traditio* 7 (1949–51) 285–86; Charles Lefebvre, "Pierre de Blois," in DDC 6:1472, and "Sicard de Cremone," in DDC 7:1008–11.

[12] Kuttner, *Repertorium*, pp. 184–87, 195–98; LAC, p. 283.

[13] Kuttner and Rathbone, "Anglo-Norman Canonists," p. 293, as well as Kuttner, *Re-*

next decade by the *Summa* of Odo of Doura.[14] Anglo-Norman canonists who were actively teaching and writing in the 1180s included Gerard Pucelle (d. 1184),[15] and Master Honorius (fl. 1184/85 ~ 1205), author of the *Summa decretalium questionum*.[16] By the 1190s, canon-law teaching was evidently flourishing at Oxford, in the hands of John of Tynmouth, Simon of Southwell, Nicholas de l'Aigle, and their associates.[17]

The Rhineland produced yet another school of canon law as early as the 1160s. The *Distinctiones Monacenses* (so-called because they are preserved in a Munich manuscript) were composed in this region between 1165 and 1169.[18] The best-known treatise of the Rhineland canonists, the *Summa "Elegantius in iure diuino"* (also known as the *Summa Coloniensis*), is thus far the only work of that school to have appeared in print.[19]

The four twelfth-century decretist schools—Bolognese, Parisian, Anglo-Norman, and Rhenish—testify that the study of canon law flourished vigorously in the half century between 1140 and 1190 (see Table 7.1 in the Appendix). Evidently Church administration during this period required numerous trained canonists.

While the four schools differed from one another in style of exposition, in emphasis, and to some degree in interpretative preferences, they shared a common body of law and a common dialectical approach to legal analysis, both of which stemmed directly from Gratian. Teachers and writers on canon law in this period, moreover, not only expounded Gratian's views of the law, but also did not hesitate to add their own ideas. The decretists proposed to their students explanations and theories about the law and structure of the Church that departed markedly from those that Gratian had adopted. The decretists also

---

pertorium, pp. 139–41; LAC, pp. 287–90; and Brian Tierney, "Two Anglo-Norman Summae," *Traditio* 15 (1959) 483–91.

[14] Kuttner, *Repertorium*, pp. 172–77; R. Naz, "Odon de Doura ou de Dour," in DDC 6:1066–67.

[15] Kuttner, *Repertorium*, p. 26; LAC, p. 287; Kuttner and Rathbone, "Anglo-Norman Canonists," pp. 296–303; Charles Lefebvre, "Gérard Pucelle," in DDC 5:955.

[16] LAC, p. 288; Kuttner and Rathbone, "Anglo-Norman Canonists," pp. 304–16.

[17] The ideas of this group are best known from a set of glosses that survive in a single manuscript, now in the library of Gonville and Caius College, Cambridge, and in the *Questiones Londinenses*, whose sole surviving copy is in the British Library in London; see Kuttner and Rathbone, "Anglo-Norman Canonists," pp. 317–21, 341, 347–53; LAC, p. 289; James A. Brundage, "The Crusade of Richard I: Two Canonical Questions," *Speculum* 38 (1963) 443–52, and "The Treatment of Marriage in the Questiones Londinenses (MS Royal 9.E.VII)," *Manuscripta* 19 (1975) 86–97.

[18] Kuttner and Rathbone, "Anglo-Norman Canonists," pp. 298–99; LAC, p. 286; Kuttner, *Repertorium*, pp. 215–16.

[19] *Summa 'Elegantius in iure diuino' seu Coloniensis*, ed. Gérard Fransen and Stephan Kuttner, MIC, Corpus glossatorum, vol. 1 (New York: Fordham University Press; Vatican City: Biblioteca Apostolica Vaticana, 1969– ; in progress).

attempted to take account of new law that had appeared since the time of Gratian and to apply both the old law, as they found it in Gratian's work, and the post-Gratian law to contemporary problems.[20]

The four canonistic schools approached many legal problems (including those involving sex, marriage, and family law) somewhat differently. The schools of Paris and Bologna, for example, adopted radically different approaches to the definition of what constituted valid marriage, as we shall see, while the Rhineland canonists took yet another position. Differences such as these were not simply theoretical, but had serious concrete consequences for property, inheritance, and other material rights. These varying approaches to the definition of valid marriage, moreover, might well lead different judges to reach conflicting conclusions as to the juridical nature of a particular couple's relationship: one might find them married, while another might hold that they were living in concubinage, and a third could decide that they were simply a prostitute and her client. Again, the consequences for the parties and their families could be quite serious.

The Early Decretists' Theories of Sex and Marriage

Most decretists, whatever their school, took a dim view of the role of sex in human life. Their negative attitudes toward sexuality reflected the opinions of the authorities that Gratian cited, particularly Jerome, Augustine, and the *Responsa Gregorii*.[21] The decretists knew also, especially from the translations of Aristotle that had begun to appear during the twelfth century, that ancient philosophers had often disapproved of sexual pleasure save in marriage and that they, as well as the Church Fathers, had strongly advised that sexual activity be limited to the minimum necessary for the reproduction of humankind.[22] Some

[20] I shall use 1190 as a dividing point in this exposition because it marks the end of the early or formative period of decretist writing; see Stephan Kuttner, "Bernardus Compostellanus Antiquus: A Study in the Glossators of the Canon Law," *Traditio* 1 (1943) 279. On the demand for canonists in this period see Charles Homer Haskins, *Studies in Medieval Culture* (Oxford: Clarendon Press, 1929), p. 47.

[21] Rudolf Weigand, "Liebe und Ehe bei den Dekretisten des 12. Jahrhunderts," in *Love and Marriage in the Twelfth Century*, ed. Willy Van Hoecke and Andries Welkenhuysen (Leuven: Leuven University Press, 1981), p. 52.

[22] Aristotle, *Rhetorica* 1.11.370a.15–29, in the anonymous Latin translation, ed. by Bernhard Schneider in *Aristoteles Latinus*, vol. 31 (Leiden: E. J. Brill, 1978), pp. 47–48; cf. the translation of the same passage by William of Moerbecke in *Aristoteles Latinus* 31:200–201. See also the "Ethica vetus" 30.10.18b.1–7, in *Ethica Nicomachea, translatio antiquissima, libr. II–III, sive "Ethica vetus," et translationis antiquioris quae supersunt sive "Ethica Nova," "Hoferiana," "Borghesiana,"*, ed. René Antoine Gauthier, in *Aristoteles Latinus*, vol. 26, no. 1–3, fasc. 2 (Leiden: E. J. Brill; Brussels: Desclée de Brouwer, 1972), p. 46. John of Salisbury, *Policraticus, sive de nugis curialium et vestigiis philosophorum libri VIII* 8.11, ed. C. C. J. Webb, 2 vols. (Oxford: Clarendon Press, 1909; repr. Frankfurt a/M.: Minerva, 1965) 2:296, likewise asserted on the authority of Zeno, Epictetus, Aristotle, and other ancient philosophers, that sex, save in marriage, is

decretists also held fast to the belief that sex was impure and unclean and that sexual relations transmitted, as it were by contagion, a state of spiritual disease.[23]

Some decretists considered sexuality part of the natural order of God's creation. This belief was bolstered by a passage in the first Distinction of Gratian's *Decretum* which referred to "the joining of man and woman" as a prime example of natural law in action.[24] But a minority, powerfully represented by Huguccio, rejected this view. Sex, according to Huguccio, was not part of natural law at all, but rather an effect of natural law. If sexual relations were decreed by natural law, Huguccio reasoned, then fornication, which is a sin, would be part of natural law as well: such a conclusion, he felt, must be rejected.[25] At the same time, however, he could scarcely overlook the evident fact that most men are stirred by sexual desires for women. To account for this, Huguccio distinguished between the sensual appetite, which made men want to experience sexual pleasure, and the reproductive urge, which made men want to mate. By distinguishing sensual appetite from reproductive sexuality, Huguccio could argue that indiscriminate sexual activity could not be excused on the grounds that it was simply the exercise of a natural function. At the same time he could consistently affirm that the use of marital sex strictly for reproduction was protected by natural law.[26]

---

always evil and that even in marriage a prudent man would be well advised to avoid it as much as possible.

[23] Rolandus, *Summa* to C. 32 q. 1 c. 12 v. *sed et hoc* and v. *impar numerus*, ed. Thaner, p. 163.

[24] Gratian, D. 1 c. 7, cites from Isidore of Seville, *Etymologiae* 5.4, a passage that states, in part: "Ius naturale est commune omnium nationum, eo quod ubique instinctu naturae, non constitutione aliqua habetur, ut uiri et feminae coniunctio, liberorum successio et educatio. . . ." Isidore's statement was a paraphrase of a passage from Ulpian (Dig. 1.1.1.3) that also appears in Justinian's Inst. 1.2 pr. The notion has deep roots in ancient philosophy; cf. Plato, *Timaeus* 91a, ed. and trans. Albert Rivaud, in Plato's *Oeuvres complètes*, 14 vols. (Paris: Les Belles Lettres, 1951–64) 10:266. The usual interpretation of this passage by the decretists identified the "joining of man and woman" specifically with sexual intercourse; see, e.g., SP to D. 1 c. 7 v. *coniunctio*, ed. McLaughlin, p. 2; *Summa 'Elegantius'* 1.5, ed. Fransen and Kuttner 1:2; and the gloss to D. 1 c. 7 v. *viri et femine coniunctio* quoted by Weigand in *Naturrechtslehre*, p. 293.

[25] Huguccio, *Summa* to D. 1 c. 7 v. *viri et femine coniunctio*, in MS lat. 2280, fol. 2 va, Biblioteca Apostolica Vaticana (hereafter cited as Vat. lat.) and Weigand, *Naturrechtslehre*, p. 290: "Est ius naturale, id est effectus eius, uel ab eo descendit ut in lege continetur ff. de iust. et iure l. i. Ius naturale [Dig. 1.1.1.3]." Likewise, Joannes Faventinus, *Summa* to D. 1 c. 4, in MS Royal 9.E.VII, fol. 2vb of the British Library in London (hereafter B.L.): "Nota quod uiri et femine coniunctio non est ius naturale sed ipsius effectus." The distinction between natural law and its effects appeared earlier in Stephen of Tournai, *Summa* to D. 1 c. 7 v. *ut viri et fem.*, ed. Schulte, p. 10.

[26] Huguccio, *Summa* to D. 1 c. 7 v. *viri et femine coniunctio*, in Vat. lat. 2280, fol. 2 va, and Weigand, *Naturrechtslehre*, p. 291: "Mihi tamen uidetur quod intelligatur de coniunctione carnali matrimoniali, non fornicaria, cum ex iure naturali peccatum non

Huguccio's teaching echoed anthropological ideas current among contemporary theologians, such as Robert of Melun (d. 1167). These notions—derived originally from St. Augustine—were accepted by other canonists of Huguccio's generation.[27] Pleasurable sensations, especially sexual pleasure, according to this scheme, were no part of God's original creation. Rather, the exquisite sensations of sex had developed after creation was complete, as a result of original sin. Genital contact between Adam and Eve in the Garden of Eden had not been accompanied by pangs of passion, since these resulted from the Fall. In Paradise, touching the genitals produced feelings no different than those produced by touching one hand with the other. After the Fall, however, the genitals became sensitized and thus became a source of intense pleasure. This pleasure, in turn, was the root of sexual sin,[28] and indirectly led to other calamities, such as the Biblical flood.[29]

This exercise in paleophysiology enabled Huguccio and his contemporaries to put a convenient distance between God and human sexuality, by relegating sexual sensations to the aftermath of the Fall from Grace. Once they defined sexual pleasure as a postlapsarian novelty, Huguccio and the rigorists could deny it any legitimate role in human life, including married life.

But the decretists found themselves bedeviled by other problems when they came to deal with Gratian's treatment of marriage formation. Gratian's marriage theory was unsatisfactory to many writers because it placed sexual relations at the very center of marriage formation. This they found offensive, and they cast about for alternatives to Gratian's theory. Three distinct approaches emerged. One approach sought to reconcile the differences between Gratian's version of the coital theory of marriage and the consensual theory, in which coitus was irrelevant to the creation of a marital union. A second approach rejected Gratian's marriage theory outright and championed a purely consensual definition of marriage. The third approach spurned both the consensual and coital theories and identified marriage with the delivery (*traditio*) of a woman to her husband. The Bolognese decretists adopted the first approach, the Parisian decretists preferred the second, and the Rhineland school, together with the Italian legist, Vacarius, opted for the third.[30]

---

possit esse; et hoc est coniunctio de iure naturali quod dicitur instinctus nature. . . ." See also the gloss to D. 1 c. 7 v. *coniunctio*, ibid., p. 299.

[27] Müller, *Lehre des hl. Augustinus*, pp. 70–71; Luscombe, *School of Pierre Abelard*, pp. 248, 294–95; Zeimentz, *Ehe nach der Lehre der Frühscholastik*, pp. 71–72.

[28] Huguccio, *Summa* to C. 32 q. 2 d.p.c. 2 v. *sine ardore*, in Admont, Stiftsbibliothek, MS 7, fol. 319va–vb, and Vat. lat. 2280, fol. 280va: "Si enim homo non peccasset, talis esset coniunctio genitalium membrorum et ita sine feruore et pruritu uoluntatis, sicut est aliorum membrorum coniunctio, sic enim membrum membro sine pruritu carnis coniungitur, sicut aliud membrum alio membro, uel tabula tabule coniungitur."

[29] Petrus Comestor, *Historia scholastica*, Liber Genesis 31, in PL 198:1081.

[30] James A. Coriden, *The Indissolubility Added to Christian Marriage by Consumma-*

The leading spokesmen for the modified coital theory were Paucapalea, Rolandus, and Rufinus. Paucapalea subscribed to Gratian's marriage formation theory without substantial change. Marriage, in Paucapalea's *Summa*, centered on the sexual union of a couple; a consensual union without consummation was no marriage, but merely a betrothal that could be terminated for good cause. Only when the union was consummated by intercourse did permanent marriage in the full sense begin.[31]

Rolandus, who made marriage law the principal focus of his *Summa*, sought to balance the two elements: he emphasized that both consent and consummation were essential to true marriage. It might be customary to refer to a union initiated by consent as a marriage, Rolandus asserted, but such a union is not permanently binding until it is consummated. Consummation, furthermore, creates a right to continued sexual relations. Prior to consummation, the man and woman were free to separate if either party wished to enter religion; after consummation such a parting required mutual consent. Marriage for Rolandus became fully binding only as a result of consummation.[32]

Rufinus, while squarely supportive of the coital theory, encountered difficulty in reconciling Gratian's position with the consensual view. He sought to avoid conflict between them by postulating that there were two sacraments of marriage, one conferred by consent when a couple agreed to marry, the other conferred by intercourse when they consummated their union.[33] Either was incomplete without the other and both were needed for a binding marriage.

An anonymous treatise on matrimony known as *In primis hominibus*, written at about the same time as Gratian's *Decretum*, also struggled with these issues. *In primis hominibus* assigned equal weight to the exchange of verbal consent and to physical consummation: marriage can be contracted, according

---

tion: An Historical Study of the Period from the End of the Patristic Age to the Death of Pope Innocent III (Rome: Officium Libri Catholici, 1961), p. 3.

[31] Paucapalea, *Summa* to C. 27 q. 1 pr. and C. 27 q. 2, ed. Schulte, pp. 112–14.

[32] Marcel Pacaut, *Alexandre III: Etude sur la conception du pouvoir pontifical dans sa pensée et dans son oeuvre*, L'église et l'état au moyen âge, vol. 11 (Paris: J. Vrin, 1956), p. 65, points out that the *Summa Rolandi* passes quickly over the 101 *Distinctiones* of Part I and also over the first fourteen *Causae* of Part II. Rolandus's commentary becomes more ample from C. 15 to C. 26; then from C. 27 to C. 36 it becomes very detailed indeed. In short, the *Tractatus de matrimonio* of the *Decretum* is the principal subject of Rolandus's *Summa*. He does not mention the *Tractatus de Poenitentia* or the *Tractatus de Consecratione* at all. Much the same concentration on marriage issues characterizes the *Sententiae Rolandi*; Pacaut, *Alexandre III*, p. 73. Note particularly Rolandus's *Summa* to C. 27 pr. and q. 2 c. 5, 16–17, 33–34, 50, ed. Thaner, pp. 114, 127, 129, 131–33; see also the *Sententiae*, p. 270.

[33] Rufinus, *Summa* to C. 27 pr., ed. Singer, pp. 430–32. Rufinus made some scathing remarks about the absurdity of the consensual theory and its supporters—he had Peter Lombard in mind—at C. 27 q. 2 pr., where he expounded his two-sacrament theory.

to this treatise, either by an exchange of consent or by intercourse between two parties who are legally capable of marrying one another.[34] Another anonymous marriage treatise of the same period, *De ortu coniugii: 'Sacramentum coniugii non ab homine,'* which survives in a single manuscript at Stuttgart, put forward no less than four definitions of marriage, two of which stressed its consensual nature, while the other two emphasized the necessity of consummation in order to create a binding marriage.[35]

The most influential and successful spokesman for consensual marriage theory in the mid-twelfth century was the Paris theologian, Peter Lombard (ca. 1095–1160). In his *Sententiae*, Peter held that the marital bond resulted from consent alone, provided that consent was given in the present tense. Consent to marriage at some future time constituted betrothal, not marriage. Future consent followed by intercourse, however, did create a marriage, according to his scheme. Intercourse was legally significant only if there had been prior agreement about a future marriage. For a couple who had exchanged present consent to marry, however, consummation was legally irrelevant. They were married, regardless of whether they had sexual intercourse or not.

For Peter Lombard and those who followed him, therefore, marriage was primarily a matter of the intention of the parties. The expression of their intention to marry through an exchange of words or signs signifying their desire to create a permanent union with each other here and now was all that was needed for marital union (see Fig. 6.1). The Lombard insisted that marital consent was separate from and independent of consent to intercourse. The one did not require the other.[36]

Peter Lombard's theory of marriage formation through present consent was,

[34] *In primis hominibus*, in B.L. MS Royal 11.B.XIII, fol. 86vb–87ra: "At uero inquirendum est quid dicat esse coniugium et forsitan sic poterit describi: suscipere mulierem in suam et uirum in suum tali consensu et uoluntate ut dum uixerint non se deserant et traddatur corpus suum in potestatem alt[er]ius ad debitum reddendum exprimendo hunc consensum uel talibus uerbis 'uolo te in uxorem' et 'te in maritum,' uel non contradicendo copulationibus eos si fuerint tales qui ualeant inter se contrahere coniugium. See also Rudolf Weigand, "Kanonistische Ehetraktate aus dem 12. Jahrhundert," in *Proceedings of the Third International Congress of Medieval Canon Law, Strasbourg, 3–6 September 1968*, ed. Stephan Kuttner, MIC, Subsidia, vol. 4 (Vatican City: Biblioteca Apostolica Vaticana, 1971; cited hereafter as *Strasbourg Proceedings*), p. 61.

[35] Quoted by Weigand, "Kanonistische Ehetraktate," pp. 66–67.

[36] Peter Lombard, *Libri IV sententiarum* 4.27.2–5, 4.28.3, 3d ed., Spicilegium Bonaventurianum, vols. 4–5 (Grottaferrata: Collegium S. Bonaventurae, 1971–81) 2:422–24, 434–35. Note that the Lombard's theory of consent differs radically from the consent theory of Roman law. Roman consent theory assumed that marital consent must be ongoing and continuing and could be revoked at any time by either party. Consent, as Peter Lombard understood it, was given once for all; once given (in the present tense, at least) it could not be revoked. See also Le Bras, "Observations sur le mariage," p. 426; Carl Gerold Fürst, "Ecclesia vivit lege Romana," ZRG, KA 61 (1975) 25; Coriden, *Indissolubility*, p. 3; Weigand, "Scheidungsproblem," p. 53; Esmein, *Mariage* 1:119–24.

in Maitland's words, "no masterpiece of human wisdom."[37] Although it would lead to many practical problems, however, the theory enjoyed great success. It attracted support initially only from the Parisian canonists; but later, as the result of papal intervention, it became the prevailing canonical marriage doctrine throughout Europe. Its triumph seriously undercut paternal authority within the family and helped to assure that the medieval family would not become a true patriarchy.[38]

In the mid-twelfth century, however, acceptance of this theory and of the Lombard's distinction between present and future consent, was still limited to theologians and canonists who taught or who received their training at Paris. The author of the *Summa Parisiensis*, for reasons that may be fortuitous, did not comment expressly on the conflict between Gratian's modified coital theory and Peter Lombard's version of the consensual theory. Still, passing references in the Paris *Summa* show that its author accepted the Lombard's formulation.[39] Stephen of Tournai refused to take sides in the conflict over marriage theories. After summarizing Gratian's theory, Stephen provided his readers with an account of Peter Lombard's alternative definition of marriage. He then declared: "We leave it to the reader whether he would prefer to accept this position."[40]

An obscure glossator who wrote in the 1160s, and whom the manuscripts refer to simply as "The Cardinal" (*Cardinalis*), identified marital consent with marital affection. A marital union, according to The Cardinal, was complete and perfect when the couple exchanged consent and sexual intercourse added nothing to the union that already existed.[41]

Joannes Faventinus, who wrote his *Summa* about 1171, proceeded cautiously in choosing between the opposing theories. Although he described Gratian's distinction between "marriage begun" (*matrimonium initiatum*) and

---

[37] Pollock and Maitland, *Hist. of English Law* 2:368.

[38] Herlihy, *Medieval Households*, pp. 81–82.

[39] SP omits discussion of C. 27–29, so that its text runs directly from C. 26 to C. 30. Since SP is known solely from one manuscript (Bamberg, Staatsbibliothek, MS Can. 36), it is possible that the lacuna may simply be an idiosyncrasy of the copyist who produced this MS. Where SP does deal with marriage formation, however, the author's preference for the Paris theory is quite plain; see SP to D. 34 c. 19; C. 30 q. 5 pr; C. 32 q. 2 pr.; C. 32 q. 7 c. 18, at pp. 33–34, 237, 241, and 248 in McLaughlin's edition. See also Terence P. McLaughlin, "The Formation of the Marriage Bond According to the *Summa Parisiensis*," *Mediaeval Studies* 15 (1953) 210–12.

[40] Stephen of Tournai, *Summa* to C. 27 q. 2 pr., ed. Schulte, pp. 235–36.

[41] Cardinalis, glosses to C. 27 q. 2 c. 3 v. *consensus*; C. 27 q. 2 c. 29 v. *coniunxerint*; C. 27 q. 2 d.p.c. 39 v. *uel effectum*; C. 27 q. 2 c. 35 v. *quam confirmat*, ed. Rudolf Weigand, "Die Glossen des Cardinalis (Magister Hubald?) zum Dekret Gratians," BMCL 3 (1973) 76, 78, 80. An anonymous gloss added that even words were not essential to express present consent: a mere nod would do; gloss to C. 27 q. 2 c. 5 v. *pactio coni.*, ibid., p. 88.

"marriage completed" (*matrimonium ratum*) as "noble," [42] he maintained that mutual assent in spirit created the marital bond that joined married couples. [43] Gandulphus, a slightly later glossator, agreed with The Cardinal and supported the consensual theory, together with the Lombard's distinction between present and future consent. By the 1180s, the consensual theory had become well established; Sicard of Cremona, who was not a daring innovator, accepted the Lombard's version of the consensual theory of marriage as a matter of course. [44]

A third analysis of the process by which marriage is contracted first emerged in the *Summa de matrimonio* written in the late 1150s by the Italian legist Vacarius (d. ca. 1200), who was at that point practicing and perhaps teaching civil law in England. Vacarius was displeased, even angry, at the way in which canonists of his generation dealt with the formation of marriage. They were, he thought, confusing the matter intolerably; their interpretations were inconsistent, useless, and rarely applied in practice. [45] Vacarius explicitly rejected Gratian's version of the coital theory. [46] While he did not comment on Peter Lombard's version of the consensual theory—understandably, since the Lombard was writing his *Sententiae* at almost precisely the same time as Vacarius composed his treatise on marriage—there is little reason to believe that he would have had much good to say of it either. Instead, Vacarius proposed that the law of marriage should rest on *traditio*, the delivery of the wife to the husband, in much the same way that the Roman law on transfer of property rested on the delivery of an object from a seller to a buyer or from a donor to a donee. [47]

Vacarius's contention that marriage took place by *traditio* clearly appealed to

[42] Joannes Faventinus, *Summa* to C. 27 q. 2 pr., in B.L. Royal 9.E.VII, fol. 134ra: "Hac distinctione nobili interiecta, scilicet de initiato et rato matrimonio. . . ."

[43] Joannes Faventinus, *Summa* to C. 27 q. 1 pr., in B.L. Royal 9.E.VII, fol. 131vb, and MS Add. 18,369, fol. 130ra–rb: "Coniunctio autem hic intelligitur non ipsa carnis commixtio, sed animorum mutua assensio, que in desponsatione contrahitur, quod cuique facile erit cognoscere, ex auctoritate ysidori que est supra d. xl. cap. sicut uiri [D. 40 c. 8]."

[44] Gandulphus, glosses to C. 27 q. 2 c. 17 v. *nuptiale ministerium* (citing Cardinalis as an authority) and C. 27 q. 2 pr., ed. Rudolf Weigand, "Gandulphusglossen zum Dekret Gratians," BMCL 7 (1977) 28, 32. Sicard of Cremona, *Summa* to C. 27 pr., in B.L., MS Add. 18,367, fol. 53v.

[45] Vacarius, *Summa de matrimonio*, pp. 270, 276; Joseph de Ghellinck, "Magister Vacarius: un juriste-théologien peu aimable pour les canonistes," *Revue d'histoire ecclésiastique* 44 (1949) 173–78. Kuttner and Rathbone, "Anglo-Norman Canonists," pp. 287–88, dated Vacarius's *Summa* between 1157 and 1159.

[46] Vacarius, *Summa de matrimonio*, pp. 271, 276, 278. Vacarius was particularly scornful of Gratian's notion of *matrimonium ratum*, a concept that he judged senseless and misleading; *Summa de matrimonio*, p. 285.

[47] Vacarius, *Summa de matrimonio*, pp. 278, 280; Charles Donahue, Jr., "The Case of the Man Who Fell into the Tiber: The Roman Law of Marriage at the Time of the Glossators," *American Journal of Legal History* 22 (1972) 23–26, 45–46. On *traditio* in Roman law see Inst. 2.1.40–46; Berger, *Encyclopedic Dictionary*, s.v. "traditio;" Jolowicz, *Historical Introduction*, pp. 143–45; Kaser, *Röm. Privatrecht* 1:351–53 and 2:197–98;

a number of his contemporaries. The idea that *traditio* makes marriage was at the heart of Bishop Henry of Winchester's opinion in the convoluted case of *Anstey c. Francheville*, which was fought out between 1158 and 1163, just as Vacarius was finishing his treatise.[48] Cardinalis seems at times to have thought along similar lines, for example, when he declared: "It is not carnal intercourse but the introduction of the bride into the house that makes a wife according to the law."[49] Vacarius's marriage theory also influenced the author of the *Summa "Elegantius in iure,"* the major treatise of the Rhineland school.[50]

The early Bolognese decretists accepted Gratian's conclusion that permanently binding, indissoluble marriage was limited to Christians and that marriages among infidels were neither *ratum* nor *perfectum*. Infidel marriages were thus subject to dissolution, according to the Bolognese masters.[51] Among the Parisian teachers, Stephen of Tournai also maintained that an infidel marriage, even though it was ratified by consummation, remained dissoluble. He added that a mixed marriage between an infidel and a Christian, even if consummated and thus ratified, could also be dissolved. Only marriages between Christians ought to be considered permanent unions, according to Stephen.[52] The Cardinal maintained, however, that consummation through sexual relations did not legally ratify marriages at all. In his view, ratification and hence indissolubility was conferred either by the priestly blessing during the wedding or else by the marital affection that the couple felt for each other.[53] Vacarius

F. de Zulueta, *The Institutes of Gaius*, 2 vols. (Oxford: Clarendon Press, 1953; repr. 1976) 2:61–62.

[48]John of Salisbury, *Letters* no. 131, ed. W. J. Millor, H. E. Butler, and C. N. L. Brooke, 2 vols., Oxford Medieval Texts (London: Thomas Nelson & Sons; Oxford: Clarendon Press, 1955–79) 1:229. John of Salisbury in this passage quotes Henry of Winchester's definition from a letter of Archbishop Theobald to Pope Alexander III. On *Anstey* see generally Patricia M. Barnes, "The Anstey Case," in *A Medieval Miscellany for Doris Mary Stenton*, ed. Patricia M. Barnes and C. F. Slade, Publications of the Pipe Roll society, n.s., vol. 36 (London: Pipe Roll Society, 1962), pp. 1–23.

[49]Cardinalis, gloss to C. 27 q. 2 d.p.c. 10, ed. Weigand, "Glossen des Cardinalis," p. 76. See also his gloss to C. 27 q. 2 c. 14 v. *desponsauerit*, ibid., p. 77.

[50]Little is known about contacts between jurists in England and their Rhineland counterparts. The Anglo-Norman canonist, Gerard Pucelle, was in Cologne while "*Elegantius*" was being written, however, and it is conceivable that Gerard might have played some role in making Vacarius's ideas known among the Rhenish canonists. Esmein, *Mariage* 1:114 n.3 and 118 n.1; Maitland, "Magister Vacarius," p. 137; Kuttner and Rathbone, "Anglo-Norman Canonists," p. 300. The marriage sections of the *Summa "Elegantius in iure diuino"* have not yet been published.

[51]Paucapalea, *Summa* to C. 28 q. 1, ed. Schulte, pp. 116–17; Rolandus, *Summa* to C. 28 q. 1 pr., ed. Thaner, pp. 133–35; Rufinus, *Summa* to C. 28 q. 1 pr., ed. Singer, p. 453.

[52]Stephen of Tournai, *Summa* to C. 28 q. 1 pr., ed. Schulte, p. 238.

[53]Cardinalis, gloss to C. 27 q. 2 c. 50 v. *de coniugali*, ed. Weigand, "Glossen des Cardinalis," p. 81.

brushed the whole controversy aside and declared roundly that Gratian's distinction was senseless. Any marriage, whether between Christians or infidels, was ratified, according to Vacarius, if the law recognized it as valid.[54]

Those who held that marriage was completed by the exchange of consent and ratified by marital affection or the nuptial blessing seem to have been motivated in part by a desire to reduce the significance of sex in marriage and to recast Christian matrimonial theory in terms of a spiritual rather than carnal union. The Cardinal expressed this notion more clearly than most when he argued that a marriage without sexual relations is better than one in which the couple have carnal intercourse. A decision to refrain from sex, he insisted, does not break the bond of marriage—indeed it makes it firmer, since the union is then based upon mutual affection, rather than upon a passion for pleasure and venereal sensations.[55]

The most trenchant and influential critic of Gratian's treatment of marriage was Huguccio, who flatly rejected Gratian's marriage formation theory as erroneous.[56] Huguccio totally abandoned Gratian's distinction between initiated and consummated marriage and opted instead for the Lombard's consensual theory. Present consent alone, Huguccio maintained, immediately created a perfect and complete marriage between a couple; the marriage was indissoluble from the moment of present consent, and sexual intercourse was not required. Huguccio also rejected the notion that parental permission, ecclesiastical ceremonies, or *traditio* were essential to the creation of marriage. Present consent, so long as it was not coerced or otherwise interfered with, and so long as the parties were legally free to marry one another, constituted the only requirement for the creation of a lifelong union. Everything else, including sexual relations, seemed irrelevant to him.[57]

With Huguccio and with the decretals of Alexander III, which we will examine in the next chapter, the victory of the consensual theory as expounded by Peter Lombard was virtually assured in the schools. Although a few writers still clung to Gratian's version of the coital theory of marriage, they were a decided minority after the time of Huguccio.[58] Consent in the present tense was almost

[54] Vacarius, *Summa de matrimonio*, pp. 285–86.

[55] Cardinalis, gloss to C. 27 q. 2 c. 16 v. *pertinere*, in Weigand, "Glossen des Cardinalis," p. 77, and more forcefully in an unsigned gloss to c. 27 q. 2 c. 10 v. *sacramentum*, ibid., p. 90.

[56] Huguccio, *Summa* to C. 27 q. 2 d.p.c. 45 v. *ex his omnibus*, in Vat. lat. 2280, fol. 262vb, as well as ed. Roman, p. 799: "Fere per totum istud § male dicit Gratianus, imo fere per totam hanc questionem."

[57] Huguccio, *Summa* to C. 27 q. 2 pr., Vat. lat. 2280, fol. 259vb, and ed. Roman, p. 746: "Si ergo inter aliquos interueniat desponsatio de presenti, statim est matrimonium inter eos perfectum et integrum, nec potest solui nisi morte uel transitu ad religionem. . . ." See also Coriden, *Indissolubility*, pp. 35–38.

[58] Notably the *Questiones Cusanae*, no. 18 and no. 33, written after the mid–1180s; see Gérard Fransen, "Les *Quaestiones Cusanae*: questions disputées sur le mariage,"

universally accepted by canonists after the late 1180s as the critical test of whether a marriage existed or not.[59] Customary law, to be sure, remained largely unaffected by the doctrinal shifts among the learned jurists; local courts continued to treat consummation as essential to the creation of a binding marriage.[60] But as the ecclesiastical courts, presided over increasingly by university-trained canonists, secured a virtual monopoly over questions relating to the formation of marriage, the consensual theory became the standard both of theory and of practice.

Disputes about marriage formation and related matters in the writings of the decretists reflected uncertainties in the ways that the popes of the second half of the twelfth century handled these problems. Papal marriage decisions of this period showed a considerable variety of opinion and practice, as we shall see in the next chapter. When Alexander III dissolved marriages on grounds of supervening affinity, and when Urban III granted a divorce to a woman whose husband had contracted leprosy and allowed remarriage when a missing man's death was presumed but not proved, so long as the first marriage had not been consummated, we are seeing the views of the Bolognese school put into practice. Before the end of the century, however, papal policy had begun to incline toward acceptance of the Parisian theory of consensual marriage, and papal decisions in marriage cases increasingly reflected this policy shift.

The displacement of the coital marriage theory by the consensual theory in the schools was probably not unrelated to the growing conviction among theo-

---

in *Convivium utriusque iuris: A. Dordett zum 60. Geburtstag* (Vienna: Wiener Dom-Verlag, 1976), pp. 216, 220.

[59] Esmein's contention in *Mariage* 1:119–21 that the triumph of the consensual position was a result of its juristic virtues is unconvincing. He asserts that the exchange of consent can readily be proved or disproved by witnesses, whereas consummation usually cannot. The weaknesses of the argument are three: first, the exchange of consent could be proved by witnesses only if witnesses were present; but since witnesses were not required for validity until the sixteenth century, a great many alleged exchanges of consent during the five hundred years between the Lombard and the Council of Trent could not in fact be proved by witnesses, and this created enormous problems, as we shall see later. Second, even when witnesses were available, their testimony could not prove the exchange of consent, but only the enunciation of words or other signs that seemed to convey consent. Parties could still deny that the words signified interior consent, and in fact they often did so. Consent, in other words, depended upon intention, and that is always difficult to demonstrate without question. Third, while eyewitnesses were rarely available to prove consummation, circumstantial evidence to corroborate the sworn testimony of the parties was often available and was used. In short, the consensual theory had no clear superiority over the coital theory so far as the law of evidence was concerned; in practice it was flawed precisely because it lacked an intrinsic basis for evidence as to whether a marriage had been contracted or not. See further the remarks of Pollock and Maitland, *Hist. of English Law* 2:369.

[60] Turlan, "Mariage dans la pratique coutumière," pp. 486, 500.

logians that Christian marriage ought to be considered a sacrament. True, Christian writers had for many centuries used the term *sacramentum* to describe marriage, but until the twelfth century the meaning of the word, particularly as applied to marriage, had never been defined with precision.[61] The clarification the concept of sacramentality and its application to marriage owed a great deal, once more, to Peter Lombard. Although he was neither the first theologian to use the term *sacramentum* specifically to describe the mechanism for securing grace under the Christian dispensation nor the first to include marriage among the sacraments of the Christian faith, the Lombard's exposition of these notions became the standard treatment that every theologian studied in the schools of the high and later Middle Ages.[62]

When canonists dealt with the sacramental nature of marriage they were less concerned with its internal spiritual effects than with its external manifestations. While Gandulphus maintained that the sacramental element in marriage is the marital union itself, other decretists criticized his approach and sought to identify the sacramentality of marriage with the inseparability and mutual dependence of the married couple, which they compared to the union between Christ and the Church.[63] Marriage can exist without children and even without fidelity, Joannes Faventinus declared, but it must have stability, otherwise it would be impossible to distinguish marriage from casual sexual unions. Further, he argued, the stability which is the essence of the sacrament of marriage must be capable of surviving temporary separations, which often occur during marriage. When the married couple are sacramentally joined, they remain married despite short-term separations. That sacramental union, Joannes argued, is at the core of the married state.[64] Huguccio agreed: "I say, therefore, that the sacrament that is the good of marriage is the inseparability of the mar-

[61] Seamus P. Heany, *The Development of the Sacramentality of Marriage from Anselm of Laon to Thomas Aquinas*, Catholic University of America, Studies in Sacred Theology, ser. 2, no. 134 (Washington: Catholic University of America, 1963), p. 1.

[62] An earlier expositor of these ideas, upon whom Peter Lombard drew freely, was Hugh of St. Victor, who wrote a treatise *De sacramentis* about 1134; see *Hugh of St. Victor on the Sacraments of the Christian Faith* 1.9.2 and 2.11.1–3, trans. Roy J. Deferrari, Mediaeval Academy of America, Publications, No. 53 (Cambridge, MA: Mediaeval Academy of America, 1951), pp. 154–59, 324–27. See also Heany, *Development of Sacramentality*, p. 70; Bailey, *Sexual Relation*, pp. 139–40.

[63] Weigand, "Gandulphusglossen," p. 28, gloss to C. 27 q. 2 c. 10 v. *sacramentum*; but see also the *Summa Lipsiensis* to C. 27 q. 2 pr., as well as the commentaries on this passage in the *Summa Tractaturus magister* and the *Summa* of Master Honorius, quoted in Weigand, "Liebe und Ehe," p. 59, n. 68–70.

[64] Joannes Faventinus, *Summa* to C. 27 pr., in B.L. Royal 9.E.VII, fol. 132ra: "Sit notandum quod coniugium sepe est sine fide et prole; perfectum quoque matrimonium nullo modo poterit sine sacramento esse. Licet enim corporaliter aliquando coniuges separantur, quod fit utriusque consensu ad tempus uel mentium promissa continentia, sacramentaliter tamen [MS: in] utroque uiuente numquam separari possunt, ut xxxii. q. vii. c. ul. [c. 28]."

ried couple."[65] Huguccio insisted that the sacrament of marriage must not be identified with carnal intercourse, since the desire for sexual relations is volatile and might pass away, while the spiritual union of the married couple persists.[66]

The author of the gloss apparatus *Ordinaturus magister* posited a further distinction between marriage and the other sacraments. While other sacraments give grace, he asserted, marriage does not, for other sacraments operate through sacred words, while marriage depends instead on the consent of the parties. Further, he continued, the other sacraments originated with canon law, while marriage originated in the law of nature.[67]

In order to explain the nature and effects of marriage, many decretists found it necessary to examine its origins and purposes as a human institution. They postulated that marriage has a dual origin: it first began in Paradise, where it was instituted for the procreation of children. After the Fall, marriage was reinstituted outside of Paradise, according to this scheme, this time for protection against fornication.[68] Just as marriage had two origins, it continues to have two

[65] Huguccio, *Summa* to C. 27 q. 2 c. 10 v. *ex peccato*, in Weigand, "Gandulphusglossen," p. 41, and Roman, p. 758.

[66] Huguccio, *Summa* to C. 27 q. 2. c. 16 v. *non pertinere ad matrimonium*, in Weigand, "Gandulphusglossen," p. 41, and *Summa* to C. 27 q. 2 pr., ed. Roman, p. 749.

[67] *Ordinaturus magister* to C. 1 q. 1 c. 101 v. *quicquid*, in Weigand, *Naturrechtslehre*, p. 286. Joannes Faventinus, *Summa* to C. 32 q. 2 d.a.c. 4 v. *non autem datur presentia spiritus sancti*, in B.L. Royal 9.E.VII, fol. 142vb, added that marital intercourse, although it did not give grace, at least did not take it away: "Id est propter coniugales illos actus gratia scilicet non datur; si tamen habetur, non amittitur, nisi in casu illo in quo modo talis culpa incurritur." Cf. SP to C. 32 q. 2 c. 4, ed. McLaughlin, p. 241. Magister Hermannus, a follower of Abelard, maintained a similar distinction; Müller, *Lehre des hl. Augustinus*, p. 74.

[68] Rolandus, *Summa* to C. 27 pr., ed. Thaner, pp. 113–14. The comments of Rufinus on C. 27 pr. were copied almost verbatim by Joannes Faventinus and Simon of Bisignano:

Rufinus (ed. cit., p. 432)	Joannes Faventinus (B.L. Royal 9. E. VII fol. 132ra	Simon of Bisignano (B.L. MS Add. 24,659, fol. 28vb)
Matrimonii vero institutio duplex fuit: una in paradiso ante peccatum, altera extra paradisum post peccatum. Prima ad officium propter sobolem propagandum, dicente Domino, 'Crescite et multiplicamini et replete terram [Gen. 1:28]'; secunda ad remedium propter fornicationem vitandam, dicente	Matrimonii uero institutio duplex fuit: una in paradiso ante peccatum, altera extra paradisum post peccatum. Prima ad officium propter sobolem propagandum, dicente Domino, 'Crescite et multiplicamini et replete terram [Gen. 1:28]'; secunda ad remedium propter fornicationem uitandam, dicente	Duplex uero est institutio matrimonii. Una fuit in paradiso ante peccatum, altera extra paradisum post peccatum. Prima concessa fuit propter sobolem, domino dicente, 'Crescite et multiplicamini'; secunda ab apostolo propter uitandam fornicationis periculum est concessa, dicente

purposes: the satisfaction of sexual desire and the begetting of offspring.[69] Of these, sexual desire was the "less honest," although, as Rolandus noted, many people nonetheless marry for that reason.[70]

The decretists agreed, however, that whatever other considerations entered into the choice of marriage partner, the avoidance of fornication was one prin-

---

apostolo, 'Ususquisque uxorem accipiat propter fornicationem [cf. 1 Cor. 7:2],' ut infirmitas prona in ruinam turpitudinis, sicut Augustinus dicit, honestate coniugii exciperetur.	apostolo 'Unusquisque propter fornicationem accipiat uxorem,' ut infirmitas prona in ruinam turpitudinis, sicut Augustinus dicit, honestate coniugii exciperetur.	apostolo, 'Unusquisque habeat suam propter fornicationem uitandam,' ut sic infirmitas prona ad ruinam turpitudinis honestate coniugii exciperetur, ut infra eodem questio, nuptiarum [C. 27 q. 1 c. 41].

See also the *Fragmentum Cantabrigiensis* to C. 27 pr., in Cambridge University Library, MS Add. 3321(1), fol. 10r: "A quo sit institutum? A deo, scilicet institutum est ut ex celsitudine institutoris dignitas sacramenti intelligatur. Ubi institutum est? In paradiso. Quando institutum est? VI. die, ut ex lectione genesis colligitur."

[69] Rolandus, *Summa* to C. 27 pr., C. 27 q. 1 c. 41 v. *in quibusdam*, and C. 32 q. 2 pr., ed. Thaner, pp. 114, 125, 164. Rufinus, *Summa* to C. 27 pr., ed. Singer, p. 432, was again followed closely by Joannes Faventinus and Simon of Bisignano:

Rufinus (ed. cit., p. 432)	Joannes Faventinus (B.L. Royal 9.E.VII, fol. 132ra)	Simon of Bisignano (B.L. MS Add. 24,659, fol. 28vb)
Denique cause coniugii alie sunt propter quas, alie per quas contrahitur; cause propter quas contrahitur alie sunt principales, alie secundarie. Et quidem principales intelliguntur susceptio prolis et vitatio fornicationis, secundarie vero ut: mulieris pulcritudo, pacis reformatio, divitiarum possessio et similia.	Denique cause coniugii alie sunt principales, alie sunt secundarie; et quidem principales intelliguntur susceptio prolis et et uitatio fornicationis, secundarie uero ut mulieris pulcritudo, pacis reformatio, dititiarum possessio et similia.	Cause uero propter quas contrahitur matrimonium alie sunt principales, alie secundarie. Principales sunt iste: susceptio prolis, uitatio fornicatinis; secundarie sunt uero mulieris pulcritudo, pacis reformatio.

Sicard of Cremona's comments in B.L. MS Add. 18,367, fol. 53vb, also bear a close resemblance to the other three: "Cause [matrimonii] alie sunt propter quas, alie per quas. Propter quas alie principales, alie secundarie. Principales due que ad duas respiciunt insitutiones, uidelicet procreatio prolis, uitatio fornicationis. Ad secundariam, secundarie que non respiciunt ad institutiones, ut mulieris pulcritudo, diuitiarum possessio, pacis reintegratio." Cf. the gloss to the *Summa* of Honorius in Weigand, "Liebe und Ehe," p. 48.

[70] Paucapalea, *Summa* to C. 27 pr., closely followed by the treatise *Sacramentum con-*

cipal goal of matrimony and that individuals ought to seek marriage partners sufficiently attractive to ward off outside temptations.[71] Other reasons for marriage, such as a desire for wealth or a need to form a family alliance, were subsidiary to fleeing fleshly temptations.[72] When the decretists spoke of mutual attraction between partners as a basic condition for marriage, they referred primarily to physical attraction, rather than to love or emotional attachment. Love, as they conceived it, was a consequence of marriage, not a cause of it.[73] At the same time, the decretists usually maintained that marriage was more than just a joining of bodies, but that it necessarily involved a joining of souls as well, to create a "solid friendship" (*firma amicitia*) in which husband and wife shared common likes and dislikes.[74]

Marriage for the decretists was more than just a contract, more than a sexual partnership for the breeding of children, and certainly more than an instrument for transmitting property and cementing ties between families. In addition to

---

iugii non ab homine. See also Weigand, "Liebe und Ehe," p. 45 n. 13; Rolandus, *Summa* to C. 31 q. 1 c. 9 v. *numerus maritorum,* ed. Thaner, p. 156; Rufinus, *Summa* to C. 31 q. 1 c. 8 v. *secundis nuptiis,* ed. Singer, p. 471; and Joannes Faventinus, *Summa* to D. 26 c. 2 v. *bigami non pecasse,* in B.L. Royal 9.E.VII, fol. 15va: "Hac ratione hic ad ueritatem, ibi ad exhortationem; uel hic de secundis qui contrahuntur causa solatii sobolis quam suscipiende, ibi de eis qui causa luxurie, sicut duobus dominis seruire non licet, scilicet christo et diabolo." An anonymous treatise on marriage, *Sacramentum coniugii non ab homine,* proposed a more elaborate analysis of reasons for marrying. Four factors enter into a woman's choice of a husband, its author wrote: strength, family, beauty, and wisdom. The important considerations for a man's choice of wife are different, according to this writer, for men take into account first a woman's beauty, then her family, her wealth, and her habits; Weigand, "Liebe und Ehe," p. 45 n. 14.

[71] Paucapalea, *Summa* to C. 27 pr., ed. Schulte, pp. 110–11; Rolandus, *Summa* to C. 31 q. 1, ed. Thaner, p. 156; and Sicard of Cremona, quoted in Francesco Salerno, "La definizione nominale del matrimonio canonico nei secoli XII–XIII," in *Ius populi Dei: Miscellanea in honorem Raymundi Bigador,* 3 vols. (Rome: Gregoriana, 1972) 3:168 n. 25.

[72] Paucapalea, *Summa* to C. 27 q. 2 c. 10, ed. Schulte, p. 115; see also n. 70 above.

[73] SP to C. 35 q. 1 pr., ed. McLaughlin, p. 258, argued that although the human race at the beginning was forced to practice endogamy, God commanded that people turn to exogamy as soon as it was practical to do so. One outcome of this, according to SP, was that people were thus compelled to expand the circle of the persons whom they loved outside of their extended families. Rufinus, *Summa* to C. 35 q. 1 pr., ed. Singer, p. 509, enlarged on this argument; see also Weigand, "Liebe und Ehe," p. 49.

[74] Rufinus, *Summa* to C. 27 pr., ed. Singer, p. 430, adopted verbatim by Joannes Faventinus, in B.L. Royal 9.E.VII, fol. 131vb, and followed closely by Simon of Bisignano, B.L. MS Add. 24,659, fol. 28va–vb. Likewise Sicard of Cremona, *Summa* to C. 27 pr., in B.L. MS Add. 18,367, fol. 53va: "Nam idem uelle et idem nolle firma est amicitia." Huguccio, *Summa* to D. 1 c. 7 v. *ut uiri et femine coniunctio,* in MS lat. 3892, fol. 2va, of the Bibliothèque National in Paris (hereafter B.N.) went even further: "Matrimonium non est nisi coniunctio animorum." See also his comments to C. 27 q. 2 pr., ed. Roman, p. 747.

these other characteristics, the decretists saw marriage as a personal relationship between husband and wife, a relationship bonded by the marital affection that was essential to the matrimonial union.[75] This enlargement of the decretists' concept of marriage was part of a broader development in the late twelfth century that has been called the discovery of the self.[76] Along with poets and theologians among their contemporaries, the decretists believed that intimate relationships should be grounded in a sharing of personal identity and outlook.[77] In marriage this shared identity included, but was not limited to, the partners' sexual activity; their shared sexual relationship must be exclusive not only because law and morality required it, but also because infidelity betrayed the trust and affection upon which marriage was grounded.[78]

The identification of marriage primarily with emotional, rather than sexual aspects of the relationship between the parties enabled the decretists to account gracefully for some anomalies in the traditional accounts of the union between the Virgin Mary and St. Joseph. Those who accepted the coital theory of marriage had great difficulty in explaining how or in what sense the Blessed Virgin and Joseph had been married, and several mid-twelfth century commentators criticized Gratian's theory of marriage formation precisely on this account.[79] Those who grounded marriage on emotional rather than sexual ties had little difficulty in interpreting the union of Mary and Joseph as a legitimate marriage.[80]

---

[75] Huguccio, *Summa* to C. 27 q. 2 c. 36 v. *quam* in Vat. lat. 2280, fol. 262rb, and ed. Roman, p. 793: "Coniunctionem, id est ex matrimonio et est personalis relatio." Vacarius argued that marital consent implies emotional bonding of heart and mind; *Summa de matrimonio*, ed. Maitland, p. 274. See also Weigand, "Liebe und Ehe," p. 42; Noonan, "Marital Affection," p. 509; and Jean-Louis Flandrin, *Les amours paysannes: amour et sexualité dans les campagnes de l'ancien France (XVIe–XIXe siècles)*, Collection archives, no. 57 (Paris: Gallimard/Julliard, 1975), pp. 25–27.

[76] Bynum, *Jesus as Mother*, p. 87.

[77] Leclercq, *Monks on Marriage*, pp. 1, 8, 29, citing the views of Egbert of Schönau (d. 1184) and Richard of St. Victor (d. 1173).

[78] Rolandus, *Summa* to C. 27 q. 2 c. 6 v. *coniuges verius*, ed. Thaner, pp. 127–28; Huguccio, *Summa* to C. 27 q. 2 c. 10 and c. 51, ed. Roman, pp. 759, 803.

[79] Rolandus, *Summa* to C. 27 q. 2 c. 10 v. *omne itaque*, ed. Thaner, p. 128; Stephen of Tournai, *Summa* to C. 27 q. 2 pr., ed. Schulte, p. 235; Rufinus, *Summa* to C. 27 q. 2 pr., ed. Singer, pp. 444–45; Cardinalis, gloss to C. 27 q. 2 d.p.c. 29 v. *simpliciter sponsa* and v. *quam Joseph*, ed. Weigand, p. 79; Huguccio, *Summa* to C. 27 q. 2 c. 9, v. *coniugium fidele* and to C. 27 q. 2 d.p.c. 39 v. *futura erat coniux*, in Weigand, "Gandulphusglossen," pp. 40, 41. See also Penny S. Gold, "The Marriage of Mary and Joseph in the Twelfth-Century Ideology of Marriage," in Vern L. Bullough and James A. Brundage, eds., *Sexual Practices and the Medieval Church* (Buffalo: Prometheus Press, 1982), pp. 102–17.

[80] Gandulphus, glosses to C. 27 q. 2 c. 3 v. *copulam* and C. 27 q. 2 c. 10, in Weigand, "Gandulphusglossen," pp. 28, 32; Vacarius, *Summa de matrimonio*, ed. Maitland, p. 279.

When the decretists described a marriage as "legitimate," they usually meant a union between persons who were legally capable of marrying one another. The decretists, like the civilians, also used "legitimate" on occasion to describe marriages contracted with the consent of the families of the parties and solemnized by a formal ceremony, but cautious writers hesitated to assign this meaning to the term. While customary law in regions as widely separated as Sicily and England required formal marriage ceremonies and dowries, the canonists did not.[81] Although they certainly did not oppose, and indeed rather favored, the use of wedding rituals and the formalization of property arrangements through dowry agreements, the decretists commonly held that none of these formalities was essential.[82] A union without these was as valid and as binding as one contracted with full pomp and circumstance, despite the problems that private, informal marriages created. Betrothal, too, was not a necessary preliminary to marriage, although it was desirable; the canonists refused to hold prenuptial betrothal agreements binding if the parties subsequently changed their minds and decided to marry someone else.[83]

Without exception, the decretists insisted that consent to marriage must be free and uncoerced; the use of force in order to secure the agreement of either party might invalidate the marriage. They maintained, too, that while parents and families had the right to make known their preferences concerning their children's marriages, elders had no right to impose those preferences on a child who objected to them.[84] The principle that marriage can only be contracted by free consent of the parties was often reiterated by decretists and Church officials.

[81] Rufinus, *Summa* to D. 34 d.p.c. 3 v. *que cessantibus legalibus instrumentis* and to C. 27 pr., ed. Singer, pp. 80, 430, closely followed by Joannes Faventinus in B.L. Royal 9.E.VII, fol. 20ra, 131vb, and MS Add. 18,369, fol. 14rb and 130rb. See also *Frag. Cantab.* to C. 27 q. 2 c. 2, in U.L.C., MS Add. 3321(1), fol. 13v: "Hic solus ponitur ad remotionem paterni consensus, et materni, et hic confutatur eorum sententia qui dicunt se non inuenire in canonibus quod sine consensu patris et matris alique possit contrahere matrimonium." See further Marongiu, "Forma religiosa," pp. 10–11; Michael M. Sheehan, "The Influence of Canon Law on the Property Rights of Married Women," *Mediaeval Studies* 25 (1963) 114.

[82] Stephen of Tournai, *Summa* to C. 3 q. 4 c. 4 v. *vel absque dotali titulo*, ed. Schulte, p. 194; Huguccio, *Summa* to C. 27 q. 2 c. 2, ed. Roman, pp. 750–51; but cf. SP to C. 3 q. 4 c. 4 v. *absque dotali*, ed. McLaughlin, p. 119, and Rufinus, *Summa* to C. 3 q. 4 c. 4 v. *absque dotali titulo*, ed. Singer, p. 265. See also Cesare Nani, *Storia del diritto privato italiano*, ed. Francesco Ruffini (Turin: Fratelli Boca, 1902; repr. Milan: Cisalpino-Goliardica, 1972), pp. 175–76; Esmein, *Mariage* 1 : 186–87.

[83] Rolandus, *Summa* to C. 31 q. 3 pr., ed. Thaner, p. 157; SP to C. 31 q. 2 pr. and q. 3 c. un. v. *si qui*, ed. McLaughlin, p. 239; Rufinus, *Summa* to C. 30 q. 2 pr. and C. 31 q. 2 pr., ed. Singer, pp. 462, 473, followed almost verbatim by Joannes Faventinus in B.L. Royal 9.E.VII, fol. 141ra, and MS Add. 18,369, fol. 139rb.

[84] Rolandus, *Summa* to C. 20 q. 3 and C. 31 q. 2, ed. Thaner, pp. 72–73, 157; Rufinus, *Summa* to C. 31 q. 2 pr., ed. Singer, p. 473; SP to C. 31 q. 2 c. 1 v. *ne ignoran-*

Families continued through the twelfth century and beyond, however, to concoct stratagems of various kinds to secure compliance with their wedding aims. A Montpellier man in 1172, for example, disinherited any daughter who failed to comply with his plans for her marriage; this ploy, with numerous variations, continued long in use. Parents even dictated marriage plans for their children in their wills: unless my daughter marries so-and-so, she shall receive no part of my estate; if she does marry him, however, then she shall receive such-and-such.[85] A person who went through a form of marriage in order to inherit an estate or to placate family members, but who never consented at heart to the union, could in theory appeal to the Church courts to be released from the marriage. Such cases were difficult to prove, but pleas of this sort occasionally succeeded.[86]

Even greater problems arose with clandestine marriages. The decretists, faithful to Gratian's teaching and to papal policy, recognized marriages that took place without formalities or witnesses as valid.[87] But jurists sought to discourage hidden marriages, because they opened the way to abuse. Rufinus, for one, taught that couples who married secretly should be presumed to be living in adultery or fornication, unless they could rebut this presumption.[88] If the parties could somehow convince a judge that they had entered the union with the intention of contracting a permanent marriage, their union was deemed to have become legitimate after the fact.[89]

---

tibus, ed. McLaughlin, p. 239; John of Salisbury, *Epist.* 131, ed. Miller, Butler, and Brooke 1:230, quoting Archbishop Theobald in the Anstey case; Leclercq, *Monks on Marriage,* p. vii.

[85] Turlan, "Mariage dans la pratique coutumière," pp. 487–91.

[86] Rolandus, *Summa* to C. 30 q. 5 c. 10, ed. Thaner, p. 154; also *Frag. Cantab.* to C. 27 pr., in U.L.C., MS Add. 3321(1), fol. 10v: "Sed quid si pactum coniugalem interfuit ubi tamen in mulierem minime consenserit, immo animo decipiendi dixerit mulieri, 'uolo te in meam,' ut scilicet eam corruptam postea deficerit. Dicit rolandus quod non minus contrahitur matrimonium." The *Questiones Cusane,* no. 21, ed. Fransen, p. 217, discussed a hypothetical situation of this sort; for actual cases, but of later date, see Richard H. Helmholz, *Marriage Litigation in Medieval England,* Cambridge Studies in English Legal History (Cambridge: At the University Press, 1974), pp. 91–93.

[87] Paucapalea, *Summa* to C. 30 q. 5, ed. Schulte, p. 123; SP C. 30 q. 5 pr., ed. McLaughlin, p. 237; Rufinus, *Summa* to C. 30 q. 5 pr., ed. Singer, p. 468, followed verbatim by Joannes Faventinus in B.L. Royal 9.E.VII., fol. 140ra.

[88] Rufinus, *Summa* to C. 30 q. 5 c. 1 v. *adulteria,* ed. Singer, p. 469, followed closely by Joannes Faventinus in B.L. MS Add. 18,369, fol. 141ra. See also Sicard of Cremona, *Summa* to C. 30 q. 5, in B.L. MS Add. 18,367, fol. 58rb: "Licet ergo sollempnitatibus priuetur, si legitima tamen testium assit probatio manifestum [*scil.*: matrimonium] preiudicat, aliter nequaquam quia super re incerta non est certa precipitanda sententia, sicut habes in hoc questionis paragrapho his ita [d.p.c. 10]."

[89] SP to C. 30 q. 5 pr., ed. McLaughlin, p. 237; Rufinus, *Summa* to C. 30 q. 5 pr., ed. Singer, p. 468; Sicard of Cremona, *Summa* to C. 30 q. 5, B.L. MS Add. 18,367, fol.

Couples who faced opposition from parents and family often married secretly in defiance of family pressure.[90] The decretists felt obliged to treat clandestine marriages as valid because of their opposition to forced marriages and their concern to implement the basic principle of canonical marriage law, namely that free consent was essential to valid marriage. If a couple exchanged consent, it was logically difficult for decretists who accepted the consensual theory to deny validity to such a marriage, despite lack of witnesses, ceremonial, and the like. Indeed, the decretists were prepared to admit almost any sort of plausible testimony that corroborated the statements of the parties as evidence for an exchange of consent.[91]

Serious problems arose when a party who had allegedly been married by a clandestine exchange of consent later married another partner publicly. If the first spouse petitioned the Church courts to adjudge the earlier union valid, it might well happen that adequate evidence could not be produced to prove the existence of a marriage, even though both partners knew perfectly well that they had exchanged consent. In situations of this sort, the courts could find themselves requiring the partners in the second marriage to continue living together in an adulterous union.[92] This was obviously unsatisfactory, but given the rules about clandestine marriage and the rules of evidence that the courts worked with, anomalous outcomes of this sort were unavoidable.[93]

An irregular but not infrequent type of marriage that twelfth-century decretists also had to cope with was the conditional marriage, where consent was contingent upon the fulfillment of a condition. Thus, "I marry you, but only on

---

58rb: "His ita respondeo: multa ab inicio non ualent que ex post facto conualescunt, sicut est coniugium alicuius cum sorore sua adoptiua et coniugia simpliciter uouentis. Similiter clandestina coniugia licet a principio non ualeant, ex postero conualescunt." McLaughlin, "Formation of the Marriage Bond," p. 210; Fransen, "Formation du lien matrimonial," p. 215; Turlan, "Mariage dans la pratique coutumière," p. 503. Rufinus also noted that while the law formerly held that the parties to clandestine marriages were subject to *infamia*, this penalty was no longer operative, because the law had been derogated by contrary custom; *Summa* to C. 3 q. 4 c. 4 v. *absque dotali titulo*, ed. Singer, p. 265.

[90] Giuseppe Ferroglio, "Raptus in parentes," *Annali della Facoltà giuridica dell'Università di Camerino* 19 (1952) 14–15; Esmein, *Mariage* 2:127.

[91] Thus the *Questiones Cusane* no. 22, ed. Fransen, p. 218, held that the evidence of witnesses who overheard a couple exchange consent in another room might prove the existence of a marriage, provided that one of the witnesses had glimpsed the couple while they were speaking the words of consent.

[92] Esmein, *Mariage* 1:189–91, 2:127–28; Pollock and Maitland, *Hist. of English Law* 2:385; Helmholz, *Marriage Litigation*, pp. 30–31.

[93] Huguccio, *Summa* to C. 27 q. 2, quoted in Jean Dauvillier, *Le mariage dans le droit classique de l'église depuis le Décret de Gratien (1140) jusqu'à la mort de Clément V (1314)* (Paris: Sirey, 1933), p. 57; *Questiones Cusane*, no. 19, ed. Fransen, pp. 216–17; Helmholz, *Marriage Litigation*, pp. 195–96.

condition that you produce a son," or "on condition that you give me a thousand gold pieces," or "on condition that your father pay the dowry that he has promised," were typical contingencies.

Conditional marriages presented the decretists with painful choices. The canonists could have adopted three possible attitudes with respect to conditional marriages. First, they could have ignored the conditions and judged the validity of the marriage without reference to them. Second the jurists could have acknowledged the existence of the conditions, but denied that the validity of the marriage depended upon their fulfillment. Third, they could have accepted the conditions as decisive for the existence of a legal marriage.[94] None of the alternatives was entirely acceptable, and no good solution to the problem was immediately apparent from the law as expounded in Gratian's *Decretum*. The problem required, in fact, both further legislation to clarify the basic law and additional discussion of the constituent issues before a consensus on the problem of conditional marriage could emerge.[95]

The Decretists and Marital Sex

The decretists' treatment of the legal implications and consequences of marital sex varied widely and depended not only upon the legal and theological presuppositions of the commentators, but also upon their understanding of contemporary ideas about medicine, physiology, and biology.[96] A few of these learned but presumably celibate jurists seemed sympathetic to the ideals of love and sex advocated by the poets who celebrated the joys of *fin'amors*.[97] A happy marriage, some decretists thought, should be a source of love and emotional satisfaction as well as a remedy for lust.[98]

Most commentators on the *Decretum* believed that sexual attraction fur-

[94] Weigand, *Bedingte Eheschliessung*, pp. 44, 176–77.

[95] Discussions of conditional marriage in the early decretists were scanty and often unclear. They provided little worthwhile guidance to the parties and their legal advisers or to the courts; see, e.g., Rolandus, *Summa* to C. 27 q. 2 c. 9, ed. Thaner, p. 128. Paucapalea, Rufinus, Stephen of Tournai, and the SP refrained from dealing with the issue at all. The gloss of Gandulphus to C. 27 q. 2 c. 8, in Weigand, "Gandulphus-glossen," p. 32, is one of the few straightforward treatments of the problem in this period. See generally Weigand, *Bedingte Eheschliessung*, pp. 414–23.

[96] Claude Thomasset, "La représentation de la sexualité et de la génération dans la pensée scientifique médiévale," in *Love and Marriage in the Twelfth Century*, p. 1.

[97] Leclercq, *Monks and Love*, p. 64.

[98] Tractatus *In primis hominibus*, in B.L. Royal 11.B.XIII, fol. 83vb: "Est [matrimonium] remedium contra delectationem libidinis qua coniugati conmiscentur, et per bona coniugii que sunt fides, proles, sacramentum. Sunt preterea alia bona nuptiarum, ut abstinere ab illicita libidine et naturalis societas que est in diuerso sexu, nec non etiam quedam [*MS canc.*: specialis; *add. in margine*: spiritualis] caritas ex illa procedens." On twelfth-century notions of happiness in marriage see Leclercq, *Monks on Love*, p. 52.

nished an unsatisfactory motive for marriage, but those who followed the Bolognese teaching considered that a sexual relationship was not merely a usual element of marriage, but an essential one.[99] Those who married because of sexual attraction acted legitimately, according to Sicard of Cremona and others, because one purpose of marriage was to provide a remedy for lust. This, said Sicard, justified marriages founded primarily upon sexual considerations.[100]

This belief that sex played a central role in the very formation of marriage helps to explain the reappearance of the marriage bed as a marital symbol. Although the bed had played a central symbolic role in early medieval wedding ceremonies, especially in Gaul, it virtually disappeared from the rituals in the late ninth century, only to reappear again late in the twelfth century. Twelfth-century manuscript paintings also began to depict the marriage bed to symbolize matrimony itself.[101]

But as noted earlier, decretist opinions about sex and its role in marriage were divided. Even writers whose ideas about the formation of marriage differed as radically as those of Rolandus and Vacarius could agree that marital sex was part of natural law.[102] And while Huguccio, as we have seen, held that sex itself was not part of natural law, he taught also that natural law implanted in man an instinct that intercourse with his lawful wife was legitimate but extramarital sex was not.[103] So also Rolandus and other decretists insisted time and

---

[99] Paucapalea, *Summa* to C. 27 pr., ed. Schulte, pp. 110–11; Stephen of Tournai, *Summa* to C. 27 pr., ed. Schulte, p. 232; Rufinus, *Summa* to C. 27 pr., ed. Singer, p. 432; Rolandus, *Summa* to C. 30 q. 5 c. 9 v. *futurarum nuptiarum* and v. *nuptialia foedera perducuntur*, ed. Thaner, pp. 151–52.

[100] Rolandus, *Summa* to C. 32 q. 2 c. 2 ed. Thaner, pp. 164–65; SP to C. 32 q. 2 pr., ed McLaughlin, p. 241; Rufinus, *Summa* to C. 32 q. 2 pr., ed. Singer, p. 479; Sicard of Cremona, *Summa* to C. 32 q. 2 pr., in B.L. MS Add 18,367, fol. 59rb-va: "De incontinentia continet ii. q. xxxii. cause, ubi queritur utrum illi qui propter incontinentiam copulantur, uel etiam copulati propter incontinentiam commiscentur dicendi sunt fornicarii uel coniuges? . . . Solutio: duplex fuit matrimonii institutio, prima in paradiso, secunda extra paradysum, prima in sobolem, secunda in remedium. . . . Quecumque capitula dicunt tales non esse coniuges locuntur de prima institutione; que uera coniuges dicunt de secunda."

[101] Chiara Frugoni, "L'iconografia del matrimonio e della coppia nel medioevo," in *Il matrimonio nella società altomedioevale* 2:962.

[102] Rolandus, *Summa* to C. 27 pr., ed. Thaner, p. 113; Vacarius, *Summa de matrimonio*, ed. Maitland, p. 274.

[103] Huguccio, *Summa* to D. 1 d.p.c. 5, in MS 72 of Pembroke College, Cambridge, fol. 117ra–rb, and Vat. lat. 2280, fol. 2va: "Michi tamen uidetur quod intelligatur de coniunctione carnali matrimoniali, non fornicaria, cum ex iure naturali peccatum non possit esse, et hec est coniunctio de iure naturali, quod dicitur instinctus nature, nec imo quod dicitur ratio. Mouetur enim homo quodam naturali appetitu sensualitatis, ut carnaliter comisceatur femine et statim succedat ratio dictans homini ut non commisceatur nisi uxori et modo legitimo, scilicet causa sobolis uel causa reddendi debitum, nam alia commixtio siue cum uxore siue cum alia non est de aliquo iure naturali."

again that marital sex was a good use of an evil thing—an Augustinian tag that epitomized their belief that marital sex was (at least sometimes) moral, while other sexual activity was always immoral.[104]

The majority of decretists agreed that the morality of marital sex depended upon the circumstances of the act and the intentions of the parties. Rufinus maintained that marital intercourse was good in itself, although it might be wrong for a couple to have sexual relations at some particular place or time, while Rolandus taught that marital sex is never tinged with the guilt of fornication, even if its purpose were not procreation.[105] Other writers were not so sure. The author of the *Summa Parisiensis*, for example, considered marital sex legitimate only if the couple specifically intended to beget a child—and even then the pleasure inherent in the experience rendered the sex act morally suspect.[106] Others were willing to concede that procreative intent always excused the evil that was an intrinsic part of all sex acts.[107]

---

[104] Rolandus, *Summa* to C. 32 q. 1 c. 11 v. *bonus usus mali*, ed. Thaner, pp. 162–63; Rufinus, *Summa* to the same passage, ed. Singer, p. 478, followed almost verbatim by Joannes Faventinus in B.L. Royal 9.E.VII, fol. 142rb; gloss to the same passage in B.L. Stowe 378, fol. 175ra: "Conueniendi carnaliter quod malum dicitur quia ex malo proueniens, id est concupiscentia carnali, uel quia facit malum, id est peccatum, uel usus mali dicatur, id est concubitus mali, id est concupiscentie. Usus tamen bonus, id est fine bono, scilicet gratia prolis."

[105] Rufinus, *Summa* to C. 27 q. 2 pr., ed. Singer, p. 446, followed verbatim by Joannes Faventinus in B.L. Royal 9.E.VII, fol. 134va–vb; Rolandus, *Summa* to C. 32 q. 2 c. 4, ed. Thaner, pp. 165–66; cf. the views of Robert of Melun, cited by Leclercq, *Monks on Marriage*, p. 21.

[106] SP to D. 5 c. 4 v. *prava* and to D. 13 c. 2 v. *peccemus*, ed. McLaughlin, pp. 5, 13; cf. John of Salisbury, *Policraticus* 8.11, ed. Webb 2:294–95.

[107] Omnebene, gloss to C. 27 q. 2 c. 5, in Müller, *Lehre des hl. Augustinus*, p. 95 n. 162: "Quidam sunt qui dormiunt secum pro habenda prole solummodo, ut nutriant in servitio Dei. Isti non offendunt, immo benefaciunt." The theologian Odo of Ourscamp, writing in the 1160s, expressed similar views (see Müller, *Lehre des hl. Augustinuus*, p. 133 n. 24), as did the Summa *Et est sciendum* to D. 1 c. 7 v. *viri et femine coniunctio*, in Weigand, *Naturrechtslehre*, p. 290. See also Rufinus, *Summa* to C. 32 q. 2 d.p.c. 2, ed. Singer, pp. 479–80, followed verbatim by Joannes Faventinus, B.L. Royal 9.E.VII, fol. 142va. Sicard of Cremona, *Summa* to C. 32 q. 2 in B.L. MS Add. 18,367, fol. 59va, adopted Rufinus's reasoning, but not his words: "Item cum alius cognoscit uxorem suam, aut exactus hoc facit aut spontaneus. Si exactus, si queret uenialiter peccat. Si spontaneus, aut facit hoc causa procreande prolis, aut propter incontinentia, aut pro explenda libidine. In primo modo nec etiam uenialiter peccat quo ad cognitionem, sed fortasse quantum ad delectationem. In secundo uenialiter peccat. Quidam dicunt quod in tertia mortaliter peccat. Ego autem dico quod uenialiter, tum propter auctoritatem superius positam, usus etc. [C. 32 q. 7 c. 14], tum etiam propter nuptiale bonum quod tripartitum est." Although procreative intention could relieve marital sex of the taint of sin and make coitus "respectable" (*honesta*), Rolandus noted that it was essential that couples make love with mutual affection, for those who copulated without affection committed quasi-adultery; Rolandus, *Summa* to C. 32 q. 2 c. 6 v. *cum qua sic cubat* and C.

Several decretists asserted that couples who intended to avoid conception were guilty of sin. Contraceptive intercourse is a species of debauchery (*luxuria*), they maintained, because it is undertaken solely for pleasure, and even in marriage this is not allowed.[108] But what if a couple were naturally sterile and unable, through no fault of their own, to have children? Could they licitly have sexual relations? This question, Simon of Bisignano noted, was difficult, but in his opinion couples in this situation could sleep together in order to preserve the virtue of marital fidelity.[109] Sterility that was deliberately induced was, of course, another matter altogether and made the person responsible for it guilty of a crime—it was, according to Rolandus, the moral equivalent of prostitution.[110]

A small but vocal minority of the decretists, however, advocated more radical restrictions on marital sex. The most powerful attack on the morality of marital intercourse came from Huguccio. There are four reasons, he declared, why married couples have sexual relations: for procreation, in order to pay the marital debt, because they wish to avoid extramarital sexual temptations, or in order to enjoy sensual pleasure. No matter what the reason, according to Huguccio, sexual relations, even in marriage, are always the source of some pleasure, and marital intercourse is always sinful to some degree.[111] To have intercourse in order to beget a child or to pay the marital debt is less sinful, to be sure, than to do so simply for pleasure, but even so some element of sin must be present.[112] Huguccio suggested one way out of this dilemma: if a man could

---

32 q. 4 c. 5 v. *honesta origo*, ed. Thaner, pp. 166, 172; also, Rufinus, *Summa* to D. 34 d.a.c. 4, ed. Singer, p. 80, followed verbatim by Joannes Faventinus in B.L. MS Add. 18,369, fol. 14rb.

[108] Stephen of Tournai, *Summa* to D. 5 c. 2 v. *voluptas*, ed. Schulte, p. 15; Rufinus, *Summa* to C. 32 q. 2 d.p.c. 2, ed. Singer, p. 480, followed verbatim by Joannes Faventinus, in B.L. Royal 9.E.VII, fol. 142vb. For the meaning of *luxuria* see the penitential manual *Homo quidam* in P. Michaud-Quantin, "Un manuel de confession archaïque dans le manuscrit Avranches 136," *Sacris erudiri* 17 (1966) 22. See also Noonan, *Contraception*, pp. 175–77, and Flandrin, *Familles*, p. 215.

[109] Simon of Bisignano, *Summa* to C. 31 q. 1, in B.L. MS Add. 24,659, fol. 32va: "Ad hoc dici potest quod licet difficile hoc potest accidere: excusaretur coitus talium propter sacramentum fidelis anime ad deum uel propter ecclesie auctoritatem, ut infra xxxiiii. q. i c. i." The citation at the end is presumably an error, since the cited passage has no evident bearing on the issue.

[110] Rolandus, *Summa* to C. 32 q. 2 c. 7 v. *illa est mariti meretrix*, ed. Thaner, p. 167; see also Rufinus, *Summa* to C. 32 q. 2 c. 7 v. *aliquando*, ed. Singer, p. 482, followed verbatim by Joannes Faventinus in B.L. Royal 9.E.VII, fol. 143ra.

[111] Huguccio, *Summa* to C. 32 q. 2 d.p.c. 2 v. *suam uxorem*, in Admont 7, fol. 319va–vb: "Notandum quod uir commiscetur uxori quatuor de causis, scilicet causa prolis, causa reddendi debitum, causa incontinentie, causa ex saturande libidinis uel explende uoluptatis."

[112] Huguccio, *Summa* to D. 5 c. 2 in Pembroke 72, fol. 119va: "Uoluptas id est delectatio que habeatur in coitu est culpa et peccatum; nunquam coitus coniugale potest exer-

manage to engage in sexual relations in order to satisfy his wife, but could refrain from orgasm himself, he might escape without sin, provided that he felt no pleasure at any time during the operation. This appears to be the earliest reference to what moralists later came to call *amplexus reservatus*.[113]

Decretists who believed that intercourse for procreation is blameless also tended to teach that sex in order to pay the marital debt is not sinful. The decretists felt bound to accept the tenet that spouses enjoyed a mutual right to sexual intercourse and that this right was a consequence of the consummation of their marriage.[114] Rolandus went so far as to hold that the partner who

---

ceri sine peccato saltem ueniale quia ad minus est feruor quidam pruritus, quedam uoluptas in corpore que est peccatum ueniale, ut xxxiii. q. iiii. uir [c. 7]." Similarly, writing on C. 32 q. 2 d.p.c.2 v. *quod enim*, in Admont 7, fol. 319va–vb, Huguccio declared: "Sed siue coitus sit peccatum siue non, numquam tamen fit sine peccato, quia semper fit et exercetur cum quodam pruritu et quodam uoluptate, nam in emissione spermatis semper subest quidam feruor, quidam pruritus, quidam uoluptas, que sine culpa esse non potest, ut xxxiii. q. iiii. uir [c. 7] et xxvii. q. ii. omne [c. 10] et c. connubia [C. 32 q. 2 c. 4], et supra eodem q. i. non enim [C. 32 q. 1 c. 11] et di. v. cum enixa [c. 1]." This passage is also edited from Munich and Bamberg MSS in Lindner, *Usus matrimonii*, p. 96 n. 21. On Huguccio's sex doctrine see also Weigand, "Liebe und Ehe," pp. 53–54; Tentler, *Sin and Confession*, pp. 166–67; and Lindner, *Usus matrimonii*, pp. 95–97.

[113] Huguccio, *Summa* to D. 13 pr., in Pembroke 72, fol. 124vb, and Vat. lat. 2280, fol. 12ra: "Unde sepe alius reddit debitum uxori ita quod ipse non explet uoluptatem suam et e contrario in premisso casu [*scil.*: ego habeo uxorem, instanter petit debitum] possum sic reddere debitum uxori, expectatiue quousque expleat uoluptatem suam. Immo sepe in tali mulier solet preuenire uirum et expleta uoluptate uxoris in carnali opere si uolo possum libere ab omni peccato discedere uoluptate mee non satisfaciens nec propagationis semen emittens. . . ." A slightly different version of this text, taken from the Munich and Bamberg MSS, appears in Lindner, *Usus matrimonii*, p. 96 n. 20; see also Rudolf Weigand, "Die Lehre der Kanonisten des 12. und 13. Jahrhunderts von den Ehezwecken," *Studia Gratiana* 12 (1967) 472 n. 141. On *amplexus reservatus* see Noonan, *Contraception*, pp. 296–98. Huguccio's views of sexual guilt were extreme, but he was not the only rigorist. The author of the *Summa Parisiensis* anticipated Huguccio's rigorism, and similar views appear in the glosses of Gandulphus and the *Summa Lipsiensis*; SP to C. 33 q. 4 c. 7 v. *sine culpa*, ed. McLaughlin, p. 252; Gandulphus, gloss to D. 13 pr. v. *item* and to D. 13 c. 3 v. *beemoth*, in Weigand, "Gandulphusglossen," pp. 20, 22. A handful of twelfth-century theological writers, notably Robert Pullen (ca. 1080–1146) and Peter the Chanter (d. 1197), supported the antipleasure position as well; Zeimentz, *Ehe nach der Lehre der Frühscholastik*, pp. 79–81; Müller, *Lehre des hl. Augustinus*, pp. 92, 151.

[114] Rolandus, *Summa* to C. 27 pr., C. 28 q. 1 c. 15 v. *prima coniugii fides*, ed. Thaner, pp. 114, 140–41; Rufinus, *Summa* to C. 27 q. 2 c. 9 v. *a prima fide desponsationis*, ed. Singer, p. 450; Simon of Bisignano, *Summa* to C. 27 q. 2 in B.L. MS Add. 24,659, fol. 29va–vb: "Item queritur si sponsa sponso debitum reddere compellatur, et dicemus eam non cogi ad soluendum debitum antequam fit, secus una caro effecta. Primo ergo coitus gratie est, non debiti. . . . A fide uero carnalis commixtionis debent sibi mutuam

rendered the debt at the other's request performed a meritorious action.[115] Most writers rejected this view. Joannes Faventinus, for example, held that rendering the marital debt did not confer positive merit, but simply avoided the penalties that refusing it would entail.[116]

Huguccio took a peculiar stand on the question of the marriage debt. While virtually all of his fellow-decretists held that the party who paid the debt did not sin in doing so, Huguccio asserted that both parties always sinned. The party who made the request for intercourse sinned by requiring something that in its very nature was sinful. The other party also sinned: if s/he denied payment, s/he committed a mortal sin; if s/he complied with the demand, s/he sinned, although only venially, because there would inevitably be pleasure in the experience and that, said Huguccio, could not happen without sin.[117] Although each party had a right to sexual relations, circumstances could limit the exercise of that right. Huguccio noted that if the wife sought sexual intercourse during her menstrual period, for example, the husband could refuse, unless there was imminent danger that she might commit fornication.[118] Rolandus also

---

seruitutem corporis, unde postquam fuerunt una caro simul effecti, nullus sine consensu alterius potest uel seruare continentiam uel ad religionem transire. . . ."

[115] Rolandus, *Summa* to C. 33 q. 5 c. 1 v. *pro sanctificatione perfecta*, ed. Thaner, p. 197: "Quasi diceret: non solum non punieris, sed imputabitur tibi ad coronam."

[116] Joannes Faventinus, *Summa* to C. 32 q. 2 d.p.c. 4 v. *non datur presentia spiritus sancti*, in B.L. Royal 9.E.VII, fol. 142vb: "Id est propter coniugales illos actus gratia scilicet non datur; si tamen habetur non amittitur, nisi in casu illo in quo modo talis culpa incurritur. Quid ergo dicitur de eo qui reddit debitum exigenti, quod computabitur ei pro sanctificatione perfecta? Intelligendum est non quoad promerendam coronam, sed ad euitandam penam." Cf. the rather similar teaching in an anonymous Vatican *Summa* reported in Müller, *Lehre des hl. Augustinus*, pp. 163–64. The obligation to provide sexual service at the demand of the other party was nearly absolute—according to Rolandus if one party demanded the marital debt during times set aside for prayer, the other spouse was bound to oblige. Likewise a wife had the right to forbid her husband to go on crusade, because his departure would deprive her of the sexual solace that he owed to her; Rolandus, *Summa* to C. 33 q. 4 pr., ed. Thaner, pp. 195–96; Rufinus, *Summa* to C. 33 q. 4 pr., ed. Singer, pp. 503–504; SP to C. 33 q. 4 pr., ed. McLaughlin, p. 252. On the crusader's wife see *Questiones Cusane*, no. 1, ed. Fransen, p. 212, as well as Brundage, "Crusader's Wife," pp. 424–41.

[117] Huguccio, *Summa* to D. 13 pr. v. *item aduersus*, in Vat. lat. 2280, fol. 12ra–rb, and Pembroke 72, fol. 124va–vb: "Item ego habeo uxorem; instanter petit debitum. Si nego, pecco mortaliter, quia facio contra preceptum, ut xxxiii. q. v. si dicat [c. 1]; si reddo, pecco saltem uenialiter, quia in quolibet coitu subest quidam pruritus, quedam delectatio que non potest non esse peccatum, ut xxxiii. q. iiii. uir cum propria uxore [c. 7]; et sic uideor esse perplexus." See also Lindner, *Usus matrimonii*, pp. 95–96, n. 20, referring to the same passage in the Bamberg and Munich MSS.

[118] Huguccio, *Summa* to D. 5 c. 4 in Vat. lat. 2280, fol. 6ra, and Pembroke 72, fol. 119vb: "Mulier ergo paciens menstrua, si uir exiget debitum revelet ei hic amodo; et si non exigit reuelet ut si illa tunc exigat ille neget; sic ergo in tali casu exigere est mortale

observed that if one spouse became unable to have intercourse, this did not give the other party any right to seek sexual satisfaction with someone else.[119]

Throughout their discussions of problems relating to the marital debt, twelfth-century decretists remained ambivalent on the issue of sexual equality. Although they maintained that husbands and wives had equal rights in regard to the conjugal debt, their discussion reflected contemporaneous social realities. Twelfth-century society generally imposed strict sexual restraints on women, while allowing great latitude to men. "Virginity is demanded from women, but not from men," Huguccio declared, adding that "even a man who had had a thousand concubines would not be denied clerical promotion."[120] The last clause was, no doubt, a rhetorical exaggeration, but Huguccio's point was well taken. The decretists felt bound to insist that women should obey their husbands in all things. The decretists declared that males enjoyed a dignity that females lacked, yet at the same time they maintained that husbands had no right to demand a standard of sexual behavior from their wives that they themselves did not observe.[121] In theory the decretists asserted that husbands and wives had equal sexual rights, but they were not consistent in the application of that principle.[122] Like many of their contemporaries, decretists were prone to believe that all women were much alike and that good ones were exceedingly rare.[123] Conventional stereotypes regarded women as even more inclined than men toward lust and sexual excess. The stereotype supported the misogynist attitudes that are so evident in the decretists' discussions of sex.[124]

---

peccatum, sed reddere non est peccatum, ar. xxxiii. q. v. manifestum [c. 11]. [Si] uoluit similiter non reddere, non est peccatum, nisi immineat periculum fornicationis; et quod de exigente hic intelligatur patet per hic quod dicitur 'accedat'."

[119] Rolandus, *Summa* to C. 32 q. 5 c. 16 v. *puto* and C. 32 q. 7 c. 18, ed. Thaner, pp. 180–81, 186.

[120] Huguccio, *Summa* to D. 26 c. 2 in Vat. lat. 2280, fol. 27va, and Pembroke, 72, fol. 137ra: "Exigitur ergo uirgiitas ex parte uxoris, sed non ex parte uiri et si ei mille habuit concubinas, non imo deest ei sacramentum et imo ratione defectus sacramenti non repellitur [a promotione]." See also Duby, "Mariage," pp. 23–24.

[121] Rolandus, *Summa* to C. 32 q. 6 c. 4, ed. Thaner, p. 182; Rufinus, *Summa* to C. 32 q. 6 pr., ed. Singer, p. 491, followed almost verbatim by Joannes Faventinus, in B.L. Royal 9.E.VII, fol. 144vb.

[122] Rolandus, *Summa* to C. 33 q. 4 c. 10, v. *Quod si factum fuerit*; C. 33 q. 5 pr. and c. 4 v. *annorum*, ed. Thaner, pp. 196–98; Rufinus, *Summa* to C. 33 q. 4 pr., ed. Singer, pp. 503–504. Cf. the remarks of Hildegard of Bingen on this matter, cited in Bynum, *Jesus as Mother*, pp. 93–94.

[123] SP to C. 32 q. 1 c. 11 v. *Non in sola*, ed. McLaughlin, pp. 240–41; *Frag. Cantab.* to C. 32 q. 7 c. 17 v. *ideo non subdit*, U.L.C., MS 3321(1), fol. 28r: "Nomine uero mulieris intelligit prestantem causam discidii, quia mulier fragilis est et fragilitas peccantis apparet post peccatum." Cf. John of Salisbury, *Policraticus* 8.11, ed. Webb 2:298, and an anonymous gloss to Matt. 10:10: "Mulier est nomen sexus et corruptionis," cited by Zeimentz, *Ehe nach der Lehre der Frühscholastik*, p. 96.

[124] To cite just a single example from many, see the twelfth-century Latin comedy, *De*

The decretists agreed with the Fathers, penitential writers, and earlier canonists that marital sex should be subject to certain limits, but the decretists defined those limits differently. Although they certainly believed that total sexual abstinence was an ideal that Christians ought to seek, the decretists realized that few married couples aspired to this goal.[125] The decretists recommended periodic sexual continence, but their comments on Gratian's scanty references to the penitential prescriptions concerning sexual abstinence during Lent and other holy seasons show no great enthusiasm for these observances.[126] The decretists stressed regular restraint in marital sex rather than periodic episodes of complete abstinence. Rigorists who taught the intrinsic sinfulness of marital intercourse insisted that lustful passion or excessive indulgence in sex is out of place in marriage and that sex for pleasure is wrong at any time.[127] Immoderate sexual intercourse is tantamount to adultery, they argued, and ought to be subject to the same penalties.[128]

---

mercatore, lines 11–14, 17–18, ed. Alphonse Dain in Gustave Cohen, *La 'comédie' latine en France au XIIe siècle,* 2 vols. (Paris: Les Belles Lettres, 1931) 2:269.

[125] Rolandus, *Summa* to C. 27 q. 1 c. 41 v. *animus Christianus* and C. 28 q. 1 c. 9 v. *nuptiis minus bono,* ed. Thaner, pp. 125, 137.

[126] Rolandus, for example, in his *Summa* to C. 33 q. 4 pr., ed. Thaner, pp. 195–96, characterized these observances as counsels of perfection, not commands, as did Rufinus, *Summa* to the same passage, ed. Singer, p. 503. Even the relatively rigoristic SP, ed. McLaughlin, p. 252, noted that the conjugal debt must be paid regardless of season, while the *Frag. Cantab.* to C. 34 q. 4 pr. v. *quod autem ⟨orationis⟩* [MS: *occasionis*], in U.L.C., MS Add. 3321(1), fol. 31v, advised that the couple's intention was the critical factor: "Hic notantum quod alii tempore ieiuniorum frequentant carnales actus causa explende libidinis, alii causa uitande proprie fornicationis, alii causa procreande sobolis in religione dei, alii causa uitande fornicationis uxoris. Illi qui causa explende libidinis uel uitande proprie fornicationis tempore ieiuniorum gerunt coniugales actus aliquando tempore pro hoc penitere debent et abstinere a corpore et sanguine domini. Illi uero qui causa procreande sobolis uel uitande fornicationis uxoris tempore ieiuniorum coniugales gerunt actus non minus secure debent accipere corpus et sanguinem domini." Huguccio, incidentally, thought he saw a connection between the practice of eating fish and abstaining from sex during penitential seasons, for he believed that fish had an anaphrodisiac effect: "Respondeo quia carnes calide sunt et immo incentive libidinis, pisces uero frigidi sunt ex maiore parte, licet quidam calidi inueniantur, et immo minus prouocant ad libidinem" (*Summa* to D. 4 c. 6, in Vat. lat. 2280, fol. 4va, and Pembroke 72, fol. 119rb).

[127] SP to C. 32 q. 2 d.p.c. 2 v. *item immoderatus* and C. 32 q. 4 c. 14, ed. McLaughlin, pp. 241, 244; Huguccio, *Summa* to C. 33 q. 4 pr. v. *quod autem,* in Lindner, *Usus matrimonii,* p. 159 n. 40; Tractatus *De ortu coniugii,* in Weigand, "Kanonistische ehetraktate," p. 65. See also gloss to C. 32 q. 4 c. 5 in B.L. Stowe 387, fol 176vb: "Ieronimus ibi iuuenem introducit in uxore proprie immoderate feruentem adeo quidem ut ad delectationis memoriam mulieribus uteretur ornamentis. De eius ergo amore quod ex origine processit honesta, quia ex coniugii gratia licet deinceps in adulteriam degeneraret uehementiam." ·

[128] Rolandus, *Summa* to C. 32 q. 4 c. 5 v. *adulter est in uxore,* ed. Thaner, p. 173; SP

But what constituted "excessive" or "immoderate" indulgence in marital sex? The decretists used three criteria. First there was a quantitative measure: sexual relations beyond that required for reproduction or to pay the conjugal debt constituted excessive or immoderate use of marital rights.[129] The second criterion was qualitative: impulsive and unrestrained sexual relations are excessive and immoderate. The decretists described this type of unacceptable marital sex as that of a man who made love to his wife as if he were commiting adultery with her.[130] The third criterion we might call technical: that is marital sex was excessive and immoderate when it deviated from what the decretists regarded as the "normal" mode of human coition. What they meant was what is now often called the "missionary position," in which the woman lies supine with the man prone above her. Any variants from this position, particularly the "dog-style" (*more canino*) approach from the rear, or any position in which the woman was superior to the man, the decretists described as unnatural and reprehensible, even in the marriage bed. Likewise, other deviations from sexual behavior the canonists regarded as normal—particularly anal intercourse or oral sex—counted as grave and unnatural offenses.[131]

The gravamen of all of these offenses lay in the twofold belief that the reason for deviations from the sexual norm was a quest for physical pleasure and that such conduct violated the order laid down by "nature" for human sexual conduct. The decretists' objections to deviant positions and practices were appar-

---

to D. 5 c. 2 v. *voluptas* and C. 32 q. 2 d.p.c. 2 v. *item immoderatus*, ed. McLaughlin, pp. 5, 241.

[129] Rolandus, *Summa* to C. 32 q. 4 c. 5 v. *amator ardentior*, ed. Thaner, p. 173; Rufinus, *Summa* to C. 32 q. 2 d.p.c. 2 v. *sed est ueniale*, ed. Singer, pp. 479–80, followed verbatim by Joannes Faventinus in B.L. Royal 9.E.VII, fol. 142va–vb. Cf. Peter Lombard, *Sententiae* 4.31.8, Quaracchi ed., 2:450–51.

[130] Rolandus, *Summa* to C. 32 q. 4 c. 5 v. *nichil est foedius*, ed. Thaner, p. 173: "Vel vehemens amator dicitur, cum in tantum quis uxorem diligit, ut apud se disponat, quod, si ipsa foret uxor alterius, non minus ei se carnaliter commisceret;" closely paraphrased in B.L. Stowe 378, fol. 176vb. Cf. Joannes Faventinus, *Summa* to C. 32 q. 4 c. 5 v. *ardentior*, in B.L. Royal 9.E.VII, fol. 144ra: "Id est indebite ardens in uxorem, intentionem scilicet habens quod si aliena esset, non minus eam cognosceret," as well as SP to D. 5 c. 2 v. *voluptas*, ed. McLaughlin, p. 5.

[131] SP to C. 32 q. 4 c. 14, ed. McLaughlin, p. 244; Rolandus, *Summa* to C. 32 q. 4 c. 14 v. *meretricum cupiuntur amplexibus* and c. 12 v. *extraordinarias uoluptates*, ed. Thaner, pp. 174, 175; Rufinus, *Summa* to C. 32 q. 2 d.p.c. 2, ed. Singer, pp. 479–80, followed verbatim by Joannes Faventinus in B.L. MS Royal 9.E.VII, fol. 142va–vb; *Frag. Cantab.* to C. 32 q. 2 c. 3 v. *quicquid*, in U.L.C., MS Add. 3321(1), fol. 23v: "Sed sic exponitur: 'Uehemens' etc., id est sua uxore contra ordinem nature utens adulter est." Also ibid./ to C. 32 q. 4 c. 5 v. *nihil interest ex qua honesta causa quis seviat*, and C. 32 q. 4 c. 12 v. *extraordinaria uoluptas*, in ibid., fol. 24v and 25v. *Summa Reginensis* to C. 32 q. 4 c. 5 v. *adulter*, quoted in Weigand, "Liebe und Ehe," p. 55; gloss to C. 27 q. 1 c. 41 v. *canino more* in B.L. Stowe 378, fol. 166ra: "Plures coeundo sicut canes, uel turbato ordine humane propagationis retrocoeant sicut subdituri sed honeste." See also Brundage, "Let Me Count the Ways," pp. 84–85.

ently grounded as much in their perception that these sexual variants promoted pleasure as in the belief that they were contraceptive. While the decretists certainly disapproved of contraceptive sex, they disapproved even more vehemently of sexual pleasure for its own sake. Pleasure might be tolerated as an accompaniment—preferably an unwanted accompaniment—of reproductive sex, but in their view carnal pleasure was absolutely intolerable in nonreproductive sex. The model of marital sex that they wanted married couples to emulate was a relationship governed by reason and discretion, in which sex served the end of reproduction, but nothing more.[132] The twelfth-century commentators on Gratian elaborated for the first time in great detail this Stoic model of marital sex, still very much alive in Roman Catholic thought.

Moralists as well as canonists sought to deter married couples from excessive or immoderate sexual behavior. Twelfth-century moral writers warned that dire consequences would result from overindulgence in sex. "Extraordinary voluptuousness," even in marriage, said Peter of Blois (fl. 1180–1200), would tempt God to impose a terrible judgment. Divine retribution might mean blindness, madness, and other infirmities in this life, as well as unimaginably dreadful penalties in the next.[133] John of Salisbury related the cautionary tale of Count Ralph of Vermandois, who died prematurely as a result of excessive intercourse with his wife, despite the warnings of his physicians.[134] And medieval physicians did, indeed, advise their patients to curtail sexual indulgence. Maimonides (who was an eminent physician as well as a philosopher) cautioned that excessive intercourse would shorten life, and later in the century Arnald of Villanova (ca 1240–1311) would turn this general advice into a very specific prescription that couples have sexual relations no more than two or at the very most three times weekly.[135] Avicenna and, in the thirteenth century Albert the Great, cautioned that excessive sexual intercourse was likely to produce numerous undesirable side effects including weakness, trembling, nervousness, ringing in the ears, protruding eyeballs, abdominal pain, and hemorrhage.[136]

Discounting the warnings of learned physicians, however, folk medicine

---

[132] Rolandus, *Summa* to C. 32 q. 4 c. 5 v. *sapiens iudicio*, ed. Thaner, p. 173: "Id est cum discretione et ratione debet amare uxorem suam, i.e. commisceri uxori suae non pro affectu, i.e. carnis appetitu, quia non est imitandus carnis appetitus in coitu scilicet, ut quotiens caro expetierit, coeatur."

[133] Peter of Blois, *De amicitia* 1.6 and 2.7, ed. M. M. Davy (Paris: E. de Boccard, 1932), pp. 130, 272–73; *Frag. Cantab.* to C. 32 q. 4 c. 5 v. *nihil interest*, in U.L.C., MS Add. 3321(1), fol. 24v: "Alii enim fiunt frenetici ex nimio studio, alii ex nimio amore, sed quantum ad imparem seuiciam nichil interest."

[134] John of Salisbury, *Historia Pontificalis: Memoirs of the Papal Court*, ed. and trans. Marjorie Chibnall, Medieval Texts Series (London: Thomas Nelson and Sons, 1956), pp. 14–15.

[135] Thomasset, Représentation," p. 16.

[136] Avicenna *Canon* 3.20.1.11, Venice: n.p., 1507, repr. Hildesheim: Georg Olms, 1964, fol. 352va–353rb; Thomasset, "Représentation," p. 8, citing Albertus Magnus, *De animalibus* 3.2.8.

taught that rigorous abstinence from sex also caused physical ailments. Even so ascetic a man as King Louis VII of France was allegedly persuaded by his physicians to have intercourse with a girl in order to cure a malady that afflicted him. The remedy was said to have produced good results.[137] Respectable medical writers also advised physicians that it was appropriate to prescribe measures designed to increase their patients' sexual pleasure and that giving advice for this purpose did not violate medical ethics.[138]

Divorce and Remarriage in the Decretists

Discussions of divorce and remarriage by the decretists mirrored their underlying disagreements concerning the formation of marriage. Thus, writers of the Bolognese school distinguished between the termination of marriages initiated by the exchange of consent and those completed by consummation. Rufinus, whose treatment of the matter is fuller than those of the other Bolognese writers, maintained that a marriage just begun (*matrimonium initiatum*) could be dissolved on eight different grounds: impotence, entry into religion, long-continued absence, intractable illness, serious crime, rape, fornication with a third party, or subsequent consummated marriage with another partner.[139] A completed marriage (*matrimonium ratum*), however, could not be dissolved at all, according to Bolognese writers. Invalid marriages were another matter—Church courts could and did separate those who married in violation of the canons concerning minimum age, competence to give consent, consanguinity, affinity, and freedom of choice, since these unions lacked legal force or effect.[140]

Decretists who held that present consent of the parties created marriage faced greater difficulties in dealing with separation and divorce. Since consensual theory maintained that sexual intercourse was not essential to the formation of the marriage bond, its advocates had difficulty in accounting for the fact that Church authorities actually did terminate marriages on the grounds of impotence or long-continued absence. Consensualists tended to argue that the grounds for granting separation ought to be limited to reasons involving capacity to marry (consanguinity, affinity, age, previous marriage, and religious vows) or defects of consent (fraud, deceit, coercion, and insanity).[141]

---

[137] Gerald of Wales, *Gemma ecclesiastica* 2.11, in his *Opera*, ed. Brewer 2:216–17; Gerald repeated this story in *De principis instructione* 1.20, ed. Warner in Gerald's *Opera* 8:132–33.

[138] Avicenna, *Canon* 3.20.2.44, fol. 358ra–rb; Thomasset, "Représentation," p. 16.

[139] Rufinus, *Summa* to C. 27 pr., ed. Singer, pp. 432–33; Rolandus, *Summa* to C. 27 pr. and C. 32 q. 7 c. 27, ed. Thaner, pp. 114–15, 187–88; Weigand, "Scheidungsproblem," pp. 54–55.

[140] Rufinus, *Summa* to C. 1 q. 7 d.a.c. 6, C. 27 q. 2 c. 9 v. *a prima fide desponsationis*, and c. 10 v. *quia nullum divortium*, as well as C. 30 q. 2 pr., ed. Singer, pp. 234, 450, 461–62; Rolandus, *Summa* to C. 35 q. 7 pr., ed. Thaner, p. 232.

[141] SP to C. 30 q. 1 pr., q. 2 pr., q. 5 pr.; C. 33 q. 1 pr., ed. McLaughlin, pp. 235–37, 249; Stephen of Tournai, *Summa* to C. 27 q. 1, ed. Schulte, pp. 232–33.

Practical reality, as both French and Bolognese decretists well knew, differed from canonistic theory. Couples in the real world often separated informally, without seeking ecclesiastical approval at all; not uncommonly they also remarried without securing permission from Church authorities. Canonists insisted that these practices were unacceptable. Couples who had separated without permission ought to reconcile and resume their married life; those who would not reunite voluntarily should be forced to do so.[142] It was easier to state this principle in a university classroom, however, than to enforce it. To be sure, we know of cases in which couples of high rank and social prominence were reconciled after informal separations, but these scattered instances may well have been reported not only because of the notoriety of the participants, but also because of the rarity of such occurrences.[143] We have no reason to doubt the observation of the author of *In primis hominibus* that persons joined in clandestine unions frequently dissolved their marriages with as little formality as they had contracted them.[144]

Decretists of both schools also knew that marriages contravening the elaborate rules on consanguinity and affinity were commonplace. Both French and Bolognese writers agreed that unions violating the incest canons ought to be dissolved, particularly when the relationship was a close one and the parties were aware of it.[145] When the relationship was distant and not generally known, however, dispensations were the preferred remedy, so as to maintain the marriages by waiving application of the law. Rolandus seems to have originated the use of the terms "diriment impediment" to characterize the first of these situations and "impedient impediment" to describe the second.[146]

[142] Rolandus, *Summa* to C. 33 q. 2 pr., ed. Thaner, p. 189; Rufinus, *Summa* to C. 33 q. 2 pr., ed. Singer, p. 498, followed almost verbatim by Joannes Faventinus in B.L. Royal 9.E.VII, fol. 146ra–rb. But cf. *Frag. Cantab.* to C. 33 q. 2 c. 2 v. *fas est*, in U.L.C., MS Add. 3321(1), fol. 29r: "Id est cum non liceat alicui subditos dampnare absque iudiciario ordine, ⟨non?⟩ licebit ei propriam uxorem dimittere pretermisso iudicio ecclesie."

[143] John of Salisbury furnishes two examples of situations of which Pope Eugene III made strenuous efforts to reconcile separated couples. One case, involving Louis VII and Eleanor of Aquitaine, was ultimately unsuccessful; his other, more successful effort involved Count Hugh of Molise and his wife, who were suing for divorce at the papal court. See *Historia pontificalis* 29, 41, ed. Chibnall, pp. 61–62, 80–82.

[144] Tractatus *In primis hominibus* in B.L. Royal 11.B.XIII, fol. 89va: "Multi enim qui occulte contraxerant coniugia dimittebant uxores suas quando displicebant eis atque hoc idem ipse ostendit hac sequenti littera."

[145] Rufinus, *Summa* to C. 1 q. 7 d.a.c. 6, ed. Singer, p. 235; Tractatus *In primis hominibus*, in B.L. Royal 11.B.XIII, fol. 85rb: "Sed queritur de coniugatis qui cognati sunt et non eis notum quamuis fortasse dicatur an inter illos sit coniugium donec iudicio ecclesie separentur. Inter tales matrimonium est quoniam si utroque uiuente alter coierit cum alia persona adulterium est neque coitus eorum inter se dampnabilis est; at tamen debent dissolui atque deinde possunt aliis copulari. Similiter et de illis quibus fuit notum se esse cognatos et tamen coniuncti sunt nisi quod coitus dampnabilis uidetur."

[146] Rufinus, *Summa* to D. 14 c. 2; C. 1 q. 7 d.a.c. 6; C. 27 q. 2 pr., ed. Singer, pp. 34–35, 234–35, 446; Cardinalis, gloss to C. 27 q. 2 c. 30 v. *copulentur*, in Weigand,

IMPOTENCE CASES

Sexual impotence vividly demonstrates the practical consequences of the differences between the marriage formation theories of the French and Italian schools. The Bolognese writers followed Gratian in supporting the Church's right to dissolve unions in which one partner proved incapable of sexual relations. As Rolandus noted, unconsummated marriages could be dissolved because the marriage bond between the couple had not yet been formed by sexual intercourse.[147] Rufinus discussed the matter at greater length than did Rolandus and made much more of the distinction, already spelled out by Gratian, between congenital, or permanent, impotence and temporary sexual incapacity caused by sorcery (*maleficium*). Rufinus saw no difficulty in dissolving a marriage where one party is congenitally impotent, but he foresaw complications if the condition proved to be temporary. Rufinus would allow divorce in both cases, but would rescind the divorce and require reconciliation of the couple if the impotent party subsequently regained sexual capacity.[148]

Writers of the French school rejected these solutions to impotence cases.[149]

"Glossen des Cardinalis," p. 79. But cf. the remarks of Duby, *Medieval Marriage*, p. 73. On diriment and impedient impediments see Rolandus, *Summa* to C. 27 q. 1 pr., ed. Thaner, p. 113; Morey, *Bartholomew of Exeter*, p. 66.

[147] Rolandus, *Summa* to C. 27 q. 2 c. 25 and C. 33 q. 1 pr., ed. Thaner, pp. 130, 188–89; see also Rolandus, *Sententiae*, ed. Gietl, pp. 281–82.

[148] Rufinus, *Summa* to C. 33 q. 1 pr., ed. Singer, pp. 496–97, followed almost verbatim by Joannes Faventinus in B.L. Royal 9.E.VII, fol. 145vb–146ra and MS Add. 18,369, fol. 148vb–149ra. Sicard of Cremona, commenting on the same passage, paraphrased and condensed Rufinus's words, but adopted all the essentials of his argument; B.L. MS Add. 18,367, fol. 61rb.

[149] Peter Lombard had not taken a clear stance on this issue, but had urged caution in dealing with impotence situations and indicated his preference that couples who were unable to consummate their marriages not separate. He clearly ruled out remarriage for persons who separated on the grounds of sexual incapacity; Peter Lombard, *Sententiae* 4.34.2, Quaracchi ed., 2:954–55. Stephen of Tournai, who had refused to choose between the French and Italian theories of marriage formation, also vacillated on the impotence question. He noted that some people hold that marriages where one party is frigid or impotent were incomplete and could be dissolved. While he did not explicitly reject this solution, Stephen indicated his preference for a solution that was more compatible with the consensual theory. Stephen's preferred solution postulated that if, after exchanging consent, one party discovered that the other could not consummate the marriage, the first party was entitled to separate and remarry because the marriage had been contracted through an error of consent. Stephen, in other words, construed sexual capacity as an essential implied condition on which marital consent was premised. Thus there had been a failure to exchange true consent; the sexually capable party had expected to get an equally capable partner and had consented to marriage on that basis. When the impotent party proved unable to perform sexually, the contract was null because of failure to fulfill an essential condition of the bargain. Impotence furnished

The author of the *Summa Parisiensis*, for example, discussed and then dismissed the Bolognese teaching. The *Summa Parisiensis* held that if sexual incapacity preceded the exchange of marital consent the marriage might be dissolved; if the condition appeared after the exchange of consent, however, the marriage must remain intact. If impotence preceding marriage was inborn and natural, the marriage could still be dissolved and the sexually capable partner could remarry. If the impotent party subsequently recovered his or her sexual capacity the *Summa Parisiensis* held that this created a presumption that the divorce had been secured through perjury; the divorce should therefore be rescinded and the marriage reinstated.[150]

Other writers who adopted French marriage formation theory were more sketchy in accounting for their rejection of the Bolognese impotence doctrine.[151] John of Salisbury, who was generally sympathetic to the teachings of the Parisian schools where he himself had been trained, added a further reason to be wary of divorces based on grounds of sexual impotence: these allegations, he observed, are easy to make, and women are often quick to accuse their husbands of sexual shortcomings when they are dissatisfied with them for other reasons. Besides, John thought it improper and even scandalous to divulge the intimate secrets of the marriage chamber publicly in the courts.[152]

Huguccio's approach was more subtle than the others. He distinguished three different causes of sexual impotence: it might result from inborn physical conditions; from mental incapacity, as in a madman; or from both mental and physical incapacity, as in a young child. Impotence might preclude true marriage, he added, but it did not necessarily do so.[153] Those who suffered from

---

grounds for pronouncing the marriage null, therefore, not because consummation was essential to marriage, but rather because the exchange of consent to marry implied a warranty of sexual capacity. See Stephen of Tournai, *Summa* to C. 33 q. 1 pr., ed. Schulte, pp. 245–46.

[150] If divorce had been grounded on impotence caused by sorcery (*per sortiarios*), however, the *Summa Parisiensis* denied that there was a necessary presumption of perjury: the divorce in such a case was not predicated on a finding that the impotent party totally lacked sexual capacity, but rather on a finding that he or she was incapable of sexual relations with a particular person—the impotence, in modern terminology, was relative, not absolute. In this case, the first marriage should not be reinstated, even though the previously impotent party was subsequently able to have sexual relations with another partner. See SP to C. 33 q. 1 pr., ed. McLaughlin, p. 249, analyzed by McLaughlin in "Formation of the Marriage Bond," p. 211.

[151] *Questiones Cusane*, no. 16, ed. Fransen, pp. 215–16; Joannes Faventinus, *Summa* to C. 27 q. 2 d.p.c. 28 v. *uel his qui aduersariis*, in B.L. Royal 9.E.VII, fol. 135vb: "In frigidis autem erat et aliud putabatur. Nam si qua mulier ei quem posse reddere debitum crederet, cum tamen reddere non posset, deciperetur et erraret et immo matrimonium a principio non constaret quo ad deum; et si ignoranter castrato nupsisset mihi uidetur hec ratio potius esse contra eos quam pro eis."

[152] John of Salisbury, *Policraticus* 8.11, ed. Webb 2:299–300.

[153] Huguccio, Summa to C. 33 q. 1 pr. in Admont 7, fol. 381ra, and Vat. lat. 2280, fol.

both mental and physical impotence, or from mental impotence alone, were incapable of contracting valid marriage, and the unions that they attempted to create were void. Physical incapacity was more difficult to evaluate and Huguccio followed the Parisian decretists in his treatment of congenital and acquired sexual impairment.[154] Huguccio added that if a married couple deliberately decided not to consummate their marriage, even though both parties were capable of intercourse, no one, including the pope, had the power to dissolve their union.[155]

Inconsistencies marked the handling of impotence problems in the decretists' commentaries. Their differences of opinion reflected the cloudy state of the law on the subject. Late twelfth-century popes were no more consistent in their treatment of these matters than were academic lawyers.[156] The discrepancies in approach to the problem also reflected differences in customary practices, particularly between the Church in France and the Roman curia, as the treatise *In primis hominibus* pointed out.[157]

PRESUMPTION OF DEATH CASES

The problem posed by the disappearing spouse, discussed in C. 34 of the *Decretum*, also highlighted the consequences of the disagreement between Paris and Bologna concerning the formation of marriage. Rolandus followed Gratian's

---

289ra: "Hic intitulatur prima questio, scilicet an impossibilitas coeundi separet matrimonium. Ad quod melius distingues notandum quod triplex est impossibilitas coeundi, scilicet animo et corpore, et hoc peruenit ratione etatis, ut in pueris, et hoc impedit matrimonium et dirimit; uel animo tantum, ut in furiosis et in ergumenis qui quidem habent potentiam coeundi sed non uoluntatem, et hoc similiter impedit et dirimit, sed non semper." Gordon, "Adnotationes," p. 206, notes a quotation from Huguccio in the *Rosarium* of Guido de Baysio (d. 1313) to C. 32 q. 7 c. 25, in which Huguccio held that neither men who were impotent (*spadones*) nor those who had been castrated (*castrati*) were capable of legitimate marriage, "quia neuter est nec esse potest potens commisceri."

[154] Huguccio, *Summa* to C. 32 q. 7 c. 18 and C. 33 q. 1 pr., ed. Roman, pp. 763, 765, 783.

[155] Huguccio, *Summa* to C. 28 q. 2 d.p.c. 2 v. *hic distinguendum* and to C. 32 q. 5 c. 18, in Rudolf Weigand, "Unauflösigkeit der Ehe und Eheauflösungen durch Päpste im 12. Jahrhundert," *Revue de droit canonique* 20 (1970) 57.

[156] See e.g., the conflicting decisions on this issue by Gregory VIII (1187) and Clement III (1187–91) in X 2.19.4, 1 Comp. 4.16.4 (X—) and X 4.15.5; Coriden, *Indissolubility*, p. 25.

[157] *In primis hominibus*, B.L. Royal 11.B.XIII, fol. 85rb: "Si autem alia causa interueniente coire non ualent matrimonium talium decreta sanctorum non dissoluunt nec romana ecclesia; et tamen condescendo fragilitati quorundam hominum permittat dissolutionem talium fieri in gallicana ecclesia et quibusdam aliis." See also Clement III in 1 Comp. 4.16.4: "[D]e Romanae ecclesiae consuetudine non erat talium matrimonium separandum." Weigand, "Unauflösigkeit," p. 64, points out the connection between the power to dissolve unconsummated marriages and the power to dispense from religious vows.

doctrine closely, as did Paucapalea, holding that a woman who believed in good faith that her missing husband had died should be allowed to remarry; she could not be charged with adultery should her belief prove mistaken. Rolandus argued further that if the first husband returned and sought to reclaim his wife, he might do so only if their marriage had been consummated. If the first marriage had not been consummated, but the second one had been, then the woman was obliged to remain with her second spouse.[158] Rufinus analyzed this problem at greater length than did Rolandus and demanded a higher degree of probability than Rolandus did that the absent husband had actually died.[159] Joannes Faventinus adopted a slightly lower standard of proof than Rufinus required.[160] Rufinus was also inclined to require restitution of the wife to her first husband, should he subsequently reappear. He did not, however, raise the issue of consummation in this connection.[161]

The *Summa Parisiensis*, by contrast, rested its discussion of presumption of death on the nature of the consent to the first marriage. The author of the Paris *Summa* paid scant attention to the degree of probability necessary to justify remarriage, but held that if the first marriage had been contracted by present consent, the wife was unconditionally obliged to return to her first husband, if he reappeared (see also Pl. 7.[162] The fragmentary Cambridge *Summa*, unlike other discussions, treated the question of evidence in some detail. The Cambridge *Summa* maintained that a bona fide belief that the husband was dead justified remarriage, provided there was adequate cause for the belief, such as

---

[158] Rolandus, *Summa* to C. 34, ed. Thaner, p. 200.

[159] Rufinus, *Summa* to C. 34 q. 1 & 2 pr., ed. Singer, p. 507, required a "strong presumption," while Rolandus required merely "reasonable evidence" of the death of the first spouse.

[160] Joannes Faventinus in B.L. Royal 9.E.VII, fol. 147 vb; "Quoniam itaque si mulier proponitur utroque simul decidatur que uiuente uiro et absente alteri nubit aut rationibus ex argumentis credit eum obiisse aut non? Si probabiliter, sibi facta fide credens eum obiisse alteri nubit, non est adulterii rea, quousque eum uiuere cognouerit. Si autem eum uiuere crediderit uel etiam nulla fide sibi facta dubitauerit et alio nupserit, adulterii pro facto rea erit." Cf. Joannes's *Summa* to C. 27 pr., in B.L. Royal 9.E.VII, fol. 131vb: "Sibi legitime coniungi putantibus, ut mulier putans uirum suum mortuum nubat alio non habenti uxorem, tunc quidam legitimum est matrimonium, propter quod et inde filii suscepti iudicabuntur legitimi." Simon of Bisignano, *Summa* to C. 34, in B.L. MS Add. 24,659, fol. 34ra, also accepted simple "belief" in the death of a missing spouse as an adequate basis for remarriage: "Queritur quando talis coitus sit licitus uel possit accusari a culpa, cum his non sit eius coniux cuius maritus constat uiuere, licet uiuere non credatur. Ad hoc dicimus quod excusatur talium coitus non per bona matrimonii, que interuenire non possit, set per ignorantiam iustam contrahentium et ecclesie permittentis auctoritatem; cum enim isti contra conscientiam non coeunt, non possunt edificare ad jehennam [sic]. Unde hic habes specialem casum ubi adulterium committitur, quia alterius thorum in ueritate uiolatur, nec tamen adulterii reatu qui hanc perpetrate tenetur obnoxium."

[161] Rufinus, *Summa* to C. 34 q. 1 & 2 pr., ed. Singer, pp. 507–508.

[162] SP to C. 34 q. 1 & 2 c. 1, ed. McLaughlin, pp. 255–56.

a report from the missing man's comrades that he had died. Even a prolonged absence without any word concerning the missing man constituted sufficient reason to believe that he was dead, according to the Cambridge author.[163] The treatise *In primis hominibus* added, however, that the wife was required to rejoin her first husband only if he wished her to do so, while Simon of Bisignano observed that if the wife did return to her first husband, the second husband was free to remarry.[164]

ADULTERY AND DIVORCE

The decretists unanimously agreed that while the Church had the power to separate a couple when one party could prove that the other had committed adultery, separation created no right of remarriage for either party so long as the original partner lived.[165] Rufinus noted that in actions brought on grounds of adultery the wife was at a legal disadvantage, since a man was entitled to

[163] *Frag. Cantab.* to C. 34 pr. v. *quidam uir*, in U.L.C., MS Add. 3321(1), fol. 34r–v: "Cum superius egisset de errore, adhuc laicus prosequitur de errore, ponens ⟨thema⟩ [MS: teuma] de ea que uirum suum ductum in captiuitate credebat defunctum, unde ad alterius transiuit copulam. Hic queritur utrum hec que sic transit ad secundum adulterium committat. Si transit sciens maritum suum uiuere, adulterium ⟨perpetrat⟩ [MS: patrat]. Si transit ad secundum sciens maritum suum mortuum uel credens maritum suum mortuum et habens iustam causam credendi eum esse mortuum, ueluti cum uenerunt socii eius eum mortuum in communi proclamantes, uel publica fama est quod mortuus sit, uel propter diutinam moram, excusatur ipsa ab adulterio et tunc utique legitima uxor est; inter eam tamen et secundum non est ⟨ratum⟩ [MS: raptum] matrimonium. Nam redeunte primo debet ipsa redire ad eum. Sed quid si ipse noluerit eam recipere, erit cogendus ut eam recipiat? Dicit rolandus quod non [*sed cf. Summa Rolandi ad C. 34 q. 2, rec. Thaner, p. 200*]. Apponit tamen medicamentum, quod si ipsa multo tempore expectauit eum et obprimebatur a multis qui passim occupabant bona sua et bona filiorum suorum et credens eum mortuum habens iustam causam credendi eum mortuum, alteri nupsit, cum redierit maritus, uelit nolit, si ipsa uoluerit ⟨debet⟩ [MS: habet] eam recipere."

[164] *In primis hominibus* in B.L. Royal 11.B.XIII, fol. 88rb: "Opponitur quod mulier cuius maritus in regno longinqua tenetur captiuus et putatur mortuus cum indigeat rectore permissione ecclesie alii copulatur, utroque tamen uiuente, sed existente [in]timatione uxoris et auorum non impu[t]ebat ille; quo redeunte secundum coniugium dissoluetur et redibi[t] ad primum si ille uolet." Simon of Bisignano, *Summa* to C. 34 in B.L. MS Add. 24,659, fol. 34ra: "Cum autem uir et maritus uerus reuertitur sicut mulier ad uirum primum redire compellitur, sic uir iste secundus ad aliam si uult potest uota transire." If a woman whose husband was missing and presumed dead chose to enter a convent rather than to remarry, the problem became still more complicated; see *Questiones Cusanae*, no. 17, ed. Fransen, p. 216.

[165] Paucapalea, *Summa* to C. 32 q. 7, ed. Schulte, pp. 128–29; Rolandus, *Summa* to C. 30 q. 1 pr., C. 32 q. 7 c. 27, ed. Thaner, pp. 145, 187–88; Rufinus, *Summa* to C. 32 q. 7 c. 22, ed. Singer, p. 495; SP to C. 33 q. 2 pr. and d.p.c. 9, ed. McLaughlin, pp. 250–51; *Frag. Cantab.* to C. 27 q. 2 c. 1 v. *non soluit*, in U.L.C., MS Add 3321(1), fol.

charge his wife with adultery on suspicion alone, while a woman could bring such a charge against her husband only with hard proof.[166] Rufinus was not prepared to agree with Peter Lombard, who taught that men could divorce their wives for adultery, but that wives could not rid themselves of their husbands on the same grounds.[167] The *Summa Parisiensis*, as an exception to the general rule, would allow husbands to dismiss their wives for adultery without formal ecclesiastical process, provided that the offense was open and notorious, but ruled out remarriage under any circumstances for either party.[168] If both parties were guilty of adultery, the decretists held, no divorce or separation should be allowed.[169]

Although the decretists often stated that married persons who indulged in excessive, immoderate, or unnatural sex were guilty of adultery, they exempted such couples from the consequences of adultery with respect to separation and divorce. This was true, one writer remarked, because of the good of marriage.[170]

The decretists expressed few disagreements about the question of whether a man and woman involved in an adulterous relationship could marry one another after the married party's spouse died. The decretists followed Gratian in holding that such a couple could marry only if they satisfied three conditions: first, they must do penance prior to marrying; second, neither of them must have been involved in procuring the death of the first spouse; and third, they must not have agreed to marry prior to the death of the first spouse.[171] Rufinus argued in favor of a fourth condition, namely that the adulterous pair could marry only if the previously married party had been repudiated by the first spouse.[172]

13v: "Hoc uerum est in adulteriis. Nam si causa adulterii aliqui separentur, non dissoluitur matrimonium."

[166] Rufinus, *Summa* to C. 32 q. 1 c. 4 v. *non ad imparia*, ed. Singer, p. 477.

[167] Peter Lombard, *Sententiae* 4.35.1, Quaracchi ed., 2:957.

[168] SP to C. 33 q. 2 pr., ed. McLaughlin, p. 250.

[169] Paucapalea, *Summa* to C. 32 q. 6, ed. Schulte, p. 128; Rufinus, *Summa* to the same passage, ed. Singer, p. 491; Rolandus, *Summa* to the same passage, ed. Thaner, pp. 182–83; SP to the same passage, ed. McLaughlin, p. 246.

[170] Rolandus, *Summa* to C. 32 q. 2 c. 3 v. *propter nuptias*, ed. Thaner, p. 165; Rufinus, *Summa* to C. 32 q. 2 d.p.c. 2, ed. Singer, p. 480: "Dicitur ergo ibi adulter non reatu illius capitalis criminis, sed similitudine adulterine libidinis: sicut enim adulter ardet in adulteram, ita iste in propriam." Followed verbatim by Joannes Faventinus in B.L. Royal 9.E.VII, fol. 142va–vb. Cf. gloss to C. 32 q. 2 c. 3 v. *adulterio*, in B.L. Stowe 378, fol. 175va: "Non tanquam adulterii uel fornicatores puniuntur propter bona nuptiarum, licet reatum fornicationis uel adulterii sic causa libidinibis incurratur. Jo." Similar observations occur in the Stowe glosses to C. 32 q. 2 c. 7 v. *prorsus* and C. 32 q. 4 c. 4 v. *nulli licet*, fol. 175vb and 176vb.

[171] Paucapalea, *Summa* to c. 31 q. 1, ed. Schulte, p. 124; Rolandus, *Summa* to the same passage, ed. Thaner, pp. 154–56; Rufinus, *Summa* to C. 31 q. 1 pr., ed. Singer, p. 470; SP to the same passage, ed. McLaughlin, p. 238.

[172] Rufinus, *Summa* to C. 31 q. 1 pr., ed. Singer, p. 470.

ENTRANCE INTO RELIGION

Discussions of the separation of married couples by mutual consent in order to enter the religious life reveal further disagreements among the decretists over the consequences of rival theories of marriage formation. Bolognese writers would allow unilateral separation so long as the marriage remained unconsummated; after consummation, however, they required mutual consent for this purpose.[173] Those who adopted the Parisian theory allowed unilateral separation after future consent, but required mutual agreement in order to sanction separation after the exchange of present consent.[174]

CONVERTS

Still another topic whose treatment reflected the differences between the Parisian and Bolognese schools concerned the marriages of converts to Christianity. Rolandus took the position that since coitus ratified marriage and made it indissoluble, a man who converted to Christianity should be considered to have ratified his earlier marriage if, at any time after baptism, he had sexual relations with his unconverted wife. New converts who wished to shed pagan spouses must avoid sexual relations after baptism. If they had sex even once with their pagan partner after conversion, that transformed their prior, non-Christian marriage into a full-fledged Christian union, which was indissoluble.[175] Those who favored the Parisian theory of marriage formation, however, took the position that since consent made marriage, the preconversion marriage was binding and could not be dissolved because of the baptism of one party into the Christian faith.[176]

As noted at the beginning of this chapter, the disagreements between decretists of the Bolognese and Parisian schools over marriage formation were not simply academic squabbles about abstract philosophical and theological principles. Rather, the differences between the two schools had important and tangible consequences for real couples and for a broad spectrum of issues, including the legitimacy of children, inheritance, marital property, and other topics. The rights of non-Christian spouses and the children of mixed marriages constitute another case in point.

[173] Paucapalea, *Summa* to C. 27 q. 2 c. 34, ed. Schulte, pp. 114–15; Rolandus, *Summa* to C. 27 q. 2 c. 19–26, ed. Thaner, p. 130; Rufinus, *Summa* to C. 27 q. 2 pr., ed. Singer, pp. 440–41.

[174] Stephen of Tournai, *Summa* to C. 27 q. 2 and to c. 13 v. *ad matrimonium*, ed. Schulte, pp. 236–37; Gandulphus, gloss to C. 27 q. 2 d.p.c. 26 v. *ecce* and to c. 19 v. *prohibuit*, in Weigand, "Gandulphusglossen," pp. 29, 33.

[175] Rolandus, *Summa* to C. 28 q. 2, ed. Thaner, pp. 141–42. Some twelfth-century theologians, e.g., Robert Pullen, adopted a similar position; Noonan, *Power to Dissolve*, p. 344.

[176] Peter the Venerable, *Epist.* 173, ed. Giles Constable, 2 vols., Harvard Historical Studies, vol. 78 (Cambridge: Harvard University Press, 1967) 1:412–13.

Concubinage in Decretist Doctrine

Concubinage and its corollary, bastardy, remained common throughout twelfth-century Europe, and decretist opinion about both matters was divided. Concubinage was practiced at all levels of society—poor couples lived together informally because they lacked incentives or means to formalize their relationships, while men of wealth often kept women of inferior social status as concubines, feeling that it was less scandalous and more convenient to retain attractive young women as companions than to marry them. And concubinage among the clergy was common as well, especially after canon law made it legally impossible for clerics in major orders to marry.[177] Some of the earliest commentators on Gratian took the position that concubinage, although permitted by human law, was forbidden by sacred law and that the Church accordingly should not recognize these unions at all.[178] More realistic writers, however, perceived that the law could not so cavalierly disregard social practice.

The author of the *Summa Parisiensis* seems to have been the earliest decretist to try to solve the concubinage problem by distinguishing between concubinage with marital affection and concubinage without it. A relationship without marital affection counted merely as an episode of fornication, no matter how long it endured or how many children it produced.[179] But if the relationship between a man and his mistress was permanent and if the two were bound together by marital affection, the situation was different. The *Summa Parisiensis* invoked the Salic Law as a basis for holding that such a relationship ought to be considered a marriage.[180]

Other writers, including Sicard of Cremona and Huguccio, adopted this dis-

---

[177] John of Salisbury, *Epist.* 87, ed. Millor, Butler, and Brooke 1:135–36, comments on the prevalence of concubinage among the Welsh and the toleration of the practice by the clergy. Examples from other regions are common: see e.g., Guibert, *Self and Society* 3.13, trans. Benton, p. 197; Robert Frank, "Marriage in Twelfth- and Thirteenth-Century Iceland," *Viator* 4 (1973) 480; Flandrin, *Familles*, pp. 176–77; Bresnier, "Mariage en Normandie," pp. 97–98.

[178] Paucapalea, *Summa* to D. 34, ed. Schulte, pp. 27–28; Rolandus, *Summa* to C. 32 q. 4 c. 4, ed. Thaner, p. 171; *Summa "Elegantius,"* 2.36, ed Fransen and Kuttner, 1:58–59; Plöchl, *Eherecht*, pp. 49–50.

[179] SP to D. 34 d.p.c. 6, ed. McLaughlin, p. 33; Cardinalis, gloss to C. 27 q. 2 c. 17, v. *nuptiale*, in B.L. Stowe 378, fol. 167ra: "Id est nuptialis affectus; non enim de carnali copula potest intelligi, cum de quadam concubina loquitur. C." quoted also by Huguccio, *Summa* to the same passage, ed. Roman p. 766, and Weigand, "Glossen des Cardinalis," p. 77.

[180] SP to D. 34 c. 4, as well as D. 33 pr., c. 1, and d.p.c. 6, C. 32 q. 2 c. 11, ed. McLaughlin, pp. 32–33, 242; Freisen, *Geschichte*, p. 70. Esmein, *Mariage* 2:114–15, argues that development of a more subtle analysis of concubinage was linked to the revival of knowledge of Roman law on the subject. Although this may be true, the decretists rarely cited Roman authorities on the matter and certainly their doctrine differed in many respects from that of the classical jurists.

tinction and identified concubinage with informal, clandestine marriage.[181] According to this view, concubinage with marital affection was not fornication and hence not a canonical offense, nor should the concubine be classed for legal or social purposes with harlots and other women of degraded status.[182] A concubine, said Huguccio, was nothing more or less than a de facto wife.[183] The usual and doubtless realistic assumption of many decretists was that servant girls routinely became involved in sexual relationships with their masters and other men of the households in which they served, but these relationships constituted fornication, not concubinage.[184]

[181] Rufinus, *Summa* to D. 34 d.p.c. 6, ed. Singer, p. 81, adopted verbatim by Joannes Faventinus in B.L. MS Add. 18,369, fol. 14rb; Stephen of Tournai, *Summa* to D. 33 pr., ed. Schulte, p. 50; Sicard of Cremona, *Summa* to D. 33 in B.L. MS Add. 18,367, fol. 8ra: "Concubina ducitur: maritali affectu que dicitur concubine quia sine solempnitatibus ducitur." Cf. Joannes Faventinus, *Summa* to D. 34 c. 4 v. *aut concubine* in B.L. MS Add. 18,369, fol. 14rb: "Coniugis, sed non sollempniter ducte," as well as *Frag. Cantab.* to C. 32 q. 2 c. 12 v. *et illa mulier*, in U.L.C., MS Add. 3321(1), fol. 24r: "Qui primo uidebatur concubina. Hic notandum quod in his capitulis non agitur de concubina que maritalis affectio asciscitur, sed de fornicaria." Huguccio, *Summa* to D. 34 d.p.c. 3 v. *concubina* in Pembroke 72, fol. 143va, and Vat. lat. 2280, fol. 35vb: "Hic determinat magister de qua concubina in superioribus capitulis debet intelligi, scilicet de concubina uxore. Uxor proprie dicitur que solemniter desponsatur et ducatur, scilicet adhibita solemni paranimforum et amicorum et sacerdotale benedictionis et nuptialis conuiuiis et huiusmodi. Sed concubina dicitur illa uxor quam quis clandestine non adhibita predicta solemnitate maritali affectu. Si copulat ut in perpetuum eam in uxorem habeat, hanc facit uxorem maritalis affectionis, ut xxxii. q. ii. solet [c. 6]. Sed dicitur concubina quia sine solemnitate accipitur et ducitur." Huguccio's comments to D. 33 pr. and c. 2 v. *unam concubinam* (Pembroke 72, fol. 143ra) also bear out this interpretation.

[182] Rufinus, *Summa* to D. 33 d.p.c. 1, ed. Singer, p. 77, followed verbatim by Joannes Faventinus in B.L. MS Add. 18,369, fol. 13va; SP to D. 33 pr., ed. McLaughlin, p. 32.

[183] Huguccio, *Summa* to D. 28 c. 2 in Pembroke 72, fol. 138va, and Vat. lat. 2280, fol. 29vb: "*Decernimus*, uerbo *uxores* de facto aut *concubinas*, sed nonne et ille uxores sunt concubine? Sic, sed ducuntur de facto et tenentur sub nomine uxorum." Sicard drew a more elaborate, threefold distinction between a concubine taken with marital affection, who ranked as a wife and with whom a union was legitimate, if not public; a concubine by mere usage, or in other words without marital affection, who ranked as a prostitute; and a concubine with whom a man maintained an exclusive sexual relationship. This last situation, Sicard thought, was irregular but should be tolerated as a matter of discretion; *Summa* to D. 33, in B.L. MS Add. 18,367, fol. 8ra: "Concunbina ducitur: maritali affectu, que dicitur concubina quia sine sollempnitatibus ducitur; his facit bigamiam, de qua supra; usu, prostitua; hanc habens non ordinetur; unica, hanc habens misericorditer toleratur." Joannes Faventinus likewise concluded that relationships with concubines, at least where there was natural affection between the parties, should be tolerated in practice; *Summa* to C. 32 q. 4 pr., in B.L. MS Add. 18,369, fol. 140vb–141ra: "Sed quomodo clandestina coniugia contrahi non debent, cum permittatur christiano habere concubinam, quam tamen naturali affectu cognoscat pro uxore, ut supra di. xxxiiii. cap. his qui, christiano [c. 4, 5]."

[184] SP to D. 33 c. 2 v. *concubinam*, ed. McLaughlin, p. 32; Rufinus, *Summa* to D. 34

The identification of long-term and exclusive sexual relationships with de facto marriage rested on the principle that the law ought to presume that cohabitation implied marriage, rather than an extra-marital relationship.[185] The decretists refused, however, to tolerate polygyny and accordingly held that the law could not allow a man to keep both a wife and a concubine at the same time.[186]

Once the decretists had identified stable and exclusive sexual relationships with marriage, other consequences followed. Concubinage of this type, for one thing, created a legal affinity that foreclosed marriage to other members of the partner's kindred.[187] Likewise a concubinage relationship itself could be broken up because of affinity contracted by a previous relationship between the concubine and a real or fictive relative of her lover, as a case debated in the *Questiones Stuttgardienses* pointed out.[188]

---

c. 15 v. *aut ancillam*, ed. Singer, p. 82, paraphrased by Joannes Faventinus in B.L. Royal 9.E.VII, fol. 20rb–va; note also the implicit assumption in Joannes Faventinus to C. 32 q. 2 c. 11 v. *ancillam* in ibid., fol. 143rb: "seu quamlibet aliam fornicariam."

[185] Huguccio, *Summa* to D. 34 c. 4 v. *concubina*, in Pembroke 72, fol. 143vb, and Vat lat. 2280, fol. 35rb: "Scilicet uxorem sine solemnitate et clandestine sibi copulatam; in huiusmodi consuetudine lex non concubinatum sed nuptias presumit et intelligit ut ff. de nuptiis, in libere [Dig. 23.2.24]; non repellatur quia uera uxor est et filii ex ea nati legitimi sunt. . . ."

[186] SP to C. 32 q. 2 d.p.c. 10, ed. McLaughlin, p. 242; cf. Peter Lombard, *Sententiae* 4.33.4, Quaracchi ed., 2:952–53.

[187] Huguccio, *Summa* to D. 1 c. 5 in Pembroke 72, fol. 117ra, and Vat. lat. 2280, fol. 2rb: "Et ualet ad probandum quod affinitas geratur per concubinam; queritur enim per uxorem . . . quare una caro cum marito efficitur, ut xxx. q. iiii. discitur, si quis unus [C. 30 q. 4 c. 3] et xxxv. q. iii. nullum, sane [C. 35 q. 2 & 3 c. 7, 14] et q. v. porro [C. 35 q. 5 c. 3]. Ergo similiter per concubinam, quia una caro cum eo efficitur, ut xxxii. q. iiii. in eo [C. 32 q. 4 c. 12] et xxxv. q. iii. de incestuos [C. 35 q. 2 & 3 c. 8]."

[188] *Questiones Stuttgardienses* in MS Add. 3321(2), fol. 30vb–31ra of the University Library, Cambridge [hereafter U.L.C.]: "Iuuenus quidam uxorem habens filiam cuiusdam de sacro fonte suscepit qui post susceptionem ex uxore sua filios generauit quos compatris filiabus copulare studuit aut in eius uxor sorti mane postea accepta quandam concubinam et aliquanto interuallo tractato in domo propria retinere placuit. Quo mortuo eius compater superstes prefatam concubinam in matrimonium sibi collocare uoluit. In hoc autem themate iii. questiones uidentur posse formari, quarum prima filii suscepti post compaternitatem uel ante compatris filiabus copulari possint? Secunda questio est utrum concubinam eius derelictam compatri in coniugium ualeat accipere? Tertia questio est an extranei ad testificationem uel accusationem consanguineorum admittendi sunt. . . . Secunda questio de facile solui potest. Idem dicitur de concubina quam de uxore; si iste qui suscepit filium uel filiam alterius uiri de sacro fonte post susceptionem fuerit effectus una caro cum concubina sua, non potest eius compater superstes ducere in matrimonium. . . ." Concubines sometimes tried to persuade their companions to regularize their relationship by a formal exchange of marriage vows. But this could also give rise to complex legal problems, particularly if the man later changed his mind and pleaded that his marital consent had been feigned, not real, as happened about 1181 in a

Although decretists by the 1160s regularly identified long-term concubinage with marital affection as informal marriage, they were inconsistent in dealing with the legal status of the children of these unions. Common opinion among the decretists classified the child of a concubine as a natural child—a venerable Roman law category—who must be legitimized by some formal act to become eligible to inherit his father's estate. Legitimation could be accomplished by formal marriage of the concubine to the child's father, even after the child's birth; this removed the taint of illegitimacy for ecclesiastical purposes, but not necessarily for secular purposes, such as inheritance. In order to qualify as legitimate under civil law, the natural child must be formally legitimized by an act of the ruler.[189] Thus the children of a concubine sometimes had the worst of both worlds. For inheritance purposes they were illegitimate, unless they obtained civil legitimation; legitimation by civil authority, however, left them illegitimate for ecclesiastical purposes, and they had to seek a dispensation in order to be eligible for ordination.[190]

Nonmarital Sex and the Decretists

The twelfth-century decretists devoted considerable attention to the chapters of Gratian's *Decretum* that dealt with sex outside marriage. Their discussions of nonmarital offenses were predicated on certain assumptions common in this period about the nature of human sexuality. Prominent among these was the belief that marital and nonmarital sex were fundamentally different in character and that while only marital sex was legitimate, both were rather splendid. Nonmarital sex was characterized as passionate, frenzied, and insistent, while marital sex was described as dispassionate, calm, and routine. Some twelfth century writers maintained that the differences between marital and non-marital sex were the result of two different kinds of love—passionate love between unmarried persons was, they thought, quite different from the gentle affection that linked married persons to one another. Both kinds of love, some poets maintained, ennobled the lovers and made them better people, even though the Church and the law considered only married love legitimate. Love as the poets described it was not merely a libidinal impulse, but also an ethical and aesthetic value involving the soul as well as the body.[191]

---

case discussed in B.N. ms. lat. 4720A, fol. 30ra–va, edited by Gérard Fransen in "Le mariage simulé: Deux questions disputées du XIIe siècle," in *Etudes de droit et de l'histoire: Mélanges Mgr. H. Wagnon* (Leuven: Bibliothèque Centrale de l'Université Catholique de Louvain, 1976), pp. 534–38.

[189] Joannes Faventinus, *Summa* to C. 32 q. 2 c. 12 v. *nec omnia filiis*, in B.L. MS Add. 18,369, fol. 145rb: "Sicut naturales, scilicet de concubina nati; qui nec filii nec legitime heredes sicut nec patri succedent nisi cum et ipsi facti fuerint forte legitimi uel per principem uel quia curie traduntur a patre, uel quando pater matrem eorum dotalibus instrumentis postea confactis in uxorem ducit."

[190] *Questiones Cusane*, no. 28, ed. Fransen, p. 219.

[191] Irving Singer, *The Nature of Love*, 2 vols. to date (Chicago: University of Chicago Press, 1966–) 2:11–12, 22–32.

Love poets and lawyers also assumed that young persons are especially prone to indulge in nonmarital sex. The heat of youth, Rolandus observed, predisposes young people to sexual excesses, and Huguccio converted this predisposition into a presumption of fact: young persons discovered in circumstances where sexual activity was possible should be presumed to have engaged in it, whereas older persons in the same circumstances should be presumed not to have done so.[192] Weakness of the flesh, though more marked in the young than in the old, was a source of concupiscence in persons of all ages, Rufinus noted, and in men, he added, the specific organic source of sexual sin lay in the testicles.[193] But both men and women were prone to commit carnal offenses—men as a result of their natural sensual appetite, which led them to seek intercourse with women at every opportunity; women, due to the weakness of their nature, burned with the fury of lust and would hardly ever remain chaste, unless they were closely watched and guarded.[194]

The seriousness of extramarital sex offenses, in the decretists' view, depended upon two considerations: the place of the offense in the scale of sexual sins and the circumstances of the offender. None of the decretists questioned seriously the scale of offenses that they found outlined in the *Decretum*, but some of them analyzed in detail the problem of aggravating and mitigating factors. The basic aggravating circumstance rested, of course, on the decision to act on sexual impulse, rather than to stifle the desire and resist temptation.[195] Other aggravating circumstances included the place of the offense and the time of its occurrence, the marital status of the parties, their ecclesiastical status, the civil relationship, if any, between them, and the extent to which the offense became public knowledge.[196] The mental state of the offender, especially his sobriety, or lack of it, might count as a mitigating circumstance and diminish his responsibility.[197] In principle the judge, like the confessor, was obliged to

---

[192] Rolandus, *Summa* to C. 32 q. 2 c. 11 v. *diffidentia aetatis*, ed. Thaner, p. 168; Huguccio, *Summa* to C. 27 q. 2 c. 19, ed. Roman, p. 768. These assumptions were not limited to canonists, of course, or for that matter to the medieval period. They presumably underlay some of the tensions between *seniores* and *juvenes* that figured so prominently in twelfth-century epics and love poems; Duby, "Structures familiales," p. 157.

[193] Rufinus, *Summa* to D. 13 c. 2 and C. 15 q. 1 pr., ed. Singer, pp. 33, 345; cf. Plato, *Timaeus* 91b–c, ed. Rivaud, pp. 226–27.

[194] Huguccio, *Summa* to D. 1 c. 7 v. *ut uiri et femine coniunctio*, in Vat. lat. 2280, fol. 2va, and B.N. lat. 3892, fol. 2 va: "Mouetur enim homo quoddam naturali appetitu sensualitatis ut carnaliter commisceatur femine." John of Salisbury, *Policraticus* 8.11, ed. Webb. 2:301; Brundage, "Carnal Delight," pp. 375–77.

[195] Stephen of Tournai, *Summa* to D. 25 c. 3 v. *nullum peccat*, ed. Schulte, p. 38; Brundage, "Carnal Delight," pp. 372–74.

[196] Rolandus, *Summa* to C. 32 q. 4 c. 4 v. *tolerabiliter*, and C. 32 q. 5 c. 12 v. *adulterium perpetratur*, ed. Thaner, pp. 171, 179–80; Rufinus, *Summa* to C. 12 q. 1 c. 18, ed. Singer, p. 322.

[197] Rolandus, *Summa* to C. 27 q. 1 c. 4, ed. Thaner, p. 119; Michaud-Quantin, "Manuel," p. 51.

weigh all of these factors when determining the punishment to be meted out.[198]

Acting on their assumption that all men and women are naturally inclined to commit sexual offenses, the decretists counselled Christians to take special precautions to avoid situations conducive to sexual temptations. Thus, neither clerics nor laymen ought to read or attend performances of comedies, which often described in word and deed the seduction of virgins and the lures of harlots and so might light the fires of lust, even in the pious.[199] These cautions were not without foundation, since twelfth-century Latin comedies, notably *De tribus puellis*, sometimes spun out sexual fantasies of considerable clinical, as well as literary, interest.[200]

Twelfth-century literary texts commonly reflected a conventional analysis of sexual attraction as a four-stage process. Visual attraction and conversation drew the lovers together. Looking and talking then led to touching, followed by kissing, and finally sexual intercourse.[201] The decretists also shared this typology of sexual involvement and described each as an increasingly grave offense. Verbal and visual dalliance, warned Rufinus, is itself sinful and leads to graver sins in turn.[202] It was especially dangerous, he added, echoing earlier penitential prescriptions, for men to bathe in the company of women. Western societies in the twelfth and thirteenth centuries discouraged nudity, because they believed that it stimulated sexual desire. Even lovers apparently did not usually see one another naked. The narrator of the comedy *De tribus puellis*, for example, expresses astonishment when the girl he is about to seduce strips off all of her clothes in preparation for lovemaking. Although some Provençal love poets of the twelfth century (William IX of Aquitaine and Bernart de Ventadorn, for example) wrote about their desire to see the beloved's naked body, their fantasies of *fin' amors* clearly involved nonmarital (and probably unconsummated) relationships. Art, literature, and law agreed during this period that decent married couples should eschew the sensual passion associated with the unclothed state. When manuscript illuminations from this period depict nudity, they do so almost invariably in contexts suggesting depravity and sin. This rejection of nudity apparently persisted until the fourteenth century.[203] (See Pls. 3 and 19.)

---

[198] Michaud-Quantin, "Manuel," pp. 35–36.

[199] Rufinus, *Summa* to D. 37 c. 2 v. *comedias*, ed. Singer, p. 87, followed verbatim by Joannes Faventinus in B.L. Royal 9.E.VII, fol. 22ra.

[200] Ian Thomson, "Latin 'Elegiac Comedy' of the Twelfth Century," in Paul G. Ruggiers, ed., *Versions of Medieval Comedy* (Norman, OK: University of Oklahoma Press, 1976), p. 54.

[201] Thomson, "Latin 'Elegiac Comedy'," p. 58. Avicenna also described the same stages of attraction; Singer, *Nature of Love* 2:43.

[202] Rufinus, *Summa* to D. 25 d.a.c. 4 §4, ed. Singer, p. 60; *Summa "Elegantius"* 1.35, ed. Fransen and Kuttner, 1:9.

[203] "De tribus puellis," ll. 249–60, ed. Paul Maury, in Cohen, *Comédie latine* 2:240–41; Singer, *Nature of Love* 2:52.

Kissing also counted as a moral danger. The treatise *Sacramentum coniugii non ab homine* included a short section on the psychology of kissing and warned that the practice quickly inflamed participants with sexual desire. A penitential in an Avranches manuscript required those guilty of erotic osculation to do penance by kissing the hand of a leper and giving him alms.[204]

The decretists warned that extramarital sex of any kind, ranging from admiring contemplation of a potential lover's beauty to actual copulation, was wrong. That such activities are common or even customary, Huguccio warned, does not excuse the crime involved in them; nor, he continued, can Christians argue that their extramarital dalliances had sacred precedents in the activities of the Old Testament prophets.[205] Immoderate familiarity with anyone of the opposite sex was an offense, even if it stopped far short of full sexual intercourse.[206]

ADULTERY AND FORNICATION

The decretists knew, of course, that transgressions against the Church's sexual code were common—the commonest of all offenses, according to Stephen of Tournai—and Huguccio lamented that few adults were innocent of fornication.[207] Despite its near universality, however, fornication, according to these writers, was an offense against natural law, if a virtually inevitable one.[208]

[204] Weigand, "Liebe und Ehe," p. 45 n. 15; Michaud-Quantin, "Manuel," p. 51.

[205] Huguccio, *Summa* to C. 32 q. 4 c. 7 v. *quando mos erat, non erat crimen*, in Weigand, *Naturrechtslehre*, p. 429; likewise Joannes Faventinus, *Summa* to D. 50 d.p.c. 12 v. *David post adulterium et homicidium*: "Nota exempla ueteris testamenti admittenda, non usquequo imitanda," (B.L. Royal 9.E.VII, fol. 29va).

[206] Huguccio, *Summa* to D. 34 c. 1 v. *mala fama*, in Pembroke 72, fol. 143va, and Vat. lat. 2280, fol. 35va–vb: "*Mala fama* non ratione criminis, scilicet quod carnaliter ad ipsam accederet, non uidetur uerisimile quod aliquis suspicaretur [MS Vat.: hoc suspicaret]. In his enim nil seui criminis naturale fedus suspicari permittit, ut C. de episcopis et clericis, eum qui [Cod. 1.3.19], sed ratione immoderate familiaritatis; uilis enim habeatur et contemptabilis cum ita se exponeret muliercule, forte tota die uolebat esse cum ea et in consilio et in colloquio et habere caput in gremio eius et sedere iuxta ea et forte osculari et amplexari; ergo illa mala nil erat nisi ab inicio uilitatis et secundum hoc non est questio quare iste non esset infamatus; non fuit purgatus, non enim erat necessaria purgatio, quia non referebatur quod de crimine notatus."

[207] Stephen of Tournai, *Summa* to D. 89 d.p.c. 5 v. *propinquis*, ed. Schulte, pp. 110–11; Huguccio, *Summa* to D. 25 d.p.c. 3 v. *sit sine peccato*, in B.N. lat. 3892, fol. 29va, and Vat. lat. 2280, fol. 26ra: "Immo pauci adulti inueniuntur sine carnali delicto, scilicet fornicationis, ut di. l. quia sanctitas [D. 50 c. 16] et ita nullus potest eligi sine peccato, unde patet quod non sic accipitur ibi in epistula pauli nomen criminis, sed sensus est ibi; see also Weigand, "Liebe und Ehe," p. 46.

[208] Simon of Bisignano, *Summa* to D. 1 c. 7 v. *uiri et femine coniunctio*; *Summa Reverentia* to the same passage; and *Summa Lipsiensis* to the same passage, all in Weigand, *Naturrechtslehre*, pp. 286, 289, 295–96; Joannes Faventinus, *Summa* to c. 32 q. 2 c. 11 v. *necessarie* in B.L. Royal 9.E.VII, fol. 143rb: "Scilicet propter necessitatem carnalis infirmitatis, quia forte continere non poterat," and cf. Rufinus, *Summa* to the same pas-

Although Gratian had taken pains to use "fornication" with some precision, the decretists used the term to describe a wide range of behavior. Fornication in their vocabulary meant not only illicit sexual intercourse, but also any wish or intention to commit such an act.[209] They used the term to describe extramarital relations by married persons as well as by unmarried ones.[210] Furthermore, fornication was used in an extended sense to describe such diverse offenses as contraceptive marital intercourse, polygyny, or any deviation from the faith (spiritual fornication).[211] To confuse matters further, decretists sometimes described illicit sex between two unmarried persons as adultery. *Stuprum* and *moechia* were all-purpose nouns that might apply to any kind of illicit sex, including both adultery and fornication.[212]

When they used the term strictly, the decretists meant by fornication any act of sexual intercourse between an unmarried man and woman.[213] The decretists held in theory that fornication in this sense was a major crime, second in seriousness only to murder; in practice, however, they often treated it as a minor

---

sage, ed. Singer, p. 483. J. F. Dedek, "Premarital Sex: The Theological Argument from Peter Lombard to Durand," *Theological Studies* 41 (1980) 644–45, claims that William of Auxerre (ca. 1150–1231) was the first theologian to argue that fornication is against the natural law.

[209] Rolandus, *Summa* to C. 32 q. 2 c. 7 *adulter uxoris,* ed. Thaner, p. 167; Joannes Faventinus, *Summa* to C. 32 q. 2 c. 7 v. *mariti meretrix est,* in B.L. Royal 9.E.VII, fol. 143ra: "Id est fornicaria, id est quantum in se est fornicatur cum marito iniuriam faciens ei. Nota quod fornicatio dicitur aliquando solo actu, ut cum quis copulatur non sue quam credit suam; aliquando dicitur reatu quis fornicari, cum actu et uoluntate uel sola uoluntate fornicatur uel cum proprie prolis necande copulatur affectu. Hoc modo dicitur ista meretrix, id est reatum contrahens ex tali copula mariti." Cf. Rufinus, *Summa* to the same passage, ed. Singer, p. 483.

[210] Rufinus, *Summa* to C. 28 q. 1 c. 5 and C. 31 q. 1 c. 9 v. *secundum veritatis rationem,* ed. Singer, pp. 453, 471–72, the latter followed verbatim by Joannes Faventinus in B.L. Royal 9.E.VII, fol. 140vb; *Summa "Elegantius"* 1.74, ed. Fransen and Kuttner, 1:25.

[211] Rufinus, *Summa* to C. 32 q. 2 c. 7 pr. and v. *mariti meretrix est,* ed. Singer, pp. 482–83, followed verbatim by Joannes Faventinus in B.L. Royal 9.E.VII, fol. 143va. Also Sicard of Cremona, *Summa* to D. 27 in B.L. MS Add. 18,367, fol. 8rb: "Inde est quidem poligamia fornicacio nomiinatur, ex poligamis penitentia dari precipitur, ut C. xxxvi. q. i. de his [*fortasse:* C. 35 q. 8 c. 1?]." In addition, SP to C. 7 q. 1 d.p.c. 18 and C. 32 q. 7 c. 15, ed. McLaughlin, pp. 136, 247; Rolandus, *Summa* to C. 27 q. 1 c. 9 v. *mater in corde,* ed. Thaner, p. 136; Stephen of Tournai, *Summa* to C. 28 q. 1 c. 4, ed. Schulte, p. 238; Michaud-Quantin, "Manuel," p. 40.

[212] Rufinus, *Summa* to C. 32 q. 4 c. 4 v. *omne stuprum adulterium est,* ed. Singer, p. 486; Stephen of Tournai, *Summa* to C. 36 q. 1 d.p.c. 2 v. *proprie virginum,* ed. Schulte, p. 257; SP to C. 32 q. 4 c. 11 v. *meretrices,* ed. McLaughlin, p. 243; Huguccio, *Summa* to C. 27 q. 2 c. 31, ed. Roman, p. 790.

[213] Rufinus, *Summa* to C. 31 q. 1 c. 9 v. *secundum veritatis rationem,* ed. Singer, pp. 471–72.

matter.[214] The degree of culpability depended to a large degree upon the circumstances and upon the persons involved.[215] The Cardinal reflected common attitudes when he remarked that people consider fornication a lesser offense for men than for women and for infidels than for Christians.[216] The status of the participants naturally affected the gravity of the offense, as did the place where it was committed, and the duration of the relationship.[217] The term "simple fornication" was sometimes used to distinguish sexual relations between two unmarried persons from "double fornication," that is sex between a married person and an unmarried one.[218]

Many people believe that simple fornication is not a serious offense, reported Bartholomew of Exeter, but he was in respectable company when he disagreed with that view.[219] Even simple fornication constituted a crime, according to the decretists, and heinous offenders might be heavily penalized.[220]

Adultery, like fornication, was common in twelfth-century society and seems

[214] Rufinus, *Summa* to D. 13 pr. v. *nisi duo mala* and D. 82 c. 5 v. *eadem quoque penitentia*, ed. Singer, pp. 32, 173. Sicard of Cremona, *Summa* to D. 13 in B.L. MS Add. 18,367, fol. 4va, echoes Rufinus's comment: "Item fornicatio minor est periurio. Sed qui iurauerit se fornicaturum, dicis eum perplexum inter fornicationem et periurium; ergo debet fornicari." But cf. Rufinus to C. 32 q. 7 c. 16, ed. Singer, pp. 492–93, followed by Joannes Faventinus in B.L. Royal 9.E.VII, fol. 145ra; Michaud-Quantin, "Manuel," p. 40.

[215] SP to C. 32 q. 7 d.p.c. 10, ed. McLaughlin, p. 247; Rufinus, *Summa* to C. 17 q. 4 c. 12 v. *et sicut maius peccatum est*, ed. Singer, p. 375; Michaud-Quantin, "Manuel," p. 26.

[216] Gloss to C. 32 q. 4 c. 3 v. *sed considera*, in B.L. Stowe 378, fol. 176vb: "Credens leuius esse delictum uiri fornicantis quam uxoris, quia leges interdicunt uxori uirum [MS: non] accusari propter suspicionem solam uel iure mariti, ut supra eodem q. i. quod si adulter [C. 32 q. 1 d.p.c. 10]. C."; Rolandus, *Summa* to C. 32 q. 4 c. 12, ed. Thaner, pp. 173–74.

[217] Rufinus, *Summa* to C. 28 q. 1 c. 5 and C. 31 q. 1 c. 7, ed. Singer, pp. 453, 470–71, followed verbatim by Joannes Faventinus in B.L. Royal 9.E.VII, fol. 140va; *Summa* "Elegantius" 3.69, ed. Fransen-Kuttner 1:146.

[218] Michaud-Quantin, "Manuel," p. 40; Joannes Faventinus, *Summa* to C. 32 q. 4 d.p.c. 10 v. *simplex fornicatio*, in B.L. Royal 9.E.VII, fol. 144ra: "Quam fecit solutus cum soluta; duplex enim est quando ligatus cum ligata uel soluta."

[219] Bartholomew of Exeter, *Penitentiale* 69, ed. Morey, pp. 236–37; Rolandus, *Summa* to C. 32 q. 4 c. 11, ed. Thaner, p. 173.

[220] Rolandus, *Summa* to C. 32 q. 4 c. 2 and c. 11, ed. Thaner, pp. 171, 173; *Summa* "Elegantius" 2.5, ed. Fransen and Kuttner 1:42. Rufinus, *Summa* to C. 2 q. 1 pr., ed. Singer p. 238, mentioned excommunication, while SP to C. 6 pr. and C. 32 pr., ed. McLaughlin, pp. 130, 240, declared that fornicators were *infames* and that the offense constituted a diriment impediment to marriage. Premarital intercourse between betrothed persons, however, was not fornication at all, according to some; under certain circumstances, of course, it could transform a betrothal into a marriage; Rolandus, *Summa* to C. 27 pr. and C. 27 q. 2 c. 50, ed. Thaner, pp. 114, 132–33; Rufinus, *Summa* to C. 27 q. 2 pr., ed. Singer, pp. 446–47; *Questiones Cusane* 2, ed. Fransen, p. 212.

in some circles to have been tacitly tolerated, so long as family honor was not jeopardized.[221] The author of the *Summa Parisiensis* claimed that adultery was horrendously common among the English, while English authors thought it terribly prevalent among the Irish.[222] A few decretists taught that adultery was prohibited by natural law, but the more frequent view maintained that the ban on adultery had been introduced by positive law.[223] The decretists fully realized that the law on adultery had undergone change through the ages. Ancient custom, Rolandus noted, had permitted married men under some circumstances to have sexual relations outside of marriage, as for example when their wives failed to produce heirs; but, he added, extramarital sex was no longer allowed for this reason (illustrated in Pl. 10).[224]

There was a clear consensus that adultery was far more heinous than simple fornication.[225] With adultery, as with fornication, intention formed an essential element of the crime. Thus if one party were unaware that the other party was married, the unwitting party might be guilty of fornication, but not of adultery.[226] In principle the consequences of adultery were supposed to be the same for men as for women, but practice was quite different.[227] The husband who

[221] John of Salisbury, *Policraticus* 8.11, ed. Webb 2:305, and *Hist. pont.* 23, ed. Chibnall, pp. 52–53; Benton, "Clio and Venus," pp. 24–28.

[222] SP to D. 56 d.p.c. 9 v. *contra Bonifacius*, ed. McLaughlin, p. 51; Mary Martin McLaughlin, "Survivors and Surrogates: Children and Parents from the Ninth to the Thirteenth Centuries," in Lloyd de Mause, ed., *History of Childhood* (New York: Psychohistory Press, 1974; repr. New York: Harper Torchbooks, 1975), p. 114.

[223] See the opinions of Huguccio, Petrus Hispanus, the Apparatus *Ordinaturus magister*, the Summa *Tractaturus magister*, the *Summa Lipsiensis*, Joannes Faventinus, and an unknown glossator (possibly Rufinus), all set forth in Weigand, *Naturrechtslehre*, pp. 414–17, 419.

[224] Rolandus, *Summa* to C. 32 q. 7 c. 27 v. *plane uxoris voluntate*, ed. Thaner, p. 188; cf. SP to C. 32 q. 4 pr., ed. McLaughlin, p. 243; Sicard of Cremona, *Summa* to C. 32 q. 7, in Weigand, *Naturrechtslehre*, p. 412; Tractatus *In primis hominibus*, in B.L. Royal 11.B.XIII, fol. 89ra-rb: "Si primus tunc poterit accipere penitentiam de precedenti adulterio et remanere cum secundo, namque tempore innocentii non erat statutum ne quis duceret illam cum [MS: con] qua fuerat adulteratus cui sententie hec sequens littera consonat."

[225] SP to C. 32 q. 7 c. 16, ed. McLaughlin, p. 247; Rufinus, *Summa* to C. 32 q. 7 c. 16, ed. Singer, pp. 492–93. The decretists' discussions of adultery are obscured, however, by the same vague use of terms that marked their discussions of fornication; Rolandus, *Summa* to C. 32 q. 4 c. 4, ed. Thaner, p. 171; SP to ibid., v. *nemo, omne stuprum*, ed. McLaughlin, p. 243; Rufinus, *Summa* to the same passage, v. *omne stuprum adulterium est* and c. 5 v. *adulter est*, ed. Singer, p. 486, followed verbatim by Joannes Faventinus in B.L. Royal 9.E.VII, fol. 143vb–144ra.

[226] Rolandus, *Summa* to C. 32 q. 5 c. 4, ed. Thaner, pp. 177–78; *Questiones Cusane* 4, ed. Fransen, p. 213; Tractatus *In primis hominibus*, in B.L. Royal 11.B.XIII, fol. 88rb: "Notandum est etiam quod si mulier ignoranter copuletur uiro habenti coniugem in aliena patria in illa non est adulterium immo coniugium, similiter et de uiro."

[227] SP to C. 32 q. 5 c. 23, ed. McLaughlin, p. 246; Rolandus, *Summa* to C. 32 q. 6 c. 4, ed. Thaner, p. 182.

discovered that his wife had engaged in an extramarital affair was obliged, according to some decretists, to turn her out: keeping her after discovery of her infidelity was both stupid and impious.[228] A wife was defiled by her husband's adultery, but she was not allowed to dismiss him for that reason.[229] The innocent party in an adulterous marriage, however, had the right to refuse to have sex with the guilty party, who lost his or her right to demand the conjugal debt.[230]

The decretists strongly opposed self-help by cuckolded husbands. Human law might allow a deceived man to kill his faithless wife, Rolandus declared, but the Church's law does not.[231] The *Summa Parisiensis* maintained that a husband who, despite this prohibition, slew his adulterous wife was entitled to plead circumstantial factors in mitigation of his guilt, and added that God might perhaps accept the wife's murder as satisfaction for her sin.[232]

The canonical consequences of adultery, according to the decretists, consisted mainly of *infamia* for lay persons, although aggravated cases might require further penalties.[233] In addition, there were conflicting opinions about an adulterous couple's right to wed after the death of the married party's spouse. The *Summa Parisiensis* held that such a couple might marry each other, but were forbidden to marry anyone else; Rolandus, however, would allow them,

[228] Rolandus, *Summa* to C. 32 q. 1, ed. Thaner, p. 160; SP to C. 22 q. 4 c. 21, ed. McLaughlin, p. 207; Stephen of Tournai, *Summa* to D. 34 c. 11 v. *dimittere*, ed. Schulte, p. 52; see also the gloss of Gandulphus to C. 22 q. 4 d.a.c. 19 v. *ecce usque laud.*, in Schulte's edition of Stephen of Tournai, p. xxix; Tractatus *In primis hominibus* in B.L. Royal 11.B.XIII, fol. 89rb: "Salamon in parabilis, 'Qui tenet adulteram stultus et impius est'[Prov. 18:22]. Quod sic exponitur: qui tenet adulteram eam non corrigendo et eius adulterio assentiendo stultus et impius est. Uel fortassis etiam si non assentiat cum illa nolit cessare et ipse possit continere tenens talem stultus et impius uidebitur."

[229] Rufinus, *Summa* to C. 32 q. 1 c. 3 v. *uxorem coinquinat*, ed. Singer, p. 476, followed verbatim by Joannes Faventinus in B.L. Royal 9.E.VII, fol. 141vb.

[230] SP to C. 32 q. 7 c. 1, ed. McLaughlin, p. 247; Cardinalis, gloss to C. 27 q. 2 c. 26 v. *nisi eand. uitam*, in Weigand, "Glossen des Cardinalis," pp. 77–78; *Questiones Cusane* 9, ed. Fransen, p. 214; Joannes Faventinus, *Summa* to C. 32 q. 1 c. 3 v. *licita sed adultera*, in B.L. Royal 9.E.VII, fol. 141vb: "Id est non est licitus uiro fornicarie exigere debitum ab uxore, sed debet abstinere ab ea tanquam ab adultera. Nam si a uiro debitum petat, reddere debet."

[231] Rolandus, *Summa* to C. 33 q. 2 c. 5 v. *adulterarum*, ed. Thaner, p. 190; Joannes Faventinus, *Summa* to C. 32 q. 1 d.p.c. 10 v. *lex iulia*, in B.L. Royal 9.E.VII, fol. 142rb, summarized, more-or-less, the provisions of the Augustan statute: "De adulteriis, quod data est a diuo augusto et temeratores aliarum nuptiarum gladio punit et eos qui nefandam libidinem in masculis exercuerunt et illos qui uirginem, uiduam, uel aliam honeste uiuentem stuprauerunt penam arrogat. Si honesti sunt, publicationem dimidie partis bonorum; si humiles cohertionem corporis cum relegatione." Secular laws in this period continued to sanction the slaying of both adulterer and adulteress; Ruiz de Conde, *Amor y matrimonio*, p. 21.

[232] SP to C. 23 q. 5 c. 6 and C. 33 q. 2 c. 5, ed. McLaughlin, pp. 218–19, 250.

[233] Rufinus, *Summa* to C. 2 q. 3 d.p.c. 7 and C. 32 q. 7 d.a.c. 19 v. *de incestuosa tant. fornic.* and v. *hii vero qui uxores*, ed. Singer, pp. 246, 493, 495.

under some circumstances, to marry others, but not to marry their partners in adultery.[234] The author of *In primis hominibus* preferred to resolve the issue on other grounds: if the adultery was public knowledge, he held, then the couple might not marry; if it was secret, they could marry, since this would not cause scandal.[235] Other writers, including Huguccio, rested their treatment of this situation on traditional grounds: if the couple had agreed to marry prior to the death of the married party's spouse or if either party were involved in plotting the death of the spouse, they were forbidden to marry. Otherwise they might be permitted to wed, although it would be preferable if they did not.[236]

PROSTITUTION

The decretists had little new to say about prostitution. Like Gratian they deplored the existence of the industry, but treated it as a minor stain on the social fabric.[237] While they advised their readers to avoid patronizing prostitutes, they

[234] SP to C. 32 q. 7 c. 22, ed. McLaughlin, p. 248; Rolandus, *Summa* to C. 31 q. 1, ed. Thaner, pp. 154–55.

[235] Tractatus *In primis hominibus*," in B.L. Royal 11.B.XIII, fol. 86va–vb: "Queritur autem de illo qui conmisit adulterium cum aliqua maritata, an marito ipsius defuncto liceat ei habere matrimonium cum illa? . . . Coniugium inter tales non admittatur si adulterium fuit publicum propter terrorem et scandalum uitandum tenet ecclesia."

[236] Rolandus, *Summa* to C. 31 q. 1, ed. Thaner, pp. 154–55; *Questiones Cusane* 12, ed. Fransen, p. 214; Simon of Bisignano, *Summa* to C. 31 pr., in B.L. MS Add. 24,659, fol. 32rb–va: "Nullus ducit in matrimonium quem polluit per adulterium. Hic ante penitentiam peractam potest intelligi. Penitentia uero peracta potest quis eam ducere in coniugium quam polluit per adulterium nisi in duobus casibus, scilicet si uiuente marito iurauit quod eandem eo mortuo duceret in uxorem, ut infra eodem questio, relatum [C. 31 q. 4 c. 4] et nisi in mortem mariti fuerat aliud machinatus, ut infra eodem questio, si quis [C. 31 q. 1 c. 5]." Sicard of Cremona, *Summa* to C. 31 q. 1 pr., in B.L. MS Add. 18,367, fol. 58vb: "Require utrum adultera prius repudiata fuit a marito uel non. Item si adulter sciebat uel ignorabat. Item si ignorabat ius aut factum. Item si peniteat uel penitencie contempnat. Item si uiuente marito fidem dederat. Item si nece defuncti machinati fuerunt. Hoc duo postrema nullam recipiant dispensationem, nam impediunt contrahendum et dirimunt contractum. . . . Unde si quis talium me consuleret, responderem quod nunquam talis cum tali contraheret, nisi forte dispensationem euidens utilitas postularet, ut forte pro bono pacis. Ubicumque autem admittitur dispensatio, cicius admititur cum repudiata quam cum nesciente uel cum penitente." Huguccio, *Summa* to C. 31 q. 1 pr., in Admont 7, fol. 312va: "Hec est questio scilicet an quis possit eam ducere in uxorem quam polluit per adulterium et dico indistincte quod potest nisi in duobus casibus, scilicet si uiuente marito fidem ei dedit quod eo mortuo duceret eam in uxorem, uel si alter illorum in mortem uiri machinatus est cum effectu. In his duobus casibus impeditur contrahendum et dirimit contractum. . . . In quolibet alio casu honestum est si non contrahant. Si tamen contrahunt, tenet et ualet."

[237] Paucapalea, *Summa* to D. 48 pr., ed. Schulte, p. 34; Rolandus, *Summa* to C. 27 q. 1 c. 41 v. *promiscuum feminarum*, ed. Thaner, p. 125.

[238] Huguccio, *Summa* to C. 32 q. 4 c. 11, in Vat. lat. 2280, fol. 283vb, and B.N. lat.

considered it only a trivial offense to have relations with a harlot.[238] Several writers enlarged slightly on Gratian's treatment of the property rights of prostitutes, developing the theme that although it is wrong for a prostitute to practice her trade, she did no wrong by accepting money for her services.[239] Writers of this period disagreed to some extent about the propriety of accepting alms from prostitutes. Huguccio, for one, was inclined to think that the Church should refuse their offerings, while Joannes Faventinus thought they might be accepted.[240]

As for marrying harlots, the decretists agreed that this practice could, under some circumstances, be considered an act of piety. Several writers, however, had misgivings about the wisdom of these marriages: Paucapalea, Rolandus, and Rufinus agreed that an unmarried man might legally marry a reformed harlot who had done penance for her shady past, but that a married man who discovered that his wife had taken to whoring was obliged to repudiate her (see Pl. 5).[241] Rolandus remarked that policy on this matter had recently changed; formerly the Church had discouraged men from marrying reformed prostitutes, "but nowadays it is considered praiseworthy."[242] Simon of Bisignano

---

3892, fol. 313va: "Ubi dicitur 'non erit meretrix de filiabus israel, neque scortator de filiis israel' . . . cum dicitur 'non erit meretrix' prohibi meretrices esse, cum enim dicitur 'non erit scortator' prohibi accedere ad meretrices." Joannes Faventinus, *Summa* to the same passage, in B.L. Royal 9.E.VII, fol. 144ra: "*Meretrices esse*: dicimus quarum publice uenialis est turpitudo." Even Andreas Capellanus, the twelfth-century codifier of the rules of love, was more urgent than most of the decretists when he advised men not to patronize prostitutes; *The Art of Courtly Love* 1.12, trans. John Jay Parry, Records of Civilization, Sources and Studies, vol. 33 (New York: Columbia University Press, 1941; repr. W. W. Norton & Co., 1969), p. 150.

[239] Rufinus, *Summa* to C. 14 q. 5 pr., ed. Singer, pp. 342–43, followed verbatim by Joannes Faventinus in B.L. MS Add. 18,369, fol. 90va; Huguccio, *Summa* to C. 14 q. 5 d.a.c. 1, in B.N. lat. 3892, fol. 119ra, and Vat. lat. 2280, fol. 205ra: "Unde dicit lex meretrix turpiter facere in eo quod est meretrix, sed nec turpiter accipit cum sit meretrix, ut ff. de consi. ob. tur. c., idem et si § quotiens [Dig. 12.5.4.2]."

[240] Huguccio, *Summa* to C. 14 q. 5 pr., in Vat. lat. 2280, fol. 205ra, and B.N. lat. 3892, fol. 119ra: "Indistincte dicunt quidam quod in nulla re illicite acquisita potest fieri elemosina, ergo nec de acquisita per furtum, uel per rapinam, uel per usurarum, uel symoniam, uel lusum, uel meretricium, uel per opus ystrionicum, uel matematicum, uel per extorsionem sicut sepe fit a rusticis, et hic ius ar. infra eodem questio, elemosinas [C. 14 q. 5 c. 7]." Cf. Rufinus, *Summa* to C. 14 q. 5 pr., ed. Singer, pp. 343–44. On the other hand see Joannes Faventinus, *Summa* to C. 14 q. 5 pr., in B.L. MS Add. 18,369, fol. 90va: "Que uero dantur ystrioni uel meretrici, licet illicite acquirantur, offere [MS: offero] tamen quia ex uoluntate dantis accipienti efficiunt, quia non turpiter, licet ex turpi officio accipiuntur. Turpiter enim facit qui est meretrix, sed ut lex dicit, non turpiter accipere cum sit meretrix; in elemosinas licite possunt expendi."

[241] Paucapalea, *Summa* to C. 32 pr. and q. 1, ed. Schulte, p. 125; Rolandus, *Summa* to C. 32 q. 1 pr., ed. Thaner, pp. 158–59; SP to C. 32 q. 1 c. 1 v. *sicut crudelis*, ed. McLaughlin, p. 240; Rufinus, *Summa* to C. 32 q. 1 pr., ed. Singer, p. 475, followed verbatim by Joannes Faventinus in B.L. Royal 9.E.VII, fol. 141va.

was more skeptical of the practice than the others: even a reformed prostitute, he thought, would find it difficult to remain virtuous, but, he added, marriage to her would nonetheless be valid.[243] Huguccio was also skeptical, but would permit marriage if the harlot had previously demonstrated that she seriously wished to reform her life.[244] In any case, Rufinus noted, a man who chose to marry a harlot, however praiseworthy his action, was barred from clerical orders.[245]

Several canonists of this period remarked that not all prostitutes are the same. The author of the *Summa Parisiensis* observed that some harlots did not choose the life voluntarily, but were forced into it and were not therefore totally accountable for what they did.[246] Even unrepentant prostitutes might be veritable paragons of piety, when it came to formal religious observances: Peter the Venerable remarked that they were especially keen in following the Church's fasting regulations and declared that their scrupulous observance provided an example that his monks ought to emulate.[247]

Pimps and panders were an altogether different matter. They incurred infamy by their very occupation, Rufinus asserted, and the faithful must shun them at all costs.[248] But even a pimp was capable of performing certain acts with legal effect—he could contract lawful marriage, for example, although if he did so the canonists felt a probably not unwarranted fear that he might force his wife into a career of sin.[249]

Prostitutes were certainly plentiful and their massive numbers compelled the Church to accommodate its rules to their presence. Prostitutes might be technically excommunicate because of their occupation, but Peter the Chanter

---

[242] Rolandus, *Summa* to C. 32 q. 1 c. 10 v. *fallax haberetur*, ed. Thaner, p. 162, closely paraphrased by Sicard of Cremona in B.L. MS Add. 18,367, fol. 58vb–59ra.

[243] Simon of Bisignano, *Summa* to D. 33 c. 2 v. *meretricem*, in B.L. Royal 10.A.III, fol. 6 va: "Nam difficile continentiam seruat, qui se illicito concubitu maculare non metuit, ut infra, distinctio proxima." Again, in his *Summa* to C. 32 q. 1 pr.: "Meretricem illam prohibemus recipere quam meretricari non desinit; quam tamen si quis acceperit, si alium non impediat, uxorem est appellanda." (B.L. MS Add. 24,659, fol. 32vb). Cf. Peter Lombard, *Sent.* 4.30; Esmein, *Mariage* 1:312–13.

[244] Huguccio, *Summa* to C. 32 q. 1 pr., in Admont 7, fol. 317ra, and Vat. lat. 2280, fol. 278vb: "Hic intitulatur prima questio, scilicet an licitum sit alicui ducere meretricem in uxorem. Breue distinguitur, aut habetur spes correctionis de meretrice aut non. Item meretrix aut ducitur animo corrigendi aut animo cum ea exercendi lenocinium. Si spes correctionis non est de ea, non licet eam ducere in uxorem. Si uero spes correctionis habetur de ea licet eam in uxorem ducere animo corrigendi, non autem turpia eam exercendi."

[245] Rufinus, *Summa* to D. 33 c. 2, ed. Singer, p. 77.

[246] SP to C. 32 q. 5 c. 1 v. *tolerabilius*, ed. McLaughlin, p. 245.

[247] Peter the Venerable, *Epist.* 161, ed. Constable 1:388.

[248] Rufinus, *Summa* to C. 2 q. 3 d.p.c. 7, ed. Singer, p. 246. For a vivid description of a twelfth-century pimp, see Thomson, "Latin 'Elegiac Comedy'," p. 56.

[249] Rolandus, *Summa* to C. 32 q. 1 c. 4, ed. Thaner, p. 160; Michaud-Quantin, "Manuel," p. 37.

advised that they should be permitted to attend Church services, lest they spend the time set aside for worship in more deplorable activities. Besides, he added on a practical note, there were simply too many prostitutes to make it feasible to exclude all of them from Church attendance.[250]

RAPE

The decretists' teachings on rape differed in several important respects from the views found in Gratian.[251] They analyzed the degrees of force employed in rape, for example, and distinguished between more grievous offence that involved violent coercion, which overpowered the victim, and the less serious offence involving moderate coercion, where the victim was induced to yield against her will, but without being physically forced to submit.[252] In either case the victim must resist or protest in order for the incident to be regarded as rape. It made no difference to the definition of the offense whether the coercive measures involved were directed against the person of the victim or against her parents and family.[253] Decretist discussions of rape also contained an early version of the notion that English and American lawyers would later call statutory rape: intercourse with a girl younger than the minimum legal age for valid consent to marriage was considered rape, even if the victim consented, and failed to protest, and no force was employed.[254]

The decretists considered prior relationship between the parties a vital fac-

[250] Nicholas M. Haring, "Peter Cantor's Views on Ecclesiastical Excommunication and Its Practical Consequences," *Mediaeval Studies* 11 (1949) 101. Medieval cities seem to have had droves of prostitutes who roamed public gathering places in search of business. For a description of harlots lining up outside of workshops to tout for clients among the workers see Jean Gimpel, *The Medieval Machine: The Industrial Revolution of the Middle Ages* (New York: Holt, Rinehart and Winston, 1976), p. 3.

[251] Note that while *raptus* may refer to the forcible theft of property as well as to abduction and sexual ravishment, the decretists restricted it primarily to mean sexual relations secured though coercion. Stephen of Tournai, *Summa* to C. 36 q. 1 pr., ed. Schulte, pp. 256–57; SP to C. 36 q. 1 ed. McLaughlin, p. 272; Rufinus, *Summa* to C. 36 q. 1 pr. and d.p.c. 3, ed. Singer, pp. 534–35, followed verbatim by Joannes Faventinus in B.L. Royal 9.E.VII, fol. 154va.

[252] Rufinus, *Summa* to C. 36 q. 1 pr., ed. Singer, p. 534, followed verbatim by Joannes Faventinus, in B.L. Royal 9.E.VII, fol. 154va. Rufinus analyzed coercion more extensively at C. 22 q. 5 c. 1, ed. Singer, pp. 400–401; see also Octavio Garcerán de Vall y Laredo, *El rapto y su jurisprudencia* (Habana: Cultural, 1945), p. 8.

[253] Stephen of Tournai, *Summa* to C. 36 q. 1 d.p.c. 2 v. *patre ad animam*, ed. Schulte, p. 257; SP to C. 36 q. 1 d.p.c. 2, ed McLaughlin, p. 272; Rufinus, *Summa* to C. 34 q. 1 & 2 c. 3 v. *legat libros*, ed. Singer, p. 508.

[254] Rufinus, *Summa* to C. 36 q. 1 d.p.c. 3 v. *et non parentibus*, ed. Singer, p. 535; cf. Joannes Faventinus, *Summa* to C. 36 q. 1 c. 3 v. *raptori consensit*, in B.L. Royal 9.E.VII, fol. 154va: "Ut fornicaretur, non ut matrimonium contrahet. Si enim ab inuito consensisset causa matrimonii dummodo nubilis esset, non redderetur patri. Si autem nondum nubilis, siue consensisset siue non, reddenda esset ei." See also Medeiros and Moreira, *Do crime de sedução*, p. 14.

tor in determining whether the crime of rape had been committed. If the parties, prior to the sexual assault, had agreed to marry in the future, or if they were actually married at the time of the incident, then the assailant could not be punished for rape, no matter how atrocious his attack. He might, however, be liable for injuries caused by his attack.[255] The Cardinal added that if a man forced his betrothed to have intercourse with him, he forfeited any future right to demand the marital debt from her.[256]

If there had been no marriage agreement between the parties prior to the assault, there was some question about whether they could subsequently marry. The early decretists noted that the law had formerly forbidden such marriages,[257] but Rufinus maintained that forcible intercourse was in itself no impediment to marriage.[258] If the girl was of age and if she consented to intercourse, then abducting her from her parents and having sexual relations with her did not bar marriage, even if the abduction involved doing violence to the parents.[259] Stephen of Tournai distinguished between abduction of a girl in order to marry her and sexual ravishment: when the rapist employed force to secure momentary sexual gratification, he and his victim could never subsequently marry.[260] In addition Rufinus and others would bar marriage if the girl had been betrothed to another man at the time of the attack or, *a fortiori*, if she had at that time been married to someone else.[261]

---

[255] Stephen of Tournai, *Summa* to C. 36 q. 1 d.p.c. 2, ed. Schulte, p. 257; Simon of Bisignano, *Summa* to C. 36 in B.L. MS Add. 24,659, fol. 35va: "Tunc enim desponsatione precedente si eam rapuerit secundum canones non dicitur raptum committere, licet alias peccauerit quia iniuriam uidetur fecisse nuptiis quas per raptum preuenit. Secus uero est secundum leges que etiam in re propria raptum et furtum dicunt posse committi, ut in Inst. iiii. t. i. § interdum [Inst. 4.1.9; *sed proprior refertur in paragraphum sequentem*]." See also the gloss to C. 36 q. 2 c. 5 in B.L. Stowe 378, fol. 204va: "Si ergo desponsatam sibi rapuerit non rapine penam incurret; secus secundum leges," and Joannes Faventinus, *Summa* to C. 27 q. 2 c. 49, in B.L. Royal 9.E.VII, fol. 136rb: "Istam legem in corpore iuris non habemus. Immo legimus quod sponsus in sponsam suam raptum potest existere et ut raptor puniendus est; ergo ibi raptus esse potest nisi prius de puelle nuptiis actum est." Ibid., v. *uel nihil fuerit*: "A raptore cum effectu. Nam si prius egit de nuptiis, id est cum ea nuptias celebrauit, non erit raptus, qui in uxorem non admitti; quamuis in sponsa propria admitti possit secundum leges, non autem secundum canones."

[256] Cardinalis, gloss to C. 27 q. 2 c. 49 v. *nupciis*, in Weigand, "Glossen des Cardinalis," p. 81.

[257] Rolandus, *Summa* to C. 27 pr., ed. Thaner, pp. 114–15; SP to C. 32 q. 7 c. 7, ed. McLaughlin, p. 247; Rufinus, *Summa* to C. 34 q. 1 c. 3, ed. Singer, pp. 507–508.

[258] Rufinus, *Summa* to C. 36 q. 2 pr. and c. 10, ed. Singer, pp. 535–36.

[259] Rolandus, *Summa* to C. 36 q. 2, ed. Thaner, pp. 233–34.

[260] Stephen of Tournai, *Summa* to C. 36 q. 2 pr., ed. Schulte, p. 257.

[261] Rufinus, *Summa* to C. 36 q. 2 c. 9 v. *nulli desponsata*, ed. Singer, pp. 535–36; gloss to C. 36 q. 2 c. 8, in B.L. Stowe 378, fol. 204vb: "Per contrarium ergo si rapta fuerit alteri desponsata, raptor eam habere non poterit. R." Ibid. to C. 36 q. 8 c. 11: "Si quis autem uxorem habere uoluerit et canonice et legaliter eam accipiat, qui uero eam

Forcible intercourse with an unwilling victim was a heinous offense and Rufinus noted with an air of satisfaction that the civil law punished it with death.[262] Canon law, of course, did not impose the death penalty; it did require that the victim be restored to her family and that the attacker submit to their will. The family head could enslave the assailant, who nonetheless retained the right to buy back his freedom if he had sufficient resources.[263] In effect this meant that the victim's family could require compensation from the attacker and that if he failed to make satisfaction, the law allowed them to seize physical control of his person. In actuality this policy simply reflected the effects of class differences: the swineherd who ravished a duchess, if by some miracle he escaped mutilation and death, would be enslaved; the duke who ravished a shepherdess, if punished at all, could make compensation by providing her with a purse full of coins as a dowry.

DEVIANT SEX

The late twelfth century was a period in which attitudes toward homosexual behavior were beginning to change. Sexual practices and preferences in this period commenced to be taken as indicators of doctrinal orthodoxy; deviance from the dominant sexual preference was thought to manifest deviance from accepted doctrine. There is some evidence that male brothels existed in Chartres, Orléans, Sens, and Paris late in the twelfth century, but overt homosexual practices attracted increasingly repressive attention from authorities, both secular and religious.[264] Peter the Chanter devoted a long chapter of his *Verbum abbreviatum* to a vigorous denunciation of the vice of sodomy, and canonists, as well as theologians, gave increasing attention to analyses and denunciations of sex practices, both homosexual and heterosexual, that they considered unnatural.[265] That these practices were widespread, according to Joannes

---

rapuerit uel furatus fuerit aut seduxerit nunquam eam habeat." But cf. Simon of Bisignano, *Summa* to C. 36, in B.L. MS Add. 24,659, fol. 35va: "Hic ergo in summa teneat quod acta penitentia de rapina, raptor potest rapte in matrimonium copulari si fuerit alteri desponsata, ut infra ii. questio, denique [C. 36 q. 2 c. 9]." The disputants in the *Questiones Cusane* discussed an interesting complication: if a parent feared that his daughter might be forcibly abducted and ravished and if, as a result, he placed her in a convent for safekeeping, might she subsequently leave the convent and return to the world when the danger had passed? The solution, according to the *Questiones*, depended upon the girl's intention. If she had never wished or intended to become a nun, she could depart and marry, but the burden of proving her intent rested upon her; *Questiones Cusanae* 3, ed. Fransen, pp. 212–13.

[262] Rufinus, *Summa* to C. 2 q. 3 d.p.c. 8 § 5, ed. Singer, pp. 247–48; SP to C. 36 pr., ed. McLaughlin, p. 271.

[263] SP to C. 36 q. 1 c. 3, ed. McLaughlin, p. 272.

[264] Boswell, CSTAH, pp. 255, 262–63, 283–84.

[265] Peter the Chanter, *Verbum abbreviatum* 138, in PL 205:333–35; SP to C. 15 q. 1 d.p.c. 3 v. *sacrae tamen legis*, ed. McLaughlin, p. 174; Rolandus, *Summa* to C. 32 q. 7 c. 12, ed. Thaner, p. 185; Michaud-Quantin, "Manuel," pp. 40–41.

Faventinus, offered no excuse for those who indulged in them. Custom could excuse many crimes, Joannes maintained, but not sexual activity "contrary to nature."[266]

The decretists had little to say about other sexual habits. Only Huguccio and Sicard of Cremona dealt explicitly with masturbation and their discussions focused mainly on defining the degrees of moral guilt in self-stimulation. For Huguccio particularly the two operative criteria were the pleasure that resulted from the sexual experience and the intention of the individual. If the pleasure was slight and not deliberately sought, as for example in nocturnal emission, the degree of guilt was correspondingly slight. But if orgasm was deliberately induced and enjoyed, the degree of guilt and the attached punishment correspondingly increased.[267]

Few decretists commented at all on cross-dressing or the biblical prohibition of transvestite practices. Stephen of Tournai, one of the minority to deal with the subject, did distinguish between respectable women who adopted male dress in order to avoid threats to their chastity, and loose women, who dressed like men in order to sin more freely.[268] None of these writers dealt with men who adopted female dress, whatever their purpose.

The Early Decretists and Clerical Sexuality

The decretists routinely reiterated conventional admonitions that clerics of all ranks, but especially those in major orders, must not only avoid living with women, but should also shun excessive familiarity with female servants and other women with whom they came in contact.[269] The *Summa "Elegantius"* particularly cautioned against eating and drinking in feminine company and observed that carnal coupling often followed conviviality at the table.[270] It is also evident that these warnings were routinely ignored by many clerics—Bishop Arnulf of Lisieux (d. 1184) reported to Pope Alexander III (1159–81), for example, that he had banished no less than seventeen concubines from the

---

[266] Joannes Faventinus, gloss to C. 32 q. 4 c. 7 v. *mos*, as well as the *Apparatus Ordinaturus magister* to C. 32 q. 4 c. 7 v. *miscebantur*, both in Weigand, *Naturrechtslehre*, p. 428.

[267] Huguccio, *Summa* to D. 6 pr., in Pembroke 72, fol. 120ra, and Vat. lat. 2280, fol. 6rb: "Credo tamen quod tale pollutio uel delectatio [*viz*: nocturna pollutio] non sit mortale peccatum, sed tantum ueniale. Et nota quod siue pollutio nocturna sit mortale peccatum siue ueniale semper tamen subest ibi quedam feruor siue pruritus, quedam uoluptas que est in quolibet coitu in emissione spermatis et talis uoluptas est peccatum ueniale, nec potest non esse peccatum, ut xxxiii. q. iiii. uir [c. 7]."

[268] Stephen of Tournai, *Summa* to D. 30 c. 3 v. *suo proposito*, ed. Schulte, p. 45, followed closely by Joannes Faventinus in B.L. Royal 9.E.VII, fol. 17rb.

[269] *Summa De multiplici iuris diuisione*, in Pembroke 72, fol. 68va: "Quod non solum extranearum mulierum cohabitatio clericis interdicta sit, sed quod etiam domesticarum personarum immoderatam familiaritatem habere non debent."

[270] *Summa "Elegantius"* 2.39, ed. Fransen and Kuttner 1:60: "Post uinum Venus, post carnem, carnalia."

chambers of his cathedral canons in a single day. Alas, the wily wenches soon sneaked back into the cathedral precincts by devious routes and under various guises. Even Arnulf's nephew, Silvester, was involved in the conspiracy to subvert the observance of clerical celibacy.[271]

Despite continued efforts by prelates and councils, clerical marriage and concubinage were by no means on the verge of extinction in the second half of the twelfth century. The majority of clerics in minor orders were married, and substantial numbers of those in major orders, including such prominent prelates as the Patriarch of Jerusalem, continued to have more or less permanent and public relationships with women. The succession of priests' sons to their fathers' clerical positions, moreover, was by no means a thing of the past.[272] Although Pope Celestine III (1191–98) referred to this latter practice as a peculiar vice of Germanic regions, there is no reason to believe that it was confined to the Teutonic world.[273] Indeed, ordinary people often preferred that their priests be married.

> The peasants say that a priest cannot live alone [reported an Alsatian chronicler] and therefore it is better that he have his own wife, for otherwise he will pursue everybody else's wives and sleep with them.[274]

Church leaders had little patience with such sentiments as these. A few diehards continued to argue and to write that the policy of compulsory clerical celibacy harmed the Church and to point out that it lacked any scriptural warrant, but they were battling in a cause already lost. The policy was fixed, although its implementation was erratic and uncertain.[275]

The decretists did not debate the issue of the desirability of celibacy as a policy. Instead they focused their efforts on trying to account for the law as they found it and on coping with problems of enforcement. One theoretical issue

[271] *The Letters of Arnulf of Lisieux*, no. 132, ed. Frank Barlow, Camden Society Publications, 3d ser., vol. 61 (London: Royal Historical Society, 1939), pp. 198–99. In *Epist.* 136 (pp. 206–207) Arnulf also recounted the case of a vicar of his diocese who took as his concubine the mother of the lord of the manor in which his parish was located.

[272] *Distinctiones Monacenses* to D. 28 c. 17, quoted in Filippo Liotta, *La continenza dei chierici nel pensiero canonistico classico da Graziano a Gregorio IX*, Quaderni di *Studi Senesi*, vol. 24 (Milan: A. Giuffrè, 1971), p. 131; John of Salisbury, *Hist. pont.* 3, ed. Chibnall, pp. 8–9; Giraldus Cambrensis, *De jure et statu Menevensis ecclesiae*, and *Speculum ecclesiae* 3.8, in his *Opera* 3:128–29 and 4:170; Volkert Pfaff, "Das kirchliche Eherecht am Ende des zwölften Jahrhunderts," ZRG, KA 63 (1977) 90. On Patriarch Heraclius of Jerusalem and his notorious womanizing see *La continuation de Guillaume de Tyr (1184–1197)*, 38–39, ed. Margaret Ruth Morgan, Documents pour servir à l'histoire des croisades, vol. 14 (Paris: Paul Geuthner, 1982), pp. 50–52.

[273] JL 17,606; 2 Comp. 3.4.3; Pfaff, "Kirchliche Eherecht," p. 87.

[274] *De rebus Alsaticis* 1, in MGH, SS 17:232; Pfaff, "Kirchliche Eherecht," p. 90.

[275] Giraldus Cambrensis, *Gemma ecclesiastica* 2.6, in his *Opera* 2:187–88; Baldwin, "Campaign to Reduce Clerical Celibacy," p. 1047; Gaudemet, "Célibat ecclésiastique," p. 30.

that did trouble them, however, was the source of the obligation. Since secular priests did not take a formal vow of celibacy, whence did their obligation to chastity arise? Rolandus proposed the hypothesis that a tacit, unarticulated vow of celibacy was somehow implied in the act of ordination and that observance of the discipline thus flowed from admission to higher orders.[276] This explanation failed to satisfy the more rigorous—and more historical-minded—decretists. Huguccio, for one, stoutly rejected the theory of the *votum adnexum*; no obligation to celibacy is inherent in ordination, he declared, for otherwise how could one explain the long-standing practice of clerical marriage in the Eastern Churches? Huguccio asserted correctly that the Western Church instituted the practice of celibacy as a disciplinary measure. Thus the obligation to observe celibacy rested upon the constitution of the Church and was not an intrinsic feature of holy orders.[277]

As for monks and others who actually did take vows of celibacy, the decretists differed about the relative seriousness of their sexual misbehavior. Rufinus argued that it is better for those who made simple vows of chastity to marry than to fornicate, but added that their offenses were more serious than adultery.[278] Paucapalea, however, had maintained that the marriage of those who took vows of celibacy, although a serious lapse, was less serious than adultery. He also criticized those who denied the validity of such marriages.[279]

Clerics in minor orders who had not taken vows of celibacy may keep concubines, according to Stephen of Tournai, so long as they do not seek promotion to higher ranks. But Rolandus maintained that their eligibility for promotion depended upon the nature of the relationship: concubinage with marital affection, he declared, created an impediment to later promotion, while simple cohabitation without marital affection did not.[280] As for priests' concubines,

---

[276] Rolandus, *Summa* to C. 27 q. 1 pr., ed. Thaner, p. 117; Gaudemet, "Célibat ecclésiastique," p. 25.

[277] Huguccio, quoted in Liotta, *Continenza dei chierici*, pp. 116–18; Gaudemet, "Célibat ecclésiastique," pp. 28–29.

[278] Rufinus, *Summa* to C. 27 q. 1 c. 41–42, ed. Singer, pp. 438–40. Others said much the same of sexually delinquent nuns; Rolandus, *Summa* to C. 27 q. 1 c. 5 and c. 21, ed. Thaner, pp. 119–21; gloss to C. 27 q. 1 c. 9, in B.L. Stowe 378, fol. 164vb: "Immo magis peccat uirgo quia a statu cadit maiore." Sicard of Cremona likewise viewed such lapses very seriously; *Summa* to C. 27 q. 1 in B.L. MS Add. 18,367, fol. 54va: "Quidam nubentes post uotum uocant adulteros. Ego autem dico quod grauiter peccant. . . . Fidei contractus inter homines nulla solet ratione dissolui; quanto magis pollicitatio domino facta sine uindicta solui non potest; item cypriano c. eodem q. nec aliqua [C. 27 q. 1 c. 4]. Si superueniens maritus sponsam suam cum adultero iacentem uiderit, indignatur et fremit et per dolorem zeli gladium portat. Nonne et domino noster Christus? Zelotes cum uirginem sibi dicatam cum adultero cernit gladium portat, quem in extremi iudicii diem omnes timere debemus."

[279] Paucapalea, *Summa* to C. 27 q. 1 c. 41, ed. Singer, pp. 112–13.

[280] Stephen of Tournai, *Summa* to D. 32 c. 8 v. *aut continentiam*, ed. Schulte, p. 49; Rolandus, *Summa* to D. 33, ed. Thaner, p. 7. Duggan, "Equity and Compassion," p. 63, passes rather lightly over the differences among the decretists on this subject; his char-

Rufinus shared the conventional opinion that they should be turned out of their consorts' dwellings, but he declared that the notion that these women should be sold into servitude was absurd and deserved no support.[281] While the decretists generally agreed that the faithful should be discouraged from frequenting services conducted by priests who lived in open concubinage, Rufinus noted that some writers taught that they should resort to this sort of boycott only after a formal complaint about the matter had been presented to the bishop, and judgment had been given against the offender. Rufinus refused to take sides on this issue and preferred to leave it to the discretion of his readers.[282]

The decretists also disagreed about the penalties that should be imposed on clerics in major orders who were guilty of concubinage or fornication. The conventional wisdom held that such clerics should lose both their offices and their benefices, but not all writers agreed with this.[283] The *Summa Parisiensis* urged that the circumstances of each case should be considered in arriving at the appropriate punishment and added that as a rule young priests should be less harshly punished than older men, in whom the fires of lust presumably burned less vigorously.[284] Rufinus maintained that in any case the old penal law was no longer observed rigorously and that it was not current practice to depose priests for sexual offenses, but merely to suspend them from their priestly functions until they reformed.[285] Fornication, he added, was only a moderately se-

---

acterization of their views accordingly rests primarily on Paucapalea, *Summa* to D. 33, ed. Schulte, p. 27, and Rufinus, *Summa* to D. 33 pr. and c. 1, ed. Singer, pp. 76–77. Huguccio, *Summa* to D. 27 pr., in Pembroke 72, fol. 137vb, points out the differences between Eastern and Western practices: "Notandum ergo quod clerici et orientales et occidentales in minoribus ordinibus constituti licite possunt contrahere matrimonium et uti contracto, ut di. xxxii. Si quis eorum [D. 32 c. 7]. . . . In hoc autem est differenciam inter orientales et occidentales: illi enim siue sint coniugati siue non promouentur ad sacros ordines, scilicet subdiaconatum et supra, etiam promissa continentia, ut di. xxxi. lex, omnino [D. 31 c. 10–11]." Others thought that in all such cases a dispensation was a necessary condition for promotion to the higher clerical grades; thus Simon of Bisignano, *Summa* to D. 33 c. 1 v. *ad concubinam*: "Ante uel post uxorem; contra enim ratione bigamie repellitur, uel fornicario more, pro quo de rigore impeditur, ex dispensatione autem potest promoueri, uide infra di. proxima fraternitas [D. 34 c. 7]." Also *Summa De multiplici iuris diuisione*, to D. 33 in Pembroke 72, fol. 68rb: "Qualiter is qui concubinam habuit post baptismum antequam ducere uxorem, post mortem uxoris ad sacri ministerii quod conscendere non possit, nisi forte ex magna dispensatione."

[281] Rufinus, *Summa* to D. 81 c. 30 v. *ideoque quecumque*, ed. Singer, p. 172.

[282] Stephen of Tournai, *Summa* to D. 32 c. 5, ed. Schulte, p. 48; *Summa "Elegantius"* 2.27–32, ed. Fransen and Kuttner 1:53–56; Rufinus, *Summa* to D. 32 c. 5, ed. Singer, p. 74.

[283] Paucapalea, *Summa* to D. 28, ed. Schulte, p. 25; *Summa "Elegantius"* 2.9 and 3.111, ed. Fransen and Kuttner, 1:44, 165–66.

[284] SP to D. 82 c. 5 v. *Si presbyter*, ed. McLaughlin, p. 66.

[285] Rufinus, *Summa* to D. 50 c. 28 v. *et potior* and D. 81 c. 12 v. *deponatur*, ed. Singer, pp. 122, 171.

rious offense for clerics and need not be harshly punished, a sentiment with which Joannes Bazianus fully agreed.[286] Even Huguccio, who was not inclined to look mildly upon carnal delicts, urged moderation in these matters, although he added that the penalties for priestly marriage ought to be more severe than those for casual fornication.[287]

Mildness and moderation did not, however, characterize the views of the decretists so far as the treatment of the sons of clerics was concerned. Instead, the decretists often treated clergymen's children more harshly than earlier writers had done. The decretists classed all children of clerics as illegitimate and thus denied them the right to inherit parental property. The severity of the decretists' treatment of the children of clerics contrasts strikingly with their relatively restrained views about the punishment of clerical transgressors. This contrast results in part, presumably, from the legal writers' concern to maintain a strict and uncompromising opposition to clerical marriage, but also reflects their concerns with Church property.[288]

The decretists by and large supported the conventional and long-standing prohibition of the ordination of twice-married men. Several of them insisted even more adamantly than Gratian and earlier writers had done that second marriages resulted from intemperate sexual desires.[289] Likewise marriage to widows, divorcées, actresses, or other women who had had multiple sexual relationships barred promotion to orders, as the *Summa "Elegantius"* noted.[290] Rufinus was the first to class constructive bigamy as an irregularity, and seems to have invented this use of the term.[291] Several decretists noted the irony and apparent inequity of allowing men who had kept concubines to be ordained, while denying orders to those who had contracted two legitimate and perfectly

---

[286] Rufinus, *Summa* to D. 50 pr., ed. Singer, p. 115; Joannes Bazianus, *Summa* to D. 32 c. 5 v. *nullus precepit*, in Liotta, *Continenza dei chierici*, p. 187.

[287] Huguccio, *Summa* to D. 28 c. 9 in Vat. lat. 2280, fol. 29vb, and Pembroke 72, fol. 139ra: "Ecce uidetur hic plus puniri sacerdos fornicans quam ductens in uxorem, sed misericorditer agit cum eo; ducens enim uxorem plus peccat quam fornicans, quia facit specialiter contra illam prohibicionem, scilicet ne quis in sacro ordine contrahat et quia illi tanto sacramento, id est matrimonio [offendat] et immo debet plus puniri, sed hic agit cum eo misericorditer." The *Summa "Elegantius"* 2.30, ed. Fransen and Kuttner 1:55, noted that even adulterous priests were not to be excommunicated.

[288] Stephen of Tournai, *Summa* to D. 56 pr., ed. Schulte, p. 84; Schimmelpfennig, "Ex fornicatione nati," p. 25.

[289] Rolandus, *Summa* to C. 31 q. 1 c. 8, ed. Thaner, p. 156; Cardinalis, gloss to C. 27 q. 2 d.p.c. 29 v. *maritus enim uidue*, in Weigand, "Glossen des Cardinalis," pp. 78–79; Rufinus, *Summa* to C. 31 q. 1 c. 8–9, ed. Singer, pp. 471–72, followed closely by Joannes Faventinus in B.L. Royal 9.E.VII, fol. 140vb.

[290] *Summa "Elegantius"* 2.33, ed. Fransen and Kuttner, 1:56–57.

[291] Rufinus, *Summa* to D. 25 d.p.c. 3, ed. Singer, p. 60; Stephan Kuttner, "Pope Lucius III and the Bigamous Archbishop of Palermo," in *Medieval Studies Presented to Aubrey Gwynn, S.J.*, ed. John A. Watt, J. B. Morrall, and F. X. Martin (Dublin: Colin O Lochlainn, 1961), p. 410.

legal marriages. Sicard of Cremona argued that the rule should be modified, at least in cases where the existence of a "bigamous" marriage was not widely known.[292]

Jurisdiction, Procedures, and Evidence in Sex Cases

By the late twelfth century, Church courts had secured jurisdiction over marriage and related matters, both in England and on the Continent. The existence and validity of marriages were generally considered matters that secular judges lacked competence to determine; such questions were routinely referred to the ecclesiastical courts for resolution, and the decision of the ecclesiastical judge was normally accepted as conclusive. The related matter of legitimacy often fell into ecclesiastical jurisdiction as well, although secular courts reserved the right to deal with questions involving marital property, succession to estates, and dowry.[293] Sex crimes and offenses were not so neatly divided between the two jurisdictions; ecclesiastical courts claimed an exclusive right to determine complaints involving sex crimes because these crimes involved sin. Some decretists, however, conceded that secular courts were competent to hear complaints involving adultery, since this crime had grave civil consequences.[294] Rape was another sex crime that frequently came before secular courts.[295]

The procedural mechanisms of the twelfth-century canonical courts were in flux. Older procedures that relied upon ordeals as instruments of proof were falling into disrepute, and several writers held that they should no longer be employed. Rather, evidence elicited from the sworn testimony of witnesses was gradually becoming the normal type of proof required in the Church's courts.[296]

[292] *Summa "Elegantius"* 2.35, ed. Fransen and Kuttner 1:57–58; Rufinus, *Summa* to D. 33 pr., ed. Singer, p. 77, followed closely by Joannes Faventinus, in B.L. Royal 9.E.VII, fol. 19rb; Sicard of Cremona, *Summa* to D. 27 in B.L. MS Add. 18,367, fol. 8rb–va: "Queritur si ualeat ordinari uel ordinatus promoueri qui cum uidua uel duabus uirginibus uel aliis fornicatur. Videtur quod non, quia si hanc nuptialis coniunctio prohibet promotionem, cur non et fornicaria? . . . Respondeo: si conuincitur aut publice confitetur, quid iuris sit in C. xv. diffinitur. Si uero crimen occultum fuerit, uel etiam si manifestum sed non ecclesiam scandalizans, peracta penitentia poterit promoueri, ut d. xxviii. prius [c. 4] et d. xxxiii. habuisse [c. 7]."

[293] Engdahl, "English Marriage Conflicts Law," p. 111; Joseph Biancalana, "The Origin of the Writs of Dower," paper presented at the XIX International Congress on Medieval Studies, Western Michigan University, 12 May 1984.

[294] Stephen of Tournai, *Summa* to C. 1 pr., ed. Schulte, p. 121.

[295] *Placita Anglo-Normannica: Law Cases from William I to Richard I*, ed. Melville Madison Bigelow (Boston: Soule and Bugbee, 1881; repr. South Hackensack, NJ: Rothman Reprints, 1970), p. 247.

[296] Stephen of Tournai, *Summa* to C. 2 q. 5 c. 25 v. *si duo*, ed. Schulte, p. 172; Cardinalis, gloss to C. 27 q. 2 c. 29 v. *per uerum iudicium*, in Weigand, "Glossen des Cardinalis," p. 78. See generally Jean Gaudemet, "Les ordalies au moyen âge: doctrine, législation, et pratique canoniques," in *La preuve*, 2 vols., Recueil de la Société Jean Bodin, vol. 17 (Brussels: Editions de la Librairie Encyclopédique, 1965) 2:99–135;

The canonists were also inclined to hold that where the facts of a case were notorious, that is where knowledge of what had transpired was widespread and virtually universal in the community, the courts could act without requiring formal proof.[297] This concept of notoriety had been unknown to Roman law and appears to have been a creation of the canonists.[298]

The canonists of this period also concerned themselves with elaborating more detailed rules than they found in Gratian concerning the right to bring accusations before the Church's courts in sex cases.[299] Criminal prosecution on adultery was subject to special restrictions: a husband who was guilty of adultery could not charge his wife with adultery; but otherwise husbands enjoyed a privileged position with respect to adultery charges, while wives were seriously disadvantaged in these cases.[300] There were further restrictions on the

---

Jean-Philippe Levy, "Le problème de la preuve dans les droits savants du moyen-âge," in *La preuve* 2:137–67; Colin Morris, "*Judicium Dei*: The Social and Political Significance of the Ordeal in the Eleventh Century," in *Church, Society, and Politics*, ed. Derek Baker, Studies in Church History, vol. 12 (Oxford: Basil Blackwell, 1975), pp. 95–111; Charles Donahue, Jr., "Proof by Witnesses in the Church Courts of Medieval England: An Imperfect Reception of the Learned Law," in *On the Laws and Customs of England: Essays in Honor of Samuel E. Thorne*, ed. Morris S. Arnold et al. (Chapel Hill: University of North Carolina Press, 1981), pp. 127–58, as well as Paul R. Hyams, "Trial by Ordeal: The Key to Proof in the Early Common Law," in ibid., pp. 90–126.

[297] Rolandus, *Summa* to C. 15 q. 7 pr., ed. Thaner, p. 36.

[298] Rosalio Castillo Lara, "Los primeros desarrollos doctrinales del 'notorium' en la canonística clásica," *Salesianum* 22 (1960) 412. The canonists also held—and this helped to mitigate some abuses that potentially inhered in the notoriety doctrine—that conviction of an offense or judicial determination of the issues, whether on the basis of notoriety, sworn testimony, or confession by the accused, was an essential precondition to a verdict of guilty and the imposition of punishment; thus *Questiones Stuttgardienses*, in U.L.C., MS Add. 3321(2), fol. 26vb–27ra: "Quidam archipresbiter crimine adulterii notatus, priusquam sit confessus aut conuictus ab ecclesia repellitur; restitutionem petit, ducitur in causam, petit inducias. Hic formatur iii. questiones: prima: si quis crimine notatus priusquam sit conuictus aut confessus sit repellendus? Secunda, si est restituendus aut postea sit dandum inducie? iii. si duo bigami uel iii. uel nimis corpore debilitatus ad eius accusationem admittantur? Prima soluitur secundum diuisionem illam que fit iii. que. ii. cause [C. 2 q. 3]." See generally Richard M. Fraher, "'Ut nullus describatur reus prius quam convincatur': Presumption of Innocence in Medieval Canon Law?" in *Berkeley Proceedings*, pp. 493–506.

[299] Certain classes of persons were barred from bringing such actions: thus, a husband who was *infamis*, for example, could not accuse his wife of adultery; SP to C. 3 q. 10 c. 3 and C. 4 q. 6 pr., ed. McLaughlin, pp. 124, 128. Rolandus also wished to ban persons involved in irregular sexual relationships from bringing criminal accusations and argued further that they could bring civil actions only where their personal interests were at issue; Rolandus, *Summa* to C. 3 q. 4, ed. Thaner, p. 18.

[300] Rufinus, *Summa* to C. 32 q. 1 d.a.c. 11 v. *publice iudicio*, ed. Singer, pp. 477–78; *Summa "Elegantius"* 4.7, ed. Fransen and Kuttner 2:4; Sicard of Cremona, *Summa* to

right to charge clerics with adultery; only those who were themselves ordained or at least qualified to enter the priesthood could charge a cleric with adultery, while persons guilty of homicide, bigamy, or adultery were specifically barred from doing so.[301] Adultery charges had to be made in writing, and both Rufinus and the *Summa "Elegantius"* provided samples of the appropriate forms.[302] Adultery accusations must also be timely; the courts were not supposed to entertain actions on such charges where the alleged misdeeds had taken place more than five years previous to the accusation.[303] Men retained the important option of accusing their wives of adultery on suspicion alone, even when definitive proof was lacking. The suspicion, however, must have some factual basis: it was not sufficient, Rufinus declared, for a husband to find his wife in the company of a comely young man and to see them wink and nod at one another. But if he were to discover his wife in bed at night with the other man, the husband had reasonable cause to suspect that they were engaged in an adulterous relationship, even if he did not witness actual sexual relations between them.[304] If a husband charged his wife with adultery and was unable to prove his case, she had the right to leave him, although she was not required to do so.[305] The courts

---

C. 32 q. 6 in B.L. MS Add. 18,367, fol. 60ra: "Uir tamen in accusando iure mariti triplici gaudet priuilegio: potest namque accusare uxorem sine inscriptione, sine metu calumpnie, et de sola suspitione." Likewise, Joannes Faventinus, *Summa* to C. 33 q. 1 d.p.c. 10 v. *hoc in mulieribus*, in B.L. Royal 9.E.VII, fol. 142ra: "Scilicet, quod ipse possit sic accusare uiros de adulterio. Sed hoc intellige ante ciuilem iudicem, nam ante ecclesiasticum possunt, sed tamen non tam facile quam uiri eas. Viri enim ex sola suspicione, legitimis tamen iudiciis approbata, accusare possunt uxores suas ante episcopum, quod feminis non conceditur."

[301] Rufinus, *Summa* to C. 2 q. 7 c. 38 v. *esse non possunt*, ed. Singer, p. 257. The *Summa Parisiensis* added that in France no layman of any sort could prefer criminal charges against a cleric, although the custom of the Roman Church was more lenient; SP to C. 2 q. 7 pr., ed. McLaughlin, p. 113.

[302] Rufinus, *Summa* to C. 2 q. 8 pr., ed. Singer, pp. 259–60; *Summa "Elegantius"* 3.93a, ed. Fransen and Kuttner 1:156.

[303] *Summa "Elegantius"* 2.9, ed. Fransen and Kuttner 1:44; the rule was based on Cod. 9.9.5.

[304] Rufinus, *Summa* to C. 32 q. 1 c. 2 v. *fornicatio*, ed. Singer, p. 476, followed verbatim by Joannes Faventinus, in B.L. Royal 9.E.VII, fol. 141vb; Stephen of Tournai, *Summa* to C. 2 q. 1 c. 13 v. *suspicionis arbitrio*, ed. Schulte, p. 161; gloss to C. 32 q. 1 c. 2 v. *suspicio* in B.L. Stowe 378, fol. 174vb: "Est suspicio mediocris ut si mulierem nutus impudicos adolescenti reddentem uideris;" Sicard of Cremona, *Summa* to C. 32 q. 6, in B.L. MS Add. 18,367, fol. 60rb: "Expressim arguit lex iulia crimen adulterii in i. q. huius c. ubi dicitur quod uir debet accusare uxorem de sola suspitione. Sciendum ergo suspicionem alia uiolenta sit si uiderit uirum cum uxore sua in lecto iacentem; alia mediocris, ut si alter alteri nutus loquatur. Prima accusationem uires exhibet sufficientes, secunda eandem eiusdem predatur."

[305] Joannes Faventinus, *Summa* to C. 32 q. 1 c. 2 v. *calumpniam faceret*, in B.L. Royal 9.E.VII, fol. 141vb: "Falso dicente uiro uxorem adulteram dimittere iubetur, sed

were also prepared in adultery cases to give weight to the testimony of persons who might otherwise not be acceptable witnesses, notably serfs and women.[306]

If one person accused another of a sex offense and the accused entered a counterclaim that the accuser was guilty of another offense, the decretists suggested procedural rules to determine the order in which the complaints should be heard. Thus an accusation of adultery took precedence over a fornication charge and accordingly must be determined first. Similarly a countercharge of pimping took precedence over an adultery accusation.[307]

Cases that involved allegations of sexual impotence posed other problems of evidence. If both parties agreed on the facts, the court might grant divorce; otherwise, at least according to the Stowe glosses, physical examination of the parties might be required in order to establish whether or not they were capable of sexual intercourse (see Pl. 14).[308] Certain kinds of sex offenses presented nearly insoluble problems of evidence. Rolandus noted that anal intercourse was virtually impossible to prove without a confession; this was also true of oral sex.[309]

Sentencing and punishment, in the opinion of Stephen of Tournai, ought to take into account the circumstances and the past record of persons convicted of sex offenses. Those guilty of repeated offenses should suffer the maximum penalties allowed. Those who were guilty of just a few offenses or of only one, however, should receive reduced punishment.[310] Defendants convicted of the most serious sex offenses, especially rape and adultery, were denied any right to appeal the first-instance decision.[311]

We are poorly informed about many practical details of the working of twelfth-century ecclesiastical courts. For one thing, we know little about litigation costs. One detailed record of expenses survives for a complex and intricate marriage case in England, *Anstey c. Francheville*, in which the proceedings ran

---

dicit Aug. hoc non esse preceptum sed permissum, causa xxviii. q. i. c. ydolatriam [c. 5]. Sub idem huius contrarietas solutionem inuenis nisi forte dicatur Aug. illum post retractasse." Cf. Rufinus, *Summa* to the same passage, ed. Singer, p. 476.

[306] Paucapalea, *Summa* to C. 4 q. 2 & 3 c. 3 v. *item servi neque pro domino neque*, ed. Schulte, p. 68; Rolandus, *Summa* to C. 15 q. 3, ed. Thaner, p. 34.

[307] Rufinus, *Summa* to C. 3 q. 11 d.p.c. 3, ed. Singer, p. 273; Stephen of Tournai, *Summa* to the same passage, v. *aliquando*, ed. Schulte, p. 199; SP to C. 3 q. 11 pr., ed. McLaughlin, p. 125.

[308] Gloss to C. 27 q. 2 c. 29 v. *per uerum iudicatum*, in B.L. Stowe 378, fol. 167vb: "Probare mulierem debet quod non possit uir cum ea coire si uult alium accipere, etiam si uir contradicat. Hic enim probo per uerum iudicium, scilicet aspectu corporis. . . . Jo." Also, Joannes Faventinus, *Summa* to C. 27 q. 1 c. 29 v. *uerum iudicari*, in B.L. Royal 9.E.VII, fol. 136ra: "Scilicet membrum eius inspiciatur a mulieribus, quia forte non est aptum carnali operi."

[309] Rolandus, *Summa* to C. 27 q. 1 c. 4, ed. Thaner, p. 119.

[310] Stephen of Tournai, *Summa* to D. 50 pr., ed. Schulte, pp. 68–69.

[311] Stephen of Tournai, *Summa* to C. 2 q. 6, ed. Schulte, p. 175.

for more than six years and costs were correspondingly large.[312] *Anstey* was by no means representative of ordinary litigation, however, and it would be misleading to generalize from the expenditures in that case. We are likewise poorly informed about how much time was likely to elapse from the commencement of an action to its termination, and the evidence of complex and notorious cases, such as *Anstey*, does not reflect ordinary experience.

Conclusions

The twelfth century has been called the century of love, because of the celebration of love in the poetry of the period.[313] The decretists who wrote in the second half of the century were probably not unaffected by contemporary beliefs and attitudes, and commentaries on the law of marriage may well reflect the influence of ideas about individualism and personal emotions current in the literature of the period. Some decretists were prepared to assert, for example, that affection between a married couple constituted a legitimate goal of marriage itself.[314] Certainly the canonists of the late twelfth century, like the theologians of the same period, ascribed a more positive value to marriage and even to sexual relations within marriage than their predecessors had usually done.[315] It would be a gross distortion to call this a sexual liberation—it was nothing of the sort. But at least some decretists implied in their analysis of married love that sexual pleasure is a positive factor, a bonding element, in the relationship.[316]

Positive valuations of love, marriage, and sexuality, however, were by no means universal or even common among canonists in this period. Huguccio, the most influential of them all, took an exceedingly dim view of sexual gratification, even in a loving and procreative matrimonial union. The differences among the decretists were most striking when they dealt with the role of sex in the formation of marriage itself. The conflict of opinion between the School of Bologna and the School of Paris on the question of whether carnal copulation was essential to create a marriage reflected the uncertainties that late twelfth-century canonists felt about the legitimacy of any kind of sexual expression. French canonists might have been expected to grant marital sexuality a more prominent place in their treatment of marriage than did their colleagues at Bologna, since the French school had adopted a definition of marriage that placed great emphasis upon the affective and personal element of consent. Yet, this failed to occur, and the most intransigent rigorists among the canonists of this age belonged to the French tradition. The Bolognese decretists, by comparison, gave greater emphasis to the sexual element in marriage.

[312] The expense accounts in the case are printed in Sir Francis Palgrave, ed., *The Rise and Progress of the English Commonwealth*, 2 vols. (London: John Murray, 1831–32) 1/2:ix–xxvii, lxxv–lxxxvii; see also Barnes, "The Anstey Case," pp. 1–23.

[313] Grévy-Pons, *Célibat et nature*, pp. 28–29.

[314] See above, pp. 273–74; Leclercq, *Monks on Marriage*, p. 12.

[315] Bynum, *Jesus as Mother*, p. 142.

[316] Leclercq, *Monks on Marriage*, pp. 69–70.

Decretist treatments both of marital and nonmarital sex were also influenced, albeit unevenly, by the development during this period of new concepts of nature. While philosophers and theologians saw nature as a liberalizing and expansive notion, the jurists employed nature, at least in regard to sex, as a restrictive principle. While twelfth-century philosophers were beginning to invoke nature as a basic cosmological principle, the canonists of the period seem to have found the concept of nature, on the whole, merely confusing.[317] Their confusion was reflected in their treatment of such matters as unusual coital positions and extravaginal intercourse in marriage, homosexuality, and other deviations from common sexual practices. This confusion, as we shall see, became even more pronounced among later generations of canonists.

Finally, the decretists' prejudices about women and beliefs about the nature of reproductive biology profoundly conditioned their treatment of sex and marriage.[318] Notions about female docility, the character and force of the female sex drive, and the natural inconstancy and intellectual inferiority of women, coupled with the clerical elite's extraordinary reverence for virginity, underlay much decretist writing about the law of marriage and sexual relations.

[317] Grévy-Pons, *Célibat et nature*, p. 28; see also Gaines Post, "The Naturalness of Society and the State," in his *Studies in Medieval Legal Thought: Public Law and the State, 1100–1322* (Princeton: Princeton University Press, 1964), pp. 494–551. The beginning of a change in the role of nature in medieval thought seems to date from the appearance of the *De planctu naturae* of Alain de Lille (1117–1203); see R. H. Green, "Alain of Lille's 'De planctu naturae,'" *Speculum* 31 (1956) 651, 665–66, and more generally Ernst R. Curtius, *European Literature in the Latin Middle Ages*, trans. Willard R. Trask (New York: Harper & Row, 1963), pp. 106–27.

[318] Erickson, *Medieval Vision*, p. 184; Vern L. Bullough, "Medieval Medical and Scientific Views of Women," *Viator* 4 (1973) 485–501. For examples of the distress that the stereotypes could cause, see Guibert, *Self and Society*, trans. Benton, pp. 38–44, 63–76, 92–97.

Plates

Plate 1. A common medieval belief about human sexual behavior held that the Devil induced sexual desires and provoked people to yield to them, as this fifteenth-century woodcut tries to make clear. (Woodcut from *Der Seelentrost* [Augsburg, 1478])

Plate 2. An alternative theory ascribed sexual desire to the influence of the planets, notably Venus. This fifteenth-century Italian woodcut illustrates her powers by showing Venus presiding over seduction in a bathtub following an intimate dinner for two, as well various episodes of amorous dalliance in the open air. (Courtesy of the Newberry Library, Chicago; from Friedrich Lippmann, *The Seven Planets*)

i menage reiaucur ueuaur uu eu euaur
s ne pozus te mande prest est du guenant
e tu dues la bataille nôme le ioz deuant
i tapareille bien car il uenta auant
Quant alixand lot si raint temautalent
A riste apela par molt grant hardement
Toute inte li donna delli quen ozient

et ripauo out le ....
G s telers te gardai a ioie z a baudoz
J ufquas bones artus ains ni soffris doloz
te soffri por uous z le uent z lardoz
L a noif z la gelee z la ruiste froidoz
s uous seruoie bien z tenoie a seignoz
Quant tu uenis des arbres ou alas a cremoz

Plate 3. Medieval bath houses were often associated with sexual license and prostitution. Respectable establishments segregated their customers by sex, as shown at the left of this marginal illumination from the Old French *Roman d'Alexandre;* but many bathing facilities, such as the one on the right, were either brothels or houses of assignation. (MS Bodley 264, fol. 75r, courtesy of the Bodleian Library, Oxford)

Plate 4. Love in a tub: another example of the role of the bathtub as an *engin d'amour* in medieval literature and art. (Fifteenth-century woodcut from an Augsburg Calendar, ca. 1480)

Plate 5. (*left*) Early medieval canon law discouraged respectable men from marrying women who had been prostitutes, but by the beginning of the thirteenth century this policy had changed. Innocent III positively encouraged charitable men to save fallen women from a life of sin by marrying them. This illumination for Causa 32 from a fourteenth-century Italian manuscript of Gratian's *Decretum* shows such a marriage. (Courtesy of the British Library, from MS Add. 15,275, fol. 89v)

Plate 6. (*right*) The exchange of free consent between the couple constituted the sole formal requirement for sacramental marriage according to the doctrine of Alexander III's decretal *Veniens ad nos*, which remained the basic law on the subject in Christian Europe from the late twelfth century up to the Council of Trent. Jan Van Eyck's painting of the marriage between Giovanni Arnolfini and Giovanna Cenami shows such an exchange between a couple, witnessed only by their dog and the two persons shown indistinctly in the mirror. (Courtesy of the Trustees of the National Gallery, London)

Plate 6. (*detail*)

Plate 7. A man who had been presumed dead returns to discover that his wife has married another. He asks a bishop to declare his wife's second marriage null and to order her to return to him. This fourteenth-century illumination depicts the hypothetical situation discussed in Causa 34 of Gratian's *Decretum*. (Courtesy of the British Library, from MS Add. 15,275, fol. 133r)

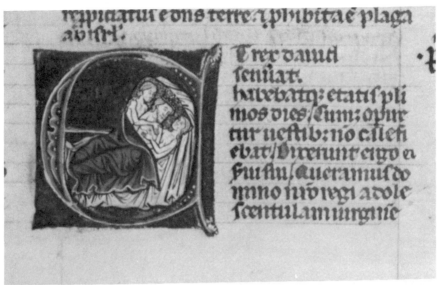

Plate 8. Canon law discouraged, but did not effectively forbid, concubinage, and nonmarital cohabitation remained common throughout medieval society. Peasant couples frequently lived together, sometimes for years, before marrying; priests and other clerics who were forbidden to marry kept concubines instead; young men of humble station who could not afford the outlays involved in marriage lived with shopgirls; servants of both sexes indulged in sexual liaisons, sometimes with one another, sometimes with their employers; young noblemen kept girls of lower status for sexual diversion; and monarchs, even married ones, might keep a concubine or two in addition to an official wife, as did Jaume II of Aragon and Catalunya. The concubinary king pictured in this fourteenth-century illumination represents King David, but he can stand for many another. (From MS Ee.2.23, fol. 98r, by permission of the Syndics of Cambridge University Library)

Plate 9. This fourteenth-century illumination from an encyclopedia known as *Omne bonum* by Jacobus Anglicus shows a cleric with his concubine and their child. The gestures of the principal figures suggest some disagreement between them, but whether over the child's parentage or arrangements for its support is not clearly apparent. (Courtesy of the British Library, from MS Royal 6.E.VI, fol. 296v)

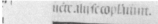

10

11

Plates 10 and 11. Adultery was a serious crime in both canon and civil law, but it was also common in medieval life and Church courts often had to unravel its consequences, including complex questions concerning the inheritance rights of children whose parentage was doubtful, as shown in these illuminations from two manuscripts of Gratian's *Decretum,* Causa 31. (Plate 10 from MS Borgh. lat. 370, fol. 269rb, courtesy of the Biblioteca Apostolica Vaticana; Plate 11 from MS Add. 15,275, fol. 87v, courtesy of the British Library)

Plate 12. Seduction of young women of well-to-do families by ardent young suitors who were unacceptable to the girl's parents furnished a common theme for medieval poets and much work for canon lawyers as well. This illumination from a fourteenth-century manuscript of Gratian's *Decretum* shows on the left the union of such a suitor and his beloved being blessed by a priest, while on the right the distressed father of the girl asks a bishop to annul the marriage. The bishop's admonishing gesture and disapproving expression suggest that he was not disposed to do so. (Courtesy of the British Library, from MS Add. 15,275, fol. 141rb)

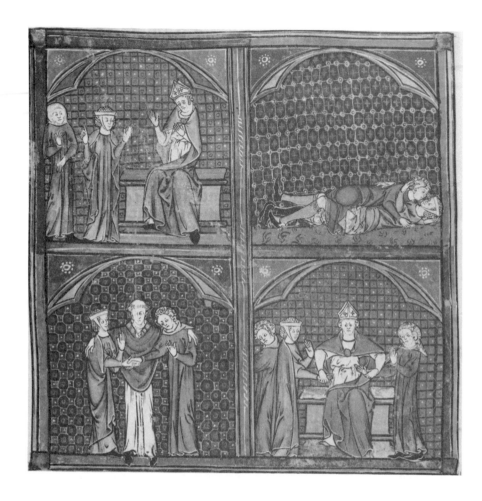

Plate 13. The illuminator of this thirteenth-century copy of the *Decretum* seems to have placed these four scenes in the wrong order, but read in proper sequence they illustrate a case of the dissolution of marriage because of impotence. In the bottom left panel a couple exchange marital consent in the presence of a priest. The episode at the upper right shows them attempting unsuccessfully to consummate their union. At the upper left the wife complains to a bishop about her husband's incapacity; and in the lower right panel the bishop symbolically annuls the marriage by disjoining the couple's hands. (Courtesy of the Syndics of the Fitzwilliam Museum, Cambridge, from MS 262, fol. 86v)

malcficuf impedituf uxon fue debmi nitte
fi potar. aluif interm elamelo eam corrupit.
a intro fuo feptra corruptoni fuo publice
nubat. Cum q amiferat in corde tm deo
2fiter. reddit huic facultraf cognofeendi
ea. repetit uxore fua. q trecepta: ut expe
diri ordini natater. 7 ut ad carnef adui

Plate 14. Canonical courts required convincing evidence of marital impotence before they would declare a marriage void. One mode of proof involved examination of the parties by experienced women, who attempted to produce sexual arousal in the allegedly impotent man. In the case illustrated here the husband had clearly failed to respond. (Courtesy of the Walters Art Gallery, Baltimore, from MS W.133, fol. 277)

Plate 15. Christ's love for the human race came to be regarded increasingly in sexual terms during the later middle ages as the humanity of Jesus became a prominent theme in Western theology. This illumination from a copy of the Song of Songs shows Jesus as a lover embracing his spouse. (Courtesy of King's College Library, Cambridge, from MS 19, fol. 21v, by the Master of the St. Albans Psalter)

Plate 16. The celebration of sensual pleasure
and carnal love became increasingly explicit
in the art of the fifteenth and sixteenth centuries, as the "Allegory of the Power of Love" by
Cristofano Robetta (1462–1522) makes plain.
(Courtesy of the Toledo Museum of Art)

Plate 17. This late fifteenth-century engraving of "Priapus and Lotis" uses a mythological episode to illustrate the horrors of the crime of forcible rape. (Courtesy of the Detroit Institute of Arts; gift of Mrs. James E. Scripps)

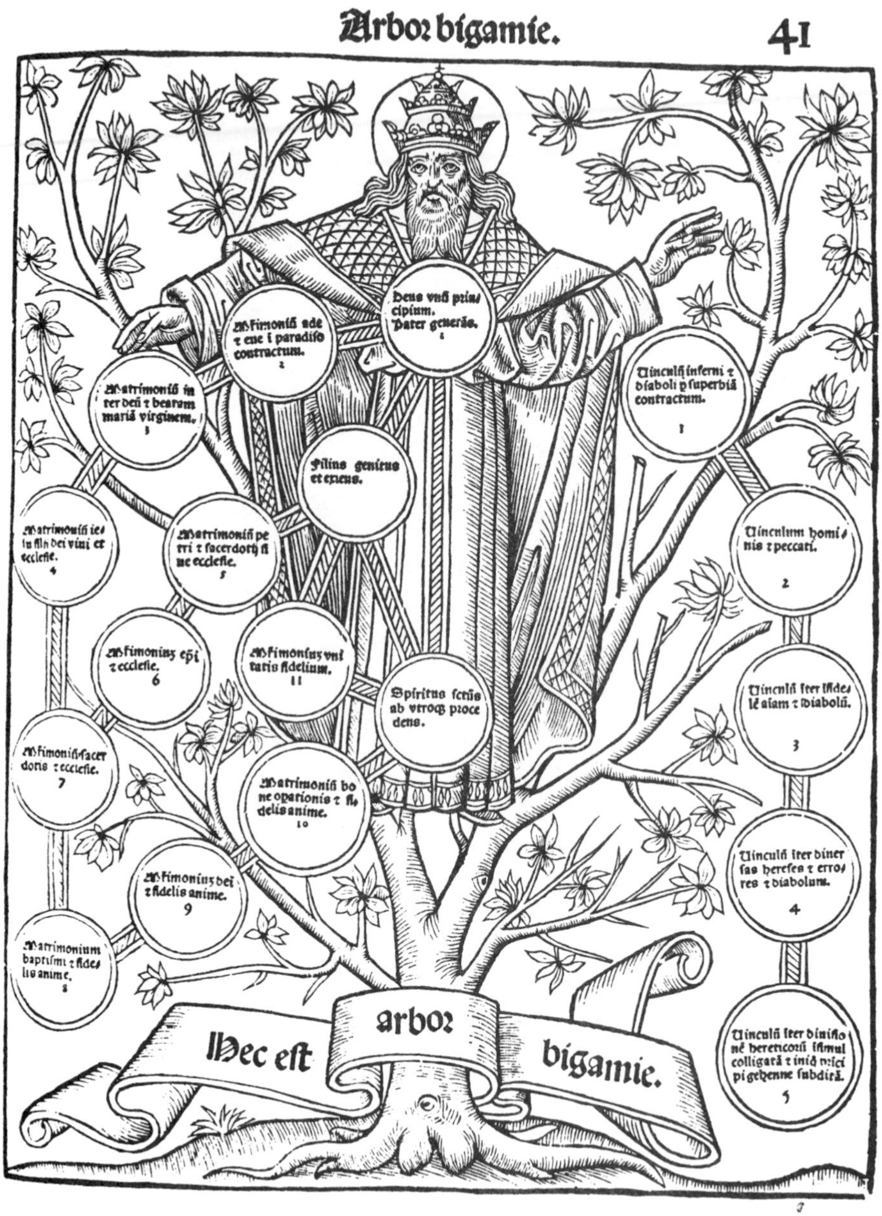

Plate 18. The "Tree of Bigamy" presents in graphic form various types of good and evil relationships, applying thirteenth-century canon law terminology to theological concepts. The woodcut is from the Lyons, 1537, edition of the *Summa aurea* of Hostiensis.

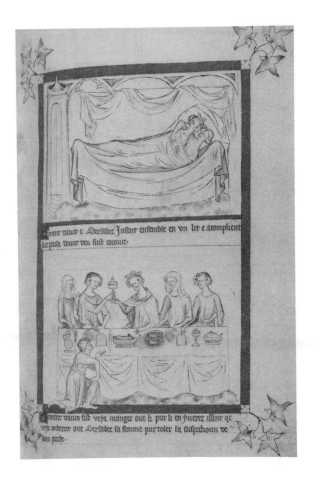

Plate 19. David and Bathsheba. Medieval moralists often cited the story of their relationship (2 Kings 11:2–27) as a classic example of the perils of sexual temptation and adultery. From Queen Mary's Psalter, an early fourteenth-century manuscript, now in the British Library, MS Royal 2.B.VII, fol. 57r. (Reproduced by courtesy of the British Library)

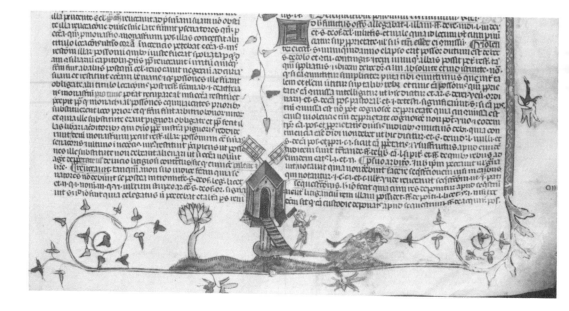

Plate 20. Privacy was at a premium in medieval communities, and couples sometimes found it impossible to be alone, even at intimate moments. This miniature from the fourteenth-century "Smithfield Decretals" illustrates a situation also documented in court records of the period. (Courtesy of the British Library, from MS Royal 10.E.IV, fol. 115r)

8

Marriage and Sex in Canon Law from Alexander III to the *Liber Extra*

Decretals, Decretalists, and Decretal Collections

The decades following the appearance of Gratian's *Decretum* witnessed a burgeoning of new canon law, much of it designed to answer questions left unresolved by Gratian or to reform the law as Gratian presented it. Most of the post-Gratian law took the form of decretals, papal letters that decided particular cases and also enunciated legal rules applicable to other cases of the same type.[1] Pope Alexander III (1159–81) and Pope Innocent III (1198–1216) were the most prolific writers of decretals in the period between Gratian and the *Liber Extra*, but every pope during these decades (even the short-lived Gregory VIII, whose pontificate lasted less than two months) produced at least a few of them. Councils and synods also added to the Church's legal *corpus*. The Third Lateran Council (1179) and the Fourth Lateran Council (1215) were particularly important, but local and regional assemblies also made significant additions to the law.

Faced with massive amounts of new law, the judges, Church administrators, and lawyers had difficulty in keeping abreast of changes. The canons of the two general councils of the period circulated widely, but the actions of local assemblies were often difficult to track down. Decretals posed even greater problems. These letters (copies of which were not always retained in the papal archives) were dispatched only to the judges and parties in the case. No system existed for collecting and distributing copies. As a result, law teachers, practitioners, judges, and officials began to collect the decretals that came to their attention and sometimes circulated their collections to others. These primitive decretal collections were often haphazard assortments of a few letters, frequently scribbled in the margins or flyleaves of the *Decretum* and other books. These early collections were unsatisfactory, because officials and practitioners

---

[1] Gérard Fransen, *Les décrétales et les collections des décrétales*, Typologie des sources du moyen âge occidental, vol. A-III.1*, fasc. 2 (Turnhout: Brépols, 1972), pp. 12–15.

needed to be able to locate relevant material quickly, without reading through an assortment of miscellaneous decretals. Users of the early collections also found that much of the verbiage in the letters consisted of routine formulas and rhetorical flourishes irrelevant to the legal pronouncements that they sought. As a result, canonists soon began to produce stripped-down, systematic decretal collections, which classified the material by topics and pruned the excess verbiage, leaving only the essential rules and principles.[2]

Bernard of Pavia (d. 1213), an Italian law teacher and bishop, about 1191 produced a systematic and analytical decretal collection entitled the *Breviarium extravagantium* (later called *Compilatio Prima*) that quickly became a standard textbook, supplementing Gratian. Bernard divided the *Breviarium* into five books, each dealing with a major facet of the law. Book One covered the sources of law, jurisdictional questions, and the legal system; Book Two treated procedural law and remedies; Book Three centered on the clergy and church property; Book Four covered marriage and related matters affecting the laity; and Book Five dealt with penal law. Each book was subdivided into titles dealing with particular themes. Within each title, Bernard provided tightly edited extracts from decretals, conciliar canons, and other sources, arranged in chronological order. The organization of the *Breviarium extravagantium* was adopted by subsequent decretal collections throughout the Middle Ages.[3]

Other collections, modeled upon Bernard's, soon appeared to help law teachers and administrators keep abreast of the latest rulings. In 1210, Pope Innocent III commissioned Pietro Beneventano to collect Innocent's own decretals. The pope published Pietro's compilation as an official textbook for use in the law faculties, where it came to be known as *Compilatio Tertia*. A few years later, John of Wales compiled a similar collection to fill the gap between *Compilatio Prima*, which had been completed before 1192, and *Compilatio Tertia*, which comprised decretals issued between 1198 and 1210. The collection of John of Wales naturally came to be known as *Compilatio Secunda* and it too became a textbook. Shortly after 1215, Johannes Teutonicus composed *Compilatio Quarta*, which included the decretals of the last six years of Innocent III's pontificate, as well as the constitutions of the Fourth Lateran Council. An-

---

[2]Fransen, *Décrétales*, pp. 19–24; LAC, pp. 222–27; Charles Duggan, *Twelfth-Century Decretal Collections and Their Importance in English History*, University of London Historical Studies, vol. 12 (London: Athlone Press, 1963), pp. 45–57. For analyses of several important early decretal collections see Emil Friedberg, *Die Canones-Sammlungen zwischen Gratian und Bernhard von Pavie* (Leipzig: B. Tauchnitz, 1897; repr. Graz: Akademische Druck- u. Verlagsanstalt, 1958); Walther Holtzmann, *Studies in the Collections of Twelfth-Century Decretals*, ed., rev., and trans. C.R. Cheney and Mary G. Cheney, MIC, Series Collectionum, vol. 3 (Vatican City: Biblioteca Apostolica Vaticana, 1979); and *Decretales ineditae saeculi XII, from the Papers of the Late Walther Holtzmann*, ed. and rev. Stanley Chodorow and Charles Duggan, series collectionum, vol. 4 (Vatican City: Biblioteca Apostolica Vaticana, 1982).

[3]*Quinque compilationes antiquae*, ed. Friedberg, pp. vi–xxiii, 1–65; Fransen, *Dé-*

other official compilation was put together by a prominent Bolognese law professor, Tancred (ca. 1185–1234/36), at the direction of Pope Honorius III (1216–1227), who published it on 2 May 1226. This collection, known as *Compilatio Quinta*, consisted principally of decretals by Honorius III, supplemented by a few constitutions of the Emperor Frederick II.[4]

These five decretal collections circulated widely and, although they competed with numerous minor collections, achieved considerable success as university textbooks and reference works. But by the late 1220s, tracking the post-Gratian law through the five compilations had itself become a tedious and time-consuming process. Accordingly, Honorius III's successor, Pope Gregory IX (1227–41), commissioned the eminent Catalan canonist Raymond of Peñafort (1175 ~ 1180–1275) to prepare an official new collection to replace the five compilations. The pope also directed Raymond to insert in the new collection any important canons that had been left out of the five compilations; the pope moreover authorized Raymond to draft new decretals to clarify existing ones. The resulting text, known as the *Liber Extra*, or the *Decretals of Gregory IX*, was massive. Gregory IX promulgated the *Liber Extra* in September 1234 and presented copies of the work to the Universities of Bologna and Paris, with directions that it be taught in the law faculties as the official decretal law of the Church. The *Liber Extra* remained in force among Roman Catholics until 1917.[5]

The period between 1190 and 1234 produced a rich harvest of learned commentaries on canon law. As the major decretal collections became textbooks in law schools, glosses and more ambitious commentaries on them soon appeared. In addition, lecturers continued to comment on the *Decretum*. Both the decretalists and the decretists—in practice often the same persons—not only tried to explicate the legal texts, but also sought to weave the varied strands of law into a coherently patterned fabric. The work of such men as Bernard

---

crétales, pp. 24–25; Van Hove, *Prolegomena*, p. 356; Stickler, *Hist. iur. can.*, pp. 225–29; LAC, pp. 227–28; Schulte, QL 1:78–82.

[4] *Quinque comp. ant.*, ed. Friedberg, pp. xxiii–xxxv, 66–186; Fransen, *Décrétales*, p. 25; Van Hove, *Prolegomena*, pp. 356–57; Stickler, *Hist. iur. can.*, pp. 232–36; LAC, pp. 230–32; Kenneth Pennington, "The Making of a Decretal Collection: The Genesis of Compilatio tertia," in *Salamanca Proceedings*, pp. 67–92.

[5] The *Liber Extra* followed the structural scheme of Bernard of Pavia's *Breviarium* and comprised 1,971 chapters, 1,756 of them taken from the five compilations. The work also included 195 decretals of Gregory IX, seven decretals of Innocent III, and two decretals of uncertain origin that had not appeared in the earlier *compilationes*. Fransen, *Décrétales*, p. 25; Van Hove, *Prolegomena*, pp. 357–61; Stickler, *Hist. iur. can.*, pp. 237–51; LAC, pp. 233–43; Stephan Kuttner, "Raymond of Peñafort as Editor: The 'Decretales' and 'Constitutiones' of Gregory IX," BMCL 12 (1982) 65–80; P. Michaud-Quantin, "Remarques sur l'oeuvre législative de Grégoire IX," in *Etudes Le Bras* 1:273–81.

of Pavia,[6] Tancred,[7] Johannes Teutonicus (d. 1245/46),[8] Vincentius Hispanus (d. 1248),[9] Laurentius Hispanus (d. 1248),[10] John of Wales,[11] Damasus Hungarus,[12] and Raymond of Peñafort,[13] produced ideas and insights that proved to

[6]Bernardus Papiensis, *Summa decretalium*, ed. E.A.T. Laspeyres (Regensburg: Josef Manz, 1860; repr. Graz: Akademische Druck- u. Verlagsanstalt, 1956); Gabriel Le Bras, "Bernard de Pavie," in DDC 2:782–89; LAC, p. 294; Kuttner, *Repertorium*, pp. 322–23; Schulte, QL 1:175–82.

[7]Tancred, *Summa de matrimonio*, ed. Agathon Wunderlich (Göttingen: Vandenhoeck & Ruprecht, 1841) and *Ordo iudiciarius*, ed. Friedrich Christian Bergmann, in *Libri de iudiciorum ordine* (Göttingen: Vandenhoeck & Ruprecht, 1842; repr. Aalen: Scientia, 1965), pp. 89–316; L. Chevailler, "Tancred," in DDC 7:1146–65; LAC, p. 299; Kuttner, *Repertorium*, pp. 327–28, 346, 358–59; Schulte, QL 1:199–205. Raymond of Peñafort edited Tancred's *Summa de matrimonio* by inserting references to the canons of the *Liber Extra* into Tancred's text. Accordingly the *Summa de matrimonio* that circulated under Raymond's name is virtually identical with Tancred's *Summa*; see n. 13 below.

[8]Johannes Teutonicus's *Glossa ordinaria* to the *Decretum*, in the version revised by Bartholomaeus Brixiensis (d. 1258), was published in numerous editions of the *Decretum* during the fifteenth, sixteenth, and early seventeenth centuries. I shall cite it from the edition published at Venice: Apud Iuntas, 1605. Johannes's *Apparatus* to the Constitutions of 4 Lateran Council appears in *Constitutiones concilii quarti Lateranensis una cum commentariis glossatorum*, ed. António García y García, MIC, Series Glossatorum, vol. 2 (Vatican City: Biblioteca Apostolica Vaticana, 1981), pp. 173–270; his *Glossa ordinaria* to 3 Comp. has begun to appear as *Apparatus glossarum in compilationem tertiam*, ed. Kenneth J. Pennington, MIC, Series Glossatorum, vol. 3 (Vatican City: Biblioteca Apostolica Vaticana, 1981–). On Johannes's life and work see generally S. Stelling-Michaud, "Jean le Teutonique," in DDC 6:120–22; Smith, *Medieval Law Teachers*, pp. 37–38; LAC, pp. 299–301; Kuttner, "Johannes Teutonicus," in *Neue deutsche Biographie* 10:571–73; *Repertorium*, pp. 93–99, 357–59, 370–71, 374–75; Schulte, QL 1:172–75.

[9]Xavier Ochoa Sanz, *Vincentius Hispanus, canonista boloñes del siglo XIII*, Cuadernos del Instituto juridico español, vol. 13 (Rome, Madrid: Consejo Superior de Investigaciones Científicas, Delegación de Roma, 1960); Stephan Kuttner, "Wo war Vincentius Hispanus Bischof?" *Traditio* 22 (1966) 471–74; R. Chabanne, "Vincent d'Espagne," in DDC 7:1507–1508; LAC, p. 298; Schulte, QL 1:191–93; Kuttner, *Repertorium*, pp. 356–57, 370, 374.

[10]Alfons M. Stickler, "Laurent d'Espagne," in DDC 6:361–64 and "Il decretista Laurentius Hispanus," *Studia Gratiana* 9 (1966), 463–549; Knut Wolfgang Nörr, "Der Apparat des Laurentius zur Compilatio III," *Traditio* 17 (1961) 542–43; António García y García, *Laurentius Hispanus: datos biográficos y estudio critica de sus obras*, Cuadernos del Instituto juridico español, vol. 6 (Rome, Madrid: Consejo Superior de Investigaciones Científicas, Delegación de Roma, 1956); LAC, pp. 297–98; Kuttner, *Repertorium*, pp. 76–80, 83–91, 326, 356.

[11]G. Oesterlé, "Jean de Galles," in DDC 6:105–106; Kuttner, *Repertorium*, pp. 345, 356; Schulte, QL 1:189.

[12]Charles Lefebvre, "Damasus," in DDC 4:1014–19; António García y García, "Observaciones sobre los Apparatus de Damaso Ungaro a las tres primeras compilaciones antiguas," *Traditio* 18 (1962) 469–71, and "Glosas de Juan Teutónico, Vicente Hispano y

have momentous influence, not only on the medieval Church, but on later notions about law, corporate organization and structure, limitations on the power of rulers, parliamentary representation, legislative consent, and constitutional government.[14]

During the decades between the *Breviarium* of Bernard of Pavia and the *Liber Extra*, the civilians (or academic commentators on Roman civil law) were exploring many of the same themes and problems that intrigued the canonists. Legists (as they were also called) such as Azo (ca. 1150–1230),[15] Accursius (ca. 1181 ~ 1186–1259 ~ 1263),[16] Placentinus (ca. 1135–1192),[17] Pillius (d. 1192),[18] and Roffredus (d. after 1243),[19] made further substantial contributions to public

---

Damaso Ungaro a los Arbores consanguinitatis et affinitatis," ZRG, KA 68 (1982) 153–85; Kuttner, *Repertorium*, pp. 393–96, 419–22, 426–28; Schulte, QL 1:194–96.

[13] In addition to the *Liber Extra*, edited by Friedberg in *Corpus iuris canonici*, vol. 2, Raymond's *Summa de penitentia* and *Summa de matrimonio* have recently been edited, together with some of his minor works, by Xavier Ochoa Sanz and Aloisio Diez, in the series Universa biblioteca iuris, vol. 1, parts B–C (Rome: Commentarium pro religiosis, 1976–78). On Raymond's life and work see generally R. Naz, "Raymond de Pennafort," in DDC 7:461–64; LAC, pp. 303–304; António García y García, "Valor y proyección histórica de la obra juridica de San Raimundo de Peñafort," *Revista española de derecho canónico* 18 (1963) 233–51; Stephan Kuttner, "Zur Entstehungsgeschichte der Summa de casibus poenitentiae des hl. Raymond von Penyafort," ZRG, KA 39 (1953) 419–34; Fernando Valls-Taberner, *San Ramón de Peñafort*, in his *Obras selectas*, vol. 1, pt. 2 (Madrid, Barcelona: Consejo Superior de Investigaciones Científicas, 1953); A. Teetaert, "Summa de matrimonio Sancti Raymundi de Penyafort," *Jus pontificium* 9 (1929) 54–61, 218–34, 312–22, and "La 'Summa de poenitentia' de Saint Raymond de Penyafort," *Ephemerides theologicae Lovanienses* 5 (1928) 49–71.

[14] See generally Brian Tierney, *Religion, Law, and the Growth of Constitutional Thought* (Cambridge: At the University Press, 1982).

[15] P. Fiorelli, "Azzone," in *Dizionario biografico degli Italiani*, ed. Alberto M. Ghisalberti (Rome: Istituto della Encyclopedia italiana, 1960– ; in progress; cited hereafter as DBI) 4:774–81; Weimar, "Legistische Literatur," in Coing, *Handbuch* 1:177, 179, 180, 183, 202–203, 205–206, 239–40; Savigny, *Gesch. d. röm. Rechts* 5:1–44.

[16] P. Fiorelli, "Accorso," in DBI 1:116–21; Erich Genzmer, "Zur Lebensgeschichte des Accursius," in *Festschrift für L. Wenger zu seinem 70. Geburtstag dargebracht von Freunden, Fachgenossen, und Schülern*, 2 vols. in 1, Münchener Beiträge zur Papyrusforschung, vol. 34/35 (Munich: C. H. Beck, 1944–45) 2:223–41; Weimar, "Legistische Literatur," in Coing, *Handbuch* 1:173–74; Savigny, *Gesch. d. röm. Rechts* 5:262–305.

[17] Charles Lefebvre, "Placentin," in DDC 7:1–10; Weimar, "Legistische Literatur," in Coing, *Handbuch* 1:178, 198, 201–205; Kantorowicz and Buckland, *Studies*, pp. 125–27, 195–99; Savigny, *Gesch. d. röm. Rechts* 4:244–85, 537–43.

[18] Charles Lefebvre, "Pillius," in DDC 6:1499–1502; Weimar, "Legistische Literatur," in Coing, *Handbuch* 1:204, 225, 230–31, 236, 247–48; Savigny, *Gesch. d. röm. Rechts* 4:312–53, 556–60.

[19] Giovanni Ferretti, "Roffredo Epifanio da Benevento," *Studi medievali*, 1st ser., 3 (1908–11) 230–87; Weimar, "Legistische Literatur," in Coing, *Handbuch* 1:194, 196, 248; Savigny, *Gesch. d. röm. Rechts* 5:184–217.

and private law. And, although canon law and civil law were often taught in separate faculties in the universities, connections between the two learned laws were close and intimate. Canonists studied civil law in order to understand their own legal system, while civilians had to pass examinations in canon law as part of their professional training.[20]

Little information survives about how courts applied canon law prior to the beginning of the thirteenth century. Court records for the period after 1200 are, however, more common, in part as a result of one of the reforms of the Fourth Lateran Council, which required ecclesiastical courts to document their actions and to file them. Although only incomplete records survive for a few localities, they nonetheless furnish evidence about practice and the actual application of academic theories.[21]

[20] Rashdall, *Universities* 1:132–34; Helmut Coing, "Die juristische Fakultät und ihr Lehrprogramm," in his *Handbuch* 1:69–80; Leonard E. Boyle, "The Curriculum of the Faculty of Canon Law at Oxford in the First Half of the Fourteenth Century," in *Oxford Studies Presented to Daniel Callus*, Oxford Historical Society Publications, n.s., vol. 16 (Oxford: At the Clarendon Press, 1964), pp. 136–38, 141–47; Gérard Fransen, "*Utrumque ius* dans les *Questiones Andegavenses*," in *Etudes Le Bras* 1:897–911; Pierre Legendre, "Le droit romain, modèle et language: De la signification de l'*Utrumque ius*," in *Etudes Le Bras* 2:913–30; Charles Munier, "Droit canonique et drot romain d'après Gratien et les décrétistes," also in *Etudes Le Bras* 2:943–54; Stephan Kuttner, "Papst Honorius III. und das Studium des Zivilrechts," in *Festschrift für Martin Wolff: Beiträge zum Zivilrecht und internationalen Privatrecht* (Tübingen: J. C. B. Mohr, 1952), pp. 89–91, 93–94; Paul Koschaker, *Europa und das römische Recht* (Munich: Biederstein, 1947), pp. 76–77; Georges Digard, "La papauté et l'étude du droit romain au moyen âge: à propos de la fausse bulle d'Innocent IV, *Dolentes*," *Bibliothèque de l'Ecole des Chartes* 51 (1890) 381–419; Haskins, *Studies in Medieval Culture*, p. 47 n. 8.

[21] 4 Lateran Council (1215) c. 38, ed. García, pp. 80–81. On this canon see generally Rudolf Weigand, "Zur mittelalterlichen kirchlichen Ehegerichtsbarkeit: Rechtsvergleichende Untersuchung," ZRG, KA 67 (1981) 213–47; Donahue, "Proof by Witnesses," p. 134. On the types of records see Helmholz, *Marriage Litigation*, pp. 6–24. Sample documents from thirteenth-century English court records can be found in *Select Cases from the Ecclesiastical Courts of the Province of Canterbury, c. 1200–1301*, ed. Norma Adams and Charles Donahue, Jr., Selden Society Publications, vol. 95 (London: Selden Society, 1981); a short run of thirteenth-century Italian records from Pisa appears in Gero Dolezalek, *Das Imbreviaturbuch des erzbischöflichen Gerichtsnotars Hubaldus aus Pisa, Mai bis August 1230*, Forschungen zur neueren Privatrechtsgeschichte (Cologne: Böhlaus, 1969). No official case records survive from the twelfth century. Hubert Silvestre, "Dix plaidoires inédites du XIIe siècle," *Traditio* 10 (1954) 373–97, published the earliest surviving set of pleadings (*allegationes*); in their present form, these seem to have been recast as academic exercises, although they are probably founded on the facts of real cases. The oldest surviving pleadings from actual lawsuits date from the early thirteenth century; see Pieter Gerbenzon, Caspar J. Van Hell, Barendma Hempenius-Van Dijk, Thea J. Veen, and Johannes A. C. J. Van de Wouw, "Allegationes Phalempinianae; Documents Bearing on Two Early Thirteenth-Century Lawsuits," *Tijdschrift voor Rechtsgeschiedenis* 49 (1981) 251–85.

Marriage Theory in Early Decretal Collections

THE CONTRIBUTIONS OF ALEXANDER III

The close of the twelfth century and the opening of the thirteenth saw developments in the European marriage market that resulted in changed marriage patterns. Men began to marry earlier in life and women later; the net result was a deterioration of the social and economic position of married women after about 1200.[22] These developments in turn produced vigorous efforts by popes and councils to resolve some uncertainties about matrimony that had bedeviled the early decretists. The preeminent contributor to the clarification of marriage law was Rolandus Bandinelli, who reigned as Pope Alexander III for the last twenty-two years of his life.

Born at Siena about 1110, Rolandus was apparently destined from his youth for an ecclesiastical career.[23] His family provided him with opportunities to study theology and law, and he clearly made good use of them, but the details of his education are poorly documented.[24] He was almost certainly not the same Rolandus who taught at Bologna and composed the *Summa* on the *Decretum*, as scholars formerly believed.[25] Rolandus Bandinelli entered the papal service in the late 1140s and rose rapidly in the curial ranks. In November 1150, Pope Eugene III (1145–53) named him a cardinal, and on 16 May 1153 he became Chancellor of the Roman Church. On 7 September 1159, he was chosen pope in a bitterly contested election and took the name of Alexander III.[26] His pontificate was turbulent, punctuated by crises and several near catastrophes that resulted from a power struggle in Italy among the papacy, the Lombard cities, Norman Sicily, and the German Emperor, Frederick Barbarossa.

Through all of these crises, Alexander maintained a calm detachment that seems to have been a fundamental characteristic of his personality. In Beryl

---

[22] Herlihy, *Medieval Households*, pp. 100–111.

[23] Boso, *Life of Alexander III*, ed. and trans. Peter Munz and G. M. Ellis (Oxford: Basil Blackwell, 1973), p. 43; Marshall W. Baldwin, *Alexander III and the Twelfth Century*, The Popes through History, vol. 3 (Glen Rock, NJ: Newman Press, 1968), pp. 4–5; Pacaut, *Alexandre III*, pp. 52–54, 58.

[24] Boso, *Life*, p. 43; Beryl Smalley, *The Becket Controversy and the Schools: A Study of Intellectuals in Politics* (Oxford: Basil Blackwell, 1973), p. 143; Pacaut, *Alexandre III*, pp. 59, 108–109; Noonan, "Who Was Rolandus?" pp. 22–25.

[25] Noonan, "Who Was Rolandus?" pp. 21, 25–44; Weigand, "Magister Rolandus," pp. 3–44.

[26] Boso, *Life*, pp. 43–46; John of Salisbury, *Hist. pont.* 36, ed. Chibnall, p. 71; *Gesta Alexandri III papae*, in *Recueil des historiens des Gaules et de la France*, ed. Martin Bouquet et al., 2d ed. rev. by Leopold Delisle, 24 vols. (Paris: V. Palme [etc.], 1840–1904; cited hereafter as RHGF) 15:720–21; Baldwin, *Alexander III*, pp. 10, 23, 45–48; Pacaut, *Alexandre III*, pp. 79, 102–105.

[27] Smalley, *Becket Controversy*, p. 149.

[28] Baldwin, *Alexander III*, pp. 213–16; Pacaut, *Alexandre III*, pp. 56, 114.

Smalley's graphic phrase, Alexander was "incapable of blowing hot and cold; he blew warm and cool."[27] He seems to have had no close friends, although he took pains once or twice to do favors for his nephews.[28] His only recorded joke was, in fact, a jibe at the use of ecclesiastical patronage—"The Lord," he said, "deprived bishops of their sons, but the devil gave them nephews."[29] Aside from a few acts of favoritism toward family members, Alexander's only apparent predilection was for promoting men of learning to the College of Cardinals and other high posts. He consistently surrounded himself with men trained in canon law, rather than in theology.[30] Perhaps he felt more at home with the canonists than with theologians. His letters certainly betray a taste for legal analysis and lawyerly phrases, many of them traceable to Gratian, with whose work Alexander was well acquainted.[31] He was an intellectual in politics, and his intellectual interests were markedly legalistic.[32]

Alexander III did much to reshape canon law and in no area was his influence more marked than in the law of marriage. During his pontificate the volume of papal decision-making increased dramatically from the levels that had been usual under his predecessors. Nearly 4,000 letters survive from the twenty-two years of Alexander's pontificate, and although many of these were no doubt drafted by his chancery clerks, the pope certainly dictated both the policy and the phrasing of many others. He served as his own chancellor for most of the first twenty years of his pontificate. When he finally filled the office of chancellor in 1178, he appointed his longtime associate, Cardinal Albert, to the post.[33] While some of the correspondence that went out under Alexander's name was routine, it is remarkable how many of his letters inaugurated new departures in policy and in law. His willingness to experiment with new solutions to old problems is particularly notable in his approach to marriage law, as is shown by the fact that more than a third of the canons dealing with marriage and family law in the *Liber Extra* originated with him (see Appendix, Table 8.1).

Although the quantity of Alexander's innovations in marriage law is impressive, even more important for long-term legal development was the quality of the changes. He clearly wished to recast the law of family relationships, and he was certainly aware that his approach differed both from that of Gratian and from the law established by his predecessors.[34] He consistently sought to free

[29] Giraldus Cambrensis, *Gemma ecclesiastica* 2.27, in his *Opera* 2:304: "Filios episcopis Dominus abstulit, nepotes autem diabolus dedit."

[30] Smalley, *Becket Controversy*, p. 143.

[31] Smalley, *Becket Controversy*, p. 159; Morey, *Bartholomew of Exeter*, pp. 67–70.

[32] Smalley, *Becket Controversy*, p. 138; Pacaut, *Alexandre III*, pp. 111, 313–17; Baldwin, *Alexander III*, p. 213.

[33] Baldwin, *Alexander III*, pp. 180–81.

[34] Alexander occasionally inserted explicit notes declaring that he was trying something new e.g., in X 4.4.3 (JL 14,091; WH 620): "[Q]uamvis alii aliter sentiant, et aliter etiam a quibusdam praedecessoribus nostris sit aliquando iudicatum. . . ." Likewise in 1 Comp. 4.4.3(5), 4(6), and 5(7); see also Charles Donahue, Jr., "The Policy of Alexander

marriages from the control of parents, families, and feudal overlords and to place the choice of marriage partners under the exclusive control of the parties themselves.[35]

The net result of Alexander III's changes was to make marriage easier to contract and more difficult to dissolve.[36] It does not necessarily follow from this, however, that Alexander III's marriage rules aimed at reconciling the law of matrimony with the sentiments of courtly love poets.[37] It is more likely that both the ethos of *fin'amors* and Alexander III's marriage decretals reflected a dawning consciousness of the importance of individual choice, coupled with a new awareness of marriage as a personal relationship—sentiments that a few decades earlier had seemed heretical, but, as we have already seen, were cautiously approved by some of Alexander III's contemporaries among the decretists.[38]

Alexander III's marriage doctrines developed gradually; he stressed different considerations at different periods, as his ideas about marriage slowly matured.[39] Early in his pontificate, Alexander III seems to have adopted the views of the French school of decretists, for he ruled that marriage resulted from the exchange of present consent, and identified future consent with betrothal.[40] Then from about 1173/74 to about 1176, his marriage decisions took a different tack: rather than concentrating on the exchange of consent, the decretals of this period focused on the solemnization of marriage. During those years, marriages that had been contracted solemnly and publicly prevailed over those that were contracted informally, secretly, or without witnesses. From about 1176 onward, Alexander's decisions entered a final stage. The decretals in the last four years of his pontificate enunciated his definitive theory of marriage, a theory that owed much to the French school but also modified the French theory

---

the Third's Consent Theory of Marriage," in *Toronto Proceedings*, p. 274. Here and later WH [= Walther Holtzmann] numbers refer to *Studies* and *Decretales ineditae*.

[35] See e.g., X 4.1.14–15; 4.2.7–9.

[36] Pollock and Maitland, *Hist. Engl. Law* 2:385; cf. Donahue, "Policy," p. 277.

[37] Donahue, "Policy," pp. 277–79; but cf. Duggan, "Equity and Compassion," p. 87.

[38] See above, pp. 273–75. One of the heretical views ascribed to Henry of Lausanne about 1135 was the teaching that the consent of the parties was all that was required for marriage; Malcolm D. Lambert, *Medieval Heresy: Popular Movements from Bogomil to Hus* (London: E. Arnold, 1977), p. 50.

[39] Gabriel Le Bras, "Le mariage dans la théologie et le droit de l'église du XIe au XIIIe siècle," *Cahiers de civilisation médiévale* 11 (1968) 191–202; Fransen, "Formation du lien," pp. 106–26; Weigand, "Unauflösigkeit," pp. 44–64; but cf. Donahue, "Policy," pp. 280–81.

[40] Marriage decretals of this period include 1 Comp. 3.28.9; 4.4.4(6); 4.4.5(7); 4.13.2; 4.16.2; 4.20.6; 2 Comp. 4.7.1; X 4.1.2; 4.3.2; 4.13.2; 4.15.2, 4; 4.17.9. On the stages in the development of Alexander III's marriage theory see Charles Donahue, Jr., "The Dating of Alexander the Third's Marriage Decretals: Dauvillier Revisited after Fifty Years," ZRG, KA 68 (1982) 102–106, as well as "Policy," pp. 255–56.

significantly. Alexander explained his mature marriage theory most clearly in the decretal *Veniens ad nos*, addressed to Bishop John of Norwich and, unfortunately, undated. *Veniens ad nos* ruled that a valid marriage might be contracted either by the free and voluntary exchange of present consent between persons of legal age who were free to marry each other, or by the free and voluntary exchange of future consent between two parties legally able to marry one another, if that consent was ratified by subsequent sexual intercourse.[41] Marriage contracted by either method was binding so long as both parties lived. Marriages that met either set of criteria might be dissolved (1) if the parties were unable to consummate the union because of sexual impotence on the part of either party;[42] or (2) by reason of a supervening affinity contracted through carnal intercourse between one party and a parent of the other prior to consummation of the marriage;[43] or again (3) by mutual agreement to enter religion, provided that the partners did so prior to consummating the marriage;[44] or still further (4) by protracted absence of a spouse under circumstances in which the absent party's death might reasonably be presumed.[45]

Thus Alexander III formally adopted the Parisian distinction between present and future consent as a central element of papal marriage law. But Alexander's final marriage theory went beyond simple acceptance of the Parisian model.[46] Although he made consent the primary consideration, Alexander also accorded an important function to sexual relations in marriage law.[47] Sexual intercourse

[41] For decisions of the second period, see X 4.1.9; 4.2.5–6; 4.4.3; 4.16.2; for *Veniens ad nos* see X 4.1.15 (JL 13,902 = 14,159), as well as Donahue, "Dating," pp. 81, 105–15, and "Policy," pp. 253–56.

[42] X 4.2.9; 4.15.2–4; *Collectio Abrincensis*, App. 13 (= JL 13,746; *Collectio Cantabrigiensis* 84), ed. Heinrich Singer, "Neue Beiträge über die Dekretalensammlungen vor und nach Bernhard von Pavia," in *Sitzungsberichte der kaiserliche Akademie der Wissenschaften in Wien*, philos.-hist. Klasse 17 (1914) 394–95; *Collectio Sangermanensis* 9.8 (= JL 14,179; cf. 2 Comp. 4.9.1 = X 4.15.3), in ibid., pp. 332–33. See also Sägmüller, "Das impedimentum impotentiae," p. 91; Donahue, "Policy," p. 252 n. 2, and "Dating," p. 80.

[43] X 4.2.4; 4.13.2. See also *Appendix Concilii Lateranensis* 50.4 and *Collectio Tanner* 7.8.10 (= JL 11,527), noted in Walther Holtzmann, "Die Register Papst Alexanders III. in den Händen der Kanonisten," *Quellen und Forschungen aus italienischen Archiven und Bibliotheken* (cited hereafter as QFIAB) 30 (1940) 24–25.

[44] X 4.1.16 (JL 13,905; WH 135); Morey, *Bartholomew of Exeter*, p. 71.

[45] *Collectio Sangermanensis* 9.13, in Singer, "Neue Beiträge," p. 334; cf. X 4.1.5, and see also Donahue, "Policy," p. 252 n. 2. A fifth exception, marriages contracted during an interdict, impeded future marriage, but did not invalidate an existing one; X 4.16.1–2.

[46] Michele Maccarrone, "Sacramentalità e indissolubilità del matrimonio nella dottrina di Innocenzo III," *Lateranum* 14 (1978) 464; Donahue, "Policy," p. 256.

[47] Alexander III's consent theory differed radically from the consent theory of marriage in Roman law. Roman notions of marriage required parental consent, as well as the consent of the parties; Inst. 1.10. pr.; Dig. 23.2.2 (Paulus). *Deductio in domum* was also necessary; Dig. 23.2.5 (Pomponius) and 35.1.15 (Ulpian). Neither of these played any

created a bond that precluded subsequent marriage between either party and members of the other party's immediate family.[48] Further, once married persons had consummated their union, Alexander was prepared to force them to continue sexual relations so long as either party desired them.[49] Even if one party contracted leprosy, the sexual obligation remained in force.[50] The pope further held that couples who had exchanged consent before reaching the minimum age for marriage were bound by their agreement if they had sexual intercourse; consummation thus outweighed the impediment of minority.[51] Likewise a conditional marriage became binding if the parties had intercourse, whether or not the stipulated condition had been fulfilled—again, sexual relations healed a defect in marital consent.[52]

Another major theme in the decretals from the close of Alexander III's pontificate involved free choice of marriage partners. Force and fear exerted by parents or others in order to secure consent to a marriage nullified that consent, provided that the force or fear in question was "sufficient to move a constant man" (*qui posset in virum constantem cadere*), a criterion that came to play a critical role in canonical jurisprudence.[53] The issue of consent likewise seems to be at the nub of Alexander's treatment of the betrothal and marriage of those who had not attained the age of puberty[54] His concern to define a minimum age for consent to marriage appears to be a special case of his general effort to maximize freedom of marital consent.

An inescapable consequence of Alexander's developed marriage doctrine was the sanction that it gave to marriages covertly contracted.[55] Alexander foresaw

---

part in Alexander's consensual theory. See generally Gaudemet, "Originalité et destin," pp. 169–77; Donahue, "Policy," pp. 253–54.

[48] 1 Comp 4.4.4(6); X 4.1.12, 13; 4.7.3; 4.13.2; 4.14.1; cf. Alexander's *Epist.* 880, in PL 200:789–90.

[49] Alexander III, *Epist.* 868 (JL 11,990), 1011, in PL 200:781–82, 891–92.

[50] X 4.8.1–2 (JL 13,773, 13,794); Delpini, "Indissolubilità," pp. 65–66. The couple had the option, of course, of taking vows of chastity.

[51] X 4.2.6 (JL 14,032; WH 204a), 8 (JL 13,767; WH 4b); Donahue, "Dating," pp. 74, 76–77.

[52] X 4.5.3 (JL 13,946; WH 808b[2]) rules that a conditional marriage is not binding unless or until the condition has been fulfilled, or unless the couple have had sexual intercourse or exchanged present consent subsequent to exchanging conditional consent. But cf. X 4.5.4 on conditional gifts of property to the Church. The theory underlying X 4.9.2, which deals with marriage between a free man and a servile woman, likewise invokes the notion of an unstated condition. There too, with reasonable consistency, Alexander held that coitus after the husband became aware of his wife's status rendered the marriage indissoluble.

[53] X 4.1.14 (JL 14,333; WH 270); 4.1.15 (JL 13,902 = 14,159; WH 1071); 4.2.9 (JL 13,969; WH 1033b). A Roman antecedent of the "constant man" test can be found in Dig. 4.2.6 (Caius).

[54] X 4.1.11 (JL 12,248); 4.2.5 (JL 13,887; WH 12).

[55] Pollock and Maitland, *Hist. Engl. Law* 2:368–69; Donahue, "Policy" pp. 258–59.

this problem and expressed concern about clandestine marriages in some of his decretals. But Alexander could not maintain that valid marriage is contracted by consent alone and avoid the consequence that such consent might be given privately. Although he ruled in *Solet frequenter* that parties who contracted clandestine marriages were anathema and that marital consent must be exchanged before witnesses, Alexander refrained from making compliance with these requirements a condition of valid marriage.[56] On the contrary, Alexander explicitly ruled in *Quod nobis* that marriages could be secretly contracted "for reasonable and legitimate cause," and in *Super eo vero* he held that a union contracted by present consent, without priest or solemnity, was nonetheless fully binding.[57] Since Alexander adhered to this policy despite his expressed concern over secret marriages, he evidently believed that some higher good could be achieved by freeing the marriage contract from requirements of form, publicity, ceremony, or witnesses. It is hard to escape the inference that this higher good was to make it possible for persons to marry despite extraneous considerations, such as financial exigency, public disapproval, or opposition from family, friends, and feudal lords.[58]

Clandestine marriages seriously undermined the stability of marriage and family relationships. Since secret marriages were just as valid as public ones, couples could marry and divorce informally without attracting public attention. Accordingly no husband or wife, even in a publicly solemnized union, could ever be sure that an earlier mate from a clandestine marriage might not someday appear on the scene to claim his or her spouse. Moreover, a person married in a secret exchange of consent could subsequently contract a bigamous public marriage. Clandestine marriage thus furnished enormous scope for misunderstanding and confusion, deliberate or fortuitous, where one party believed that s/he was married to another person, who believed that s/he was not married.[59]

Historians have found little to commend in Alexander III's marriage doctrine, even though freedom to choose one's marriage partner was often in serious danger from family interests during the twelfth century, and the pope's concern to provide legal safeguards against interference with this freedom was hardly trivial or unfounded. Further, the consistency with which Alexander's successors adhered to his marriage system, despite the social costs that it entailed, indicates a continuing awareness of the problem of both formal and informal coercion and a commitment to the goal of free consent.

[56] 1 Comp. 4.4.4 (JL 14,162; WH 990); Duggan, "Equity and Compassion," p. 83. The public celebration of marriage at the doorway of the church was, however, the usual practice for most couples, at least in France. For the ceremonies used in this period, see Jean–Baptiste Molin and Protain Mutembe, *Le rituel du mariage en France du XIIe au XVIe siècle*, Théologie historique, no. 26 (Paris: Beauchesne, 1974), pp. 32–37.

[57] X 4.3.2 (JL 13,774; WH 819); 1 Comp. 4.4.6(8)(JL 14,234; WH 954e); and cf. WH 911a (JL—) in *Decretales ineditae* 98, pp. 173–74; Germain Lesage, "La 'Ratio canonica' d'après Alexandre III," in *Toronto Proceedings*, p. 102.

[58] Donahue, "Policy," p. 259.

[59] Donahue, "Policy," pp. 259, 267.

Alexander III's immediate successors made only modest additions to the Church's marriage law. The next major phase in the maturation of medieval matrimonial legislation commenced a decade after Alexander's death, when the College of Cardinals elected its youngest member, the thirty-seven-year-old Lothario dei Segni, as Pope Innocent III. No pope before or since has been more forceful in his defense of papal power, none faced greater challenges, political or intellectual, to that power, and few have left so lasting an imprint on their office or on the Christian Church.

THE CONTRIBUTIONS OF INNOCENT III

Innocent was an extraordinary figure in an extraordinary age. When he took the papal throne, towns and cities throughout Europe were growing daily in size and wealth. These urban centers increasingly challenged established political relationships and social values. At the same time, each of the major European kingdoms was ruled by a man of talent and ambition—Richard Lion-Heart in England, Philip Augustus in France, Henry VI in Germany. Dissatisfied with traditional feudal monarchy, they and their successors sought to centralize their governments, to increase royal revenues, to concentrate power in the king's hands—all policies that threatened the independence and power of the Church. And in the universities, philosophers and theologians seemed bewitched by the novelties of the heathen—they seemed to find more inspiration in the pages of Aristotle and Averroës than they did in Holy Writ or the writings of the Fathers.

But Innocent III faced even more direct and open challenges to the Church and to papal authority than those from intellectuals, kings, and burghers. Europe in 1198 was spotted with festering patches of heresy. In the manufacturing towns of northern Italy and southern France the unordained and untrained followers of Peter Waldo were preaching and teaching an alarming brand of Christianity that denied the special authority of the clergy and cast doubt on the spiritual value of the sacraments. Elsewhere, Cathar heretics attacked the benevolence of the Creator by proclaiming that the material world was intrinsically evil; they maintained that only the spiritual realm, on which they seemed to feel they had a monopoly, had been created by an all-good deity.

None of these challenges appeared to daunt the new pope. Self-assured, industrious, a man of keen intellect, infectious charm, and intellectual audacity, Innocent seemed certain that he was God's chosen agent on earth. Secure in that belief, he was ready to deal with everyone and everything that came his way.[60]

[60] The literature dealing with Innocent III and his pontificate is large. A helpful basic introduction is James M. Powell, *Innocent III: Vicar of Christ or Lord of the World?* (Boston: D. C. Heath and Company, 1963). An old but still valuable study is Friedrich von Hurter-Ammann, *Geschichte Papst Innocenz des Dritten und seiner Zeitgenossen*, 3d ed., 4 vols. (Hamburg: F. Perthes, 1841); the standard modern biography is Helene Tillmann, *Papst Innozenz III.*, Bonner historische Forschungen, vol. 3 (Bonn: Ludwig

Countless crises crowded the eighteen years of his pontificate, but Innocent made time nearly every day to deal with the flood of legal business referred to the papal court. Indeed this was the papal function that he appeared to enjoy with greatest zest. Among the hundreds of cases that Innocent decided were numerous marriage cases, and he was by all odds the most daring of Alexander III's immediate successors in adopting new departures in marriage law. Nonetheless Innocent stood firmly by the basic tenets of Alexander's marriage formation doctrine. The new pope insisted more fiercely than Alexander had on the principle that Catholic marriage law must be uniform and that local variations on fundamental issues must be discouraged. Innocent firmly maintained the consensual doctrine as Alexander had framed it and was adamant in defending it against other models of Christian marriage.[61]

Innocent nevertheless did modify some features of the Alexandrine marriage law. He rejected the doctrine that a present consent marriage might be dissolved on the grounds of supervening affinity.[62] In addition he explicitly denied that abduction followed by carnal intercourse created an impediment to marriage; he thus cleared the way for marriage between the abductor and his victim, provided that both parties consented freely to the union.[63] Innocent also clarified the elements of conditional marriages. In the decretal *Per tuas* he held that a couple who exchanged conditional consent should be presumed to be married if they had sexual relations following the exchange of consent, even if the condition had not yet been fulfilled at the time when intercourse took place.[64] Sex thus became a constitutive element in conditional marriage, since

---

Röhrscheid, 1954). Important specialized treatments of particular aspects of Innocent's life and career include Michele Maccarrone, "Innocenzo III prima del pontificato," *Archivio della R. Deputazione romana di Storia Patria*, n.s. 9 (1943) 59–134; Kenneth J. Pennington, "The Legal Education of Pope Innocent III," BMCL 4 (1974) 70–77; and Christopher R. Cheney, *Pope Innocent III and England*, Päpste und Papsttum, vol. 9 (Stuttgart: Hiersemann, 1976). An abundant literature deals with Innocent's treatment of church-state relationships; see especially Brian Tierney, "'Tria quippe distinguit iudicia': A Note on Innocent III's Decretal *Per venerabilem*," *Speculum* 37 (1962) 48–59; Kenneth J. Pennington, "Pope Innocent III's Views on Church and State: A Gloss to *Per venerabilem*," in *Law, Church, and Society*, pp. 49–67; Friedrich Kempf, *Papsttum und Kaisertum bei Innocenz III.: die geistigen und rechtlichen Grundlagen seiner Thronstreitpolitik*, Miscellanea historiae pontificiae, vol. 58 (Rome: Pontificia Università Gregoriana, 1954); Sergio Mochi Onory, *Fonti canonistiche dell'idea moderna dello stato: imperium spirituale, iurisdictio diviso, sovranità*, Pubblicazioni dell'Università cattolica del Sacro Cuore, n.s., vol. 38 (Milan: Società editrice "Vita e pensiero", 1951); and Michele Maccarrone, *Chiesa e stato nella dottrina di Innocenzo III* (Rome: Lateranum, 1940).

[61] See especially X 4.1.25; 4.4.5; 4.5.6; Coriden, *Indissolubility*, pp. 49–50; Maccarrone, "Sacramentalità," pp. 472–74, 514.

[62] X 4.13.6 (Po 1182).

[63] X 5.17.7 (Po 1066); cf. X. 4.1.6 (JL 14,235); Maccarrone, "Sacramentalità." p. 476.

[64] X 4.5.6; Maccarrone, "Sacramentalità," pp. 476–77.

Innocent construed consent to sexual intimacy as abrogating the condition on which the original consent had been premised. In this ruling he contradicted the position taken by Huguccio, whose pupil he is often said to have been.[65] In other respects, however, Innocent remained sympathetic to Huguccio's rigoristic approach.[66]

A major unresolved problem that figured in the marriage decretals of this age concerned the dissolution of marriages in which one party suffered from impotence or frigidity. On this matter, French and Roman practice differed. Gallic tradition accepted either permanent or temporary impotence as adequate grounds for dissolving a marriage. In these cases, accordingly, French bishops allowed either party to remarry without penalty. Roman custom, however, restricted dissolution to cases of permanent impotence alone and allowed only the sexually capable partner to remarry. The early decretists, as we have seen, were divided on this question, and variance in practice persisted. Alexander III in an early decretal affirmed the Roman rule, but he later declared that the French custom might be tolerated.[67] Clement III in 1190–91 reaffirmed the Roman position, which left the law as confused as before.[68]

In 1206, Innocent III attempted to clarify the matter in a decretal that dealt with a case in which the couple could not consummate their marriage because of a gross disparity of size between their genital organs. Innocent ruled that the marriage might be ended, and the parties might remarry. But he added that if surgery or intercourse with a second husband later made it possible for the woman to accommodate her first husband, then she must return to the first husband and reinstate the prior marriage. The woman's second husband was presumably free to remarry, although Innocent did not explicitly rule on that issue.[69] Innocent III's successor, Honorius III, decided that inability to consummate a marriage after three years of vain efforts constituted sufficient proof that the condition was real.[70] Honorius's decision left unresolved, however, the procedure to be followed when the condition was cured after the marriage was dissolved, as well as the difficulties posed by what would now be called relative impotence—where a man was unable to have sex with a particular woman, but was perfectly capable of intercourse with others.

Late twelfth- and early thirteenth-century pontiffs also acted on problems

[65] On the problematical question of Innocent's legal training see Pennington, "Legal Education," pp. 70–77.

[66] See esp. his treatise *De miseria humanae conditionis* 1.3.1, ed. Michele Maccarrone (Lugano: Thesaurus mundi, 1955), p. 10, a work that Innocent wrote prior to his election as pope. See also Müller, *Lehre des hl. Augustinus*, p. 147.

[67] 1 Comp. 4.16.2 (JL 14,075; WH 188b); X 4.15.2 (JL 11,866; WH 822a); Maccarrone, "Sacramentalità." pp. 489–91; Pfaff, "Kirchliche Eherecht," pp. 110–11.

[68] 1 Comp. 4.16.4 (JL 16,650).

[69] X 4.15.6 (Po 2836); cf. *Registrum* 7.38, in PL 215:320 (Po 2166). See also the discussion of this problem by Laurentius and Vincentius in Tancred's *Apparatus* to 3 Comp. 4.11.1 v. *utrum debeat*, in Caius MS 28/17, p. 290b.

[70] X 4.15.7 (Po 7832); Coriden, *Indissolubility*, p. 25.

raised by infidel marriages. Celestine III held that a Saracen who converted to the Christian faith might marry a Christian woman even if he had a Saracen wife at the time of his conversion.[71] Innocent III took a more rigorous position on this matter: infidel marriages were indissoluble under the same conditions that applied to Christian marriages; that is, the parties must have consented freely, and they must have ratified their consent by sexual intercourse.[72] Soon thereafter, however, Innocent reconsidered some of the implications of his earlier verdict. In *Quanto te* he held that if one party to an infidel marriage converted to Christianity, the convert could remarry in his new faith, provided that his unconverted spouse refused to cohabit with him after his conversion or that she made it difficult for him to fulfill his new religious obligations.[73] In the decretal *Gaudemus*, dated in 1201, Innocent imposed further limitations on remarriage. Infidels who had married within the degrees of relationship forbidden by canon law were not permitted to dismiss their earlier wives solely on that account after baptism. The canonical prohibitions were a matter of ecclesiastical positive law and did not stem from natural or divine law, Innocent declared. Converts who had infringed the prohibitions prior to baptism were not required to conform to them later. Further, a convert who had more than one wife at the time of his conversion should retain his earliest mate and dismiss all the others. Those who had divorced and remarried while still infidels, Innocent added, must send away their later partners and return to the first one. Should this be impossible—perhaps because the first partner had remarried—the convert must remain unmarried until his first spouse died.[74]

While Innocent's decretals concerning the marriages of converts clarified some of the uncertainties that clouded this topic, they failed to supply a reliable guide for handling other situations where the law remained unclear.[75] Problems of this sort were on the rise during the early thirteenth century in Europe's frontier regions, such as Livonia, where Innocent III campaigned to suppress levirate marriage, which apparently was practiced among the pagan Balts, and where Honorius III cautioned judges to be wary of Russian clerics who pretended to dissolve the marriages of converts to Latin Christianity.[76]

Late twelfth- and early thirteenth-century popes often called on local authorities to instill respect for Catholic marriage law in their flocks. Both new converts and the faithful in regions where Christianity had long been established were all too prone, Roman authorities believed, to regard marriage as a private matter and to ignore canonical rules that conflicted with personal pref-

[71] X 3.33.1 (JL 17,649); Pfaff, "Kirchliche Eherecht," p. 109.

[72] X 4.14.4 (Po 507); Maccarrone, "Sacramentalità," pp. 454–55.

[73] X 4.19.7 (Po 684); Noonan, *Power to Dissolve*, pp. 344–46.

[74] X 4.19.8 (Po 1325).

[75] Noonan, *Power to Dissolve*, p. 347; Maccarrone, "Sacramentalità," pp. 459–60.

[76] Honorius III in *Sēnas Latvijas vēstures avoti*, no. 101, ed. A. Svabe, 2 vols. (Riga: Latvijas vēstures Institūta Apgādiens, 1937) 1:77; Innocent III in X 4.19.9 (Po 1323).

erence or family interest. Marriages that failed to conform to canon law, Alexander III warned, cannot be tolerated. Local authorities must compel the faithful to obey the law. Failure to do so was an offense against reason and the Church's authority.[77] Likewise people must not dissolve their marriages informally or without reasonable and evident cause, he declared in another decretal. People must realize, he continued, that marriage was a serious business, instituted by God, not man.[78] Alexander himself several times attempted to reconcile estranged couples who had separated without the permission of Church authorities.[79]

The popes of this era, particularly Alexander III, were willing, even eager, to accommodate marriage law to social reality. There were limitations, naturally, to the law's elasticity: divine commands must be obeyed, but human law could be bent with due discretion in order to achieve equitable results. "It is more tolerable," Alexander III declared, "to allow some people to remain joined contrary to human ordinances than to disjoin legitimately married persons contrary to the Lord's law."[80] This equitable principle accounts for many of the inconsistencies among the marriage decretals of this period.

Concubinage and Nonmarital Sex

Alexander III and his successors shared their predecessors' ambiguity toward concubinage among the laity. Indeed Alexander's marriage formation doctrine made it more difficult to distinguish clandestine marriage from simple concubinage. Even the participants were probably not sure of their own status in some cases, since marriage depended so much upon intentions and attitudes that the couple may never have defined clearly in their own minds.

Alexander III was determined to penalize men who deserted their wives in order to take up with a mistress. Such men, he declared, must be forced to take back their legitimate wives and treat them with marital affection. But difficulties sometimes arose when a man claimed that he had exchanged informal marital consent with his mistress prior to his public marriage to another spouse. Under those circumstances a court might hold that the publicly married wife was a concubine and the apparent mistress was a legitimate wife.[81]

---

[77] X 4.1.4 (JL 13,137); Lesage, "Ratio canonica," p. 105.

[78] X 1.29.16 (JL 11,867); Lesage, "Ratio canonica," p. 102.

[79] Alexander III, *Epist.* 78, 370, in RHGF 15:795–96, 942; also *Epist.* 1484 in PL 200:1285–86; Gilbert Foliot, *Letters and Charters*, no. 162–64, ed. Z. N. Brooke, Adrian Morey, and C. N. L. Brooke (Cambridge: At the University Press, 1967), pp. 214–18.

[80] 1 Comp. 4.19.3; JL 14,214; Morey, *Bartholomew of Exeter*, pp. 67–68: "Tolerabilius est enim aliquos contra statuta hominum copulatos relinquere, quam coniunctos quoslibet legitime contra statuta domini separare."

[81] 1 Comp. 2.20.21 (JL 13,823); Duggan, "Equity and Compassion," p. 72; Dauvillier, *Mariage*, p. 102.

Late twelfth-century popes were generally conservative in dealing with non-marital sex.[82] The law in this area was reasonably clear, but measures for enforcing it were so poorly developed and ineffective that many people remained unaware, for example, that simple fornication was an offense.[83] Prostitution was likewise little affected by decretal legislation. Popes and other churchmen in this period did not attempt to repress prostitution (which they had apparently concluded was a hopeless task), but rather aimed to make it easier for women to leave the trade, either through marriage or entrance into religion.[84] In consequence religious houses and even whole orders dedicated to the reform of prostitutes thrived during these decades.[85]

Clerical Marriage and Concubinage

The decretals of this period dealt more often with clerical marriage and concubinage than they did with sex offenses among the laity, but here, too, there was little innovation. The new law, for the most part, elaborated existing rules.

Although Gerald of Wales reported that Alexander III personally opposed mandatory clerical celibacy and considered changing the law, no hint of that inclination appears in the pope's decretals. It is likely that Gerald's report was based on wishful thinking, not hard evidence.[86] On the contrary, Alexander III publicly deplored the frequency with which the ban on clerical concubinage and marriage was violated and urged bishops to strip clerical sex offenders of their offices and positions.[87] It is also clear from Innocent III's decretals, as well as from other sources, that the popes were fighting an uphill battle in the attempt to enforce clerical celibacy.[88]

Decretals in this period reiterated earlier bans on clerical marriage and

---

[82]Thus, e.g., although 1 Comp. devoted a whole title (5.13) to adultery and fornication, only one of its six chapters represented recent legislation; the rest were excerpts from pre-Gratian sources. The adultery titles of the other major decretal collections are very brief: 3 Comp. 5.8 includes only two decretals, both of which reiterated earlier law, while the single chapter of 5 Comp. 5.8 deals with dowry rights following marital separation on account of adultery. Likewise Alexander III's lengthy letter to the Archbishop of Upsala on sexual offenses did little more than restate earlier law on these matters; see *Epist.* 975, in PL 200:850–52 (JL 12,113).

[83]E.g., *De rebus Alsaticis* 14, in MGH, SS 17:236.

[84]X 4.1.20 (Po 114).

[85]Jacques de Vitry, *Historia occidentalis* 8, ed. John F. Hinnebusch, Spicilegium Friburgensis, vol. 17 (Fribourg: The University Press, 1972), pp. 99–100; *De rebus Alsaticis* 6, in MGH, SS 17:254; Max Heimbucher, *Die Orden und Kongregationen der katholischen Kirche*, 3d ed., 2 vols. (Munich: F. Schöningh, 1965) 1:646–48; Milton R. Gutsch, "A Twelfth-Century Preacher—Fulk of Neuilly," in *The Crusades and Other Essays in Honor of Dana Carleton Munro* (New York: Appleton-Century-Crofts, 1928), pp. 190–91.

[86]Giraldus Cambrensis, *Gemma ecclesiastica* 2.6, in his *Opera* 2:187.

[87]1 Comp. 3.2.9 (JL 13,910) and 3.3.6 (JL 16,090); X 3.3.3 (JL 10,608).

[88]X 3.3.5 (Po 1944); Gaudemet, "Célibat ecclésiastique," p. 29.

called on clerics in major orders to separate from their wives.[89] Alexander III ruled that the marriages of clerics in major orders were nothing more than simple cohabitation (*contubernium*), equivalent to the temporary unions of Roman slaves.[90] He also demanded that concubinary clerics renounce their mistresses, and repeated the pleas of earlier pontiffs that the faithful abstain from attending Masses celebrated by priests who kept concubines.[91] None of this was new. The decretals of the late twelfth century on clerical sexuality did little more than reaffirm positions that had become standard teaching since the Gregorian reform. As was true of sex crimes, however, the enforcement process lagged far behind the lawmaking process. Implementation of the celibacy rules remained patchy and erratic.

Second Marriages

The decretals that dealt with second marriages offered slightly more novelty than the decretals dealing with sex offenses and clerical sexuality. Alexander III, for one thing, forbade clerics to give the nuptial blessing to couples if one spouse had been married previously.[92] The decretal made no attempt to provide a rationale for the ruling, which was puzzling, in view of the church's long-standing disapproval of those who condemned second and subsequent marriages. In another decretal Alexander ruled that a man who contracted a bigamous marriage during the lifetime of his first wife, should not be allowed to separate from his second wife after his first wife's death.[93] This case further illustrates Alexander's willingness to overrule earlier precedents in order to find equitable solutions to difficult problems.[94]

---

[89] X 4.6.1 (JL 14,076) and 4.6.2 (JL 13,841); Alexander III, *Epist.* 403 (JL 11,281) and 1478 (JL 14,222), in PL 200:418–19, 1280–81.

[90] Alexander III, *Epist.* 1050, in PL 200:930 (JL 12,254); Mary G. Cheney, "Pope Alexander III and Roger, Bishop of Worcester, 1164–1179," in *Toronto Proceedings*, pp. 211–12.

[91] 1 Comp. 3.2.6 (JL 12,254); 3.2.9 (JL 13,810); 3.2.10 (JL 14,184); 3.2.11 (JL 14,135); cf. 1 Comp. 3.2.2, Council of Poitiers (1078), c. 9, in Mansi 20:499. He likewise deprived married or concubinary clerics of their benefices: 2 Comp. 1.8.3 (JL 16,617); *Collectio Sangermanensis* 9.39, ed. Singer, p. 339; Alexander III, *Epist.* 1050, in PL 200:930 (JL 12,254). In addition, monks and nuns who had taken solemn vows were declared ineligible to marry, although married religious who were bound only by simple vows could retain their wives, provided that they left their religious communities; X 4.6.3 (JL 13,162); 4.6.4 (JL 14,005); 4.6.5 (JL 14,165).

[92] X 4.21.1 (JL 14,180).

[93] X 4.7.1 (JL 12,636).

[94] Although the second marriage was in theory null because it was bigamous, Alexander ruled as he did in order to prevent the husband from benefiting from his disobedience to the canons. The decretal also specified that the second wife could divorce the man, despite the fact that he could not divorce her. This part of the ruling was also inconsistent with the logic of established law, and evidently represented a further attempt by the pope to penalize the man for disobedience. Celestine III, in another decretal,

Legitimacy and Marital Property

Two late twelfth-century decretals asserted sweeping claims to ecclesiastical jurisdiction over legitimacy and marital property issues. Both decretals originated in English cases involving claims to decedents' estates in which the outcome hinged on the question of the legitimacy of one party. In both decretals, Alexander III claimed for the Church courts an exclusive right to adjudicate the legitimacy issue and denied the competence of secular tribunals in this matter.[95] Alexander also claimed the right to determine the circumstances under which a natural child might be legitimized, not only for ecclesiastical purposes, but also for inheritance and succession.[96]

In particular the pope insisted that children born to a couple prior to their marriage were legitimized by the subsequent marriage of their parents and that this legitimation was effective in the secular as well as the ecclesiastical forum. Moreover, Alexander held that while the child of an adulterous union was illegitimate, the child of a valid clandestine marriage was not.[97] In yet another case he ruled that when a marriage was pronounced null by an ecclesiastical court, a child born or conceived prior to final judgment was legitimate and had full inheritance and succession rights.[98] The same decretal also asserted that legitimate children had a right to support from their parents, even if the parents' marriage was subsequently held invalid. This child-support doctrine extended significant new protection to the children of divorced and separated parents, a subject that the law up to this point had largely ignored. Alexander also upheld the legitimacy of the children of a second marriage following a nullity judgment against a prior marriage. The status of these children had previously been unclear.[99]

Alexander III dealt with the special property concerns of married crusaders in two other letters. One of these, addressed to King Louis VII of France, held that a crusader, unlike other married men, could alienate property inherited by his wife without first obtaining his wife's consent—a decision that substantially broadened the property rights conferred on crusaders by Pope Eugene III in *Quantum predecessores*.[100] In a later ruling, however, Alexander limited this augmented right of alienation to property that did not form part of the wife's

---

held that a concubine did not count as a wife so far as the irregularity of digamy was concerned. This ruling confirmed a sixth-century conciliar canon that appeared in Bernard of Pavia's *Breviarium*; 2 Comp. 1.11.1 (JL 17,663); cf. 3 Council of Orleans (538) c. 9 in 1 Comp. 1.13.1.

[95] X 4.17.5 (JL 14,281) and 4.17.7 (JL 14,002); Morey, *Bartholomew of Exeter*, pp. 68–69, explains the background of X 4.17.7, which arose out of the case of Arderne c. Arderne.

[96] X 4.17.1 (JL 14,167) and 4.17.6 (JL 13,917).

[97] X 4.17.4 (JL 13,932) and 4.17.9 (JL 13,774).

[98] X 4.17.2 (JL 14,194).

[99] X 4.17.8 (JL 11,871).

[100] Alexander III, *Epist.* 65, in RHGF 15:789–90 (JL 10,796). On alienation rights in

dowry. A crusader who sold or mortgaged dowry property, even for the purpose of financing a crusade, was compelled to make immediate restitution, under pain of severe punishment.[101]

Jurisdiction, Evidence, and Procedures

Alexander III, who was a major innovator in these areas, strongly encouraged judges to base their decisions on the testimony of witnesses, rather than on the unexamined statements of oath-helpers or the outcome of ordeals.[102] This policy attests the influence of Roman law ideas on the formation of Alexander's attitudes; it probably reflects, as well, his consciousness of the changes in society during his pontificate.[103]

While he preferred to base judgments upon sworn testimony, Alexander III insisted that the evidence of more than one witness was necessary, particularly when marital separation or nullity was at issue. Marriages were not to be dissolved on the testimony of a single witness unless that evidence was corroborated by public notoriety or further proof.[104] Where two or more witnesses agreed, however, even if they were interested parties, Alexander was prepared to rule that their testimony established a presumption of fact, a presumption that could be rebutted only by the opposing evidence of a greater number of credible persons.[105]

In *Veniens ad nos*, Alexander III defined the standard of proof required to warrant a finding that marital consent had been invalidated by force and fear— he required that the force or threats involved must be sufficient "to move a constant man," a fictional creature who became almost as ubiquitous in canon law as his younger cousin, "the reasonable man," in the common law of torts.[106]

Other basic procedural rules that date from the pontificate of Alexander III dealt with the hitherto cloudy status of parties whose marriages were *sub judice*. Alexander declared that where the validity of a marriage was contested on grounds of consanguinity, the parties must separate and remain separated until a final judgment had been pronounced.[107] In cases that involved an alleged clan-

---

Quantum predecessores see Brundage, *Medieval Canon Law and the Crusader*, pp. 176–77.

[101] Alexander III, *Epist.* 239, in RHGF 15:870–71 (JL 11,465).

[102] X 4.18.1 (JL 14,052).

[103] Baldwin, *Alexander III*, p. 210; on social change and the older forms of proof, see Hyams, "Trial by Ordeal," pp. 101–106, 124–26.

[104] X 4.13.3 (JL 14,044).

[105] X 4.17.3 (JL 14,086).

[106] X 4.1.15 (JL 13,902, 14,159; WH 1071); Donahue, "Policy," p. 272; Helmholz, *Marriage Litigation*, pp. 90–94. For the reasonable man see William L. Prosser, *The Law of Torts*, 5th ed. by W. Page Keeton et al. (St. Paul, MN: West, 1984), pp. 173–85, and the classic exposition in the fictional case of Fardell v. Potts, in A. P. Herbert, *Uncommon Law* (London: Eyre Methuen, 1977), pp. 1–6.

[107] X 4.16.3 (JL 14,235).

destine marriage and in which the parties disagreed as to whether they had consented to marriage or not, Alexander held that the couple might be permitted to separate, *lite pendente*, although they were not required to do so.[108] Neither party to a contested marriage, no matter what the grounds, might contract a new marriage while judgment on the previous one was still pending or during an appeal from a first instance nullity decision.[109]

Sex Law and Marriage in the Decretals

The decretals of the late twelfth and early thirteenth centuries, as we have seen, significantly altered the Church's law on marriage and made important adjustments in the law concerning other types of sexual relationships. Alexander III played a critical role in this process, for the most basic and sweeping changes occurred during his pontificate. Alexander gave Western marriage law a form that was to endure for the greater part of four centuries. His rules remained in effect, by and large, until the Council of Trent—and even then were abandoned only with reluctance.[110]

Legal Scholarship in the Late Twelfth and Early Thirteenth Centuries

This burgeoning new body of decretal law took shape during the generations when academic institutions in the West were just beginning to emerge as universities—the earliest universities, in a strict sense of the term, anywhere.[111] While Bologna's law students created a corporate structure for themselves shortly after the middle of the twelfth century, Parisian law teachers apparently did not organize formally until late in the century.[112] Canon law was certainly being taught at Oxford at about the same time, although precisely when a formal law faculty emerged there is difficult to say.[113] Shortly after the beginning of the thirteenth century a university appeared at Cambridge, and by the late 1220s or the early 1230s a canon law faculty was functioning.[114] Other university centers began to appear at about the same time on the Continent: in Palencia between 1208 and 1214, in Salamanca about 1218/19, in Padua in 1222, and in

[108] X 4.3.2 (JL 13,774; WH 819).

[109] X 4.4.4 (JL 13,969; WH 1033a).

[110] Charles Donahue, Jr., "The Canon Law on the Formation of Marriage and Social Practice in the Later Middle Ages," *Journal of Family History* 8 (1983) 146–47.

[111] Rashdall, *Universities* 1:2–17.

[112] Coing, "Juristische Fakultät," in *Handbuch* 1:42; Gaines Post, "Parisian Masters as a Corporation, 1200–1246," in his *Studies in Medieval Legal Thought*, pp. 27–60; Rashdall, *Universities* 1:323, 437–39.

[113] Rashdall, *Universities* 3:32–33; R.W. Southern, "From Schools to University," and Leonard E. Boyle, "Canon Law before 1380," in *The History of the University of Oxford*, ed. T. H. Aston, vol. 1: The Early Oxford Schools, ed. J. I. Catto (Oxford: Clarendon Press, 1984), pp. 12–21, 531–36.

[114] M. B. Hackett, *The Original Statutes of Cambridge University: The Text and its History* (Cambridge: At the University Press, 1970), pp. 29, 131.

Orléans and Angers during the 1230s.[115] Elsewhere, outside of the new universities, law books circulated briskly and were consulted avidly, even by those who lacked formal instruction in the law.[116]

In the new universities, teachers of law lectured both on Gratian and on the decretal collections that supplemented the older body of law. The four decades that elapsed between the appearance of Bernard of Pavia's *Breviarium extravagantium* and the publication of the *Liber Extra* were a period of bustling activity in university classrooms, and the lectures delivered in them circulated in written form to audiences throughout Europe. Decretists continued to reexamine and reinterpret Gratian in the light of the new law that poured in ever increasing volume from the papal chancery, while the lecturers and writers who dealt with the decretals tried to organize the swelling mass of new rules into intelligible form and to guide fledgling lawyers, judges, and prelates in applying the new law to the cases that came before them.

In these decades, university law teachers transformed canon law from an inchoate jumble of regulations that lacked comprehensible form into something that can fairly be called legal science. Canon law by the beginning of the thirteenth century had become a transnational discipline, closely linked to Roman law and sharing with it a common terminology and method. Legal scholars in the universities cultivated canon law as an independent discipline, one that borrowed from, but was also distinct from, civil law, rhetoric, and theology. They sought to formulate a body of principles upon which the new science of canon law rested and approached their subject as a systematic intellectual discipline, rather than merely as a trade or craft, although it was that, too. The canon law faculties were producing both a new branch of knowledge and a new type of professional lawyer that Europeans had not seen before.[117]

These decades, then, were a period of rapid multiplication of legal commentaries but also a period of consolidation; academic lawyers were trying to facilitate analysis of the canons, while at the same time they sought to make it easier for their students to assimilate the growing mass of legal literature.

While law teachers were commenting on the new law as it appeared, they also needed to impose system and coherence on the thousands of glosses and explications of the *Decretum Gratiani* already in circulation. Johannes Teutonicus was a critically important figure in both processes. Johannes came to Bologna from Germany to study canon law. When he had completed his course of study, he stayed on to teach. After a successful career as a law professor, Johannes returned to Germany to become an ecclesiastical dignitary and administrator. During his years as a teacher Johannes assembled a massive collection of comments on the *Decretum* by all of the major and many of the minor decretists. Johannes ultimately published his anthology, and it became a huge success. So successful was it, indeed, that it was designated the Ordinary Gloss

---

[115] Coing, "Juristische Fakultät," in *Handbuch* 1:42, 46–47.

[116] *De rebus Alsaticis* 2, in MGH, SS 17:232.

[117] Berman, *Law and Revolution*, pp. 161–64.

(*Glossa ordinaria*), or standard commentary on Gratian's text. The Ordinary Gloss was used for centuries as a supplemental textbook in canon law faculties, where it attained an authority only slightly less exalted than the *Decretum* itself. In addition to compiling the Ordinary Gloss, Johannes also edited *Compilatio quarta*, on which he not only wrote a commentary, but also compiled a gloss apparatus; beyond this, he wrote a substantial gloss apparatus to the constitutions of the Fourth Lateran Council.[118] Although Johannes Teutonicus was unusually industrious and successful, he was representative of a large group of his contemporaries who were both decretists and decretalists and who were trying to master the new law and integrate it with the old into a single coherent legal system.

SEX AND MARRIAGE IN THE NEW LEGAL SCHOLARSHIP

One of the urgent tasks of the new legal scholarship at the end of the twelfth century was to assimilate the massive changes in marriage and sex law that began with the pontificate of Alexander III. The canonists of this period, like their predecessors, did not agree on the question of whether sexual relations should be considered part of the natural law or not. Johannes Teutonicus held in the *Glossa ordinaria* that sexual intercourse was a product of humankind's sensual nature and hence that it was a result of the operation of natural law.[119] Other authors were more cautious. The Apparatus *Ecce vicit leo*, for example, conceded that mankind shared with brute beasts a natural instinct for copulation, but shrank from identifying this with natural law, reasoning that sexual intercourse often amounted to fornication, which was a sin, and hence should not be considered part of natural law.[120] Similar arguments appeared in the *Apparatus* of Alanus Anglicus, the *Summa Duacensis*, and Accursius's Ordinary Gloss to the Digest.[121] Elsewhere, however, the Ordinary Gloss on the *Decretum* identified the source of sexual desire not as "nature" but as diabolical suggestions,

[118] See above, n. 8.

[119] *Glos. ord.* to D. 1 c. 7 v. *coniunctio*. The *glos. ord.* to the *Decretum* (and to the rest of the *Corpus iuris canonici*) will be cited from the edition published at Venice: Apud Iuntas, 1605. See also the *Apparatus Animal est substantia*, to D. 1 c. 7 v. *viri et femine coniunctio* and Laurentius's gloss on the same passage in Weigand, *Naturrechtslehre*, pp. 299, 302–303.

[120] *Ecce vicit leo* to D. 1 c. 7 v. *coniunctio* and to C. 32 q. 4 c. 3 v. *non adulteriam demonstrauerit*, in Weigand, *Naturrechtslehre*, pp. 287, 301–302, 418; cf. the *Glossa Palatina* to C. 32 q. 5 c. 14 v. *libidinis instinctu*, in MS O.10.2 of Trinity College, Cambridge, fol. 59va: "Ut cum appetit et instigat aliquem ad coitum." See also the marginal gloss to Rom. 1:26 v. *passiones* in Trinity B.1.6, fol. 3r: "Id est uoluptas, que et si delectent sunt passiones nature."

[121] Accursius, *Glos. ord.* to Dig. 1.1.1.3 v. *coniugatio*; Alanus, *Apparatus* to D. 1 c. 7 and C. 32 q. 4 c. 3 v. *uidebatur*, and *Summa Duacensis* to D. 1 c. 7 v. *viri et femini coniunctio*, all in Weigand, *Naturrechtslehre*, pp. 82, 297–98, 300, 417; Antonio Rota, "Il decretista Egidius e la sua concezione del diritto naturale," *Studia Gratiana* 2 (1954) 245–46.

originating in the testicles.[122] This inconsistency may be accounted for by the belief that the pleasurable sensations associated with sex had a different origin than sexual activity itself. The thrill of sexual pleasure, according to an argument familiar to earlier decretists, was a product of man's fall from grace. Sin brought sexual pleasure into the world, and this pleasure made all sexual activity sinful, according to this reasoning.[123]

Because sexual sensations were so attractive and the pleasure they afforded so intense, sex amounted to a kind of insanity, according to Thomas of Chobham (ca. 1158 ~ 1168–after 1233), who completed his *Summa confessorum* about the same time that Johannes Teutonicus finished the Ordinary Gloss. The insanity of love and sexual attraction, Thomas argued, required vigorous treatment in order to cure those stricken with it. To illustrate this he described the case of a woman who was cured of her morbid love for a priest by a clever bishop. The bishop tricked the priest into appearing publicly with another woman; his female admirer, after seeing them, "began to hate the priest so much that she desired never to see him again," and thus was cured of her affliction. Another wily prelate, an archbishop this time, achieved the same goal by confining a priest and his lady friend together in a small chamber, never allowing them to leave one another, day or night. After a few days of this, the priest was cured of his romantic passion and begged to be separated from his former mistress.[124]

Canonistic writers of this period shared the gloomy forebodings of their predecessors about the awful results of sexual desire. Lust, like the sirens of ancient fable, lures the souls of men to death and destruction, warned an Anglo-Norman glossator.[125] Other writers alluded to the old notion that sex was a source of ritual pollution, an intimate enemy of man's higher nature.[126] The sex urge was fed and nurtured by immodesty and the cultivation of other sensual pleasures, particularly indulgence in food and drink.[127] Talking with women, es-

[122] *Glos. ord.* to D. 13 c. 2 v. *nervi, testiculorum.* Cf. Rufinus, *Summa* to D. 13 c. 2, ed. Singer, p. 33, and Plato, *Timaeus* 91b-c, ed. Rivaud, pp. 226–27.

[123] *Glos. ord.* to c. 32 q. 2 d.p.c. 2 v. *sine ardore.* This passage depends heavily upon Huguccio; see above, p. 262. See also Thomas of Chobham, *Summa confessorum* 7.2.5.3, ed. F. Broomfield, Analecta mediaevalia Namuricensia, vol. 25 (Louvain: Editions Nauwelaerts, 1968), p. 343.

[124] Chobham, *Summa* 7.2.17.2, ed. Broomfield, pp. 389–90; cf. Nov. 74.4 pr.

[125] Gloss to C. 32 q. 5 c. 11 v. *syrene* in MS 283/676, fol. 193vb, of Gonville and Caius College, Cambridge: "Sirene monstra marina fuerunt, que cantus sui dulcedine naues attractas periclitari faciunt, per quas designantur concupiscentie, quarum periculosa uoluptas mortem animabus infligit."

[126] Chobham, *Summa* 7.2.2.3, ed. Broomfield, p. 339; Lothario dei Segni, *De miseria humanae conditionis* 2.22–23, ed. Maccarrone, pp. 56–57. Similar notions were current among Jewish thinkers in the same period; see Maimonides (1135–1204), *Guide for the Perplexed* 3.49, trans. Shlomo Pines (Chicago: University of Chicago Press, 1963), pp. 606, 609.

[127] *Glos. ord.* to C. 32 q. 5 c. 11 v. *aliam; Ecce vicit leo* to C. 32 q. 2 c. 3 v. *immod-*

pecially discussing and joking about sexual subjects, poisoned the soul and might lead to spiritual death.[128] Young men were so susceptible to sexual allures that some authorities declared that youths were by nature incapable of sexual purity.[129] Even when students go to church, the Ordinary Gloss remarked, they often do so not to worship but to ogle women.[130] Allowances had to be made for the circumstances of individual offenders: it was a lesser offense, according to Alain de Lille (1117–1203), for a man to have illicit sex with a beautiful woman than with an ugly one—the greater the temptation, the less the offense.[131]

As for women, it was commonly agreed that continence was more difficult for virgins than for sexually experienced women—the less they knew about sex, the more attractive they thought it was.[132] Other stereotypes of female sexuality abound in the canonical literature as well as the poetic literature of the period—the myth that women are naturally frail and prone to sin, stories of women's insatiable sexual appetite, together with the idealization of female chastity as something more than merely human.[133] Yet at the same time can-

---

estum, in Trinity O.5.17, fol. 126rb: "Scilicet naturale causa incontinencie, uel exscitandi causa libidinis." *Glossa Palatina* to C. 32 q. 4 c. 12 v. *immunditia,* in Trinity O.10.2, fol. 57va: "Que attenditur serua usum illicitum membrorum luxuria attenditur in cibo et potu, cum utitur delicatis et calidis ut aptior sit ad immundiciam." A similar observation occurs in *Glos. ord.* to Cod. 9.9.28(29) v. *intemperantiae.* Cf. the elaborate prescriptions for sexual modesty in Maimonides, *Code, Book Five: The Book of Holiness* 1.21.16–25, trans. Louis I. Rabinowitz and Philip Grossman, Yale Judaica Series, vol. 16 (New Haven: Yale University Press, 1965), pp. 137–39, and *Guide* 3.49, trans. Pines, p. 608.

[128] Benencasa, *Casus* to C. 32 q. 5 c. 12; Accursius, *Glos. ord.* to Cod. 5.27.1.1 v. *venenis;* cf. Maimonides, *Guide* 3.49, trans. Pines, p. 604, and *Code* 5.1.21.1–6, trans. Rabinowitz and Grossman, pp. 133–34. For examples of the gross sexual puns and double entendres that were part of the stock of twelfth-century humor see Betsy Bowden, "The Art of Courtly Copulation," *Medievalia et humanistica,* n.s. 9 (1979) 67–85.

[129] John of Tynemouth, gloss to C. 28 q. 1 c. 9 in Caius 283/676, fol. 184va: "Num ergo inuitus tenetur continere, quia continentia res uoti est, non precepti. Num igitur si iuuenis est et continere non potest, potuit eam cognoscere, etiam si non potest cohabitare." See also Raymond of Peñafort, *Summa de mat.* 9.1, ed. Ochoa and Diez, col. 948–49.

[130] *Glos. ord.* to C. 24 q. 1 c. 28 v. *sed suas.*

[131] Alain de Lille, *Liber poenitentialis* 1.27, ed. Jean Longère, 2 vols., Analecta medievalia Namuricensia, vols. 17–18 (Louvain: Editions Nauwelaerts, 1965) 2:34. See also Winthrop Wetherbee, "Alain of Lille," in DMA 1:1119–20.

[132] *Glos. ord.* to C. 27 q. 1 c. 2 v. *viae sunt.*

[133] Backeljauw, "De uxoris statu sociali," pp. 271–72. A classic literary expression of the myth of woman's sexual voracity can be found in the poem "De coniuge non ducenda," attributed to Golias, esp. ll. 85–88, 145–65, in *The Latin Poems Commonly Attributed to Walter Mapes,* ed. Thomas Wright (London: Camden Society, 1841; repr. Hildesheim: Georg Olms, 1968), pp. 80, 83. Guibert of Nogent, *Self and Society* 2.5,

onists maintained that a higher standard of sexual purity was demanded from women than from men, a view that Tancred and others explained in terms of the spiritual symbolism of the union of Christ and the Church.[134]

Diversity of opinion on sexual issues was as marked among unorthodox thinkers as it was among those who subscribed to conventional doctrine. Some heretics surpassed even the most rigorous Catholic writers and condemned all sexual relations, marital and nonmarital alike, as sinful, while orthodox writers commonly described other heretics, notably the Cathars, as indulging in indiscriminate adultery, fornication, and lurid sexual orgies.[135] Latins believed also that Muslims, no less than Christian heretics, advocated and practiced promiscuous sex.[136]

THE FORMATION OF MARRIAGE

Canonists in the late twelfth and early thirteenth centuries speculated, as had their teachers, about the place of marriage in Christian life. The Summa *Prima*

---

ed. Benton, p. 138, also warns of the perils of female sexual rapacity in his story of a man driven into the monastery in order to escape the sexual demands of his wife. The exaltation of virginity is well illustrated by the casual remark in the *Glossa Palatina* to C. 32 q. 1 c. 12, Trinity O.10.2, fol. 56v: "Non ideo hoc dicit ut sole uirgines habeant paradisum, sed quia facilius, ar. infra prox. q. v quintum [C. 33 q. 5 c. 5], uel quia uirginitas soror est angelorum. . . ."

[134] Tancred to 3 Comp. 1.14.2 v. *uitam*, Caius 28/17, p. 173b, and Vat. lat. 1377, fol. 176r: "Queritur quare exigitur maior castitas in uxore quam in uiro, quoniam maritus corrupte uel ab alio cognite promoueri non potest, ut xxxiiii. di. curandum, precipimus, si cuius, laici [D. 34 c. 9–12]; sed ille qui post uxorem habuit concubinam potest promoueri, ut eodem di. fraternitatis [c. 7]. Hugo dixit quod uir significat ecclesiam, que in parte sepe adulteratur recedendo a christo et exorbitando a fide, et ideo non deest sacramenti significatio in uiro, quamuis non sit uirgo; uxor uero significat christum qui numquam ecclesiam dimisit quoniam ipse est fons uiuus cui non communicat alienus. Alii dicunt, et credo melius, quod uir significat christum qui copulauit sibi synagogam et postea ecclesiam, et ideo non nocet si uir diuisit carnem suam in duas; uxor uero significat ecclesiam que semper uirgo permansit, saltem mente, unde apostolus: 'desponi enim uos uni uirgo,' etc. [2 Cor. 11:2], ut xxvii. q. i nuptiarum [c. 41]; et ideo exigitur quod uxor carnem suam non diuiserit in duos, quod si fecit, deest in coniuge significatio sacramenti unitatis. t⟨ancredus⟩." I am grateful, here and elsewhere, to Professor Kenneth Pennington for supplying me with his readings of the Vatican and Admont MSS.

[135] Paul Alphandéry, *Les idées morales chez les hétérodoxes latins au début du XIIIe siècle*, Bibliothèque de l'Ecole des hautes études, sciences religieuses, vol. 16 (Paris: Ernest Leroux, 1903), pp. 63–67, 162 n. 1; Müller, *Lehre des hl. Augustinus*, pp. 89, 101–102; Kuttner, "Gratian and Plato," pp. 97–98; Robert E. Lerner, *The Heresy of the Free Spirit in the Later Middle Ages* (Berkeley and Los Angeles: University of California Press, 1972), pp. 10–34.

[136] Jacques de Vitry, *Historia Iherosolimitana 1*, in *Gesta Dei per Francos, sive orientalium expeditionum et Francorum Hierosolimitani historia*, ed. Jacques Bongars, 2 vols. (Hannover: Typis Wechelianis, apud heredes Ioan. Aubrii, 1611) 1:1055.

primi argued that matrimony enjoyed a special dignity in the sacramental system, since it was the only sacrament coeval with the human race.[137] Others, however, stressed the inferiority of marriage to continence, and *Ecce vicit leo* characterized marriage as the least worthy among the sacraments.[138] The value of marriage, according to the Ordinary Gloss, sprang not from the marital relationship, but from the fact that marriage provided a cure for fornication and a means of producing children. In itself marriage was not something to be desired.[139]

Several writers challenged this view. In addition to the contractual obligation that it created, they asserted, matrimony also involved a social bonding of the couple through their mutual love and fidelity, symbolized by the wedding ring.[140] Interpretations such as this consorted well with the emphasis on consent that appeared in the later marriage decretals of Alexander III. Consent was the efficient cause of marriage, declared *Prima primi*, and Tancred, among others, emphasized that as soon as marital consent was expressed, in words, by signs, or even by silence, marriage was complete and binding.[141] Several writers

[137] *Prima primi* to C. 27 q. 1 in B.L. Royal 11.D.II, fol. 331ra: "Hoc sacramentum preeminit ceteris temporis, locis, rei signate, dignitate; cum enim cetera sacramenta habuerunt originem uel a uetri testamento, ut in unctio regum et episcoporum, ut ii di. ca. [?], uel a nouo, ut eucharistia, baptisma; solum matrimonium humane nature coeuum."

[138] Gloss to C. 27 q. 1 c. 41 v. *celle*, Caius 283/676, fol. 180va: "Q.d. non dapnatur is qui uouit quia suscipitur autem matrimonium, quia est bonus inferius continencie bono, sed quia cadit a bono superiore, scilicet continencie." Cf. the marginal gloss to 1 Cor. 7:35 v. *non ut laqueum uobis inuitam*, in Trinity B.1.6, fol. 40v: "Sed ad id tendens. Dico quod honestum est ut homo sit castus corpore et animo, non quod turpe sit coniugio, sed hoc honestius est et quod facilitatem habeat." *Ecce vicit leo* to C. 27 pr., in Salamanca, Biblioteca de la Universidad Civil, MS 2491, fol. 129ra: "Prior tamen agit de sacramento matrimonii, quominus indignius sit quam alia sacramenta."

[139] *Glos. ord.* to C. 31 q. 1 c. 10 v. *per se*: "Matrimonium enim propter se non appetitur, quia non ducit ad vitam; sed tamen est appetendum causa vitande fornicationis et propter prolem, infra prox. causa c. 2 § his ita [C. 32 q. 2 d.p.c. 2]."

[140] *Ecce vicit leo* to C. 27 pr., Salamanca 2491, fol. 129ra: "Si queritur quid sit matrimonium in sui natura, dicunt quidam quod sit relatio, siue qualitas que est in duobus, sicut biuari, qui sic est in duobus quod in neutro dictis lapidis, scilicet uirgo et uxore duplex est non unde matrimonio, sed duo, ita quod in neutro. Alii dicunt quod est quedam uinculum quod ligat duos ad inuicem, ar. infra xxxii. q. vii. tantum [c. 27]." Gloss to C. 28 q. 2, Caius 283/676, fol. 185ra: "Sed secundum hoc oportet dicere quod tria sunt matrimonia in quolibet matrimonio: unum in uiro per se, altera in muliere, tercium quod durante matrimonio dicitur uinculum sociale; sed quoniam hoc dicere est absurdum, dicemus quod matrimonium semper est uinculum sociale, nec unquam stabit matrimonium ex altera parte tantum." *Glossa Palatina* to C. 30 q. 5 c. 3 v. *anulo*, Trinity O.10.2, fol. 53v: "Anulo qui significat mutuum amorem et fidem coniugalem esse seruandum ut infra eodem femine [c. 7]."

[141] Tancred, *Summa de matrimonio*, tit. 8, ed. Wunderlich, p. 12, which is identical with Raymond of Peñafort, *Summa de matrimonio* 2.2, ed. Ochoa-Diez, col. 912. Also Tancred to 3 Comp. 4.1.3 v. *matrimonialiter*, in Caius 28/17, p. 285a, and Vat. lat. 1377,

noted pointedly that marriage was both a formless contract and a formless sacrament.[142] Neither consummation nor *traditio* was necessary to make marriage binding for life,[143] although there were serious differences of opinion on this point, especially among the Anglo-Normans.[144] Both actual cases and academic

fol. 252v: "Sed hec erat dubitatio huius capituli, quia cum alexander expresserit certam formam uerborum per quam contrahitur matrimonium, supra de spons. du., licet, lib. i [1 Comp. 4.4.3 = X 4.4.3], et dicitur infra e.c. ult. [3 Comp. 4.1.5 = X 4.1.25] quod necessaria sunt uerba quantum ad ecclesiam, quia si detrahitur, id est subicietur uerbum, non sit sacramentum, ut i. q. i detrahere [C. 1 q. 1 c. 54]. Uidebatur quod mutus contrahere non possit, sed non est ita, quia matrimonium solo consensu contrahitur legitimo, ut xxvii. q. ii. sufficiat [c. 2]; unde qui potest consentire, potest matrimonium contrahere, sed non omnis qui potest loqui, ut xxx. q. ii. ubi non est [c. 1] et supra de frigi., quod sedem lib. i. [1 Comp. 4.16.3 = X 4.15.2]. t⟨ancredus⟩." Ibid., to 3 Comp. 5.2.5 v. *non prebere*, Caius 28/17, p. 301b, and Vat. lat. 1377, fol. 263v: "Quia sepe qui tacet consentire uidetur, ut liiii. di. si seruus sciente [c. 20]; C. de nupt., sicut proponis [Cod. 5.4.5]. Sicut e conuerso, de con. di. iiii. cum paruulis [c. 77]; ff. de seruit. urb. ru. ⟨pre.⟩ [MS: Vat. male], inuitum. [Dig. 8.2.5(4)]; supra de baptismo et eius effectu, c. i. l.e. [3 Comp. 3.34.1 = X 3.42.3]. t⟨ancredus⟩."

[142] *Prima primi* to D. 27 pr., B.L. Royal 11.D.II, fol. 331ra: "Causa efficiens matrimonii est consensus matrimonialis, ut infra eodem q. i. sufficit [C. 27 q. 2 c.2?]." *Argumentum quod religiosi* to C. 32 q. 2, in MS 101 of Pembroke College, Cambridge, fol. 60va: "Nota nullam sollempnitatem uel formam necessariam ad matrimonii suberam, ut c. solet [c. 6] et di. xxiiii. c.ii. et iii. et B. lxiiii. de fra.[?]." See also the *questio disputata* of the French school, ca. 1181, in Fransen, "Mariage simulé," p. 537.

[143] Tancred to 1 Comp. 4.1.10 v. *consenserit*, in Caius 28/17, p. 88a, and Admont 22, fol. 55r: "Uidetur tamen quod secundum leges tradicio faciat de sponsa uxorem, ut C. de donat. ante nup., cum in te [Cod. 5.3.6]; ff. de ritu nup., denique [Dig. 23.2.6]. Sed secundum canones dico solum consensum facere uxorem, ut xxvii. q. ii. coniuges [c. 6]. R⟨ichardus?⟩. Sed et dici potest secundum canones per traductionem matrimonium contrahi, ar. infra de sponsa duorum, c. ult [1 Comp. 4.4.7 = X 4.4.4]; ar. infra de coniugi. leprosorum, litteras [1 Comp. 4.8.3 = X 4.8.3]. Erat ergo dubitatio istius decretalis quia secundum leges non uidebatur ista uxor, quia traducta non fuerat, ff. de ritu nup., mulierem [Dig. 23.2.5]; xxxiiii. di. uidua, sed secus est secundum canones, ut hic. lau⟨rentius⟩." *Ecce vicit leo* to C. 27 q. 2 c. 42 v. *lege coniugii*, in Trinity O.5.17, fol. 119vb: "Id est nondum carnaliter cognita." See also Raymond of Peñafort, *Summa de mat.* 2.2, ed. Ochoa and Diez, col. 912.

[144] Gloss to C. 33 q. 1 d.p.c. 3 in Caius 283/676, fol. 196rb: "Quidam fornicarius laborans in extremis nolens decedere ⟨ut⟩ fornicator ducit concubinam suam. Cum tamen sciat se nunquam posse eam cognoscere de cetero, num est matrimonium? Jo⟨annes de⟩ Cornub⟨io⟩ dicit quod matrimonium est; consensus enim presens trahitur ad cohitum preteritum, non quod habuit [?] illum, quia hoc esset impius, sed quia eo suffragante per hunc consensum fit matrimonium, sicut alias consensus de futuro legitimat cohitus subsequente, et facit matrimonium; ar. ad hoc sunt ff. his ubi dicitur, quod numquam [?] et 5 q. 6 qui nunc consenciant in matrimonium [?]. Si ante hoc tempus numquam fuerunt una caro, ualet matrimonium? Jo⟨annes⟩. de ti⟨nemuth⟩ dicit non ualere. Sed num filii prius suscepti habebuntur pro legitimis? Hoc uidetur quantum enim in contrahentibus fuit, matrimonium fuit."

speculation suggest, however, that whatever the law might say about the validity of marriage without witnesses or ceremony, their absence caused serious difficulties.[145]

"Consent means a joining of souls," said Tancred, and internal consent was essential to marriage.[146] But a determined seducer could easily simulate consent, while an exterior show of consent might be forced or maneuvered from an unwilling bride or groom.[147] Consent to marriage need not be explicit: it might be presumed from consent to intercourse following an agreement about future marriage—this doctrine, which originated with academic commentators, was soon adopted by the pope.[148]

All of this clouded the role, if any, of intercourse in the formation of marriage. Intercourse was usually said to consummate marriage, although the marriage of the Blessed Virgin and St. Joseph was held to have been consummated by means other than carnal union.[149] Writers of this period seem to have been

---

[145] *Select Cases*, ed. Adams and Donahue, A.7, pp. 25–28.

[146] Tancred to 3 Comp. 1.14.2 v. *consensus*, in Caius 28/17, p. 173b: "Scilicet coniunctio animarum. t⟨ancredus⟩."

[147] Gloss to C. 31 q. 2 pr. v. *cogenda*, in Caius 283/676, fol. 189rb: "Et hoc uerum adeo quod si per coactionem fiat matrimonium non ualet, quia supra prox. q. 5 c. 1 [C. 30 q. 5 c. 1?] et hoc speciale in matrimonio, secus enim in aliis contractibus metu factis, quia ualent." Raymond of Peñafort, *Summa de mat.* 11.2, ed. Ochoa and Diez, col. 956.

[148] Gloss to C. 27 q. 2 pr. in Caius 283/676, fol. 181ra: "Sponsalia fit mentio futurarum nuptiarum seu repromissio, D. de sponsalibus l. i. [Dig. 23.1.1], qui si contrahuntur inter alios ut solet fieri per uerba de futuro. Sponsus et sponsa modo dicuntur sed inter hos non est matrimonium nec uelimus dicere spe futurorum nec re presentum. Si autem sequitur copula carnalis necdum est matrimonium ibi, sed tamen ecclesia presumit esse. In Extra de sponsalia in futuro cognita, ueniens qui s. [1 Comp. 4.1.5?], que secundum jo⟨annem de⟩ ti⟨nemuth⟩ fornicata est ex illa uel enim pro socio uel marito et admittatur probatio in contrarium; potest autem probari copulam carnalis non interuenisse officium maritalis, sed ⟨modo⟩ [MS: motu] fornicatiuo." Tancred to 1 Comp. 4.4.1 v. *si permiserit*, in Caius 28/17, p. 93b, and Admont 22, fol. 58v: "Hec condicio turpis est si de fornicario coitu intelligatur, et ideo ea abiecta tenent simpliciter sponsalia, ut infra de condi. apo. c. i. lib.eodem [1 Comp. 4.5.1]. Unde si postea rem secum habuerit confirmatur matrimonium, ar. supra de spon. de illis [1 Comp. 4.1.4]. Si de coitu legitimo intellecta fuit multo forcius per sequentem coitum matrimonium confirmatur; potius enim est hortatio quam condicio, ut sit simile, ff. de tutel., muto [Dig. 26.1.6]. ala ⟨nus⟩. Ego credo quod istud si non continetur conditionaliter sed causatiue notat enim causam quia in omni matrimonio hec causa, scilicet carnalis copula, debet interuenire, saltem quo ad propositum, ut xxvii. q. ii. § cum ergo, uer. 'beata maria' [C. 27 q.2 c. 3], et expone si id est quia permiserit etc.; simile si habetur, supra de elec., significasti [1 Comp. 1.4.21(18) = X 1.6.4], ff. quando dies legat. cedat, quando ticio § quedam [Dig. 36.2.22.1]. t⟨ancredus⟩." This doctrine was adopted by Gregory IX in X 4.1.30.

[149] Gloss to C. 27 q. 2 c. 5, in Caius 283/676, fol. 181ra: "Queritur de beata uirgine et Joseph. Respondeo dici potest quod matrimonium inter eos fuit consummatum non per carnis copulam, sed propter rem signi, quia in aula beate uirginis facta est unio deitatis ad carnem; non ergo signum facit matrimonium consumari multo fortius ipsa res signi,

uncertain as to whether consummation was ever required for valid marriage. They agreed that, once sexual consummation had taken place, the duty to pay the conjugal debt was thenceforth in force and that reluctant spouses could be compelled to have sexual relations with their mates.[150]

Canonists assumed that marriage was a lifelong union, but the *Glossa Palatina* noted that marriage also resembled limited-term agreements, such as partnerships *(societates)*, since, like a partnership, marriage could be contracted by proxy.[151] Tancred observed that the law in his day sought to hold couples to betrothal agreements more firmly than it had in the past, although the Church did not require specific performance when one party refused to honor a promise of future marriage.[152]

CONSANGUINITY AND AFFINITY

Consanguinity and affinity underwent radical and much-needed change during this period. For centuries the canons had defined marriages within seven degrees of relationship as incestuous. Consequently, persons who knowingly mar-

---

quia res est dignior suo signo. Quod ergo dici solet eorum matrimonium non fuisse consummatum, exaudi 'per carnis commixtionem'."

[150] Gloss to C. 31 q. 2 pr., in Caius 283/676, fol. 189rb: "Duplex est traditio, ad desponsationem scilicet et ad carnalis copulam. Ad primam nullum ⟨nulla?⟩ est cogenda; sed post consensum in primam, secundum quosdam, cogi potest ad secundam, ar. 74 ubi [D.74 c. 7] et 92 si quis episcopus [D. 92 c. 7]. Sed non potest cogi ubi subest alternatio. In extra, ex publico [1 Comp. 3.28.7 = X 3.32.7; JL 13,787]."

[151] *Glos. ord.* to C. 32 q. 2 c. 6 v. *si usque ad mortem.* But see *Glossa Palatina* to C. 27 q. 2 c. 11 v. *quibusdam aliis,* Trinity O.10.2, fol. 45vb: "Potest ergo matrimonium contrahi inter absentes, sicut et societas, ff. pro socio l. iiii. [Dig. 17.2.4]; ar. xxx. q. iiii. nec illud [?]." Likewise the gloss to C. 30 q. 5 c. 8 v. *uxor* in Caius 283/676, fol. 188rb: "Ar. matrimonium per procuratorem contrahi posse, 32 q. 2 honorantur [C. 32 q. 2 c. 13] pro et contra, tamen hic uxor futura sit."

[152] Tancred to 1 Comp. 4.4.1 v. *priori,* in Caius 28/17, p. 93b, and Admont 22, fol. 58v: "Non obstante illa consuetudine mala que olim uiguit in ecclesia bononiensis et mutinensis que hodie reprobata est, tam de iure quam de facto, ut infra e.t. c. i. lib. iii. [3 Comp. 4.1.1. = X 4.1.22], infra eodem t. c. licet preter sollicitudini [1 Comp. 4.4.3 = X 4.4.3; JL 14,091; WH 620]." Damasus asserted in his *Questiones,* in MS Vat. Borgh. lat. 261, fol. 38vb, that even a mundane excuse, such as the other party's poverty, could justify breaking off sponsalia: "Pone quod mulier que promisit c. uergat ad inopiam nec possit soluere, queritur utrum sit conpellandus cum ea contrahere, et uidetur quod sic. . . . Solutio: Forte dicendum esset unum non esse conpellendum quia inuite nupcie malos euentus consueuerunt habere, ut extra i. e. requisiuit [1 Comp. 4.1.12 = X 4.1.17]." See also Johannes Teutonicus to 4 Comp. 4.1.1 v. *desponsaret,* in Caius 44/150, fol. 140va: "Si iste desponsauit tamen quibuslibetcumque uerbis usus fuerit, pocius est considerandum quid fuerit factum quam quid fuerit dictum, ut extra ii. de ap. ad audienciam [2 Comp. 2.19.7 = X 2.28.34]; extra ii. de uer. sig., in hiis [2 Comp. 5.23.1 = X 5.40.15]; C. plus ualere quod agitur, l. si quis [Cod. 4.22.4]." See also Thomas of Chobham, *Summa* 7.2.13, ed. Broomfield, pp. 370–71.

ried within the seven-degree limit must either secure a dispensation or accept the risk that their marriage might be annulled. Since seven degrees of relationship computed according to canonical rules could encompass thousands of persons, the incest rules created potentially serious problems for individual couples and for society as a whole.[153] In 1215, the Fourth Lateran Council reduced the forbidden degrees of kinship from seven to four, declaring that "the urgent necessity or evident utility" of the Church required alteration of the former law.[154] The new law sizeably increased the number of potential partners that any given individual could marry and decreased the need for dispensations in order to legitimize marriages between cousins.

Pope Celestine III held that sexual relations between two persons created a legal affinity that barred subsequent marriage between either party and any close relative of the other—the affinity was similar to that created by acting as godparent to a child.[155] Commentators generally interpreted this decretal restrictively, so as to limit affinity contracted by coitus to the smallest number of cases. Thus they held, for example, that *coitus interruptus* did not create affinity, nor did "unnatural" intercourse, so long as there was no ejaculation of semen within the vulva.[156] A number of writers also discussed related problems, such as the implications of marriage within the forbidden degrees for the marital debt,[157] and the advisability of construing the law more leniently for young couples than for old folk, in order to accommodate the fiery sex drive of youth.[158]

[153] Bernard of Pavia, *Summa* 4.14.7, ed. Laspeyres, pp. 166–67; Champeaux, "Jus sanguinis," pp. 241–90; Flandrin, *Amours paysannes*, pp. 33–34. The way in which the consanguinity rules might affect political events is well illustrated by the case of King Amaury of Jerusalem, whose succession to the throne was compromised by his marriage to his cousin-german, Agnes. The couple divorced and both remarried before the problem was resolved; *Continuation de Guillaume de Tyr* 3, ed. Morgan, pp. 19–20.

[154] 4 Lateran Council (1215) c. 50, ed. García y García, pp. 90–91.

[155] 2 Comp. 4.7.4 = X 4.13.5; JL 16,643. Alexander III had also held, but more tentatively, that illicit coitus with a close relative might create a supervening affinity; see above, p. 334.

[156] Bernard of Pavia, *Summa* 4.14.17, ed. Laspeyres, p. 173; *Glossa Palatina* to C. 35 q, 2 & 3 c. 11 v. *impedire*, Trinity O.10.2, fol. 81vb: "Talis enim pollutio que fit extra uuluam non facit sanguinis commixtionem nec carnis unitatem; sed quid si quis frangit claustrum pudoris, sed non spermatizat ibi uel si spermatizat, non cum ipsa? Dico cum h. per talem coitum unitatem carnis non fieri nec sanguinis commixtionem, nec impediri ob hoc consanguineorum ab eius copula si constare possit. Jo. et R. legant hanc causam sub alio sensu, quia talis pollutio non impedit nisi sit in tanta uel nisi fiat maritalis affectio, sed hoc superfluit una negatio."

[157] Gérard Fransen, "Les 'Questiones' des canonistes: essai de dépouillement et de classement (IV)," no. Bb.80, *Traditio* 20 (1964) 500. See also *Glos. ord.* to C. 32 q. 7 c. 21 v. *neutram.*

[158] Gloss to C. 31 q. 1 pr., in Caius 283/676, fol. 188vb: "Quid autem si mechus et mecha iuuenes sint? Num si inuicem contraxerint, matrimonium est? Ar. 33 q. 2 interfectores [c. 5]. Sed certe iuuenilis etas non eadem ius prodest ut sit inter eos matri-

Canonists in this period also insisted that marriages contracted before the parties reached the age of puberty were not binding unless the individuals were capable both of assenting to marital obligations and of fulfilling them.[159] Alanus favored adopting a further distinction based on Roman law that would have made the validity of marriage depend upon the parties having reached "full puberty," which civil law set at age seventeen, rather than "incomplete puberty," which girls were presumed to reach at twelve and boys at fourteen.[160] Alanus's proposal found little support, and most commentators continued to assert that twelve and fourteen were the canonical minimum ages.[161] Some writers even advocated Huguccio's argument in favor of recognizing the betrothal of children who had not yet reached the minimum age, on the grounds that intent, not chronological age, was what counted.[162]

---

monium quod alias non esset matrimonium si maturiores essent; sed eatenus confert iuuenilis etas ut cum aliis contrahant, qui alias sine spe coniugii manerent."

[159] Statutes of Winchester I (1224) c. 60, in *Councils and Synods with Other Documents Relating to the English Church*, A.D. 1205–1313, ed. Frederick M. Powicke and Christopher R. Cheney, 2 vols. (Oxford: At the Clarendon Press, 1964; cited hereafter as Powicke and Cheney) 1:135; *Glossa Palatina* to C. 30 q. 5 c. 3, Trinity O.10.II, fol. 53vb: "Si fuerit in etate adulta que nuptiis apta deputata; alias non esset matrimonium, ff. de ritu nup., minorem [Dig. 23.2.4]. Si scilicet ante xiv. annos eam traduceret." Cf. *Glos. ord.* to the same passage, v. *apto.* Tancred to 1 Comp. 4.2.4 v. *consensus*, in Caius 28/17, p. 91a, Admont 22, fol. 56r: "Etas legibus definita quo ad sponsalia est vii. annorum, ut infra eodem, litteras [1 Comp. 4.2.5 = X 4.2.4]; quo ad matrimonium, xii. annorum in puella, et xiiii. in masculo, ut infra eodem si puella lib.e. [1 Comp. 4.2.11; JL 14,126; WH 310c & d]; et de utraque congrue intelligitur quod hic dicitur. Sed quare prohibetur ante tempus legitimum coniugari? Respondeo quia sepe inter tales solet discordia oriri et dimittendis [A: diuertentes] consanguineis alterius copulantur, quod fieri non debet, ut supra titulo proximo, iuuenis [1 Comp. 4.1.18 = X 4.1.3; JL 9655]. t⟨ancredus⟩." Cf. Tancred to 3 Comp. 4.2.2 v. *tunc nubilis erat*, in Caius 28/17, p. 286a, and Vat. lat. 1377, fol. 253r: "Et nihilominus exigitur quod sit uir potens, scilicet quod prudencia suppleat etatem, ut infra sequitur et supra e.t. puberes [1 Comp. 4.2.7] et hoc perpenditur ex qualitate corporis ita quod generare possit, ut supra e.t. manifestum [1 Comp. 4.2.3] et c. de illis l. 1 [1 Comp. 4.2.9 = X 4.2.7; JL 13,767]. Qualiter autem cognoscantur ista, non potest iure aliquo declarari, sed iudicis arbitrio relinquitur, ut ff. de iure deliberan. l. ii. [Dig. 28.8.2] et supra de donat., apostolice l.e. [3 Comp. 3.18.6 = X 3.24.9; Po. 3077]."

[160] Alanus to 1 Comp. 4.2.5, in B.N. lat. 3932, fol. 49rb: "Nota quod est pubertas plena, scilicet cum quis est xvii. annorum, ut in institu. de adopt. § minorem [Inst. 1.1.4], ff. de alimentis uel cibariis legatis l. ⟨certe⟩[Dig. 34.1.14.1], xxviii. dis. de his [D. 28 c. 5]. Est pubertas semiplena ut in xii. anno in feminis, in xiiii. anno in masculis, ut infra proximo c. [1 Comp. 4.2.6]. W."

[161] See generally Onclin, "L'âge requis pour le mariage," pp. 240–43.

[162] Johannes Teutonicus to 4 Comp. 3.10.1 v. *prudentia*, in Caius 44/150, fol. 137vb: "Hic canonicatur opinio h. qui dicit quod sicut doli capax se potest obligare diabolo, ut extra i. de delic. pu., pueris [1 Comp. 5.20.1 = X 5.23.1] Sic dico quod sicut in matrimonio carnali malicia supplet etatem, ut supra de sponsal. impu. l. i. manifestum [1

Contraception

Writers in this period paid far more attention than had those of the previous generation to problems raised by marital contraception. An intention to avoid having children might even invalidate a marriage, according to the Ordinary Gloss, and a conditional marriage entered into with express contraceptive intent ought to be held null, in the same way that any other contract would be vitiated by an illegal condition. Other writers, however, held that although such a marriage would be illegal, it was nonetheless binding and that couples could not separate on the grounds that they had married with contraceptive intentions.[163] In addition, contraceptive intercourse constituted a species of ritual pollution, according to both the *Glossa Palatina* and Johannes Teutonicus.[164] Contraceptive intercourse was sometimes compared to adultery, as well, even if the couple were legitimately married.[165] Neither canonists nor moral writers detailed the contraceptive methods they had in mind, although *coitus interruptus* was presumably the most effective technique available in this period.

Conjugal Debt

Like their predecessors, canonists of the late twelfth and early thirteenth centuries maintained that husbands and wives had equal rights to marital sex. They acknowledged, however, that women were less likely to insist on their sexual

---

Comp. 4.2.3], sic et in spirituali contractum tamen consueuit dici ab aliis ut notaui xx. q. i. in summa [*Glos. ord.* to C. 20 q. 1 pr. v. *infra annos*]. Jo⟨hannes⟩."

[163] *Glos. ord.* to C. 32 q. 2 c. 6 v. *noluit* and to C. 32 q. 2 c. 7 v. *et si ab initio* and *coniuges non sunt.* See also X 4.5.7 and Raymond of Peñafort, *Summa de mat.* 4.3, ed. Ochoa and Diez, col. 929. Likewise, *Argumentum quod religiosi* to C. 32 q. 2, Pembroke 101, fol. 60va: "Nota quod non sunt coniuges qui eo animo iuncti sunt ut prolis generatio impediretur et quod in eodem coniugali opere unus peccat, alter non, et quod matrimonium aliquando ex una tantum parte tenet, ut c. aliquando [c. 7], ut infra q. v proposito [c. 5]." Similarly, gloss to C. 32 q. 2 c. 6, in Pembroke 162, fol. 266r: "Habes ergo hic quod uitatio prolis uel propositum uitandi filios impedit matrimonium, et c. proximo."

[164] *Glos. ord.* to C. 32 q. 4 c. 12 v. *immunditia; Glossa Palatina* to C. 32 q. 4, in Trinity O.10.2, fol. 57va, and Salzburg, Stiftsbibliothek St. Peter, MS a.XII.9, fol. 201v [I am grateful to Professor Kenneth Pennington for this and other readings from the *Palatina Salzburgensis*]: "Ar. opera nuptiarum que non sunt causa liberorum mortalia esse, quia luxuria et immunditia nominantur, ut infra c. liberorum [c. 14]; sed hoc dicitur non quo ad reatum mortalis uicii, sed quo ad speciem facti; speciem enim et similitudine luxurie et immundicie pretendunt [*T corr. ex* predetendant]." Likewise *Argumentum quod religiosi* to C. 32 q. 4, in Pembroke 101, fol. 60vb: "Ar. quod opera nuptiarum que non fiunt causa liberorum mortalia esse, quia luxuria et immundicia nominantur, ut c. In eo, in finem [C. 32 q. 4 c. 12] et c. liberorum [C. 32 q. 4 c. 14]." A contemporary scriptural gloss to 1 Cor. 7:4 v. *uir sui corporis potestatem non habet*, in Trinity B.1.6, fol. 38v, however, held contraceptive intercourse only venially sinful: "Quod preter intentionem generationis non est nuptiarum malum, sed ueniale propter nuptiarum bonum."

[165] Benencasa, *Casus* to C. 32 q. 2 c. 7.

rights.[166] The parity of sexual rights in marriage was the foundation for discussions of conjugal debt that pushed the right to claim the debt to extremes undreamed of by earlier generations of canonists. The right of a married person to have intercourse on demand took precedence over most other duties. According to Alanus, whose treatment of the topic relied upon Huguccio, a married serf whose wife demanded that he make love to her at the same time that his manorial lord required his services in the field ought to obey his lord, unless there was imminent danger that his wife might commit fornication. If the wife insisted, however, he was obliged to comply with her demand—the wife's rights took precedence over the lord's.[167] The right to the conjugal debt was so basic that even an excommunicate, who otherwise was ineligible to prosecute actions in court, might be allowed to sue for the restitution of marital rights if his wife refused to have intercourse with him.[168] The obligation of the marital debt was so serious that in the view of one Anglo-Norman glossator it constituted a telling argument against polygyny, for, he declared, no man could hope to satisfy more than one woman.[169]

A radical legislative innovation concerning the marital debt during this period occurred in a decretal of Innocent III. Prior to Innocent's time, a man who wished to go on Crusade must secure his wife's permission, since during his absence she would be deprived of his sexual services and might be led to commit adultery. Although Innocent III decided to allow married men to make Crusade vows without the consent of their wives, academic canonists found this ruling so anomalous that they generally passed over it in silence when they lectured.[170]

Only two circumstances excused a failure to pay the marital debt. If the spouse who made the demand had been guilty of adultery, the innocent partner

---

[166] *Glos. ord.* to C. 32 q. 1 c. 4 v. *non ad imparia* and C. 32 q. 6 c. 2 v. *intactam*; Flandrin, *Familles*, pp. 158–59.

[167] Alanus to 1 Comp. 4.9.1, in B.N. lat. 3932, fol. 50va: "Secundum huguccionem, si dominus seruicium exigat et uxor debitum eodem tempore, domino est pocius obediendum, quod uerum puto, nisi periculum fornicacionis in uxore timeatur uel magnum fiat preiudicium uxori, quo casu intelligatur illud c., et hoc ideo quia seruus prius fuit domino obligatus cum eodem honore [?] transit ad uxorem." Tancred said much the same thing in his *Apparatus* to 1 Comp. 4.9.1 v. *seruicia*, Caius 28/17, p. 98b.

[168] *Glossa Palatina* to C. 4 q. 6 c. 2 v. *omnibus*, in Elizabeth Vodola, *Excommunication and the Legal Status of the Excommunicate* (Berkeley and Los Angeles: University of California Press, 1985), p. 85 n. 66.

[169] Gloss to C. 32 q. 4 c. 7, in Caius 283/676, fol. 192va: "Unica tamen fuit uxor quia nullus maritus potest obligari pluribus uxoribus ad matronalem continenciam." Also to C. 32 q. 2 pr., fol. 190vb: "Item mulier debet uiro suo seruitutem corporis ne ipse incidat in fornicationem, ut in hec causa quicquid [C. 33 q. 2 c. 3] in finem. Ergo uir potest exigere debitum propter fornicationem uitandam, ut 33 q. 5 secundum [c. 5]. Ergo potest uti exacto sine peccato, nam id solum possumus quod de natura possumus."

[170] X 3.34.9; James A. Brundage, "The Crusader's Wife Revisited," *Studia Gratiana* 14 (1967) 241–52.

had the right to refuse payment until the guilty party had done penance.[171] The other situation in which a married person might be justified in refusing a request for sexual relations arose if s/he were conscious of some legal affinity that was unknown to the party who made the demand.[172] This might happen if the husband, for example, secretly had sex with his wife's sister or mother and thus contracted an occult supervening affinity. In this situation he was required to refuse to have intercourse with his wife until he had received absolution and done penance for his misdeed.

MARRIAGES OF SERFS

Writers of the generation between Bernard of Pavia and the *Liber Extra* were more interested than their predecessors had been in the marital rights of unfree persons. In addition to discussing the serf's right to claim the conjugal debt, they considered the conflicts of interest that might arise when a servile marriage deprived a lord of property rights. In general the canonists maintained that servile marriage was as valid and as binding as the marriage of free persons. Problems arose, however, when one partner was free and the other a serf. Under most circumstances the canonists resolved these questions in favor of the freedom to marry, but they qualified this stance in two important respects. Where such a marriage would deprive the owner of property, they maintained that the marriage was valid but that the free party incurred a liability for the damages that resulted from the loss of labor. When marriages crossed class boundaries the canonists also allowed owners to separate the couple if there had been deceit or concealment of the servile party's true status prior to or at the time of the exchange of consent.

---

[171] *Glos. ord.* to C. 32 q. 1 c. 3 v. *licita*; Raymond of Peñafort, *Summa de pen.* 3.3.5, ed. Ochoa and Diez, col. 582 and *Summa de mat.* 2.11, ed. Ochoa and Diez, col. 918–19; *Argumentum quod religiosi* to C. 32 q. 1, in Pembroke 101, fol. 60va: "Ar. quod mortaliter uir peccat debitum reddendo uxori adultere ante completam penitentiam, ut c. i., ii., iii., iiii., vi. et di. xxxiiii. si laici uxor [c. 12]." But cf. *Glossa Palatina* to C. 32 q. 1 c. 3 v. *ut non sit licita*, in Trinity O.10.2, fol. 56rb, Salzburg fol. 198v: "Nota secundum b., secus esset quando aliquis adulteratur, quia tunc non priuetur iure petendi debitum si occultum est, sed tantum ubi notorium, et tunc etiam non peccanti non est licitum reddere debitum, nec etiam exigere, nisi post penitentiam uel nisi non possit continere." See also Tancred to 1 Comp. 4.11.2 v. *ex malicia*, in Caius MS 28/17, p. 99b: "Numquid iste potest exigere debitum? Uidetur quod sic, quia non inuenitur prohibitum; uel dic quod si unus solus coniugum sit in culpa, non potest exigere, ut infra de secundis nuptiis, Comes W. l. ii. [2 Comp. 4.13.2; JL 16,611]. Si uero ambo, uterque potest exigere, ar. xxx. q. i. de eo [c. 5] Vin⟨centius⟩."

[172] *Glossa Palatina* to C. 32 q. 1 c. 3 v. *ut non sit licita*, Trinity O.10.2, fol. 56r: "Ubi uero contrahitur affinitas spiritualis, siue sit occultum siue manifestum, priuatur delinquens iure petendi debitum, sed tamen siue sit occultum siue manifestum etiam ante penitentiam qui non delinquid absque peccato potest reddere et exigere debitum si uult, nec est necessaria hic penitentia sicut ubi est adulterium, quia ibi peccatum reddit eam illicitam, que purgatur per penitentiam."

Secular law writers were less tolerant than the canonists of marriages between free and unfree persons. Carlo de Tocco, who wrote a gloss apparatus to
the Lombard laws early in the thirteenth century, took a particularly dim view
of marriage between a free woman and a serf. A woman committed a more serious offense by contracting such a marriage, he declared, than she would have
done by fornicating with a free man. Her father, he added, had just cause for
disinheriting her and would also be within his rights if he had her bound and
beaten—though not to death.[173]

RELIGIOUSLY MIXED MARRIAGES

Discussions of the law concerning religiously mixed marriages during this period contained few novelties. *Prima primi* asserted that non-Christian marriages
were generally valid, but admitted a few exceptions to the rule.[174] Tancred argued that one exception involved marriage among Jews, for since Jewish law
allowed marriages to be dissolved by a bill of repudiation, it followed that Jewish marriages were in some sense incomplete because they were not indissoluble, as Christian marriages were.[175] Benencasa also asserted that Christians
should not marry non-Christians, even if the marriage was premised on the
condition that the non-Christian convert to Christianity.[176]

CLANDESTINE MARRIAGE

Perhaps the most thorny issue in discussions of marriage formation during this
period continued to be clandestine marriage, since the law itself contained internal contradictions that could not readily be resolved. As we have seen,

[173] Gérard Fransen, "Les 'Questiones' des canonistes," pts. I and II, no. 1.33 and
3.12, in *Traditio* 12 (1956) 577 and 13 (1957) 483; also "La structure des Questiones," no.
B.46, *Traditio* 23 (1967) 526. See also *Argumentum quod religiosi* to C. 29 q. 2 in
Pembroke 101, fol. 60rb: "Ar. quod non sit matrimonium inter seruum et ancillam et
quod separari possint si uoluntate dominorum non fuerint coniuncti, ut c. dictum est [c.
8]; contrarium autem in quoddam decreto Adriani pape quod non est in hoc uolumine [1
Comp. 4.9.1 = X 4.9.1]." And ibid. to C. 30 q. 2: "Ar. quod ille qui imprudens ancillam
duxerit in uxorem cogitur eam redimere si potest, ut c. si quis ingenuus [C. 29 q. 2 c. 4].
Ar. quod qui ignorans ancillam duxerit in uxorem dimittere eam potest, cum sciuerit nec
redimere cogitur, ut c. si femina [C. 29 q. 2 c. 5]." *Leges Longobardorum cum ar-
gutissimis glossis Carlo de Tocco* 1.31.1 v. *vindictam* (Venice: Domenico Giglio e Fratelli, 1537; repr. Turin: Bottega d'Erasmo, 1964), fol. 83va, and Hans Van de Wouw,
"Questiones aus Orleans aus der Zeit vor Jacques de Revigny," no. 4, *Tijdschrift voor
Rechtsgeschiedenis* 48 (1980) 47–48.

[174] *Prima primi* to C. 28 pr., in B.L. Royal 11.D.II, fol. 331rb: "Hic primo probat
Gratianus quod inter infideles non est matrimonium, postea contrarium. Et certum est
quod inter eos est matrimonium."

[175] Tancred to 3 Comp. 4.10.1 [= X 4.14.4] v. *non seperaret*, in Caius 28/17, p. 289a,
followed almost verbatim, but without Tancred's *siglum*, in *Glos. ord.* to X 4.14.4 v. *esse
matrimonium inter eos*.

[176] Benencasa, *Casus* to C. 32 q. 8 c. 1.

canon law by the 1190s required only the consent of the parties to create a marriage and neither ceremonies, witnesses, dowry, publicity, nor family consent were necessary for validity. But at the same time the popes also insisted that marriages should be public and made secret marriages illegal.[177]

The Fourth Lateran Council required couples to announce their intention to marry prior to the wedding, so that their neighbors might know about their plans and raise timely objections if need be. The Council insisted, moreover, that the wedding itself must take place publicly. Those who failed to conform to these rules were subject to ecclesiastical penalties, and their children might be declared illegitimate.[178] But the Council stopped short of making the validity of marriages depend upon the fulfillment of these requirements. The result was confusion in both policy and practice. "Secret waters are sweeter," said Bernard of Pavia, and people perversely continued to contract secret marriages, despite reiterated prohibitions.[179] The law seems to have assumed an unstated premise that it was important to define as many relationships as possible as marriages. Unions that failed to meet the minimum requirements for publicity were nonetheless treated as marriages, despite the fact that they violated the law. *Honestas*, Johannes Teutonicus observed, took priority over *liceitas* in marriage law.[180]

The most difficult practical problem that clandestine marriage posed arose from the lack of proof that the parties had ever exchanged consent. When secret marriages were contested, as they often were, the evidence of the parties often conflicted on this point.[181] Sometimes, no doubt, this arose from genuine

---

[177] *Prima primi* to C. 30 q. 5 c. 6, in B.L. Royal 11.D.II, fol. 331rb: "Hic autem pro constanti sumpto docet quod matrimonia non sunt clam contrahenda. Queritur quamuis fuit uera, ecclesia de eis postea dubitante, eis manifeste preiudicant, ut i.e. his ⟨ita⟩ [MS itaque] respondetur [C. 30 q. 5 d.p.c. 9] et c. sequentibus. Clandestina ergo coniugia non sunt contrahenda, sed contracta non dissoluuntur." Likewise the *Distinctiones Cantabrigienses*, in U.L.C., MS Add. 3321(1), fol. 38r: "Huic multa obuiant, cum multa sint que non debent fieri, que tamen ex post facto conualescunt, ut est illud clandestinorum coniugium, que fieri non debent, que tamen si fiant rata habentur."

[178] 4 Lateran Council (1215) c. 51, ed. García y García, pp. 91–92. The *Apparatus* of Johannes Teutonicus on this canon, v. *penitus inhibimus*, nonetheless made a point of insisting on the validity of clandestine marriages; *Constitutiones*, ed. García y García, p. 258. See also Sheehan, "Marriage Theory and Practice," pp. 432–33, 438, 440. Etienne Diebold, "L'application en France du canon 51 du IVe concile de Latran d'après les anciens statuts synodaux," *L'année canonique* 2 (1953) 187–95.

[179] Bernard of Pavia, *Summa decretalium* 4.3 pr., ed. Laspeyres, p. 141; the allusion is to Prov. 9:17.

[180] Johannes Teutonicus, *Apparatus* to 4 Lateran c. 50 v. *de sobole suscepta*, ed. García y García, p. 257.

[181] Raymond de Peñafort, *Summa de mat.* 2.14, ed. Ochoa and Diez, col. 921–22; *Ecce vicit leo* to C. 30 q. 5 pr., Salamanca 2491, fol. 139ra: "Et quamuis tali matrimonium probari non possit, nichilominus ibi uerum est matrimonium nec deficit in ius sed iuris probatio; et adulter est qui clam contraxit et aliam ea uiuente cum qua contraxit ducit. Non autem debent fieri clandestina matrimonia, ne sub hoc pretextu fornicatio uel adul-

differences in intent, sometimes from discrepancies of perception, sometimes from difficulty in recalling long-past events; more than occasionally, however, conflicts of testimony resulted from fraud and deception. Ecclesiastical judges, who were not gifted with second sight, found it difficult, often impossible, to be certain that litigants were dealing honestly with the court.

Academic commentators noted that there was no presumption in favor of clandestine marriages and that relationships in which matrimonial consent could not be proved should be presumed to be adultery, not marriage.[182] Only if witnesses or other evidence could be produced were the courts supposed to give legal recognition to secret marriages. If evidence was forthcoming, however, a prior secret marriage would invalidate any subsequent union, no matter how solemn and well-attested it might have been.[183] In the nature of things, clandestine marriages were no doubt more common among the lower orders of society where large property interests were not at issue, than they were among the wealthy. The upper classes sought to make their marriages as public and as splendid as possible, not only as a matter of honor and social obligation, but also to assure that property transactions connected with the marriage would be honored.[184]

---

terium committitur." For an example from actual practice see Theodora c. Palmerio (10 May 1230) in *Imbreviaturbuch*, no. 6, ed. Dolezalek, p. 94.

[182] Tancred to 1 Comp. 4.3.1 v. *manifeste*, Caius 28/17, p. 93b, Admont 22, fol. 58v: "Si clandestinum matrimonium inter aliquos contractum est et eorum alter monasterium ingreditur, numquid si uterque confiteatur extrahendus est? Ita, quia confessio probatio est, infra de raptoribus, cum causam [1 Comp. 5.14.4 =X 5.17.6]. . . . Presumit autem canon clandestinum matrimonium adulterium esse, xxx. q. v. aliter [c. 1]; sed contra ff. de ritu nup., in libere [Dig. 23.2.24], sed illa lex corrigitur per aut. quibus modis naturales § quantum et § ult [Auth. 6.1.4 in Cod.; Nov. 74]." Tancred to 1 Comp. 4.18.5 v. *comprobare*, Caius 28/17, p. 104b, also quoted a gloss of Laurentius to the same effect. See also *Argumentum quod religiosi* to C. 30 q. 5, Pembroke 101, fol. 60rc: "Ar. quod non presumitur matrimonium, sed potius adulterium ubi sollempnia desunt uel manifesta iudicia adsunt, ut c. aliter [c. 1]."

[183] Gloss to C. 30 q. 5 pr. in Caius 283/676, fol. 187vb: "De principali autem uerum est quod clandestinum coniugium preiudicat manifesto, si probari potest; in extra de clandestinis, quod nobis [1 Comp. 4.3.3 = X 4.3.2]; peccant tamen mortaliter qui clam contrahunt, quia contrahere interdictum est." Cf. *Ecce vicit leo* to C. 30 q. 5 pr., Salamanca 2491, fol. 139ra: "Quod hic intitulatur q. v. . . . . utrum clandestina desponsatio in manifesta desponsatio preiudicet, et hec non est dubium si manifestum non precessit, quia solus consensus facit matrimonium, xxvii. q. ii." Likewise *Prima primi* to C. 27 q. 2, B.L. Royal 11.D.II, fol. 331rb: "Quod clandestina coniugia, si de eis possit constare, manifestas preiudicent apparet in decretales de sponsa duorum, super eo [1 Comp. 4.4.6(8); JL 14,234; WH 954 e–f], et de clandestina desponsatione, quod autem nobis [1 Comp. 4.3.3 = X 4.3.2]."

[184] Gloss to C. 30 q. 5 c. 3, in Caius 283/676, fol. 188ra: "Sed quod hic dicitur uerum est de quibusdam si defuit, ut est dos et instrumentum dotale inter modicis personas et pauperes; i.e. § sed obiicitur [C. 30 q. 5 d,p.c. 8] unde de hoc leuiter loquitur canon, D.

The concern that impelled both lawmakers and law writers to uphold the validity of clandestine marriages arose from their commitment to freedom of contract and their wish to enable persons to marry despite opposition from their families. This was the mainspring that powered their stiff opposition to making the validity of marriage depend upon publicity.[185] While Roman law permitted parents to dictate the marriage choices of their children, especially their daughters, canon law refused to concede that power to them.[186] Cases from this period record several successful efforts by thirteenth-century women to assert their canonical right to refuse husbands chosen for them by their families.[187]

SEXUAL BEHAVIOR IN MARRIAGE

Although some canonists and theologians continued to repeat the views of Huguccio and others who maintained that marital sex always involved some sin, common opinion during this period shifted away from the rigorism of earlier generations.[188] Johannes Teutonicus formulated the mainstream view that dominated canonistic discussions of marital sex. Although Johannes reported the rigorist view in the *Glossa ordinaria*, he relegated it to incidental notes and plainly did not share it.[189] As Johannes explained matters, marital sex with re- productive intention was never sinful, nor was marital coitus sinful for the party paying the conjugal debt.[190] His view was shared by other canonists, both

---

de uentere inspic. l. i. § quod autem parentes [*Collectio Dunelmensis secunda* 112 = JK +384?]

[185] Bernard of Pavia, *Summa decretalium* 1.30.1–3, ed. Laspeyres, pp. 26–27; cf. Accursius, *Glos. ord.* to Dig. 4.2.7 v. *nec timorem infamie.*

[186] Tancred to 1 Comp. 4.2.2 v. *non posse*, Caius 28/17, p. 91a, Admont 22, fol. 56v: "Nec etiam secundum leges potest pater compellere filium familias inuitum contrahere, ut ff. de sponsa., filiofamilias [Dig. 23.1.13]. Secus de filia, nam illa contradicere non potest, nisi pater dederit sibi sponsum turpem uel moribus suis indignum, ut ff. de sponsa., sed ea que [Dig. 23.1.12]. Secus tamen secundum canones, ut supra eodem, cum locum [1 Comp. 4.1.19 = X 4.1.14], xxvii. q. ii. sufficiat [C. 27 q. 2 c. 2]. R⟨ichardus⟩."

[187] Dolezalek, *Imbreviaturbuch*, no. 15, 17, pp. 101–103, both from May, 1230.

[188] Lindner, *Usus matrimonii*, p. 102; Müller, *Lehre des hl. Augustinus*, p. 119; *Glossa Palatina* to C. 33 q. 4 c. 7 v. *uoluptate*, Trinity O.10.2, fol. 78rb: "Et ita non potest fieri sine peccato; hic sumit ergo h⟨uguccio⟩ opinionem suam quod nunquam opus coniugale potest sine peccato exerceri, unde etiam qui debitum reddit peccat uenialiter quia semper est ibi quidam pruritus et ⟨uoluptas⟩ [*MS* uoluntas] in emissione spermatis." Cf. *Glos. ord.* to C. 33 q. 4 c. 7 v. *uoluptate*. The *Glos. ord.* adds, however that "p⟨etrus⟩ manducator dixit contra ut nota xiii. di. nerui [c. 2]." Thomas of Chobham, *Summa* 7.2.2.1, ed. Broomfield, pp. 333–34, reported Augustine's belief that a "holy man" could somehow ignore the pleasure of sexual orgasm and thus avoid sin.

[189] *Glos. ord.* to C. 33 q. 4 c. 7 v. *uoluptate*, as well as to D. 13 d.a.c. 1 v. *item aduersus*; D. 13 c. 2 v. *et quia*; D. 25 d.p.c. 3 v. *excepto*; and C. 27 q. 2 c. 10 v. *non poterat*.

[190] *Glos. ord.* to C. 32 q. 2 c. 3 v. *Ab adulterio*; Weigand, "Liebe und Ehe," p. 54;

among the Bolognese masters and the Anglo-Norman glossators.[191] Alanus even saw positive virtues in marital sex, which he described as a necessary element of marriage.[192] Tancred likewise maintained that marital consent was most convincingly expressed through sexual relations; the couple's physical union ratified and confirmed their verbal agreement to marry.[193] John of Tynemouth was even more positive in his assessment of the role of sex in marriage. He affirmed that marital sex was not merely allowed, but was morally good, even if the goal of a couple's lovemaking was to avoid extramarital temptations, rather than procreation.[194]

Raymond of Peñafort, *Summa de mat.* 2.10, ed. Ochoa and Diez, col. 917–18; Lindner, *Usus matrimonii*, p. 133.

[191] Gloss to D. 1 c. 7 v. *coniunctio*, in Weigand, *Naturrechtslehre*, p. 294; gloss to C. 32 q. 2 pr. in Caius 283/676, fol. 190va:

Actus coniugalis: Numquam sine uoluptate et pruritu carnis, imo nec sine peccato ut quosdam ar. 33 q. 4 uir cum [c. 7]; 27 q. 2 omne [c. 10]; D. 5 ca. 1; secundum alios non semper qualiter uoluptas comitem habet peccatum; et in comedendo uoluptas et delectatio est, interdum ubi comedet non peccat, ergo potest actus coniugalis iam esse legitimus et modestus et in modo agendi et intentione agencium, quod sine omni peccato erat. . . .

—Contra naturam, semper est mortale peccatum, 32 q. 7 adulterii [c. 11]

—Bonus et uere uidetur meritorius si exactus reddiderit, 33 q. 5 si dicat [c. 1]. Item si causa prolis procreande et ad clerum Dei regenerande, D. 13 nerui [c. 2].

Male et peccatum:

—Secundum naturam: Mortale si causa libidinis explende, 34 q. 4 origo [c. 5]. Ueniale quando causa fornicationis euitande, D. 25 nunc autem [d.p.c. 3].

[192] In addition to the glosses of Alanus in Weigand, "Liebe und Ehe," pp. 54–55, note also his gloss to 1 Comp. 4.1.3 v. *recepit*, B.N. lat. 3932, fol. 48va: "Scilicet quod ei coheserit carnaliter. Est itaque hic ar. quod nec iuramentum nec subarratio facit matrimonium, ar. xxvii. q. ii. non dubium [c. 16], sicut nec ruda rei traditio facit dominium, ut ff. de acquirenda rerum dominio, l. nunquam [Dig. 41.1.31]."

[193] Tancred to 1 Comp. 4.1.3 v. *processerit*, Caius 28/17, p. 86b, Admont 22, fol. 54r: "Scilicet per carnalem copulam, quia tunc esset matrimonium cum prima, ut infra cap. prox., in fine t⟨ancredus⟩." Likewise to 4.1.17 v. *cognosci*, p. 89b and fol. 56r: "Si uero permisisset se ab eo cognosci, ex quo semel in carnalem copulam consensisset, ulterius non audiretur quod inuita fuisset, ut infra qui matrimonium accusare pos., insuper lib. ii. [2 Comp. 4.12.3 = X 4.18.4]; infra de eo qui duxit in matrimonium quam polluit, significauit in e. [1 Comp. 4.7.2 = X 4.7.2]. t⟨ancredus⟩." also to 4.2.12 v. *consensisse*, p. 93a and fol. 58r: "Per carnalem copulam, supra eodem continebatur [1 Comp. 4.2.8 = X 4.2.6]. § Pone quod puella habeat xi. annos et dimidium dum desponsatur et traducitur et antequam ueniat complementum erit xii. anni reclamet, numquid iudicandum est ibi matrimonium? Respondeo si carnalis copula interuenit cum malicia uideatur suppleuisse etatem, iudicandum est pro matrimonio ut hic, alias non; supra eodem, capitulo proximo. t⟨ancredus⟩."

[194] Gloss to C. 32 q. 2 pr, Caius 283/676, fol. 190vb: "Immo secundum Jo⟨annem de⟩ Ti⟨nemuth⟩ nullum est peccatum quia contrahere est bonum, uitare fornicacionem est bonum, ergo contrahere causa fornicationis uitande est bonum. Pari ratione et cog-

But even canonists who saw moral value in marital sex, however, were not prepared to see coitus as a source of grace. An Anglo-Norman glossator noted that the Holy Spirit disappeared while married couples made love, but added that this was because of the sensual itch that accompanied coitus, not because of the act of love.[195] The *Glossa Palatina* stated that disciplined and saintly couples could be said to practice marital chastity, even when they made love.[196] This did not mean that they should not enjoy sex or that married couples were bound to observe a rigid and unbending decorum in each other's presence.[197] Instead they ought to aim at a balanced regimen in their sex life, as in their other habits. In the same vein, authors cautioned married Christians to be careful of their diet, lest excessive food and drink lure them into sexual indulgence.[198]

Writers continued to warn against immoderate marital lovemaking,[199] but

---

noscere causa fornicationis uitande est bonum; sed dices multa licita sunt que tamen in condicionem deduci non possunt, infra q. 5 Quam pia [?]. Ita est hic forte bonum coire, bonum uitare fornicationem, nec tamen hic illo fine facere bonum non est, sed probat aliter." Further on in the same passage: "Matrimonium est institutum ab apostolo causa fornicationis uitande, ergo nec contrahere nec coire hoc fine peccatum est. Item mulier debet uiro suo seruitutem corporis, ne ipse incidat in fornicatione, ut in hac capitula quicquid in finem [C. 32 q. 2 c. 22]; ergo uir potest exigere debitum propter fornicationis uitandum, ut 33 q. 5 secundum [c. 5]. Ergo potest uti exacto sine peccato, nam id solum possumus quod de iure possumus. Item nemo potest esse perplexus inter duo peccata. Sic ergo si uir non potest continere, oportet ut fornicetur uel suam cognoscit propter fornicationem. Manifestum est ergo hac causa cognoscere non esse peccatum propter illud Augustini, Quicquid [C. 32 q. 2 c. 3]; ius sit quod nisi fieret recte reprehenditur, non est peccatum."

[195] Gloss to C. 32 q. 2 c. 4, Caius 283/676, fol. 191ra: "Uel non dabitur gratia spiritus sancti hic habito respectum ad pruritum, non ad ipsum actum quando fit ex caritate."

[196] *Glossa Palatina* to C. 31 q. 1 c. 11 v. *obtrectatores*, Trinity O.10.2, fol. 55ra: "Ergo castitas est inter coniuges qui sancti dicuntur, xxx.di. hec scripsimus [c. 16]; potest ergo eorum concubitus dici castitas, ut ar. supra di. xxxi. Nicena [c. 12]." Also the gloss to 1 Comp. 3.3.5 in Caius 44/150, fol. 34rb: "Contra, continentia coniugalis dicitur castitas, ut xxxi. c. Nicena [c. 12]."

[197] *Prima primi* to C. 32 q. 5, B.L. Royal 11.D.II, fol. 331va: "Pudicitia duplex: § uirtum scilicet anime qualitatis; animi hoc per uiolentiam non aufertur, ut infra eodem c. 7. § Qualitas corporis, et hec proprie integritas carnis appellatur. Hec amittitur per oppressionem, ut infra eodem c. 1. Hanc pudicitiam coniuges seruare non tenentur, ut supra ⟨27⟩ [MS 75] q. 1 nuptiarum [c. 41]."

[198] Gloss to C. 33 q. 4 c. 1, Pembroke 162, fol. 195v: "Decreta ergo illa que prohibent carnes agni comedere tempore amplexus loquuntur in eo casu quando cognoscit explende libidinis causa; cetera uero loquuntur in aliis casibus. Hec distinctio potest haberi ex illo decreto uir cum propria [C. 33 q. 4 c. 7]." See also *Glossa Palatina* to C. 32 q. 2 c. 7 v. *immunditia*, in n. 127 above.

[199] Johannes Teutonicus, *Glos. ord.* to D. 13 c. 2 v. *maiora*; C. 27 q. 1 c. 20 v. *peiores*; C. 32 q. 4 c. 5 v. *amator, adulter*. Cf. the strikingly similar observations of Maimonides, *Code* 5.1.21.11, trans. Rabinowitz and Grossman, p. 136. See also *Glossa Palatina* to C.

there was a shift in the treatment of this admonition toward the end of the twelfth century. In addition to seeing Jerome's admonitions against excessive or too ardent love as a caution against too frequent intercourse, writers at the end of the century also interpreted his words as a prohibition of "unnatural" marital intercourse, by which they meant among other things the use of unusual coital positions. They assumed that the proper posture for marital sex ought to be the one in which the man lay atop his wife. Deviations from this posture were perversions, motivated by a quest for unusual pleasures (*extraordinaria voluptas*).[200] Sexual experimentation was thus equated with attempts to surpass the order that nature had dictated for marital relations.[201]

Unconventional sexual techniques were thought to imitate in marriage the unsavory practices of harlots and adulterers.[202] The gravest disapproval was reserved for coitus from the rear,[203] apparently on the grounds that this position was common in animal copulation and that it was inappropriate for humans to imitate the beasts of the field. Even if variations from the conventional coital position were customary or common, Johannes Teutonicus declared that this would not excuse their use or make them acceptable.[204] The canonists and theologians of this period made no references to oral sex, but a number of them spoke gingerly about anal intercourse, of which they disapproved most strongly indeed—so much so that the *Glossa Palatina* would allow a wife to divorce her husband if he demanded anal sex from her.[205]

Few canonists active in this period had much to say about the traditional proscriptions of marital intercourse during forbidden periods of the liturgical

---

32 q. 4 c. 5 v. *magnitudo*, Trinity O.10.2, fol. 57ra: "Immoderata exactio pro nimio ardore libidinis," as well as *Glos. ord.* to the same passage.

[200] For explicit descriptions of deviant coital positions see Johannes Teutonicus, *Glos. ord.* to C. 32 q. 5 c. 11 v. *et posteriora*, to C. 32 q. 7 c. 13 v. *que si omnes*, and Benencasa, *Casus* to C. 32 q. 7 c. 14, as well as the anonymous Dominican *Summa* quoted in Müller, *Lehre des hl. Augustinus*, pp. 205 n. 74 and 207 n. 77. By contrast see Maimonides, *Code* 5.1.21.9, trans. Rabinowitz and Grossman, p. 135.

[201] Thomas of Chobham, *Summa* 7.2.2.3, ed. Broomfield, pp. 335–36.

[202] Johannes Teutonicus, *Glos. ord.* to C. 32 q. 7 c. 7 v. *sodomita*; Benencasa, *Casus* to C. 32 q. 7 c. 14. Robert of Flamborough, *Poenitentiale* 4.244, ed. Firth, p. 196, cautioned against describing these practices in detail, lest this give lewd inspiration to those who had never considered these possibilities.

[203] *Glos. ord.* to C. 32 q. 5 c. 11 v. *et posteriora*.

[204] *Glos. ord.* to C. 32 q. 7 c. 13 v. *que si omnes*; *Glossa Palatina* to C. 27 q. 2 c. 6 v. *si poterat*, Trinity O.10.2, fol. 48va: "Hinc elicitur quod coitus cum uxore numquam potest esse illicitus sine peccato, ar. xxxiii. q. iiii. uir cum propria [c. 7]; ar. contra xiii. di nerui [c. 2]." But cf. *Glos. ord.* to C. 27 q. 2 c. 10 v. *non poterat*.

[205] *Glossa Palatina* to C. 32 q. 7 c. 7 v. *sodomita*, Trinity O.10.2, fol. 59va: "Ar. quod propter opus sodomiticum possit uxor dimittere uirum; est enim pessimum genus fornicationis et est uerum, ar. supra eodem q. iv. in eo [c. 12]. But cf. *Glos. ord.* to the same passage.

year or the wife's physiological cycle. Johannes Teutonicus, for example, referred to these prohibitions in the *Glossa ordinaria*, but advised that they were counsels of perfection, not legal requirements. In discussing periodic sexual abstinence, he also distinguished between coitus for procreation and coitus to avert adultery.[206]

Moralists and penitential writers were more inclined than canonists to insist that couples must observe the earlier discipline.[207] The discrepancy between canonist and moralist teaching suggests that the old discipline was not widely observed by the early thirteenth century. Some took the view that if one spouse demanded the marital debt during a proscribed period, the other party was bound to comply and did not sin by so doing.[208]

It would seem that the same logic should apply if an excommunicated husband demanded the debt from his wife, and this was the solution preferred by Gandulph and John of Tynemouth.[209] The rigoristic author of *Ecce vicit leo*, on the other hand, held that the innocent party was bound to pay the debt, even though doing so was sinful.[210] Thomas of Chobham advised married women to use sexual attraction to reform their errant husbands:

[206] *Glos. ord.* to D. 5 c. 4 v. *ablactetur* and to C. 33 q. 4 pr. v. *quod autem*; Raymond of Peñafort, *Summa de mat.* 2.10, ed. Ochoa and Diez, col. 917–18. The author of the marginal gloss to Lev. 20:18 v. *Qui coierit*, Trinity B.1.31, fol. 115v, concluded that the purpose of the marital abstinence prescriptions was to lead couples to abandon marital sex altogether: "Intendit legislator continenciam suadere, ne more pecorum continue mulieribus misceantur, sed uel coacti ⟨uel⟩ ad usum continendi paulatim ueniamus."

[207] Alain de Lille, *Poenitentiale* 1.4, ed. Longère 2:27; Thomas of Chobham, *Summa* 7.2.2.2–3 and 7.2.10, ed. Broomfield, pp. 334–39, 364–66; Robert of Flamborough, *Poenitentiale* 5.285, ed. Firth, p. 237. Cf. the discussion of these topics by Maimonides, *Code* 5.1.4.1–22 and 5.1.21.11, trans. Rabinowitz and Grossman, pp. 25–31, 135. Thomas of Chobham, *Summa* 7.2.2.3, ed. Broomfield, pp. 338–39, admonished confessors to inquire closely into the details of married penitents' sexual habits in order to frighten them out of doing such things.

[208] *Distinctiones Cantabrigienses*, U.L.C. Add. 3321(1), fol. 39v: "Sed dicimus quod lex canonum nemini prestat auctoritatem peccandi. . . . Sicuti et lex canonum dicit poscenti debitum carnale soluendum, si tamen quis preter spem prolis uxori debitum reddat, non hoc facit legis auctoritate, sed uoluntate proprie temeritatis, ut cum indiscrete quis preceps fertur ad coitum uel que precipitanter affectat coitum, uel ex utriusque infirmitate uel alterius corruptela."

[209] Gloss to C. 11 q. 3 c. 103 v. *quoniam*, Caius 283/676, fol. 116ra: "Sed d. G⟨andulphus⟩ and Jo⟨annes de⟩ Ti⟨nemuth⟩ dicunt in debita reddendo tantum ad paria iudicari, ita quod sicut uxor reddens debitum uiro petenti excommunicato excusatur, ita uir uxori excommunicate; in aliis uero secus."

[210] *Ecce vicit leo* to C. 28 q. 1, Salamanca 2491, fol. 136rb–va: "Sed queritur an liceat contrahere cum excommunicata, ⟨dices⟩ [*MS* dicens] quod non, quia non est ei communicandus nisi in illo que pertinet ad correctionem uel in casu necessitatis, ut vi. q. iii. quando [*fortasse* C. 11 q. 3 c. 23]; tamen si contraxit licet peccaret contrahendo sed post teneretur debitum reddere, tamen peccaret debitum reddendo."

In the bedchamber and in the midst of their embraces she ought to speak softly to him, and if he is a hard-hearted and merciless oppressor of the poor, she should urge him to be merciful.[211]

CONCUBINAGE

Canonists of this period found the legal status of concubines perplexing. They considered concubinage immoral, but doubted that it was illegal, since both civil law and the Old Testament tolerated the institution.[212] The distinction between concubinage and marriage was hazy. If a man called his concubine his wife, *Argumentum quod religiosi* declared, then that is what she was.[213] From this it followed, according to some, that a concubine must be faithful to her lover, and their relationship created an affinity that precluded subsequent liaisons with other members of the lover's family.[214]

But canonists were uncomfortable with the policy of tolerating concubinage and advised couples to regularize their unions. The Church also fashioned a mechanism for encouraging this result: abjuration under pain of marriage. Church courts could require couples who lived in open concubinage to swear an oath that they would not subsequently have sexual relations with one another. If they were later discovered keeping company, they were subject to the penalties for perjury, unless they immediately solemnized their union by formal marriage.[215] Married men who kept concubines were required to renounce

---

[211] Thomas of Chobham, *Summa* 7.2.15, ed. Broomfield, p. 375.

[212] Johannes Teutonicus, *Glos. ord.* to D. 34 d.p.c. 3 v. *coniunctione* and C. 32 q. 4 c. 4 v. *de legibus*; Placentinus, *Summa Codicis* 5.26 (Mainz: Ivo Schoeffer, 1536; repr. Turin: Bottega d'Erasmo, 1962), p. 218; *Glossa Palatina* to C. 32 q. 2 c. 6, Trinity O.10.2, fol. 57rb: "Hic uidetur surgere quedam inextricabilis contrarietas, nam in deuteronomio licitum erat habere concubinam et contrahere cum ea postea uel dare ei pretium sue pudicitie ⟨et⟩ eam dimittere; sed in decalogo secundum interpretatione augustini prohibita fuit omnis fornicatio, ut hic dicit. H⟨uguccio⟩ dicit quod non sunt contraria, nam aliud est permissio de qua in deuteronomio, aliud preceptum de quo in decalogo. Sed hec solutio nulla uidetur quia circa illud non possit habere locum permissio et preceptum siue prohibitio immo dicendum illud intelligi de comparatiua permissione, simile infra xxxiii. q. ii. si quod uerius [c. 9], nam in ueritate illud semper fuit peccatum, extra de diuortiis, gaudemus [3 Comp. 4.14.2 = X 4.19.8]."

[213] *Argumentum quod religiosi* to C. 32 q. 4, Pembroke 101, fol. 60vb: "Ar. quod concubinam uxorem facit qui eam uxorem nominat. Nam desinit esse adulter, ut c. dicat [C. 32 q. 4 c. 9]."

[214] Rudolf Weigand, "Quaestionen aus den Schule des Rolandus und Metellus," *Archiv für katholisches Kirchenrecht* 138 (1969) 87.

[215] Johannes Teutonicus, *Glos. ord.* to C. 31 q. 1 c. 3 v. *claudatur*; Statutes of Winchester I (1224?) c. 54, 58, and Statutes of Coventry (1224 ~ 1237) c. 15, in Powicke and Cheney, *Councils and Synods* 1:134–35, 213; Thomas of Chobham, *Summa* 7.2.5.5, ed. Broomfield, pp. 345–46; Sheehan, "Marriage and Family," p. 209; and see generally Richard H. Helmholz, "Abjuration *sub pena nubendi* in the Church Courts of Medieval England," *Jurist* 32 (1970) 80–90.

their mistresses under pain of fines, excommunication, and other penalties.[216]

Despite efforts to discourage the practice, men of wealth and power continued to have concubines. Their companions were usually women of lower social status, and marriage to them would have been scandalous or even illegal by civil law. The canonists refused, as their predecessors had done for centuries, to accept disparity of social status as an impediment to marriage; but the use of limitations on marriage to support class distinctions still persisted, as some civilians noted with apparent complacency.[217] Occasionally the rights of the concubine and her lover were spelled out in formal contracts. Such a contract between King James I of Aragon and Countess Aurembaix of Urgel, dated 23 October 1228, for example, made detailed provisions for the status of any children they might have, property-sharing between the principals, and the disposition of assets owned jointly.[218] No churchman apparently cared to declare this contract void.

DIVORCE AND REMARRIAGE

Late twelfth-century canonists were dissatisfied with the theory of separation, divorce, and remarriage that they inherited. The critical issue was indissolubility. Popes and theologians in the West had insisted since the eleventh century that valid marriages were indissoluble; canonists wanted to reconcile that principle with the realities of practice. Some authorities believed that the pope could under certain circumstances dissolve a valid marriage. Tancred reported an argument that held that the Church could dissolve a valid marriage if a grave impediment arose after the exchange of consent.[219] But popes were reluctant to use this power, even if they had it—a reluctance that accounts in part for their disinclination to hold clandestine marriages null.[220]

Civilians and canonists both knew that Roman law allowed civil authorities,

---

[216] For actual cases see Vitalis c. Guida in Dolezalek, *Imbreviaturbuch*, no. 9, pp. 96–97 (1230), and Ferraria c. Arnaldo (1225), "Dos causas de divorcio en el siglo XIII," in *Miscellanea Mons. José Rius Serra*, 2 vols. (San Cugat del Valles: Instituto internacional de cultura romanica, 1964) 2:701–703.

[217] Placentinus, *Summa* to Cod. 5.26, 1536 ed., p. 218; Accursius, *Glos. ord.* to Dig. 25.7.1 v. *stuprum non committitur.* Some canonists observed that marriages across social boundaries were less scandalous than consanguineous unions; *Quaestiones dominorum Bononiensium* 147, ed. Palmiero 1:239–40.

[218] Ferran Soldevila, *Els primers temps de Jaume I*, Institut d'estudis catalans, Memòries de la secció histórico-arqueològica, vol. 27 (Barcelona: Institut d'estudis catalans, 1968), pp. 298–300. On the complex marital and amorous career of James I see generally Robert I. Burns, "The Spiritual Life of James the Conqueror, King of Arago-Catalonia, 1208–1276: Portrait and Self-Portrait," *Catholic Historical Review* 62 (1976) 1–35.

[219] Tancred to 1 Comp. 4.2.9 v. *iudicio*, Caius 28/17, p. 92b: "Ar. sponsalia per iudicium ecclesie dissolui debere quia matrimonium est et eo usque tenet quousque ea dissoluerit ecclesia, nisi forcius impedimentum superuenerit, ut est matrimonium et sollempne uotum, tunc enim ipso iure dissoluitur. R⟨ichardus⟩."

[220] 2 Comp. 4.10.1; JL 16,639; Pfaff, "Kirchliche Eherecht," pp. 91–92.

or even the parties themselves, to dissolve marriages on a variety of grounds, or on none at all.[221] They also knew that Mosaic law allowed the dissolution of marriages.[222] Whether this could be done under the Christian dispensation was another question. The author of the *Glossa Palatina* (probably Laurentius Hispanus),[223] acknowledged that the Mosaic law permitted divorce and remarriage because of adultery, but declared that canon law no longer allowed this.[224] It was easy enough to distinguish the dissolution of marriage from repudiation of a betrothal; the latter was perfectly legal and could be done by mutual consent of the parties and their families.[225] But terminating a marriage was more complicated.

Divortium in canonistic language meant either a declaration of nullity (that a valid marriage had never existed) or else permission for a married couple to separate and establish independent households, but not to remarry. Both of these actions could also be differentiated from dissolving a valid marriage, and the Church's power to do both was not in question. Nonetheless, the law on marital separation was also in flux, since the circumstances that justified separation were by no means universally agreed. Bernard of Pavia, for example, held that the Church should authorize separation only if one party committed adultery.[226] Others believed that the Church had broader discretion to grant separations: *Argumentum quod religiosi*, for example, maintained that a married person could rightfully seek a separation for any major failing on the spouse's part. Most writers were unwilling to stretch the law this far.[227]

---

[221] Accursius, *Glos. ord.* to Dig. 24.2 rubric; gloss to C. 33 q. 2 c. 2 v. *non prohibet*, in Pembroke 162, fol. 273r: "In Auth. licet matri uel auie § causas [Auth. 8.13 = Nov. 117.9]; lex humana admittet diuorcium propter multas alias causas."

[222] Gloss to C. 31 q. 1 d.p.c. 7, in Caius 283/676, fol. 189ra: "Johannes Crisostomus super hoc locum Matthei [*In Matt. homil.* 17.4, in PG 57:259]: 'Qui uoluit dimitere uxorem, det libellum repudii et dimittat eam,' [cf. Matt. 5:31; 19:7] exponens ait: 'Moyses permisit eis dare libellum repudii ne sanguinus fundaretur innoxius'; permisit minora ne fient grauiora."

[223] Alfons M. Stickler, "Il decretista Laurentius Hispanus," *Studia Gratiana* 9 (1966) 463–549.

[224] *Glossa Palatina* to C. 31 q. 1 c. 9 pr., Trinity O.10.2, fol. 54vb: "Casus in ueterem testamentum facta fuit a moyse permissio dandi repudii et aliam ducendi uiuente prima. In nouo uero testamento fuit ab apostolo alia permissio de ducenda uxore, 'habeat unusquisque suam propter fornicationem' [cf. 1 Cor. 7:2]; in hoc ergo capitulum crisostomus comparat istas duos permissiones inter se, Mosaycum et apostolicum, et ostendit eos similes esse et dissimiles; et hec sunt similes quia uterque permittit minus malum ut maius uitetur; mosayca adulterium ut uitetur homicidium, apostolica coitum ut uitetur fornicatio." Cf. Benencasa, *Casus* to the same passage.

[225] Gloss to C. 32 q. 7 c. 1 v. *repudium*, in Pembroke 162, fol. 270vb: "Id est diuortium, nam repudium proprie est inter sponsos, ut ff. de adulteriis, rite nuptiarum § 2 [Dig. 24.2.2.2?]."

[226] Bernard of Pavia, *Summa decretalium* 4.20.1, ed. Laspeyres, p. 187.

[227] *Argumentum quod religiosi* to C. 28 q. 1, Pembroke 101, fol. 60rb: "Ar. quod pro

Canonists commonly maintained in this period that separation, but not re-marriage, might be authorized because of physical or spiritual infidelity by the spouse.[228] Yet the law did not require a husband to leave his wife because of her extramarital affairs.[229] And under some circumstances, as Bernard of Pavia re-minded his readers, husbands were forbidden to separate from their adulterous spouses—if, for example, a husband had forced his wife into prostitution, or if he himself had been guilty of extramarital sexual adventures.[230]

There was general agreement that separation, with or without remarriage, required a formal judgment from an ecclesiastical court.[231] Informal separation by mutual consent was not acceptable, and Laurentius declared that the law presumed those separations lacked reasonable grounds.[232] Thomas of Chobham,

---

qualibet mortali culpa potest uir uxorem dimittere et e contrario si ad hoc eum com-pellat, ut c. uxor [C. 32 q. 7 c. 17] et c. ydolatria [C. 27 q. 1 c. 5]."

[228] Gloss to C. 28 q. 1 c. 4, Caius 283/676, fol. 183rb: "Gan⟨dulphus⟩ . . . dicit quod non solum pro infidelitate sed etiam pro qualibet spirituali fornicatione ad quam uxor trahit uirum, uxor potest a uiro dimitti." Also ibid. to C. 28 q. 1 c. 5, fol. 183va: "Uehe-menter uidetur Augustinus inclinare se ad illam opinionem ut pro qualibet fornicatione, siue corporali siue spirituali, que est mortale peccatum, libere possit uir uxorem dimit-tere, quod tamen tantum est peligro, ut est uideri supra in illa distinctione fornicatio [?]." Likewise *Ecce vicit leo* to C. 33 q. 1 pr. v. *fornicationis,* Trinity O.5.17, fol. 128vb: "Scilicet spiritualis uel carnalis," and Tancred to 1 Comp. 4.20.2 v. *Quesiuit,* Caius 28/17, p. 106a, Admont 22, fol. 66r: "Ad intelligenciam huius capituli et similium nota quod . . . istud matrimonium quod est ratum nunquam soluitur post carnalem copulam; tamen maritus potest dimittere uxorem et uxor uirum pro sola fornicatione tam carnali quam spirituali . . . ita quod aliud non ducat. . . . t⟨ancredus⟩." Cf. Engdahl, "English Marriage Law," pp. 116–17.

[229] *Argumentum quod religiosi* to C. 33 q. 1, Pembroke 101, fol. 60rb: "Ar. quod non tenetur quis causa fornicationis dimittere uxorem nisi noluerit, ut c. ydolatria [C. 33 q. 1 c. 5], uerbo permisit, non iussit. Ar. contra causa xxxii. c. ii. [sic]." *Prima primi* to C. 27 pr., B.L. Royal 11.D.II, fol. 331ra: "Item propter fornicationem potest dimittere uel reconciliare secundum Apostolum, ut 31 q. 7 apostolus [c. 3]."

[230] Bernard of Pavia, *Summa decretalium* 4.20.3, ed. Laspeyres, pp. 188–89; Ray-mond of Peñafort, *Summa de mat.* 22.3, ed. Ochoa and Diez, col. 987–88.

[231] Johannes Teutonicus, *Glos. ord.* to C. 33 q. 2 c. 2 v. *comperimus.* But cf. *Ecce vicit leo* to C. 32 q. 7 c. 18, Trinity O.5.17, fol. 128rb: "Argumentum quod statim probata adulterio uir possit dimittere uxorem, nec teneatur reddere dicte uxori dimisse propter fornicationem."

[232] Tancred to 1 Comp. 2.20.21 v. *rationabili,* Caius 28/17, p. 46a: "Id est semper pre-sumitur sine causa rationabili dimittere nisi eam dimittat iudicio ecclesie, ut xxxv. q. ii. seculares [C. 33 q. 2 c. 1], xxxv. q. vi. multorum [c. 10]; etiam si manifestum sit impedi-mentum inter eos, ut infra de diuor., porro l.e. [1 Comp. 4.20.3 = X 4.19.3]. la⟨uren-tius⟩." This was especially true for couples joined in informal clandestine marriages; *Ar-gumentum quod religiosi* to C. 34 q. 1, Pembroke 101, fol. 61ra: "Ar. quod non potest contrahere matrimonium qui uel de facto ⟨uel de iure⟩ habet uxorem nisi prius coram ecclesia fuerit separatus, ut c. cum in captiuitate [C. 34 q. 1 c. 2], et in causa pariter q. v. multorum [C. 35 q. 6 c. 10?]."

writing about 1216, also warned couples against attempts to hoodwink the Church's courts in separation cases and discussed two examples that he apparently drew from actual situations.[233]

Separation, even when sanctioned by the courts, did not terminate marriage, but simply relieved the parties of their obligation to live together and cancelled their right to the marital debt. If the separated couple reconciled, however, marital rights, including sexual ones, were fully restored.[234]

A priori separated persons were not allowed to remarry—although Johannes Teutonicus hinted that in exceptional circumstances even this might be permitted.[235] Parties whose petition for separation was still in litigation were of course barred from remarriage.[236] A series of rulings by Alexander III, Clement III, and Innocent III established guidelines for dealing with marriages contracted while one party was still bound to a previous spouse.[237] A man who separated from his wife was better advised, some writers said, to remarry bigamously than to commit fornication.[238] But after Clement III ruled that a separated wife could reinstate her marriage if her husband committed fornication after their separation, this seemed rather dubious advice.[239]

The change in the rules about the forbidden degrees of kinship adopted by the Fourth Lateran Council brought the law on that subject into line with matrimonial practice.[240] Reducing the radius of the circle of relationship within which marriage was barred meant that after 1215 fewer unions were open to attack on grounds of consanguinity or affinity. While academic canonists continued to treat this complex area of the law in considerable detail, petitions for nullity declarations on these grounds appear only infrequently in the scanty records of marriage litigation that survive from this period.[241] Affinity cases also

[233] Thomas of Chobham, *Summa* 7.2.14.4, ed. Broomfield, pp. 373–74.

[234] *Argumentum quod religiosi* to C. 27 q. 2, Pembroke 101, fol. 60ra: "Ar. quod per reconciliationem coniugii redditur fornicanti potestas in corpore alterius, ut c. scripsit [C. 27 q. 2 c. 26]. Alioquin teberga sine uoluntate lotharii conuerti posset."

[235] *Glos. ord.* to C. 32 q. 7 c. 18 v. *nubat*; see also Benencasa, *Casus* to C. 32 q. 7 c. 28; and gloss to C. 28 q. 2 c. 2, Caius 283/676, fol. 185ra: "Uidetur ergo quod uxor relinquens maritum ob contumeliam cum autem remanent ligati lege matrimonii et ius matrimonii stabit ex altera parte tantum, quod quidam concedunt, ar. 29 q. 2 si quis ⟨liber⟩ [*MS* igitur; c. 29 q. 2 c. 2]; ar. 32 q. 2 aliquando [c. 7]."

[236] X 4.4.4; JL 13,969; WH 1033a.

[237] X 4.7.1 (JL 12,636), 4.7.3 (JL 13,773), 4.7.4 (JL 16,602), 4.7.5 (JL 17,678), 4.7.6 (Po 106).

[238] Gloss to C. 32 q. 7 c. 2 v. *licite*, Caius 283/676, fol. 194vb: "Ar. magis peccat qui uxore dimissa causa fornicationis fornicatur cum alia quam si aliam de facto duxisset; supra 28 presbyter [D. 28 c. 9]; ar. immo potius contrarium uidetur B. li. 2 presbyter si uxorem [?]."

[239] X 4.19.5 (JL 16,645, wrongly ascribed to Alexander III).

[240] Duby, *Medieval Marriage*, pp. 80–81.

[241] *Select Cases* A.8, ed. Adams and Donahue, pp. 29–30 (ca. 1200); Fransen, "Questiones des canonistes (II)," no. 3.40 and 3.47, pp. 488, 490; also ibid., pt. 3, no. 23, p. 523.

dwindled as the result of the growing disenchantment of canonists with supervening affinity and their inclination to interpret strictly the law on this matter.[242]

The greater emphasis on consent in matrimonial law after Alexander III meant that nullity cases increasingly centered on defects of consent resulting from force and fear, or because one party was under the minimum age for marriage, or as a result of incapacity to consent because of a previous valid marriage or religious vows.[243]

Early thirteenth-century canonists paid special attention to the complications that arose when a spouse disappeared without a trace, as often happened in war. Roman law had automatically terminated the marriages of prisoners of war and men missing in action, but the canonists rejected this rule.[244] Alexander III had established a ten-year waiting period before remarriage,[245] but Lucius III ruled that the death of the first husband must be clearly demonstrated before his widow could remarry. If the missing man reappeared, his marriage remained in force and his wife, even if she had remarried, must return to him.[246] Pope Celestine III shortened the waiting period to seven years. If the missing husband failed to return within that time, his wife might remarry. If her first husband reappeared later, and if the first marriage had been consummated, she must go back to him. If the first marriage was unconsummated, however, she could remain with her new husband.[247] Vincentius Hispanus maintained that *Ad liberandum*, the crusading canon of the Fourth Lateran Council, required persuasive proof of the missing man's death before remarriage, but his inter-

---

[242] Tancred to 3 Comp. 4.9.3 v. *separatis*, Caius 28/17, p. 288b, and Vat. lat 1377, fol 254v: "Nota quod affinitas superueniens sponsalibus rumpit ea, supra de eo qui cog. consan. uxo. suo, ueniens l. i [1Comp. 4.13.3]. Sed non est ita si superueniat in matrimonio, supra eodem titulo c. i l. i [1 Comp. 4.13.1]; supra xxxiiii. q. ult., in lectum [C. 34 q. 1 & 2 c. 6]. Vin⟨centius⟩."

[243] *Select Cases* A.1, ed. Adams and Donahue, pp. 1–3 (1198 ~ 1204); Dolezalek, *Imbreviaturbuch*, no. 45, 47, 51, pp. 132–34, 136–37.

[244] Albertus to 2 Comp. 4.1.3, B.N. lat. 3932, fol. 93rb: "ff. de diuor., uxores [Dig. 24.2.6] contra, ubi dicitur quod cum incertum est uirum captum uiuere, post quinquennium expectetur. Solutio: illud secundum leges antiquos, sed authenticum C. de repudi., aut hodie [Cod. Auth. 5.17.9] et secundum canones per quos hodie reguntur matrimonium tenet, quod hic dictum, ii. q. iii. § hinc colligitur [C. 2 q. 3 d.p.c. 7]; extra⟨uagantes⟩ titulos de secundis nuptiis [1 Comp. 4.22; 2 Comp. 4.15]; xxxiiii. q. ii. cum per bellicum [C. 34 q. 1 & 2 c. 1]. Sponsa uero triennio expectat sponsum, C. de repu. l. ii. [Cod. 5.17.2], et hoc cum sola uoluntate absens est; si uero iusta causa, quamdiu causa illa durat, ff. de sponsa., sepe [Dig. 23.1.17], nisi per absentem ante recessum steterit, ar. 8. de spon. de ill. au. et i. [?]" In addition see above, pp. 201.

[245] Holtzmann, *Decretales ineditae*, p. 55, no. 32; also followed by Celestine III; Walther Holtzmann, "La 'Collectio Seguntina' et les décrétales de Clément III et de Célestin III," *Revue d'histoire ecclésiastique* 50 (1955) 438, no. 68(c).

[246] 1 Comp. 4.22.3 = X 4.21.2, JL 15,211.

[247] Holtzmann, "Collectio Seguntina," RHE 50 (1955) 438, no. 60; see generally, Pfaff, "Kirchliche Eherecht," p. 93.

pretation strained the words of the canon, which did not specify the degree of certainty.[248] Laurentius Hispanus believed that the putative widow must actively inquire about her missing husband. If her investigation produced no evidence of his fate, Laurentius held that the wife could remarry.[249]

Separation of married couples in order to enter religion also troubled canonists and legislators. While no one denied a couple's right to take this step, popes during the late twelfth and early thirteenth centuries limited the practice stringently—as the twenty-one decretals on this subject in the title *De conversione coniugatorum* of the *Liber Extra* attest.[250] While the canonists insisted that couples who wished to separate in order to enter religion must do so before consummating their marriage,[251] the decretals themselves show that popes sometimes allowed separation after consummation.[252] Repeated insistence that both parties must enter religious communities and that neither of them could remain in the world, probably indicates that this condition, too, was breached with some frequency.[253] Thomas of Chobham cautioned women to be wary of priests and monks who tried to persuade their husbands to assume the religious habit on their deathbeds. The wife who allowed this, he warned,

[248] Vincentius to 4 Lat. c. 71 v. *certissime cognoscatur*, ed. García y García, p. 383.

[249] Tancred to 1 Comp. 4.22.3 v. *uita*, Caius 28/17, p. 107b, Admont 22, fol. 67r: "Tunc enim constat ei de morte uiri ex quo per quinquennium expectauit, ut ff. de diuor, uxores [Dig. 24.2.6]. Sed contra C. de repudi. aut. hodie [Auth. Cod. 5.17.7] et infra de spon., in presencia [2 Comp. 4.1.3]. Sed quid faciet si nec per magistrum militum ut ibidem dicitur certificari poterit de morte uiri, sicut sepe accidit in magnis preliis et precipue sarracenorum et christianorum, ubi multi pereunt, de quibus nichil nouerunt hii qui ducebant exercitum? Mittat ad uicinas ciuitates si potest; alias contrahat. la⟨urentius⟩."

[250] The authors of the decretals in X 3.32 are:

Pope	Chapters	Number	Percent
Alexander III	1–8	8	38.1
Urban III	9	1	4.8
Clement III	10	1	4.8
Celestine III	11–12	2	9.5
Innocent III	13–18	6	28.5
Gregory IX	19–20*bis*	3	14.3

[251] Raymond of Peñafort, *Summa de pen.* 1.8.8, ed. Ochoa and Diez, col. 350–51; Thomas of Chobham, *Summa* 7.2.14.1, ed. Broomfield, p. 371; *Ecce vicit leo* to C. 27 q. 2 d.p.c. 1, Salamanca 2491, fol. 132ra: "Non potest sponsa recedere ante carnalem copulam nisi in unico casu, scilicet causa religionis."

[252] E.g., X 3.32.3, 5, 11, 13, 17. See also the case of an English priest who entered the Templar order together with his wife; *Records of the Templars in England in the Twelfth Century: The Inquest of 1185 with Illustrative Charters and Documents*, ed. B. A. Lees, Records of the Social and Economic History of England and Wales, vol. 9 (London: British Academy, 1935), p. 38; Peter Partner, *The Murdered Magicians: The Templars and Their Myth* (Oxford: Oxford University Press, 1982), p. 12.

[253] X 3.32.16.

would find herself obliged to practice perpetual continence after her husband's death, a consequence that clerical recruiters might not make clear.[254]

IMPOTENCE AND FRIGIDITY

The canonists were fascinated by the legal problems that sexual incapacity created. So, too, were the artists who illuminated canonistic texts (see Pl. 14). This topic raised basic questions both about the role of sexual relations in marriage and also about the scope of papal authority over marriage. One issue concerned the pope's power to dissolve unconsummated unions and the basis of that power. Earlier Bolognese decretists, as we have seen, considered the proposition that the pope could dissolve an unconsummated marriage almost self evident, since according to Gratian such a marriage is imperfect and incomplete. Once Alexander III had rested matrimonial validity squarely on consent, however, the legal significance of inability to consummate a marriage became problematical. Accordingly canonists between 1190 and 1234 were wary of ascribing to the pope a power to end unconsummated unions. Several writers, among them Laurentius Hispanus and Tancred, denied that the pontiff had any such power and maintained that decretals claiming to exercise this right were in error.[255] Alanus and Tancred were equally skeptical about terminating marriages because of senile impotence. They argued that elderly men who could not consummate their marriages remained validly married nonetheless. Tancred also observed that senile impotence might well prove intermittent and able to be cured by proper diet and medication.[256] Tancred held that vaginal constriction, however, furnished adequate grounds for declaring a marriage null. If the condition later disappeared, moreover, the prior marriage need not be reinstated.[257]

Other writers saw things differently. Alanus maintained that the pope had absolute power to dissolve unconsummated marriages because the binding power of these unions rested on the constitution of the Church, not on divine

---

[254] Thomas of Chobham, *Summa* 7.2.14.3, ed. Broomfield, p. 373.

[255] Tancred to 2 Comp. 3.20.2 v. *contumelia* and Laurentius to the same passage, v. *et liber aditus*, both in Weigand, "Unauflösigkeit," pp. 58–59.

[256] Tancred to 1 Comp. 4.16.3 v. *impotentes*, Caius 28/17, p. 101b, Admont 22, fol. 63v: "Hac ratione perpensa uidetur quod senex quem etatis frigiditas minus ydoneum fecit, contrahere non possit cum tamen secus sit C. de nupt., sancimus [Cod. 5.4.27], xxxi. q. i. aperiant, quod si dormierit [C. 31 q. 1 c. 11, 13]. ala⟨nus⟩. Sed tu dic impotentes perpetuo impedimento quoniam licet senex sit naturali calore derelictus, beneficio tamen diete uel alicuius medicine aliquando ad coitum moueretur. t⟨ancredus⟩."

[257] Tancred to 3 Comp. 4.11 un. v. *cuius simili*, Caius 28/17, p. 290a: "Sic xxxiii. q. i. requisisti, et inuenitur hic et in fine huius capituli [3 Comp. 4.11.1 in fin.] quod si prior uir non posset eam cognoscere sine incommoditate, quia forte homo est magne carnis, quod non sit reddenda primo uiro licet ex post facto per consuetudinem secundi uiri iam possit a primo uiro cognosci, quod uincentius et johannes concedunt, quia non fuit matrimonium inter eam et primum uirum. t⟨ancredus⟩."

or natural law. Hence the pope's power to dissolve these marriages was not constrained by higher authority.[258] John of Tynemouth simply declared that natural frigidity rendered a marriage dissoluble, as did emasculation; however he proposed no theory to account for his conclusion.[259] Richardus Anglicus presented an elaborate analysis of various types of impotence and concluded that sexual incapacity nullified marriage only if the condition was permanent and preceded the exchange of consent. Like John of Tynemouth, however, Richardus advanced no theory to account for the Church's power to dissolve these unions.[260] Johannes Teutonicus adopted much of Richardus's analysis and noted that opinions differed as to whether a marriage could be dissolved on these grounds. He believed that this was permissible, and that the parties could remarry, although he considered it better if they did not.[261]

Writers who held that impotence justified dissolving marriages usually cautioned their readers to be careful with these cases, since divorcing one wife often seemed to restore a man's sexual capacity, whereupon he married again. When a divorce was granted on grounds of sexual incapacity, therefore, the Caius glosses maintained that the judge should deny the man permission to take another wife.[262] The Caius glosses also recognized, however, that men

[258] Weigand, "Unauflösigkeit," pp. 54–55, 62.

[259] Gloss to C. 32 q. 7 c. 27, Caius 283/676, fol. 195vb: "In hoc articulo Jo⟨annes de⟩ Ti⟨nmuth⟩ fauet sententie Jo⟨annis⟩ Fau⟨entini⟩ et hic habet rationem. Cum enim frigiditas que est impossibilitas de iure, tale dissoluat matrimonium, multo forcius truncatio membrorum quod est impossibilitas de facto."

[260] In his *Distinctiones decretorum* to C. 33 q. 1 pr. (B.L. Royal 10.C.III, fol. 39v), Richardus Anglicus distinguishes three fundamental types of 'impossibilitas coeundi': (1) 'animo et corpore', (2) 'anime tantum', and (3) 'corpore tantum'. The first type of impotence, he writes, 'prouenit ratione etatis, ut in pueris; hec dirimit contractum, ut xxx. q. iiii. his qui neque [?]'. The second type occurs 'ut in furiosis et energumenis; hic dirimit contractum, supra prox.' Richardus subdivides the third type into two categories: 'accidentalis' and 'naturalis'. He disposes briefly of natural (i.e., congenital) bodily impotence, observing 'Hec impedit et dirimit matrimonium, ut hic c. i, ii.' He subdivides accidental bodily impotence into two sub-categories, 'ex sectione' and 'ex maleficio'. Under the sub-category 'ex sectione' Richardus distinguishes between cutting which preceded marriage and cutting subsequent to marriage and comments: 'Si precedit, impedit et dirimit matrimonium, Extra de frig. Quod sedem in fin. [1 Comp. 4.16.3]. Si sequitur, non dirimit, ut supra prox Q. vii. ille qui [C. 32 q. 7 c. 7]'. As for accidental bodily impotence that results 'ex maleficio', Richardus again distinguishes between situations in which the condition commenced before marriage and those in which the condition began after marriage. Accidental bodily impotence 'ex maleficio' that preceeded marriage, he says, is either temporary or permanent: 'Si temporale est, non dirimit, i.e. Si per sortiarias [C. 33 q. 1 c. 4]. Si perpetua est, nihil agitur.' But if accidental bodily impotence 'ex maleficio' followed marriage, then 'non fiet diuortium'.

[261] *Glos. ord.* to C. 32 q. 7 c. 25 v. *ex secti*; C. 33 q. 1 pr. v. *quod autem*; and C. 33 q. 1 c. 2 v. *naturaliter*.

[262] Gloss to C. 33 q. 1 pr., Caius 283/676, fol. 196rb: "Queritur si uiro ob frigiditate ab uxore sua separato uxor alii nupserit, et uiro postea restituatur facilitas coeundi, quid fiet, quia eius iuramento iterum non creditur, sed nec licentiam dabit ei ecclesia aliam

might be impotent only with one particular woman, but might be perfectly capable of coitus with others. This is the result of sorcery, not congenital impotence, he declared, and remarriage could be authorized because the man would be able to consummate his marriage to another woman.[263]

Tancred discussed with evident relish the case of a woman whose first marriage was dissolved on the grounds that she could not consummate it. She then remarried and had sex successfully with her second husband. Should she return to her first husband so that he could try once more to consummate their marriage? Tancred believed that she should, but added that if the attempt were unsuccessful she ought to go back to her second husband. But how many times could this process be repeated? Tancred thought that the first husband should be limited to three attempts to consummate the marriage with his ex-wife. Johannes Teutonicus, however, argued against setting any limit at all and was prepared to see the wife shuttle back and forth between her first and second husbands in perpetuity.[264]

----

ducere." Damasus, *Questiones*, Vat. Borgh. lat. 261, fol. 61ra, found it difficult to give a flat answer: "Solutio: quidam dicunt perpetuum, alii quod non sit perpetuum, et dicunt illud c. si per sorciarias [C. 33 q. 1 c. 4] non tenere."

[263] Gloss to C. 33 q. 1 c. 4 v. *prioribus*, Caius 283/676, fol. 196va: "Solutio: Manifesta est diuersitas frigiditatis et maleficii, quia qui naturaliter frigidus est nec suam nec aliam numquam cognoscere potest. Unde si sua dimissa ob hanc causam, aliam ducit postea presumitur a canone quod suam sicut aliam posset cognoscere et immo quasi ecclesia circumuenta ad suam cogitur redire. Maleficium autem quandoque id efficit ut tantum unam quis nullo modo unquam possit cognoscere, alias autem bene, uel aliter." Damasus, *Questiones*, Vat. Borgh. lat. 261, fol. 61ra-rb, agreed.

[264] Tancred to 1 Comp. 4.16.4 v. *habitare*, Caius 28/17, p. 102a, Admont 22, fol. 63v: "Queritur de hoc capitulo quomodo stare possit ex quo eam cognoscere non potest. Respondeo secundum illos qui dicunt quod nullum maleficium impedit uel dirimit planum est, et abrogatum est illud capitulum, xxxiii. q. i. si per sorciarias [c. 4]. Secundum alios dicendum est quod impedimentum istud secutum est matrimonium, non precessit, et illud 'si per sorciarias' intelligitur quando precessit. Nostra tamen est opinio quod omne perpetuum maleficium impedit matrimonium ipso iure, non autem ex constitutione ecclesie; secus si ad tempus: tunc enim non separentur, Hug⟨uccio⟩. Et nota quod aliud est in frigido, aliud in maleficiato. Si enim aliquis est frigidus ad unam, est frigidus ad omnes; unde si dicat se frigidum et separetur et postea habeat accessum ad aliam, reducitur ad primam, xxxiii. q. i. requisisti [c. 2]. Sed maleficiatus ad unam, aliam cognoscere [MS C: non] potest, unde si separetur ab una licet aliam cognoscat non cogitur redire ad illam, ut in illo capitulo 'si per sorciarias' [C. 33 q. 1 c. 4]. Item nota quod omne maleficium a principio presumitur temporale, sed post triennium presumitur perpetuum, et precesisse matrimonium, ar. aut. de nupt., § qui per occasionem [Auth. 4.1.6 = Nov. 22.6], infra eodem laudabilem [2 Comp. 4.9.3]. Vinc⟨entius⟩." Also, Tancred to 3 Comp. 4.11. un. v. *perpetuum*, Caius 28/17, p. 290a: "Ego dico aliquando maleficium esse perpetuum et insanabilem, nam ex quo cohabitauerit uiro spacio trium annorum et dedit operam copule carnali studiose, si non poterunt commisceri presumitur impedimentum esse perpetuum et postea possunt separari, ut supra eodem titulo laudabilem l. ii. [2 Comp. 4.9.3], et in authenticum de nuptiis § per occasionem

MIXED MARRIAGES

The Anglo-Norman canonists advanced some interesting speculations about marriages between Christians and non-Christians. John of Tynemouth dealt with the problem of a pagan wife who deserted her Christian husband because of religious antagonism, but who subsequently converted to Christianity herself. Could she then demand reinstatement of the marriage that she had been instrumental in breaking off? Huguccio discussed this situation and concluded that she could do so. John disagreed; he argued by analogy that since a woman dismissed by her husband for adultery had no right to reinstate her prior marriage, even after she had done penance, the desertion of a Christian husband by a non-Christian wife must also shatter the nuptial bond.[265] The Caius glosses quoted an unnamed Anglo-Norman commentator who held that baptism itself broke the marriage bond, although the bond could be mended, as it were, if the convert had intercourse with the non-Christian spouse after baptism.[266]

[Auth. 4.1.6 = Nov. 22.6], et potest utroque eorum nubere alteri, ut xxxiii. q. i. si per sorciarias [c. 4], quia potest esse aliquis maleficiatus cum una muliere et non cum alia, sicut tales quando⟨que⟩ uidi et hoc est uerum quando impedimentum illud precessit matrimonium. Si uero post contractum matrimonium superueniat maleficium uel aliquid aliud impedimentum, non debet separari matrimonium prius contractum, ut supra xxxiii. di. illi qui sani [?]. t⟨ancredus⟩." Further, Tancred to 3 Comp. 4.11. un. v. *pretextu fornicationis*, Caius 28/17, p. 290a, and Vat. lat. 1377, fol. 255v: "Ad hoc dicas quod sicut ex sequenti euento apparet matrimonium, ut dicitur in fine, sic ex sequenti euentu apparet retro fuisse factam iniuriam priori uiro, sic ff. de capti. et postlimi. reuersis, in bello § 1 [Dig. 49.15.12.1] et ff. ad macedoni. l. i. [Dig. 14.6.1]. Sed quid si post primum coitum cum secundo reserate sunt sere mulieris, prior ceperit eam et dicat se nolle separari cum adhuc sit apta amplexibus suis? Dico quod ei est reddenda et si non inuenit eam aptam, est secundo uiro reddenda; et post iterum in secundo coitu repetit eam prior ut experiatur an sit apta ei, et si non sit ei apta, iterum restituatur secundo et sic in infinitum. Jo⟨hannes⟩. Ego dico hanc infinitatem uitandam, ut ff. de contrahen. empt., rutilia polla [Dig. 18.1.69]. Undo dico eam restituendam priori uiro ad plus tribus uicibus, quia tantum due sententie post primam sunt ferende, quia non licet tertio appellare, ut ii. q. vi. Si quis in quacumque [c. 41?]. t⟨ancredus⟩." Cf. also Bernard of Parma, *Glos. ord.* to X 4.15.6 v. *fornicario modo*.

[265] Gloss to C. 28 q. 2 c. 2, Caius 283/676, fol. 185ra: "Queritur utrum si mulier que relinquit uirum suum ob odium fidei christiane, postea post annum uel plus uel minus conuertatur ad fidem possit petere uirum suum? Hug⟨uccio⟩ dicit etiam, ar. ff. de re. uen. quando., Celsus [Dig. 18.5.1] et 61 secundum his omnibus [?] in fi. Secundum Jo⟨hannem de⟩ ti⟨nemuth⟩ petere non potest quia maritus uxorem propter adulterium dimissam, peracta penitentia, repetere non potest, ar. 27 q. 2 agathosa [c. 21] et preterea ruptum fuit uinculum matrimonii inter eos."

[266] Gloss to C. 28 q. 1 c. 9, Caius 283/676, fol. 184rb: "In arbitrio uiri fidelis est ⟨cum⟩ uxore infideli cohabitare, ⟨seu⟩ dimittere uel non. Si dimittit, non tenetur ei coitus reddere; num ergo in eius arbitrio est utrum uinculum mutue seruitutis rumpitur an non? Respondeo, non est in eius uoluntate utrum obligetur an non, C. de contrah. empt., in uendentis, etc. [Cod. 4.38.13], quia uinculum istud rumpitur in instanti quo ille bap-

Innocent III dealt with the law on interfaith marriages in two important decretals. In *Quanto te* (1199), Innocent ruled that marriage between a Christian
convert and his infidel wife might be dissolved, but that if one party to a Christian marriage renounced Christianity, the marriage nonetheless remained in
force. This ruling, which contradicted a decretal of Celestine III, was apparently designed to prevent men who wished to rid themselves of their wives
from fraudulently simulating a reversion to paganism or a lapse into heresy in
order to accomplish their purpose.[267] Two years later in *Gaudemus* (1201), Innocent affirmed that non-Christian marriages were sacramental. He added that
infidels who married within the degrees of relationship forbidden by the Church
were not, on that account, to be separated from their wives—a clear contradiction of the position taken by the Caius gloss.[268] *Gaudemus* also required polygynous pagan men to become monogamous upon conversion. Previously divorced
and remarried converts were left free to choose which mate they preferred to
live with after baptism, a position at odds with the teaching of other contemporary writers.[269]

FORNICATION

It has been maintained that Western theologians did not clearly take the position that sexual relations between unmarried men and women constituted a
deadly sin until the late twelfth century.[270] If this is true, theologians lagged
well behind canonists in the development of their doctrine about nonmarital
sex. As we have already seen, Gratian and the early decretists made it clear that
any sort of extramarital use of the sex organs constituted a canonical offense.
The canonists of the late twelfth and early thirteenth centuries built upon that
premise.[271]

Johannes Teutonicus observed almost wistfully that nearly everyone com-

---

tizatur et illa non. Uidetur autem renodari et regenerari facere duobus modis, scilicet si
ille eam adhuc cohabitare uolentem uelit secum habere et eam cognoscat, sicut si uir
post compertum adulterium, si uir criminem sciens postea eam cognoscat, ipsa re-
cuperat quod amisit. . . ."

[267] X 4.19.7; Noonan, *Power to Dissolve*, pp. 345–46.

[268] X 4.19.8; cf. *Raymundiana seu documenta quae pertinent ad S. Raymundi de Pen-
naforti vitam et scripta*, no. 18, ed. F. Balme, C. Paban, and I. Collumb, 2 vols., Monumenta Ordinis Fratrum Praedicatorum Historica, vols. 4 and 6 (Rome: In domo Gener-
alitia; Stuttgart: Jos. Roth, 1898–1901) 2:32–33.

[269] See the remarks on Christian-Jewish marriages in Raymond of Peñafort, *Summa de
pen.* 1.4.8, ed. Ochoa and Diez, col. 316–17, and *Argumentum quod religiosi* to C. 33
q. 1, Pembroke 101, fol. 6orb: "Ar. quod fidelis uxorem potest dimittere iudeam, etiam
cohabitare uolentem, et aliam ducere illa uiuente, ut c. iudei [C. 27 q. 1 c. 10]."

[270] Dedek, "Premarital Sex," pp. 644–46.

[271] The Anglo-Norman gloss to C. 28 q. 1 pr. in Caius 283/676, fol. 183ra, furnishes an
elaborate analysis of the species of fornication, distinguishing between carnal and spiritual fornication, and then between numerous sub-types of each of these.

mits fornication, and people are more prone to this offense than to any other failing.[272] For this reason, Johannes continued, canon law punishes fornication less severely than other offenses.[273] Moralists, however, considered fornication a powerful subverter of Christian morality, and Thomas of Chobham termed it the master builder of the Devil's temple.[274]

Canonists and moral writers of this period often described sexual relations between two unmarried persons as "simple fornication"; they occasionally used "compound fornication" to designate intercourse between a married person and an unmarried partner.[275] Simple fornication, the canonists maintained, was a canonical crime, even though it was not an offense in civil law, but this distinction was not widely understood or accepted among the laity. The synod of Salisbury, for example, urged the clergy to drive home the message that fornication is a mortal sin and commanded them to repeat this teaching in confession and in sermons, particularly on solemn feast days. Priests who failed to do this might themselves be punished as fornicators.[276] Writers on penance often reiterated this message, since their readers routinely dealt with ill-informed penitents who refused to believe that so commonplace an activity could possibly be a serious sin.[277] Those who maintained that fornication is either a minor transgression or no sin at all, according to Thomas of Chobham, were guilty of a far graver sin than fornication itself.[278] Penance for fornication, Thomas added, should vary according to the circumstances—the confessor ought to take into account whether the offense was secret or notorious, continuous or intermittent, with one partner or with many.[279]

Circumstances, however, could sometimes make fornication no sin at all: a

---

[272] *Glos. ord.* to c. 15 q. 8 c. 1 v. *caetera* and to D. 2 de pen. c. 5 v. *ex qua minus.*

[273] *Glos. ord.* to C. 32 q. 4 c. 12 v. *edificet*; cf. the marginal gloss to Lev. 18:24 v. *his quibus*, Trinity B.1.31, fol. 105v: "Demones qui propter multitudinem dicuntur grege qui cum omni peccato gaudeant, precipue fornicatio et idolatria, quia in his et corpus et anima maculatur et totus homo qui traditur, sed uisitat deus terram, id est hominum genus."

[274] Thomas of Chobham, *Summa* 7.2.5.1, ed. Broomfield, p. 341.

[275] *Glos. ord.* to C. 32 q. 4 c. 4 v. *uxore*; gloss to C. 34 q. 1 & 2 d.p.c. 7, Pembroke 162, fol. 297v: "Simplex fornicatio consideratur inter personas que nullo maritali legis uinculo colligate sunt uel copulate."

[276] Statutes of Salisbury I (1217 X 1219) c. 35, in Powicke and Cheney, 1:72; *Argumentum quod religiosi* to C. 32 q. 4, in Pembroke 101, fol. 60vb: "Hic nota simplicem fornicationem esse canonicum crimen, id est per canones, non per leges crimen esse, ut c. Nemo [c. 4] in principio. Nota quoniam maius esse peccatum manifeste quam occulte peccare, ut c. eodem."

[277] Thomas of Chobham, *Summa* 7.2.5.2, ed. Broomfield, pp. 341–42; Raymond of Peñafort, *Summa de pen.* 3.34.22, ed. Ochoa and Diez, col. 817.

[278] Thomas of Chobham, *Summa* 7.2.5.3, ed. Broomfield, p. 344.

[279] Thomas of Chobham, *Summa* 7.2.5.4, ed. Broomfield, pp. 344–45; Johannes Teutonicus, *Glos. ord.* to C. 32 q. 7 d.p.c. 24 v. *inane*; gloss to C. 31 q. 1 c. 10 v. *unius*, Caius 283/676, fol. 189ra: "Ar. minus malum est cum una ter fornicari quam cum tribus ter."

man who mistakenly slept with a woman thinking that she was his wife, for example, was held blameless. Carlo di Tocco argued in addition that sexual relations with a concubine or a harlot did not qualify as fornication.[280] The Caius glosses also noted that a woman whose husband had deserted her did no wrong if she had sex with another man.[281]

Sexual relations, whether licit or illicit, meant that the partners became one flesh.[282] Hence some canonists concluded that all sexual relations, even if illegal, created affinity, although Johannes Teutonicus denied this.[283] The doctrine that fornication created affinity furnished the basis for rulings (such as Innocent III's decretal *Ex litteris*) that prohibited marriage between the fornicator and close relatives of his partner in crime.[284]

Innocent III also addressed the complications that resulted from fornication

---

[280] Gloss to C. 29 q. 2 c. 4 v. *scieverat*, Caius 283/676, fol. 186ra: "Queritur de talium coitu num fornicatus sit? Respondeo etiam quoad actum, non quoad reatum, 34 causa in lectum [C. 34 q. 1 & 2 c. 6." Carlo di Tocco, gloss to *Leg. Lomb.* 1.31.1 v. *si puella* and *de fornicatione*, fol. 83rb–va.

[281] Gloss to c. 27 q. 2 c. 21 v. *quodam*, Caius 283/676, fol. 181vb: "Bene dicit 'quodam', quia si post discessum uiri fornicata esset, non imputaretur ei ubi non posset uirum repetere, quia uir uideretur prestitisse causa eius delicti, infra eodem, Si tu abstines [C. 27 q. 2 c. 24], in extra de diuorcio propter adulterium, significasti, et capitula sequenti [1 Comp. 4.20.4–5]."

[282] Gloss to C. 32 q. 4 c. 12 v. *fornicator*, Caius 283/676, fol. 193ra: "Ar. fornicarium et fornicariam unam carnem effici, quod uerum est, sed aliter quam uirum et uxorem."

[283] *Glos. ord.* to C. 32 q. 4 c. 12 v. *erunt* and C. 35 q. 2 & 3 c. 8 v. *concubitu*; also gloss to C. 32 q. 4 c. 12 v. *carne una*, Caius 283/676, fol. 193ra: "Per coitum fornicarium contrahitur affinitas, sed non ualet quia hic 'in una carne' id est in unica carnis commixtione feda non est; contra 34 q. 3 De incestu [c. 8], Nec eam [c. 10]." *Glossa Palatina* to C. 35 q. 2 & 3 c. 11 v. *in naturalibus*: "Ar. affinitatem contrahi fornicario coitu sicut et legitime, ar. supra prox. c. nec eam [C. 34 q. 2 & 3 c. 10]." Tancred to 1 Comp. 4.5.1 pr., Caius 28/17, p. 101a: "Quod si ex fornicario coitu huius⟨modi⟩ proles sit suscepta, numquid idem est impedimentum? Notauit laurentius quod non est impedimentum. Ego contra per sequentem cap. et quia ita contrahitur affinitas per fornicarium coitum sicut per legitimum, extra iii. de eo qui cognouit consanguineam uxoris, discretionem [3 Comp. 4.9.1]. t⟨ancredus⟩." Tancred to 3 Comp. 4.9.1 v. *affinitas*, Caius 28/17, p. 288b, and Vat. lat. 1377, fol. 254v: "Hic reprobatur opinio illorum qui dicunt quod per fornicarium coitum non contrahitur affinitas, sic infra t. prox. tue fraternitas [3 Comp. 4.10.3 = X 4.13.10], ar. supra xxx(i)v. q. iii. nec eam [c. 10]; ar. contra ff. de gradibus, non facile § sciendum et § efficies [Dig. 38.10.4]. Sed est uerum per talem coitum affinitatem contrahi. t⟨ancredus⟩." But see Vincentius to 3 Comp. 4.9.1 v. *affinitas*, B.N. lat. 14,611, fol. 120rb: "Affinitas ergo per fornicarium coitum contrahitur, quod concedit Hug⟨uccio⟩, sed secundum hoc consanguinea matrimonium in secundo gradu non potest contrahere cum eo qui cognouit consanguineam meam, quod non credo." On the other hand, see *Glos. ord.* to C. 35 q. 1 pr.

[284] 3 Comp. 4.9.3 = X 4.13.8 (Po. 1942); also 1 Comp. 4.13.1 = X 4.13.1, from the *Decretum Vermeriense* c. 11 (758 ~ 768?), in MGH, Capitularia 1:41; Burchard, *Decretum* 19.5, in PL 140:966. Alexander III and Celestine III had previously dealt with some aspects of this situation.

by a betrothed person. In *Quemadmodum*, Innocent ruled that fornication by a betrothed man with a close relative of his fiancée prior to the time of their betrothal did not bar marriage between the two principals, but that the same offense committed after betrothal would do so.[285] *Quemadmodum* suggests that legislation on this point aimed to discourage intrafamilial sexual rivalries.

The major decretal collections of the period showed that many contemporaries found Gratian's treatment of fornication unsatisfactory. Bernard of Pavia not only devoted an entire title of his *Breviarium* to adultery and fornication, but he also drew five of the six chapters in that title from sources that had been available to Gratian.[286] Raymond of Peñafort incorporated all of the material in Bernard's title on fornication into the *Liber Extra*, although he assigned one of Bernard's chapters to a different title.[287]

Bernard of Pavia, like other canonists of his generation, equated fornication with the Roman delict of *stuprum*. The identification was only half-true—but this was not the first (and certainly not the last) time that historical half-truths, or even downright fables, furnished foundations for legal doctrines.[288] If *stu-*

[285] 3 Comp. 2.15.11 = X 2.24.25 (Po 3168); Tancred to 1 Comp. 4.1.9 v. *filios et filias*, Caius 28/17, p. 87b, Admont 22, fol. 54v: "Hic queritur de eo qui iurauit ducere unam de filiabus Lotharii et postmodum stuprauit unam ex eis; queritur an precise illam ducere teneatur, cum aliam ducere non possit? Ar. quod sic, ff. de contrahen. emp., si in emptione § si emptor [Dig. 18.1.34.3], ff. de solutio., stichum, an pamphilium [Dig. 46.3.95 pr.]; preterea ipse se coartauit, ff. si quis cau., l. iii [Dig. 2.11.3], xv. q. i. si quis insaniens [c. 12]; immo uidetur quod statim sit matrimonium, ex quo eam cognouit tanquam desponsatione precedente, ar. infra de eo qui duxit in matrimonium quam prius polluit, Significauit [1 Comp. 4.7.2 = X 4.7.2], s.e. de illis [1 Comp. 4.1.4 = X 4.1.5]; ar. contra ff. de ritu nup., generandi [Dig. 23.2.34] § si quis caut., sed et si quis rei [Dig. 2.11.4], ff. de usur., quociens [Dig. 22.1?] ar. contra. Solutio: Dicunt quidam eum non compellendum quia inuite nup., etc.; xxxi. q. ii. § i et c. i; ego contra, quia ut fiat uolens compelletur, ar. i. de eo qui duxit in matrimonium quam prius polluit [1 Comp. 4.7], causa xxiii q. vi. uides [c. 3]. lau⟨rentius⟩."

[286] 1 Comp. 5.13. It contains:

Chapter	Incipit	Source
c. 1	Si seduxerit	Exod. 22:16–17
c. 2	Peruenit ad nos	Gregory I, *Reg.* 3.42, JE 1246
c. 3	Si uir sciens	Hermas, *Pastor*, Mand. 4.1.4–5
c. 4	Perniciosa	Synod of Rome (898) c. 12
c. 5	Maritis etiam	Cod. Theod. 9.7.2 interp.
c. 6	Significasti nobis	Alexander III, JL 12,183

[287] 1 Comp. 5.13.1–3 = X 5.16.1–3; 5.13.4 = X 1.31.1; 5.13.5–6 = X 5.16.4–5.

[288] For a striking instance in the field of matrimonial law see Regina v. Millis, [1843] 10 Clark and Finelley 534 at 655, 720, 8 English Reports 844 at 889, 913, where the House of Lords held that the presence of an ordained clergyman has been necessary for the formation of a valid marriage in England according to both common law and ecclesiastical law since the earliest times. This remarkable conclusion was affirmed in Beamish v. Beamish [1861], 9 House of Lords Cases 274 at 336, 11 Eng. Rep. 735 at 760. Another egregious example is the finding in the court of King's Bench on 10 May 1727

prum meant any sexual congress between unmarried persons, then it was possible to maintain that fornication had from time out of mind been contrary both to civil law and to the law of the Church.[289]

The law, according to Richardus Anglicus, imposed excommunication on fornicators in order to persuade the peccant parties to marry one another.[290] If they would not, or could not, marry, they must renounce further relations with one another and do penance for their misdeeds. If one party agreed to reform and the other refused, the repentant one was required to denounce his partner as part of his own rehabilitation.[291] Those whose sexual failings were public knowledge might be pressured through other sanctions to mend their wicked ways. Notorious fornicators were barred from preferring criminal charges against others, although according to some writers they were still entitled to bring civil actions to protect their own property.[292] Civil law also penalized unmarried women who were guilty of sexual indiscretions.[293] In principle, neither civil nor canon law courts would enforce contracts that required one party to give sexual

that King Alfred was the founder of University College, Oxford; Rashdall, *Universities* 3:179; James Parker, *The Early History of Oxford, 727–1100, Preceded by a Sketch of the Mythical Origin of the City and University*, Oxford Historical Society Publications, vol. 3 (Oxford: Oxford Historical Society, 1885), pp. 53–57, 62; William Carr, *University College* (London: F. E. Robinson, 1902), pp. 173–74; James K. Ingram, *Memorials of Oxford*, 3 vols. (Oxford: J. H. Parker, H. Slatter, and W. Graham, 1837), University College 1:6.

[289] Bernard of Pavia, *Summa decretalium* 5.13.2, ed. Laspeyres, p. 227; *glos. ord.* to C. 32 q. 4 c. 4 v. *stuprum* and C. 36 q. 1 d.p.c. 2 v. *non revocante*; Thomas of Chobham, *Summa* 7.2.8, ed. Broomfield, pp. 355–56.

[290] Tancred to 1 Comp. 5.13.2 v. *excommunicatus*, Caius 28/17, p. 118b: "Quo ad sacramentorum communicationem et intelligo tam grauem penam fuisse appositam ut eius metu acceperet eam in uxorem. R⟨ichardus⟩,"

[291] Tancred to 1 Comp. 5.13.3 v. *reus erit*, in Caius 28/17, p. 118b, Admont 22, fol. 75v: "Presumitur enim consentire, uel dico quod mortaliter peccat si eam ad penitenciam non denunciat, ut ii. q. i. si peccauerit [c. 19], infra de iureiurando, quemadmodum in l. iii [3 comp. 2.15.11]. R⟨ichardus⟩."

[292] Johannes Teutonicus, *Glos. ord.* to C. 31 q. 2 c. 4 v. *innocens*; note also his *Apparatus* to 4 Comp. 5.1.1 v. *concubinarios*, Caius 44/150, fol. 142rb: "Sed nonne isti persequuntur iniuriam suam? Quare ergo non admittuntur quantumcumque criminosi, ut iiii. q. vi. omnibus [c. 2]? Respondeo: criminosus admittitur ad accusandum, sed non ad denunciandum; sed loquitur de notoriis fornicatoribus, qui sunt sicut privati ingressu ecclesie, ut xxxii. di. uerum [d.p.c. 6], sicut et aliis accusationibus ut uidetur."

[293] *Tractatus de legibus et consuetudinibus regni Anglie qui Glanvilla vocatur* 7.12, ed. and trans. G. D. G. Hall (London: Nelson, 1965; cited hereafter as Glanvill), pp. 86–87. The author of this treatise cannot be identified with certainty. It is unlikely that it was actually written by its supposed author, Ranulf Glanvill, one of Henry II's justiciars. Maitland suggested that Glanvill's nephew, Archbishop Hubert Walter, might have composed the work, but this ascription poses other problems; see Christopher R. Cheney, *Hubert Walter* (London: Thomas Nelson and Sons, 1967), pp. 22–23.

favors to the other.[294] Had this rule been followed in practice, then concubinage agreements, such as the one between James the Conqueror and Countess Aurembaix, would have resulted in the union being classed as a marriage.[295]

Fornication also created problems of ecclesiastical status, especially for women. The *Glossa Palatina* carefully distinguished various situations: a woman whose hymen ruptured during masturbation or foreplay still counted as a virgin for ecclesiastical purposes. But if her hymen were broken as the result of penetration, however slight, by a penis, she irrevocably lost her virgin status and could never become a consecrated virgin or a choir nun, although she could still take the veil as a lay sister.[296]

The perils of extramarital sex were not limited to legal penalties. Physicians cautioned their patients to abstain from nonmarital sex, warning that it would expose them to numerous diseases and afflictions, especially leprosy.[297]

ADULTERY

Adultery, like fornication, could be committed in the mind, as Johannes Teutonicus noted, but both were primarily crimes against the body.[298] Adulterers of either sex sinned both against their own bodies and the bodies of their spouses.[299]

---

[294] Tancred to 1 Comp. 4.4.1 v. *si promiserit*, Caius 28/17, p. 93b: "Hec conditio turpis est si de fornicario coitu intelligatur, et ideo ea abiecta teneat simpliciter sponsalia, ut infra de condi. appo. c. i. l.e. [1 Comp. 4.5.1 = X 4.5.1], unde si postea rem secum habuit, confirmatur matrimonium, ar. supra de spon., de illis [1 Comp. 4.1.4 = X 4.5.3]. Si de coitu legitimo intellecta fuit, multo forcius per sequentem coitum matrimonium confirmatur; potius enim est hortacio quam odium, ut sit simile ff. de tutel., muto [Dig. 26.1.6]. ala⟨nus⟩. Ego credo quod istud si non tenetur condicionaliter sed tentatiue notat enim causam, quia in omni matrimonio hec causa, scilicet carnalis copula, debet interuenire, saltem quo ad propositum, ut xxvii. q. ii. § cum ergo [d.p.c. 2] uerbo 'beata maria' et expone si i. quia promiserit etc., simile si habeatur; supra de elect., significasti [1 Comp. 1.4.2 = X 1.6.4], ff. quando dies legat. cedat, ⟨si⟩ [MS quando] ticio, § quedam [Dig. 36.2.22.1]. t⟨ancredus⟩."

[295] See above, p. 370.

[296] *Glossa Palatina* to C. 32 q. 5 c. 9 v. *carne non utitur*, Trinity O.10.2, fol. 58ra, Salzburg, fol. 202r: "Ar. quod puella que corrupta est, si talis etatis sit que non possit libidinose agere, si cum manu uel palo confracta esset, non impeditur ut inter uirgines consecratur; secus si membro uirili licet inuita, etiam si talis sit qui spermatizare non possit."

[297] Thomasset, "Représentation," pp. 8–9.

[298] *Glos. ord.* to C. 32 q. 5 c. 13 v. *studiosa;* cf. Azo, *Summa super Codicem* 9.9, Corpus glossatorum juris civilis, vol. 2 (Pavia: Bernardinus et Ambrosius fratres de Rouellis, 1506; repr. Turin: Bottega d'Erasmo, 1966), p. 329.

[299] *Glos. ord.* to C. 32 q. 1 c. 4 v. *si quis* and C. 32 q. 7 c. 6 v. *causam fornicationis; Ecce vicit leo* to C. 32 q. 1 c. 3 v. *quecumque peccata*, Trinity O.5.17, fol. 125vb: "Scilicet alia a fornicatione, quia qui fornicatur in corpus suum peccat, id est in uxorem cum qua est unum corpus." Likewise the gloss to the same passage in Caius 283/676, fol.

The adulterer is not much different from a harlot, declared *Ecce vicit leo*, and the two were often compared, usually to the harlot's advantage.[300] The crime of adultery is more detestable when committed by a woman than when committed by a man, added Johannes Teutonicus, whose sentiment reflected the common belief in the peculiar sexual rapacity of women.[301] Besides, as Benencasa of Arezzo (d. 1206) noted in his *Casus* on the *Decretum*, it is much more common for a man to accuse his wife of adultery than for a woman to accuse her husband of this crime. Benencasa added that other reasons might account for this, namely feminine reluctance to air sordid charges against their husbands, the greater care that women took to conceal their love affairs, and the fact that pregnancy often made a woman's adultery easier to prove than a man's.[302] Common belief held that a wife's adultery was often due to her husband's sexual shortcomings, which may also have made men reluctant to press charges.[303]

Although legal writers continued to complain that their sources used the terms adultery, fornication, and *stuprum* loosely and inconsistently, they themselves usually distinguished adultery from other sex offenses with some precision.[304] Canonists by 1190 had largely abandoned the earlier practice of using "adultery" to designate any type of sexual misdemeanor and reserved the term to describe sexual intercourse by a married person with anyone other than the spouse.[305] Although, strictly speaking, adultery was a married person's crime, Johannes Teutonicus was willing to stretch the concept of adultery sufficiently

---

190ra: "Quia qui fornicatur in corpus suum peccat; uxor autem pars corporis sui est, 33 q. 2 ammonere [c. 8]."

[300] Gloss to C. 32 pr., Trinity O.5.17, fol. 125va: "In precedenti causa tractatum est qualiter quis possit uel non possit sibi copulare illam quam prius polluit adulterio; sed quia meretrix non multum distat ab adultera, immo adnectat causam in quam ostendit an meretrix possit uel non possit duci in uxorem."

[301] *Glos. ord.* to C. 12 q. 2 d.p.c. 58 v. *capituli*: "Quia detestabilius est hoc crimen in muliere quam in uiro. Jo⟨hannes⟩." Bartholomew of Brescia, who revised and expanded the *Glos. ord.* ca. 1245, disagreed with Johannes on this point: "Male dicit Jo. quia accusari potest mulier et vir si cum ancilla sua fornicetur, aut femina si adulterium committat, ut extra de diuor., ex litteris [X 4.19.5]. B⟨artholomeus⟩." Johannes's statement reflected the beliefs more pungently expressed by Golias in the poem 'De uxore non ducenda'; see esp. ll. 85–100 in *The Latin Poems Commonly Attributed to Walter Mapes*, ed. Thomas Wright, Camden Society Publications, vol. 50 (London: Camden Society, 1841), pp. 80–81; similarly see Maimonides, *Guide* 3.49, trans. Pines, pp. 601–603.

[302] Benencasa, *Casus* to C. 32 q. 5 c. 23.

[303] E.g., Guibert of Nogent, *Self and Society* 3.3, trans. Benton, pp. 148–49.

[304] Accursius, *Glos. ord.* to Cod. 9.9. pr. and 9.9.28(29) v. *quae adulterium*. Johannes Teutonicus, *Glos. ord.* to C. 32 q. 4 c. 4 v. *stuprum, adulterium*, lists no less than six meanings assigned to *adulterium* in the *Decretum*.

[305] Bernard of Pavia, *Summa decretalium* 5.13.1, ed. Laspeyres, p. 227; Johannes Teutonicus, *Glos. ord.* to C. 32 q. 4 c. 4 v. *de legibus* and v. *sed omne*; Accursius, *Glos. ord.* to Cod. 9.9.1 v. *declarat*; Azo, *Summa* to Cod. 9.9; Thomas of Chobham, *Summa* 7.2.9.1, ed. Broomfield, pp. 356–57.

to include the marriage of a person bound by a vow of chastity.[306] The definition of adultery raised further questions: did a woman whose marriage had not been consummated commit adultery if she had sex with a man other than her husband?[307] Did a party to an invalid marriage commit adultery by sleeping with someone else?[308] Was it adultery for a woman who was legally separated from her husband to have an affair with another man?[309] What if the husband committed sodomy with another man—was that adultery?[310] Various writers addressed each of these questions.

Yet another aspect of adultery that attracted canonistic attention during this period was malice. Adultery can only be committed if the offender knowingly has sex with someone other than the lawful spouse.[311] Thus a married man in an extramarital affair might be guilty of adultery, while his girlfriend committed only simple fornication if she was unaware that her lover was married.[312]

Other circumstances might mitigate the seriousness of the deed. Some canonists considered adultery an occupational hazard for women employed in taverns and therefore held that a husband who allowed his wife to work as a barmaid could not charge her with adultery if she succumbed to the temptations associated with her calling.[313] Furthermore, a married woman who was sexually assaulted by force or by guile was also immune from adultery charges.[314] A hypothetical question often used by law professors when they discussed mitigating circumstances in adultery cases involved a gravely ill man whose physician would treat him only on condition that the patient allow the physician to sleep with the patient's wife. The invalid reluctantly agreed, the deed was done, the patient treated, and the illness cured. What should happen in this case, the law teachers asked, if the recovered husband then accused his wife of committing adultery? The question provided ample scope for examining the ramifications

---

[306] *Glos. ord.* to C. 27 q. 1 c. 41 v. *adulteria* and C. 32 q. 5 c. 15 v. *qui preter suam.*

[307] Tancred to 3 Comp. 4.9.1 v. *adulterii*, Caius 28/17, p. 288b, and Vat. lat. 1377, fol. 254v: "Cum primus sit ei maritus et non secundus et est hoc notabile quid committitur adulterium cum sponsa alterius de presenti, licet non sit cognita a uiro suo. t⟨ancredus⟩."

[308] Tancred to 3 Comp. 4.8.1 v. *videbatur*, Caius 28/17, p. 288a and Vat. lat. 1377, fol. 254r: "Quo ad opinionem omnium ita quod quamuis in ueritate nullum esset adulterium quia nullum erat matrimonium, tamen poterat sicut uxori accursari, ut ff. ad leg. Iuliam de adulter. [*MS C*: aquil.] si uxor [Dig. 48.5.14(13)]. t⟨ancredus⟩."

[309] *Glossa Palatina* to C. 27 q. 2 pr., Trinity O.10.2, fol. 45rb: "Ibi non est adulter, separatus enim maritus est, licet aliam ducit, uel hoc intellige quo ad possessionem ciuilem qua quis possidet uxorem, nam animo non corpore quis amittit possessionem, ff. de acq. pos. l. i. [Dig. 41.2.1]."

[310] Anonymous gloss on *Glos. ord.* to C. 32 q. 7 c. 13 v. *sodomitarum*, in Vat. Borgh. lat. 370, fol. 277vb: "Adde hanc sententiam dicunt hu. et lau. esse ueram . . . scilicet adulter sodomita. Non enim propter alia potest dimitti secuundum hoc. . . ."

[311] Johannes Teutonicus, *Glos. ord.* to C. 32 q. 5 c. 1 v. *adulterari.*

[312] Johannes Teutonicus, *Glos. ord.* to C. 32 q. 5 c. 4 v. *unus admisit* and C. 34 q. 2 c. 6 v. *in lectum.*

[313] Bernard of Pavia, *Summa decretalium* 5.13.10, ed. Laspeyres, p. 230.

[314] Fransen, "Questiones (IV)," no. Bb.98, *Traditio* 20 (1964) 502.

of adultery law and distinguishing the shades and degrees of guilt assigned to the parties.[315]

There was general agreement that adultery was a serious crime and that it often led to further crimes.[316] The canonists stressed that although folklaw might permit a husband to slay his wife if he discovered her in bed with another man, canon law absolutely denied him this right.[317] Thomas of Chobham asserted, on the basis of John 8:3–11, that Jesus himself had abolished the death penalty for adultery.[318] Johannes Teutonicus even claimed that it was a greater offense for a man to kill his adulterous wife than to kill his mother.[319] Moreover, he added, even the old law that permitted husbands to kill their unfaithful wives penalized the husband by depriving him of his wife's dowry.[320] But despite the protests of canonists, customary practice usually held husbands blameless in these situations.[321]

While the canonists forbade husbands to take revenge on their faithless wives, their legal system provided other remedies, both civil and criminal, for the offense.[322] In addition to the standard canonical penalties—deposition of adulterous clerics, excommunication of adulterous laypersons, and separation on grounds of adultery[323]—Johannes Teutonicus noted that it was usual to mete out other punishments, such as shaving the heads of adulterous women, parading them ignominiously with torn clothes through public places, and whipping them publicly (this last was administered by civil, not ecclesiastical, authorities).[324] Beyond this, the aggrieved husband had the right to expel his wife from

[315] Johannes Teutonicus, *Glos. ord.* to C. 32 q. 7 c. 23 v. *si se continere*; Fransen, "Questiones (III)," no. 25, *Traditio* 19 (1963) 523.

[316] Bernard of Pavia, *Summa decretalium* 1.27.3, ed. Laspeyres, p. 22; Johannes Teutonicus, *Glos. ord.* to C. 32 q. 7 c. 16 v. *grauius*; Azo, *Summa* to Cod. 9.9; Thomas of Chobham, *Summa* 7.2.9.1, ed. Broomfield, pp. 357–58.

[317] *Glos. ord.* to C. 33 q. 2 c. 6 v. *liceat*; *Argumentum quod religiosi* to C. 33 q. 2, Pembroke 101, fol. 60vc: "Ar. quod non sit reus homicidii qui deprehensam in adulterio uxorem occidit, ut c. Interfectores [c. 5] et c. Quicumque [c. 6] et Admonere [c. 8], uer. sine causa mortis. Ar. contra c. Inter hec [c. 7] et c. Si qui [c. 9]. Ex eodem collige quod in his que sunt de genere criminum sola secularis legis permissio non excusat a culpa, ut in usuris; secus si hec et lex diuina permittit in legis ministris maxime, ut supra c. xxiii. q. v. Sunt quedam [c. 39] et c. Rex [c. 40] et c. Si homicidium [c. 41] et c. Sunt homines [c. 42]." Cf. *Glos. ord.* to Dig. 4.2.7 v. *quamquam adulter.*

[318] Thomas of Chobham, *Summa* 7.2.9.3, ed. Broomfield, p. 362.

[319] *Glos. ord.* to C. 33 q. 2 c. 8 v. *penitentia.*

[320] *Glos. ord.* to C. 33 q. 2 c. 6 v. *liceat.*

[321] E.g., *El fuero de Estella según el manuscrito 944 de la Biblioteca del Palacio de Madrid*, 51, ed. Gustav Holmér, Leges hispanicae medii aevi, vol. 10 (Karlshamm: E. G. Johansson, 1963), p. 51.

[322] Bernard of Pavia, *Summa decretalium* 5.13.9, ed. Laspeyres, p. 230.

[323] Bernard of Pavia, *Summa decretalium* 5.13.6, ed. Laspeyres, p. 229.

[324] *Glos. ord.* to C. 32 q. 1 c. 5 v. *et calvatas*; Thomas of Chobham, *Summa* 7.2.11, ed. Broomfield, p. 368.

the matrimonial home and to keep her dowry.[325] Neither party could remarry during the lifetime of the other, although after separation the innocent party could enter a religious community, with or without permission of the other.[326]

All of these provisions operated only if the infidelity became known to the innocent party. When the spouse remained ignorant of the affair, adultery was a matter for the confessional, not the courts, and moralists cautioned confessors to assign penances in such a fashion that the spouse would not become aware of the transgression. The public adulterer, on the other hand, could be punished publicly if he refused to abandon the adulterous liaison. In extreme cases he might be barred from communion so long as his legal spouse lived.[327]

Canonical doctrine concerning the marriage of couples guilty of adultery changed markedly in the decades following 1190. While the early decretists, notably Huguccio, had held that these couples are permanently barred from marrying each other, even after the death of their earlier wives or husbands, Bernard of Pavia characterized this teaching as old-fashioned and declared that nowadays such marriages are allowed. Johannes Teutonicus also rejected the earlier teaching, while other writers distinguished between the consequences of notorious adultery (following which marriage was forbidden) and secret adultery (following which marriage was allowed).[328]

PROSTITUTES, PIMPS, AND PANDERS

Harlots, Accursius declared, are not worth the law's notice; nonetheless both civilians and canonists paid considerable attention to prostitution and its social consequences.[329] Canonists of this period, like their predecessors, identified

---

[325] Johannes Teutonicus, *Glos. ord.* to C. 32 q. 7 c. 18 v. *culpa.*

[326] 1 Comp. 4.20.4 = X 4.19.4; JL 14,107; Bernard of Pavia, *Summa decretalium* 4.1.14, ed. Laspeyres, pp. 134–35; Raymond of Peñafort, *Summa de penitentia* 1.8.12, ed. Ochoa and Diez, col. 357.

[327] Thomas of Chobham, *Summa* 7.2.9.3, ed. Broomfield, pp. 361–63; Johannes Teutonicus, *Glos. ord.* to C. 32 q. 7 c. 8 v. *exierit.*

[328] Bernard of Pavia, *Summa decretalium* 4.1.15 and 4.7, ed. Laspeyres, pp. 135, 151; Johannes Teutonicus, *Glos. ord.* to C. 31 q. 1 c. 1 v. *adulterio* and C. 31 q. 1 c. 4 v. *violasse;* gloss to C. 31 q. 1 pr. in B.N., nouv. acq. lat. 2508, fol. 272va: "Cardinalis uult distinguere inter publicum adulterium, ut tunc non possit ducere eam, uel priuatum uel occultum, ut tunc possit, sed hoc non ⟨ap⟩probauit l⟨aurentius⟩, io⟨hannes⟩." Bartholomew of Brescia added: "Hodie autem si quis uxore uiuente alie fidem dederit uel eam contraxit de facto, si nec ante nec post cognouerit eam, post mortem uxoris cum ea contrahere potest, ut extra de eo qui duxit c. ult [X 4.7.7]. b⟨artholomeus⟩," *Ecce uicit leo* to C. 31 q. 1 pr., Salamanca 2491, fol. 139vb: "Aut sint manifestum aut occultum. Si manifestum non possit contrahere adulter cum adultera et si contrahit non tenet. Si occultum similiter non debet contrahere sed si contraxit tenet et imponetur penitentia pro istis."

[329] Accursius, *Glos. ord.* to Dig. 12.5.4. v. *sed noua ratione.* See also Leah Lydia Otis, *Prostitution in Medieval Society: The History of an Urban Institution in Languedoc* (Chicago: University of Chicago Press, 1985), p. 17.

prostitution with public sexual promiscuity.[330] Authorities disagreed, however, on the fine points of definition: just how many lovers must a woman have had before the law classed her as a whore? Johannes Teutonicus declared that she must have slept with "more than a few" men and suggested that this could mean a minimum of 23,000! Johannes did not take this figure altogether seriously, however, for he suggested elsewhere that sixty, or possibly even forty, lovers qualified a woman as a prostitute. Even these figures were much higher than those in some Spanish *Fueros*, which suggested that a woman who had five or more lovers was legally a prostitute. Thomas of Chobham argued that a woman who is secretly promiscuous or who engages only in long-term liaisons with a number of men should not be classed as a harlot. Accursius added that accepting money or other consideration is not an essential element of prostitution, even though that was normal practice.[331]

Prostitution, like other illicit sexual activities, was condemned as an offense against natural law.[332] Moreover a prostitute who had intercourse with any man who came along ran the risk of commiting adultery or incest or sleeping with a monk, which made her calling even more despicable.[333]

Despite this, the Church rarely took vigorous measures to suppress prostitution. Thomas of Chobham argued that toleration was necessary because the people of his generation were exceptionally prone to sexual excess. Besides, he continued, referring to the classical Augustinian rationale, if prostitution were suppressed even worse evils would arise—among them murders and sexual perversion.[334] The known incidence of murder and buggery in such thirteenth-century cities as Paris and Oxford undermines this rationalization, however, since prostitution flourished in both cities, together with a burgeoning crime rate.

Jacques de Vitry, writing in the first quarter of the thirteenth century, penned a lively description of Parisian prostitutes in his day. Strumpets were everywhere in the city, Jacques complained, soliciting passing clerics to patronize their brothels and crying out "Sodomite!" after those who chose not to sample their delights. Both a brothel and a school might occupy the same

---

[330] Johannes Teutonicus, *Glos. ord.* to D. 33 c. 6 v. *Si non pellicem*, C. 27 q. 1 c. 41 v. *promiscuum*, and C. 32 q. 4 c. 11 v. *quarum*.

[331] Johannes Teutonicus, *Glos. ord.* to D. 34 c. 16 v. *quae multorum* and D. 45 c. 9 v. *paucorum*; Thomas of Chobham, *Summa* 7.2.6.1, ed. Broomfield, pp. 346–47; Accursius, *Glos. ord.* to Dig. 3.2.4 v. *quaestuaria*; and cf. Maimonides, *Code* 5.1.18.1–6, trans. Rabinowitz and Grossman, pp. 113–15.

[332] Johannes Teutonicus, *Glos. ord.* to D. 1 c. 7 v. *ius naturale* and C. 32 q. 1 c. 11 v. *usus mali*. Maimonides, on the other hand, taught that before the time of Moses there had been no distinction between intercourse with a prostitute and intercourse with one's spouse; *Guide* 3.49, trans. Pines, pp. 603–604.

[333] Robert of Flamborough, *Poenitentiale* 4.228, ed. Firth, p. 198.

[334] Thomas of Chobham, *Summa* 7.2.6.2, ed. Broomfield, pp. 347–48.

[335] Jacques de Vitry, *Hist. occidentalis* 7, ed. Hinnebusch, p. 91.

house, he continued, with the master giving lessons above, while the bawds entertained their clients below. Whores and pimps quarreled on one floor, while scholars disputed fine points of law and philosophy on the other.[335] An anonymous preacher described Parisian streetwalkers who strutted along the city's main thoroughfares, displaying their attractions and crying out, "Look at me! Look at me! Who would like to straddle a body like this!"[336] With their bouncing curls, gold jewelry, and strings of pearls, the ladies of the street not only advertised their trade but also, as moralists complained, set a flashy standard of dress that respectable women were far too eager to imitate.[337]

Nor were Europe's capitals and university towns the only places where thirteenth-century harlots plied their trade. They boldly importuned pilgrims, Crusaders, and sailors visiting the shrines of the Holy Land itself. In the army camp at Damietta during the fifth Crusade, the whores slipped silently from tent to tent during the night, proffering their costly solaces to the soldiers of the Cross, feeling aggrieved if they left a client with the shirt on his back.[338] During periods of crisis, mortal fear, and high moral fervor, the Crusading heroes banished the ladies of the evening from their camps, as had their predecessors on earlier expeditions, but welcomed them back as soon as danger receded.[339]

Although prostitution seemed inevitable, canonists considered this no excuse for its practitioners. A man might be excused for stealing because he was hungry, but hunger and poverty did not justify a woman in selling her body.[340] On the other hand there was little sentiment for penalizing her harshly. King Roger of Sicily, for one, commanded that prostitutes in his kingdom should not be mistreated, although he forbade them to live in neighborhoods frequented by decent women.[341] Actresses and barmaids were presumed to be prostitutes and fell under the same ban.[342]

[336] Quoted from a sermon in B.N. lat. 16,498 by Albert Lecoy de la Marche, *La chaire française au moyen âge, spécialement au XIIIe siècle, d'après les manuscrits contemporains*, 2d ed. (Paris: Renouard, 1886), pp. 414–15.

[337] Jacques de Vitry, *Hist. occidentalis* 4, ed. Hinnebusch, pp. 82–83.

[338] Quoted from a sermon of Jacques de Vitry in B.N. lat. 17,509, fol. 101, 130, by Lecoy de la Marche, *Chaire*, p. 415.

[339] Jacques de Vitry, *Epist.* 5, ed. Huygens, pp. 117–18; Brundage, "Prostitution, Miscegenation, and Sexual Purity," p. 59.

[340] Johannes Teutonicus, *Glos. ord.* to C. 32 q. 5 c. 3 v. *consentire*; see also the glosses of Laurentius and Vincentius in Stephan Kuttner, *Kanonistische Schuldlehre von Gratian bis auf die Dekretalen Gregors IX.*, Studi e testi, vol. 64 (Vatican City: Biblioteca Apostolica Vaticana, 1935; repr. 1961), p. 298 n. 1.

[341] Frederick II, *Constitutiones regni Siciliae* 3.77, in Jean L.A. Huillard-Bréholles, *Historia diplomatica Friderici secundi*, 7 vols. in 11 (Paris: Plon, 1852–61; hereafter *Hist. dip.*) 4/1:169–70; also in *Die Konstitutionen Friedrichs II. von Hohenstaufen für sein Königreich Sizilien nach einer lateinischen Handschrift des 13. Jahrhunderts*, ed. Hermann Conrad, Thea von der Lieck-Buyken, and Wolfgang Wagner, Studien und Quellen zur Welt Kaiser Friedrichs II., vol. 2 (Cologne: Böhlau, 1973), p. 336.

[342] Accursius, *Glos. ord.* to Cod. 5.4.23.1 v. *scenicis*.

Both civilians and secular officials were harsher on those who forced women into prostitution than they were on prostitutes themselves. Azo reminded his readers of the stern penalties that Justinian had prescribed for pandering, while Roger of Sicily ordered that mothers who sold their daughters into harlotry should have their noses cut off.[343] The canonists did not go quite this far, but they made their disapproval equally plain. Pimps and panders were by definition *infames* and were personally accountable for every transgression committed by the women under their control. Persons who promoted prostitution, such as those who helped to adorn harlots and to bestow on them a beauty that God had not given them, were likewise guilty, though to a lesser extent.[344] The owners of premises in which prostitution was practiced could also be punished.[345] The canonists were especially critical of husbands who allowed their wives or servants to become prostitutes. Although a husband could not charge his wife with adultery if she turned to whoring, he was obliged either to compel her to reform or to divorce her. Complaisant husbands were guilty of pandering and subject to the penalties for pimps.[346]

Nor did law writers overlook the brothels found in virtually every city, town, and hamlet. True, as Johannes Teutonicus observed, the brothels themselves were not infamous, since only persons could suffer *infamia*, but sporting houses were wicked places, and decent persons, including judges, should avoid them.[347] Raymond of Peñafort pointedly noted the Roman ban on holding court sessions in brothels.[348] Bathhouses often doubled as brothels, and are frequently so depicted in late medieval art (see Pls. 3 and 4). No doubt because of this association, Johannes Teutonicus and Benencasa warned against the moral dangers of bathing in mixed company, "for even pagans scarcely tolerate this practice."[349] Municipal bathhouses in Spain customarily segregated the sexes by setting aside certain days of the week for male bathers and others for female patrons, but these restrictions failed to rehabilitate their reputation as dens of iniquity.[350]

---

[343] Azo, *Summa* to Cod. 11.41; Frederick II, *Constitutiones* 3.80, 85, in Huillard-Bréholles, *Hist. dip.* 4/1:170, 173, and ed. Conrad et al., *Konst. Friedrichs II.*, pp. 338, 342

[344] Accursius, *Glos. ord.* to Dig. 3.2.4. v. *ait pretor, non in officina*; Thomas of Chobham, *Summa* 7.2.20, ed. Broomfield, pp. 403–404.

[345] Azo, *Summa* to Cod. 11.41.

[346] 1 Comp. 5.13.3 = X 5.16.3; Johannes Teutonicus, *Glos. ord.* to C. 32 q. 1 d.p.c. 10 v. *adulterio uxorem*; Azo, *Summa* to Cod. 9.9; Accursius, *Glos. ord.* to Cod. 9.9.2 v. *crimen lenocinii* and to Cod. 9.9.28(29) v. et *stupri et adulterii.*; Thomas of Chobham, *Summa*, 7.2.3, 11, 20, ed. Broomfield, pp. 339–40, 366–68, 404; Frederick II, *Constitutiones* 3.74, 3.76, 3.79, 3.84, ed. Huillard-Bréholles, *Hist. dip.* 4/1:168–70, 172, and ed. Conrad et al., *Konst. Friedrichs II.*, pp. 334, 336, 338, 342.

[347] *Glos. ord.* to C. 32 q. 6 c. 1 v. *lupanaria.*

[348] Raymond of Peñafort, *Summa de pen.* 2.8.3, ed. Ochoa and Diez, col. 562.

[349] *Glos. ord.* to D. 81 c. 28 v. *omnino*, and *Casus* to ibid.

[350] James F. Powers, "Frontier Municipal Baths and Social Interaction in Thirteenth-Century Spain," *American Historical Review* 84 (1979) 657–59.

Folklore taught that prostitutes cared only for money, and preachers warned their hearers against the mercenary guile of immoral women.[351] Both lawyers and moralists continued to maintain, as earlier writers had done, that the property that a prostitute received in return for her services was rightfully hers. A prostitute's right to her earnings could be questioned only if she made herself out to be something that she was not. If deceit was involved, the prostitute might be obliged to make restitution. Otherwise she could keep what she got.[352] She had no recourse, however, if a client failed to pay the fee that he had agreed to—a point on which Duke Leopold VI of Austria handed down a ruling in 1192.[353] If a client slapped a harlot in the face or cut off her hair, and if she could prove this by credible witnesses, then the attacker was liable for damages.[354]

Learned opinion was divided over the question of whether the Church should accept alms from whores. A substantial body of opinion held that since harlots acquired their property from the practice of an immoral trade, the Church ought to refuse their gifts—Huguccio had argued that gifts from anyone in a state of mortal sin should be rejected, which probably would have reduced the Church's income rather sharply. Peter of Blois, Accursius, and Johannes Teutonicus disputed Huguccio's argument. Some ill-gotten gains ought to be refused, they maintained, such as gifts from the proceeds of theft or usury. But harlots, unlike thieves or usurers, had a legal right to keep their earnings, and therefore could give them away.[355] In practice, authorities only occasionally refused their offerings. Thomas of Chobham relates that the whores of Paris habitually thronged to the Cathedral of Notre Dame on Saturday afternoons and offered gifts of candles for the altars, although they were not permitted to make contributions during Mass, "lest they mingle the stench of the stews with the odor of sacrifice." When a group of harlots offered to donate a "noble glass window" to Notre Dame, the bishop also felt obliged to refuse their gift, lest by accepting it he seem to condone their activities.[356]

Disagreements arose over the tithe liability of prostitutes. Some argued that it was unseemly to take money from them, as that would amount to the Church living on the proceeds of prostitution. Moreover, this argument continued, acceptance was forbidden by the Scriptures (Deut. 23:18). The majority view, however, justified imposing tithes on harlots on the same basis as it justified

[351] Jacques de Vitry, *Hist. occidentalis* 8, ed. Hinnebusch, p. 99.

[352] Johannes Teutonicus, *Glos. ord.* to D. 86 c. 7 v. *talibus* and c. 8 v. *meretricibus*; Azo, *Summa* to Cod. 4.7; Robert of Flamborough, *Poenitentiale* 4.208, ed. Firth, p. 185; Thomas of Chobham, *Summa* 7.2.6.4, ed. Broomfield, pp. 351–52.

[353] Quoted in Josef Schrank, *Die Prostitution in Wien in historischer, administrativer und hygenischer Beziehung* (Vienna: privately printed, 1886), p. 517; Azo, *Summa* to Cod. 4.7, and Accursius, *Glos. ord.* to Cod. 5.3.5 v. *non potes*.

[354] Johannes Teutonicus, *Glos. ord.* to D. 90 c. 2 v. *dona*.

[355] Peter of Blois, *Summa*, B.L. Royal 10.B.IV, fol. 16v; Accursius, *Glos. ord.* to Dig. 27.10.15 v. *et mulieri*; Johannes Teutonicus, *Glos. ord.* to C. 1 q. 1 c. 27 v. *ex illicitis rebus* and C. 14 q. 5 pr. v. *quod vero*.

[356] Thomas of Chobham, *Summa* 7.2.6.2, ed. Broomfield, pp. 348–49.

accepting charitable donations from them. Besides, some authorities added, it was better to take their tax money and use it for pious purposes than to leave it in their hands to be spent on vanities.[357]

Throughout these discussions of the Church's use of property acquired from harlots, there ran a common thread: the ancient notion that sex creates pollution. Arguments over accepting gifts and taxes from harlots implicitly assumed that their money was tainted by its association with sexual intercourse. The underlying premise of the discussion by canonists and moralists held that this pollution could be transmitted through contact, even indirect, with the participants.

Although the law commonly protected prostitutes against robbery, theft, and assault, legal writers were dubious about whether they ought to be protected against sexual assaults, since by the nature of their trade harlots made themselves generally available to whoever wanted them. Accursius held that a whore was not entitled to redress against a customer who forced her to have sex with him, and the municipal law of Vienna (1221) also adopted this view.[358] In Sicily and South Italy, however, the Constitutions of Melfi (1231) protected whores against rape and prescribed the death penalty for men who ravished them by force, provided that the victim made a timely complaint.[359]

Harlots were unable to initiate criminal accusations, save for personal injury, although the canonists did allow them to lay complaints against laymen who were guilty of simony.[360] Pimps suffered many of the same disabilities as prostitutes, although Accursius noted that a harlot, unlike a pimp, was not *ipso iure* infamous, unless she was caught in the act of adultery with a married man.[361]

---

[357] Robert of Flamborough, *Poenitentiale* 4.213, ed. Firth, p. 188; Johannes Teutonicus, *Glos. ord.* to C. 16 q. 1 c. 66 v. *negotio* and *App.* to 3 Comp. 3.23.5 v. *de lucro*, Admont 22, fol. 209r: "Set numquid meretrix uel ystrio dabit decimam? Non uidetur, quia ut dixi honorandus est dominus de iustis laboribus, et decime tantum de licitis dantur, ut supra eodem, Ex transmissa, lib. ii. [2 Comp. 3.17.7]. Item quia scriptum est,'Non accipies mercedem prostibuli' [Deut. 23:18], et est arg. ad hoc xiiii. q. v. Elemosina [c. 7] et xxxii. q. iiii. Sic non sunt [c. 10]. Nam illicite quesita non sunt in bonis nostris, ut ff. pro socio, Cum duobus § ult. [Dig. 17.2.52.18]. Ad hoc dicunt quidam quod a talibus non est sumenda decima, ne ecclesia uidetur approbare delictum eorum, arg. ad hoc xxiii. q. i. Paratus, in fine [c. 2]. Alii dicunt quod decima sumenda est potius ab eis quam apud eos remaneat, arg. xxii. q. i. Considera [c. 8]. Melius dicas quod si transfertur dominium in aliquos ita quod non competit repetitio licet illi peccent, tamen tenentur dare decimas. Et licet ecclesia petat decimam a talibus, non tamen approbat officium eorum quia conuenit eos tamquam quemlibet possessorem lucri, unde de iustis spoliis danda est decima exemplo Abrahe, ut xxiii. q. v. Dicat [c. 25]. Jo⟨hannes⟩." My thanks to Professor Kenneth Pennington for readings from Admont 22.

[358] *Glos. ord.* to Cod. 9.13.1 v. *virginum honestarum*; Schrank, *Prostitution in Wien*, p. 51.

[359] Frederick II, *Constitutiones* 1.21, in Huillard-Bréholles, *Hist. dip.* 4/1:23–24 and ed. Conrad et al., *Konst. Friedrichs II.*, p. 32.

[360] 1 Comp. 5.2.7 = X 5.3.8; 4 Comp. 5.1.1 = X 5.1.20; Johannes Teutonicus, *Glos. ord.* to C. 6 q. 1 pr. v. *quod autem.*

[361] *Glos. ord.* to Dig. 37.12.3 pr. v. *meretricem.*

Both moralists and canonists in this period were much concerned with rehabilitating repentant prostitutes. Thomas of Chobham furnished guidance for
confessors who dealt with such women. The confessor should require them to
do penance for adultery, incest, and "every uncleanness and debauchery that
they might have incurred." He should also be sure to absolve them from any
excommunications that they might have been subject to, even unwittingly.
Thomas remembered that he had seen harlots doing penance with shaven heads
and he approved of this as well, "since they cannot purge themselves of carnal
uncleanness without many afflictions of the flesh." Once shriven, the reformed
prostitute was freed from the legal disabilities attached to her former trade.[362]

Fulk of Neuilly, a popular preacher, launched a campaign early in the thirteenth century to induce Parisian prostitutes to reform. Many of the women
whom Fulk rescued from a life of sin entered houses of religion, at least for a
time. To accommodate them, Fulk was instrumental in founding near Paris a
Cistercian convent dedicated to St. Anthony the Hermit.[363] In the Rhineland,
meanwhile, Rudolph of Worms, chaplain of the papal legate, Conrad of Zäh-
ringen, was founding the Order of St. Mary Magdalen as a refuge for repentant
harlots. The Magdalen Order was a great success; Gregory IX granted papal
approval in 1227, and houses of the order sprang up in a number of cities,
mainly in France and Germany. The sisters wore a white habit, whence they
were often known as the White Ladies, and followed the Augustinian Rule.[364]
Reformed harlots often preferred to marry rather than to remain nuns, and
Magdalen convents apparently served many of them as something like halfway
houses on the road to rehabilitation.[365]

Reformers encouraged former prostitutes to marry, once they had shown evidence of a firm purpose of amendment. Fulk of Neuilly induced the bourgeoisie
of Paris to subscribe more than a thousand *livres* to create a dowry fund for
reformed prostitutes, and the university students of the city scraped up a further 250 *livres* to augment the fund.[366] Accursius warned of the pitfalls in such
schemes, however: if the woman took the money but persisted in her sinful
ways, he cautioned, the donors had no legal recourse to recover it from her.[367]

Innocent III actively encouraged the reform campaign: in the decretal *Inter
opera caritatis* (1198) the pope declared that men who married prostitutes were

[362]Thomas of Chobham, *Summa* 7.2.6.3, ed. Broomfield, pp. 349–51.

[363]Jacques de Vitry, *Hist. occidentalis* 8, ed. Hinnebusch, pp. 99–100; Milton R.
Gutsch, "A Twelfth-Century Preacher—Fulk de Neuilly," in *The Crusades and Other
Essays Presented to Dana Carleton Munro*, ed. Louis John Paetow (New York: Appleton,
Century, 1928), pp. 190–91; Bullough, *Hist. of Prostitution*, p. 115.

[364]Max Josef Heimbucher, *Die Orden und Kongregationen der katholischen Kirche*,
2d ed., 3 vols. (Paderborn: F. Schöningh, 1907–1908) 1:646–48; Bloch, *Prostitution*
1:819–21.

[365]Otis, "Prostitution and Repentance," p. 151.

[366]Leclercq, *Monks on Marriage*, p. 91.

[367]*Glos. ord.* to Dig. 12.5.4 v. *sed quod meretrici.*

performing a pious work, one that "is not the least among the works of charity." Their action, he added, would count toward the remission of their own sins.[368]

RAPE, ABDUCTION, AND ELOPEMENT

"Rape," declared Thomas of Chobham, "is a detestable crime, according to both divine and secular law." On that account, he continued, rape is punishable by death.[369] The canonists were less rhetorical and more systematic in their analysis of the crime.[370] The victim of the crime might be either the woman or her parents—it rarely happens, Accursius added, that a woman rapes a man, although in law, if not often in life, that was also possible.[371]

Rape involved illicit sex, but the offense was far more serious than voluntary sex crimes.[372] It was of the essence of forcible rape that the victim did not consent, and in practice this meant that she must resist and protest audibly: silence signified consent, Johannes Teutonicus noted.[373] Several canonists held that once a woman had consented to sex with her husband or fiancé, subsequent abduction or assault by them was not punishable as rape, although civil law held otherwise.[374] A married woman who was forcibly ravished by someone

---

[368] 2 Comp. 4.1.5 = X 4.1.20. Lea, *Hist. of Auricular Confession* 3:188 refers to this as an indulgence, but strictly speaking, it was not.

[369] Thomas of Chobham, *Summa* 7.2.7.1, ed. Broomfield, p. 353.

[370] Bernard of Pavia, *Summa decretalium* 5.14.1, ed. Laspeyres, p. 231; Raymond of Peñafort, *Summa de pen.* 2.5.1, ed. Ochoa and Diez, col. 464–65. Cf. the discussions by Glanvill 14.6, ed. Hall, pp. 175–76, and Carlo di Tocco, gloss to *Leg. Lomb.* 1.30.2 v. *faciat*, fol. 8ova. Zurowski, "Einflüsse," pp. 358–59, describes the situation in Poland, where during this period there was a concerted effort to repress forcible abduction, while permitting elopement. See also Kalifa, "Singularités matrimoniales," p. 217.

[371] *Glos. ord.* to Cod. 9.13.1 v. *sponsam.*

[372] *Glos. ord.* to C. 36 q. 1 c. 1 v. *qui raptu*; Benencasa, *Casus* to C. 36 q. 1 d.p.c. 3; Alain de Lille, *Poenitentiale* 1.28, ed. Longère 2:34.

[373] *Glos. ord.* to C. 32 q. 5 c. 3 v. *putaverit* and C. 34 q. 1 c. 3 *et non clamaverit.* Johannes added that a girl who had not attained the age of marital consent was legally unable to agree either to elopement or to sexual relations; hence any abduction of an underage girl was violent rape, regardless of whether she resisted. Here we have the elements of the offense that later came to be called statutory rape; *Glos. ord.* to C. 36 q. 2 c. 1 v. *eos qui rapiunt.*

[374] Johannes Teutonicus, *Glos. ord.* to C. 36 q. 1 c. 2 v. *lex illa; Argumentum quod religiosi* to C. 27 q. 2, Pembroke 101, fol. 6ora: "Ar. quod sit raptus in sponsam propriam secundum canones, ut c. lex illa [c. 2] et C. xxxvi. cap. iiii. et v. [sic!]." But cf. *Argumentum quod religiosi* to C. 36 q. 1, fol. 61rc–va: "Ar. quod in sponsam propriam quis raptum non committit, ut c. lex [c. 2] et c. de puellis [C. 36 q. 2 c. 4] et c. si quis uirginem [C. 36 q. 2 c. 5]." See also Tancred to 1 Comp. 5.14.4 v. *admitti*, Caius 28/17, p. 119b, and Admont 22, fol. 76r: "Secundum leges etiam in sponsa propria raptus committitur, ut C. de raptu uirginum l. i. in medio [Cod. 9.13.1]. ala⟨nus⟩. Sed canon preiudicat ut hic et xxvii. q. ii. §. i. et c. lex illa [C. 36 q. 1 c. 2]; quicquid tamen sit raptor potest contrahere cum rapta, ⟨x⟩xxvi. q. ii. tria sunt, infra eodem tit. c. i., lib. iii. t⟨ancredus⟩."

other than her husband was not guilty of adultery, even if she voluntarily placed herself in the situation that led to the assault.[375]

Women were morally justified in using deceptive stratagems to forestall sexual attackers. Faced with an assault upon her virtue, an unmarried woman could rightfully pretend that she was married, according to Raymond of Peñafort: the lie involved was only a minor sin.[376] A woman who promised to pay a would-be attacker in order to persuade him to desist had no obligation to keep her promise, and if the assailant tried to enforce the promise, the law would not require her to pay.[377]

In keeping with the Church's policy of enabling couples to marry despite opposition from their families, legislators and canonists sought to eliminate abduction as a marriage impediment. Johannes Teutonicus noted that the law had formerly forbidden an abductor to marry his victim, but added that nowadays things are different.[378] His claim rested on decretals of Lucius III and Innocent III that greatly enhanced the opportunities for couples to marry in the face of parental disapproval.[379] Johannes Teutonicus observed that although civil law would punish a woman who consented to elopement, the canons rejected that policy.[380] A father was entitled to disinherit a daughter under the age of twenty-five who married against his will. But he was still obliged to furnish her with a dowry, provided that she married a man of an appropriate social class.[381]

The easing of older prohibitions against marriage following abduction soon altered the practice of the courts. One twelfth-century case illustrates some of the practical issues in these situations. The plaintiff complained that his fiancée had been abducted by a rival, who had subsequently married her; on this account the plaintiff petitioned the court for redress. The defendant denied that he had abducted the girl. He admitted that he and the alleged victim had married hastily, but he maintained that they had done so in proper form. Moreover, he asserted that prior to the alleged abduction he had proposed marriage and had discussed the matter with the girl's family; he further claimed that credible witnesses could prove these negotiations. Going over to the offensive, the defendant counterclaimed that the plaintiff had laid his charges out of vindic-

---

[375] Johannes Teutonicus, *Glos. ord.* to C. 32 q. 5 c. 4 v. *adultera* and c. 6 v. *ipsa potest*, as well as Benencasa, *Casus* to c. 4.

[376] Raymond of Peñafort, *Summa de pen.* 1.10.3, ed. Ochoa and Diez, col. 382.

[377] Accursius, *Glos. ord.* to Dig. 4.2.8. v. *quod si dederit.*

[378] *Glos. ord.* to C. 31 q. 2 c. 1 v. *temperamus.*

[379] 1 Comp. 5.14.4 = X 5.17.6; 3 Comp. 5.9.1 = X 5.17.7.

[380] Tancred to 3 Comp. 5.9.1 v. *cum raptore*, Caius 28/17, p. 207a: "Licet secundum antiquas canones et secundum leges raptor non possit contrahere cum rapta, ut xxxvi. q. ii. de puellis [c. 4], si autem [c. 10], et c. placuit [c.11], et C. de raptu uirginum l. i. § Si tamen [Cod. 9.13.1.2]; hodie secus est, ut hic et xxxvi. q. ii. denique [c. 9] et tria legitima [MS sunt; c. 8]. Jo⟨hannes⟩."

[381] Johannes Teutonicus, *Glos. ord.* to C. 36 q. 1 c. 3 v. *excusata* and C. 36 q. 2 c. 4 v. *nullatenus.*

tiveness and asked the court to penalize the plaintiff for bringing a baseless action. He further requested that the same penalties be imposed on the plaintiff that the defendant would have suffered had he been found guilty.[382] Those penalties were not negligible. Forcible rape was a capital crime at civil law. Canon law punished it by excommunication, jailing, whipping, and the loss of up to half of the convicted man's assets. If the guilty party was a cleric, he also forfeited his clerical position and was permanently confined in a monastery.[383] The mixture of penalties in a particular case depended on the circumstances, particularly on the degree of violence involved, whether fraud or deceit had been employed, and whether the offender showed signs of sorrow for his offense.[384]

HOMOSEXUALITY, BESTIALITY, MASTURBATION

Legal and moral literature during this period had little to say about sexual practices that theologians regarded as deviant, although comments on these matters were often more explicit than those in previous generations. Raymond of Peñafort attempted to define the term "unnatural" as it applied to sexual practices. Unnatural sex, he declared, meant any sort of sexual activity "save for that between man and woman using the appropriate organs." Only heterosexual vaginal intercourse, therefore, was natural.[385] All other sex practices, Benencasa declared, are rejected and punished by everyone, and several of his contemporaries elaborated on that theme, citing Justinian's declaration (Nov. 77 pr.) that sexual deviance is responsible for disasters such as famine, pestilence, and earth-

---

[382] Silvestre, "Dix plaidoires," pp. 384–88.

[383] Bernardus Papiensis, *Summa decretalium* 5.13.7 and 5.14.2, ed. Laspeyres, pp. 229–31; Thomas of Chobham, *Summa* 7.2.7.2, ed. Broomfield, pp. 354–55. Raymond of Peñafort, *Summa de pen.* 2.5.3, ed. Ochoa and Diez, col. 466–67, after outlining the canonical penalties, recommended that in especially heinous cases the offender should be handed over to royal authorities for mutilation or execution.

[384] Raymond of Peñafort, *Summa de pen.* 2.5.45, ed. Ochoa and Diez, col. 527. Rapists could take tenuous comfort, perhaps, in the thought that they were eligible for ecclesiastical sanctuary; *Argumentum quod religiosi* to C. 36 q. 1, Pembroke 101, fol. 61va: "Nota raptores ecclesie priuilegio impunitatem mereri si ad ipsam confugerint, ut c. de raptoribus [c. 3]." Johannes Teutonicus offered consolation for victims as well, noting that they were not required to do penance and their virtue was not deemed to have been forfeited, even if they had lost their virginity; *Glos. ord.* to C. 32 q. 5 pr. v. *quod autem,* C. 32 q. 5 c. 11 v. *suscitare,* and C. 36 q. 2 c. 10 v. *publicam;* Tancredus to 3 Comp. 4.2.1 v. *interdicimus,* Caius 28/17, p. 285b, and Vat. lat. 1377, fol. 252v: "Ita quod sit per extorsionem uel uiolentiam quicquam fieret in preiudicium puelle, non preiudicaretur ei, et ita non est contra supra de matrimonio contracto contra interdictum ecclesie, c. ult., l. i [1 Comp. 4.17.3], et supra de spon., de muliere, in fi., l. i [1 Comp. 4.1.5]. . . . vin⟨centius⟩."

[385] Raymond of Peñafort, *Summa de pen.* 3.34.44, ed. Ochoa and Diez, col. 845; Thomas of Chobham, *Summa* 7.2.19.1, ed. Broomfield, pp. 398–99.

quakes.[386] From this time forward, Justinian's comment became a stock item in the rhetoric of medieval vituperation.[387]

Popular writers sometimes associated sodomitical practices with Islam, and Jacques de Vitry declared that Muhammad himself had introduced sodomy to the Arab world.[388] Perhaps because of this association, Vincentius Hispanus pointedly declared that homosexuals were not wanted in the army of the Crusade.[389] Sodomy was also associated with heresy, as well as with Islam; the Cathars, in particular, were suspected of unnatural sexual preferences, in part no doubt because of their negative attitude toward marriage.[390]

The Third Lateran Council (1179) thought it necessary to adopt a canon specifically prohibiting "that incontinence which is against nature" and decreed that clerics guilty of unnatural vice must either forfeit clerical status or be confined indefinitely in a monastery. Laymen, the canon continued, were to be excommunicated and entirely excluded from society.[391] Elaborating on these prescriptions, canonists concluded that sodomy is the most serious sexual offense—even worse than incest between mother and son, according to Raymond of Peñafort. Raymond added that the vice is so dreadful that even hearing about it could cause pollution. He therefore cautioned confessors to be exceptionally careful in questioning penitents about these matters.[392] Robert of Flamborough noted that his own practice in confession was to allude to unnatural sex only in the most vague and general terms, in order to avoid giving penitents ideas that had not already occurred to them. Rather inconsistently he added that everyone knows that these things are sinful, which implies that everyone knows about them anyway.[393]

Although the canonists condemned sexual deviance as an exceptionally horrid crime, the canonical penalties, while serious, were not extraordinarily se-

---

[386] Benencasa, *Casus* to C. 32 q. 7 c. 13; Lothario dei Segni (Innocent III), *De miseria humanae conditionis* 2.24–25, ed. Michele Maccarrone (Lugano: Thesaurus Mundi, 1955), pp. 57–58; Maimonides, *Guide* 3.49, trans. Pines, p. 606, and *Code* 5.1.1.14, trans. Rabinowitz and Grossman, p. 13.

[387] Johannes Teutonicus, *Glos. ord.* to C. 32 q. 4 c. 12 v. *polluerentur*; Vincentius, to 4 Lat. c. 14 v. *libidinis uitio* and Damasus, to the same passage, ed. García y García, pp. 309, 426.

[388] Jacques de Vitry, *Hist. Iherosol.* 5, ed. Bongars 1: 1055–56.

[389] Vincentius Hispanus, to 4 Lat. c. 71 v. *uiros idoneos destinauerint*, ed. García y García, p. 384.

[390] Lerner, *Heresy of the Free Spirit*, pp. 10–34; Michael Goodich, "Sodomy in Medieval Secular Law," *Journal of Homosexuality* 1 (1976) 295–302.

[391] 3 Lateran Council (1179) c. 11, in COD, pp. 193–94; X 5.31.4. Religious communities prescribed their own special penalties for sodomy; see e.g., Indrikis Sterns, "Crime and Punishment among the Teutonic Knights," *Speculum* 57 (1982) 91–92.

[392] Raymond of Peñafort, *Summa de pen.* 3.34.44, ed. Ochoa and Diez, col. 845; Benencasa, *Casus* to C. 32 q. 7 c. 13 and 14.

[393] Robert of Flamborough, *Poenitentiale* 4.224, ed. Firth, p. 196; Raymond of Peñafort, *Summa de pen.* 3.44.44, ed. Ochoa and Diez, col. 845.

vere; civil law, as Johannes Teutonicus noted, punished sexual perversion more harshly than did canon law.[394] Those guilty of sodomy, said Damasus, are automatically *infames*, but legal opinion was divided on the question of whether this constituted sufficient grounds for marital separation or divorce.[395] Bernard of Pavia was of the opinion that in any event it did not create affinity and thus constituted no impediment to marriage.[396]

Writers of this period rarely mentioned lesbianism. The few references that do occur indicate that sexual relationships between women were thought more shocking than male homosexual relationships.[397] Despite this, however, canonists apparently did not perceive lesbian practices as a major problem or as a serious threat to the social order.

Bestiality concerned moral writers of this period much less than it had the authors of penitentials. The most detailed treatment of bestiality in the early thirteenth century was provided by Thomas of Chobham, who counseled that when a case of this kind was detected, the animal should be killed and its carcass burnt or buried. The human offender should be required to go barefoot for the rest of his or her life, should be permanently barred from entering the church, and should practice lifelong abstinence from meat, fish, and intoxicants.[398]

Masturbation had no legal consequences, was dealt with in confession, not the courts, and hence did not concern the canonists of this generation. Moral writers, however, continued to denounce it as a serious sin.[399] Thomas of Chobham devoted no less than four chapters of his *Summa* to nocturnal emis-

---

[394] *Glos. ord.* to c. 32 q. 7 c. 13 v. *perversitate.*

[395] Damasus, to 4 Lat. c. 14 v. *libidinis vitio*, ed. García y García, p. 426; *Glos. ord.* to C. 32 q. 7 c. 7 v. *sodomita*; gloss to C. 32 q. 7 c. 11, Caius 283/676, fol. 195ra: "Queritur si uir cognoscat uxorem suam in membro ad hoc non concesso, num possit tamquam adulter dimitti? Respondeo potest, si hec manifestum sit, supra eodem Omnes causationes in med. [c. 7] ar." But cf. *Prima primi* to C. 27 pr., B.L. Royal 11.D.II, fol. 331ra: "Item non potest allegari enormitas delicti, quia non propter homicidium uel coitum cum bruto animali fieret separatio."

[396] Bernard of Pavia, *Summa decretalium* 4.14.7, ed. Laspeyres, p. 173.

[397] Robert of Flamborough, *Poenitentiale* 5.272, ed. Firth, p. 229 (cf. Ivo, *Decretum* 9.85–87, in PL 161:681); also Maimonides, *Code* 5.1.21.8, trans. Rabinowitz and Grossman, p. 135.

[398] Thomas of Chobham, *Summa* 7.2.19.2, ed. Broomfield, pp. 402–403; Robert of Flamborough, *Poenitentiale* 5.272, ed. Firth, p. 229 (cf. Ivo, *Decretum* 9.90, in PL 161:682); interlinear gloss to Lev. 18:23 v. *cum omne pecore non coibis*, Trinity B.1.31, fol. 105r: "Cum actionibus scilicet bestialium, ut nefandis uoluptatibus polluaris." Cf. Maimonides, *Code* 5.1.1.16–17, trans. Rabinowitz and Grossman, pp. 14–15.

[399] Thomas of Chobham, *Summa* 7.2.1.1, ed. Broomfield, p. 331; Robert of Flamborough, *Poenitentiale* 4.224, 5.294, ed. Firth, pp. 196–97, 242. Maimonides, the most eminent Jewish moralist of the period, even held that masturbation was as serious an offense as murder, a view that no Christian writer at this time supported; *Code* 5.1.21.18, trans. Rabinowitz and Grossman, p. 137. A century later, however, Christian moralists would treat masturbation as a far more serious matter; Jean-Louis Flandrin,

sion, a problem of great concern in clerical circles, but again a matter for confession, not a public adjudication.[400]

Clerical Celibacy and Clerical Sexuality

Involvement with women discolors clerical life, declared Bernard of Pavia, who went on to warn clergymen against sharing living quarters or even talking with any woman whose presence might cause scandal.[401] The Dominican Constitutions commanded members of that order not to make a practice of gazing at women or conversing with them, save when hearing their confessions.[402] Johannes Teutonicus held that while members of religious communities could bathe in public bathhouses, they must never do so when women, or even non-Christian men, might be present.[403] Since drinking tended to excite lust, the Fourth Lateran Council cautioned clerics to be temperate in their libations, lest they stumble into sexual sins while tipsy.[404] Raymond of Peñafort was inclined to think that clerics who disobeyed these rules could be presumed to be unchaste and should be punished accordingly.[405] Johannes Teutonicus adopted a much more lenient view: such behavior, he thought, should always be interpreted benignly. If a cleric was seen embracing a woman, said Johannes, he should be presumed to be blessing her![406]

Although mandatory clerical celibacy was by this time well established as a matter of law, if not of practice, the policy continued to come under attack both from the clergy themselves and from the laity. Thomas of Chobham, who was certainly no moral laxist, strongly criticized the celibacy policy, arguing that the

---

"Mariage tardif et vie sexuelle: discussions et hypothèses de recherche," *Annales: é.s.c.* 27 (1972) 1359.

[400] Thomas concluded that involuntary spermatic emissions were not mortally sinful unless they were stimulated by erotic daydreams and fantasies; *Summa* 7.2.1.1–4, ed. Broomfield, pp. 330–33.

[401] Bernard of Pavia, *Summa decretalium* 3.2. pr., 1, ed. Laspeyres, pp. 67–68; Tancred to 3 Comp. 3.2.1 v. *non ex evidenti*, Caius 28/17, p. 237a, and Vat. lat. 1377, fol. 220v: "Sed constet aliquem haberet suspectam mulierem secum in domo, eo ipso probata est ei fornicatio, supra eodem titulo, ut nullus [1 Comp. 3.2.2]. Ergo si publice eam detinet, eo ipso convictus est. . . . Alias illud opus uix notorium esset rei euidentia cum semper latebras querat. la⟨urentius⟩." Decretal collections reiterated the prohibitions often (e.g., 1 Comp. 3.2.1–12; 2 Comp. 3.1.1; 3 Comp. 3.2.1–2), as did local authorities (e.g., Powicke and Cheney 2:26, 132, 187).

[402] Heinrich Denifle, ed., "Die Constitutionen des Predigerordens in der Redaction Raimunds von Peñafort," *Archiv für Literatur- und Kirchengeschichte des Mittelalters* 5 (1889) 545–46. The Teutonic Knights had similar regulations; see Sterns, "Crime and Punishment," p. 89.

[403] *Glos. ord.* to C. 24 q. 1 c. 24 v. *balneas.*

[404] 4 Lateran Council (1215) c. 15 = X 3.1.14; reiterated in English synodal statutes (1222 ~ 1225?) c. 64, in Powicke and Cheney 1:151.

[405] Raymond of Peñafort, *Summa de pen.* 3.30.10, ed. Ochoa and Diez, col. 711.

[406] *Glos. ord.* to C. 11 q. 3 c. 14 v. *sinistrum.*

clergy had not consented to it, that it was not required by the Eastern Church, and that, since God and the Apostles allowed marriage, it was temerarious to forbid it to the clergy. He rejected the theory that a vow of continence was somehow annexed to the sacrament of holy orders. "But," he concluded, "it is foolish to dispute in this way, for we are obliged to obey the decisions of the Holy Roman Church."[407] Other critics were not so resigned. An anonymous poet writing shortly after 1215 harshly criticized the Fourth Lateran Council's attempt to enforce clerical celibacy. The result, declared the poet, will be an increase in fornication and adultery:

> Priests who lack a girl to cherish
> Won't be mindful lest they perish.
> They will take whom'er they find
> Married, single—never mind![408]

He raged particularly against Innocent III, arguing that separating priests from their wives or concubines was a crime both against Scripture and against natural law:

> Innocent? No sweetheart he,
> He's just as deadly as can be!
> What God established, he'll destroy,
> Our knavish, Roman bully boy.
> Our Lord decreed we should have wives;
> Our pope demurs—and spoils our lives.[409]

Despite the protests and laments of critics, however, the celibacy policy remained in place, and the Fourth Lateran Council ordered bishops to make renewed efforts to enforce it.[410] The Council even penalized clerics in minor orders who took wives by decreeing that those who did so should forfeit their benefices.[411]

Thomas of Chobham thought that this was going too far. He advised confessors that they could counsel minor clerics to wed secretly and to keep quiet

---

[407] Thomas of Chobham, *Summa* 7.2.16.1, ed. Broomfield, pp. 377–78.

[408] My translation of "De concubinis sacerdotum," ll. 9–12, in Wright, *Latin Poems*, p. 171:

> Quid agunt presbyteri propria carentes?
> alienas violant clanculo molentes,
> nullis pro conjugiis foeminis parcentes,
> poenam vel infamiam nihil metuentes.

[409] My paraphrase of ibid., ll. 29–32, p. 172:

> Non est Innocens, immo nocens vere,
> qui quod Deus docuit, studet abolere;
> jussit enim Dominus foeminas habere,
> sed hoc noster pontifex jussit prohibere.

[410] 4 Lateran Council (1215) c. 7, 31, ed. García y García, pp. 53–54, 75.

[411] Ibid., c. 14, pp. 62–63.

about their marriages. It would only be a trivial sin, and Thomas considered it morally better for minor clerics to marry secretly and keep their benefices (so long as they were discreet about it) than for them to fornicate openly. If the cleric's superiors later demanded that he take major orders, Thomas still thought it better for him to keep his secret wife, rather than to fornicate with other women, assuming that he would in any event be unable to restrain his sexual desires completely.[412] Thomas's advice ran counter both to official policy and to the opinions of the jurists. It is better, an anonymous glossator declared, for those bound by vows *not* to marry than to burn, while Johannes Teutonicus held that clerics in major orders sinned more seriously by marrying than by fornicating.[413]

Many clerics were unwilling or unable to observe the law of celibacy. Odo, the conscientious Bishop of Rouen, recorded that about one-eighth of the clerics in his diocese were gravely suspect of sexual incontinence, indicating that this figure is more likely to underestimate than to exaggerate the problem.[414] Vincentius Hispanus complained that some favored groups—he had the Templars in mind—got off scot free, even though the pope was well aware that they habitually broke the celibacy rule.[415] In practice, both popes and lawyers knew that strict enforcement of the celibacy policy was not working and was perhaps not workable. Enforcement procedures were gradually modified to take account of the realities. Although the law continued to prescribe stern punishment for married or concubinary priests,[416] some decretals of the late twelfth and early thirteenth century tolerated clerical fornication so long as it was discreet, directing prelates to take action only against notorious offenders.[417] The legal writers treated this policy of selective enforcement as a dispensation from

---

[412] Thomas of Chobham, *Summa* 7.2.16.1, ed. Broomfield, pp. 376–77.

[413] Gloss to C. 27 q. 1 d.p.c. 40, Pembroke 162, fol. 253r: "In uouentibus melius est non nubere quam uri." *Glos. ord.* to C. 32 q. 2 d.p.c. 2 v. *coniugii.*

[414] Gabriel Le Bras, *Institutions ecclésiastiques de la chrétienté médiévale*, Histoire de l'église depuis les origines jusqu'à nos jours, vol. 12 (Paris: Bloud et Gay, 1959), p. 168, n. 6.

[415] Tancred to 1 Comp. 5.28.3 v. *robor auctoritatis episcopalis*, Córdoba, Biblioteca del cabildo, MS 10, fol. 88r: "Alii dicunt quod nullo modo potest eos aliquis punire, nam papa istud reseruauit sibi quod sic probatur: nonne papa scit quod templarii in aliena prouincia semper sunt, utique et scit quod delinquunt, et tamen dicit quod non puniuntur, ut infra eodem, Sane [1 Comp. 5.28.8; JL 13,745]." I should like to thank Professor Kenneth Pennington for this reference to the Córdoba MS. The Teutonic Knights had a similar problem with persistent infractions of the celibacy rules and the Order's internal disciplinary system never managed to cope with it adequately; Sterns, "Crime and Punishment," pp. 97–98.

[416] Johannes Teutonicus, *Glos. ord.* to D. 32 c. 5 v. *audiat* et c. 10 v. *eos qui*; Statutes of Salisbury I (1217 ~ 1219) c. 8, in Powicke and Cheney 1:62. Secular customary law occasionally reinforced the canonical celibacy policy; e.g., *Fuero de Estrella* 52, ed. Holmér, p. 51.

[417] 2 Comp. 3.1.1 (X 3.2.7); X 1.11.17 and 3.2.10.

the full rigor of the law and thus achieved a precarious harmony between principle and practice.[418]

If clerical marriage remained a problem despite generations of campaigns against it, clerical concubinage was an even greater one. In England, particularly in the northern province, clerical concubinage was the rule, not the exception. The practice was also common in France, Spain, and Norway. As for Germany and Italy, Benencasa lamented that in these lands "priests, deacons, and subdeacons keep their concubines publicly," and concluded that the old law forbidding clerics who kept concubines from holding ecclesiastical office was no longer in force.[419] This last was a considerable exaggeration, however, for councils and synods reiterated the ban with increasing frequency throughout this period. But, as with clerical marriage, enforcement was selective. Notorious offenders might be prosecuted, but unless the situation was scandalous, authorities usually preferred not to make an issue of the matter.[420] Notorious or manifest offenses meant those of which the offender had been convicted or to which he had publicly confessed; in addition a cleric who openly flaunted his relationship with a suspect woman and kept her in his house might be deemed a notorious offender.[421] Where concubinage was not open or manifest, however, bishops were advised to warn clerics suspected of keeping concubines that they must give up their mistresses. If, after the warning, the cleric failed to mend his ways, he might be suspended, deposed, or excommunicated.[422] The offense was transformed, in effect, from a sexual offense (i.e., concubinage) into an offense against ecclesiastical discipline (i.e., disobedience).

[418] Bernard of Pavia, *Summa decretalium* 3.2.2–3, ed. Laspeyres, p. 68; Raymond of Peñafort, *Summa de pen.* 1.8.3, ed. Ochoa and Diez, col. 341–42.

[419] Benencasa, *Casus* to D. 81 c. 15 v. *Si qui*; Liotta, *Continenza*, p. 190; Le Bras, *Institutions ecclésiastiques*, p. 168.

[420] 3 Lateran Council (1179) c. 11, in COD, pp. 193–94; Council of Westminster (1175) c. 1 and Council of Westminster (1200) c. 10, in Whitelock, Brett, and Brooke, *Councils and Synods* 1:983–84, 1067; Canterbury I (1213/14) c. 3–4, Salisbury I (1217 ~ 1219) c. 7, Oxford (1222) c. 34, Winchester I (1224) c. 37–40, Exeter I (1225 ~ 1237) c. 5, in Powicke and Cheney 1:25, 62, 117, 132, 229–30; X 3.2.6; Bernard of Pavia, *Summa decretalium* 3.2.2–3, ed. Laspeyres, p. 68; Tancred to 1 Comp. 3.2.2 v. *concubinaria*, Caius 28/17, p. 53a: "Est enim ipso iure suspensus si notorium est, ut supra xxxii. di. preter hoc nullus [c. 6], supra di. lxxxi. si qui sunt [c. 15], presbyter [c. 12], infra eodem titulo uerum dixit [?]. t⟨ancredus⟩." See also Boelens, "Klerikerehe," pp. 600–601.

[421] 2 Comp. 3.1.1 = X 3.2.7; X 3.2.10. See also the comments of Alanus, Petrus Hispanus, and Ambrosius, quoted in Liotta, *Continenza*, pp. 217–18, 302, and 357–58; Boelens, "Klerikerehe," pp. 603–604. In those circumstances a man might be subject to the penalties formally pronounced against concubinary clerics and his parishioners might lawfully abstain from attending services at which he officiated; in addition he might be forbidden to prefer criminal charges against others; 4 Comp. 5.1.1 = X 5.1.20; Raymond of Peñafort, *Summa de pen.* 3.30.7, ed. Ochoa and Diez, col. 706.

[422] 1 Comp. 3.2.4–5 =X 3.2.3–4; Gulielmus Vasco to D. 32 c. 5 v. *indubitanter*, in Liotta, *Continenza*, p. 298; Raymond of Peñafort, *Summa de pen.* 3.30.9, ed. Ochoa and Diez, col. 708–710; Thomas of Chobham, *Summa* 7.2.16.4, ed. Broomfield, p. 382.

As for concubines themselves, Thomas of Chobham observed that the harsh punishments prescribed in the old canons—notably enslavement—were no longer enforced and that bishops usually ignored the problem so far as they could. In Thomas's opinion bishops ought to deal more firmly with the concubines of their priests; they should at least forbid these women to be given the kiss of peace during Mass and several English synodal statutes of the early thirteenth century prescribed just that punishment.[423] Others had sterner ideas: some synods, both English and Continental, prescribed shaving the heads of priests' concubines, denying them the sacraments, ostracizing them socially, and the like.[424] In the opinion of Laurentius Hispanus, the concubines of clerics should not be allowed to receive legacies or bequests from their lovers, although he was willing to allow clerics during their lifetimes to give their concubines gifts inspired by affection.[425] Much of the fervor seems to have gone out of the campaign against the concubines of clerics, and Church officials during this period at last abandoned the strategy of discouraging clerical concubinage by penalizing the women who were really its victims.

Multiple Marriages

Writers of this period added little to the treatment of the ordination of men who married more than once.[426] Nonetheless, a series of decretals reaffirmed the old

[423] Thomas of Chobham, *Summa* 7.2.16.7, ed. Broomfield, pp. 385–87; Salisbury I (1217 ~ 1219) c. 9; Canterbury decree (1225), and Worcester II (1229) c. 60, in Powicke and Cheney 1:62–63, 154–55, 180.

[424] Council of Rouen (1231) c. 11, in Mansi 23:215; *Constitutiones cuiusdam episcopi* (1225 ~ 1230) c. 35, and Council of Oxford (1222) c. 34, in Powicke and Cheney 1:117, 187; Boelens, "Klerikerehe," p. 604.

[425] Tancred to 1 Comp. 3.2.9 v. *fornicarias*, Caius 28/17, p. 53b, and Admont 22, fol. 33r: "Et certe huiusmodi fornicarie nichil possunt optinere [uel exigere *om.* A] ab eis nec inter uiuos facta donatione, ar. C. de donat. inter uir. et uxor., Si ancillam [Cod. 5.16.2], nec in testamento a clericis, sed quod relictum est fisco, id est ecclesie, applicabitur, ar. ff. de dona. inter uir. et uxo., cum hic status [Dig. 24.1.32] in fi.; sed nec a militibus nisi iure militari testantur, alias optinere possunt quod eis relinquerunt, ar. ff. de his que ut indig. habetur, aufertur, mulierem [Dig. 34.9.2, 14]; in aliis autem omnibus optinet quod dicit lex, quia inhonestes donaciones affectionis gratia, ut circa meretrices, non sunt prohibite, ff. de donati., affectionis [Dig. 39.5.5]. lau⟨rentius⟩." Similarly, Damasus, *Questiones* in Vat. Borgh. lat. 261, fol. 33vb–34ra, disallowed gifts to the concubines of clerics.

[426] E.g., Bernard of Pavia, *Summa decretalium* 1.13.1, 4.22.1, 5.13.12, ed. Laspeyres, pp. 15, 194, 230; Johannes Teutonicus, *Glos. ord.* to C. 31 q. 1 c. 8 v. *ducunt*; Benencasa, *Casus* to C. 31 q. 1 c. 8. The gloss to C. 27 q. 1 c. 24 in Caius 283/676, fol. 179vb, distinguishes six kinds of bigamists: "Reputatur bigamus: Qui 2. legitimas habuit uxores, 26 Nemo [*fortasse* D. 32 c. 12?]; qui unam legitimam et aliam illegitimam, 31 q. 1 Quomodo [c. 10]; bruta alia, 32. q. 1 Nuptie [c. 12]; qui bis baptizatur, infra de con. 4 Quis bis [c. 117]; qui post nuptias spirituales carnales contraxit, hic; cuius uxor adulterata est, 34 si cuius [c. 11], uel qui uiduam duxit, 34 Si quis uiduam [c. 13]." A similar list appears in a gloss to 2 Comp. 1.11, Caius 44/150, fol. 85v. Johannes Teutonicus noted

rules and clarified minor problems of interpretation.[427] Inconsistencies continued to abound. Innocent III, for example, held that the survivor of an unconsummated marriage did not commit digamy if he remarried, but Alanus maintained that even premarital relations with a woman whom one later married were regarded as digamous and, in fact, constituted canonical bigamy.[428] This predilection for seeing sexual relationships as a central issue in determining eligibility for ordination resulted from the belief that sex imparted spiritual pollution.

Since the ban on the ordination of men who had engaged in multiple sexual relationships rested on apostolic authority, the power to dispense from it was problematical. Richardus Anglicus believed that the pope or any bishop could dispense candidates for ordination up to the rank of subdeacon from the irregularity of bigamy, but that no one, including the pope, could dispense for ordination beyond that point. Tancred was less sure. He thought that the pope might be able to dispense candidates for ordination to higher orders, since the pope had greater administrative authority than St. Paul had enjoyed.[429]

Robert of Flamborough's discussion of a case involving a cleric who was married four times illustrates the complications latent in these situations. The

---

the irony of the rules that forbade men who entered a second marriage to be ordained, while those who had committed fornication countless times were perfectly eligible to become priests; *Glos. ord.* to D. 34 c. 7 v. *non patitur* and C. 32 q. 1 c. 12 v. *unde.*

[427] 1 Comp. 1.13.1–3; 2 Comp. 1.11.1–2; 3 Comp. 1.14.1–2; 4 Comp. 1.10.1; X 1.21.7.

[428] 3 Comp. 1.14.2 = X 1.21.5; Tancred to 1 Comp. 3.3.3 v. *virginem*, Caius 28/17, p. 54b, Admont 22, fol. 33v: "Ar. quod qui corrumpit uxorem suam antequam eam duceret, promoueri non debet, xxxiiii. di. curandum [c. 9]. al⟨anus⟩." Cf. Tancred to 3 Comp. 4.1.2 v. *non cognouit*, Caius 28/17, p. 294b: "Nota quod ille si ordinari uellet non repellitur quasi bigamus, licet priorem uxorem habuit et non cognouerit post matrimonium, supra de bigamis non ordinandis c. i. l.e. [3 comp. 1.14.1 = X 1.21.4]. uin⟨centius⟩." See also Robert of Flamborough, *Penitentiale* 3.168, ed. Firth, pp. 162–63; Trümmer, "Bigamie als Irregularitätsgrund," p. 396.

[429] Tancred to 1 Comp. 1.13.3 v. *dispensari*, Caius 28/17, p. 14a and Admont 22, fol. 8r: "Secundum xxxiiii. di. lector [c. 18] contra. Solutio: ibi ostendit martinus quid liceat pape aut quid aliis episcopis scilicet dispensare cum bigamo usque ad subdiachonatum, quod non est contra apostolum. Sed usque ad diachonatum non posset, per hoc c. sicut michi uidetur. R⟨ichardus⟩. § Uideo enim quod apostolus [A: episcopus] prohibuit criminosum ordinari, ut xxv. § nunc autem [d.p.c. 3], et quod episcopis liceat dispensare cum criminosis, scilicet cum adulteris, et in minoribus criminibus implicatis, est arg. de iudic., at si clerici [1 Comp. 2.1.6 = X 2.1.4], et non est contra apostolum, sed preter apostolum. Quidam tamen dicunt quod episcopis nullo modo licet dispensare cum bigamo, et si ordinaretur non reciperet caracterem, sicut nec asinus, et dicunt quod martinus non fuit papa sed capra. Videtur quibusdam et mihi quod dominus papa directe contra apostolum dispensare possit, quoniam maior est amministracione quam fuerat paulus, et fertur; sed scriptum non uidi quod lucius papa dispensauit cum bigamo usque ad sacerdocium. t⟨ancredus⟩." Cf. Robert of Flamborough, *Poenitentiale*, Appendix, ed. Firth, p. 281.

cleric's first union was with a nine-year-old girl, with whom he could not have intercourse. Next, he was forced to marry an older virgin, with whom he lived and had sexual relations up to the time of her death. After his second wife died, the cleric married another virgin, voluntarily this time, and lived with her until she died. Subsequently he married a widow, but never had sex with her. After the death of his fourth wife he sought ordination. Robert analyzed this case at length and concluded that the cleric could be validly ordained, since he did not "divide his flesh" and hence was not a bigamist, despite four ventures into matrimony and despite the fact that he had sexual relations with two of his wives.[430]

As for simultaneous bigamy (that is marriage to two spouses at the same time, as opposed to constructive bigamy, or marriage to two spouses sequentially), the canonists agreed that it was unlawful and immoral—save when the practice was permitted by divine inspiration. In that case, in the words of Alanus Anglicus, "sex with the second wife or concubine was allowed by a divine miracle, although it would be contrary to the natural law."[431]

The canonists' main concern with second and subsequent marriages was to assure that they were contracted freely and not dictated by family or feudal lords. The marriages of widows who held property in fee posed particularly acute difficulties. The lord commonly claimed not only the right to require the widow to remarry, but also to select her husband. Family members also often opposed these marriages.[432] Canonists criticized those who tried to restrict either the widow's right to determine whether she would remarry at all or her right to a free choice of marriage partner.[433]

---

[430] Robert of Flamborough, *Poenitentiale* 3.188–95, ed. Firth, pp. 173–78.

[431] Alanus, gloss to C. 32 q. 4 c. 7 v. *crimen non*, in Weigand, *Naturrechtslehre*, p. 423; see also the *Summa Duacensis*, ibid., p. 425, and the similar opinion of Laurentius in Tancred to 3 Comp. 1.14.1 v. *conuenit*, Caius 28/17, p. 173a: "Q.d. de facto contraxit cum secunda, quia de iure non potuit, tamquam duas simul uxores habere licuerit, quod numquam licuit nisi ex reuelacione spiritus sancti concessum fuit, ut infra de diuor., gaudemus [3 Comp. 4.14.2]. la⟨urentius⟩." Cf. Tancred, *Summa de mat.* 27, ed Wunderlich, p. 49, and Raymond of Peñafort, *Summa de mat.* 13 pr., ed. Ochoa and Diez, col. 958. The reference to divine permission for bigamy is to the story of Lamech in Gen. 4:19–24.

[432] These rules were particularly strict in the law of the Latin Kingdom of Jerusalem, where the need to have fiefs occupied by fighting men was acute; *Le livre au roi* c. 30–31, in RHC, Lois 1:626–27. On family opposition see Janet Senderowitz Loengard, "'Of the Gift of Her Husband': English Dower and its Consequences in the Year 1200," in *Women of the Medieval World: Essays in Honor of John H. Mundy*, ed. Suzanne Wemple and Julius Kirshner (Oxford: Basil Blackwell, 1985), p. 237.

[433] Johannes Teutonicus, *Glos. ord.* to C. 31 q. 2 pr. v. *quod autem*, citing 1 Cor. 7:39; but cf. Noonan, "Power to Choose," pp. 419, 433–34. The canonists' insistence on freedom of choice ultimately influenced royal law: the provisions of the final version of Magna Carta (1217) relating to the rights of widows, for example, clearly reflected canonistic doctrine; Magna Carta, reissues of 1217 (c. 7, 8, 22) and 1225 (c. 7, 8, 18), in

Legitimacy and Property Issues

A series of decretals from this period claimed ecclesiastical jurisdiction over the division of marital property following divorce or separation.[434] Kings were reluctant to concede this claim, since resolution of marital property disputes normally fell within their jurisdiction. Customary and royal laws on these matters were in the process of change during this period, however, and some rulers accommodated the Church's policies by incorporating principles enunciated in the decretals. Thus, for example, Glanvill stated as a rule of Common Law the principle that a wife who was separated from her husband on account of her adultery forfeited her dowry, a rule that echoed the position adopted by canonists and asserted by a decretal of Clement III.[435] Ecclesiastical courts also successfully required the parents of illegitimate children to support their offspring and protected the claims of the natural children of concubines to share in the estates of both parents.[436]

Several decretals of this period asserted the canon law's right to judge issues concerning parentage and legitimacy, but the Church's success in making good this claim was variable (see Pl. 9).[437] When canonists dealt with the ecclesiastical consequences of legitimacy—for example with respect to a child's eligibility for ordination—secular rulers and courts were not apt to challenge their jurisdiction.[438] When canonists claimed that their courts could regulate the

---

William Stubbs, ed., *Select Charters and Other Illustrations of English Constitutional History from the Earliest Times to the Reign of Edward the First*, 9th ed., rev. by H. W. C. Davis (Oxford: At the Clarendon Press, 1913), pp. 341–42, 350; Michael M. Sheehan, "The Influence of Canon Law on the Property Rights of Married Women in England," *Mediaeval Studies* 25 (1963) 117.

[434] 1 Comp. 4.21.1–3; 2 Comp. 4.14.1–2; 3 Comp. 4.15.1–3; X 4.20.8; Sheehan, "Influence of Canon Law," p. 110.

[435] Glanvill 6.17, ed. Hall, p. 68; cf. 2 Comp. 4.14.2 = X 4.20.4. See also Loengard, "'Of the Gift of Her Husband'," pp. 216–20.

[436] 1 Comp. 4.18.4 = X 4.17.4; 2 Comp. 4.5.2 = X 4.7.5; Raymond of Peñafort, *Summa de pen.* 2.5.11, ed. Ochoa and Diez, col. 476–77; Tancred to 1 Comp. 4.18.6 v. *hereditate*, Caius 28/17, p. 104b, and Admont 22, fol. 65r: "Alii sunt legitimi tantum, ut adoptiui uel abrogati; alii sunt legitimi et naturales, ut nati ex matrimonio uero uel putatiuo; hii scilicet primi et secundi succedunt parentibus in omnibus bonis, ut supra eodem cum inter [1 Comp. 4.18.2 = X 4.17.2], C. de suis et leg. here. per totum [Cod. 6.55]; alii sunt naturales et non legitimi, ut nati ex concubinis que in domibus habentur; hii succedunt in duabus unciis tantum, ab intestato, ut C. de naturalibus liberis, aut. licet patri [Auth. Cod. 5.27.8; Nov. 89.12, 15]; alii sunt spurii, ut nati ab adulterio et uulgo concepti, ut ff. de statu hominum, uulgo [Dig. 1.5.23]; hii in nullo succedunt, nec etiam pasci debent a patre, ut in predicta aut. et xxxii. q. iiii. dicat aliquis [c. 9]. t⟨ancredus⟩." Icelandic, Norwegian, and Swedish laws conformed closely to canonical prescriptions; Jochens, "Church and Sexuality," p. 381; Jacobsen, "Sexual Irregularities," pp. 74–75, 78, 80, 83.

[437] 1 Comp. 4.18.5 = X 4.17.5; JL 14,218.

[438] 1 Comp. 1.9.1 = X 1.17.1; Bernard of Pavia, *Summa decretalium* 1.9.pr., ed. Laspeyres, p. 11.

legitimation of children for inheritance purposes, however, there was stout resistance.[439] A decretal of Alexander III, as noted earlier, maintained that the children of clandestine marriages were legitimate. Secular judges found this teaching more tolerable than legitimation by subsequent marriage.[440]

Canonists approved of the paternal feeling that moved fathers to provide for their illegitimate children—save when it was a matter of the illegitimate off-spring of fornicating clerics.[441] Even in these cases, thirteenth-century writers moderated the disabilities that previous generations had imposed on the illegitimate children of clergymen.[442]

Jurisdiction, Procedures, and Evidence

Writers on secular law during this period by and large accepted canonistic claims to exclusive jurisdiction over marriage, with the significant exception of claims involving inheritance and property, as noted above. Thus Glanvill, for example, while denying the canonists' right to rule on legitimacy, acknowledged that English royal courts routinely referred questions concerning the validity of marriages to ecclesiastical tribunals, while reserving to themselves jurisdiction over property questions.[443] Criminal complaints about sexual behavior might in practice be heard by royal courts, by local customary law courts, or by canonical courts, although the canonists claimed exclusive jurisdiction over adultery.[444] Alexander III preferred that ecclesiastical judges hear complaints involving rape and other sex crimes, although he was prepared to have them do this as delegates of secular authorities.[445]

Canonical tribunals became more professional and their proceedings more systematic throughout this period. Jurisdiction over minor sex offenses remained for the most part in the hands of rural deans. Litigation concerning divorce and separation, however, was beginning to be reserved to higher levels of the Church's judicial system. In England the commissary courts of bishops and the Courts of Audience claimed cognizance of divorce or separation cases after about 1225, and the lower courts were forbidden to handle these matters.[446]

---

[439] 1 Comp. 4.18.6 = X 4.17.6; 3 Comp. 4.12.1 = X 4.17.12; Bernard of Pavia, *Summa decretalium* 4.18.12, ed. Laspeyres, p. 182; Fransen, "Questiones (IV)," no. Bb95, in *Traditio* 20 (1964) 501, and "Deux collections des questiones," p. 496; Azo, *Summa* to Cod. 5.26. pr., 1; *Questiones dominorum Bononensium*, no. 111, 114, ed. Palmiero 1:229.

[440] 1 Comp. 4.3.3 = X 4.17.9; JL 13,774; WH 819.

[441] Tancred to 1 Comp. 4.18.3 v. *standum*, Caius 28/17, p. 103b, and Admont 22, fol. 64v: "Tunc quia in possessione filiationis non fuit, tum quia presumitur quod si filius esset paterna pietas super ipso moueretur, supra de presumptionibus, auferte [1 Comp. 2.16.2 = X 2.23.2], C. de nat. l., si mater [*fortasse* Cod. 5.27.2]. ala⟨nus⟩."

[442] Thomas of Chobham, *Summa* 7.2.16.6, ed. Broomfield, pp. 384–85.

[443] Glanvill 7.15, ed. Hall, p. 88.

[444] Johannes Teutonicus, *Glos. ord.* to C. 32 q. 5 c. 23 v. *apud sacerdotes*.

[445] 1 Comp. 5.14.3 = X 5.17.4, JL 14,044.

[446] English Synodal Statutes (1222 ~ 1225) c. 42, in Powicke and Cheney 1:147; Colin

Marriage and separation actions were normally initiated by a complaint from one of the parties (instance cases), but from the early thirteenth century onward, increasing use was made of *ex officio* prosecutions to bring morals offenses and even some marriage cases before the judges.[447] Parties in both types of cases during the course of the century increasingly employed professional canonists to represent and advise them in the course of litigation.[448]

The increase in the use of professional counsel resulted in part from the greater complexity of canonical procedures during this period. Standards for evidence were spelled out more clearly by law writers. Johannes Teutonicus catalogued the types of circumstantial evidence that judges should admit in divorce or separation actions grounded on adultery. Mere suspicion was no longer adequate, for canonists had begun to insist that plaintiffs produce evidence to show a reasonable foundation for their suspicions.[449] Celestine III ruled in *Laudabilem* that a husband who believed that his wife had been unfaithful must not separate from her or leave the matrimonial home until he had proved his suspicions to the satisfaction of an ecclesiastical magistrate.[450] Legal writers also attempted to discourage frivolous and ill-founded separation actions and prescribed with increasing rigor the circumstances under which these actions might be initiated.

Increased procedural complexity expanded the opportunities for canon lawyers to use procedural devices in order to manipulate proceedings. The wife whose husband sought to dismiss her on grounds of infidelity, for example, could delay matters by interposing an exception to the charge—she could, perhaps, allege that her husband was also guilty of adultery—and determination of the separation issue must then await the judge's ruling on the exception. If he found her exception proved, the separation action was dismissed; if the evidence failed to support her exception, the court then tried the main issue, namely the adultery charge against her.[451] The tactical use of exceptions and other procedural devices made it more expensive, more time-consuming, and more hazardous for husbands to rid themselves of disagreeable wives and probably gave married women a greater measure of protection than the looser procedures of earlier times had done. The Council of Oxford in 1222 found it

---

E. Morris, "The Commissary of the Bishop in the Diocese of Lincoln," *Journal of Ecclesiastical History* 10 (1959) 51, 56, 62.

[447] 1 Comp. 5.1.11 = X 5.1.9; Helmholz, *Marriage Litigation*, p. 70.

[448] 3 Comp. 1.22.1 = X 1.38.5, Po 2656.

[449] Bernard of Pavia, *Summa decretalium* 5.13.3, 11, ed. Laspeyres, pp. 227–28, 230; *Glos. ord.* to C. 32 q. 1 c. 2 v. *suspicio* and d.p.c. 10 v. *accusationem*, as well as C. 33 q. 2 c. 1 v. *probabiliter*; Raymond of Peñafort, *Summa de mat.* 22.1–2, ed. Ochoa and Diez, col. 985–86; Donahue, "Proof by Witnesses," pp. 127–28.

[450] 2 Comp. 2.9.2 = X 2.16.3, JL 17,649.

[451] Bernard of Pavia, *Summa decretalium* 5.13.5, ed. Laspeyres, pp. 228–29; Johannes Teutonicus, *Glos. ord.* to C. 31 q. 2 c. 4 v. *innocens*, C. 32 q. 1 d.p.c. 10 v. *privilegium*, C. 32 q. 6 pr. v. *sed ponatur*, and also c. 1 v. *convincitur*.

necessary to warn advocates against abuses and sharp practice in handling marriage matters.[452]

Canonists repeatedly insisted that married women could initiate separation and divorce actions against their husbands, even though civil law denied them this right. For the most part the evidential requirements were the same for actions initiated by women as for those initiated by men—with the significant difference that women could not seek separation on circumstantial evidence alone. In this respect, women were seriously disadvantaged in marriage litigation.[453] The canonists also continued to be suspicious of women's testimony and to consider their evidence less credible than that given by men.[454] Canonists of this period also permitted third parties to initiate actions to separate married persons—marital irregularities were, Vincentius noted, "popular causes," since the entire community had a stake in preserving the sanctity of matrimony; hence any member of the community was entitled to denounce irregular unions.[455] Further, unlike most other civil actions, matrimonial cases could not be settled by compromise between the parties, but must be determined one way or another by the court itself.[456]

While civil law required that actions for separation or divorce based on grounds of adultery must be filed within five years of the alleged offense, the canonists rejected this constraint.[457] They did recognize other limitations on the right to initiate these actions, however: if the spouse had done penance for his or her adultery, for example, no separation action could later be based on the past offense. The law forbade ex-spouses to rake up old adultery charges once the court had authorized separation.[458]

Although canonists of this period believed that judges should rely primarily on the evidence of witnesses, they were prepared to accept public fame or notoriety as a type of proof. Notoriety was particularly significant in adultery, clerical concubinage, and fornication cases. A decretal of Innocent III held that nei-

---

[452] Council of Oxford (1222) c. 4, in Powicke and Cheney 1:107.

[453] Johannes Teutonicus, *Glos. ord.* to C. 32 q. 1 d.p.c. 10 v. *privilegium*, C. 32 q. 5 c. 23 v. *detegatur*, C. 32 q. 6 c. 1 v. *convincitur*, C. 33 q. 2 c. 4 v. *reddita*. The civilians continued to bar wives from charging their husbands with adultery; Accursius, *Glos. ord.* to Cod. 9.9.1 v. *violata*.

[454] 1 Comp. 5.36.10 = X 5.40.10, ad fin.

[455] Bernard of Pavia, *Summa decretalium* 4.19.4, ed. Laspeyres, p. 185; Vincentius Hispanus to 4 Lat. c. 51 v. *qui uoluerit et ualuerit* and Damasus to 4 Lat. c. 51 v. *impedimentum opponat*, ed. García y García, pp. 362, 449; cf. Accursius, *Glos. ord.* to Cod. 9.9.6 v. *iure mariti*.

[456] Statues of Winchester I (1224) c. 59, in Powicke and Cheney 1:135.

[457] Bernard of Pavia, *Summa decretalium* 5.13.4, ed. Laspeyres, p. 228; Johannes Teutonicus to 4 Comp. 4.3.3 v. *de longinquitate*, Caius 44/150, fol. 142ra: "Et sic hodie non currit prescriptio contra accusatores matrimonii, licet olim currebat, extra iii. qui matrimonium accus. non pos., per tuas [3 Comp. 4.13.2]."

[458] Johannes Teutonicus, *Glos. ord.* to C. 32 q. 1 c. 7 v. *poenitentia* and C. 32 q. 7 c. 3 v. *viro*.

ther accusers nor witnesses were required in order to take action against clerics who were generally known to be living in concubinage. If the situation was notorious and plainly evident to everyone in the community, a bishop was justified in proceeding against the offender without proving specific acts of sexual intercourse.[459] The Fourth Lateran Council extended the use of common fame (or notoriety) to cases involving consanguinity and affinity.[460] Not all canonists were pleased with this innovation, however, and several writers, including Laurentius, Vincentius, and the anonymous author of the Apparatus *Militant siquidem patroni* urged restrictions on the use of notoriety. They argued that notoriety must be distinguished carefully from mere suspicion. Ex officio action against known offenders who had previously been warned to mend their ways might justifiably be based on common fame; otherwise, however, common report alone proved nothing.[461]

Common fame, while not adequate proof of wrongdoing by itself, could certainly establish presumptions of fact, as Laurentius Hispanus noted, and might corroborate circumstantial evidence to prove the existence of a marriage when credible direct evidence was not available.[462] Cohabitation did not create a presumption of marriage in canon law, as we have seen. Canonists, unlike civilians, normally presumed that cohabiting couples were not married unless they could produce some evidence, such as a wedding ring, to substantiate their married status.[463] Tancred reminded his readers that statements made by par-

---

[459]3 Comp. 3.2.1 = X 3.2.8; Bernard of Pavia, *Summa decretalium* 2.17.4, ed. Laspeyres, p. 52; Johannes Teutonicus, *Glos. ord.* to C. 32 q. 1 c. 4 v. *si quis; Militant siquidem patroni* to 1 Comp. 3.2.3 v. *sacerdotis,* in Liotta, *Continenza,* p. 277. Cf. 1 Comp. 2.20.20 = X 2.28.15 on notoriety in adultery cases.

[460]4 Lateran Council (1215) c. 52, ed. García y García, pp. 93–94; Johannes Teutonicus, *Glos. ord.* to C. 32 q. 7 c. 19 v. *illi vero.*

[461]*Militant siquidem patroni* to 1 Comp. 3.2.1 v. *inhibendum est,* as well as the Casus *Scribit dominus papa* to 3 Comp. 3.2.1 v. *tua,* in Liotta, *Continenza,* pp. 276, 359; Tancred to 1 Comp. 4.1.14 v. *si fama,* Caius 28/17, p. 89a: "Ar. quod sufficit fama ad probationem, quod Azo dicit; quid tamen si dubitetur famam fuisse qualiter probatur? Respondeo per duos testes, infra, qui matrimonium accusare possunt, Peruenire [1 Comp. 4.19.3], supra de presumptionibus, Quia in similitudinem [*fortasse* 1 Comp. 2.16.11]. Vin⟨centius⟩." Tancred to 3 Comp. 5.1.3 v. *fama,* Caius 28/17, p. 297b: "Ar. fama nichil per se probare, supra xxxv. q. vi. si duo [c. 4], supra de eo qui cog. consan. uxo. sue, super eo, l. ii. [2 Comp. 4.7.1]; licet Jo⟨hannes⟩ dixerit contra, supra iiii. q. iii. § item in criminale, uer. sepe [*Glos. ord.* to C. 4 q. 2 & 3 c. 3 v. *sepe*]. la⟨urentius⟩." See also Carlo di Tocco, gloss to *Leg. Lomb.* 1.32.2 v. *purificare,* fol. 84va–85ra.

[462]Tancred to 1 Comp. 4.1.14, Caius 28/17, p. 89a: "Id est si nichil obiciatur contra instrumentum et probetur quod iam obiciebatur uel pre. i. maxime [?]. Nam sola fama bene probat matrimonium, nam uiolenta est eius presumptio, ar. supra de testibus c. ii [1 Comp. 2.13.2?]. lau⟨rentius⟩."

[463]Tancred to 1 Comp. 4.1.14 v. *uxorem,* Caius 28/17, p. 89a, Admont 22, fol. 55v: "Quare alia exigitur probatio, cum cohabitatio [A: habitatio] sufficiat ad presumptionem [A: probationem] matrimonii, quousque probetur contrarium, ut ff. de ritu nup., in libere [Dig. 23.2.24]. Respondeo illa presumptio est legis; canon uero contra presumit,

ties to divorce or separation actions carried little weight and that corroborative evidence is always required.[464]

Surviving documents from actual marriage cases of the early thirteenth century by and large bear out the statements of the academic jurists. In *Iacopina c. Bonfiliolum Lanaiolum*, a case from Pisa in 1230, for example, the complainant wife sought to show that Buonfiglio (*Bonfiliolus*) had married her. She produced three witnesses who testified that the couple had cohabited, had had a child, and were commonly believed by their neighbors to be married—she relied, in other words, on circumstantial evidence coupled with common fame to prove her case.[465] Similarly in *Alice c. John the Blacksmith*, an English case heard in the Court of Arches about 1200, Alice sought to prove marriage by future consent ratified by coitus. She relied on the testimony of witnesses who stated that they knew that the couple had been betrothed and that they had subsequently seen the pair in bed together on several occasions. John's defense is unknown; perhaps he denied intercourse, but the record fails to show his side of the story. Alice's case, however, clearly rested on a presumption of sexual intercourse corroborated by circumstantial evidence.[466]

Petitions for dissolution of a marriage on grounds of impotence presented formidable problems of evidence, particularly if the defendant denied the allegation.[467] The testimony of witnesses might be produced to show that the couple had lived together and hearsay accounts of their unsuccessful attempts to consummate their marriage might also be admitted. In addition, as we have seen, the courts might order physical examination of one or both parties in order to determine whether they were physically capable of intercourse.[468]

---

scilicet non esse matrimonium etiam inter cohabitantes nisi probetur esse contrarium, et hoc propter anime periculum, ut xxx. q. v. c. i. ala⟨nus⟩." Same passage, v. *anulos*: "Nota quod si anulus datur mulieri in ecclesia uel in domo sponsi presumitur matrimonium, xxx. q. v. femine [c. 7]; si coram parentibus suis presumitur sponsalia, xxx. q. v. utantes [*fortasse* C. 30 q. 5 c. 3]. . . . vin⟨centius⟩."

[464] Tancred to 1 Comp. 5.13.6 v. *confessio*, Caius 28/17, p. 119b: "Item nota quod quamcumque confitentur coniuges ad dissolutionem matrimonii tunc non creditur illis, xxxv. q. vi. si duo [c. 4], xxxiii. q. i. requisisti [c. 2], infra de eo qui cogno. consangui. uxoris, super eo, l. iii [*recte* 2 Comp. 4.7.1]."

[465] Dolezalek, *Imbreviaturbuch* no. 44, pp. 129–32.

[466] Adams and Donahue, *Select Cases* A.7, pp. 25–28.

[467] *Argumentum quod religiosi* to C. 27 q. 2, Pembroke 101, fol. 60ra: "Ar. quod ubi discordia est de coniugali coitu, probatio defertur mulieri si per uerum iudicium probare ualet, ut c. Quod autem [c. 29] et supra q. i. nec aliqua [C. 27 q. 1 c. 4]. Nam in uerisimile defertur probatio uiri, ut infra C. 33 q. i. Si quis accepit [c. 3]." Tancred to 1 Comp. 4.16.2 v. *consuetudo*, Caius 28/17, p. 101b: "Ubi dubium est ut eam esse frigidam consueuit hoc facere romana ecclesia [*scil.*: ut ipsam habeat sicut sororem]. Si enim constat nec conseutudo nec constitutio posset facere quod ibi esset matrimonium, adeo est naturale impedimentum frigiditatis quoniam talis non potest ostendere quod sit uir, in aut. de nupt. § per occasionem [Auth. 4.1.6 = Nov. 22.6]. t⟨ancredus⟩."

[468] Johannes Teutonicus, *Glos. ord.* to C. 27 q. 1 c. 4 v. *obstetricum*; Tancred to 3

Other intricate problems in separation or divorce cases arose from allegations of force and fear. Canonists of this period approached these problems cautiously and rarely went much beyond hesitant attempts to define the degree of apprehension required to invalidate matrimonial consent.[469] Fuller development of the jurisprudence on this issue had to await the work of later generations of writers.

Conclusions

The rethinking of doctrine and the restructuring of law concerning sex and marriage, during the closing decade of the twelfth and first three decades of the thirteenth centuries, reflected changes in European social structure and culture. Poets, canonists, civilians, and theologians were all beginning to take interest in facets of human behavior, including sexual actions, that earlier generations had often ignored. The new views about the place of sex in human life involved serious reappraisal of earlier ideas about marriage. Canonists were among the earliest writers in this age to give serious attention to the personal and social consequences that flowed from marriage. More than most poets or theologians, the canonists focused their attention on the practical results of marriage, not only for the couple but also for their offspring and their families. They made conscientious, if not always successful, efforts to balance the conflicting interests involved in marriage and to create a system that would respect the needs of the parties as well as of the social networks to which they belonged. The consequences of developments in matrimonial law during this period were profound.[470]

The key element in this restructuring of marriage law was, of course, the final acceptance of consensual marriage theory in the version formulated in *Veniens ad nos.* When marriage was conceived as a relationship created by the agreement of the parties, the focus of marriage law shifted dramatically to the intentions of the couple. Upon the assessment of those psychic factors depended the validity of their union, the legitimacy of their children, their own and their descendants' property rights, and the relationship of their families. Central to the consensual theory was free choice of matrimonial partners, which thenceforth took ascendancy over family interest and parental wishes in Catholic marriage law. This legal doctrine produced basic changes in the definition of family relationships and had enormous consequences for the subsequent history of marriage and family throughout the West.

The consensual theory also produced some oddities. The new marriage law

---

Comp. 4.11.1 v. *per errorem,* Caius 28/17, p. 290a: "Id est aspectum corporis, ut supra de probationibus, postulasti, l. ii [*recte* 2 Comp. 2.10.2], quia manus obstetric⟨is⟩ et oculus sepe fallitur, xxvii. q. i. nec aliam [C. 27 q. 1 c.4], et sic patet quod sententia a qua non est appellatum retractatur."

[469] Raymond of Peñafort, *Summa de mat.* 11.2.4, ed. Ochoa and Diez, col. 956–57.

[470] Sheehan, "Marriage Theory and Practice," p. 457.

legitimized an array of irregular unions, particularly clandestine marriages. Since the consent of the parties was the only essential requirement for marriage, it seemed inconsistent to limit a couple's freedom of consent by requiring as a condition of validity that marriages must be public and announced in advance to all parties who might be interested. For nearly half a millennium European marriage law wrestled with this tension between the insistence on preserving the couple's right to contract freely by simple consent and society's interest in requiring persons to marry openly. Efforts to restrain clandestine contracts, notably the attempt by the Fourth Lateran Council to require publication of banns prior to marriage and the celebration of marriages in public, failed to solve the problem, despite the efforts of popes, prelates, and judges to enforce these rules.[471]

Law writers during this period were not agreed about the role that sex ought to play in married life. A few of them valued marital sex more positively than had previous generations of canonists, but suspicion about the impurity of sex continued to trouble the writers of this period. They believed that the exercise of sexual rights in marriage should be restrained, but they approached the problem differently than had their predecessors. A few canonists, to be sure, fell back on earlier rules about periodic abstinence from sex, but writers of this generation more frequently concentrated on the quality and character, rather than the frequency, of sexual encounters—their discussions of coital positions reflect that concern.

Legal authorities in this period said little that was new about the intrinsic evils of marital sex. They were far more concerned than their predecessors with the role of sex in the emotional bonding of the couple. A telling symbol of the new attitudes toward marital sex appeared in this period. Wedding rituals after the mid-twelfth century reintroduced a half-forgotten element of older ceremonies: the blessing of the bridal chamber and the marriage bed, which from this time began to assume increasing importance in the iconography of marriage in medieval art.[472]

The increased prominence of impotence and frigidity as grounds for divorce in canonical jurisprudence during these decades also points to a renewed awareness of the importance of sex in marriage. Although sexual intercourse was no longer essential to the formation of marriage, the capacity to have sexual relations was deemed so central that where it was absent an otherwise valid marriage could be dissolved.

Canonistic commentators of this generation tried to clarify the process of terminating unsuccessful unions, either through divorce (which was increasingly restricted) or through separation of the parties without the right to remarry. Divorce and separation law was considerably affected, too, by the action

---

[471] Diebold, "Application," p. 195.

[472] Molin and Mutembe, *Rituel du mariage*, pp. 37–39, 257, 259. This rite had been used as early as the sixth century, but then fell out of general use. It reappears in twelfth century marriage rituals; ibid., pp. 255–56.

of the Fourth Lateran Council in reducing the forbidden degrees of consanguinity and affinity from seven to four.

The law concerning sex offenses changed less during this generation than did marriage law, although sex offenses constituted a major part of the case load of the ecclesiastical courts, especially at the lower levels of the system. Fornication was reduced to a minor offense, dealt with routinely by imposing small fines and ritual humiliations on offenders. Adultery, because of its greater social consequences, remained a major offense, although its importance, too, seems to have diminished in the minds of the law writers of the period.

Clerical sex continued to present problems. Clerical marriage was no longer a central issue, since married men could no longer be ordained, and marriage by men already in major orders was invalid. But clerical concubinage remained common, and no effective means to combat it were devised, despite numerous efforts. The law concentrated during this generation on efforts to penalize the concubinary cleric himself, through suspension, deposition, and deprivation. Efforts to deal with the problem by harsh treatment of concubines diminished during this era.

Finally the law concerning procedure and evidence in sex cases, as in other matters, became more precise and comprehensive. Ordeals and other nonrational modes of proof are scarcely mentioned by the law writers of this age. They focused instead on problems of evaluating the testimony of witnesses.

The generation that spanned the decades from the end of the pontificate of Alexander III to the publication of the *Liber Extra* left a permanent imprint on the Western Church's legal system. Canon law by the end of this period had become a more supple and sophisticated tool for implementing the policies of the Church's leaders than it had been at the beginning. Succeeding generations made good use of the new foundations.

9
Sex, Marriage, and the Legal Commentators, 1234–1348

Sources and Literature of the Law from the *Liber Extra* to the Black Death

The century between the promulgation of the *Liber Extra* and the death of Johannes Andrea during the first major outbreak of the Black Death was a period of consolidation and systematization in canon law. Three major figures, sometimes called "The Princes", dominated canonistic scholarship during that century: Sinibaldo dei Fieschi, better known as Pope Innocent IV (d. 1254),[1] Henry of Segusio, cardinal bishop of Ostia, usually called Hostiensis (d. 1271),[2] and Johannes Andreae (d. 1348), the first layman to make a significant contribution to canon law.[3] The three Princes were enormously hardworking men, who coupled keen intellects with wide-ranging scholarship. Numerous lesser jurists of the period also left lasting marks on the law's development, among them Bernard of Parma,[4] who compiled the *Glossa ordinaria* on the *Liber Extra*, Geoffrey of Trani (d. 1245),[5] who wrote an influential *Summa super titulis de-*

---

[1] LAC pp. 311–12; J.A. Cantini and Charles Lefebvre, "Sinibalde dei Fieschi (Innocent IV)," in DDC 7:1029–62; Elisabeth Vodola, "Innocent IV" in DMA 6:465–67; Schulte, QL 2:91–94.

[2] LAC, pp. 312–14; Charles Lefebvre, "Hostiensis," in DDC 5:1211–27; Elisabeth Vodola, "Hostiensis," in DMA 6:298–99 Schulte, QL 2:123–29; and three articles by Noel Didier: "Henri de Suse en Angleterre (1236?–1244)," in *Studi in onore di Vincenzo Arangio-Ruiz nel XLV anno del suo insegnamento*, 4 vols. (Naples: Jovene, 1953) 2:333–51; "Henri de Suse, évêque de Sisteron (1244–50)," RHDF, 4th ser., 31 (1953) 244–70, 409–29; "Henri de Suse, prieur d'Antibes, prévôt de Grasse (1235?–1245)," SG 2 (1954) 595–617.

[3] LAC, pp. 327–28; Svein Stelling-Michaud, "Jean d'André," in DDC 6:89–92; Schulte, QL 2:205–29. Johannes Andreae was not the first layman to teach canon law at Bologna, however; that honor belongs to Egidio Foscarari (d. 1289), who was thrice-married and had four sons, one of them a bastard; LAC, p. 316; Schulte, QL 2:139–43.

[4] LAC, p. 309; Paul Ourliac, "Bernard de Parme ou de Botone," in DDC 2:781–82; Schulte, QL 2:114–17; Stephan Kuttner and Beryl Smalley, "The 'Glossa ordinaria' to the Gregorian Decretals," *English Historical Review* 60 (1945) 97–105; Stephan Kuttner, "Notes on the *Glossa ordinaria* of Bernard of Parma," BMCL 11 (1981) 86–93.

[5] LAC, p. 308; R. Naz, "Geoffroy de Trani," in DDC 5:952; Schulte, QL 2:88–91.

cretalium, William Durand (d. 1296),[6] called "The Speculator," the greatest procedural authority of the later middle ages, Bernard of Montemirato (d. 1296),[7] a Benedictine monk who was commonly called "The Old Abbot" (*Abbas Antiquus*) and whose legal writing was marked by a keen critical sense, and Guido of Baysio (d. 1311), also known as the Archdeacon, the most important commentator on Gratian's *Decretum* during this century.[8]

The period also saw continued growth in the numbers of universities and consequently in the numbers of canon lawyers who taught in them and who wrote commentaries on canonistic texts and themes.[9] Within these new universities, as also in the older *studia generalia*, the faculties of canon law claimed increasing autonomy from civil law faculties and from theology. Graduates of these faculties followed a wide variety of careers: many became ecclesiastical functionaries, considerable numbers of them became bishops, and a few ended their careers as cardinals or even as popes—notably Innocent IV and Boniface VIII. But large numbers made careers in secular government as well: in England, for example, a majority of those middle-level administrators about whose training we have information in the government of Edward I (1272–1307) had studied canon law.[10] Still others became judges or practiced as advocates or proctors in the burgeoning courts of this age. Canon law had a well-deserved reputation as an avenue to wealth as well as to power.[11]

The period between 1234 and 1348 witnessed further additions to the body of canon law. Decretal letters continued to pour forth from Rome and, during

---

[6]LAC, pp. 319–21; L. Falletti, "Guillaume Durand," in DDC 5:1014–75; Ronald J. Zawilla, "Durand, William," in DMA 4:314–15; Schulte, QL 2:144–56.

[7]LAC, p. 315; A. Villien, "Abbas," in DDC 1:1–2; Schulte, QL 2:130–32.

[8]LAC, pp. 326–27; G. Mollat, "Gui de Baysio," in DDC 5:1007–1008; Schulte, QL 2:186–90; Filippo Liotta, "Appunti per una biografia del canonista Guido da Baisio, arcidiacono di Bologna (con appendice di documenti)," *Studi Senesi*, 3d ser., 13 (1964) 7–52.

[9]In France new centers of juristic study and teaching appeared at Avignon (ca. 1256), Montpellier (ca. 1260), Orange (ca. 1265), and Cahors (before 1332), while in Italy universities developed at Rome (1244/45), Perugia (1307), Treviso (1318), and Pisa (1339). New universities were also being created in the Iberian peninsula at Valladolid (before 1293), Lérida (1300), and Coimbra (1290). The first university east of the Rhine was founded at Prague in 1348; Coing, "Juristische Fakultät," pp. 42, 46–47; Rashdall, *Universities* 3:65, n. 2.

[10]Tierney, *Religion, Law, and Constitutional Thought*, p. 11.

[11]Stephan Kuttner, "Dat Galienus opes et sanctio Justiniana," in *Linguistic and Literary Studies in Honor of Helmut A. Hatzfeld*, ed. Alessandro S. Crisafulli (Washington, D.C.: Catholic University of America Press, 1964), pp. 237–46; James A. Brundage, "English-Trained Canonists in the Middle Ages: A Statistical Analysis of a Social Group," in *Law-Making and Law-Makers in British History*, ed. Alan Harding (London: Royal Historical Society, 1980), pp. 64–78; T. H. Aston, "Oxford's Medieval Alumni," *Past and Present* 74 (1977) 11–16, 19, 22–23, 27–31; T. H. Aston, G.D. Duncan, and T. A. R. Evans, "The Medieval Alumni of the University of Cambridge," *Past and Present* 86 (1980) 57–63, 70–83.

the latter part of the period, from Avignon, where the popes resided between 1309 and 1378. Three general councils—1 Lyon (1245), 2 Lyon (1274), and Vienne (1311–12)—added ninety-six new constitutions and decrees to the Church's legal arsenal, and numerous local councils and synods adopted many times that number of new canons. Much of the new law was collected, arranged in systematic order, and disseminated in canonistic collections, the most important of them issued by the papacy itself. Innocent IV published no less than three collections of *Novellae* (1245, 1246, and 1253), and Gregory X (1271–76) issued the *Novissimae*, consisting mainly of the constitutions of 2 Lyon in 1276. The most comprehensive official collection of the period was the *Liber Sextus* of Boniface VIII (1294–1303), which incorporated most of Innocent's *Novellae* and Gregory's *Novissimae*, along with much else, and was promulgated in 1298. Not long after the beginning of the new century a much smaller collection, the *Constitutiones Clementinae*, was published by order of Pope John XXII (1316–34).[12]

Although a great deal was added to the already bulging storehouse of ecclesiastical law, there was during this period far less fundamental innovation in the canon law concerning marriage and sexual behavior than in the preceding century. The basic changes had already been made. Marriage law remained relatively static; so, too, did the law concerning clerical sexuality and sex offenses. This was an age not of innovation but of consolidation and refinement in the canon law about sex. Canonists during the late thirteenth and early fourteenth centuries were far more concerned with enforcing the existing sex laws of the Church than with creating new law. While academic legal commentators wrote at length about sexual behavior, much of what they said echoed earlier conclusions. The most striking novelties of the age had to do with procedures and evidence, not with innovations in the substantive law on sex and marriage.

Social and Political Context

The period from 1234 to 1348 saw further social as well as legal change in Western Europe. Population growth slackened and by the closing decades of the thirteenth century had come to a halt. There was probably some fall in population early in the fourteenth century, even before the demographic disaster of the Black Death. City populations continued to outpace rural populations, and the bourgeoisie almost everywhere greatly enhanced its social and political power. The upper ranks of the urban population—well-to-do merchants, craftsmen, and professional people, especially lawyers—were beginning to acquire real influence in politics and society. The growth of the size, wealth, and power of cities meant that lawyers, including canon lawyers, played increasingly central roles in society and politics, for the lawyers as a group enjoyed a special status in urban society. Their skills and expertise became ever more critical for

[12] LAC, pp. 243–56; Van Hove, *Prolegomena*, pp. 361–68; Stickler, *Hist. iur. can.*, pp. 251–72.

commercial entrepreneurs in the cities, and both ecclesiastical and royal administrators also depended increasingly on them for advice and counsel.[13]

Growing activism of municipal authorities with respect to sexual behavior and marriage was notable during this century. Municipal statutes dealt with sexual matters much more often. The authorities of towns and communes asserted their competence to regulate prostitution, to punish adultery and sodomy, and to determine the property consequences of divorce and separation. The statutes that embodied these assertions of municipal power and authority were themselves often redacted by lawyers for municipal governments, cases arising under these statutes were prosecuted by lawyers serving city authorities, and the results of prosecutions were determined with increasing frequency by judges trained in one or both of the learned laws.[14]

The Black Death ended an era in several senses. The death of Johannes Andrea, the most important canonist of his generation, and the passing a few years later of his younger and even more able contemporary among the civilians, Bartolus of Sassoferrato (1314–57), left a void that the following generation proved unable to fill.[15] Both population and prosperity suffered from the effects of the great plague, which for three centuries continued to return at frequent intervals with devastating results.[16]

Sex, Society, and Social Thought

Some thirteenth-century canonists and theologians attempted to modify older ideas concerning sexuality, particularly marital sexuality.[17] Legislators, at the

[13] See generally Johannes Fried, *Die Entstehung des Juristenstandes im 12. Jahrhundert: Zur sozialen Stellung und politischen Bedeutung gelehrter Juristen in Bologna und Modena*, Forschungen zur neueren Privatrechtsgeschichte, vol. 21 (Cologne: Böhlau, 1974), esp. pp. 87–139, 158–71, 187–224, and 237–45; William J. Bouwsma, "Lawyers in Early Modern Culture," *American Historical Review* 78 (1973) 305–27; Franklin J. Pegues, *The Lawyers of the Last Capetians* (Princeton: Princeton University Press, 1962). On rural population growth and its implications for both the peasant economy and sexual mores see J. Z. Titow, "Some Differences between Manors and Their Effects on the Condition of the Peasant in the Thirteenth Century," *Agricultural History Review* 10 (1962) 4, 6–7; P. P. A. Biller, "Birth-Control in the West in the Thirteenth and Fourteenth Centuries," *Past and Present* 94 (1982) 20.

[14] Fried, *Entstehung des Juristenstandes*, pp. 115–39, 218–23.

[15] C. N. S. Woolf, *Bartolus of Sassoferrato: His Position in the History of Medieval Political Thought* (Cambridge: At the University Press, 1913); Julius Kirschner, "Bartolo da Sassoferrato," in DMA 2:114–16; Anna T. Sheedy, *Bartolus on Social Conditions in the Fourteenth Century*, Studies in History, Economics, and Public Law, no. 495 (New York: Columbia University Press, 1942).

[16] See generally Robert S. Gottfried, *The Black Death: A Natural and Human Disaster in Medieval Europe* (New York: Free Press, 1983), and "Black Death," in DMA 2:257–67; Philip Ziegler, *The Black Death* (London: Collins, 1969).

[17] Jacques Rossiaud, "Prostitution, Youth, and Society in the Towns of Southeastern France in the Fifteenth Century," in *Deviants and the Abandoned in French Society: Selections from the Annales: économies, sociétés, civilisations*, ed. Robert Forster and

same time, sought to implement more effectively the restraints on extramarital sex that the law decreed and to punish offenders more consistently.[18] The growth during this period of interest in and information—or pseudo-information—about reproductive biology also influenced treatments of sexual problems by canonistic and theological writers.[19]

While most authors maintained the conventional view that sex in Paradise was radically different from sex in this sinful world,[20] some challenged the received wisdom on this matter. St. Albert the Great (ca. 1208–80) dismissed this as an empty assertion. Sex, Albert held, was a natural act and its nature did not change as a result of original sin. Certainly the biology of sex was the same, he maintained, and sexual arousal and desire had not been fundamentally different in Eden than in the postlapsarian world.[21] Albert's view that sex was part of God's original creation, rather than a result of man's rebellion against the creator, formed the basis for a naturalistic approach that characterized his treatment of sexual morality.

Albert the Great's innovative views failed to attract a significant following. Even his most famous pupil, Thomas Aquinas (1224–74), rejected Albert's sexual teachings and clung instead to the Augustinian-Stoic tradition that viewed sexual desire and venereal pleasure as results of sin.[22] Thomas repeatedly argued that lust was a disorder because it undermined reason, and this in turn

Orest Ranum, trans. Elborg Forster and Patricia M. Ranum (Baltimore: Johns Hopkins University Press, 1978), p. 28.

[18] Sheehan, "Marriage and Family," pp. 208–209.

[19] Helen Rodnite Lemay, "William of Saliceto on Human Sexuality," *Viator* 12 (1981) 169; Vern L. Bullough, "Medieval Medical and Scientific Views of Women," *Viator* 4 (1973) 493–94, 500–501; Brundage, "Carnal Delight," pp. 376–77.

[20] Guido de Baysio, *Rosarium* to C. 32 q. 7 c. 12 v. *coire* (Lyon: Apud Hugonem a Porta, 1549), fol. 350va; Nicholas de Lyra, *Postilla super totam Bibliam*, 4 vols. (Strasbourg: Johann Grüninger, 1492; repr. Frankfurt a/M.: Minerva, 1971; unpaginated) to Gen. 2:25 v. *erant autem uterque nudus*. The theme also surfaces in some of the poets of this period, e.g., Matfré Ermengau, *Breviari d'amor*, ll. 8355–85, ed. Gabriel Azaïs, 2 vols. (Béziers: Sécrétariat de la Société archéologique, scientifique, et littéraire de Béziers, 1862–81) 1:288–89.

[21] Albertus Magnus, *Summa* 2.18.122.1.4, in his *Opera omnia*, ed. A. Borgnet, 38 vols. (Paris: Louis Vives, 1890–99).; Müller, *Lehre des hl. Augustinus*, p. 239; but the *Summa* was written during the final decade of Albert's life and some scholars question its authenticity; cf. John J. Clifford, "The Ethics of Conjugal Intimacy According to St. Albert the Great," *Theological Studies* 3 (1942) 10. On this point, at least, Albert's *Summa* agreed with the love poet, Jean de Meung, who insisted in his continuation of the *Roman de la rose* on the natural character of the sex urge; Grévy-Pons, *Célibat et nature*, p. 39. A few writers of this period, notably Richard Fishacre and Peter John Olivi, taught that sexual pleasure before the fall was even greater than it is nowadays; Müller, *Lehre des hl. Augustinus*, p. 209; Burr, "Olivi on Marriage," p. 185.

[22] Thomas Aquinas, *Summa Theologica* (cited hereafter as ST) 1.98.2.ad 3 (I have used several editions of ST, most frequently the edition in 8 vols. [Paris: Bloud et Baral, 1885]). Aquinas did concede, however, that Adam and Eve had copulated in Paradise,

caused it to corrupt both morals and judgment. These views were echoed by Nicholas of Lyra (d. 1349?) and Guido of Baysio among others.[23] The lusts of the flesh, Nicholas observed, were so powerful that they survived baptism, and thus few Christians ever attained complete sexual denial.[24]

The ubiquity of sexual sin was a favorite topic of late thirteenth-century preachers and moralists who decried the pervasiveness of lechery even among faithful Christians. The sermons of Humbert de Romans (d. 1277), Master-General of the Dominicans, for example, abound with denunciations of carnality. Humbert gave special prominence to sexual improprieties among married couples, but he also excoriated the loose morals of the fornicators and adulterers who abounded in thirteenth-century Europe.[25] Humbert was scarcely alone in targeting sexual license for homiletical attack. Collections of anecdotes for preachers show a constant preoccupation with sexual sins.[26]

The perception that sexual license abounded was not solely the product of the fevered imaginations of a few celibate clerics. Those who sought examples needed to look only at the career of James the Conqueror, King of Aragon and Catalunya (1208–76). While he was married to Princess Violant of Hungary (the second of his four wives), by whom he had nine children, James was also involved with four mistresses, by whom he sired three more children.[27] James

---

but added that prelapsarian sex lacked the lustful pleasure that was born of sin. See also Noonan, *Contraception*, pp. 252–54.

[23] ST 1-2.33.4 and 34.1. ad 1; ST 2-2.55.8 ad 1; also Aquinas, *On Kingship to the King of Cyprus* 2.8.144, 147, trans. Gerald B. Phelan, rev. I. Th. Eschmann (Toronto: Pontifical Institute of Mediaeval Studies, 1949), pp. 78–80; Müller, *Lehre des hl. Augustinus*, p. 257; Nicholas of Lyra, *Postilla* to Gen. 3:7 v. *et fecerunt sibi perizomata*; Guido of Baysio, *Rosarium* to C. 32 q. 7 c. 12, fol. 350va.

[24] Nicholas of Lyra, *Postilla* to 1 Cor. 7:2 v. *propter fornicationem*.

[25] Alexander Murray, "Religion among the Poor in Thirteenth-Century France: The Testimony of Humbert de Romans," *Traditio* 30 (1974) 314.

[26] Frederic C. Tubach, *Index exemplorum: A Handbook of Medieval Religious Tales*, Finnish Academy of Sciences, Communications, no. 204 (Helsinki: Suomalainen Tiedeakatemia, 1969) shows these frequencies for explicit sexual themes:

Theme	Entries
Harlots	42
Adultery	30
Incest	13
Fornication	8
Rape	7
Seduction	4
Homosexuality	1
Pimps	1

By way of comparison, monks receive 190 entries, wives 90, usury 74, marriage 33, widows 26, husbands 22, and widowers only one.

[27] Burns, "Spiritual Life of James the Conqueror," pp. 26–27.

was outstanding, even in a heroic age of lechery, but his determined pursuit of sexual variety was by no means unique.

The inquisitors at the village of Montaillou, not far across the Pyrenees from James' domains, discovered astonishingly complex networks of sexual involvement among people at all levels of the social hierarchy. Either men or women might initiate these affairs and they did not confine themselves to partners of their own social class.[28] The inquisitors interested themselves in the people of Montaillou because they suspected (with good reason, it turned out) that many villagers belonged to the Cathar sect. The struggle against Cathars who held marriage worthless and procreation sinful colored Catholic writing and thinking about sexual topics in the thirteenth and fourteenth centuries. Opposition to Catharism led Catholic authorities to insist even more urgently than before that marriage was a sacrament and procreation its primary goal.[29]

Some popular writers of the period described sex as a manifestation of the forces of nature, which they personified as a subordinate female deity who operated in her own way according to rules that did not necessarily conform to those of the Creator—this view surfaces plainly in the *Roman de la Rose*, for example, especially in the continuation of the poem by Jean de Meung (d. ca. 1305).[30] A remarkable synthesis of Catholic theology and *fin'amors* appears in the *Breviari d'amor* of the Franciscan, Matfré Ermengau (d. 1322). Matfré described a veritable theology of love. In Matfré's poem, love figured as the offspring of nature and the narrator used the metaphor of the tree of nature to explain his cosmology. Atop the tree, the source of all else, was God; beneath him was nature, who ruled all created beings. Nature, in turn, was the source of natural law and of the *jus gentium*. Sexual love descended from natural law, of which it was a product. Sexual attraction in Matfré's cosmology was an intrinsic element in God's design for the world, and he clearly rejected the belief that sex resulted from sinful defiance of the Creator's will.[31]

A few theologians took positions akin to those of the love poets, but conven-

---

[28] Emmanuel Le Roy Ladurie, *Montaillou: The Promised Land of Error*, trans. Barbara Bray (New York: George Braziller, 1978), pp. 16–17. Ladurie's account is seriously flawed, however, and must be used with caution; see the catalogue of errors by Leonard E. Boyle, "Montaillou Revisited: *Mentalité* and Methodology," in *Pathways to Mediaeval Peasants*, ed. J. Ambrose Raftis, Papers in Mediaeval Studies, no. 2 (Toronto: Pontifical Institute of Mediaeval Studies, 1981), pp. 119–140.

[29] On Catharism see generally A. Borst, *Die Katharer*, MGH, Schriften, vol. 12 (Stuttgart: A. Hiersemann, 1953); Fredric L. Cheyette, "Cathars," in DMA 3:181–91, and other works cited there. Fuchs, *Sexual Desire and Love*, p. 126, argues that the struggle against the Cathars made it necessary for thirteenth-century writers to reexamine the whole system of Christian sexual ethics.

[30] *Roman de la rose*, ll. 15,893–16,148, 19,865–68, 20,637–44, ed. Félix Lecoy, 3 vols. (Paris: H. Champion, 1969–70); Grévy-Pons, *Célibat et nature*, pp. 36–37.

[31] Matfré Ermengau, *Breviari*, ll. 32,644–33,045; Grévy-Pons, *Célibat et nature*, pp. 31–2.

tional theologians and canonists distanced themselves from such fancies. Sex, Hostiensis was inclined to think, was a nuisance and a distraction. He quoted with approval Jerome's statement that men who had sex easily available would not be able to give their minds wholeheartedly to God.[32] St. Bonaventure (ca. 1217–74) was even more emphatic: "The sexual act itself," he wrote, "is diseased, for it cannot be performed without disorder," that is without perturbation of body and spirit.[33] No one denied that sex was pleasant: that was its snare, for attached to the pleasure were shame, defilement, and in the aftermath a depression that resulted, as Nicholas of Lyra believed, from the strength of carnal passion.[34] The Archdeacon, Guido de Baysio, agreed and added that it mattered not whether a married couple performed the sex act or whether it conformed to the prescriptions of nature: in any case sex invariably resulted in shame and defilement.[35] According to the civilian Oldradus da Ponte (d. after 1337), sex was a kind of madness; thus, Oldradus added, a man in the throes of passion could not be charged with perjury if he subsequently failed to fulfill commitments that he made under oath while in that fevered condition.[36]

Sexual pleasure was dangerous for yet another reason: experiencing even a little of it kindled a burning desire for more. By its nature sex was a greedy pleasure: just as a tiny spark can ignite a pile of dry wood, so the slightest sexual tingle could set off a burst of insatiable passion. Sexual moderation, if not impossible, was at least highly improbable and therein lay the peril of exposing oneself to any sort of titillation.[37] The taboo against nudity seems to have been particularly strong. Representation of the naked body in this period usually oc-

[32] Hostiensis, *In quinque Decretalium libri commentaria* to X 2.23.15 § 3, 5 vols. in 2 (Venice: Apud Iuntas, 1581; repr. Turin: Bottega d'Erasmo, 1965; cited hereafter as *Lectura*).

[33] St. Bonaventure, *Commentarium in quattuor libros Sententiarum* 4.31.2.1, in his *Opera omnia*, ed. A. C. Peltier, 15 vols. (Paris: L. Vivès, 1864–71) 6:277; cf. Clifford, "Ethics of Conjugal Intimacy," pp. 5–6, and Børresen, *Subordination and Equivalence*, p. 327. On Bonaventure generally see J. F. Quinn, "Bonaventure, St.," in DMA 2:313–19 and the literature cited there.

[34] Nicholas of Lyra, *Postilla* to Gen. 3:16 v. *multiplicabo erumnas tuas et conceptus tuos* and Exod. 19:15 v. *ne appropinquetis uxoribus vestris*.

[35] Guido de Baysio, *Rosarium* to C. 32 q. 4 c. 12; William of Pagula, *Summa summarum* 5.16, in Pembroke MS 201, fol. 239ra: "Luxuria autem dicitur in cibus uel potu cum utitur delicatis et calidis ut apcior sit ad immundiciam [*viz.*: usum illicitum membrorum], xxxii. q. iiii. in eo [c. 12], in glo. que attenditur." Cf. Clifford, "Ethics of Conjugal Intimacy," p. 16. On William of Pagula see Leonard E. Boyle, "The *Oculus sacerdotis* and Some Other Works of William of Pagula," *Transactions of the Royal Historical Society*, 5th ser., 5 (1955) 81–110, and "The 'Summa summarum' and Some Other English Works of Canon Law," in *Boston Proceedings*, pp. 415–56.

[36] Quoted in Woldemar Engelmann, *Die Schuldlehre der Postglossatoren und ihre Fortentwicklung*, 2d ed. (Leipzig: K. F. Koehler, 1895; repr. Aalen: Scientia Verlag, 1965), p. 34. I should like to thank my colleague, Professor John F. McGovern, for bringing this reference to my attention.

[37] Thomas Aquinas, *On Kingship* 2.8.145, trans. Phelan, p. 79.

curred in scenes depicting debauchery and sexual licentiousness (see Pl. 19). Bishop William Durantis (1237–96) thought that decent artists should follow what he described as the Greek practice of representing persons only from the waist up, "in order to remove occasion for foolish thoughts."[38] Moralists even cautioned husbands and wives, as we have noted earlier, not to look upon one another's naked bodies, lest they arouse the spirit of lust, which was inappropriate in the marital relationship. The contrast with the celebration of nudity in ancient art and its subsequent reappearance in renaissance art after about 1400 is striking.[39]

Sexual indulgence held still further dangers, Aquinas warned. Those who indulged in sex, married or not, were weakened and debilitated as a result. Thus in wartime wise commanders cast women forth from their camps, so that soldiers might not spend their strength in carnal indulgence.[40] Bonaventure was convinced that frequent intercourse was dangerous to the health and that every sex act helped to shorten one's life.[41] Here Bonaventure, himself the son of a physician, differed from the prevailing medical views of his time, for physicians commonly taught that regular sexual intercourse was essential for health. This was the view of Galen, who had described celibacy as unnatural and commended the example of the Cynic, Diogenes, who had prescribed masturbation as a relief from the unhealthy tensions of continence. Galen taught that people had a natural need for sexual relief and compared this to the need for bowel movements and urination. Medieval medical authorities respected Galen's teachings, but found themselves troubled by the resulting conflict between the demands of health and morals.[42]

Dangerous as it might be, sex was inescapably woven into the fabric of the universe.[43] Moreover the sexual distinction between men and women was part of the human constitution and was, Nicholas of Lyra asserted, a requirement for human perfection.[44] Of the two sexes, men were the more perfect. Aquinas agreed. Women, he declared, were created for the subordinate role of assisting men to carry out the divine plan, specifically by making possible the continuation of the human race. Aquinas accepted the Augustinian belief that the pri-

[38] William Durantis, *Rationale divinorum officiorum* 1.3.2, quoted in Leo Steinberg, *The Sexuality of Christ in Renaissance Art and in Modern Oblivion* (New York: Pantheon, 1983), p. 27.

[39] See above, p. 302.

[40] Thomas Aquinas, *On Kingship* 2.8.146, trans. Phelan, p. 79. This seems to be a rationalization of military practices that were probably based originally on fear that sexual defilement would attract divine wrath.

[41] Bonaventure, *Comm.* to 2 Sent. 30.3.1.

[42] Cadden, "Medieval Scientific and Medical Views," p. 12; LeMay, "William of Saliceto," p. 177.

[43] Popular belief, indeed, sometimes ascribed sexual activities to God himself, a notion that orthodox thinkers strenuously rejected; LeRoy Ladurie, *Montaillou*, p. 144.

[44] Nicholas of Lyra, *Postilla* to Matt. 19:4 v. *masculum et feminam* and 1 Cor. 7:2 v. *propter fornicationem*.

mary function of the female was procreation, while her lack of strength, both mental and physical, meant that she was unfit for more central roles in human affairs.[45] His contemporaries, canonists and theologians alike, shared these views. Bernard of Parma put the matter bluntly in his *Glossa ordinaria* on the *Liber Extra*:

> A woman on the other hand should not have [jurisdictional] power. . . . because she is not made in the image of God; rather man is the image and glory of God and woman ought to be subject to man and, as it were, like his servant, since man is the head of the woman and not the other way about.[46]

Men were fitted to rule, the argument ran, because their mental faculties were more acute than those of women.[47]

Female inferiority resulted from women's biological constitution. Women were stout and wide below, but slender and more graceful above the waist, according to the unflattering description of Nicholas of Lyra. These anatomical differences, in turn, resulted from women's natural coldness, which allowed their nutriments to pass downward and settle in the lower parts of their bodies. Men, on the other hand, were naturally endowed with greater heat, which resulted in their having wider chests, broader shoulders, and larger heads than women. In consequence the food that men consumed was quickly processed in the upper part of their bodies, so that they tended to be hefty above and slender below the waist. Women, because they were cooler, took longer to digest their food, so that it wound up in the lower part of their bodies.[48] These anatomical stereotypes, which sometimes appear in late medieval and renaissance art (see for example Pls. 16 and 17) were held to account for other attributes commonly ascribed to women. They were said to be variable and changeable because of the delicacy of their physical constitution and, for the same reason, softhearted and yielding.[49]

At the same time, women were expected to be shy, retiring, coy, and modest about sexual matters. Women usually blush when sex is mentioned, said Hostiensis,[50] and both Aquinas and Bonaventure agreed that women preferred to

---

[45] ST 1.92.1 ad 2; Nicholas of Lyra, *Postilla* to Eph. 5:22 v. *mulieres viris suis subdite sint*; Børresen, *Subordination and Equivalence*, pp. 256–58, 260–61, 340–41; Backeljauw, "De uxoris statu sociali," p. 272.

[46] *Glos. ord.* to X 1.33.12 v. *iurisdictionis*. Cf. Johannes Andreae, *In quinque decretalium libros novella commentaria* to X 1.33.12 § 6, 5 vols. in 4 (Venice: Apud Franciscum Franciscium, 1581; repr. Turin: Bottega d'Erasmo, 1963; cited hereafter as *Novella*).

[47] Nicholas of Lyra, *Postilla* to 1 Pet. 3:1 v. *viris suis*.

[48] Nicholas of Lyra, *Postilla* to Gen. 2:22 v. *et edificavit*.

[49] Hostiensis, *Lectura* to X 3.33.2 § 10.

[50] Hostiensis, *Lectura* to X 4.13.11 § 2 v. *carnis stimulis*; adopted almost verbatim by Johannes Andreae, *Novella* to X 4.13.11 § 1 v. *supplicavit*.

speak about sex in circumlocutions. Thus when a woman says that she yearns for a baby, what she really means is that she lusts for sex.[51] Married men needed to be sensitive to this shyness, since their wives may be in need of sexual intercourse yet too shy to say so. Husbands should not wait for their wives to make outright demands for sex, but should be sensitive to their unspoken signs, according to William of Pagula (fl. 1314–31).[52]

Behind the veil of modesty lurked the specter of insatiable female sexual appetite. The argument from anatomy was used to justify the belief that women in general, and young women in particular, found sensual stimulation irresistible.[53] Hostiensis described this forthrightly. Women are always ready for sex, he declared, and they need no preparation for it. A priest who journeyed with two young women, so that one rode in front of him and the other behind, could never swear that the one in back was a virgin. Men, he continued, are differently constituted, although he acknowledged that a few sexually precocious males could do astounding things.[54]

But despite these common beliefs about female lustiness, canonists nonetheless maintained that both law and morality required a higher standard of sexual restraint from women than from men. Innocent IV sought to account for this by arguing that men were like Christ, who was joined first to the synagogue and then to the Church. Thus no harm was done if a man "divided his flesh" between several women. But women, Innocent continued, were like the Church, which always remained a virgin, at least mentally, and hence a woman who "divided her flesh" between several men betrayed her symbolic archetype.[55]

Women, accordingly, had a duty to maintain a higher degree of sexual modesty than was demanded of men. Modesty is woman's peculiar strength, accord-

[51] Thomas Aquinas, *Commentaria in Sententias* 4.34.1.2, Expositio, in his *Opera omnia ut sunt in indice Thomistico*, ed. Roberto Busa, 7 vols. (Holzboog: Friedrich Fromann, 1980); Bonaventura, *Comm. in 4 Sent.* 34.3.3.2; Gordon, "Adnotationes," p. 201.

[52] William of Pagula, *Summa summarum* 4.1, Pembroke 201, fol. 202vb: "An uir teneatur abinde reddere debitum uxori? Dic quod non solum debet uir reddere debitum uxori quando ipsa expresse petit debitum, sed etiam quando per signa apparet eam hoc uelle; non tamen est iudicium de petitione uiri quia mulieres magis solent uerecundari petendo debitum quam uiri, secundum tho. et pe."

[53] Hostiensis, *Lectura* to X 2.13.10 § 13.

[54] Hostiensis cited the example of the nine-year-old lad mentioned in one of Pope Gregory's *Dialogues* who got his nurse pregnant. "I myself," Hostiensis continued, "have known such a case involving a boy of eleven or twelve;" *Lectura* to X 4.13.11 § 1, citing Geoffrey of Trani; repeated with minor variations by Johannes Andreae, *Novella* to X 4.13.11 § 5.

[55] Innocent VI, *Apparatus toto orbe celebrandus super quinque libros Decretalium* to X 1.21.5. § 3 (Frankfurt a/M: Sigismund Feyerabendt, 1570; repr. Frankfurt a/M: Minerva, 1968); cf. Hostiensis, *Summa aurea*, lib. 1, tit. *De bigamis* (Lyon: Johannes de Lambray, 1537; repr. Aalen: Scientia Verlag, 1962), fol. 40vb. Cf. the earlier use of this symbolic argument by Tancred; see above, pp. 350–51.

ing to Johannes Andreae, and immodest women might cause men to commit murder and other horrid crimes, as David did when he was bewitched by the sight of Bathsheba bathing.[56]

Given the dangers on both sides, legal and theological writers of this period wished to see contact between men and women restricted and closely supervised. It was possible for men to be led astray by looking at women or talking to them; one anonymous commentator recalled the advice of Gregory the Great that one should love women as if they were sisters, but flee from them as if they were enemies.[57] Confessors needed to be especially careful about their conduct with women. They must avoid conversation that might seem suggestive or that might put ideas for more adventurous sins into the heads of penitents.[58] Nicholas of Lyra likewise noted with approval the custom practiced in royal households of keeping young women of the ruling family locked up out of sight, so that sexual temptations would be minimized.[59] Married women, regardless of class, Nicholas added, should be subject to their husbands, but as companions, not as slaves.[60]

The pervasiveness of sexual sins and the temptation to commit them were not entirely due to human perversity nor were they wholly under the individual's control, according to many writers. Arabic astrological treatises, several of which circulated widely in Latin translations, maintained that sexual preferences, the size and condition of the genital organs, the extent of sexual activity, and other aspects of sexual behavior were determined by the positions of the planets, especially Venus and Mars, at the time of the individual's birth.[61] Inborn proclivities could, however, be modified by medical intervention, according to physicians of this period. Several writers prescribed anaphrodisiac measures that could reduce the sex drive and thus make life easier for those who sought chastity.[62] In any case, Nicholas of Lyra advised his readers, the problem

[56] Johannes Andreae, *Novella* to X prol. § 7; Nicholas of Lyra, *Postilla* to 2 Kings 11:2 v. *viditque mulierem se lavantem.*

[57] *Flores Decretorum* to D. 32, in Law MS F.6, Library of Congress, Washington, D.C. (hereafter L.C.), fol. 3ra, amplifying D. 32 c. 18: "Feminam quam bene uideris conuersantem, mente dilige, non coporali frequentia; sed bonum est mulierem non tangere, malum est ergo tangere: 'presbiter uxorem suam quasi sororem diligat et quasi hostem fugiat'."

[58] Hostiensis, *Summa aurea*, lib. 5, tit. *De penitentia et remissione* § 49.

[59] Nicholas of Lyra, *Postilla* to 2 Kings 13:2 v. *quia cum esset virgo.*

[60] Nicholas of Lyra, *Postilla* to Gen. 2:22 v. *costam quam tulerat*; to 1 Cor. 11:9 v. *etenim non est creatus uir propter mulierem*; and to Col. 3:19 v. *et nolite amari esse ad illos.*

[61] Helen Rodnite Lemay, "The Stars and Human Sexuality: Some Medieval Scientific Views," *Isis* 71 (1980) 127–28.

[62] Cadden, "Medieval Scientific and Medical Views," p. 10, citing Magnino of Milan (fl. ca. 1330), the *Canon of Medicine* by Avicenna (ca. 980–1037), and Dame Trotula (fl. 11th century).

would sooner or later take care of itself, for after the age of sixty, he declared, lust cools off, and sexual temptation fades away.[63]

Several sectarian groups in this period rejected the views of the established Church concerning the sinfulness of sex, either marital or nonmarital. The belief that pleasure was no sin and that sexual relations carried no moral stigma, so long as they were agreeable to both parties, apparently continued to persist, especially in rural communities. The Runcarian heretics, who held that whatever was done below the belt was no sin, allegedly made this a part of their teaching. Exponents of orthodoxy, in turn, insisted all the more vehemently that sex of any kind outside of marriage, as well as many kinds of sex within marriage, were grievously sinful. Sexual beliefs and practices, therefore, became tests of religious orthodoxy.[64]

While Catholic theologians universally condemned the view that sex was not sinful, one author of unquestioned orthodoxy questioned the conventional belief that pleasure of any kind was a moral failing. Richard Middleton, a Franciscan theologian who wrote about 1272, reported the opinion of "certain" unnamed theologians that pleasure was a legitimate human goal. Although he did not explicitly advocate this position, Middleton reported the view without censure. According to Middleton, advocates of the legitimacy of pleasure argued that Augustine's use of the term "fault" (*culpa*) to describe pleasure did not mean that pleasure was sinful, but rather that it was less than perfect. Further, Middleton reported, those anonymous theologians who supported the legitimacy of pleasure maintained that what was morally wrong was not pleasure itself, but the compulsive, unrestrained pursuit of it—"Man does not sin," they declared, "every time he takes a bite of food in order to savor its taste." Similarly marital sex was free from blame so long as it was enjoyed in moderation. Marriage was not ordained for reproduction alone; in addition to its procreative purpose, marriage prevented fornication by channeling sexual desire into the acceptable outlet of marital relations. Further, having sex with one's wife in order to promote one's own bodily health was no sin either.[65] Like the views of Albert the Great, however, those reported by Richard Middleton failed to command widespread acceptance among the learned. Much more common was the argument that although sex itself was morally indifferent, the pleasure that accompanied it was wicked. Hence marital sex was free from sin only so long as no one enjoyed it.[66]

[63] Nicholas of Lyra, *Postilla* to 1 Tim. 5:9 v. *non minus lx. annorum.*

[64] William of Auxerre, *Summa aurea in quattuor libros Sententiarum* (Paris: P. Pigouchetti, 1500; repr. Frankfurt a/M: Minerva, 1964), fol. 18rb–va; Albertus Magnus, *Summa theologica* 2.18.122.1.1, in his *Opera*, ed. Pierre Jammy, 21 vols. (Lyon: Claudius Prost [etc.], 1651); LeRoy Ladurie, *Montaillou*, p. 151; Lerner, *Heresy of the Free Spirit*, pp. 17–18; Alphandery, *Les idées morales*, p. 185 n. 1.

[65] Richard Middleton, *Commentarium super quarto Sententiarum* 31.3.2 and resp. ad 4 (Venice: Bonetus Locatellus, 1499), fol. 207vb; Noonan, *Contraception*, p. 295.

[66] Lindner, *Usus matrimonii*, pp. 117–18; Noonan, *Contraception*, pp. 198, 293.

Writers of the late thirteenth century laid greater emphasis than their predecessors had on the notion that marriage and marital sex were directed not only toward procreation but also toward child rearing. Thus Nicholas of Lyra argued by analogy with the animal world that monogamy was commanded because of the necessity of cooperation between mates in order to nourish, educate, and provide for the welfare of their offspring. Among animals such as dogs, Nicholas observed, the female alone cares for the pups, and promiscuity is normal. But among other creatures, such as doves, successful nurture of the young requires the cooperation of both parents. Hence, Nicholas argued, the mating pattern among those animals, and also among humans, requires permanent union of the male and female. Promiscuity cannot be tolerated because it conflicts with the needs of the offspring.[67] Major writers such as Aquinas and Nicholas of Lyra, as well as such lesser figures as Humbert de Prully, Johann von Sterngassen, and Hugh of Newcastle, observed that although both parents were necessary for the proper upbringing of the young, the tie between mother and child was closer than that between father and child.[68] Besides, one author wryly added, maternity was a matter of fact, but paternity was a matter of opinion.[69]

The Formation of Marriage

Theories of marriage formation during the late thirteenth and early fourteenth centuries emphasized, as had those current in the previous generation, that intimacy and fidelity were central to marriage.[70] Sexual attraction motivated some marriages and, William of Pagula declared, it is not always sinful to marry a woman because of her beauty; but if her physical attractions were the principal reason, the marriage might be considered seriously sinful.[71] Spouses do many things for each other besides providing sexual partnership, and for this reason if sexual attraction waned or if sex became impossible, the marriage did not necessarily end.[72] Indeed Pierre de La Palude (ca. 1277–1342) declared that sex often confused the basic issues. He supported this observation with an etymological argument that derived the Latin noun *nuptiae* from *nubes*, mean-

[67] Nicholas of Lyra, *Postilla* to 1 Cor. 7:2 v. *mulierem non tangere* and *propter fornicationem.*

[68] Aquinas, ST Supp. 41.1 in c.; Nicholas of Lyra, *Postilla* to Matt. 19:4 v. *qui respondens* and Matt. 19:6 v. *homo non separet*; the opinions of the lesser writers are quoted in F. Salerno, "La definizione nominale del matrimonio canonico nei secoli XII–XIII," in *Ius populi Dei* 3:161 n. 20.

[69] Salerno, "Definizione nominale," p. 167 n. 24, citing Brussels MS 1542 (11,614), fol. 223ra.

[70] Nicholas of Lyra, *Postilla* to Eph. 5:25 v. *viri diligite uxores vestras.*

[71] William of Pagula, *Summa summarum* 4.1, Pembroke 201, fol. 202va: "An peccatum sit contrahere cum aliqua muliere propter pulchritudinem? Dic quod hoc potest esse sine peccato et quandoque cum peccato ueniali. Si autem libido pulchritudinis esset causa principalis non excusaretur a peccato mortali, sed esset effrenata multitudo secundum tho. in scrip."

[72] Guido de Baysio, *Rosarium* to C. 32 q. 5 c. 18, fol. 349rb.

ing clouds.[73] Marriage was not necessarily full of joy and pleasure, Nicholas of Lyra added, and it often led to tears and sadness.[74]

Despite it all, people persisted in marrying and often did so with a love and affection that surpassed the emotional ties between parent and child.[75] Indeed Bernard of Montemirato (ca. 1225–1296) declared that marriage was a basic right and added that a son whose father refused to allow him to marry had grounds for an action against his father. Bartolus of Sassoferrato argued that daughters had a similar right and that under some circumstances they could force their fathers to provide them with dowries so that they could marry.[76] Both in law and reality, marriage for love was not only conceivable but also practiced, at least by men and at least in some regions of medieval Europe.[77] "Everyone should know that a good marriage is highly pleasing to God—and highly profitable to man," declared the *Assises de la cour des bourgeois* in the Latin Kingdom of Jerusalem, and the profit that the author had in mind was spiritual and emotional, as well as mundane.[78]

The more positive attitude toward marriage adopted by Catholic writers in the thirteenth and fourteenth centuries was partly a reaction against the Cathar heresy, which as we have seen held marriage worthless. The Cathars likewise denied that marriage was a sacrament. Those who supported that position often found themselves suspected of heresy.[79] Notable among these dissidents was Peter Olivi (1248–98), one of the most original theologians among the Spiritual Franciscans and, ironically, the principal begetter of the theory of papal infallibility.[80] Olivi's views about many matters, including infallibility, troubled orthodox authorities, who in 1279 appointed a committee of theologians to examine his writings for heresy. They seized upon his doubt about the sacramentality of

[73] Pierre de La Palude (Petrus Paludanus), *Lucubrationum opus in quartum Sententiarum* 26.1.1 (Salamanca: Andreas a Portonariis, 1552), p. 321.

[74] Nicholas of Lyra, *Postilla* to 1 Cor. 7:30 v. *et qui flent*.

[75] Guido de Baysio, *Rosarium* to C. 35 q. 10 c. 1.

[76] Bernardus de Montemirato, *Commentarium* to X 4.1.11 v. *non est vobis*, in *Abbatis antiqui, Bernardi Compostellani, Guidonis Pape, et Joannis a Capistrano commentaria ad libros decretalium* (Venice: Apud Iuntas, 1588), fol. 124rb; Bartolus, *Commentaria* to Dig. 44.7.51, in his *Opera*, 8 vols. (Venice: Apud Giuntas, 1580–81) 5:163rb-va. In his *Consilia* 1.124 Bartolus also argued that a woman could provide her own dowry if her father failed to do so; see his *Consilia, quaestiones et tractatus* (Lyon: Thomas Bertellus, 1547), fol. 38vb–39rb. See also Sheedy, *Bartolus on Social Conditions*, pp. 60–61.

[77] LeRoy Ladurie, *Montaillou*, p. 189; Alan Macfarlane, *The Origins of English Individualism: The Family, Property, and Social Transition* (New York: Cambridge University Press, 1979), pp. 197–98.

[78] *Assises de la cour des bourgeois* 159, in RHC, Lois 2:108.

[79] Johann Joseph Ignaz von Döllinger, *Beiträge zur Sektengeschichte des Mittelalters*, 2 vols. (Munich: Beck, 1890; repr. New York: Burt Franklin, 1966) 2:23.

[80] Brian Tierney, *Origins of Papal Infallibility, 1150–1350: A Study on the Concepts of Infallibility, Sovereignty, and Tradition in the Middle Ages*, Studies in the History of Christian Thought, vol. 6 (Leiden: E. J. Brill, 1972), pp. 93–96.

marriage. In an effort to escape condemnation Olivi defended his views by evading the issue. He retracted, without formally admitting, earlier statements that marriage was not a sacrament. But he then tried to distinguish marriage as less perfect and less virtuous than the other sacraments. Further Olivi seemed to believe that matrimony, unlike the other sacraments, did not confer grace. Pressed to clarify what he meant by this, Olivi distinguished: marriage conferred grace, he conceded, but not in the same manner as the other sacraments. Therefore, he claimed, the Church merely tolerates marriage, but does not advocate it, because although marriage is a sacrament, it is contaminated by worldly considerations—desire for property, for family alliances, for enhancement of social standing or political interest—as well as by sexual attraction. To bolster his position, Olivi further declared that marriage differs from the other sacraments because it does not imprint a "character" on the soul, as do baptism and holy orders, and hence could lawfully be received many times.[81] Although Olivi was forced to modify his views of marriage, he remained skeptical of its sacramental role in the scheme of salvation. Some of his Franciscan followers, notably Pierre de La Palude and Durand de St.-Pourçain, continued to uphold his views.[82]

Even thoroughly orthodox teachers sometimes expressed reservations about the sacramentality of marriage. Albert the Great maintained that marriage was a sacrament, and he also distinguished between it and the others. Albert held that while marriage did confer grace, it did so only in the limited sense that the power of the sacrament helped married persons to achieve the goals of marriage, such as raising children and getting on with one's spouse. He failed to make it clear, however, just why he considered the grace imparted by marriage to be so limited.[83]

John Duns Scotus (1270–1308) took another tack. He distinguished between the sacrament of marriage and the marriage contract. As Scotus saw it, not every marriage was sacramental. A couple could enter into marriage by mutual consent, and this created a perfectly legitimate and binding, but not sacramental union. The couple received the sacrament of marriage only when their contract was ratified by the Church. For Scotus, then, the sacrament of marriage was conferred by the nuptial blessing, not by the mere fact of the marriage contract.[84] Other writers linked the sacramental character of marriage to sexual

---

[81] Anneliese Maier, "Per la storia del processo contro l'Olivi," in *Ausgehendes Mittelalter: gesammelte Aufsätze zur Geistesgeschichte des 14. Jahrhunderts*, 3 vols., Storia e Letteratura, no. 105 (Rome: Storia e Letteratura, 1964–77) 2:241–42, 244–46; David Burr, "Olivi on Marriage: The Conservative as Prophet," *Journal of Medieval and Renaissance Studies* 2 (1972) 187–90; Esteban Pérez, "¿Todo matrimonio entre cristianos es sacramento?" *Escritos del Vedat* (1976) 11.

[82] Pierre de La Palude, *Lucubrationum* 26.4.1, pp. 327–28; Maier, "Per la storia del processo," pp. 252–53.

[83] Clifford, "Ethics of Conjugal Intimacy," pp. 12–14; Noonan, *Contraception*, pp. 286–88.

[84] John Duns Scotus, *Quaestiones in IV libros Sententiarum* 4.26.14, in his *Opera*

consummation. On this theory there were two stages in the reception of the matrimonial sacrament: one occurred when the couple exchanged consent, the other when they physically consummated their union. This view resurrected Gratian's distinction between initiated and ratified marriage.[85]

The teaching of Aquinas and others in this period, however, affirmed that marriage was a sacrament and that the exchange of consent itself conferred grace in the same way that other sacraments did. This view was adopted as a dogmatic truth by the Council of Florence; the Council of Trent ultimately condemned contrary views as heresy.[86]

In order to marry validly, the couple must be of age, they must consent freely, and they must not be too closely related.[87] Canonists continued to refine the rules concerning each of these matters. The anonymous Notabilia *Aliter debet* cautioned against too literal an interpretation of the rule of twelve for girls, fourteen for boys. A couple who had not quite attained the minimum age, but who were within six months of it, could marry validly, according to this writer.[88]

---

omnia, 26 vols. (Paris: Louis Vives, 1891–95; repr. Farnborough: Gregg, 1969) 19:168; Pérez, "¿Todo matrimonio?" pp. 11–12.

[85] Vincentius Hispanus, *Lectura* to X 1.21.5, Salamanca 2186, fol. 47vb: "Queritur utrum in quolibet matrimonio significetur hoc sacramentum et dico quod sic ante carnalem commixtionem; queritur autem an desinat hoc esse sacramentum quem cito carnalis cohabitus intentone, dic uel induret uel remaneat et potest esse quod sic, uel dic melius forte quod non consensus enim animarum qui uariabilis erunt postea efficiuntur rati et confirmati sed non est modo fidelem animam et quia quamdiu est in hoc seculo anima diuertere potest." Cf. the anonymous *Questiones de bigamis* in Caius MS 54/31, fol. 151rb–va: "Nota quod in matrimonio attenditur duplex sacramentum propter duplicem coniunctionem que in eo est, saltem in matrimonio per carnalem copulam consummato. Prima est coniunctio animorum, secunda corporum. Prima significat coniunctionem fidelis anime ad deum; hec dissoluitur per ⟨sub⟩sequens peccatum, sicut et illa ante carnalem copulam per religionis ingressum. Secunda scilicet coniunctio corporum significat coniunctionem Christi et ecclesie; hec fuit matrimonium initiatum in prophetis et patriarchis, ratum enim in tempore gratie, scilicet in natiuitate, quoniam ipse lapsus angelorum temptat edificare ecclesiam unam de iudeis aliam de gentilibus parietem erigens. Consummatum in cruce; uel ratum fuit in cruce, consummatum in patria."

[86] 1 Synod of Salisbury (1217 ~ 1219) c. 15, in Powicke and Cheney 1:65, counted marriage among the sacraments and added that it conferred grace but did not take away sin, as other sacraments did; Thomas Aquinas, ST 2–2 q. 100 a. 2 ad 6; Sheehan, "Marriage Theory and Practice," pp. 415–16; Kosnik et al., *Human Sexuality*, p. 41; Heany, *Development of the Sacramentality of Marriage*, pp. 197–98. See also Council of Florence (1431–46), sess. 8, *Bulla unionis Armenorum*, as well as Council of Trent (1545–63), sess. 7 (1547) c. 6–8 and sess. 24 (1563) proem., in COD, pp. 517, 660–61, 730.

[87] *Assises des bourgeois* 158, in RHC, Lois 2:107.

[88] *Aliter debet* to X 4.2.6, in Caius MS 23/12, fol. 45rb: "Statur iuramento ũiri semper ubi per aspectum corporis uirginitatem probet et uidetur si lamigo [?] est necessaria ad hoc ut dicatur mulier uiri potens. Item tunc dicitur quis proximus etati quando deficiunt

But Hostiensis reminded his readers that the real criterion of readiness for marriage was sexual capacity; a girl who was able and willing to consummate a sexual union was fit for marriage, whatever her chronological age, and boys who were fit for sex were likewise capable of contracting marriage.[89] Civil authorities sometimes adopted the canonical minimum age for marriage as the age of majority for other actions, such as fief-holding.[90]

Hostiensis puzzled over the question of why women attained puberty at an earlier age than boys. He accounted for the difference on a biological basis: the female, he said, was colder and more adaptable than the male. On this account she matured more quickly, but also tended to die at an earlier age, like weeds, which grow faster than useful plants. He added that sexual intercourse was easier for women than for men, since the female role was passive and less demanding than the active role of the male.[91]

The noble jurists of the Latin Kingdom of Jerusalem, where legal expertise and forensic skill were highly prized qualities, reasoned that since the law established a minimum age for marriage, both intellectual symmetry and practical considerations demanded a maximum age as well, one beyond which parents or liege lords could no longer demand that a person take on the burdens of marriage. Jean d'Ibelin pointed out that the law excused male vassals from military service after they attained the age of sixty. He argued that by analogy women over that age should not be required to marry and that a feudal lord who required an elderly man or woman to marry acted against God and reason. He added that it was the "usage, custom, law, or reason" of the Kingdoms of Jerusalem and Cyprus to exempt the elderly both from marriage and from military service, but that those who claimed this exemption were also bound to guard their chastity and not to indulge in sexual debauchery.[92]

As for incest, the four-degree rule adopted by the Fourth Lateran Council was re-enacted and adopted by numerous local synods and by secular authori-

---

vi. menses et ⟨licet⟩ etas quo ad matrimonium debet esse complete et non incepta et sufficit aliqua presumptio etatis ad iudicantum pro matrimonio." On *Aliter debet* see Kuttner, *Repertorium*, p. 414 n. 1.

[89] Hostiensis, *Lectura* to X 4.2.1 § 3; Petrus de Samsone, *Lectura* to X 4.1.3, in MS Ripoll 30 of the Archivo de la Corona de Aragón in Barcelona (hereafter A.C.A.), fol. 115ra: "Doli enim capax erat quia ad carnalem copulam aspirabat." But cf. *Aliter debet* to X 4.2.6, Caius 23/12, fol. 45rb: "Item cum mulier permisit super se uirum ascendere dubitari potest quod sic uiri potens est."

[90] *Livre de Jean d'Ibelin* 171, in RHC, Lois 1:263–64, and *Assises des bourgeois* 158–59, in RHC, Lois 2:107–108; Hans Ankem, "Le mariage et les conventions matrimoniales des mineurs: Etude sur le statut juridique des enfants mineurs dans l'histoire du droit privé néerlandais à partir du trezième siècle," *Tijdschrift voor rechtsgeschiedenis* 46 (1978) 203–49.

[91] Hostiensis, *Lectura* to X 4.2.4 § 2; Pierre de La Palude, *Lucubrationum* 27.1.2, p. 331.

[92] *Livre de Jean d'Ibelin* 228, in RHC, Lois 1:362–64.

ties as well.[93] A considerable body of evidence suggests that the rule was generally observed, although Beaumanoir (ca. 1250–96) claimed that simple people remained ignorant of the niceties of the incest prohibitions. Studies of marriage practices in English villages during the late thirteenth and early fourteenth centuries indicate that marriage was a common vehicle of mobility and that women often married outside their villages of origin. Presumably this happened in part at least to avoid marriage with relatives. Court records also suggest, contrary to Beaumanoir, that the ban on consanguine and affine marriages may even have been more scrupulously observed among the peasantry than among the higher nobility.[94] It is certainly true that marriage litigation involving consanguinity and affinity was relatively uncommon in England during this period.[95] Studies of Occitan and north Italian urban marriage patterns show similar results.[96] The laws of the Latins in the Levant required that persons who proposed to marry must make a sworn declaration that they were free to do so and that they were not related by ties of affinity or consanguinity to their prospective marriage partners.[97]

Only the pope, according to Pierre de La Palude, was empowered to dispense couples from the rules governing consanguinity and affinity. Joannes Andreae observed that these rules had been established in order to avoid the quarrels and frictions that arose in marriages between closely related persons.[98]

Canonists, theologians, and civilians continued throughout this period to in-

---

[93] Hostiensis, *Summa aurea*, lib. 5, tit. *De adulteriis et stupro* § 12, fol. 245ra; Magister Serlo, *Summa de penitentia* 26, ed. J. Goering in *Mediaeval Studies* 38 (1976) 33–36; *Assises des bourgeois* 158–59, 161, in RHC, Lois 2:107–11; Sheehan, "Marriage Theory and Practice," p. 420.

[94] Philippe de Beaumanoir, *Coutumes de Beauvaisis* § 585, ed. A. Salmon, 2 vols., Collection des textes pour servir à l'étude et à l'enseignement de l'histoire (Paris: A. & J. Picard, 1899–1900; repr. 1970) 1:284; J. Ambrose Raftis, *Tenure and Mobility: Studies in the Social History of the Medieval Village*, Studies and Texts, vol. 8 (Toronto: Pontifical Institute of Mediaeval Studies, 1964), pp. 178–82; Helmholz, *Marriage Litigation*, p. 80.

[95] Helmholz, *Marriage Litigation*, pp. 86–87. Adams and Donahue, *Select Cases* D.2, pp. 350–65, present the documents in Alice de Marescal c. Elias de Suffolk (1292–93), a case in which the central issue on appeal was Elias's claim that his alleged marriage to Alice was null because of affinity contracted as a result of his sexual relations with Christine de Thorley, a blood relative of Alice. This is one of the few cases based on this issue and also one of the even smaller number of cases in which we know the outcome: the judge found Elias's exception proved.

[96] LeRoy Ladurie, *Montaillou*, pp. 182–83; Jacques Heers, *Family Clans in the Middle Ages: A Study of Political and Social Structures in Urban Areas* (Amsterdam: North-Holland, 1976), p. 56.

[97] *Assises des bourgeois* 162, in RHC, Lois 2:111–12.

[98] Pierre de La Palude, *Tractatus de potestate papae* 2.2.4, ed. P. T. Stella, Textus et studia in historiam scholasticae, vol. 2 (Zurich: Pos-Verlag, 1966), p. 127; Joannes Andreae, *Novella* to X 4.1.3; Nicholas of Lyra, *Postilla* to Matt. 19:5 v. *propter hoc*.

sist that neither party could unilaterally cancel a promise of future marriage. Synods in England also demanded that betrothal, like marriage, be celebrated publicly and in the presence of a priest, although there is little evidence that this demand was systematically enforced.[99] Either betrothal or marriage could be contracted by proxy, provided that the agents had received a sufficient mandate from their principals.[100] If a couple exchanged promises of future marriage and subsequently had sexual relations, this created either a binding marriage, according to some authors, or a presumption of marriage, according to others.[101] Bartolus noted that simple cohabitation by partners of equal social status established a presumptive marriage in civil law, even without a promise of future marriage; he added, however, that the canonists required some exchange of consent before they would recognize these unions as marriages.[102] In actual practice the records of the Cerisy court make it clear that at least in Normandy couples treated betrothal as a trial marriage and normally slept together once

[99] 1 Canterbury (1213/14) c. 55, 2 Winchester (1247?) c. 51, 3 Winchester (1262 ~ 1265) c. 26, Coventry (1224 ~ 1237) c. 13, in Powicke and Cheney 1:34–35, 212, 410, 707; Sheehan, "Marriage Theory and Practice," pp. 425–26. On the dissolution of *sponsalia* see Synod of Liège (1287) 9.9, in Edmond Martène and Ursin Durand, eds., *Thesaurus novus anecdotorum*, 5 vols. (Paris: Florence Delalune, 1717; repr. New York: Burt Franklin, 1968) 4:848–49; Bernardus de Montemirato, *Comm.* to X 4.1.2 and 5, fol. 123vb; Joannes Andreae, *Novella* to X 4.1.2; *Assises des bourgeois* 163, in RHC, Lois 2:112.

[100] Gloss to Geoffrey of Trani, *Summa super titulos* 4.1. pr., in MS McLean 137, fol. 168ra, of the Fitzwilliam Museum, Cambridge: "Nota quod matrimonium potest contrahi inter absentes, et sponsalia."

[101] Bernardus de Montemirato, *Comm.* to X 4.1.15, fol. 124rb, held that intercourse following future consent created a *matrimonium verum*, as did Pedro de Albalat, *Summa septem sacramentorum*, ed. Peter Linehan in *Hispania sacra* 22 (1963) 26. *Aliter debet* to X 4.4.1, Caius 23/12, fol. 45va, thought that this was true even if their intention was to commit fornication. William of Pagula, *Summa summarum* 4.1, Pembroke 201, fol. 203rb, however, understood the matter differently: "An uir cognoscens carnaliter sponsam de futuro peccet? Dic quod si cognoscat eam fornicario affectum tunc est peccatum mortale nec facit uerum matrimonium huiusmodi copula carnale, sed facit matrimonium presumptum." Vincentius Hispanus, *Lectura* to X 4.1.31, Salamanca 2186, fol. 173vb, thought that coitus following future consent established a presumption of marriage, regardless of the couple's intention: "Item copula carnalis non facit matrimonium ⟨sed⟩ presumptio⟨nem⟩ tamen, nisi ubi fuit prestita fides solute de futuro, supra c. i., ubi due mulieres prestent eundem maritum et probaretur equaliter de intentione sua et una probaret amplius coitum: illa que coitum allegat potius uidetur habere, quia presumitur pro illa, iiii. q. iii. item in criminali [d.p.c. 2] et supra de testibus, licet [X 2.20.23?]." See also Dauvillier, *Mariage*, pp. 61, 67; Sheehan, "Marriage Theory and Practice", pp. 429–30.

[102] Bartolus, *Super Auth.* 6.2.5 (= Nov. 74.4) in his *Opera* 10:29vb–30ra; Sheedy, *Bartolus*, pp. 56–57; Paul Ourliac, "Note sur le mariage à Avignon au XVe siècle," in *Recueil de mémoires et travaux publiés par la Société d'histoire du droit et des institutions des anciens pays de droit écrit* 1 (1948) 59.

they had exchanged future consent. If the relationship failed to work out satisfactorily, couples often contrived to create an impediment to marriage, for example by becoming co-godparents of a child, in order to cancel their obligation to marry.[103] Similar customs were common elsewhere in Europe, and while some thirteenth-century English synods legislated against these practices it is not clear that they succeeded in suppressing them.[104]

Although custom often insisted that sexual consummation was essential to complete a marriage, canonists and theologians continued to insist that only present consent was needed to create a valid and indissoluble union.[105] Authorities disagreed over whether tacit consent was adequate to seal a binding marriage.[106] Whether spoken or tacit, all authorities agreed that free consent to marriage was essential for, as Bartholomew of Brescia remarked, coerced marriages rarely turned out well.[107] Despite the canonists' efforts to discourage par-

---

[103] "Le registre de l'officialité de Cerisy, 1314–1457," ed. M. G. Dupont, in *Mémoires de la Société des antiquaires de Normandie*, 3d ser., 10 (1880) 602; Jean-Luc Dufresne, "Les comportements amoureux d'après le registre de l'officialité de Cerisy," *Bulletin philologique et historique (jusqu'à 1610) du Comité des travaux historiques et scientifiques* (1973), pp. 134–35.

[104] 3 Worcester (1240) c. 28, in Powicke and Cheney 1:302; Sheehan, "Marriage Theory and Practice," p. 431; Turlan, "Recherches," pp. 485–86; Madeleine-Rose Marin-Muracciole, *L'honneur des femmes en Corse du XIIIe siècle à nos jours* (Paris: Cujas, 1964), p. 73.

[105] Bernardus de Montemirato, *Comm.* to X 4.1.3, fol. 123vb. The consensual principle was likewise accepted by some secular law-makers, e.g., *Assises des bourgeois* 158–59, in RHC, Lois 2:107–108, and *Las siete partidas del don Alfonso el Sabio . . . glosadas por Gregorio Lopez* 4.2.5, ed. J. de Vargas y Ponce, 3 vols. (Paris: Rosa Bouret, 1851) 3:20–21. William of Pagula cautioned, however, that marital consent must be deliberate and adequately considered before it could be deemed binding; *Summa summarum* 4.1, Pembroke 201, fol. 199ra: "Quid enim si duo uadunt per uiam et sibi inuicem complacent et unus in alterum consentit matrimonialiter? Absurdum esset dicere inter tales esse matrimonium."

[106] Hostiensis, *Lectura* to X 4.1.7 and *Summa aurea*, lib. 4, tit. *De matrimoniis* § 13, fol. 195va–vb; Bernard of Parma, *Glos. ord.* to X 4.1.25 v. *verba*; Geoffrey of Trani, *Summa super titulis* 4.1.14. William of Pagula, once again, was inclined to be cautious; *Summa summarum* 4.1, Pembroke 201, fol. 199ra: "An matrimonium potest contrahi solo consensu sine uerbis? Johannes, Goffredus, et ber. dicunt quod uerba sunt necessaria ad matrimonium inter illis personis qui loqui possunt. Dicit magister sententiarum quod solus consensus interior non facit matrimonium, sed requiritur expressio uerborum, quia sacramentum est res sensibilis, unde non sufficit actus interior adesse satis, sed requiritur exterius signum expressum. Expressio autem conueniencior non [?] fit per uerba et hoc dicit Innoc. qui reddit hanc rationem, quia sic statutum est ab ecclesia [*App.* to X 4.1.25 v. *consensum*] et merito, alias multa pericula imminuerent."

[107] Bartholomew of Brescia, *Questiones dominicales* 29.5, in *Tractatus universi juris*, 22 vols. in 28 (Venice: Franciscus Zilettus, 1584–86; cited hereafter as TUJ) 17:38ra. I have also used the earlier edition of TUJ, 18 vols. (Lyon: Petrus Fradin, 1548–49), hereafter cited as TUJ*.

ents from choosing wives and husbands for their children, and despite municipal statutes in some areas that made it an offense to attempt to force unwilling persons to marry, parents and public authorities often pressured couples into contracting marriage. In regions outside of the mainstream of legal institutions, such as Corsica and Iceland, for example, canonical doctrines about freedom of choice had little influence, and parental consent continued to be required for marriage.[108] Even where the canonical principle of free consent was in force, marriage remained part of the larger social process of the community and was often treated as a family matter to be decided in light of the common interests of the group, not merely of the contracting parties.[109]

Family and community were not the only sources of constraint on the free choice of marriage partners. Feudal lords demanded that widows and heiresses who controlled property for which they owed military service must marry men who were capable of making good the obligation. This concern, as we have seen, was especially acute in the Levant. Philippe de Novarre, who finished his legal treatise about 1260, explained that the early monarchs of the Latin Kingdom had allowed women to choose their own marriage partners freely. The kings soon discovered, however, that heiresses did not always choose husbands who would or could serve the needs of their lords. Consequently, Philip continued, the Latin kings insisted that no widow or heiress be allowed to marry without first securing the consent of the lord from whom she held property. But marriageable women and their families protested at this, and the Latins of the Levant arrived at a compromise solution.[110] Seigneurs demanded that eligible

---

[108] Hostiensis, *Summa aurea*, lib. 4, tit. *De sponsa duorum* § 7, fol. 203ra; for a case of attempted judicial coercion see *Recueil des lettres des officialités de Marseille et d'Aix (XIVe–XVe s.): Contribution à l'histoire des officialités au moyen-âge*, ed. Roger Aubenas, 2 vols. (Paris: Auguste Picard, 1937–38) 2:31–32. The municipal statutes of Sarzana (redacted in 1330, but modeled closely on the statutes of 1269) made it an offense, punishable by a heavy fine, to force anyone into an undesired marriage; *Gli statuti di Sarzana di 1330* 2.53, ed. Ida Gianfranceschi, Collana storica della Liguria orientale, vol. 3 (Cuneo: Istituto internazionale di studi Liguri, 1965), p. 140. On the other hand, the 1327 redaction of the Modena statutes forbade any couples to contract betrothal or marriage without first obtaining the consent of the fathers of both parties; *Statuta civitatis Mutine, anno 1327 reformata* 4.27, Monumenti di storia patria delle provincie Modenesi, Serie degli statuti, vol. 1 (Parma: Pietro Fiaccadori, 1864), p. 397. On parental consent in Corsica see Marin-Muracciole, *L'honneur des femmes*, pp. 74–75, and for Iceland see Frank, "Marriage in Iceland," p. 477; but cf. Sheehan, "Marriage Theory and Practice," pp. 427.

[109] LeRoy Ladurie, *Montaillou*, pp. 179, 182; Heers, *Family Clans*, p. 120; Diane Owen Hughes, "Urban Growth and Family Structure in Medieval Genoa," *Past and Present* 66 (1975) 26; Sue Sheridan Walker, "Free Consent and Marriage of Feudal Wards in Medieval England," JMH 8 (1982) 123–34; Dufresne, "Comportements amoureux," p. 136.

[110] *Le Livre de Philippe de Novarre* 86, in RHC, Lois 1:558–59; Jean Richard, "Le statut de la femme dans l'Orient Latin," *Recueils de la Société Jean Bodin* 12 (1962) 379.

women marry only men acceptable to their lords, for whom the right to approve these marriages was extremely profitable. Seigneurs however undertook not to force women to marry against their wills.[111] Women who did not wish to marry could not be summarily dispossessed; they had a right to be summoned, to explain their reasons for refusing to marry, and to be represented by counsel at their hearing.[112] If the lord insisted that the woman marry, he must give her a choice from among three suitable candidates. Should none of them be acceptable to her, she was entitled to demand a second slate of three candidates. Once she received their names, she had a year and a day to make up her mind.[113] Should she still refuse to marry any of the men proposed by her lord, he could, at the end of the statutory term, dispossess her.[114] Jean d'Ibelin, who wrote at about the same time as Philippe de Novarre, carefully detailed tactics that widows and heiresses could use to escape the exercise of their lords' marriage rights over them.[115] These complex regulations were neither a mere figment of the jurists' imaginations nor a simple subterfuge to enable lords to do as they pleased. Peter I of Cyprus discovered this the hard way when he attempted to circumvent these rules and as a result precipitated a revolt in 1369 that nearly toppled him from the throne.[116]

No Western monarchy seems to have adopted the tactics used by the Latins in the East to shield feudal heiresses and widows from the matrimonial schemes of feudal overlords, but even in the West, feudal control of a woman's marriage was not necessarily inconsistent with a free choice of marriage partners. The Church, both East and West, provided a safeguard against the more blatant types of coercion, since its courts were prepared to annul marriages when coercion could be proved. In practice complaints that feudal lords forced women into marriages were rare. Feudal heiresses and widows in the West often made up their own minds about whom they would marry or whether they wanted to marry at all and then paid fines to their overlords for permission to exercise that choice.[117]

The interests of families and feudal lords in regulating the marriages of those under their control required that couples marry publicly, so that their marital status would not be in doubt. Although the Western Church prescribed no uniform marriage rite and tolerated a wide degree of variance in wedding rituals, marriage ceremonies in France became far more uniform during the thirteenth

[111] Jean d'Ibelin 171, 177, 229, and Philippe de Novarre 86, in RHC, Lois 1:264–65, 279, 364, 559.
[112] Jean d'Ibelin 227–28, in RHC, Lois 1:359–60, 362.
[113] Jean d'Ibelin 171, 227, in RHC, Lois 1:265, 359, 361.
[114] Jean d'Ibelin 229–30 and Philippe de Novarre 86, in RHC, Lois 1:365–66, 559.
[115] Jean d'Ibelin 179, in RHC, Lois 1:281–82.
[116] Richard, "Statut de la femme," pp. 379–80.
[117] Walker, "Free Consent," pp. 24–25; Pierre Petot, "Le mariage des vassales," RHDF, 4th ser., 56 (1978) 29–47, shows that in France seigneurs rarely exercised feudal marriage rights after the time of Philip Augustus.

century. In Italy, however, local variations continued to proliferate and even when controls were ultimately imposed, practices there were far less uniform than in France.[118]

Town governments, both in Italy and in France, began during this period to restrict expenditures for weddings. Local ordinances on this subject often limited the numbers of people who could be invited to nuptial ceremonies and the lavish feasts provided for them.[119] Italian cities also introduced during this period a practice, uncommon north of the Alps, of having present consent exchanged in the presence of a notary, who made a formal public record of the event. The notary often played an active role in the proceedings, putting questions to the couple, which he recorded together with their answers.[120] Regardless of the form employed—and the canonists were prepared to accept any intelligible formula for the exchange of consent—families and communities wished to assure that weddings were properly witnessed and often demanded more witnesses and greater formality than Church law required.[121]

Weddings were accompanied almost everywhere by feasts and drinking bouts, often marked by excess. Ecclesiastical authorities objected to these carouses and complained that they led to unseemly tumults and disorders. The Second Council of Westminster demanded that couples forego the practice of holding their wedding ceremonies in taverns. Other English synods condemned the practice of staging mock weddings in drinking establishments, and warned that this custom sometimes resulted in people being bound by matrimonial ties that they had never seriously considered or desired.[122]

The growing efforts of municipalities to control and regulate weddings reflects the continuing problem of secret unions. Canonical writers and secular lawgivers attempted to define clandestine marriage more precisely. Hostiensis, for example, distinguished no less than six types. These included secret mar-

---

[118] Christiane Klapisch-Zuber, "Zacharie, ou le père évincé: Les rites nuptiaux toscans entre Giotto et le concile de Trente," *Annales é.s.c.* 34 (1979) 1217, also in her *Women, Family, and Ritual in Renaissance Italy*, trans. Lydia Cochrane (Chicago and London: University of Chicago Press, 1985), p. 180; Sheehan, "Marriage Theory and Practice," p. 424. Pedro de Albalat, *Summa septem sacramentorum*, ed. Linehan, p. 25, described in some detail the form of marriage current in Tarragona at this period and Lecoy de la Marche, *Chaire française*, pp. 431–33, gives detailed descriptions of northern French practices.

[119] Heers, *Family Clans*, p. 76.

[120] Peter Leischung, "Eheschliessung vor dem Notar im 13. Jahrhundert," ZRG, KA 94 (1977) 34–46.

[121] Bartholomew of Brescia, *Questiones dominicales* 26.4, in TUJ 17:37rb; Alberto dei Gandini, *Questiones statutorum* 339, ed. Heinrich Solmi in *Scripta anecdota glossatorum* 3:174.

[122] 1 Salisbury (1217 ~ 1219) c. 83 and 2 Council of Westminster (1247?) c. 56, in Powicke and Cheney 1:87, 411–12; Synod of Avignon (1337) c. 3–4, in Martène and Durand, *Thesaurus* 4:560–61; Synod of St.-Luc (1277), quoted in Diebold, "L'application," p. 191; Sheehan, "Marriage Theory and Practice," p. 416.

riages in the rigor of the term, where there were either no witnesses or very few witnesses to the exchange of consent; marriages celebrated without the nuptial blessing; marriages between minors without prior dispensation or between persons bound by a previous marriage or religious vows; marriages celebrated during an ecclesiastical interdict; and marriages celebrated without prior proclamation of the banns.[123] Nonetheless all of these marriages, save for those between under-age persons and persons bound by vows or previous marriages, were valid, even though they were contrary to law.[124] The fact that a couple married secretly provided no grounds for divorce or separation and if a clandestine marriage preceded a public one, the clandestine union prevailed over the formal marriage.[125] Although lawgivers complained about clandestine marriages and repeatedly condemned them, they refused to strip clandestine marriage of legal force.[126]

[123] Hostiensis, *Lectura* to X 4.3.1; see also John of Fribourg, gloss to Raymond of Peñafort, *Summa de mat.* 2.4 v. *matrimonium iudicari*, in *Summa Sancti Raymundi de Peniafort de poenitentia et matrimonio cum glossis Ioannes de Fribourgo* (Rome: Ioannes Tallinus, 1603; repr. Farnborough: Gregg, 1967), p. 512; *Siete partidas* 4.3.1, ed. Vargas y Ponce 3:35–36; Diebold, "L'application," p. 189.

[124] Bernardus de Montemirato, *Comm.* to X 4.3.2, fol. 126ra; Pierre de La Palude, *Lucubrationum* 28.2.4, p. 352; *Magister Gratianus uolens compilare* to C. 30 q. 5, in Peterhouse MS 169(2), fol. 26va–vb: "In quintam soluitur quod clandestina fieri non debent, sed si fiant et probari possunt et ualent, alias non; nec debet pro malis leuis aliquis condempnari, infra eodem § his ita [C. 30 q. 5 d.p.c. 9] et c. incerta et al. c. [?] et § se.usque in finem questionis." See also Synod of Wells (1258) c. 11, Carlisle (1258/59) c. 11, and 2 York (1259) c. 11, in Powicke and Cheney 1:597–98, 626–27, 658–59, as well as Sheehan, "Choice of Marriage Partner," p. 17, and "Marriage Theory and Practice," p. 451.

[125] Petrus de Salinis, *Lectura* to C. 30 q. 5 pr., in B.L., MS Arundel 435, fol. 152vb: "In themate fuit proposita v. questio an clandestina ⟨desponsatio⟩ [*MS* dispensatio] preiudicet manifestam et deductum est quod preiudicat si de ea constet; non enim deficit ius sed probacio. . . ." Ibid. to d.p.c. 8: "Supra dictum est in § hiis omnibus [d.p.c. 6] quod clandestina coniugia pro infectis haberi debent; nunc allegat gratianus pro contraria parte dicens quod multa fieri non debent, facta tamen non rumpuntur, ut matrimonia simpliciter uouencium. Sic et clandestina coniugia fieri non debent, facta tamen tenent et ad hoc inducit lex sequens."

[126] Synod of Liège (1287) 9.1, 4–6, in Martène and Durand, *Thesaurus* 4:847. For England see Synod of Coventry (1224 ~ 1237) c. 13; Lincoln (1239) c. 42; Norwich (1240 ~ 1243) c. 39; 2 Winchester (1247?) c. 51, 57; Wells (1258) c. 10; Statutes of Bishop Fulk Basset (1245 ~ 1259) c. 1–2; 2 Exeter (1287) c. 7, in Powicke and Cheney 1:212, 274, 351, 410, 412, 597, 630–31, and 2:997–99. For Spain see Pedro de Albalat, *Summa*, ed. Linehan, p. 25, and *Siete partidas* 4.3 pr., 3, 5, ed. Vargas y Ponce 3:34–35, 37–39. See also Sheehan, "Marriage Theory and Practice," pp. 423, 443, 449–50; Diebold, "L'application," pp. 188–91; Ruiz de Conde, *Amor y matrimonio secreto*, pp. 8, 12, 29. For a case that illustrates strikingly the complications that arose in attempting to prove the celebration of a clandestine marriage see Norman c. Proudfoot (1269–72) in Adams and Donahue, *Select Cases* C.2, pp. 102–12. William of Pagula, *Summa summarum* 4.1, Pembroke 201, fol. 203rb, concluded that those who contracted clandestine marriages

Civic authorities occasionally legislated on this subject, too. The Ferrara statutes of 1287, for example, imposed heavy fines on parties to secret marriages and levied further penalties upon anyone assisting at such affairs.[127] The kings of Sicily went even further. In marked contrast to the usual rules elsewhere in Europe and in flat contradiction to canon law, the law of Sicily and southern Italy required the presence of a priest and the bestowal of a nuptial blessing: marriages that lacked these formalities were devoid of juridical effect in the Two Sicilies.[128] The Sicilian pattern remained unique in the West, however, and reflects the continuing influence in that area of Byzantine customs, which also required the presence of a priest and a sacerdotal blessing as a condition of matrimonial validity.[129]

Elsewhere in Western Europe, valid clandestine marriages presented the Church, secular governments, and individuals with innumerable problems. Since secret marriages were illegal, though not invalid, both canonists and theologians urged parties to celebrate their marriages publicly. Conscientious officials sometimes insisted that couples who intended to marry furnish certificates that the banns had been read and couples anxious to secure their marriage against possible legal attack saw these certificates as safeguards for their own interests.[130] But not all officials were conscientous, nor did all couples insist on having their marriages documented. Pierre de La Palude enumerated six situations in which dispensations from the requirement for publication of the banns and public marriage were usually granted:

> 1. Marriages of great nobles, since these marriages were usually considered carefully and discussed in advance with family, friends, and associates.

---

sinned mortally in so doing, unless they were ignorant of the law; he also detailed mitigating circumstances that might justify dispensations from the law. The penances imposed on those who contracted clandestinely were sometimes severe, as is shown by the case of a Norman squire, William Daubeuf (1266), who was required to undertake pilgrimages to Rome, to Bari, and to St.-Gilles in order to expiate his guilt; see *The Register of Eudes of Rouen*, trans. Sidney M. Brown, ed. Jeremiah F. O'Sullivan, Records of Civilization, Sources and Studies, no. 72 (New York: Columbia University Press, 1964), pp. 622–23.

[127] *Statuta Ferrariae anno MCCLXXXVII* 4.55bis, ed. William Montorsi (Ferrara: Casa di Risparmio di Ferrara, 1955), p. 271.

[128] Antonio Marongiu, "La forma religiosa del matrimonio nel diritto del regno di Napoli," in *Studi in memoria di Romualdo Trifone*, (Sapri: n.p., 1963) 1:9–10, reprinted with original pagination in Marongiu's *Byzantine, Norman, Swabian, and Later Institutions in Southern Italy.*

[129] Marongiu, "La forma religiosa del matrimonio nel diritto bizantino," p. 1.

[130] For examples of these documents see *The Letter-Book of Wiilliam of Hoo, Sacrist of Bury St. Edmunds, 1280–1294*, no. 101–2, 171, 173, ed. Antonia Gransden, Suffolk Records Society, Publications, vol. 5 (Ipswich: Suffolk Records Society, 1963), pp. 65, 90–91.

2. Marriage between a person of noble rank and a non-noble, since these unions excited opposition and scandal.

3. Marriage of a rich person to a poor one, as these upset the social order.

4. Marriages in which one of the parties was very old.

5. Marriages in which there was reason to fear parental wrath and where the parties had already exchanged informal consent.

6. Marriages in which the couple had been living together for a long time and wished to regularize their relationship.[131]

Although dispensations were readily available for secret marriages in these circumstances, a great many people ignored the legal requirements and married informally without dispensation. This was so common that Sir Gerard de Gommegnyes could declare casually in a petition to Pope Clement VI (1342–52) that it was not customary in his part of the world to bother about the banns at all; there is little reason to think that he was exaggerating.[132] Clandestine weddings were by all indications commonplace, and the number of them was sufficiently large that certain places achieved notoriety as rendezvous for clandestine nuptials. A more or less organized trade provided couples who wished to marry on the sly with complaisant clergymen prepared to furnish the semblance of a formal service and nuptial blessing, without the irritation of awaiting the proclamation of banns or the fuss and bother of finding witnesses.[133] Undoubtedly many, perhaps most, clandestine marriages were contracted in this way in order to avoid opposition from parents or family.[134] Faced with the *fait accompli* of a valid, if irregular, marriage, families often chose to make the best of the situation. Those who sought to break up the union faced a formidable struggle. Poets and preachers in this period hinted rather broadly that ecclesiastical judges were sometimes not above taking bribes from families who wished to secure a canonical judgment against a marriage, but it is difficult to determine how well founded those allegations may have been.[135] Pierre de La Palude counseled parents to put up with these situations with as much grace as they could muster and warned fathers that they themselves committed an offense if they expressed their displeasure with a clandestine marriage by disinheriting their sons or daughters.[136]

[131] Pierre de La Palude, *Lucubrationum* 28.2.3, p. 352.

[132] *Suppliques de Clément VI (1342–52)*, no. 413, ed. Ursmer Berlière, Analecta Vaticano-Belgica, vol. 1 (Rome: Institut historique belge, 1906), p. 91.

[133] Turlan, "Mariage dans la pratique coutumière," p. 515. LeRoy Ladurie, *Montaillou*, p. 100, constructs a description of the celebration of a clandestine wedding between Raymonde Piquier and Pierre Mary.

[134] Thus at Modena a municipal statute that forbade marriage without paternal consent also prohibited clandestine marriages; Modena, *Statuti* (1327) 4.27, p. 398.

[135] Gerald R. Owst, *Literature and Pulpit in Medieval England: A Neglected Chapter in the History of English Letters and of the English People*, 2d ed. (Oxford: Basil Blackwell, 1961), p. 254.

[136] Pierre de La Palude, *Lucubrationum* 28.2.4, p. 353.

Concubinage among the Laity

Clandestine marriage raised problems closely related to concubinage. Canonists usually read marriage law restrictively; this led them to classify as concubinage all cases of long-continued cohabitation where evidence of matrimonial intent was not apparent.[137] The civilians were more lenient. Bartolus preferred to view concubinage as quasi-marriage and to treat the children of such unions as legitimate, a position that Odofredus (d. 1265) had adopted earlier.[138] Odofredus was even more concerned than Bartolus to uphold the legitimacy of concubinage, even when marriage could not be presumed, although he was careful to draw the line at plural concubinage or concubinage by married men.[139] Another leading civilian of the period, Cino da Pistoia (1270–1336/37), similarly maintained that concubinage was licit and not subject to legal penalties.[140] Concubinage, like marriage, was a social fact that created bonds of relationship between the parties and their families, according to the legists, so that a son was forbidden to marry his father's concubine and, in the Latin East at any rate, sons who slept with their father's concubines might be ineligible to inherit the paternal estate.[141]

The legists' toleration of concubinage was not shared by all of their contemporaries. From the early fourteenth century onward, municipalities began to enact statutes forbidding concubinage and imposing penalties upon men who openly cohabited with women to whom they were not married.[142] Some canonists and theologians, while acknowledging the different position taken by civil law,[143] declared that concubinage was forbidden by the canons, while

[137] Hostiensis, *Lectura* to X 1.21.6 v. *non incurrerint*; Helmholz, *Marriage Litigation*, p. 46.

[138] Bartolus, *Comm.* to Dig. 25.7.3.1–3 and Cod. 5.4.6; Odofredus, *Lectura super Digesto vetero* to Dig. 23.2.24, 2 vols. (Lyon: Joannes Pullen, 1552; repr. Bologna: A. Forni, 1968); Sheedy, *Bartolus on Social Conditions*, pp. 57–59; Esmein, *Mariage* 2:114; Udo Wolter, *Ius canonicum in iure civili: Studien zur Rechtsquellenlehre in der neueren Privatrechtsgeschichte*, Forschungen zur neueren Privatrechtsgeschichte, vol. 23 (Cologne: Böhlau, 1975), pp. 48–49.

[139] Odofredus, *Lectura super Codice* to Cod. 5.26, 3 vols. in 2 (Lyon: Franciscus et Claudius Marchant, 1550–52; repr. Bologna: A. Forni, 1968), and *Lectura super Dig. vet.* 24.2.11. Church officials took action on occasion to force married men to give up their concubines; see William Hoo, *Letter-Book*, no. 124, pp. 73–74, for an example.

[140] Cino da Pistoia, *In Codicem et aliquot titulos primi Pandectorum tomi, id est Digesti veteris, doctissima commentaria* to Cod. 5.4.4, 2 vols. (Frankfurt a/M: Johannes Feyerabend, 1578; repr. Turin: Bottega d'Erasmo, 1964).

[141] Cino, *Comm.* to Cod. 5.4.4; Odofredus, *Lectura* to the same passage; Joshua Prawer, *Crusader Institutions* (Oxford: Clarendon Press, 1980), pp. 442, 448, 453; LeRoy Ladurie, *Montaillou*, p. 57.

[142] Bologna, *Statuti* 4.33, ed. Fasoli and Sella 1:197; Löwenstein, *Bekämpfung*, p. 20.

[143] Guido de Baysio, *Rosarium* to C. 35 q. 3 c. 17, fol. 376rb; William of Pagula, *Summa summarum* 5.16, Pembroke 201, fol. 239ra: "An sit licita habere concubinam?

Thomas Aquinas declared that it was contrary to natural law as well.[144] Canonistic opinion was divided: some authorities wished to extend legal toleration to concubinage, as they did to prostitution, although they disapproved of both on moral grounds.[145] Guido de Baysio argued, however, that the Church should not allow divorced or separated men to take concubines in place of their legal wives.[146]

Court records make it clear that, despite the reservations of academic lawyers and theologians, concubinage was common in many regions. Most concubinage cases that appear in the court registers of Cerisy, for example, involved couples who lived together for short periods prior to marriage, but some reports deal with what were obviously long-term relationships, such as the case of Jean Dupont, who had six children by his concubine, and Pierre de Limengais, whose concubine was pregnant with their third child when they appeared in court.[147] In one Cerisy case a single man kept two widows, both of them related to him, as concubines,[148] while on the manor of Halesowen in Worcestershire, Margery Port seems to have been the concubine of two men simultaneously.[149] The inquisitorial records of Carcassonne show that about ten percent of the couples in the village of Montaillou during the years from 1300 to 1320 were living in concubinage.[150] In Spain both Church and state seem to have tolerated *barragania* among the laity and men were rarely penalized on account

---

Dic quod non, quia fornicator tollit membra Christi et facit ea membra meretricis, xxxii. q. iiii. meretrices [c. 11] et c. in eo [c. 12]; xxxiiii. di. audite [c. 6] palam est."

[144] Hostiensis, *Lectura* to X 3.26 and X 4.17.5; Thomas Aquinas, *Comm.* to Sent. 4.33.1.3.

[145] *Magister Gratianus uolens compilare* to D. 34, Peterhouse 169(2), fol. 4va: "In secunda dicit quod qui habet legalem concubinam, id est uxorem sine sollempnitate, non peccat, in eodem is qui non habet [D. 34 c. 4]." The *Questiones de bigamis* in Caius 54/31, fol. 151va, on the other hand, denied that concubinage was equivalent to marriage and hence held that a man who took a concubine after his wife's death was not guilty of digamy: "Item queritur cum consecratio episcopi maior sit et dignior quam consecratio uirginum, quare potest in episcopum consecrari qui non solum uxorem habuit, sed etiam post uxorem habuit concubinam. Et si qua fuerit corrupta uel ante baptismum uel post, sponte uel ui, cum peccato uel sine peccato, non potest inter sacratas uirgines ⟨consecrari⟩ [MS consecratur]. § Ad hoc respondeo, sacrata uirgo significat ecclesiam triumphantem, que sine macula et ruga est, sed episcopus ecclesiam militantem, in qua sunt boni et mali."

[146] Guido de Baysio, *Rosarium* to C. 32 q. 5 c. 21, fol. 349va.

[147] *Registre de Cerisy*, no. 75a, 261d, ed. Dupont, pp. 334, 457; Dufresne, "Comportements amoureux," pp. 136–40.

[148] *Registre de Cerisy*, no. 199c, ed. Dupont, p. 421.

[149] *Court Rolls of the Manor of Hales, 1272–1307*, ed. John Amphlett and Sidney Graves Hamilton, 3 vols., Worcestershire Historical Society Publications, vol. 28 (Oxford: James Parker, 1910–33) 3:564.

[150] LeRoy Ladurie, *Montaillou*, p. 169. LeRoy Ladurie adds (p. 172) that while the Cathars may have encouraged concubinage, they certainly did not introduce the prac-

of these relationships.[151] Likewise in Italy concubinage remained common throughout this period and was sometimes formalized by contractual agreements between the partners, agreements that included promises of sexual fidelity, stipulations about support obligations, and provisions for care of the concubine in case of illness. At least one such contract was made for the lifetime of the parties, but the more usual practice seems to have been to limit the agreement to a specified term, at the end of which it could be renewed if both parties agreed.[152]

Although some medieval canonists, as well as some modern scholars, assumed that men took concubines because they were not content with a single sexual partner and wished to indulge their taste for sensual pleasure, other factors helped to account for the frequency with which concubinage appears in thirteenth and fourteenth-century records. Economic and social considerations almost certainly made concubinage a useful alternative to marriage for many families. Families who dreaded or who could not afford the loss of property that dowry entailed found it preferable to encourage their daughters to agree to concubinage relationships, which may well have had the additional attraction of attaching the woman's family to the political and social networks of wealthier and more prominent men than they could have hoped to attract into marriage.[153] In some cases concubinage ultimately led to marriage; certainly canonists considered this a realistic possibility.[154]

---

tice into Montaillou, where it had been part of local usage long before the heretics arrived.

[151] *Siete partidas* 4.14 pr., 1–2, ed. Vargas y Ponce 3:126–29; Winterer, "Zur Priesterehe in Spanien," p. 371; Eugen Wohlhaupter, "Germanische Rechtsgedanken in Familien- und Erbrecht des Libro de los Fueros de Castiella," *Historisches Jahrbuch* 55 (1935) 242–43; Burns," Spiritual Life of James the Conqueror," pp. 28–29; António Aunós Pérez, *El derecho catalán en el siglo XIII* (Barcelona: Helios, 1926), pp. 69–70. The Council of Valladolid (1322) did excommunicate married men who kept concubines and any men, married or not, who kept infidel mistresses, but took no action at all against other concubinary laymen; Mansi 25:720; Henry Ansgar Kelly, *Canon Law and the Archpriest of Hita*, Medieval & Renaissance Texts and Studies, vol. 27 (Binghamton, NY: Center for Medieval & Early Renaissance Studies, 1984), p. 84.

[152] Antonio Marongiu, *La famiglia nell'Italia meridionale (sec. VIII–XIII)*, Biblioteca dell'Unione cattolica per le scienze sociale, vol. 9 (Milan: "Vita e Pensiero," 1944), p. 89; Gian Luigi Barni, "Un contrato di concubinato in Corsica nel XIII secolo," *Rivista di storia del diritto italiano* 22 (1949) 131–55; Marin-Muracciole, *L'honneur des femmes*, pp. 384–85; William Boulting, *Woman in Italy, from the Introduction of the Chivalrous Service of Love to the Appearance of the Professional Actress* (London: Methuen, 1910), pp. 278–79.

[153] Guido de Baysio, *Rosarium* to C. 32 q. 2 c. 11, fol. 346va; Jean-Louis Flandrin, "Contraception, mariage et relations amoureuses dans l'Occident chrétien," *Annales é.s.c.* 24 (1969) 1379; LeRoy Ladurie, *Montaillou*, p. 36.

[154] *Magister Gratianus uolens compilare* to C. 32 q. 2, Peterhouse 169(2), fol. 27ra: "In vi.a [*scil.*: parte huius questionis] dicit quod si aliquis aliquam mulierem concubinam sibi habuit ad tempus et eam in legitimam uxorem ⟨duxit⟩[*MS* ac] non peccat,

Despite the willingness of many academic lawyers to view concubinage as a tolerable, if not desirable, institution, ecclesiastical authorities continued to discourage the practice. They commonly did so through some variety of abjuration *sub pena nubendi*. Bishop Peter des Roches at Winchester, for example, required men whom he discovered to be living with a concubine to agree to a conditional marriage with their mistresses. In effect the agreement forced the man either to marry his *amasia* or to agree that further sexual relations with her would constitute marriage. The bishop enforced these agreements by requiring the parties to swear an oath before witnesses that they would honor the commitment; if they were reluctant to do this, he demanded a promise with sureties that if the man and his mistress were found together in future they would be subject to a fine.[155]

SEXUAL BEHAVIOR IN MARRIAGE

Both canonists and theologians remained commited to the well-established principle that husband and wife enjoyed equal sexual rights in marriage.[156] In other aspects of the marriage relationship the husband continued to be held superior to the wife, although some writers emphasized that woman was created to be man's companion, not his servant.[157] Nicholas of Lyra observed that mutual pleasure in marital intercourse created a bond of attraction that helped to keep married couples together. A married man, he wrote, gladly returns to his wife because of the sexual delights that she will provide for him, while Hos-

---

infra c. ancillam et c. non omnis [c. 11–12]." Likewise *Aliter debet* to X 4.7.3, Caius 23/12, fol. 46ra: "Cognoscere aliquam ut concubinam non impedit quamuis possit eam ducere post mortem ⟨sue⟩ uxoris. . . ."

[155] Sheehan, "Marriage and Family," pp. 209–10. English synods often prescribed abjuration *sub pena nubendi*; see 2 Salisbury (1238 ~ 1244) c. 53; Wells (1258?) c. 13; Statutes of Fulk Basset (1245 ~ 1259) c. 3; 2 London (1245 ~ 1259) c. 80; 2 Exeter (1287) c. 7, in Powicke and Cheney 1:385–86, 598, 631, 650, and 2:999. For the court record of one such case, Wood c. Clapton (1269–71), see Adams and Donahue, *Select Cases*, C.1, pp. 96–103; and see generally Helmholz, "Abjuration *sub pena nubendi*." For other regions see also Marongiu, *La famiglia nell'Italia meridionale*, pp. 91–93; Rudolf Weigand, "Die Einführung der Formpflicht für die Eheschliessung durch das Tridentinum und die bedingte Eheschliessung," *Würzburger Diözesansgeschichtsblätter* 35/36 (1974) 266.

[156] Hostiensis, *Lectura* to X 5.16.6 v. *in utroque*; Thomas Aquinas, *Comm. in Sent* 4.32.1.3; Børresen, *Subordination and Equivalence*, pp. 204–205. Joannes de Deo, *Summa de dispensationibus*, in Peterhouse MS 42(2), fol. 8rb, summed up the teaching in a verse:

Uir caput uxoris
Uero est mulier potioris.
Femina merita mari
Conditione pari
Quo ad thorum.

[157] See the authorities cited in Salerno, "Definizione nominale," pp. 197–98;

tiensis observed that women whose husbands were absent pined and sighed until their men returned.[158] It was generally agreed that a satisfactory sexual relationship between spouses was a desirable, even necessary, ingredient of marriage and that a union predicated on an agreement that the partners would never have intercourse was not binding. Nonetheless Aquinas warned couples not to place too great an emphasis on the pleasures of the marriage bed. He added that a man who had intercourse with his wife solely for enjoyment was treating her as if she were a whore.[159]

Although a few heretics maintained that marital sex was sinful under all circumstances, orthodox writers in the thirteenth and fourteenth centuries increasingly rejected this teaching.[160] All of the major theologians and canonists of the period taught that marital relations were free from sin under some circumstances, although they failed to agree just what those circumstances might be.[161] Albert the Great and a few others went so far as to contend that marital sex was good in itself and might even be spiritually meritorious if approached in the spirit of love and with procreative intentions.[162] This view was by no means universally accepted, however, for the older notion that sex was evil and a source of moral and spiritual impurity remained very much a part of theological belief.[163]

Leading authorities distinguished between situations in which marital sex was sinful from those in which it was not. The Franciscan theologian, Alexander of Hales (d. 1245), whose *Summa theologica*, Roger Bacon complained, was heavier than a horse, identified three situations in which marital relations were without sin. It was no sin, according to Alexander, for a couple to have sex in order to conceive a child, to pay the conjugal debt, or to avoid danger of fornication. If a couple had relations just for pleasure, however, the act was sinful; how

---

[158] Nicholas of Lyra, *Postilla* to 1 Cor. 7:2 v. *propter fornicationem*; Hostiensis, *Lectura* to X 3.34.7 § 15.

[159] Thomas Aquinas, ST Supp. 49.6 ad 1; Guido de Baysio, *Rosarium* to C. 27 q. 2 d.p.c. 2 v. *an uterque*, fol. 331rb; Sheehan, "Marriage Theory and Practice," pp. 447–48; Noonan, *Power to Dissolve*, pp. 80–89.

[160] Döllinger, *Beiträge zur Sektengeschichte* 2:23–24.

[161] Thomas Aquinas, ST 2–2.153.2; Albertus Magnus, *Comm.in* Sent. 4.31.19; Clifford, "Ethics of Conjugal Intimacy," pp. 2–4. See also the additional authorities quoted in Müller, *Lehre des hl. Augustinus*, pp. 191–95, and Lindner, *Usus matrimonii*, pp. 123–27.

[162] Albertus Magnus, *Comm. in* Sent. 4.31.19; Pierre de La Palude, *Lucubrationum* 26.2.1 and 31.3.1, pp. 323, 367; William of Pagula, *Summa summarum* 4.1, Pembroke 201, fol. 202vb: "An actus coniugalis possit esse meritorius? Dic quod ad actum meritorium sufficiunt tria, scilicet status mentis, forma intentionis debite, et honestas operis. Cum ad actum coniugale que fit in caritate causa prolis procurande uel reddendi debitum, hec tria concurrunt, actus ille non est solus excusabilis a malo, sed meritorius in bono per se."

[163] E.g., Guido de Baysio, *Rosarium* to C. 27 q. 2 c. 10 v. *pudenda*, fol. 331va: "Pudenda, id est feda propter feditatem que fit in coitu alibi. Alia causa assignatus quare Christus nasci voluit de virgine, xxxii. q. ii. pudor [c. 1]." See also Tentler, *Sin and Confession*, pp. 227–28.

sinful depended upon whether both parties agreed to the act. If it proceeded from mutual agreement, the sin was venial; but a lustful husband who took his wife to bed against her will sinned mortally.[164] Another Franciscan, St. Bonaventure (1221–74), rejected the two extreme positions on the sinfulness of marital sex. Bonaventure reminded his readers of the rigorist teaching of Huguccio that marital sex was sinless only if it was not pleasurable, but added that he found this teaching too harsh (*nimis dura*). Married men could enjoy their wives so long as they did so with marital affection; although this was venially sinful, it was saved from being mortally sinful because of the good of marriage.[165] Aquinas took a moderate position, rejecting the rigorist doctrine, but holding that marital sex for pleasure alone, so long as it remained within the bounds of proper matrimonial behavior (*infra limites matrimonii*), was only venially sinful.[166] Albert the Great maintained that the sinfulness of marital sex depended on the intention of the parties. If one of them initiated the sex act out of lust, but also had a conscious hope of conceiving a child, the act was venially sinful. If the couple went to bed solely in order to conceive and "endured" the pleasure because it was unavoidable, their act was not sinful and might be meritorious. But if pleasure was the only reason for coitus, this was a serious sin, although not actually mortal.[167] Other teachers proposed even more elaborate analyses. The Dominican, Roland of Cremona (d. 1271), distinguished five legitimate reasons for marital sex. In addition to the four reasons usually cited (payment of marital debt, procreation, avoiding incontinence for one's self, preventing incontinence by the spouse), Roland added as a further acceptable reason the intention of avoiding the anger of one's wife, since anger might lead her into mortal sin; it is well known, Roland added, that sex diminishes women's anger.[168] On the other hand some reasons for marital intercourse, even though virtuous in themselves, were not adequate to overcome the evil inherent in the sex act. Thus, according to William of Pagula, a man who had intercourse with his wife in order to regain his own bodily health, sinned by doing so.[169]

Several English synods of the thirteenth century sought to discourage a

[164] Alexander of Hales, *Glossa in quattuor libris Sententiarum Petri Lombardi* 4.30.11, 4 vols., Bibliotheca Franciscana scholastica medii aevi, vol. 12–15 (Quaracchi: Collegium S. Bonaventurae, 1951–57); *Siete Partidas* 4.2.9, ed. Vargas y Ponce 3:26; Nicholas of Lyra, *Postilla* to 1 Cor. 7:6. For Bacon's comment see Etienne Gilson, *History of Christian Philosophy in the Middle Ages* (New York: Random House, 1955), p. 327.

[165] Bonaventure, *Comm.* to Sent. 4.31.2.3; Müller, *Lehre des hl. Augustinus*, pp. 229–39. William of Auxerre, *Summa aurea*, fol. 288ra, on the other hand, still subscribed to the rigorist position.

[166] Thomas Aquinas, *Comm.* to Sent. 4.31.2, 3.

[167] Albertus Magnus, *Comm.* to Sent. 4.31.21; Müller, *Lehre des hl. Augustinus*, p. 254; Clifford, "Ethics of Conjugal Intimacy," pp. 6, 11.

[168] Roland of Cremona, *Summa*, quoted in Müller, *Lehre des hl. Augustinus*, p. 190.

[169] William of Pagula, *Summa summarum* 4.1, Pembroke 201, fol. 202vb: "An cognoscere carnaliter mulierem propter sanitatem corporalem sit peccatum? Dic quod sic, quia querit sanitatem corporalem conseruandi uel recuperandi per hoc quod ad hoc non

popular belief that married persons who received the sacrament of extreme unction committed a mortal sin if they later had sexual relations for any reason whatever. The synodal canons enjoined priests to make it clear to their parishioners that this notion was erroneous, for, the lawmakers believed, married folk who thought that extreme unction meant the end of marital sex often refused to receive the sacrament, even when laboring in their final agony.[170]

The conventional opinion of canonists and theologians was thus fairly clear. Marital sex was permissible, but only provided that the partners brought the proper intentions to the act. Marital relations required forethought, deliberation, and conscious reflection if one wished to avoid serious sin. Above all, married persons must observe moderation in their sexual habits, and they should not use their marital rights to achieve improper ends, such as physical pleasure.[171] Given these guidelines, few married persons can have escaped sinning through lust, excessive affection, or a desire for pleasure. The constant danger of committing sin in daily contacts with one's husband or wife obviously troubled many people. Jacques de Vitry was no doubt right when he observed that marriage was morally more demanding than the monastic life.[172]

Medical writers took a different view of marital sex. Coitus, they believed, furnished both husband and wife with healthy pleasure, and William of Saliceto's *Summa conservationis* described in detail methods for enhancing the enjoyment of both parties. Avicenna, followed by James of Forli and a few other Latin authors, gave special attention to methods for ensuring the wife's orgasm.[173] Female orgasm seemed critical not only to medical writers but also to theologians who relied on their expertise in such matters, since they believed that only when a woman "emitted her seed" could conception occur. Failure of either partner to achieve orgasm rendered intercourse nonprocreative and thus presented a moral problem, particularly if the woman deliberately refrained from yielding to sexual pleasure.[174] On the other hand, those who wished to

---

est ordinatum, sicut qui sacramentum baptismi querit propter salutem corporalem secundum tho. in quadam questione de quolibet."

[170] 1 Salisbury (1217 ~ 1219) c. 94; 2 Canterbury (1222 ~ 1228) c. 94; 1 Durham (1228 ~ 1236) c. 94; Durham peculiars (1241 ~ 1249) c. 55; *Constitutiones cuiusdam episcopi* c. 55; 2 London (1245 ~ 1259) c. 53; 2 Salisbury (1238 ~ 1244) c. 18; 1 Chichester (1245 ~ 1252) c. 32; 3 Worcester (1240) c. 37; 3 Winchester (1262 ~ 1265) c. 25; 2 Exeter (1287) c. 6, all in Powicke and Cheney 1:90–91, 166, 190, 201, 305, 372–73, 444, 457, 645, 707; 2:995–96; Sheehan, "Marriage Theory and Practice," pp. 453–54.

[171] Guido de Baysio, *Rosarium* to C. 32 q. 4 c. 5, fol. 347va; Hostiensis, *Summa aurea*, lib. 4, tit. *De conditionibus appositis in desponsatione vel aliis contractibus* § 12, fol. 204ra. See also Biller, "Birth Control," pp. 21–22, citing Dante, *Paradiso* 15.11.106–8.

[172] Quoted in Lindner, *Usus matrimonii*, pp. 161–62.

[173] Lemay, "William of Saliceto," pp. 166, 171; Jean-Louis Flandrin, *Le sexe et l'Occident* (Paris: Seuil, 1981), p. 131.

[174] Jean-Louis Flandrin, "La vie sexuelle des gens mariés dans l'ancienne société: de la doctrine de l'église à la réalité des comportements," in *Sexualités occidentales*, p. 105,

avoid conception were advised to try to inhibit orgasm during intercourse. Pierre de La Palude, writing early in the fourteenth century, advised couples who already had as many children as they could support to practice *coitus interruptus* if they were unable to achieve complete sexual continence.[175]

According to the *Summa Astensis* it was the more common opinion among theologians of this era that sexual pleasure in marriage was always a venial sin, although the author added, "Some say that there is no sin at all in it."[176] There was almost universal agreement, however, that kissing and "indecent touching" between married persons was sinful, although some would tolerate such behavior as a prelude to intercourse, provided that the couple's intention was procreative, and there was no danger of premature ejaculation.[177] The pseudonymous treatise *De secretis mulierum*, ascribed to Albert the Great, gave detailed instructions for the technique of marital coitus. The spouses should prepare themselves physically and mentally: they should not make love immediately after eating and they ought to make sure that bladder and bowels were empty. Some foreplay—kissing, embracing, and fondling of "the lower parts"—was prescribed, since the author considered it essential to raise the woman's body heat to the proper level. The husband would know that the critical moment had arrived when his wife commenced "to speak as if she were babbling." The husband should immediately commence intercourse when this happened and the woman was instructed to lie absolutely still, since if she moved the seed might divide with the result that a defective child would be conceived. The woman should also pay attention to what was going on and not let her thoughts wander to other matters, since if she were musing at the critical moment about, say, a cow, her child might turn out to resemble the animal.[178]

Earlier prohibitions against intercourse during pregnancy and menstruation produced a rich casuistry to deal with doubts about these practices, but most thirteenth- and fourteenth-century writers treated ritual purity as a minor issue.[179] Albert the Great thought that sex during pregnancy ought to be

---

reports that of the fifteen writers whose opinions he examined, eight concluded that the woman sinned mortally by refraining from orgasm, four thought that she sinned venially, and three believed that she did not sin at all.

[175] Pierre de La Palude, *Lucubrationum* 4.31.3.2, p. 367; Flandrin, "La vie sexuelle," p. 104 and "L'attitude à l'égard du petit enfant et les conduites sexuelles dans la civilisation occidentale: structures anciennes et évolution," *Annales de démographie historique* (1973) 146 (also reprinted in his *Sexe et l'Occident*).

[176] *Summa Astensis* 8.9.2, quoted in Lindner, *Usus matrimonii*, p. 145 n. 100.

[177] Pierre de La Palude, *Lucubrationum* 31.3.2, p. 368; Albertus Magnus, *Summa theologica* 2.18.122.1.4; Flandrin, "La vie sexuelle," p. 107 and *Sexe et l'Occident*, p. 133.

[178] *De secretis virorum et mulierum* (Rouen: J. Mauditier for Raulin Gaultier, 1508; unpaginated); Helen Rodnite Lemay, "Some Thirteen and Fourteenth Century Lectures on Female Sexuality," *International Journal of Women's Studies* 1 (1978) 397–98.

[179] In addition to the references cited in Lindner, *Usus matrimonii*, pp. 151–52, see also Pierre de La Palude, *Lucubrationum* 26.2.1. and 31.3.2, pp. 323, 367; Nicholas of

excused, since he believed that the fetus stimulated the expectant mother's nerves, which made her hunger for sexual satisfaction. "A woman," he declared, "never desires sex so much as she does when she is pregnant," and he believed that this furnished ample reason for allowing coitus during this period, since "Medicine is most needed in the time of greatest illness."[180]

Many theological and canonical authorities of this period repeated earlier censures against the use of unconventional coital positions. Alexander of Hales, for example, considered coitus *a tergo* unnatural. It was, he declared, a very serious sin and was never allowed for any reason. Other variations from the missionary position were also sinful, he believed, but less seriously so than penetration from the rear.[181] Alexander's views were shared by many others.[182] Some thought that preferences for particular coital positions might be inborn as a result of the configuration of the planets at the time of a person's birth, although extraterrestrial influences seem not to have been considered seriously by writers on moral questions.[183] The author of *De secretis mulierum* suggested that using nonstandard coital positions might result in birth defects in children conceived during their parents' experiments.[184]

During the latter part of the thirteenth century and the first half of the fourteenth, however, modifications of earlier opinions about irregular coital positions began to surface, and several respected theologians and canonists questioned whether these practices were sinful at all. The best-known questioner was Albert the Great. Albert described five coital positions (missionary, side-by-side, seated, standing, and *a tergo*) and maintained, conventionally enough, that the missionary position was the most natural of these. He considered use of the other four morally questionable, but not mortally sinful.[185]

Lyra, *Postilla* to 2 Reg. 11:4 v. *statimque sanctificata*. William of Pagula, *Summa summarum* 4.1, Pembroke 201, fol. 199rb–203ra, also dealt with these matters in detail.

[180] Albertus Magnus, *Comm. in Sent.* 4.31.22.1, as well as Ps.-Albertus, *Secreta mulierum*, and Lindner, *Usus matrimonii*, p. 150. Albert likewise believed that married persons might pay the conjugal debt to their spouses without sin during penitential seasons or on feast days although the spouse who demanded sex at those times was guilty of a venial sin; *Comm. in Sent.* 4.31.23.

[181] Alexander of Hales, *Summa theologica . . . cura PP. Collegii S. Bonaventurae*, 2–2.3.5.2.1.8.3, 4 vols. (Quaracchi: Ex typographia Collegii S. Bonaventurae, 1924–48).

[182] Thomas Aquinas, ST 1.98.2 and 2–2.159.11; Guido de Baysio, *Rosarium* to C. 32 q. 4 c. 5 v. *non affectu* and c. 12 v. *extraordinarias*, fol. 347va, 348ra; Magister Serlo, *Summa de penitentia* 27, ed. Goering, p. 39; Hostiensis, *Summa aurea*, lib. 5, tit. *De penitentia et remissione* § 19, fol. 278va–vb; Noonan, *Contraception*, p. 224.

[183] Lemay, "Stars and Human Sexuality," p. 133.

[184] *De secretis mulierum* (unpaginated) and Lemay, "Some Thirteenth and Fourteenth Century Lectures," p. 397.

[185] Albertus Magnus, *Comm. in Sent.* 4.31.24; William of Pagula, *Summa summarum* 4.1, Pembroke 201, fol. 203ra, follows this passage almost verbatim; see also Tentler, *Sin and Confession*, pp. 189–90; Clifford, "Ethics of Conjugal Intimacy," p. 21; Flandrin, "Vie sexuelle," p. 107; Noonan, *Contraception*, p. 241.

Albert and a few other writers observed, moreover, that use of unconventional positions could be perfectly justified and not sinful at all in certain situations. Where one party was grossly obese, for example, the missionary position might be impractical and one of the others might be substituted. Pregnancy was another contingency that justified the use of unusual coital positions, since there was fear that coitus in the missionary position might harm the fetus. Use of aberrant coital positions was seriously sinful only if they were adopted in order to heighten sexual pleasure.[186]

Intimate details of the sexual habits of married persons rarely came before the courts, although one case in the Cerisy court register refers in oblique language to what may have been a complaint about use of strange coital postures.[187] Confessors presumably heard about such practices more often than judges did.

Other facets of the sex lives of married persons, however, did crop up in the courts with considerable frequency. The most common was the charge that one party refused to pay the marital debt. In many, probably most, of these cases the underlying issue was in fact desertion—the commonest situation was one in which the husband had left his wife (often in order to set up housekeeping with another woman). The wife then came to court petitioning for payment of the conjugal debt. In effect she was asking the court to order her husband to return to her. Actions for payment of the conjugal debt furnished a procedural mechanism for dealing with this situation.[188]

SEPARATION, DIVORCE, AND REMARRIAGE

Legal modes of terminating marriages between living partners had by this period effectively been reduced to two: separation from bed and board (*a mensa et thoro*) and nullification of invalid unions. The first carried with it no right of remarriage, but in the second, when marriage was annulled, the parties could, if they wished, marry someone else.[189] Canonists repeatedly asserted that marital separation was never permitted without a formal ecclesiastical decree, but this was difficult to enforce. Actual cases show many examples of parties who not only separated but also remarried without seeking, much less securing, any sort of judgment. These situations entered the record, of course, only when the

---

[186] Pierre de La Palude, *Lucubrationum* 31.3.2, p. 367; William of Rennes, gloss to Raymond of Peñafort, *Summa de mat.* 4.2.13 v. *nihil fedius.*

[187] *Registre de Cerisy*, no. 75b, ed. Dupont, p. 335.

[188] 2 Synod of Exeter (1287) c. 7, in Powicke and Cheney 2:999; Bernard of Parma, *Glos. ord.* to X 5.16.7 v. *fornicationis;* Pierre de La Palude, *Lucubrationum* 32.1.1, p. 368; Nicholas of Lyra, *Postilla* to 1 Cor. 7:3; Guido de Baysio, *Rosarium* to C. 27 q. 2 pr., C. 32 q. 1 c. 3 v. *ius exigendi,* and C. 32 q. 4 c. 5 v. *amator,* fol. 331ra, 343rb, and 347va. For some cases see *Registre de Cerisy*, no. 95c, 124b, 261b, ed. Dupont, pp. 350, 371, 456. See also Sheehan, "Theory and Practice," p. 252; Flandrin, "Vie sexuelle," p. 105.

[189] Joannes Andreae, *Novella* to X 5.16.4 v. *plus caeteris;* Pierre de La Palude, *Lucubrationum* 42.2.3, p. 435.

matter arose in the course of other litigation, often when a subsequent marriage came before the courts. In practice the laity, at least on the lower socio-economic levels, exercised far greater control over marriage and divorce than academic commentators acknowledged or than the Church's lawgivers were prepared to concede.[190]

But records of marriage litigation in England during this period show that practice more often conformed rather closely to ecclesiastical marriage law. Certainly this seems to have been true for the law on consanguinity and affinity, and cases in which those problems were at issue were quite uncommon. Since marriage cases tended to be strenuously contested, it is difficult to believe that these issues would have been passed over in silence had there been grounds for raising them.[191]

Recent studies of the particularly rich English records also indicate that marriage cases that came into the courts almost always centered on issues involving consent. The issues raised in most of the cases studied involved either pre-contract (i.e., exchange of consent between one of the couple and a third party prior to the time of the contested marriage), force and fear, or incapacity to consent (usually because one party was allegedly under age at the time of marriage).[192]

Discussions of these issues by canonists in the late thirteenth and early fourteenth centuries followed long-established patterns.[193] Adultery and fornication

---

[190] Bernardus de Montemirato, *Comm.* to X 4.19.3, fol. 131rb: Helmholz, *Marriage Litigation*, p. 59; Dufresne, "Comportements amoureux," p. 137. An anonymous gloss to X 4.19.6 v. *conpellendam* in U.L.C., MS Ee.5.4(B), fol. 177rb, held that husbands may dismiss their wives without formal process for fornication: "Nota secundum host⟨iensem⟩ quod uir potest dimittere uxorem suam sine iudicio ecclesie propter fornicationem, ut pater Augustinus dixit: Si uxor alicuius fornicationem fecit licitum est uiro istam dimittere, xxxii. q. iii. § Dixit dominus [*recte* D. 4 de pen. c. 3]. Ad hanc tamen quod mulier dotem amittat post mortem uiri sui necessaria est sentencia diuorcii." For the Hostiensis reference see *Summa aurea*, lib. 4, tit. *De divortiis* § 7, fol. 218va; but on the other hand see ibid. § 13, fol. 219rb. *Magister Gratianus uolens compilare* to C. 33 q. 2, Peterhouse 169(2), fol. 27vb–28ra, maintained that couples who separated informally might be forced to reconcile when their situation came to the attention of authorities. William of Pagula, *Summa summarum* 4.19, Pembroke 201, fol. 215vb, disposed of the contradiction by a distinction: "Dic quod uxor fornicans potest dimitti dupliciter: aut quo ad thorum solum, aut quo ad thorum et cohabitationem. Primo modo potest uir uxorem de cuius fornicatione sibi constat dimittere propria auctoritate et debitum ei denegare quousque compellatur auctoritate ecclesie. . . . Secundo autem modo non licet uiro uxorem dimittere sine iudicio ecclesie, et si dimissa fuerit, debet cogi uir ad cohabitandum nisi incontinenti uir fornicationem probare possit, secundum tho. et pe. in scrip."

[191] Helmholz, *Marriage Litigation*, p. 79.

[192] Helmholz, *Marriage Litigation*, pp. 74–77, 90–99; Sheehan, "Formation and Stability," pp. 257–62; Donahue, "Policy," p. 267.

[193] These include among others stock assertions that men and women should be treated equally in marriage, reiteration of the "constant man" standard for force-and-fear

were in practice not often cited as grounds. By this period, of course, adultery no longer justified dissolution of marriage and consequently remarriage following separation for this reason was, at least in theory, not allowed.[194] Innocent IV, followed by Guido de Baysio, maintained that a wife was entitled to separate from her husband if he attempted to persuade her to consent to anal intercourse, although she could not secure a separation if her husband practiced sodomy with other persons of either sex.[195] Another basis for separation from bed and board that began to appear in the record during the late thirteenth century was cruelty (*saevitia*), which justified separation when the spouse's cruelty had become unbearable. This cause for separation was created by practice, not by legislation. By about 1300, *saevitia* had emerged as a common cause for canonical separation and was recognized in the civil law of some regions as well.[196]

Judicial determination that a marriage had ceased to exist was often grounded on presumption of death. Remarriage in these cases was permitted, although some authorities in the late thirteenth century took less liberal attitudes toward presumption-of-death situations than their predecessors had done. Both Hostiensis and Bernard of Montemirato, for example, cautioned their readers to be wary of these cases. Hostiensis noted that although earlier canons had prescribed that a woman who remarried might be subject to the penalties for adul-

---

cases, and the like. See, e.g., Alexander of Hales, *Glos. in Sent.* 4.29.1; Thomas Aquinas, *Comm.* to Sent. 4.35.1.4; Pierre de La Palude, *Lucubrationum* 35.1.5, pp. 391–92; Bernardus de Montemirato, *Comm.* to X 4.1.5, 21, fol. 124ra–va.

[194]Thomas Aquinas, *Comm.* to Sent. 4.35.1.1; Gulielumus Durantis, *Speculum iudiciale* 4.4.4–5 (Frankfurt a/M: Sumptibus heredum J. Wechli et J. Gymnici, 1592), p. 477; Nicholas of Lyra, *Postilla* to Matt. 19:9 v. *nisi ob fornicationem, mechatur*, and 1 Cor. 7:11 v. *quod si discesserit*; Pierre de La Palude, *Lucubrationum* 35.2.1, p. 392; Guido de Baysio, *Rosarium* to C. 32 q. 5 c. 16, fol. 349rb; William of Pagula, *Summa summarum* 4.1, Pembroke 201, fol. 198va: "Ut matrimonium non separetur, licet enim thori diuisio fiat propter adulterium, tamen non separetur matrimonium." Similar statements occur, e.g., in the marginal gloss to Geoffrey of Trani, *Summa decretalium* 4.3, Fitzwilliam Museum, McLean 137, fol. 173v, and the *Flores decretorum* to C. 32 q. 7 c. 3 in L.C., Foreign Law MS F.6, fol. 30va. On practice in England see Helmholz, *Marriage Litigation*, pp. 100–101. Part of the record of Arnald c. Ferraria, a Spanish case brought on these grounds, appears in Rius Serra, "Dos causas," pp. 1221–23.

[195]Innocent IV, *App.* to X 5.16.1; Guido de Baysio, *Rosarium* to C. 32 q. 7 c. 7, fol. 350rb.

[196]Helmholz, *Marriage Litigation*, pp. 100–101, 105; Esmein, *Mariage* 2:93–94. The doctrine appears also in the *Assises des bourgeois* 175, RHC, Lois 2:118, with the novel provision that before granting a separation petition on grounds of cruelty the court should require the couple to live together in a house with three good women for two weeks or a month. The court was then to question the good women about the behavior of the party against whom the complaint had been lodged. If their testimony supported the allegations, the defendant might be required to enter religion, while the plaintiff could remarry. This seems a practical solution to a difficult problem, but it presented formidable doctrinal difficulties, both theological and canonical.

tery if her missing husband returned, this was applied in his day only when remarriage had taken place despite reasonable belief that the first spouse still lived.[197] In this respect, too, civil law in some regions followed the lead of the canonists.[198]

Divorce with the right to remarry was largely restricted in this period to nonconsummation cases. Several authors dealt with the problems of men who were incapable of consummating their marriages because they had been castrated. Pierre de La Palude believed that so long as the castrated man was able to achieve an erection and penetrate the vagina, he was capable of contracting a valid marriage. Pierre thus advised that marriages of such men should not be considered void, despite the fact that they were unable to ejaculate semen or conceive a child.[199] Other authorities disputed this conclusion. William of Pagula and the author of *Aliter debet*, for example, held that *castrati* were unable to contract valid marriages. If a man was castrated after marriage, however, his marriage remained valid.[200] Both Thomas Aquinas and Bonaventure, on the other hand, held that permanent incapacity to copulate created a bar to marriage, no matter what the origin of the disability, while Bernard of Montemirato maintained that both capacity to have intercourse and ability to inseminate were necessary for valid marriage.[201]

[197] Hostiensis, *Summa aurea*, lib. 4, tit. *De sponsa duorum* § 6, fol. 203ra; Bernardus de Montemirato, *Comm.* to X 4.21.2, fol. 132rb; Beaumanoir § 1636, ed. Salmon 2:337.

[198] Bresnier, "Mariage en Normandie," p. 85.

[199] Pierre de La Palude, *Lucubrationum* 34.2.1, p. 387.

[200] William of Pagula, *Summa summarum* 4.13, Pembroke 201, fol. 211vb: "Dic quod tales quibus utriusque testiculos abscissus est, quia inepti sunt ad reddendum debitum matrimonium contrahere non possunt, sicut nec ⟨im⟩puberi, extra de frigidis et maleficiis, quod sedem [X 4.15.2], et si contraxerunt dimittendi sunt, quoniam nullum est matrimonium. Si uero matrimonium precessit sectionem, non separatur, licet uir factus sit ineptus ad reddendum debitum, ut xxxii. q. vii. illi qui [c. 25]. . . . Secundum autem legistas spado potest contrahere matrimonium et adoptare, licet non potest generare, sicut notat hug. xxxii. q. vii. hii qui [c. 25], sed host. hanc reprobat quia spado emittit semen, licet sit inualidus ad generandum secundum Ray. § iii. [Raymond of Peñafort, *Summa de mat.* 8.3] set secundum host. e.t. unde accidentalis [Hostiensis, *Summa aurea*, lib. 4, tit. *De frigidis et maleficiatis* § 7]." *Aliter debet* to X 4.1.3 v. *iuuenis*, Caius 23/12, fol. 44vb: "Item contrahere potest matrimonium qui in carnalem copulam consentire potest, nisi sit minor uel carens utroque testiculo uel furiosus."

[201] Thomas Aquinas, *Comm. in Sent.* 4.34.1.2, as well as his *Questiones quodlibetales* 11.9.2; Bonaventure, *Comm.* to Sent. 4.34.2.1. See also Bernardus de Montemirato, *Comm.* to X 4.1.30 and 4.13.7, fol. 125ra, 128va. Vincentius Hispanus, *Lectura* to X 4.1.32, Salamanca 2186, fol. 174ra, on the other hand, believed that penetration, even without ejaculation, was all that was essential, and *Aliter debet* to X 4.2.6 v. *continebatur*, Caius 23/12, fol. 45rb, agreed. Petrus de Sampsone, *Lectura* to X 4.1.30, A.C.A., Ripoll 30, fol. 116ra, held that insemination without penetration constituted consummation: "Ita quid si quis seminet in aras mulieris et non intrabit nunquam consummatur matrimonium? Respondeo quod sic. . . . Ecce ergo . . . matrimonium consummari posse sine effractione claustri pudoris."

Writers continued to debate the distinction between natural, inborn impotence, which they considered permanent, and impotence caused by sorcery, which might be temporary. Impotence that lasted for three years was presumed to be permanent and justified an annulment with right of remarriage.[202] Proof of impotence or frigidity (*impotentia coeundi* and *frigiditas* could refer to sexual incapacity in persons of either sex) continued to be troublesome. The three conventional modes of proof found in earlier literature (physical examination of the parties, sworn testimony of neighbors, and evidence of three years of cohabitation) continued in use. While earlier writers usually assumed that physical examination was used primarily to determine whether the woman's hymen was intact or not, Bernard of Montemirato advised inspection of the man's genitalia as well, to discover whether he showed evidence of immaturity or physical abnormalities that might warrant a finding of impotence.[203] The practice of the English courts went a step further: they sometimes employed "honest women" to determine the man's ability to copulate by attempting to arouse him sexually. The examiners bared their breasts, kissed and fondled him, stroked his penis and testicles, and generally attempted to entice erection. Men who failed to respond to these provocations were presumed to be incapable of sexual intercourse. Under the stressful circumstances of such an inspection, men who were being examined might well have failed to show arousal—particularly after being cursed for failure by the examiners—regardless of their sexual capacities in less frightening situations.[204] A miniature painting of the period depicted the conduct of such an examination (see Pl. 14).

[202] Alexander of Hales, *Glos. in Sent.* 4.34.5; Bonaventure, *Comm.* to Sent. 4.34.2.2; Bernardus de Montemirato, *Comm.* to X 4.15.1, 7, fol. 129va; Pierre de La Palude, *Lucubrationum* 34.2.1, p. 388; *Siete partidas* 3.8.1, ed. Vargas y Ponce, 3:61; William of Pagula, *Summa summarum* 4.13, Pembroke 201, fol. 211vb: "Qualiter cognoscetur an maleficium sit perpetuum uel temporale? Dic quod a principio quod licet maleficium presumitur temporale, quia omnis homo pubes creditur potens ad coitum; sed ex quo per triennium cohabitauerunt uel dantes operam studiosum carnali copule, ubi adhuc durat impedimentum presumitur maleficium perpetuum, extra e.t. ult. [X 4.15.7] secundum Ray⟨mundum de Peñafort⟩ [*Summa de mat.* 16.3] et host⟨iensem⟩ [*Summa aurea*, lib. 4, tit. *De frigidis et maleficiatis* § 9]." Both Hostiensis and William of Pagula follow the text of Raymond of Peñafort's discussion almost verbatim, while Raymond's text, in turn, was essentially that of Tancred. See also Klaus Lüdicke, "Die Rechtswirkungen der heilbaren Impotenz: Überlegungen zu einem übersehen Ehenichtigkeitsgrund," *Archiv für katholisches Kirchenrecht* 146 (1977) 89–90.

[203] Bernardus de Montemirato, *Comm.* to X 4.1.30 and 4.15.5, fol. 125ra, 129va–vb; Joannes Andreae, *Novella* to X 4.2.3; *Aliter debet* to X 4.15.1, Caius 23/12, fol. 46rb: "Item nota tria esse necessaria ad probationem frigiditatis, scilicet aspectus corporis, iura merita cum vii. manu propinquorum, et triennium cohabitatio. Potest tamen esse quod unum sufficiat secundum prouidenciam iudicantis, licet sit melius quod super hoc uideret probationes propter periculum anime." See also Gordon, "Adnotationes," pp. 184–86; Lemay, "William of Saliceto," pp. 175–76.

[204] Helmholz, *Marriage Litigation*, p. 89.

Female impotence resulting from vaginal constriction was considered more amenable to treatment than male impotence, as well it might have been, since many cases so described presumably resulted from what physicians and sex therapists now call vaginismus. William of Pagula advised surgical hymenotomy as a possible treatment if the difficulty was simply due to indurated membrane that was impervious to male thrusting.[205] If there was gross disparity of genital size between the parties, however, that treatment would do little to relieve the situation, as William acknowledged; in such cases the only hope was that further maturation and perhaps repeated intercourse with another partner more closely adapted to the woman's vaginal capacity might enable her to accommodate her husband. If intercourse did become possible, writers of this period differed, as earlier authors had done, over the question of reinstating the original marriage.[206] Jacobus Butrigarius and Odofredus dealt with the further difficult question, ignored by most other writers, of the partition of dowry property in cases where a marriage was dissolved because of impotence. Both authors maintained that in such a situation the woman had a right to restitution of her dowry, regardless of which party suffered from sexual incapacity.[207]

In practice, divorce grounded on impotence appears fairly often in litigation during this period, although by no means all cases where nonconsummation was at issue involved impotence. Nor were all separations because of impotence brought before the courts; many couples parted informally, without ceremony or judicial intervention.[208] Formal proceedings were far more common when the parties were socially prominent and when large amounts of property were at issue, as happened, for example in the well-documented case of *Alvaro de Urgel c. Constanza de Moncada* (1261), where the alleged impotence of Alvaro was fiercely contested in an action that involved some of the most eminent personages of the Kingdom of Aragon, including King James I and Raymond of Peñafort. The Moncada divorce was scarcely typical, but it illustrates the ways in which a plea of impotence might to used to secure release from a union that had ceased to serve the interests of the parties.[209]

[205] William of Pagula, *Summa summarum* 4.13, Pembroke 201, fol. 212rb: "Quid si non potest cum uirginem copulari, sed cum corrupta? Dic quod tunc medicinaliter aliquo instrumento possent claustra pudicitie frangi, nec esset contra matrimonium quia non fit ⟨propter concupiscentiam⟩ [*MS* contra] sed ad medicamentum, secundum tho. in scrip."

[206] Bernardus de Montemirato, *Comm.* to X 4.15.3, fol. 129va; Pierre de La Palude, *Lucubrationum* 34.2.1, p. 387; Ludicke, "Rechtswirkungen," pp. 90–93, 98–100.

[207] Jacobus de Butrigario, *De dote* 21–22, in TUJ 9:448vb; Odofredus, *De dotis restitutione* 17, in TUJ 9:472vb.

[208] See e.g., Ricca c. Gaitano (Pisa, 1241), in Dolezalek, *Imbreviaturbuch*, no. 61, p. 154; William Tristram c. Isabella de Wacton (Norwich? 1271), in Adams and Donahue, *Select Cases* C.5, pp. 123–27; H. Tracy Sturcken, "The Unconsummated Marriage of Jaime of Aragon and Leonor of Castile," JMH 5 (1979) 185–201; LeRoy Ladurie, *Montaillou*, p. 202.

[209] A.C.A., Cancillería. ser. 2, legajo 2 (*olim* Urgel E. 168–69). See also James A.

FORNICATION AND ADULTERY

Although Western theologians were aware that the Greek Church considered simple fornication between two unmarried persons no sin, this belief was formally condemned as a heresy in 1277, during the controversy over Averroist teaching at the University of Paris.[210] Several leading theologians, including Aquinas, held that fornication was prohibited by natural law. This was so, St. Thomas argued, not because the sex act itself was evil, but rather because natural law forbade sex outside of marriage.[211]

Lawmakers during this period for the first time sought to implement the ban on fornication by institutionalizing procedures for systematic reporting of sex offenses. An English synodal decree dated between 1238 and 1244 provides an early example of the type of system that was developing: it charged parish clergymen with the task of reporting to their rural deans notorious fornicators and men who openly lived with concubines. The dean in turn was to prefer a formal complaint against the offenders to the archdeacon, who was empowered to summon the accused and to determine whether the complaint had substance. If he found that it did, the archdeacon could either punish the parties by fines and censures or, preferably, induce them to marry one another voluntarily, provided that they were legally free to do so. If they refused, the archdeacon could require them to abjure further relations with one another under penalty of marriage.[212]

Not all authorities were prepared to go so far as this, particularly with cases involving casual sexual contacts. Bernard of Parma, for example, characterized fornication by separated persons as a minor offense and Hostiensis observed that many circumstances might excuse fornication or mitigate the penalties attached to it.[213] Although lawmakers might decree heavy penalties, as the Synod of Winchester did, on the grounds that small fines were inadequate to discourage sex offenders, the courts often disposed of fornication complaints by imposing small fines and public humiliation on offenders. Only in aggravated cases, where multiple relationships were involved, or where the relationship lasted

Brundage, "Matrimonial Politics in Thirteenth-Century Aragon: Moncada c. Urgel," *Journal of Ecclesiastical History* 31 (1980) 271–82.

[210] *Chartularium universitatis Parisiensis*, ed. Heinrich Denifle and Emile Chatelain, 4 vols. (Paris: Delain Frères, 1889–97) 1:553, no. 183; Lerner, *Heresy of the Free Spirit*, pp. 21, 24, 126; Deno Geanakopolis, "Bonaventura, the Two Mendicant Orders, and the Greeks at Lyon," *Studies in Church History* 13 (1976) 190.

[211] Thomas Aquinas, ST 2–2.154.2; Albertus Magnus, *Summa theologica* 2.18.122.1.4; Pierre de La Palude, *Lucubrationum* 33.1.3, p. 377; Dedek, "Premarital Sex," pp. 658, 660.

[212] 2 Salisbury (1238 ∼ 1244) c. 53; 2 Winchester (1247?) c. 53, in Powicke and Cheney 1:385–86, 411; Sheehan, Marriage and Family," p. 210.

[213] Bernard of Parma, *Glos. ord.* to X 4.15.6 v. *fornicario modo*; Hostiensis, *Lectura* to X 4.15.6 §10.

for a protracted period and caused public scandal, for example, were more serious penalties invoked. Even then it was not unheard-of for the convicted fornicator to settle the case with a cash payment in lieu of flogging or other serious
penalties.[214]

Certainly one reason why the courts treated fornication and other kinds of
extramarital sex as minor offenses had to do with the enormous numbers of
these cases that came before them as the enforcement system improved. The
registers of the Cerisy court, for example, show that fornication and adultery
accounted for about seventy percent of the court's business. Further, the incidence of sex offenses in relationship to the total population was very high. The
parish of Deux-Jumeaux, for example, produced eleven fornication or adultery
cases in 1314, although the parish contained only forty households. This was an
usually high incidence, to be sure, but other parishes in the region were not
far behind. The ratio of sex offenses to households in Cerisy itself during that
same year amounted to 1:6 and even in the placid parish of Litry it stood at
about 1:8.[215]

Although an academic observer such as Nicholas of Lyra might profess astonishment and dismay that people would fornicate publicly and in plain sight (a
practice, he declared, that not even pagans tolerated), people who lived in rural
communities in the thirteenth century were apparently not overly zealous to
conceal even their illegal sexual activities from their neighbors. In *Wood c.
Clapton* (1270), for example, three witnesses asserted that while on their way to
a tavern they had observed Richard Wood copulating with Matilda Goderhele
in a neighbor's croft.[216] Similar testimony in two cases from Aragon, one of them
a sodomy case, shows that there, too, concealment of even very heinous activities from public gaze was at best imperfect and sometimes disdained.[217] Illuminations in legal manuscripts of the period confirm the documentary evidence
that copulation in public places was not unusual; see for example Pl. 20. Under
circumstances where privacy was difficult to secure, it is not surprising that

---

[214] 2 Winchester (1247?) c. 55, in Powicke and Cheney 1:411; *Registre de Cerisy* 17b,
60a, 75b, ed. Dupont, pp. 300, 325–26, 335; Amphlett, *Court Rolls of Hales*, p. 564; C.
Eveleigh Woodruff, "Notes from a Fourteenth-Century Act-Book of the Consistory
Court of Canterbury," *Archaeologia Cantiana* 40 (1928) 56; Georg May, *Die geistliche
Gerichtsbarkeit des Erzbischofs von Mainz im Thüringen des späten Mittelalters*, Er-
furter theologische Studien, vol. 2 (Leipzig: St. Benno Verlag, 1956), p. 223.

[215] Dufresne, "Les comportements amoureux," pp. 133–34, 139.

[216] Nicholas of Lyra, *Postilla* to 1 Cor. 5:1 v. *ita ut vir*; Richard de Bosco c. Johanne de
Clapton (1270), testimony of William Le Muner, Roger le Cannevere, and Nicolas
Piscator de Clapton, in Adams and Donahue, *Select Cases*, pp. 100–101.

[217] Rex c. Pons Hugo de Ampurias (1311), in A.C.A., Cancillería, Procesos, ser. 2,
legajo 5, proc. 24, fol. 2r–3v, 7v–8v; for an analysis of the case see my study "The Politics of Sodomy: Rex c. Pons Hugo de Ampurias," forthcoming in *Festschrift in Memory
of Schafer Williams*. Maria Isabel Simó Rodriguez, "Un conflicto entre Ponce Hugo VI,
conde de Ampurias, y los Venecianos," *Historia, instituciones, documentos* 4 (1977)
583–96, deals with some aspects of the case, but does not address the sodomy issue.

court records show high levels of detection of extramarital sexual dalliance.

The penalties attached to fornication varied greatly. The canonists generally sought to repair the damage caused by seduction by requiring the couple to marry, provided that both parties agreed and that the woman's family also consented; Hostiensis indicated that some degree of coercion might be applied, if necessary, to induce the man to agree.[218] Where marriage was impossible because of some canonical impediment, or where one party withheld consent, the seducer might be obliged to provide an appropriate dowry for the woman.[219] Men who refused to marry their partners in crime and who were unable or unwilling to provide a dowry for them might be subject to corporal punishment in place of the normal canonical remedies.[220] Customary practice was often considerably harsher than this, and vengeance killings were not uncommon.[221] By the end of the thirteenth century, a few municipalities were also beginning to prescribe penalties, usually fines, for men found guilty of fornication with unmarried women of respectable social status.[222] The aim of the canonists, however, was characteristically to heal the social wounds that fornication caused by inducing the couple of marry, if possible, rather than simply to punish them for their behavior.[223] One major exception to this rule concerned fornication between Christians and non-Christians, mainly Jews or Saracens. Penalties for miscegenation with non-Christians were often harsh: commentators on Bartolus thought the death penalty was appropriate, and their opinion agreed with

[218] Bernard of Parma, *Glos. ord.* to X 5.16.1 v. *uxorem*; Hostiensis, *Lectura* to X 5.16.1 v. *noluerit*.

[219] Bernard of Parma, *Glos. ord.* to X 5.16.1 v. *et dotabit eam*; Hostiensis, *Lectura* to X 5.16.1 v. *iuxta modum*, 5.16.2 v. *poena*, 5.23.11 v. *et qualiter puniatur*, as well as *Summa aurea*, lib. 5, tit. *De adulteriis et stupro* § 11, fol. 244vb–245ra; Nicholas of Lyra, *Postilla* to Deut. 22:30 v. *si invenerit vir*; William of Pagula, *Summa summarum* 5.16, Pembroke 201, fol. 239rb: "Quid iudicetur si quis seduxerit uirginem et eam corrupit? Dic quod eam dotabit et in uxorem habebit. Si autem pater puelle noluerit ei dare in uxorem, reddet pecuniam iuxta modum dotis, nam estimabitur dos iuxta facultates illius uiri et dignitatem puelle, extra e.t. c. i et in glo. ult. [*Glos. ord.* ad X 4.20.1 v. *totam*]." The same practice was observed in the customary law of Corsica and, no doubt, elsewhere as well; Marin-Muracciole, *L'honneur des femmes*, p. 197.

[220] Hostiensis, *Lectura* to X 5.16.2 v. *corporaliter*.

[221] Thus, e.g., Eric Glipping, King of Denmark (1259–86), was assassinated by a group of noblemen who claimed that the king had seduced their wives; see William Urban, *The Baltic Crusade* (DeKalb, IL: Northern Illinois University Press, 1957), p. 242.

[222] Sarzana, *Statuti* (1330) 2.11, ed. Gianfranceschi, pp. 110–11; *Statuti de Bologna dell'anno 1288*, 4.30, ed. Gina Fasoli and Pietro Sella, 2 vols., Studi e testi, vol. 73, 85 (Vatican City: Biblioteca Apostolica Vaticana, 1937–39) 1:195; Modena, *Statuti* (1327) 4.27, p. 398; *Archives de la ville de Lectoure: coutumes, statuts, et records du XIIIe siècle*, a.55, ed. P. Druilhet, Archives historiques de Gascogne, fasc. 9 (Paris: H. Champion, 1885), p. 45; Flandrin, "Mariage tardif," p. 1371; Bennecke, *Strafrechtliche Lehre von Ehebruch* 1:129; May *Geistliche Gerichtsbarkeit*, p. 169.

[223] Joannes Andreae, *Novella* to X 5.16.2 v. *agat*; Bernard of Parma, *Glos. ord.* to X 5.16.2 v. *excommunicatusque*; Bernardus de Montemirato, *Comm.* to X 5.16.1.

customary practice. The *Fueros* of Sepúlveda, Teruel, and Cuenca prescribed execution of religiously mixed couples who were caught *in flagrante delicto*, either by burning them alive or by hurling them from a precipice. If they were not taken in the act, however, they were to be flogged in public and sent into exile. The laws of the Latin Kingdom of Jerusalem were equally stern toward Latin colonists who took Muslim sexual partners.[224]

Adultery, while not so common as fornication, was certainly a pervasive social problem. Several reported cases involved multiple relationships, some of them long-continued, which considerably complicated the difficulties.[225] Preachers thundered warnings about the awful consequences of adultery, and reinforced their admonitions with such cautionary tales as the one about a moralistic lion who hunted down adulterers and tore them to shreds. None of this seems to have diminished very seriously the rate at which married folk yielded to extramarital temptations.[226]

Canonists and theologians were not entirely agreed whether adulterous men were more culpable than adulterous women. Thomas Aquinas argued that women should be more severely punished for adultery because of the danger that they might furtively introduce into their families children conceived by their lovers. Master Serlo and William of Pagula, on the other hand, felt that the adulterous man offended more seriously and deserved stricter punishment, a position that Hostiensis apparently shared.[227] Customary law, however, generally penalized women far more severely than men for adultery. Some Spanish *fueros* allowed husbands, and sometimes other family members, too, to slay women caught in the act. Old notions that female adultery dishonored husbands and their kinsmen remained very much part of popular morality during

---

[224] *El fuero de Teruel* 497, ed. Max Gorsch, Leges hispanicae medii aevi, vol. 1 (Stockholm: Almqvist & Wiksell, 1950; cited hereafter as FTeruel), p. 301; Dillard, "Women in Reconquest Castile," in *Women in Medieval Society*, ed. Stuard, pp. 85–86; Sheedy, *Bartolus on Social Conditions*, p. 238; Brundage, "Prostitution, Miscegenation and Sexual Purity," pp. 60–61. If the Christian party was unaware that his or her sexual partner was non-Christian, however, punishment might be reduced or dispensed with altogether, according to William of Pagula, *Summa summarum* 5.16, Pembroke 201, fol. 239rb, relying on *Glos. ord.* to X 5.6.15 v. *erroris*.

[225] *Registre de Cerisy*, no. 42c, 63, ed. Dupont, pp. 316, 328; Amphlett, *Court Rolls of Hales*, pp. 403–404; Dufresne, "Les comportements amoureux," pp. 137–38.

[226] Alexander of Hales, *Summa* 2–2.3.4.2.1.7.2–3; Tubach, *Index exemplorum*, no. 58, p. 13; John Bromyard, *Summa predicantium omnibus diuini eloquij propagatoribus vsui accommodatissima*, s.v. *adulterium* (Nuremburg: Johann Stuchs, 1518), fol. 20va.

[227] Thomas Aquinas, ST Supp. 62.4 ad 5; cf. 2–2.154.8; Bromyard, *Summa predicantium* s.v. *adulterium*, fol. 20rb; Magister Serlo, *Summa de penitentia* 25, ed. Goering, p. 33; Hostiensis, *Lectura* to X 5.16.6 v. *eam*; William of Pagula, *Summa summarum* 5.16, Pembroke 201, fol. 239vb: "An uir sit grauius puniendus pro adulterio quam uxor? Dic quod sic, quia uir est caput mulieris et debet uxorem regere, xxxii. q. vi. indigantur [c. 4] et c. se." See also Børresen, *Subordination and Equivalence*, pp. 206–208.

this period.[228] In principle canon law equalized one of its penalties for adultery by insisting that a prior adulterous relationship constituted an impediment to subsequent marriage, but the canonists themselves usually interpreted this impediment restrictively, and few actual cases mention prior adultery as an issue.[229]

PROSTITUTES, PIMPS, AND PANDERS

Late thirteenth- and fourteenth-century canonists and theologians remained by and large faithful to the traditional concept that prostitution was a species of fornication, although a few writers noted differences between canon and civil law on this point.[230] While the Ordinary Gloss to the Bible observed that the Scriptures forbade men to have sexual relations with prostitutes, and both ecclesiastical and royal authorities occasionally penalized men who violated this prohibition, legal action was usually directed against bawds, not their clients.[231] A few cities decreed that all prostitutes were to be expelled—Bologna did so in 1259, Venice in 1266 and again in 1314, and Modena in 1327—but there is little evidence that these actions ever had more than a short-term effect.[232] Most legal writers and theologians continued to advocate a policy of practical toleration. The prostitute had a certain public usefulness, they believed, and what

[228] FTeruel 479, ed. Gorsch, p. 296; Beaumanoir §§ 930, 933, 1637, ed. Salmon 1:470, 472–73, and 2:337–38; Dillard, "Women in Reconquest Castile," p. 81.

[229] 1 Salisbury (1217 ~ 1219) c. 79, in Powicke and Cheney 1:85–86; William of Pagula, *Summa summarum* 4.1, Pembroke 201, fol. 203rb: "An intencio non seruandi fidem excludat matrimonium? Dic quod de bono fidei duo actus sunt: unus essentialis, scilicet non negare usum sui corporis coniugi, et intencio opponita huic excludit matrimonium; alter accessorius, scilicet non exhibere corpus suum alteri quam coniugi, et imo intencio huic opposita non excludit matrimonium, quia si alius contrahit matrimonium et tamen habet propositum adulterandi, nihilominus tenet matrimonium. . . . Si uero habeat propositum numquam reddendi debitum, si hoc deducitur in peccatum non est matrimonium secundum pe. Quidam tamen dicunt quod contrahitur matrimonium in hac casu." See also Sheehan, "Marriage Theory and Practice," p. 420, and Helmholz, *Marriage Litigation*, pp. 94–95.

[230] Hostiensis, *Summa aurea*, lib. 5, tit. *De adulteriis et stupro* § 9; Guido de Baysio, *Rosarium* to C. 32 q. 4 c. 11 v. *accedere*; Bloch, *Prostitution* 1:20; Leopold Brandl, *Die Sexualethik des heiligen Albertus Magnus: Eine moralgeschichtliche Untersuchung*, Studien zur Geschichte der katholischen Moraltheologie, vol. 2 (Regensburg: F. Pustet, 1955), p. 244; LeRoy Ladurie, *Montaillou*, pp. 150–51.

[231] *Glos. ord.* to Deut 23:17 v. *non*; *Registre de Cerisy*, no. 410h, ed. Dupont, p. 607; Joinville, *Life of St. Louis* 140.702, trans. Hague, p. 205; *Ordonnances des roys de France de la troisième race*, 23 vols. (Paris: Imprimerie Royale, 1723–1849; repr. Farnsborough, Hants.: Gregg Press, 1967–68) 1:74 § 34 (1254) and 1:105 § 5 (1269).

[232] Bologna, *Statuti* 12.4, ed. Frati and Sella 3:509–10; Modena, *Statuti* 4.76, pp. 428–29; *Leggi e memorie Venete sulla prostituzione finito alla caduta della Republica* (Venice: n.p., 1870–72), p. 30; Elizabeth Pavan, "Police des moeurs, société, et politique à Venise à la fin du moyen âge," *Revue historique* 264 (1980) 243.

was required was to set limits to her practice, rather than to eliminate her from society.[233]

In practice, prostitution was and remained a flourishing part of the medieval social system and provided a marginally acceptable outlet for male sexuality.[234] Legal commentators often speculated on the causes that led women into harlotry. Some laid the blame on poverty and the necessity for poor girls to make a living, both matters about which attitudes seem to have been changing during this period.[235] Whereas twelfth- and early thirteenth-century writers tended to treat poverty as a misfortune that was also spiritually virtuous, late thirteenth-century writers had begun to see it as a menace, a condition to be viewed with suspicion and alarm. The poor were becoming a distinct social class, particularly in cities, where the criminal courts often treated them harshly. The result was the emergence in some cities, such as Bologna, or a criminal underworld, whose social centers were often located in one or more of the city's taverns or in the baths. Both of these tended to be the haunts of prostitutes, who thus became increasingly identified with urban criminals.[236] Other theories abounded to account for the prostitute's choice of vocation. Thomas Aquinas believed that women were attracted into the life because of their greed; Hostiensis, on the other hand, seemed to think that prostitutes were exceptionally lustful, a view that was contradicted by medical writers, who taught that prostitutes did not enjoy sex and were sterile.[237] Others laid the blame on astrological influences at the time of the woman's birth, thus relieving her of some blame for the life that she led.[238] Hostiensis could see no excuse for the prostitute. It might be possible, he declared, to pardon some crimes, even homicide, that were committed accidentally or in order to protect one's self; but these considerations did not apply to a woman who voluntarily consented to sex with a man to whom she was not married. The harlot's only excuse was that she had been forced into the life against her will.[239]

Promiscuity remained the defining feature of prostitution for legal writers of

---

[233] Guido de Baysio, *Rosarium* to C. 32 q. 4 c. 3; Hostiensis, *Lectura* to X 4.1.20 § 7; Thomas Aquinas, ST 2–2.1011 *conclusio*, and cf. 1–2.101.3 ad 2; Nicholas of Lyra, *Postilla*, praefatio in quatuor evangelistas; Post, *Studies in Medieval Legal Thought*, p. 553, n. 151; Lea, *Hist. of Auricular Confession* 1:253; Bullough, *Hist. of Prostitution*, p. 116.

[234] Rossiaud, "Prostitution, Youth, and Society," pp. 29–31.

[235] Bernard of Parma, *Glos. ord.* to X 4.1.20 v. *publicas*; Bartholomew of Brescia, *Questiones dominicales* 82.4, in TUJ 17:49rb; Hostiensis, *Lectura* to X 4.1.20 § 6 and 5.18.3 §§ 2–4.

[236] Sarah R. Blanshei, "Crime and Law Enforcement in Medieval Bologna," *Journal of Social History* 16 (1982) 121–23.

[237] Thomas Aquinas, ST 2–2.118.8 ad 4; Hostiensis, *Lectura* to X 4.19.4 § 3; Thomasset, "Représentation," pp. 4–5, 11.

[238] Lemay, "Stars and Human Sexuality," p. 131.

[239] Hostiensis, *Lectura* to X 5.18.3 § 9.

this period. So long as a woman made herself available to anyone who wanted her, she was a prostitute; Odofredus, however, maintained that a woman who confined herself to one or two lovers did not qualify as a prostitute, even if they paid for her sexual services.[240] Local authorities sometimes tried to define the matter more precisely. The statutes of Savigliano in 1305 declared that a woman who had four or more lovers was a prostitute; several Spanish *fueros* set the minimum number at five, while the *fuero* of Alfambra stipulated a minimum of eleven. Cremona, on the other hand, cast the net much wider: its statutes classed any woman who had sex with two or more men as a harlot.[241]

Although canonists considered the prostitute's profession demeaning and contemptible, harlots occasionally gained a degree of civic recognition and sometimes participated marginally in the life of their communities. The prostitutes of Paris are said to have organized a guild under the patronage of St. Mary Magdalen, while the prostitutes of Perugia played a colorful role in celebrating their city's conquest of Arezzo in 1335—they seized the victory banner, attended the victory Mass as a group, and dressed in scarlet finery to bear their banner in triumph through the conquered city.[242]

As for the financial implications of prostitution, Guido de Baysio, for one, puzzled over the question of whether a man who paid a prostitute for her services committed an additional wrong by rewarding her. After reviewing the opinions of his predecessors, Guido concluded that it was wrong to pay a prostitute only if payment was promised in advance in order to persuade her to do what otherwise she might have refused to do. If payment was made after the event, there was no harm either in the client offering or in the harlot accepting her fee; indeed, it was only right to compensate her for her labor.[243] On the other hand she could not sue to collect a promised fee, as the *maggior consiglio* of Venice ruled in 1303.[244] Authorities continued to disagree over the tithe obligations of harlots. Hostiensis thought that they had no obligation to pay, while

---

[240] Odofredus, *Lectura super Dig. vet.* to Dig. 23.2.43.

[241] *Fuero de Cuenca* 11.43, ed. Rafael; de Ureña Semenjaud (Madrid: Tipografía de Archivos, 1939; hereafter FCuenca), p. 238; *Statuta civitatis Cremonae* c. 109 (Cremona: Apud C. Draconium & P. Bozolam et socios, 1578), p. 40; Bloch, *Prostitution* 1:18; Boulting, *Woman in Italy*, p. 293; Luigi Cibrario, *Economie politique du moyen âge*, 2 vols. (Paris: Guillaumin, 1859) 2:1141 Leah Lydia Otis, *Prostitution in Medieval Society: The History of an Urban Institution in Languedoc* (Chicago: University of Chicago Press, 1985), pp. 71–72.

[242] Expressions of contempt for prostitutes are commonplace; see, e.g., Hostiensis, *Lectura* to X 3.2.9 § 1, repeated verbatim by Joannes Andreae, *Novella* to the same passage. For the prostitutes' guild see Bullough, *Hist. of Prostitution*, p. 112, and for the Perugian victory celebration see Boulting, *Woman in Italy*, p. 297. On the socioeconomic status of Parisian prostitutes see Bronislav Geremek, *Les marginaux parisiens au XIVe et XVe siècles*, trans. Daniel Beauvois (Paris: Flammarion, 1976), pp. 241–45.

[243] Guido de Baysio, *Rosarium* to D. 36 c. 8; Hostiensis, *Lectura* to X 3.30.23 § 7.

[244] Venice, *Leggi e memorie*, p. 30.

Thomas Aquinas held that they must pay, but that the Church should not accept their payments until they had reformed.[245]

Similar doubts arose concerning other religious obligations of whores. Hostiensis discussed the intriguing case of a prostitute who had vowed to go on crusade. Should she be required to fulfill her promise? Or should she be made to redeem it by a money payment in lieu of personal service? If she went on crusade, he argued, many men could follow her and this would certainly help the Holy Land, although the good faith of her followers might be questioned. He concluded that she could not personally participate in a crusade and that her offerings in compensation for her failure to accompany the expedition should also be refused.[246] In actual practice, large numbers of prostitutes regularly did attend crusading armies, although whether they actually made crusading vows remains uncertain. During St. Louis's Crusade in Egypt, for example, the king felt obliged to dismiss a considerable number of his followers because they were operating brothels within a stone's throw of his tent.[247]

Both law writers and law makers continued to limit the ability of prostitutes to protect themselves from violence and abuse. Bernard of Parma thought that they should be barred from accusing others of crimes, and the statutes of Bologna, like the *fueros* of Sepúlveda and Cuenca, gave legislative force to this opinion by exempting assaults on prostitutes, pimps, and panders from the remedies provided against battery. Prostitutes were particularly exposed to the danger of rape, from which authorities were frequently unwilling to protect them. Hostiensis declared that the penalties for rape applied only to attacks on honest women, and Alberto de Gandino (d. ca. 1300), discussing a Mantua rape case, concluded that if the victim hired out her body, as the attacker claimed, her assailant could not be punished.[248] Vienna was more vigilant than most cities in protecting its strumpets from rape and other assaults.[249]

Even attacks on the property of harlots might be ignored, as Alberto de Gandino pointed out, recalling the classical Roman ruling that a man who smashed the door of a harlot's house and thus made it possible for thieves to make away with her goods could not be held responsible for the loss, since the doorbreaker's motive was lust, not greed.[250] Further, according to Bernard of

---

[245] Hostiensis, *Lectura* to X 3.30.23 § 2; Thomas Aquinas, ST 2–2.87.2 ad 2; cf. *Glos. ord.* to Deut. 23:18 v. *non offeres*.

[246] Hostiensis, *Summa aurea*, lib. 3, tit. *De voto et voti redemptione* § 11, fol. 177rb.

[247] Joinville, *Life of St. Louis* 36.171, trans. Hague, p. 66.

[248] Hostiensis, *Summa aurea*, lib. 5, tit. *De penis raptorum corporum*, pr., fol. 245vb; Alberto de Gandino, *Tractatus de maleficiis*, ed. Hermann Kantorowicz in *Albertus Gandinus und das Strafrecht der Scholastik*, 2 vols. (Berlin: J. Guttentag, W. De Gruyter, 1907–26) 2:360–61; Powers, "Frontier Municipal Baths," pp. 659–60.

[249] Bernard of Parma, *Glos. ord.* to X 5.1.20 v. *concubinarios*; Bologna, *Statuti* 4.47, ed. Fasoli and Sella 1:210; Dillard, "Women in Reconquest Castile," p. 86; Boulting, *Woman in Italy*, p. 293; Schrank, *Prostitution in Wien*, pp. 52, 54. quoting a law of Duke Friedrich II, 1 July 1244 § 8.

[250] Alberto de Gandino, *Tractatus de maleficiis*, ed. Kantorowicz 2:214, recalling Ulpian in Dig. 47.2.39.

Parma, a whore who was charged with an offense should not be allowed to answer the charge in person; instead, like a madman, she must appoint a proctor to present her defense to the court.[251] Given the many restrictions on their civic rights and the lack of protection that society generally afforded to them, it is not surprising that harlots were commonly believed to harbor grievances that they might work out in peculiar ways. Pseudo-Albertus, for example, related a version of the ancient male anxiety myth of the *vagina dentata*—the vagina with teeth. Pseudo-Albertus's version featured prostitutes who hid sharp pieces of iron in their vaginas in order to lacerate their clients' penises. Etienne de Bourbon, a popular preacher, warned captains not to allow whores on board their ships, since the presence of a harlot would cause storms at sea.[252]

The civic disabilities incurred by prostitutes often applied as well to their pimps, panders, and procurers. These occupations were broadly defined so as to include anyone who encouraged, promoted, or profited from prostitution. Traditionally any man who failed to expel his adulterous wife or who attempted to conceal her crimes was classed as a pimp. A woman who concealed her husband's infidelities, however, was not considered guilty of pandering or procuring.[253] The Cerisy registers suggest that authorities in rural Normandy may have been more assiduous in prosecuting procurers, pimps, and keepers of bawdy houses than they were in dealing with prostitutes themselves, while Alberto de Gandino apparently conducted a brief campaign against promoters of prostitution at Bologna in 1289.[254] A civic ordinance at York in 1301 ordered that brothels discovered in that city were to be destroyed and their proprietors imprisoned (though only for a day and a night). But fits of civic rectitude such as these seem to have been sporadic, short-lived, and generally ineffective.[255] Most cities strove for the more modest goal of controlling the activities in their brothels and bathhouses by forbidding gambling in them, as Avignon did in

[251] Bernard of Parma, *Glos. ord.* to X 2.1.14 v. *factum proferat.*

[252] Ps.-Albertus, *Secreta mulierum* (unpaginated); Lemay, "Some Thirteenth and Fourteenth Century Lectures," p. 395; Tubach, *Index exemplorum*, no. 4648, p. 352.

[253] Bernard of Parma, *Glos. ord.* to X 5.16.3 v. *reus erit*; Geoffrey of Trani, *Summa super titulis* to X 5.16 § 4; Hostiensis, *Summa aurea*, lib. 5, tit. *De adulteriis* §§ 14–15, fol. 245ra; Guido de Baysio, *Rosarium* to C. 32 q. 1 d.p.c. 10 v. *crimen*; William of Pagula, *Summa summarum* 5.16, Pembroke 201, fol. 238vb: "Quot modis committitur lenocinium? Dic quod committitur lenocinium qui habet mancipia questuaria, quia hic non est minus quam proprio corpore questum facere. Item leno est qui scienter ducit dampnatam adulteram uel qui reconciliauit sibi eam uel qui scienter tenet adulteram, uel qui recepit pecuniam pro adulterio secundum glo. [Glos. ord., supra]." See also LeRoy Ladurie, *Montaillou*, p. 91.

[254] *Registre de Cerisy*, no. 75b, 76, 95b–c, 110b, 181, 285c, 286, ed. Dupont, pp. 334–35, 350, 358, 360, 399–400, 474–75; Kantorowicz, *Albertus Gandinus*, doc. 30, 35, 1:243–44, 252–54.

[255] *York Civic Ordinances, 1301*, ed. Michael Prestwich, Borthwick Papers, no. 49 (York: Borthwick Institute of Historical Research, 1976), pp. 16–17; for a similar investigation of prostitution and illicit sex at Bury St. Edmunds a few years earlier, see William Hoo, *Letter-Book*, no. 29, pp. 41–42.

1243, or by forbidding harlots to frequent the public baths, save on certain days of the week, as Marseille did somewhat later in the century. At Paris, supervision of the city's prostitutes and enforcement of the regulations concerning their behavior was entrusted to a royal official, the *roi des ribauds*, who had counterparts in many other French towns and cities.[256] Small towns and villages, such as Montaillou, rarely had brothels at all, but prostitutes were sufficiently common that those who required their services could easily find them in nearby communities. A few French cities—Paris, Chartres, Sens, and Orleans—apparently had male homosexual brothels, in addition to the usual heterosexual establishments, but nothing is known about their operations.[257]

Canonists of this period believed that prostitutes should be distinguished from respectable women by their style of dress and Bernard of Parma pointedly referred to an ancient civil law text in which Paulus had declared that matrons who dressed like whores lost their social privileges.[258] Town statutes sought to implement this strategy by prescribing dress codes to mark out harlots from other women. A tactic often used in German-speaking lands required prostitutes to wear clothes of a distinctive color: in Augsburg the designated color was green, in Vienna and Leipzig it was yellow, in Zurich, red.[259] Other cities preferred to mark out their whores by the style and cut of the clothes they were permitted to wear. Statutes sometimes even prescribed the fabrics from which their clothing could be made. Some towns also restricted the use of certain types of headdress and jewelry to prostitutes.[260] An increasingly popular stratagem was to segregate prostitutes from respectable women by forbidding harlots to live or even to walk in certain parts of a city.[261] An Avignon statute of 1243

[256] Avignon, Statutes of 1243, c. 77, in L. Le Pilleur, *La prostitution du XIIIe au XVIIe siècle: Documents tirés des archives d'Avignon, du comitat Venaissin, de la principauté d'Orange, et de la ville libre impériale de Besançon* (Paris: Honoré Champion, 1908), p. 1; Marseille, municipal statutes (second half of the thirteenth century), lib. 5, c. 13, in Hippolyte Mireur, *La prostitution à Marseille: Histoire, administration, et police, hygiène* (Paris: E. Dentu; Marseille: Librairie Marseillaise, 1882), pp. 366–67; Anne Terroine, "Le roi des ribauds de l'Hôtel du roi et les prostituées parisiennes," RHDF, 4th ser., 56 (1978) 253–67.

[257] LeRoy Ladurie, *Montaillou*, p. 7; Boswell, CSTAH, p. 262.

[258] Bernard of Parma, *Glos. ord.* to X 5.39.5 v. *meretricali*, citing Dig. 23.2.47; see also Hostiensis, *Lectura* to X 5.6.15 § 4, citing Labeo in Dig. 47.10.15.15.

[259] Jung, *Geschlechtsmoral*, p. 219.

[260] Sarzana, *Statuti* (1330) 2.21, ed. Gianfranceschi, pp. 115–16; Marseille, *Statutes* (late thirteenth century), lib. 5 c. 12, in Mireur, *Prostitution*, pp. 365–66; Gustav Schönfeld, *Beiträge zur Geschichte des Pauperismus und der Prostitution in Hamburg*, Socialgeschichtliche Forschungen, vol. 2 (Weimar: Emil Felber, 1897), p. 92; Geremek, *Marginaux*, pp. 246–47; Diane Owen Hughes, "Distinguishing Signs: Ear-Rings, Jews, and Franciscan Rhetoric in the Italian Renaissance City," *Past and Present* 112 (1986) 3–59. Tubach, *Index exemplorum*, no. 2453, p. 194, reports a tale in which a prostitute ridicules a respectable woman because of her simple, unadorned dress.

[261] Bologna, *Statuti* (1288) 4.34, ed. Fasoli and Sella 1:197–98; Sarzana, *Statuti* (1330)

went so far as to forbid whores and Jews to touch bread or fruit put up for sale in the marketplace and required them to buy any item on which they laid a finger.[262] A few cities designated a civic official to supervise local prostitutes and made him responsible for enforcing the rules governing the dress and behavior of the town's harlots. In Augsburg, the municipal hangman was assigned this duty on holidays and Saturday evenings, when presumably he was not occupied with more demanding tasks.[263] In England the royal marshal employed a clerk and a serjeant specifically for the purpose of keeping harlots out of the households of the king and queen and the royal children. Strumpets apprehended in the forbidden precincts were to be let off with a warning the first time; if they reappeared they could be imprisoned; a third offense resulted in a shaved head; if they were so foolhardy as to make a fourth appearance, their upper lips were to be cut off; this presumably diminished their ability to carry on their trade.[264]

Efforts to encourage the reform of prostitutes continued to receive support during this period, especially from Louis IX of France, who endowed a number of convents for reformed harlots.[265] Not all prostitutes, by any means, entered the trade willingly, and the eminent proceduralist William Durand included in his *Speculum iudiciale* instructions for dealing with petitions from women who wished to be liberated from the stews, together with models of the documents needed in these cases.[266] Canonists also continued to encourage men to marry prostitutes who wished to reform and characterized this as a meritorious action—although Bernard of Montemirato added that it was not nearly as meritorious as going on a Crusade.[267]

RAPE AND ABDUCTION OF WOMEN

Abduction and rape of women, particularly wealthy ones, remained a serious but not common crime; it does not appear nearly so frequently in civic court records as larceny, burglary, theft, or even homicide. It is likely, however, that

---

2.20, ed. Gianfranceschi, p. 115; Avignon, *Statutes* (1243) c. 96, ed. LePilleur, *Prostitution*, p. 2; Otis, *Prostitution*, pp. 25, 28–31.

[262] Avignon, *Statutes* (1243) c. 137, ed. LePilleur, *Prostitution* p. 2.

[263] Schrank, *Prostitution in Wien*, p. 54, citing an ordinance of Rudolf von Habsburg for Augsburg, 9 March 1276.

[264] *Fleta* 2.5, ed. and trans. H. G. Richardson and G. O. Sayles, Selden Society Publications, vols. 72, 89, 99 (London: Bernard Quaritch, 1955–83) 2:114–15.

[265] Joinville, *Life of St. Louis* 142.725, trans. Hague, p. 210. See also Otis, *Prostitution*, pp. 72–75, on similar convents in Languedoc.

[266] Gulielmus Durantis, *Speculum iudiciale* 4.4.8–9 (Frankfurt a/M: Sumptibus heredum A. Wechli et J. Gymnici, 1592), p. 477.

[267] Bernard of Parma, *Glos. ord.* to X 4.1.20 v. *in uxores*; Innocent IV, *Apparatus* to X 4.1.20 v. *remissionem*; Hostiensis, *Lectura* to X 3.32.19 § 3 and 4.1.20 § 8; Bernardus de Montemirato, *Comm.* to X 4.1.20 v. *peccatorum*; Pierre de La Palude, *Lucubrationum* 26.2.3, p. 324.

then, as now, rape was seriously under-reported.[268] Men tended to be skeptical about rape complaints, and defendants often claimed that the woman had invited the attack, but courts rarely found the charges wholly without merit.[269]

The French customary law writer, Beaumanoir, furnished the most lucid discussion in the legal literature of this period of the problem of defining the degree of force and the level of resistance necessary to constitute rape. Beaumanoir outlined the nucleus of a resistance standard for rape. He deemed that the victim must at least show that she had protested, that she had attempted to escape, and that her abductor had threatened her life or the lives of members of her family.[270] If there had been a prior marriage agreement, however, the canonists maintained that the penalties for rape were inappropriate.[271]

There was no general agreement on the question of whether abduction, with or without carnal knowledge, was an impediment to subsequent marriage between attacker and victim.[272] Oldradus da Ponte (d. 1335) described a case in point. A certain John from the diocese of Utrecht wished to marry a girl named Margaret. She refused to marry him and John then abducted her by force and violence. Once John had her under his control, he compelled Margaret to exchange words of present consent with him, under threat that he would kill her if

[268] *Registre de Cerisy* no. 3, 205, 235b–d, 292–94, 371, ed. Dupont, pp. 287–89, 428, 442–43, 480–81, 545; Dufresne, "Comportements amoureaux," pp. 144–45; Barbara A. Hannawalt, "The Female Felon in Fourteenth-Century England," in Stuard, *Women in Medieval Society*, p. 137; LeRoy Ladurie, *Montaillou*, p. 149, Synod of Liège (1287) 9.9, in Martène and Durand, *Thesaurus* 4:848.

[269] Bartholomew of Brescia, *Questiones dominicales* 80.3, in TUJ* 17:48vb; Tubach, *Index exemplorum*, no. 4035, p. 310; Thomasset, "Représentation," p. 11. The only actual case of a finding that a rape accusation was false and malicious that has come to my attention is in *Registre de Cerisy*, no. 394h, ed. Dupont, p. 591.

[270] Beaumanoir § 929, ed. Salmon 1:469–70; Bernard of Parma, *Glos. ord.* to X 5.17.6 v. *dicatur admitti*; William of Pagula, *Summa summarum* 5.17, Pembroke 201, fol. 239vb, 240va: "An rapiens puellam excusatur a pena si rapta que est nubilis etatis ei consenserit? Dic quod liberatur a pena corporali, non tamen a pena pecuniaria quam sustinere debet, xxxvi. q. i. de raptoribus [c.3] et in prin. glo. . . . An potest dici raptor qui habet consensum mulieris? Dic quod non, extra e.t. cum causam [X 5.17.6]." See also Walker, "Free Consent," p. 127; Wohlhaupter, "Germanistische Rechtsgedanken," p. 238; Giuseppe Ferroglio, "Studi in tema di 'impedimentum raptus,'"*Annali della Facoltà giuridica dell'Università di Studi di Camerino* 20 (1935) 175.

[271] Hostiensis, *Lectura* to X 5.17.6 v. *dicatur admitti*; William of Rennes, gloss to Raymond of Peñafort, *Summa de pen.* 2.5.4 v. *contrahere potest*, p. 168; Esmein, *Mariage* 1:392.

[272] Bernard of Parma, *Glos. ord.* to X 5.17.7 v. *cum raptore*; Hostiensis, *Lectura* to the same passage; Bernardus de Montemirato, *Comm.* to X 5.17.6 v. *cum causa*; Joannes Andreae, *Novella* to X 5.17.6; Esmein, *Mariage* 1:392–93. Indeed, rather than considering rape as an impediment to marriage, popular belief often considered marriage an alternative to the death penalty for the rapist; Tubach, *Index exemplorum*, no. 3037, 4040, p. 310. In the following century municipal statutes sometimes offered that alternative; see below, p. 531.

she refused. Once she had uttered the required words, John locked Margaret up in a secluded house, where he had intercourse with her repeatedly over the course of twelve days. Finally Margaret seized a chance to escape and fled to complain to the authorities. In discussing this case, Oldradus gave special weight to the circumstances of the escape and concluded that Margaret's flight proved that the exchange of consent was a sham and had no force in law. The simulated marriage, Oldradus declared, was null, and Margaret, or her family, was free to prosecute John for rape.[273] Had the words of consent been valid, however, Margaret would have had no case, since the canonists refused to admit the possibility that a husband could rape his wife.[274]

If Margaret had been married to another man, her husband would probably have had grounds for action against John for "criminal diversion" of his spouse— English statutes, for example, expressly granted an action for these cases. The husband, if successful, might be awarded damages by the royal courts; the ecclesiastical courts, although they were prepared to entertain such complaints, could do no more than order the wife restored to her husband and impose a penance upon the abductor. Understandably, therefore, English husbands in this situation normally resorted to the royal courts.[275]

In rape cases where the victim was unmarried, the ecclesiastical courts had other remedies to offer. They might impose fines or order the offender to be flogged (at least so long as the whipping drew no blood).[276] The convicted rapist might also be denied Christian burial when he died.[277] Secular tribunals offered a choice of penalties, ranging from the death penalty through mutilation (castration was an obvious favorite, although by the end of the thirteenth century it had begun to fade out of fashion), exile, forfeiture of property, fines, compensation for the victim or her family, imprisonment, and, of course, flogging (but without the limits imposed by canon law).[278] Accessories to the crime could also

[273] Oldradus da Ponte, *Consilia: aurea quidem sunt haec ac pene divina responsa*, no. 35 (Lyon: Compagnie des Libraires, 1550), fol. 13va–vb.

[274] Innocent IV, *Apparatus* to X 5.17.6 § 1; Bartholomew of Brescia, *Questiones dominicales* 80.2, in TUJ* 17:48vb.

[275] Statute of Westminster I c. 13, 3 Edw. I (1275), in *Statutes of the Realm, Printed by Command of His Majesty King George the Third*, 9 vols. in 10 (London: G. Eyre & A. Stahan) 1:29; Helmholz, *Marriage Litigation*, pp. 109–10.

[276] Bernard of Parma, *Glos. ord.* to X 5.17.4 v. *pecuniaria poteris, flagellis*; Hostiensis, *Summa aurea*, lib. 5, tit. *De penis raptorum corporum* § 1, fol. 245vb–246ra.

[277] Hostiensis, *Summa aurea*, lib. 5, tit. *De penis raptorum corporum* § 3, fol. 246ra–rb; Joannes Andreae, *Novella* to X 5.17.2 v. *super eo*.

[278] Bologna, *Statuti* (1288) 4.32, ed. Fasoli and Sella 1:196; Ferrara, *Statuta* (1287) 4.48, 54, and 6.68, ed. Montorsi, pp. 269–71, 396; Beaumanoir §§ 920–27, ed. Salmon 1:467–68; FTeruel 474, 476–77; Statute of Westminster I (3 Edw. I) c. 13; Edmund Gibson, *Codex iuris anglicani* 47.4 (London: Printed by J. Baskett, 1713), p. 1125; John C. Bellamy, *Crime and Public Order in England in the Later Middle Ages* (London: Routledge & Kegan Paul; Toronto: University of Toronto Press, 1973), p. 181; LeRoy Ladurie, *Montaillou*, p. 45; Garcerán de Vall, *El rapto y su jurisprudencia*, pp. 2–3.

be punished, although usually more lightly than principals.[279] Clerics guilty of rape or abduction were, in addition, liable to be deprived of clerical preferment, which, at least in theory, they could not regain without papal license.[280] In practice, ravishment and abduction were rarely punished with anything like the severity that either secular or ecclesiastical law prescribed. This was especially true, of course, when the victim consented to abduction and, as sometimes happened, even cooperated in the affair.[281]

SODOMY AND SEXUAL DEVIANCE

The second half of the thirteenth century witnessed a sharp growth of legislation about homosexual relationships. Municipal statutes, during this period prescribed far more savage penalties for deviant sexual behavior than appear earlier. The new hostility toward homosexuals may have stemmed in part from fear that their presence might trigger a salvo of divine wrath against the whole community—at least such fears are often cited as a rationale for imposing horrendous penalties upon sexual deviants.[282] Popular belief identified sodomy as a particularly common vice among the clergy, and also as a peculiarity of urban populations.[283] Perhaps the fashion for imposing exemplary penalties upon men convicted of sodomy stemmed in part from anticlerical sentiments; the fact that the most savage penalties occur in city statutes and ordinances, however, makes it improbable that the phenomenon reflected antiurban prejudice.[284]

While moralists, theologians, and canonists usually assumed that sexual deviance resulted from moral defects, medical writers attempted to account for this behavior on the basis of physical abnormalities. Rhazes described male homosexuality as inborn, while William of Saliceto identified the causes of lesbianism as either uterine prolapse or abnormal enlargement of the clitoris.[285]

While Master Serlo incorporated in his penitential a list of old-fashioned prescriptions—primarily fasting and other ascetic disciplines—for homosexuality, others favored drastic action against homosexual offenders. The Templars and Teutonic Knights were supposed to expel those guilty of sexual deviance

---

[279] Ferrara, *Statuta* (1287) 4.46 and 6.65, ed. Montorsi, pp. 268, 395.

[280] Joannes Andreae, *Novella* to X 5.17.2 v. *irrecuperabiliter.*

[281] LeRoy Ladurie, *Montaillou*, p. 150.

[282] William M. Bowsky, "The Medieval Commune and Internal Violence: Police Power and Public Safety in Siena, 1287–1355," *American Historical Review* 73 (1967) 5.

[283] Hostiensis, *Summa aurea*, lib. 5, tit. *De excessibus prelatorum* § 2, fol. 259vb; *Roman de la rose*, ll. 20,028–30; Lea, *Hist. of Auricular Confession* 1:243; LeRoy Ladurie, *Montaillou*, p. 149. Boswell, CSTAH, pp. 207–41, argues strongly—perhaps more strongly than the evidence warrants—for the identification of gay sexuality with urban life-styles.

[284] LeRoy Ladurie, *Montaillou*, p. 146, notes that although most of the homosexuals cited in the inquisitorial records lived in cities, they had strong ties with the rural communities of the Pamiers region.

[285] Lemay, "William of Saliceto," pp. 178–80; William was one of the few writers of this period to deal with lesbianism at all.

from their orders, while the diocesan statutes of Cambrai (1300 ~ 1310) treated these crimes as reserved sins that ordinary confessors could not forgive and that required recourse to the bishop. "Manual pollution," according to these statutes, was also reserved to diocesan penitentiaries. Parish priests in Cambrai were left to deal only with fornication, masturbation by boys under fourteen and by girls under twenty-five, together with "irregular" heterosexual intercourse, which meant either coitus in unusual positions or anal and oral sex.[286] Municipal laws were far more bloodthirsty. The Bologna statutes of 1288 replaced the earlier fine levied for homosexual offenses with death by burning; thirteenth-century Portuguese practice, adapted from the *Fuero real* of Alfonso the Wise, prescribed castration for male homosexuals, followed (three days later) by hanging by the legs until death; Siena also prescribed hanging, but "by the virile members," while the customs of Tortosa prescribed the death penalty without specifying the means.[287]

Also striking is the frequency with which homosexual behavior comes to be identified with heresy. The charge of sodomy became a more or less routine ingredient of political and social invective just when secular penalties for homosexual practices were becoming markedly more savage. The Knights Templars were suppressed, in part for practicing sodomy; William of Nogaret included sodomy among the numerous other vices that he ascribed to Pope Boniface VIII and to Bishop Guichard of Troyes; the sodomy charges preferred by King James II of Aragon against Count Alvaro of Urgel were a potent weapon in a political vendetta; if these charges also had some foundation in fact, that was a convenient coincidence.[288]

Other sexual practices considered deviant in this period were heatedly denounced, but seldom prosecuted. Bestiality, which Alexander of Hales characterized as the most grievous kind of unnatural sex crime, hardly ever appears in the records, while cross-dressing seems to have carried no penalties at all— Cypriot knights were described as fighting tournaments while dressed as women and, although this was treated as peculiar, it was not criminal.[289]

Sex practices deemed unnatural apparently did not diminish as a result of

[286] Magister Serlo, *Summa de penitentia* 27, ed. Goering, pp. 39–42; Sterns, "Crime and Punishment," p. 91; Flandrin, "Contraception," p. 1376, "Mariage tardif," p. 1356, and *Sexe et l'Occident*, pp. 114–15. Jean de Meung also classified masturbation as a crime against nature; *Roman de la rose*, ll. 20,039–44.

[287] Bologna, *Statuti* (1288) 4.31, ed. Fasoli and Sella 1:196; *Costums de Tortosa* 9.24.3, in Bienvenido Oliver, *Historia del derecho en Cataluña, Mallorca y Valencia*, 4 vols. (Madrid: Miguel Ginesta, 1876–81) 4:333; A. H. de Oliveira Marques, *Daily Life in Portugal in the Middle Ages*, trans. S. S. Wyatt (Madison: University of Wisconsin Press, 1971), pp. 180–81.

[288] Partner, *Murdered Magicians*, pp. 53–54; Brundage, "Politics of Sodomy" (forthcoming); Boswell, CSTAH,. pp. 283–86.

[289] Alexander of Hales, *Summa* 2–2.3.5.2.1.8.1; Hostiensis, *Summa aurea*, lib. 5, tit. *De adulteriis* § 15, fol. 245ra–rb; Nicholas of Lyra, *Postilla* to Rom. 1:24 v. *propter quod*; Tubach, *Index exemplorum*, no. 3834, p. 296; David Jacoby, "The Diffusion of

the greatly increased penalties attached to them. Indeed Pierre de La Palude even found it necessary to explain at length why the Church did not allow homosexuals to marry one another, which may indicate that he was aware, or at least fearful, of attempts to extend social recognition to same-sex relationships through some type of wedding ritual.[290]

SEXUAL BEHAVIOR OF THE CLERGY

In a circular letter to his archdeacons written about 1244, Bishop Robert Grosseteste of Lincoln (d. 1253) lamented that many parish priests in his diocese continued, despite all the rules against it, to live publicly with concubines. Grosseteste acknowledged, however, that they had the good grace, not to say prudence, to send them away when he visited their parishes. Grosseteste instructed his archdeacons to remain vigilant and to report to him any cases that they detected.[291] It is unlikely that Grosseteste's efforts met with much success. Clerical concubinage and fornication remained persistent problems throughout the fourteenth century, and priests seem to have lived with their female companions almost as openly and as often as had their eleventh-century predecessors. The chief difference was that, as we have seen, these unions were no longer legitimized as marriages, and so clerical couples lived in sin, under threat of suspension and deposition if a vigilant archdeacon or a reforming bishop should find them out. Not all bishops took great pains to ferret out such cases, since some of them were doing much as their priests did: Bishop Henry of Gelders at Liège, to take a flagrant example, boasted that he had sired fourteen sons in twenty-two months. A recent study has shown that in Norway and Sweden during the early fourteenth century large numbers of the clergy were themselves illegitimate sons of priests, and it is not unreasonable to assume that many of them in turn had children of their own.[292] Those whose incontinence was detected, moreover, could often rely upon their colleagues to help fend off punishment. William Bordenn, rector of Wittersham, in 1342 found twenty-two clerics willing to act as compurgators in clearing him of charges of sexual irregularities, as well as kicking and beating one of his parishioners in the parish church during Mass.[293] Others simply defied the courts and challenged their authority to punish clerics for fornication.[294]

Despite their predecessors' lack of success in implementing the policy of

---

Knightly Values in the Crusader States of the Eastern Mediterranean," paper presented at the XVI International Congress of Medieval Studies, Kalamazoo, MI, 8 May 1981.

[290] Pierre de La Palude, *Lucubrationum* 26.1.2, p. 322.

[291] Robert Grosseteste, *Epistolae* 107, ed. Henry R. Luard, Rolls Series, no. 25 (London: Longman, Green, Longman, and Roberts, 1861), p. 317; cf. Statutes of 2 Salisbury (1238 ~ 1244) c. 34, in Powicke and Cheney 1:380.

[292] Schimmelpfennig, "Ex fornicatione nati," pp. 33, 40–41.

[293] Woodruff, "Notes from a Fourteenth-Century Act-Book," p. 59.

[294] *Registre de Cerisy*, no. 276a, ed. Dupont, pp. 470–71.

mandatory clerical celibacy, legal commentators and synodal lawmakers continued to insist that the policy must be enforced; they continued to adopt additional, often redundant, enactments requiring clerics to give up their concubines, and sought to devise new penalties in the apparent hope that sooner or later they would hit on an enforcement mechanism that would work. But the new remedies failed just about as regularly as the old ones.[295]

Some authorities were resigned to ignoring clerical fornication and concubinage, at least so long as it was not notorious, and attempted enforcement only where an offender caused public scandal that could no longer be ignored.[296] Synods also tried to prevent clerics from leaving legacies to their concubines and from buying or building houses for them; these enactments further reinforce the impression that many clerics lived in relatively stable relationships over long periods of time and treated their companions as de facto wives.[297]

[295] Joannes Andreae, *Novella* to X 3.2.4; Odofredus, *Lectura* to Cod. 5.26; *Siete partidas* 1.6.43–44, ed. Vargas y Ponce 1:249–50; Vincentius Hispanus, *Lectura* to X 3.2.2 v. *canonice*, Salamanca 2186, fol. 128rb: "Id est in monasterio trudatur, xxxiii. alii exponuntur: id est in seruitutem redigatur, xxxii. eos quibus [?]; si fuit ex concubina iniungetur ei penitentia pro adulterio et sacrilegio, xxvii. q. i. que Christo [c. 10]; si uero publice ducta fuit in uxorem magis punietur, quia ipsa uxor et proles in seruitutem redigentur et ita intelligo lxxxi. di. quidam [c. 30], xi. q. ult. cum multe [*recte* C. 15 q. 8 c. 3] de uxoribus etiam non concubinis." Synodal statutes are numerous, especially in England; see Lincoln (1239?) c. 10, 3 Worcester (1240) c. 100, Norwich (1240 ~ 1243) c. 9–10, 2 Salisbury (1238 ~ 1244) c. 37, 2 Winchester (1247?) c. 13, 2 Durham (1241 ~ 1249) c. 20–21, 1 Chichester (1245 ~ 1252) c. 58, 1 York (1241 ~ 1255) c. 7, 2 Lincoln (1245 ~ 1259) c. 55, 3 Winchester (1262 ~ 1265) c. 43, Legatine Council of London (1268) c. 8, 2 Exeter (1287) c. 18, 2 Chichester (1289) c. 2, all in Powicke and Cheney 1:269, 320, 346–47, 380–81, 405, 427–28, 463, 486, 645–46, 710, 756–57, and 2:1013–14, 1083. On the Continent see, e.g., Constitutions of Fiesole (1306) and Florence (1310), in Richard C. Trexler, *Synodal Law in Florence and Fiesole, 1306–1518*, Studi e testi, vol. 268 (Vatican City: Biblioteca Apostolica Vaticana, 1971), pp. 189, 220, 247–48; Council of Valladolid (1322) c. 7 in Mansi 25:700–703, and Winterer, "Zur Priesterehe in Spanien," p. 376.

[296] Joannes Andreae, *Novella* to X 3.2.7; Gulielmus Durantis, *Speculum iudiciale* 4.2, tit. *De cohabitatione clericorum et mulierum*; *Magister Gratianus uolens compilare* to D. 28, Peterhouse 169, fol. 3vb: "In xi.a probat quod possumus audire missam a presbitero concubinario quamdiu toleratur, quod laici non iudicent clericos licet mali sint, infra eodem consulendum [D. 28 c. 17]." In 1322, at the Council of Valladolid, Cardinal William Godin abrogated the excommunication of concubinary priests; Mansi 25:703; Kelly, *Canon Law and the Archpriest of Hita*, p. 83. In England a priest who failed to abjure his mistress after being commanded to do so might be required to undertake a penitential pilgrimage; William of Hoo, *Letter-Book*, no. 152, p. 81.

[297] 3 Winchester (1262 ~ 1265) c. 44–45, in Powicke and Cheney 1:710–11; William of Pagula, *Summa summarum* 3.2, Pembroke 201, fol. 139va: "An clericus beneficiatus potest aliquid relinquere concubine sue in suo testamento? Dic quod non, et si fecerit hoc quod legauit debet conuerti in usus ecclesie quo rexit defunctus." A concubinage contract between a priest and his mistress is summarized in *Le registre d'inquisition de Jacques Fournier, évêque de Pamiers (1318–1325)*, ed. Jean Duvernoy, 2 vols., Bibli-

Efforts to penalize the concubines themselves persisted. Although Church officials had long since ceased their efforts to enslave the concubines of priests, they continued to demand that these women be excommunicated, that they be forbidden to enter churches, that parishioners refuse them either social or business relations, and that at death they be consigned to the "burial of asses" outside of consecrated precincts.[298] Spanish authorities went so far as to require that priests' concubines observe the sumptuary laws that applied to prostitutes, so that their status would be immediately apparent to all who saw them.[299] How effective any of these measures may have been in humiliating and disadvantaging the consorts of priests is uncertain; what is clear is that they did not greatly decrease the incidence of clerical concubinage.

It would have been surprising had these measures met with success, for some communities—upon whom these measures depended for their effectiveness—not only supported the wives and children of their clerics, but even forced priests to take a concubine in order to protect their own women.[300] Intellectual opposition to the celibacy policy surfaced occasionally during this period. Jean de Meung described celibacy in the *Roman de la rose* as an unnatural state, while William Durand questioned the value of the policy and concluded that it ought to be repealed. Durand and other opponents of the celibacy rule sometimes cited in support of their position the fact that the Byzantine Church allowed clerical marriage. When substantial numbers of married Greek clergy officiated side by side with Latins, as happened in Sicily and southern Italy, this doubtless created acute problems both of morals and morale.[301] There is no evi-

---

othèque méridionale, ser. 2, vol. 41 (Toulouse: E. Privat, 1965) 1:252–53. Henry Ansgar Kelly, *Love and Marriage in the Age of Chaucer* (Ithaca, NY: Cornell University Press, 1975), pp. 200–201, treats clerical concubinage as "non-sacramental marriage," a term which has the virtue of implying that these unions were often stable, long-term affairs, but which suffers from the double vices of being hopelessly anachronistic and palpably unfaithful to the legal categories used by contemporary jurists.

[298] Joannes Andreae, *Novella* to X 3.2.2 in fin.; 2 Durham (1241 ~ 1249) c. 22, 1 Chichester (1245 ~ 1252) c. 59, 1 York (1241 ~ 1255) c. 5, Legatine Council of London (1237) c. 16, 4 Salisbury (1257) c. 13, Wells (1258?) c. 24, 2 Exeter (1287) c. 18, and 2 Chichester (1289) c. 5, in Powicke and Cheney 1:252–53, 428, 463, 486, 555, 603, and 2:1015, 1083; Synod of Cologne (1280) c. 2 and Synod of Gerona (1274) c. 26 (repeating and reenacting the canons of the Synod of Lérida [1257]), in Mansi 23:346–37, 936.

[299] Winterer, "Zur Priesterehe in Spanien," p. 379.

[300] The Council of Valladolid (1322) c. 7, in Mansi 25:703, excommunicated laymen who did this; see also Schimmelpfennig, "Ex fornicatione nati," p. 32, and Kelly, *Canon Law and the Archpriest of Hita*, pp. 83–84.

[301] Bartholomew of Brescia, *Questiones dominicales* 30, in B.L., Arundel 435, fol. 230ra: "Sacerdos quidam grecus cum uxore sua se transtulit ad latinos ibique moram faciens, cum bene sciret latinam et officium latinorum uolebat diuinum officium celebrare et uti uxore sua. Queritur an sit permittendus cum sit notus et de eius uita constet? . . . Solutio: satis credo quod non sit prohibendus sacerdos iste ministrare. Idem dicit t⟨ancredus⟩." See generally James A. Brundage, "The Decretalists and the Greek

dence, however, that the popes of this period ever seriously entertained proposals to alter the celibacy policy. Since the popes were reluctant to abandon
mandatory celibacy, some unknown forger attempted to do it for them by fab-
ricating a spurious papal constitution, ascribed to Pope Boniface VIII and dated
13 May 1297, rescinding the existing policy and authorizing clerical marriage
once more.[302] How widely this forgery circulated and how many people may
have been taken in by it cannot, unfortunately, be established.

DIGAMY, BIGAMY, AND POLYGAMY

Multiple marriages attracted considerable interest among canonists and other
law writers during the late thirteenth and early fourteenth centuries. The remarriages of widowers apparently resulted in more numerous expressions of
popular hostility during this period than they had earlier. In addition, bigamy
and polygamy seemed more pressing problems to writers of this generation
than they had to their predecessors. Perhaps bigamy had become more common as a result of the proliferation of clandestine marriages. Beyond that, some
canonists were dissatisfied with the categories and concepts traditionally used
in discussing these matters.

Authoritative writers continued to support the church's long-established policy of recognizing second and subsequent marriages of widows and widowers as
perfectly valid and lawful—even the thousandth remarriage would be licit,
Hostiensis declared.[303] Some restrictions were attached to remarriage, however: secular law occasionally specified a mandatory mourning period that must
elapse between the death of one spouse and marriage to another, and widows
who remarried might lose custody of the children of their first marriages as a
result of remarriage.[304] St. Bonaventure believed, in addition, that although
second marriages were lawful, they were also sacramentally incomplete. That
was the reason, he declared, why no nuptial blessing was given to those who
married for a second time.[305] Popular resentment also ran deep against second
marriages, particularly unions between elderly widowers and much younger

---

Church of South Italy," in *La chiesa greca in Italia dall'VIII al XVI secolo*, 3 vols.
(Padua: Antenore, 1973) 3:1075–81.

[302] Gulielmus Durantis, *Tractatus de modo generalis concilii celebrandi* 2.4 (Lyon: J.
Crispinus, 1531), fol. 16ra; *Roman de la rose*, ll. 8990–95, 14,091–96, 15,800–15,807;
Grévy-Pons, *Célibat et nature*, p. 38; Schimmelpfennig, "Ex fornicatione nati," pp.
47–49, prints the text of the forged constitution.

[303] Hostiensis, *Summa aurea*, lib. 4, tit. *De secundis nuptiis* §§ 1–2, fol. 224va–vb;
Bonaventure, *Comm.* to Sent. 4.42.3.1; Pierre de La Palude, *Lucubrationum* 42.3.1,
p. 436.

[304] *Assises des bourgeois* 166–67, in RHC, Lois 2:113–14; Pierre de La Palude, *Lucubrationum* 42.3.1, p. 436.

[305] Bonaventure, *Comm.* to Sent. 4.42.3.2; Hostiensis, *Summa aurea*, lib. 4, tit. *De
secundis nuptiis* § 2, fol. 224vb; Bernardus de Montemirato, *Comm.* to X 4.21.1.

brides. This animosity reflected competition among young men for attractive and desirable young women and anger at seeing an older, previously married rival remove an eligible candidate from the pool of choices. The problem was more critical in country districts than in cities, but outpourings of rage and resentment occurred in both urban and rural communities. The wrath of young bachelors who saw an elderly man take off one of their potential brides found expression in *charivaris*, organized harassment of the newly married couple. These affairs were often frightening and sometimes degenerated into violence against the newlyweds, occasionally culminating in gang rape of the bride. Both civic authorities and Church officials condemned these goings-on and imposed penalties upon participants, but episodic reports of *charivaris* surfaced throughout the later middle ages and the early modern period.[306]

The law concerning second marriages was considerably confused by the conventional habit of using the same term, bigamy, to refer indifferently to simultaneous marriage to two spouses and to remarriage following the death of an earlier spouse. Hostiensis attempted to clarify matters by distinguishing between true bigamy (two spouses at once) and interpretative bigamy (remarriage after death or divorce from the first spouse). An elaborate diagram of the "Tree of Bigamy" attempted to relate these concepts to theological issues (see Pl. 18).[307]

Doctrinal writers unanimously rejected true bigamy and other forms of polygyny, as their predecessors had done for centuries. Thomas Aquinas maintained that polygyny was contrary to natural law, although he conceded that under some circumstances the practice was allowed, since it had plainly been practiced by the Old Testament patriarchs. Aquinas maintained on a more practical level that any type of polygamy was undesirable, since it tended to create family stress and complicated marital relationships.[308] St. Bonaventure asserted that the practice of polygyny by Lamech had produced such intolerable complications that God responded by sending the great flood to straighten things out.[309]

Canonical prohibitions of simultaneous bigamy were reinforced by municipal laws that imposed substantial fines upon persons guilty of contracting bigamous marriages—a further example of the extension of municipal jurisdiction into areas that previously had been dealt with almost exclusively by canonical processes.[310]

---

[306] Natalie Zemon Davis, "The Reasons of Misrule: Youth Groups and Charivaris in Sixteenth-Century France," *Past and Present* 50 (1971) 45, 53–54, 65–66.

[307] Hostiensis, *Summa aurea*, lib. 1, tit. *De bigamis* §3, fol. 40va–rb.

[308] Thomas Aquinas, *Comm.* to Sent. 4.33.1.1–2 and ST Supp. 65.1 in c.; likewise Alexander of Hales, glos. to Sent. 4.33.1.1 and *Summa* 2–2.3.4.2.1.7.3; Pierre de La Palude, *Lucubrationum* 33.1.1, pp. 374–75; Nicholas of Lyra, *Postilla* to Deut. 24:4 v. *ne peccare faciat*; Hostiensis, *Summa aurea*, lib. 4, tit. *De sponsa duorum* § 5, fol. 202vb–203ra; Joannes Andreae, *Novella* to X 4.1.30; Salerno, "Definizione nominale," p. 188.

[309] Bonaventure, *Sermo XV in Hexameron*, in his *Opera*, ed. Peltier 9:99.

[310] Bologna, *Statuti* (1288) 4.33, ed. Fasoli and Sella 1:197; Ferrara, *Statuta* (1287) 4.55, ed. Montorsi, p. 271.

Digamy, or constructive bigamy, remained a concern for canonists, while secular lawmakers ignored it. Canonistic commentators continued to explicate the tangled web of rules that their predecessors had woven around St. Paul's declaration that "A bishop should be a man of one wife." The complexity of the regulations bewildered ordinary clerics and even some bishops. A thirteenth-century Orléans professor described his confrontation with "a great ass," whose asininity consisted in misunderstanding the digamy rules. The fool asserted that a digamist could not be validly ordained and that even the pope was unable to dispense from this canonical impediment. When the professor contradicted these assertions, the ass denounced him as a heretic to three bishops, who were themselves in doubt as to what the rules required and had to be instructed in them by a theological expert, retained at great cost for the occasion.[311]

Property Consequences of Sexual Relationships

Sexual relationships, marital and nonmarital, often had property consequences that concerned both ecclesiastical and secular courts. Canonists claimed that the jurisdiction of the Church's tribunals reached beyond questions of separation or nullity and included the right to determine the division of property between spouses when a marriage broke up. Both the decretals themselves and also the canonistic commentaries on them attempted to accommodate the principles of ecclesiastical law to variations in local custom and law in different parts of the Western world. In northern France, where marital property law was undergoing basic change during this period, the Church's courts treated the spouses as joint tenants of property acquired during their marriage (acquest property) and required that such property be divided equally when the marriage ended. In England, Normandy, Flanders, and much of southern France, however, where local law gave preference to the husband and eldest son in the division of acquests, canonical tribunals adopted the customary usage of the region.[312] Beaumanoir pointed out, however, that men were often unwilling to make provision for their former wives and dependents, despite the requirements of the law, and the courts often had to intervene in order to protect disadvantaged women and children. Canonists and civilians alike held that husbands incurred a continuing obligation to maintain their wives, not only during marriage, but also after its termination. This principle found expression in pro-

---

[311] See esp. the anonymous *Questiones de bigamis* of the late thirteenth or early fourteenth century in Caius MS 54/31, fol. 151rb–vb, for the kinds of problems deemed important during this period. For the incident of the "great ass" see Martin Bertram, "Kirchenrechtliche Vorlesungen aus Orléans (1285/7)," *Francia* 2 (1974) 230.

[312] Beaumanoir § 1626, ed. Salmon 2:331–32; *Assises des bourgeois* 181, 183, in RHC, Lois 2:121–23; Pierre de La Palude, *Lucubrationum* 42.3.2, p. 436; Sheehan, "Influence of Canon Law on Property Rights," pp. 110–11; Donahue, "What Causes Fundamental Legal Ideas?" pp. 64–69; Emmanuel LeRoy Ladurie, "Système de la coutume: Structures familiales et coutume d'héritage en France au XVIe siècle," *Annales é.s.c.* 27 (1972) 825–46.

visions for alimony support, although the sums alloted were often quite small and could be terminated altogether if the separated wife became a prostitute or led a disorderly life.[313]

Dowry property that the wife brought to the marriage presented further problems for the courts. Canonists held that when a marriage was annulled the wife was entitled to restitution of her dowry. If the couple were separated because of desertion by the wife or because she was guilty of adultery, however, she forfeited her right to the dowry, which remained in the hands of her husband. Even in these circumstances, however, the husband had some residual obligations toward her. He was at least expected to see to it that she did not starve to death, for as Beaumanoir said, "It would be too great an act of cruelty to allow her to die of hunger."[314]

Child support was another continuing obligation, and the decretals required parents to furnish the necessities of life to all of their children, whether born in wedlock or outside of it. Common usage dictated that minor children remain with their mother when the marriage ended, but their father was obliged to contribute to their support within his means. The same principle applied to illegitimate children and Church courts asserted wide-ranging judicial discretion in framing child support orders so as to take account of individual circumstances. Court records do not suggest that judges were overly generous in providing for the maintenance of minor children. Support orders tended to be small, but even so judges often had to intervene with both moral suasion and penal sanctions in order to secure payment as ordered.[315]

Inheritance and succession laws invariably disadvantaged illegitimate children. Customary law usually barred them altogether from succession, although civilians and canonists both maintained that small bequests could properly be left to illegitimate offspring in a will. A mistress or concubine could likewise receive gifts and legacies, although she had little chance of enforcing promises made to her, should her lover change his mind. Property conveyed to a mistress, however, was deemed to be validly transferred and legal writers argued that the courts should protect whatever property she received.[316]

[313] Beaumanoir § 1630, ed. Salmon 2:334; Bartolus, *Tractatus de alimentis* §§ 48–49, in his *Opera* 12:127rb; Pierre de La Palude, *Lucubrationum* 42.2.1, p. 434; *Assises des bourgeois* 174, in RHC, Lois 2:117; Sheedy, *Bartolus on Social Conditions*, p. 62.

[314] Beaumanoir § 931, ed. Salmon 1:471; see also Bartholomew of Brescia, *Questiones dominicales* 8.4, 43.1, in TUJ* 17:33rb, 45ra; Pierre de La Palude, *Lucubrationum* 42.2.3 and 42.3.3, pp. 435, 437; *Assises des bourgeois* 176, in RHC, Lois 2:118–19.

[315] Bernard of Parma, *Glos. ord.* to X 4.7.5 v. *secundum facultates*; Bartolus, *Comm.* to Cod. 4.28.5 and 5.5 (Auth. Ex complexus, Nov. 89.15); *Assises des bourgeois* 177, in RHC, Lois 2:119; Richard H. Helmholz, "Support Orders, Church Courts, and the Rule of *Filius nullius*: A Reassessment of the Common Law," *Virginia Law Review* 63 (1977) 433–34, 443, 446.

[316] Vincentius Hispanus, *Lectura* to X 1.17.1 v. *ex fornicatione*, Salamanca 2186, fol. 45rb: "Id est de spuriis qui patrem ostendere non possunt, qui uulgo sunt quesiti uel cum patrem habent quem habere non licet, ut ff. de statu monachorum [?]; uulgo illegitimus prohibetur successio hereditaria, hoc quedam in eorum consuetudo habent,

Evidence, Procedure, and Jurisdiction in Sex and Marriage Cases

Court records show that jurisdiction over sexual behavior and marriage accounted for most of the case load of local ecclesiastical tribunals during this period, at least in England. Fragmentary records from the court of the Official of the Archdeacon of Sudbury in the late thirteenth century, for example, show that sex and marriage cases accounted for nearly two-thirds of the actions there, while sex and marriage accounted for nearly ninety percent of the cases heard in a rural dean's court in the diocese of Worcester in 1300. Other jurisdictions had a somewhat lower incidence of sex and marriage matters, but in virtually every court that has been studied these cases make up a majority of the actions for which records survive. Fornication was typically the most common criminal offense dealt with, followed by adultery and prostitution. Rape, concubinage, and enforcement of marital debt figure less prominently in the records. Marriage and divorce were everywhere the leading type of civil action in Church courts at the intermediate level of the judicial hierarchy.[317] These patterns are

---

sed multum est in conuerso, xv. q. ult. cum multe [C. 15 q. 8 c. 3] et in aut. qui. mo. na. ef. legi. § ult. [Auth 6.1; Nov. 74.6. ep.]." See also Bartolus, *Comm.* to Cod. 5.5.6 [Nov. 89.15]; Odofredus, *Lectura* to Dig. 39.5.31; *Assises des bourgeois* 178, in RHC, Lois 2:119–20; Pierre de La Palude, *Lucubrationum* 42.3.2, pp. 436–47; Helmholz, "Support Orders," p. 437. Customary law on the Continent, however, usually denied that the fathers of natural children had any enforceable obligation to furnish child support; *Siete partidas* 4.19.5, ed. Vargas y Ponce 3:169; Chevailler, "Observations," p. 385. An anonymous fourteenth-century gloss to D. 26 c. 3 in L.C., Law MS G.7, fol. 20v, however, reverted to an ancient Roman rule, for the writer declared that if a man named any or all of his concubine's children as his heirs in his will, he thereby legitimized them all (the reference is to Cod. 5.27.3).

[317] Antonia Grandsden, "Some Late Thirteenth-Century Records of an Ecclesiastical Court in the Archdeaconry of Sudbury," *Bulletin of the Institute of Historical Research* 32 (1959) 62–69; Frank S. Pearson, "Records of a Ruridecanal Court of 1300," in *Collectanea*, ed. Sidney G. Hamilton, Worcester Historical Society Publications 31 (1912) 69–80; Henry Ansgar Kelly, "Clandestine Marriage and Chaucer's 'Troilus'," *Viator* 4 (1973) 439–40. The Cerisy register for the decade 1314–23, for example, shows 170 cases involving sexual offenses (excluding marital nullity and separation cases), distributed as follows:

Offense	Number of Cases	Percent
Fornication	103	60.5
Adultery	46	26.5
Procuring, brothel-keeping	8	5.0
Cohabitation	6	4.0
Concubinage	3	2.0
Prostitution	1	0.5
Marital debt	1	0.5
Rape	1	0.5
Incontinence with wife	1	0.5
TOTAL	170	100

That sex cases accounted for the greater part of the business of the ecclesiastical

best documented in English records, but fragmentary evidence from the Continent, such as the Cerisy registers, shows roughly similar patterns there as well.

It is likely, moreover, that court records under-represent the frequency of sex offenses, perhaps by a considerable margin. Some incidents were almost certainly dealt with informally, when detected at all, and there are complaints from contemporaneous preachers—how well founded it is impossible to tell—that adulterers and fornicators often escaped prosecution and punishment by bribing summoners and other officials, including judges.[318] Beaumanoir, an experienced and sensible lawyer not given to hyperbole, remarked casually that marriage cases were contrived with many frauds, while two thirteenth-century English synods criticized sharp practices among advocates and proctors in divorce and separation proceedings.[319]

There was little disagreement during this period over the competence of Church courts and judges to deal with litigation concerning separation, divorce, and the validity of marriage. The Church's jurisdiction over adultery and fornication remained important, although municipalities were beginning to assert their own rights to deal with these matters.[320] The sex crime over which jurisdictional claims were most often disputed was rape. Secular courts could and often did deal with rape charges, while the canonists showed a certain diffidence about asserting their claims to deal with this matter. Bernard of Parma took the position that there was mixed civil and ecclesiastical jurisdiction over

---

courts was well known, of course, to contemporaries; see Chaucer's comment in the Friar's Tale, 11. 1301–1320; Dorothy M. Owen, "Ecclesiastical Jurisdiction in England, 1300–1550: The Records and Their Interpretation," *Studies in Church History* 11 (1975) 199.

[318]John Bromyard, *Summa predicantium*, s.v. *adulterium, ministratio*, fol. 20vb; Owst, *Literature and Pulpit*, p. 252.

[319]Beaumanoir § 1051, ed. Salmon 2:29; Statues of Wells (1258) c. 72 and 2 Exeter (1287) c. 7, in Powicke and Cheney 1:622 and 2:999.

[320]Beaumanoir §§ 313, 586, 588–89, ed. Salmon 1:154, 285–88; *Assises des bourgeois* 159, 181, in RHC, Lois 2:108, 121; Bartolus, *Comm.* to Cod. 11.8.7; Hostiensis, *Summa aurea*, lib. 5, tit. *De adulteriis* § 2, fol. 243vb; statute of Bishop Hugh of Ely on archidiaconal jurisdiction (1276), in U.L.C., MS Add. 3468 (the so-called Black Book of Ely), fol. 14r: "Uxores tamen eorum [*scil.* scholarium] super crimine adulterii uel alio cuius cognitio et correctio ad archidiaconum spectant in casu consimili in personis aliis sibi subditorum diffamate . . . archidiacono sint subiecti in omnibus et singulis sicut ceteri alii laici municipii Cantabrigie et tocius nostro diocesis Eliensis." See also Gibson, *Codex juris anglicani* 22.5, 47.5, 1:510, 2:128; Bellamy, *Crime and Public Order*, pp. 155–56; Engdahl, "Full Faith and Credit," pp. 8–9, 18–19, and "English Marriage Law Conflicts," p. 133; Sheedy, *Bartolus on Social Conditions*, p. 56. In Spain the jurisdiction of the courts of archpriests over marriage cases was disputed; in the Diocese of Salamanca they were forbidden to hear marriage cases at all and these matters were reserved to the bishop's court; Kelly, *Canon Law and the Archpriest of Hita*, pp. 39–40. On French practice see Juliette M. Turlan and Pierre Claude Timbal, "Justice laique et lien matrimonial en France au moyen âge," RDC 30 (1980) 347–63.

rape. He was prepared to concede that when Church courts handled such cases they did so as delegates of the civil authorities, subject to the restriction that if the case involved issues in which a sentence of death or mutilation might be prescribed, clerics should not presume to deal with it.[321] Hostiensis was more assertive in defending canonical jurisdiction. While he agreed that clerics should not impose sentences that involved bloodshed, Hostiensis observed that they could convert sanguinary penalties into fines or order whippings that stopped short of drawing blood. When neither tactic seemed appropriate, they ought to turn the convicted perpetrator over to civil authorities for punishment.[322]

There were only modest refinements during this period in legal doctrine concerning evidence. Compurgation continued to be used frequently as a defense to adultery charges, both in marriage litigation and in criminal proceedings.[323] Canonists rightly tended to be skeptical about the evidential value of self-serving declarations by the parties to divorce and separation. They were similarly skeptical concerning the testimony of a man that the girl he had seduced was no virgin.[324] Although academic writers continued to insist that women should either not testify at all or that at best their evidence should be treated with great skepticism, the courts in practice ignored this teaching. The court in *Attebury c. LaLeye* was even willing to accept the testimony of a prostitute who alleged that a man had married her, despite his denial.[325]

Canonists and others sought to articulate more precisely their doctrine concerning the timeliness of actions for redress of wrongs, in order to limit the period that elapsed between an alleged event and the time when the matter was brought to court. Bernard of Parma, for example, noted that a husband must bring an adultery action against his wife within sixty days; if he delayed longer, and was unsuccessful in proving his charge, he might be liable to the penalties

---

[321] Bernard of Parma, *Glos. ord.* to X 5.17.4 v. *commiserit puniendos.*

[322] Hostiensis, *Summa aurea*, lib. 5, tit. *De penis raptorum corporum* § 2, fol. 246ra; Joannes Andreae, *Novella* to X 5.17.1 v. *de illis et ad locum* and X 5.17.4 v. *in archiepiscopatu* and *in iurisdictione*; Bologna, *Statuti* (1288) 2.10, ed. Fasoli and Sella 1:63.

[323] William of Hoo, *Letter-Book*, no. 5, p. 28.

[324] Vincentius Hispanus, *Lectura* to X 5.16.1 and 5.17.6, Salamanca 2186, fol. 205rb, 206rb: "Quid si dicat uir non esse uirginem? Non audietur, sibi imputet quia uiolenter fuit usus ea. . . . Item nota quod quandocumque confiterentur coniuges ad dissolutionem non creditur eis, xxxv. q. vi. si duo [c. 4] et xxxiii. q. i. requisisti [c. 2], infra de eo qui cog. consan., super eo [X 4.13.5], nisi uero agit ad dissolutionem mutue seruitutis confessio, ut si confiteatur se comisisse adulterium, supra de clandes. despon., ex litteris [*fortasse* X 4.19.5]. uincentius." See also Joannes Andreae, *Novellae* to X 5.16.1; Bernardus de Montemirato, *Comm.* to X 5.16.5; Helmholz, *Marriage Litigation*, p. 71, and "Crime, Compurgation, and the Courts of the Medieval Church," *Law and History Review* 1 (1983) 1–26.

[325] Adam Attebury c. Matilda LaLeye (1270–72), in Adams and Donahue, *Select Cases* C.4, pp. 118–23; cf. Hostiensis, *Lectura* to X 5.40.10; Bartolus, *Comm.* to Dig. 48.18.10.14; Sheedy, *Bartolus on Social Conditions*, pp. 52–53.

for calumny.[326] A charge of *stuprum*, according to Hostiensis, had a far longer lifetime: it could be brought as late as five years after the event, unless force was involved, in which case there was no limit on the life of the action.[327] Local statutes of limitation sometimes differed strikingly from these standards. At Ferrara, for example, the 1287 statutes provided that a rape charge must be brought within fifteen days of the event; otherwise the municipal courts would not hear it.[328] A doctrine of limitations likewise applied to divorce actions brought on the grounds that force and fear had been used to coerce consent to marriage. Here the limit was eighteen months; as William of Pagula summed up the law, after a year-and-a-half prudent men could presume that consent had been forthcoming. He also noted Raymond of Peñafort's opinion that if a woman had had an opportunity to protest and nevertheless allowed her husband to have sex with her, she ought to be presumed to have consented to the marriage. If he used physical force to compel her to submit to him, however, her consent could not be presumed either to intercourse or to marriage.[329]

Much of what the canonists of this period had to say about the law of evidence, like many of their observations about marriage, concubinage, prostitution, and sex offenses, was patently biased in favor of men. Canonists in this period appear to have been more conscious of this than their predecessors were: at least they discussed the matter freely and occasionally in terms that seem to indicate that they found this situation puzzling, even embarrassing. Hostiensis in particular examined the subject in some detail. "The condition of women," he declared, "is worse than that of men in many particulars." He then specified some female disabilities: women cannot be judges or arbitrators; like-

---

[326] Bernard of Parma, *Glos. ord.* to X 5.16.4 v. *plus caeteris*; likewise Hostiensis, *Summa aurea*, lib. 5, tit. *De adulteriis* §3, fol. 243vb–244ra.

[327] Hostiensis, *Summa aurea*, lib. 5, tit. *De adulteriis* § 10, fol. 244vb.

[328] Ferrara, *Statuta* 4.53, ed. Montorsi, p. 270.

[329] William of Pagula, *Summa summarum* 4.1, Pembroke 201, fol. 204ra: "Quid si mulier post consensum coactum moram trahit in domum mariti, uel permittit se ab eo cognosci? Dic quantumcunque sit metus uel uiolencia matrimonio contrahendo, si mulier que allegat metum steterit per annum et dimidium cum marito uel consensit etiam in carnalem copulam, non debet postea audiri si allegat metum uel uiolenciam, ex. de spon. ad id quod [X 4.1.21], ex. qui matri. accusat. pos., mulier [?]. Et quod dicitur 'per annum et dimidium' idem intelligas de minore tempore si tamen iuxta arbitrium boni uiri tantum tempore sit quod presumi debeat pro consensu, ut predico c. ad id quod secundum glo. [Bernardus Parmensis, *Glos. ord.* in X 4.1.21 v. *per annum et dimidium*] et host⟨iensem⟩ [*Summa aurea*, lib. 5, tit. *De matrimonio* §26, fol. 197rb] et secundum Ray⟨mundum⟩ in ti. de impedimento ui §ult. [*Summa de mat.* 11.4, col. 957]. Sed de muliere que post coactum consensum carnaliter cognoscitur, dicit pe. quod si habita opportunitate reclamandi se cognosci permittit, presumitur tacite consentire in matrimonium; si autem cogitur ad carnalem copulam, aut hanc erat per uim absolutam, et tunc non est matrimonium aut per metum [*MS rep.* aut ergo] sufficientem [*MS rep.* et sic non est matrimonium] aut insufficientem et tunc in iudicio fori presumitur matrimonium. Si tamen uere non consensit non est matrimonium secundum pe. in scrip."

wise they cannot teach, preach, hear confessions, or exercise other types of spiritual power, nor may they receive holy orders, plead in court, or act as notaries or guardians (save for their own children). In addition they cannot bring criminal accusations, adopt children, hold public office, act as agents, be witnesses to wills, or work as silversmiths. They are, in short, subject to men, as signified by St. Paul's dictum that they should be veiled in the churches, for they were not formed in God's image, as men were. Hostiensis added, however, that in a few situations the juridical position of women was superior to that of men—but he seemed able to think of only three examples: women were advantaged, he believed, in acting as sureties for debts (although he admitted that there, too, others considered their situation worse than a man's), in the fact that they were sometimes presumed not to know the law, and in securing the discharge of unqualified guardians for their minor sons. "There are many other examples," he added lamely, "but these will suffice in order to keep the discussion brief."[330]

Summary and Conclusions

The years between 1234 and 1348 were a period of substantial change in both law and society, change that affected the law of sex and marriage, as well as other aspects of human relationships. Both canon law and secular law grew in volume, but the balance between the two shifted markedly. Between 1140 and 1234 the development of canon law had been spectacular. It had grown from a rudimentary and confused jumble of conflicting and often obscure regulations into an all-embracing and intellectually sophisticated legal system. During that same period, however, royal and customary law developed at much lower levels of intellectual refinement. In the years between 1234 and 1348, canon law continued to grow in volume, but showed fewer novel insights, less innovation in fundamental ideas than in the preceding period. So far as the regulation of sexual behavior was concerned, perhaps there was little need for further innovation at this point. By the mid-thirteenth century Western churchmen had arrived at a fairly clear consensus about the goals of the Church's sexual policy, and canon law had devised workable solutions to many of the commonest difficulties.

During that same period municipal and royal law made notable strides toward comprehensiveness and maturity. In the process, royal and municipal lawmakers had begun to interest themselves in kinds of problems, including problems of sexual behavior, that previously had been the exclusive domain of the canonists. Since the goals of municipal lawmakers were not always identical with those of the Church's leaders, civic law on sexual matters sometimes departed fairly radically from canonical prescriptions.

[330] Hostiensis, *Lectura* to X 1.43.4 §§5–6. Cf. the much briefer discussion by Joannes Andreae, *Glos. ord.* to VI 1.6.44 v. *verecundiam* and 2.1.2 v. *prohibemus*, and note also Thomas Aquinas's remarks on the subjection of women to men in ST 1.92.1 ad 2.

This was particularly striking in the regulation of prostitution. Control of the activities and behavior of prostitutes, pimps, and panders increasingly became a concern of municipal authorities, while canonists had little new to say about this problem and concentrated instead on rehabilitating repentant whores. Rape is another sex offense in which municipal and royal authorities took greater interest during this period. Also striking and significant is the increased involvement of secular authorities in the repression of homosexual behavior, which commenced to be defined as a major capital crime and attracted a far greater degree of attention than ever before from municipal law-makers.

Europe's long-term rise in population ended in 1348 with a catastrophe of gigantic dimensions: the Black Death. The dislocations that resulted from that disaster radically altered established social and economic relationships and in the process subjected European legal systems to enormous stresses. The legal mechanisms for the control of marriage and sexual relationships were sorely tested by these events but emerged from them remarkably intact. In the process, however, some significant readjustments took place. The following chapter will examine both what survived and what perished in the process.

10

Sex, Marriage, and the Law from the Black Death to the Reformation, 1348–1517

The period between the demographic disaster of the Black Death and the religious revolution of the sixteenth century saw surprisingly little change in the law and theology of sex and marriage. This relative stability is unexpected, since one might suppose that the disappearance of between a quarter and a third of Europe's population during the mid–fourteenth-century epidemics would have produced drastic changes in the ways society dealt with sex, marriage, and reproduction. Ideas about sex, however, remained remarkably stable, and major alterations in European sex law and doctrine did not not appear until the sixteenth century.

This is not to say that no changes occurred in sex and marriage law. But innovations during this period had more to do with the administration of the law, with its enforcement, and with the formal sources of sex and marriage law than with the basic principles, on which there seemed to be general agreement by this time.

Two developments in this period were particularly striking. One was the greatly increased activism of royal and especially municipal governments in regulating sexual behavior. We have seen evidence of the beginning of this development during the preceding period, but it became far more pronounced during the late fourteenth and fifteenth centuries. A second notable innovation was the public takeover of the prostitution industry, notably in northern Italy, southern France, and southern Germany. In those regions, though rarely elsewhere, publicly owned brothels suddenly appeared in many towns—only to vanish abruptly in the sixteenth century.

The Social Context

This century and a half was marked by continuing crises, both religious and political. The return of the popes from Avignon to Rome sparked new convulsions in the great schism (1378–1417) and the struggle over conciliarism, as successive councils attempted to impose limits on papal power. The Church faced insistent demands for reform. Critics proposed numerous, sometimes conflicting, remedies for the Church's ills, including abolition of pluralism, curbing of papal provisions, elimination of peculation and corruption, either effective implementation or abandonment of mandatory clerical celibacy, reform of marriage law, elimination of clandestine marriages, and disciplinary renewal in the religious orders. Many of these proposals originated with publicists, intellectuals, or mystics, and a few schemes received support from kings and other secular rulers.

Some reformers went beyond the bounds that Catholic orthodoxy would willingly tolerate. In England, John Wyclif (ca. 1328–1384) and his followers called for such wholesale restructuring both of traditional theology and ecclesiastical institutions that their movement was branded heretical, although Wyclif himself escaped direct punishment. The Bohemian reformer, John Hus (ca. 1369–1415), was not so lucky; despite guarantees of his personal safety, the Church burnt him for heresy at the Council of Constance.

This was also an age of political turmoil and endemic warfare. The Ottoman Turks seized the heartland of the ancient Byzantine Empire in Anatolia, and in 1453 they crowned their achievement by capturing Constantinople. From this base they launched attacks upon the Balkans and spurred their armies into the heartland of central Europe. By 1529, they would be at the gates of Vienna. The Hundred Years' War (1338–1453) sapped the strength of the French monarchy, drained England of men and money, and contributed mightily to the discontents that resulted in the Peasants' Revolt of 1381. Spain saw the culmination of four centuries of sporadic struggles between Christians and Muslims in 1492 with the capture of the last Moorish capitol at Granada and the union of the Crowns of Aragon and Castile.

War and violence complicated the social dislocations that resulted from the Black Death. The great pandemic of 1348/49 was not an isolated episode, for plague outbreaks continued to recur with considerable frequency throughout the remainder of the fourteenth century—indeed, local outbreaks continued until the second half of the seventeenth century. Population levels recovered slowly following 1348/49; but not until the second half of the fifteenth century did population growth again become general on the Continent. Such sharp demographic changes resulted in a considerable measure of social realignment and stress. Labor suddenly became scarce in many regions, and the economy adapted to this new situation by concentrating investment in less labor-intensive types of enterprise. It is no coincidence that the period from the mid-fourteenth to the early sixteenth centuries was an age of technological innovation. Agricultural workers, for example, even in areas only lightly touched by the epidemics, found their lives radically altered by changes in farming strategies adopted by landlords in quest of greater productivity using fewer workers. Skilled workers, artisans, and craftsmen saw demand for their talents soar and, at least in some areas, improved their wages and status accordingly. Governments, too, had to readjust to the new situation. As revenue sources changed, along with military and other technologies, new tax systems were sought to increase royal revenues. Social structure, economic systems, and political institutions were all affected by the consequences of the plague epidemics.[1]

The legal system felt the impact of these social changes in a variety of ways, some of them at first glance surprising. The period between 1348 and the end of the fifteenth century saw a dramatic expansion in the numbers of European universities, despite the calamities of plague, war, famine, and social turmoil. France gained five new universities in this period and Burgundy produced four more, while Italy saw three new universities appear in the same period.[2] Three universities (St. Andrews, Glasgow, and Aberdeen) were founded in Scotland as well. The greatest explosion in higher education, however, took place in Germany and Scandinavia. Prior to 1348, Prague had the only university east of the Rhine. Between 1364 and 1506 no less than fourteen additional universities sprang up across the Holy Roman Empire and Eastern Europe, plus two others in Scandinavia.[3] All offered instruction in either civil or canon law, and most of them taught both. Legal education also continued to flourish in the older universities, where law faculties attracted numerous students, many of whom became prominent in later life, not only as judges and advocates, but also as political and civic leaders, diplomats, or men of wealth. In addition, dispropor-

---

[1] See particularly Bernard Guenée, *L'Occident au XIVe et XVe siècles: Les états*, Nouvelle Clio, no. 22 (Paris: Presses universitaires de France, 1971), and Jacques Heers, *L'Occident au XIVe et XVe siècles: Aspects économiques et sociaux*, 2d ed., Nouvelle Clio, no. 23 (Paris: Presses universitaires de France, 1966). Good general treatments of the period in English include Denys Hay, *Europe in the Fourteenth and Fifteenth Centuries* (London: Longmans; New York: Holt, Rinehart and Winston, 1966); Robert L. Reynolds, *Europe Emerges, Transition Toward an Industrial World-Wide Society, 600–1700* (Madison: University of Wisconsin Press, 1967), esp. pp. 389–434; and Myron P. Gilmore, *The World of Humanism, 1453–1517* (New York: Harper, 1952; repr. 1962). On population changes the best introductions are Russell, *Late Ancient and Medieval Population*, pp. 113–31, and David Herlihy, "Demography," in DMA 4:136–48. For a more detailed treatment see Roger Mols, *Introduction à la démographie historique des villes d'Europe du XIVe au XVIIIe siècle*, 3 vols., University of Louvain, Recueil des travaux d'histoire et de philologie, ser. 4, fasc. 1 (Gembloux: J. Duclot, 1954–56). For a closely focused study of the impact of the Black Death on a single small community see Zvi Razi, *Life, Marriage, and Death in a Medieval Parish: Economy, Society, and Demography in Halesowen, 1270–1400* (Cambridge: At the University Press, 1980).

[2] The French universities were: Poitiers (1431), Caen (1432), Bordeaux (1441), Nantes (1460), and Bourges (1464). In Burgundy new universities appeared at Avignon (1303), Aix (1409), Dole (1422), and Valence (1452). Italy produced universities at Pavia (1361), Ferrara (1391) and Turin (1405).

[3] In Eastern Europe and the Empire, universities appeared at Cracow (1364), Vienna (1365), Pecs (1367), Heidelberg (1385), Leipzig (1409), Rostock (1419), Louvain (1426), Greifswald (1456), Trier (1454), Ingolstad (1459), Mainz (1476), Pressburg (1465), Wittenberg (1502), and Frankfurt a/Oder (1506). The two Scandinavian universities were Copenhagen (1478) and Uppsala (1477). See generally Coing, "Juristische Fakultät," pp. 47–48; Rashdall, *Universities* 1:261–62; 2:51–57, 173–81, 186–206, 211–324.

tionately large numbers of men trained in law emerged as intellectual leaders during this period—surprising numbers of renaissance poets, historians, and classical scholars, both north and south of the Alps, had trained in law during their youth, and many practiced their profession while they were active in literature, scholarship and the arts.[4]

Styles of academic legal discourse changed during this period as well, and new styles of legal writing became prominent. The fourteenth and fifteenth centuries were the age of the treatise, the commentary, and the *consilium* in legal literature. The commentary—a voluminous, often multivolumed, explication of a legal text—replaced the older Summas and gloss Apparatuses. Commentaries tended to be much longer than the earlier types of exposition and were not as closely tied to the text of the work they explicated as the Summas and Apparatuses had been. The treatise, a detailed and closely focused analysis and exposition of the law on some specialized topic—dowries or betrothal or wills, for example—was a new expository form. By the beginning of the fifteenth century the sources of law had become so voluminous and the content of law so complex that ordinary practitioners, to say nothing of students and judges, found these specialized treatments indispensible. The *consilium* was a legal opinion rendered by a legal expert—often a teacher of law—in response to a request from a litigant, another lawyer, or a judge who needed guidance in applying the law to a particular case. Commentaries, treatises, and *consilia*, like legal services in this period, were both more specialized and more costly than their predecessors had been.

Sex and Society in the Fourteenth and Fifteenth Centuries

Legal writers throughout this period continued to treat sex as a social problem and to take a dim view of physical beauty and sensual pleasure. As a proverb current in the period put it: "Beautiful women end up in the brothel and handsome men on the gallows."[5] Lechery attacked both body and soul, according to St. John Fisher (ca. 1459–1535), and sexual orgasm, the end result of "the fylthy lust of the flesshe," robbed men of vital energy and exposed them to dangers both moral and physical. "Physycyens saye," according to Fisher, "that a

[4] Bouwsma, "Lawyers in Early Modern Culture," pp. 305–27, furnishes a good introduction. See generally Donald R. Kelley, *Foundations of Modern Historical Scholarship: Language, Law, and History in the French Renaissance* (New York: Columbia University Press, 1970), and Lauro Martines, *Lawyers and Statecraft in Renaissance Florence* (Princeton: Princeton University Press, 1968); Bernard Guenée, *Tribunaux et gens de justice dans le baillage de Senlis à la fin du moyen âge (vers 1380–vers 1550)*, Publications de la Faculté des lettres de l'Université de Strasbourg, fasc. 144 (Paris: Les Belles Lettres, 1963), esp. pp. 185–217, 277–309.

[5] Giovanni Nevizzani, *Silva nuptialis, in qua . . . plurime questiones . . . in materia matrimonii, filiationis, adulterii, originis, successionis, et monitorialium, una cum remediis ad sedandum factiones de Guelfis et Giebellinis* (Lyon: Impressa per J. Moylinal's de Cambray, 1524), fol. 47va: "[P]roverbium rusticorum dicit pulchrum mulierem destinatam ad prostibulum, pulchrum virum ad patibulum."

man taketh more hurte by the effusyon of a lytell sede than by shedynge of ten tymes so moche blode."[6] Moreover, as Nicholas of Plowe (writing between 1427 and 1438) reminded his readers, Aristotle had warned that coitus robbed both men and women of the use of reason, subverted the intellect, and weakened the mind by draining away its strength.[7]

These warnings did little to change behavior. People stubbornly continued to chase after sexual pleasure with undiminished energy, despite (or perhaps because of) plague, war, political upheaval, and social turmoil. In Venice, for example, there was no decrease in the total number of sex crimes during the plague years, even though more than one-third of the city's inhabitants perished in the epidemic. This may well indicate that one of the reactions to the plague in Venice—and perhaps elsewhere as well—was to cause authorities to hunt out and prosecute sexual offenders more vigorously than they had previously, on the theory that sexual licentiousness had brought the disaster on the community. This conclusion is reinforced by other evidence showing that sex crimes were more harshly punished in the years immediately following the plague than in earlier decades.[8] It is also possible that people terrified by the mysterious epidemic and fearful that they, like their neighbors, might fall victim to it, sought relief, consolation, and pleasure in sex, legal or illegal, to ward off their terror. And indeed the poor, the deprived and the disadvantaged, as another peasant proverb noted, had no better relief from their troubles than venery.[9]

Many towns and cities in the post-plague years adopted new statutes restricting sexual activities and discouraging illicit sexual adventures. A Perugia statute dating from before 1400, for example, forbade men between the ages of fifteen and forty to stand around the city's churches on Sundays and feast days in order to admire the women attending services. It imposed heavy fines on any man who dared to insinuate himself into portions of the church reserved for female worshippers.[10] The age specification in the Perugia statute reflects a belief, articulated more explicitly in a Rieti statute, that although men of all ages are inclined to sexual wickedness, young men are particularly likely to commit

[6] St. John Fisher, *Sermon on Ps. 38* in his *English Works*, ed. J. E. B. Mayer, Early English Text Society Publications, Extra Series, no. 27 (London: N. Trubner, 1876; repr. New York: Kraus, 1975), p. 64. I should like to thank Professor William Craft for calling my attention to this sermon.

[7] Nicholas de Plowe, *Tractatus de sacramentis et eorum administratione* 7.2.5, in TUJ 3:44r.

[8] Guido Ruggiero, "Sexual Criminality in the Early Renaissance: Venice, 1338–1358," *Journal of Social History* 8 (1974/75) 24–25, and more recently, *The Boundaries of Eros: Sex Crime and Sexuality in Renaissance Venice* (New York: Oxford University Press, 1985), pp. 6–7, 93, 112–14.

[9] Nevizzani, *Silva nuptialis*, fol. 84ra: "[I]ta illa rustica dicebat quod pauperes nullum aliud pasatempus habent quam copulam."

[10] *Primum [-quartum] volumen statutorum Perusiae* 1.39, 4 vols. in 1 (Perugia: In aedibus H. F. Chartularii, 1523–48) 1:25vb.

these offenses and must be more strictly monitored and curbed than the rest of the population.[11] A statute of Reggio Emilia attempted to restrain men of every age from making verbal approaches to women on the streets, from touching them, following them through the city, or standing around outside their houses. The statute made these actions criminal offenses, punishable by a £10 fine.[12] Lucca similarly imposed fines on men over the age of eighteen who infiltrated parties and celebrations held by women or tried to engage women in conversation or to joke with them.[13] Statutes such as these reflect both popular beliefs and the teachings of theologians and canonists on the dangers of familiarity between the sexes, and enacted into law the warnings of moralists against kisses, embraces, "dishonest touching," or even the exchange of soulful glances between men and women.[14]

Statutes from this period also show the influence of popular ideas about differences in sex drive between men and women. The widely held belief that women are sexually more voracious than men, that they desire intercourse more ardently and enjoy it more, and that in consequence their sexual behavior requires stricter supervision than that of men, is mirrored in a Belluno statute of 1428 which stipulated that no women over the age of twenty ought to be presumed to be a virgin unless her chastity could be proved, at least by circumstantial evidence.[15]

The experience of the criminal courts of the period supported the belief that age and gender largely determined the incidence of sexual misconduct. Criminal court records also show, however, that social status was an important element in determining who committed—or at least who was charged with committing—sex offenses. An analysis of the Venetian criminal records of this period shows that the nobility of the Republic appeared as sex offenders out of all proportion to their numbers. The nobility accounted for between three and seven percent of the Venetian population, but were charged with twenty-one percent of the sex crimes during the period examined. This astonishing disproportion can presumably be accounted for in part by the assumption that the nobility were more likely than others to be charged because, as well-known figures, they were easy to identify and apprehend. It may also be that their

---

[11] *Statuta, siue constitutiones ciuitatis Reatae super ciuilibus et criminalibus causis aeditae* 1, prol. (Rome: Apud A. Bladium, 1549), fol. 1r; cf. Ruggiero, "Sexual Criminality," pp. 25–26.

[12] *Statuta magnificae communitatis Regii* 3.53 (Reggio Emilia: Apud H. Bartholum, 1582), fol. 160r–v.

[13] *Lucensis civitatis statuta nuperrime castigata* 4.207 (Lucca: Impressit I. B. Phaellus, 1539), fol. 255r–v.

[14] Nevizzani, *Sylva nuptialis*, fol. 69ra, 83va; Guy de Roye, *Le doctrinal de sapience* (Paris: Alain Lotrian, n.d.), fol. 52v–53r; cf. John Gower, *Confessio amantis* 7.5, ll. 4257–78, ed. G. C. Macaulay in Gower's *Complete Works*, 4 vols. (Oxford: Clarendon Press, 1899–1902) 3:354–55.

[15] *Ius municipale bellunensium*, lib. 3, tit. *De adulteriis*, c. 18 (Venice: F. de Thomasiis, 1525), fol. 83r; Nevizzani, *Sylva nuptialis*, fol. 71va–vb.

wealth made it more profitable for authorities to levy fines against them. Probably, too, the high incidence of noble sex offenders reflects marriage patterns among the nobility, who tended to marry later in life than members of other social groups.[16]

Not only were men of certain ages and social groups more likely to be accused of sex crimes, but also certain places seem to have been favored venues for "the foule and fylthy pleasure of the body."[17] Sexual offenses most commonly occurred in the victim's home, which is perhaps not unexpected, given that women of all classes tended to spend most of their lives in their homes. Other places, however, appear frequently in the criminal records as the scene of sex offenses—empty houses, convents, jails, even a ducal palace. Boats seem to have been much favored, again for obvious reasons, by Venetian rapists, many of whom were boatmen by occupation.[18] But no one and no place was entirely safe for those who wished to avoid sexual assault or sexual temptation. We have frequent references to illicit copulation in churches and cemeteries. The city fathers of Perugia felt it necessary to enact a statute specifically forbidding women to have sex with the city's lepers.[19]

Although municipal statutes, customary law, and the canons all prescribed heavy penalties for sexual transgressions, practice was considerably milder than statutory language would suggest. Certainly the canonical courts treated the usual run of sexual offenses rather lightly—considerably less harshly than offenses against ecclesiastical institutions and church property.[20]

This leniency in practice was all the more notable because of the widespread belief during this period that loose sexual habits were the peculiar traits of heretics, who were thought to look with indifference or even approval on all types of sexual indulgence. The sectarians known as the Men of Intelligence, and the associated group of Brethren of the Free Spirit, were particularly notorious for sexual exploits with the women associated with their movements. Inquisitors elicited from members of these groups confessions of a wide range of sexual aberrations. Buggery, sodomy, incest, adultery, and indiscriminate fornication were, according to informants, commonplace among the heretics, who considered these activities no sin at all but natural enjoyment of the pleasures of paradise. Although aberrant sex routinely appeared among the charges against heretics, the Church courts dealt with these matters surprisingly lightly.[21] It is

[16] Ruggiero, "Sexual Criminality," pp. 28–29, *Boundaries of Eros*, pp. 13–14.

[17] Fisher, *Sermon on Ps. 38*, ed. Mayer, p. 64.

[18] Ruggiero, "Sexual Criminality," pp. 27–28.

[19] Perugia, *Statuta* 3.91, fol. 34vb–35ra. The statute may have been envisioned as a public health measure to prevent the spread of the disease and was probably intended to apply primarily to prostitutes.

[20] May, *Geistliche Gerichtsbarkeit*, p. 224; Rossiaud, "Prostitution, Youth, and Society," p. 8; Ruggiero, *Boundaries of Eros*, pp. 20 (Table 1), 52 (Table 2), 94 (Table 5).

[21] Lerner, *Heresy of the Free Spirit*, pp. 109, 137; Michel De Waha, "Note sur l'usage de moyens contraceptifs à Bruxelles au début du XVe siècle," *Annales de la Société belge d'histoire des hôpitaux* 13 (1975) 10, 20; Ruggiero, *Boundaries of Eros*, pp. 143–44.

questionable, of course, whether heretics were anything like as addicted to irregular sex as authorities said they were. Confessions of prisoners held by the inquisition need to be treated with great skepticism, since accused persons commonly tell interrogators whatever they believe the interrogators want to hear.

Marriage Theory and Practice

Beginning in the fifteenth century, detailed information concerning actual marriage practices survives from several communities, most of them in northern Italy. These records show that late medieval marriage patterns were highly diverse. The Florentine *catasto* of 1427, for example, reveals that nuclear families constituted a bare majority of the households in that city. A remarkable forty-three percent of households consisted either of a woman with her children but without a husband or else a single person living alone. Slightly less than half of the Florentine men between the ages of twenty-eight and thirty-two were married. Comparable figures from other cities show far different patterns: at Arezzo about sixty percent of the city's adult men were married, while at Pistoia the proportion rose to slightly more than seventy percent. Many men delayed marriage until they were thirty or older and quite substantial numbers apparently never married at all. These patterns were apparently peculiar to cities. Evidence from rural areas shows that a substantially greater proportion of the farm population married, and at much younger ages, than town-dwellers.[22]

The reasons for these marriage patterns were primarily economic. Many fifteenth-century Italian townspeople simply could not afford to marry. Women faced the problem of finding a dowry, and men were unable to afford the expense of maintaining a wife and children. The result was that women often married downward in the social hierarchy. Some family groups pooled resources to provide dowries for poor relatives, and the government of Florence in 1425 sought to alleviate the problem by establishing the *Monte delle doti* to furnish dowries for young women who would otherwise have been unable to marry.[23] But economic hardships do not explain all. The *catasto* of Pistoia in 1428 shows that men who belonged to wealthy households tended to marry even later than men from poor families.[24] Presumably these cases reflect other factors, including family policy and parental pressure, rather than economic necessity, as reasons for delayed entry into the married state.

While we do not have comparable records in any quantity from other parts of fifteenth-century Europe, sixteenth-century data from England show fea-

---

[22] Hughes, "Urban Growth and Family Structure," pp. 4–5; David Herlihy, "Marriage at Pistoia in the Fifteenth Century," *Bullettino storico pistoiese* 74 (1972) 9–11; Ruggiero, *Boundaries of Eros*, pp. 13–14; Heers, *Family Clans*, pp. 57–58.

[23] Heers, *Family Clans*, pp. 60–61; Herlihy, *Medieval Households*, pp. 154–55; Julius Kirschner and A. Molho, "The Dowry Fund and the Marriage Market in Early Quattrocento Florence," *Journal of Modern History* 50 (1978) 403–38.

[24] Herlihy, "Marriage at Pistoia," p. 13.

tures similar to those found earlier in Italy: a high incidence of celibacy, delay in marriage until the mid-twenties or later, and differences in marriage patterns between town and country.[25] Fifteenth-century evidence from Dijon shows something else that was probably common: a striking disparity of age between married couples. In Dijon, at any rate, men in their thirties generally had wives who were eight to sixteen years younger. Men in their forties and fifties often had wives between twenty and thirty years their juniors. Over all, more than a third of marriageable women wound up with substantially older husbands. This meant that young bachelors in Dijon faced strong competition for brides from older men, many well established in the civic hierarchy and able to bring pressure to bear on families to give them the girls they desired. That situation could lead men to identify strongly with others of their own age group and to show hostility to rivals in other age groups by indulging in demonstrations known as *charivaris*.[26] Both civic and Church authorities condemned these demonstrations and ordered participants punished, but the practice continued.[27] Municipalities ordered stiff penalties for participants, and these sanctions no doubt reflected fears and personal concerns of lawmakers, who tended to be mature males and likely targets for such demonstrations.[28]

The fact that a good many men delayed marriage until a relatively late age, and that many people of both sexes never married at all, helps explain several features of late medieval society, especially the rigorist sexual doctrines common among theologians and canonists. Since sexual repression was apparently inevitable for a great many people through a large part of their adult lives, an ascetic sexual morality served a useful social function, inasmuch as it rationalized the situation and attributed spiritual value to it. Theologians and canonists who disapproved of sex on moral grounds bolstered the social order by teaching a sexual ethic well adapted to social practice and economic conditions.[29]

[25] Macfarlane, *Origins of English Individualism*, pp. 158–59.

[26] Rossiaud, "Prostitution, Youth, and Society," p. 10.

[27] Synod of Bourges (1368) c. 8; Meaux (1365) c. 1; Tréguier (1365) c. 2, 8, all in Martène and Durand, *Thesaurus* 4:654, 923–24, 1118–20. See also Martine Grinberg, "Charivaris au moyen-âge et à la renaissance: Condemnation des remariages ou rites d'inversion du temps?" and François LeBrun, "Le charivari à travers les condemnations des autorités ecclésiastiques en France du XIVe au XVIIIe siècles," in *Le charivari: Actes de la table ronde organisée à Paris (25–27 avril 1977) par l'Ecole des Hautes Etudes en Sciences Sociales et le Centre National de Recherche Scientifique*, ed. Jacques LeGoff and Jean-Claude Schmitt, Civilisations et sociétés, no. 67 (Paris: Mouton, 1981), pp. 142, 221.

[28] Borgosesia, *Statuta* 100, ed. Mor, p. 179; *Corpus statutorum communis Cunei, 1380* 3.250, ed. Piero Camilla, Biblioteca della Società per gli studi storici, archeologici e artistici della provincia di Cuneo, vol. 12 (Cuneo: Stabilimento tipografico, 1970), pp. 133–34; LeBrun, "Charivari," pp. 223–24; Grinberg,"Charivaris au moyen âge," p. 141; Christiane Klapisch-Zuber, *Women, Family, and Ritual in Renaissance Italy*, trans. Lydia Cochrane (Chicago and London: University of Chicago Press, 1985), pp. 261–82.

[29] Tentler, *Sin and Confession*, p. 221.

The pattern of postponed marriage for many, and lack of any marriage prospects for others, helps explain the popularity and wide circulation of antimatrimonial tracts and misogynist propaganda during this period. Chaucer (ca. 1340–1400) described the genre and one of its devotees in the *Canterbury Tales*. Jankyn, the latest husband of the Wife of Bath:

> . . . Every nyght and day was his custume,
> Whan he hadde leyser and vocacioun
> From oother worldly occupacioun,
> To reden on this book of wikked wyves,
> He knew of hem mo legendes and lyves
> Than been of good wyves in the bible.
> For trusteth wel, it is an impossible
> That any clerk wol speke good of wyves. . . . [30]

Poor imprudent Jankyn got his comeuppance when the Wife of Bath snatched the "book of wikked wyves" from his hands, tore out three pages, and burnt the rest. Jankyn personifies an undoubtedly wide audience who found it comforting to reflect that postponement of marriage was, after all, perhaps not such a bad thing and that avoidance of it altogether might be a stroke of luck.[31] The people of Provence, according to Jean Montaigne, considered it folly to get married at all because of the countless burdens that marriage imposed on both men and women. His report reflects a rationalization common throughout the period.[32]

Humanist writers in the fourteenth and fifteenth centuries, on the other hand, often esteemed the married life and praised the joys of domestic bliss. They described the married man as the ideal human type and marriage as the foundation of social order.[33]

Critics who thought less well of marriage raised once again the question of its sacramental character—a question that most theologians during the preceding three centuries had considered essentially closed. Yet, at the very end of the fifteenth and the beginning of the sixteenth centuries, the subject revived once more. Erasmus (ca. 1466–1536), although he concluded that marriage could be counted among the sacraments, nonetheless distinguished it from all others. He refused to extend sacramentality to clandestine marriages, which he

---

[30] Geoffrey Chaucer, Wife of Bath's Prologue, ll. 682–91, in his *Poetical Works*, ed. F. N. Robinson (Boston: Houghton Mifflin Co., The Riverside Press, 1933), p. 99.

[31] Robert A. Pratt, "Jankyn's Book of Wikked Wyves: Medieval Antimatrimonial Propaganda in the Universities," *Annuale medievale* 3 (1962) 5–17; Francis Lee Utley, *The Crooked Rib: An Analytical Index to the Argument about Women in English and Scots Literature to the End of the Year 1568* (Columbus: Ohio State University Press, 1944; repr. New York: Octagon Books, 1970). A striking specimen of the genre is the *Alphabetum malarum mulierum* in MS Lat. 43, fol. 2r–6v, of the University of Pennsylvania Library.

[32] Jean Montaigne, *De bigamia* 2.7, in TUJ* 14:107vb–108ra.

[33] Herlihy, *Medieval Households*, pp. 116–17, citing among others Coluccio Salutati, Leonardo Bruni, and Francesco Barbaro.

considered invalid because they were usually contracted under the influence of sexual attraction, because the parties were often drunk when they exchanged consent, and because these unions could be manipulated by persons who stood to profit from them.[34] Peter of Ancharano (ca. 1330–1416) noted that marriage was not "strictly speaking" a sacrament, while the theologian, Melchior Cano (1509–60), thought marriages became sacramental only when a priest officiated. Cano questioned the sacramentality of marriages by proxy as well, a view that Cardinal Cajetan (1469–1534) strongly upheld.[35]

Despite doubts about its sacramental status and despite the propaganda attacking it, however, marriage remained the connective tissue of late medieval society.[36] Most people continued to marry, apparently without overmuch worry about the reservations of canonists and theologians or the gloomy picture purveyed by misogynist writers. When they married, persons from the more prominent and prosperous levels of society continued to do so with considerable forethought, preparation, and formality. Marriages at this social level were usually negotiated far in advance of the actual wedding, and negotiations were normally conducted by parents and other senior family members. Despite the preoccupation with political and economic matters that often dictated marital choice, however, it also seems clear that many of these marriages ripened into warm and affectionate personal relationships.[37]

The prospective bride and groom were usually not present at betrothal negotiations and might not even be informed about them until after an agreement had been reached. In Tuscany, family agreement on a prospective marriage was usually followed by a formal betrothal at which the couple were present and during which they exchanged future consent. The wedding ring was often given to the prospective bride at this point as a token of her new status as a *sponsa*.[38] The couple sometimes met for the first time at the betrothal ceremony for, as Peter of Ancharano remarked, there was no legal requirement that they know or understand each other in order to contract either betrothal or marriage.[39] Nor did the couple have to be present in person, either for betrothal or marriage; either or both could be contracted quite legally through duly appointed

[34] Desiderius Erasmus, *Opera omnia*, 10 vols. in 11 (Leiden: Petrus Van der Aa, 1703–1706; repr. Hildesheim: Georg Olms, 1961) 6:855 n. 37; Perez, "¿Todo matrimonio?" p. 15. Herlihy observes, however, that Erasmus also had highly positive things to say about marriage as compared with the monastic life; *Medieval Households*, p. 117.

[35] Petrus de Ancharano, *In quinque decretalium libros facundissima commentaria* to X 4.21.1, 5 vols. (Bologna: Apud Societatem typographiae Bononiensis, 1580–81) 4:175; Perez, "¿Todo matrimonio?" pp. 14, 20–21.

[36] Madeleine Jeay, "Sexuality and Family in Fifteenth-Century France: Are Literary Sources a Mask or a Mirror?" *Journal of Family History* 4 (1979) 334.

[37] Joel T. Rosenthal, "Aristocratic Marriage and the English Peerage, 1350–1500: Social Institution and Personal Bond," *Journal of Medieval History* 10 (1984) 181–94.

[38] Klapisch-Zuber, *Women, Family, and Ritual*, pp. 185–87.

[39] Petrus de Ancharano, *Comm.* to X 4.1.7, 1580/81 ed. 4:6.

proxies (usually parents).[40] Communities, as well as the Church, began during this period to reimpose controls upon the process of betrothal and to penalize those who failed to conform to regulations.[41] Betrothal, once formalized, was binding on both parties. John Mirc, writing about 1450, cautioned parish priests that they must not allow couples to break engagements without formal process:

> He that wole chese hym a fere,
> And seyt to hyre on thys manere,
> 'Here I take the to my wedded wyf,
> And there-to I plyghte þe my trowþe
> Wyth-owten cowpulle or fleschly dede,
> He þat wommon mote wedde nede;
> For þage he or ho a-nother take,
> That word wole deuors make.[42]

If both parties wished to be released from betrothal, there was little problem in securing permission; but if only one wished to escape from the engagement, he or she must be prepared to prove adequate grounds. One way around this difficulty was for the party who wished to terminate the betrothal to contract a clandestine marriage with someone else and thus present his or her ex-fiancé with a fait accompli. This practice helps to account for the frequency with which clandestine unions appear in late medieval court records.[43]

Betrothed couples who wished to proceed with their marriages, on the other hand, usually did so with some formality, although the ceremonies were often family affairs and did not necessarily involve participation by the clergy. In Tuscany, for example, fourteenth-century marriage ceremonies among the wealthy featured a ritual procession of the bride and her family to the house of the groom's family, where the bride was formally delivered to her new husband and the couple exchanged present consent. This was followed by a ritual banquet and, in particularly pious households, by the nuptial blessing. A notarized record was frequently made of the event. Following this the couple consummated their marriage.[44]

Although the church had centuries earlier rejected the requirement of parental consent to marriage, a strong feeling still persisted that couples who married against the wishes of their families acted wrongly. Such a practice was

[40] Felino Sandeo, *Consilium* no. 39, in *Consilia sive responsa clarissimorum suo tempore iurisconsultorum et in iure praesertim canonico primas partes tenentium* . . . (Venice: Apud Bernardum Iuntam & fratres, 1582), fol. 40ra.

[41] Reggio Emilia, *Statuta* 3.57, fol. 161r.

[42] John Mirc, *Instructions for Parish Priests*, ll. 190–97, ed. Edward Peacock, Early English Text Society Publications, Original Series, no. 31a (London: Kegan Paul, Trench, Trübner & Co., 1902), pp. 6–7. For an example of a court decision in such a case see Aubenas, *Recueil* 2:123–25.

[43] Anne Lefebvre-Teillard, "Règle et réalité dans le droit matrimonial à la fin du moyen-âge, RDC 30 (1980) 46–47.

[44] Klapisch-Zuber, *Women, Family, and Ritual*, pp. 184–87.

contrary to good morals, declared Felino Sandeo (1444–1503) and municipal statutes imposed heavy fines on couples who married without first obtaining parental consent.[45] Still, the Church remained committed to the principle that individuals could choose their marriage partners freely, whether their parents consented or not, and Petrus de Monte (d. 1457) maintained that the courts could compel reluctant parents to approve the marriages of their children.[46]

Some towns penalized women who chose to marry men who lived outside the city limits.[47] People who wished to evade this and other restrictions could marry secretly, and clandestine marriage continued to be a serious problem throughout the period.[48] Ecclesiastical prohibitions of secret marriage were well established in canon law, but synods nonetheless continued to condemn the practice and to remind the faithful of the penalties attached to it.[49] Canonists and moral writers tried to classify various forms of clandestinity—St. Antoninus (1389–1459), the Archbishop of Florence, distinguished six varieties— and disagreed about how many witnesses it took to make a marriage public.[50] Ordinary people, meanwhile, continued to disregard rules against clandestine unions. Courts usually dealt with that reality by ordering the parties to regularize their union with a formal wedding.[51] Some clandestine unions were cele-

[45] Felino Sandeo, *Consilium* no. 26, in *Consilia seu responsa*, fol. 26va; *Statuta civitatis Parmae* 3.76 (Parma: Angelus Ugoletus, 1494), fol. 132v–133r; *Statuta ciuitatis Pisauri* 2.107 (Pesaro: Impressa per B. q. Francini de Carthularis, 1531), fol. 40r.

[46] Petrus de Monte, *Repertorium utriusque iuris*, s.v. *mulier* (Padua: Johannes Hereot, 1480), fol. 76ra. Serfs likewise had the right to marry without the consent, or even the knowledge, of their lords; Petrus de Ancharano, *Comm.* to X 4.9.1, 1580/81 ed. 4:77. Rossiaud, "Prostitution, sexualité, société," pp. 82–83, claims that effective freedom of choice became more common, especially for young women, during the early sixteenth century than it had previously been, but the evidence for this conclusion seems rather weak.

[47] *Statuta et capitula Canisculi* (1405) 71; *Statuta concessa communitati ex hominibus Romani* (1515) 6; *Statuta et ordinamenta communis et hominum ac universitatis loci Fabricii* (1422) 88, all in *Corpus statutorum Canavisii*, ed. Giuseppe Frola, 3 vols., Biblioteca della Società Storica Subalpina, vol. 92–94 (Turin: Scuola tipografia Salesiana, 1918) 2:50, 346, and 3:184.

[48] Rudolf Weigand, "Die Rechtssprechung des Regensburger Gerichts in Ehesachen unter besonderer Berücksichtigung der bedingte Eheschliessung nach Gerichtsbüchern aus dem Ende des 15. Jahrhunderts," *Archiv für katholisches Kirchenrecht* 137 (1968) 428–29.

[49] Provincial Council of Narbonne (before 1310) c. 8; Synod of Nantes (ca. 1350) c. 3; Bourges (1368) c. 25; Nantes (1389) c. 2; Strasbourg (1435) c. 13; Avignon (1447) c. 4; Lyon (1449) c. 14, all in Martène and Durand, *Thesaurus* 4:378, 533, 589, 647, 960, 990–92.

[50] St. Antoninus, *De censuris; De sponsalibus et matrimonio* 19 (Venice: Johannes de Colonia & Johann Uanten, 1474; unpaginated); Antonio de Rosellis, *De legitimatione* 5.5, in TUJ* 6:271ra; Joannes ab Imola, *Consilia*, no. 135 (Venice: Apud Damianum Zenarum, 1581), fol. 78ra–vb.

[51] *The Courts of the Archdeaconry of Buckingham, 1483–1523*, no. 214, ed. E. M. Elvey, Publications of the Buckinghamshire Record Society, vol. 19 (Welwyn Garden

brated in the presence of a priest, but without the publication of the banns and other formalities required by law; in these cases the normal practice was to punish the offending priest, usually by temporary suspension from his office.[52] The parties themselves could be excommunicated *latae sententiae* if they failed to obey a court order to solemnize their marriage.[53] A few cities asserted their civic interest in discouraging clandestine marriages by fining those discovered to have contracted such unions.[54] Families sometimes meted out less formal, but perhaps more effective, penalties to children who ignored their parents' warnings and married informally. Thus when seventeen-year-old Margery Paston secretly married the bailiff, her parents sequestered her on one of the family estates and kept her incommunicado for two years. The matter ultimately came to the attention of the Bishop of Norwich, who ruled that her marriage was valid and ordered that she be reunited with her husband. The family reluctantly complied, but expelled Margery from the family home and thenceforth treated her as if she were dead.[55] More prominent offenders, such as Joan

City: Buckinghamshire Record Society, 1975), p. 148; Ferdinand Fronsdorf, "Ein Urtheilsbuch des geistlichen Gerichts zu Augsburg aus dem 14. Jahrhundert," *Deutsche Zeitschrift für Kirchenrecht* 10 (1871) 17; Jean-Philippe Lévy, "L'officialité de Paris et les questions familiales à la fin du XIVe siècle," in *Etudes LeBras* 2:1266 n. 7. Two common situations are illustrated by cases from the Commissary Court of Ely: (1) "Henricus Docher de Herdewykis citatus coram nobis . . . super contractu matrimonio inter ipsum et Alic' commorantem cum Johannem Warde de Whyte Well in parochia de Derton clandestine nutis fama publica referente et dictus Henricus coram nobis per se comparens vii. kalendis septembris anno domini supradicto [1374] fatetur se matrimonium contraxisse cum prefata Alicia per verba de presenti mutuum consensum eorumdem exprimente clandestine cum carnalis copula subsequenta. Et quia . . . non sunt aliunde coniuncti nec subest impedimentum . . . mandauimus uicarium de Dertoun ad solempnizandum matrimonium inter eos, bannis prius editis, si nullum subsit impedimentum." (Ely Diocesan Records [hereafter E.D.R.] D/2/1, fol. 11v). (2) "Thomas Humbleton de Cantabr', taillor, et Agnes ffolnyle de eadem citati coram nobis . . . [17 Dec. 1375] super carnali copula inter eosdem commissa et diutius continuata ac super contractu matrimoniali inter eos clandestine nuto. Comparent personaliter coram nobis et . . . fatebantur se matrimonium adinuicem contraxisse per uerba de presenti, mutuum consensum eorundem exprimende, carnali copula subsecuta. Inquisiti an sciant quicquum dicere quare non debeat adiudicari pro matrimonio inter eos dicunt se nichil scire dicere seu proponere . . . et pronunciamus pro matrimonio inter eos determinantes matrimonium inter eosdem fore in facie ecclesie Sancti Dunstani Cantabr' cuius sunt parochi solempniter bannis prius editis si nullum subsit impedimentum pro loco et tempore oportunis." (E.D.R. D/2/1, fol. 35r).

[52] E.D.R. D/2/1 (1377), fol. 82v–84r, 85r–v.

[53] Aubenas, *Recueil* 1:104–105; 2:82–83.

[54] Lucca, *Statuta* 4.199, fol. 251v; *Statuta et decreta civitatis Placentie* 5.23 (Brescia?: Bernardinus Misina? 1495; unpaginated); *Statuta ciuitatis Vrbini* 2.49 (Pesaro: Impressa per B. Caesanum, 1599), fol. 61r.

[55] Ann S. Haskell, "The Paston Women on Marriage in Fifteenth-Century England," *Viator* 4 (1973) 467–68.

Plantagenet, the Fair Maid of Kent, seem to have escaped such harsh treatment: Joan entered two clandestine marriages (the second one with the Prince of Wales), as well as a bigamous public marriage, which was ultimately declared invalid by the Roman Rota. While her conduct was scandalous, there is no evidence that she was ever seriously penalized for her marital adventures.[56]

But clandestine marriage was far commoner among ordinary folk than among the rich and well-born. Secret marriages made up a sizeable part of the case load in many ecclesiastical courts. The Synod of Nantes in 1386 complained that clandestine unions occurred daily and the records show that this was no exaggeration.[57] Nearly half of the mid-fifteenth-century marriage cases heard by the Augsburg court, for example, involved clandestine marriages, as did about one-third of the Regensburg cases in 1490.[58] As we have already noted, clandestine marriage provided escape from an unwelcome betrothal. Beyond this the availability of clandestine marriage proved to be an effective check on the principle of indissolubility, which may have been dear to the hearts of theologians and canonists but which many layfolk saw as an intolerable nuisance. In practice clandestine marriage made it possible for people to contract and dissolve their own marriages. If a couple made promises to each other privately in the future tense, and then settled down together, there was no effective way to prevent them from separating and marrying again should the experiment not work out. If one party haled the other into court to try to hold the union together, there was often so little evidence available that the judge had no choice but to separate them legally, even if they had children.[59]

[56] Karl P. Wentersdorf, "The Clandestine Marriage of the Fair Maid of Kent," JMH 5 (1979) 203–31.

[57] Synod of Nantes (1386) c. 2, in Martène and Durand, *Thesaurus* 4:960; Diebold, "Application," p. 192.

[58] Weigand, "Zur mittelalterlichen kirchlichen Ehegerichtsbarkeit," pp. 217–20, and "Rechtssprechung des Regensburger Gerichts," pp. 407–408, 413; Ruiz de Conde, *El amor y el matrimonio*, p. 14; Ourliac, "Notes sur le mariage," p. 57; G. Laribière, "Le mariage à Toulouse au XIVe et XVe siècles," *Annales du Midi* 79 (1967) 341.

[59] Lefebvre-Teillard, "Règle et réalité," p. 50; Sheehan, "Choice of Marriage Partner," p. 18. Beatrice Gottlieb, "The Meaning of Clandestine Marriage," in Wheaton and Hareven, *Family and Sexuality*, pp. 70–72, argues that clandestine marriage was not marriage at all, but rather nothing more than informal betrothal and that court actions involving these unions were in effect suits for breach of promise of marriage. Clandestine marriage was, according to Gottlieb, "a legal abstraction." Gottlieb's interpretation of the records she has used—principally a series of marriage litigation documents from the diocese of Troyes between 1475 and 1525—is neither plausible nor well founded. Popes and academic lawyers clearly meant that clandestine marriage was true marriage, and the courts regularly took them at their word: this was no abstraction, legal or theological. Contrary to Gottlieb's confident but unwarranted assertion, many clandestine unions lasted for years, and couples had often produced children, sometimes a good many of them, before they were haled into court. In England both royal and ecclesiastical courts routinely determined property issues on the premise that private exchange of consent constituted real marriage; see, e.g., Hog v. Latton (1267/68), Hykel-

The exchange of promises of future consent followed by sexual intercourse remained throughout this period a widely practiced method of creating a marriage, despite the fact that lawyers and theologians had insisted for centuries that marriage was more properly contracted by present consent. In popular opinion, however, marriage required sexual consummation and, despite the theoretical triumph of the consensual model of marriage, couples and their families continued to act as if consummation was essential. Delivery of the bride to the groom's home, and her voluntary election to remain there, were taken in fourteenth-century Florence to establish a presumption that the couple had consummated their marriage, although that presumption could be rebutted by proof that the bride remained a virgin.[60] Some authorities held that the gift of a ring by a man to a woman created a presumption that they were married, although Baldus (1327?–1400) considered that it did so only if the gift was made in the man's house or in a church.[61] If a man described a woman as his wife when he spoke to others, this also created a presumption that they were married.[62]

The formalities and rituals that surrounded the marriage contract varied considerably from one place to another. Fourteenth- and fifteenth-century English synods insisted that marriage ought to take place in church, which was also the common practice in France. In northern Italy, however, nuptials were usually celebrated in the home, and it was not common for couples to receive the nuptial blessing as part of the wedding rite. At Florence, when the nuptial blessing was given, the bride often received it alone, since the groom did not usually accompany her to the church. Even in the same region or city, wedding practices varied considerably between different classes of the population. Clergymen typically played more prominent roles in the weddings of lower-class North Italian couples, for example, than they did in weddings among the upper classes. Wealthy and prominent persons usually had their marital consent wit-

---

ing v. Valeyns (1286), Child v. Oyldebuf (1287), Brok v. Nastok (1290), Stodleye v. Parson of Wolwardinton (1301), all reported in Palmer, "Contexts of Marriage," pp. 43–47, 52–53. The Gottlieb thesis can be sustained only by disregarding a large body of evidence.

[60] Klapisch-Zuber, *Women, Family, and Ritual*, pp. 190–92; cf. the anonymous fourteenth-century gloss to X 4.1.21, in L.C. Foreign Law MS D.41, fol. 140rb:

> Effuge dum poteris
> Ne consensisse puteris.
> Nam si persisteris
> Tu sua speris.

[61] Baldus degli Ubaldi, *Ad tres priores libros Decretalium commentaria* to X 2.23.11 §3 (Lyon: n.p., 1585; repr. Aalen: Scientia, 1970), fol. 219rb; Ludovicus Sardus, *De naturalibus liberis* 6.14, in TUJ* 6:251vb; Klapisch-Zuber, *Women, Family, and Ritual*, pp. 196–97.

[62] Felino Sandeo, *Consilia* no. 19, fol. 18ra.

nessed by a notary; their humbler neighbors were much more likely to exchange consent in the presence of a priest.[63]

SEXUAL BEHAVIOR IN MARRIAGE

Discussions of sexual behavior in marriage during the fourteenth and fifteenth centuries centered upon the moral dangers inherent in marital intercourse, save for reproduction. John Bromyard (d. ca. 1390), an English Dominican, pictured marriage as "a life-long curbing of desire," punctuated occasionally by serious and solemn attempts to conceive a child.[64] Sexual pleasure in marriage should be feared and shunned; when experienced, it troubled the conscience, lest enjoyment be found to have been, after all, the principal goal of coitus. A married woman who prepared a love potion in order to stimulate her husband's sexual interest in her was open to severe condemnation.[65] A few writers, particularly among the Franciscans, adopted a less condemnatory approach to marital sex, but theirs was a minority position. Marcus von Weide (ca. 1450–ca. 1516), a Dominican, agreed with the conventional view that sexual sins in marriage were a daily occurrence and that scarcely any married persons were free from them. But unlike most contemporaries, Marcus believed that daily marital offenses were minor matters that did not require either confession or formal penance. They were forgiven and penance paid for them by blessing oneself with holy water or saying an "Our Father."[66] But this was an exceptionally permissive approach to the matter.

How far these attitudes got through to the general run of people is hard to say. On the one hand, Egidio of Bellamera (d. 1392) related that the people of Angers were scandalized when a Mendicant preacher told them that sexual pleasure in marriage was a sin, which would seem to indicate that the rigorist teachings common among the learned had failed to take root in the popular conscience.[67] On the other hand, Margery Kempe (ca. 1373–after 1439), a shrewd but illiterate townswoman and self-proclaimed mystic, was convinced that her

---

[63] Petrus de Ancharano, *Comm.* to X 4.1.1, 1581/82 ed. 4:2; Petrus Ravennus, *De consuetudine* 46, in TUJ 1:112r–v; Sheehan, "Marriage Theory and Practice," p. 444; Klapisch-Zuber, *Women, Family, and Ritual*, pp. 194–97; Heers, *Family Clans*, p. 227.

[64] Bromyard, *Summa predicantium*, s.v. *matrimonium*, fol. 202ra–203ra; John Colet, *Ennaratio in primam epistolam S. Pauli ad Corinthios* 7:9, ed. and trans. J. H. Lupton (London: Bell, 1874), pp. 90–91; Owst, *Literature and Pulpit*, pp. 378–79.

[65] Felino Sandeo, *Consilia* no. 15, fol. 13va; Tentler, *Sin and Confession*, pp. 231–32.

[66] Quoted in Lindner, *Usus matrimonii*, p. 162; cf. Jean Gerson, *Sermon contre la luxure*, in his *Oeuvres complètes*, ed. P. Glorieux, 10 vols. (Paris: Desclée, 1960–73) 7:819. Joannes a Capistrano, *Summa de matrimonio* 354 (Venice: Apud Iuntas, 1588), fol. 382rb–va, held that marital coitus might even, under some circumstances, be meritorious. See also Flandrin, "Vie sexuelle," p. 103, and Rossiaud, "Prostitution," p. 80.

[67] Quoted in Kelly, *Love and Marriage*, p. 261 n. 49.

sexual relations with her husband amounted to incontinence. She browbeat
him into agreeing that they should both take vows of chastity for their souls'
sake. Once they had done so, she reported that her neighbors were scandalized
when she returned to her husband's house to care for him after he suffered
a serious accident, for everyone assumed that they had gone back to their
"unclennesse." Granted that Margery was uncommonly obsessed with the nas-
tiness of sex, she was also soaked in the popular piety of her age. She apparently reflected notions of sexual morality common among the people of King's
Lynn in her day. Chaucer's Parson corroborated her evidence when he reproved
married couples who "Assemble oonly for amorous love and . . . for to accomplice thilke brennynge delit, they rekke nevere how ofte. Soothly it is deedly
synne; and yet, with sorwe, somme folk wol peynen hem moore to doon than to
hire appetit suffiseth."[68] The differences in perception between Marcus von
Weide and Margery Kempe testify to the fact that there was no broad general
consensus about the morality of marital sex in this period.

Both clergy and laity generally believed, however, that the ability to have
sexual relations was essential to marriage and that those unable to have sex
could not marry validly.[69] Couples were not supposed to have sexual relations,
of course, until after marriage and spiritual counselors advised that even after
marriage they should not do so until they had spent their first three days and
nights together in prayer and meditation. Then they should approach consummation in a spirit of solemn devotion and with the fear of God in their minds.[70]
While this may have been the practice of a pious few, many more couples probably consummated their marriages in advance of any formal ceremony. Among
the well-to-do in Florence, at any rate, this practice seems to have become
more common, not less so, during the fifteenth century. Consummation was
also frequently linked to property considerations. In Italian towns couples often
initiated conjugal relations only when the dowry had been paid.[71] For the mon-
eyed classes of society, marital sex, especially its commencement, was in many
respects a social event, rather than the private business of the newlyweds.[72]

Several canonists in this period felt that marriage was not completed or per-

[68] *The Book of Margery Kempe*, ed. S. B. Meech and H. E. Allen, Early English Text
Society Publications, vol. 212 (London: EETS, 1940), pp. 23, 179; Chaucer, Parson's
Tale, l. 942, ed. Robinson, p. 308.

[69] Johannes Bosch, *De nuptiis* 1.17, and Antonio de Rosellis, *De legitimatione* 2.33, in
TUJ* 6:2vb, 266rb; Martín de Azpilceuta, *Consilia* 4.2.4.4, in his *Opera hactenus inedita*, 3 vols. (Lyon: Apud haeredes Gulielmi Rovilii, 1589–94) 3/2:14.

[70] Synod of Nantes (ca. 1350) c. 3, in Martène and Durand, *Thesaurus* 4:960–61; St.
Bernardino, *Le prediche volgari* 20, ed. Piero Bargellini (Milan, Rome: Rizzoli, 1936),
pp. 439–40; C. N. L. Brooke, "Aspetti del matrimonio e della famiglia nel mondo di
Santa Catarina e di San Bernardino," in *Atti del simposio internazionale Cateriniano-
Bernardiniano* (Siena: Accademia senesi degli intronati, 1982), p. 888.

[71] Klapisch-Zuber, *Women, Family, and Ritual*, pp. 191–92; Heers, *Family Clans*,
p. 59.

[72] Jeay, "Sexuality and Family," p. 336.

fected until the couple had consummated it.[73] There was, as noted earlier, a tendency to go back to Gratian's belief that coitus was not only an important element of marriage but a necessary one. A few canonists accordingly gave consummation great prominence in their definitions of marriage. Peter of Ancharano in particular explored the topic in detail. It was possible, he wrote, for a couple to consummate their marriage even prior to the time when the wife attained the age of puberty. A marriage so consummated should, in his view, be treated as complete and valid. Consummation was, according to his reasoning, the defining term, and because it was the central element in marriage, its presence outweighed in importance defects of age and consent. Peter was also more concerned than his predecessors with the question of whether insemination, as well as penetration, was essential for consummation. Could a man who, for example, in his first marriage had managed to penetrate the vagina, but who failed to ejaculate during intercourse, claim that the marriage was unconsummated and marry again? Or, at the other extreme, should a marriage be deemed consummated when the man ejaculated in the vulva, but failed to penetrate the vagina? Both questions had been canvassed by earlier writers—notably Joannes Andreae—but these problems fascinated several writers of this age, including Egidio of Bellamera and Niccolo de' Tudeschi, commonly known as Panormitanus (1386–1445), in addition to Peter of Ancharano.[74] This increased attention to the definition of consummation arguably indicated the beginning of a return to the view that consent alone did not make a complete marriage.

Canonists of this period attempted to define ever more precisely the circumstances under which Courts Christian might intervene in order to compel married couples to fulfill their conjugal debt obligations.[75] No doubt this reflected the fact, evident from court records, that this was a period of vigorous judicial activism in enforcing the marital debt. Orders requiring husbands and wives to treat each other with marital affection and to pay the conjugal debt became common and were issued even when the couple no longer lived together. Thus in one separation decree the court stated:

> We hold the defendant bound to pay the conjugal debt to the plaintiff in her father's house one night each week and to keep [this obligation] faithfully, until we shall order otherwise.[76]

---

[73] Felino Sandeo, *Consilia* 26, fol. 25va–vb; Johannes Bosch, *De nuptiis* 1.16, and Ludovicus Sardus, *De naturalibus liberis* 1.7, in TUJ* 6:2vb, 249ra; Lefebvre-Teillard, "Règle et réalité," p. 48; Ourliac, "Notes sur le mariage," p. 58.

[74] Petrus de Ancharano, *Comm.* to 4.1.2, 32; 4.2.6, 1580/81 ed., 4:3, 32, 37; Aegidius de Bellamera, *Comm.* to C. 35 q. 2 & 3 c. 11, 1550 ed. 3:92rb; Panormitanus, *Commentaria* to X 4.1.32 § 3 and 4.13.7 §§ 4–5, in his *Omnia quae extant commentaria*, 9 vols. (Venice: Apud Iuntas, 1588) 7:20rb–va, 51ra–rb.

[75] Petrus de Ancharano, *Comm.* to X 4.7.4 and 4.13.4, 11, 1580/81 ed., 4:73, 86, 89; Aegidius de Bellamera, *Comm.* to C. 32 q. 7 c. 10, 1550 ed. 3:54vb; Panormitanus, *Comm.* to X 4.13.4 §§ 2, 7, 1588 ed. 7:49rb.

[76] "Dicimus ream teneri ad reddendum debitum coniugale actori in domo patris una

Marital affection orders were routinely used to terminate informal separations or de facto divorces and required couples to reestablish a marital relationship with one another under pain of excommunication or other serious penalty; they served, in other words, many of the functions that in Common Law might be served by an injunction.[77] Here too we find fifteenth-century towns involving themselves in matters that earlier had been an exclusive concern of the Church. Thus the Faenza statutes, for example, provided:

> We decree and ordain that anyone in the city, county, or district of Faenza who does not keep his wife in his house and who fails to treat her with marital affection shall forfeit half of the dowry of his said wife. . . . And, on the other hand, if a wife fails to treat her husband with wifely affection, but lives dishonorably, commits adultery, or wanders about without her husband's permission, she shall lose her dowry and her husband may profit thereby. In order to sustain [charges on] these matters common knowledge proved by five witnesses shall suffice.[78]

Courts did not concern themselves with husbands occasionally absent from home on business, but preachers and moralists did, on the no doubt sensible ground that such disruptions created strains in the marital relationship and exposed the parties to sexual temptations. St. Bernardino identified merchants as particular offenders and encouraged the wives of tradesmen to use every means to force their husbands to return home at frequent intervals. He added that he was not concerned with brief absences—a week or two, or a month at a time— but with absences of two or three years, which he said were displeasing to God. Precisely such prolonged absences were, however, a common feature of mercantile careers. Resident factors for Italian traders in the Levant, for example, typically remained overseas, almost always separated from wives and children, for years on end. Other young women, particularly those from prominent fami-

---

nocte semel in hebdomada adhibita fideli custodia quousque aliter ordinabimus." Quoted by Anne Lefebvre-Teillard, *Les officialités à la vielle du Concile de Trente*, Bibliothèque d'histoire du droit et droit romain, no. 19 (Paris: R. Pichon et R. Durano-Auzias, 1973), p. 199 n. 265; Weigand, "Zur mittelalterlichen kirchlichen Ehegerichtsbarkeit," p. 245.

[77] For other examples see Aubenas, *Recueil* 1:72, 75–76; A. T. Bannister, "Visitation Returns of the Diocese of Hereford in 1397," *English Historical Review* 44 (1929) 281, 283, 449, and 45 (1930) 94, 450. Some forms for orders of this kind appear in E.D.R., F/5/32, fol. 7r, 25v, 30r, and are common in form-books elsewhere. For the forms used in the papal curia see Peter Herde, *Audientia litterarum contradictarum: Untersuchungen über die päpstlichen Justizbriefe und die päpstliche Delegationsgerichtsbarkeit vom 13. bis zum Beginn des 16. Jahrhunderts*, no. K.157, 159–60, 2 vols. (Tübingen: Max Niemeyer, 1970) 2:302–304.

[78] *Magnificae ciuitatis Fauentie ordinamenta nouissime recognita* 3.27 (Faenza: I.M. de Simonetis, 1527); see also Pesaro, *Statuta* 3.50, fol. 54v.

lies, found themselves "widowed" by the exile of their husbands for political reasons. Communes often intensified the pain of exile by preventing family members from joining the exiled miscreant. Such episodes as these, however, affected only a tiny segment of society. Commercial activities undoubtedly disrupted the lives of many more families than political factionalism did.[79]

Sexual relations in other families might end by the unilateral decision of one family member, often a wife who had borne as many children as she could endure. Voluntary unilateral termination of marital sex was sometimes based on religious grounds, too, despite the often reiterated prohibitions of such conduct by both canonists and theologians. Still a determined spouse could often find a way to secure what he or she wanted.

The self-revelations of Margery Kempe once more give insight into the domestic drama surrounding such occurrences. Margery was atypical, to be sure, but a good part of her atypicality consisted in her extraordinarily frank and detailed recording of her experiences. Margery tells us that she heard a heavenly song while lying abed one morning and, on the strength of that experience, decided that heaven was so splendid that she must make sure that she got there. She therefore determined to cease having sexual relations with her husband,

> for þe dette of matrimony was so abhominabyl to hir þat she had leuar hir trowt etyn or drynkyn þwose, þe mukke in þchanel, þan to consentyn to any fleschly comownyng. . . .

Having come to this decision, she told her husband that their sex life was finished. He was not amused. When he finally realized that Margery was serious, he was furious and demanded that she have intercourse with him then and there. Margery protested, but "He wold haue hys wylle." He brushed aside her objections, "And so he vysd her as he had do be-for, for he wold not spar," despite the fact that Margery shrieked, wept, and howled at the top of her voice on this and every subsequent occasion when he took her against her will. At length, worn down by her persistent protests and rejections, he desisted from marital rape and agreed to join Margery in taking a vow of chastity.[80] It is highly unlikely that this was the only story of its kind, though just how common such episodes were we will never know.

Writers on moral problems during this period often repeated earlier injunctions against variations in the sexual techniques that married couples used, but

---

[79] St. Bernardino, *Sermo* 32.7.3, in his *Opera omnia* 5 vols. (Florence: Ad Claras Aquas, 1950–56) 4:158–59; James Bruce Ross, "The Middle-Class Child in Urban Italy, Fourteenth to Early Sixteenth Century," in *History of Childhood*, ed. Lloyd de Mause (New York: Psychohistory Press, 1974; repr. New York: Harper Torchbooks, 1975), p. 200; Eliyahu Ashtor, *Levant Trade in the Middle Ages* (Princeton: Princeton University Press, 1984), pp. 404–409.

[80] *The Book of Margery Kempe*, pp. 11–12.

rarely dealt specifically with anal or oral sex. Although variant sexual practices were condemned both because they might be contraceptive and also because they promoted sexual pleasure as an end in itself, writers of the period rarely distinguished explicitly between the two reasons for their disapproval.

A few authors criticized critics of deviant coital positions. The most outspoken of them, Silvester Prierias Mazzolini (1460–1523), denied that variations from the "missionary position" were contraceptive, as Pierre de La Palude had claimed. Silvester also argued that even if couples employed unusual coital postures in order to enhance their pleasure, this was not in itself sinful.[81] Injunctions to married folk to abstain from sexual relations during the solemn liturgical seasons, pregnancy, and menstruation also recur in the moralistic literature of the period, but violations of these rules ranked low in the scale of sexual offenses. A surprising development in this respect was the resurrection of the old rule against intercourse during lactation. This prohibition had largely disappeared from the literature on marital sex during the high middle ages, but suddenly reappeared toward the end of the fourteenth century.[82] On the other hand, the ban on sexual foreplay, which a number of earlier authorities had taught was mortally sinful, found little support among fourteenth- and fifteenth-century authors. The *Sylvestrina*, which this time agreed with the teaching of Pierre de La Palude, maintained that erotic stimulation prior to marital intercourse was not sinful, so long as it was not indulged in for pleasure alone and so long as it was "completed" by intercourse. St. Bernardino, on the other hand, sternly warned audiences that they must avoid excessive sexual stimulus as a prelude to marital relations, for such practices were contrary to the ethics of Christian marriage. Couples, he declared, must avoid lascivious kisses and fondling, they should on no account touch one another's genitals, and they must never see their spouses naked or allow their own bare bodies to be seen by their mates.[83]

As for contraception, probably the most effective technique available during this period continued to be *coitus interruptus*, a practice that was apparently common in some regions. Writers from northern Italy seem to have been particularly sensitive about this issue and more inclined to condemn it explicitly than did those from other areas. This may well reflect concerns that stemmed from the relatively high birth rate in this region during the late fourteenth century. Elsewhere *coitus interruptus* seems not to have been perceived as a par-

---

[81] Silvestro Prierias Mazzolini, *Sylvestrinae summa quae summa summarum merito nuncupatur*, s.v. *Debitum coniugale*, 2 vols. in 1 (Lyon: Apud Ioannem & Franciscum Frellonios fratres, 1546) 1:226–27; Nicolaus de Plowe, *Tractatus de sacramentis* 7.4.2, in TUJ 3:45r; Tentler, *Sin and Confession*, pp. 190–91, 201–202; Flandrin, "L'attitude," pp. 150–51.

[82] Tentler, *Sin and Confession*, pp. 208, 214–15; Flandrin, "L'attitude," p. 190.

[83] *Sylvestrina*, s.v. *Debitum coniugale*, 1:228; but cf. St. Bernardino, *Sermo* 18.3.1, in his *Opera* 1:222–23; Tentler, *Sin and Confession*, pp. 188–89, 205.

ticularly grave issue until the sixteenth century, when for the first time it became a common theme in the literature on moral problems.[84]

DIVORCE AND REMARRIAGE

Canonists during the fourteenth and fifteenth centuries were commonly much more concerned with divorce and remarriage than with marital sex. This no doubt reflected the relatively high frequency with which marital conflicts appeared in ecclesiastical courts. The experience of Courts Christian in England seems to have differed from that of ecclesiastical tribunals on the Continent. An analysis of cases that came before the Canterbury Consistory Court in the late fourteenth-century, for example, showed that matrimonial causes accounted for approximately one-third of the total business. During the fifteenth century, however, the proportion of matrimonial cases declined precipitously. In 1373/74, for example, more than thirty marriage cases were introduced per year; after 1400 cases declined to less than ten. After 1500, the number of marriage cases rose once again. This decline does not appear to have been characteristic of the experience of canonical courts on the Continent, however, and therefore it presumably reflects social and legal developments peculiar to England.[85]

The grounds on which marriage cases were brought to court also differed from England to the Continent. Most marriage litigation in French canonical tribunals consisted of suits to enforce promises of future marriage, whereas the Courts Christian in England more often dealt with cases of present consent marriage, sometimes followed by consummation, sometimes not. But even here patterns varied. The practice of courts in the south of France resembled that found in England much more closely than it did that of northern French courts.[86]

---

[84] *Sylvestrina*, s.v. *Debitum coniugale*, 1:228. Canonistic and theological treatments of coitus interruptus present serious difficulties of interpretation, since passages that condemn "unnatural" coitus may possibly refer to this practice, but they are often so vaguely worded as to leave the author's precise meaning uncertain. Noonan, *Contraception*, pp. 226–28, 236–38, 348, interprets many of these vague denunciations as references to *coitus interruptus*; Flandrin, "La vie sexuelle," p. 104, and "L'attitude," p. 147, tends to think that these passages may refer to other issues. De Waha, "Note," pp. 11, 13, interprets an enigmatic mention of a *modum specialem coëundi* practiced by the fifteenth-century heretic, Aegidius Cantor, and which Aegidius claimed was used by Adam in Paradise, as a reference to coitus interruptus, but the meaning is far from clear. And what is one to make of a statement such as that of Guy de Roye, *Doctrinal de sapience*, fol. 64v: "Pour la reverence du mariage que dieu a tant honnore ilz se doibvent bien garder de user deshonneument contra lordonnance de nature, car ilz pecheroient mortellement"? On birthrates in northern Italy see Herlihy, *Medieval Households*, pp. 146–49, and Heers, *Family Clans*, p. 61.

[85] Brian L. Woodcock, *Medieval Ecclesiastical Courts in the Diocese of Canterbury* (London: Oxford University Press, 1952), p. 85; Helmholz, *Marriage Litigation*, pp. 166–68; Weigand, "Zur mittelalterlichen kirchlichen Ehegerichtsbarkeit," p. 246.

[86] Donahue, "Canon Law on the Formation of Marriage," pp. 149–53.

English litigants presented matrimonial problems to the courts much more often to establish the validity of an alleged marriage than to secure a nullity decree rescinding an acknowledged union.[87] Although preachers and poets lamented the frequency with which false divorces were obtained, and the ease with which courts could be corrupted, litigation records do not bear out those complaints. The volume of nullity cases during this period was not large, but they were often hard-fought. Although evidence may have been fabricated from time to time and advocates no doubt coached witnesses on occasion, the records furnish little basis for the suspicions that were voiced about judicial corruption.[88]

Canonistic opinion remained divided on the question of papal power to terminate marriages. Martín de Azpilceuta (1492–1596), for example, was confident, as most of his predecessors had been, that the pope could dissolve unconsummated marriages for good cause.[89] When it came to dissolving valid consummated marriages the problem was far more difficult. Egidio of Bellamera (d. 1392), after reviewing conflicting opinions on the matter, concluded that the pope lacked this power, but Peter of Ravenna (fl. 1497–1508) thought otherwise. The saying of Jesus, "What God has joined together let no man put asunder," did not apply to the pope, Peter declared, because he is the vicar of Christ: when he dissolves a marriage it is not man who sunders the nuptial tie, but God acting through the pope.[90]

In any event canonical courts at every level were in practice less rigorous than legal theory required and on occasion granted divorces that ruptured the bond of marriage, even though theorists claimed that they could not do so. They also granted separations and nullity decrees on grounds that had no foundation in the canons.[91] When Luther complained that Church courts authorized separations for reasons not specified in Scripture he was certainly reporting accurately.[92] The clearest example of a situation in which the courts created new grounds for separation was the introduction of cruelty or mistreatment (*saevitia*) as a basis for separation, which the courts began to use during the late

[87] Helmholz, *Marriage Litigation*, pp. 74–75.

[88] John Bromyard, *Summa praedicantium*, s.v. *iuramentum*, fol. 177ra; *Piers Plowman*, B text, pass. 2.174–77 and pass. 15.239–43, ed. G. Kane and E. Talbot Donaldson (London: Athlone Press, 1960), pp. 265, 548–49; also in the C text, pass. 22.136–39, ed. Derek Pearsall (Berkeley and Los Angeles: University of California Press, 1979), p. 367; Owst, *Literature and Pulpit*, pp. 254, 281; Helmholz, *Marriage Litigation*, pp. 146–47, and "Ethical Standards for Advocates and Proctors in Theory and Practice," in *Toronto Proceedings*, pp. 293–99.

[89] Martín de Azpilceuta, *Consilia* 4.1.3.2, in his *Opera* 3/2:3.

[90] Aegidius Bellamera, *Consilia* 28 (Lyon, Joannes de Campray, 1512), fol. 49va–50vb; Petrus Ravennas, *De consuetudine* 72, in TUJ 1:112v–113r.

[91] Ourliac, "Notes sur le mariage," p. 59; Lefebvre-Teillard, "Règle et réalité," pp. 51–53.

[92] Martin Luther, *Vom ehelichen Leben* (1522), in his *Werke: kritische Gesamtausgabe* (Weimar: H. Böhlaus, 1883– ; cited hereafter as WA) 10/2:280–87.

thirteenth century (as mentioned previously); it began to become prominent in the commentaries during this period. Legal scholars tended to be conservative on this issue but held that where a petitioner could show that his or her spouse had made death threats, or had acted in ways that constituted a danger to life and limb, canonical separation was warranted.[93] Courts, however, did not always require such critical situations before they would take action. They granted separation, for example, on grounds of habitual drunkenness, as well as cruelty and mistreatment, although mere quarrelsomeness and bad temper apparently did not furnish adequate basis for so drastic a remedy. *Saevitia* became a common basis for separation decrees during this period—the Augsburg court granted fourteen such decrees in 1350 alone, while at Regensburg more than a third of the fifty-two separations granted in 1490 were based on this.[94] Another innovation in practice was the granting of separation of residence but not immunity from the marriage debt. Again this appears to have no clear basis in the canons—at least not until the practice was sanctioned by the Council of Trent—but it was certainly common by the end of the fourteenth century. This type of separation was usually granted because of hatred (*odium*), quarrels (*rancores*), fiscal irresponsibility (*dilapidatio seu dissipatio bonorum*), or stinginess (*austeritas*). Decrees dealing with this type of separation usually specified that marital rights were reserved (*iure thori reservato*) and, as we have already seen, courts might specify the times, places, frequency, and circumstances under which sexual rights were to be exercised.[95] Couples were sometimes forbidden to have sexual relations while litigation concerning their marriage was pending, but opinion about the propriety of this was by no means unanimous.[96]

Other causes for separation or divorce were better grounded in the canons. Although academic lawyers devoted a great deal of time and ingenuity to discussions of consanguinity and affinity, these grounds rarely appeared in practice and affected only insignificant numbers of cases.[97] Force and fear were likewise

[93] Felino Sandeo, *Consilium* 14, fol. 13ra; Petrus de Ancharano, *Comm.* to X 4.19.1, 1580/81 ed., 4:135.

[94] Weigand, "Zur mittelalterlichen kirchlichen Ehegerichtsbarkeit," pp. 241–43; Elvey, *Courts of the Archdeaconry of Buckingham*, no. 212, 245, 248B, pp. 144, 174, 176; In re Willelmus at Hill, an ex officio case from the diocese of Rochester in 1444, is noted also in B.L., MS Add. 11,821, fol. 7r.

[95] Council of Trent, Sess. 24 (1563) c. 8, in COD, p. 731; Lefebvre-Teillard, "Règle et réalité," pp. 53–54; Helmholz, *Marriage Litigation*, pp. 100–103.

[96] Elvey, *Courts of the Archdeaconry of Buckingham*, no. 386, p. 308; Petrus de Ancharano, *Comm.* to X 4.9.2, 1580/81 ed., 4:78. Remarriage during the course of litigation was, of course, also forbidden; Joannes ab Imola, *Consilia* 125, fol. 73rb–va.

[97] Helmholz, *Marriage Litigation*, pp. 79–87; Lefebvre-Teillard, "Règle et réalité," pp. 50–51; Weigand, "Zur mittelalterlichen kirchlichen Ehegerichtsbarkeit," pp. 231–33. Cases of consanguinity and affinity might also be brought to the attention of authorities by third parties, e.g., during the visitation of a parish, as happened at Kingston (Hereford) in 1379; Bannister, "Visitation Returns," p. 445; cases were sometimes prosecuted ex officio, e.g., a Rochester case of 8 April 1436, in B.L., MS Add. 11,821, fol. 1r.

not a common basis for nullity, in part no doubt because of the stringent standards of proof required.[98] Pre-contract continued to be a common basis for annulment, and multiparty suits for enforcement of a marriage also appear in the records with some frequency. These cases often involved clandestine marriage and presented difficult problems in the evaluation of evidence.[99]

Impotence also remained a common basis for nullity. Here, too, one finds occasional discrepancies between theory and practice. Although academic commentators taught that a castrated man could not marry, an Augsburg judge thought otherwise, for he held in a case on 9 March 1350 that a eunuch (*spado*) had successfully consummated his marriage.[100] Courts seem to have been as skeptical as commentators about the evidence supporting impotence pleas. Thus, for example, in the Poynant case (1378–80) at Ely, John Poynant received a divorce on the grounds that he was impotent. After the divorce John successfully consummated a second marriage with another woman, who testified that he was potent enough, not only to have intercourse but also to beget a child, with whom she was pregnant when the matter came to court. The court then rescinded John's divorce from his first wife, quashed both his and his wife's second marriages, and commanded John and his first wife to resume married life together and to treat each other with marital affection. What happened to John's second wife and their child does not appear in the record.[101]

Courts might also bend their own rules and treat prostitutes and other women as credible witnesses in impotence cases. They continued, as well, to rely on testimony from medical experts, physical examination by midwives, and other forms of expert evidence in dealing with these cases.[102] Complaints of impotence caused by sorcery and magic also continued to trouble both the commentators and the courts in this period.[103]

---

[98] Helmholz, *Marriage Litigation*, pp. 90–94; Weigand, "Zur mittelalterlichen kirchlichen Ehegerichtsbarkeit," pp. 238–39; for two additional Augsburg cases see Frensdorff, "Ein Urtheilsbuch," pp. 18–19.

[99] Helmholz, *Marriage Litigation*, pp. 57–62, 76–77; Weigand, "Zur mittelalterlichen kirchlichen Ehegerichtsbarkeit," p. 230.

[100] Helmholz, *Marriage Litigation*, pp. 87–90; Weigand, "Zur mittelalterlichen kirchlichen Ehegerichtsbarkeit," pp. 234–35; Petrus de Ancharano, *Comm.* to X 4.15.2, 1580/81 ed. 4:97.

[101] *In re* Poynant (1378–80), E.D.R. D/2/1, fol. 100r–102v, 105v, 110r, 130r, 134v, 136r, 140v, 142r–v.

[102] Petrus de Ancharano, *Comm.* to X 4.15.1, 7, 1580/81 ed., 4:96, 103; Etienne Aufréri, *Decisiones capelle sedis archiepiscopalis Tholose* no. 380 (Lyon: Venundantur ab Stephano Gueynard, 1508), fol. 94v–96v; Mario Ascheri, "'Consilium sapientis', perizia medica, e 'res iudicata': Diritto dei 'dottori' e instituzioni comunali," in *Salamanca Proceedings*, pp. 534–35, 537.

[103] Petrus de Ancharano, *Comm.* to X 4.15.2, 1580/81 ed., 4:97; *Depositions and Other Ecclesiastical Proceedings from the Courts of Durham Extending from 1311 to the Reign of Elizabeth*, ed. James Raine, Surtees Society Publications, vol. 21 (London: J. B. Nichols and Son, 1847), p. 27.

Marital separation because of adultery was an infrequent cause of action. The *Officialis* of Paris, when dealing with such cases, sometimes awarded the complainant a share of the assets of the marriage, without granting a decree of separation.[104] One reason for the comparative rarity of adultery litigation may well have been the feeling that bringing such a cause to the courts was itself shameful:

> Only humble and powerless men bring their [adultery] cases before a judge [wrote Paulus de Castro] for according to common reckoning no small amount of shame flows from these actions and the complainant who does not avenge himself with his own hands but waits for a judge to vindicate him is considered a vile cuckold. Even the judges often do not do right by him, but smirk and chuckle and snigger, so that a husband is right not to have recourse to the judge, but is better off dealing with the affront on his own authority.[105]

Another consideration that may well have dissuaded many potential plaintiffs from bringing separation actions on the grounds of adultery was the fact that the defendant spouse might well react with a countercharge of adultery. Moreover even if, say, a husband secured a separation from his wife on grounds of her adultery, and if she subsequently discovered that he was sexually involved with another woman, the separated wife could have the separation quashed and a court could well require him to return to live with her. This might, to say the least, create an awkward situation.[106]

The Roman Church remained strongly opposed throughout this period to the practice of granting absolute divorces, with the right of remarriage, on grounds of adultery, despite the fact that in earlier times this had often been done.[107] This matter became an issue in negotiations over reunion between Rome and various Eastern Orthodox communities. Despite the difficulties that the issue presented, however, the papacy refused to compromise, and Pope Eu-

---

[104] Lévy, "L'officialité de Paris," pp. 1277–78.

[105] Paulus de Castro, *Consilia et allegationes* no. 192 (Venice: Paganinus de Paganinis, 1489; unpaginated): "[N]on solet querela proprii coram iudice nisi per uiles homines et impotentes quia de verecundia penes homines et vulgus non currant cum secundum iudicium vulgarium non parva sequeretur ex hoc verecundia quia reputarentur viles et cornuti qui propriis manibus de talibus se non vindicant sed expectant per iudicem vindicari. Sed nec iudices de talibus solent ius reddere sed trufari et cachinari et ridere unde iustam habuit occasionem maritus si ad iudicem non habuit recursus, sed propria auctoritate disposuit iniuriam repellere et propulsare quam sine gravi verecundia pati non poterat, ff. quod vi aut clam, si alius § bellissime in fi. [Dig. 43.24.7.3], et ibi nota glos. puta si iudicis non habet copiam etc. [*Glos. ord.* to Dig. 43.24.7.3 v. *Ex magna*]. Et quod nota C. de iude. l. nullus [Cod. 1.9.14] et l. ait praetor § si debitorem, ff. de privi. credi. [?]." See also Nevizzani, *Sylva nuptialis*, fol. 9rb.

[106] Petrus de Ancharano, *Comm.* to X 4.19.5, 1580/81 ed. 4:138; Frensdorff, "Urtheilsbuch," p. 34, presents documents from an Augsburg case of 25 May 1350.

[107] See above, pp. 95, 143, 199–201.

gene IV (elected 1431, suspended 1438, deposed 1439, d. 1447) inserted in the Decree for the Armenian Church a specific affirmation of Rome's position on the subject.[108]

Canonists continued to condemn the practice of informal divorce, and couples who simply separated and went their own ways were occasionally haled before courts and ordered to resume married life. The problem of desertion and informal separation also became the subject of legislation in a few cities, which imposed fines on couples who parted without formal process.[109]

CONCUBINAGE AMONG THE LAITY

Legal writers in the fourteenth and fifteenth centuries were more concerned about concubinage among the laity than were previous generations. Although earlier authorities generally did not treat concubinage as a punishable offense, several writers of this period questioned whether it was equitable to punish fornicators and prostitutes while tolerating men who kept concubines.[110] Some went further and concluded that while concubinage had formerly been permitted, canon law no longer allowed this and should force men to dismiss their concubines. This finally became official policy early in the sixteenth century, when the Fifth Lateran Council (1514) prohibited concubinage among the laity.[111] But well before 1514, sentiment for abolishing concubinage had per-

---

[108] Council of Florence, Sess. 8 (1439), *Bulla unionis Armenorum*, in COD, p. 526; De Sanctis, "Coniuge abbandonato," p. 218.

[109] Petrus de Ancharano, *Comm.* to X 4.1.20, 1580/81 ed., 4:18; Elvey, *Courts of the Archdeaconry of Buckingham*, no. 344, p. 250; *In re* Blair, an ex officio Rochester case from 1439/40, is reported in B.L., MS Add. 11,821, fol. 2r–v; Rieti, *Statuta* 3.18, fol. 38v; *Statuta Burgi Sexii, MCCCLXXXXVII* § 164–65, ed. Carlo Guido Mor, in *Statuti della Valsesia*, pp. 203–204. Canonists of this period had little new to say about remarriage of widows and widowers. While they deplored remarriage on the grounds that it displayed an unseemly desire for continued sex after the death of a prior spouse, authorities admitted that remarriages were commonplace, that they were preferable to fornication, and that they were permitted by ecclesiastical law; Joannes Garonis, *De secundis nuptiis*, in TUJ* 6:82va–87rb; Johannes Bosch, *De nuptiis* 2:36–37, in TUJ* 6:4vb–5ra.

[110] Fortunius García de Erzilia, *Tractatus de ultimo fine iuris canonici et civilis* §§ 126, 128, in TUJ 1:13ra; Albericus de Rosate, *Vocabularius utriusque iuris longe castigatissimus*, s.v. *concubinatus* (Paris Johannes Cornilleau, 1525), fol. 51vb–52ra; Ludovicus Sardus, *De naturalibus liberis* 1.13, in TUJ* 6:249rb; Egidio Bossi, *Tractatus varii, qui omnem fere criminalem materiam excellenti doctrina complectuntur*, tit. *De coitu damnato* 76 (Venice: Apud Heredes I. M. Bonelli, 1574), fol. 189ra; Hieronymus Olives, *Commentaria et glossa* in Eleanora of Arborea, *Carta de logu, legum et ordinationum Sardarum* 50 (Calari: I. B. Canauera, 1708), p. 91.

[111] Nevizzani, *Sylva nuptialis*, fol. 69ra; *Sylvestrina* s.v. *concubinatus*, 1546 ed. 1:154; Ludovicus Sardus, *De naturalibus liberis* 1.9 and Antonio de Rosellis, *De legitimatione* 2.2, in TUJ* 6:249ra, 264vb–265ra; Rochus Curtius, *Tractatus de consuetudine* 84, in TUJ 1:127v; 5 Lateran Council (1514), Constitution *Supernae dispositionis*, in COD, p. 599.

suaded towns and cities in many regions to outlaw the practice and to impose sanctions on men who continued to cohabit with women to whom they were not married. As early as 1387, Cremona had forbidden men to keep harlots as concubines, and in many cities during the fifteenth century it became a crime to keep a concubine.[112] The offense was compounded and the penalties increased if the offender was a married man.[113] Both Courts Christian and secular tribunals regularly took action against couples suspected of living in sin. Those convicted—and convictions were routine—were usually punished by fines, sometimes supplemented by public penitential acts, such as offering a candle during Mass or marching barefoot and in penitential garb around the Church during services on Sundays or feast days.[114]

It was presumably no coincidence that precisely during the period when concubinage was beginning to be regarded as illegal, the practice of dealing with these relationships by abjuration *sub pena nubendi* commenced to disappear. Although not uncommon, at least in fourteenth-century English courts, abjuration diminished in frequency from about the beginning of the fifteenth century. By the end of that century it had virtually vanished.[115] Fifteenth-century canonists, instead, departed from the doctrine of their predecessors and began to teach that long-continued cohabitation created a presumption of

[112] *Statuta civitatis Cremonae* 117 (Cremona: Apud C. Draconium & P. Bozolam et socios, 1578), p. 42 (but cf. c. 112, p. 40); *Statuta communitatis Bergomi* 9.74 (Brescia: Angelus et Jacobus Britannicus, 1490), fol. 143v; Reggio Emilia, *Statuta* 7.5, fol. 291v; Urbino, *Statuta* 4.39, fol. 91r; Avignon, police ordinances (1458) art. 9, in LePilleur, *Prostitution*, p. 13; Löwenstein, *Bekämpfung*, pp. 19–22, cites similar statutes from Ulm (1364), Würzburg (1393), Schlettstatt in Alsace (1418), Frankfurt a/M (15th cent.), Bern (1459), and Basel (1448, 1498). See also Albericus de Rosate, *Vocabularium*, s.v. *concubinatus*, fol. 52ra, and Boulting, *Woman in Italy*, p. 279.

[113] Borgosesia, *Statuta* 163, ed. Mor, p. 203; Faenza, *Ordinamenta* 4.23, fol. 41r; Lucca, *Statuta* 4.106, fol. 217v; Perugia, *Statuta* 3.83, fol. 33va; Rieti, *Statuta* 3.18, fol. 38v; *Statuti di Forli* 3.18, quoted in Evelina Rinaldi, "La donna negli statuti del commune di Forli, sec. XIV," *Studi storici* 18 (1909) 191 n. 1; edict of the Bishop of Avignon (1448) in LePilleur, *Prostitution*, p. 10; Bossi, *Tractatus varii*, tit. *De coitu damnato* 22, 26, fol. 186rb–vb.

[114] Venice, decree of the Council of Ten, 17 June 1355, in *Leggi e memorie*, p. 203; Lévy, "L'officialité de Paris," p. 1283 n. 134; Ourliac, "Notes sur le mariage," p. 61; Raine, *Depositions*, pp. 34, 53–54; Elvey, *Courts of the Archdeaconry of Buckingham*, no. 338, p. 246; Bannister, "Visitation Returns," 44 (1929) 281–82, 288–89, and 45 (1930) 100, 444, 449–50; *Before the Bawdy Court: Selections from Church Court and Other Records Relating to the Correction of Moral Offences in England, Scotland, and New England, 1300–1800*, ed. Paul Hair, no. 36, 519 (London: Elek, 1972), pp. 45, 200. Saustra c. Barbo was a concubinage case of some complexity, in which the couple had lived together, parted, and then reconciled; there was some question as to whether they had married clandestinely and there was an appeal to Canterbury, which was declared frivolous; see E.D.R., D/2/1, fol. 39v–40r, 87r, 91v.

[115] Helmholz, *Marriage Litigation*, pp. 180–81.

marriage, a presumption that in many cases must have been virtually impossible to rebut.[116]

In addition to facing penances and secular sanctions, men who kept concubines might find themselves disadvantaged in other ways. According to Bartolomeo Cipolla (d. 1477), for example, a tenant who introduced his concubine into premises that he had leased thereby violated an implicit term of his agreement and was liable to lose his title to the leased property and to be summarily evicted by his landlord.[117] A married man who kept a concubine might also pay dearly for his pleasure since, according to an opinion of Paulus de Castro (fl. 1400), this entitled his wife to secure a separation and to recover her dowry in full.[118] Concubines themselves were already disadvantaged, but their situation worsened during this period. Fourteenth-century Sardinian customary law as embodied in the *Carta de logu*, for example, incorporated a Roman law rule that a concubine who removed property from premises that belonged to her consort was guilty of theft.[119] She was forbidden to testify in court and, at least in theory, ineligible to receive legacies or to inherit from her lover's estate, although it is clear that in practice this last provision was not regularly enforced.[120] Her children were also theoretically ineligible to benefit from their father's estate unless, of course, she had regularized their relationship by marriage.[121]

The volume of cases in the courts, however, suggests that concubinage remained common long after systematic measures were taken to repress it. This suggests that the institution met a continuing social need. It is reasonable to suspect that in many cases concubinage represented a viable alternative to marriage for those who lacked the resources to enter into more formal and conventional relationships.[122] Certainly this was not always true, however, for some

---

[116] Panormitanus, *Comm.* to X 1.21.6; Bartolomeo Cipolla, *Tractatus cautelarum* 251.3, in his *Varii et perutiles tractatus* (Venice: Apud haeredes Petri Dehucini, 1586), fol. 310ra.

[117] Cipolla, *Tractatus de servitutis urbanae* 5.5, in *Varii et perutiles tractatus*, fol. 6rb–va.

[118] Paulus de Castro, *Consilia* 392.

[119] *Carta de logu* 50, p. 91; the lover was also obliged to respect his concubine's property, however.

[120] Baldus, *Comm.* to X 1.33.7 § 4 and 2.20.24 § 3, fol. 119va, 198va; Simone da Borsano, *Lectura* to Clem., proem., pars prima, ed. Domenico Maffei, "Dottori e studenti nel pensiero di Simone da Borsano," *Studia Gratiana* 15 (1972) 242; Boulting, *Woman in Italy*, p. 279.

[121] Baldus, *Comm.* to X 1.6.20 § 10, fol. 64ra; Cipolla, *Tractatus cautelarum* 250.1, fol. 309rb; Martino Garazzi, *De legitimatione* 48, in TUJ* 6:281ra.

[122] Jeay, "Sexuality and Family," p. 339. This was certainly true; for example, in Sardinia, the poor continued until quite recently to live in concubinage because they could not afford marriage. Centuries of denunciation by Church authorities also wrought little change in Sardinian marriage customs; John Day, "On the Status of Women in Medieval Sardinia," in *Women of the Medieval World*, pp. 312–13.

men were able to furnish dowries for their concubines and to provide them with annual pensions.[123]

Sexual Offenses in the Fourteenth and Fifteenth Centuries
FORNICATION AND ADULTERY

The popular belief that simple fornication between unmarried persons was neither a sin nor a crime persisted, although this had been classified formally as heresy since 1287. Inquisitors almost routinely noted that persons of unorthodox religious persuasion professed this belief; but it is quite possible that those who did so were merely reflecting a notion nearly as widespread among faithful Catholics as among the heterodox.[124] It must have been common knowledge by this period, however, even among the simple and unlettered, that Church courts required men who seduced unmarried women to provide them with dowries and likewise to make reparation for their action. In addition, the Courts Christian routinely imposed fines, whippings, and participation in penitential processions upon those found guilty of illicit sex.[125] Such actions were commonplace in the lower ecclesiastical courts, and it is difficult to believe that many people were ignorant of this.[126]

Although it had long been true that Church courts exercised jurisdiction over simple fornication, the late fourteenth and fifteenth centuries saw the intrusion of secular law into this domain as well as into the others previously mentioned. A good many cities adopted local statutes and ordinances providing punishment for adultery, fornication, and other common types of nonmarital sex.[127] In addition, towns often expressly prohibited fornication in certain spe-

[123] Philippe Wolff, "Quelques actes notariés concernant famille et mariage (XIVe–XVe siècles)," *Annales du Midi* 78 (1966) 122–23.

[124] Jean Gerson, *Sermon contre la luxure*, ed. Glorieux 7:817; Andrea Alciati, *Tractatus de praesumptioibus* 3.26.2 (Venice: Apud C. de Tridino Montisferrati, 1564), fol. 122vb. San Bernardino, *Le prediche volgari* 20, p. 433; *Sylvestrina*, s.v. *Luxuria*, 2:163; Etienne Aufréri, *Decisiones* 346, fol. 83r–v; Lerner, *Heresy of the Free Spirit*, pp. 150, 176; De Waha, "Note," pp. 9–10; Y.-B. Brissaud, "L'infanticide à la fin du moyen âge, ses motivations psychologiques et sa répression," RHDF, 4th ser., 50 (1972) 232; Lea, *Hist. of Auricular Confession* 2:420, 253 n. 4.

[125] Nevizzani, *Sylva nuptialis*, fol. 56vb–57rb; Petrus de Ancharano, *Comm.* to X 5.16.1, 1580/81 ed. 5:87; Richard M. Wunderli, *London Church Courts and Society on the Eve of the Reformation*, Speculum Anniversary Monoographs, no. 7 (Cambridge, MA: Medieval Academy of America, 1981), pp. 15, 33.

[126] E.g., Raine, *Depositions*, pp. 26–28, 35–36, 47–48; Elvey, *Courts of the Archdeaconry of Buckingham*, nos. 20, 112, 117, 268, 358, pp. 22, 81, 123, 188, 269; Paulus de Castro, *Consilia*, no. 228.

[127] Paulus Grillandus, *De penis* 9.3, in TUJ* 10:31rb; Fortunius García, *Tractatus de ultimo fine iuris*, 124, in TUJ 1:12vb–13ra; *Constitutiones siue statuta magnificae ciuitatis Anconae, nouissime decreto Senatus impressa* 3.12 (Ancona: Excudebat A. de

cial situations—Agliè and Lesolo, for example, penalized fornication in the house of one's lord or employer, and other cities made it an offense to seduce or have intercourse with the servants of another.[128] Belluno, however, specifically exempted from punishment men who had sex with servant women in their own households, at least so long as the women agreed to their masters' proposition.[129] Still other cities only penalized fornicators who belonged to specific occupational groups—jailers, for example, were prohibited from having sexual intercourse with women prisoners; Perugia banned fornication by doctors, barbers, tailors, and other craftsmen who visited the houses of their clients, while at Rieti millers were specifically forbidden to molest female patrons.[130] Fornication with non-Christians was severely punished: sex between Christians and Jews, for example, carried a fine of £1000 at Perugia, payable within twenty days of conviction; those who failed to pay might be burnt alive. Modena imposed the death penalty and confiscation of all assets for intercourse with Saracens; if the offender was a public prostitute, however, the penalty was mitigated to life imprisonment and forfeiture of all property.[131] Still, even so rigidly orthodox a writer as Martín de Azpilcueta (1492–1586) could advise his readers that it was better for a Catholic to fornicate with a heretic than to marry one.[132] Belluno prescribed the death penalty for men who had sex with girls under the age of ten, but levied only a fine for sexual molestation if they stopped short of intercourse.[133] That city also adopted special statutes penalizing fornication with widows or virgins and sex play of any sort with a woman who was married to another man.[134] Conviction rates on fornication charges, however, were sometimes very low. The London commisary courts of the late fifteenth century showed convictions in less than twenty percent of the fornication cases that they heard, although after 1500 the conviction rate rose to about one-third of the cases.[135]

Grandis, 1566), p. 84; Bergamo, *Statuta* 9.72, fol. 143v; Cremona, *Statuta* 109, pp. 39–40; Cuneo, *Corpus statutorum* 6.429, ed. Camilla, p. 225; Faenza, *Ordinamenta* 4.23, fol. 41v; Lucca, *Statuta* 4.102, 105, fol. 215v, 217v; *Libri quinque statutorum inclytae civitatis Mutinae* 3.65 (Modena: Excudebat I. de Nicolis, 1547), fol. 80v–81r; Pesaro, *Statuta* 4.38, fol. 54r–v; Urbino, *Statuta* 4.39, fol. 90v.

[128] *Capitula et statuta terre Alladij* 45 and *Statuta et capitula loci Lezuli* 5, in *Corpus statutorum Canavisii* 1:116, 2:413; Lucca, *Statuta* 4:103–105, fol. 216v–217r; Urbino, *Statuta* 4.39, fol. 91r–v.

[129] Belluno, *Ius municipale*, lib. 3, tit. *De adulteriis*, c. 19, fol. 83v.

[130] Bossi, *Tractatus varii*, tit. *De coitu damnato* 40, fol. 187va; Petrus Grillandus, *De penis* 13.1, in TUJ* 10:33vb; Perugia, *Statuta* 3.90, fol. 34vb; Rieti, *Statuta* 3.58, fol. 50r.

[131] Perugia, *Statuta* 3.91, fol. 35ra; Modena, *Statuta* 3.63, fol. 80r.

[132] Martín de Azpilceuta, *Consilia* 4.1.5.10, in his *Opera hactenus inedita*, 3 vols. (Lyon: Apud haeredes Gulielmi Rovilii, 1589–94) 3/2:5.

[133] Belluno, *Ius municipale*, lib. 3, tit. *De adulteriis*, c. 12, 15, fol. 82v–83r.

[134] Belluno, *Ius municipale*, lib. 3, tit. *De adulteriis*, c. 8, 16, fol. 82v, 83v.

[135] Wunderli, *London Church Courts*, p. 92.

In theory, at least, adultery continued to be a much more serious offense than simple fornication—Alessandro Tartagni (1424–71) held that it was more serious than rape, while Egidio Bellamera considered it the most heinous of all sex crimes, comparable in gravity to heresy.[136] Even animals show indignation at those who made sexual advances to their mates, declared Giovanni Nevizzani, who regretfully noted that adultery was no longer punishable by death.[137]

In reality, adultery was rarely punished as severely as either ecclesiastical or civic authorities said it should be. The sixteenth-century Neapolitan jurist, Paulus Grillandus, accurately reflected current practice when he numbered it among the lesser crimes. Offenders convicted of adultery were often punished no more severely than those found guilty of simple fornication—fines, penitential processions, and public whippings were the commonest penalties, although in aggravated cases, especially with prominent families involved, the death penalty was occasionally imposed.[138] Several authorities maintained that when a woman committed adultery, her husband was at fault and should be punished as much or more than she was, but I have yet to see a case in which that was done.[139] It was not altogether uncommon, however, for the male adulterer to be charged, while his female accomplice was not. This does not necessarily mean, however, that she escaped scot free, but rather may indicate that it was customary in many places for adulteresses to be dealt with privately by their husbands or families, while the man was turned over to the courts. Adulteresses who were brought to court tended to be punished more severely than their male companions, as Eleanora of Arborea (ca. 1350–ca. 1403) noted.[140] Legal commentators reflected common practice when they stated that actual intercourse was not essential to the crime of adultery—wanton kisses and embraces, fondling of the breasts, and other types of sex play were sufficient to sustain a complaint of adultery, according to Baldus degli Ubaldi (ca. 1327–1400). In practice, finding a married woman alone with another man was sufficient proof of

[136]Alessandro Tartagni, *Consilia* 24, 62 (Venice: Bernardinus Stagninus, 1488), fol. 16va, 67rb; Aegidius Bellamera, *Comm.* to C. 32 q. 7 c. 15, 1580 ed. 3:55rb.

[137]Nevizzani, *Silva nuptialis*, fol. 9ra, 14vb.

[138]Grillandus, *De penis* 6.6, in TUJ* 10:29vb; Helmholz, *Marriage Litigation*, pp. 182–83, 185, and "Infanticide in the Province of Canterbury During the Fifteenth Century," *History of Childhood Quarterly* 2 (1975) 384; Wunderli, *London Church Courts*, p. 88; Gottlieb, "Meaning of Clandestine Marriage," p. 67; Werner L. Gundesheimer, *Ferrara: The Style of a Renaissance Despotism* (Princeton: Princeton University Press, 1973), pp. 78–79; Ruggiero, "Sexual Criminality," p. 24, and *Boundaries of Eros*, pp. 45–64.

[139]Gerson, *Sermon contre la luxure*, ed. Glorieux 7:819; Nevizzani, *Silva nuptialis*, fol. 85rb; Joannes Montaigne, *De bigamia* 2.8, in TUJ* 14:108ra.

[140]Hieronimus Olives, *Comm.* to *Carta de logu* 22, p. 58. Ruggiero, *Boundaries of Eros*, pp. 54–55, shows that Venetian practice in this respect changed fairly suddenly in the mid-fourteenth century. Prior to that time the adulteress was rarely charged; after the beginning of the 1360s, however, it became increasingly common to penalize her as well as her partner in crime.

adultery to satisfy many courts.[141] Even the fact that a married woman went out alone at night or attended parties without her husband might be adequate foundation for an adultery charge, according to Giovanni Nevizzani.[142]

In a continuing extramarital affair, each act of intercourse or sex play theoretically counted as a separate offense and lies told in order to hide the offense could also be taken into account when determining punishment. On this last point, Martín de Azpilceuta maintained that a woman whose husband, sword in hand, threatened to kill her for adultery was entitled to lie in order to save her life.[143] In Sardinian customary law, the location where adultery took place affected the penalty imposed: a married woman who slept with another man in the man's house was punished more lightly than if she received her lover in her husband's dwelling.[144]

In addition to other penalties, adultery could result in substantial financial loss. Adulterous wives forfeited their claims to the estates of their husbands, and their offense also revoked any *inter vivos* gifts they had received from him prior to marriage.[145] On the other hand a husband who killed his adulterous wife, while he escaped criminal penalties for homicide, also forfeited his claims to her dowry.[146] A male adulterer whose married mistress conceived a child, moreover, was obliged to compensate his paramour's husband for expenses incurred in raising the child. If the child was placed in an orphanage, the adulterer was obliged to defray the institution's costs. But Silvestro Mazzolini added, "If the adulterer is in doubt, because the woman is flighty and has committed adultery with others, this may be left to God's judgment."[147]

A great many municipalities during this period enacted criminal statutes against adultery. Male adulterers were subject to a fine, often quite a heavy one, while their mistresses frequently became liable to physical punishment—whipping was common—and might have their heads shaved or be exiled from the city for a period of time; the dowry was usually forfeited to the husband.[148]

[141] Baldus, *Comm.* to X 1.38.5 § 4, fol. 127ra; Bossi, *Tractatus varii,* tit. *De coitu damnato* 57, fol. 188ra; Nevizzani, *Silva nuptialis,* fol. 15vb–16ra; Hieronymus Olives, *Comm.* to *Carta de Logu* 22, pp. 57–58; Ourliac, "Notes," p. 60.

[142] Nevizzani, *Silva nuptialis,* fol. 79rb.

[143] Martín de Azpilceuta, *Comm.* to C. 22 q. 5 c. 11, in his *Opera* 1:422–23; Baldus, *Comm.* to X 2.20.9 § 3, fol. 195ra; Rochus Curtius, *Tractatus de consuetudine* 72, in TUJ 1:127v.

[144] Eleanora of Arborea, *Carta de logu* 22, p. 58.

[145] Baldus, *Comm.* to X 1.14.10 §§ 6–7 and 1.38.5 § 4, fol. 52va, 127ra; *Die Summa legum brevis, levis, et utilis des sogenannten Doctor Raymundus von Wiener-Neustadt* 1.30, 2.36, ed. Alexander Gál, 2 vols. (Weimar: Hermann Böhlaus Nachfolger, 1926) 1:187–91, 300; *Sylvestrina,* s.v. *Adulterium,* 1:31.

[146] Ulrich Zasius, *In celeberrimos aliquot titulos ff. ennarationes, non modo ad iuris veteris lucem cogitationemque, sed et aeque ad palatiorum et fori praxim supra fide conferentes* to Dig. 24.3.10.1 § 6 (Lyon: Excudebat N. Bonhomme, 1548), fol. 16va.

[147] *Sylvestrina,* s.v. *Adulterium,* 1:31: "Si autem dubitat adulter ex eo quod mulier sit levis et cum aliis adulteratur, relinquatur iudicio Dei."

[148] Ancona, *Constitutiones* 3.12, p. 83; Belluno, *Ius municipale,* lib. 3, tit. *De adulter-*

Perugia's statutes limited the number of times that a man might be penalized for adultery to once per month—the purpose, apparently, was to prevent men who carried on long-term affairs with married women from being charged with a separate offense for each contact.[149]

PROSTITUTION AS A PUBLIC UTILITY

The legal status of prostitution changed radically during the late fourteenth and fifteenth centuries. Efforts to reform prostitutes diminished sharply during this era, and penalties attached to the practice of prostitution became little more than anachronisms in many places.[150] Most striking of all was the transformation of prostitution into a public utility[151] and the involvement of town and city governments, particularly in southern Europe, in the ownership and operation of brothels.

Prostitutes during this period fell into four distinct categories. The top tier consisted of the inmates of public brothels, which had been almost unheard-of in medieval Europe prior to this time. These institutions were owned by a municipality and managed by public officials. As municipal enterprises, these houses received official protection, and their inmates in effect worked for the community. Towns often realized significant profits from these operations. The second class comprised those who worked in bathhouses, or stews. Bathhouses were usually privately owned, operated for profit, and frequently attracted investment from respectable persons of rank and social standing. Third came the strumpets who worked in bordellos, small-scale operations kept by madames who were usually retired whores. Bordellos were privately owned, often by the

---

iis, c. 7, fol. 82r–v; Lucca, *Statuta* 4.56, 99, fol. 201v, 214v–215r; *Consuetudines nobilis civitatis Messanae suisque districtus* 43 (Venice: D. & G. B. Guerra, sumptibus L. Pelugi, 1575), p. 18; Modena, *Statuta* 3.64, fol. 80r–v; *Reformationes et decreta civitatis Vrbiueteris super mercedibus officialium* 3.26 (Rome: Apud heredes A. Bladij, 1581?), p. 174; Perugia, *Statuta* 3.81, 83, fol. 33ra–va; Piacenza, *Statuta* 5.41; Reggio Emilia, *Statuta* 3.53, fol. 159v–160r; Urbino, *Statuta* 4.39, fol. 90r; Valsesia, *Statuta* 4.180, 184, pp. 105–106; Cuneo, *Corpus statutorum* 6.429, pp. 224–25; *Statuti communis et hominum Sancti Georgii* 35 (second recension), in *Corpus statutorum Canavisii* 3:285; Rinaldi, "La donna negli statuti di Forlì," p. 189; Oliveira Marques, *Daily Life in Portugal*, pp. 177–78.

[149] Perugia, *Statuta* 3.82, fol. 33rb: "Quicumque vero cognoverit uxorem alterius solvat communi perusii pene nomine CC. lib. den. etiam si de pluribus vicibus accusetur in eadem accusatione, nec accusari nec condemnari possit nisi pro una commissione adulterii mense quolibet."

[150] Geremek, "Marginaux," pp. 240–41. In London relatively few women were charged with prostitution—they averaged less than nine a year between 1471 and 1514—and of the 377 charges brought in that period, only ten resulted in convictions; Wunderli, *London Church Courts*, p. 100.

[151] The notion that the prostitute served a useful public function was, of course, an old one and earlier authors sometimes used the term *publica utilitas* to describe her. See above, pp. 463–64.

madames themselves. At the lowest end of the scale were the streetwalkers, essentially individual entrepreneurs although frequently managed by and dependent on a pimp, who was simultaneously their protector, business manager, lover, parasite, and abuser.[152]

Both the social and the legal situation of the prostitute depended upon which category she belonged to. Prostitutes who worked in municipal brothels were not merely tolerated, but often enjoyed protection and even some civic privileges. Lucca accorded them the right of citizenship in 1534.[153] Other prostitutes were not usually so well treated as their sisters in Lucca, but toleration was the general rule. When the *Adel* and burghers of Oberhanheim were quarreling over the division of the income from their whorehouse in 1517, the legal opinion in the case observed that it was the universal practice to tolerate these institutions because, "It is a lesser evil that lecherous men take out their lust on common women or whores than on the wives and daughters of the citizens."[154]

Official prostitutes, who worked in municipal brothels or were licensed by civic authorities, were presumably only a fraction, possibly quite a small fraction, of the women whose sexual services could be had on a commercial basis. It is difficult to estimate the numbers of prostitutes active at any given place and time, since their numbers varied considerably depending upon the way in which the category was defined. At Venice a directory of local harlots was published early in the sixteenth century, giving their names, addresses, and fees. The guide listed 210 women, whose price per "trick" ranged from one-half *scudo* (Elena Rossi) to thirty *scudi* (Paulina Filla Canevo).[155] The list is probably incomplete, for the number of entries is extraordinarily low for a city the size of Venice in this period. A recent study of prostitutes at Dijon in the fifteenth century showed that most were local women and roughly four-fifths were the daughters or widows of artisans or manual laborers. Most of the Dijon whores entered the life at about age seventeen and nearly half reported that they had been forced into prostitution. Almost a quarter of the group were apparently prostituted by their families and more than a quarter had been victims of rape.[156] London's regulated brothels were located across the river from the city

---

[152] Rossiaud, "Prostitution, Youth, and Society," pp. 2–4; Carlo M. Cipolla, *Before the Industrial Revolution: European Society and Economy, 1000–1700* (New York: W.W. Norton, 1976), p. 84.

[153] Boulting, *Woman in Italy*, p. 295.

[154] Quoted in Schrank, *Prostitution in Wien*, p. 66: "Minus autem mali esse, ut libidinem suam incontinentes expleant in vulgaribus mulieribus sive prostibulis, quam in alienis matronis et filiabus." See also Petrus de Ancharano, *Comm.* to X 4.1.20, 1580/81 ed., 4:18; Oliveira Marques, *Daily Life in Portugal*, pp. 178–79.

[155] *Leggi e memorie Venete*, pp. 3–9; Boulting, *Woman in Italy*, p. 310.

[156] Rossiaud, "Prostitution, Youth, and Society," p. 19; Leah Lydia Otis, *Prostitution in Medieval Society: The History of an Urban Institution in Languedoc* (Chicago: University of Chicago Press, 1985), pp. 63–72; Cipolla, *Before the Industrial Revolution*, pp. 85–86; Carol Z. Wiener, "Sex Roles and Crime in Late Elizabethan Hertfordshire,"

in a section of Southwark known as Stewside, where eighteen establishments were situated at the end of the fifteenth century.[157] We know little about the working conditions and social history of prostitutes in rural areas.

Economic details of late medieval prostitution are difficult to pin down, but municipal brothels often produced profits and the operators of bathhouses apparently realized substantial returns. Small-scale private establishments apparently were less attractive investments—Florentine tax records show, for example, that in 1433 Antonia and Piero di Simone Brunelleschi, a mother and son who owned two houses inhabited by prostitutes, made four florins a month. A well-connected entrepreneur, Rosso di Giovanni di Niccolo de' Medici, who let out six rooms to prostitutes in one of the houses that he owned, got between ten and thirteen lire per month.[158] The income of individual harlots was presumably highly variable. Giovanni Nevizzani observed that beauties could be had for a trifling price and he was probably right. Moralists decreed that prostitutes must charge no more than a just price for their services, but they failed to specify how that price could be determined.[159]

Legal writers continued to maintain that the law should protect the property that prostitutes gained from their occupation. Francis de Platea (d. 1460), while discussing prostitutes' property rights, addressed the intriguing question of the ownership of property acquired by a nun who was also a prostitute. He concluded that she ought to remit her fees to her convent; the convent, however, should not retain the money, but should use it to support pious causes.[160] The earnings of prostitutes were generally subject to taxes levied by municipal authorities; ecclesiastical bodies also taxed prostitutes occasionally for the benefit of religious causes.[161]

Journal of Social History 8 (1974/75) 41–42; Rashdall, *Universities* 1:578 n. 1; Gene A. Brucker, *The Society of Renaissance Florence: A Documentary Study* (New York: Harper Torchbooks, 1971), pp. 196–97; Bernard Guillemain, *La cour pontifical d'Avignon, 1309–1376: Etude d'une société* (Paris: E. de Boccard, 1966), p. 540.

[157] Wunderli, *London Church Courts*, p. 97. For a splendid contemporary description of a London harlot see John Skelton's "The Tunning of Elinor Rumming," in his *Complete English Poems*, ed. John Scattergood (Harmondsworth, Middlesex: Penguin, 1983), pp. 214–30.

[158] Brucker, *Society of Renaissance Florence*, pp. 190–91.

[159] Nevizzani, *Silva nuptialis*, fol. 8vb; Dennis Doherty, *The Sexual Doctrine of Cardinal Cajetan*, Studien zur Geschichte der katholischen Moraltheologie, vol. 12 (Regensburg: F. Pustet, 1966), p. 102 n. 35.

[160] Franciscus de Platea, *Opus restitutionum* 52–53 (Venice: Johannes de Colonia & Johann Manthen, 1474; unfoliated); Nevizzani, *Silva nuptialis*, fol. 41rb. Evidence about the lively sex life of some Venetian convents in this era indicates that this problem was neither fanciful nor trivial; Ruggiero, *Boundaries of Eros*, pp. 75–81.

[161] Perugia, *Statuta* 1.422, fol. 104vb; Salvatore di Giacomo, *La prostituzione in Napoli nei secoli XV, XVI, e XVII: Documenti inediti* (Naples: Riccardo Marghieri, 1899), pp. 38–40; Cipolla, *Before the Industrial Revolution*, p. 87.

Some cities restricted the financial activities of their prostitutes. Venice, for example, imposed a limit on the debts that prostitutes could assume. Should they fail to repay their obligations on schedule, they might be jailed.[162]

Despite financial limitations, lively competition for trade, and generally low fees for their services, some late medieval harlots accumulated substantial amounts of property. The last will and testament of Claudie Fabrie, a whore in the brothel of Beaucaire, dated 1 July 1492, shows that she was reasonably prosperous. Her will gave directions for her funeral, together with bequests for that service and for the priest who heard her last confession, stipends for anniversary Masses, and a number of charitable bequests. In addition she left legacies to another harlot, Agnes Cornegrasse, to her brother, who was a notary, to her husband, and to one Jacques Torrelli, alias Cassolet, whom she described as her "faithful friend" and who may well have been her pimp.[163]

Prostitution in many parts of Europe was regulated during this period by confining prostitutes to specified sections of cities, by dictating the kinds of clothing they could wear, and by limiting some other aspects of their trade.[164] Restrictions on dwelling places of harlots were common throughout the fourteenth and fifteenth centuries. Statutes designated specific neighborhoods where whores could legally dwell and often provided that those who set up shop elsewhere could be expelled from their houses if their neighbors filed a complaint. A few towns required all prostitutes to live in the public brothel, presumably in an effort to secure a monopoly. The quarter set aside for prostitutes was often a region with a high crime rate and civic authorities seem to have hoped to confine noise, rowdiness, and disturbances to a single zone within the city. Piacenza attempted to deal with the problem by exiling its prostitutes to the suburbs, but how well this worked is unclear.[165] Many cities regulated the appearance of their whores. Sumptuary statutes often specified that respectable women were forbidden to wear the particular colors, types of cloth, or styles of dress reserved for trollops. A few places also required women of ill-

[162] *Leggi e memorie Venete*, p. 40; Petrus de Monte, *Repertorium*, s.v. *Meretrix*, fol. 55ra.

[163] Text in LePilleur, *Prostitution*, pp. 139–41; see also Otis, *Prostitution*, pp. 65–66, for other examples of well-to-do-prostitutes.

[164] Bullough, *Hist. of Prostitution*, p. 114; Rossiaud, "Prostitution, sexualité, société," p. 70.

[165] Ancona, *Constitutiones* 4.10, p. 123; Bergamo, *Statuta* 10.50, fol. 178r; Cremona, *Statuta* 114, p. 41; *Statuta Mediolani*, 2 vols. (Milan: Impressum apud A. Minutianum, impensis P.M. & B. fratrum de Bugatis, 1512) 2:146r–147v; Modena, *Statuta* 3.67, fol. 81r; *Statuta Novariae*, lib. 1, tit. *Quod meretrices expelluntur* (Milan: Impressum per J. de Castelliono, 1511), fol. 83v; Parma, *Statuta* 4.81, fol. 157r; Perugia, *Statuta* 4.109, fol. 30rb–va; Piacenza, *Statuta* 1.36; Reggio Emilia, *Statuta* 7.3, 4, 7, fol. 290r–292v; Urbino, *Statuta* 5.35, fol. 108r; *Ordonnances des rois* 6:611; LePilleur, *Prostitution*, pp. 12–13; Oliveira Marques, *Daily Life in Portugal*, p. 179; Bellamy, *Crime and Public Order*, pp. 60–61; Bullough, *Hist. of Prostitution*, pp. 113–14.

repute to wear an arm band or other insignia when they appeared in public. The rationale advanced for these regulations was usually that they would protect honest girls and matrons from importunings and propositions by lechers on the streets.[166] Several towns forbade prostitutes to appear in public during certain seasons. Nîmes required them to stay indoors during Holy Week under pain of a fine. Todi banned them from the streets every day of the week save Saturday, and those who showed themselves on other days might be publicly whipped. French towns closed their brothels during periods of epidemic disease as a public health measure.[167] A few places tried to limit the length of time that any particular prostitute might spend in the town.[168] Public solicitation by prostitutes troubled authorities in several cities. One way of controlling this was to exclude harlots from taverns and public eating-places. Venice seems to have been particularly sensitive on this issue, for the Senate of the Republic not only forbade prostitutes to eat or drink in public places, but also prohibited them from sleeping in taverns or hostels and denied them the right to sell wine in the city's brothels.[169] Florence finally forbade its prostitutes to engage in any other trade at all.[170]

Some cities also attempted to limit the clientele to whom prostitutes could offer their services. Avignon forbade Jews to enter public brothels under pain of losing a foot and forfeiting twenty-five *livres* for each offense. A synodal statute at Avignon also made it an offense for clerics or married men to frequent brothels: the penalty was excommunication plus a fine of twenty marks if the visit was at night. The fine was reduced to ten marks for daytime visits.[171] Ulm attempted to keep youngsters out of its sporting houses by penalizing boys under

[166] Ancona, *Constitutiones* 3.55, p. 99; Bergamo, *Statuta* 10.48, fol. 178r; Milan, *Statuta* 2:146v–147r; Orvieto, *Reformationes et decreta* 5.29, pp. 260–61; Reggio Emilia, *Statuta* 7.1, fol. 285r–289v; Venice, *Leggi e memorie*, pp. 35–36; *Ordonnances de rois* 7:327; LePilleur, *Prostitution*, pp. 4–5, 10–12, 32–33, 135–36; Hermann Kantorowicz and N. Denholm-Young, "De ornatu mulierum: A Consilium of Antonio de Rosellis with an Introduction on Fifteenth-Century Sumptuary Legislation," in Kantorowicz's *Rechtshistorische Schriften*, pp. 341–76; Oliveira Marques, *Daily Life in Portugal*, p. 179.

[167] Municipal edict of Nîmes, 1353, in LèPilleur, *Prostitution*, pp. 135–36; *Statuta civitatis Tudertine* 4.121 (Todi: Impressum per P.M. Thesori, 1549), fol. 125v–126r; Rossiaud, "Prostitution, sexualité, société," p. 69.

[168] The police statutes of Le Banoux (1407) required them to be on their way after one night, while the Bishop of Avignon in 1488 allowed them to stay at Barbentane for up to one week; LePilleur, *Prostitution*, pp. 6, 10.

[169] Albiano, *Statuta* (2d recension) 55, in *Corpus statutorum Canavisii* 1:40; Cremona, *Statuta* 123, p. 43; Cuneo, *Corpus statutorum* 3.210, pp. 116–17; Venice, *Leggi e memorie*, pp. 34, 42; Trexler, *Synodal Law*, p. 123.

[170] Florence (1558), *Legge delle meretrici del comprare da loro* (Florence: Giorgio Marescotti, 1575), pp. 3–4.

[171] LePilleur, *Prostitution*, pp. 6–7, 15–16, 33; Bossi, *Tractatus varii*, tit. *De coitu damnato* 24, fol. 186va; Hieronymus Olives, *Comm.* to *Carta de logu* 22, p. 58.

age fourteen who visited them.[172] In general, however, the clients of prostitutes were usually immune from prosecution or punishment, although Avignon attempted to prevent its brothels from being used as houses of assignation by forbidding proprietors of these establishments to allow men to bring their mistresses onto the premises for immoral purposes.[173] This curious solicitude for public morality was not unlike complaints made by the public prostitutes of Tarascon and Dijon, who apparently feared competition from free-lance practitioners outside of the public brothel and demanded that civic authorities take steps to curb debauchery.[174] Avignon seemingly witnessed fierce competition between public purveyors of sex as well, for the police ordinances of 1458 included a provision that forbade whores to drag men by force into brothels and to keep them against their will.[175]

The fifteenth century seems to have been the heyday of publicly operated prostitution. During this period a good many cities authorized public expenditure to build, maintain, and enlarge municipal brothels, while taking little interest in other types of public investment. A fair number of cities that operated public houses of prostitution, for instance, had no municipal schools. Both public and private brothels thrived during this century. Thus Dijon, for example, with a population numbering only about 2,500 in the city proper and less than 10,000 in the *baillage*, in 1485 not only maintained a public brothel, but also eighteen private bordellos, which seem to have been tolerated by their neighbors and were in no way marginal either to the civic or the economic life of the town.[176] At Seville early in the following century, brothels were clustered in the low-lying area next to the river and were clearly seen as profitable and respectable investments. Their owners included not only the town itself, but also several ecclesiastical corporations, including the cathedral chapter, religious communities, and hospitals, which leased them to private operators. A generation or two later Seville's public executioner leased no less than twenty brothels, which he sublet to individuals who operated them under the supervision of a municipal brothel manager. The city government, in other words, licensed individuals to keep houses of prostitution and required those who received licenses to take an oath to uphold the statutes governing their operation. The owners and operators of these establishments were esteemed as respectable citizens and described themselves as good Christians with no hint of embarrassment.[177] Similar situations were common in other European cities during

[172] Jung, *Geschlechtsmoral*, p. 218.

[173] Nevizzani, *Silva nuptialis*, fol. 57ra; LePilleur, *Prostitution*, p. 15.

[174] Rossiaud, "Prostitution, Youth, and Society," p. 5.

[175] Text in LePilleur, *Prostitution*, p. 15.

[176] Rossiaud, "Prostitution, sexualité, société," pp. 68, 78, 80; Otis, *Prostitution*, pp. 31–39, 51–52.

[177] Ruth Pike, *Aristocrats and Traders: Sevillian Society in the Sixteenth Century* (Ithaca, NY: Cornell University Press, 1972), pp. 203–206; Mary Elizabeth Perry, *Crime and Society in Early Modern Seville* (Hanover, NH: University Press of New England, 1980), pp. 192, 227–28, 231–32.

this period.[178] Not only did civic authorities operate and supervise brothels, but they also treated them as communal enterprises for civic purposes. Thus, when the Emperor Sigismund stopped at Bern on his way to the Council of Constance in 1414, the city fathers welcomed him and his entourage by opening the city's brothels to the emperor and his men free of charge. Similarly in 1509 Venice dispatched a thousand of its prostitutes at public expense to care for the sexual needs of its army at Mestre.[179]

Private establishments, especially "dishonest" bathhouses that doubled as brothels, were often in direct competition with the public facilities. The association between bathhouses and the practice of prostitution was notorious, and the expression "to go to the bathhouse" required no explanation—it had little to do with cleansing the body. The inventory of one fifteenth-century Avignonese bathhouse disclosed that the facility had a great many beds, but no bathtubs at all.[180] The identification was so close, indeed, that genuine bathing facilities had to distinguish themselves sharply from the commoner kind of bathhouse. Thus a new bathhouse at Avignon about 1446 spelled out the propriety of its operation with great care:

> Let everyone of whatever rank be aware that Genin de Geline or de Helme, otherwise known as de la Cerveleria, has established behind his house at Helme good and honest stews for bathing by good and honest women and that these are quite separate from the men's bath of de la Cerveleria . . . and that women will be well received and taken care of here by trustworthy ladies.[181]

Since town governments considered prostitution a civic industry, they were anxious to curb the activities of entrepreneurs who were not part of the local establishment. Statutes prohibited pimps from extorting money from prosti-

---

[178] Cremona, *Statuta* 110, 112, pp. 40, 42; Faenza, *Ordinamenta* 4.58, fol. 48v; Milan, *Statuta* 2:147r; Todi, *Statuta* 4.120, 123, fol. 125v–126r; Venice, *Leggi e memorie*, pp. 31–32; LePilleur, *Prostitution*, pp. 5, 18–19. Indeed, in 1608 the Dominicans of Perpignan were collecting alms to refurbish the city's brothel and allegedly described the building of sporting houses as "pious, holy, and deserving work"; Otis, "Prostitution and Repentance," p. 137.

[179] LePilleur, *Prostitution*, pp. 19–20, 70–71, 137; Elizabeth Pavan, "Police des moeurs, société et politique à Venise à la fin du moyen âge," *Revue historique* 264 (1980) 242, 257; Schrank, *Prostitution in Wien*, pp. 61, 73; Jung, *Geschlechtsmoral*, pp. 220, 222; Gustav Wustmann, "Frauenhäuser und freie Frauen in Leipzig im Mittelalter," *Archiv für Kulturgeschichte* 5 (1907) 469–82; Brucker, *Society of Renaissance Florence*, p. 190; Rossiaud, "Prostitution, Youth, and Society," pp. 4–5, 13; Otis, *Prostitution*, pp. 71–72.

[180] Rossiaud, "Prostitution, Youth, and Society," pp. 3–4; Lewinsohn, *Hist. of Sexual Customs*, p. 148.

[181] Text in LePilleur, *Prostitution*, p. 8: "Item quod tota persona de qualque istat ho condition que sié saupe que Genin de Geline ho de Helme, aliàs de la Cerveleria, a fait fire darier son hostal de Helme, estubas belas et honestas per estubar donas honorablas et honestas, lasqualas totalmen son desemparadas de las estubas de los homes de la Cer-

tutes and attempted to limit the activities of the men and women who recruited girls for the brothels. It is unlikely that this regulatory activity accomplished a great deal, for private brothels and streetwalkers seem to have been controlled almost everywhere by thugs and ruffians who lived off the earnings of prostitutes and practiced various kinds of extortion not only on the harlots, but also on their customers.[182] It is likewise doubtful whether occasional civic efforts to halt the process of selling women to the brothels—parents often did this—and forcibly holding them there resulted in any great diminution in the practice.[183]

By and large, prostitutes were not often prosecuted during this period for simply practicing their trade. Such prosecutions as there were seem to have been confined to England, where civic prostitution never caught on. The City of London even expelled its prostitutes in 1485 in an endeavor "to eschewe the stynkyng and horrible Synne of Lechery." As they settled just across the Thames in Southwark, the expulsion probably did little to achieve its nominal purpose. This fastidiousness was distinctly unusual: when prostitutes were prosecuted elsewhere in this period the circumstances usually suggest that the defendant had been guilty of setting up business without complying with local ordinances governing prostitutes.

Prostitutes were still disadvantaged, to be sure, but the disadvantages they suffered were in this period more often inflicted on them by their families than by public authorities.[184] Nor is there much evidence that the clients of prosti-

---

veleria, en las qualz se estubant homes, lasqualas estubas de donas an lor intrado devant l'ostal de Maistre Anthoni Carbonel, bédel de l'Estudi, per que touta dona honesta que l'y plaira de se anar estubar l'en poyria anar, car aqui sera recuillida ben et honestmen et bon merchant per donas honestas." See also Otis, *Prostitution*, pp. 98–99.

[182] *Constitutiones Marchiae Anconitanae* 1.8 (Faenza: Per I.M. de Simonetis, 1524), fol. 5r–v; Bergamo, *Statuta* 10.49, fol. 178r; Cremona, *Statuta* 118, 124, pp. 442–43; Faenza, *Ordinamenta* 1.8; Lucca, *Statuta* 4.108, fol. 222v; Modena, *Statuta* 3.66, fol. 81r; Orvieto, *Reformationes et decreta* 3.28, p. 175; Perugia, *Statuta* 3.88, fol. 34vb; Reggio Emilia, *Statuta* 7.6, 8, fol. 291v–293r; Urbino, *Statuta* 4.39, fol. 91r; LePilleur, *Prostitution*, p. 14; Elvey, *Courts of the Archdeaconry of Buckingham*, no. 292, p. 207; Hair, *Before the Bawdy Court*, no. 241, 533, pp. 110, 205; Brucker, *Society of Renaissance Florence*, pp. 199–201; DeLloyd J. Guth, "Enforcing Late-Medieval Law: Patterns in Litigation during Henry VII's Reign, in *Legal Records and the Historian: Papers Presented to the Cambridge Conference on Legal History, 7–10 July 1975*, ed. J. H. Baker (London: Royal Historical Society, 1978), pp. 92–93; Wunderli, *London Church Courts*, pp. 93–95; Marin-Muracciole, *L'honneur des femmes en Corse*, pp. 272–74; Oliveira Marques, *Daily Life in Portugal*, pp. 179–80; Rossiaud, "Prostitution, sexualité, société," p. 72; Pike, *Aristocrats and Traders*, p. 195.

[183] Cremona, *Statuta* 115–16, p. 41; Orvieto, *Reformationes et decreta* 3.19, p. 175; Parma, *Statuta* 6.54, fol. 128r; Rieti, *Statuta* 3.98, fol. 55r; Todi, *Statuta* 3.112, fol. 75r–v; Nevizzani, *Silva nuptialis*, fol. 74rb.

[184] *Calendar of Letter-Books Preserved Among the Archives of the City of London at the Guildhall: Letter-Book L, temp. Henry IV–Henry VII*, ed. Reginald L. Sharpe (Lon-

tutes were punished or harassed. Frequenting the brothel carried with it little or no dishonor or shame in fifteenth-century society, although clerics who did so openly might be reprimanded by Church authorities.[185] But public officials in this period were generally more interested in giving public protection to prostitutes, particularly those working in civic brothels, than in punishing them.

While legal writers continued to maintain that forcible ravishment of a whore was not rape, secular authorities acted differently. Prostitutes were frequently beaten, occasionally stabbed, and otherwise abused by clients; but the very fact that such assaults appear in court records and that some towns adopted ordinances forbidding attacks on harlots suggested that the whore who was assaulted had at least some recourse.[186]

Attempts to rescue prostitutes from a life of sin became less popular during the fourteenth and fifteenth centuries than earlier; perhaps they were also less successful. There is occasional evidence of reform at work—the city council of Avignon, for example, administered a small fund for rehabilitating prostitutes—but this is uncommon. One Florentine prostitute was offered money by her neighbors to relinquish her trade, but she refused to take it on the grounds that the sum was insufficient. At Paris, when Jean Tisserand established a refuge for reformed prostitutes in 1490, some poor women of the city set themselves up as

---

don: Printed by Order of the Corporation, 1912), p. 206; Elvey, *Courts of the Archdeaconry of Buckingham*, no. 103, 173, pp. 76, 121; Margaret Bowker, "Some Archdeacons' Court Books and the Commons' Supplication against the Ordinaries of 1532," in *The Study of Medieval Records: Essays in Honour of Kathleen Major*, ed. D. A. Bullough and R. L. Storey (Oxford: At the Clarendon Press, 1971), p. 306; Hair, *Before the Bawdy Court*, no. 67, 410, pp. 54, 167; Luigi Cibrario, *Economie politique au moyen âge*, 2 vols. (Paris: Guillaumin, 1859) 2:114; Boulting, *Woman in Italy*, p. 293; Guth, "Enforcing the Law," p. 12; Raymundus von Wiener-Neustadt, *Summa legum* 2.58, pp. 342–43.

[185] Ancona, *Constitutiones* 3.12, p. 54; Rossiaud, "Prostitution, sexualité, société," p. 70; Hair, *Before the Bawdy Court*, no. 456, p. 180. Bellamy, *Crime and Public Order*, p. 169, notes that one of medieval London's prisons, the Tun of Cornhill, was used almost exclusively for holding prostitutes, their employers, and their clients; see also his remarks on the punishment of prostitutes in England, pp. 182, 184–85.

[186] Petrus de Ancharano, *Comm.* to X 5.16.1, 1580/81 ed., 5:88; Nevizzani, *Silva nuptialis*, fol. 57ra, 74rb; Bossi, *Tractatus varii*, tit. *De raptu mulieris* 10, fol. 182vb; Petrus de Monte, *Repertorium*, s.v. *Meretrix, Raptor*, fol. 55ra–rb, 221va; Hieronymus Olives, *Comm.* to *Carta de logu* 21, p. 57. While Urbino, *Statuta* 4.40, fol. 91v, specifically disallowed penalties or claims for damages as a result of attacks on prostitutes or their property, other cities were more generous in granting harlots redress for injuries done to their persons and belongings; see Bergamo, *Statuta* 9.69, fol. 143r; Todi, *Statuta* 4.122, fol. 126r; Ruth Pike, "Crime and Criminals in Sixteenth-Century Seville," *Sixteenth Century Journal* 6 (1975) 9–10; Rossiaud, "Prostitution, sexualité, société," pp. 77–78.

harlots in order to qualify for admission to the institution.[187] Zeal for reform of bawdy women was distinctly on the wane in this era.[188]

RAPE AND ABDUCTION

The incidence of rape and abduction varied considerably between different areas of Europe in the late fourteenth and fifteenth centuries. In Venice, forcible coitus, abduction, and similar assaults were by far the most frequently entered sex offenses in the criminal records. Dijon, with a population well below 10,000, recorded twenty or more rape cases annually. Rape and abduction were also common in English records for the same period.[189] In Seville, on the other hand, abduction and rape seem to have been relatively rare, although perhaps they were simply underreported.[190] Rape and abduction charges seem to have been brought against upper-class males far more frequently than their numbers in the total population would warrant. We may infer from this that sexual attacks were more often reported when the perpetrator was wealthy and prominent than when the assailant belonged to the humbler orders. In any event, punishment of convicted rapists was often much less severe than the statutes prescribed. Fines, imprisonment for brief periods, or some combination of the two were the commonest penalties decreed by Venetian courts for convicted rapists. When compared with the savage mutilations and death sentences routinely handed down for robbery and other kinds of assault, these were very mild punishments indeed.[191] But there seems to have been a marked class bias in these cases: the higher the social status of the victim, the more severe the punishment. The courts dealt with sexual assaults on lower-class women as relatively trivial crimes, but treated sexual attacks upon women of the upper classes as a social peril that required savage reprisal.[192]

---

[187] LePilleur, *Prostitution*, p. 36; Rossiaud, "Prostitution, sexualité, société," p. 81; Brucker, *Society of Renaissance Florence*, pp. 191–95. Legal writers continued to repeat stock remarks about the spiritual merit of helping prostitutes to reform; see, e.g., Panormitanus, *Comm.* to X 4.1.20.

[188] The decline in the numbers of sisters in the Magdalen Convent at Perpignan after 1430, for example, bears this out, although it is impossible to say with certainty how general such declines may have been; Otis, "Prostitution and Repentance," p. 150.

[189] Rossiaud, "Prostitution, Youth, and Society," p. 6; Ruggiero, "Sexual Criminality," p. 20; Bellamy, *Crime and Public Order*, p. 58.

[190] Pike, "Crime and Criminals," pp. 10–11.

[191] Ruggiero, "Sexual Criminality," p. 20, and *Boundaries of Eros*, pp. 94–96. Sentences were not greatly different in England; John Jordan of London, for example, got off with a fine and banishment from the City for raping a fourteen-year-old girl in 1472; *Calendar of Letter-Books . . . Letter Book E*, p. 103.

[192] Egidio Bossi, *Tractatus varii*, tit. *De raptu mulieris* 1, fol. 181vb–182ra; Petrus Grillandus, *De penis* 10.1, in TUJ* 10:31va–vb; Petrus de Monte, *Repertorium* s.v. *Raptor*, fol. 221rb; Bellamy, *Crime and Public Order*, pp. 33, 194; Ruggiero, "Sexual Criminality," pp. 18, 20–21, 30; Rossiaud, "Prostitution, Youth, and Society," pp. 6–8.

Victims of sexual assaults were always women. The commentators declared that sexual attacks on men by women were either impossible or at least very unlikely, and the criminal records of the period agree. On the other hand, academic lawyers and some legislators also maintained that sexual assaults on all women—save for prostitutes—merited equal penalties, but courts failed to apply this egalitarian doctrine in practice.[193]

Municipalities often legislated extensively about rape, abduction, and related matters. Many prescribed the death penalty for most or all of these offenses. Belluno, after experimenting with lesser penalties, reinstated capital punishment for rape in 1428. A few towns, among them Agliè, Bergamo, and Faenza, prescribed graduated scales of punishment, calibrated to fit the circumstances of different cases. Penalties varied according to the marital status of the victim and of the perpetrator, the time and place of the offense, and the degree of malice involved. The customary law of Sardinia prescribed only a fine for rape, but provided that if the full amount of the fine was not paid within fifteen days of conviction the offender would lose a foot.[194] Jean LeCoq (d. ca. 1400) noted a rape case in which the defendant demanded the right to fight a duel with his accuser; the court rejected his demand, however, because the defendant was a cleric.[195] Several communities adopted statutes that voided rape prosecutions if both parties were unmarried and were willing to marry each other, provided that the woman's parents approved the match.[196] Academic lawyers taught that sexual molestation of a girl who had not yet reached puberty merited the death penalty under any circumstances. Lesser sexual assaults, such as kissing or fondling a woman without her consent, were also penalized, but did not warrant the death penalty. The statues of Bergamo provided that

[193] Ancona, *Constitutiones* 3.12, p. 83; Perugia, *Statuta* 3.82, fol. 33rb; Nevizzani, *Silva nuptialis*, fol. 52rb, 74ra; Bossi, *Tractatus varii*, tit. *De raptu mulieris* 10, fol. 183ra; Albericus de Rosate, *Vocabularius* s.v. *Raptus*, fol. 94rb–va; Petrus Grillandus, *De penis* 10.23, in TUJ* 10:32vb.

[194] Agliè, *Capitula et statuta* 50, in *Corpus statutorum Canavisii* 1:117; Ancona, *Constitutiones* 3.12, p. 83; Belluno, *Ius municipale*, lib. 3, tit. *De adulteriis*, c. 1, 2, 6, fol. 81v–82r; Bergamo, *Statuta* 9.67, fol. 142v–143r; Borgosesia, *Statuta* 38, ed. Mor, p. 159; Caluso, *Statuta* 30, in *Corpus statutorum Canavisii* 2:11; Cremona, *Statuta* c. 108, 111, pp. 39–40; Cuneo, *Corpus statutorum* 6.429, ed. Camilla, p. 225; Faenza, *Ordinamenta* 4.23, fol. 41r; Lessolo, *Statuta* 12, in *Corpus statutorum Canavisii* 2:414; Lucca, *Statuta* 4.99, 103, 104, fol. 214v, 216v–217r; Messina, *Consuetudines* 58, p. 24; Modena, *Statuta* 3.60, fol. 79r–v; Perugia, *Statuta* 3.82, fol. 33rb; Piacenza, *Statuta* 5.42; Urbino, *Statuta* 4.39, fol. 90r; Valsesia, *Statuta* 4.182, ed. Mor, p. 105; *Carta de logu* 21, p. 56; Wunderli, *London Church Courts*, p. 91.

[195] Jean LeCoq, *Questiones Johannis Galli*, no. 80, ed. Marguerite Boulett, Bibliothèque des écoles françaises d'Athènes et de Rome, fasc. 156 (Paris: E. de Boccard, 1944), pp. 95–97.

[196] Lucca, *Statuta* 4.102, fol. 215v; Parma, *Statuta* 3.57, fol. 128v; Reggio Emilia, *Statuta* 3.52, fol. 159r–v; Spoleto, *Statuta* 2.46, fol. 33r–v; Petrus de Ancharano, *Comm.* to X 5.16.2, 1580/81 ed. 5:88: Johannes Bosch, *De nuptiis* 2.22, in TUJ* 6:4rb.

there was a presumption against rape if intercourse took place in the house of a third party, provided that the woman entered the house of her own free will.[197]

Treatment of rape and related crimes depended greatly on the victim's resistance to the advances of the offender. Egidio Bossi (1487–1546) noted that even if the woman consented to intercourse, the incident still counted as rape if violence was employed to induce her consent. The municipal statutes of Belluno (1428) specified, however, that admiring phrases, persuasive speeches, and promises uttered in order to persuade a woman to have sex did not constitute violence.[198] On the other hand if the woman wept, wailed, and protested, according to Bossi, this established a presumption that she did not consent to the advances. Further, even if she consented after the fact, a rape charge could still be pressed against the assailant. Bossi also noted that rape was a crime against her parents as well as against the victim and that abduction and the moving of the unwilling victim from one place to another were of the essence of the crime.[199]

Attempted rape was usually punished less severely than a completed attack—Bossi suggested deportation as an appropriate remedy, although some cities imposed fines and other sanctions for this crime.[200] Lucca and Modena prescribed the same penalties for accessories and accomplices as for the principal offender, but in practice they generally got off with milder penalties.[201]

Legal writers generally agreed that it was rape to have sex with one's fiancé by force, but that forcible coitus with one's wife was not a crime. A rape charge was warranted, according to Giovanni Nevizzani, only when carnal knowledge was the principal objective of the attack. Thus if a woman was forcibly abducted and held prisoner, this action would not be punishable as *raptus* unless the abductor had intercourse with her against her will.[202]

The labels "rape" or "ravishment" can be misleading, for the terms described a variety of situations. When a minor child, for example, was abducted by her mother or father and married to a man of whom the child's legal guardian

---

[197] Bossi, *Tractatus varii*, tit. *De coitu damnato* 67–68 and *De extraordinariis criminibus* 3, fol. 188va–vb, 229rb–va; Belluno, *Ius municipale* lib. 3, tit. *De adulteriis* 14, fol. 83r; Bergamo, *Statuta* 9.68, fol. 143r.

[198] Bossi, *Tractatus varii*, tit. *De raptu mulieris* 7–8, 15, and *De coitu damnato* 66, fol. 182rb–va, 183rb–va, 188rb; Belluno, *Ius municipale* lib. 3, tit. *De adulteriis*, c. 18, fol. 83r; Hieronymus Olives, *Comm.* to *Carta de logu* c. 21, p. 57; Martín de Azpilceuta, *Consilia* 5.17.1.1, in his *Opera* 3/2:156; Ruggiero, "Sexual Criminality," p. 21.

[199] Bossi, *Tractatus varii*, tit. *De raptu mulieris* 3–5, 21, fol. 182ra–rb, 183va, 184rb; Nevizzani, *Silva nuptialis*, fol. 73vb–74ra; Gibson, *Codex iuris anglicani* 22.3, p. 504.

[200] Bossi, *Tractatus varii*, tit. *De coitu damnato* 70, fol. 188vb; Belluno, *Ius municipale*, lib. 3, tit. *De adulteriis*, c. 5, fol. 82r.

[201] Lucca, *Statuta* 4.99, fol. 215r; Modena, *Statuta* 3.60, fol. 79r–v; Ruggiero, "Sexual Criminality," pp. 21–22.

[202] Nevizzani, *Silva nuptialis*, fol. 73vb; Panormitanus, *Comm.* to X 4.13.6 § 3; Bossi, *Tractatus varii*, tit. *De raptu mulieris* 20, fol. 184ra; Petrus de Monte, *Repertorium* s.v. *Raptor*, fol. 221va; Modena, *Statuta* 3.60, fol. 79r–v.

did not approve, this might well be classed as ravishment, although it certainly is not in any ordinary sense rape. Parents in these situations no doubt acted for a variety of reasons. In some cases the mother may have been motivated by concern for the child's well-being, but in others the abducting mother seems to have been more concerned with profiting from her child's marriage than with anything else. In order to discourage this sort of conduct, Richard II of England approved a statute that disinherited women who were "ravished" in this way, so that the "ravisher" would not profit from the crime. The legislation, however, did not seem to diminish the frequency of the offense.[203]

SINS AGAINST NATURE

Secular and religious lawmakers, as well as law writers, were greatly concerned during this period about "unnatural" sex, particularly homosexuality and masturbation. Their interest was reflected in the vastly increased volume of municipal law dealing with homosexual behavior. Some ecclesiastical writers also treated masturbation as a major contravention of natural and divine law.

For reasons that may be linked to concern over the population crisis following the Black Death, lawmakers in the generation after 1348 suddenly seem to have perceived sodomy as a grave threat to society and visited upon those convicted of deviant sexual practices severe and gruesome punishments. "Sodomy is a most detestable vice," declared Egidio Bossi, and municipal authorities clearly agreed. In 1432, Florence even created a special magistrate, the Official of the Curfew and the Convents, to deal with sodomy cases. The magistrate's title illustrates one feature of popular views of homosexuality, namely that the vice was most prevalent among students and clergy.[204] Writers on moral questions lumped together as sodomy any and all sexual practices that they considered unnatural, including masturbation, mutual masturbation, oral sex, and anal sex, either homosexual or heterosexual. Although most sodomy legislation referred specifically to sexual contacts between men, legal theorists contended that sodomy had begun historically with the practices of the women of Sodom and Gomorrah, the "mothers of lust," as Bossi called them, who were not satisfied with the sexual pleasure of intercourse with men and consequently in-

[203] 6 Rich. II § 1.6; Sue Sheridan Walter, "Widow and Ward: The Feudal Law of Child Custody in Medieval England," in *Women in Medieval Society*, ed. Stuard, pp. 164–65.

[204] Bossi, *Tractatus varii*, tit. *De stupro detestabili in masculos* 1, fol. 189vb; Brucker, *Society of Renaissance Florence*, pp. 201–204; Ruggiero, "Sexual Criminality," pp. 22–23, and *Boundaries of Eros*, pp. 109–45; E. William Monter, "La sodomie à l'époque moderne en Suisse romande," *Annales é.s.c.* 29 (1974) 1024–25; Rossiaud, "Prostitution, sexualité, société," p. 82; Tentler, *Sin and Confession*, p. 207; De Waha, "Note," p. 14; Michael Goodich, "Sodomy in Ecclesiastical Law and Theory," *Journal of Homosexuality* 2 (1976) 427–29. London court records, however, show a surprisingly low incidence of sodomy charges: out of 21,000 defendants recorded between 1470 and 1516, only one was charged with sodomy, and he was excommunicated merely for nonappearance; Wunderli, *London Church Courts*, pp. 83–84.

vented new and perverse pleasures to appease their lust. Men, according to this pseudohistory, had been all too ready to take up these womanly perversions, and thus unnatural vice spread through the world.[205]

Although conservative clerics, such as John Mirc (fl. ca. 1450), cautioned preachers that they should avoid mentioning sodomy and other sexual sins in their sermons, St. Bernardino of Siena threw timidity to the winds and dedicated one of his Lenten sermons specifically to sins against nature. He aimed his denunciations squarely at the insanity (as he called it) of homosexual desire, which he believed deranged reason as no other vice could do.[206] Either sodomy or masturbation, he declared, furnished more than adequate grounds for a divorce, a novel conclusion that several legal writers adopted.[207]

Municipal statutes often envisioned grisly punishments for homosexuals. Burning alive was by far the most common, although a few towns substituted beheading for burning under some circumstances. Several cities adopted complex scales of punishment. Perugia, for example, prescribed heavy fines for the first two convictions and burning alive only for the third, provided that the offender was an adult. Perugian boys between the ages of twelve and fifteen who consented to sodomy could be jailed for three months; boys above fifteen were fined £50 in addition to their jail sentences. Age was often a major factor in determining the punishment for sodomy, as was the role, active or passive, played by the convicted person. Other cities distinguished between sodomy committed by married men and by unmarried men. Todi fined both parties to a homosexual act £100, provided that they were under the age of twenty-five. If they failed to pay within ten days, they were to be stripped, tied by the genitals, paraded naked through the city, beaten, and expelled from town. If the culprit was between twenty-five and thirty-three, the fine rose to £200, with the same penalty for nonpayment. A culprit over the age of thirty-three was to be burnt publicly and all his property forfeited to the city. Bergamo not merely required a public burning, but also insisted that the condemned man's family be compelled to witness the execution and that they not be permitted to leave until the fire was extinguished.[208] Case records show that the most horrendous

[205] Bossi, *Tractatus varii*, tit. *De stupro detestabilis in masculos* 4, fol. 190ra–rb; Jean Gerson, *De confessione mollitiei*, ed. Glorieux 8:72; Paulus Grillandus, *De penis* 2.1–2, in TUJ* 10:28ra.

[206] John Mirc, *Instructions*, ll. 222–25, ed. Peacock, p. 7; St. Bernardino, *Sermo* 15.1–3, in his *Opera* 3:267–82.

[207] St. Bernardino, *Sermo* 15.2.2, in his *Opera* 3:277; Aegidius Bellamera, *Comm.* to C. 32 q. 7 c. 7, d.p.c. 10, and C. 35 q. 2 & 3 c. 11, 1580 ed. 3:54va–55ra, 92ra–rb; Petrus de Ancharano, *Comm.* to X 5.16.4, 1580/81 ed. 5:88–89; Bossi, *Tractatus varii*, tit. *De stupro detestabili in masculos* 6, fol. 190rb.

[208] Ancona, *Constitutiones* 3.12, p. 84; Belluno, *Ius municipale*, lib. 3, tit. *De adulteriis* c. 13, fol. 82v; Bergamo, *Statuta* 9.76, fol. 143v–144r; Cremona, *Statuta* 113, p. 41; Faenza, *Ordinamenta* 4.23, fol. 41r; Lucca, *Statuta* 4.107, fol. 217v–222v; Modena, *Statuta* 3.63, fol. 80r; Orvieto, *Reformationes et decreta* 3.27, pp. 174–75; Parma, *Statuta* 3.33, fol. 124v; Perugia, *Statuta* 3.18, 214, fol. 17rb–va, 63vb–64ra; Reggio Emilia,

statutory punishments were reserved for particularly vicious cases, such as homosexual rape and that ordinary offenders were more likely to be whipped, fined, and exiled.[209] Men accused of sodomy, like defendants in other serious criminal cases, were denied the right of counsel in presenting their defense. If convicted, their property was usually confiscated and their wills declared void.[210]

Masturbation, although classed as an unnatural sex act by moralists, was not subject to public prosecution, and where evidence of it emerged in the course of proceedings for other sex offenses, authorities ignored it.[211] Instead, masturbation was a matter for the internal forum of confession. Guy de Roye (ca. 1345–1409), Archbishop of Sens, considered masturbation so serious a matter that he classified it as a reserved sin, for which absolution could be granted only by a bishop or diocesan penitentiary, but this doctrine appears to have been peculiar to Guy, for no other authority of the period took a similar stand.[212] Indeed, Jean Gerson (1363–1429), who wrote a special treatise on hearing the confessions of masturbators, nowhere indicated that he was dealing with a matter reserved to bishops, although he, too, considered it a grave moral vice. While masturbation was serious, Gerson knew that it was also extremely common. Boys, he observed, often begin to masturbate at the age of five, or even as early as three. By the time they have grown old enough to appreciate the seriousness of their actions, he declared, they are so addicted to the pleasure it produces that they continue to manipulate their genitals anyway, despite the fact that continued masturbation may lead to even more heinous sex crimes, such as sodomy. Even adults, Gerson added, may continue to practice masturbation, and many of them never confess this fact. Gerson advised confessors to question penitents cautiously in order to ferret out secret masturbators and bring them to repent. Gerson suggested that penitents be encouraged to seek good company, to practice abstinence in food and drink, accompanied by frequent prayer, flagellation, sprinkling with cold water, and spitting on the ground while renouncing the devil.[213]

Statuta 3.58, fol. 161r–v; Spoleto, Statuta 2.47, fol. 33v; Todi, Statuta 3.113 and Reformationes, rubr. 52, fol. 75v, XVIv; Urbino, Statuta 4.39, fol. 91r; Valsesia, Statuta 1.181, ed. Mor, p. 105; Elizabeth W. Marvick, "Nature Versus Nurture: Patterns and Trends in Seventeenth-Century French Child-Rearing," in DeMause, History of Childhood, p. 280; Gibson, Codex iuris anglicani 47.3, p. 1122.

[209] Brucker, Society of Renaissance Florence, pp. 204–206; Ladislao Münster, "Un processo per sodomia a Venezia e una perizia medica relativa ad esso," in Frascastoro: Studi e memorie per il IV centenario della morte (Verona: Ghidini Fiorini, 1954), pp. 82–84.

[210] Bossi, Tractatus varii, tit. De stupro detestabilis in masculos 2, 5, fol. 190ra–rb.

[211] See the case reported by Ruggiero, Boundaries of Eros, pp. 114–15.

[212] Guy de Roye, Doctrinal de sapience, fol. 53r; Flandrin, "Mariage tardif," p. 1359, and "Repression and Change," p. 206.

[213] Jean Gerson, De arte audiendi confessiones 6, 14, 15, and De confessione mollitiei, ed. Glorieux 8:11, 13–14, 71–73; Tentler, Sin and Confession, pp. 91–93, 228.

Other deviant sexual practices attracted scant attention from legal writers, moralists, or lawmakers during this period, although municipal authorities sometimes legislated against sexual relations with animals, which they classed with sodomy. The city fathers of Reggio Emilia felt sufficiently threatened by cross-dressing to impose a £50 fine on transvestites. Their concern, however, seemed to have been primarily that randy men might disguise themselves as women in order to make their way into sections of the churches reserved for females, in order to flirt with the wives and daughters of respectable citizens.[214]

Sex and the Clergy

Poets and preachers continued to insist on the well-established literary commonplace that few clerics actually remained celibate, although for centuries they had been legally bound to the discipline. The Dominican preacher, John Bromyard, roundly declared that the unchastity of priests was a scandal and a cause of ruin, while John Gower described as typical the lecherous priest who prowled through his parish like a wolf around a sheepfold, searching out attractive young women whom he might seduce:

> So the lecherous parson,
> With his lustful gaze,
> Teaches simple layfolk
> Foul abandon's ways.[215]

These complaints were not simply the vaporings of superheated rhetoric. The documentary evidence of visitations, petitions to the pope, and court records bears out the impression that clerical incontinence was an open scandal in many parts of Western Christendom.[216] Poets and preachers may have exaggerated the seriousness of the problem for rhetorical effect, but reforming polemicists did not have to search diligently to discover ample evidence that the Catholic clergy often felt that although celibacy might require them not to

---

[214] Reggio Emilia, *Statuta* 3.53, fol. 160r–v.

[215] John Gower, *Vox clamantis* 3.21, ll. 1624–25, in his *Works*, ed. Macaulay 4:51: "Sic et in incastis exemplis presbiterorum / Indoctis laicis feda libido nocet." See also ll. 1515–24, 1597–1600, 1681–86, ed. Macaulay 4:147–48, 150, 152. John Bromyard, *Summa praedicantium* s.v. *Luxuria*; Owst, *Literature and Pulpit*, p. 260; Martin Boelens, "Die Klerikerehe in der kirchlichen Gesetzgebung vom II. Laterankonzil bis zum Konzil von Basel," in *Ius sacrum: Klaus Mörsdorf zum 60. Geburtstag*, ed. Audomar Scheuermann and Georg May (Munich: F. Schöningh, 1969), p. 610.

[216] Peter Heath, *English Parish Clergy on the Eve of the Reformation*, Studies in Social History (London: Routledge & Kegan Paul, 1969), pp. 104–108, 118–19; Canice Mooney, *The Church in Gaelic Ireland: Thirteenth to Fifteenth Centuries*, A History of Irish Catholicism, vol. 2 (Dublin: Gill & Macmillan, 1969), pp. 56–60; *The Book of Llan Dâv*, ed. J. G. Evans (Oxford: Privately printed, 1893), pp. 274–80; Elvey, *Courts of the Archdeaconry of Buckingham*, no. 388, p. 311; Bannister, "Visitation Returns," pp. 287, 451; Hair, *Before the Bawdy Court*, no. 175, p. 90; Schimmelpfennig, "Ex fornicatione nati," pp. 32–33; Oliveira Marques, *Daily Life in Portugal*, p. 176.

marry, it did not oblige them to renounce sex. The English reformer, Robert
Barnes (1495–1540) reported that a London notary told him of having written a
thousand dispensations during his career to allow the sons of priests to be ordained and estimated that less than a third of the English clergy observed the
celibacy rule.[217]

Official opposition to clerical marriage and concubinage remained essentially
unchanged through the pre-Reformation period. The Council of Basel in 1435
reiterated the longstanding condemnnation of clerical concubinage in ringing
terms. Clerics who retained their concubines and refused to renounce them
within two months of the publication of the Council's decree were to be deprived of their benefices, suspended from clerical status, and to lose any titles,
dignities, or offices they might hold. Local synods were directed to adopt this
decree and to enforce its provisions. A good many of them did the one and attempted the other. At Reims, Camin, Avignon, Seville, Florence, Tournai, and
Augsburg, bishops and their clergy re-enacted the Basel decree and added fines
and other punishments of their own to those decreed by the general council.[218]
It might not be accurate to say that all this effort had no effect, but its results
were certainly modest. The energies of local reformers, at any rate, seem to
have been directed primarily at avoiding scandal and only secondarily at controlling clerical carnality. By the end of the fifteenth century many Churchmen
had concluded that further attempts to enforce celibacy were futile: the best
they could do was to confine the clergy's sexual activities within tolerable
limits.[219]

Rulers, too, were concerned about the enforcement of clerical celibacy. Nicolaus Boerius (1469–1539) declared that temporal authorities had the right to
penalize clerics who lived in open and notorious concubinage, and at least a few
towns enacted statutes for this purpose. How effectively they were enforced,
however, remains questionable. No evidence suggests that secular courts had
greater success in this matter than did their ecclesiastical counterparts.[220]

---

[217] John K. Yost, "The Reformation Defense of Clerical Marriage in the Reigns of
Henry VIII and Edward VI," *Church History* 50 (1981) 157; Fuchs, *Sexual Desire and
Love*, p. 135.

[218] Council of Basel, Sess. 20 (1435), in COD, pp. 461–63; Martin Boelens, "Die
Klerikerehe in der kirchlichen Gesetzgebung zwischen den Konzilien von Basel und Tri-
ent," *Archiv für katholisches Kirchenrecht* 138 (1969) 62–63, 66–68; Trexler, *Synodal
Law*, pp. 49–50.

[219] Trexler, *Synodal Law*, pp. 50–51.

[220] *Concubinatum clericorum: Bedenken der Concubinen Wegen* (1589), in MS Lea
376 (Ger) of the University of Pennsylvania Library, Philadelphia, fol. 2r, cites Decis. 72
of Nicolaus Boerius, who "Expresse tenet, quantum in casu notorii concubinatus, sub-
diti scandalizati, querelas offerunt, quod tunc clerici et abbates concubinarii per offi-
ciales Regios (et sic magistratum secularem) iubentur sub certa poena seu emenda, a
conuersatione concubinarum abstinere, et si non parcant, puniantur per saeculares."
This short treatise is a legal opinion rendered for Count Fugger by a jurist who signed
himself "H. F." Statutes in point include Faenza, *Ordinamenta*, Constitutiones domini

Sixteenth-century reformers would see the failure to enforce celibacy as proof of the policy's theological unsoundness and would argue that God had sanctioned marriage precisely to provide a remedy for sexual temptations and an outlet for sexual passions, from neither of which the clergy were immune. Every major figure of the Reformation rejected celibacy as a mistaken and ill-conceived policy.[221]

Those criticisms were nothing new: arguments that celibacy ought to be abolished had been advanced in every generation since the policy was adopted by earlier Church reformers in the eleventh century. The criticisms continued unabated through the fourteenth and fifteenth centuries. The agenda of the Council of Constance contained a proposal that clerical marriage be permitted, and in 1440, at the Council of Basel, the Polish physician and humanist, Jan de Ludzisko, argued that clerical celibacy should be abandoned in theory because it had long since been disregarded in practice, a position supported by Johann Schele, Bishop of Lübeck.[222] Their arguments may have owed some of their substance to the *Lamentacio humane nature adversus Nicenam constitucionem* of Guillaume Saignet (ca. 1364 ~ 1369–1444), who argued that clerical celibacy was unnatural and called for its rejection.

A generation earlier, however, St. Birgitta of Sweden (1303–73) had been shocked to encounter an archbishop who declared that if he were pope he would allow all clerics, including priests, to marry and who claimed that this would be more acceptable to God than having clerics who lived sexually dissolute lives, as most of them currently did. Birgitta was indignant and dismayed:

> Know this [she replied to the archbishop], that if any pope were to give priests permission to contract carnal marriage, God would condemn him with a spiritual penalty similar to that meted out to men who have committed heinous offenses, for by secular law they should pluck out his eyes, cut off his tongue and lips, his nose and ears, chop off his hands and feet, and let all the blood drain out of his body so that he becomes cold. And then his exsanguinated corpse should be thrown to the dogs and other wild beasts that they may devour it. This is the sort of thing that will happen—spiritually, of course—to that pope who grants such a license to priests for contracting marriage against the foreordained will of God.[223]

---

papae vicarium 3.13, and Perugia, *Statuta* 3.82, fol. 33rb; see also May, *Geistliche Gerichtsbarkeit*, p. 223.

[221] Yost, "Reformation Defense of Clerical Marriage," pp. 155–56.

[222] *Capitula agendorum in concilio generali Constanciensi* 13, in *Acta concilii Constanciensis*, ed. Heinrich Finke, 4 vols. (Münster i/W.: Regensburg, 1896–1928) 4:569–70; Grévy-Pons, *Célibat et nature*, pp. 52–53.

[223] Guillaume Saignet's *Lamentacio* is edited by Grévy-Pons, *Célibat et nature*, pp. 135–61; on St. Birgitta see ibid., p. 52; the quotation is from her *Revelationes* 7.10 (Nuremberg: Anton Koberger, 1500; unpaginated).

Fourteenth- and fifteenth-century writers continued to advocate the time-honored cures that had proved so ineffective in the past. But none of the conventional remedies worked.[224] Nor was a cleric who felt inclined to take a concubine likely to be dissuaded when he learned that if he murdered his mistress's husband he would automatically forfeit his clerical privileges.[225] "One should not force a cleric to swear that he will not go back to his concubine," concluded Giovanni Nevizzani, "for because of human frailty he will not keep his word."[226] Authorities may not have been altogether keen to see clerical celibacy actually enforced, for they might well have feared that, as an anonymous critic threatened, effective enforcement would simply result in an exodus of priests from their ministry.[227]

By the fifteenth century, Church authorities had largely abandoned attempts to penalize women who became sexually involved with clerics. Legislation about clerical sexuality during this period was silent on the subject and Giovanni Bossi considered earlier penal provisions aimed at punishing concubines to be a dead letter in his day.[228]

Multiple Marriages

If the clergy could not legally marry at all, some laymen redressed the balance by marrying many times. While this was legally permitted, of course, so long as the multiple marriages followed one another in sequence, both civil and Church authorities penalized those who took more than one spouse at a time. Court records for the period show a low incidence of bigamy, and the practice was certainly no threat to the established social order anywhere in Europe.[229] A

---

[224] Panormitanus, *Comm.* to X 1.21.6, in his *Opera* 2:96vb; Joannes a Capistrano, *Comm.* to X 3.2.2, 4, 7, fol. 325ra–vb, 327va; St. Antoninus, *De censuris* 94; Nevizzani, *Silva nuptialis*, fol. 83ra; Hippolytus de Marsiliis, *Tractatus de fideiussoribus*, in Benvenuto Straccha, *De mercatura decisiones et tractatus varii* (Lyon: Expensis Petri Tandry, 1610; repr. Turin: Bottega d'Erasmo, 1971), p. 689; *Domini de Rota decisiones novae, antiquae, et antiquiores*, no. 26 (Turin: Apud Heredes Nicolai Bevilaquae, 1579), p. 272; *Directorium concubinarum saluberrimum quo quedam stupenda et quasi inaudita pericula quam apertissime resoluuntur nedum clericis aut etiam laicis hoc crimine pollutis necessarius* (Cologne: Quentell, 1509), fol. 2r; cf. Mirc, *Instructiones*, ll. 57–60, ed. Peacock, p. 3, and Gower, *Vox clamantis* 4.11, ll. 431–90, ed. Macaulay 4:178.

[225] Jean LeCoq, *Questiones*, no. 379, pp. 472–74.

[226] Nevizzani, *Silva nuptialis*, fol. 17rb.

[227] *Carmina prose et rithmi editi in laudem pudicicie sacerdotalis contra prosam excusare conantem scandalosissimum concubinatum* (Strasbourg: Johann Prüss fils, 1512), fol. 1v: "Si clerum deficere: vides non miabere carna sumpta, / Non est sicut angelus: neque velut spiritus; lege tua sis cautus ne sit ceca. / Membra quam debilia: corpora quam fragilia, omnia considera hec predicta." See also *Archiv für Reformationsgeschichte* 22 (1925) 117–22.

[228] Bossi, *Tractatus varii*, tit. *De coitu damnato* 15–18, fol. 185vb–186ra.

[229] Elvey, *Courts of the Archdeaconry of Buckingham*, for example, shows six cases

handful of cities adopted statutes prohibiting bigamous marriages and imposing penalties upon offenders; the usual punishment involved a substantial fine, although at Reggio Emilia, bigamy was made a capital crime if the second marriage was consummated. At Belluno the bigamist who failed to pay his £200 fine within a month could be castrated; he might also lose one hand to the executioner.[230] Women were not usually punished for bigamy at all, a fact that Jean Montaigne put down to the well-known frailty of their sex; it may also have been a result of the fact that in many cases the woman was unaware that her husband still had another living wife.[231]

The Church continued to consider sequential or constructive bigamy an obstacle to ordination, but more boisterous and immediate reaction to the remarriage of widows and widowers was likely to come from young people, who, despite continuing censures from both Church and civic authorities, continued to intimidate and harass couples with *charivaris* or, as they were known in Tuscany, *scampanate*. These youthful brigades found plenty of victims, for widowers and widows made up a substantial part of city populations during this period, and many widowers remarried, almost always to younger women. Although this often earned them the dubious attentions of local youth groups, the young men could generally be persuaded to abandon their tambourines, rattles, and horns in return for a suitable offering from their victims.[232]

Property Consequences of Sexual Relationships

Municipal lawmakers were concerned during this period about the consequences of marriage and other sexual relationships for the property rights of the parties and the issue of their union. Although canon law had for centuries recognized marriage without dowry, communities strongly disapproved of unions

---

over a twenty-five-year period. Bigamy charges sometimes arose out of uncertainty about the legitimacy of a divorce, as happened in the case of John Guy at Durham in 1451; Raine, *Depositions*, pp. 30–31. Bossi, *Tractatus varii*, tit. *De coitu damnato* 78, fol. 189ra–rb, related the tale of a Frenchman with four wives; he kept marrying in hope of finding an agreeable wife, but every time he failed. See generally Etienne Aufréri, *Decisiones* no. 253–55, fol. 60r–v; *Domini de Rota decisiones*, no. 447, p. 77; Jean Montaigne, *De bigamia*, esp. 1.3, 4.5, in TUJ* 14:105va, 109rb; Albericus de Rosate, *Vocabularius*, s.v. *Bigamus*, fol. 35va–36ra.

[230] Belluno, *Ius municipale*, lib. 3, tit. *De adulteriis*, c. 20, fol. 83v; Perugia, *Statuta* 3.84, fol. 33va–vb; Pesaro, *Statuta* 3.51, fol. 54v; Reggio Emilia, *Statuta* 3.56, fol. 160v–161r.

[231] Jean Montaigne, *De bigamia* 5.33, in TUJ* 14:112rb; Petrus de Ancharano, *Comm.* to X 4.7.4, 1580/81 ed., 4:73.

[232] Natalie Z. Davis, "Some Tasks and Themes in the Study of Popular Religion," in *The Pursuit of Holiness in Late Medieval and Renaissance Religion*, ed. Charles Trinkaus and Heiko A. Obermann Studies in Medieval and Reformation Thought, vol. 10 (Leiden: E. J. Brill, 1974), p. 323, and "Reasons of Misrule," pp. 52–53; Herlihy, "Marriage at Pistoia," p. 10.

lacking dowry—Florentines considered it far more shameful to marry without dowry than to marry without the blessing of a priest.[233] "Since it is in the interest of the government to have rich citizens and subjects, and to eliminate the causes of their impoverishment," declared the Reggio Emilia statutes, it seemed necessary to impose strict limits upon the amount of property that families might give as dowry. No one might dower his daughter with more than fifteen percent of his total assets, nor might any dowry exceed a maximum of 400 gold ducats, according to the statute.[234] Such limitations had implications for the groom's family as well, since the contribution by the man's family to the newlyweds was liable to be approximately equal to the contribution of the bride's family.[235] Cities were anxious that these arrangements be settled in writing, or at least that agreements concerning them be attested by witnesses.[236] Italian towns also tried to see to it that the dowries given to marriageable daughters did not disadvantage other family members. For this reason several of them incorporated in their statutes what had long been a common practice, namely that a woman who received a dowry at the time of marriage was excluded from any further share in her family's estate.[237]

Dowry represented the married woman's claim to financial security, but that security might be jeopardized by her own actions or those of her husband. The married woman who committed adultery stood to lose her dowry, and the beneficiary in that case was her husband, who received part or all of it as compensation for his humiliation.[238] Giovanni Nevizzani held that even exchanging a sexy kiss with a man to whom she was not married might cause a married woman to forfeit her dowry, but other authorities were unwilling to push the point this far. Ulrich Zasius maintained that a woman convicted of adultery on circumstantial evidence alone should not be deprived of her dowry. Martín de Azpilceuta also argued in favor of an unmarried woman's prospective rights in a dowry promised to her and declared that even if she had an illicit affair her parents or other benefactor could not on that account deny her the promised

---

[233] Christiane Klapisch-Zuber, "Le complexe de Griselda: Dot et dons de mariage au Quattrocento," *Mélanges de l'Ecole française de Rome: Moyen âge–temps modernes* 94 (1982) 8; also in *Women, Family and Ritual*, p. 214.

[234] Reggio Emilia, *Statuta* 7.2, fol. 289v–290r.

[235] Reggio Emilia, *Statuta* 2.79, fol. 122v–123r; Klapisch-Zuber, *Women, Family, and Ritual*, pp. 218–24.

[236] Novara, *Statuta*, lib. 2, tit. *De dotibus mulierum*.

[237] Borgosesia, *Statuta*, 46, pp. 161–62; Caluso, *Statuta* 15, Favria, *Statuta* 89, and Romano, *Statuta* 19, in *Corpus statutorum Canavisii* 2:8, 347, and 3:188; Valsesia, *Statuta* 1.68, p. 55.

[238] Bossi, *Tractatus varii*, tit. *De coitu damnato* 54, fol. 188ra; Franciscus de Platea, *Opus restitutionum* 59; St. Antoninus, *De sponsalibus* 36; Ulrich Zasius, *In celeberrimos aliquot titulos*, to Dig. 24.3.2 §22, fol. 4ra; Paulus de Castro, *Consilia* 121; Johannes Bosch, *De nuptiis* 2.11, in TUJ* 6:3vb–4ra; Joannes Campegius, *De petitione et restitutione dotis* 223, in TUJ* 6:105ra; Giovanni Pietro Ferrari, *Practica nova judicialis* (Venice: Jacobinus Suigus, 1487), fol. 128va.

settlement at the time of marriage.[239] Men had to be careful, too. A husband who expelled his wife without legal cause might be required not only to repay her dowry, but also to add up to a quarter of his own assets to her financial settlement. If a man committed fornication with a widow, he stood to lose any legacy left to him by her late husband. If both parties to a marriage were guilty of sexual misconduct, the wife was entitled to repossess her dowry and the husband to take all other marital property when their marriage terminated.[240] If a man received gifts from a married woman with whom he had committed adultery, however, he was obliged to restore that property to her husband as a condition for reconciliation with the Church.[241]

The property claims that resulted from adulterous relationships were so complicated, and might be so disruptive, that some couples were willing to overlook or to bear with their marital discords in order to conserve their financial interests by avoiding the economic penalties that separation or divorce entailed.[242]

Both canonists and secular authorities sought to protect women whose financial interests were threatened by the carelessness, incompetence, or neglect of spendthrift husbands. They provided a process whereby the wife might secure a separation from her husband if she could show that he was endangering her financial security and that his conduct tended to impoverish her. In these cases the wife was entitled to sue for restitution of her dowry, as was also true in some jurisdictions if her husband was convicted of a crime.[243]

Secular writers also attempted to spell out in detail the rights of surviving spouses in the estates of their deceased partners. If the wife died before the husband, he was normally entitled to a share in her dowry, whether there were children from the marriage or not. If there were children, they received the residue of their mother's dowry; if there were no children, the residue usually returned to the wife's family of origin. Where the husband predeceased the wife, she was normally entitled to claim all of her dowry. If there were children of the marriage, the widow commonly had to divide with them her interest in the husband's property and in any acquests. If there were no children she received a portion of her husband's estate proportional to the value of the dowry she had brought to the marriage.[244]

---

[239] Nevizzani, *Silva nuptialis*, fol. 69ra; Zasius, *In celeberrimos aliquot titulos*, to Dig. 24.3.2 § 23, fol. 4ra; Martín de Azpilceuta, *Consilia* 4.5.2.1, in his *Opera* 3/2:23.

[240] Nevizzani, *Silva nuptialis*, fol. 9va–vb, 38ra; Joannes Campegius, *De petitione et restitutione dotis* 230, in TUJ* 6:105va; Paulus de Castro, *Consilia* 128.

[241] Franciscus de Platea, *Opus restitutionum* § 54.

[242] Baptista de Sancto Blasio, *De privilegiis dotalibus* 72, in TUJ* 6:235vb–236ra; Nevizzani, *Silva nuptialis*, fol. 9ra.

[243] Orvieto, *Reformationes et decreta* 2.71, 75–76, pp. 140, 142–43; Ourliac, "Notes sur le mariage," p. 60; Julius Kirshner, "Wives' Claims against Insolvent Husbands in Late Medieval Italy," in *Women of the Medieval World*, pp. 260–302.

[244] Alix, *Statuta* 24–25; Caluso, *Statuta* 16; and San Giorgio, *Statuta* 5, all in *Corpus statutorum Canavisii* 1:73–74, 2:8, and 3:253; Orvieto, *Reformationes et decreta* 2.74,

Some civic authorities shared the ecclesiastical courts' concern about alimony and child support following divorce or separation. The *Concilio maggiore* of Venice declared in 1374, for example, that it was prepared to deal with complaints about these matters and to require husbands to make appropriate financial arrangements to care for their estranged wives and children.[245]

Legitimation of Children

Church authorities had long maintained their right to determine the circumstances under which illegitimate children could be legitimized and thus, as Peter of Ravenna put it, transformed from nonpersons into persons. Secular authorities during this period asserted an increased interest in gaining control of this process, and the result was jurisdictional conflict over such matters.[246] In practice a great deal depended on the interest of the fathers. Some fathers clearly felt a personal concern for their illegitimate offspring and took pains to see that they were properly reared and given the advantages that their parents' status could afford.[247] These were probably exceptional, however, and bastard children commonly suffered considerable economic and social disadvantages as a result of the circumstances of their birth.[248]

Among legal writers, the canonists seem to have been more solicitous to improve the lot of bastard children than were civic authorities. Thus, for example, Simone da Borsano (d. 1381) maintained that illegitimate boys had as much right to be promoted to the academic rank of doctor as their legitimate siblings, since "Knowledge is a gift of the Holy Spirit, who bloweth where he listeth."[249] The city fathers of Novara, however, barred bastards from membership in the skilled craft guilds of their city and forbade them admission to the city council or to other positions of trust and honor in the town.[250] Canonists were also more

---

pp. 141–42; Todi, *Statuta* 2:52–53, fol. 43v; Valsesia, *Statuta* 1.69, p. 55; *Statuta Veneta emendatissima* 1.62 (Venice: B. Benalio & Compagno, 1528), fol. 30v–31r; Heers, *Family Clans*, p. 212; Janet Senderowitz Loengard, "'Of the Gift of Her Husband': English Dower and Its Consequences in the Year 1200," in *Women of the Medieval World*, pp. 215–55, summarizes the English rules, which were still largely intact at this period.

[245] Venice, *Statuta emendatissima*, Consulta 8, fol. 177r; Helmholz, *Marriage Litigation*, pp. 106–108.

[246] Petrus Ravennatus, *De consuetudine* 27, in TUJ 1:112r; Baldus, *Comm.* to X 2.23.11 § 3, fol. 219ra; Chevailler, "Observations," p. 396.

[247] Ross, "The Middle-Class Child," pp. 197, 207, cites the case of the illegitimate child of an Italian merchant and a Tartar slave girl, who was cared for and taught by both parents and ultimately married in high style.

[248] Baldus, *Comm.* to X 1.6.20 § 10, fol. 64ra; Fortunius García, *Tractatus de ultimo fine juris*, 126, 133, in TUJ 1:13ra, va; Petrus de Ancharano, *Comm.* to X 4.17.1, 1580/81 ed. 4:106; Chevailler, "Observations," p. 404.

[249] Simone da Borsano, *Lectura in Clem.*, proem., pars prima, in Maffei, "Dottori e studenti," p. 234.

[250] Novara, *Statuta*, lib. 2, tit. *De naturalibus et artistis ad officium consulatus non admittendis*, fol. 51v.

apt than civilians to insist that the child of a married woman, even a prostitute, was presumed to be legitimate. The child of a married woman who lived as the public concubine of a man other than her husband, however, was presumed to be a bastard.[251] Paulus de Castro remarked with apparent approval on the case of an unmarried woman who bore a son to her lover. The woman's mother raised the child and refused to allow the natural father to see him, in order to bring pressure on the boy's father to marry her daughter. Whether this stratagem succeeded, however, Paulus does not tell us.[252] The fourteenth-century records of the *Officialis* of the diocese of Paris contain a number of cases in which the ecclesiastical courts issued support orders requiring the fathers of natural children to contribute to their support, and other cases have been reported from England in this period.[253]

The city of Lucca enacted unusually detailed provisions for limiting the portion of an estate that illegitimate children could inherit. The wording of the statute shows that the influence of Roman law on this matter was still very much alive.[254] Both customary law and statutes often limited the rights of bastards to make valid wills and otherwise to dispose of property, although there was considerable diversity in the way that this matter was handled. In France one group of customs allowed bastards virtually complete freedom to devise property by testament. A second group of customs limited the testamentary rights of bastards to the disposition of certain kinds of property, while a third group of customs, mainly in the south, severely curtailed their testamentary rights—one or two customary law jurisdictions denied bastards the right to make wills at all, but this was exceptional.[255] English common law was more inflexible than any of the French customs. The common law, according to the rule confirmed by the Statute of Merton (1236) held that once a bastard, always a bastard, and refused to recognize canonical legitimation.[256]

Jurisdiction, Procedures, and Evidence in Sex Cases

"Carnal crime is as frequent as it is damnable," declared Paulus Grillandus, and certainly the courts, like the rest of late medieval society, seem to have been preoccupied with the norms of sexual behavior.[257] While the proportion of mat-

---

[251] Marcello Crescenzi, *Decisiones Rotae Romanae* (Rome: Apud Typographos Camerales, 1601), p. 207; Bossi, *Tractatus varii*, tit. *De coitu damnato* 51, 77, fol. 188ra, 189ra; Hippolytus de Marsiliis, *Tractatus de fideiussoribus*, p. 689.

[252] Paulus de Castro, *Consilia* no. 228.

[253] Lévy, "L'officialité de Paris," p. 1285; Helmholz, *Marriage Litigation*, pp. 108–109.

[254] Lucca, *Statuta* 2.7, fol. 86r.

[255] Laurent Chevailler, "Note sur le testament du bâtard dans les coutumes du Nord," *Revue du Nord* 40 (1958) 207–208.

[256] J. H. Baker, *An Introduction to English Legal History* (London: Butterworths, 1971), p. 263. English law on this point was changed only by the Legitimacy Act of 1926.

[257] Paulus Grillandus, *De penis* 1.1, in TUJ* 10:26va; Wunderli, *London Church Courts*, pp. 78–79.

rimonial litigation and sex offense cases varied considerably from one region to another during the later Middle Ages, in most jurisdictions whose records have been studied, marriage and sex issues accounted for a majority, often a large majority, of the total business of the Church's lower-level courts. At Regensburg, for example, marriage matters accounted for more than sixty-eight percent of the total cases recorded in 1350, while at Bridgenorth between 1470 and 1523, sexual offenses and keeping suspicious company accounted for about three-quarters of the case load. At Lichfield in 1466, fully ninety percent of the offenders haled before the court were charged with adultery or fornication. In the Archdeaconry of Buckingham, however, only about one-eighth of the cases reported between 1484/85 and 1520 involved either marriage or sex offenses. By contrast, nearly seventy percent of the ex officio cases heard in the Canterbury Consistory court in 1478 involved sex charges, while these matters accounted for about two-thirds of the business of the London commisary courts.[258]

It is obviously difficult to generalize from these data, since the practice of courts varied widely, the survival of records is at best haphazard, and there was considerable fluctuation in the types of business that courts took cognizance of. There were regional differences, too, in the ways that ecclesiastical courts approached problems. As a general rule, French ecclesiastical courts dealt with most types of marriage problems as criminal matters, whereas English Courts Christian treated them as civil causes.[259] There was a notable decline in the volume of marriage cases brought before the Courts Christian in England during the fifteenth century, but French practice showed no such decline during the same period.[260]

It does appear to be true, at least on the limited evidence available, that canonical courts both in England and on the Continent followed the theories of academic canonists fairly closely, even though custom dictated deviations from strict canonical theory on some scores. In practice, canonical courts often treated sexual intercourse as an essential defining element in marriage, although the Church had been committed to the consensual definition of marriage since the time of Alexander III. The records of both Continental and English courts also show numerous examples of what amounted to separations by mutual consent, although in strict law these certainly should not have been allowed. Still, taking one thing with another, the teachings of academic lawyers clearly influenced the practice of the courts and were often decisive in determining how cases

---

[258] Weigand, "Rechtssprechung," p. 411; Anne Lefebvre-Teillard, "Ad matrimoniuum contrahere compellitur," RDC 28 (1978) 213; Guth, "Enforcing the Law," pp. 9–10, 12; Bowker, "Some Archdeacons' Court Books," pp. 291, 309; Woodcock, *Medieval Ecclesiastical Courts*, p. 79; Wunderli, *London Church Courts*, p. 81. Pike, "Crime and Criminals," p. 5, found it impossible to determine from the Seville records what proportion of sex offenses were dealt with by the Church courts there, although she found very few such cases in the municipal courts.

[259] Donahue, "Canon Law on the Formation of Marriage," pp. 148–49, 154 n. 40.

[260] Helmholz, *Marriage Litigation*, pp. 166–67.

were handled. There seems to have been remarkably little judicial freewheeling and a great deal more respectful attention to legal doctrine than one might have expected in a system that lacked provisions for systematic review of the actions of lower courts by appellate tribunals.[261]

Secular courts were experimenting during this period with their procedures in sex offenses and matrimonial matters. At Cremona, motivated perhaps by the large volume of business, the city fathers decreed that prosecutions of sex cases, particularly those involving pimps and prostitutes, should follow a summary procedure, stripped of the customary forms and solemnities.[262] A number of Italian towns limited to certain family members the right to prefer sex complaints, particularly in cases of adultery, fornication, or incest. A Faenza statute alleged that this had to be done in order to prevent a flood of false accusations, and an Ancona statute also complained that unfounded denunciations of alleged sexual offenders presented problems both for judicial administration and for civic tranquillity.[263]

Although canonical courts had well-established rules of evidence—not always followed in practice, however—for dealing with the proof of marriage by the testimony of witnesses, municipal lawmakers were not eager to imitate canonistic models. At Lucca, the city statutes required that marriage be proved in the old-fashioned way, that is by documentary evidence concerning dowry and other property transactions related to the alleged marriage. Even in the Church's own courts the defense of choice in response to charges of adultery, fornication, and infanticide, even as late as the fifteenth century, was compurgation, rather than the alternatives stipulated in the decretals.[264]

Conclusions

During the period between the Black Death and the beginning of the sixteenth century, royal and municipal law became more deeply involved in the legal control of marriage and sexual behavior than they previously had been. This phenomenon was particularly marked in the towns of northern Italy, but it was by no means confined either to towns or to Italy.

The new activism of civil governments in dealing with sexual problems was in part a response to the social and demographic dislocation that resulted from

[261] Ourliac, "Notes sur le mariage," p. 55; Helmholz, *Marriage Litigation*, pp. 2–3, 134–35, 187; Wunderli, *London Church Courts*, p. 60.

[262] Cremona, *Statuta* 121, p. 42.

[263] March of Ancona, *Constitutiones* 4.41, fol. 40v; Faenza, *Ordinamenta*, Constitutiones domini papae vicarium 4.41; Modena, *Statuta* 3.64, fol. 80v; Urbino, *Statuta* 4.39, fol. 91v.

[264] Lucca, *Statuta* 1.100, fol. 48v; Felino Sandeo, *Consilia* 19, fol. 18ra–rb; Aufréri, *Decisiones* 309, fol. 74r; Helmholz, "Infanticide," p. 383, and "Crime, Compurgation, and the Courts," pp. 13–18. The procedural shortcomings of the courts probably had a great deal to do with the apparent ineffectiveness of prosecutions for sex offenses; Wunderli, *London Church Courts*, pp. 34–39.

the epidemics of 1348 and after. Efforts to control sexual behavior were also symptomatic of the growing strength of political and constitutional institutions during the later Middle Ages and may, to some degree, also have reflected a growing disenchantment among Western Europeans, including rulers, with the capacity of ecclesiastical institutions to deal adequately and fairly with marital problems and sexual behavior.

The Church was not prepared, however, to step aside from its traditional role as the arbiter of Christian sexuality. Church courts continued, perhaps even expanded, their efforts to cope with the sex among the faithful. They remained the primary tribunals for dealing with marriage, divorce, and separation litigation; in addition they continued to deal routinely with concubinage, violations of clerical celibacy, and a wide range of sex crimes and offenses, including adultery, fornication, rape, prostitution, and homosexual activities. But in all of these problem areas, Church courts during this period faced growing competition from civil courts.

We are far better informed about the actual practices of European courts, both secular and ecclesiastical, during the years between 1348 and 1517 than for any earlier period of human history. Judicial records survive from this period in quantities unparalleled in earlier generations. While this was in part due to improvements in record-keeping routines, it probably also reflects an actual increase in the activities of courts at all levels throughout Western Europe.

As a result of the relatively abundant survival of documents of practice from this period, we are for the first time in a position to reach informed judgments about the relationship between the teachings of the law faculties and the practice of courts. Comparisons between what the law and its commentators said ought to be happening and what the courts were actually doing show that in large measure practice reflected academic doctrine. The gap between the views of academic jurists and the actions of the ecclesiastical judges was fairly narrow, at least in the law of sex crime and domestic relations.

During this period, too, we have evidence about population characteristics, family organization, and social structure (at least for a few places and for short spans of time) that does not exist for earlier periods. Studies of these demographic and social records provide information about the social context in which the law of sexual behavior operated. This hard information about family structure shows a fairly high degree of conformity between marriage practices and the norms that were taught in the faculties of theology and canon law.

But there were striking and important divergences, too. While the courts usually applied the norms of consensual marriage theory to the cases that came before them, the evidence of practice makes it plain that people by and large had not fully accepted the premise that consent alone made a marriage. The general public remained convinced that a marriage had to be consummated sexually before it was "real." In addition, people often married in ways that emphasized *traditio* and the transfer of property between families, despite the insistence of lawmakers and jurists that the essence of marriage lay in free consent to wed a partner freely chosen. Similarly, academic commentators took a dim view of concubinage, but this institution clearly persisted in practice far more widely than one might have thought from reading statute books and academic treatises. Divorce and separation also showed discrepancies between social reality and legal theory. The courts granted divorces with the right of remarriage when the law said they could not do so, they granted separations on grounds that the canons did not recognize, and conversely some of the grounds for separation that are most elaborately discussed in the commentaries appear very infrequently in practice.

There was relatively little that was new in the law of this period concerning adultery and fornication, the commonest sex offenses. Municipal legislation shows that civic lawmakers in this period perceived sodomy and homosexual behavior as ominous threats to society and attempted to penalize them with great severity.

Prostitution flourished on a large scale and the involvement of towns and cities in the operation of brothels was a striking novelty of the age. The flourishing of prostitution in the fourteenth and fifteenth centuries may have reflected reactions to the demographic changes resulting from the Black Death, and other disasters, including the Hundred Years War and the other conflicts that fill the pages of chroniclers and political historians. Population decline as a result of pestilence, war, and famine may well have made it even more difficult for men to marry at an early age. Indeed the shortage of suitable partners may have made it impossible, or excessively expensive, for considerable numbers of them to marry at all. In addition, disproportionately large numbers of prostitutes may well have perished from the Black Death, and a shortage of them could help to explain the concern of town governments to foster the trade by providing civic patronage for its practice.[265] The comparative respectability implied by civic management of prostitution may also have helped to mitigate the discontent of those who wanted wives but could not afford them. It is scarcely surprising that this period of public promotion of prostitution witnessed a perceptible slackening of campaigns to reform prostitutes.

Underpinning much of the legislation, legal commentary, and practice of this age were a number of premises that were not often articulated expressly by writers or judges but that seem to have formed the basis for a good deal of what they wrote and did. Among these was a set of assumptions about female sexuality—the belief that women possessed unquenchable sexual appetites, that they were more likely than men to seek illicit sexual satisfaction, and that they were more often than not the root and source of marriage problems and sexual immorality.[266] "The laws presume that all women are usually bad, because they

[265] Otis, *Prostitution*, pp. 101–102.

[266] Strongly antifeminist beliefs appeared in many writers of this period. See, for example, the *Miroir de mariage* of Eustache Deschamps (ca. 1346–ca. 1406), ed. Gaston Raynaud in vol. 9 of Deschamps' *Oeuvres complètes*, 11 vols. (Paris: Firmin Didot,

are so full of mischief and vices that are difficult to describe," wrote Giovanni Nevizzani, and his statement summarized assumptions that many lawmakers and law writers shared.[267] For a few purposes the law assumed that women were equal to men, but those purposes were restricted to a handful of situations—sex rights in marriage and child custody, primarily. It is also true that in one or two situations the law treated women more leniently than men, but these were exceptional.[268] Women were generally handicapped by the law, not favored by it, and this was notably true in the law concerning sexual behavior. Even the way in which women dressed might be prescribed in minute detail by municipal law—sumptuary statutes to regulate male fashions are rare.[269]

Another assumption that runs through the legislation, legal commentaries, and judicial actions of this period is the moral and legal disavowal of pleasure, and sexual pleasure in particular, as a legitimate human goal. True, many of the canons and statutes that dealt with adultery, fornication, and homosexual activity were motivated in part by the conviction that these behaviors, if unchecked, would disrupt the social order and therefore that society's interests required that they be restrained and regulated in minute detail. But the underlying belief that sex was evil because it was pleasurable was clearly a factor in giving sex law the shape that it took. Allied to this was another ancient belief, namely that sex dirtied and defiled those who engaged in it. Overt references to ritual pollution and the need to cleanse oneself from it occur only rarely in legal writing during this period, but belief in these mechanisms clearly underlies a good deal of the sex law of the age.

Finally this age saw the beginning of a novel kind of sexual behavior that did not attract much attention from legal writers before 1500, although it was to become an important issue for later generations. I refer to pornography. The Middle Ages produced very little explicitly sex-oriented literature, and this may have been true because prior to the end of the thirteenth century reading almost always meant reading aloud. When silent reading began to become common, as it gradually did in the fourteenth and fifteenth centuries, this tended to

1878–1903; repr. New York: Johnson Reprint Corp., 1966); *The Fifteen Joys of Marriage*, trans. Elisabeth Abbott (New York: Bramhall House, 1959); Archbishop Giovanni della Casa (1503–56), *Se s'abbia da prender moglie (An uxor sit ducenda)*, 17–18, ed. and trans. Ugo Enrico Paoli (Florence: F. LeMonnier, 1946), pp. 168–83. Similar stereotypes of good and bad women appear in Gower's *Vox clamantis* 5.6, ll. 293–468, ed. Macaulay 4:209–13. Among the canonists of the period Joannes a Capistrano, *Comm.* to X 3.2.6, fol. 327ra–rb, most clearly shows the influence of these beliefs, although occasional references show up in many other writers as well. See also Jeay, "Sexuality and Family," p. 329.

[267] Giovanni Nevizzani, *Silva nuptialis*, fol. 21va.

[268] Venice, *Statuta emendatissima* 2.15, fol. 43v; Ancona, *Constitutiones* 3.37, p. 93; see also above, pp. 484–85.

[269] I have seen only one such statute: Todi, *Statuta* 3.233, fol. 99r.

encourage, for the first time since late antiquity, the writing and copying of erotic tales and stories, sometimes accompanied by explicit illustrations.[270]

Sex law in Western Christendom on the eve of the Reformation was founded on assumptions and beliefs that had developed slowly over the previous millennium. The legal system that had evolved for dealing with sexual behavior and marital problems translated the ideals and finespun speculations of theologians and moralists into cruder forms needed for coping with the actual behavior of real people. The religious shocks that resulted from the Reformation produced major readjustments in this system. But, as we shall see, the Reformation also left much of the framework of medieval sex law intact, and sizable portions remain in force in modern times.

[270] Paul Saenger, "Silent Reading: Its Impact on Late Medieval Script and Society," *Viator* 13 (1982) 412–13.

11

Sexual Issues in the Age of the Reformation: Ninety-Five Theses to *Tametsi*, 1517–1563

Religious unrest and dissent from the doctrines and discipline of the established Church were far from unusual in medieval Europe. The criticisms of Church practices and beliefs made by the early sixteenth-century reformers were not particularly novel. What was unprecedented was the success these critics achieved in securing a hearing, the breadth of support their criticisms attracted, and the Roman Church's inability to silence this set of adversaries as it had others. Sixteenth-century reformers were by no means united among themselves. They disagreed about objectives, adopted different priorities, and failed to present anything like a common front to the authorities they attacked. The Reformation was not a single movement, but rather a concatenation of protests by reformers with diverse agendas, both theological and practical. Not all of Rome's critics in this period ended up in the Protestant camp. Some of the most vociferous foes of ecclesiastical abuses, such as Erasmus, remained within the Roman obedience and sought to reform the establishment from inside.[1]

[1] On the Reformation and Counter-Reformation, see generally G. R. Elton, *Reformation Europe* (New York: Harper & Row, 1963); Owen Chadwick, *The Reformation*, Pelican History of the Church, vol. 3 (Harmondsworth: Penguin, 1964); H. G. Koenigsberger and George L. Mosse, *Europe in the Sixteenth Century* (London: Longmans, Green and Co.; New York: Holt, Rinehart and Winston, 1968); Harold J. Grimm, *The Reformation Era, 1500–1560*, 2d ed. (New York: Macmillan, 1973); Pierre Janelle, *The Catholic Reformation* (Milwaukee: Bruce Publishing Co., 1949); A. G. Dickens, *The Counter Reformation* (New York: Harcourt, Brace & World, 1969); Hubert Jedin, *Katholische Reformation oder Gegenreformation? Ein Versuch zur Klärung der Begriffe nebst einem Jubiläumsbetractung über das Trienter Konzil* (Lucerne: J. Stocker, 1946); Henry O. Evennett, *The Spirit of the Counter-Reformation*, ed. John Bossy (Cambridge: At the University Press, 1968). On Luther see particularly E. G. Rupp, *Luther's Progress to the Diet of Worms* (New York: Harper & Row, 1964); Roland H. Bainton, *Here I Stand: A Life of Martin Luther* (New York: Abingdon-Cokesbury Press, 1950); Edgar M. Carlson, *The Reinterpretation of Luther* (Philadelphia: Westminster Press, 1948); and Erik H. Erikson, *Young Man Luther: A Study in Psychoanalysis and History* (New York: W. W. Norton & Co., 1958). The best general treatment of Calvin is still François Wendel, *Calvin: The Origins and Development of His Religious Thought*, trans.

Major Protestant reformers, notably Luther, Calvin, and Zwingli, attacked three facets of traditional Roman Catholicism: its ecclesiology, its theology, and its morality. The ecclesiological strictures of the reformers centered on papal power and the relationship of the pope to bishops and to Church councils. The reformers also rejected Catholicism's distinction between clergy and laity and the roles of those groups in the governance of the Western Church. Theological issues that the reformers raised included the problems of grace and free will, the relationship between faith and good works in the Christian scheme of salvation, the nature and number of the sacraments, the concept of indulgences, confession, penance for sins, and related matters.

Sexual behavior was prominent among the moral and disciplinary issues that concerned reformers. They rejected the belief that marriage was a sacrament, repudiated the mandatory practice of celibacy, argued that the clergy should be free to marry, criticized the Church's marriage law particularly for its tolerance of clandestine marriage and lay concubinage, and discarded much of the medieval Church's teaching about the role of sex in marriage. Most reformers were prepared under some circumstances to tolerate divorce followed by remarriage.

At a more fundamental level, Protestant writers placed a different value on erotic love than did their Catholic counterparts. While they were keenly aware that sexual love could disrupt human relations, engender violence, and distract people from spiritual issues, reformed theologians characteristically adopted a more positive attitude toward sex than was traditional in Catholic thought. The reformers insisted that sex must be used responsibly, but they also looked upon it as a source of joy and strength, a force for good in married life, a blessing bestowed by the Creator, not a flaw in human nature engendered by sin.[2]

The Reformers and Sexual Issues
MARRIAGE

Sixteenth-century reformers rejected many features of medieval marriage practice. Like earlier critics—not all of them heretics—Luther, Calvin, and Zwingli deplored the prevalence of clandestine marriage and the Alexandrine theory of marriage by present consent alone, which made clandestine unions so easy to contract. Luther insisted not only that marriage must be public, but that consent of the parents of both parties was essential for Christian marriage, a stance that Martin Bucer (1491–1551) strongly supported as well.[3] Disobedience to one's parents, Luther claimed, was rebellion against God. Christian authorities,

---

Philip Mairet (New York: Harper & Row, 1963). On Calvin's sexual views see André Biéler, *L'homme et la femme dans la morale calviniste: La doctrine réformé sur l'amour, le mariage, le célibat, le divorce, l'adultère, et la prostitution, considérée dans son cadre historique* (Geneva: Labor et Fides, 1963).

[2] Fuchs, *Sexual Desire and Love*, pp. 157–63.

[3] Bucer, *De regno Christi libri duo* 2.18, ed. François Wendel in *Martini Bvceri opera latina*, vol. 15 (Paris: Presses universitaires de France, 1955), pp. 157–62.

Luther believed, should not merely forbid marriages contracted without parental consent, but should hold them invalid.[4] Calvin agreed. Calvin's legislation at Geneva included a provision that rescinded marriages contracted by young people without the blessings of their parents,[5] while the marriage court that Zwingli established in Zürich also held such marriages invalid.[6]

An even more basic break with the past was the resounding rejection by every major reformer of the Roman Catholic doctrine that marriage was a sacrament. Calvin knew that this belief had appeared during the medieval period (although he credited it erroneously to Pope Gregory VII). He denounced the notion as a corruption that arose from misunderstanding the reference in Eph. 5:32 to marriage as a mystery (St. Jerome had translated *mysterion* as *sacramentum* in the Vulgate). Moreover, Calvin observed, it was hardly consistent for Catholic theologians to maintain that marriage was a sacrament and then to vilify marital sex as unclean pollution and carnal filth. This, Calvin thought, was absurd; indeed, it verged on the grotesque.[7] Luther also rejected the sacramentality of marriage and was, if anything, even more scornful of the teaching. In his 1520 treatise *On the Babylonian Captivity of the Church*, Luther maintained that marriage was a product of the natural order and in no sense a sacrament of the Christian religion.[8] Philip Melanchthon (1497–1560), whom Luther respected more than any other contemporary theologian, delighted his admirer by seconding his rejection of the sacramentality of marriage.[9] Radical reformers, such as the Anabaptists, whom Luther emphatically did not admire, at least agreed with him on this point.[10]

---

[4] Martin Luther, *Von den Ehesachen* (1530), in his *Werke, kritische Gesamtausgabe* (Weimar: Hermann Böhlaus, 1883– ; repr. Graz: Akademische Druck- u. Verlagsanstalt, 1966; cited hereafter as WA) 30/3:198–248, and *Das Eltern die Kinder zur Ehe nicht zwingen noch hindern, und die Kinder ohne der Eltern willen sich nicht verloben sollen* (1524) in WA 15:155–69; Steven Ozment, *When Fathers Ruled: Family Life in Reformation Europe* (Cambridge, MA: Harvard University Press, 1983), pp. 36–44.

[5] John Calvin, *Ecclesiastical Ordinances of 1561*, quoted in Fuchs, *Sexual Desire and Love*, pp. 143–44.

[6] Ulrich Zwingli, Zurich Marrriage Ordinance (1525), in his *Selected Works*, ed. Samuel Macauley Jackson (Philadelphia: University of Pennsylvania Press, 1901; repr. 1972), p. 121.

[7] Calvin, *Institutes of the Christian Religion* 4.19.34–36, ed. John T. McNeill, trans. Ford Lewis Battles, 2 vols., Library of Christian Classics, vol. 20–21 (Philadelphia: Westminster Press, 1960) 2:1480–83. © 1960 W. L. Jenkins. Excerpts reprinted and used by permission of The Westminster Press, Philadelphia, PA.

[8] Luther, *De captivitate Babylonica ecclesiae praeludium*, in WA 6:550–53; Ozment, *When Fathers Ruled*, pp. 31–33.

[9] Melanchthon, *Loci communes*, Signs, in *Melanchthon and Bucer*, ed. and trans. Wilhelm Pauck, Library of Christian Classics, vol. 19 (Philadelphia: Westminster Press, 1969), pp. 135–36.

[10] Sebastian Franck, Letter to John Campanus, in *Spiritual and Anabaptist Writers: Documents Illustrative of the Radical Reform*, ed. George Huntston Williams, Library of Christian Classics, vol. 25 (Philadelphia: Westminster Press, 1957), pp. 148–49.

CLERICAL CELIBACY

Having rejected the belief that marriage was a sacrament, the reformers advocated abolition of clerical celibacy. The clergy ought to be free to marry, Luther declared in his address *To the Christian Nobility of the German Nation* (1520). He characterized Catholic insistence on celibacy as tyrannical, arbitrary, and wanton, adding that celibacy was not God's commandment and certainly not necessary for salvation.[11] Calvin heartily agreed with the other reform leaders on this score:

> Surely the forbidding of marriage to priests came about by an impious tyranny not only against God's word but also against all equity. First, to forbid what the Lord left free was by no means lawful to men. Again, that the Lord expressly took care by his Word that this freedom should not be infringed upon is too clear to require a long proof.[12]

Moreover, Calvin continued, celibacy, as a late development in Catholic practice, could not be justified by appeal to ancient custom or immemorial tradition.[13] Not only was celibacy unsupported by scripture or ancient practice, but the reformers agreed that it engendered moral corruption. Priests and other clerics bound in theory to celibacy found the discipline in practice untenable, the reformers maintained. Hence Roman clerics often kept concubines or, even worse, indulged in unnatural sexual passions with other men. Ironically, Melanchthon declared, celibacy did not promote sexual purity at all, since married persons were often more chaste than their celibate clergy.[14] The sexual habits of the Roman Catholic clergy, according to reformers, were a sewer of iniquity, a scandal to the laity, and a threat of damnation to the clergy themselves. Bucer, too, considered it an offense against God to deny men the right to marry.[15] Zwingli, like Bucer, maintained that the clergy had a perfect right to marry if they wished to, just as other Christians did. To deny them the exercise of that right was a perversion of Christian doctrine and moral order. The Reformation accordingly offered priests who lived with concubines the opportunity to regularize their domestic situations and to legitimize their offspring at the same time. It was an opportunity that sizable numbers of clerics accepted. It must have presented a sore temptation to many others who, for one reason or another, chose not to avail themselves of it.[16]

---

[11] Luther, *An den Christlichen Adel deutscher Nation von des christliches Standes Besserung*, in WA 6:442; Ozment, *When Fathers Ruled*, pp. 1–12.

[12] Calvin, *Institutes* 4.12.23, McNeill and Battles 2:1250.

[13] Calvin, *Institutes* 4.12.26–27, McNeill and Battles 2:1252–53.

[14] Melanchthon, *Loci communes*, Vows of monks, p. 59.

[15] Bucer, *De regno Christi* 2.45, pp. 226–31.

[16] Luther, *Von den Ehesachen*, in WA 30/3:222; Calvin, *Institutes* 4.5.14, 4.12.28, in McNeill and Battles 2:1097, 1253–54; Zwingli, *Selected Works*, pp. 25–39, 73–75, 114. Yost, "Reformation Defense of Clerical Marriage," pp. 152–54.

Luther, however, was no uncritical admirer of the married state. There was truth, he said, in the proverb that "It takes a brave man to wed a wife." But although marriage might entail misery, the married man was still better off than his unwillingly celibate brother: "In any case marriage is preferable, for it is better to be unhappy without sinning than to sin without unhappiness, much less to sin and also be unhappy."[17] Sexual feelings, according to Luther, were inborn, part of our essential human nature. It was folly, he asserted, to talk of sexual feelings as if they were something voluntary: we experience sexual feelings, whether we want them or not. Men and women must learn to confront their sexuality and deal with it as an inescapable part of being human.[18] Not only was it not shameful to feel sexual desire, but there was no intrinsic wrong in satisfying it, since sex was essential to human health.[19]

MARITAL SEX

Both Luther and Calvin rejected the teaching that marital sex must be specifically directed toward procreation in order to be without sin. Calvin conceded that there might be some reason to believe that when married couples yielded to lust and had sex just for venereal pleasure they fell short of Christian perfection; but he added that God pardons whatever sin might be involved because of the value of holy matrimony. Marriage, he thought, was so good that it overcame the sexual depravity inherent in conjugal relations. Calvin, in effect, stood the standard Roman view about marital sex and celibacy on its head. Marriage was the greater good, benevolent and conducive to holiness, while celibacy was a rare condition, always morally suspect, which usually led to unhappiness and sin.[20]

Bucer adopted a position similar to Calvin's, but without some of the qualifications that Calvin insisted upon. It was blasphemy, Bucer maintained, to call marital sex sinful.[21]

Luther explicitly rejected Jerome's condemnation of the married man who burned with sexual desire for his wife:

> The old teachers used to quote the heathen saying: 'The too-ardent lover commits adultery with his own wife.' But a pagan said that and accordingly I pay it no heed and maintain that it is not true. No man can commit adultery with his own wife, unless he does not treat her as his wife or caresses her as if she were not his wife.[22]

[17] Luther, *Das siebente Kapitel aus der Epistel S. Pauli zu den Chorinthern* (1523) in WA 12:100: "Eyntmal es yhe besser ist, unlust on sunde, denn sunde on unlust, ia sunde mit unlust datzu."

[18] Luther, *Vom ehelichen Leben* (1522), in WA 10/2:276.

[19] Luther, *Vom ehelichen Leben*, in WA 10/2:301.

[20] Calvin, *Commentaria* to Deut. 24:5 and 1 Cor. 7:5, quoted in Fuchs, *Sexual Desire and Love*, pp. 141–42.

[21] Bucer, *De regno Christi* 2.46, p. 232.

[22] Luther, *Siebente Kapitel zu den Chorinthern*, in WA 12:101–102: "Es haben wol

Calvin, however, was unwilling to reject this time-honored formula, for he feared that to do so might leave the way open for wanton and unrestrained romping in the matrimonial bed. Instead, he admonished married couples to remember that their union was blessed by God and that they must therefore refrain from "uncontrolled and dissolute lust" in conjugal relations:

> Therefore let not married persons think that all things are permitted to them, but let each man have his own wife soberly, and each wife her own husband. So doing let them not admit anything at all that is unworthy of the honorableness and temperance of marriage. For it is fitting that thus wedlock contracted in the Lord be recalled to measure and modesty so as not to wallow in extreme lewdness.[23]

Marital sex was virtuous in Calvin's eyes only so long as the couple observed the limits of modesty and propriety. Even so, Calvin considered marriage "a good and holy ordinance of God" and indignantly rejected the opinions of those who described marital sex as unclean and a source of defilement.[24]

Anabaptists and other radical reformers saw marital sex in much the same way that Calvin did. Like him, they considered sexual lust a serious impediment to the spiritual life and felt that married persons should be wary of creaturely things, lest they be led astray from the straight and narrow path to salvation.[25] Nonetheless they deemed marriage a laudable institution and found in it the most appropriate metaphor to describe the relationship between believers and God.[26]

Although the major reformers demoted marriage from sacramental status, they nonetheless considered it a great good, the spiritually preferable state of life for most people in this world.[27] Sex, they believed, was a necessary part of any marriage. Marital sex both symbolized and embodied conjugal affection.[28] The virtue of sex in marriage, as the reformers viewed things, was not that it led to procreation, but rather that it expressed and increased the couple's love for one another. It was the affectionate and loving relationship between married persons that constituted the good of marriage and lay at the heart of the marital

---

ettlich alte lerer den heydnischen spruch gefuret: 'Wer zu hitzig ist ynn der liebe, der ist an seynem eygen weybe eyn ehebrecher.' Aber eyn hyde hatts geredt, darumb acht ich seyn nicht, und sage, es sey nicht war. Es kan freylich niemant an seynem weybe eyn ehebrecher werden, er wolt sie denn nicht sur seyn weyb hallten, odder nicht als seyn weyb berüren."

[23] Calvin, *Institutes* 2.8.44, McNeill and Battles 1:407–408.

[24] Calvin, *Institutes* 4.12.24–25, McNeill and Battles 2:1250–51.

[25] Thus, for example, Thomas Müntzer, Sermon Before the Princes (1524), in *Spiritual and Anabaptist Writers*, p. 60.

[26] Thus, for example, Melchior Hoffmann, The Ordinance of God (1530), in *Spiritual and Anabaptist Writers*, pp. 185–203.

[27] Fuchs, *Sexual Desire and Love*, p. 142.

[28] Bucer, *De regno Christi* 2.21, pp. 164–65; Biéler, *L'homme et la femme*, pp. 42–44.

state. Procreation, in their scheme of things, was a second-order virtue in married life.[29]

EXTRAMARITAL SEX

While the reformers considered marital sex blameless, they were no more prepared than their Roman counterparts to countenance sex outside of marriage. Indeed, the reformers and their followers treated nonmarital sex with considerable harshness and had no patience with the resigned tolerance of some Catholic writers. Fornication, Luther declared, was evil: it was bad for body, soul, family, fortune, and honor.[30] Zwingli also opposed sexual license and made seduction subject to stiff penalties at Zürich.[31] Calvin, to be sure, thought that extramarital sex had a place, of sorts, in the scheme of salvation. The sordid squalor of extramarital sex, particularly with prostitutes, he argued, made manifest the fallen condition of mankind. Prostitution, Calvin believed, was thus a God-given sign of the consequences of sin, and the harlot played a role in the design of salvation, since the spectacle of her depraved life should incite God-fearing Christians to reform their own lives.[32]

Some of Calvin's Puritan followers took a considerably less benign view. They saw adultery and prostitution as both physical and spiritual offenses that merited stern retribution, physical and spiritual, in this life as well as hereafter. Fornication or adultery, they believed, resulted from serious mental and spiritual shortcomings. Christians must keep their hearts and minds pure and avoid situations that might lure them to pursue fleshly desires outside of marriage. Those who yielded to sexual temptation or enticed others to yield deserved no mercy.[33] Bucer argued that civil authorities ought to punish adultery by death. Calvin's followers added that if civil authorities failed to do their duty in this regard, God would intervene directly. The Lord demanded that sexual sins receive exemplary punishment in this world so as to deter others from similar behavior. Thus Samuel Saxey, who published his *Straunge and Wonderfull Example of the Iudgement of almighty God, shewed vpon two adulterous persons in London* in 1583, related the cautionary tale of a couple who kept an adulterous rendezvous in St. Bride's Church, whereupon a fire broke out and burned the pair to death. Divine judgment had decreed, according to Saxey, that the couple who had been consumed by the fires of illicit passion must then be incinerated physically. Saxey also found spiritual uplift in the case of a prostitute hanged for adultery. Her fate, he maintained, was not at all disproportionate to her offense, and, moreover, it might dissuade others from wallowing in carnal

---

[29] Fuchs, *Sexual Desire and Love*, p. 142.

[30] Luther, *Vom ehelichen Leben*, in WA 10/2:299.

[31] Zwingli, *Selected Works*, p. 121.

[32] Biéler, *L'homme et la femme*, pp. 42–44.

[33] Robert V. Schnucker, "La position puritaine à l'égard de l'adultère," *Annales: é.s.c.* 27 (1972) 1382. I should like to thank my colleague, Professor Carole Shammas, for calling this article to my attention.

sin.[34] But Saxey's views were puritan and extreme. It was, in fact, more common practice in Calvinist circles to imprison adulterers and prostitutes than to burn or hang them.[35]

DIVORCE AND REMARRIAGE

Reformers further differed from their opponents in their approach to divorce and remarriage. While Roman Catholic canonists and theologians, as we have seen, had severely restricted the grounds on which marriages could be dissolved and allowed annulments only when the validity of supposed marriages was seriously in doubt, sixteenth-century reformers contenanced the outright dissolution of failed marriages and allowed the innocent party to remarry. This difference resulted from the reformers' rejection of the sacramentality of marriage. Since Luther, Calvin, and others denied that marriage was a sacrament, they felt less constrained than writers of the Roman persuasion in determining when and under what circumstances a marriage between Christians might legitimately be dissolved.

Luther was particularly indignant about traditional canon law on marriage and divorce:

> The cursed papal law [he wrote] has created such confusion and distress, while the negligence of both the spiritual and temporal powers has caused such awful abuses and dreadful situations, that I would much prefer to ignore the whole problem and not to hear about it.[36]

Despite this, he plunged straightway into a scathing denunciation of the errors and hypocrisy of canon law on divorce, which he described as "A net for gold and silver and a noose for the soul."[37] While he lamented the breakup of marriages and denied that he was in favor of divorce, Luther nonetheless maintained that in some situations not only was divorce unavoidable, but remarriage was also to be encouraged, since the natural appetite for sex made it unlikely that the couple would be able to live apart in chastity.[38] Luther specified some grounds for divorce that carried a right or even a duty of remarriage: when the partners were unable to have intercourse with one another, when one party

[34] Schnucker, "Position puritaine," p. 1380.

[35] Bellamy, *Crime and Public Order*, p. 166. Luther also believed that the death penalty should be imposed on adulterers, and regretted that authorities were unlikely to implement this ideal; *Vom ehelichen Leben*, in WA 10/2:289.

[36] Luther, *Vom ehelichen Leben*, in WA 10/2:275: "Denn der iamer durch Bepstlich verdampte gesetz alsso schendlich verwyrret ist, datzu durch hynlessig regiment, beyde geystlichs und welltlichs schwerts sso viel grewlicher missbreuch und irriger felle sich drynnen begeben haben, das ich nicht gern dreyn sehe, noch gern davon höre."

[37] Luther, *Vom ehelichen Leben*, in WA 10/2:280: "Unnd tzwar er sie auch selb nicht fester noch stercker hellt, den biss man sie mit gollt und silber umbstosse, Und sie auch nur datzu erfunden sind, das sie gelltnetz und seelstrick seyn sollten, 1 Pet. 2."

[38] Luther, *Vom ehelichen Leben*, in WA 10/2:280.

committed adultery, or refused to have sexual relations or interposed so many objections to sex that marital relations became a struggle, then the couple ought to divorce and the partners should enter new marriages in the hope that these might work out more satisfactorily.[39] Luther also favored retaining the canonical grounds of *saevitia*, but for separation only, without the right of remarriage by either partner. A man who found himself with a shrewish mate, said Luther, had no claim to remarry, since his wife, disagreeable as she might otherwise be, had not refused to have sex with him. He might well be justified in separating from her, lest he yield to the temptation to do something worse, but since he had not been deprived of conjugal rights, he could not remarry in order to satisfy his sexual desires—"He who wants the heat must put up with the smoke."[40] The same reasoning presumably applied to battered wives as to henpecked husbands.

Whereas Luther grounded his teachings about divorce and remarriage on elemental feelings about sex, and rejected Catholic views on the matter with fiery defiance, Calvin was cooler and more reasoned in the exposition of his divorce doctrine. Calvin, like Luther, would allow divorce under certain circumstances, but for him the right to remarry following divorce was not so much a matter of sexual need as of freedom of conscience. Religious judges had no right to require a man or woman whose spouse committed adultery either to continue in a broken marriage or to endure involuntary celibacy. Religious authorities, Calvin noted, could not possibly restrain every vice. They must take account of what people are able to do and not impose unreasonable or impossible limitations on personal conduct, especially limitations that are nowhere prescribed by Scripture.[41]

Other reform leaders were also prepared to countenance divorce and remarriage. Bucer argued that the Scriptures clearly authorized divorce on account of adultery. Like Zwingli, Bucer added that if either party suffered from incurable sexual impotence, leprosy, or insanity, civil authorities were justified in permitting divorce on those grounds as well.[42] It was an essential condition of marriage, Bucer thought, that the spouses must maintain a common life. Catholics were wrong, he declared, in teaching that the marital bond persisted after a couple had separated.[43] Accordingly, if either spouse deserted the other without cause, the innocent party had the right to remarry, according to Bucer.[44] Moreover, since marital sex was also essential to married life, Bucer

[39] Ibid. 10/2:287–91.

[40] Ibid. 10/2:291: "Wer des fewers haben will, muss den rauch auch leyden."

[41] Zwingli's Marriage Court at Zürich was also empowered to grant divorces, with the right of remarriage, on a variety of grounds, including adultery, insanity, desertion, leprosy, and other health problems; *Selected Works*, pp. 121–22; Fuchs, *Sexual Desire and Love*, p. 138.

[42] Bucer, *De regno Christi* 2.7.31–32, 35–37, 42, pp. 186–88, 197–204, 217–20.

[43] Ibid. 2.7.38, p. 206.

[44] Ibid. 2.7.41, pp. 206–207.

contended that if either partner persistently refused to have conjugal relations with the other, the couple were no longer married.[45]

Anabaptists and other radical reformers, however, considered these teachings as shocking departures from the revealed word of God. Divorce and remarriage might be permitted solely on grounds of adultery, according to them, and no other reason could justify the dissolution of Christian marriage. True, if one party to a marriage deviated from the truths of Christian faith as the Anabaptists understood those truths, the other party might be obliged to sever their relationship, but that was shunning, not divorce, in the Anabaptist view of things.[46]

THE PLACE OF WOMEN

The positive value that many reformers attributed to human sexuality also led them to reject some misogynist tenets of medieval anthropology. Luther, as usual, was colorful and forthright in stating his views. Earlier writers, he declared, spoke of women as sources of irritation, annoyance, and temptation, but nonetheless necessary for all of that. This attitude, Luther declared, verged on blasphemy, for womankind was a deliberate creation of God and had not sprung spontaneously into being. Hence to grumble and complain that women were unfortunate and irritating aberrations in a man's world was to criticize the work of the Creator. "But I suppose," he added, "that if women were to write books, they would say much the same sorts of things about men."[47] Neither sex, however, has any monopoly on virtue. We are what God made us and neither man nor woman ought to disparage the Creator's work:

> Thus we are: I a man, you a woman, just as God made us, to be honored and respected as Godly work. Man has no right to despise or scoff at woman's body or character, nor has woman any right to denigrate man. Rather each should honor the appearance and body of the other as a divine good work, an achievement that is pleasing even to God Himself.[48]

Such words as these should not be taken to mean, however, that reform leaders necessarily saw women as men's equals. For Bucer, Calvin, and others

[45] Ibid. 2.7.38, p. 208.

[46] Menno Simons, On the Ban (1550), in *Spiritual and Anabaptist Writers*, p. 265.

[47] Luther, *Vom ehelichen Leben*, in WA 10/2:292–93: "Ich hallt auch, wenn die weyber sollten bücher schreyben, sso wurden sie von mannen auch der gleychen schreyben."

[48] Ibid. 10/2:276: "[SS]o sint wyr, ich eyn man, du eyn weyb, und solch gutte gemecht will er geehrt und unveracht haben als seyn gottlich werck, das der man das weybs bild odder glid nicht verachte noch spotte. Widderumb das weyb den man nicht, ssondern eyn iglich ehre des andern bild und leyb als eyn gottlich gutt werck, das gott selbs wol gefellet."

women remained the weaker sex, frail, vain, and lightheaded, more prone than men to succumb to sexual temptation. Hence women must be guided and controlled by their fathers and husbands lest they stray into foolishness and sin.[49]

Catholic Reform and Counter-Reform

Many problems that troubled sixteenth-century Protestant leaders also bothered conscientious Catholics. In consequence during the first three-quarters of the century both a Catholic Reformation (that is, a movement among Roman Catholics to reform their Church from within) and a Counter-Reformation (that is a Catholic reaction against, and attack upon, the Protestant reformers) were going on simultaneously. The two movements were interrelated, and the line of demarcation between them was by no means clear-cut. But for purposes of analysis and description it is useful to treat them as separate movements.[50]

Roman Catholic reformers such as Erasmus (ca. 1466–1536), Gian Matteo Gilberti (Bishop of Verona, 1524–43), Cardinal Gaspar Contarini (1483–1542), and St. Philip Neri (1515–95) were troubled by many of the same issues that outraged Protestant leaders. Abuse of papal power, corruption in the distribution of church offices, scandals arising from clandestine marriages, doubts about the wisdom of mandatory celibacy for the clergy, reservations about long-standing policies concerning divorce, annulment, separation, and remarriage, questions about morally dubious money-raising schemes, such as the commercialization of indulgences—all of these issues were on the agendas of Catholic reformers. But much as they deplored the shortcomings and corruption of individual popes and bishops, and much as they criticized Church policies, these men were not prepared to reject papal authority and the traditional hierarchical structure of the medieval church.

Counter-Reformers, on the other hand, included such diverse figures as St. Peter Canisius (1521–97), Gian Pietro Caraffa (Pope Paul IV, 1555–59), and St. Vincent de Paul (ca. 1580–1660). While these men conceded that the Roman Church must clean its house, they viewed reform primarily as a tactic in the war against the Protestants. Counter-Reformers focused their energies and attention primarily on the struggle to safeguard the papacy and Roman doctrine from their Reformation critics. In the process the Counter-Reformation forces were prepared, even eager, to combat Protestants and Protestantism both physically and intellectually. Counter-Reformers were determined to win back the religious allegiance of those who had gone over to the Protestant movement; and in some regions (notably Poland) they succeeded in achieving that goal. In order to achieve success, the Counter-Reformers knew that they must not only attack the teachings of the opposition, but that they must also suppress

[49] Bucer, *De regno Christi* 2.9.55, pp. 261–62; Calvin, *Commentary on the Epistles of Paul the Apostle to the Corinthians*, to 1 Cor. 7:5, quoted in Fuchs, *Sexual Desire and Love*, pp. 141–42.

[50] Dickens, *Counter Reformation*, pp. 7–8; Jedin, *Katholische Reformation*.

the scandals and reform the abuses that had paved the way for Protestant victories.

The Council of Trent

Both Catholic Reformers and Counter-Reformers agreed that a general council was essential in order to frame an ambitious program of church reform and give it unassailable legitimacy, but resistance to proposals for summoning such a council were strong, particularly at the papal court. Curial officials were suspicious of both general councils and reform movements, however earnest and well-intentioned they might be. Curialists suspected—not without reason— that a reforming council would try to strip them of their powers and prerogatives and would inevitably attack the well-worn and profitable routines of papal administration. Members of the curia found it hard to believe that the Protestant movement had been as successful as it actually was and, long after large regions of Western and Central Europe had renounced allegiance to Rome, curial officials remained convinced that the Reformation would soon pass away as people grew tired of its novelties. The whole business would evaporate, they thought, leaving papal administration essentially unaltered and the traditional religious system much as it had been before Luther, Calvin, and the rest began their tiresome attacks upon established authority. The curialists were therefore prepared to postpone the summoning of a council as long as possible, preferably forever, and their inertia was matched by that of the early sixteenth-century popes themselves.[51]

Not until the election of Pope Paul III (1534–49) did the proposal to summon a reforming council become a serious proposition in Rome. Even then the pope moved cautiously. In the summer of 1536 he appointed a commission of cardinals to survey the needs of the Church and the problems to be dealt with by a council—if and when it were called. Since the members of the commission were drawn almost exclusively from the ranks of the Catholic reform movement, the body soon completed its work. It submitted a confidential report to the pope in March, 1537. In its report the commission documented frankly and in detail the record of past abuses of ecclesiastical power, including papal power. Although this explosive document was intended for the eyes of the pope and his chief advisers alone, rumors about its contents soon leaked out. Within a few months a purloined copy was published; it quickly became a best seller,

---

[51] The best current treatment of the Council of Trent is the magisterial work of Hubert Jedin, *Geschichte des Konzils von Trient*, 6 vols. (Freiburg i/Br.: Herder, 1949–75), of which a partial English translation is also available: *History of the Council of Trent*, trans. Ernest Graf, 2 vols. (London: Nelson, 1957–61). The authoritative edition of the massive documentation pertaining to the Council is *Concilium Tridentinum: Diariorum, actorum, epistularum, tractatuum nova collectio*, ed. by the Görres-Gesellschaft (Freiburg i/Br.: Herder, 1901–). A particularly useful collection of studies is *Das Weltkonzil von Trient: Sein Werden und Wirken*, ed. Georg Schreiber, 2 vols. (Freiburg i/Br.: Herder, 1951).

and Luther considered it so devastating to the papal cause that he translated it into German and published it, together with his own acid comments.[52]

Once the report of the commission had been made public, pressure on the pope to summon a reforming council mounted rapidly. But Paul III and his advisers continued to delay the formal proclamation of the council, while struggles continued behind the scenes over its venue (the curial party wanted it to meet in Rome, where it would be relatively easy to control), over its agenda, and over the question of whether and how seriously it should try to make peace with the Protestant leaders.

The long-awaited council finally convened on 13 December 1545 at Trent, a small city not far south of the Brenner Pass, on Italian soil, but also subject to the German Emperor, Charles V (1519–56), who insisted that the council must meet in his territories. Even when it finally opened, there was protracted wrangling over the council's agenda—Paul III and the curia wanted to concentrate on condemning the heresies of Luther, Calvin, and other reformers, while the Emperor, anxious to heal religious divisions in Germany, insisted that disciplinary problems must be dealt with first and that doctrinal issues could be settled later. As a compromise, it was agreed to deal with both doctrine and discipline simultaneously. As often happens with forced compromises, neither side was happy with the result.

MARRIAGE REFORM AT TRENT

The Council of Trent found it easier to compromise on disciplinary issues than on dogmatic ones. Although the council rejected all of the basic theological or ecclesiological criticisms leveled against Roman Catholicism by Protestant leaders, it was willing to make some modifications in the Catholic disciplinary system. One major area of reform was marriage law. The marriage reforms of Trent were embodied in the decree *Tametsi*, which the Council finally adopted after more than fifteen years of discussion, in its twenty-fourth session, 11 November 1563.[53] The final version of *Tametsi* revolutionized earlier practice and

---

[52] *Consilium delectorum cardinalium et aliorum praelatorum de emendanda ecclesia* (n.p.: 1549?); Luther, *Ratschlag eines Ausschuffes etlicher Kardinäle Papst Paulo III., auf seinem Befehl geschrieben und überantwortet* (1538), in WA 50:284–308.

[53] The final version of *Tametsi* may be found in *Concilium Tridentinum* 9:968–71, as well as in COD, pp. 731–35. The debates and discussions that led up to the final decree were long and intricate; see Giuseppe Di Mattia, "Il decreto *Tametsi* e le sue radici nel concilio di Bologna," *Apollinaris* 53 (1980) 476–500; Gaetano Cozzi, "Padri, figli e matrimoni clandestini (metà sec. XVI–metà sec. XVIII)," *La cultura* 2 (1976) 169–213; Reinhard Lettmann, *Die Diskussion über die klandestinen Ehen und die Einführung einer zur Gültigkeit verpflichtenden Eheschliessungsform auf dem Konzil von Trient: Eine kanonistische Untersuchung*, Münsterische Beiträge zur Theologie, vol. 51 (Münster: Aschendorff, 1967); Jean Bernhard, "Le décret *Tametsi* du concile de Trente: Triomphe du consensualisme matrimonial ou institution de la forme solennelle du mariage?" RDC 30 (1980) 209–33.

doctrine. While the canon explicitly, even defiantly, reiterated the long-standing teaching that the essence of marriage consisted in the free exchange of marital consent between parties competent to marry one another, *Tametsi* added the further critical requirement that in order to be valid the exchange of consent must take place in the presence of witnesses and that these witnesses must include the pastor of the parish where the parties made their promises. Marriages that failed to meet these requirements would from the time of the promulgation of the decree be considered invalid and of no effect. The Council further required parish priests to keep written records of marriages in their parishes.[54] These provisions of *Tametsi* sought to remove the conditions under which clandestine exchange of consent had for so long remained a viable option for those who wished to avoid public knowledge of their marriages. *Tametsi* made it impossible henceforth for secret marriages to compromise publicly celebrated nuptials. Although the council expressly stated that parental consent was not required for valid marriage—as both Luther and Calvin had argued it should be—the effect of the canon was to restore to parents greater legal control over the marriages of their offspring than they had enjoyed for many centuries in Catholic Europe.

Trent's marriage legislation also tidied up numerous loose ends. *Tametsi* instituted controls over the marriages of persons without fixed addresses, prohibited forced marriages, regulated the times at which weddings might be celebrated, abolished the rule that sexual intercourse created affinity, and made some technical adjustments in the law concerning consanguinity and affinity.[55] In addition, the council reiterated the ban on concubinage among the laity adopted by the Fifth Lateran Council and imposed stiff penalties on men who refused to give up their mistresses.[56]

In the aftermath of the council, the interpretation of the Tridentine rules and the elaboration of the post-Tridentine theology and canon law on marriage were dominated by the work of the erudite but aloof Spanish Jesuit, Tomás Sánchez (1550–1610). His *De sancti matrimonii sacramento* remained a standard Roman Catholic guide to marriage problems until the mid-twentieth century. Sánchez, an intelligent and enormously learned jurist, approached marriage law as he might have approached a complicated tax code. A shrewd master of the rules of the game, an inventor of ingenious solutions to many of its puzzles, Sánchez seems to have been utterly uninterested in human emotions or their consequences for relationships in real life. Catholic confessors and counselors relied for centuries on Sánchez's treatment of the Tridentine

[54] Council of Trent, Sess. 24 (1563) c. 1 in COD, pp. 731–32; Hermann Conrad, "Das tridentinische Konzil und die Entwicklung des kirchlichen und weltlichen Eherechts," in *Weltkonzil* 1 : 297–324.

[55] Council of Trent, Sess. 24, c. 2, 4–5, 7, 9–10, in COD, pp. 733–35.

[56] Council of Trent, Sess. 24, c. 8, in COD, pp. 734–35; E. Hillman, "Polygamy and the Council of Trent," *Jurist* 33 (1973) 358–76; Baumann, *Zivilrechtliche Bedeutung*, p. 19; Esmein, *Mariage* 2 : 310–14.

marriage law, and like their master, treated marriage as a particularly arid and abstract branch of the law of obligations.[57] A few Catholic writers, such as Sánchez's contemporary, Basilio Ponce de León (1570–1629), who put the emotional bond between married couples at the heart of their relationship, were either ignored or denounced as laxists who were liable to lead souls into spiritual danger.[58] Post-Tridentine Catholic marriage law enjoyed the considerable virtue of resting on clear principles and well-defined procedures. Its defects— notably its rigid incapacity to adapt to social change, the stupefying complexity of its jurisprudence, and the opportunities for cynical manipulation that the system afforded those who possessed wealth, social standing, and few scruples— mirrored problems endemic in civil institutions throughout early modern Europe.

Trent's most significant action on marriage law was its abolition of the loopholes that had made clandestine marriage such a problem for the medieval Church. But this measure was only partially successful: numbers of clandestine marriages diminished, certainly, in the decades after 1563, but the phenomenon by no means disappeared from the Catholic world. *Tametsi* provided that its regulations would become binding only after they had been promulgated and explained to the faithful. In many regions of Europe, however, *Tametsi* was neither published nor explained for generations after its adoption at Trent and hence did not become binding law for those areas until much later. In Normandy, for example, *Tametsi* was not received until the seventeenth century; it was not published and received by English Catholics until the nineteenth century.[59]

MARITAL SEX AND TRIDENTINE CATHOLICISM

The legislation of the Council of Trent gave no explicit attention to problems of marital sexuality, but those who interpreted Trent's marriage law found it necessary to deal with marital sex. In some respects, the commentators—Sánchez

---

[57] Tomás Sánchez, *De sancto matrimonii sacramento disputationum tomi tres*, 3 vols. in 1 (Lyon: Sumptibus Societatis typographorum, 1621). On Sánchez' career see Schulte, QL 3:737–38; Noonan, *Contraception*, pp. 323–26, and *Power to Dissolve*, pp. 31–32; R. Naz, "Sanchez, Thomas" in DDC 7:864–70.

[58] Sabino Ardito, "La dottrina matrimoniale di Basilio Ponce de Leon (1570–1629) e la letteratura ecclesiastica posteriore fino al Concilio Vaticano II," *Salesianum* 43 (1981) 757–815.

[59] Martín de Azpilceuta, *Consilia* 4.1.4.2, in his *Opera* 3/2:4; Cozzi, "Padri, figli e matrimoni," p. 172; Jean Gaudemet, "Législation canonique et attitudes seculières à l'égard du lien matrimonial au XVII siècle," *XVIIe siècle* 102/103 (1974) 28; Bresnier, "Mariage en Normandie," p. 110; Otto Erwin Koegel, *Common Law Marriage and Its Development in the United States* (Washington, D.C.: John Byrne & Co., 1922), pp. 22–23. In remote areas, such as the Scottish Highlands, archaic marriage practices survived among Catholics and Protestants alike, until the seventeenth and eighteenth centuries; see W. D. H. Sellar, "Marriage, Divorce, and Concubinage in Gaelic Scotland," *Transactions of the Gaelic Society of Inverness* 51 (1978/80) 464–93.

above all—were less restrictive of sexual enjoyment in marriage than their pre-Reformation predecessors. Sánchez, for example, taught that it was appropriate for married persons to take pleasure in seeing one another's bodies and even in touching each other, although he modified this principle by distinctions based on the intentions of the actors. If a couple touched and fondled each other in order to secure arousal as a prelude to coitus, then their actions constituted no sin. If, however, they took to touching and feeling one another in order to heighten their pleasure after arousal, this was sinful, though only venially so.[60] Likewise Sánchez held that it was not gravely sinful for married persons to daydream about the sexual pleasures that they experienced with their mates, although he suspected that all sexual fantasies entailed some degree of sin.[61] There was danger, after all, that contemplating sexual delights with one's proper spouse might lead to arousal, which was always sinful, although the sin was not always mortal.[62] In general, however, Sánchez and his followers believed that married couples might do as they pleased in their sexual relations, so long as they did not impede or preclude conception; at worst they would be guilty of venial sin.[63] The pleasure that married couples experienced during sex, Sánchez taught, was not sinful in itself; indeed, once intercourse had begun, the couple had a moral obligation to continue until both parties achieved orgasm, for it was wrong for one to attain satisfaction without assuring that the other did so too.[64]

Sánchez analyzed in detail the problem of coital positions used by married couples. The missionary position, he maintained, was "natural," and all deviations from it were therefore to some degree "unnatural" and thus sinful, unless excused by a just cause.[65] This was so, he explained, because changes in coital position inverted the order of nature and also tended to make conception less likely. Sánchez suspected that couples usually experimented with deviant coital positions in order to enhance their sexual pleasure. This goal, he felt, did not constitute a legitimate cause for departing from the "natural" way of doing things. Accordingly Sánchez classed variations in coital position as serious venial sins, although they fell short of being deadly sins. He was inclined, however, to count intercourse with the woman on top of her husband as a mortal sin, because it significantly inverted the natural order. After all, he recalled, it was on account of this perversion that God had sent the Biblical Flood—an arcane bit of lore that he had picked up from Petrus Comestor.[66]

Sánchez and other post-Tridentine canonists were prepared to tolerate other slight variations from what they regarded as the normal and natural course of

[60] Sánchez, *De sancto matrimonio* 9.44.2.8–11.
[61] Ibid. 9.44.3.
[62] Ibid. 9.44.4–5.
[63] Ibid. 9.16.4; Flandrin, "Vie sexuelle," p. 103.
[64] Sánchez, *De sancto matrimonio* 9.17.11.
[65] Ibid. 9.16.1, 3, 7.
[66] Ibid. 9.16.1, 3; Flandrin, *Sexe et l'occident*, p. 130.

marital sex. Sánchez, for example, was more tolerant than most in his treatment of such lovemaking practices as the wife licking or sucking her husband's penis or allowing anal penetration. So long as these practices were used as a prelude to "natural" intercourse, Sánchez allowed them. If couples did these things just for pleasure, the actions were venially sinful; if they experienced orgasm during foreplay, however, the sin was mortal.[67]

DIVORCE, SEPARATION, AND REMARRIAGE

Since Protestant reformers, particularly Luther, had rejected Catholic law concerning divorce, separation, and remarriage, the Council of Trent was bound to deal with these issues. After lengthy deliberations and after considering a number of alternatives, the council adopted a canon that held that adultery did not dissolve the marriage bond and hence was not an acceptable basis for divorce.[68] This was a studied rejection of Luther's argument that Matt. 5:32 and 19:9 authorized dissolution of marriages, with the right of remarriage, because of adultery. The Fathers of the council were aware when they adopted this position that patristic writings substantially supported Luther's contentions. The majority felt, nonetheless, that they must stand by a teaching that had become traditional since the late twelfth century, in part at least because failure to do so would seem tantamount to a confession that earlier rulings had been incorrect. The text of the canon was deliberately framed in such a way as to avoid pronouncing on the question of whether the Church had the power to dissolve a valid marriage or not.[69]

SEX AND THE CLERGY

The Fathers of the Council of Trent were, of course, painfully aware that Protestant reformers had attacked the policy of mandatory clerical celibacy, which had itself been introduced into Catholicism by the earlier reform movement in the eleventh century. The Fathers knew also that the principal Protestant leaders and many of their sympathizers had personally renounced celibacy and had married. Indeed, during the Council the papacy twice authorized papal nuncios and legates to recognize marriages contracted by priests, provided that the married priests ceased to exercise their sacerdotal functions in public.[70] Moreover members of the council repeatedly stated during its deliberations that the policy of clerical celibacy was not working, that in practice priests commonly kept concubines, and that celibacy in many areas accomplished little more than

[67] Sánchez, *De sancto matrimonio* 9.17.1.4–5; 9.44.2.14–16.

[68] Council of Trent, Sess. 24, *Doctrina de sacramento matrimonii* and *Canones de sacramento matrimonii*, c. 8, in COD, pp. 729–31; Piet Fransen, "Divorce on the Ground of Adultery—The Council of Trent (1563)," *Concilium* 7 (1970) 95–96; De Sanctis, "Il pensiero della Chiesa sul problema del coniuge abbandonato," pp. 201–21.

[69] Fransen, "Divorce on the Ground of Adultery."

[70] Lynch, "Marriage and Celibacy," p. 210.

to assure that priests' de facto wives and children received no share in their estates. The Duke of Bavaria's representative, for example, declared publicly during the council that a recent visitation had shown that ninety-six or ninety-seven Bavarian priests out of a hundred had concubines or clandestine wives.[71]

Celibacy was a sore issue. All Protestant reformers had rejected it and most members of the council knew that observance of the discipline was at best uneven and in many regions might fairly be described as unusual. Many members of the council felt that it was time to rescind the policy and to restore to clerics the right to marry, as they had done in the early history of the Church. As the Bavarian representative put it:

> Many other men who are aware of the current state of affairs in Germany . . . believe that chaste marriage would be preferable to sullied celibacy. They further warn that the most able and knowledgeable men in the population would rather have wives without ecclesiastical benefices than benefices without wives.[72]

But the prospect of changing this long-standing policy made most council Fathers uneasy. Some, perhaps, remembered the chilling threats of St. Birgitta about the likely fate of prelates who took responsibility for abandoning mandatory celibacy.[73] Many changed their minds repeatedly, in the style of Pope Pius II, who prior to his election as pope had favored allowing the clergy to marry, but after his election felt obliged to reverse his position.[74]

In the end the council reaffirmed the policy of mandatory celibacy, reiterated penalties earlier imposed on concubinary clerics, and re-enacted older canons penalizing the bastard children of the clergy.[75] Little in this bundle of legislation was new, and a reading of it would furnish scant reason to believe that Trent's reaffirmation of mandatory celibacy would result in any significant change. In fact, however, Trent would be far more successful than any previous council had been in securing general, if not universal, observance of celibacy. The secret of its success lay not in canons dealing with clerical sexuality, but rather in prescriptions concerning clerical education. In the summer of 1563, a

[71] *Concilium Tridentinum* 8:622 (27 June 1562). A year earlier Ioannes Franciscus Commendonus reported to Cardinal Charles Borromeo on his discussions with the Duke of Cleves about conciliar business and noted: "Di più pensa, esser necessario il connubio de sacerdoti, et afferma, non essere in tutti i suoi stati cinque preti senza publiche concubine"; *Concilium Tridentinum* 8:202.

[72] *Concilium Tridentinum* 8:624: "Ceterum existimant plerique viri rerum Germanicarum periti, tale nunc esse in Germania . . . ut plerique omnes castum matrimonium contaminato coelibatu praeferendum arbitrentur. Quamobrem animadvertitur passim, praeclara ingenia doctissimosque homines ducere uxores malle, ut careant ecclesiasticis beneficiis, quam ecclesiastica beneficia acceptare et carere uxoribus. . . ."

[73] St. Birgitta, *Revelationes* 7.10; see above, p. 538.

[74] *Concilium Tridentinum* 9:652.

[75] Council of Trent, Sess. 22 (1562) c. 1; Sess. 25 (1563) c. 14–15, in COD, pp. 713–14, 768–70.

few months before final adoption of *Tametsi*, the council approved another decree, *Cum adolescentium aetas*, which became the cornerstone of the seminary system of clerical education. The seminaries created under the provisions of *Cum adolescentium aetas* provided the intellectual and moral formation of the post-Reformation Catholic clergy. Seminaries systematically instilled the practice of celibacy into aspirants for the priesthood and attempted, with some success, to weed out those unwilling or unable to accept responsibility for a celibate lifestyle. While scandals over clerical sex were certainly not unknown in post-Tridentine Catholicism, the seminary system proved to be a powerful and often effective instrument for inculcating would-be priests with a reverence for the virtue of celibacy and for conditioning them from an early age to minimize sexual temptations and resist the allures of the flesh.[76]

EXTRAMARITAL SEX AMONG THE LAITY

Trent made no significant changes in the canon law dealing with sex outside of marriage and the council Fathers apparently felt that existing law was adequate to deal with these problems. There does seem to have been a major change, however, in the way in which laws dealing with extramarital sex were enforced in the years after Trent. Protestant preachers inveighed against the sexual vices of the old order and warned their flocks to abjure the loose moral standards that they claimed characterized popery. Catholic reformers, for their part, sought to police sexual behavior more vigorously and to repress undesirable sexual activity more systematically than earlier generations had done.

The new moral climate was particularly hard on the practice of prostitution. Reformers, both Catholic and Protestant, denounced the wickedness of both harlot and client, while fulminating against the involvement of municipalities in operating public brothels. Public opinion, in consequence, seems to have turned against the old policy of tolerating prostitution, and people began to consider it shameful to patronize the brothels that their ancestors had established. Toward the close of the sixteenth century, municipal brothels began to close their doors in one town after another. The activities of private prostitutes also came under censorious scrutiny from officials, who commenced to banish them from public places and to penalize them for what had formerly been a recognized, if not honored, trade.[77]

Sánchez and other post-Tridentine Roman Catholic commentators on sex offenses were, like their Protestant counterparts, much concerned with strengthening parental control over the marriages of young people. Sánchez, for ex-

---

[76] Lynch, "Marriage and Celibacy," pp. 209–10.

[77] Alessandro de' Medici, Archbishop of Florence, *Editto delle prohibizioni dell'ingresso delle meretrici in alcune chiese ed altri luoghi pij della città e diocesi di Firenze* (Florence: I Giunti, 1577); Bernardus Coveronius, *De publicis concubinariis*, in TUJ 11/1:167va § 1; Otis, *Prostitution*, pp. 40–45; Rossiaud, "Prostitution, sexualité, société," p. 83.

ample, analyzed abduction, forcible intercourse, and marriage by coercion in minute detail. Any abduction of a young woman, so far as Sánchez was concerned, constituted *raptus*, provided that the victim was in her parents' custody at the time of her abduction. Whether the victim consented or not was beside the point. *Raptus*, according to Sánchez, was a twofold crime: since it involved extramarital sex it was an offense against chastity, and since it involved forcible abduction of a girl from her parents it was a crime against natural justice.[78] Whether abduction without sexual intercourse constituted *raptus* was a question about which Sánchez's authorities differed. He concluded that nonsexual abduction was a less serious form of the crime, for which lesser penalties were appropriate.[79] Sánchez added that *raptus* was not an exclusively male crime, for it could also be perpetrated by a woman either against a man or another woman, although he acknowledged that neither case was common. Female rapists, he thought, should be subject only to the noncapital punishments prescribed for this crime.[80] More important, Sánchez broadened the definition of *raptus* by arguing that passionate and importunate pleading by a perpetrator who implored his victim to run away with him or begged tearfully for her sexual favors, constituted the force necessary to qualify the act as *raptus*. Sánchez carefully specified that what he had in mind was not just the usual kind of persuasion that passionate young men employed with their girl friends, but pleading so ardent and extreme that it amounted to verbal violence and made it emotionally impossible for the victim to resist.[81] Moreover Sánchez believed—unlike most medieval canonists—that the crime of *raptus* should include abduction and forcible sexual relations with a prostitute. *Raptus*, he asserted, was radically different from simple fornication because it involved an element of violence, either physical or moral. A man who used violence against a woman (regardless of her social status) in order to have sex with her, committed a crime against justice and that, so far as Sánchez was concerned, made *raptus* a heinous crime.[82]

DEVIANT SEXUALITY

Sixteenth- and seventeenth-century canon law and theology showed few novelties in their treatment of deviant sexual behavior. By and large the older condemnations continued in force, and both Catholic and Protestant writers agreed that homosexual acts should be punished severely. Writers and judges seem to have been more concerned with lesbian behavior in this period than was true earlier. Some scattered sixteenth-century prosecutions for sexual relations between women have come to light in recent years and, while there are not many of them, they greatly outnumber those known from any earlier century in the

[78] Sánchez, *De sancto matrimonio* 12.7.12.30.

[79] Ibid. 12.7.18.

[80] Ibid. 12.7.24–25.

[81] Ibid. 7.12.10, 12.7.32.

[82] Ibid. 12.7.23, 37.

Middle Ages.[83] Similarly, transvestite behavior seems to have concerned authorities during this period and to have been punished much more severely than was common previously.[84]

Post-Tridentine moral and canonical commentators on sex problems also gave great prominence to masturbation, which they classed as a more serious moral problem than fornication. Masturbation, they reasoned, was contrary to nature, and people engaged in it solely in order to feel the pleasure of orgasm. Hence, the argument ran, masturbation was akin to sodomy and ought to merit more severe penalties than fornication or even adultery—although none of the authorities went quite so far as to prescribe the death penalty for it.[85] Sánchez believed that even spontaneous orgasm, where no conscious self-stimulation was involved, was wrong and should be fended off, if at all possible. A person who felt a sexual climax coming on, save during marital intercourse, should lie still, taking care to avoid touching the genitals, should make the sign of the cross, accompanied by fervent prayers beseeching God not to allow him to slip into orgasmic pleasure.[86] Sánchez's treatment of spontaneous orgasm makes it plain that the notion of sex as impurity remained an important element in his thought on sex and sexual problems, as did his identification of pleasure with immorality.

JURISDICTION AND COURTS

Protestant writers almost unanimously criticized the treatment of marriage and sex offences by medieval Church courts. Some, like Martin Bucer, maintained that ecclesiastical tribunals should have no jurisdiction over marriage at all. Instead, Bucer argued, matrimonial causes rightfully belonged in the royal courts, since marriage is a civil matter.[87] Bucer's stance became the norm in much of Protestant Europe, where princely and municipal courts extended their jurisdiction over offenses against sexual morality and marriage law, while ecclesiastical courts either ceased to exist or restricted themselves to settling disputes involving church property and similar matters.[88]

England long remained a notable exception to the general rule among Prot-

---

[83] The best documented of them, the case of Benedetta Carlini, is described by Judith C. Brown, *Immodest Acts: The Life of a Lesbian Nun in Renaissance Italy* (New York: Oxford University Press, 1986), pp. 117–28. Other cases from this period are briefly noted in Brown, *Immodest Acts*, pp. 133–35 and 165–70, n. 5; see also Louis Crompton, "The Myth of Lesbian Impunity: Capital Laws from 1270 to 1591," *Journal of Homosexuality* 6 (1980/81) 11–25.

[84] Brown, *Immodest Acts*, pp. 134 and 204 nn. 4–5; Patricia Labalme, "Sodomy and Venetian Justice to the Renaissance," TRG 52 (1984) 249–53.

[85] Sánchez, *De sancto matrimonio* 9.17.15; Coveronius, *De publicis concubinariis* § 14, in TUJ 11/1:159rb.

[86] Sánchez, *De sancto matrimonio* 9.17.16.

[87] Bucer, *De regno Christi* 2.7.15, pp. 152–53.

[88] Schulte, QL 3/2:3–5, 14–17.

estant nations. Anglican Courts Christian continued for generations following the Reformation to function in ways not radically different from those that had obtained before the break with Rome. Although Henry VIII asserted royal control over ecclesiastical matters, including Church courts, he failed to achieve the substantial revision of canon law that at one time he envisioned. Instead he and his successessors left the medieval canonical system basically intact, although modified in some details by a series of royal injunctions, parliamentary statutes, and the Canons Ecclesiastical of 1603. Marriage and sexual behavior remained subject primarily to ecclesiastical courts whose rules and procedures differed only marginally from those of medieval Catholicism.[89] The pre-Tridentine practice of consensual marriage, for example, continued to flourish in England and in the seventeenth century roughly ten percent of English marriages were clandestine. Only in 1753 did Hardwicke's Act effectively do for Anglicans what *Tametsi* had done for Catholics.[90] Marriage remained in principle indissoluble in English law, although Parliament occasionally did revoke the marriages of peers and influential persons by private bills. Divorce in the modern sense of the term did not become available to ordinary people in England until the Marriage Act of 1857.

In Roman Catholic Europe, the most striking result of Trent's judicial reforms was the increased centralization of Church law and courts. The Tridentine papacy systematically attempted to discourage local customs and vigorously suppressed variations, even minor ones, from Roman usage in all aspects of Catholic life.

In keeping with the papacy's general policy of imposing uniform observance, the central papal courts, the Rota, the Signatura, and the Penitentiary, became increasingly busy appellate tribunals in the period following Trent. Local canonical courts, of course, continued to function and in many regions their case loads expanded dramatically in the wake of the council's reforms and the flood of decrees that issued from the newly created Roman dicasteries. But the deci-

---

[89] *The Constitutions and Canons Ecclesiastical (Made in the Year 1603 and Amended in the Years 1865, 1887, 1936, 1946, and 1948)* (London: S.P.C.K., 1961); *The Canon Law of the Church of England, Being the Report of the Archbishops' Commission on Canon Law* (London: S.P.C.K., 1947); Eric Waldram Kemp, *An Introduction to Canon Law in the Church of England* (London: Hodder and Stoughton, 1957). On sixteenth-century Anglican canon law see particularly Ronald A. Marchant, *The Church under the Law: Justice, Administration, and Discipline in the Diocese of York, 1560–1640* (Cambridge: At the University Press, 1969), pp. 140–41, 240–43, and Ralph Houlbrooke, *Church Courts and the People during the English Reformation, 1520–1570* (Oxford: Oxford University Press, 1979), pp. 55–88.

[90] Anglican divines and common lawyers had, of course, long voiced dismay at clandestine unions and their consequences. In 1696, however, the government imposed a tax on marriages, as a result of which secret weddings flourished even more. When Hardwicke's Act made these invalid, the effect was to cut the poor off from cheap marriages and to drive them into concubinage; Lasch, "Suppression of Clandestine Marriage," pp. 90–109.

sions of the Roman tribunals increasingly dominated the thought and practice of local ecclesiastical judges.[91] The jurisprudence of the Rota was particularly important for the law of matrimony and sexual morality in Tridentine Catholicism. Unlike other Roman tribunals, the Rota's decisions spelled out the reasoning on which they were grounded and thus provided guidance for other ecclesiastical judges. While the Rota did not publish its decisions systematically, individuals (including some judges of the Rota) compiled private collections of selected Rotal decisions and these became standard reference works for canonists throughout the world.[92] Although the Rota never formally adopted a *stare decisis* rule, Roman authorities expected the decisions of local Church courts to adhere to the *stylus*, or practice, of the Rota. Canonical judges at the local level often cited Rotal decisions as the basis for their rulings and frequently assigned them greater weight than papal decretals and most other sources of Church law.[93]

Canonical marriage jurisprudence after Trent reflected the new divisions in Christendom. Mixed marriages between Catholics and Protestants confronted the Church's courts with complex problems, both practical and theoretical. In dealing with these issues, ecclesiastical judges drew upon medieval law concerning marriages with Jews, Saracens, and pagans, but the new situation posed difficulties for which the older law provided few guidelines. Canonical courts needed to decide, for example, whether and under what conditions they should consider marriages between baptized Protestants binding. Likewise, since most Protestant groups held that legitimate marriages could be dissolved under some circumstances, Catholic canonists had to determine whether, for example, a Catholic could lawfully marry a former Protestant who had been divorced and subsequently converted to Catholicism. And since civil authorities in predominantly Protestant regions often granted divorces without regard to the religion of the parties, canonists with increasing frequency had to wrestle with cases of Catholics who had secured civil divorces and later wished to remarry with the blessing of their own Church. Or if one party entered marriage with the intention of seeking divorce should the union fail to work out, did that intention itself invalidate the marriage? If so, how could such an "intention against permanence" be proved? Moreover, since the Council of Trent required the announcement of banns, the presence of the parish priest, and a prescribed ceremony as essential conditions for valid marriage, a wide range of cases involving what canonists called "defects of form" also came before the Church's tribunals for adjudication.

Post-Tridentine writers on matrimonial law were greatly concerned, too,

---

[91] Francis Morrisey, *The Canonical Significance of Papal and Curial Pronouncements* (Hartford, CT: Canon Law Society of America, 1974); Schulte, QL 3:11–19; Stickler, *Historia*, pp. 338–46.

[92] Gero Dolezalek and Knut Wolfgang Nörr, "Die Rechtssprechungssammlungen der mittelalterlichen Rota," in Coing, *Handbuch* 1:849–56.

[93] Noonan, *Power to Dissolve*, pp. 26–27.

with reproductive intention in marital relations. Catholic theologians and canonists in the sixteenth and seventeenth centuries held sharply conflicting opinions on this matter. Sánchez, among others, argued that married couples need not intend to conceive a child each time they had conjugal relations, but also maintained that if a person married with a firm intention to avoid having any children at all, the marriage could be annulled.[94] In practice, however, this issue seems not to have come before the Church's courts with any regularity prior to the twentieth century.[95]

The role of canonical courts in dealing with sex offenses declined precipitously in the period following the Council of Trent. Municipalities and royal governments in many parts of the West assumed greater responsibility for the regulation of public morality, while theologians increasingly viewed the internal forum of the confessional as a more appropriate venue than the courts for the chastisement of sex offenses that took place in private. In some regions, principally Spain and Italy, the Inquisition, rather than the local Church courts, took cognizance of the most heinous and scandalous types of sexual misbehavior. By the eighteenth century ordinary ecclesiastical courts no longer played a major role in the enforcement of sexual morals, save perhaps in the papal states. Canon law continued to enunciate standards of sexual behavior for Catholic Christians, but enforcement of those standards had passed into other hands.

Conclusions

The sixteenth century Reformation was not entirely centered on abstract issues of theology, such as justification by faith, or on ecclesiological problems, such as the plenitude of papal power or the priesthood of all believers. Problems involving sexual conduct were also at issue in the struggles between Protestant and Catholic.

Roman Catholic and Protestant beliefs differed sharply on questions about the sacramentality of marriage, clerical celibacy, divorce and remarriage, and ultimately about the aims and purposes of human sexuality itself. The Catholic reaction, both in its reform mode and in its Counter-Reformation mode, tended to sharpen rather than blunt the differences between the two camps. After Trent, Roman authorities insisted even more vehemently than before upon the role of sex as a disruptive force in society. Catholic writers insisted that sex created a spiritual defilement from which individuals must be cleansed in order to become pure. Some held that marital sex was morally tolerable only if ordered toward reproduction or the avoidance of fornication, but all agreed that the highest and most worthy type of Christian life required celibate renunciation of sex altogether. Although Roman Catholic doctrine insisted that marriage was a sacrament, it was a marginal sacrament because of its links with the unholy combination of sex and pleasure.

[94] Sánchez, *De sancto matrimonio* 5.13.5.

[95] On conflicting doctrinal opinions see Noonan, *Contraception*, pp. 303–83; for an analysis of decisions involving this issue in the early twentieth century, see also p. 435.

Protestant divines, by contrast, flatly and unequivocally rejected the sacramentality of marriage, but paradoxically held matrimony in higher esteem than their Catholic counterparts. The Protestant clergy were, with few exceptions, married men, and most Protestants regarded celibacy as an oddity, graced with no special prestige or privilege. Protestant writers treated sex as a normal part of conjugal relationships, a sign of love between husband and wife, rather than a failing that required a procreative purpose to excuse it. For Protestants, marriage was a basic Christian institution, approved by Scriptures, and integral to a full human life. Reformers praised the beauty, dignity, and morality of married life as a central feature of Christian society; but at the same time, they also taught that marriages could be terminated for good cause. Since marriage for them was no sacrament, questions that troubled Roman Catholic writers when dealing with divorce and remarriage created fewer difficulties for Protestant theologians.[96]

Since the mid-sixteenth century, sex legislation in Western nations has reflected the divergent views of sexual ethics that emerged from the religious polemics of the Reformation. The sex law of predominantly Roman Catholic nations has assumed that sex is impure, that all nonmarital sex is wrong, that contraceptive practices should be illegal, that marriage is indissoluble, and that divorce should therefore be banned. Predominantly Protestant societies, on the other hand, have based much of their sex law on the sexual ethics of the sixteenth- and seventeenth-century reformers. Thus their marriage law has characteristically emphasized society's interest in promoting the family and its welfare, but has left many issues relating to marital sex and contraception to the conscience of the individual, rather than trying to enact norms on these matters into law. Predominantly Protestant societies attempted to discourage divorce, but, unlike traditional Catholic societies, they have also been willing to tolerate it as an unfortunate necessity.

While these differences are significant, they are outweighed by the similarities between Catholic and Protestant attitudes toward sex. The principal features of medieval sex law have not only remained intact in post-Tridentine Roman Catholicism but have also been assimilated within Protestantism. Substantial parts of medieval law on sexual behavior, moreover, not only survived the religious struggles of the sixteenth and seventeenth centuries, but have also found their way into the legal systems of modern secular states.

[96] Nonetheless, the Reformed churches incorporated substantial elements of Catholic canon law, including the canon law of marriage, in their own disciplinary systems. See generally Wilhelm Maurer, "Reste des kanonischen Rechtes im Frühprotestantismus," ZRG, KA 51 (1965) 190–253.

12

Medieval Sex Law and Modern Society: Recapitulation, Reflections, and Conclusions

Recapitulation

From Hammurabi to Augustus, diverse sexual beliefs and practices abounded in ancient Mediterranean societies. Roman moralists and lawgivers adopted some of the sex lore of earlier societies into their own system, at the same time as they rejected other sexual attitudes as incompatible with their way of life.

Christianity brought still further diversity into Mediterranean ideas about the role of sex in human life, as the Church attempted to integrate the mental habits and practices of late ancient culture into its heritage of biblical revelation and Jewish law. As the western half of the Roman Empire crumbled, Latin Christians needed to rethink their sexual theories once again to take account of the customs and practices of Germanic, Celtic, and Oriental peoples. Thus began the long, laborious process through which medieval men and women gradually created the sexual ethos that has become central to the traditional value systems of Western societies.

Long before the time of Jesus, philosophers and rulers had learned to be wary of sex. This fiery passion must be controlled lest it disrupt settled household and property arrangements and undermine the social harmony of communities. Pre-Christian societies had also glimpsed the fundamental connections of sex with life, with heaven, and with the gods. From primitive fertility cults and temple prostitution to the world-weary disenchantment of the Epicureans, the ancient world alternately yearned for carnal ecstasy and foreswore it with cold disdain.

Jesus of Nazareth said little about sex. His Roman and Jewish contemporaries discussed sexual ethics in some detail, but Jesus provided little explicit guidance on sexual conduct. His followers soon incorporated into the new religion elements drawn from Jewish law and practice, but early Christians lacked any uniquely characteristic approach to sexual conduct. By the early fourth century, however, a swelling tide of converts required the growing Church to refine its teachings on many subjects, and in the process to define exactly what they believed. Christian teaching about the morality of sexual conduct was one topic that required clarification. Gradually a body of sexual doctrine took shape, as the Church became assimilated into the Roman political and social establishment.

Philosophical speculations of late antiquity largely shaped the views of the Christian Fathers on sexual issues. Abstinence and adherence to the aims of nature became basic tenets of Christian sexual teaching. No sex at all should be the highest Christian ideal, the Fathers taught, although grimly joyless and responsible copulation was acceptable for those determined to marry and breed children or tormented by carnal temptation. The Fathers adopted much of this from the late Stoics. Nature and the natural became the norms that governed marital sex, which was held to be authorized primarily for the conception and nurturing of offspring and secondarily for the avoidance of fornication. The Fathers frowned upon delight in fleshly pleasure. They praised virginity as meritorious and splendid, and cherished chastity as the preeminent Christian virtue.

Political events during the late fourth and fifth centuries disrupted the Church's application of its newly fashioned sexual doctrine. Germanic successor-states made a shambles of the Christian Empire's administrative routines. The Church's organizational unity crumbled with the empire that had fostered it, while regional authorities supplanted the older organs of ecclesiastical government, as a rural and Germanic West grew increasingly estranged from an urban, imperial, and still Roman East. These new circumstances seriously limited the ability of Church authorities to discipline Christians who flouted ecclesiastical norms of any kind, including sexual norms. Yet despite the provincialism of the early Middle Ages, the main lines of the older sexual doctrine remained intact. The patristic bias against sexual pleasure informed the penitential manuals that passed on to spiritual authorities in succeeding generations the stern and joyless visions of the past.

But early medieval Church authorities had a limited capacity to regulate the behavior of the laity. Germanic kings and their followers were accustomed to marrying early and often. Polygyny was common among wealthy men, who sometimes kept flocks of concubines as well as a number of official wives. The new spiritual leaders of recently baptized Germans and Celts found it difficult to persuade the laity to alter their matrimonial habits.

Changes in society and economy following the invasions, however, soon transformed the traditional household structure of antiquity into something new. The disappearance of large-scale slavery and the emergence of peasant agriculture led to the appearance of the monogamous nuclear family as a basic social unit in the early middle ages. One consequence of the new social structure founded on the family unit was the gradual adoption of Christian ideals of sexual conduct among rich and poor alike. By the mid-eighth century the new type of family household and sexual morality was becoming well established in most parts of Western Christendom.

Europe entered upon a new phase of economic, political, and social development shortly after A.D. 1000. The Church also achieved new levels of spiritual and intellectual leadership early in the new millennium. The Gregorian reformers not only demanded that priests and prelates foreswear marriage and concubinage, but also required observance of stricter standards of sexual conduct from the Christian laity as well. Leaders of the reform movement were aware that in order to impose these standards on an unwilling world they would need to use sturdier tools than their predecessors had possessed. They found what they needed in canon law.

Canon law was transformed into an effective instrument for Church government and discipline during the twelfth century. The *Decretum* of Gratian gave Western Churchmen for the first time a coherent battery of rules for the governance of the Church and for regulating the behavior of its members. Gratian gathered his rules from old sources—biblical, patristic, conciliar, and papal— but he put them together in a new way that made sense out of the patchwork of venerable material that went into his *Decretum*. Gratian's work gave popes and bishops a workable, if still unpolished, implement for controlling, among other things, the sexual mores of clergy and laity.

The *Decretum* also furnished law teachers with a basic textbook that allowed them to explain canon law systematically to ever increasing numbers of law students who began filling the law faculties of Europe's new universities. By the end of the twelfth century the teaching and study of canon law became a growth industry. Law professors spun out treatises and commentaries that became something akin to best-sellers, while clever young men with their eyes on the main chance guessed that one reliable road to high office, power, and considerable emoluments began in university law faculties. The clever young men guessed right. At the same time the pace of legislation quickened rapidly. Popes, councils, and synods poured out a seemingly endless stream of new rulings and regulations, which the law faculties soon incorporated into their curricula, thus lengthening the course of studies and creating still greater need for professionally trained canonists to cope with it all.

Sex, both within marriage and outside of it, was a prominent concern of the new law and the new lawyers. Marriage law grew rapidly in volume and complexity. Law teachers soon incorporated into their commentaries on marriage law insights gleaned from the revived Roman jurisprudence that the civilians were studying. Meanwhile popes, notably Alexander III, sought to refashion the institution of matrimony in ways calculated to diminish the power of parents to control the marriages of their children and to permit individuals to choose their own spouses. The law of separation, annulment, and divorce was also being refashioned, as was the penal law that restricted nonmarital sex. The new legal guidelines had immediate repercussions on the disposition of property and on the political and social alliances that were customarily sealed by intermarriage between members of powerful clans.

The thirteenth and fourteenth centuries witnessed the expansion and consolidation of canonical marriage law. During the same period canon law became increasingly concerned with other aspects of sexual behavior. Nonmarital sex became a problem of growing interest to the Church's lawyers, as did the law of evidence and procedures in sex cases.

After 1350, however, competition from secular governments began to erode the Church's monopoly on sex law. Royal and municipal courts successfully asserted jurisdiction over rape, prostitution, incest, adultery, fornication, and sexual deviance. Some secular judges even tried to bring marriage and divorce cases before their courts.

The Protestant Reformation and Catholic reactions to it resulted in a critical reexamination of medieval sex doctrines during the sixteenth and seventeenth centuries. For a time, Protestant reformers hovered on the brink of a radical transformation of sexual mores. They downplayed the spiritual value of virginity and denied the necessity of sacerdotal celibacy, while they also rejected sacramental status of matrimony. Catholics struck back by reaffirming that marriage was a sacrament, but at the same time totally revamped their own marriage law and in the process redefined what constituted marriage.

By the end of the seventeenth century, however, Protestant Puritans and Catholic Jansenists had resurrected some of the most Draconian provisions of medieval sex law and enshrined them in statutes and casuistic manuals, where many lingered until the second half of the twentieth century. The Reformation and its aftermath did not result in abandonment of the views about sex that had become traditional in the medieval Church. Instead medieval sexual morality became the paradigm for modern Western assumptions about human sexuality that remain by and large intact.

Reflections: Medieval Christianity and Modern Sexual Norms

Our survey of medieval teachings about sex and marriage has shown that the medieval Church continually modified its teachings on these matters and at several critical junctures revised its doctrines quite radically. Major changes in sex doctrines often represented responses to unorthodox beliefs, especially dualist teachings, such as those of the Manichaeans in the fourth century or the Albigensians in the thirteenth, which challenged the established Church's doctrinal authority. In the process the Western Church suffered, as it were, a dualistic intoxication, from which it never fully recovered. The two-valued logic and dichotomous oppositions—spirit and matter, mind and body, good and evil, God and the Devil—that are so characteristic of Catholic moral teaching represent in part Catholicism's hangover from its combat with the dualists.[1]

Throughout the Middle Ages Church authorities continued to rely upon the three basic approaches to sexuality outlined in the introduction to this book, although the ratio of the mixture varied from one period to another. From the mid-twelfth century onward Church authorities increasingly relied upon canon

---

[1] Antonio Hortelano, "Rivoluzione sessuale e famiglia," *Concilium* 20 (1984) 99–100; Joseph C. Smith, "The Sword and Shield of Perseus: Some Mythological Dimensions of the Law," typescript of a paper presented to the Faculty of Law of the University of British Columbia, 11 December 1983, pp. 19–20. These oppositions are also common among Protestant Fundamentalists; George M. Marsden, *Fundamentalism and American Culture: The Shaping of Twentieth-Century Evangelicalism, 1870–1925* (New York: Oxford University Press, 1980), p. 26.

law and canonical courts as tools for imposing their sexual views upon society. Not even the religious upheavals of the sixteenth century could loosen Europe's adherence to those doctrinal approaches or its reliance on the law as a primary instrument for social control of sexual behavior.

The model of sexuality that defines sex primarily as a reproductive mechanism, and therefore staunchly opposes contraception has demonstrated great hardiness. This view assumes that procreativity is the principal measure of the moral acceptability of each act of intercourse and, more broadly, of all sexual behavior. Writers who place primary emphasis on sex as reproduction, therefore, condemn homosexual relations as well as heterosexual oral and anal sex practices and often maintain that even the postures used in marital sex are morally good or bad depending on whether they hinder or promote conception. Those who consider reproduction the primary criterion of sexual morality usually deny any positive value to sexual pleasure and often assume that pleasure in sexual encounters varies in inverse proportion to reproductive potential. Partisans of procreation also argue that marriage must be permanent and indissoluble in order to maximize parental capacity for nurturing and rearing children. Those who take this view often picture marital sex as an unfortunate necessity to achieve a laudable goal—a good use of a bad thing, as St. Augustine called it. Hence they minimize the value of sexual satisfaction as a binding mechanism in marriage. The primary force that holds married couples together, in their scheme of things, should be the welfare of their children, and moral duty will dictate that couples remain together, whether they care to or not. Those who favor the procreative emphasis almost invariably regard any form of nonmarital sex as wrong.

Writers who take reproduction as the sole or primary goal of sex have virtually without exception dealt with human sexuality from an exclusively male perspective. Men are normally fertile from puberty to late old age, and male orgasm accompanies the emission of sperm. Thus the view that sex and reproduction are inextricably joined together reflects the experience of most men. Women experience sex differently. Females are fertile only for a fraction of their adult life, from puberty to menopause.[2] The biological cycle of the human female, unlike that of most other mammals, does not involve a close link between ovulation and the female sex drive. Moreover, orgasm for women is primarily a function of the clitoris, which has no reproductive function at all. Thus the link between sexual satisfaction and reproduction is relatively weak from a woman's viewpoint. Reproductionist writers about sexual morality have historically rejected this point of view. Indeed, they have rarely even considered it.[3]

---

[2] It is of course true that in pre-industrial societies substantial numbers of women died before reaching menopause, so that sex was linked to reproduction throughout their adult lives. Hence the reproductionist view of sex probably reflected mature women's experience somewhat better in the Middle Ages than it does in more recent times.

[3] Barbara Andolsen, "Il leale dissenso dei credenti: rapporto dagli Stati Uniti," *Concilium* 20 (1984) 164–66.

The model of sexuality that lays primary emphasis on the impurity of sex also remains vigorous. This view entails some of the same consequences as the first one. Like the first model, the impurity school condemns nonmarital sex as morally wrong. Those who see sex as impure, like advocates of the reproductive model, attach no positive value to sexual pleasure, but rather consider it a lure that tempts men and women to debauchery. Supporters of both models often consider marriage indissoluble, but those who subscribe to the impurity school also oppose second marriages following the death of a first spouse. Adherents of the sex-is-dirty school of thought, unlike the children-first school, see little difference between various sexual techniques and coital positions: all of them corrupt and defile mind, soul, and body. The distinctions between one variety of sex and another seem to them relatively minor.

Advocates of the pollution model of sex attach only secondary importance to procreation; hence they tend not to emphasize "nature" as a criterion of sexual morality, nor are they greatly concerned about contraception. Unlike procreationists, pollutionists strongly favor limiting marital sexual relations by restricting the times, seasons, places, and circumstances in which sex is allowed. They are also much concerned with the question of who initiates sexual encounters, for they tend to view the party who takes the initiative as guilty of a more serious fault than the one who simply complies with a partner's demand for sexual relations. Those who identify sex with pollution reverence virginity as the highest, purest, and most perfect state of life. They relegate marriage (save perhaps for unconsummated unions) to the inferior status of a lesser form of Christian life, suitable only for those who cannot measure up to the heroic demands of virginity.

The third model of sexuality views marital sex as a source of intimacy and affection, as both a symbol and a source of conjugal love. Subscribers to this school of thought regard sexual pleasure more positively than do adherents of the other two models. A few writers of this third persuasion even endow marital sex with spiritual virtue. Proponents of this view usually reject efforts to restrict sexual relations to certain seasons. They argue instead that the frequency of marital sex ought to depend on the needs and desires of the married couple, not on fluctuations of the liturgical calendar or the menstrual cycle. They oppose asexual marriages and tend to regard virginity as an unusual vocation, one to which a few Christians may feel called, but which confers no special privileged status on those who respond to that call.

Advocates of this third view maintain that Christians ordinarily have a right to marry, a right that some consider almost a duty. Those who take this stand deny that sexual relations in marriage detract from spiritual virtue; instead they see the marital relationship, including its sexual component, as an exemplar of the spiritual bond between Christ and his Church. Proponents of this model of sexuality are generally indifferent to the use of "nature" as a criterion of sexual morality and either approve or at least do not seriously criticize experimentation and variation in sexual techniques practiced by married couples. Advocates of marital-sex-as-bonding commonly see no harm in second marriages and tend to be neutral on the issue of contraception, since in their view the mutual love that sexual intimacy fosters between spouses outranks procreation as the primary goal of conjugal relations.

Writers at different periods during the Middle Ages adopted elements of each of these models of human sexuality, as we have seen, in varying combinations and with varying degrees of enthusiasm. In early medieval Europe, Christian writers and Church authorities placed greatest stress on the impurity model, but sometimes adopted ideas characteristic of the reproduction model. From the mid-twelfth century, the age of Gratian and Peter Lombard, many canonists and theologians gave greater prominence to the reproductive model of sex. Adopting some notions characteristic of the third approach (sex-as-intimacy), they reduced considerably the prominence of the second view (sex-as-defilement). A minority of thirteenth and fourteenth century writers varied this mixture by stressing the third approach, while somewhat downplaying the importance of reproduction. This group, however, remained outside the mainstream of late medieval theories about sex.

Since the Reformation, Protestant Christians have often emphasized the third model of sexuality, although some Protestant authorities (notably the Puritans) stressed the impurity view. Catholic theologians and canonists after the Reformation, and especially since the nineteenth century, have increasingly advocated the reproductive view, but with a strong subordinate emphasis on defilement. Until quite recently Catholic theologians have paid little attention to the third model, which they sometimes characterized as a theological error that stemmed from Protestantism or rationalism.[4] During the Second Vatican Council (1962–65), however, many bishops demanded reconsideration of the Church's teachings about marital sexuality. In the Constitution *Gaudium et spes* they made it clear that they felt that more attention needed to be paid to emotional bonds in marriage, including the sexual intimacy of spouses, than to procreation and the formal aspects of marital union that Catholic teaching had com-

---

[4]A reasonably typical summary of the then prevailing Catholic view stated: "Surrender to the physical passions is a debasement for men. But among these passions the one that works the greatest havoc is the sex passion, and the reaction against it finds expression in the idea of impurity: all that relates to the sex passion has something dangerous and degrading about it." Jacques Leclercq, *Marriage and the Family*, trans. Thomas R. Hanley, 2d ed. (New York: Pustet, 1948), p. 145; see also pp. 119–29 and Richard Ginder, *Binding with Briars: Sex and Sin in the Catholic Church* (Englewood Cliffs, NJ: Prentice-Hall, 1975), p. 51, as well as Edwin F. Healy, *Marriage Guidance: A Study of the Problems of the Married and Those Contemplating Marriage* (Chicago: Loyola University Press, 1948), pp. 130–39, 159; Conan Gallagher, "Sexual Pleasure: Its Proper Setting in Christian Marriage," *American Ecclesiastical Review* 146 (1962) 315–26; B. Laband, "The Interpretation of the Conjugal Act in the Theology of Marriage," *Thomist* 1 (1939) 360–80; Francesco Roberti, *Dictionary of Moral Theology*, ed. Pietro Palazzini, trans. Henry J. Yannone (London: Burns & Oates, 1962), s.v. "Marriage, Nature," "Marriage, Use of," and "Protestantism, Theology of," pp. 731–34, 743–44, 978–80.

monly emphasized during the nineteenth and early twentieth centuries.[5] Since Vatican II there has also been a significant reorientation of jurisprudence in Catholic matrimonial tribunals. During the past twenty years Church courts have laid far greater emphasis on marriage as an affective relationship than previously.[6] The judges who sit in these tribunals, both in Rome and elsewhere, have often been more responsive and sympathetic to the relational aspect of marriage than have postconciliar popes.[7]

Catholic tradition has consistently opposed many varieties of sexual expression—it condemns premarital and extramarital relationships, remarriage following divorce, and all types of deviant sexual practices, including oral and anal intercourse (either homosexual or heterosexual) and masturbation—and classifies them as grievous sins. Some Catholic writers have called for a drastic reconsideration of their Church's sexual policies and her theology of sex. A few Catholic authorities have argued that the Church should relax its long-standing condemnation of persons tainted by sexual irregularities. But Catholic leaders remain firmly opposed to these views.[8]

[5] 2 Vatican Council, Constitution on the Church and the Modern World, *Gaudium et spes* §§ 48–50, in *Acta Apostolicae Sedis* 58 (1966) 1025–1120 (cited hereafter as AAS); English trans. in *The Documents of Vatican II*, ed. Walter M. Abbot (New York: America Press, 1966), pp. 250–55; see also the comments of Robert McAfee Brown on the marriage doctrine of *Gaudium et spes* in *Documents of Vatican II*, pp. 314–15.

[6] William LaDue, "Conjugal Love and the Juridical Structure of Christian Marriage," *Jurist* 34 (1974) 36–67; Peter Hocken, "The Developing Theology of Marriage," *Law and Justice* 46/47 (1975) 29–37; Theodore Mackin, "Conjugal Love and the Magisterium," *Jurist* 36 (1976) 263–301; Aldo M. Arena, "The Jurisprudence of the Sacred Roman Rota: Its Development and Direction after the Second Vatican Council," *Studia canonica* 12 (1978) 165–93. Canonical tribunals in the U.S. have been especially active in this development; texts of selected decisions can be found in *The Tribunal Reporter*, ed. A. Maida (Huntington, IN: *Our Sunday Visitor*, 1970), and in the continuing series, *Matrimonial Jurisprudence, U.S.* (Toledo, OH: Canon Law Society of America, 1968– ; 5 vols. to date). Tribunals in the U.K., by contrast, are far more cautious than their U.S. counterparts; see generally *Matrimonial Decisions for England and Wales* (London: Canon Law Society of Great Britain and Ireland, 1967–); since 1980 this series has been retitled *Matrimonial Decisions of Great Britain and Ireland*.

[7] Arena, "Jurisprudence of the Rota," pp. 265–93. Three landmark Rotal decisions, *Coram De Jorio* (20 Dec. 1967), *Coram Pinto* (18 Dec. 1979) and *Coram Colagiovanni* (15 Dec. 1979) can conveniently be found in Thomas P. Doyle, "Rotal Jurisprudence," in his *Marriage Studies* 2 : 159–99. On the development of matrimonial jurisprudence in U.S. tribunals see also Doyle, "Matrimonial Jurisprudence in the United States," *Marriage Studies* 2 : 111–58, and C. J. Hettinger, "Matrimonial Jurisprudence: The Second Postconciliar Decade," *Jurist* 37 (1977) 358–75.

[8] Charles E. Curran, "Divorce—From the Perspective of Moral Theology," in Canon Law Society of America, *Proceedings* 36 (1974) 1–24; William E. May, "Marriage, Divorce and Remarriage," *Jurist* 37 (1977) 266–86; James J. Young, ed., *Ministering to the Divorced Catholic* (New York: Paulist Press, 1979), Francesco Javier Urrutia, "The 'Internal Forum Solution': Some Comments," *Jurist* 40 (1980) 128–40; James H. Provost, "Intolerable Marriage Situations Revisited," in *Jurist* 40 (1980) 141–96. Victor J. Pos-

Protestant Christians since the sixteenth century have often tolerated some practices—notably divorce and remarriage—that Catholics condemn, and Protestant opposition to most kinds of nonmarital sex has diminished notably since the 1950s. Civil law in the Western industrialized nations has also become increasingly neutral on most of these issues. Divorce and subsequent remarriage are now permitted by law virtually everywhere in the West, even in traditional strongholds of Catholic intransigence, such as Italy and Spain. Virtually nowhere in Western Europe, save in Ireland, is access to contraceptive devices seriously restricted by law.

In the United States the intervention of the federal courts has caused even strongholds of sexual conservatism to permit the sale of what some statutes used to refer to as "indecent articles."[9] Homosexual practices between consenting adults are no longer subject to criminal prosecution in most of the Western

---

pishill, *Divorce and Remarriage: Towards a New Catholic Teaching* (New York: Herder and Herder, 1967), suggested, partly on historical grounds, a basic restructuring of Catholic doctrine and policy, but his proposals received little welcome from the Roman authorities. Other radical proposals were offered by Morris L. West and Robert Francis, *Scandal in the Assembly: A Bill of Complaints and a Proposal for Reform in the Matrimonial Laws and Tribunals of the Roman Catholic Church* (New York: William Morrow and Company, 1970), but their proposals, even less conventional than those of Msgr. Pospishill, found correspondingly less favor at Rome. In the Irish Republic, where civil law does not recognize even Roman annulments, the voters at the urging of the Catholic bishops have recently rejected by a large majority an attempt to lift the ban on divorce; *New York Times*, Saturday, 28 June 1986, pp. 1, 5, and Sunday, 29 June 1986, sect. 1, p. 3. Modifications in traditional moral condemnations of homosexuals have been suggested by the Dutch *New Catechism*, English translation (New York: Herder and Herder, 1969), pp. 384–85; John Coleman, "La rivoluzione omosessuale," *Concilium* 20 (1984) 216–24; Letha Scanzoni, *Is the Homosexual My Neighbor? Another Christian View* (San Francisco: Harper & Row, 1978); Robin Scroggs, *The New Testament and Homosexuality: Contextual Background for Contemporary Debate* (Philadelphia: Fortress Press, 1983), and Ginder, *Binding with Briars*, pp. 129–48, 183–97, among others. In the present climate of ecclesiastical opinion, however, Roman authorities seem unlikely to take these suggestions with great seriousness either. Even modest proposals for relatively minor relaxation of the taboos that have become traditional among Catholics during the past two centuries and more have been brusquely rejected by the Roman leadership in recent years; *Times* (London), 3 Sept. 1980, p. 4; *National Catholic Reporter*, 28 Sept. 1984, pp. 7, 25, and 5 Oct. 1984, p. 7; Elaine Sciolino, "American Catholics: A Time for Challenge," *New York Times Magazine*, 4 Nov. 1984, pp. 40, 70, 74–5, 84–5, 93, 100–1.

[9]Thus Wis. Stat. §450.11(1) [1973]. In Baird v. Lynch, 390 F. Supp. 740 (1974), however, the U.S. District Court for the Western District of Wisconsin ruled that the provisions of this statute that prohibited the sale or gift of contraceptive materials to unmarried persons violated the constitutional right of privacy. Accordingly Wis. Stat. § 450.11 [1975] was amended to delete the unconstitutional provisions and, in the process, the reference to "indecent articles" also disappeared.

world, except again in Ireland and some parts of the United States.[10] Adultery and fornication, although still statutory crimes in some American jurisdictions, are in practice almost never prosecuted when practiced discreetly and in private.[11] Even so, private sexual relationships between consenting adults remain theoretically subject to legal restrictions in most Western nations.[12]

Why have medieval Christian beliefs and policies concerning sex endured so persistently? Three factors provide at least partial explanations. The first has to do with the large-scale stability of long-term social conditions in Western Europe between about 1100 and the industrial revolution. Medieval sexual doctrine, as it developed in its classic form during the twelfth and thirteenth centuries, responded to problems in a society that was becoming increasingly urban and economically diversified. Those social characteristics persisted into the modern era, as have sexual doctrines adapted to respond to them. Secondly, medieval canonists and theologians, the principal architects of sexual doctrine, were conscious that sex is in some mysterious way connected with the wellsprings of salvation and the bliss of heaven, that it is both wonderful and terrible. They considered those who contravene the limits that religion sets on sexual behavior as trespassers in a sacred realm. This perception (by no means unique either to Western Europeans or the Middle Ages) has also persisted and helps to explain why modern societies continue to find so many medieval Christian sexual doctrines viable. Third, medieval writers who dealt with sexual

---

[10] In the U.K. the Sexual Offenses Act 1967 § 1(1) lifted criminal sanctions against homosexual relations between consenting adults, except in Northern Ireland. By a peculiar quirk of the statute, however, sodomy between a man and a woman (including husband and wife) remains punishable by life imprisonment; S.O.A. 1967 § 12(1); Anthony M. Honoré, *Sex Law* (London: Duckworth, 1978), pp. 24, 91–101. In the U.S. statutes penalizing homosexual acts remain current law in twenty-six states. The U.S. Supreme Court recently affirmed in Bowers v. Hardwick (30 June 1986) that States have the power to penalize homosexual sodomy. The Hardwick judgment reversed a series of Federal Appellate decisions that had extended the right of privacy to cover homosexual acts between consenting adults; *New York Times*, 1 July 1986, pp. 1, 10–11; Baker v. Wade, 553 F. Supp. 1121 (1982); Bowers v. Hardwick (slip opinion).

[11] Several lower courts in recent years have taken the position that the Supreme Court's decision in Eisenstadt v. Baird brought all private, voluntary, and noncommercial sexual relationships under the protection of the right of privacy; see Eisenstadt v. Baird, 405 U.S. 431, 92 S.Ct. 1029, 31 L.Ed.2d 349 (1972); Doe v. Commander, Wheaton Police Dept., 273 Md. 262 at 272, 329 A.2d 35 at 41 (1975); Montgomery County, Md. v. Walsh, 274 Md. 502 at 513, 336 A.2d 97 at 105 (1975); State v. Pilcher, 242 N.W.2d 348 (Ia., 1976); State v. Bateman, 547 P.2d 6 at 9 (Ariz., 1976); Baker v. Wade, 553 F. Supp. 1121 (Texas, 1982). The effects of these decisions extend well beyond the area of criminal law and may affect, among other things, contracts, testamentary issues, and property arrangements of all kinds; Kay and Amyx, "*Marvin v. Marvin*: Preserving the Options," pp. 937–77; Dwyer, "Immoral Contracts," pp. 386–88.

[12] Honoré, *Sex Law*, pp. 24–34, 59–76, 94–101, 117–32. Schnucker, "La position puritaine," pp. 1380–81, 1386; Stone, "Family History in the 1980s," pp. 78–79.

problems assigned to law and legal processes a paramount role in controlling sexual behavior. They counted on lawgivers, lawyers, the courts, and civic officials (in modern times, especially the police) to keep at bay those who profane the holy. Law is by and large a conservative force in society, for law seeks to assure continuity and preservation. The legal profession, moreover, came into being in something resembling its modern form during the thirteenth century, just at the time that a consensus among religious teachers about the basic elements of Christian sexual morality was taking shape. Jurists, in collaboration with moralists, have been instrumental in securing the continued acceptance of the medieval sexual ethos during the past seven centuries.

These three factors—the continuity of the socioeconomic environment, the continuing identification of the erotic with the sacred, and the inertia of the law and its institutions—not only help to explain the continuity of medieval sexual teaching, but are useful in understanding the historical development of that teaching itself.

One aspect of socioeconomic continuity requires special mention. Modern historians sometimes claim that one of the principal contrasts between late medieval society and modern society is in family structure. The "modern" family, they say, centers on the nuclear unit of father-mother-children, and this type of family first emerged between 1680 and 1850. But as we have seen, the nuclear family had already become the primary social unit in many parts of Europe before A.D. 800. Some other characteristics of the so-called "modern" family— including free choice of marriage partner, the rejection of parental permission as a necessary precondition for the marriage of adults, the ideal of conjugal bonding through mutual affection—were also promoted and championed by medieval lawyers and theologians a half-millennium before 1680.[13]

This is not to cast the medieval Church in the role of a disinterested champion of liberty in its marriage law: the development of canonistic theories about marital formation makes that a highly dubious proposition. But at least in this respect the Church successfully anticipated the needs of later European society.

The suggestion has recently been advanced, not for the first time, that the medieval Church tried to keep a tight grip on sexual behavior in order to advance its own economic interests. Medieval marriage law certainly tended in some respects to secure economic advantages for the Church. At least some of the Church's leaders may have perceived that this was true. The virtual monopoly that the medieval Church enjoyed over the legal determination of who was married and who was not meant that the Church was in a position to influence patterns of inheritance in the medieval West. That Church leaders sometimes

---

[13] Lawrence Stone, *The Family, Sex, and Marriage in England, 1500–1800*, abridged ed. (Harmondsworth: Penguin, 1979), pp. 21–22, 407–14, and his "Family History in the 1980s: Past Achievements and Future Trends," *Journal of Interdisciplinary History* 12 (1981) 73–75; Jack Goody, *The Development of the Family and Marriage in Europe* (Cambridge: At the University Press, 1983), p. 24.

used that position in ways calculated to benefit their institution seems very likely indeed.

It is a great deal less likely, however, that the Church and its leaders were either cunning enough or farsighted enough to have implemented a long-range scheme to shape Christian marriage law so as to maximize the Church's material benefits. It would have required a better-organized and more efficient system of centralized planning than the medieval Church ever enjoyed to have projected and implemented such a strategy.

While the medieval Church's marriage and sex policies may have helped to increase ecclesiastical wealth, it does not necessarily follow that the system was designed in order to achieve that goal, although some Protestant reformers suspected that it had been.[14] We are more likely dealing with an unintended result of the Church's urge to protect the sanctity of sex, rather than with policy consciously created to enrich the ecclesiastical establishment.

The leaders of the medieval Church, although occasionally sensitive to the problems and moral dilemmas of their flocks, were often indifferent to the social implications that their policies created. Nowhere was their indifference more marked than in matters concerning reproduction and family life.[15] Twentieth-century spokesmen have also maintained that Christians should ignore the pain and suffering that may result from the application of their moral principles, and have repeatedly disclaimed responsibility for the results of their moral teachings.[16]

The third factor in our explanatory scheme—the persistent control of sexual conduct by the legal establishment—holds the key to explaining several anomalies in the historical development of sexual beliefs. Virtually all restrictions that now apply to sexual behavior in Western societies stem from moral convictions enshrined in medieval canonical jurisprudence. The attitudes and beliefs of canonists and theologians about marriage, divorce, family structure, women's status, human psychology, gender roles, and a host of other controversial topics are woven into the very fabric of our legal system. In recent decades, legislative bodies and courts have begun to eliminate some vestiges of the medieval Christian world view from secular law. Despite this, substantial parts of our medieval religious heritage remain embedded in Western law because they still reflect a broad consensus about the most desirable ways of shaping institutions and controlling human behavior. The committment of Western societies to the principle of monogamy is one vestige of medieval Christendom that remains

[14] Luther, *Von ehelichen Leben* in WA 10/2:280.

[15] Flandrin, *Familles*, p. 175; James Muldoon, "Missionaries and the Marriages of Infidels: The Case of the Mongol Mission," *Jurist* 35 (1975) 141.

[16] Basil Mitchell, *Law, Morality, and Religion in a Secular Society* (London: Oxford University Press, 1970), p. 110; Peter Nichols, *The Pope's Divisions: The Roman Catholic Church Today* (London: Faber and Faber, 1981; repr. Harmondsworth: Penguin, 1982), pp. 263–64; Fuchs, *Sexual Desire and Love*, pp. 168–70.

intact. The institution of marriage itself retains a generous measure of its medieval antecedents, even in the most secularized Western societies, and again there is little evidence that significant numbers of people wish to see it altered in any fundamental way.

To stress the primacy of law as a means of sexual control is not to maintain that there has been harmonious compliance with its regulations, or universal agreement with its strictures. Indeed, medieval canon law's record in securing obedience to its marriage policies was decidedly mixed. Flandrin is surely right when he asserts that the medieval Church never entirely succeeded in securing acceptance of its views on reproductive policy. Yet the Church often did secure compliance with many aspects of its marriage law. Its consensual marriage theory was generally accepted, although sometimes modified in practice; its attempts to secure freedom of choice in the selection of marriage partners were often implemented; certainly its efforts to make marriage easy to contract were generally successful, although the price paid for this achievement—the prevalence of clandestine marriage and the consequent uncertainties that surrounded even solemnized marriages—seems excessively high.[17] It is striking that where surviving court records make it possible to compare the practices of judges with the prescriptions of the law and the academic commentators, the agreement between practice and theory is by and large rather close.[18] It is much more difficult to tell to what degree ordinary people may have internalized the prescriptions of canonists and theologians on marital practices. Thus it is nearly impossible to determine what degree of success the Church may have had in forming people's perceptions and shaping their consciences on sexual matters.

Marriage and the family are such central social institutions that rules governing the methods of contracting, terminating, and supporting marital units will continue to be legislated, and governments will try to enforce them in any foreseeable circumstances. But the relationship between restrictive sex laws and the social price we pay for them remains a matter for basic disagreement. Those who subscribe to a functionalist anthropology, as many people do in the late twentieth century, insist that restrictions on sexual behavior can be justified only if they serve identifiable social goals—bolstering the institutions of family and kinship, for example, or avoiding harm to children. Many other people, however, reject this functionalist view and believe that society has a duty to restrain sexual behavior in obedience to enduring moral and religious values. Those who take this view maintain that a moral society must impose stringent limitations upon sexual freedom: they believe that sex should be permitted only at certain times, under certain circumstances, or for certain purposes—such as within marriage, in the missionary position, and with the goal of reproduction, for example.

[17] Flandrin, *Familles*, p. 76; Ariès, "Le mariage indissoluble," p. 130. Goody, *Development of the Family*, p. 185; Pollock and Maitland, *History of English Law* 2:368–69, 385; Howard, *History of Matrimonial Institutions* 1:324, 334; Sheehan, "Marriage and Family in English Conciliar Legislation," p. 213.

[18] Helmholz, *Marriage Litigation*, pp. 187–89; Flandrin, "La vie sexuelle," p. 111.

Many twentieth century societies, however, lack a broad consensus about either religious beliefs or the proper role of law in enforcing sexual morals. Those who operate on functionalist assumptions find the limitations that medieval religious beliefs imposed on sexual conduct indefensible and argue that they should be repealed because they no longer serve a social purpose. Those who continue to subscribe to traditional Christian religious beliefs, however, feel that legal restraints premised on their views of sexual propriety should remain in place and warn that to relax those restraints will mean abandoning the central values that have historically held Western societies together.

It is certainly true that twentieth-century attitudes toward sex often betray a continuing, frequently unconscious, acceptance of the medieval sexual ethos. This shows up in the expressions that we use to refer to sex, in the concepts and categories employed in analyzing sexual behavior, and in the feelings that most adults in our society share about their sexual experiences. Although many people in late twentieth-century society (especially, but not exclusively, in the United States) are prepared to tolerate public discussions of sexual issues that nineteenth- and early twentieth-century society would have found objectionable in the extreme, it remains true that, as Gagnon and Simon observed, "learning about sex in our society is learning about guilt; conversely, learning how to manage sexuality constitutes learning how to manage guilt."[19] The guilt that we attach to all kinds of sexual behavior is beyond serious doubt an artifact of medieval Christian beliefs about personal morality. Technical legal discourse in particular still employs language—"crime against nature," "unnatural act," and "sodomy" for example—that implicitly assumes medieval beliefs about the nature of sex and its role in human life (see Appendix 3).

Our sexual assumptions, moreover, still rely heavily on beliefs and rhetoric that stem from late ancient psychology and anthropology. Medieval and modern analyses of sexuality usually assume more or less absolute dichotomies between body and soul, matter and spirit, reason and passion, mind and feelings. None of these ideas is self-evident, and none is supported by indisputable (or even terribly persuasive) proof. Another common assumption, sometimes openly expressed, more often tacitly implied, holds that human instincts and feelings are at best morally suspect, if not downright evil, a notion that stems from the belief in original sin. This view identifies sexuality with passion and animality which are tainted with wickedness, impurity, and sin. These themes were highly developed in medieval theology and law, as we have seen, and the sentiments, even the metaphors and phrases of medieval thinkers, still figure in the pronouncements of religious authorities, notably the modern popes.[20]

[19] John H. Gagnon and William Simon, *Sexual Conduct: The Social Sources of Human Sexuality* (Chicago: Aldine, 1973), p. 42.

[20] Thus, for example, Pope John Paul II in an audience on 8 October 1980 reiterated as his own belief the dictum that St. Jerome borrowed from Sextus Empiricus to the effect that married men who felt sexual desire for their own wives were guilty of adultery; Nichols, *Pope's Divisions*, p. 254; that John Paul should resurrect this patristic topos is not entirely surprising in the light of his scholarly work, prior to becoming pope, on the

Like their medieval models, twentieth century Catholic sex theories typically deny that pleasure has spiritual value and treat sex as an unfortunate consequence of sin. Some Catholic writers in this century have cautiously moved away from this position, to assert that sexuality may not, after all, have been one of the Creator's blunders or, alternatively, a punishment for sin. By and large, however, Catholic thinkers have hesitated to adopt this position. In view of the disapproval visited on its proponents by the Sacred Congregation of the Doctrine of the Faith (otherwise known as the Holy Office, the successor of the Roman Inquisition) their hesitation is understandable.[21]

Protestant writers in this century have often been more willing than their Catholic counterparts to emphasize the positive role of sex as a symbol and an expression of married love. Few Christian theologians of any persuasion, however, challenge the historical antipathy of their religious tradition toward nonmarital sex, either homosexual or heterosexual.[22]

The persistence of these ancient positions has meant that Christians, especially those in the Catholic tradition, still tend to separate sex from love. Catholic spokesmen have occasionally asserted that the two are related and that conjugal sexuality has a positive value in the marital relationship. But those who assert this usually wrap their statements in reservations and qualifications so convoluted and obscure that the message is liable to be lost in the noise that accompanies it.[23] The effects of this separation of love from sex have been and

---

Gdansk *Abbreviatio* of Gratian's *Decretum*; Karol Wojtyla, "Le traité de 'Penitentia' de Gratien dans l'abrégé de Gdansk mar. F. 275," *Studia Gratiana* 7 (1959) 355–90. Note, too, Pope Paul VI's remarks about married couples' "tendencies of instinct or passion," which, the pope declared, must be dominated by reason and will, a process that, as he saw it, "will undoubtedly require ascetical practices." *Humanae vitae* §§ 10, 21, in AAS 60 (1968) 481–503. The declaration of Pope Innocent XI on 2 March 1679 that it was heresy to teach that married couples might have sexual relations for pleasure and do so without sin apparently still represents the policy of the Roman authorities; *Decisiones sanctae sedis de usu et abusu matrimonii*, 2d ed. (Turin: Marietti, 1944), p. 12.

[21] S. Congregation for the Doctrine of the Faith, "Declaration on . . . Sexual Ethics" §§ 12–13, (1976).

[22] Fuchs, *Sexual Desire and Love*, pp. 204–5.

[23] G. de Broglie, "Le fondement de l'amour conjugal," *Doctor Communis* 23 (1970) 192–216; Fuchs, *Sexual Desire and Love*, pp. 153–54, 168; Flandrin, "La vie sexuelle," p. 107; Goody, *Development of the Family*, p. 77. Recent Catholic pronouncements on the matter are often inconsistent. Thus, for example, Pope John Paul II in a statement at an audience on 17 January 1980 implied strongly that there was a positive connection between marital sex and conjugal love. "The human body with its sex and its masculinity and its femininity," the pope declared, "is not only directed towards fruitfulness and procreation, but towards the capacity to express love, that love in which the man-person becomes a gift and, by means of this gift, actuates the very sense of his being and his existence." Thus, he continued, married couples are "free to give each other to each other and love each other mutually in full mastery of themselves." *Osservatore Romano*, English ed., no. 616 (21 Jan. 1980), quoted in Nichols, *Pope's Divisions*, p. 251. This

continue to be tragic for thousands of Christians. Clinical studies make it clear, for example, that vaginismus and orgasmic dysfunction among women and secondary impotence among men are closely related to religious piety and conformity among persons of Judeo-Christian upbringing.[24] The usual response of religious authorities to findings of this sort has been to denounce scientific sex research as subversive of morality, "leading to the loss of serenity" and "opening the way to vice."[25]

The negative attitudes toward sex that are commonplace among Christian religious writers and teachers are also related to the misogynism entrenched in so much Christian belief and practice. The belief that sex is nasty, indecent, and impure has often tempted Christian theologians and canonists—virtually all of them male—to identify these characteristics with women, whom they see as the embodiment of sexual allure and temptation. Some elements of this misogynist tradition can be traced to Christianity's Judaic origins; but Christian religious leaders have powerfully reinforced and amplified the distrust of female sexuality latent in their Jewish heritage. They have, partly for this reason, systematically excluded women from primary roles of power and authority in the Christian religious establishment. That these effects are related to a belief in the danger and impurity of female sexuality seems highly probable.[26]

---

murky statement was interpreted as hinting that there might, after all, be some positive value in marital sexuality; the pope's more recent declarations, however, as well as the guidelines on sex education subsequently issued by the Sacred Congregation for Catholic Education, raise serious doubts about this interpretation; *Osservatore Romano*, English ed. no. 812 (5 December 1983), pp. 5–9.

[24] William H. Masters and Virginia E. Johnson, *Human Sexual Inadequacy* (Boston: Little, Brown and Company, 1970), pp. 117, 138–39, 174–75, 179, 213, 229–30, 252. Earlier survey research had suggested a strong link between religious attitudes and various sexual dysfunctions; see esp. Alfred C. Kinsey, Wardell B. Pomeroy, and Clyde E. Martin, *Sexual Behavior in the Human Male* (Philadelphia: W. B. Saunders Company, 1948), pp. 465–87, and Alfred C. Kinsey, Wardell B. Pomeroy, Clyde E. Martin, and Paul H. Gebhard, *Sexual Behavior in the Human Female* (Philadelphia: W. B. Saunders Company, 1953), pp. 381–82. More recent surveys indicate that religious practice and convictions may have had a decreasing influence on sexual behavior among members of the generation after Kinsey's sample; see Morton M. Hunt, *Sexual Behavior in the 1970s* (Chicago: Playboy Press, 1974), pp. 29–30, 194, 259, 264; John DeLamater and Patricia MacCorquodale, *Premarital Sexuality: Attitudes, Relationships, Behavior* (Madison: University of Wisconsin Press, 1979), p. 232; for a report of an English study see Michael Schofield, *The Sexual Behaviour of Young People* (Harmondsworth: Penguin, 1968), pp. 72–3, 101–2, 107, 124, 190, 201. Despite this it may be significant—it is impossible to ascertain because of her research design—that Shere Hite reported that more than 95% of the women surveyed in her study indicated they had been brought up believe sex was an unmentionable subject and sexuality was inherently bad or wrong; *The Hite Report* (New York: Macmillan, 1976; repr. New York: Dell, 1977), p. 39.

[25] Pope John Paul II, *Familiaris consortio* § 37.

[26] Fuchs, *Sexual Desire and Love*, pp. 110–13; Joseph C. Smith, "Sword and Shield of Perseus," p. 24; cf. the perceptive remarks of another Smith, the eighteenth-century

Religion and law have served past societies as means for enunciating social consensus about acceptable outlets for sexual urges and for imposing both formal and informal controls on the acting out of sexual fantasies and desires. Medieval Church leaders saw that these two modalities of social control could be fused with one another, that religious prohibitions could be enforced by legal sanctions, while legal doctrines could be shaped by religious values. Although it is impossible to divorce law from morality—and it would be undesirable to do so, even if it were possible—it does not follow that law need be so intimately concerned with sexual morals as it commonly is and has been in Western thought. H. L. A. Hart was no doubt correct when he asserted that certain "universal values" (by which he meant generally accepted values) are necessary to the survival of any society, but there is no need to suppose that the sexual beliefs and attitudes of medieval Christendom are among those values or that abandonment of late ancient Stoic and medieval Christian beliefs about anthropology and sexual morals would destroy the foundations of Western society.[27]

The Christian churches continue to enjoy a legally and politically privileged position, even in what is sometimes called a secular age. Within the churches, however, and particularly among their intellectual elite, ideas about the proper role of sex in Christian life are very much in flux. The three traditional models of sexuality that have dominated Christian discussions of the subject since patristic times continue to attract, in one combination or another, the allegiance both of professed Christians and of many whose ties to organized religion are casual or nonexistent. Some theologians and canonists are anxious to break away from traditional attitudes and doctrines on sexual matters. Discontent with accepted orthodoxies is particularly keen among Catholic intellectuals, many of whom wish to see their Church give real weight in its law and doctrine to the concept of marriage as a relationship bonded by intimacy. Catholic writers who champion change on such issues as contraception and abortion, however, have met stiff resistance both from the Roman curia and from recent popes. Modification of the Roman leadership's views about sex seems unlikely in the near term.[28]

---

economist and moral philosopher, Adam Smith, in *Lectures on Jurisprudence*, ed. R. Meek, D. Rapheal, and Peter Stein, in vol. 5 of the Glasgow edition of Smith's *Works* (Oxford: Clarendon Press, 1978), p. 147.

[27] H. L. A. Hart, *Concept of Law* (Oxford: Clarendon Press, 1961), pp. 188–95, and his *Law, Liberty, and Morality* (Stanford: Stanford University Press, 1963), pp. 17–24; Mitchell, *Law, Morality, and Religion*, p. 24.

[28] The bishops assembled in the Second Vatican Council both astonished and frightened conservative Catholic leaders by their openness to change in this area and their willingness to consider significant modifications of the prevailing orthodoxies. Since 1965, intransigents in the Catholic hierarchy have settled into the doctrinal trenches, prepared to fight a war of attrition in order to foreclose substantial change. The Catholic faithful, meanwhile—particularly in West Germany, the Netherlands, and the United States—have tended either to ignore Roman fulminations altogether or else to pay them only polite lip service. Those who wish to see some re-ordering of priorities in Catholic

While diversity of thought, teaching, and opinion on sexual matters offends the stereotype of a monolithic Roman Church, many Protestant Christians take positive pride in their tradition's capacity to tolerate disagreement on basic issues. Mainline Protestant churches have typically adopted a relatively permissive stance on sexual morality. Most of them will tolerate divorce and remarriage among their members without imposing disciplinary sanctions. Although most Protestants disapprove of casual fornication and still more strongly of marital infidelity, premarital intercourse between engaged couples is usually accorded tacit acceptance as a prelude to formal marriage.[29] Masturbation no longer ranks as a significant moral offense in the minds of most Protestant writers, a startling shift from Protestant views in the nineteenth century and the first half of this century. Considerable numbers of mainstream Protestants are now prepared to tolerate homosexual relationships. A few congregations accept clergymen who make no secret of their homosexual life styles.[30]

Among fundamentalist and evangelical Christians, however, sexual activity and expression remains more rigidly controlled. While only the more intransigent fundamentalists flatly condemn remarriage following divorce and even fewer punish divorced persons by banishing them from their fellowship, fundamentalists and evangelicals consider divorce a moral evil and strongly disapprove of remarriage of divorced persons. Extramarital sex of all kinds remains nearly as taboo among fundamentalists as it is among traditional Catholics. Much the same is true of attitudes toward homosexuality and other deviant sexual practices. In the United Kingdom the Revere Ian Paisley's campaign to "Save Ulster from sodomy" echoes hostilities and fears that remain strong in the United States among Southern Baptists, evangelicals, fundamentalists and Pentecostals. But Dr. Paisley and other militant Orangemen probably share more beliefs and sentiments with conservative elements in Catholicism than members of either group would care to acknowledge, even to themselves.[31]

---

sexual doctrine seem to assume that the people will prevail and that Rome will sooner or later accept what it cannot change, as it has done often enough in the past. In no other aspect of contemporary Catholic life does the myth of the monolithic Church so obviously misrepresent reality as in the theology and canon law of sexuality. See, e.g., Andolsen, "Leale dissenso," pp. 160–69; Peter Nichols, *The Politics of the Vatican* (New York: Frederick A. Praeger, 1968), p. 279; John F. Dedek, *Contemporary Sexual Morality* (New York: Sheed and Ward, 1971), pp. 19–23 and 44–65, but cf. pp. 92–161; Pohier, *Chrétien, plaisir, sexualité*, pp. 90–115.

[29] *Times* (London), 3 June 1983, pp. 3, 13; 13 June 1983, p. 1; *Sex and Morality: A Report to the British Council of Churches* (Philadelphia: Fortress Press, 1966); Hodgson, *Sex and Christian Freedom*, pp. 38–84.

[30] David J. Atkinson, *Homosexuals in the Christian Community* (Grand Rapids, MI: Eerdmans, 1981); *Towards a Theology of Gay Liberation*, ed. Malcom Macourt (London: SCM Press, 1977); *Times* (London), 10 June 1982, p. 3.

[31] James Barr, *Fundamentalism* (London: SCM Press, 1977), p. 320, maintains that these attitudes are not central to fundamentalists, at least in Britain. Sexual issues are prominent, however, in U.S. fundamentalism; Marsden, *Fundamentalism and American*

The diverse views of contemporary Christians about sexual behavior reflect familiar mixtures of the three models of sexuality that we found in the writings of medieval canonists and theologians. The themes of reproduction, purity, and affection, together with subsidiary propositions deduced from them, flourish almost as vigorously in the twentieth century as they did in the twelfth. And in the present century, as in earlier eras, Church leaders insist that governments have a moral obligation to enact into law Christian religious prescriptions about sexual conduct.[32]

Conclusions

The history of changing concepts among Christian leaders and intellectuals about the nature of human sexuality and about the kinds and varieties of sexual practices that are consistent with Christian belief suggests that dogmatic assertions about the unity, consistency, and invariability of Christian sexual morality must be treated with skepticism. "Christian sexual morality" has encompassed a wide range of inconsistent views.

The history of medieval attempts to modify patterns of sexual activity through law suggests that past efforts in this direction have been successful only when society as a whole has perceived that the hoped-for modifications will meet needs other than purely moral and spiritual ones. The early medieval Church succeeded, for example, in imposing monogamy upon the Germanic invaders whose previous marriage practices had favored polygyny, at least among the rich, the strong, and the well born. Monogamy ultimately prevailed, but it did so only after a long struggle. In the final analysis its victory probably owed as much to material considerations relating to the conservation of heritable property, succession to political power, the disappearance of slavery, and the emergence of peasant agriculture as it did to moral and ethical concerns. The triumph of monogamy has been reasonably complete and permanent. It was also the most complete victory that Christian beliefs about sexual morality and family structure ever won. The history of the struggles to win acceptance of the principle of matrimonial indissolubility or the contest over the rules limiting endogamy, for example, show far more limited successes, and in the long run

---

Culture, p. 26; Gary K. Clabaugh, *Thunder on the Right: The Protestant Fundamentalists* (Chicago: Nelson-Hall, 1974), pp. 5–31. The sexual attitudes of Protestant evangelicals, fundamentalists, latter-day Puritans, and traditionalist Catholics seem to mirror long-held Mediterranean value systems that are to some degree independent of religious affiliations, for they are as common among Cypriot Highlanders and Algerian herdsmen as they are among Andalucian Catholics; see Jean G. Péristani, ed., *Honour and Shame: The Values of Mediterranean Society* (London: Weidenfeld and Nicholson; Chicago: University of Chicago Press, 1960), pp. 42–52, 86–88, 180–82, 224–28.

[32] United States Catholic Conference, "Statement on Role of the Church in Politics," *New York Times*, 14 Oct. 1984, p. 13; and cf. Alfredo Ottaviani, *Institutiones iuris publici ecclesiastici*, 4th ed. by Giuseppe Dannizia, 2 vols. (Vatican City: Typis Polyglottis Vaticanis, 1958–60) 2:98–99.

even those proved transitory. The history of efforts to legislate bans on prostitution demonstrated that the capacity of religious leaders to implement their moral beliefs through legal regulation was severely limited; it also underscored the wisdom of those Church leaders who opted for a policy of practical toleration for behavior that they disapproved of but that they perceived might meet some wider social needs. The failure of medieval efforts to eradicate fornication, concubinage, premarital cohabitation, adultery, and sodomy through legal prescriptions, even where those prescriptions were backed by serious enforcement efforts, is rather sobering. It suggests that simply enacting theological principles into law is not likely to be a rewarding exercise.

The Christian Church and Western governments in the past have accommodated their sexual teachings and their sex laws to the social needs and intellectual perceptions of successive eras. Attempts to enunciate permanent and unchanging prescriptions for sexual behavior are not likely, on the past record, to rise above the level of vain and transient fads. Even basic institutions, such as marriage and the family, change over time, as they respond to changes in society, the economy, and intellectual perceptions. No system of law and regulation can adequately prescribe the bounds and limits of human sexual conduct, for there is no single right and proper way for humans to respond sexually to each other. Human sexuality remains, at the end, a mystery suffused with wonder and with terror, the foundation of our existence as individuals and as a species, but also an explosive force that can tear us apart and pit us one against the other as readily as it can join us together in cozy and rapturous intimacy.

Law is a tool that societies legitimately use to set boundaries, to protect some forms of sexual expression while discouraging others. Law can legitimately penalize sexual behaviors that endanger life, health, and public safety. It can in some measure protect the disadvantaged from the cruder kinds of sexual exploitation. What law cannot do effectively is to impose a uniform sexual morality, to compel the public to conform to a single ideal of sexual ethics, however noble that ideal may be.

Law is a crude, if indispensable, tool of social policy; but it is also a fragile one. To force it beyond its limits is not only to invite failure to achieve the intended goal, but also to inspire disrespect for the legitimate social functions of law and ultimately for society itself. Sex law presents powerful temptations to force law beyond its limits. Societies do well to resist those temptations.

Appendix 1
Tables

Table 4.1 Early Medieval Legal Sources

Germanic Laws	Councils and Synods	Capitularies	Canonical Collections
466 ~ 485 *Codex Euricianus*			498 ~ 514 *Dionysiana*
501 ~ 515 *Lex Burgundionum*			
597 ~ 604 Laws of Ethelbert of Kent			
613 *Pactus legis Alamannorum*			633 (?) *Hispana*
643 *Edictum Rotharii*	664 Whitby		
717 ~ 719 *Lex Alamannorum*			
744 ~ 748 *Lex Baiwariorum*	744 Soissons		
	756 Verberie		
	757 Compiègne		
		768 Charlemagne, *Capitularium primum*	774 *Dionysio-Hadriana*
785 *Lex Saxonum*	795 London	789 *Admonitio generalis*	
	796/97 Friuli		
	802 Aachen		
	813 Metz		
	813 Tours		
	825 Paris	827 Ansegis, *Capitularium*	840 *Collectio Dacheriana*
	Before 850 Ingelheim		847 ~ 852 Pseudo-Isidorian Decretals
			882 *Collectio Anselmo dedicata*
			906 Regino of Prüm
			1008 ~ 1010 Burchard of Worms

Table 4.2   Major Penitential Collections

Penitential	Date	Texts
	Celtic	
Finnian	late 6th cent.	Wasserschleben 108–19; Schmitz 1:502–9; Bieler 74–5; McNeill and Gamer, 87–97
Columban	late 6th cent.	Wasserschleben 353–60; Schmitz 1:588–602; Bieler 96–107; McNeill and Gamer 249–57
Cummean	7th/8th cent.	Bieler 108–35; McNeill and Gamer 99–117
Canones Hiberniae	ca. 675	Wasserschleben 136–44; Bieler 160–75; McNeill and Gamer 118–30
Collectio canonum Hibernenses	ca. 725	*Irische Kanonensammlung,* McNeill and Gamer 139–42
Old-Irish Penitential	ca. 780	Bieler 258–74; McNeill and Gamer 157–68
	Anglo-Saxon	
Canones Gregorii Capitula	690 ~ 710	Wasserschleben 160–80; Haddan and Stubbs 3:207–9
Theodore	690 ~ 710	Wasserschleben 182–219; Schmitz 1:524–50; Haddan and Stubbs 3:173–204; McNeill and Gamer 182–215
Bede	before 735?	Wasserschleben 220–30; Schmitz 1:550–64; Haddan and Stubbs 3:326–34; McNeill and Gamer 233–37
Egbert	ca. 750	Wasserschleben 231–47; Schmitz 1:565–87; Haddan and Stubbs 3:416–31; McNeill and Gamer 237–38
Pseudo-Bede	8th cent.	Wasserschleben 248–82
Pseudo-Egbert	8th cent.	Wasserschleben 300–48; McNeill and Gamer 243–48
	Continental: Pre-Carolingian	
Bigotianum	700 ~ 725	Wasserschleben 441–60; Bieler 198–239; McNeill and Gamer 148–55
Hubertense	before 750	Wasserschleben 377–86
Fleury	775 ~ 800	Wasserschleben 422–25; McNeill and Gamer 280–82
Merseburgense		
(a)	680 ~ 780	Wasserschleben 387–407
(b)	680 ~ 780	Wasserschleben 429–33

Table 4.2   (*continued*)

Penitential	Date	Texts
Continental: Pre-Carolingian, cont.		
Escarpsus Cummeani	8th cent.	Wasserschleben 465–93; Schmitz 1:615–45
Remense	8th cent.	Wasserschleben 497–504; Schmitz 1:645–53
Vindobonense (b)	8th cent.?	Wasserschleben 493–97
Sangallense Tripartita	2d half of 8th cent.	Schmitz 2:175–89
Capitula iudiciorum	2d half of 8th cent.	Wasserschleben 505–26; Schmitz 1:653–76
Valicellanum II	late 8th ~ early 9th cent.	Wasserschleben 547–50; Schmitz 1:239–42
Martenianum	8th ~ 9th cent.	Wasserschleben 282–300
Parisiense	9th cent.	Schmitz 1:677–97
Continental: Carolingian		
Dacheriana	first half of 9th cent.	*Spicilegium*, 2d ed., 1:509–64
Halitgar	817 ~ 831	Schmitz 1:719–33; McNeill and Gamer 295–314; PL 105:649–64
Pseudo-Theodore	830 ~ 847	Wasserschleben 566–622
Rabanus	ca. 841	PL 110:467–94
Continental: Post-Carolingian		
Pseudo-Gregory III	late 9th ~ early 10th cent.	Wasserschleben 535–47
Cassinense	ca. 900	Schmitz 1:388–432
Vallicellanum II	9th cent.	Wasserschleben 550–66; Schmitz 1:350–88
Arundel	10th cent.	Schmitz 1:432–65
Pseudo-Egbert	10th cent.	Wasserschleben 318–48
Pseudo-Edgar	10th cent.	PL 138:499–514
Regino	906	PL 132:185–370
Burchard and Later		
Burchard, *Corrector*	ca. 1010	Wasserschleben 624–82
Burchard, *Decretum*, Book 19	ca. 1010	PL 140:949–1014
Sangermanense	11th cent.	Wasserschleben 348–52
Laurentianum	11th cent.	Schmitz 1:786–91; McNeill and Gamer 352–53
Ivo of Chartres, *Decretum*, Pt. 15	ca. 1094	PL 161:893–95
Thorlac Thorhallson	1133 ~ 1193	Schmitz 1:707–15; McNeill and Gamer 354–58

Table 4.3 Penances for Selected Sexual Offenses

	Fornication	Adultery	Masturbation	Anal Sex	Oral Sex	Bestiality
Finnian	12 y.# 7 y.$,&		1 d. 9 psalms	4 y.@ 7 y.*	4 y.@ 7 y.*	
Columban	12 y.# 3–7 y.& 1 y.+	7 y.	3 y.& 2 y.⟨	10 y. 7 y.+		2 y.⟨ 3 y.&
Cummean	12 y.# 7 y.$,&	1 y.		7 y.	3 y.@ 7 y.*	1 y.⟩ 40 d.⟨
Theodore	1 y.	4 y.	40 d.	7 y.@ 10 y.* 15 y.&	7 y. 15 y. 22 y.	
Bede	1 y.+ 3 y.$ 7 y.&	3 y.	40 d.⟩	4 y.@ 7 y.*		1 y.+ 2 y.$
Egbert	4 y.+ 5–10 y.& 12 y.#	4 y.+ 5–10 y.& 12 y.#		5 y.+ 7–12 y.& 14 y.#		3 y.
Bigotianum	3 y.	7 y. 3 y.	3 w.& 100 d.@ 1 y.*		4 y.@ 7 y.*	10 y.*
Halitgar		7 y.		15 y.⟩ 25 y.⟨		15 y.⟩ 25 y.⟨
Regino	3 y.	2–7 y.	40–100 d.⟩ 20 d.+ 30 d.&			1–10 y.
Burchard, *Decretum*	20 d.	7–15 y.	10–20 d.		10 y.@ 12 y.*	7–10 y.

Note: y. year; d. day; w. week; * habitual; @ first offense; # bishop; $ monk; & cleric; + layman; ⟨ child; ⟩ adult

Table 4.4 Abstinence from Marital Sex: Physiological Cycle and Weekdays

	Menstru-ation	Pregnancy	Lactation	Sun.	Wed.	Fri.	Sat.
Finnian		X		X			
Cummean	X	X	X	X			X
Columban							
Theodore	40 d.	40 d.	X				
Egbert		20–40 d.	20–40 d.	26 s.	26 s.	26 s.	26 s.
Pseudo-Egbert	40 d.	20–40 d.	40 d.	3 d.			
Bigotianum		X	X				
Halitgar		X	X				
Regino	40 d.	X	X	X	X	X	
Burchard, *Decretum*	10 d.	10–20 d.	20 d.	40 d.			

Note: X mentioned; d. pence; s. shilling (= 12 pence)

Table 4.5 Abstinence from Marital Sex: Liturgical Cycle

	Lent	Advent	Pente-cost	During Penance	Other Fasts	Easter	Other Feasts	Before Commu-nion	Wedding Night
Finnian	X	X	X						
Cummean	X	X	X						
Columban				X					
Theodore	1 y.					X		X	X
Egbert	26 s.	26 s.	26 s.						
Pseudo-Egbert									
Bigotianum	X					X		X	
Halitgar	X					X			X
Regino	X	X	X						X
Burchard, *Decretum*	40 d.	40 d.	X	X	40 d.		40 d.	X	X

Note: X mentioned; d. pence; s. shillings (= 12 d.); y. year

Table 5.1 Consanguinity and Affinity in Canonical Collections of the Church Reform Movement and in Gratian

Canon	Burchard, *Decretum*	Hinschius, DPI	Anselm of Lucca	Ivo, *Decr.*	Ivo, *Panor.*	Gratian
Aequaliter				4.41		C. 35 q. 2 c. 13
Beatus vir Isidorus	7.10			9.46	7.76	C. 35 q. 4 c. 1, C. 35 q. 5 c. 1
Coniunctiones	7.1	140	11.77	9.22		C. 3 q. 4 c. 4
Cum noverca		738–39		9.28		
De eo quod	17.24			9.82	7.66	C. 30 q. 1 c. 5
De his qui	7.3	347		9.329		C. 35 q. 2 c. 9
De incestis coniunctionibus	7.4	336		9.25, 9.40		C. 35 q. 2 c. 8
Dictum etiam	17.23			9.81	7.65	C. 30 q. 1 c. 4
Hi qui incesta	7.3	347		9.29		C. 35 q. 2 c. 9
Illud etiam	17.46			9.97		C. 30 q. 3 c. 7
In copulatione	7.2			9.39		C. 35 q. 2 c. 18
Incestuosi dum	7.5			9.41		C. 35 q. 8 c. 3
Inter eas				9.1		
Interrogatum est si pater	17.21			9.79		
Interrogatum est si quis	17.20			9.78		
Isidorus	7.9			9.45		
Ita diligere				9.34	6.123	C. 30 q. 3 c. 1
Item judi-catum	17.15			9.75		
Mulier si	17.1	263		9.67		
Nam et haec	7.6	353		9.42		C. 31 q. 1 c. 2
Nec concu-binae				8.10	6.45	C. 31 q. 1 c. 2, C. 32 q. 2 c. 5
Nulli ex	7.13			9.48	7.78	C. 35 q. 2 c. 19
Nullum in	7.14			9.49	7.80	C. 35 q. 2 c. 7
Nullus de				9.15		
Nullus fide-lium	7.12			9.47		
Nullus pro-prium	17.25			9.83		
Progeniem	7.11	751		9.26	7.77	C. 35 1 & 2 c. 16
Quam detes-tabile	17.26			9.84		

Table 5.1 *(continued)*

Canon	Burchard, *Decretum*	Hinschius, DPI	Anselm of Lucca	Ivo, *Decr.*	Ivo, *Panor.*	Gratian
Que spiritu-alem habet	17.45			9.96	7.67	C. 30 q. 4 c. 4
Qui consan-guinitatis				9.12		
Qui dormierit	17.3			9.69		C. 27 q. 2 c. 30
Quid est				9.18		C. 35 q. 7 c. 1
Quidam de-sponsavit	17.49			9.100		C. 27 q. 2 c. 31
Quidam for-nicatus est	17.16			9.76		C. 34 q. 1 c. 10
Quidam sponsam		263		9.24		
Scripsisti				9.37		
Si cum ea				9.2		
Si frater cum	17.14			9.74		
Si homo	7.13			9.73		C. 35 q. 2 c. 6
Si qua mulier	17.2	432		9.68		
Si quis com-matrem		754				
Si quis cum duabus				9.31		C. 33 q. 2 c. 16
Si quis cum matre	17.12			9.72		C. 34 q. 1 c. 9
Si quis cum muliere				8.36		
Si quis filias-trum	17.22			9.80	6.125	C. 30 q. 1 c. 2
Si quis forni-catus	17.8			9.70		
Si quis fratris		754				
Si quis ne-farium				9.3		
Si quis no-vercam		754				
Si quis viduam	17.9	9.77		9.71		C. 32 q. 7 c. 20
Terribile	17.47			9.98		
Ut definitum				9.11		
Ut omnibus	7.17					

Table 5.2 Sexual Abstinence in the Canonists

Period and Canon	Hinschius, DPI	Burchard, *Decretum*	Ivo, *Decretum*	Ivo, *Panormia*	Gratian
Advent:					
In tribus quadragesimis		19.155	15.163		
Lent:					
Abstinendum est		13.4	4.47		
Coinquinatus es cum		19.5			
In tribus quadragesimis		19.155	15.163		
Qui in quadragesima		19.75	15.88		
Rogation days:					
Fornicari omnibus			8.89		C. 33 q. 4 c. 5
Si causa procreandorum			8.84	6.21	C. 33 q. 4 c. 4
During penance:					
In primis ut		6.1			
Parricidium		6.35			
Pentecost:					
In tribus quadragesimis		19.155	15.163		
Feast Days:					
Si causa procreandorum			8.84	6.21	C. 33 q. 4 c. 4
Before communion:					
In perceptione corporis			2.24		
Omnis homo ante		5.22	2.32	1.51	D. 2 de cons. c.21
Sciatis fratres			8.87		C. 33 q. 4 c. 1
Sundays:					
Concubuisti cum uxore		19.5			
Consuetis praeterea			8.83		
Wednesdays:					
In tribus quadragesimis		19.155	15.163		
Fridays:					
In tribus quadragesimis		19.155	15.163		
Menstruation:					
Ad enixae mulieris			8.88		D. 5 c. 4
Iunxisti te uxori		19.5			
Observet unusquisque	64		19.119		
Pregnancy:					
Concubuisti cum uxore		19.5			
In tribus quadragesimis		19.155	15.163		
Post Partum:					
In tribus quadragesimis		19.155	15.163		
Lactation:					
Ad enixas mulieris			8.88		D. 5 c. 4
Wedding Night:					
Sponsus et sponsa	87–88	9.5	8.6, 8.143	6.20	D. 23 c. 33, C. 30 q. 5 c. 5
Ut sponsus et sponsa		9.7	8.145		

Table 8.1 Marriage Decretals of Alexander III in the *Liber Extra*

Number and Title	Total Number	Number by Alex. III	Percent
1 De sponsalibus et matrimonio	22	13	59.0
2 De desponsatione impuberum	14	6	42.6
3 De clandestina desponsatione	3	1	33.3
4 De sponsa duorum	5	2	40.0
5 De conditionibus appositis in desponsatione	7	2	28.6
6 Qui clerici vel voventes matrimonium contrahere possunt	7	5	71.4
7 De eo qui duxit in matrimonium quam polluit per adulterium	8	3	37.5
8 De coniugio leprosorum	3	2	66.7
9 De coniugio servorum	4	1	25.0
10 De natis ex libero ventre	1	0	00.0
11 De cognatione spirituali	8	3	37.5
12 De cognatione legali	1	0	00.0
13 De eo qui cognovit consanguineam uxoris suae vel sponsae	11	2	18.2
14 De consanguinitate et affinitate	9	1	11.1
15 De frigidis et maleficiatis et impotentia coeundi	7	2	28.8
16 De matrimonio contracto contra interdictum ecclesiae	3	3	100.0
17 Qui filii sint legitimi	15	9	60.0
18 Qui matrimonium accusare possunt	6	1	16.1
19 De divortiis	9	35	33.3
20 De donationibus inter virum et uxorem et de dote post divortium restituenda	8	0	00.0
21 De secundis nuptils	5	1	20.0
Total	156	60	38.5

Appendix 2
Marriage Law and the Economic Interests of the Medieval Church

Jack Goody's thesis that the medieval Church's control over marriage enhanced its economic power is only partly consistent with the evidence.[1] The Church's policy of promoting exogamy and discouraging endogamy through the rules concerning consanguinity had the effect of breaking up closely held concentrations of real property; this was a major reason why the law on consanguineous marriage generated resistance among the propertied classes. The extension of these principles to affinal relationships may have been motivated by a similar desire among the Church's leaders to achieve a wider distribution of power and property by preventing marriages between families linked to one another by godparenthood, as well as by social, political, and economic interests.[2]

The almost total disappearance in medieval Europe of adoption as a strategy for supplying childless couples with a means to assure their family's existence and to preserve the continuity of their property holdings seems to support Goody's argument.[3] His supposition that ecclesiastical opposition to concubinage, either among the clergy or the laity was consistent and effective, however, finds little foundation in the evidence. There was no formal prohibition of lay concubinage until the sixteenth century and, although the canons certainly discouraged the practice, they did not flatly forbid it.[4] Further, the disadvantages visited upon illegitimate children, with respect to both inheritance and other matters, originated primarily in secular, rather than ecclesiastical, law. If concubinage was, as Goody argues, inimical to the economic interests of the Church, then the Church was not particularly successful in defending this aspect of its property interests.[5]

The Church's defense of its economic interests did not, in fact, always reach

[1] Goody, *Development of the Family*, pp. 154–56.
[2] Ibid. pp. 134–46.
[3] Ibid. pp. 68–84.
[4] 5 Lateran Council (1514), Constitution *Supernae dispositionis*, in COD, p. 599; see above pp. 514–17, as against Goody, *Development of the Family*, pp. 75–81.
[5] Goody, *Development of the Family*, pp. 75–81, 134; but see above, pp. 543–44, as well as Brundage, "Concubinage and Marriage," pp. 1–17.

a high level of effectiveness. The strenuous efforts that the eleventh-century reformers had to make in order to recover property that the Church had lost to lay owners testified eloquently to this. Goody's conclusion that ecclesiastical marriage policies resulted in substantial numbers of families in any given generation being left without legitimate male heirs may be correct, but the figure of forty percent that he proposes as an estimate of the proportional frequency of this result is difficult to test.[6]

[6]Goody, *Development of the Family*, pp. 44, 214–16, 220–21; cf. the similar criticisms made by Herlihy in *Medieval Households*, p. 13.

Appendix 3

Survivals of Medieval Sex Law in the United States and the Western World

Both Puritan and Catholic divines have often maintained that government has an obligation to enforce Christian religious prescriptions about sexual morality. This belief has been especially influential in the United States, where a long-standing Puritan tradition has coexisted since the mid-nineteenth century with a sizable Catholic population, many of whose leaders bear the imprint of Jansenist rigorism. As a result, United States legislators have been more zealous than most in attempting to bring a broad spectrum of sexual behavior under legal control.

Perhaps the most striking example of the American penchant for public regulation of private sexual behavior occurs in criminal statutes dealing with fornication and adultery. Voluntary noncommercial sex between consenting adults who are not married to each other constituted a criminal offense as of 1984 in seventeen states, the Commonwealth of Puerto Rico, and the District of Columbia. Most of the remaining States formerly considered adultery and fornication crimes, but decriminalized them during the previous two decades.[1] Neither adultery nor fornication was a crime at common law, although both were violations of ecclesiastical law.[2] In England, adultery (but not fornication) be-

[1] Alabama, Code (1975) § 13.8.1; Arizona, Rev. Stat. Ann. § 13.1408–9; Connecticut, Gen. Stat. Ann. 53a–81; District of Columbia Code Ann. (1981) § 22.301; Florida, Stat. Ann. § 798.01, 798.03; Georgia, Code Ann. § 16–6–18, 19; Idaho, Code § 18–6601–4; Illinois, Smith-Hurd Ann. Stat., Ch. 38, § 11–7, 8; Kansas, Stat. Ann. 21–3507; Maryland, Ann. Code §§ 1, 4; Massachusetts, Ann. Laws, G.L., ch. 272 §§ 14, 16, 18; Minnesota, Stat. Ann. § 609.34, 36; Nebraska, Rev. Stat. 1943 (1977 reissue) § 28–704; New Hampshire, Rev. Stat. Ann. § 645.1, 3; New York, McKinney's Cons. Laws Ann., Penal § 255.17; North Dakota, Cent. Code 12.1–20–09; Puerto Rico, Laws Ann. 33 § 4147; South Carolina, Code Ann. § 16–15–60; Utah, Code Ann. § 76–7–103–4; West Virginia, Code § 61.8.3. California's criminal statute against adultery (Penal Code § 269a, b) was repealed by Statutes 1975 c. 1 §§ 5–6, while Wisconsin repealed its criminal penalties for fornication (Stat. 944.15–16, 20) in 1983 (Act no. 17, published 5/11/83), but defeated measures in a related bill to repeal penalties for adultery and concubinage. Wisconsin also rejected a 1983 effort to exclude consensual sex acts between married persons from the criminal sanctions for sexual perversion (S.B. 113).

[2] State v. Lash, 1 Harrison 380 (N.J. 1838) at 386; Commonwealth v. Call, 38 Mass.

came a felony, punishable by death, under the Puritan Commonwealth in 1650. Adultery had been made a crime even earlier in the Massachusetts Bay Colony, where it was punished by a severe whipping. In 1631, Massachusetts went further and authorized the death penalty for adultery, although the extreme sentence seems not to have been imposed with any regularity. In colonial Massachusetts and Connecticut sexual relations between a betrothed woman and any man other than her fiancé also counted as adultery and made her subject to the death penalty.[3] Such extreme measures against sexual offenders gradually gave way to milder ones, but adultery and fornication remained criminal offenses almost everywhere in the United States until the 1960s.

In practice the courts dealt with charges under these statutes rather gingerly. Although adultery and fornication are usually considered "crimes of darkness and secrecy,"[4] U.S. courts have often held that these offenses must be open, notorious, and habitual in order to be subject to statutory criminal penalties—a construction of the statutes that makes successful prosecution unlikely in most cases.[5] American adultery and fornication statutes originally sought, beyond much doubt, to use the criminal law in order to enforce, or at least to enunciate, Christian moral standards. A South Carolina prosecutor in the early nineteenth century, for example, argued that even though his state had no statute prohibiting adultery, extramarital sex involving a married person nonetheless must have been a crime at common law because it offended Christian morals. The indictment that he based upon this premise expressed common sentiment in strikingly grandiose terms when it charged that the defendants

> being persons of ill-fame and reputation and of wicked, corrupt, and depraved dispositions, and wholly lost to all sense of morality, decency, and religion, and intending, as much as in them lay, to corrupt and vitiate the morals of the good citizens of this State, and to bring into disgrace and disrepute the honorable estate of matrimony, with force and arms . . . did and still do live in open lewdness,

---

(21 Pick.) 509 (1839); Commonwealth v. Elwell, 2 Metcalf 190 (1840); Pollard v. Lyon, 91 U.S. 225 (1875). Although fornication is not an offense at common law and is not expressly prohibited by statute, Darling J. declared nonetheless in Pearce v. Brooks [1911] 1 K.B. 511, that "Fornication is therefore illegal in the sense that it is contrary to the law as recognized in various statutes, and it is immoral," in support of which he cited the Statute of 13 Edw. I c. 4.2 (1284/85) and the Ecclesiastical Suits Act of 1784 (27 Geo. III c. 44), among others. See also John L. Dwyer, "Immoral Contracts," *Law Quarterly Review* 93 (1977) 388.

[3] Ohlson, "Adultery" pp. 350, 353–57, 361–62.

[4] Bodfield v. State, 5 So. 559 at 560 (Ala., 1889).

[5] State v. Bess, 20 Mo. 419 (1855); State v. Marvin, 12 Iowa 499 (1861); Carotti v. State, 42 Miss. 344 (1868); Bodfield v. State, 5 So. 559 (Ala., 1889); People v. Bright, 238 P. 71 at 73 (Colo., 1925); People v. Potter, 319 Ill. App. 409, 49 N.E.2d 307 (1943); City of Chicago v. Murray, 333 Ill. App. 233, 77 N.E.2d 452 (1947); People v. Cessna, 42 Ill. App.3d 746, 356 N.E.2d 621 (1976); but see also State v. Byrum, 60 Neb. 384 (1900); State v. Brooks, 254 N.W. 374 at 375 (Wis., 1934); Ohlson, "Adultery," pp. 576–77.

whoredom and adultery, to the great displeasure of Almighty God, the evil example of all others in like cases offending, to the great corruption of the morals and manners of the citizens of this State, and against the peace and dignity of the same State aforesaid.[6]

But this heady rhetoric failed to convince the Supreme Court of South Carolina. The court found that the offenses charged belonged under the jurisdiction of the spiritual forum and accordingly granted the defendants the arrest of judgment that they sought. In the second half of this century, however, Justice Goldberg, concurring in the majority opinion of the U.S. Supreme Court in *Griswold v. Connecticut* (1965), maintained that the constitutionality of state statutes prohibiting adultery and fornication was "beyond doubt" and his opinion has recently been supported by Justice White, writing for the majority of the court in *Bowers v. Hardwick* (1986).[7] The New Jersey Supreme Court had previously questioned the constitutionality of such statutes and a Federal district court in Texas had held that the right of privacy shields consenting adults from prosecution for voluntary noncommercial sexual relations.[8] American law on these matters still remains in flux; the recent contention of the Attorney General of the State of Georgia that no one has a right to engage in sexual intercourse outside of marriage, goes against a substantial body of contrary decisions and is not likely to be the final word on the matter.[9]

In actual practice, few complaints were filed under the old adultery and fornication statutes and even fewer resulted in convictions—the statutes were simply not enforced, which raised the question of what function they were thought to serve. Apparently the answer is that they were intended to articulate the moral standards that the community hoped its members would observe, but that prosecution of those who failed to meet those standards was

[6]State v. Brunson and Miller, 17 S.C.L. (1 Bail.) 149 (1831).

[7]Griswold v. Connecticut, 381 U.S. 479 (1965); Bowers v. Hardwick, Slip Op., as well as *New York Times*, 1 July 1986, p. 10. See also Robert A. Brazener, "Validity of Statute Making Adultery and Fornication Criminal Offenses," 41 A.L.R.3d 1338–42.

[8]State v. Saunder, 75 N.J. 200 at 203, 381 A.2d 333 at 339–40 (1977); Baker v. Wade, 553 F. Supp. 1121 (1982).

[9]Bowers v. Hardwick (No. 85–140), argued on 31 March 1986, decided on 30 June 1986, slip op.; also *New York Times*, 1 April 1986, p. 19, and 1 July 1986 pp. 1, 10–11. The defendant, Michael Hardwick, was arrested for committing sodomy with another man in the privacy of his own bedroom. The police had entered his dwelling in order to arrest Hardwick for failure to pay a fine for drinking in public. The U.S. Court of Appeals held that the State of Georgia failed to show a compelling interest in restricting the right of privacy as it applied to sexual relations between consenting adults. The Supreme Court, however, ruled that the right of privacy does not extend to homosexual sodomy. Chief Justice Burger in a concurring decision pointedly noted that legislation prohibiting homosexual acts sprang from Judeo-Christian religious beliefs about morality, which in his view the states have every right to enforce by law. Justice Blackmun, however, in a strongly argued dissenting opinion, rejected the Chief Justice's reasoning, asserting that "A state can no more punish private behavior because of religious intolerance than it can punish such behavior because of racial animus."

thought unseemly and indecorous. As Slovenko put it, these laws "are unenforced because we want to continue our conduct, and unrepealed because we want to preserve our morals."[10] The recent rash of repeals of statutes that imposed criminal penalties on adulterers and fornicators—and repeals of such measures are not limited to the United States, although they are particularly common here—presumably indicates some change in the level of anxiety about moral standards, as well perhaps as a feeling that the enforcement of sexual morality through the criminal process may be inappropriate as well as ineffective.[11]

The medieval Church's marriage law clearly lies at the base of common law doctrine that forcible sexual intercourse between man and wife is no crime and that marriage therefore furnishes an affirmative defense to criminal prosecutions for rape. This doctrine continues to be current law in thirty-eight states, Puerto Rico, the Virgin Islands, and the District of Columbia, as well as in the United Kingdom. The spousal exception in rape cases remains a clear example of the pervasive influence that medieval canon law continues to exert on Western attitudes toward sex and marriage. Even though all of the jurisdictions that recognize the spousal exception provide by statute for divorce and acknowledge the right of parties to dissolve their marriages under some circumstances, it is still current law that marital consent conveys a comprehensive right to sexual relations at the will of either party—a notion founded on the medieval exegesis of 1 Cor. 7:4–5 and the doctrine of marital debt.[12]

---

[10] Ralph Slovenko, "Sex Mores and the Enforcement of the Law of Sex Crimes: A Study of the Status Quo," *Kansas Law Review* 15 (1967) 271; Larry E. Joplin, "An Examination of the Oklahoma Laws Concerning Sexual Behavior," *Oklahoma Law Review* 23 (1970) 462, 470.

[11] The Greek Parliament, for example, recently abolished the practice of public shaming for adulterers and removed adultery from the offenses in the penal code; the Code previously provided not only a one-year prison term for those convicted of adultery, but also prohibited marriages between convicted adulterers, which likewise reflected the canonical tradition; *Times* (London), 27 July 1982, p. 7. The contention that criminal law is an inappropriate means to enforce beliefs about sexual morality is, of course, by no means a twentieth-century innovation; see for example Bernard Mandeville (1670–1733), *A Modest Defence of Public Stews: Or, an Essay upon Whoring as it is now Practic'd in These Kingdoms . . . Written by a Layman* (London: Printed by A. Moore near St. Paul's, 1724; repr. Los Angeles: William Andrews Clark Memorial Library, 1973), p. 70.

[12] The spousal exclusion is currently recognized by explicit statutory provision in Alabama, Code § 13A-6-60(4); Alaska, Stat. § 11.41.445(a); Arizona, Rev. Stat. Ann. § 13–1401(4); Colorado, Rev. Stat. § 18–3–409(1); Connecticut, Gen. Stat. Ann. § 53a–65(2); District of Columbia, Code Ann. § 22–2801; Georgia, Code Ann. § 26–1001, 10018; Hawaii, Rev. Stat. § 707–700(9), (11); Idaho, Code § 18–6107; Illinois, Smith-Hurd Ann. Stat., ch. 38 § 11–1; Indiana, Code Ann. § 35–42–4–1(b); Kansas, Stat. Ann § 1–3502, 3503, 3505; Kentucky, Rev. Stat. Ann. § 510.010(1), (8); Louisiana, Rev. Stat. Ann. § 14:41; Maine, Rev. Stat. Ann, tit. 17A, Ch. 11, Supp. 1979, note at 99; Maryland, Ann. Code, Art. 27 § 464D; Massachusetts, Ann. Laws, G.L., Ch. 265 § 23; Michigan, Comp. Laws Ann. § 750.5201; Missouri, Rev. Stat. § 566.010(2); Montana, Rev.

A similar example of the unacknowledged incorporation of medieval canon law into modern statutes occurs in jurisdictions that prohibit "sodomy" and refer to the offense not only by that biblical title, but also call it a "crime against nature" or "unnatural act"—terms that remain common in current law, both in the United States and Great Britain. At least twelve American states use the medieval terminology—usually in the form hallowed by Sir Edward Coke (1552–1634)—while twenty-two other States impose criminal penalties specifically upon those who participate in oral or anal sex acts, whether homosexual or heterosexual.[13] Persistence of the concept that these activities should be penalized because they are "contrary to nature" is by no means confined to legislators. Both state and federal courts in the United States continue to employ suppositions about proper sexual conduct that would have been perfectly recognizable to any thirteenth-century theologian.[14] A recent California case,

---

Code Ann. § 45–5–502(1), 503(1); Nevada, Rev. Stat. § 200.373; New Hampshire, Rev. Stat. s. 632A:5; New Mexico, Stat. Ann. § 30–9–11; New York, McKinney's Cons. Laws Ann., Penal Law § 130.10(4); North Carolina, Gen. Stat. § 4–27.8; North Dakota, Cent. Code § 12.1–20–01(2); Ohio, Rev. Code Ann. § 2907.02A, .03A, .04A, .05A, .06A, .12A; Oklahoma, Stat. Ann., tit. 21 § 1111; Pennsylvania, Stat. Ann., tit. 18 §§ 3121, 3122, 3123; Puerto Rico, Laws Ann., tit. 33 § 4061; Rhode Island, Gen. Laws § 11–37–2; South Carolina, Code § 16–3–652, 653; South Dakota, Comp. Laws Ann § 22–22–7; Tennessee, Code Ann. §§ 39–3701 to 3710; Texas, Vernon's Codes Ann., Penal Code, tit. 5 § 21.12; Utah, Code Ann. §§ 76–5–401, 407; Vermont, Stat. Ann., tit. 13 § 3252; Virgin Islands, Code Ann., tit. 14 §§ 1701, 1702, 1703; Washington, Rev. Code § 9.A.44.40, 50, 60; West Virginia, Code § 61–8B1(2); Wyoming, Stat. § 6–4–307; and see generally Leigh Bienen, "Rape IV," *Women's Rights Law Reporter* 6 Supp. (1980) 1–61. For the spousal exclusion in England see generally *Halsbury's Laws of England*, 4th ed. by Lord Hailsham (London: Butterworth, 1973– ; in progress) 11:652–53 § 1227, and *Sexual Offenses: A Report of the Cambridge Department of Criminal Science* (London: Macmillan, 1957), pp. 324–25. While the law of the United Kingdom does not reckon forcible intercourse by a man with his wife to be rape, it may be punishable as assault; for other restrictions on the exclusion see also Rex v. Clarke [1949] 2 All E.R. 448, 33 Cr. App. 216, and Regina v. Miller [1954] 2 Q.B. 282, 2 W.L.R. 138. In the United States it has been held that the spousal exclusion applies even to couples joined in informal, common law marriages; People v. Pizzura, 178 N.W. 235 (Mich., 1920).

[13] Coke, *Third Institute*, c. 10, 4th ed. (London: Printed for A. Crooke, W. Leake, A. Roper, et al., 1669), p. 58, drawing in part on the Statute of 25 Hen. VIII, c. 26, in *Statutes of the Realm* 3:441. U.S. Statutes that refer to oral or anal sexual practices as "unnatural," or "the crime against nature," include Ala., Code § 13.1.110; Ariz., Rev. Stat. Ann. § 13.1411, 1412; La., Rev. Stat. Ann. § 14:89; Idaho, Code § 18–6605; Mass., Ann. Laws, G.L., Ch. 272 § 34, 35; Miss., Code § 97–29–59; Nevada, Rev. Stat. 201.190; N.C., Gen. Stat. § 14–177; Okla., Stat. Ann., tit. 21 § 886, 887; R. I., Gen. Laws, § 11–5–1; Tenn., Code Ann. § 39–3714; Va., Code § 18.2–361. A similar provision in the Texas Penal Code § 21.06 was struck down as unconstitutional in Baker v. Wade, 553 F. Supp. 1121 (1982).

[14] See for example Balthazar v. Superior Court of Massachusetts, 428 F. Supp. 425 at 433, 434 (1977); Commonwealth v. Gallant, 369 N.E.2d 707 at 712 (Mass., 1977);

People v. Baldwin (1974), furnished a conspicuous example. In *Baldwin* the Court of Appeals rejected the defendant's argument that the sodomy statute enacted Judeo-Christian religious taboos into public law and hence that it breached the constitutional separation of Church and State. In denying the defendant's claim, the court asserted that the statute reflected a general public consensus about homosexual behavior. While the justices conceded that this consensus had religious foundations, they held that the statute did not enact religious doctrine.[15]

The court's reasoning was less than compelling and its distinction between religious doctrine and community consensus was certainly no model of clarity. The ruling may have satisfied the majority of the court, but it did not deal squarely with Baldwin's contention that the California Penal Code, as it then stood, incorporated Christian religious beliefs and that those, in turn, rested on assumptions about the character of human sexuality that were, to say the least, debatable. Since the Baldwin ruling, the California legislature has altered its statutes to meet many of the points that Baldwin raised, for legislation has now eliminated references to the "crime against nature" and decriminalized private oral and anal sex acts between consenting adults.[16] Other states have similarly modified their treatment of oral and anal sex in recent years. In several jurisdictions the courts have ruled that sodomy statutes may not apply to sexual relations between husband and wife, although some earlier decisions had held the opposite.[17] The recent rulings mark a clear break with medieval ecclesiastical notions about permissible marital sex practices—views that Catholic authorities continue to reiterate, although in practice many Catholics have rejected them, as have liberal Protestants, Jews, and most non-Christians.[18]

Williams v. State, 316 So.2d 362 (Ala., 1975); Wainwright v. Stone, 414 U.S. 21, 94 S.Ct. 190, 38 L.Ed.2d 179 (1976); State v. Larsen, 81 Idaho 90, 337 P.2d 1, cert. den. 361 U.S. 882, 80 S.Ct. 154, 4 L.Ed.2d 119 (1959); People v. Smith, 256 P.2d 586 at 587 (1953); People v. Babb, 229 P.2d 843 at 846 (1951); State v. Attwater, 29 Idaho 107, 157 P. 256 (1916).

[15] People v. Baldwin, 37 Cal. App.3d 388, 112 Cal. Rptr. 290 at 291–92.

[16] Ann. Cal. Codes, Penal Code § 286, amended 1975, 1976, 1977, 1978, 1980, 1981.

[17] Mentek v. State, 71 Wis.2d 799, 238 N.W.2d 752 (1976); State v. Pilcher, 242 N.W.2d 348 at 358 (Ia., 1976); Jones v. State, 55 Wis.2d 742, 200 N.W.2d (1972) 587; and Poe v. Ullman, 367 U.S. 497, 81 S.Ct. 1752, 6 L.Ed.2d 989 (1961). But see State v. Schmit, 273 Minn. 78, 139 N.W.2d. 800 (1965); Cole v. State, 175 P.2d 376 (Okla., 1946); State v. Nelson, 199 Minn. 86 at 94, 271 N.W. 114 at 118 (1937).

[18] S. Congreg. for the Doctrine of the Faith, *Declaration on . . . Sexual Ethics*, §§ 8, 11 (Hales Corners, Wis.: Priests of the Sacred Heart, 1976); repr. from *L'Osservatore Romano*, English ed., 408 (22 Jan. 1976), 5, 11–12, and AAS 68 (1976) 77–96. For other views see Michael F. Valente, *Sex: The Radical View of a Catholic Theologian* (New York: Bruce Publishing Co., 1970); Pohier, *Chrétien, plaisir, sexualité*; Albert Donval, *Un avenir pour l'amour: une nouvelle éthique de sexualité dans le changement aujourd'hui* (Paris: Le Centurion, 1976), pp. 39–42, 75–85; Marcel Eck, *Sodome: essai sur l'homosexualité* (Paris: Fayard, 1966), esp. pp. 260–300. For some modern Protestant views see

Other types of legislation on sexual matters, both in the United States and elsewhere, continue to rely upon modified versions of medieval Christian views about sexual propriety. In some respects American statutes often seem more rigid and uncompromising than the policies enunciated in medieval law. The contrast is particularly marked in statutes dealing with prostitution, brothels, pandering, and other aspects of commercial sex. Where medieval authorities typically regarded prostitution as an evil to be tolerated in order to avoid still graver social problems, current statutes in all American states, with the exception of Nevada, ban prostitution, penalize pimps, panderers, and brothel-keepers, and sometimes prescribe penalties for the clients of prostitutes, as well as for the prostitutes themselves.[19] These statutes are notoriously ineffec-

---

Fuchs, *Sexual Desire and Love*, pp. 172–209; W. Norman Pittenger, *Making Sexuality Human* (Philadelphia: Pilgrim Press, 1970), pp. 29–58, 69–96.

[19] The canonical dictum that equates promiscuity with prostitution, whether the prostitute charges a fee or not, apparently is still treated as law in some parts of the U.S.; see People v. Brandt, 306 P.2d 1069 at 1072 (Cal., 1956); Bayrouth v. State, 294 P.2d 856 (Okla., 1956); Salt Lake City v. Allred, 430 P.2d 371 (Utah, 1967). Current statutes banning prostitution include: Ala., Code § 13.7.1–2; Alaska, Stat. § 11.66.100, 110–130, 150; Ariz., Rev. Stat. Ann. § 13.3201 to 3212; Ark., Stat. § 41–3001 to 3006, 3051; Cal., Codes Ann., Penal Code §§ 266, 309; Colo., Rev. Stat. 18–7–101 to 208; Conn., Gen. Stat. Ann. § 53a–82 to 89; Del., Code Ann., tit. 11 §§ 1342–1344, 1355–1356; District of Columbia, Code Ann. § 22–2701, 2704, 2705, 2707, 2708, 2712, 2722; Fla., Stat. Ann. §§ 796.01, .03–.07; Ga., Code Ann. §§ 16–6–9 to 12, 16–6–16; Hawaii, Rev. Stat. §§ 712–1200 to 1202; Idaho, Code §§ 18–5602, 5606, 5608 to 5610, 5612 to 5614; Ill., Smith-Hurd Ann. Stat., Ch. 38, §§ 11–14 to 19; Ind., Code Ann. §§ 35–45–2 to 4; Iowa, Code Ann. §§ 725.1–3; Kans., Stat. Ann. §§ 21–3512 to 3515; Ky., Rev. Stat. Ann. §§ 529.20 to .070; La., Rev. Stat. Ann § 14:82 to 86; Me., Rev. Stat. Ann., tit. 17, §§ 851 to 853B, 855; Md., Ann. Code, art. 27 §§ 15 to 17; Mass., Ann. Laws, G.L., Ch. 272 §§ 2, 6, 7, 24, 53; Mich., Comp. Laws Ann. §§ 750.448 to 449a; Minn., Stat. Ann. §§ 609.321, 323, 324; Miss., Code Ann. §§ 97–29–49 to 53; Mo., Stat. Ann. § 567; Mont., Rev. Code Ann. §§ 45–5–601 to 603; Nebr., Rev. Stat. §§ 28–801 to 804; N.H., Rev. Stat. Ann. § 645:2; N.J., Stat. Ann. § 2C:34–1; N.M., Stat. Ann. §§ 30–9–2 to 4; N.Y., McKinney's Cons. Laws Ann., Penal Law §§ 230.00 to .03, .15, .20, .25, .30, .32, .40; N.C., Gen. Stat. §§ 14.203–14, 204 to 208; N.D., Cent. Code §§ 12.1–29–01 to 03; Ohio, Rev. Code Ann. § 2907.21 to .25; Okla., Stat. Ann., tit. 21 §§ 1025, 1028, 1029; Or., Rev. Stat. § 167.002, .007, .012, .017; Pa., Stat. Ann., tit. 18 § 5902; Puerto Rico, Laws Ann., tit. 33 §§ 4070 to 4072; R.I., Gen. Laws §§ 11–34–1 to 5; S.C., Code §§ 16–15–90 to 110; S.D., Comp. Laws Ann. § 22–23–1 to 8; Tenn., Code Ann. §§ 39–3504, 3505; Tex., Vernon's Codes Ann., Penal Code § 43.02 to .05; Utah, Code Ann. § 76–10–1302 to 1306; Vt., Stat. Ann., tit. 13 § 2632; Virgin Islands, Code Ann., tit. 14 §§ 1622 to 1625; Va., Code Ann. §§ 18.2–346 to 349, 355 to 358; Wash., Rev. Code Ann. §§ 9A.88.0.0 to .090; W. Va., Code Ann. §§ 61–8–5 to 8; Wis., Stat. Ann. §§ 944.30 to 34; Wyo., Stat. Ann. §§ 6–5–103 to 105, 109, 110. In Nevada, where prostitution is no crime, the statutes restrict many details of its practice; thus Rev. Stat. § 201.380 forbids operating a brothel within 400 yards of a school or church and § 201.390 prescribes that property located on principal streets or those zoned for business must

tive, however, and in many jurisdictions are largely ignored, save during those occasional spasms of moral self–righteousness that seem to afflict Americans as intensely and unpredictably as they do Englishmen.[20]

The influence of Christian moral doctrine is even more obvious in modern marriage law, since the definition of the conjugal unit draws directly from Christian theology. An obvious example is the insistence throughout the Western world that marriage must be monogamous. Western prohibitions of polygamy are clearly religious and rooted firmly in medieval canon law. The history of the admission of Utah to the United States furnishes a striking example of the determination of modern Western governments not to compromise on this basic principle of family structure. In this struggle federal authorities successfully demanded that Utah's Mormons sacrifice their religious principles as a necessary condition of incorporation into the Union, and the courts upheld the constitutionality of the whole proceeding.[21]

The consensual marriage theory of the canonists has also impressed itself deeply into the matrimonial jurisprudence of many modern states. In England the pre-Tridentine canon law of marriage remained in effect until the passage in 1753 of Lord Hardwicke's Act. Since that date, consensual marriage—often referred to as "common law marriage," despite the fact that its historical roots lie in canon law—has not been recognized in England.[22] In the United States,

---

not be rented for purposes of prostitution. Moreover, pandering is a felony in Nevada, as is living from the earnings of a prostitute, Rev. Stat. §§ 201.300, 320. Enforcement of these statutes, however, appears to be even more haphazard than the enforcement of similar statutes in other jurisdictions. In France, where the practice of prostitution has in recent times been prosecuted under art. 334 of the *Code pénal* as "conduct tending to lead to debauchery" (*attitude de nature à provoquer la debauche*), prostitutes staged a nationwide strike in June, 1975, to protest what they characterized as harassment by the police. They also demanded freedom to carry on their occupation without penalty and asserted a right to be included under the national social security scheme, which would guarantee them health benefits and pensions. A public opinion poll conducted by the French Institute of Public Opinion in Lyon during the strike showed that the attitudes reflected in medieval legislation on prostitution are alive and well: 65 percent of those polled favored prostitution in publicly regulated brothels, while 93 percent believed that prostitution will always exist and that efforts to suppress it are futile; *Figaro* (Paris), 10 June 1975, p. 9.

[20] Lord Macauley, "Moore's Life of Lord Byron," in Macauley's *Complete Writings*, 20 vols. (Boston: Houghton-Mifflin, 1899–1900) 12:193: "We know of no spectacle so ridiculous as the British public in one of its periodic fits of morality."

[21] Reynolds v. U.S., 98 U.S. 145, 25 L.Ed. 244 (1878); Musser v. Utah, 333 U.S. 95, 68 S.Ct. 397, 92 L.Ed. 562 (1948); Sidney L. W. Mellen, *The Evolution of Love* (San Francisco: W. H. Freeman, 1981), p. 272; T. A. Lacey, *Marriage in Church and State*, rev. ed. by R. C. Mortiner (London: S.P.C.K., 1959), pp. 93–94; Lecky, *Hist. of European Morals* 2:351; Mitchell, *Law, Morality, and Religion*, pp. 25–30.

[22] Lord Hodson, "Common Law Marriage," *International and Comparative Law Quarterly* 7 (1958) 206; Christopher Lasch, "The Suppression of Clandestine Marriage

however, the simple exchange of marital consent, even if done in private—in short, clandestine marriage as the medieval canonists knew it—long remained a perfectly acceptable type of marital union and is still recognized in thirteen states. In 1884 the United States Supreme Court declared that

> Under our law a marriage depends solely upon the mutual consent of the contracting parties. They may enter into the marriage secretly, and the fact may be unknown to all save the man and the woman. . . . [A] marriage is valid without witnesses and no ceremony is necessary.[23]

Virtually the whole gamut of medieval theological and canonical opinion about marriage formation has been incorporated at some point or other in the civil jurisprudence of the United States. Several states that uphold (or upheld) the validity of common law marriages replaced the rule that consent, not coitus, makes a marriage (*consensus non concubitus facit matrimonium*) with the coital marriage theory that intercourse makes marriage (*concubitus facit matrimonium*). Still other states were at one time prepared to accept future consent followed by coitus as valid marriage for civil purposes, although apparently no state does so currently.[24] While nineteenth-century American judges revived medieval clandestine marriage, English judges rewrote the history of consensual marriage law. With a great show of learning the House of Lords in *Regina v. Millis* reached the historically indefensible conclusion that marriage by present consent of the parties alone had never existed in England and that the presence of an ordained clergyman had always been required for valid marriages in the English kingdom.[25]

Twentieth-century American courts continue to wrestle with other problems familiar to their twelfth- and thirteenth-century predecessors, such as the

---

in England: The Marriage Act of 1753," *Salmagundi* 26 (1974) 90–109; Koegel, *Common Law Marriage*, pp. 9, 32–36.

[23] Murphy v. Ramsey, 114 U.S. 15, 5 S.Ct. 747, 29 L.Ed. 47 (1884).

[24] Tartt v. Negus, 127 Ala. 201, 28 So. 713 at 715 (1900); Carey v. Hulett, 69 N.W. 31 (Minn., 1896); Franklin v. Franklin, 154 Mass. 515,28 N.E. 681 at 682 (1891); U.S. v. Simpson, 4 Utah 227 at 229, 7 P. 257 at 258 (1885); Dumarely v. Fishly, 10 Ky. (A. K. Marsh) 1198 at 1199 (1821); Londonderry v. Chester, 2 N.H. 268 at 278 (1820); Robert C. Casad, "Unmarried Couples and Unjust Enrichment: From Status to Contract and Back Again?" *Michigan Law Review* 77 (1978) 47; Michael Grossberg, "Guarding the Altar: Physiological Restriction and the Rise of State Intervention in Matrimony," *American Journal of Legal History* 26 (1982) 206, 212; Koegel, *Common Law Marriage*, pp. 9–10, 106–107.

[25] Regina v. Millis, 10 Clark and Finnelly 534 at 655, 720, 8 Eng. Rep. 844 at 889, 913 (1843); Beamish v. Beamish, 9 H.L.C. 274 at 336, 11 Eng. Rep. 735 at 760 (1861). In the United States, however, the New Hampshire Supreme Court declared in 1820 that the notion that marriage requires "the presence and aid of a priest" was a consequence of the belief that marriage was a sacrament, a notion that the court characterized as "one of the corruptions of popery"; Londonderry v. Chester, 2 N.H. 268 at 278 (1820).

problem of the equitable treatment of the financial interests of a concubine. The leading issues in *Marvin v. Marvin* (1976) were tolerably familiar to medieval commentators and the solution that the California Court of Appeals arrived at would scarcely have astounded them, although the amount of property at issue might well have done so.[26] Modern civil law jurisdictions have struggled with these same issues and in many cases, notably in Latin America, have borrowed heavily from medieval canon law in resolving them.[27] In France, even though the Civil Code ignored the existence of concubinage, twentieth-century legislators and judges have found it necessary to deal with the problem and, consciously or not, have followed lines of reasoning similar to those of the canonists in resolving the problems of concubines and their children.[28]

Divorce is yet another department of modern domestic-relations law where the influence of canon law remains visible, although during the past quarter-century the canonical element in divorce law has steadily diminished. Still, in many jurisdictions the grounds for divorce and even the processes, procedures, and administrative paraphernalia of divorce were closely linked until recently to medieval law.[29]

As these examples show, the medieval Church's doctrines concerning marriage and sex not only furnished the antecedents from which modern law grew, but continue to exert a powerful influence on both law and practice. The modern secular state is neither as modern nor as secular as it is often thought to be. Medieval Christian value systems remain pervasive and prominent in legal treatments of sexual matters, in and out of marriage.

---

[26] Marvin v. Marvin, 18 Cal.3d 660, 134 Cal. Rptr. 814, 557 P.2d 106 (1976). *Marvin* rejected the previously held doctrine in California (and elsewhere) that effectively invalidated property arrangements between parties whose relationship would be described as "meretricious" because they had a nonmarital sexual relationship with one another; see Hill v. Westbrook's Estate, 39 Cal.2d 458, 247 P.2d 19 (1952) and Trutalli v. Meraviglia, 215 Cal. 698, 12 P.2d 430 (1932); Casad, "Unmarried Couples," p. 48; Herma Hill Kay and Carol Amyx, "*Marvin v. Marvin*: Preserving the Options," *California Law Review* 65 (1977) 937–77.

[27] Edgard de Moura Bittencourt, *O concubinato no direito*, 2d ed., 4 vols. (Rio de Janeiro: Ed. Juridica e Universitaria, 1969), esp. 1:104–105, 109–13; Gustavo A. Bossert, *Concubinato: Doctrina, legislación, jurisprudencia* (Rosario, Argentina: Ediciones Juridicas Orbir, 1968); Eduardo A. Zannoni, *El concubinato en el derecho civil argintino y comparado latino-Americano* (Buenos Aires: De Palma, 1970).

[28] Baumann, *Zivilrechtliche Bedeutung*, p. 20; Colette Holstein-Brunswic, *Le droit et l'amour* (Paris: Flammarion, 1970), pp. 32, 58–59.

[29] The links are particularly obvious in England, where Probate, Divorce, and Admiralty are formally joined together as a division of the High Court in recognition of the common roots of these three branches of English law in the romano-canonical tradition, which remained a living part of the English legal system until the dispersion of Doctors' Commons under the terms of the Court of Probate Act of 1857; G. D. Squibb, *Doctors' Commons: A History of the College of Advocates and Doctors of Law* (Oxford: Clarendon Press, 1977), pp. 102–109.

List of Manuscripts Cited

Admont, Stiftsbibliothek
MS 7
Huguccio, *Summa.*
MS 22
Tancred, *Apparatus to 1 Comp.*
Johannes Teutonicus, *Apparatus to 3 Comp.*

Barcelona, Archivo de la Corona de Aragón
Cancillería, Procesos, ser. 2, legajo 2
Moncada c. Urgel.
Cancillería, Procesos, ser. 2, legajo 4
Rex c. Pons Hugo de Ampurias.
MS Ripoll 30
Petrus de Samsone, *Lectura to Liber Extra.*

Cambridge, Fitzwilliam Museum
MS McLean 137
Geoffrey of Trani, *Summa super titulos decretalium* with glosses.

Cambridge, Gonville and Caius College
MS 23/12
Notabilia Aliter debet.
MS 28/16
Tancred, *Apparatus to 1 Comp.*
Tancred, *Apparatus to 3 Comp.*
MS 44/150
Johannes Teutonicus, *Apparatus to 4 Comp.*
MS 54/31
Questiones de bigamis.
MS 283/676
Decretum Gratiani with Anglo-Norman glosses.

Cambridge, Pembroke College
MS 72
Huguccio, *Summa.*
MS 101
Argumentum quod religiosi.
MS 162
Decretum Gratiani with glosses.
MS 201
William of Pagula, *Summa summarum.*

Cambridge, Peterhouse
MS 42(2)
Joannes de Deo, *Summa de dispensationibus.*
MS 169(2)
Breviarium Decreti, "*Magister Gratianus uolens compilare.*"

Cambridge, Trinity College
MS B.1.6.
Biblical glosses (New Testament).
MS B.1.31
Biblical glosses (Old Testament).
MS O.5.17
Apparatus "*Ecce vicit leo.*"
MS O.10.2
Glossa Palatina.

Cambridge, University Library
Ely Diocesan Records D/2/1
Registrum causarum consistorii Eliensis.
MS Add. 3321(1)
Fragmentum Cantabrigiensis.
Distinctiones Cantabrigiensis.

MS Add. 3321(2)
  Questiones Stuttgardienses
MS Add. 3468
  The Black Book of Ely
MS Ee.5.4.(B)
  Liber Extra with glosses

Códoba, Biblioteca del Cabildo
MS 10
  Tancred, *Apparatus to 1 Comp.*

London, British Library
MS Add. 11,821
  Extracts from the Rochester Act
  Book.
MS Add. 18,367
  Sicard of Cremona, *Summa.*
MS Add. 18,369
  Joannes Faventinus, *Summa.*
MS Add. 24,659
  Simon of Bisignano,
  Summa.
MS Arundel 435
  Petrus de Salinis, *Lectura to the De-*
  cretum Gratiani.
  Bartholomew of Brescia, *Questiones*
  dominicales.
MS Royal 9.E.VII
  Joannes Faventinus, *Summa.*
MS Royal 10.A.III
  Simon of Bisignano, *Summa.*
MS Royal 10.C.III
  Ricardus Anglicus, *Distinctiones*
  decretorum.
MS Royal 11.B.XIII
  Tractatus "In primis hominibus."
MS Royal 11.D.II
  Summa "Prima primi."
MS Stowe 378
  Decretum Gratiani with glosses.

Paris, Bibliothèque Nationale
MS lat. 3892
  Huguccio, *Summa.*

MS lat. 3932
  Alanus, *Apparatus to 1 Comp.*
  Albertus, *Apparatus to 2 Comp.*
MS lat, 14,611
  Vincentius, *Apparatus to 3 Comp.*
MS nouv. acq. lat. 2508
  Decretum Gratiani with glosses.

Philadelphia, University of Pennsylvania
Libraries
MS Lea 376 (Ger)
  Concubinatum clericorum.

Salamanca, Biblioteca de la Universidad
Civil
MS 2168
  Vincentius Hispanus, *Lectura to the*
  Liber Extra.
MS 2491
  Apparatus "Ecce vicit leo."

Salzburg, Stiftsbibliothek St. Peter
MS a.xii.9
  Glossa Palatina.

Vatican City, Biblioteca Apostolica
Vaticana
MS Borgh. lat. 261
  Damasus, *Questiones.*
MS Borgh. lat. 370
  Decretum Gratiani with glosses.
MS lat. 1377
  Tancredus, *Apparatus to 3 Comp.*
MS lat. 2280
  Huguccio, *Summa.*

Washington, D.C., Library of Congress,
Law Library
MS D.41
  Liber Extra with glosses.
MS F.6
  Flores decretorum.
MS G.7
  Decretum Gratiani with glosses.

Select Secondary References

A comprehensive bibliography for this study would occupy a volume in itself and, in any event, the notes supply full bibliographical details for works cited in this book. This list is highly selective: it comprises less than one-tenth of the works that appear in my notes.

This list includes only those secondary works dealing with the law of sex and marriage that I have consulted repeatedly in preparing this study or that present particularly novel information or ideas. I have, however, omitted articles published in the specialized periodicals and reference works on legal history (such as BMCL, DDC, JEH, JMH, LQR, RDC, RHDF, SDHI, SG, TRG, and ZRG) that appear in the Abbreviations List.

Adami, Franco Edoardo. "Precizazioni in tema di consenso matrimoniale nel pensiero patristico." *Il diritto ecclesiastico* 76 (1965) 206–41.

Aldous, Joan, and Reuben Hill. *International Bibliography of Research in Marriage and the Family.* Minneapolis: University of Minnesota Press, 1967.

Alesandro, John A. *Gratian's Notion of Marital Consummation.* Rome: Officium Libri Catholici, 1971.

Alphandéry, Paul. *Les idées morales chez les hétérodoxes latins au début du XIIIe siècle.* Paris: Ernest Leroux, 1903.

Atkinson, Clarissa W. "Precious Balsam in a Fragile Glass: The Ideology of Virginity in the Later Middle Ages." *Journal of Family History* 8 (1983) 131–43.

Backeljauw, Joris. "De uxoris statu sociali in iure canonico medii aevi." *Divus Thomas* 89 (1968) 271–96.

Bailey, Derrick Sherwin. *Sexual Relation in Christian Thought.* New York: Harper Brothers, 1959.

Barstow, Anne Llewellyn. *Married Priests and the Reforming Papacy.* New York: Edwin Mellen, 1982.

Basset, William W., ed. *The Bond of Marriage: An Ecumenical and Interdisciplinary Study.* Notre Dame: University of Notre Dame Press, 1968.

Baumann, Alexis. *Die zivilrechtliche Bedeutung des Konkubinates in rechtsvergleichender Darstellung unter besonderer Berücksichtigung des schweizerischen, deutschen, österreichischen und französischen Privatrechtes.* Coburg: Gedruckt im Tageblatt-Haus, 1932.

Béraudy, Roger. "Le mariage des chrétiens: Etude historique." *Nouvelle revue théologique* 114 (1982) 50–69.

Berkner, Lutz K. "Recent Research on the History of the Family in Western Europe." *Journal of Marriage and the Family* 25 (1973) 395–405.

Berrouard, Marie-Françoise. "Saint Augustin et l'indissolubilité du mariage: Evolution de sa pensée." *Recherches Augustiniennes* 5 (1968) 139–55.

Biller, P. P. A. "Birth-Control in the West in the Thirteenth and Early Fourteenth Centuries." *Past and Present* 94 (1982) 3–26.

Bloch, Iwan. *Die Prostitution.* 2 vols. Berlin: Louis Markus, 1912–25.

Boelens, Martin. *Die Klerikerehe in der Gesetzgebung der Kirche unter besonderer Berücksichtigung der Strafe: Eine rechtsgeschichtliche Untersuchung von den Anfängen der Kirche bis zum Jahre 1139.* Paderborn: F. Schöningh, 1968.

Bonnet, Piero Antonio. "Amor coniugalis matrimoniumque in fieri prout Vetus et Novum Testamentum significant." *Periodica de re morali, canonica, liturgica* 65 (1976) 587–611.

Børresen, Kari Elisabeth. *Subordination and Equivalence: The Nature and Role of Women in Augustine and Thomas Aquinas.* Translated by Charles H. Talbot. Washington, D.C.: University Press of America, 1981.

Bowden, Betsy. "The Art of Courtly Copulation." *Medievalia et humanistica*, n.s. 9 (1979) 67–85.

Briffault, Robert. *Sin and Sex.* London: Allen & Unwin, 1931; repr. New York: Haskell House, 1973.

Broglie, G. de. "Le fondement de l'amour conjugal." *Doctor communis* 23 (1970) 192–216.

Brooke, Christopher N.L. "The Gregorian Reform in Action: Clerical Marriage in England, 1050–1200." *Cambridge Historical Journal* 12 (1956) 1–20.

———. *Marriage in Christian History: An Inaugural Lecture.* Cambridge: At the University Press, 1978.

———. "Married Men among the English Higher Clergy, 1066–1200." *Cambridge Historical Journal* 12 (1956) 187–88.

Broudéhoux, Jean-Paul. *Mariage et famille chez Clément d'Alexandrie.* Paris: Beauchesne, 1970.

Browe, Peter. *Beiträge zur Sexualethik des Mittelalters.* Breslau: Müller & Seiffert, 1932.

Brundage, James A. "'Allas! That Evere Love Was Synne': Sex and Medieval Canon Law." *Catholic Historical Review* 72 (1986) 1–13.

———. "Marriage Law in the Latin Kingdom of Jerusalem." In *Outremer—Studies in the History of the Crusading Kingdom of Jerusalem Presented to Joshua Prawer*, pp. 258–71. Edited by Benjamin Z. Kedar, Hans Eberhard Mayer, and R. C. Smail. Jerusalem: Yad Izhak Ben Zvi Institute, 1982.

———. "The Treatment of Marriage in the Questiones Londinenses (MS Royal 9. E. VII)." *Manuscripta* 19 (1975) 86–97.

Bruns, Berhnard. *Ehescheidung und Wiederheirat im Fall von Ehebruch.* Munich: F. Schöningh, 1976.

Buckstaff, Florence Griswold. "Married Women's Property in Anglo-Saxon and Anglo-Norman Law and the Origin of the Common Law of Dower." *Annals of the American Academy of Political and Social Science* 4 (1893–94) 233–64.

Bugge, John. *Virginitas: An Essay in the History of a Medieval Ideal.* The Hague: Martinus Nijhoff, 1975.

Bullough, Vern L. *The History of Prostitution.* New Hyde Park, NY: University Books, 1964.

———. "Medieval Medical and Scientific Views of Women." *Viator* 4 (1973) 485–501.

———. *Sexual Variance in Society and History.* Chicago: University of Chicago Press, 1980.

——— and James A. Brundage, eds. *Sexual Practices and the Medieval Church.* Buffalo, NY: Prometheus, 1982.

——— and Cameron Campbell. "Female Longevity and Diet in the Middle Ages." *Speculum* 55 (1980) 317–25.

Burge, William. *The Comparative Law of Marriage and Divorce.* Edited by Alexander Wood Renton and George Grenville Phillimore. London: Sweet & Maxwell, 1910.

Burr, David. "Olivi on Marriage: The Conservative as Prophet." *Journal of Medieval and Renaissance Studies* 2 (1972) 183–204.

Caselli, Gian Carlo. "*Concubina pro uxore*: Osservazioni in merito al c. 17 del primo concilio di Toledo." *Rivista di storia del diritto italiano* 37/38 (1964/65) 163–220.

Castelli, Guglielmo. "Il concubinato e la legislazione Augustea." *Bullettino dell'Istituto di diritto romano* 27 (1914) 55–71.

Clifford, John J. "The Ethics of Conjugal Intimacy According to St. Albert the Great." *Theological Studies* 3 (1942) 1–26.

Corbett, Percy E. *The Roman Law of Marriage.* Oxford: Clarendon Press, 1930.

Coriden, James A. *The Indissolubility Added to Christian Marriage by Consummation: An Historical Study of the Period from the End of the Patristic Age to the Death of Pope Innocent III.* Rome: Officium libri Catholici, 1961.

Csillag, Pál. *The Augustan Laws on Family Relations.* Budapest: Akadémiai Kiadó, 1976.

Daudet, Pierre. *L'établissement de la compétence de l'église en matière de divorce et consanguinité (France, Xème–XIIème siècles).* Paris: Sirey, 1941.

Dauvillier, Jean. *Le mariage dans le droit classique de l'église, depuis de Décret de Gratien (1140) jusqu'à le mort de Clément V (1314).* Paris: Sirey, 1933.

Dedek, John F. "Premarital Sex: The Theological Argument from Peter Lombard to Durand." *Theological Studies* 41 (1980) 643–67.

Delpini, F. "L'indissolubilità matrimoniale nei documenti ecclesiastici nell'età medioevale." *Sacra doctrina* 49 (1968) 61–120.

DeSanctis, Carlo. "Il pensiero della chiesa sul problema del coniuge abbandonato senza colpa." *Apollinaris* 48 (1975) 201–21.

Deviants and the Abandoned in French Society: Selections from the Annales: économies, sociétés, civilisations. Edited by Robert Forster and Orest Ranum. Translated by Elborg Forster and Patricia M. Ranum. Baltimore: John Hopkins University Press, 1978.

Donahue, Charles, Jr. "The Canon Law on the Formation of Marriage and Social Practice in the Later Middle Ages." *Journal of Family History* 8 (1983) 144–58.

———. "The Case of the Man Who Fell into the Tiber: The Roman Law of Marriage at the Time of the Glossators." *American Journal of Legal History* 22 (1978) 1–53.

———. "Lyndwood's Gloss *propriarum uxorum*: Marital Property and the *ius commune* in Fifteenth-Century England." In *Europäisches Rechtsdenken in Geschichte und Gegenwart: Festschrift für Helmut Coing,* pp. 19–37. Munich: C. H. Beck, 1982.

———. "Proof by Witnesses in the Church Courts of Medieval England: An Imperfect Reception of the Learned Law." In *On the Laws and Customs of England: Essays in Honor of Samuel E. Thorne,* edited by Morris S. Arnold et al., pp. 127–58. Chapel Hill: University of North Carolina Press, 1981.

———. "What Causes Fundamental Legal Ideas? Marital Property in England and

France in the Thirteenth Century." *Michigan Law Review* 78 (1979) 59–88.

Dortel-Claudot, Michel. "Le prêtre et le mariage: Evolution de la législation canonique dès origines au XIIe siècle." *L'année canonique* 17 (1973) 319–44.

Douglas, Mary. *Purity and Danger: An Analysis of Concepts of Pollution and Taboo.* New York: Frederick A. Praeger, 1966.

Doyle, Thomas P., ed. *Marriage Studies: Reflections in Canon Law and Theology.* Toledo, Ohio: Canon Law Society of America, 1980– ; in progress; 3 vols. to date.

Duby, Georges. *The Knight, the Lady, and the Priest: The Making of Marriage in Medieval France.* Translated by Barbara Bray. New York: Pantheon, 1983.

——. *Medieval Marriage: Two Models from Twelfth-Century France.* Translated by Elborg Forster. Baltimore: Johns Hopkins University Press, 1978.

Dufresne, Jean-Luc. "Les comportements amoureux d'après le registre de l'officialité de Cerisy." *Bulletin philologique et historique (jusqu'à 1610) du Comité des travaux historiques et scientifiques* (1973) 131–56.

Engdahl, D. E. "English Marriage Conflicts Law before the Time of Bracton." *American Journal of Comparative Law* 15 (1967) 109–35.

——. "Full Faith and Credit in Merrie Olde England: New Insight for Marriage Conflicts Law from the Thirteenth Century." *Valparaiso University Law Review* 5 (1970) 1–25.

Epstein, Louis M. "The Institution of Concubinage among the Jews." *Proceedings of the American Academy for Jewish Research* 6 (1935) 153–88.

——. *Marriage Laws in the Bible and the Talmud.* Cambridge: Harvard University Press, 1942.

——. *Sex Laws in Judaism.* New York: Ktav, 1967.

Esmein, Adhémar. *Le mariage en droit canonique.* 2d ed. 2 vols. Paris: Sirey, 1929–35.

Etudes d'histoire de droit canonique dédiées à Gabriel LeBras. 2 vols. Paris: Sirey, 1965.

Falcão, Miguel. "Atitude de Igreja perante as uniões conjugais da Roma clásica." *Theologica* 8 (1973) 1–26.

——. *Las prohibiciones matrimoniales de caracter social en el Imperio Romano.* Pamplona: EUNSA, 1973.

Family and Sexuality in French History. Edited by Robert Wheaton and Tamara K. Hareven. Philadelphia: University of Pennsylvania Press, 1980.

Ferretti, Walter. "Il matrimonio in San Pier Damiani." *Sacra doctrina* 82 (1976) 529–43.

Ferroglio, Giuseppe. "Raptus in parentes." *Annali della Facoltà giuridica dell'Università di Camerino* 19 (1952) 3–34.

——. "Studi in tema di 'impedimentum raptus'." *Annali della Facoltà giuridica dell'Università di Camerino* 20 (1953) 145–234.

Flandrin, Jean-Louis. *Les amours paysannes: Amour et sexualité dans les campagnes de l'ancien France (XVI–XIXe siècles).* Paris: Gallimard/Julliard, 1975.

——. "Contraception, mariage et relations amoureuses dans l'Occident chrétien." *Annales: économies, sociétés, civilisations* 24 (1969) 1370–90.

——. *Families in Former Times: Kinship, Household, and Sexuality.* Translated by Richard Southern. Cambridge: At the University Press, 1979.

——. *Le sexe et l'occident.* Paris: Editions du Seuil, 1981.

——. *Un temps pour embrasser: Aux origines de la morale sexuelle occidentale (VIe–XIe siècle).* Paris: Editions du Seuil, 1983.

Foucault, Michel. *Histoire de la sexualité.* Paris: Gallimard, 1976– ; 3 vols. to date.

Frank, Roberta. "Marriage in Twelfth- and Thirteenth-Century Iceland." *Viator* 4 (1973) 473–84.

Fransen, Gérard. "Le mariage simulé: Deux questions disputées du XIIe siècle." In *Etudes de droit et d'histoire: Mélanges Mgr. H. Wagnon*, pp. 530–41. Louvain: Bibliothèque centrale de l'Université Catholique de Louvain, 1976.

———. "Les Quaestiones Cusanae: questions disputées sur le mariage." In *Convivium utriusque iuris: A. Dordett zum 60. Geburtstag*, pp. 109–21. Viena: Wiener Dom-Verlag, 1976.

———. "Les 'questiones' des canonistes: Essai de depouillement et de classement (I–IV)." *Traditio* 12 (1956) 566–91; 13 (1957) 481–501; 19 (1963) 516–31; 20 (1964) 495–502.

Freisen, Joseph. *Geschichte des kanonischen Eherechts bis zum Verfall der Glossenliteratur.* 2d ed. Paderborn: F. Schöningh, 1893; repr. Aalen: Scientia, 1963.

Friedberg, Emil. *Das Recht der Eheschliessung in seiner geschichtlichen Entwicklung.* Leipzig: B. Tauchnitz, 1865; repr. Aalen: Scientia, 1965.

Fuchs, Eric. *Sexual Desire and Love: Origins and History of the Christian Ethic of Sexuality and Marriage.* Translated by Marsha Daigle. Cambridge: James Clarke & Co., 1983.

Gaudemet, Jean. *L'église dans l'empire romain (IVe–Ve siècles).* Paris: Sirey, 1958.

———. *La société ecclésiastique dans l'Occident médiéval.* London: Variorum, 1980.

———. *Sociétés et mariage.* Strasbourg: CERDIC, 1980.

Génestal, R. *Histoire de la légitimation des enfants naturels en droit canonique.* Paris: E. Leroux, 1905.

Gide, Paul. *Etude sur la condition privée de la femme dans le droit ancien et moderne et en particulier sur le sénatus-consulte velléien.* 2d ed. by A. Esmein. Paris: L. Larose et Forcel, 1885.

Goodich, Michael. *The Unmentionable Vice: Homosexuality in the Later Medieval Period.* Santa Barbara: ABC-Clio, 1979.

Goody, Jack. *The Development of the Family and Marriage in Europe.* Cambridge: At the University Press, 1983.

Gordon, Ignatius. "Adnotationes quaedam de valore matrimonii virorum qui ex toto secti sunt a tempore Gratiani usque ad Breve 'Cum frequenter'." *Periodica de re morali, canonica, liturgica* 66 (1977) 171–247.

Grévy-Pons, Nicole. *Célibat et nature: une controverse médiévale; à propos d'un traité du début du XVe siècle.* Paris: Centre National de la Recherche Scientifique, 1975.

Gryson, Roger. *Les origines du célibat ecclésiastique du première au septième siècle.* Gembloux: J. Duclot, 1970.

Haskins, George L. "The Development of Common Law Dower." *Harvard Law Review* 62 (1948) 42–55.

Heany, Seamus P. *The Development of the Sacramentality of Marriage from Anselm of Laon to Thomas Aquinas.* Washington, D.C.: Catholic University of America Press, 1963.

Heers, Jacques. *Family Clans in the Middle Ages: A Study of Political and Social Structures in Urban Areas.* Amsterdam: North-Holland, 1976.

Helmholz, Richard H. "Abjuration *sub pena nubendi* in the Church Courts of Medieval England." *The Jurist* 32 (1970) 80–90.

———. "Crime, Compurgation, and the Courts of the Medieval Church." *Law and History Review* 1 (1985) 1–26.

———. "*Legitim* in English Legal History." *University of Illinois Law Review* (1984) 659–74.

————. *Marriage Litigation in Medieval England.* Cambridge: At the University Press, 1974.

————. "The Roman Law of Guardianship in England, 1300–1600." *Tulane Law Review* 52 (1978) 223–57.

————. "Support Orders, Church Courts, and the Rule of *Filius nullius*: A Reassessment of the Common Law." *Virginia Law Review* 63 (1977) 431–48.

Herlihy, David. "Life Expectancies for Women in Medieval Society." In *The Role of Women in the Middle Ages,* edited by Rosemarie T. Morewedge, pp. 1–22. Albany: State University of New York Press, 1975.

————. "The Making of the Medieval Family: Symmetry, Structure, and Sentiment." *Journal of Family History* 8 (1983) 116–30.

————. "Marriage at Pistoia in the Fifteenth Century." *Bullettino storico pistoiese* 74 (1972) 3–21.

————. *Medieval Households.* Cambridge: Harvard University Press, 1985.

————. "The Medieval Marriage Market." *Medieval and Renaissance Studies* 6 (1976) 3–27.

Hermann, Horst. *Die Stellung unehelicher Kinder nach kanonischem Recht.* Amsterdam: B. R. Grüner, 1971.

Herter, Hans. "Die Soziologie der antiken Prostitution im Lichte des heidnischen und christlichen Schrifttums." *Jahrbuch für Antike und Christentum* 3 (1960) 70–111.

Hinschius, Paul. "Das Ehescheidungsrecht nach den angelsächsischen und fränkischen Bussordnungen." *Zeitschrift für deutsches Recht* 20 (1861) 66–87.

Howard, George Elliott. *A History of Matrimonial Institutions, Chiefly in England and the United States.* 2 vols. Chicago: University of Chicago Press, 1904.

Hughes, Diane Owen. "From Brideprice to Dowry in Mediterranean Europe." *Journal of Family History* 3 (1978) 262–96.

————. "Urban Growth and Family Structure in Medieval Genoa." *Past and Present* 66 (1975) 1–28.

Jeay, Madeleine. "Sexuality and Family in Fifteenth-Century France: Are Literary Sources a Mask or a Mirror?" *Journal of Family History* 4 (1979) 328–45.

Jolly, Jules. *Des seconds mariages: Etude historique sur la législation des seconds et subséquents mariages.* Paris: A. Rousseau, 1896.

Kajanto, Iiro. "On Divorce Among the Common People of Rome." *Revue des études latines* 47 (1969) 99–113.

Kantorowicz, Hermann. *Rechtshistorische Schriften.* Edited by Helmut Coing and Gerhard Immel. Karlsruhe: C. F. Müller, 1970.

————, and Buckland, W. W. *Studies in the Glossators of the Roman Law: Newly Discovered Writings of the Twelfth Century.* Cambridge: At the University Press, 1938.

Kelly, Henry Ansgar. *Canon Law and the Archpriest of Hita.* Binghamton: Center for Medieval & Early Renaissance Studies, 1984.

————. *Love and Marriage in the Age of Chaucer.* Ithaca, NY: Cornell University Press, 1975.

————. *The Matrimonial Trials of Henry VIII.* Stanford: Stanford University Press, 1976.

Klapisch-Zuber, Christiane. *Women, Family, and Ritual in Renaissance Italy.* Translated by Lydia Cochrane. Chicago: University of Chicago Press, 1985.

Koegel, Otto Erwin. *Common Law Marriage and Its Development in the United States.* Washington, D.C.: John Byrne & Co., 1922.

Kornfeld, Walter. "L'adultère dans l'Orient antique." *Revue biblique* 57 (1970) 92–109.

Kosmer, Ellen. "The 'noyous humoure of lecherie'." *Art Bulletin* 55 (1975) 1–8.

Kosnik, Anthony, et al. *Human Sexuality: New Directions in American Catholic Thought.* New York: Paulist Press, 1977.

Kuttner, Stephan G. *Kanonistische Schuldlehre von Gratian bis auf die Dekretalen Gregors IX.* Vatican City: Biblioteca Apostolica Vaticana, 1935.

———. "Pope Lucius III and the Bigamous Archbishop of Palermo." In *Medieval Studies Presented to Aubrey Gwynn, S. J.*, edited by John A. Watt, J. B. Morrall, and F. X. Martin, pp. 409–53. Dublin: Colin O Lochlainn, 1961.

———. *Repertorium der Kanonistik (1140–1234): Prodromus corporis glossarum.* Vatican City: Biblioteca Apostolica Vaticana, 1937.

———, and Rathbone, Eleanor. "Anglo-Norman Canonists of the Twelfth Century: An Introductory Study." *Traditio* 7 (1949/51) 279–358.

Lacombe, Paul. *La famille dans la société romaine: Etude de moralité comparée.* Paris: Lecrosnier et Babé, 1889.

Laeuchli, Samuel. *Power and Sexuality: The Emergence of Canon Law at the Synod of Elvira.* Philadelphia: Temple University Press, 1972.

Landau, Peter. *Die Entstehung des kanonischen Infamiebegriffs von Gratian bis zur Glossa ordinaria.* Cologne: H. Böhlau, 1966.

LeBras, Gabriel. *Institutions ecclésiastiques de la chrétienté médiévale.* Paris: Bloud et Gay, 1959.

———. "Le mariage dans la théologie et le droit de l'église du XIe et XIIIe siècle." *Cahiers de civilisation médiévale* 11 (1968) 191–202.

Lecky, W. E. H. *A History of European Morals from Augustus to Charlemagne.* 2 vols. in 1. London: Longmans, 1859; repr. New York: George Braziller, 1955.

Leclercq, Jean. *Monks and Love in Twelfth-Century France: Psycho-Historical Essays.* Oxford: Clarendon Press, 1979.

———. *Monks on Marriage: A Twelfth-Century View.* New York: Seabury Press, 1982.

Lecoy de La Marche, Albert. *La chaire française au moyen âge, spécialement au XIIIe siècle, d'après les manuscrits contemporains.* 2d ed. Paris: Renouard, 1886.

Lefebvre-Teillard, Anne. *Les officialités à la veille du Concile de Trente.* Paris: R. Pichon et R. Durant-Auzias, 1973.

Légasse, S. "Jésus et les prostituées." *Revue théologique de Louvain* 7 (1976) 137–54.

Lemay, Helen Rodnite. "Some Thirteenth and Fourteenth Century Lectures on Female Sexuality." *International Journal of Women's Studies* 1 (1978) 391–400.

———. "The Stars and Human Sexuality: Some Medieval Scientific Views." *Isis* 71 (1980) 127–37.

———. "William of Saliceto on Human Sexuality." *Viator* 12 (1981) 165–81.

Lettmann, Reinhard. *Die Diskussion über die klandestinen Ehen und die Einführung einer zur Gültigkeit verpflichtenden Eheschliessungsform auf dem Konzil von Trient: Eine kanonistische Untersuchung.* Münster: Aschendorff, 1967.

Lightman, Marjorie, and Zeisel, William. "*Univira*: An Example of Continuity and Change in Roman Society." *Church History* 46 (1977) 19–32.

Lindner, Dominikus. *Der Usus matrimonii: Eine Untersuchung über seine sittliche Bewertung in der katholischen Moraltheologie alter und neuer Zeit.* Munich: Josef Kösel und Friedrich Pustet, 1929.

Liotta, Filippo. *La continenza dei chierici nel pensiero canonistico classico da Graziano a Gregorio IX.* Milan: A. Giuffrè, 1971.

Löffler, Josef. *Die Störingen des geschlechtlichen Vermögens in der Literatur der auctoritativen Theologie des Mittelalters: Ein Beitrag zur Geschichte der Impotenz und des medizinischen Sachverständigenbeweises im kanonischen Impotenzprozess.* Mainz: Akademie der Wissenschaften und der Literatur, 1958.

Löwenstein, Eduard Max. *Die Bekämpfung des Konkubinates in der Rechtsentwicklung.* Breslau [Wrocław]: Schletter'sche Buchhandlung, 1919.

Lorenz, Egon. *Das Dotalstatut in der italienischen Zivilrechtslehre des 13. bis 16. Jahrhunderts.* Cologne: H. Böhlau, 1965.

Love and Marriage in the Twelfth Century. Edited by Willy Van Hoecke and Andries Welkenhuysen. Louvain [Leuven]: Leuven University Press, 1981.

Lüdicke, Klaus. "Die Rechtswirkungen der heilbaren Impotenz: Überlegungen zu einem übersehen Ehenichtigkeitsgrund." *Archiv für katholisches Kirchenrecht* 146 (1977) 74–128.

Lynch, John E. "Marriage and Celibacy of the Clergy: The Discipline of the Western Church; an Historico-Canonical Synopsis." *The Jurist* 32 (1972) 14–38, 189–212.

Maccarrone, Michele. "Sacramentalità e indissolubilità del matrimonio nella dottrina di Innocenzo III." *Lateranum* 14 (1978) 449–514.

Machielsen, Lambertus. "Les spurii de S. Grégoire le Grand en matière matrimoniale, dans les collections canoniques jusqu'au Décret de Gratien." *Sacris eruditi* 14 (1963) 251–70.

McLaughlin, Terence P. "The Formation of the Marriage Bond According to the *Summa Parisiensis.*" *Mediaeval Studies* 15 (1953) 208–12.

———. "The Prohibition of Marriage against Canons in the Early Twelfth Century." *Mediaeval Studies* 3 (1941) 94–100.

McNamara, JoAnn. "Cornelia's Daughters: Paula and Eustochium." *Women's Studies* 11 (1984) 9–27.

———. "Muffled Voices: The Lives of Consecrated Women in the Fourth Century." In *Medieval Religious Women*, edited by John A. Nichols and Lillian Thomas Shank, pp. 11–29. Kalamazoo, MI: Cistercian Publications, 1984.

Mañaricua y Nuere, Andrès E. de. *El matrimonio de los esclavos: Estudio histórico-jurídico hasta la fijación de la disciplina en el derecho canónico.* Rome: Apud aedes Universitatis Gregorianae, 1940.

Marin-Muracciole, Madeleine-Rose. *L'honneur des femmes en Corse du XIIIe siècle à nos jours.* Paris: Editions Cujas, 1964.

Marongiu, Antonio. *Byzantine, Norman, Swabian, and Later Institutions in Southern Italy.* London: Variorum, 1972.

———. *La famiglia nell'Italia meridionale (sec. VIII–XIII).* Milan: Società editrice 'Vita e pensiero', 1944.

———. "Matrimoni e convivenze 'more uxorio' in Sardegna prima e dopo il Concilio di Trento." In *Studi in onore di Ugo Gualazzini*, 2:313–325. Milan: A. Giuffrè, 1981.

Il matrimonio nella società altomedievale. 2 vols. Spoleto: Centro Italiano di Studi sull'alto medioevo, 1977.

May, Georg. *Die geistliche Gerichtsbarkeit des Erzbischoffs von Mainz im Thüringen des späten Mittelalters.* Leipzig: St. Benno Verlag, 1956.

The Meaning of Courtly Love: Papers of the First Annual Conference of the Center for Medieval and Early Renaissance Studies, State University of New York at Binghamton, March 17–18, 1967. Edited by F. X. Newman. Albany: State University of New York Press, 1972.

Meyer, Paul Martin. *Der römische Konkubinat nach den Rechtsquellen und den Inschriften.* Leipzig: B. G. Teubner, 1895; repr. Aalen: Scientia, 1966.

Meyvaert, Paul. "Les 'responsiones' de S. Grégoire le Grand à S. Augustin de Cantorbéry." *Revue d'histoire ecclésiastique* 54 (1959) 879–94.

Michaud-Quantin, Pierre. *Sommes de casuistique et manuels de confession au moyen âge (XIIe–XVIe siècles).* Louvain: Nauwelaerts, 1962.

Millon, David. "Ecclesiastical Jurisdiction in Medieval England." *University of Illinois Law Review* (1984) 621–38.

Molin, Jean-Baptiste, and Mutembe, Protais. *Le rituel du mariage en France du XIIe au XVIe siècle.* Paris: Beauchesne, 1974.

Montan, A. "Alle origini della disciplina matrimoniale canonica: contributi per la ricerca." *Apollinaris* 54 (1981) 151–82.

———. "La legislazione romana sul divorzio: Aspetti evolutivi e influssi cristiani." *Apollinaris* 53 (1980) 167–94.

Monter, E. William. "La sodomie à l'époque moderne en Suisse romande." *Annales: économies, sociétés, civilisations* 29 (1974) 1023–33.

Müller, Michael. *Die Lehre des hl. Augustinus von der Paradiesesehe und ihre Auswirkung in der Sexualethik des 12. und 13. Jahrhunderts bis Thomas von Aquin.* Regensburg: Friedrich Pustet, 1954.

Muldoon, James. "Missionaries and the Marriages of Infidels: The Case of the Mongol Mission." *The Jurist* 35 (1975) 125–41.

———. *Popes, Lawyers, and Infidels: The Church and the Non-Christian World, 1250–1550.* Philadelphia: University of Pennsylvania Press, 1979.

Mullenders, Joannes. *Le mariage présumé.* Rome: Università Gregoriana, 1971.

Murray, Alexander Callander. *Germanic Kinship Structure: Studies in Law and Society in Antiquity and the Early Middle Ages.* Toronto: Pontifical Institute of Mediaeval Studies, 1983.

Neusner, Jacob. *The Idea of Purity in Ancient Judaism.* Leiden: E. J. Brill, 1973.

Nock, Arthur Darby. *Essays on Religion and the Ancient World.* Edited by Zeph Stewart. 2 vols. Oxford: Clarendon Press, 1972.

Noonan, John T., Jr. *Contraception: A History of Its Treatment by the Catholic Theologians and Canonists.* Cambridge: Harvard University Press, Belknap Press, 1965.

———. "Power to Choose." *Viator* 4 (1973) 419–34.

———. *Power to Dissolve: Lawyers and Marriages in the Courts of the Roman Curia.* Cambridge: Harvard University Press, Belknap Press, 1972.

Nygren, Anders. *Agape and Eros.* Translated by Philip S. Watson. New York: Harper, 1969.

Orestano, Riccardo. *La struttura giuridica del matrimonio romano dal diritto classico al diritto giustinianeo.* Milan: A. Giuffrè, 1951.

Otis, Leah Lydia. *Prostitution in Medieval Society: The History of an Urban Institution in Languedoc.* Chicago: University of Chicago Press, 1985.

Ozment, Steven. *When Fathers Ruled: Family Life in Reformation Europe.* Cambridge: Harvard University Press, 1983.

Padgug, Robert A. "Sexual Matters: On Conceptualizing Sexuality in History." *Radical History Review* 20 (1979) 3–23.

Palazzini, Pietro. "S. Pier Damiani e la polemica anticelebataria." *Divinitas* 14 (1970) 127–33.

Palmer, Robert C. "Contexts of Marriage in Medieval England: Evidence from the King's Court circa 1300." *Speculum* 59 (1984) 42–67.

Patlagean, Evelyne. "L'histoire de la femme déguisée en moine et l'évolution de la sainteté féminine à Byzance." *Studi medievali,* 3d ser., 17 (1976) 597–623.

Pavan, Elisabeth. "Police des moeurs, société et politique à Venise à la fin du moyen âge." *Revue historique* 264 (1980) 241–88.

Payer, Pierre J. *Sex and the Penitentials.* Toronto: University of Toronto Press, 1984.

Pérez, Esteban. "¿Todo matrimonio entre cristianos es sacramento?" *Escritos de Vedat* (1976) 9–50.

Pierrugues, Pierre. *Glossarium eroticum linguae latinae sive theogoniae, legum et morum nuptialium apud Romanos explanatio nova.* Paris: A. F. & P. Dondey-Dupré, 1826; repr. Amsterdam: Adolf M. Hakkert, 1965.

Plöchl, Willibald. *Das Eherecht des Magisters Gratianus.* Leipzig: F. Deuticke, 1935.

Pollock, Sir Frederick, and Maitland, Frederic William. *The History of English Law before the Time of Edward I.* 2d ed., rev. by S. F. C. Milsom. 2 vols. Cambridge: At the University Press, 1968.

Pomeroy, Sarah B. *Goddesses, Whores, Wives, and Slaves: Women in Classical Antiquity.* New York: Schocken Books, 1975.

Post, J. B. "Ravishment of Women and the Statutes of Westminster." In *Legal Records and the Historian,* edited by John H. Baker, pp. 150–64. London: Royal Historical Society, 1978.

Powell, Chilton Latham. *English Domestic Relations, 1487–1653: A Study of Matrimony and Family Life in Theory and Practice.* New York: Columbia University Press, 1917.

Powers, James F. "Frontier Municipal Baths and Social Interaction in Thirteenth-Century Spain." *American Historical Review* 84 (1979) 649–67.

Pratt, Robert A. "Jankyn's Book of Wikked Wyves: Medieval Antimatrimonial Propaganda in the Universities." *Annuale medievale* 3 (1962) 5–27.

Rasi, Piero. "Il diritto matrimoniale nei glossatori." In *Studi di storia e diritto in onore di Carlo Calisse* 1:129–58. Milan: A. Giuffrè, 1940.

Rawson, Beryl. "Roman Concubinage and Other *de facto* Marriages." *Transactions of the American Philological Association* 104 (1974) 279–305.

Regatillo, Eduardo Fernándo. "El derecho matrimonial en las Partidas y en las Decretales." In *Acta Congressus iuridici internationalis VII saeculo a decretalibus Gregorii IX et XIV a Codice Iustiniano promulgatis* 3:315–84. Rome: Pontificium Institutum Utriusque Iuris, 1935–37.

Reinhardt, Heinrich J. *Die Ehelehre der Schule des Anselm von Laon.* Münster: Verlag Aschendorff, 1974.

Richard, Jean. "Le statut de la femme dans l'Orient Latin." *Recueils de la Société Jean Bodin* 12 (1962) 377–88.

Richlin, Amy. "Approaches to the Sources on Adultery at Rome." *Women's Studies* 8 (1981) 225–50.

Rinaldi, Evelina. "La donna negli statuti del commune di Forli, sec. XVI." *Studi storici* 18 (1909) 185–200.

Ritzer, Karl. *Le mariage dans les églises chrétiennes du Ier au XIe siècle.* Paris: Editions du Cerf, 1970.

Roberti, Melchiorre. "'Delictum' e 'peccatum' nelle fonti romane e cristiane: Contributo allo studio dell'influenza del cristianesimo sul diritto romano." In *Studi di storia e diritto in onore di Carlo Calisse* 1:159–76. Milan: A. Giuffrè, 1940.

Rossi, Guido. "Statut juridique de la femme dans l'histoire du droit italien, époque médiévale et moderne." *Recueils de la Société Jean Bodin* 12 (1962) 115–34.

Ruggiero, Guido. *The Boundaries of Eros: Sex Crime and Sexuality in Renaissance Venice.* Oxford: Oxord University Press, 1985.

———. "Sexual Criminality in the Early Renaissance: Venice, 1338–1358." *Journal of Social History* 8 (1974/75) 18–37.

Ruiz de Conde, Justina. *El amor y el matrimonio secreto en los libros de caballerias.* Madrid: M. Aguilar, 1948.

Ruiz, Humberto. *El concubinato como fuente de relaciones jurídicas.* Cali: Deptal, 1960 [?].

Ryan, J. Joseph. *Saint Peter Damiani and His Canonical Sources: A Preliminary Study in the Antecedents of the Gregorian Reform.* Toronto: Pontifical Institute of Mediaeval Studies, 1956.

Sägmüller, Johannes Baptista. "Das 'Impedimentum impotentiae' bei der Frau vor Alexander III." *Theologische Quartalschrift* 93 (1911) 90–126.

———. "Nochmals das 'Impedimentum impotentiae' bei der Frau vor Alexander III." *Theologische Quartalschrift* 95 (1913) 565–611.

Saldón, Eutiquiano; Rincón, Tomás; and Tejero, Eloy. *El matrimonio, misterio y signo.* 3 vols. Pamplona: EUNSA, 1971.

Salerno, Francesco. *La definizione del matrimonio canonico nella dottrina giuridica e teologica dei sec. XII–XIII.* Milan: A. Giuffrè, 1965.

Sauerwein, E. *Der Ursprung des Rechtsinstitutes der päpstlichen Dispens von der nicht vollzogenen Ehe: Eine Interpretation der Dekretalen Alexanders III. und Urbans III.* Rome: Università Gregoriana, 1980.

Schadt, H. "Die Arbores bigamiae als heilsgeschichtliche Schemata: Zum Verhältnis von Kanonistik und Kunstgeschichte." In *Kunst als Bedeutungsträger: Gedenkschrift für Günter Bandmann,* edited by Werner Busch, Reiner Hausherr, and Eduard Trier, pp. 129–47. Berlin: Mann, 1978.

Scheurl, Adolf von. *Die Entwicklung des kirchlichen Eheschliessungsrechts.* Erlangen: A. Deichert, 1877.

Schimmelpfennig, Bernhard. "*Ex fornicatione nati*: Studies on the Position of Priests' Sons from the Twelfth to the Fourteenth Century." *Studies in Medieval and Renaissance History* 2 (1980) 3–50.

Scholtens, J. E. "Maintenance of Illegitimate Children and the *Exceptio plurium concubentium.*" *South African Law Journal* 72 (1955) 144–51.

Schubart-Fikentscher, Gertrud. *Das Eherecht im Brünner Schöffenbuch.* Stuttgart: W. Kohlhammer, 1935.

Sellar, W. D. H. "Marriage, Divorce, and Concubinage in Gaelic Scotland." *Transactions of the Gaelic Society of Inverness* 51 (1978/80) 464–93.

Sexual Behavior and the Law. Edited by Ralph Slovenko. Springfield, IL: Thomas Publishing Company, 1965.

Sexualités occidentales. Paris: Editions du Seuil, 1982.

Shaw, Brett D., and Saller, Richard P. "Close Kin Marriage in Roman Society?" *Man: The Journal of the Royal Anthropological Society* 19 (1984) 432–44.

Sheedy, Anna Toole. *Bartolus on Social Conditions in the Fourteenth Century.* New York: Columbia University Press, 1942.

Sheehan, Michael M. "Choice of Marriage Partner in the Middle Ages: Development and Mode of Application of a Theory of Marriage." *Studies in Medieval and Renaissance History,* n.s. 1 (1978) 3–33.

———. *Family and Marriage in Medieval Europe: A Working Bibliography.* Vancouver: Medieval Studies Committee, 1976.

———. "The Formation and Stability of Marriage in Fourteenth-Century England: Evidence of an Ely Register." *Mediaeval Studies* 33 (1971) 228–63.

———. "The Influence of Canon Law on the Property Rights of Married Women in England." *Mediaeval Studies* 25 (1963) 109–24.

———. "Marriage and Family in English Conciliar and Synodal Legislation." In *Essays in Honour of Anton Charles Pegis*, edited by J. Reginald O'Donnell, pp. 205–14. Toronto: Pontifical Institute of Mediaeval Studies, 1974.

———. "Marriage Theory and Practice in the Conciliar Legislation and Diocesan Statutes of Medieval England." *Mediaeval Studies* 40 (1978) 408–60.

Singer, Irving. *The Nature of Love.* Chicago: University of Chicago Press, 1966– ; 2 vols. to date.

Slovenko, Ralph. "Sex Mores and the Enforcement of the Law on Sex Crimes: A Study of the Status Quo." *Kansas Law Review* 15 (1967) 265–86.

Sohm, Rudolf. *Das Recht der Eheschliessung aus dem deutschen und kanonischen Recht geschichtliche entwickelt: Eine Antwort auf die Frage nach dem Verhältnis der kirchlichen Trauung zur Zivilehe.* Weimar: Hermann Böhlau, 1875; repr. Aalen: Scientia, 1966.

Soliday, Gerald L. et al. *History of the Family and Kinship: A Select International Bibliography.* Millwood, NY: Kraus International Publications, 1980.

Steinberg, Leo. *The Sexuality of Christ in Renaissance Art and in Modern Oblivion.* New York: Pantheon Books, 1983.

Stone, Lawrence. "Family History in the 1980s: Past Achievements and Future Trends." *Journal of Interdisciplinary History* 12 (1981) 51–87.

Stückradt, Volker. *Rechtswirkungen eheähnlicher Verhältnisse.* Cologne: [privately printed], 1964.

Taviani, Huguette. "Le mariage dans l'hérésie de l'an mil." *Annales: économies, sociétés, civilisations* 32 (1977) 1074–89.

Tejero, Eloy. "La sacramentalidad del matrimonio en la historia del pensamiento cristiano." *Ius canonicum* 14 (1974) 11–31; 20 (1980) 285–327.

Tentler, Thomas N. *Sin and Confession on the Eve of the Reformation.* Princeton: Princeton University Press, 1977.

Theories of Property, Aristotle to the Present. Edited by Anthony Parel and Thomas Flanagan. Waterloo, Ont.: Wilfrid Laurier University Press, 1979.

Thomas, J. A. C. "Lex julia de adulteriis coercendis." *Études offertes à Jean Macqueron,* pp. 635–44. Aix-en-Provence: Faculté de droit et des sciences économiques, 1970.

Tierney, Brian. "*Natura id est Deus*: A Case of Juristic Pantheism?" *Journal of the History of Ideas* 24 (1963) 307–22. Reprinted with original pagination in his *Church, Law, and Constitutional Thought in the Middle Ages.* London: Variorum, 1979.

———. *Religion, Law, and the Growth of Constitutional Thought.* Cambridge: At the University Press, 1982.

Tomulescu, C. St. "Justinien et le concubinat." In *Studi in onore di Gaetano Scherillo* 1:299–326. Milan: Istituto Editoriale Cisalpina 'La Goliardica," 1972.

Torrella Niubo, Francisco. "Significado social de la ropas suntuarias durante de edad media en la Corona de Aragón." *Estudios de historia social de España* 3 (1955) 769–89.

Trexler, Robert C. "Le célibat à la fin du moyen âge: les religieuses de Florence." *Annales: économies, sociétés, civilisations* 27 (1972) 1329–50

———. "La prostitution Florentine au XVe siècle: Patronages et clientèles." *Annales: économies, sociétés, civilisations* 36 (1981) 983–1015

———. *Synodal Law in Florence and Fiesole, 1306–1518.* Vatican City: Biblioteca Apostolica Vaticana, 1971.

Trümmer, Josef. "Bigamie als Irregularitätsgrund nach der Lehre der alten Kanonistik." In *Speculum iuris et ecclesiarum: Festschrift für Willibald M. Plöchl zum 60. Geburtstag*, edited by Hans Lentze and Inge Gampl, pp. 393–409. Vienna: Herder, 1967.

Turlan, Juliette. "Instigante diabolo." In *Mélanges offerts à Jean Dauvilier*, pp. 803–808. Toulouse: Centre d'histoire juridique méridionale, 1979.

Visky, Károly. "Le divorce dans la législation de Justinien." *Revue internationale des droits de l'antiquité*, 3d ser., 23 (1976) 239–64.

Vitali, Enrico G. "Premesse romanistiche a uno studio sull' 'impedimentum criminis' (adulterio e divieti matrimoniali)." In *Studi in onore di Gaetano Scherillo* 1:274–98. Milan: Istituto editoriale cisalpino 'La Goliardica,' 1972.

Volterra, Edoardo. *La conception du mariage d'après les juristes romains*. Padua: La Garangola, 1940.

———. "Per la storia del reato di bigamia in diritto romano." In *Studi in memoria di Umberto Ratti*, edited by Emilio Albertario, pp. 387–447. Milan: A. Giuffrè, 1934.

Walker, Sue Sheridan. "Common Law Juries and Feudal Marriage Customs in Medieval England: The Pleas of Ravishment." *University of Illinois Law Review* (1984) 705–18.

Watkins, Oscar D. *A History of Penance*. 2 vols. London: Longmans, Green & Co., 1920; repr. New York: Ben Franklin, 1961.

Weigand, Rudolf. *Die bedingte Eheschliessung im kanonischen Recht*. Munich: Max Hueber, 1963.

———. "Die Einführung der Formpflicht für die Eheschliessung durch das Tridentinum und die bedingte Eheschliessung." *Würzburger Diözesangeschichtsblätter* 35/36 (1974) 261–73.

———. "Magister Rolandus und Papst Alexander III." *Archiv für katholisches Kirchenrecht* 149 (1980) 3–44.

———. *Die Naturrechtslehre der Legisten und Dekretisten von Irnerius bis Accursius und von Gratian bis Johannes Teutonicus*. Munich: Max Hueber, 1967.

———. "Quaestionen aus den Schule des Rolandus und Metellus." *Archiv für katholisches Kirchenrecht* 138 (1969) 82–94.

———. "Die Rechtssprechung des Regensburger Gerichts in Ehesachen unter besonderer Berücksichtigung der bedingten Eheschliessung nach Gerichtsbüchern aus dem Ende des 15. Jahrhunderts." *Archiv für katholisches Kirchenrecht* 137 (1968) 403–63.

———. "Das Scheidungsproblem in der mittelalterlichen Kanonistik." *Theologische Quartalschrift* 151 (1971) 52–60.

Wemple, Suzanne Fonay. "The Medieval Family: European and North American Research Directions." *Trends in History* 3 (1985) 27–44.

———. *Women in Frankish Society: Marriage and the Cloister, 500 to 900*. Philadelphia: University of Pennsylvania Press, 1981.

Williams, Gordon. "Some Aspects of Roman Marriage Ceremonies and Ideals." *Journal of Roman Studies* 48 (1958) 16–29.

Wolff, Hans Julius. *Written and Unwritten Marriages in Hellenistic and Postclassical Roman Law*. Haverford, PA: American Philological Association, 1939.

Wolff, Philippe. "Quelques actes notariés concernant famille et mariage (XIVe–XVe siècles)." *Annales du Midi* 78 (1966) 115–23.

Women in Medieval Society. Edited by Susan Mosher Stuard. Philadelphia: University of Pennsylvania Press, 1976.

Women in Western European History: A Select Chronological, Geographical, and Topical Bibliography, from Antiquity to the French Revolution. Edited by Linda Frey, Marsha Frey, and Joanne Schneider. Westport, CT: Greenwood, 1982.

Women of the Medieval World: Essays in Honor of John H. Mundy. Edited by Julius Kirshner and Suzanne F. Wemple. Oxford: Basil Blackwell, 1985.

Wood, Charles T. "The Doctors' Dilemma: Sin, Salvation, and the Menstrual Cycle in Medieval Thought." *Speculum* 56 (1981) 710–27.

Wunderli, Richard M. *London Church Courts and Society on the Eve of the Reformation.* Cambridge, MA: Medieval Academy of America, 1981.

Wustmann, Gustav. "Frauenhäuser und freie Frauen in Leipzig im Mittelalter." *Archiv für Kulturgeschichte* 5 (1907) 469–82.

Zeimentz, Hans. *Ehe nach der Lehre der Frühscholastik: Eine moralgeschichtliche Untersuchung zur Anthropologie und Theologie der Ehe in der Schule Anselms von Laon und Wilhelms von Champeaux, bei Hugo von St. Viktor, Walter von Mortagne und Petrus Lombardus.* Düsseldorf: Patmos-Verlag, 1974.

Ziegler, Josef Georg. *Die Ehelehre der Pönitentialsummen von 1200–1350: Eine Untersuchung zur Geschichte der Moral- und Pastoraltheologie.* Regensburg: Friedrich Pustet, 1956.

Zurowski, Marian. "Einflüsse des kanonischen Rechts auf das ursprüngliche polnische Eherecht." *Oesterreichisches Archiv für Kirchenrecht* 25 (1974) 354–65.

Index of Cases Cited

General Index

Index of Biblical Citations

Index of Legal Citations

Ivo, *Panormia* (continued)
6.37, 206
6.40, 196
6.43, 206
6.45, 195
6.49–50, 206
6.55, 209
6.56, 210
6.57, 212
6.59–62, 196
6.67, 191, 196
6.74, 201
6.76–78, 203
6.82, 202
6.83–85, 203
6.86–91, 201
6.92, 195, 201
6.93, 201
6.103, 200
6.106, 200
6.107, 187
6.109, 209
6.112–18, 202
6.119, 202, 224
6.120, 202, 208
6.125, 194, 206
7.1, 200
7.3, 198
7.4–7, 200
7.9–10, 203, 208
7.11–12, 208
7.14–15, 208
7.19, 207
7.20–21, 208
7.22–23, 207
7.27, 207
7.35–38, 200
7.41, 200
7.52, 239
7.65–66, 193
7.67, 193
7.70, 200
7.89, 200
8.36, 195
8.40–41, 189
8.43, 200
8.82, 197
8.142, 218
8.232, 200
8.235, 200
8.263, 198
9.37, 195
17.24, 193

17.26, 193
17.46, 193

Decretum Gratiani
D. 1 c. 4, 261
D. 1 c. 5, 299
D. 1 d.p.c. 5, 250, 279
D. 1 c. 7, 235, 261–62,
   280, 301, 303, 348, 365,
   390
D. 1 d.p.c. 12, 246
D. 1 d.p.c. 15, 251
D. 1 d.p.c. 18, 250
D. 4 c. 6, 285
D. 4 c. 77, 353
D. 5 d.a.c. 1, 240
D. 5 c. 1, 282
D. 5 c. 2, 240, 281, 286
D. 5 c. 4, 242, 280, 283,
   368
D. 6 pr., 314
D. 6 c. 1–3, 246
D. 6 d.p.c. 3, 246
D. 8 pr., 235
D. 8 c. 1, 235
D. 13 pr., 282–83, 305, 364
D. 13 c. 2, 280, 301, 349,
   364, 366
D. 13 c. 3, 282, 293
D. 14 c. 2, 289
D. 24 c. 2–3, 353
D. 25 c. 3, 301
D. 25 d.p.c. 3, 241, 246,
   218, 302, 303, 318, 364
D. 25 d.p.c. 7, 241
D. 26 d.p.c. 4, 252
D. 26 c. 2, 284
D. 26 c. 1, 252
D. 26 c. 2, 252, 273, 284
D. 26 c. 3, 252, 481
D. 26 c. 4, 244
D. 26 d.p.c. 4, 252
D. 26 c. 5, 252
D. 27–36, 231
D. 27 c. 8, 251
D. 27 c. 9, 252
D. 28 c. 2, 251, 298
D. 28 c. 4, 319
D. 28 c. 5, 357
D. 28 c. 9, 251, 318, 373
D. 28 c. 17, 315
D. 30 c. 3, 245, 314
D. 30 c. 6, 251

D. 30 c. 12, 235
D. 30 c. 14, 245
D. 31 c. 8–9, 235
D. 31 c. 10–11, 317
D. 32 c. 5, 317–18,
   403–404
D. 32 c. 6, 251, 404
D. 32 c. 7, 317
D. 32 c. 8, 316
D. 32 c. 10, 251
D. 32 c. 11, 251
D. 32 c. 12, 252, 405
D. 32 c. 16, 251
D. 32 c. 17, 251
D. 32 c. 18, 251
D. 33 pr., 251, 297, 319
D. 33 c. 1, 251–52, 297,
   317
D. 33 d.p.c. 1, 298
D. 33 c. 2, 252, 298, 310
D. 33 c. 6, 252, 390
D. 33 d.p.c. 6, 252
D. 33 c. 7, 252, 319
D. 33 c. 17, 252, 297
D. 34 c. 1, 251, 303
D. 34 d.p.c. 3, 239, 245,
   275, 281, 298, 369
D. 34 c. 4, 245, 299
D. 34 c. 5, 245
D. 34 c. 6, 245, 445
D. 34 d.p.c. 6, 297–98
D. 34 c. 7, 253, 351, 406
D. 34 d.p.c. 8, 249
D. 34 c. 9–12, 351
D. 34 c. 11, 307, 405
D. 34 d.p.c. 12, 252
D. 34 c. 13, 405
D. 34 d.p.c. 14, 252
D. 34 c. 15, 298–99
D. 34 c. 16, 248, 395
D. 34 c. 18, 253
D. 34 c. 19, 265
D. 37 c. 2, 302
D. 40 c. 8, 266
D. 45 c. 9, 390
D. 48 pr., 308
D. 50 d.p.c. 12, 303
D. 50 c. 16, 303
D. 50 c. 28, 317
D. 50 c. 29, 252
D. 50 c. 33, 252
D. 50 d.p.c. 36, 248